DEMOCRAT
$3 TRILLION
SPENDING PLAN

DEMOCRAT $3 TRILLION SPENDING PLAN

HEALTH AND ECONOMIC RECOVERY OMNIBUS EMERGENCY SOLUTIONS ACT (HEROES ACT, H.R. 6800)

116th CONGRESS
2d Session

Thirteen Colony Press

Thirteen Colony Press
c/o Sastrugi Press LLC
PO Box 1297, Jackson, WY 83001, United States
www.sastrugipress.com

CIP data available
U.S. Congress House of Representatives
Democrat $3 Trillion Spending plan: Health and Economic Recovery Omnibus Emergency Solutions Act (HEROES Act, H.R. 6800) / U.S. Congress House of Representatives —1st United States edition

p. cm.

1. Civics 2. Politics 3. Government
Democrat partisan bill proposal for appropriating $3 trillion dollars for the COVID-19 pandemic of 2020 and other unrelated matters.

Thirteen Colony Press is an imprint of Sastrugi Press LLC.

ISBN-13: 978-1-64922-014-1(paperback)
Printed in the United States of America when bought in the United States of America.
10 9 8 7 6 5 4 3 2 1
Sastrugi Press
00221

PUBLISHER'S NOTE

The original Congressional appropriations bill has been reformatted to fit the digital and print copies as you see here for easier reading. Thank you for choosing Thirteen Colony Press.

Contents

Contents

CONTENTS

CONTENTS

CONTENTS

CONTENTS

Health and Economic Recovery Omnibus Emergency Solutions Act (HEROES Act, H.R. 6800), House Committee on Appropriations Press Release

House Democrats Introduce The Heroes Act

May 12, 2020 Press Release

Bold, Transformative Legislation Meets the Challenge of the Coronavirus Pandemic
House Democrats today introduced The Heroes Act, a bold and comprehensive coronavirus response bill that will meet the challenge this pandemic poses to our nation.

The more than $3 trillion legislation protects the lives and livelihoods of the American people. Among its many provisions, the bill:

- **Honors our heroes**, by providing nearly $1 trillion to state, local, territorial and tribal governments who desperately need funds to pay vital workers like first responders, health workers, and teachers who keep us safe and are in danger of losing their jobs
- **Establishes a Heroes' Fund for essential workers**, with $200 billion to ensure that essential workers who have risked their lives working during the pandemic receive hazard pay
- **Supports testing, tracing and treatment**, by providing another $75 billion for coronavirus testing, contact tracing and isolation measures, ensuring every American can access free coronavirus treatment, and supporting hospitals and providers
- **Provides additional direct payments**, cushioning the economic blow of the coronavirus crisis with a second round of more substantial economic impact payments of $1,200 per family member, up to $6,000 per household
- **Protects payrolls**, by enhancing the new employee retention tax credit that encourages employers to keep employees on payroll, allowing 60 million Americans to remain connected to their paychecks and benefits
- **Ensures worker safety**, by requiring OSHA to issue a strong, enforceable standard within seven days to require all workplaces to develop and implement infection control plans based on CDC expertise, and prevents employers from retaliating against workers who report infection control problems
- **Supports small businesses and nonprofits**, by strengthening the Payroll Protection Program to ensure that it reaches underserved communities, nonprofits of all sizes and types and responds flexibly to small businesses by providing $10 billion for Covid-19 emergency grants through the Economic Injury Disaster Loan program
- **Preserves health coverage**, by protecting Americans losing their employer-provided health insurance with COBRA subsidies to maintain their coverage and creating a special enrollment period in the ACA exchanges for uninsured Americans
- **Extends unemployment benefits**, ensuring weekly $600 federal unemployment payments through next January, providing a vital safety net for the record number of Americans who are unemployed
- **Bolsters housing assistance**, helping struggling families afford a safe place to live with $175 billion in new supports to assist renters and homeowners make monthly rent, mortgage and utility payments and other housing-related costs
- **Strengthens food security**, addressing rising hunger with a 15 percent increase to the maximum SNAP benefit and additional funding for nutrition programs that help families put food on the table

- **Safeguards our democracy**, with new resources to ensure safe elections, an accurate Census, and preserve the Postal Service

The Heroes Act was introduced by Appropriations Committee Chairwoman Nita M. Lowey (D-NY) and co-sponsored by Education and Labor Committee Chairman Robert C. "Bobby" Scott (D-VA), Energy and Commerce Committee Chairman Frank Pallone, Jr. (D-NJ), Financial Services Committee Chairwoman Maxine Waters (D-CA), Foreign Affairs Committee Chairman Eliot L. Engel (D-NY), Judiciary Committee Chairman Jerrold Nadler (D-NY), Natural Resources Committee Chairman Raúl M. Grijalva (D-AZ), Oversight and Reform Committee Chairwoman Carolyn B. Maloney (D-NY), Small Business Committee Chairwoman Nydia M. Velázquez (D-NY), Veterans Affairs Committee Chairman Mark Takano (D-CA) and Ways and Means Committee Chairman Richard E. Neal (D-MA).

The legislation follows the Paycheck Protection Program and Health Care Enhancement Act enacted on April 24; the Coronavirus Aid, Relief, and Economic Security (CARES) Act, enacted on March 27; the Families First Coronavirus Response Act, enacted on March 18; and the Coronavirus Preparedness and Response Supplemental Appropriations Act enacted on March 6.

The text of The Heroes Act, H.R. 6800, is here. A one pager on the legislation is here. A section-by-section summary is here. A resource on the state and local relief provisions is here.

116th Congress

Health and Economic Recovery Omnibus Emergency Solutions Act (HEROES Act, H.R. 6800), Title-By-Title Summary

H.R. 6800, The Heroes Act

Title-By-Title Summary

DIVISION A – Coronavirus Recovery Supplemental Appropriations Act, 2020

Prepared by the Democratic staff of the House Committee on Appropriations

Title I – Agriculture, Rural Development, Food and Drug Administration, and Related Agencies

Supplemental Nutrition Assistance Program (SNAP) – Provides $10 billion to support anticipated increases in participation and to cover program cost increases related to flexibilities provided to SNAP by the Families First Coronavirus Response Act.

Special Supplemental Nutrition Program for Women Infants and Children (WIC) – Provides an additional $1.1 billion to provide access to nutritious foods to low-income pregnant women or mothers with young children who lose their jobs or are laid off due to the COVID-19 emergency.

The Emergency Food Assistance Program (TEFAP) – Includes $150 million to help local food banks meet increased demand for low-income Americans during the emergency. Including funding provided by the Families First Coronavirus Response Act and the Coronavirus Aid, Relief, and Economic Security Act (CARES Act), TEFAP has received a total of $1 billion.

Child Nutrition Programs – Includes $3 billion in additional funding to provide emergency financial relief to school meal providers and USDA's Child and Adult Care Food Program.

Farm and Ranch Stress Assistance Network program – Provides $20 million to strengthen activities and services that connect farmers and ranchers to stress assistance resources and programs.

USDA Office of Inspector General – Provides $2.5 million to increase monitoring and oversight activities.

Title II – Commerce, Justice, Science, and Related Agencies

Census Bureau, Periodic Censuses and Programs – $400 million for expenses due to delays in the 2020 Decennial Census in response to the coronavirus.

Census Bureau, Current Surveys and Programs – $10 million for expenses incurred as a result of the coronavirus.

National Oceanic and Atmospheric Administration (NOAA) – $100 million for Fishery Disaster Assistance for tribal, subsistence, commercial, and charter fishery participants, in response to economic injury precipitated by the coronavirus.

Department of Commerce, Office of Inspector General – $1 million for auditing and oversight of supplemental funds provided to the Commerce Department in the earlier CARES Act and this Act.

Bureau of Prisons – $200 million to prevent, prepare for, and respond to coronavirus in Federal prisons, including funding for medical testing and services, personal protective equipment, hygiene supplies and services, and sanitation services

Violence Against Women Act (VAWA) programs – $100 million, with a waiver of the local match requirement, including $30 million for grants to combat violence against women, $15 million for transitional housing assistance grants, $15 million for sexual assault victims assistance, $10 million for rural domestic violence and child abuse enforcement assistance, $10 million for legal assistance for victims, $4 million for assistance to tribal governments, and $16 million to support families in the justice system.

Byrne Justice Assistance Grants – $300 million to help prevent, prepare for, and respond to coronavirus, including for purchasing personal protective equipment and controlling outbreaks of coronavirus at prisons, with waivers of the local match and non-supplanting requirements.

Public defender funding is also an authorized use of Byrne-JAG grants. The bill additionally prevents the Department of Justice from preventing these funds from going to sanctuary jurisdictions.

Community Oriented Policing Services (COPS) – $300 million for law enforcement hiring grants and for the purchase of personal protective equipment, with waivers of the local match and non-supplanting requirements.

Second Chance Act grants – $250 million for grants to help facilitate the reintegration of ex- prisoners back into society and to prevent recidivism.

Pandemic Justice Response Act Grants – $600 million, including: (1) $500 million to prevent, detect, and stop the presence of COVID-19 in correctional institutions, and for pre-trial citation and release grants, (2) $25 million for Rapid COVID-19 Testing at correctional institutions, and (3) $75 million for Juvenile Specific Services.

National Science Foundation (NSF) Research and Related Activities – $125 million to prevent, prepare for, and respond to coronavirus.

Legal Services Corporation – $50 million to address legal needs arising from coronavirus.

Department of Justice, Office of Inspector General – $3 million to prevent, prepare for, and respond to coronavirus, including by providing auditing and oversight of supplemental funds provided to the Justice Department.

Title III – Financial Services and General Government

State Fiscal Relief – $500 billion in funding to assist state governments with the fiscal impacts
from the public health emergency caused by the coronavirus.

Local Fiscal Relief – $375 billion in funding to assist local governments with the fiscal impacts from the public health emergency caused by the coronavirus.

Tribal Fiscal Relief – $20 billion in funding to assist Tribal governments with the fiscal impacts from the public health emergency caused by the coronavirus.

Fiscal Relief for Territories – $20 billion in funding to assist governments of the Territories with the fiscal impacts from the public health emergency caused by the coronavirus.

CARES Act Coronavirus Relief Fund Repayment to DC – Provides an additional $755 million for the District of Columbia to assist with the fiscal impacts from the public health emergency caused by the coronavirus

Treasury Inspector Generals – $35 million for the Treasury Inspector General for oversight of Coronavirus Fiscal Relief Fund payments to state and local governments, and $2.5 million for the Treasury Inspector General for Tax Administration for oversight of IRS payments.

Community Development Financial Institutions (CDFI) – $1 billion for economic support and recovery in distressed communities by providing financial and technical assistance to CDFIs.

Tax Credit Implementation – $599 million for implementation of additional payments to individuals.

Assistance to Homeowners--$75 billion to states, territories, and tribes to address the ongoing needs of homeowners struggling to afford their housing due directly or indirectly to the impacts of the pandemic by providing direct assistance with mortgage payments, property taxes, property insurance, utilities, and other housing related costs.

Elections – $3.6 billion for grants to States for contingency planning, preparation, and resilience of elections for Federal office.

Broadband – $1.5 billion to close the homework gap by providing funding for Wi-Fi hotspots and connected devices for students and library patrons, and $4 billion for emergency home connectivity needs.

Assisting Small Businesses – $10 billion in grants to small businesses that have suffered 3
financial losses as a result of the coronavirus outbreak.

Office of Personnel Management Inspector General Office (OPM IG) – $1 million for the OPM IG to combat healthcare fraud associated with COVID-19.

General Services Administration Technology Modernization Fund – $1 billion in funding for technology-related modernization activities to prevent, prepare for, and respond to coronavirus.

Postal Service – $25 billion for revenue forgone due to the coronavirus pandemic, plus language providing additional protections to Postal workers. An additional $15 million is provided for the Postal Service Inspector General for oversight of this funding.

Title IV – Homeland Security

Federal Emergency Management Agency – $1.3 billion to prevent, prepare for, and respond to coronavirus, including $200 million for the Emergency Food and Shelter Program; $500 million for Assistance to Firefighter Grants (AFG); $500 million for Staffing for Adequate Fire and Emergency Response (SAFER) grants; and $100 million for Emergency Management Performance Grants (EMPG).
In addition –
• Prohibits the use of funds provided in the bill from being used for other purposes.
• For AFG and SAFER, waives cost sharing requirements for cash-strapped fire departments and waives certain other program requirements in order to help expedite grant awards.

Office of Inspector General – $3 million for oversight of the Department of Homeland Security's pandemic response activities.

Title V – Interior, Environment, and Related Agencies

Fish and Wildlife Service – $71 million to support activities related to wildlife-borne disease prevention, with $50 million for grants through the State and Tribal Wildlife grant program.

United States Geological Survey – $40 million for biosurveillance and research related to wildlife-borne disease.

Bureau of Indian Affairs – $900 million to meet Tribal government needs necessary to prevent, prepare for, and respond to coronavirus, including:
• $780 million to continue Tribal government operations and programs and to clean Tribal facilities.
• $100 million to address overcrowded housing which is prohibiting social isolation. 4
• $20 million for sanitation needs to provide for water hydration and hygiene issues

to mitigate and respond to coronavirus.

Department of the Interior – $1 billion for building hospitals and critical infrastructure in the Insular Areas, as well as for general technical assistance in responding to Coronavirus; and $5 million to perform oversight, accountability, and evaluation of programs, projects, or activities in the Department of the Interior pandemic response.

Environmental Protection Agency – $50 million for environmental justice grants, including investigating links between pollution exposure and the transmission and health outcomes of coronavirus in environmental justice communities.

Indian Health Service – $2.1 billion to address health care needs related to coronavirus for Native Americans, including:

• $1 billion to account for lost third party revenues as a result of reduced medical care.

• $64 million to assist Urban Indian Organizations.

• $10 million to assist with sanitation, hydration and hygiene needs in Indian Country

necessary to prevent, prepare for, and respond to coronavirus.

• $500 million to provide health care, including telehealth services to Native Americans,

and to purchase medical supplies and personal protective equipment.

• $140 million to expand broadband infrastructure and information technology for telehealth and electronic health records system purposes.

• $20 million to provide health care, housing and isolation units for domestic violence

victims and homeless Native Americans.

• No less than $366 million to provide isolation or quarantine space.

National Endowment for the Arts- $10 million for the National Endowment for the Arts for grants to support the general operations of recipients and language to permit the waiver of matching requirements.

National Endowment for the Humanities- $10 million for the National Endowment for the Humanities for grants to support the general operations of recipients and language to permit the waiver of matching requirements.

Title VI – Labor, Health and Human Services, Education, and Related Agencies

Department of Labor – $3.1 billion to support workforce training and worker protection activities related to coronavirus, including:

• $2 billion to support worker training;

• $25 million for migrant and seasonal farmworkers, including emergency supportive

services;

• $925 million to assist States in processing unemployment insurance claims;

• $15 million for the federal administration of unemployment insurance activities;

• $100 million for the Occupational Safety and Health Administration for workplace protection and enforcement activities in response to coronavirus, including $25 million for Susan Harwood training grants that protect and educate workers;

• $6.5 million for the Wage and Hour Division to support enforcement and outreach activities for paid leave benefits; and

• $5 million for the Office of the Inspector General.

Health Resources and Services Administration – $7.6 billion to support expanded health care
services for underserved populations, including:
- $7.6 billion for Health Centers to expand the capacity to provide testing, triage, and care for COVID-19 and other health care services at approximately 1,000 existing health centers across the country; and
- $10 million to Ryan White HIV/AIDS clinics to support extended operational hours, increased staffing hours, additional equipment, and additional home delivered meals and transportation needs of clients, who disproportionately suffer from co-morbidities and underlying immunosuppression that puts them at greater risk for COVID-19 complications.

Centers for Disease Control and Prevention – $2.1 billion to support federal, state, and local public health agencies to prevent, prepare for, and respond to the coronavirus, including:
- $2 billion for State, local, Territorial, and Tribal Public Health Departments and
- $130 million for public health data surveillance and analytics infrastructure modernization.

National Institutes of Health – $4.745 billion to expand COVID-19-related research on the NIH campus and at academic institutions across the country and to support the shutdown and startup costs of biomedical research laboratories nationwide.

Assistant Secretary for Preparedness and Response – $4.575 billion to respond to coronavirus, including:
- $3.5billion for Biomedical Advanced Research and Development Authority (BARDA) for therapeutics and vaccines;
- $500 million for BARDA to support U.S.-based next generation manufacturing facilities;
- $500 million for BARDA to promote innovation in antibacterial research and development; and
- $75 million for the Office of Inspector General.

Public Health and Social Services Emergency Fund – $175 billion to reimburse for health care related expenses or lost revenue attributable to the coronavirus, as well as to support testing and contact tracing to effectively monitor and suppress COVID-19, including:
- $100 billion in grants for hospital and health care providers to be reimbursed health care related expenses or lost revenue directly attributable to the public health emergency resulting from coronavirus; and
- $75 billion for testing, contact tracing, and other activities necessary to effectively monitor and suppress COVID-19.

Substance Abuse and Mental Health Services Administration – $3 billion to increase mental health support during this challenging time, to support substance abuse treatment, and to offer increased outreach, including:
- $1.5 billion for the Substance Abuse Prevention and Treatment Block Grant;
- $1 billion for the Community Mental Health Services Block Grant;
- $100 million for services to homeless individuals;
- $100 million for Project AWARE to identify students and connect them with mental
health services;

• $10 million for the National Child Traumatic Stress Network;
• $265 million for emergency response grants to address immediate behavioral health
needs as a result of COVID-19;
• $25 million for the Suicide Lifeline and Disaster Distress Helpline; and
• Not less $150 million for tribes, tribal organizations, urban Indian health organizations,
or health service providers to tribes across a variety of programs.

Centers for Medicare & Medicaid Services – Nursing Strike Team – $150 million for States to establish and implement strike teams to deploy to skilled nursing facilities or nursing facilities within 72 hours of three residents or employees being diagnosed with or suspected of having COVID-19.

Administration for Children and Families – $10.1 billion to provide supportive and social services for families and children through programs including:
• $7 billion for Child Care and Development Block Grants;
• $1.5 billion for the Low-Income Home Energy Assistance Program (LIHEAP);
• $1.5 billion to support paying water bills for low income families;
• $50 million for Family Violence Prevention and Services;
• $20 million for Child Abuse Prevention and Treatment Act (CAPTA) State Grants; and
• $20 million for Community Based-Child Abuse Prevention Grants.

Administration for Community Living – $100 million to provide direct services such as home- delivered and prepackaged meals, and supportive services for seniors and disabled individuals, and their caregivers.

Department of Education – $100.15 billion to support the educational needs of States, school districts, and institutions of higher education in response to coronavirus, including:
• $90 billion for a State Fiscal Stabilization Fund for grants to States to support statewide and local funding for elementary and secondary schools and public postsecondary institutions. This flexible funding can support:
o costs associated with making up instructional time, including teacher, school leader, and classified school employee personnel costs;
o providing school-based supports for impacted students, families, and staff, including counseling, mental health services, family engagement efforts, and the coordination of physical health services;
o costs associated with sanitation and cleaning for schools and school transportation;
o professional development for school-based staff on trauma-informed care to restore the learning environment;
o purchasing educational technology, including assistive technology, that aids in regular and substantive interactions between students and their classroom instructor;
o coordination efforts between State educational agencies and public health departments for emergency planning, response, and recovery;
o authorized activities under education statutes including ESEA, IDEA, McKinney-Vento Homeless Assistance Act, the Adult Education and Family Literacy Act, and the Perkins Act;
o training and professional development for college and university faculty and staff

to use technology and services related to distance education;

o general expenditures for institutions of higher education for expenses associated with a disruption in services or operations related to coronavirus, including defraying expenses due to lost revenue, reimbursement for expenses already incurred, and payroll; and,

o emergency financial aid to postsecondary students for housing, food, technology, health care, and child care.

• $10.15 billion to help alleviate burdens associated with the coronavirus for both colleges and students, including $1.7 billion for Historically Black Colleges and Universities and Minority Serving Institutions, $20 million for Howard University, $11 million for Gallaudet University, $11 million for the National Technical Institute for the Deaf, and $8.4 billion for other institutions of higher education.

Institute for Museum and Library Services – $5 million to support libraries and museums with costs and expenses associated with coronavirus, including operational supports and providing technology and resources for their communities.

Railroad Retirement Board – $5 million to support the processing of unemployment benefits under the Railroad Unemployment Insurance Act, including $500,000 for the Office of the Inspector General.

Title VII – Legislative Branch

House of Representatives – $5 million to support an upgraded imaging solution required to expediently and efficiently meet the demand for House imaged laptops due to COVID-19. In addition, this funding will support an increase in inventory of satellite phone, Mobile Wi-Fi Hotspots, and updated satellite bandwidth technologies to meet escalating demand of District Offices during COVID-19, as well as provide funding for the newly formed Select Committee that will provide oversight of the funds provided for coronavirus and economic aid.

Government Accountability Office (GAO) – $30 million for GAO to conduct oversight of funding provided to federal departments and agencies for coronavirus response and recovery efforts.

Title VIII – State, Foreign Operations, and Related Programs Oversight – $2 million to the Department of State Inspector General to conduct oversight of coronavirus response activities.

Title IX – Transportation, Housing and Urban Development, and Related Agencies

Department of Transportation (DOT)

FAA, Operations – $75 million for additional janitorial services at air traffic control towers and other FAA facilities; hazard pay, and overtime pay to prevent, prepare for, and respond to coronavirus; and a study on mitigating pathogens in airliner cabin air.

Airport and Airway Trust Fund Relief (AATF) – The combination of reduced air passenger traffic and the suspension of certain aviation taxes through January 2021 in the Coronavirus Aid, Relief, and Economic Security Act (CARES Act) (P.L. 116-136) will significantly reduce aviation-related excise tax revenue remitted to the AATF and may result in the AATF being unable to rely solely on aviation taxes to meet its obligations, such as grants to airports, air traffic control operations, and research in fiscal year 2020. Section 10901 ensures that the AATF can meets its obligations using the General Fund of the Treasury.

Highways – $15 billion for grants to support the ongoing work of State, Tribal, and Territorial Departments of Transportation and certain local governments to mitigate the effects of coronavirus including the salaries of staff and other administrative expenses.

Transit Emergency Relief – $15.75 billion for operating assistance grants to support the transit agencies that require significant additional assistance to maintain basic transit services. Of these amounts $11.75 billion will be distributed by formula and $4 billion will be available to any grantee or sub-recipient by application to the Secretary.

Department of Housing and Urban Development (HUD)

Tenant-Based Rental Assistance – $4 billion to allow public housing agencies (PHAs) to respond to coronavirus and the ability to keep over 2.2 million families stably housed even when facing a loss of income, including $1 billion for new, temporary, vouchers for individuals and families who are homeless or at risk of becoming homeless, or fleeing domestic violence. Allows PHAs the flexibility necessary for the safe and effective administration of these funds while maintaining fair housing, nondiscrimination, labor standards, and environmental protections.

Public Housing Operating Fund – $2 billion for PHAs to carry out coronavirus response for the operation and management of almost 1 million public housing units. Allows PHAs the flexibility necessary for the safe and effective administration of these funds while maintaining fair housing, nondiscrimination, labor standards, and environmental protections.

Housing for Persons with AIDS – $15 million to maintain operations, rental assistance, supportive services, and other necessary actions to mitigate the impact of coronavirus on low- income persons with HIV/AIDS.

Community Development Block Grant – $5 billion for coronavirus response and to mitigate the impacts in our communities to be distributed by formula to current grantees. The legislation continues to waive the public services cap to allow communities to respond to the impacts of the pandemic.

Homeless Assistance Grants – $11.5 billion for Emergency Solutions Grants to address the impact of coronavirus among individuals and families who are homeless or at risk of homelessness and to support additional homeless assistance, prevention, and diversion activities to mitigate the impacts of the pandemic.

Emergency Rental Assistance – $100 billion to provide emergency assistance to help low- income renters at risk of homelessness avoid eviction due to the economic impact of the coronavirus pandemic.

Project-Based Rental Assistance – $750 million to ensure the continuation of housing assistance for low-income individuals and families living in project-based rental assistance properties, and to ensure housing providers can take the necessary actions to prevent, prepare for, and respond to the pandemic.

Housing for the Elderly – $500 million to maintain operations at properties providing affordable housing for low-income seniors and to ensure housing providers can take the necessary actions to prevent, prepare for, and respond to the coronavirus pandemic. To ensure access to supportive services for this vulnerable population, this includes $300 million for service coordinators and the continuation of existing congregate service grants for residents of assisted housing projects.

Housing for Persons with Disabilities – $200 million to maintain operations at properties providing affordable housing for low-income persons with disabilities, and to ensure housing providers can take the necessary actions to prevent, prepare for, and respond to the coronavirus pandemic.

Housing Counseling Assistance – $100 million to enable housing counselors to respond to the surge of demand for services, which include foreclosure and eviction mitigation counseling, in light of the economic impact of the COVID-19 pandemic. The bill allows the purchase of technology and equipment so services can be provided through electronic means.

Office of Fair Housing and Equal Opportunity – $14 million to address fair housing issues resulting from coronavirus. This includes $4 million for Fair Housing Organization Initiative grants and $10 million for Education and Outreach grants to educate the public and the housing industry about fair housing rights and responsibilities during the COVID-19 pandemic.

Title X – General Provisions DIVISION B – Revenue Provisions
Prepared by the Democratic staff of the House Committee on Ways and Means
Sec. 20001. Short title; table of contents.
Titles this division the "COVID-19 Tax Relief Act of 2020."

Title I – Economic Stimulus
SUBTITLE A – 2020 RECOVERY REBATE IMPROVEMENTS
Sec. 20101. Dependents taken into account in determining credit and rebates.
Makes all dependents eligible for the $500 qualifying child amount in the Economic Impact Payments made under the CARES Act, previously only applicable to children below age 17. This allows households with dependents who are full-time students below age 24 and adult dependents to also receive the $500 amount. This provision is effective retroactive to the date of enactment of the CARES Act.

Sec. 20102. Individuals providing taxpayer identification numbers taken into account in determining credit and rebates.
Allows Economic Impact Payments to be made to an individual who provides a Taxpayer Identification Number, rather than a Social Security Number. This provision is effective retroactive to the date of enactment of the CARES Act.

Sec. 20103. 2020 recovery rebates not subject to reduction or offset with respect to past-due support.
Exempts Economic Impact Payments from reduction or offset with respect to past-due child support.

Sec. 20104. Protection of 2020 Economic Impact Payments.
Protects Economic Impact Payments from any form of transfer, assignment, execution, levy, attachment, garnishment, legal process, bankruptcy or insolvency law, and any other means of capture prohibited for payments made under Chapter 7 Subchapter 2 of the Social Security Act.

Sec. 20105. Payments to representative payees and fiduciaries.
Amends the CARES Act to clarify that, for an individual whose Economic Impact Payment was paid based on a Social Security Benefit Statement or Social Security Equivalent Benefit Statement, any Economic Impact Payment made to a representative payee or fiduciary shall only be used for the benefit of the person for whom the payment was intended. This provision is effective retroactive to the date of enactment of the CARES Act.
Technical budgetary provisions.

Sec. 20106. Application to taxpayers with respect to whom advance payment has already been made.

When the amendments to the Economic Impact Payments described above increase the amount of advance payments a taxpayer is eligible for, Treasury shall issue a rebate equal to the taxpayers' redetermined rebate less the previously issued rebate.

SUBTITLE B – ADDDITIONAL RECOVERY REBATES TO INDIVIDUALS

Sec. 20111. Additional recovery rebates to individuals.

Provides a $1,200 refundable tax credit for each family member that shall be paid out in advance payments, similar to the Economic Impact Payments in the CARES Act. The credit is $1,200 for a single taxpayer ($2,400 for joint filers), in addition to $1,200 per dependent up to a maximum of 3 dependents. The credit phases out starting at $75,000 of modified adjusted gross income ($112,500 for head of household filers and $150,000 for joint filers) at a rate of $5 per $100 of income. Treasury shall issue this credit as an advance payment based on the information on 2018 or 2019 tax returns. Treasury shall issue advance payments for Social Security Old-Age, Survivors, and Disability Insurance beneficiaries, Supplemental Security Income recipients, Railroad Retirement Board beneficiaries, and Veterans Administration beneficiaries who did not file returns for 2018 or 2019 based on information provided by the Social Security Administration, the Railroad Retirement Board, and the Veterans Administration. Treasury shall conduct outreach to non-filers to inform them of how to file for their advance payment. Taxpayers receiving an advance payment that exceeds their maximum eligible credit based on 2020 information will not be required to repay any amount of the payment to the Treasury. If the credit based on 2020 information exceeds the amount of the advance payment, taxpayers can claim the difference on their 2020 tax returns.

The recovery rebate improvements in sections 201 through 205 of this division generally apply to these additional rebates. Additionally, Treasury is instructed to make payments to the territories that relate to the cost of providing the credits for each territory.

SUBTITLE C – EARNED INCOME TAX CREDIT

Sec. 20121. Strengthening the earned income tax credit for individuals with no qualifying children for 2020.

Expands the eligibility and the amount of the earned income tax credit for taxpayers with no qualifying children (the "childless EITC") for 2020. In particular, the minimum age to claim the childless EITC is reduced from 25 to 19 (except for full-time students) and the upper age limit for the childless EITC is increased from age 65 to age 66. This section also increases childless EITC amount by increasing the credit percentage and phaseout percentage from 7.65 to 15.3 percent, increasing the earned income amount to $9,720, increasing the phaseout amount to $11,490. Under these parameters, the maximum credit amount in 2020 increases from $538 to $1,487.

Sec. 20122. Taxpayer eligible for childless earned income credit in case of qualifying children who fail to meet certain identification requirements.

Repeals the provision prohibiting an EITC-eligible taxpayer with qualifying children from taking the childless EITC if he or she cannot claim the EITC with respect to qualifying children due to failure to meet child identification requirements (including a valid SSN for qualifying children). Accordingly, individuals who do not claim the EITC with respect to qualifying children due to failure to meet identification requirements would now be able claim the childless EITC.

Sec. 20123. Credit allowed in case of certain separated spouses.

Allows a married but separated individual to be treated as not married for purposes of the EITC if a joint return is not filed. Thus, the EITC may be claimed by the individual on a separate return. This rule only applies if the taxpayer lives with a qualifying child for more than one-half of the taxable year and either does not have the same principal place of abode as his or her spouse for the last six months of the year, or has a separation decree, instrument, or agreement and doesn't live with his or her spouse by the end of the taxable year. This change aligns the EITC eligibility requirements with present-day family law practice.

Sec. 20124. Elimination of disqualified investment income test.

Eliminates the disqualified investment income test so that individuals are able to claim the EITC without regard to the amount of certain investment income.

Sec. 20125. Application of earned income tax credit in possessions of the United States.

Instructs Treasury to make payments to the territories that relate to the cost of each territory's EITC. The possessions must provide Treasury with annual reports on the estimate of costs and a statement of costs with respect to the preceding year.

Sec. 20126. Temporary special rule for determining earned income for purposes of earned income tax credit.

Allows taxpayers in 2020, for purposes of computing the EITC, to substitute their 2019 earned income for their 2020 earned income if their 2020 earned income is less than their 2019 earned income.

SUBTITLE D – CHILD TAX CREDIT

Sec. 20131. Child tax credit improvements for 2020.

Makes the child tax credit ("CTC") fully refundable for 2020 and increases the amount to $3,000 per child ($3,600 for a child under age 6). The provision also makes 17-year-olds qualifying children. The provision requires the Secretary to make best efforts to provide the enhanced credit in the form of an advanced payment.

Sec. 20132. Application of child tax credit in territories.

Instructs Treasury to make payments to each "mirror code" territory for the cost of the territories' CTC. This amount is determined by Treasury based on information provided by the territorial governments. Puerto Rico, which does not have a mirror code, will receive the refundable CTC by having its residents file for the CTC with the IRS. For American Samoa, which does not have a mirror code, Treasury is instructed to make payments in an amount estimated by Treasury as being equal to the aggregate benefits that would have been provided if American Samoa had a mirror code in place.

SUBTITLE E – DEPENDENT CARE ASSISTANCE

Sec. 20141. Refundability and enhancement of child and dependent care tax credit for 2020.

Makes the child and dependent care tax credit ("CDCTC") fully refundable for 2020 and increases the maximum credit rate to 50 percent. Amends the phaseout threshold to begin at $120,000 instead of $15,000. Doubles the amount of child and dependent care expenses that are eligible for the credit to $6,000 for one qualifying individual and $12,000 for two or more qualifying individuals.

Sec. 20142. Increase in exclusion for employer-provided dependent care assistance for 2020.

Increases the exclusion for employer-provided dependent care assistance from $5,000 to $10,500 (from $2,500 to $5,250 in the case of a separate return filed by a married individual) for 2020.

SUBTITLE F – FLEXIBILITY FOR CERTAIN EMPLOYEE BENEFITS

Sec. 20151. Increase in carryover for health flexible spending arrangements in 2020. Permits cafeteria plans and health flexible spending arrangements to allow participants to carry over up to $2,750 in unused benefits or contributions from 2020 to 2021.

Sec. 20152. Carryover for dependent care flexible spending arrangements in 2020.

Permits cafeteria plans and dependent care flexible spending arrangements to allow participants to carry over up to the annual maximum amount of unused dependent care assistance benefits or contributions from 2020 to 2021.

Sec. 20153. Carryover of paid time off in 2020.

Permits cafeteria plans to allow participants to carry over unused paid time off from 2020 to 2021.

Sec. 20154. Change in election amount in 2020.

Permits cafeteria plans and health flexible spending arrangements to allow participants to make one-time elections for any reason to a health FSA or to the amount of paid time off. Such one- time election is allowed between the date of enactment and December 31, 2020.

Sec. 20155. Extension of grace periods, etc. in 2020.

Permits cafeteria plans, health flexible spending arrangements, and dependent care flexible spending arrangements to provide an extension of the grace period for the 2020 plan year to 12 months after the end of the 2020 plan year. Extension of the grace period will allow benefits or contributions from these plans or arrangements to be used for expenses incurred up to 12 months after the end of the plan year. Permits cafeteria plans and health flexible spending arrangements to allow employees who cease participation in the plan (e.g. due to being terminated) to continue to receive reimbursements from unused contributions for the rest of the plan year (including the grace period as extended above).

Sec. 20156. Plan amendments.

Permits retroactive amendments to cafeteria plans, health flexible spending arrangements, and dependent care arrangements for the purposes of this subtitle.

SUBTITLE G – DEDUCTION OF STATE AND LOCAL TAXES

Sec. 20161. Elimination for 2020 and 2021 of limitation on deduction of state and local taxes.

Eliminates the limitation on the deduction for state and local taxes for taxable years beginning on or after January 1, 2020 and on or before December 31, 2021.

Title II – Additional Relief For Workers

SUBTITLE A – ADDITIONAL RELIEF

Sec. 20201. Increase in above-the-line deduction for certain expenses of elementary and secondary school teachers.

Doubles the above-the-line deduction for certain unreimbursed out-of-pocket expenses for elementary and secondary school teachers from $250 to $500. This amount is adjusted for inflation.

Sec. 20202. Above-the-line deduction allowed for certain expenses of first responders.

Provides a $500 above-the-line deduction for unreimbursed expenses of professional first responders related to the cost of uniforms or tuition and fees related to training. This deduction is indexed to inflation.

Sec. 20203. Temporary above-the-line deduction for supplies and equipment of first responders and COVID-19 front-line employees.

Provides a $500 above-the-line deduction for 2020 for the uniforms, supplies, and equipment of first responders and COVID-19 front-line employees. COVID-19 front-line employees are those that perform at least 1,000 hours of essential work, as defined for pandemic premium pay reimbursable from the COVID-19 Heroes Fund.

Sec. 20204. Payroll credit for certain pandemic-related employee benefit expenses paid by employers.

Provides a 30% refundable payroll tax credit for expenses reimbursed or paid for the benefit of an employee for reasonable and necessary personal, family, living, or funeral expenses incurred as a result of the presidentially declared disaster related to COVID-19. The credit percentage is 50% for expenses paid to employees if a substantial portion of the services performed by the employee is essential work, as defined for pandemic premium pay reimbursable from the COVID-19 Heroes Fund. No credit is allowed if the expenses are provided in a manner which discriminates in favor of highly compensated employees. The Social Security and Railroad Retirement trust funds are held harmless under this provision, through a General Fund transfer of lost receipts as a result of this credit.

SUBTITLE B – TAX CREDITS TO PREVENT BUSINESS INTERUPTION

Sec. 20211. Improvements to employee retention credit.

Increases the applicable percentage of qualified wages reimbursed through the employee retention credit from 50% to 80%.

Modifies the gross receipts requirement to allow a partial credit, phased in for a decline in gross receipts between 10% and 50% compared to the same calendar quarter of the previous year.

Increases the limit on wages taken into account per employee from $10,000 for the year to $15,000 per quarter (limited to $45,000 for the calendar year).

Replaces the 100-employee delineation for determining the relevant qualified wage base with a definition of large employer. A large employer is an employer with greater than 1,500 full time employees and gross receipts of greater than $41,500,000 in 2019.

Allows state and local governments and certain federal instrumentalities to claim the credit in the event they are paying wages to employees while their operations are fully or partially shut down.

Clarifies that group health plan expenses can be considered qualified wages even when no other wages are paid to the employee, consistent with recent revisions to IRS guidance on this issue. This provision also clarifies that wages paid by an employer for lost tips will not trigger the wage limitation in section 2301(c)(3)(B) of the CARES Acts.

All provisions apply retroactively to the effective date included in section 2301 of the CARES Act.

Sec. 20212. Payroll credit for certain fixed expenses of employers subject to closure by reason of COVID-19.

Provides a 50% refundable payroll tax credit for qualified fixed costs. Qualified fixed costs include covered rent obligations, covered mortgage obligations, and covered utility payments. These terms have the same definitions as the definitions provided in section 1106 of the CARES Act, relating to forgiveness of Paycheck Protection Program loans. For each quarter, qualified expenses eligible for this credit are limited to 25% of qualified wages (as defined in the employee retention credit) or 6.25% of 2019 gross receipts (which annualizes to 25%), with a maximum of $50,000.

This credit is limited to employers with no more than 1,500 full-time equivalent employees or no more than $41,500,000 in gross receipts in 2019. Additionally, employers must be subject to a full or partial suspension due to a COVID-19 government order or have a decline in gross receipts of at least 20% compared to the same calendar quarter of the preceding year. This credit is phased in for employers with a decline in gross receipts between 10% and 50%.

The Social Security and Railroad Retirement trust funds are held harmless under this provision, through a General Fund transfer of lost receipts as a result of this credit.

The section applies to qualified fixed expenses paid or accrued from March 12, 2020 until December 31, 2020.

Sec. 20213. Business interruption credit for the self-employed.

Provides a 90% refundable individual income tax credit for certain self-employed individuals who have experienced a significant loss of income. The credit may be claimed on "qualified self-employment income" which is the loss in gross income for self-employment that exceeds a 10% reduction from 2019 to 2020, scaled using the ratio of net earnings from self-employment to gross income from self-employment in 2019. The amount of qualified self-employment income taken into account cannot exceed the reduction in adjusted gross income from 2019 to 2020, and is capped at $45,000. The credit phases out starting at $60,000 of adjusted gross income ($120,000 for married filing jointly) at a rate of $50 for every $100 of income.

SUBTITLE C – CREDITS FOR PAID SICK AND FAMILY LEAVE

Sec. 20221. Extension of credits.

Extends the refundable payroll tax credits for paid sick and family leave, enacted in the Families First Coronavirus Response Act, through the end of 2021. This provision is effective as if included in FFCRA.

Sec. 20222. Repeal of reduced rate of credit for certain leave.

Coordinates changes made to the requirement to provide paid sick time to allow employers to claim up to $511 per day, rather than $200 per day for leave for caregivers of individuals subject to a coronavirus related stay at home order and parents providing for children affected by a coronavirus related school closure. This provision applies to days on or after the date of enactment of this Act.

Sec. 20223. Increase in limitations on credits for paid family leave.

Coordinates changes made to the requirement to provide emergency paid family and medical leave to allow employers to claim up to $12,000 in refundable payroll tax credits, rather than $10,000. Allows individuals to claim the credit for a maximum of 60 days (corresponding to the $12,000 amount) rather than 50 days. This provision is effective as if included in FFCRA.

Sec. 20224. Election to use prior year net earnings from self-employment in determining average daily self-employment income.

Allows individuals to elect to use their average daily self-employment income from 2019 rather than 2020 to compute the credit. This provision is effective as if included in FFCRA.

Sec. 20225. Federal, state, and local governments allowed tax credits for paid sick and paid family and medical leave.

Removes the exclusion disallowing the paid sick and family leave credits enacted in the Families First Coronavirus Response Act for Federal, state, and local governments. It makes conforming changes to the definition of qualified wages to align the credit with the intent that the credit cover the leave required by the respective mandates. This provision is effective as if included in FFCRA.

Sec. 20226. Certain technical improvements.

Makes technical changes coordinating the definitions of qualified wages within the paid sick leave, paid family and medical leave, and the exclusion of such leave from employer OASDI tax. This provision is effective as if included in FFCRA.

Sec. 20227. Credits not allowed for certain large employers.

Provides that, notwithstanding other changes in this Act requiring that employers with 500 or more employees provide required paid sick leave and paid family and medical leave, these employers are not eligible for payroll tax credits for these wages. This restriction does not apply to federal, state, and local governments. This provision applies to wages paid after the date of enactment.

SUBTITLE D – OTHER RELIEF

Sec. 20231. Payroll tax deferral allowed for recipients of certain loan forgiveness.

Allows businesses receiving Paycheck Protection Program loan forgiveness to defer payment of payroll taxes under Section 2302 of the CARES Act.

Sec. 20232. Emergency financial aid grants.

Excludes emergency financial aid grants made to students from gross income and holds students harmless for purposes of determining eligibility for higher education tax incentives.

Sec. 20233. Certain loan forgiveness and other business financial assistance under CARES Act not includable in gross income.

Excludes certain loan forgiveness by the Small Business Administration, emergency EIDL grants, and certain loan payments from the gross income of the ultimate recipient.

Sec. 20234. Authority to waive certain information reporting requirements.

Provides the Secretary of the Treasury with the authority to waive information reporting requirements under Chapter 61 of the Code with respect to income that is exempt from tax as excludible loan forgiveness under the Paycheck Protection Program or under sections 332 or 333 of this Act.

Sec. 20235. Clarification of treatment of expenses paid or incurred with proceeds from certain grants and loans.

Clarifies that expenses paid or incurred with proceeds from Payment Protection Program loans that are forgiven pursuant to section 1106(b) of the CARES Act and certain loan forgiveness by Small Business Administration, emergency EIDL grants, and certain loan payments that are not included in gross income under section 333 of this Act do not result in a denial of any deduction or basis of any asset for federal tax purposes This provision also clarifies the order in which section 1106(i) of the CARES Act and relevant provisions of the Internal Revenue Code apply.

Sec. 20236. Reinstatement of certain protections for taxpayer return information.

Restores certain taxpayer protections under Section 6103 of the Internal Revenue Code that were modified by the CARES Act, retroactively effective as of the date of the FUTURE Act.

Title III – Net Operating Losses

Sec. 20301. Limitation on excess businesses losses of non-corporate taxpayers restored and made permanent.

Amends changes made by the CARES Act to section 461(l) of the Code, which provides that an excess business loss of a taxpayer (other than a corporation) is not allowed for a taxable year. Excess business losses are treated as net operating losses in the next succeeding taxable year. An excess business loss exists if taxpayer's total deductions from all trades or businesses exceed all income from such trades or businesses, plus $250,000 ($500,000 for joint filers). The CARES Act suspended this provision for taxable years beginning in 2018, 2019 and 2020. Under current law (as amended by CARES), this provision applies for taxable years beginning on or after January 1, 2021, and beginning before December 31, 2025. This section amends current law to apply the provision to taxable years beginning on or after January 1, 2018, as was the case before CARES passed. In addition, this section makes the provision permanent, and repeals section 461(j) of the Code as a deadwood provision. This provision is made effective retroactive to the date of enactment of the CARES Act.

Sec. 20302. Certain taxpayers allowed carryback of net operating losses arising in 2019 and 2020.

Amends the CARES Act changes to section 172 of the Code. Under current law (as amended by CARES), taxpayers with a loss in 2018, 2019 or 2020 may apply those losses to the preceding five taxable years. This section amends the provisions of CARES that provide for net operating loss carrybacks by limiting carrybacks to taxable years beginning on or after January 1, 2018. In addition, this provision prohibits taxpayers with excessive executive compensation or excessive stock buybacks and dividends from carrying back losses. This provision is made effective retroactive to the date of enactment of the CARES Act.

DIVISION C – Health Provisions

Prepared by the Democratic staff of the House Committees on Energy and Commerce, Ways and Means, and Education and Labor

Title I – Medicaid

Section 30101. FMAP increase. Increases Federal Medical Assistance Percentage (FMAP) payments to state Medicaid programs by a total of 14 percentage points starting July 1, 2020 through June 30, 2021.

Section 30102. MFAR. Prevents the Secretary of Health and Human Services (HHS) from finalizing the Medicaid Fiscal Accountability Regulation (MFAR) until the end of the COVID- 19 public health emergency.

Section 30103. Home and Community Based Services. Increases the federal payments to state Medicaid programs by an additional 10 percentage points starting July 1, 2020 through June 30, 2021 to support activities that strengthen their home- and community-based services (HCBS) benefit.

Section 30104. No cost-sharing for COVID-19 treatment. Eliminates cost sharing for Medicaid beneficiaries for COVID-19 treatment and vaccines during the COVID-19 public health emergency.

Section 30105. Covering the uninsured for COVID-19 treatment. Ensures that uninsured individuals whom states opt to cover through the new Medicaid eligibility pathway will be able to receive treatment for COVID-19 without cost-sharing during the COVID-19 public health emergency.

Section 30106. Temporary extension of 100 percent FMAP to Indian health providers.
Clarifies that services received through urban Indian providers are matched at 100 percent FMAP through June 30, 2021.

Section 30107. Medicaid coverage for citizens of Freely-Associated States.
Restores Medicaid eligibility to individuals who are residents of the freely-associated states.

Section 30108. Increase DSH payments. Temporarily increases Medicaid disproportionate share hospital (DSH) allotments by 2.5 percent.

Section30109. Extension of existing section 1115 demonstration projects.
Authorizes states with section 1115 demonstration projects that expire on or before February 28, 2021 to extend them through December 31, 2021.

Section 30110. Allowance for medical assistance under Medicaid for inmates during 30-day period preceding release. Provides Medicaid eligibility to incarcerated individuals 30 days prior to their release.

Section 30111. Non-emergency medical transportation. Codifies the regulatory requirement that state Medicaid programs cover non-emergency medical transportation (NEMT).

Title II – Medicare

Section 30201. Hold Medicare beneficiaries harmless for specified COVID-19 treatment services furnished under Part A or Part B of the Medicare program. Establishes zero cost- sharing (out-of-pocket costs) for COVID-19 treatment under Medicare Parts A and B during the COVID-19 public health emergency.

Section 30202. Ensure communications accessibility for residents of skilled nursing facilities during the COVID-19 emergency period. Ensures skilled nursing facilities provide a means for residents to conduct "televisitation" with loved ones while in-person visits are not possible during the COVID-19 public health emergency.

Section 30203. Medicare hospital inpatient prospective payment system expanded outlier payment for COVID-19 patients. Provides an outlier payment for inpatient claims for any amount over the traditional Medicare payment to cover excess costs hospitals incur for more expensive COVID-19 patients until January 31, 2021.

Section30204. Coverage of treatments for COVID–19 at no cost sharing under the Medicare Advantage program. Establishes zero cost-sharing (out-of-pocket costs) for COVID- 19 treatment under Medicare Advantage during the COVID-19 public health emergency.

Section 30205. Coverage under Prescription Drug Plans (PDPs) and Medicare Advantage- Prescription Drug plans (MA-PDPs) without cost-sharing. Requires coverage under Medicare PDPs and MA-PDPs without cost-sharing or Utilization Management Requirements for drugs intended to treat COVID-19 during the COVID-19 public health emergency.

Section 30206. Improve the Accelerated and Advance Payment Program. Lowers the interest rate for loans to Medicare providers made under the Accelerated and Advance Payment Program, reduces the per-claim recoupment percentage, and extends the period before repayment begins.

Section 30207. Create a new special enrollment period for Medicare. Creates a new special enrollment period for Medicare Parts A & B eligible individuals during the COVID-19 public health emergency.

Section 30208. Skilled nursing facility incentive payments. Provides incentives for nursing facilities to create COVID-19-specific facilities and includes safety and quality protections for patients.

Section 30209. Nursing home strike teams. Directs HHS to allocate money to the states to create strike teams to help facilities manage outbreaks when they occur.

Section 30210. Infection control in nursing facilities. Requires the Secretary of HHS to provide additional assistance to facilities struggling with infection control through Medicare's Quality Improvement Organizations (QIOs).

Section 30211. Nursing homes demographic data reporting. Requires HHS to collect data on COVID-19 in nursing homes and to publicly report demographic data on COVID-19 cases in nursing homes on *Nursing Home Compare*.

Section 30212. Imputed Rural Floor. Requires the Centers for Medicare and Medicaid Services (CMS) to re-establish a rural floor for the Medicare hospital area wage index for hospitals in all-urban states.

Title III – Private Insurance

Section 30301. Special enrollment period through exchanges; federal exchange outreach and Activities. Provides for a two-month open enrollment period to allow individuals who are uninsured, for whatever reason, to enroll in coverage. Currently, Americans can only enroll in an Affordable Care Act (ACA) plan during open enrollment period, or because of a qualifying life event if they were previously insured.

Section 30302. Ensuring access to COVID-19 prevention care. Requires the Advisory Committee on Immunization Practices (ACIP) to meet and provide a recommendation no later than 15 days after a COVID-19 vaccine is listed under the Public Health Service Act.

Section 30303. Coverage of COVID-19 related treatment at no cost sharing. Requires coverage of items and services related to the treatment of COVID-19 in group and individual market health plans and waives cost-sharing requirements for consumers during the COVID-19 public health emergency.

Section 30304. Requiring prescription drug refill notifications during emergencies. Requires group and individual market health plans to notify consumers if their plan permits advance prescription drug refills during an emergency period.

Section 30305. Improvement of certain notifications provided to qualified beneficiaries by group health plans in the case of qualifying events. Improves the information provided to workers who lose their employer-sponsored coverage so that they are aware of all affordable coverage options, including coverage available under the ACA.

Section 30306. Earlier coverage of testing for COVID-19. Makes the requirement for free coverage of COVID-19 testing retroactive to the beginning of the COVID-19 public health emergency.

Section 30307. Preserving health benefits for workers. Provides full premium subsidies, through January 2021, to allow workers to maintain their employer-sponsored coverage if they are eligible for COBRA due to a layoff or reduction in hours, and for workers who have been furloughed but are still active in their employer-sponsored plan.

Title IV – Other Health Provisions

Section 30401. Coverage of COVID-19 related treatment at no cost sharing in TRICARE.
Establishes zero cost-sharing (out-of-pocket costs) for COVID-19 treatment under TRICARE.

Section 30402. Coverage of COVID-19 related treatment at no cost sharing for Veterans.
Establishes zero cost-sharing (out-of-pocket costs) for COVID-19 treatment under the Department of Veterans Affairs health plans.

Section 30403. Coverage of COVID-19 related treatment at no cost sharing for Federal Civilians. Establishes zero cost-sharing (out-of-pocket costs) for COVID-19 treatment under the Federal Employee Health Benefit Program.

Title V – Public Health Subtitle A—Supply Chain Improvements

Section 30511. Medical Supplies Response Coordinator. Requires the President to appoint a Medical Supplies Response Coordinator. A Medical Supplies Response Coordinator would serve as the point of contact for the health care system, supply chain officials, and states on medical supplies, including personal protective equipment (PPE), medical devices, drugs, and vaccines. The appointee is required to have health care training and an understanding of medical supply chain logistics.

Section 30512. Information to be included in list of devices determined to be in shortage.
Clarifies that the medical device identifier or national product code shall be included with any required shortage reporting, which will help facilitate identification of acceptable alternatives.

Section 30513. Device shelf life dates. Provides authority to the Food and Drug Administration (FDA) to require manufacturers to provide the agency with information pertinent to an extension of medical device shelf life dates in cases of shortages or material slowdowns during public health emergencies.

Section 30514. Authority to destroy counterfeit devices. Extends FDA's administrative destruction authority to medical devices. This would allow FDA to destroy certain imported medical devices, such as counterfeit tests or masks, in instances where FDA believes such medical devices are adulterated, misbranded, or unapproved and may pose a threat to the public health as they currently do for drugs.

Section 30515. Reporting requirement for drug manufacturers. Requires drug manufacturers to report foreign drug manufacturing sites and to report quarterly on the volume of drugs manufactured.

Section 30516. Recommendations to encourage domestic manufacturing of critical drugs.
Requires National Academies of Science, Engineering, and Medicine (NASEM) to conduct a symposium of experts to discuss recommendations to encourage domestic manufacturing of critical drugs and devices of greatest priority to providing health care.

Section 30517. Failure to notify of a permanent discontinuance or an interruption. Provides FDA with an enforcement mechanism to require timely notifications related to a permanent discontinuance or interruption in the manufacturing of certain drugs and the reasons for such discontinuance or interruption, as required under current law.

Section 30518. Failure to develop risk management plan. Provides FDA with an enforcement mechanism to require drug manufacturers to develop a risk management plan, as required under current law

Section 30519. National Centers of Excellence in Continuous Pharmaceutical Manufacturing. Directs FDA to designate National Centers of Excellence in Continuous Pharmaceutical Manufacturing (NCEs). NCEs will work with FDA and industry to craft a national framework for the implementation of continuous manufacturing of drugs, including supporting additional research and development of this technology, workforce development, standardization, and collaborating with manufacturers to support adoption of continuous manufacturing of drugs.

Section 30520. Vaccine manufacturing and administration capacity. Requires the Secretary of HHS to award contracts, grants, cooperative agreements, and enter into other transactions, as appropriate, to expand and enhance manufacturing capacity of vaccines and vaccine candidates to prevent the spread of COVID-19. It also requires a report on the vaccine supply necessary to stop the spread of COVID-19, the manufacturing capacity to produce vaccines, activities conducted to enhance such capacity, and plans for continued support of vaccine manufacturing and administration.

Subtitle B—Strategic National Stockpile Improvements

Section 30531. Equipment maintenance. Requires the Secretary of HHS to ensure that contents of the Strategic National Stockpile (SNS) are in good working order and, as necessary, conduct maintenance on contests of the stockpile.

Section 30532. Supply chain flexibility manufacturing pilot. Improves the SNS domestic product availability by enhancing medical supply chain elasticity, improving the domestic production of PPE, and partnering with industry to refresh and replenish existing stocks of medical supplies.

Section 30533. Reimbursable transfers from Strategic National Stockpile. Improves the SNS financial security by allowing the SNS to sell products to other Federal departments or agencies within six months of product expiration.

Section 30534. Strategic National Stockpile action reporting. Requires the SNS to report to Congress about every request made to the SNS during the COVID-19 public health emergency and details regarding the outcomes of every request.

Section 30535. Improved, transparent processes for the Strategic National Stockpile.
Requires the SNS to develop improved, transparent processes for SNS requests and identify clear plans for future communication between the SNS and States.

Section 30536. GAO study on the feasibility and benefits of a Strategic National

Stockpile user fee agreement. Requires the Government Accountability Office (GAO) to conduct a study to investigate the public sector procurement process for single source materials from the SNS.

Subtitle C—Testing and Testing Infrastructure Improvements

Section 30541. COVID–19 testing strategy. Requires the Secretary of HHS to update the COVID-19 strategic testing plan required under the Paycheck Protection Program and Health Care Enhancement Act no later than June 15, 2020. The updated plan shall identify the types and levels of testing necessary to monitor and contribute to the control of COVID-19 and inform any reduction in social distancing. In addition, the updated strategic testing plan must include specific plans and benchmarks with clear timelines, regarding how to ensure sufficient availability and allocation of all testing materials and supplies, sufficient laboratory and personnel capacity, and specific guidelines to ensure adequate testing in vulnerable populations and populations at increased risk related to COVID-19, including older individuals, and rural and other underserved areas. This plan must also involve testing capacity in non-health care settings in order to help expand testing availability and make testing more accessible, as well as how to implement the testing strategy in a manner that will help to reduce disparities with respect to COVID-19.

Section 30542. Centralized testing information website. Requires the Secretary of HHS to establish and maintain a public, searchable website that lists all in vitro diagnostic and serological tests used in the United States to analyze critical specimens for detection of COVID- 19 or antibodies for the virus. The website will also list relevant information about the tests, including the sensitivity and specificity of the test and the numbers of tests available.

Section 30543. Manufacturer reporting of test distribution. Requires in vitro diagnostic test manufacturers to notify the Secretary of HHS with information regarding distribution of tests, including quantity distributed.

Section 30544. State testing report. Requires States authorizing the development of in vitro COVID-19 tests to provide the Secretary of HHS with a weekly report identifying all authorized laboratories and providing relevant information about the laboratories, including their testing capacity, listing of all authorized tests, and providing relevant information about such tests.

Section 30545. State listing of testing sites. Requires States receiving funding through this Act to establish a public, searchable webpage identifying and providing contact information for COVID-19 testing sites within the State.

Section 30546. Reporting of COVID–19 testing results. Requires every laboratory that performs or analyzes COVID-19 tests to submit daily reports to the Secretary of HHS. This information would then be required to be made available to the public in a searchable, electronic format.

Section 30547. GAO report on diagnostic tests. Requires a GAO report on the response of laboratories, diagnostic test manufacturers, state, local, Tribal, and territorial governments, and relevant federal agencies, related to the COVID-19 epidemic with respect to the development, regulatory evaluation, and deployment of diagnostic tests.

Section 30548. Public health data system transformation. Requires HHS to expand, enhance, and improve public health data systems used by the Centers for Disease Control and Prevention (CDC). This includes: grants to State, local, Tribal, or territorial public health departments for the modernization of public health data systems in order to assist public health departments in assessing current data infrastructure capabilities and gaps; to improve secure public health data collection, transmission, exchange, maintenance, and analysis; to enhance the interoperability of public health data systems; to support and train related personnel; to support earlier disease and health condition detection; and to develop and disseminate related information and improved electronic case reporting.

Section 30549. Pilot program to improve laboratory infrastructure. Authorizes grants to states and localities to improve, renovate, or modernize clinical laboratory infrastructure in order to help increase COVID-19 testing capacities.

Section 30551. Core public health infrastructure and activities for CDC. Authorizes $1 billion for CDC to expand and improve their core public health infrastructure and activities in order to address unmet and emerging public health needs.

Section 30550. Core public health infrastructure for State, local, and Tribal health departments. Authorizes $6 billion for public health departments to expand workforce, improve laboratory systems, health information systems, disease surveillance, and contact tracing capacity to account for the unprecedented spread of COVID-19.

Subtitle D—COVID-19 National Testing and Contact Tracing (CONTACT) Initiative

Section 30561. National system for COVID-19 testing, contact tracing, surveillance, containment and mitigation. Requires CDC to coordinate with State, local, Tribal, and territorial health departments to establish and implement a national evidence-based system for testing, contact tracing, surveillance, containment and mitigation of COVID-19, including offering guidance on voluntary isolation and quarantine of positive COVID-19 cases.

Section 30562. COVID-19 testing, contact tracing, surveillance, containment, and mitigation grants. Requires CDC to award grants to State, local, Tribal, and territorial health departments to carry out evidence-based systems for testing, contact tracing, surveillance, containment and mitigation of COVID-19. CDC shall provide a minimum level of funding for all State, local, Tribal, and territorial health departments, and prioritize additional funding for areas with high number of cases of COVID-19, areas with a surge in cases of COVID-19, and those proposing to serve high numbers of low-income and uninsured populations, including underserved populations. Funding shall be used to leverage or modernize existing systems, identify specific strategies for testing in medically underserved populations, establish culturally competent and multilingual strategies for contact tracing, hire and compensate a locally-sourced workforce, and support individuals who have been infected with or exposed to COVID-19.

Section 30563. COVID-19 testing, contact tracing, surveillance, containment, and mitigation guidance. Requires CDC and other relevant agencies to issue guidance, provide technical assistance and information, and establish clear communication pathways for State, local, Tribal, and territorial health departments for the establishment and maintenance of their testing, contact tracing, surveillance, containment, and mitigation systems.

Section 30564. Awareness campaign. Provides grants for a multilingual and culturally appropriate national, science-based COVID-19 campaign, to include information related to availability of testing and promote the importance of contact tracing. Grants can be issued to public or private entities, including faith-based organizations.

Section 30565. Research and development. Requires CDC, in collaboration with the National Institutes of Health (NIH), the Agency for Healthcare Research and Quality (AHRQ), FDA, and CMS to support research and development on efficient and effective testing, contact tracing, and surveillance strategies.

Section 30566. Grants to the Local Workforce Development System and Community-based Organizations. Authorizes grants to support the recruitment, placement, and training of individuals in COVID-19 contact tracing and related positions, with a focus on
recruiting from impacted local communities and building a culturally competent workforce. This section also provides for transitional assistance and support post-employment.

Section 30568. Authorization of Appropriations. Authorizes $75 billion for these efforts. **Subtitle E—Demographic Data and Supply Reporting Related to COVID-19**

Section 30571. COVID-19 reporting portal. Requires the Secretary of HHS, within 15 days, to establish and maintain an online portal for health entities to track and transmit data regarding their inventory and capacity related to COVID-19. This portal will enable hospitals and long- term care facilities to report their inventory related to PPE, medical supplies (like available ventilators and beds), and facility capacity (like number of needed doctors, nurses, and lab personnel). Facilities should be required to report these figures on a biweekly basis.

Section 30572. Regular CDC reporting on demographic data. Requires the Secretary of HHS, no later than 14 days following enactment, to update and make publicly available the report to Congress required by the Paycheck Protection and Health Care Enhancement Act on the collection of data on race, ethnicity, age, sex, and gender of individuals diagnosed with COVID- 19. The updated report must include how the Secretary will provide technical assistance to State, local, and territorial health departments to improve collection and reporting of demographic data, and requirements for the report to be updated every 30 days and to identify any barriers for such health departments in collecting such data.

Section 30573. Federal modernization for health inequities data. Authorizes funding to AHRQ, CDC, CMS, FDA, the Office of the National Coordinator for Health Information Technology, and NIH to modernize their data collection methods and infrastructure in order to increase data collection related health inequities.

Section 30574. Modernization of state and local health inequities data. Authorizes grants to state, local, and territorial health departments in order to support the modernization of data collection methods and infrastructure in order to increase data collection related health inequities.

Section 30575. Tribal funding to research health inequities, including COVID-19. Requires the Indian Health Service (IHS), in coordination with CDC and NIH, to conduct research and field studies to improve understanding of tribal health inequities.

Section 30576. CDC field studies pertaining to specific health inequities. Requires CDC to establish field studies to better understand health inequities that are not currently tracked by the Secretary of HHS.

Section 30577. Additional reporting to Congress on the race and ethnicity rates of COVID- 19 testing, hospitalization, and mortalities. Requires the Secretary of HHS, by August 1, to expand on the report to Congress as required by the Paycheck Protection Program and Health Care Enhancement Act describing the testing, positive diagnoses, hospitalization, intensive care admissions, mortality rates, associated with COVID–19, disaggregated by race, ethnicity, age, sex, and gender. The Secretary of HHS must also now propose evidence-based response strategies to reduce disparities related to COVID-19 and a final report in 2024.

Subtitle F— Miscellaneous

Makes technical corrections to the CARES Act.

Title VI – Public Health Assistance Subtitle A—Assistance to Providers and Health System

Section 30611. Health Care Provider Relief Fund. Codifies the CARES Act health care provider relief fund for the purposes of reimbursing eligible health care providers for expenses related to preventing, preparing for, and responding to COVID-19, as well as lost revenues that have resulted from the COVID-19 pandemic.

Section 30612. Public Health Workforce Loan Repayment Program. Establishes a loan repayment program to enhance recruitment and retention of state, local, tribal, and territorial public health department workforce.

Section 30613. Expanding capacity for health outcomes. Authorizes grants to expand the use of technology-enabled collaborative learning and capacity building models to respond to COVID-19. To be eligible for funding under this section, health entities must have experience providing services to rural, frontier, health professional shortage areas, medically underserved populations, or Indian Tribes.

Section 30614. Additional funding for Medical Reserve Corps. Authorizes additional funding for the Medical Reserve Corps (MRC), which is a national network of local volunteer units who engage their local communities to strengthen public health, reduce vulnerability, build resilience, and improve preparedness, response, and recovery capabilities.

Section 30615. Grants for schools of medicine in diverse and underserved areas. Authorizes grants to schools of medicine in rural, underserved, or Minority-Serving Institutions. Grants can be used to build new schools of medicine and expand, enhance, modernize, support existing schools of medicine. Funding priority is given to rural, underserved, or Minority-Serving Institutions, including Historically Black Colleges and Universities, Hispanic-Serving Institutions, Tribal Colleges and Universities, and Asian American and Pacific Islander Serving Institutions.

Section 30617. Longitudinal study on the impact of COVID-19 on recovered patients.

Directs NIH to carry out a study on the short- and long-term impact of COVID-19 on infected and recovered individuals.

Section 30618. Research on the mental health impact of COVID–19. Directs the NIH's National Institute of Mental Health to support research on the mental health consequences of COVID-19, including the impact on health care providers.

Section 30616. GAO study on public health workforce. Requires the GAO to conduct a study to investigate gaps, challenges, and recommended steps for improvement associated with the Federal, State, local, Tribal, and territorial public health workforce.

Section 30619. Emergency mental health and substance use training and technical assistance center. Establishes a technical assistance center at the Substance Abuse and Mental Health Services Administration (SAMHSA) that will support public or nonprofit entities and public health professionals seeking to establish or expand access to mental health and substance use services associated with the COVID-19 public health emergency.

Section 30620. Importance of the blood plasma supply. Updates the blood donation public awareness campaign authorized by the CARES Act to include blood plasma.

Subtitle B— Assistance for Individuals and Families

Section 30631. Reimbursement for additional health services relating to coronavirus.
Authorizes COVID-19 treatment to be reimbursed for uninsured individuals.

Section 30632. Centers for Disease Control and Prevention COVID–19 response line.
Requires CDC to maintain a toll-free telephone number to address public health questions related to COVID-19.

Section 30633. Grants to address substance use during COVID-19. Authorizes SAMHSA to award grants to support local, tribal, and state substance use efforts that need further assistance as a result of COVID-19.

Section 30634. Grants to support increased behavioral health needs due to COVID-19.
Authorizes SAMHSA to award grants to States, tribes, and community-based entities to enable such entities to increase capacity and support or enhance behavioral health services.

Subtitle C —Public Health Assistance to Tribes

Section 30641. Improving State, local, and Tribal public health security. Extends eligibility
for the CDC's Public Health Emergency Preparedness (PHEP) program to Tribes.

Section 30642. Provision of items to Indian programs and facilities. Guarantees IHS and other Tribal health organizations direct access to the Strategic National Stockpile, just like all 50 other states.

Section 30643. Ensure parity for urban Native veterans. Allows the Urban Indian Health Organizations (UIHO) to bill VA for care provided to qualified urban native veterans.

Section 30644. Ensure coverage for Native veterans. Clarifies VA coverage for Native Veterans who qualify for both VA benefits and IHS services.

DIVISION D – Retirement Provisions

Prepared by the Democratic staff of the House Committees on Ways and Means and Education and Labor

Sec. 100. Short title. The short title of the legislation is the Emergency Pension Plan Relief Act of 2020 ("EPPRA").

Title I – Relief for Multiemployer Pension Plans

Sec. 101. Special Partition Relief. About 10 million Americans participate in multiemployer pension plans and about 1.3 million of them are in plans that are quickly running out of money. Many of these troubled multiemployer plans cover workers who are on the front lines of the COVID-19 public health crisis, such as trucking, food processing, grocery store workers, and others. Even before the pandemic, workers, businesses, and retirees faced a crisis and were in dire need of our help. With work drying up around the country and the market downturn, the economic catastrophe resulting from COVID-19 has exacerbated the multiemployer pension crisis and threatened the hard-earned pensions of even more workers and retirees. This threatens to bankrupt the Pension Benefit Guaranty Corporation ("PBGC"), impose damaging liabilities on thousands of businesses, and devastate communities across the country.

Under current law, PBGC has limited authority to partition certain troubled multiemployer pension plans. In a partition, PBGC takes on the financial responsibility of some of the benefits of an eligible plan, so that the plan can stay solvent. EPPRA creates a special partition program that would expand PBGC's existing authority, increase the number of eligible plans, and simplify the application process—allowing more troubled plans to obtain much-needed relief. Just like the bipartisan Butch Lewis Act (H.R. 397), eligible plans would include: plans in critical and declining status, plans with significant underfunding with more retirees than active workers, plans that have suspended benefits, and certain plans that have already become insolvent. In contrast, EPPRA allows plans to become eligible for the special partition program through 2024. Because the COVID-19 crisis has already caused significant investment losses to pension plan assets and decreased the number of hours worked, plan funding may deteriorate over time. Consequently, plans may need to access the special partition relief program in coming years.

PBGC is required to issue regulations within 120 days of enactment of this legislation and may prioritize the processing of applications of plans most in need. A qualifying plan may apply to PBGC and, upon approval, would receive financial assistance. Under the special partition program, a plan would receive enough financial assistance to keep it solvent and well-funded for thirty years—with no cuts to the earned benefits of participants and beneficiaries. Plans that previously cut benefits would have to restore them to the retirees who earned them. In exchange for the financial assistance, each plan would have to comply with certain conditions, and would be required to file regular comprehensive reports to PBGC and to the Congressional committees of jurisdiction.

This legislation also includes important accountability and transparency provisions. PBGC would be required to annually report to Congress. The Government Accountability Office ("GAO") would be required to regularly evaluate PBGC's implementation and administration of the special partition relief program. PBGC's Inspector General would receive funding to audit the special partition relief program to prevent against waste, fraud, and abuse. PBGC would be required to establish and regularly update a user-friendly website so that plan administrators, employers, participants, beneficiaries, interested stakeholders, and the public can track the implementation and administration of the special partition relief program. Because PBGC currently receives no appropriations, the legislation includes additional funding to cover the costs of the program.

By stabilizing these pensions, the special partition relief program would protect retirees who worked for decades to earn their benefits. It would also help businesses avoid crushing liabilities and support communities around the country.

Sec. 102. Repeal of Benefit Suspensions for Multiemployer Plans in Critical and Declining Status. Upon date of enactment, no plan would be permitted to apply, or be approved, for a suspension of benefits under the Multiemployer Pension Reform Act ("MPRA"). This restores the promise of a secure retirement for millions of workers currently in danger. Going forward, no participant or beneficiary in a multiemployer pension plan would suffer a cut to their earned benefits under MPRA.

Sec. 103. Temporary Delay of Designation of Multiemployer Plans as in Endangered, Critical, or Critical and Declining Status. Under the legislation, a plan could retain its funding zone status as of a plan year beginning in 2019 for plan years that begin in 2020 or 2021. A plan in endangered or critical status would not have to update its plan or schedules until the plan year beginning March 1, 2021. This would provide a plan with flexibility and ease an administrative burden given the economic and financial turmoil resulting from the COVID-19 public health crisis.

Sec. 104. Temporary Extension of the Funding Improvement and Rehabilitation Periods for Multiemployer Pension Plans in Critical and Endangered Status for 2020 or 2021. Under the bill, a plan in endangered or critical status for a plan year beginning in 2020 or 2021 could extend its rehabilitation period by five years. This would give a plan additional time to improve its contribution rates, limit benefit accruals, and maintain plan funding—all on its own terms. This provision is effective for plan years beginning after December 31, 2019.

Sec. 105. Adjustments to Funding Standard Account Rules. Funding shortfalls as a result of investment losses are generally required to be made up over a period of 15 years. Following the financial crisis of 2008, multiemployer plans were allowed to amortize investment losses from 2008 or 2009 over a period of 30 years. Now, the market downturn resulting from the COVID-19 pandemic is already damaging the funding of multiemployer pension plans. Under the legislation, for investment losses in plan years beginning in 2019 and 2020, a plan could use a 30-year amortization base to spread out losses over time. Pension plans, participants, and plan sponsors need more stability and a longer period over which to pay for long-term liabilities that can stretch out for decades. This would help a plan weather this economic and financial storm. This provision is effective for plan years ending on or after February 29, 2020.

Sec. 106. PBGC Guarantee for Participants in Multiemployer Plans. PBGC provides a maximum guaranteed benefit of $12,870 to a participant in a multiemployer plan, if that participant had 30 years of service. The guarantee is 100% of the first $11 of the monthly benefit rate, plus 75% of the next $33 of the monthly benefit rate, multiplied by the participant's years of credited service. This legislation would double the guarantee to 100% of the first $15 in monthly benefits per year of service and 75% of the next $70 in monthly benefits per year of service, and indexes it thereafter. This would help participants and beneficiaries receive more of the benefits they earned through their hard work and service. All plans receiving financial assistance beginning December 16, 2014, would see the improved guarantee take effect. A plan that becomes insolvent in the future would be subject to the increased guarantee in the calendar year in which it becomes insolvent.

Title II – Relief for Single Employer Pension Plans

Sec. 201. Extended Amortization for Single Employer Plans. In light of an ongoing pattern of interest rate and market volatility due to the COVID-19 public health crisis, the current law requirement to amortize funding shortfalls over seven years is no longer appropriate. Pension plans, participants, and plan sponsors need more stability and a longer period over which to pay for long-term liabilities that can stretch out for more than 50 years. Accordingly, under the bill, the following rules would apply to all single employer pension plans, effective for plan years beginning after December 31, 2019:

All shortfall amortization bases for all plan years beginning before January 1, 2020 (and all shortfall amortization installments determined with respect to such bases) would be reduced to zero.

All shortfalls would be amortized over 15 years, rather than seven years.

Sec. 202. Extension of Pension Funding Stabilization Percentages for Single Employer Plans. In 2012, 2014, and 2015, Congress provided for pension interest rate smoothing in order to address concerns that historically low interest rates were creating inflated pension funding obligations, diverting corporate assets away from jobs and business recovery. Under interest rate smoothing, the interest rates used to value pension liabilities must be within 10% of 25-year interest rate averages. The smoothed interest rates would begin phasing out in 2021, with the 10% corridor around the 25-year interest rate averages increasing five percentage points each year until interest rates need only be within 30% of the 25-year averages. Because of this phase- out, smoothing would soon cease to have much effect. In order to preserve the stabilizing effects of smoothing:

The 10% interest rate corridor would be reduced to 5%, effective in 2020.

The phase-out of the 5% corridor would be delayed until 2026, at which point the corridor would, as under current law, increase by 5 percentage points each year until it attains 30% in 2030, where it would stay.

A 5% floor would be put on the 25-year interest rate averages. This floor would establish stability and predictability on a longer-term basis, so that interest rate variations do not create excessive volatility. In addition, this floor would protect funding rules from the extremes of interest rate movements.

This provision is effective for plan years beginning after December 31, 2019.

Title III – Other Retirement Related Provisions

Sec. 301. Waiver of Required Minimum Distributions for 2019. Under current law, generally
at the age of 72, individuals must take a required minimum distribution ("RMD") from their defined contribution plans and IRAs. Due to the market downturn resulting from the COVID-19 pandemic, the balances in these accounts have sharply decreased – in many instances, the market has reduced taxpayers' accounts more than what their RMD would have been. Therefore, the recently enacted CARES Act waived RMDs for 2020, allowing individuals to keep funds in their retirement plans. This provision expands this relief further by providing that 2019 RMDs would be waived for defined contribution plans and IRAs.

Sec. 302. Waiver of 60-Day Rule in case of Rollover of Otherwise Required Minimum Distributions in 2019 and 2020. This provision further expands the 2020 RMD relief in the CARES Act by providing that:

• The RMDs made for 2019 would be permitted to be rolled back to a plan or IRA without regard to the 60-day requirement if the rollover is made by November 30,

2020.

- RMDs made for 2020 would be permitted to be rolled back to a plan or IRA without regard to the 60-day requirement if the rollover is made by November 30, 2020.

Sec. 303. Employee Certification as to Eligibility for Increased CARES Act Loan Limits from Employer Plan. The CARES Act permits eligible retirement plans to rely on an employee's certification that the employee qualifies to receive a coronavirus-related distribution. Technically, it appears that a plan cannot rely on such a certification for purposes of determining whether an employee is eligible for the special loan rules. In past disaster relief, the IRS has generally permitted reliance on reasonable representations by an employee in a similar context, absent actual knowledge to the contrary. But in the past, the statute has not had a specific employee certification provision that applies for distributions but not loans. This provision provides a statutory clarification.

Sec. 304. Exclusion of Benefits Provided to Volunteer Firefighters and Emergency Medical Responders Made Permanent. Almost 70 percent of firefighters and emergency medical services ("EMS") personnel are volunteers, 71 percent of fire departments are exclusively staffed by volunteers, and 91 percent of all US fire department use volunteer firefighters and EMTs to some degree. Therefore, at the end of last year, the SECURE Act reinstated for one year the exclusionsforqualifiedStateorlocaltaxbenefitsand qualifiedreimbursementpayments provided to members of qualified volunteer emergency response organizations and increases the exclusion for qualified reimbursement payments to $50 for each month during which a volunteer performs services. This would allow volunteer fire and EMS personnel for 2020 to receive nominal recruitment and retention incentives without those incentives being considered as taxable income. The COVID-19 pandemic places an enormous amount of strain on these volunteer personnel as they are exposing themselves to COVID-19 and are responding to a much higher than normal call volume. Therefore, the provision would make permanent these amendments to Code Section 139B.

Sec. 305. Application of Special Rules to Money Purchase Pension Plans. The CARES Act provided for early distribution and loan relief for retirement plans during the coronavirus relief period. While this relief was intended to apply to all qualified retirement plans, there were questions as to whether it would apply to money purchase pension plans ("MPPP"). MPPPs are a type of defined-contribution retirement plan offered by some employers. This provision would clarify that MPPPs would benefit from the legislation.

Sec. 306. Grants to Assist Low-Income Women and Survivors of Domestic Violence in Obtaining Qualified Domestic Relations Orders. Certain states under stay-at-home orders have seen domestic violence rates rise as much as 30 percent since the beginning of the COVID- 19 pandemic. This provision directs the Secretary of Labor, acting through the Director of the Women's Bureau in conjunction with the Assistant Secretary of the Employee Benefits Security Administration, to award grants of at least $250,000 to established community-based organizations on a competitive basis to assist low-income women and survivors of domestic violence in obtaining qualified domestic relations orders to ensure that these women actually obtain the benefits to which they are entitled through those orders.

Sec. 307. Modification of Special Rules for Minimum Funding Standards for Community Newspaper Plans. Community newspapers are generally family-owned, non-publicly traded, independent newspapers. The recently enacted SECURE Act provided pension funding relief for a number of community newspaper plan sponsors by increasing the interest rate to calculate those funding obligations to 8%. Additionally, the SECURE Act provided for a longer amortization period of 30 years from 7 years. These two changes enable struggling community newspapers to stretch out their required pension plan contributions over a longer time period. The legislation would expand the SECURE Act relief to additional community newspapers.

Sec. 308. Minimum Rate of Interest for Certain Determinations Related to Life Insurance Contracts. In order to qualify as life insurance contracts for tax purposes, permanent life insurance policies must meet several requirements under Internal Revenue Code section 7702. These requirements include two interest rate assumptions for determining the premiums that can be used to fund the contracts. The interest rate assumptions were set by statute at 4 percent and 6 percent when the requirements were put in place in 1984. At the time, the average long-term Treasury rate was around 12 percent. The recent public health and economic crisis has prompted the Federal Reserve to reduce already persistently low interest rates to around 0 percent, and the daily long-term Treasury rate has hovered at 1 percent. Without adjusting the section 7702 interest rates to reflect economic realities, consumer access to financial security via permanent life insurance policies—which represent approximately 60 percent of the individual life insurance market—could decrease significantly. This legislation updates section 7702 to reflect the interest rate environment that has been exacerbated by the current crisis, and ensures that the rates will continue to appropriately reflect economic conditions, by tying the rates to either a floating rate prescribed in the National Association of Insurance Commissioners' Standard Valuation Law or a floating rate based on the average applicable Federal mid-term rates over a 60-month period.

DIVISION E – Continued Assistance to Unemployed Workers
Prepared by the Democratic staff of the House Committee on Ways and Means
Sec. 101. Extension of Federal Pandemic Unemployment Compensation (FPUC).
Subsection (a).
This subsection would extend the $600 per week FPUC supplement to state and federal unemployment benefits through January 31, 2021. It would also add a transition rule (sometimes called a "soft cutoff") to allow individuals already receiving regular state unemployment benefits on January 31 to continue receiving the FPUC supplement until the end of the period of benefits to which they are entitled so long as they would end by March 31, 2021.
Subsection (b).
This subsection would require federal programs and state and local programs which receive any federal funding to disregard FPUC payments when calculating income for the purposes of determining eligibility for benefits or assistance, and to exclude it from resource limits for 9 months following receipt.
Sec. 102. Extension and benefit phaseout rule for Pandemic Unemployment Assistance.

This section would extend Pandemic Unemployment Assistance benefits (PUA) provided to workers who do not qualify for regular unemployment compensation through January 31, 2021. Under this provision, workers would be able to apply for PUA through January 31, 2021. Individuals would receive all of the weeks of benefits they so long as they are for weeks ending by March 31, 2021.

Sec. 103. Extension and benefit phaseout rule for Pandemic Extended Unemployment Compensation. This section would extend Pandemic Extended Unemployment Compensation (PEUC), which provides 13 additional weeks of unemployment benefits to individuals who have exhausted other benefits, through January 31, 2021. Workers would be able to apply for PEUC through January 31, 2021, and to receive the full 13 weeks so long as they are for weeks ending no later than March 31, 2021.

Sec. 104. Extension of full federal funding for the first week of compensable regular unemployment for states with no waiting week. This section would extend the provision in the CARES Act which reimbursed states that waived the "waiting week" for the first week of regular unemployment compensation through January 31, 2021.

Sec. 105. Extension of emergency relief and technical corrections for governmental entities and nonprofit organizations. This section would extend the financial relief provided to reimbursable employers in the CARES Act through January 31, 2021, and make technical corrections to ensure that states can simply waive 50 percent of the amount owed by such employers.

Sec. 106. Reduction of state administrative burden in determination of amount of Pandemic Unemployment Assistance (PUA). This clarifies state flexibility to use the most readily available sources of income verification for PUA applicants, including data from the mobile apps used by many gig workers.

Sec. 107. Extension of temporary assistance to states with advances. The Families First Coronavirus Response Act provided states with interest-free loans through December 31, 2020. This provision extends that duration through June 30, 2021.

Sec. 108. Extension of full federal funding of extended unemployment compensation. The Families First Coronavirus Response Act increased federal reimbursement for extended unemployment compensation (EB) from 50 percent to 100 percent for benefits provided through December 31, 2020. This section extends the 100 percent reimbursement to cover benefits paid through June 30, 2021.

Sec. 109. Extension of temporary financing of Short-Time Compensation payments to states with programs in law. This section would extend the period in which payments under short-time compensation programs in state law were 100 percent federally reimbursable through January 31, 2021.

Sec. 110. Extension of temporary financing of Short-Time Compensation payments. This section would extend the 50 percent reimbursement for Short-Time Compensation payments not made under a state law through January 31, 2021.

Sec. 111. Grace period for full financing of new short-time compensation programs. This provision ensures that any states that enacts a short-time compensation (STC) law will receive full federal financing for all agreements in place after March 29, even if agreement began before a new state STC law became effective.

DIVISION F – Assistance to Agricultural Producers and Other Matters Relating

to Agriculture
Prepared by the Democratic staff of the House Committee on Agriculture
Title I – Livestock
Section 60101. Ensures livestock producers are paid for their animals by requiring dealer trusts, for the benefit of all unpaid cash sellers of livestock.
Section 60102. Provides emergency assistance to support livestock producers who are forced to euthanize market-ready livestock due to local processing plant disruptions because of COVID- 19.
Section 60103. Provides $300 million to support improved animal health surveillance and laboratories, some of which are performing COVID-19 tests in this public health emergency.
Title II – Dairy
Section 60201. Establishes a direct dairy donation program to prevent dumped milk and
facilitate rapid donations of displaced dairy products directly to feeding programs. Milk associated with donated products would be reimbursed at current Class I prices.
Section 60202. Provides necessary cash flow assistance to small and mid-sized dairies that have grown over the last seven years by establishing supplemental margin coverage based on the difference between 2019 actual production and Dairy Margin Coverage production history.
Section 60203. Authorizes an USDA recourse loan program for dairy processors, packagers, merchants, marketers, wholesalers, and distributors.
Section 60204. Reduces the cost of Dairy Margin Coverage premiums for operations that commit to participating in the program for 2021-2023 by providing a payment worth 15% of annual premium costs.
Title III – Specialty Crops and Other Commodities
Section 60301. Provides $100 million in additional funding to address COVID-19 specialty crop supply chain issues at the state level via Specialty Crop Block Grant Program. Temporarily waives matching requirements for these additional funds.
Section 60302. Provides $50 million in additional funding to support local farmers, farmers markets, and other local food outlets who are impacted by COVID-19 market disruptions. Temporarily waives matching requirements for these additional funds.
Section 60303. Provides $50 million to support beginning farmers and ranchers with financial, operational, and marketing advice in this difficult market. Temporarily waives matching requirements for these additional funds.
Section 60304. Provides $28 million to be distributed as block grants to State departments of agriculture for use to support existing farm stress programs.
Section 60305. Provides support for renewable fuels and cotton textile mills.
Section 60306. Provides $16.5 billion for direct payments to agricultural producers.
Title IV – Commodity Credit Corporation
Section 60401. Amends the CCC Charter Act to add authority for the Secretary to deal with removal and disposal of livestock and poultry due to supply chain interruption during a public health emergency. Amends the CCC Charter Act to add authority to provide assistance to agricultural processing plants in the event of a public health emergency in order to assure the continuation of markets for

agricultural commodities

Section 60402. Amends the CCC Charter Act to require Congressional notification before disbursement of CCC funding.

Title V – Conservation

Section 60501. Expands the Conservation Reserve Program Soil Health Incentive Pilot Program to 5 million acres.

Title VI – Nutrition

Section 60601. Definitions.

Section 60602. Provides $25 million for Farm to Food Bank and makes program improvements
for these additional funds.

Section 60603. Waives the non-Federal match requirement for TEFAP administrative funds.

Section 60604. Provides additional administrative flexibilities for the Senior Farmers Market Nutrition Program.

Section 60605. Provides flexibilities for the Food Distribution Program on Indian Reservations.

Section 60606. Increases the SNAP benefit level by 15%. Excludes the Pandemic Unemployment Compensation as countable income for SNAP benefit calculation. Increases the minimum SNAP benefit to $30 per month. Waives all work requirements for SNAP and prevents funding for USDA to implement or finalize the Able-Bodied Adults Without Dependents, Broad Based Categorical Eligibility, and Standard Utility Allowance rules. Provides additional funding to States for SNAP administration this fiscal year, to meet the increased need for SNAP.

Section 60607. Directs USDA to allow the use of SNAP to purchase hot foods or hot food products ready for immediate consumption from authorized retail food stores.

Section 60608. Provides flexibility for SNAP Nutrition Education.

DIVISION G – Accountability and Government Operations

Prepared by the Democratic staff of the House Committee on Oversight and Reform

Title I – Accountability

Sec. 70101. Membership of the Pandemic Response Accountability Committee.
This section would provide the Chair of the Council of the Inspectors General for Accountability and Efficiency greater flexibility in choosing a Chair of the Committee by expanding the Inspectors General eligible to be named Chair of the Committee to all Inspectors General on the Committee.

Sec. 70102. Congressional Notification of Change in Status of Inspector General.
This section would require the President to notify Congress 30 days prior to placing an Inspector General in paid or unpaid non-duty status (administrative leave).

Sec. 70103. Presidential Explanation of Failure to Nominate an Inspector General.
This section would require the President to inform Congress of the reasons for not filling a vacancy in an Inspector General position if that position is vacant for more than 210 days.

Sec. 70104. Inspector General Independence.
This section would allow an Inspector General to be removed only for specified

causes including permanent incapacity, inefficiency, neglect of duty, malfeasance, conviction of a felony or conduct involving moral turpitude, knowing violation of a law, rule, or regulation, gross mismanagement, gross waste of funds, or abuse of authority.

Sec. 70105. U.S. Postal Service Inspector General Oversight Responsibilities.

This section would require the Postal Service Inspector General to conduct audits and investigations of activities carried out with funds provided by this Act.

Title II – Census Matters

Sec. 70201. Modification of 2020 Census Deadlines and Tabulation of Population

This section would implement an Administration request to allow a delay of the publication of apportionment and state redistricting data by 120 days. The delay is necessary due to the postponement of major census operations caused by the coronavirus. The section also requires the Census Bureau to use the same data quality standards used for the 2010 Census.

Sec. 70202. Reporting Requirement for the 2020 Census.

This section would require monthly reporting by the Census Bureau to the House Committee on Oversight and Reform, the Senate Committee on Homeland Security and Governmental Affairs, the Appropriations Committees of the House and Senate of detailed operational information about the 2020 Census.

Sec. 70203. Providing the Bureau of the Census Access to Information from Institutions of Higher Education.

This section would clarify that colleges and universities are permitted to provide the Census Bureau information about students living on campus for purposes of responding to the 2020 Census. With many colleges closed due to the coronavirus outbreak, this section would ensure that the Census Bureau will still be able to get an accurate of count of students by receiving information directly from schools. This section would require schools to provide ten days public notice and an opportunity for students to opt-out before transmitting this information. This section would apply only to the 2020 Census.

Sec. 70204. Limitation on Producing Non-Census Data in Connection with 2020 Census.

This section would prohibit the compiling or production of any data products in connection with the 2020 Census based on data that is not collected during the 2020 Census, except for data products that are required by 13 U.S.C. 141(b) and (c), use the same methodology as a tabulation produced by the Census Bureau prior to January 1, 2019, or use a methodology finalized and made public prior to January 1, 2018.

Title III – Federal Workforce

Sec. 70301. Teleworking Requirements for Federal Employees.

This section would require agency leaders to allow telework for all eligible federal employees during the coronavirus pandemic. The provisions would require agencies to expand telework by creating incentives to increase its use and disincentives to reducing it.

Sec. 70302. Retirement for Certain Employees

This section would allow federal first responders to stay in their current retirement plans if they are unable to meet the physical requirements of their position due to exposure to the coronavirus and are moved to other jobs in the civil service as a result.

Sec. 70303. Workers' Compensation for Certain Federal Employees Diagnosed with Coronavirus. This section would create a presumption that the coronavirus was contracted in the workplace for employees whose duties require substantial contact with the public.

Title IV – Federal Contractors

Sec. 70401. Mandatory Telework.

This section would mandate that agencies allow contractor personnel to telework during the coronavirus health emergency if their work can be conducted remotely and to provide periodic reports to Congress.

Sec. 70402. Guidance on the Implementation of Section 3610 of the CARES Act. This section would require OMB to issue governmentwide guidance to implement Section 3610 of the CARES Act, which allows agencies to reimburse contractors to keep their employees and subcontractors in a ready state.

Sec. 70403. Past Performance Ratings.

This section would ensure that contractors are not penalized by adverse performance ratings due to contract disruptions caused by the coronavirus crisis.

Sec. 70404. Accelerated Payments.

This section would require contracting officers to pay prime contractors within 15 days of the submission of an invoice.

Title V – District of Columbia

Sec. 70501. Special Borrowing Authority by the District of Columbia.

This section would authorize the District of Columbia to participate in the Municipal Liquidity Facility (MLF) established by the Federal Reserve to support lending to states, cities, and counties in response to the coronavirus, as well as in any future such facilities. Under the rules of the MLF, the District is expressly eligible to participate, but the District Home Rule Act does not authorize the District to so.

Title VI – Other Matters

Sec. 70601. Estimates of Aggregate Economic Growth Across Income Groups

This section would require the Bureau of Economic Analysis to include in its quarterly and annual reports on Gross Domestic Product and estimate of the impact on each decile of income and the highest 1% of income.

Sec. 70602. Waiver of Matching Funds Requirement for the Drug Free Community Support Program.

This section would allow the Administrator of the Office of National Drug Control Policy to modify or waive the matching requirements for Drug Free Community grants for the duration of the coronavirus emergency.

Sec. 70603. U.S. Postal Service Borrowing Authority

This section would repeal certain restrictions on the $10 billion in borrowing authority provided to the U.S. Postal Service in the CARES Act.

DIVISION H – Veterans and Servicemembers Provisions

Prepared by the Democratic staff of the House Committee on Veterans' Affairs

Section 80001. Technical correction authorizing existing salaries for senior health care leaders at VA. Clarifies a conflict in the law that caused senior VA health care leaders to be paid at a rate above a statutory pay cap for over 10 years.

Section 80002. Increase in aid and attendance for disabled veterans during the COVID-19 public health emergency. Increases by 25% the amount being paid to disabled veterans to assist with daily activities including purchase of personal protective equipment for veterans and their caregivers or home health aides.

Section 80003. No copays for COVID-19 preventative services at VA medical facilities.
Eliminates the payment of copays or cost-sharing for preventative treatment or services for COVID-19, including the administration of a vaccine.

Section 80004. Grant Per Diem for children of homeless veterans. Authorizes VA to provide reimbursements to social service providers receiving grants for the costs of services for minor children of homeless veterans. This provision would modify the calculation of grants to providers to ensure children are included in calculations.

Section 80005. Streamlining payment of emergency care claims to community providers during the COVID-19 public health emergency. Grants prior authorization for any emergency care sought by veterans at non-VA hospitals, including COVID-19-related diagnosis and treatment, and ambulance transportation.

Section 80006. Flexibility for the VA to care for homeless veterans during the COVID-19 public health emergency. Allows VA to provide transportation, purchase food, shelter, telecommunication equipment, clothing, blankets, and toiletry items for homeless veterans.

Authorizes VA to setup homeless encampments on the grounds of VAMCs during a public health emergency, and make improvements to allow homeless veterans to stay temporarily in VA parking lots.

Amends the CARES Act to expedite additional funding for Grant Per Diem (GPD) providers and the award of additional grants to service providers. Authorizes Grant Per Diem providers to use per diem payments for food, basic supplies, and housing to assist homeless veterans and formerly homeless veterans to self-isolate during a public health emergency.

Section 80007. Streamlining provision of HUD-VASH vouchers to homeless veterans during the COVID-19 pandemic. Allows public housing agencies administering HUD-VASH rental assistance vouchers to process applications electronically and waive in-person inspection requirements to rapidly house veterans during the COVID-19 public health emergency.

Section 80008. Lease protections for military servicemembers under stop-movement orders during the COVID-19 pandemic. Allows servicemembers to terminate home and vehicle leases, without penalty when a servicemember under orders to report to a new duty station receives a stop movement order of at least 30 days.

Section 80009. Cable, internet, and telephone contract protections for military servicemembers under stop-movement orders during the COVID-19 pandemic. Allows servicemembers to terminate cable, internet, and phone contracts without penalty when a servicemember under orders to report to a new duty station receives a stop movement order of at least 30 days.

Section 80010. Cable, internet, and telephone contract protections for military servicemembers and their families due to death or catastrophic disability. Authorizes the families of fallen and catastrophically injured servicemembers to terminate their phone, television, or internet contracts, without being financially penalized.

Section 80011. Housing and vehicle lease protections for military servicemembers and their families due to death or catastrophic disability. Authorizes the families of fallen and catastrophically injured servicemembers to terminate their housing and vehicle leases without being financially penalized.

Section 80012. Suspension of VA debt collection activities during the COVID-19 public health emergency. Prohibits the Secretary from taking enforcement actions to collect payments for benefit debts, establishing new benefit debts, sending notices regarding benefit debts to individuals or consumer reporting agencies, allowing interest to accrue on benefit debts, or applying administrative fees on benefit debts. Suspension of debt collection applies for 60 days past the end of the COVID-19 public health emergency.

Section 80013. Extending deadlines for veterans to file claims and appeals for VA benefits.
Extends the deadline for veterans to file claims and appeals for VA benefits, including disability compensation, during the COVID-19 public health emergency and 90 days after the emergency has ended.

Section 80014. VA health care for veterans without health insurance. Authorizes veterans without a disability but determined to have a financial hardship to qualify for enrollment in VA's health care system, and be exempt from payment of hospital and medical care copays.

Section 80015. Coverage of COVID-19 related treatment at no cost sharing for Veterans.
Establishes zero cost-sharing (out-of-pocket costs) for COVID-19 treatment under the Department of Veterans Affairs health plans.

Section 80016. Vet Center mental health care and services for National Guard and Reserve members responding to the COVID-19 public health emergency.
Permits any National Guard or Reserve member to receive mental health care at Vet Centers if deployed for more than 14 days in support of the COVID-19 public health emergency.

DIVISION I – Small Business Provisions
Prepared by the Democratic staff of the House Committee on Small Business
Section 90001: Amendments to PPP.
- (a) Extension of the covered period from June 30 to December 31;
- (b) Clarifies the definition of a tribal business concern to prevent them from being held to inapplicable HUBZone requirements;
- (c) Makes a technical clarification to ensure hospitals in bankruptcy still qualify for PPP
loans due to the essential nature of their operations;
- (d) Extends eligibility to all nonprofits of all sizes and clarifies the eligibility of housing
cooperatives;
- (e) Clarifies the inclusion of small, local news broadcast entities;
- (f) Clarifies that loan terms extend through the end of the covered period;
- (g) Establishes a minimum maturity on PPP loans of 5 years to enable borrowers to
amortize loans over a longer period of time, which lowers monthly payments;
- (h) Clarifies that PPP loans cannot be calculated on a compound basis, saving borrowers

money over the long-term;

• (i) Modifications to PPP Funds, including

o A carve out of 25% of the existing funds on the date of enactment to be used specifically for small businesses with 10 or fewer employees to guarantee they are fully able to access PPP assistance;

o A carve out of 25% of the existing funds on the date of enactment solely for the use of all nonprofits, no matter their size or type but requiring that at least half this amount go to small nonprofits under the 500-employee threshold;

o Establishes an additional set aside of existing funds of the lesser of 25% or $10 billion specifically for community financial institutions, such as Community Development Financial Institutions (CDFIs), Minority Development Institutions (MDIs), SBA microlenders, and SBA Certified Development Companies (CDCs); and

o Mandates that any returned amounts due to the cancellation of a covered loan shall be redistributed through loans to small businesses with 10 or fewer employees.

• (j) Alleviates burdens to borrowers deemed ineligible due to prior criminal history; and

• (k) Establishes technical assistance grants for small community financial institutions and

small depository institutions and credits with assets of less than $10 billion; and •

(l) Makes a technical amendment to a section title.

Section 90002: Commitments for PPP. Bifurcates the SBA's traditional lending authority in the 7(a) program from that of the PPP authority to certify the 7(a) lending program continues operation after PPP appropriations run out.

Section 90003: Inclusion of SCORE and Veteran Business Outreach Centers in Entrepreneurial Development Programs. Includes SCORE and Veteran Business Outreach Centers (VBOCs) as eligible SBA entrepreneurial development resource partners so they can access $10 million each in previously appropriated sums for the purpose of assisting businesses during the pandemic.

Section 90004: Amendments to PPP Loan Forgiveness.

• (a) Adds flexibility in the covered period for borrowers by extending the 8-week period to 24 weeks and extends the covered period from June 30 to December 31;

• (b) Harmonizes the use of proceeds with forgiveness;

• (c) Mandates forgiveness data collection and reporting;

• (d) Creates a safe harbor for borrowers who cannot rehire in the prescribed timeframe;

• (e) Eliminates the 75/25 rule on use of loan proceeds; and

• (f) Clarifies the hold harmless provision for lenders.

Section 90005: Improved Coordination Between PPP and Employee Retention Tax Credit.

Clarifies the coordination between the Employee Retention Tax Credit and the PPP loans to ensure borrowers can take advantage of both types of assistance.

Section 90006: Taxability of Subsidy for Certain Loan Payments. Ensures the principal and interest loan assistance is not treated as taxable income to small business borrowers.

Section 90007: Prohibiting Conflicts of Interest for Small Business Programs under the CARES ACT. Clarifies that the conflict of interest standards set forth in the law apply to PPP funds.

Section 90008: Flexibility in Deferral of Payments of 7(a) Loans. Allows the SBA Administrator to give lenders the ability to extend loan deferments, including payment of principal and interest for one year if the borrower provides documentation justifying the additional deferment and gives the Administrator the ability to purchase the loan in order to provide the stated relief if the loan cannot be purchased on the secondary market.

Section 90009: Certain Criminal Violations and Disaster Loan Applications. Alleviates burdens to disaster loan borrowers deemed ineligible due to prior criminal history.

Section 90010: Temporary Fee Reductions. Reduces the cost of capital by waiving fees associated with the SBA 7(a) and 504 loan programs for borrowers and lenders, including the Community Advantage and Export loan programs.

Section 90011: Guarantee Amounts. Incentivizes lenders to make loans by temporarily increasing the guarantee up to 90% on 7(a) loans and for 504 loans, increasing the guarantee to 90% on loans up to $350,000 and 75% on loans greater than $350,000.

Section 90012: Maximum Loan Amount for 7(a) Loans. Expands the pool of availability capital for small firms by increasing the annual lending limit of the 7(a) program from $30 billion to $75 billion.

Section 90013: Maximum Loan Amount for 504 Loans. Enhances the 504 refinance program to reach more small businesses who need to refinance expensive fixed assets and lower their payments.

Section 90014: Recovery Assistance Under the Microloan Program. Boosts the SBA microloan program with an additional $72 million in loans, increase how much each lender can loan from $6 million to $10 million, and give borrowers an extra two years to repay.

Section 90015: Cybersecurity Awareness Reporting. Strengthens the cybersecurity of the Small Business Administration by directing SBA to issue reports that assess its cybersecurity infrastructure and reporting cyber-threats, breaches, and cyber-attacks.

Section 90016: Reporting on Small Business Programs under the CARES Act. Requires mandatory regular reporting by the SBA on a number of specific demographic, industry, size, and geographic data points for PPP loans and EIDL loans and grants.

Section 90017: Funding for Resources and Services in Languages other than English. Mandates the SBA use previously allocated funds for purposes of translations services for all materials, applications, and websites related to COVID-19.

Section 90018: Direct Appropriations. Directs appropriations of $500 million to carry out fee waivers and guarantee increases for the traditional SBA 7(a) and 504 programs. It also appropriates $57 million for microloans and technical assistance.

DIVISION J – Support for Essential Workers, At-Risk Individuals, Families, and Communities

Prepared by the Democratic staff of the House Committee on Ways and Means
Title I – Family Care for Essential Workers Sec. 100101. Family Care for Essential Workers.

Subsection (a). Increase in Funding.

This section increases the overall authorization level for the Social Services Block Grant (SSBG) to $12.15 billion in 2020 and directly appropriates $850 million to SSBG to fund child and family care for essential workers.

Subsection (b). Rules Governing Use of Additional Funds.

This section specifies that states can only use the $850 million appropriated in this section to provide care for members of the households of essential workers that are incapable of self-care, including children and adult family members who require daytime care.

The section gives states several options for providing care, including reimbursing workers directly for care they obtain themselves, paying child care and adult care providers, and setting up emergency child care. It specifies that there is no income test for receiving this emergency child care help, and waives some existing SSBG funding restrictions that prevent states from working directly with health care facilities or otherwise providing these services.

In cases where the state works with child care providers or sets up child care facilities, they would be required to follow state and local licensing laws unless the state determined that a specific requirement would prevent them from providing the services, in which case they are required to report specifically to the Secretary on the requirement and why it is an impediment.

The section specifies that states cannot supplant state funding used for child care with these new federal dollars, or exclude essential workers by requiring a means test for services.

Finally, the section defines "essential worker" to include:

• Health care sector workers
• Emergency response workers
• Sanitation workers
• Workers at businesses which state or local officials have determined must stay open to serve the public during the COVID-19 emergency
• Any other worker who cannot telework and who the State or local government deems to be essential during the COVID-19 pandemic

Title II – Pandemic Emergency Assistance and Services

Sec. 100201. Funding to States, Localities, and Community-Based Organizations for Emergency Aid and Services.

Subsection (a). Funding for States.

This subsection directly appropriates $9.6 billion to the Social Services Block Grant for the sole purpose of providing emergency aid and services to disadvantaged children, families, and households. It requires the Department of Health and Human Services to distribute the funds to all 50 states, the District of Columbia, and all U.S. Territories within 45 days, and requires states and territories to obligate the funds by December 31, 2020.

Under this section, states would be required to pass through at least 50 percent of the funds to county governments, local governments working in partnership with community-based organizations, or directly to community-based organizations with experience serving disadvantaged individuals or families. States are required to distribute the funds expeditiously, ensure that the pass-through funds are distributed to sub-state areas based on the area's share of disadvantaged individuals, and report to HHS on their plan for distribution within 90 days.

The funds could be used to provide basic economic and well-being necessities, provide necessary supplies to protect against infection, help connect individuals and families to payments and services for which they are eligible, provide short-term cash, non-cash, or in-kind disaster relief, and pay operational costs directly related to providing the services and maintaining local social service operations to assist needy families.

This section also prohibits imposition of burdensome individual eligibility determinations for emergency assistance and waives section 2005(a)(2) and 2005(a)(8) of the Social Security Act to allow emergency payments.

Finally, it prohibits states from using any of the funds to supplant existing state spending or to pay for services which would be reimbursed by the Federal Emergency Management Agency.

Subsection (b). Funding for Federally Recognized Indian Tribes and Tribal Organizations.

This subsection provides $400 million to federally recognized Indian Tribes and Tribal organizations to fund emergency aid and services for disadvantaged individuals and families. Funds would be distributed on the basis of population and could not be used for services that would be reimbursed by the Federal Emergency Management Agency.

Sec. 100202. Emergency Assistance to Older Foster Youth.

Subsection (a). Funding Increases.

This section increases fiscal year 2020 funding for the John H. Chafee Foster Care Independence Program, which serves older youth who were in foster care at age 14, by $50 million for 2020. It also increases authorized funding for the specific program that provides Education and Training Vouchers (ETV) to these youth by 30 percent, and provides flexibility to better serve youth.

Subsection (b). Programmatic Flexibility.

This section provides states with various temporary flexibilities needed to serve vulnerable older foster youth during the COVID-19 pandemic. Those include:
• Eliminating the age limit on receiving Chafee-funded services, so states can serve more former foster youth in need
• Suspending work and educational progress requirements for older youth receiving assistance due to current or past foster care during the time period in which they may be impossible to comply with
• Giving states authority to waive limits on providing housing assistance to older youth,
who may have lost their current housing due to university and other closings
•
• Waiving educational progress and employment requirements for older foster youth who
are unable to work or go to school during the pandemic All flexibilities expire January 31, 2021.

Sec. 100203. Emergency Assistance to Families Through Home Visiting Programs.

This section temporarily allows home visiting programs funded under the Maternal, Infant, and Early Childhood Home Visiting program (MIECHV) to
• Conduct virtual home visits, when needed to comply with public health directives
47
o Help families acquire needed technology to participate in virtual home visits

o Train home visitors in conducting virtual home visits
• Train home visitors to assist families with emergency preparedness and response
• Provide emergency supplies to families, such as diapers, formula, non-perishable food,
water, soap, and hand sanitizer.
• Provide prepaid debit cards to families to help meet emergency needs.
The section also provides an additional $100 million for home visiting in 2020, and allows HHS to extend contracts and delay reporting deadlines as is reasonable during the COVID-19 pandemic.
The flexibilities end January 31, 2021.

Title III – Program Flexibility During the Pandemic Sec. 100301. Emergency Flexibility for Child Welfare Programs.
This section provides state child welfare programs with flexibility to provide services, including caseworker visits, virtually when necessary to comply with public health directives.

Sec. 100302. Emergency Flexibility for Child Support Programs.
This section provides states with the option to suspend penalties for non-custodial parents for inability to pay child support during the COVID-19 pandemic, since some courts have suspended non-emergency proceedings, including those related to modifying child support orders. It also suspends federal requirements to penalize custodial parents (via TANF) and non-custodial parents (via Child Support Enforcement) for failure to comply with paternity establishment rules, since paternity establishment requires in-person action which may not be possible during the pandemic. In some states, using this flexibility may require a change in state law.
The section does not change that the state's duty to make all reasonable efforts to deliver child support funds to custodial parents, but does suspend financial penalties and generally holds states financially harmless for failure to meet strict targets and state plan and operational requirements during the pandemic. The flexibility means states can continue to receive federal child support incentive payments even if they fall below the 90 percent paternity establishment threshold. The section also allows the Secretary of HHS to, wherever possible, provide tribal child support programs with the same flexibilities as those afforded to state programs.
The flexibilities expire January 31, 2021.

Sec. 100303. Emergency Flexibility for TANF Programs.
In order to allow compliance with social distancing, shelter-in-place, and other public health guidance, this section suspends the federal work participation rate requirements and the federal time limit for the federal Temporary Assistance for Needy Families (TANF) Program during the COVID-19 emergency, and creates penalties for any state or Tribal TANF program that fails to "stop the clock" on federal time limits for families, and/or that sanctions families for failure to work or participate in "work participation" activities. The policy suspensions expire January 31, 2021.

DIVISION K – COVID-19 HERO Act
Prepared by the Democratic staff of the House Committees on Financial Services and Judiciary
Sec. 110001. Short title; table of contents.

• Establishes the short title of the bill and provides a table of contents

Title I – Providing Medical Equipment for First Responders and Essential Workers

Sec. 110101. COVID–19 Emergency Medical Supplies Enhancement.

• This section would expand the use and oversight of Defense Production Act (DPA) authorities to: increase the production and supply of critical medical supplies and equipment, such as diagnostic tests and personal protection equipment; focus efforts on supply chain mobilization; decrease the disruption of critical deliveries to state and local governments; and require assessments for both immediate and longer term needs and plans to meet those needs, as well as requiring longer-term planning to ensure that the United States is better prepared for future pandemics.

Title II – Protecting Renters and Homeowners from Evictions and Foreclosures

Sec. 110201. Emergency rental assistance.

This section would authorize $100 billion for an Emergency Rental Assistance program that would allocate funding to states, territories, counties, and cities to help renters pay their rent and utility bills during the COVID-19 pandemic, and help rental property owners of all sizes continue to cover their costs.

Sec. 110202. Homeowner Assistance Fund.

This section provides $75 billion to states, territories, and tribes to address the ongoing needs of homeowners struggling to afford their housing due directly or indirectly to the impacts of the COVID-19 pandemic by providing direct assistance with mortgage payments, property taxes, property insurance, utilities, and other housing related costs.

Sec. 110203. Protecting renters and homeowners from evictions and foreclosures.

This section extends and expands the eviction moratorium and foreclosure moratorium in the CARES Act to include all renters and homeowners, improves the forbearance provided under the CARES Act, and specifies the loan modifications and loss mitigation that should be available to homeowners following a moratorium to prevent any homeowner from facing a lump sum payment that they cannot afford.

Additionally, this section protects federal relief payments from being taken in bankruptcy proceedings, ensuring that homeowners in bankruptcy proceedings can participate in the mortgage forbearance program created by the CARES Act and other COVID-19 mortgage assistance; increases the amount of home equity protected in the bankruptcy process to $100,000; makes it easier for homeowners to exit bankruptcy so they can resume normal economic activity and continue paying off their mortgages; and opens Chapter 13 to more homeowners and small businesses by raising the limits for debt to qualify for a bankruptcy through Chapter 13.

Sec. 110204. Liquidity for mortgage servicers and residential rental property owners.

This section would require the Federal Reserve facility established by Section 4003 of the CARES Act to be implemented for the benefit of mortgage servicers and residential rental property owners, contingent on compliance with certain reporting requirements and protections for borrowers and renters.

Sec. 110205. Rural rental assistance.

This section would authorize $309 million in supplemental funding for USDA's rental assistance programs, including $25 million for rural vouchers, to absorb reductions in tenant rent contributions and to provide rental assistance to unassisted households living in USDA subsidized properties who are struggling to pay rent during the COVID-19 pandemic.

Sec. 110206. Funding for public housing and tenant-based rental assistance.

This section would authorize $2 billion for the public housing operating fund and $3 billion for the Housing Choice Voucher program, including $500 million for administrative fees, to help public housing authorities (PHAs) absorb reductions in tenant rent contributions and mitigate other costs associated with the COVID-19 pandemic.

110207. Supplemental funding for supportive housing for the elderly, supportive housing for persons with disabilities, supportive housing for persons with aids, and project- based section 8 rental assistance.

• This section would authorize $500 million in funding for the HUD Section 202 Supportive Housing for the Elderly program to ensure sufficient staffing, services, and other resources for 3,500 senior and disabled resident communities during the COVID-19 pandemic. This section would also authorize $200 million in funding for the HUD Section 811 Supportive Housing for Persons with Disabilities program, $15 million for the Housing Opportunities for People with AIDS program (HOPWA), and $750 million for Project-Based Section 8 rental assistance.

Sec. 110208. Fair Housing.

This section authorizes $14 million to ensure individuals are protected from housing- related hate crimes and increasing forms of housing discrimination from Coronavirus- motivated bias through adequate and accessible housing discrimination complaint intake, investigations, and public education of housing rights.

Sec. 110209. Funding for housing counseling services.

This section would authorize $100 million in funding to support housing counseling services that help homeowners, renters, and people experiencing or at-risk of homelessness navigate their housing options and rights, including protections and resources provided through COVID-19 relief legislation.

Title III – Protecting People Experiencing Homelessness

Sec. 110301. Homeless assistance funding.

This section would authorize $11.5 billion for the Emergency Solutions Grants program to enable state and local governments to finance housing and health related services for the hundreds of thousands of people currently experiencing homelessness.

Sec. 110302. Emergency rental assistance voucher program.

This section would authorize $1 billion for Housing Choice Vouchers targeted to people experiencing or at risk of homelessness and survivors of domestic violence.

Sec. 110401. Reporting of information during major disasters.

This section would suspend negative consumer credit reporting during the COVID-19 pandemic and other declared major disasters plus 120 days. Credit score furnishers would be prohibited from implementing new credit scoring models that would lower existing consumer credit scores during the COVID-19 pandemic or during other major disaster periods. This section also permanently bans the reporting of medical debt arising out of COVID-19 treatments.

Sec. 110402. Restrictions on collections of debt during a national disaster or emergency.

This legislation provides a temporary moratorium on consumer debt collection during this COVID-19 crisis, and for 120 days thereafter.

Sec. 110403. Repayment period and forbearance for consumers.

This section ensures reasonable forbearance and repayment options for consumers when payments resume following the moratorium provided by Section 402, including simply maintaining the same payment schedule by extending the maturity by the same period of time payments were suspended under Section 402.

Sec. 110404. Credit facility.

This section provides creditors access to a Federal Reserve facility to receive a low- interest, long-term loan where payments would be deferred until a borrower resumes making payments to the creditor pursuant to the debt collection moratorium and forbearance provided in this title.

Title IV – Suspending Negative Credit Reporting and Strengthening Consumer Protections

Title V – Forgiving Student Loan Debt and Protecting Student Borrowers

Sec. 110501. Payments for private education loan borrowers as a result of the COVID–19 national emergency.

• This section extends existing CARES Act student loan payment and consumer protections, such as debt collection prohibitions, to private loan borrowers, who are currently not covered by the CARES Act, and provides up to $10,000 in debt relief to be applied to a private student loan. The Treasury Department will make monthly payments on behalf of the borrower up to $10,000 until September 2021.

Sec. 110502. Additional protections for private student loan borrowers.

As Treasury will be making payments on behalf of borrowers under this title, this section requires private student servicing companies that receive funds to offer income driven repayment plans, and payments or forbearance under this title will not impact applicable State statutes of limitation. Furthermore, this section instructs Treasury to apply any unused portion of the up to $10,000 forgiveness amount to any remaining outstanding private loan balance when borrower payments resume.

Title VI – Standing Up For Small Businesses, Minority-Owned Businesses, and Non- Profits

Sec. 110602. Repayment period and forbearance for small businesses and nonprofit organizations.

• This section ensures reasonable forbearance and repayment options for small businesses and nonprofit organizations when payments resume following the debt collection moratorium provided by Section 601.

Sec. 110603. Credit facility.

Sec. 110601. Restrictions on collections of debt during a national disaster or emergency.

This legislation provides a temporary moratorium on small business and nonprofit debt collection during this COVID-19 crisis, and for 120 days thereafter.

This section provides creditors access to a Federal Reserve facility to receive a low- interest, long-term loan where payments would be deferred until a borrower resumes making payments to the creditor pursuant to the debt collection moratorium and forbearance provided in this title.

Sec. 110604. Main Street Lending Program requirements.

This section mandates that the Federal Reserve's Main Street Lending Program, which was established utilizing CARES Act funds and is backstopped by the Treasury Department, include non-profit organizations as eligible borrowers, and stipulates that the Fed immediately offer a low-cost loan option tailored to the unique needs of non-profit organizations with deferred payments, and the loan may be forgiven solely for non- profits predominantly serving low-income communities that are ineligible for a PPP loan.

• This section mandates that the Federal Reserve, through the Main Street Lending Program, shall provide at least one low-cost loan option that small businesses and small non-profits are eligible for that does not have a minimum loan size, overriding the current $500,000 minimum loan size to participate in the program.

Sec. Program.

110605. Options for small businesses and non-profits under the Main Street Lending

Sec. 110606. SAFE Banking.

This section would allow cannabis-related legitimate businesses, that in many states have remained open during the COVID-19 pandemic as essential services, along with their service providers, to access banking services and products, as well as insurance. This section also requires reports to Congress on access to financial services and barriers to marketplace entry for potential and existing minority-owned cannabis-related legitimate businesses.

Title VII – Empowering Community Financial Institutions

Sec. 110701. Community Development Financial Institutions Fund.

This section authorizes an emergency appropriation of $2 billion to the Community Development Financial Institutions (CDFI) Fund, of which $800 million would be set aside for minority-owned lenders, including minority depository institutions (MDIs), to support small businesses, minority-owned businesses and underserved communities.

Sec. 110702. Ensuring diversity in community banking

This section strengthens MDIs, CDFIs, and newly designated "impact banks" that predominantly serve low-income communities through partnerships, technical assistance, and Federal deposits, and is similar to H.R. 5322, Ensuring Diversity in Community Banking Act.

Title VIII – Providing Assistance for State, Territory, Tribal, and Local Governments

Sec. 110801. Emergency relief for State, territorial, Tribal, and local governments.

This section expands the Federal Reserve's assistance to local governments by allowing U.S. territories, as well as a greater number of cities and counties, to be eligible issuers in the Federal Reserve's municipal liquidity facility.

Sec. 110802. Community development block grants.

This section would authorize $5 billion in Community Development Block Grant funding to provide states and local governments with additional flexible resources to mitigate and address the health and economic impacts of COVID-19.

Title IX – Providing Oversight and Protecting Taxpayers

Sec. 110901. Mandatory Reports to Congress.

This section would amend the Act by requiring the Treasury Secretary to provide the same reports to Congress for its programs that the Federal Reserve submits for Federal Reserve programs under Section 13(3)(C) of the Federal Reserve Act and to submit to Congress and the Special Inspector General for Pandemic Recovery monthly summaries of Treasury's CARES Act and related activities.

Sec. 110902. Discretionary reports to Congress.
This section would amend the Act by authorizing the Congressional Oversight Commission to share additional information with the Financial Services Committee beyond the existing specifications listed under "Regular Reports" (Section 4020(b)(2)) .

Sec. 110903. Definition of appropriate congressional committees.
This section would amend the Act by adding the Financial Services Committee to the list of appropriate congressional committees that receive reports from (1) the Pandemic Response Accountability Committee and (2) the GAO.

Sec. 110904. Reporting by inspectors general.
This section would (1) require inspectors general at certain federal agencies to include in their semiannual reports information about their respective agencies' COVID-related rulemaking, supervisory, and oversight activities and (2) in addition to reporting such information in their semiannual report, Inspectors General must also provide such information to the Special Inspector General for Pandemic Recovery, the Pandemic Response Accountability Committee, and the Congressional Oversight Commission.

DIVISION L – Families, Workers, and Community Support Provisions
Prepared by the Democratic staff of the House Committee on Education and Labor
Title I – Amendments to Emergency Family and Medical Leave Expansion Act and Emergency Paid Sick Leave Act
Subtitle A - Emergency Family and Medical Leave Expansion Act Amendments
Sec. 120101. References.
Sec. 120102. Employee Eligibility and Employer Clarification. This section temporarily suspends, until December 31, 2022, the current 1,250 hour eligibility requirement and reduces the tenure eligibility requirement from 12 months to 90 days under non-emergency Family and Medical Leave Act (FMLA). This will ensure rampant unemployment and furloughs do not leave workers unable to qualify for FMLA benefits in the near future. This section also clarifies that public agencies are covered under the Family and Medical Leave Act of 1993, regardless of the number of employees.

Sec. 120103. Emergency Leave Extension. This section extends the availability of Emergency Family and Medical Leave benefits from December 31, 2020 to December 31, 2021.

Sec. 120104. Emergency Leave Definitions. This section
• Provides private sector and public sector employees who have been on the job for at least
30 calendar days with the right take up to 12 weeks of job-protected paid leave under the
Family and Medical Leave Act, *regardless of the size of their employers.*
• Employees can take this leave to: (1) self-isolate because they were diagnosed with COVID-19, (2) obtain a medical diagnosis or to care for symptoms of COVID-19, (3) comply with a recommendation or order to self-isolate because physical

presence at work
would jeopardize the health of the employee, other employees, or a person in the employee's household, (4) care for a family member who is self-isolating, (5) care for a child whose school has closed or child care provider is unavailable due to COVID-19, or (6) care for a family member who is individual with a disability or senior citizen whose place of care or direct care provider is unavailable.

Sec. 120105. Regulatory Authorities. This section removes the Secretary of Labor's authority to issue regulations, authorized under Families First Coronavirus Response Act, to exempt employees of businesses with fewer than 50 employees, or to issue regulations to exempt health care providers and emergency responders from the right to paid leave. Any regulations that have been issued under that previous authority shall have no effect.

Sec. 120106. Paid Leave. This section ensures that workers are provided with a full 12 weeks of paid emergency FMLA leave and such leave does not count towards an employee's 12 weeks of non-emergency unpaid FMLA leave. This section also clarifies that only the employee can decide to take emergency FMLA leave concurrently with any other paid leave they have available.

Sec. 120107. Wage Rate. This section ensures employees will receive a benefit from their employers that will be no less than two-thirds of the employee's usual pay, up to $200 a day, but no less than the applicable minimum wage in their area.

Sec. 120108. Notice. This section requires that employees provide their employers with notice as soon as is practicable.

Sec. 120109. Intermittent Leave. This section clarifies that employees can take leave intermittently or on a reduced work schedule, regardless of a previous agreement between an employer and employee.

Sec. 120110. Certification. This section states employers may require requests for emergency leave to be supported by basic documentation, but not before five weeks after the employee has started the leave.

Sec. 120111. Authority of the Director of the Office of Management and Budget to Exclude Certain Federal Employees. This section eliminates the authority of the Director of the Office of Management and Budget to exclude certain federal employees from paid leave.

Sec. 120112. Technical Amendments. This section makes technical amendments.

Sec. 120113. Amendments to the Families First Emergency Family and Medical Leave Expansion Act.

• Clarifies that employees who work under a multiemployer collective bargaining agreement and whose employers pay into a multiemployer plan are provided with leave.

• Eliminates provisions that allow employers of health care providers and emergency responders the ability to exclude their employees from emergency FMLA leave.

• Eliminates provisions that restrict employees from exercising a private right of action against employers, with fewer than 50 employees.

Subtitle B – Emergency Paid Sick Leave Act Amendments Sec. 120114. References.

Sec. 120115. Paid Sick Time Requirement. This section—

• Allows eligible employees to use paid sick leave for the uses allowed under the emergency FMLA (see above).

• For each 12-month period, entitles eligible full-time employees to two workweeks (80 hours) of emergency paid sick leave. For each 12-month period, eligible part-time employees are entitled to the hours of emergency paid sick leave that equals the typical number of hours that they work in a typical two-week period.

• Ensures employees receive emergency paid sick leave in addition to any existing employer-provided paid leave.

• Clarifies that employees can take leave intermittently or on a reduced work schedule, regardless of a previous agreement between an employer and employee.

• Allows employers to require requests for paid sick leave to be supported by basic documentation, but not before 7 days after the employee has returned to work.

• Requires employees to provide their employers with notice of need to take leave as soon as is practicable.

• Clarifies that full emergency paid sick leave is available to employees where they begin employment with a new employer.

• Requires employers to restore employees to their positions after returning from paid sick leave.

Sec. 120116. Sunset. This section extends the availability of emergency paid sick leave from December 31, 2020 to December 31, 2021.

Sec. 120117. Definitions. This section eliminates the large employer exemption and clarifies that nonprofit organizations are covered employers. This section ensures that full-time and part-time employees earn full wage replacement (up to $511 per day) for all emergency paid sick leave uses.

Sec. 120118. Emergency Paid Sick Leave for Employees of the Department of Veterans Affairs and the Transportation Security Administration for Purposes Relating to COVID- 19. This section ensures employees of the Department of Veterans Affairs and Transportation Security Administration are eligible for paid sick days.

Sec. 120119. Authority of the Director of the Office of Management and Budget to Exclude Certain Federal Employees. This section eliminates the authority of the Director of the Office of Management and Budget to exclude certain federal employees from paid sick leave.

Sec. 120120. Regulatory Authorities. This section eliminates the Secretary of Labor's authority to issue regulations, provided under the Families First Coronavirus Response Act, to exempt certain employers with fewer than 50 employees, health care providers, and emergency responders from the emergency paid sick leave provisions. This section also eliminates the Secretary's authority to issue regulations to align Divisions C (Emergency Family and Medical Leave Act), E (Emergency Paid Sick Leave Act) and G (Tax Credits for Paid Sick and Paid Family and Medical Leave) of the Family First Coronavirus Response Act. Any such regulations issued by the Department shall have no force and effect.

Title II – COVID-19 Workforce Development Response Activities

Section 120201. Definitions and Special Rule: Defines coronavirus, COVID-19 national emergency, "Secretary" as the Secretary of Labor, apprenticeship programs as Registered Apprenticeship programs. Requires that any funds used under this Act for apprenticeships are used only for Registered Apprenticeships.

Section 120202. Job Corps Response to the COVID–19 National Emergency: Provides additional programmatic flexibilities, including for eligibility, enrollment length, advanced career training programs, counseling, job placement and assessments, and transition support for Job Corps participants.

Section 120203. Native American Programs Responding to the COVID-19 National Emergency: Authorizes a 1-year extension on the 4-year grant cycle due to the COVID- 19 national emergency.

Section 120204. Migrant and Seasonal Farmworkers Program Response: Authorizes a 1-year extension on the 4-year grant cycle due to the COVID-19 national emergency, and expands eligibility to individuals not exceeding 150 percent of the poverty line.

Section 120205. YouthBuild Activities Responding to the COVID-19 National Emergency: Expands eligibility for individuals who turned 25 during the COVID-19 national emergency, and expands enrollment length beyond 2 years for individuals participating in the program during the COVID-19 national emergency.

Section 120206. Apprenticeship Support During the COVID-19 National Emergency: Requires the Secretary to identify and disseminate strategies and tools to support virtual and online learning and training within 30 days of bill enactment.

Title III – COVID–19 Every Worker Protection Act of 2020".

Sec. 120301. Short Title. This division may be cited as the "COVID–19 Every Worker

Protection Act of 2020".

Sec. 120302. Emergency Temporary and Permanent Standards.

Requires OSHA to issue an emergency temporary standard (ETS) within 7 days of enactment to protect health care and other workers at occupational risk of exposure to COVID-19. The ETS:

• Requires employers to develop and implement a comprehensive infectious disease exposure control plan to protect workers from exposure to the SARS-CoV-2 virus that causes COVID-19.

• Incorporates, as appropriate, guidance issued by the Centers for Disease Control and Prevention, the National Institute for Occupational Safety and Health, and OSHA which are designed to prevent the transmission of infectious agents in healthcare settings and relevant scientific research on novel pathogens.

• Requires the ETS to be no less protective than the infectious disease precautions for novel pathogens issued by any OSHA state plan.

• Permits OSHA to exercise enforcement discretion in the event of equipment shortages.

• Requires OSHA state plan states to adopt an ETS within 14 days of enactment.

• Covers public employees in the 24 states where they are not currently covered by OSHA

• Requires OSHA to issue a permanent infectious disease standard within 24 months of enactment.

• Requires employers to comply with existing OSHA recordkeeping regulations.

• Prohibits employers from retaliating against workers for reporting or publicizing health and safety hazards, or for using their own more protective personal protective equipment if not provided by the employer.

Sec. 120303. Surveillance, Tracking, And Investigation of Work-Related Cases of COVID– 19.

Requires the CDC, in conjunction with the National Institute for Occupational Safety and Health, to collect and, as appropriate, investigate reports of work-related transmission of COVID-19 to health care and other workers, and make recommendations on needed actions or guidance based on those reports and investigations.

Title IV – Community and Family Support Community and Family Support Sec. 120401. Matching Funds Waiver for Formula Grants and Subgrants Under the Family Violence Prevention and Services Act. This section waives the matching requirement for grantees and subgrantees under the Family Violence Prevention and Services Act (FVPSA) during the COVID-19 pandemic. This will provide relief to domestic violence providers who rely on volunteer support to meet their matching requirements, but have been unable to maintain volunteers due to the pandemic.

Sec. 120402. Distribution of Certain Funds Appropriated for the Community Services Block Grant Act. This section ensures that all states receive the appropriate share of Community Services Block Grant (CSBG) funds under the Coronavirus Aid, Relief, and Economic Security Act (CARES Act), raises the poverty line for all CSBG funds appropriated during fiscal years 2020-2022 to 200 percent, and ensures that states distribute CSBG funds received under the CARES Act to local community action agencies in a timely manner.

Sec. 120403. Low Income Home Energy Assistance Program (LIHEAP)

This section expands energy assistance for low-income families, reduces barriers to LIHEAP participation during the COVID-19 emergency, and temporarily increases LIHEAP agencies' administrative resources to process the higher volume of applications remotely.

Title V – COVID-19 Protections under the Longshore and Harbor Workers' Compensation Act

Sec. 120501. Compensation Pursuant to the Longshore and Harbor Workers' Compensation Act.—Establishes a presumption that COVID-19 is work related and authorizes eligibility for benefits under the LHWCA to those maritime employees who were employed between January 27, 2020 and January 27, 2022 who are diagnosed with COVID-19, or who were ordered not to return to work by the employer or by a public health agency because of exposure or risk of exposure in the workplace to 1 or more individuals diagnosed with COVID- 19.

An employer or carrier is entitled to reimbursement for the costs of compensation paid for COVID-19 claims from the Special Fund established under the LHWCA Section 44, provided such employer is in compliance with requirements and guidance related to the prevention of exposure to COVID-19 issued by the Occupational Safety and Health Administration, Centers for Disease Control, the U.S. Coast Guard, or state or local health authority related. Insurance premiums and experience ratings cannot be adjusted based upon compensation paid by the carrier, if the carrier is reimbursed for the costs of claim from the Special Fund for purposes of this Title. Claims for reimbursement shall be submitted to the Department of Labor pursuant to regulations established under the War Hazards Compensation Act.

Funds are appropriated to the Special Fund. DOL shall report to Congress on claims paid, claims denied and claims pending, and expenditures from the Special Fund related to COVID-19 claims under this Title.

DIVISION M – Consumer Protection and Telecommunications Provisions
Prepared by the Democratic staff of the House Committee on Energy and Commerce

Title I – Covid-19 Price Gouging Prevention

Sec. 101. Short Title. Stipulates that the short title of this section is the "COVID-19 Price Gouging Prevention Act".

Sec. 102. Prevention of Price Gouging. Prohibits the sale of consumer goods and services at unconscionably excessive prices. Goods and services include personal protective equipment, drugs, hand sanitizers, and healthcare services, among others. It also authorizes the Federal Trade Commission and State attorneys general to enforce the law and impose civil penalties on price gougers. No state laws would be preempted by the title.

Title II – E-Rate Support for Wi-Fi Hotspots, Other Equipment, and Connected Devices

Sec. 201. E-Rate Support for Wi-Fi Hotspots, Other Equipment, and Connected Devices

During Emergency Periods Related to COVID-19.

authorized are set aside to help serve schools and libraries that serve people living on tribal lands.

Title III – Emergency Benefit for Broadband Service

Sec. 301. Benefit for Broadband Service During Emergency Periods Relating to COVID-19.

Sec. 302. Enhanced Lifeline Benefits During Emergency Periods.

Title IV – Continued Connectivity

Section 401. Continued Connectivity During Emergency Periods Relating to COVID-19.

Prohibits broadband and telephone providers from terminating service due to a customer's inability to pay their bill because of financial hardships caused by the COVID-19 pandemic or imposing late fees incurred because of hardships caused by the COVID-19 pandemic. It also prohibits broadband providers from employing data caps or charging customers from going over data caps and requires them to open Wi-Fi hotspots to the public at no cost during the COVID-19 public health emergency.

Title V – Don't Break Up the T-Band

Section 501. Repeal of Requirement to Reallocate and Auction T-Band Spectrum. Allows public safety organizations to continue using a portion of the airwaves critical for their radios, specifically, the T-Band.

Authorizes $5 billion in funding for a

temporary disbursement to be administered through the Federal Communications Commission's (FCC) E-rate Program for schools and libraries to provide internet service in a technologically neutral way to students and teachers, prioritizing those without internet access at home. It allows authorized funding to be used for internet service and providing connected devices, like laptops and tablets, Wi-Fi hotspots, modems, and routers, to students and teachers to help keep them in the digital classroom during the COVID-19 pandemic. Five percent of the emergency funds.   Entitles households in which a member has been laid off or furloughed to get a $50 benefit, or a $75 benefit on tribal lands, to put toward the monthly price of internet service during the COVID-19 public health emergency. Internet service providers would be required to provide eligible households service at a price reduced by an amount up to the emergency benefit, and

those providers can seek a reimbursement from the FCC for such amount. This would authorize nearly $9 billion to cover the costs of reimbursements. Providers make unlimited minutes and unlimited data available to those that rely on the Lifeline

program to stay connected to phone or internet service and provides additional support.

Sec. 303. Grants to States to Strengthen National Lifeline Eligibility Verifier. Authorizes $200 million in funding to help states participate in the National Lifeline Eligibility Verifier.

Requires that Lifeline

Title VI – National Suicide Hotline Designation

Sec. 601. Findings. Includes findings related to suicide and mental health crisis counseling and the importance of designating a three-digit code for the National Suicide Prevention Lifeline.

Sec. 602. Universal Telephone Number for National Suicide Prevention and Mental Health Crisis Hotline System. Designates 9-8-8 as the universal dialing code for the National Suicide Prevention Lifeline.

Sec. 603. State Authority Over Fees. Allows states to impose a fee or charge on voice service subscribers' bills for the support or implementation of 9-8-8 services for the support of the National Suicide Prevention Lifeline.

Sec. 604. Location Identification Report. Requires the FCC to evaluate and submit a report to Congress on the feasibility and cost of automatically providing the dispatchable location of calls to 9-8-8.

Sec. 605. Report on Certain Training Programs. Requires the Assistant Secretary for Mental Health and Substance Use to submit a report to Congress that details a strategy for offering support or providing technical assistance for training programs for National Suicide Prevention Lifeline counselors to increase competency in serving LGBTQ youth.

Title VII – COVID-19 Compassion and Martha Wright Prison Phone Justice

Sec. 701. Findings. Includes findings regarding the need to connect families and incarcerated

family members, particularly during the COVID-19 pandemic.

Sec. 702. Requirement for Confinement Facility Communications Services, During the Covid-19 Pandemic and Other Times. Sets a mandatory, immediate, interim cap on all rates charged in connection with voice calls and video calls made to or from prisons or jails —both for calls within a state and calls between states — of .04 cents per-minute for debit calls and .05 cents per-minute for collect calls. It also gives the FCC the authority to set rates in connection with voice calls and video calls in prisons and jails both for calls within a state and calls between states. Finally, it requires the FCC to adopt rules to replace the mandatory interim caps within 18 months of passage and to review those rates every two years. Prohibits prisons or jails from charging site commissions.

Sec. 703. Authority. Preempts any state law that permits a higher rate for voice or video calling but allows state laws mandating a lower rate to persist.

Title VIII – Healthcare Broadband Expansion During COVID-19
Section 801. Expansion of Rural Health Care Program of FCC in Response to COVID-19.

Authorizes $2 billion for a temporary expansion of the FCC's Rural Health Care Program (RHCP) to partially subsidize their health care providers' broadband service. Authorized subsidies would flow to all nonprofit and public hospitals, not just rural ones. Increases the broadband subsidy rate from 65 percent to 85 percent. Also uses authorized funds to expand eligibility of the RHCP to ensure mobile and temporary health care delivery sites are eligible and temporarily modifies administrative processes to ensure funding is delivered expediently.

DIVISION N – Giving Retirement Options to Workers Act
Prepared by the Democratic staff of the House Committee on Education and Labor

Sec.___0001. Short Title: This division may be cited as the "COVID-19 Protections under the Longshore and Harbor Workers' Compensation Act."
Sec.___0002. Composite Plans

The section changes the multiemployer pension system by authorizing what is referred to as a "composite plan." This new plan is composed of features of a traditional defined benefit plan and of a 401(k)-style defined contribution plan. A composite plan may be a stand-alone plan or a part of an existing multiemployer plan as long as such plan is not in critical status or anticipated to be in critical status in the next five years. An eligible existing plan (referred to as a "legacy plan") that establishes a composite plan must satisfy certain requirements for funding the composite plan. Whether it is a stand-alone plan or part of an existing multiemployer plan, a composite plan must be professionally managed and must maintain a projected funding ratio of 120 percent on a 15-year going forward basis. If the amount of plan assets is not enough to pay 120 percent of participants' promised benefits, the plan would have to take remedial action by adopting what is referred to as a "realignment program." The realignment program consists of several tiers of options to be undertaken by the plan to enable it to achieve a 120 percent funding ratio. The first options include increasing contribution rates (negotiated by the bargaining parties), reducing future accrual rates, and reducing adjustable benefits for non-retirees. If necessary, the last option is reducing retiree benefits. Consequently, a participant's benefit may increase or decrease depending on the funding level of the composite plan. Ensuring that a composite plan maintains a 120 percent funding target is viewed as beneficial and could help mitigate against the kind of volatility in the financial markets that has occurred during the COVID-19 public health crisis.

There are requirements to provide annual notices to composite plan participants. Composite plans do not pay PBGC premiums and are not covered by the PBGC guarantee. If a composite plan were to become insolvent, it could not obtain financial assistance from PBGC, and its participants and beneficiaries would not be covered by the PBGC guarantee. Those employers who contribute to a composite plan negotiate a fixed contribution rate and do not have withdrawal liability, which is a payment or series of payments by an employer that no longer participates in a multiemployer plan. A legacy plan that establishes a composite plan, however, must continue to pay PBGC premiums and comply with existing funding rules, among other requirements. Participants and beneficiaries in a legacy plan continue to be covered by PBGC and their benefits would be covered by the PBGC guarantee.

DIVISION O – Education Provisions and Other Programs

Prepared by the Democratic staff of the House Committee on Education and Labor

Title I – Higher Education Provisions

Sec. 150101. Definitions.

This section provides definitions for terms such as "award year", "authorizing committees", and "FAFSA", which stands for the Free Application for Federal Student Aid.

Subtitle A – CARES Act Amendments

Sec. 150102. Application of Waiver to Participating Nonprofit Employers.

This section clarifies that the Secretary will waive the non-federal match requirement for non- profit employers for award years 2019-2020 and 2020-2021.

Sec. 150103. Extension of Federal Work-Study During a Qualifying Emergency.

This section extends flexibility into the fall that allows institutions of higher education (institutions) to pay federal work-study students even if they are unable to complete their jobs due to COVID-19.

Sec. 150104. Continuing Education at Affected Foreign Institutions.

This section clarifies that a foreign institution is eligible to offer courses via distance education based on a declaration of an emergency in the applicable country rather than the qualifying emergency in the United States. Further, it allows foreign institutions to enter into agreements with US based institutions for the duration of the emergency in the applicable country as well as in the United States.

Sec. 150105. Funding for HBCU Capital Financing.

This section replaces the $62 million cap on mandatory funding provided for the Historically Black Colleges and Universities (HBCU) Capital Financing program with "such sums."

Sec. 150106. Waiver Authority for Institutional Aid

This section repeals a provision in the *Coronavirus Aid, Relief, and Economic Security Act* (CARES Act) that allows the Secretary of Education to waive the special allotment rule for HBCUs with direct HEA appropriations.

Sec. 150107. Scope of Modifications to Required and Allowable Uses.

This section clarifies that the Department of Education cannot use the authority provided under the CARES Act to grant waivers that would allow grant funds to be used in a way that deviates from the overall purpose of the grant program. This section additionally allows the Secretary of Education to grant waivers related to the required and allowable uses for the Minority Science and Engineering Improvement Program.

Subtitle B – Financial Aid Access

Sec. 150108. Emergency Financial Aid Grants Excluded from Need Analysis.

This section specifies that emergency financial aid grants shall not be included as income or assets for the purposes of calculating a student's expected family contribution (EFC) or treated as estimated financial assistance not received under Title IV of the *Higher Education Act of 1965* (HEA). As a result, emergency financial aid provided to a student in response to the COVID-19 emergency will not impact that student's eligibility for federal financial aid.

The term "emergency financial aid grant" includes emergency aid awarded under the Higher Education Emergency Relief Fund of the CARES Act, emergency aid supported with Supplemental Educational Opportunity Grant (SEOG) program funds, and any other emergency aid provided by a Federal agency, state, Indian tribe, institution, or scholarship-granting organization for the purpose of providing relief in response to a qualifying emergency.

Sec. 150109. Facilitating Access to Financial Aid for Recently Unemployed Students.

This section specifies that any individual who has applied for, or is receiving, unemployment benefits at the time that they submit an application for federal financial aid will be treated as a dislocated worker on the FAFSA, which can qualify a FAFSA applicant for the simplified needs test or an automatic zero EFC. This provision is effective for the duration of the COVID-19 emergency and the following award year. The Department of Education is required to implement this provision within 30 days of enactment.

This section also requires the Department of Education to work with the Department of Labor and institutions to provide guidance and conduct outreach to recently unemployed individuals informing them of their potential eligibility for aid, including their treatment as dislocated workers on the FAFSA. The Department of Education is additionally required to work with institutions to inform applicants for federal student aid of the availability of other means-tested federal benefit programs and to inform institutions of their authority to share information from a student's FAFSA (with the student's consent) with organizations that assist students in applying for and receiving Federal, State, local, or tribal assistance.

This section specifies that guidance released by the Department of Education on May 8, 2009, shall be effective for the duration of the COVID-19 emergency and the following award year, including guidance regarding the ability of financial aid administrators to conduct professional judgement for recently unemployed students and adjustments to the Department of Education's risk-based model for selecting institutions for program reviews.

Sec. 150110. Student Eligibility for Higher Education Emergency Relief Fund

This section prohibits the Secretary of Education from imposing restrictions on the populations of students who may receive funds under section 18004 of the CARES Act, which creates the Higher Education Emergency Relief Fund. This section specifies that the Personal Responsibility and *Work Opportunity Reconciliation Act of 1996* does not apply to funds made available under section 18004 of the CARES Act.

Sec. 150111. Definition of Distance Education.

This section applies the definition of distance education that was included in the Department of Education's proposed rule on Distance Education and Innovation published on April 2, 2020 that was reached by consensus, to programs that begin on or after August 15, 2020. Distance education is defined as education that uses technology to deliver instruction to students who are separated from the instructor(s) and to support regular and substantive interaction between the students and the instructor(s), either synchronously or asynchronously. This provision is effective until the end of the 2020-2021 award year.

Sec. 150112. Institutional Stabilization Program.

This section creates the Institutional Stabilization Program (ISP) which allows eligible institutions, in lieu of submitting a letter of credit to be considered financially responsible in order to participate in title IV, to enter into a COVID-19 provisional program participation agreement (CVPPPA) after meeting certain requirements.

To participate in the ISP, a non-profit institution, that offered on campus classes during award year 2018-2019, must have a composite score below 1.0 and a liquidity level of 180 days or below. An institution that does not currently have a composite score below 1.0 but estimates that it will have a composite score below 1.0 for the following year can also opt into the program if it meets the liquidity threshold. Institutions with a liquidity level above 180 days are not eligible to participate.

An eligible institution must submit an application to the Secretary of Education no later than December 31, 2020 and include in the application: an estimated liquidity level; assurance that the institution will submit a record management plan and teach-out plan; and an assurance that the institution will meet the requirements of the teach-out agreement if applicable. Eligible institutions that want to opt into the ISP have 10 days to notify the institutional state authorizer and accreditor of such application and 60 days to procure an auditor attestation of its liquidity level (calculated under the FASB ASU 2016-14) and submit a teach-out plan and record management plan as approved by the Department of Education and the institution's accreditor. If the institution closes, it must release all financial holds placed on student records and provide access to transcripts at no cost for three years after the institution closes. Institutions with 90 days or less in liquidity must meet additional requirements after the application is approved. While applications are pending, the Secretary of Education cannot collect a letter of credit. The Secretary of Education is required to approve or deny complete applications within 10 days of receiving them and institutions must notify the state authorizer and accreditor within 5 days of such decision.

All institutions must also meet other eligibility requirements regarding administrative capability and cash reserve requirements under the HEA. The institution will be required to meet the teach-out plan or agreement requirement based on the liquidity level verified by the auditor – not the institution's estimate in the initial application. Once the institution is in the program, changes in liquidity level will no longer impact eligibility or treatment under the program, until it is up for renewal. However, if there is a consistent decline in liquidity, the Secretary may require an institution to make substantial progress on a teach-out agreement.

After an institution has met the above requirements, the institution is now approved to enter the ISP under a COVID-19 Provisional Program Participation Agreement (CVPPPA). Institutions with 90 days or less in liquidity must additionally make sufficient progress on the teach-out agreement (requiring that a minimum of 75% of students are covered) within 30 days of being approved for the CVPPPA and must submit updates on subsequent progress every 14 days as determined by its accreditor thereafter until the teach-out agreement(s) covers all students. All participating institutions must also report regularly (i.e. every 15 days for those with 90 days or below in liquidity and every 30 days for those with 91-180 days in liquidity) to the Secretary of Education regarding liquidity and student enrollment. If these requirements are not met, the institution is no longer eligible for the CVPPPA and the Secretary can collect a letter of credit.

The CVPPPA may be renewed through June 30, 2022, and if the Secretary of Education determines that it is in the benefit of the institution to extend such participation, the agreements may be renewed through June 30, 2024. The Secretary of Education must also submit reports to Congress with a summary of each agreement 90 days after enactment and every 90 days thereafter until all agreements have expired or been terminated.

If a student attending an institution participating in a CVPPPA at the time of closure, and 120 days prior, is entitled to an automatic closed school discharge if such student has not re- enrollment in a new institution within three years of such closure.

This section also defines "liquidity level", "teach-out agreement", "teach-out institution", and "teach-out plan".

The Secretary is authorized $300 million to provide grants to participating institutions that meet the CVPPPA requirements.

Subtitle C – Federal Student Loan Relief

Part A – Temporary Relief for Federal student Loan Borrowers Under the CARES Act

Sec. 150113. Expanding Loan Relief to all Federal Student Loan Borrowers.

This section amends the CARES Act to define the term "Federal student loan" to include Direct Loans, Department- and commercially-held Federal Family Education Loans (FFEL), Department- and institutionally-held Perkins loans, and Health and Human Services (HHS) student loans under subpart II of part A of Title VII and part E of Title VIII of the *Public Health Service Act* that are eligible for consolidation with Direct Loans under the HEA.

Sec. 150114. Extending the Length of Borrower Relief due to the Coronavirus Emergency.

This section amends the CARES Act to extend suspension of payments for Federal student loans through September 30, 2021 and adds a 30-day transition period where any missed payments after payment suspension ends do not result in collection fees and are not reported to consumer reporting agencies. Adds a provision that requires the Secretary or, as applicable, the HHS Secretary to make the borrowers with loans that were excluded from the CARES Act (i.e., commercially-held FFEL, institutionally-held Perkins loans, and HHS student loans) whole as if those loans were part of the original CARES Act. Allows borrowers repaying under an income- driven repayment plan to not recertify their income or family size until after December 30, 2021.

Sec. 150115. No Interest Accrual.

This section amends the CARES Act to extend no interest accrual on Federal student loans (regardless of repayment status) until September 30, 2021 or until the economy shows initial signs of recovery (as defined in the Act), whichever is longer. For commercially-held FFEL and institutionally-held Perkins loans, the Secretary is required to pay the amount of interest due on the unpaid principal to the holder on a monthly basis. The payments cannot affect payment calculations under the special allowance rules in the HEA. The HHS Secretary must also pay the amount of interest due on the unpaid principal to the holder of the loan on a monthly basis. Adds a provision that requires the Secretary or, as applicable, the HHS Secretary to make the borrowers with loans that were excluded from the CARES Act (i.e., commercially-held FFEL, institutionally-held Perkins loans, and

HHS student loans) whole as if those loans were part of the original CARES Act. Clarifies that accrued interest prior to March 13, 2020 cannot be capitalized as a consequence of the implementation of pause payments or the no interest accrual provisions.

Sec. 150116. Notice to Borrowers.

This section makes conforming amendments to the CARES Act such as requiring the HHS Secretary to notify HHS borrowers that the benefits provided to them under the CARES Act, as amended in this Act will end. Also requires the Secretary of Education and, as applicable, the HHS Secretary to notify Perkins loan and HHS borrowers of income-driven repayment plans available to them if they consolidate.

Sec. 150117. Writing Down Balances for Federal Student Loan Borrowers.

This section amends the CARES Act to provide $10,000 of up-front debt relief for all Department of Education loan borrowers. Borrowers owing less than $10,000 will receive up to the amount owed on their balance. Unless otherwise requested by the borrower, the discharge is applied first toward the loan with the highest interest rate. Borrowers with the same interest rate on all loans, the discharge is applied first toward the loan with the highest principal balance. The discharged amount is excluded from gross income and not required to be reported to the Internal Revenue Services.

Sec. 150118. Implementation.

This section amends the CARES Act to facilitate implementation of the temporary relief provided to borrowers. Requires holders of commercially-held FFEL, institutionally-held Perkins loans, and HHS loans to report information that allows the Secretary of Education and, as applicable, the HHS Secretary to verify borrower payments that are to be provided or suspended and calculate the amount of interest due to the holder for reimbursement.

Sec. 150119. Effective Date.

This section requires that the amendments made under this Part take effect as if enacted as part of the CARES Act.

Part B – Consolidation Loans and Public Service Loan Forgiveness

Sec. 150120. Special Rules Relating to Federal Direct Consolidation Loans.

This section establishes special rules for borrowers consolidating loans between the date of enactment and September 30, 2021 or until the economy shows initial signs of recovery (as defined in this Act), whichever is longer. The special rule allows borrowers to consolidate without losing prior payments for purposes of Public Service Loan Forgiveness (PSLF) and income-driven repayment plans. To determine the number of monthly qualifying payments, the Secretary of Education must calculate the weighted factor of each component loan, determine the number of qualifying monthly payments made on each component loan before consolidation, add the number of qualifying monthly payments on each loan, and round to the nearest whole number. When determining the new interest rate, the standard rules for consolidation apply except that the Secretary must not round up the weighted average of the interest rate. The Secretary of Education and the HHS Secretary must undertake a campaign to alert borrowers on the benefits of consolidating.

This section also requires the Government Accountability Office to submit a report within six months after the date of enactment of this Act on the implementation of this section.

Sec. 150121. Treatment of PSLF.

This section removes the requirement that a borrower must be employed in a public service employer at the time of forgiveness under PSLF. This section also allows a borrower with a full- time job as a health care practitioner working at a public or non-profit hospital or health care facility but prohibited by State law from being employed directly by the hospital or health care facility to be eligible for PSLF.

Part C – Emergency Relief for Defrauded Borrowers

Sec. 150122. Emergency Relief for Defrauded Borrowers.

This section provides full student loan relief to borrowers who attended an institution that, according to findings made by the Department of Education on or before the date of enactment of this Act, made a false or misleading job placement representation. Full student loan relief is also provided to borrowers who attended an institution that, according to findings made by the Department of Education on or before the date of enactment, made a false or misleading guaranteed employment or credit transferability representation and submitted a claim to the Department of Education. Under this section, borrowers covered under these findings who have already received partial relief are entitled to the rest of relief on their loans.

Not later than 30 days after enactment, the Secretary of Education must notify each eligible borrower with information about the relief, the borrower's eligibility to receive federal financial aid, and any additional relief the Secretary deems appropriate. Not later than 45 days after enactment, the Secretary of Education will cancel or repay the full balance of interest and principle (including fees and charges) and refund the borrower with the full amount of payments such borrower made on their loans. Not later than 60 days after enactment, the Secretary of Education is required to remove all adverse credit history related to such loans. Additionally, this section requires the Secretary of Education to adjudicate claims submitted by State Attorneys General (AGs) within 180 days of enactment. For each claim where the State AG proves misrepresentation and the borrower has not yet received full relief, the Secretary of Education is required to provide full relief. While the claims are being adjudicated, the Secretary of Education must suspend payments, involuntary collections and interest on the eligible loans. Further, not later than 10 days after relief is provided, the Secretary of Education must notify borrowers. The Secretary of Education must provide detailed documents to the authorizing committees regarding claims pertaining to 20 or more individuals not later than 10 days after the claims are adjudicated.

Regarding each loan cancelled or repaid under this section, the Secretary of Education shall initiate an appropriate proceeding to require the institution whose act or omission resulted in relief provided to the borrowers in this section to repay the Secretary of Education.

Relief provided under this section is excluded from gross income and not required to be reported to the Internal Revenue Services.

Subtitle D – Notifications and Reporting Relating to Higher Education

Sec. 150123. Notification Related to Non-CARES Act Flexibilities

This section requires the Secretary of Education to submit written notification to the authorizing committees each time an HEA provision (including regulation or subregulatory guidance) will be modified or waived due to COVID-19, other than a provision authorized to modify or waive under the CARES Act. This notification must also be published online. Each notification must include certain elements outlined in the Act. The Secretary of Education must also submit quarterly reports through the end of the first fiscal year after the qualifying emergency ends. For flexibilities already granted prior to enactment of this Act, the Secretary must submit a report outlining those flexibilities and include the elements outlined in the Act.

This section also requires institutions that exercise an authority provided under specific sections in the CARES Act to submit to the Secretary of Education a report that describes how the institution used the authority and the number of students affected by the use of such authority. The Secretary of Education is then required to submit a summary of this information to the authorizing committees, along with other information as outlined in this Act.

The Secretary of Education must submit a report to the authorizing committees summarizing modifications to any contracts with servicers and amendments to program participation agreements with institutions. The Secretary of Education must also submit randomly selected sample copies of program participation agreements.

This section amends other sections in the CARES Act to add certain reporting requirements.

Title II – Other Programs

Subtitle A - Carl D. Perkins Career and Technical Education Act of 2006 and Adult Education and Literacy COVID–19 National Emergency Response

Sec. 150201. Definitions.

This section defines "apprenticeship" and "apprenticeship program", "coronavirus", "COVID-19 national emergency", and "Secretary" as the Secretary of Education.

Sec. 150202. COVID-19 Career and Technical Education Response Flexibility.

This section provides legislative flexibility for programs under the *Perkins Career and Technical Education Act of 2006* (Perkins CTE) in response to COVID-19 such as allowing Perkins CTE entities to retain funds at the local level instead of returning unspent academic year funds to the state.

Sec. 150203. Adult Education and Literacy Response Activities.

This section provides legislative flexibility for the *Adult Education and Family Literacy Act* to allow for program administration and state leadership funds to be used for online service delivery and requires the Secretary of Education to provide guidance on virtual proctoring of adult education.

Sec. 150204. General Provisions.

This section allows Perkins CTE and Adult Education eligible agencies to apply for waivers under the General Education Provisions Act for the 2019-2020 academic year.

Subtitle B - Corporation for National and Community Service COVID–19 Response Activities

Sec. 150201. Definitions.

This section defines "apprenticeship, apprenticeship program", "coronavirus", "COVID-19 national emergency" and "Secretary" as the Secretary of Education.

Sec. 150202. COVID-19 Career and Technical Education Response Flexibility.

This section provides legislative flexibility for programs under the *Perkins Career and Technical Education Act of 2006* (Perkins CTE) in response to COVID-19 such as allowing Perkins CTE entities to retain funds at the local level instead of returning unspent academic year funds to the state.

Sec. 150203. Adult Education and Literacy Response Activities.

This section provides legislative flexibility for the *Adult Education and Family Literacy Act* to allow for program administration and state leadership funds to be used for online service delivery and requires the Secretary of Education to provide guidance on virtual proctoring of adult education.

Sec. 150204. General Provisions.

This section allows Perkins CTE and Adult Education eligible agencies to apply for waivers under the General Education Provisions Act for the 2019-2020 academic year.

Subtitle C - Corporation for National and Community Service COVID-19 Response Activities

Sec. 150205. Corporation for National and Community Service Provisions.

This section provides a technical correction to the CARES Act to provide for the stipend available to AmeriCorps volunteers whose service was interrupted by the COVID-19 national emergency.

Sec. 150206. National Service Expansion Feasibility Study.

This section requires CNCS to conduct a study on the feasibility of increasing the capacity of national service programs to respond to the economic and social impacts of COVID-19.

Sec. 150207. Definitions.

This section provides definitions, including definitions from the Domestic Volunteer Service Act of 1973.

DIVISION P – ACCESS Act

Prepared by the Democratic staff of the Committee on House Administration

Section 160001: Short Title. The "American Coronavirus/COVID-19 Election Safety and Security Act" or the "ACCESS Act".

Section 160002. Requirements for Federal Election Contingency Plans In Response To Natural Disasters And Emergencies.

• Requires states and jurisdictions to establish and make publicly available contingency plans that enable voting in federal elections during a state of emergency, public health emergency or national emergency and to update such plans at least every 5 years.

• Requires contingency plans to include initiatives to provide equipment and resources necessary to protect the health and safety of poll workers and voters and to recruit poll workers from resilient and unaffected populations.

• Permits the Attorney General to bring a civil action in an appropriate United States District Court as may be necessary to carry out the requirements of this section and permits a private right of action.

Section 160003. Early Voting and Voting by Mail.

• Requires at least 15 consecutive days of early voting for federal elections. Goes into effect in the November 2020 election and for each succeeding federal election.

o Requires the early voting period to be no less than 10 hours each day, to have uniform hours for each day, and to allow for voting prior to 9:00am and after 5:00pm.

o Requires polling places with early voting periods to be located within walking distance of a stop on a public transportation route and to be available in rural areas of states.

o Directs the Election Assistance Commission to issue election administration standards for early voting that include standards for nondiscriminatory geographic placement of polling places and that permit deviation (provided there is adequate public notice) in the case of unforeseen circumstances.

o Requires states to begin processing and scanning ballots cast during the early voting period at least 14 days prior to election day.

• Ensures that every voter can access no-excuse absentee vote-by-mail. Goes into effect in the November 2020 election and for each succeeding federal election.

o Prohibits states from imposing additional conditions or requirements for eligibility to vote by absentee ballot upon individuals who are already eligible voters.

o Prohibits states from requiring any form of identification to obtain an absentee ballot, although requiring a signed affirmation of identity is permitted.

o Prohibits states from requiring notarization or witness signatures to obtain or cast an absentee ballot.

o Ensures that voters can opt-in to voting permanently by absentee ballot by mail in their absentee voting applications.

o Requires states that conduct signature verification of voters submitting an absentee ballot to provide due process protections that must include a notice and an opportunity to cure a discrepancy in signatures or a missing signature. Provides voters with a 10-day period to cure which begins on the date the voter is notified.

o Requires states to submit a report to Congress containing information on invalidated ballots no later than 120 days after each federal election cycle.

o Ensures that every voter can submit an online request for an absentee ballot.

o Requires states to deliver an absentee ballot and related voting materials to voters prior to election day if the request for such materials is received prior to 5 days before election day.

• With respect to the COVID-19 pandemic and all future emergencies declared between 120 days before election day and 30 days before election day, requires states to automatically mail absentee ballots and balloting materials to all registered voters no later than two weeks before election day (and for states that do not register voters, to all voters in the state's central voter file). Requires a voter to attest that the voter has not and will not cast another ballot.

• Provides standards for absentee ballots cast by mail.

o Ensures that absentee ballots and related voting materials are accessible to voters with disabilities.

o Requires that submitted absentee ballots be accepted and processed if postmarked,
signed or otherwise indicated by the United States Postal Service to have been mailed on or before election day and if received within ten days after election day. o Permits voters to return absentee ballots by mail, by casting it at a polling place on election day, by submitting it at a designated ballot drop-off location, or by designating another person to return the ballot to the post office, a ballot drop-off location, a tribally designated building or an election office.

o Requires states to begin processing and scanning ballots cast by mail at least 14 days prior to election day.

• Requires states to establish an absentee ballot tracking program. Goes into effect in the November 2020 election and for each succeeding federal election.

• Ensures that notwithstanding the precinct or polling place at which a provisional ballot is cast within the state, the appropriate election official shall count each vote on such ballot for each election in which the individual who cast such ballot is eligible to vote. Goes into effect in the November 2020 election and for each succeeding federal election.

• Provides voters with a private right of action for violations of requirements under Subtitle C of Title III under the Help America Vote Act of 2002.

Section 160004. Permitting Use of Sworn Written Statement To Meet Identification Requirements For Voting.

• Provides that if a state has a voter identification requirement to cast a ballot in-person or by mail, an individual may make a sworn written statement attesting to their identity to fulfill the identification requirement. Does not affect the Help America Vote Act's requirements for certain first-time voters who submitted their voter registration by mail.

Section 160005. Voting Materials Postage.

• Ensures that voter registration application forms, absentee ballot application forms, and absentee ballots in federal elections are mailed to voters expeditiously with self-sealing envelopes and prepaid postage.

Section 160006. Requiring Transmission of Blank Absentee Ballots Under UOCAVA To Certain Voters.

• Amends the Uniformed and Overseas Citizens Absentee Voting Act (UOCAVA) to require states to transmit blank absentee ballots electronically to certain qualified individuals and prohibits electronic return of such marked ballots. Goes into effect in the November 2020 election and for each succeeding federal election.

o Defines qualified individuals as voters who have requested an absentee ballot but have not received it at least 2 days before election day, voters who reside in an area where an emergency has been declared within 5 days of election day and have not already requested an absentee ballot, voters who will be absent on election day due to professional or volunteer service in response to an emergency or disaster, voters who are hospitalized or expect to be on election day, or voters who have a disability and reside in a state that does not offer secure remote ballot marking.

• Requires blank absentee ballots transmitted to qualified voters to comply with the language requirements under section 203 of the Voting Rights Act of 1965 and the disability requirements under section 508 of the Rehabilitation Act of 1973.

• Requires qualified individuals to provide the state with an attestation in electronic form that they are qualified, that they have not and will not cast another ballot and that they acknowledge the consequences of stating a material misstatement of fact.

• Requires electronic blank absentee ballots transmitted to qualified individuals to have prepaid return postage.

• Prohibits states from refusing to accept and process an absentee ballot from a qualified individual based on notarization or witness signature, paper type, or envelope type requirements.

Section 160007. Voter Registration.

• Amends the National Voter Registration Act of 1993 to ensure that voters can register to vote online, can submit an EAC-prescribed mail voter registration application online, and can update their voter registration information online.

o Requires states to establish technological security measures to protect information provided through online voter registration services.

o Ensures that online voter registrations services are available to individuals with disabilities.

o Ensures that online voter registration services are also available through the use of an automated telephone-based system.

• Amends the Help America Vote Act of 2002 to ensure that all eligible individuals can register to vote on the same day that they vote. Goes into effect in the November 2020 election and for each succeeding federal election.

• Amends the National Voter Registration Act of 1993 to prohibit states from requiring voter registration applicants to provide more than the last 4 digits of their social security numbers. Goes into effect in the November 2020 election and for each succeeding federal election.

Section 160008. Accommodations for Voters Residing in Indian Lands.

• Permits an Indian Tribe to designate buildings as ballot pickup and collection locations and to designate one building per precinct located within Indian lands at no cost to the Indian Tribe.

• Requires states or political subdivisions to collect ballots from designated locations and to provide Indian Tribes with accurate precinct maps for all precincts located within Indian lands at least 60 days before an election.

• Requires states or political subdivisions to provide absentee ballots for federal elections to each individual who is registered to vote and who resides on Indian lands without requiring a residential address or a mail-in or absentee ballot request.

• Ensures that voters living on Indian lands may use the address of a designated building for ballot pickup and collection as their residential and mailing address if such building is in the same precinct of the voter, and if the building is not in the same precinct, may use the address of another tribally designated building within Indian lands.

• Requires that states or political subdivisions covered under section 203 of the Voting Rights Act of 1965 provide all applicable language accessibility requirements.

• Permits the Attorney General to bring a civil action in an appropriate United States District Court as may be necessary to carry out the requirements of this section and permits a private right of action.

• Goes into effect in the November 2020 election and for each succeeding federal election. **Section 160009. Payments by Election Assistance Commission to States to Assist with Costs of Compliance.**

• Requires the Election Assistance Commission to make payments to eligible states for the costs of complying with the ACCESS Act, including the costs for pre-paying the postage on absentee ballots and balloting material, for public education campaigns regarding the requirements of the ACCESS Act, and for voluntarily electing to comply with the ACCESS Act in the 2020 primary elections.

• For party-run primaries, requires the Election Assistance Commission to make payments to eligible political parties for costs incurred in transmitting absentee ballots and balloting materials in accordance with the ACCESS Act in the 2020 primary elections.

• Requires states to pass through funds to local jurisdictions or Tribal Governments.

• Requires states and political parties of states to submit an application to the Election
Assistance Commission to receive payment assistance.
• In the case of an emergency, permits states to submit a payment request to the Election Assistance Commission and requires that payment be made to the states no later than 7 days after receipt of the request.
• Prohibits funding for costs attributable to the electronic return of marked ballots.
• Requires states to submit reports to the Election Assistance Commission no later than 6 months after the end of each fiscal year on the activities conducted with the funds provided.
• Requires the Election Assistance Commission to submit a report on such payments each fiscal year to the Committee on House Administration of the House of Representatives and the Committee on Rules and Administration of the Senate.

Section 160010. Grants to States for Conducting Risk-Limiting Audits of Results of Elections.
• Permits the Election Assistance Commission to make grants to eligible states to conduct risk-limiting audits with respect to federal general elections. Goes into effect in the November 2020 election and for each succeeding federal election.
• Authorizes the appropriation of $20 million for fiscal year 2020 for risk-limiting audit grants.
• Authorizes a GAO analysis no later than 6 months after the first grants are awarded on the extent to which risk-limiting audits improve the administration and security of elections.

Section 160011. Additional Appropriations tor the Election Assistance Commission.
• Authorizes the additional appropriation of $3 million to the Election Assistance Commission for fiscal year 2020 in order for the Commission to provide additional assistance and resources to states to improve election administration.

Section 160012: Definition.
• Clarifies that the definition of election for Federal office in Titles I to III in the Help America Vote Act apply to primaries, special, runoff and general elections.

DIVISION Q – COVID–19 Heroes Fund Act of 2020
Prepared by the Democratic staff of the House Committee on Education and Labor, the House Committee on Ways and Means, and the House Committee on Oversight and Reform

Title I – Provisions Relating to State, Local, Tribal, And Private Sector Workers
Section 170101. Definitions. This section defines key terms under Title I, including "essential work employers" and "essential work." "Essential work" (1) is performed during the COVID–19 Public Health Emergency, (2) is not performed while teleworking, (3) involves regular interaction with others or items handled by others, and (4) is work in any of the 33 enumerated areas of work (*e.g.,* health care, first responders, grocery stores, transportation, etc.)

Section 170102. Pandemic premium pay for essential workers. This section provides that employers that apply for and receive grants will pay essential workers $13 per hour premium pay on top of regular wages. Essential workers are eligible for up to $10,000 ("highly compensated" essential workers earning above $200,000, up to $5,000) for work performed from January 27, 2020 until 60 days after the last day of the COVID–19 Public Health Emergency. If an essential worker develops symptoms of COVID–19 and dies, the worker's next of kin receives the remainder of the premium pay as a lump sum.

Section 170103. COVID–19 Heroes Fund. This section establishes the COVID–19 Heroes Fund in the Treasury of the United States and to be administered by the Secretary of Treasury.

Section 170104. COVID–19 Heroes Fund grants. This section directs the Secretary of the Treasury to award grants to essential work employers who choose to apply for grants for the purpose of providing premium pay to essential workers. Essential work employers are eligible for grants of $10,000 per essential worker ($5,000 for highly compensated essential workers) to cover the entire cost of premium pay, including employer payroll taxes for premium pay. Employer payroll taxes include the employer portion of Medicare Hospital Insurance tax (and the corresponding part of the Railroad Retirement Board (RRB) tier 1 tax), federal unemployment tax, and state and local employment taxes. Unused funds must be returned to the Treasury.

Section 170105. Enforcement and outreach. This section grants the Secretary of Labor authority to enforce payment requirements and to conduct outreach to employers. Failure to adhere to payment requirements are treated as violations of overtime requirements under the Fair Labor Standards Act.

Section 170106. Funding for the Department of the Treasury Office of Inspector General.
This section appropriates $1 million to the Inspector General of the Department of the Treasury to conduct oversight.

Section 170107. Authorization and appropriations. This section appropriates $190 billion to carry out Title I.

Title II – Provisions Relating to Federal Employees And COVID–19

Section 170201. Definitions. This section provides definitions of agency, employee, covered duty, covered period. The definition of agency includes any entity within the executive, legislative, and judicial branches of the federal government except for the Postal Service or the Postal Regulatory Commission. (The Postal Service is covered under Title I.) The definition of employee includes employees in all federal personnel systems but does not include political appointees, Members of Congress. or Congressional staff. It also includes employees of federally funded Tribal programs. Covered duty is defined as duty that requires an employee to have regular or routine contact with the public or the reporting of an employee to a worksite at which social distancing is not possible, consistent with the regularly assigned duties of the position of the employee and other preventative measures with respect to COVID–19 are not available. It does not include duty performed while teleworking from a residence. The covered period is the period from January 27, 2020, to the date that is 60 days after the end of the national public health emergency.

Section 170202. Pandemic duty differential. Federal employees will be eligible for the same premium pay as is available to employees in the state/local/tribal/ private sectors. OPM (or the employing agency that is not in the executive branch) is required to develop criteria for determining eligibility for premium pay and implementing regulations, which shall apply equally to all federal agencies.

Section 170203. Limitation on premium pay. This section provides that pandemic premium pay is in addition to other premium pay that may be available for federal employees, except that aggregate pay may not exceed the annual rate of pay available in any calendar year for Level II of the Executive Schedule.

Section 170204. Authorization and Appropriation. This section appropriates $10 billion to carry out Title II.

Title III – Coordination Of Benefits With Other Programs And Laws

Section 170301. Coordination with other benefits. This section provides that payments under this Act are not regarded as income for the purposes of determining eligibility for federal, state, or local benefits or assistance. For purposes of determining health insurance premium tax credit amounts, household income is generally reduced by premium pay received. This section also provides that premium pay shall not be considered wages for purposes of the employer portion of Social Security tax, as well as the corresponding rates for RRB tier 1 tax and self-employment tax. The Social Security trust funds and the Social Security Benefit Account are held harmless.

Section 170302. Clarification of coordination with other laws. This section clarifies that nothing in this Act allows noncompliance with or diminishes any rights or benefits under federal, state, or local laws, collective bargaining agreements, or employer policies.

Section 170303. Applicability of Fair Labor Standards Act of 1938 to sovereign Tribal employers. This section clarifies that receipt of funds by a sovereign Tribal employer under this Act will not expand, constrict, or alter the application of the Fair Labor Standards Act of 1938 such sovereign Tribal employer.

DIVISION R – Child Nutrition and Related Programs

Prepared by the Democratic staff of the House Committee on Education and Labor

Sec. 180001. Short Title: Child Nutrition and Related Programs Recovery Act.

Sec. 180002. Emergency Costs for Child Nutrition Programs During COVID-19 Pandemic.

This section provides emergency funding to the school meal and child adult care food programs to help cover operational costs during COVID-19. These programs operate on a per-meal reimbursement, making additional funding necessary to cover fixed costs at a time when the number of meals served is drastically reduced due to the pandemic. This funding will help to ensure that these child nutrition programs have sufficient funding to continue feeding children in need. The funding will be administered by states and distributed to providers based on a formula that takes into account the typical level of reimbursement a program would receive to operate the program, and the reimbursement being received during the pandemic.

Sec. 180003. Amendments to the Pandemic EBT Act. This section extends the Pandemic EBT program (which provides resources to families with children who would have otherwise received free or reduced price meals in school but for pandemic-related school closures) through the summer and until schools reopen, and allows states to include children who would have otherwise received meals through child care.

Sec. 180004. Fresh Produce for Kids in Need. This section extends the waiver authority provided to the Department of Agriculture under the Families First Coronavirus Response Act to the Fresh Fruit and Vegetable Program (FFVP). FFVP provides fresh fruit and vegetable snacks to children in low-income schools. This waiver authority will provide more flexibility for schools to serve FFVP foods, such as serving in bulk.

Sec. 180005. WIC Benefit Flexibility During COVID-19 Act. This section allows the Secretary of Agriculture to increase the value of the WIC Cash Value Voucher (CVV) from $9 for children and $11 for women per month to $35 per month for women and children though the end of fiscal year 2020. The WIC CVV may be used to purchase fruits and vegetables.

Sec. 180006. Calculation of Payments and Reimbursements for Certain Child Nutrition Programs. This section ensures that certain calculations under the Richard B. Russell National School Lunch Act and the Child Nutrition Act that are based on reimbursements for school year 2019-2020, such as commodity allocations and administrative funding amounts, may not be less than the amounts provided for school year 2018-2019.

Sec. 180007. Reporting on Waiver Authority. This section requires the Secretary of Agriculture to make public all child nutrition waiver applications authorized by the Families First Coronavirus Response Act, as well as the Department's response to such applications in a timely manner. It also requires all guidance related to such waivers to be dated to avoid confusion among child nutrition providers.

DIVISION S – Other Matters

Prepared by the Democratic staff of the House Committees on Natural Resources, Transportation and Infrastructure, Energy and Commerce, and Judiciary

Title I — Health Care Access for Urban Native Veterans Act

Sec. 190101. Short Title. This title may be cited as the "Health Care Access for Urban Native
Veterans Act."

Sec. 190102. Sharing Arrangements with Federal Agencies. Authorizes the Indian Health Service (IHS), Department of Veterans Affairs (VA), and the Department of Defense (DOD) to enter into arrangements for the sharing of medical facilities and services with urban Native American organizations. The VA and DOD shall also reimburse an urban Native American organization where services are provided to beneficiaries eligible for services from either department.

Title II — Tribal School Federal Insurance Parity

Sec. 190201. Short Title. This title may be cited as the "Tribal School Federal Insurance Parity Act."

Sec. 190202. Amendment to The Indian Health Care Improvement Act. Clarifies that schools that receive grants under the Tribally Controlled Schools Act of 1988 can participate in the Federal Employee Health Benefits program (FEHB) program and the Federal Employees Group Life Insurance (FEGLI) program.

Title III — PRC for Native Veterans Act 79

Sec. 190301. Short Title. This title may be cited as the "Proper and Reimbursed Care for Native Veterans Act" or the "PRC for Native Veterans Act."

Sec. 190302. Clarification of Requirement of Department of Veterans Affairs and Department of Defense to Reimburse Indian Health Service for Certain Health Care Services. Requires the Veterans Health Administration (VHA) to reimburse Indian Health Service (IHS) and Tribally-run health facilities for Purchased/Referred Care (PRC) used for treating Native American veterans.

Title IV — Wildlife-Borne Disease Prevention

Section 190401. Short Title. This title may be cited as the "Wildlife-Borne Disease 5 Prevention Act of 2020."

Section 190402. Measures to address species that pose a risk to human health. This section authorizes $21,000,000 for U.S. wildlife agencies to work with the CDC to identify wildlife species that pose a risk to human health and to perform risk analyses to determine which species should be listed as "injurious" under the Lacey Act in order to limit trade of such species.

Section 190403. Trade of injurious species and species that pose a risk to human health. This section amends the Lacey Act of 1900 to allow for species that transmit pathogens that pose risks to human health to be listed as "injurious," which would prohibit the import and transport of those species, and to allow for emergency listings in the case of threats to human health. It also prohibits transportation of injurious species across state lines to limit spread of disease.

Section 190404. National Wildlife Health Center. This section directs the U.S. Geological Service's National Wildlife Health Center to establish a national database for wildlife diseases, including diseases that have the potential to infect humans, and to provide technical and scientific support for surveillance of emerging wildlife-borne diseases with the potential to infect humans, to coordinate surveillance, and to provide models and risk assessments of species and diseases.

Section 190405. Surveillance by States, Tribes, and Insular Areas. This section directs the Fish and Wildlife Service to provide funds to States, the District of Columbia, Tribes, and territories to conduct surveillance of emerging wildlife-borne diseases with the potential to infect humans.

Title V — Pandemic Relief for Aviation Workers and Passengers

Sec. 190501. Pandemic relief for aviation workers. Extends the prohibition on involuntary furloughs of employees of airlines or contractors that receive financial assistance (i.e., payroll grant) under the CARES Act through full exhaustion of such assistance, rather than ending on September 30, 2020. Clarifies that the CARES Act prohibition on the Treasury Department conditioning airline and contractor payroll grants on changes to current collective bargaining agreements applies regardless of when the grants are issued.

Sec. 190502. Transparency of financial assistance. Improves transparency of the Treasury Department's issuance of payroll grants to airlines and contractors under the CARES Act by requiring the Department to publish descriptions of each issued grant, including the grant recipient and amount, on the Department's public website within 72 hours of issuance. The Department will also be required to submit this information to Congress.

Sec. 190503. Air carrier maintenance outsourcing. Prohibits airlines that receive a loan or loan guarantee under the CARES Act from increasing their share of heavy maintenance work done overseas.

Sec. 190504. National aviation preparedness plan. Requires the Department of Transportation, in coordination with heads of other Federal departments and agencies, to develop a national aviation preparedness plan for communicable disease outbreaks, as the Government Accountability Office recommended in 2015, to ensure that Federal, State, and local governments, airports, airlines, and other aviation industry and labor stakeholders are better prepared for a future public health crisis.

Sec. 190505. Working and travel conditions. Mandates that airlines, during the COVID-19 pandemic: (1) require flight attendants and passengers on airplanes to wear masks or other face coverings; (2) require pilots to wear a mask or face covering while outside the flight deck and submit to the Federal Aviation Administration a proposal and safety risk assessment to allow pilots to wear such materials while in the flight deck; (3) provide pilots, flight attendants, and customer-facing employees with masks or protective face coverings, gloves, hand sanitizer, and alcohol wipes; (4) ensure aircraft and enclosed facilities are cleaned, disinfected, and sanitized frequently in accordance with Centers for Disease Control and Prevention guidance; (5) ensure cleaning workers are provided masks or protective face coverings and gloves; and (6) establish guidelines for notifying employees of a confirmed COVID-19 diagnosis.

Sec. 190506. Protection of certain Federal Aviation Administration employees. Mandates that the Federal Aviation Administration, during the COVID-19 pandemic: (1) provide air traffic controllers and airway transportation systems specialists with masks or protective face coverings, gloves, hand sanitizer, and alcohol wipes; (2) ensure air traffic control facilities are cleaned, disinfected, and sanitized frequently in accordance with Centers for Disease Control and Prevention guidance; and (3) ensure cleaning workers are provided masks or protective face coverings and gloves.

Title VI — Amtrak and Rail Workers

Sec. 190601. Amtrak COVID-19 Requirements. This provision provides that, for the duration of the COVID-19 pandemic, Amtrak must require passengers and employees to wear masks or protective face coverings while onboard an Amtrak train. Amtrak must also provide masks or protective face coverings, gloves, hand sanitizer, and wipes to all employees whose job responsibilities include passenger interaction. It also ensures that Amtrak trains, stations, and enclosed facilities are frequently cleaned and disinfected, and that employees who do this work are provided masks or protective face coverings and gloves.

Sec. 190602. Additional Enhanced Benefits Under the Railroad Unemployment Insurance Act. For railroad workers receiving unemployment benefits under the Railroad Unemployment Insurance Act, this provision would extend the temporary recovery benefit that provides $1,200 every two weeks (per registration period) in addition to regular benefits, creating parity for railroad workers.

Sec. 190603. Treatment of Payments from the Railroad Unemployment Insurance Account.
This provision would eliminate the Balanced Budget and Emergency Deficit Control Act sequester that automatically cuts unemployment and sickness benefits provided to railroad workers under the Railroad Unemployment Insurance Act. This change would allow railroad workers to receive the full benefit amounts to which they are entitled and would create parity with the treatment of other unemployment insurance benefit programs.

Sec. 190604. Technical Correction for Extended Unemployment Benefits under the Railroad Unemployment Insurance Act. Provides a technical correction to a provision in the CARES Act that extended railroad unemployment benefits to allow for easier implementation of the extended benefits.

Sec. 190605. Technical Correction. Provides a technical correction to a provision in the CARES Act by fixing an incorrect title reference to the Railroad Retirement Act.

Sec. 190606. Clarification of Oversight and Implementation of Relief for

Workers Affected by Coronavirus Act. Provides a technical correction to ensure that the Railroad Retirement Board (RRB) and its Inspector General have implementation and oversight authority over the RUIA-related provisions of the CARES Act.

Title VII — Energy and Environment Provisions

Section 190701. Home Energy and Water Service Continuity. Requires states and utilities receiving federal emergency funds to adopt or maintain in force policies to prevent shutoffs and ensure safety and continuity of home energy and water services to residential customers during the COVID-19 public health emergency.

Section 190702. Grants for Environmental Justice Communities Disproportionally Affected by COVID-19. Authorizes the Environmental Protection Agency's (EPA) environmental justice grants and provides up to $50 million in additional FY 2020 funds for the sole purpose of investigating or addressing the disproportionate impacts of COVID-19 in environmental communities.

Section 190703. Low-Income Household Drinking Water and Wastewater Assistance.
Provides financial assistance to low income and other adversely affected consumers to assist with payments for drinking water and wastewater expenses by authorizing $1.5 billion for grants to states, territories and Indian Tribes.

Section 190704. Water Service Continuity. Adds additional requirements to protect water services to residential customers during the COVID-19 public health emergency. Ensures all occupied residences are connected to water services throughout the emergency's duration, and that any reconnections are conducted in a manner that minimizes health risks. It also prohibits providers from assessing late fees for nonpayment occurring during the emergency period.

Title VIII — Death and Disability Benefits for Public Safety Officers Impacted by COVID-19

Sec. 190802. Death and Disability Benefits for Public Safety Officers Impacted by COVID- 19- Amends the Public Safety Officers' Benefits Program (PSOB) to establish a presumption that officers who die or are disabled because of COVID-19 infection are eligible to receive disability and death benefits. Ensures that officers who were injured or disabled during or because of the September 11, 2001 attacks, and whose injuries in combination with a COVID-19 illness result in disability or death, may apply for PSOB disability or death benefits.

Title IX — Victims of Crime Act Amendments

Sec. 190901. Short Title. This title may be cited as the "Victims of Crime Act Fix Act of 2020."

Sec. 190902. Victims of Crime Act Fix of 2020. Directs funding from deferred prosecution agreements and non-prosecution agreements to support victims of crime and waives state- matching requirement during the COVID-19 pandemic.

Sec. 190903. Waiver of Matching Requirement. Waives state matching requirement during the COVID-19 pandemic.

Title X — Jabara-Heyer NO HATE Act

The "No HATE Act": This Act would provide grant funding incentives to state and local law enforcement agencies for the collection of hate crimes data and reporting it to the Department of Justice, which would report the data to Congress.

Sec 191001. Short Title. This section contains the short title, the "Jabara-Heyer

National Opposition to Hate, Assault, and Threats to Equality Act of 2019, or "Jabara-Heyer NO HATE Act"

Sec 191002. Findings. This section makes a number of findings related to the recent rise of violent hate crimes and problems concerning inaccurate and incomplete hate crimes data.

Sec 191003. Definitions. This section defines several terms, including "priority agency" relevant to funding under this provision

Sec 191004. Reporting of Hate Crimes. This section authorizes the Attorney General to give grants to States and local governments to assist in implementing the National Incident-Based Reporting System (NIBRS) and to train employees to identify and classify hate crimes in NIBRS.

Sec 191005. Grants for State-Run Hate Crime Hotlines. This section authorizes the Attorney General to give grants to States to create hate crime hotlines.

Sec 191006. Information Collection by States and Units of Local Government. This section authorizes the Attorney General to give grants to local law enforcement agencies to conduct law enforcement activities or crime reduction programs to prevent, address, or otherwise respond to hate crimes, particularly related to reporting hate crimes.

Sec 191007. Requirements of the Attorney General. This section requires the Attorney General to collect and analyze information submitted by States and local governments for the purposes of developing policies related to the provision of accurate data.

Sec 191008. Alternative Sentencing. For individuals convicted under the Matthew Shepard and James Byrd, Jr. Hate Crimes Prevention Act, Section 8 allows a condition of supervised release where the defendant takes educational classes or performs community service directly related to the community harmed by the defendant's offense.

Title XI — Prisons and Jails

Sec. 191102. Emergency Community Supervision Act- During a declared national emergency relating to a communicable disease, mandates the release into community supervision of federal prisoners and pretrial detainees who are non-violent and, for instance, pregnant women, juveniles, older prisoners and detainees, and those with certain medical conditions. Modifies probation and supervised release policies to avoid unnecessary in-person contact with probation officers and to reduce the numbers of those supervised and those imprisoned for violations. Mandates the release of non-violent pretrial defendants on their own recognizance.

Sec. 191103. Court Authority to Reduce Sentences and Temporary Release Authority- During the COVID-19 emergency, expands court authority to order compassionate release for federal prisoners and to reduce sentences, and removes administrative barriers that slow the ability of prisoners to seek compassionate release. Authorizes courts to temporarily release persons who have been sentenced, but have not yet been transported to a Bureau of Prisons facility, to protect them from COVID-19.

Sec. 191104. Exemption for Prisoners from Exhausting Administrative Remedies- Exempts individuals from having to exhaust administrative remedies before bringing their concerns to a judge about conditions of incarceration that present a significant risk of harm during the COVID- 19 emergency.

Sec. 191105. Increasing Availability of Home Detention for Elderly Offenders- Increases the availability of home detention for non-violent elderly prisoners by ensuring that participants in the elderly prisoner home confinement pilot program get credit for good conduct time earned and lowers the eligibility for participation during the COVID-19 emergency period.

Sec. 191106. Effective Assistance of Counsel in the Digital Era Act- Directs the Attorney General to put in place an electronic communication system to be used by persons in federal custody that ensures confidential communication between those in custody and their attorneys.

Sec. 191107. COVID-19 Correctional Facility Emergency Response Act- Provides $600 million in funding to address the COVID-19 crisis in state and local prisons and jails, including $500 million to states and local governments that operate correctional facilities to provide testing and treatment of COVID-19 for incarcerated individuals by creating two grant programs—one focused on the release of low-risk individuals who are currently incarcerated and another aimed at reducing COVID-19 exposure for those individuals who are arrested; $75 million in funding to a new grant program to encourage states and localities to adopt practices that promote juvenile safety and rehabilitation without unnecessarily exposing youth to incarceration during this crisis; and $25 million for a grant program for state and local governments that operate correctional facilities for rapid testing of inmates who are leaving correctional custody.

Sec. 191108. Moratorium on Fees and Fines- Authorizes the establishment of a grant program that distributes funds directly to state and local courts, with the condition that they impose a moratorium on the imposition and collection of court-imposed fees and fines during the COVID-19 crisis.

Sec. 191109. Definition- Defines the "emergency covered period" consistent with the CARES Act.

Sec. 191110. Severability- Includes a severability clause for this title. **Title XII — Immigration Matters**

Sec. 191201. Extension of Filing and Other Deadlines. This section creates protections for certain noncitizens in the United States, as well as certain immigrant visa applicants, affected by processing delays and travel restrictions related to the COVID-19 public health emergency. Certain noncitizens who were lawfully present in the United States when HHS declared a public health emergency are protected from negative immigration consequences due to the inability to meet filing deadlines or leave the country. Temporary immigration status or work authorization that is set to expire during the emergency is automatically extended for a temporary period. Expiration dates of issued immigrant visas are extended for the duration of the emergency. Immigrant visa numbers that go unused at the end of the fiscal year are rolled over for use in subsequent fiscal years. And voluntary departure deadlines are extended for the duration of the emergency.

Sec. 191202. Temporary Accommodations for Naturalization Oath Ceremonies Due to Public Health Emergency. This section requires the Secretary of Homeland Security to establish procedures for remotely administering naturalization oath ceremonies during the COVID-19 emergency. Individuals who have been approved for naturalization may opt to participate in a remote swearing-in ceremony given the current suspension of in-person public ceremonies. The Department of Homeland Security (DHS) must provide written notice to eligible individuals and, to the greatest extent practicable, ensure that remote oath ceremonies are held expeditiously. The Secretary must also submit a report to Congress 180 days after the end of the public health emergency providing statistics on the use of remote oath ceremonies.

Sec. 191203. Temporary Protections for Essential Critical Infrastructure Workers. This section provides temporary protections to undocumented workers in the United States engaged in essential critical infrastructure work, as defined by DHS-issued guidance, during the COVID-19 emergency. Such workers are deemed to be in a period of deferred action and to be authorized for employment, and employers are shielded from certain immigration-related violations for employing such workers.

Sec. 191204. Supplementing the COVID response workforce. This section would temporarily ease certain immigration-related restrictions to allow immigrant physicians and other critical healthcare workers to better assist in the fight against COVID-19. This section would:

• Allow immigrant physicians who have lived and worked lawfully in the United States for years, and who have been approved for immigrant visas but are stuck in visa backlogs, to immediately apply for green cards if they will engage in COVID-19 work.

• Require DHS and the Department of State to expedite the processing of nonimmigrant petitions and visa applications for medical professionals and researchers who will engage in COVID-19 work.

• Provide flexibility to hospitals, medical facilities, and other employers of healthcare workers to quickly transfer employees to administer direct patient care or telemedicine in COVID-19 hot spots, engage in research and development of COVID-19 vaccines and cures, and provide other services as needed to address the emergency.

• Permanently authorize the "Conrad 30" Waiver Program, which allows States to sponsor immigrant physicians to work in medically underserved areas in exchange for a waiver of the physicians' 2-year foreign residence requirement. The base number of annual Conrad waivers available to each State is increased from 30 to 35, with a demand-based sliding scale to determine the number of available waivers in future years.

• Provide independent temporary work authorization documents to nonimmigrant physicians and other healthcare workers, giving them maximum mobility and flexibility to engage in COVID-19 work during the present emergency.

• Provide special immigrant status for certain nonimmigrant COVID-19 workers and ensure that the spouses and children of such workers are not subject to removal if the worker dies.

Section 191205. ICE Detention. This section requires DHS to review the immigration files of all individuals in the custody of Immigration and Customs Enforcement (ICE) to assess the need for continued detention. Individuals who are not subject to mandatory detention shall be prioritized for release, either on recognizance or into an alternative to detention program, unless the individual is a threat to public safety or national security. DHS shall also ensure that all individuals who continue to be detained by ICE:

• Have access to free telephonic and video communications, including unmonitored telephone calls with attorneys.

- May receive legal correspondence by fax or email.
- Are provided sufficient soap, hand sanitizer and other hygiene products.
Have access to virtual "know your rights" and legal orientation programming conducted by approved nonprofit organizations.

Title XIII — Coronavirus Relief Fund Amendments
Sec. 191301. Congressional Intent Relating to Tribal Governments Eligible for Coronavirus Relief Fund Payments. Clarifies that only federally recognized tribal governments are eligible for payments in CARES and the Heroes Act.
Sec. 191302. Redistribution of Amounts Recovered or Recouped from Payments for Tribal Governments; Reporting Requirements. Establishes procedures to recoup and/or repay amounts to tribal governments.
Sec. 191303. Use of Relief Funds. Expands the use of funds to cover lost, delayed, or decreased revenue stemming from the COVID-19 public health emergency.

Title XIV — Rural Digital Opportunity
Sec. 191401. Acceleration of Rural Digital Opportunity Fund Phase I Auction. This section requires the FCC to expedite its Rural Digital Opportunity Fund auction to fast-track the build out of high-speed, gigabit internet service to rural America. This fast-track would only be available to uncontested applicants that can build networks that can provide service within a year of having funding authorized.
Sec. 191402. Ensuring the FCC Creates Accurate Service Maps. This section sets a firm
deadline for implementing the Broadband DATA Act and authorizes funding for that purpose.

Subtitle A

Title XV — Foreign Affairs Provisions
SEC. 191501. MITIGATION PLAN TO ASSIST FEDERAL VOTERS OVERSEAS IMPACTED BY COVID-19.– this section would require the State Department, in consultation with the Defense Department, to submit to Congress and make widely available its plans to mitigate any COVID-19 related impacts on overseas voters seeking to return their mail-in ballots ahead of the 2020 federal election.
SEC. 191502. REPORT ON EFFORTS OF THE CORONAVIRUS REPATRIATION TASK FORCE.– this section would require an after-action report by the State Department on their efforts to repatriate Americans back to the United States during the COVID-19 crisis.

Subtitle B
- **GLOBAL HEALTH SECURITY ACT OF 2020**- requires the President to establish a U.S. Global Health Security Coordinator, a position previously located at the National Security Council, which the Administration eliminated in 2018. It also establishes an interagency review council to ensure global health security is prioritized within the Executive Branch, and would require a global health security strategy to help other countries strengthen their health care systems and detect and mitigate outbreaks early.

Subtitle C
SECURING AMERICA FROM EPIDEMICS ACT – this would authorize the US to participate in the Coalition for Epidemic Preparedness Innovations (CEPI), a consortium which has led on developing vaccines for high priority epidemic threats, including Ebola and COVID- 19.

Subtitle D

SEC. 191515. AUTHORIZATION TO EXTEND MILLENNIUM CHALLENGE COMPACTS – this section would notwithstand the statutory 5 year limit on MCC, allowing MCC to continue working with countries to complete compact agreements which were interrupted by COVID for up to one additional year.

DIVISION T – Additional Other Matters

Prepared by the Democratic staff of the House Committees on Transportation and Infrastructure and House Administration

Sec. 200001. Application of Law. Temporarily waives prohibition on using federal funds to pay for consultants or counsel to allow EDA grantees to pay consultants to help develop grant applications for funds under the CARES Act.

Sec. 200002. Disaster Recovery Office. Grants EDA disaster hiring authority, which it currently does not have, and defederalizes the EDA revolving loan funds, which are vital lifelines to small, family-owned businesses.

Sec. 200003. Application of Buy American. The Stafford Act has a Buy American requirement limited only to Washington, D.C., Puerto Rico, the U.S. Virgin Islands, and American Samoa. This provides a waiver – only during the COVID-19 pandemic – so these four entities may source crucial personal protective and medical equipment internationally, if necessary, just as other States can.

Sec. 200004. Premium Pay Authority. Expands the premium pay cap waiver for FEMA employees for 2020 and 2021 due to heightened operational activity from Stafford Act-declared major disasters and emergencies.

88

Sec. 200005. Cost Share. Adjusts the cost share for assistance provided under any Stafford Act declaration for the COVID-19 pandemic from 75% Federal/25% non-Federal to 100% Federal.

Sec. 200006. Clarification of Assistance. Provides assistance for activities, costs, and purchases of States, local, or eligible private non-profits, including activities eligible under the Stafford Act including, but not limited to: backfill costs for first responders, increased operating costs for essential government services, costs of providing public guidance and information, costs for establishing virtual services and operating remote test sites, training provided in anticipation of, or response to, to the next emergency declaration, personal protective equipment for first responders, public health and medical supplies, non-congregate sheltering, food preparation and delivery to impacted communities, and funeral benefits.

Sec. 200007. Safety Upgrades in GSA Facilities. Requires the General Services Administration (GSA) to take action to prevent airborne transmission of COVID–19 through air conditioning, heating, ventilating, and water systems in facilities owned or leased by the GSA to ensure safe and healthy indoor environments for Federal employees. It also states that GSA should prioritize indoor air and water environmental quality in facilities and energy-saving building technologies and products.

Sec. 200008. Non-Federal Tenants in GSA Facilities. Prohibits GSA from referring any non- Federal tenants in GSA-owned facilities to a debt collection agency during the COVID–19 pandemic, and requires GSA to submit to Congress a report containing all requests for rent deferrals related to COVID–19 from non-Federal tenants of facilities owned by the GSA.

Sec. 200009. Transit COVID-19 Requirements. This section applies to large transit agencies in urbanized areas with at least 500,000 individuals (covered transit agencies) and would: (1) for covered transit agencies, require public transit passengers to wear masks or other face coverings; (2) require covered transit agencies to provide all customer-facing employees with masks or protective face coverings, gloves, and hand sanitizer and wipes with sufficient alcohol content; (3) ensure that public transit vehicles are sanitized frequently in accordance with CDC guidance; (4) ensure that transit stations and facilities in which transit employees work are sanitized on a regular basis in accordance with CDC guidelines; and (5) require covered transit agencies to establish or adhere to applicable guidelines for notifying employees of confirmed COVID-19 diagnoses.

Sec. 200010. Regulation of Anchorage and Movement of Vessels During National Emergency. Expands the Coast Guard's authority under 46 USC 70051 (formerly part of the Magnuson Act under 50 USC 191) to go beyond strict war/national security type incidents to also include public health emergencies.

Sec. 200011. MSP Operating Vessels. Waives the minimum vessel operating days for Maritime Security Program (MSP) operators for FY20-21 to ensure the MSP stipend is paid in full to all 60 enrolled vessels to keep critical U.S.-flag national and economic security assets available.

Sec. 200012. Library of Congress. This section authorizes the Library of Congress to extend the period of performance or delivery of services under severable service contracts for an additional twelve months if the contract is delayed or otherwise affected by the COVID-19 pandemic.

Sec. 200013. Architect of the Capitol. This section authorizes the Architect of the Capitol to, in the case of an emergency, reimburse employees for commuting costs between their residence and place of employment. This section is intended to mitigate against the significant reduction in public transportation services in the National Capitol Region for workers essential to the operations of the Legislative Branch.

Sec. 200014. Reports on Suicide Among Members of the Armed Forces During the COVID–19 Public Health Emergency. Requires the Secretary of Defense, no later than 90 days following enactment, to submit a report to Congress on suicide among members of the Armed Forces during the COVID-19 public health emergency. The report will also include a research agenda for the Secretary of Defense to establish suicide prevention treatment for Armed Forces during a public health emergency.

Sec. 200015. Modification to Maintenance of Effort Requirement for Temporary Increase in Medicaid FMAP. Modifies provisions in the Families First Coronavirus Response Act to ensure that states are able to receive FMAP funds irrespective of changes made to their Medicaid programs that went into effect in early April.

Health and Economic Recovery Omnibus Emergency Solutions Act (HEROES Act, H.R. 6800), Complete Bill Text

116th CONGRESS

2d Session

H. R. 6800

Making emergency supplemental appropriations for the fiscal year ending September 30, 2020, and for other purposes.

IN THE HOUSE OF REPRESENTATIVES

May 12, 2020

Mrs. Lowey (for herself, Mr. Engel, Mrs. Carolyn B. Maloney of New York, Mr. Nadler, Mr. Neal, Mr. Pallone, Mr. Scott of Virginia, Mr. Takano, Ms. Velázquez, Ms. Waters, Mr. Grijalva, and Ms. Lofgren) introduced the following bill; which was referred to the Committee on Appropriations, and in addition to the Committees on the Budget, and Ways and Means, for a period to be subsequently determined by the Speaker, in each case for consideration of such provisions as fall within the jurisdiction of the committee concerned

A BILL

Making emergency supplemental appropriations for the fiscal year ending September 30, 2020, and for other purposes.

Be it enacted by the Senate and House of Representatives of the United States of America in Congress assembled,

SHORT TITLE

Section 1.

This Act may be cited as the "Health and Economic Recovery Omnibus Emergency Solutions Act" or the "HEROES Act".

TABLE OF CONTENTS

SEC. 2.

The table of contents is as follows:

SEC. 3.

Except as expressly provided otherwise, any reference to "this Act" contained in any division of this Act shall be treated as referring only to the provisions of that division.

DIVISION A—CORONAVIRUS RECOVERY SUPPLEMENTAL APPROPRIATIONS ACT, 2020

The following sums are hereby appropriated, out of any money in the Treasury not otherwise appropriated, for the fiscal year ending September 30, 2020, and for other purposes, namely:

TITLE I

—AGRICULTURE, RURAL DEVELOPMENT, FOOD AND DRUG ADMINISTRA-TION, AND RELATED AGENCIES
DEPARTMENT OF AGRICULTURE
AGRICULTURAL PROGRAMS

Office Of Inspector General

For an additional amount for "Office of Inspector General", $2,500,000, to remain available until September 30, 2021, to prevent, prepare for, and respond to coronavirus, domestically or internationally: Provided, That the funding made available under this heading in this Act shall be used for conducting audits and investigations of projects and activities carried out with funds made available to the Department of Agriculture to prevent, prepare for, and respond to coronavirus, domestically or internationally: Provided further, That such amount is designated by the Congress as being for an emergency requirement pursuant to section 251(b)(2)(A)(i) of the Balanced Budget and Emergency Deficit Control Act of 1985.

DOMESTIC FOOD PROGRAMS

Food And Nutrition Service

child nutrition programs

For an additional amount for "Child Nutrition Programs", $3,000,000,000 to remain available until September 30, 2021, to prevent, prepare for, and respond to coronavirus, domestically or internationally: Provided, That the amount provided under this heading is for the purposes of carrying out section 180002 of the "Child Nutrition and Related Programs Recovery Act": Provided further, That such amount is designated by the Congress as being for an emergency requirement pursuant to section 251(b)(2)(A)(i) of the Balanced Budget and Emergency Deficit Control Act of 1985.

special supplemental nutrition program for women, infants, and children (wic)

For an additional amount for the "Special Supplemental Nutrition Program for Women, Infants, and Children", $1,100,000,000, to remain available through September 30, 2022: Provided, That such amount is designated by the Congress as being for an emergency requirement pursuant to section 251(b)(2)(A)(i) of the Balanced Budget and Emergency Deficit Control Act of 1985.

supplemental nutrition assistance program

For an additional amount for "Supplemental Nutrition Assistance Program", $10,000,000,000, to remain available until September 30, 2021, to prevent, prepare for, and respond to coronavirus: Provided, That such amount is designated by the Congress as being for an emergency requirement pursuant to section 251(b)(2)(A)(i) of the Balanced Budget and Emergency Deficit Control Act of 1985.

commodity assistance program

For an additional amount for "Commodity Assistance Program", $150,000,000, to remain available through September 30, 2021, for the emergency food assistance program as authorized by section 27(a) of the Food and Nutrition Act of 2008 (7 U.S.C. 2036(a)) and section 204(a)(1) of the Emergency Food Assistance Act of 1983 (7 U.S.C. 7508(a)(1)): Provided, That such amount is designated by the Congress as being for an emergency requirement pursuant to section 251(b)(2)(A)(i) of the Balanced Budget and Emergency Deficit Control Act of 1985.

GENERAL PROVISIONS—THIS TITLE

SEC. 10101.

For an additional amount for the Commonwealth of the Northern Mariana Islands, $1,822,000, to remain available until September 30, 2021, for nutrition assistance to prevent, prepare for, and respond to coronavirus: Provided, That such amount is designated by the Congress as being for an emergency requirement pursuant to section 251(b)(2)(A)(i) of the Balanced Budget and Emergency Deficit Control Act of 1985.

SEC. 10102.

Under the heading "Commodity Assistance Program" in the Coronavirus Aid, Relief, and Economic Security Act (Public Law 116–136), strike "to prevent, prepare for, and respond to coronavirus, domestically or internationally,": Provided, That the amounts repurposed in this section that were previously designated by the Congress as an emergency requirement pursuant to the Balanced Budget and Emergency Deficit Control Act of 1985 are designated by the Congress as an emergency requirement pursuant to section 251(b)(2)(A)(i) of the Balanced Budget and Emergency Deficit Control Act of 1985.

SEC. 10103.

For an additional amount for the program established under 7 U.S.C. 5936, to prevent, prepare for, and respond to coronavirus, $20,000,000, to remain available until September 30, 2021: Provided, That such amount is designated by the Congress as being for an emergency requirement pursuant to section 251(b)(2)(A)(i) of the Balanced Budget and Emergency Deficit Control Act of 1985.

TITLE II

—COMMERCE, JUSTICE, SCIENCE, AND RELATED AGENCIES
DEPARTMENT OF COMMERCE
Bureau Of The Census
current surveys and programs
(including transfer of funds)
For an additional amount for "Current Surveys and Programs", $10,000,000: Provided, That such sums may be transferred to the Bureau of the Census Working Capital Fund for necessary expenses incurred as a result of the coronavirus, including for payment of salaries and leave to Bureau of the Census staff resulting from the suspension of data collection for reimbursable surveys conducted for other Federal agencies: Provided further, That such amount is designated by the Congress as being for an emergency requirement pursuant to section 251(b)(2)(A)(i) of the Balanced Budget and Emergency Deficit Control Act of 1985.
periodic censuses and programs
For an additional amount for "Periodic Censuses and Programs", $400,000,000, to remain available until September 30, 2022, to prevent, prepare for, and respond to coronavirus: Provided, That such amount is designated by the Congress as being for an emergency requirement pursuant to section 251(b)(2)(A)(i) of the Balanced Budget and Emergency Deficit Control Act of 1985.
National Oceanic And Atmospheric Administration
assistance to fishery participants
Pursuant to section 12005 of the Coronavirus Aid, Relief, and Economic Security Act of 2020 (Public Law 116–136), for an additional amount for "Assistance to Fishery Participants", $100,000,000, to remain available until September 30, 2021, for necessary expenses to provide assistance to Tribal, subsistence, commercial, and charter fishery participants affected by the novel coronavirus (COVID–19), which may include direct relief payments: Provided, That such amount is designated by the Congress as being for an emergency requirement pursuant to section 251(b)(2)(A)(i) of the Balanced Budget and Emergency Deficit Control Act of 1985.
Departmental Management

office of inspector general

For an additional amount for "Office of Inspector General", $1,000,000, to remain available until expended to prevent, prepare for, and respond to coronavirus, including the impact of coronavirus on the work of the Department of Commerce and to carry out investigations and audits related to the funding made available for the Department of Commerce in this Act and in title II of division B of Public Law 116–136: Provided, That such amount is designated by the Congress as being for an emergency requirement pursuant to section 251(b)(2)(A)(i) of the Balanced Budget and Emergency Deficit Control Act of 1985.

administrative provision—department of commerce

SEC. 10201.

Notwithstanding any other provision of law, the Federal share for grants provided by the Economic Development Administration under this Act, Public Law 116–93, Public Law 116–20, and Public Law 116–136 shall be 100 percent: Provided, That the amounts repurposed in this section that were previously designated by the Congress as an emergency requirement pursuant to the Balanced Budget and Emergency Deficit Control Act of 1985 are designated by the Congress as an emergency requirement pursuant to section 251(b)(2)(A)(i) of the Balanced Budget and Emergency Deficit Control Act of 1985.

DEPARTMENT OF JUSTICE

Federal Prison System

salaries and expenses

For an additional amount for "Salaries and Expenses", $200,000,000, to remain available until September 30, 2021, to prevent, prepare for, and respond to coronavirus, including the impact of coronavirus on the work of the Department of Justice, to include funding for medical testing and services, personal protective equipment, hygiene supplies and services, and sanitation services: Provided, That such amount is designated by the Congress as being for an emergency requirement pursuant to section 251(b)(2)(A)(i) of the Balanced Budget and Emergency Deficit Control Act of 1985.

Office Of Inspector General

For an additional amount for "Office of Inspector General", $3,000,000, to remain available until expended to prevent, prepare for, and respond to coronavirus, including the impact of coronavirus on the work of the Department of Justice and to carry out investigations and audits related to the funding made available for the Department of Justice in this Act: Provided, That such amount is designated by the Congress as being for an emergency requirement pursuant to section 251(b)(2)(A)(i) of the Balanced Budget and Emergency Deficit Control Act of 1985.

State And Local Law Enforcement Activities

Office On Violence Against Women

violence against women prevention and prosecution programs

For an additional amount for "Violence Against Women Prevention and Prosecution Programs", $100,000,000, to remain available until expended, of which—

(1) $30,000,000 is for grants to combat violence against women, as authorized by part T of the Omnibus Crime Control and Safe Streets Acts of 1968;

(2) $15,000,000 is for transitional housing assistance grants for victims of domestic violence, dating violence, stalking, or sexual assault, as authorized by section 40299 of the Violent Crime Control and Law Enforcement Act of 1994 (Public Law 103–322;

"1994 Act");

(3) $15,000,000 is for sexual assault victims assistance, as authorized by section 41601 of the 1994 Act;

(4) $10,000,000 is for rural domestic violence and child abuse enforcement assistance grants, as authorized by section 40295 of the 1994 Act;

(5) $10,000,000 is for legal assistance for victims, as authorized by section 1201 of the Victims of Trafficking and Violence Protection Act of 2000 (Public Law 106–386; "2000 Act");

(6) $4,000,000 is for grants to assist tribal governments in exercising special domestic violence criminal jurisdiction, as authorized by section 904 of the Violence Against Women Reauthorization Act of 2013; and

(7) $16,000,000 is for grants to support families in the justice system, as authorized by section 1301 of the 2000 Act:

Provided, That funds made available under this heading shall be made available without any otherwise applicable requirement that a recipient of such funds provide any other Federal funds, or any non-Federal funds, as a condition to receive the funds made available under this heading: Provided further, That such amount is designated by the Congress as being for an emergency requirement pursuant to section 251(b)(2)(A)(i) of the Balanced Budget and Emergency Deficit Control Act of 1985.

Office Of Justice Programs

state and local law enforcement assistance

For an additional amount for "State and Local Law Enforcement Assistance", $300,000,000, to remain available until expended, for the same purposes and subject to the same conditions as the appropriations for fiscal year 2020 under this heading in title II of division B of Public Law 116–136, including for the purchase of personal protective equipment, and for costs related to preventing and controlling coronavirus at correctional institutions: Provided, That, notwithstanding section 502(a)(1) of the Omnibus Crime Control and Safe Streets Act of 1968 (34 U.S.C. 10153), funds provided under this heading in both this Act and title II of division B of Public Law 116–136 may be used to supplant State or local funds: Provided further, That funds made available under this heading in both this Act and title II of division B of Public Law 116–136 shall be made available without any otherwise applicable requirement that a recipient of such funds provide any other Federal funds, or any non-Federal funds, as a condition to receive the funds made available under such heading: Provided further, That such amount is designated by the Congress as being for an emergency requirement pursuant to section 251(b)(2)(A)(i) of the Balanced Budget and Emergency Deficit Control Act of 1985.

For an additional amount for "State and Local Law Enforcement Assistance", $250,000,000, to remain available until expended, for offender reentry programs and research, as authorized by the Second Chance Act of 2007 (Public Law 110–199) and by the Second Chance Reauthorization Act of 2018 (Public Law 115–391), without regard to the time limitations specified at section 6(1) of such Act, to prevent, prepare for, and respond to coronavirus: Provided, That, notwithstanding any other provision of law, funds provided under this heading may be used to supplant State or local funds: Provided further, That funds made available under this heading shall be made available without any otherwise applicable requirement that a recipient of such funds provide any other Federal funds, or any non-Federal funds, as a condition to receive the funds made available under this heading: Provided further, That

such amount is designated by the Congress as being for an emergency requirement pursuant to section 251(b)(2)(A)(i) of the Balanced Budget and Emergency Deficit Control Act of 1985.

For an additional amount for "State and Local Law Enforcement Assistance", $600,000,000, to remain available until expended, for grants, contracts, cooperative agreements, and other assistance as authorized by the Pandemic Justice Response Act ("the Act"): Provided, That $500,000,000 is to establish and implement policies and procedures to prevent, detect, and stop the presence and spread of COVID–19 among arrestees, detainees, inmates, correctional facility staff, and visitors to the facilities; and for pretrial citation and release grants, as authorized by the Act: Provided further, That $25,000,000 is for Rapid COVID–19 Testing, as authorized by the Act: Provided further, That $75,000,000 is for grants for Juvenile Specific Services, as authorized by the Act: Provided further, That, notwithstanding any other provision of law, funds provided under this heading may be used to supplant State or local funds: Provided further, That funds made available under this heading shall be made available without any otherwise applicable requirement that a recipient of such funds provide any other Federal funds, or any non-Federal funds, as a condition to receive the funds made available under this heading: Provided further, That such amount is designated by the Congress as being for an emergency requirement pursuant to section 251(b)(2)(A)(i) of the Balanced Budget and Emergency Deficit Control Act of 1985.

Community Oriented Policing Services

community oriented policing services programs

For an additional amount for "Community Oriented Policing Services", $300,000,000, to remain available until expended, for grants under section 1701 of title I of the 1968 Omnibus Crime Control and Safe Streets Act (34 U.S.C. 10381) for hiring and rehiring of additional career law enforcement officers under part Q of such title, notwithstanding subsection (i) of such section, and including for the purchase of personal protective equipment: Provided, That, notwithstanding 34 U.S.C. 10384, funds provided under this heading may be used to supplant State or local funds and may be used to retain career law enforcement officers: Provided further, That funds made available under this heading shall be made available without any otherwise applicable requirement that a recipient of such funds provide any other Federal funds, or any non-Federal funds, as a condition to receive the funds made available under this heading: Provided further, That such amount is designated by the Congress as being for an emergency requirement pursuant to section 251(b)(2)(A)(i) of the Balanced Budget and Emergency Deficit Control Act of 1985.

SCIENCE

National Science Foundation

research and related activities

(including transfer of funds)

For an additional amount for "Research and Related Activities", $125,000,000, to remain available until September 30, 2022, to prevent, prepare for, and respond to coronavirus, including to fund research grants, of which $1,000,000 shall be for a study on the spread of COVID–19 related disinformation: Provided further, That, within the amount appropriated under this heading in this Act, up to 2 percent of funds may be transferred to the "Agency Operations and Award Management" account for management, administration, and oversight of funds provided under this heading in this Act: Provided further, That such amount is designated by the Congress as being for an emergency requirement pursuant to section 251(b)(2)(A)(i) of the Balanced Budget and Emergency Deficit Control Act of 1985.

RELATED AGENCIES

Legal Services Corporation

payment to the legal services corporation

For an additional amount for "Payment to the Legal Services Corporation", $50,000,000, for the same purposes and subject to the same conditions as the appropriations for fiscal year 2020 under this heading in title II of division B of Public Law 116–136: Provided, That such amount is designated by the Congress as being for an emergency requirement pursuant to section 251(b)(2)(A)(i) of the Balanced Budget and Emergency Deficit Control Act of 1985.

TITLE III

—FINANCIAL SERVICES AND GENERAL GOVERNMENT

DEPARTMENT OF THE TREASURY

Departmental Offices

office of inspector general

salaries and expenses

For an additional amount for "Salaries and Expenses", $35,000,000, to remain available until expended, to conduct monitoring and oversight of the receipt, disbursement, and use of funds made available under the "Coronavirus State Fiscal Relief Fund" and the "Coronavirus Local Fiscal Relief Fund" (collectively, "Fiscal Relief Funds"): Provided, That, if the Inspector General of the Department of the Treasury determines that an entity receiving a payment from amounts provided by the Fiscal Relief Funds has failed to comply with the provisions governing the use of such funding, the Inspector General shall transmit any relevant information related to such determination to the Committees on Appropriations of the House of Representatives and the Senate not later than 5 days after any such determination is made: Provided further, That such amount is designated by the Congress as being for an emergency requirement pursuant to section 251(b)(2)(A)(i) of the Balanced Budget and Emergency Deficit Control Act of 1985.

treasury inspector general for tax administration

salaries and expenses

For an additional amount for "Salaries and Expenses", $2,500,000, to remain available until expended, to prevent, prepare for, and respond to coronavirus, domestically or internationally: Provided, That such amount is designated by the Congress as being for an emergency requirement pursuant to section 251(b)(2)(A)(i) of the Balanced Budget and Emergency Deficit Control Act of 1985.

homeowner assistance fund

For activities and assistance authorized in section 110202 of the "COVID–19 HERO Act" , $75,000,000,000, to remain available until expended: Provided, That such amount is designated by the Congress as being for an emergency requirement pursuant to section 251(b)(2)(A)(i) of the Balanced Budget and Emergency Deficit Control Act of 1985.

Bureau Of The Fiscal Service

salaries and expenses

For an additional amount for "Salaries and Expenses", $78,650,000, to remain available until September 30, 2021, to prevent, prepare for, and respond to coronavirus, domestically or internationally: Provided, That such amount is designated by the Congress as being for an emergency requirement pursuant to section 251(b)(2)(A)(i) of the Balanced Budget and Emergency Deficit Control Act of 1985.

coronavirus state fiscal relief fund

For making payments to States, territories, and Tribal governments to mitigate the fiscal effects stemming from the public health emergency with respect to the Coronavirus Disease (COVID–19), $540,000,000,000 to remain available until expended, which shall be in addition to any other amounts available for making payments to States, territories, and Tribal governments for any purpose (including payments made under section 601 of the Social Security Act), of which:

(1) $20,000,000,000 shall be for making payments to the Commonwealth of Puerto Rico, United States Virgin Islands, Guam, Commonwealth of the Northern Mariana Islands, and American Samoa: Provided, That of the amount made available in this paragraph, half shall be allocated equally among each entity specified in this paragraph, and half shall be allocated as an additional amount to each such entity in an amount which bears the same proportion to half of the total amount provided under this paragraph as the relative population of each such entity bears to the total population of all such entities;

(2) $20,000,000,000 shall be for making payments to Tribal governments: Provided, That payments of amounts made available in this paragraph shall be made to each Tribal Government in an amount determined by the Secretary of the Treasury, in consultation with the Secretary of the Interior and Indian Tribes, that is based on increased aggregate expenditures of each such Tribal government (or a tribally-owned entity of such Tribal government) in fiscal year 2020 relative to aggregate expenditures in fiscal year 2019 by the Tribal government (or tribally-owned entity) and determined in such manner as the Secretary determines appropriate to ensure that all amounts available pursuant to the preceding proviso for fiscal year 2020 are distributed to Tribal governments:

(3) $250,000,000,000 shall be for making initial payments to each of the 50 States and the District of Columbia, of which—

(A) $51,000,000,000 shall be allocated equally between each of the 50 States and the District of Columbia;

(B) $150,000,000,000 shall be allocated as an additional amount to each such entity in an amount which bears the same proportion to the total amount provided under this subparagraph as the relative population of each such entity bears to the total population of all such entities;

(C) $49,000,000,000 shall be allocated as additional amounts among each of the 50 States and the District of Columbia in an amount which bears the same proportion to the total amount provided under this subparagraph as the relative prevalence of COVID–19 within each such entity bears to the total prevalence of COVID–19 within all such entities: Provided, That the relative prevalence of COVID–19 shall be calculated using the most recent data on the number of confirmed and probable cases as published on the Internet by the Centers for Disease Control and Prevention for each entity specified in the preceding proviso;

(4) $250,000,000,000 shall be for making an additional payment to each of the 50 States and the District of Columbia, of which—

(A) $51,000,000,000 shall be allocated equally between each of the 50 States and the District of Columbia; and

(B) $199,000,000,000 shall be allocated between each such entity in an additional amount which bears the same proportion to the total amount provided under this subparagraph as the average estimated number of seasonally-adjusted unemployed individuals (as measured by the Bureau of Labor Statistics Local Area Unemployment Statistics program) in each such entity over the 3-month period ending in March 2021 bears to the average estimated number of seasonally-adjusted unemployed individuals in all such entities over the same period.

Provided further, That any entity receiving a payment from funds made available under this heading in this Act shall only use such amounts to respond to, mitigate, cover costs or replace foregone revenues not projected on January 31, 2020 stemming from the public health emergency, or its negative economic impacts, with respect to the Coronavirus Disease (COVID–19): Provided further, That if the Inspector General of the Department of the Treasury determines that an entity receiving a payment from amounts provided under this heading has failed to comply with the preceding proviso, the amount equal to the amount of funds used in violation of such subsection shall be booked as a debt of such entity owed to the Federal Government, and any amounts recovered under this subsection shall be deposited into the general fund of the Treasury as discretionary offsetting receipts: Provided further, That for purposes of the preceding provisos under this heading in this Act, the population of each entity described in any such proviso shall be determined based on the most recent year for which data are available from the Bureau of the Census, or in the case of an Indian tribe, shall be determined based on data certified by the Tribal government: Provided further, That as used under this heading in this Act, the terms "Tribal government" and "Indian Tribe" have the same meanings as specified in section 601(g) of the Social Security Act (42 U.S.C. 601(g)), as added by section 5001 of the CARES Act (Public Law 116–136) and amended by section 191301 of division X of this Act, and the term "State" means one of the 50 States: Provided further, That the Secretary of Treasury shall make all payments required pursuant to paragraphs (1), (2), and (3) not later than 30 days after the date of enactment of this Act, and shall make all payments required pursuant to paragraph (4) not later than May 3, 2021: Provided further, That such amount is designated by the Congress as being for an emergency requirement pursuant to section 251(b)(2)(A)(i) of the Balanced Budget and Emergency Deficit Control Act of 1985.

coronavirus local fiscal relief fund

For making payments to metropolitan cities, counties, and other units of general local government to mitigate the fiscal effects stemming from the public health emergency with respect to the Coronavirus Disease (COVID–19), $375,000,000,000, to remain available until expended, which shall be in addition to any other amounts available for making payments to metropolitan cities, counties, and other units of general local government (including payments made under section 601 of the Social Security Act), of which—

(1) $187,500,000,000 shall be for making payments to metropolitan cities and other units of general local government (as those terms are defined in section 102 of the Housing and Community Development Act of 1974 (42 U.S.C. 5302)), of which—

(A) $131,250,000,000 shall be allocated pursuant to the formula under section 106(b)(1) of the Housing and Community Development Act of 1974 (42 U.S.C. 5306(b)(1)) to metropolitan cities (as defined in section 102(a)(4) of such Act (42 U.S.C. 5302(a)(4)), including metropolitan cities that have relinquished or deferred their status as a metropolitan city as of the date of enactment of this Act: Provided, That $87,500,000,000 of the funds provided under this subparagraph shall be paid not later than 30 days after the date of enactment of this Act: Provided further, That $43,750,000,000 of the funds provided under this subparagraph shall be paid not earlier than April 15, 2021, but not later than May 3, 2021; and

(B) $56,250,000,000 shall be distributed to each State (as that term is defined in section 102 of the Housing and Community Development Act of 1974 (42 U.S.C. 5302)) for use by units of general local government, other than counties or parishes, in non-entitlement areas (as defined in such section 102) of such States in an amount which bears the same proportion to the total amount provided under this subparagraph as the total population of such units of general local government within the State bears to the total population of all such units of general local government in all such States: Provided, That two-thirds of the funds provided under this subparagraph and allocated to each such unit of general local government shall be distributed to each such unit of general local government not later than 30 days after the date of enactment of this Act: Provided further, That the remainder of the funds provided under this subparagraph and allocated to each such unit of general local government shall be distributed to each such unit of general local government not earlier than April 15, 2021, but not later than May 3, 2021: Provided further, That a State shall pass-through the amounts received under this subparagraph, within 30 days of receipt, to each such unit of general local government in an amount that bears the same proportion to the amount distributed to each such State as the population of such unit of general local government bears to the total population of all such units of general local government within each such State: Provided further, That if a State has not elected to distribute amounts allocated under this paragraph, the Secretary of the Treasury shall pay the applicable amounts under this subparagraph to such units of general local government in the State not later than 30 days after the date on which the State would otherwise have received the amounts from the Secretary; and

(2) $187,500,000,000 shall be paid directly to counties within the 50 States, the District of Columbia, the Commonwealth of Puerto Rico, the United States Virgin Islands, Guam, the Commonwealth of the Northern Mariana Islands, and American Samoa in an amount which bears the same proportion to the total amount provided under this paragraph as the relative population of each such county bears to the total population of all such entities: Provided, That two-thirds of the funds provided under this paragraph and allocated to each such county shall be distributed to each such county not later than 30 days after the date of enactment of this Act: Provided further, That the remainder of the amount allocated to each such county under this paragraph shall be distributed to each such county not earlier than April 15, 2021, but not later than May 3, 2021: Provided further, That no county that is an "urban county" (as defined in section 102 of the Housing and Community Development Act of 1974 (42 U.S.C. 5302)) shall receive less than the amount the county would otherwise receive if the amount distributed under this paragraph were allocated to metropolitan cities and urban counties under section 106(b) of the Housing and Community Development Act of 1974 (42 U.S.C. 5306(b)): Provided further, That in the case of an amount to be paid to a county that is not a unit of general local government, the amount shall instead be paid to the State in which such county is located, and such State shall distribute such amount to units of general local government within such county in an amounts that bear the same proportion as the population of such units of general

local government bear to the total population of such county:
Provided further, That any entity receiving a payment from funds made available under this heading in this Act shall only use such amounts to respond to, mitigate, cover costs or replace foregone revenues not projected on January 31, 2020 stemming from the public health emergency, or its negative economic impacts, with respect to the Coronavirus Disease (COVID–19): Provided further, That if the Inspector General of the Department of the Treasury determines that an entity receiving a payment from amounts provided under this heading has failed to comply with the preceding proviso, the amount equal to the amount of funds used in violation of such subsection shall be booked as a debt of such entity owed to the Federal Government, and any amounts recovered under this subsection shall be deposited into the general fund of the Treasury as discretionary offsetting receipts: Provided further, That nothing in paragraph (1) or (2) shall be construed as prohibiting a unit of general local government that has formed a consolidated government, or that is geographically contained (in full or in part) within the boundaries of another unit of general local government from receiving a distribution under each of subparagraphs (A) and (B) under paragraph (1) or under paragraph (2), as applicable, based on the respective formulas specified contained therein: Provided further, That the amounts otherwise determined for distribution to units of local government under each of subparagraphs (A) and (B) under paragraph (1) and under paragraph (2) shall each be adjusted by the Secretary of the Treasury on a pro rata basis to the extent necessary to comply with the amount appropriated and the requirements specified in each paragraph and subparagraph, as applicable: Provided further, That as used under this heading in this Act, the term "county" means a county, parish, or other equivalent county division (as defined by the Bureau of the Census): Provided further, That for purposes of the preceding provisos under this heading in this Act, the population of an entity shall be determined based on the most recent year for which data are available from the Bureau of the Census: Provided further, That such amount is designated by Congress as being for an emergency requirement pursuant to section 251(b)(2)(A)(i) of the Balanced Budget and Emergency Deficit Control Act of 1985.

Community Development Financial Institutions Fund Program Account
(including transfer of funds)

For an additional amount for the "Community Development Financial Institutions Fund Program Account", $1,000,000,000, to remain available until September 30, 2021, to prevent, prepare for, and respond to coronavirus: Provided , That the Community Development Financial Institutions Fund (CDFI) shall provide grants using a formula that takes into account criteria such as certification status, financial and compliance performance, portfolio and balance sheet strength, and program capacity: Provided further , That no less than $25,000,000 may be for financial assistance, technical assistance, and training and outreach programs designed to benefit Native American, Native Hawaiian, and Alaska Native communities: Provided further , That the CDFI Fund shall make funds available under this subsection within 60 days of the date of enactment of this Act: Provided further , That funds made available under this heading may be used for administrative expenses, including administration of CDFI Fund programs and the New Markets Tax Credit Program: Provided further , That such amount is designated by the Congress as being for an emergency requirement pursuant to section 251(b)(2)(A)(i) of the Balanced Budget and Emergency Deficit Control Act of 1985.

administrative provision—internal revenue service
(including transfer of funds)

SEC. 10301.

In addition to the amounts otherwise available to the Internal Revenue Service in fiscal year 2020, $520,000,000, to remain available until September 30, 2021, shall be available to prevent, prepare for, and respond to coronavirus, including for costs associated with the extended filing season: Provided, That such funds may be transferred by the Commissioner to the "Taxpayer Services", "Enforcement", or "Operations Support" accounts of the Internal Revenue Service for an additional amount to be used solely to prevent, prepare for, and respond to coronavirus, domestically or internationally: Provided further, That the Committees on Appropriations of the House of Representatives and the Senate shall be notified in advance of any such transfer: Provided further, That such transfer authority is in addition to any other transfer authority provided by law: Provided further, That not later than 30 days after the date of enactment of this Act, the Commissioner shall submit to the Committees on Appropriations of the House of Representatives and the Senate a spending plan for such funds: Provided further, That such amount is designated by the Congress as being for an emergency requirement pursuant to section 251(b)(2)(A)(i) of the Balanced Budget and Emergency Deficit Control Act of 1985.

INDEPENDENT AGENCIES

Election Assistance Commission

election resilience grants

(including transfer of funds)

For an additional amount for payments by the Election Assistance Commission to States for contingency planning, preparation, and resilience of elections for Federal office, $3,600,000,000, to remain available until September 30, 2021: Provided, That of the amount provided under this heading, up to $5,000,000 may be transferred to and merged with "Election Assistance Commission—Salaries and Expenses": Provided further, That under this heading the term "State" means each of the 50 States, the District of Columbia, the Commonwealth of Puerto Rico, Guam, American Samoa, the United States Virgin Islands, and the Commonwealth of the Northern Mariana Islands: Provided further, That the amount of the payments made to a State under this heading shall be consistent with section 103 of the Help America Vote Act of 2002 (52 U.S.C. 20903): Provided further, That for the purposes of the preceding proviso, each reference to "$5,000,000" in such section 103 shall be deemed to refer to "$7,500,000": Provided further, That not later than 30 days after the date of enactment of this Act, the Election Assistance Commission shall obligate the funds to States under this heading in this Act: Provided further, That not less than 50 percent of the amount of the payment made to a State under this heading in this Act shall be allocated in cash or in kind to the units of local government which are responsible for the administration of elections for Federal office in the State: Provided further, That such amount is designated by the Congress as being for an emergency requirement pursuant to section 251(b)(2)(A)(i) of the Balanced Budget and Emergency Deficit Control Act of 1985.

administrative provision—election assistance commission

SEC. 10302.

(a) The last proviso under the heading "Election Assistance Commission—Election

Security Grants" in the Financial Services and General Government Appropriations Act, 2020 (division C of Public Law 116–93; 133 Stat. 2461) shall not apply with respect to any payment made to a State using funds appropriated or otherwise made available to the Election Assistance Commission under the Coronavirus Aid, Relief, and Economic Security Act (Public Law 116–136).

(b) The first proviso under the heading "Election Assistance Commission—Election Security Grants" in the Coronavirus Aid, Relief, and Economic Security Act (Public Law 116–136) is amended by striking "within 20 days of each election in the 2020 Federal election cycle in that State," and inserting "not later than October 30, 2021,".

(c) The fourth proviso under the heading "Election Assistance Commission—Election Security Grants" in the Coronavirus Aid, Relief, and Economic Security Act (Public Law 116–136) is amended by striking "December 31, 2020" and inserting "September 30, 2021".

(d) Notwithstanding any requirement that a State legislature appropriate and release any funds made available under the Help America Vote Act of 2002, the chief election official of each State shall have access to the funds made available under the heading "Election Assistance Commission—Election Security Grants" in the Coronavirus Aid, Relief, and Economic Security Act (Public Law 116–136) without any such action by the State legislature.

(e) A State may elect to reallocate funds allocated under the heading "Election Assistance Commission—Election Security Grants" in the Coronavirus Aid, Relief, and Economic Security Act (Public Law 116–136) as funds allocated under the heading "Election Assistance Commission—Election Security Grants" in the Financial Services and General Government Appropriations Act, 2020 (division C of Public Law 116–93; 133 Stat. 2461) that were spent to prevent, prepare for, and respond to coronavirus, domestically or internationally, for the 2020 Federal election cycle; or funds allocated under the heading "Election Assistance Commission—Election Reform Program" in the Financial Services and Government Appropriations Act, 2018 (division E of Public Law 115–141) that were spent to prevent, prepare for, and respond to coronavirus, domestically or internationally, for the 2020 Federal election cycle.

(f) This section shall take effect as if included in the enactment of the Coronavirus Aid, Relief, and Economic Security Act (Public Law 116–136).

(g) The amounts repurposed in this section that were previously designated by the Congress as an emergency requirement pursuant to the Balanced Budget and Emergency Deficit Control Act of 1985 are designated by the Congress as an emergency requirement pursuant to section 251(b)(2)(A)(i) of the Balanced Budget and Emergency Deficit Control Act of 1985.

Federal Communications Commission

salaries and expenses

For an additional amount for "Salaries and Expenses", $24,000,000, to remain available until September 30, 2021, for implementing title VIII of the Communications Act of 1934 (47 U.S.C. 641 et seq.), as added by the Broadband DATA Act (Public Law 116–130): Provided, That such amount is designated by the Congress as being for an emergency requirement pursuant to section 251(b)(2)(A)(i) of the Balanced Budget and Emergency Deficit Control Act of 1985.

emergency connectivity fund

For an additional amount for the "Emergency Connectivity Fund", $1,500,000,000, to remain available until September 30, 2021, to prevent, prepare for, and respond to coronavirus, domestically or internationally, through the provision of funding for Wi-fi hotspots, other equipment, connected devices, and advanced telecommunications and information services to schools and libraries as authorized in section 130201: Provided, That such amount is designated by the Congress as being for an emergency requirement pursuant to section 251(b)(2)(A)(i) of the Balanced Budget and Emergency Deficit Control Act of 1985.

emergency broadband connectivity fund

For an additional amount for the "Emergency Broadband Connectivity Fund", $4,000,000,000, to remain available until September 30, 2021, to prevent, prepare for, and respond to coronavirus, domestically or internationally, through the provision of an emergency benefit for broadband service as authorized in section 130301: Provided, That such amount is designated by the Congress as being for an emergency requirement pursuant to section 251(b)(2)(A)(i) of the Balanced Budget and Emergency Deficit Control Act of 1985.

General Services Administration

technology modernization fund

For an additional amount for the "Technology Modernization Fund", $1,000,000,000, to remain available until September 30, 2022, for technology-related modernization activities to prevent, prepare for, and respond to coronavirus, domestically or internationally: Provided, That such amount is designated by the Congress as being for an emergency requirement pursuant to section 251(b)(2)(A)(i) of the Balanced Budget and Emergency Deficit Control Act of 1985.

Office Of Personnel Management

office of inspector general

salaries and expenses

For an additional amount for "Salaries and Expenses", $1,000,000, to remain available until expended to prevent, prepare for, and respond to coronavirus, domestically or internationally: Provided, That such amount is designated by the Congress as being for an emergency requirement pursuant to section 251(b)(2)(A)(i) of the Balanced Budget and Emergency Deficit Control Act of 1985.

Small Business Administration

emergency eidl grants

For an additional amount for "Emergency EIDL Grants" for the cost of emergency EIDL grants authorized by section 1110 of division A of the CARES Act (Public Law 116–136), $10,000,000,000, to remain available until expended, to prevent, prepare for, and respond to coronavirus, domestically or internationally: Provided, That such amount is designated by the Congress as being for an emergency requirement pursuant to section 251(b)(2)(A)(i) of the Balanced Budget and Emergency Deficit Control Act of 1985.

administrative provisions—small business administration

SEC. 10303.

(a) The third proviso under the heading "Small Business Administration—Business Loans Program Account" the Financial Services and General Government Appropriations Act, 2020 (division C of Public Law 116–93) is amended by striking "$30,000,000,000" and inserting "$75,000,000,000".

(b) The sixth proviso under the heading "Small Business Administration—Business Loans Program Account" the Financial Services and General Government Appropriations Act, 2020 (division C of Public Law 116–93) is amended by striking

"$12,000,000,000" and inserting "$35,000,000,000".

United States Postal Service

payment to postal service fund

For an additional payment to the "Postal Service Fund", for revenue forgone due to coronavirus, $25,000,000,000, to remain available until September 30, 2022: Provided , That the Postal Service, during the coronavirus emergency, shall prioritize the purchase of, and make available to all Postal Service employees and facilities, personal protective equipment, including gloves, masks, and sanitizers, and shall conduct additional cleaning and sanitizing of Postal Service facilities and delivery vehicles: Provided further , That such amount is designated by the Congress as being for an emergency requirement pursuant to section 251(b)(2)(A)(i) of the Balanced Budget and Emergency Deficit Control Act of 1985.

office of inspector general

salaries and expenses

For an additional amount for "Salaries and Expenses", $15,000,000, to remain available until expended, to prevent, prepare for, and respond to coronavirus, domestically or internationally: Provided , That such amount is designated by the Congress as being for an emergency requirement pursuant to section 251(b)(2)(A)(i) of the Balanced Budget and Emergency Deficit Control Act of 1985.

general provisions—this title

SEC. 10304.

(a) Title V of division B of the CARES Act (Public Law 116–136) is amended in the first proviso under the heading "Independent Agencies—Pandemic Response Accountability Committee" by inserting "or any other Act (including Acts other than appropriations Acts)" after "provided in this Act".

(b) Amounts repurposed under this section that were previously designated by the Congress, respectively, as an emergency requirement or as being for disaster relief pursuant to the Balanced Budget and Emergency Deficit Control Act are designated by the Congress as being for an emergency requirement pursuant to section 251(b)(2)(A)(i) of the Balanced Budget and Emergency Deficit Control Act of 1985 or as being for disaster relief pursuant to section 251(b)(2)(D) of the Balanced Budget and Emergency Deficit Control Act of 1985.

SEC. 10305.

Title V of division B of the CARES Act (Public Law 116–136) is amended by striking the fifth proviso under the heading "General Services Administration—Real Property Activities—Federal Buildings Fund": Provided, That the amounts repurposed in this section that were previously designated by the Congress as an emergency requirement pursuant to the Balanced Budget and Emergency Deficit Control Act of 1985 are designated by the Congress as an emergency requirement pursuant to section 251(b)(2)(A)(i) of the Balanced Budget and Emergency Deficit Control Act of 1985.

SEC. 10306.

For an additional amount for "Department of the Treasury—Departmental Offices—Coronavirus Relief Fund", an amount equal to—

(1) $1,250,000,000; less

(2) the amount allocated for the District of Columbia pursuant to section 601(c)(6) of the Social Security Act:

Provided, That such amounts shall only be available for making a payment to the

District of Columbia, and shall be in addition to any other funds available for such purpose: Provided further , That the Secretary of the Treasury shall pay all amounts provided by this section directly to the District of Columbia not less than 5 days after the date of enactment of this Act: Provided further , That the District of Columbia shall use such amounts only to cover costs or replace foregone revenues stemming from the public health emergency with respect to the Coronavirus Disease (COVID–19): Provided further , That such amount is designated by Congress as being for an emergency requirement pursuant to section 251(b)(2)(A)(i) of the Balanced Budget and Emergency Deficit Control Act of 1985.

TITLE IV

—HOMELAND SECURITY
DEPARTMENT OF HOMELAND SECURITY
Office Of Inspector General
operations and support
For an additional amount for "Operations and Support", $3,000,000, to remain available until September 30, 2022, for oversight of activities of the Department of Homeland Security funded in this Act and in title VI of division B of Public Law 116–136 to prevent, prepare for, and respond to coronavirus: Provided, That such amount is designated by the Congress as being for an emergency requirement pursuant to section 251(b)(2)(A)(i) of the Balanced Budget and Emergency Deficit Control Act of 1985.
Federal Emergency Management Agency
federal assistance
For an additional amount for "Federal Assistance", $1,300,000,000, to remain available until September 30, 2021, to prevent, prepare for, and respond to coronavirus, of which $500,000,000 shall be for Assistance to Firefighter Grants for the purchase of personal protective equipment and related supplies, mental health evaluations, training, and temporary infectious disease de-contamination or sanitizing facilities and equipment; of which $500,000,000 shall be for Staffing for Adequate Fire and Emergency Response Grants; of which $100,000,000 shall be for Emergency Management Performance Grants; and of which $200,000,000 shall be for the Emergency Food and Shelter Program: Provided, That such amount is designated by the Congress as being for an emergency requirement pursuant to section 251(b)(2)(A)(i) of the Balanced Budget and Emergency Deficit Control Act of 1985.
General Provisions—This Title

SEC. 10401.
Notwithstanding any other provision of law, funds made available under "Federal Emergency Management Agency—Federal Assistance" shall only be used for the purposes specifically described under that heading.

SEC. 10402.
(a) Subsections (c)(2), (f), (g)(1), (h)(1)–(4), (h)(6), and (k) of section 33 of the Federal Fire Prevention and Control Act of 1974 (15 U.S.C. 2229) shall not apply to amounts appropriated for "Federal Emergency Management Agency – Federal Assistance" for Assistance to Firefighter Grants in this Act and in division D, title III of the Consolidated Appropriations Act, 2020 (Public Law 116–93).
(b) Subsection (k) of section 33 of the Federal Fire Prevention and Control Act of 1974 (15 U.S.C. 2229) shall not apply to Amounts provided for "Federal Emergency

Management Agency–Federal Assistance" for Assistance to Firefighter Grants in title VI of division B of Public Law 116–136.

(c) Amounts repurposed under this section that were previously designated by the Congress, respectively, as an emergency requirement or as being for disaster relief pursuant to the Balanced Budget and Emergency Deficit Control Act are designated by the Congress as being for an emergency requirement pursuant to section 251(b)(2)(A)(i) of the Balanced Budget and Emergency Deficit Control Act of 1985 or as being for disaster relief pursuant to section 251(b)(2)(D) of the Balanced Budget and Emergency Deficit Control Act of 1985.

SEC. 10403.

Subsections (a)(1)(A), (a)(1)(B), (a)(1)(E), (a)(1)(G), (c)(1), (c)(2), and (c)(4) of section 34 of the Federal Fire Prevention and Control Act of 1974 (15 U.S.C. 2229a) shall not apply to amounts appropriated for "Federal Emergency Management Agency – Federal Assistance" for Staffing for Adequate Fire and Emergency Response Grants in this Act and in division D, title III of the Consolidated Appropriations Act, 2020 (Public Law 116–93).

TITLE V

—INTERIOR, ENVIRONMENT, AND RELATED AGENCIES
DEPARTMENT OF THE INTERIOR
United States Fish And Wildlife Service
resource management

For an additional amount for "Resource Management", $21,000,000, to remain available until expended for research; listing injurious species; electronic permitting system development; operation and maintenance; law enforcement interdiction and inspections; and other support activities, as described in sections 190402, 190403, and 190404 of division S of this Act: Provided, That amounts may be transferred to "Surveys, Investigations and Research" in the United States Geological Survey; "National Oceanic and Atmospheric Administration" in the Department of Commerce; and the "Center for Disease Control" in the Department of Health and Human Services: Provided further, That such amount is designated by the Congress as being for an emergency requirement pursuant to section 251(b)(2)(A)(i) of the Balanced Budget and Emergency Deficit Control Act of 1985.

state and tribal wildlife grants

For an additional amount for "State and Tribal Wildlife Grants", $50,000,000, to remain available until expended, for a onetime grant program to remain available until expended, as described in section 190405 of division S of this Act: Provided, That such amount is designated by the Congress as being for an emergency requirement pursuant to section 251(b)(2)(A)(i) of the Balanced Budget and Emergency Deficit Control Act of 1985.

United States Geological Survey
surveys, investigations, and research

For an additional amount for "Surveys, Investigations, and Research", $40,000,000, to remain available until September 30, 2021, for technical assistance, biosurveillance of wildlife and environmental persistence studies and related research, database development, and accompanying activities as described in section 190404 of division S of this Act: Provided, That such amount is designated by the Congress as being for an emergency requirement pursuant to section 251(b)(2)(A)(i) of the Balanced Budget and Emergency Deficit Control Act of 1985.

Bureau Of Indian Affairs

operation of indian programs

For an additional amount for "Operation of Indian Programs", $900,000,000, to remain available until September 30, 2021, to prevent, prepare for, and respond to coronavirus, of which—

(1) $100,000,000 shall be for housing improvement;

(2) $780,000,000 shall be for providing Tribal government services, for Tribal government employee salaries to maintain operations, and cleaning and sanitization of Tribally owned and operated facilities; and

(3) $20,000,000 shall be used to provide and deliver potable water; and,

Provided, That none of the funds appropriated herein shall be obligated until 3 days after the Bureau of Indian Affairs provides a detailed spend plan, which includes distribution and use of funds by Tribe, to the Committees on Appropriations of the House of Representatives and the Senate: Provided further, That the Bureau shall notify the Committees on Appropriations of the House of Representatives and the Senate quarterly on the obligations and expenditures of the funds provided by this Act: Provided further, That assistance received herein shall not be included in the calculation of funds received by those Tribal governments who participate in the 'Small and Needy' program: Provided further, That such amounts, if transferred to Indian Tribes and Tribal organizations under the Indian Self-Determination and Education Assistance Act (1) will be transferred on a one-time basis, (2) are non-recurring funds that are not part of the amount required by 25 U.S.C. 5325, and (3) may only be used for the purposes identified under this heading in this Act, notwithstanding any other provision of law: Provided further, That section 11008 of this Act shall not apply to tribal contracts entered into by the Bureau of Indian Affairs with this appropriation: Provided further, That such amount is designated by the Congress as being for an emergency requirement pursuant to section 251(b)(2)(A)(i) of the Balanced Budget and Emergency Deficit Control Act of 1985.

Departmental Offices

Insular Affairs

assistance to territories

For an additional amount for "Assistance to Territories", $1,000,000,000, to remain available until expended, to prevent, prepare for, and respond to coronavirus, of which (1) $945,000,000 is for Capital Improvement Project grants for hospitals and other critical infrastructure; and (2) $55,000,000 is for territorial assistance, including general technical assistance: Provided, That any appropriation for disaster assistance under this heading in this Act or previous appropriations Acts may be used as non-Federal matching funds for the purpose of hazard mitigation grants provided pursuant to section 404 of the Robert T. Stafford Disaster Relief and Emergency Assistance Act (42 U.S.C. 5170c): Provided further , That amounts repurposed in this section that were previously designated by the Congress as an emergency requirement pursuant to the Balanced Budget and Emergency Deficit Control Act of 1985 are designated by the Congress as an emergency requirement pursuant to section 251(b)(2)(A)(i) of the Balanced Budget and Emergency Deficit Control Act of 1985: Provided further , That such amount is designated by the Congress as being for an emergency requirement pursuant to section 251(b)(2)(A)(i) of the Balanced Budget and Emergency Deficit

Control Act of 1985.

Office Of Inspector General

salaries and expenses

For an additional amount for "Salaries and Expenses" , $5,000,000, to remain available until expended: Provided, That such amount is designated by the Congress as being for an emergency requirement pursuant to section 251(b)(2)(A)(i) of the Balanced Budget and Emergency Deficit Control Act of 1985.

Environmental Protection Agency

environmental programs and management

For an additional amount for "Environmental Programs and Management", $50,000,000, to remain available until September 30, 2021, for environmental justice grants to prevent, prepare for, and respond to coronavirus: Provided, That such amount shall be used to monitor or study links between pollution exposure and the transmission and health outcomes of coronavirus as described in section 190702 of division S of this Act: Provided further, That such amount is designated by the Congress as being for an emergency requirement pursuant to section 251(b)(2)(A)(i) of the Balanced Budget and Emergency Deficit Control Act of 1985.

DEPARTMENT OF HEALTH AND HUMAN SERVICES

Indian Health Service

indian health services

(including transfer of funds)

For an additional amount for "Indian Health Services", $2,100,000,000, to remain available until expended, to prevent, prepare for, respond to, and provide health services related to coronavirus, of which—

(1) $1,000,000,000 shall be used to supplement reduced third party revenue collections;

(2) $500,000,000 shall be used for direct health and telehealth services, including to purchase supplies and personal protective equipment;

(3) $140,000,000 shall be used to expand broadband infrastructure and information technology for telehealth and electronic health record system purposes;

(4) $20,000,000 shall be used to address the needs of domestic violence victims and homeless individuals and families;

(5) not less than $64,000,000 shall be for Urban Indian Organizations; and,

(6) not less than $10,000,000 shall be used to provide and deliver potable water:

Provided, That such funds shall be allocated at the discretion of the Director of the Indian Health Service: Provided further, That of the funds provided herein, not less than $366,000,000 shall be transferred to and merged with 'Indian Health Service—Indian Health Facilities' at the discretion of the Director to modify existing health facilities to provide isolation or quarantine space, to purchase and install updated equipment necessary, and for maintenance and improvement projects necessary to the purposes specified in this Act: Provided further, That such amounts may be used to supplement amounts otherwise available for such purposes under 'Indian Health Facilities': Provided further, That such amounts, if transferred to Tribes and Tribal organizations under the Indian Self-Determination and Education Assistance Act, will be transferred on a one-time basis and that these non-recurring funds are not part of the amount required by 25 U.S.C. 5325, and that such amounts may only be used for the purposes identified under this heading notwithstanding any other provision of law: Provided further, That none of the funds appropriated herein for telehealth broadband activities shall be available for obligation until 3 days after the Indian Health Service provides to the Committees on Appropriations of the House of Representatives and the Senate, a detailed spend plan that includes the cost, location, and expected completion date of each activity: Provided further, That the Indian Health Service shall notify the Committees on Appropriations of the House of Representatives and the Senate quarterly on the obligations and expenditures of the funds provided by this Act: Provided further, That section 11008 of this Act shall not apply to tribal contracts entered into by the Bureau of Indian Affairs with this appropriation: Provided further, That such amount is designated by the Congress as being for an emergency requirement pursuant to section 251(b)(2)(A)(i) of the Balanced Budget and Emergency Deficit Control Act of 1985.

National Foundation On The Arts And Humanities

National Endowment For The Arts

grants and administration

For an additional amount for "Grants and Administration", $10,000,000 to remain available until September 30, 2021, for grants to respond to the impacts of coronavirus: Provided, That such funds are available under the same terms and conditions as grant funding appropriated to this heading in Public Law 116–94: Provided further, That 40 percent of such funds shall be distributed to State arts agencies and regional arts organizations and 60 percent of such funds shall be for direct grants: Provided further, That notwithstanding any other provision of law, such funds may also be used by the recipients of such grants for purposes of the general operations of such recipients: Provided further, That the matching requirements under subsections (e), (g)(4)(A), and (p)(3) of section 5 of the National Foundation on the Arts and Humanities Act of 1965 (20 U.S.C. 954) may be waived with respect to such grants: Provided further, That such amount is designated by the Congress as being for an emergency requirement pursuant to section 251(b)(2)(A)(i) of the Balanced Budget and Emergency Deficit Control Act of 1985.

National Endowment For The Humanities

grants and administration

For an additional amount for "Grants and Administration", $10,000,000 to remain available until September 30, 2021, for grants to respond to the impacts of coronavirus: Provided, That such funds are available under the same terms and conditions as grant funding appropriated to this heading in Public Law 116–94: Provided further, That 40 percent of such funds shall be distributed to state humanities councils and 60 percent of such funds shall be for direct grants: Provided further, That notwithstanding any other provision of law, such funds may also be used by the recipients of such grants for purposes of the general operations of such recipients: Provided further, That the matching requirements under subsection (h)(2)(A) of section 7 of the National Foundation on the Arts and Humanities Act of 1965 may be waived with respect to such grants: Provided further, That such amount is designated by the Congress as being for an emergency requirement pursuant to section 251(b)(2)(A)(i) of the Balanced Budget and Emergency Deficit Control Act of 1985.

TITLE VI

—DEPARTMENTS OF LABOR, HEALTH AND HUMAN SERVICES, AND EDUCATION, AND RELATED AGENCIES

DEPARTMENT OF LABOR

Employment And Training Administration
training and employment services
(including transfer of funds)

For an additional amount for "Training and Employment Services", $2,040,000,000, to prevent, prepare for, and respond to coronavirus, of which $15,000,000 shall be transferred to "Program Administration" to carry out activities in this Act, Public Law 116–127 and Public Law 116–136 for full-time equivalent employees, information technology upgrades needed to expedite payments and support implementation, including to expedite policy guidance and disbursement of funds, technical assistance and other assistance to States and territories to speed payment of Federal and State unemployment benefits,and of which the remaining amounts shall be used to carry out activities under the Workforce Innovation and Opportunity Act (referred to in this Act as "WIOA") as follows:

(1) $485,000,000 for grants to the States for adult employment and training activities, including incumbent worker trainings, transitional jobs, on-the-job training, individualized career services, supportive services, needs-related payments, and to facilitate remote access to training services provided through a one-stop delivery system through the use of technology, to remain available until June 30, 2021: Provided, That an adult shall not be required to meet the requirements of section 134(c)(3)(B) of the WIOA: Provided further, That an adult who meets the requirements described in section 2102(a)(3)(A) of Public Law 116–136 may be eligible for participation: Provided further, That priority may be given to individuals who are adversely impacted by economic changes due to the coronavirus, including individuals seeking employment, dislocated workers, individuals with barriers to employment, individuals who are unemployed, or individuals who are underemployed;

(2) $518,000,000 for grants to the States for youth activities, including supportive services, summer employment for youth, and to facilitate remote access to training services provided through a one-stop delivery system through the use of technology, to remain available until June 30, 2021: Provided, That individuals described in section 2102(a)(3)(A) of Public Law 116–136 may be eligible for participation as an out-of-school youth if they meet the requirements of clauses (i) and (ii) of section 129(a)(1)(B) or as in-school youth if they meet the requirements of clauses (i) and (iii) of section 129(a)(1)(C) of the WIOA; Provided further, That priority shall be given for out-of-school youth and youth with multiple barriers to employment: Provided further, That funds shall support employer partnerships for youth employment and subsidized employment, and partnerships with community-based organizations to support such employment;

(3) $597,000,000 for grants to States for dislocated worker employment and training activities, including incumbent worker trainings, transitional jobs, on-the-job training, individualized career services, supportive services, needs-related payments, and to facilitate remote access to training services provided through a one-stop delivery system through the use of technology, to remain available until June 30, 2021: Provided, That a dislocated worker shall not be required to meet the requirements of section 134(c)(3)(B) of the WIOA: Provided further, That a dislocated worker who meets the requirements described in section 2102(a)(3)(A) of Public Law 116–136 may be eligible for participation;

(4) $400,000,000 for the dislocated workers assistance national reserve to remain available until September 30, 2023; and

(5) $25,000,000 for migrant and seasonal farmworker programs under section 167 of the WIOA, including emergency supportive services, to remain available until June 30, 2021, of which no less than $500,000 shall be for the collection and dissemination of electronic and printed materials related to coronavirus to the migrant and seasonal farmworker population nationwide, including Puerto Rico, through a cooperative agreement;

Provided, That the impact of the COVID–19 national emergency may be considered as an additional factor for reimbursement for on-the-job training under section 134(c)(3)(H) of the WIOA and as a factor in determining the employer's portion of the costs of providing customized training under section 3(14) of the WIOA: Provided further, That notwithstanding section 134(d)(5) of the WIOA, a local board may use 40 percent of funds received under paragraphs (1) and (3) for transitional jobs: Provided further, That notwithstanding section 194(10) of the WIOA, that funds used to support transitional jobs may also be used to support public service employment: Provided further, That sections 127(b)(1)(C)(iv)(III), 132(b)(1)(B)(iv)(III), and 132(b)(2)(B)(iii)(II) shall not apply to funds appropriated under this heading: Provided further, That such amount is designated by the Congress as being for an emergency requirement pursuant to section 251(b)(2)(A)(i) of the Balanced Budget and Emergency Deficit Control Act of 1985.

Wage And Hour Division

salaries and expenses

For an additional amount for "Wage and Hour Division", $6,500,000, to remain available until September 30, 2021, to prevent, prepare for, and respond to coronavirus, including for the administration, oversight, and coordination of worker protection activities related thereto: Provided, That the Secretary of Labor shall use funds provided under this heading to support enforcement activities and outreach efforts to make individuals, particularly low-wage workers, aware of their rights under division C and division E of Public Law 116–127: Provided further, That such amount is designated by the Congress as being for an emergency requirement pursuant to section 251(b)(2)(A)(i) of the Balanced Budget and Emergency Deficit Control Act of 1985.

Occupational Safety And Health Administration

salaries and expenses

For an additional amount for "Occupational Safety and Health Administration", $100,000,000, to remain available until September 30, 2021, for worker protection and enforcement activities to prevent, prepare for, and respond to coronavirus, of which $25,000,000 shall be for Susan Harwood training grants and at least $70,000,000 shall be to hire additional compliance safety and health officers, and for state plan enforcement, to protect workers from coronavirus by enforcing all applicable standards and directives, including 29 CFR 1910.132, 29 CFR 1910.134, Section 5(a)(1) of the Occupational Safety and Health Act of 1970, and 29 CFR 1910.1030: Provided, That activities to protect workers from coronavirus supported by funds provided under this heading includes additional enforcement of standards and directives referenced in the preceding proviso at slaughterhouses, poultry processing plants, and agricultural workplaces: Provided further, That within 15 days of the date of enactment of this Act, the Secretary of Labor shall submit a spending and hiring plan for the funds made available under this heading, and a monthly staffing report until all funds are expended, to the Committees on Appropriations of the House of Representatives and the Senate: Provided further, That within 15 days of the date of enactment of this Act, the Secretary of Labor shall submit a plan for the additional enforcement activities described in the third proviso to the Committees on Appropriations of the House of Representatives and the Senate: Provided further, That such amount is designated by the Congress as being for an emergency requirement pursuant to section 251(b)(2)(A)(i) of the Balanced Budget and Emergency Deficit Control Act of 1985.

Office Of Inspector General

For an additional amount for "Office of Inspector General", $5,000,000, to remain available until expended, to prevent, prepare for, and respond to coronavirus. Provided, That such amount is designated by the Congress as being for an emergency requirement pursuant to section 251(b)(2)(A)(i) of the Balanced Budget and Emergency Deficit Control Act of 1985.

administrative provision—department of labor

SEC. 10601.

There is hereby appropriated for fiscal year 2021 for "Department of Labor—Employment Training Administration—State Unemployment Insurance and Employment Service Operations", $28,600,000, to be expended from the Employment Security Administration Account in the Unemployment Trust Fund ("the Trust Fund") to carry out title III of the Social Security Act: Provided, That such amount shall only become available for obligation if the Average Weekly Insured Unemployment ("AWIU") for fiscal year 2021 is projected, by the Department of Labor during fiscal year 2021 to exceed 1,728,000: Provided further, That to the extent that the AWIU for fiscal year 2021 is projected by the Department of Labor to exceed 1,728,000, an additional $28,600,000 from the Trust Fund shall be made available for obligation during fiscal year 2021 for every 100,000 increase in the AWIU level (including a pro rata amount for any increment less than 100,000): Provided further, That, except as specified in this section, amounts provided herein shall be available under the same authority and conditions applicable to funds provided to carry out title III of the Social Security Act under the heading "Department of Labor—Employment Training Administration—State Unemployment Insurance and Employment Service Operations" in division A of Public Law 116–94: Provided further, That such amounts shall be in addition to any other funds made available in any fiscal year for such purposes: Provided further, That such amount is designated by the Congress as being for an emergency requirement pursuant to section 251(b)(2)(A)(i) of the Balanced Budget and Emergency Deficit Control Act of 1985.

DEPARTMENT OF HEALTH AND HUMAN SERVICES

Health Resources And Services Administration

primary health care

For an additional amount for "Primary Health Care", $7,600,000,000, to remain available until September 30, 2025, for necessary expenses to prevent, prepare for, and respond to coronavirus, for grants and cooperative agreements under the Health Centers Program, as defined by section 330 of the Public Health Service Act, and for grants to Federally qualified health centers, as defined in section 1861(aa)(4)(B) of the Social Security Act, and for eligible entities under the Native Hawaiian Health Care Improvement Act, including maintenance or expansion of health center and system capacity and staffing levels: Provided, That sections 330(r)(2)(B), 330(e)(6)(A)(iii), and 330(e)(6)(B)(iii) shall not apply to funds provided under this heading in this Act: Provided further, That funds provided under this heading in this Act may be used to (1) purchase equipment and supplies to conduct mobile testing for SARS–CoV–2 or

COVID–19; (2) purchase and maintain mobile vehicles and equipment to conduct such testing; and (3) hire and train laboratory personnel and other staff to conduct such mobile testing: Provided further, That such amount is designated by the Congress as being for an emergency requirement pursuant to section 251(b)(2)(A)(i) of the Balanced Budget and Emergency Deficit Control Act of 1985.

ryan white hiv/aids program

For an additional amount for "Ryan White HIV/AIDS Program", $10,000,000, to remain available until September 30, 2022, to prevent, prepare for, and respond to coronavirus: Provided, That awards from funds provided under this heading in this Act shall be through modifications to existing contracts and supplements to existing grants and cooperative agreements under parts A, B, C, D, F, and section 2692(a) of title XXVI of the Public Health Service Act: Provided further, That such supplements shall be awarded using a data-driven methodology determined by the Secretary of Health and Human Services: Provided further, That sections 2604(c), 2612(b), and 2651(c) of the Public Health Service Act shall not apply to funds provided under this heading in this Act: Provided further, That the Secretary may waive any penalties and administrative requirements as necessary to ensure that the funds may be used efficiently: Provided further, That such amount is designated by the Congress as being for an emergency requirement pursuant to section 251(b)(2)(A)(i) of the Balanced Budget and Emergency Deficit Control Act of 1985.

Centers For Disease Control And Prevention

cdc–wide activities and program support

For an additional amount for "CDC–Wide Activities and Program Support", $2,130,000,000, to remain available until September 30, 2024, to prevent, prepare for, and respond to coronavirus, domestically or internationally: Provided, That of the amount provided under this heading in this Act, $1,000,000,000 shall be for Public Health Emergency Preparedness cooperative agreements under section 319C–1 of the Public Health Service Act: Provided further, That, of the amount provided under this heading in this Act, $1,000,000,000 shall be for necessary expenses for grants for core public health infrastructure for State, local, Territorial, or Tribal health departments as described in section 30550 of division C of this Act: Provided further, That of the amount made available under this heading in this Act for specified programs, not less than $100,000,000 shall be allocated to tribes, tribal organizations, urban Indian health organizations, or health service providers to tribes: Provided further, That of the amount provided under this heading in this Act, $130,000,000 shall be for public health data surveillance and analytics infrastructure modernization: Provided further, That funds appropriated under this heading in this Act for grants may be used for the rent, lease, purchase, acquisition, construction, alteration, or renovation of non-Federally owned facilities to improve preparedness and response capability at the State and local level: Provided further, That all construction, alteration, or renovation work, carried out, in whole or in part, with funds appropriated under this heading in this Act, or under this heading in the CARES ACT (P.L. 116–136), shall be subject to the requirements of 42 U.S.C. 300s-1(b)(1)(I): Provided further, That such amount is designated by the Congress as being for an emergency requirement pursuant to section 251(b)(2)(A)(i) of the Balanced Budget and Emergency Deficit Control Act of 1985.

National Institutes Of Health

national institute of allergy and infectious diseases

For an additional amount for "National Institute of Allergy and Infectious Diseases",

$500,000,000, to remain available until September 30, 2024, to prevent, prepare for, and respond to coronavirus: Provided, That such amount is designated by the Congress as being for an emergency requirement pursuant to section 251(b)(2)(A)(i) of the Balanced Budget and Emergency Deficit Control Act of 1985.

national institute of mental health

For an additional amount for "National Institute of Mental Health", $200,000,000, to remain available until September 30, 2024, to prevent, prepare for, and respond to coronavirus: Provided, That such amount is designated by the Congress as being for an emergency requirement pursuant to section 251(b)(2)(A)(i) of the Balanced Budget and Emergency Deficit Control Act of 1985.

office of the director

(including transfer of funds)

For an additional amount for "Office of the Director", $4,021,000,000, to remain available until September 30, 2024, to prevent, prepare for, and respond to coronavirus, domestically or internationally: Provided. That not less than $3,000,000,000 of the amount provided under this heading in this Act shall be for offsetting the costs related to reductions in lab productivity resulting from the coronavirus pandemic or public health measures related to the coronavirus pandemic: Provided further, That up to $1,021,000,000 of the amount provided under this heading in this Act shall be to support additional scientific research or the programs and platforms that support research: Provided further, That funds made available under this heading in this Act may be transferred to the accounts of the Institutes and Centers of the National Institutes of Health ("NIH"): Provided further, That this transfer authority is in addition to any other transfer authority available to the NIH: Provided further, That such amount is designated by the Congress as being for an emergency requirement pursuant to section 251(b)(2)(A)(i) of the Balanced Budget and Emergency Deficit Control Act of 1985.

Substance Abuse And Mental Health Services Administration

health surveillance and program support

For an additional amount for "Health Surveillance and Program Support", $3,000,000,000, to remain available until September 30, 2021, to prevent, prepare for, and respond to coronavirus: Provided, That of the funds made available under this heading in this Act, $1,500,000,000 shall be for grants for the substance abuse prevention and treatment block grant program under subpart II of part B of title XIX of the Public Health Service Act ("PHS Act"): Provided further, That of the funds made available under this heading in this Act, $1,000,000,000 shall be for grants for the community mental health services block grant program under subpart I of part B of title XIX of the PHS Act: Provided further, That of the funds made available under this heading in this Act, $100,000,000 shall be for services to the homeless population: Provided further, That of the funds made available under this heading in this Act, $100,000,000 shall be for activities and services under Project AWARE: Provided further, That of the funds made available under this heading in this Act, $10,000,000 shall be for the National Child Traumatic Stress Network: Provided further, That of the amount made available under this heading in this Act, $265,000,000 is available for activities authorized under section 501(o) of the Public Health Service Act: Provided further, That of the amount made available under this heading in this Act, $25,000,000 shall be for the Suicide Lifeline and Disaster Distress Helpline: Provided further, That of the amount made available under this heading in this Act for specified programs, not less than $150,000,000 shall be allocated to tribes, tribal organizations, urban Indian health organizations, or health or behavioral health service providers to tribes: Provided further, That the Substance Abuse and Mental Health Services Administration has flexibility to amend allowable activities, timelines, and reporting requirements for the Substance Abuse Prevention and Treatment Block Grant and the Community Mental Health Services Block Grant pursuant to the public health emergency declaration: Provided further, That such amount is designated by the Congress as being for an emergency requirement pursuant to section 251(b)(2)(A)(i) of the Balanced Budget and Emergency Deficit Control Act of 1985.

Centers For Medicare & Medicaid Services

program management

For an additional amount for "Program Management", $150,000,000, to remain available through September 30, 2022, to prevent, prepare for, and respond to coronavirus, for State strike teams for resident and employee safety in skilled nursing facilities and nursing facilities, including activities to support clinical care, infection control, and staffing: Provided, That such amount is designated by the Congress as being for an emergency requirement pursuant to section 251(b)(2)(A)(i) of the Balanced Budget and Emergency Deficit Control Act of 1985.

Administration For Children And Families

low income home energy assistance

For an additional amount for "Low Income Home Energy Assistance", $1,500,000,000, to remain available until September 30, 2021, to prevent, prepare for, and respond to coronavirus, for making payments under subsection (b) of section 2602 of the Low-Income Home Energy Assistance Act of 1981 (42 U.S.C. 8621 et seq.): Provided, That of the amount provided under this heading in this Act, $750,000,000 shall be allocated as though the total appropriation for such payments for fiscal year 2020 was less than $1,975,000,000: Provided further, That each grantee that receives an allotment of funds made available under this heading in this Act shall, for purposes of income eligibility, deem to be eligible any household that documents job loss or severe income loss dated after February 29, 2020, such as a layoff or furlough notice or verification of application for unemployment benefits: Provided further, That the limitation in section 2605(b)(9)(A) of the Low-Income Home Energy Assistance Act of 1981, regarding planning and administering the use of funds, shall apply to funds provided under this heading in this Act by substituting "12.5 percent" for "10 percent": Provided further, That section 2607(b)(2)(B) of such Act (42 U.S.C. 8626(b)(2)(B)) shall not apply to funds made available under this heading in this Act: Provided further, That such amount is designated by the Congress as being for an emergency requirement pursuant to section 251(b)(2)(A)(i) of the Balanced Budget and Emergency Deficit Control Act of 1985.

payments to states for the child care and development block grant

For an additional amount for "Payments to States for the Child Care and Development Block Grant", $7,000,000,000, to remain available until September 30, 2021, to prevent, prepare for, and respond to coronavirus, including for Federal administrative expenses, which shall be used to supplement, not supplant State, Territory, and Tribal general revenue funds for child care assistance for low-income families within the United States (including territories) without regard to requirements in sections 658E(c)(3)(D)–(E) or section 658G of the Child Care and Development Block Grant Act: Provided, That funds provided under this heading in this Act may be used for costs of providing relief from copayments and tuition payments for families and for paying that portion of the child care provider's cost ordinarily paid through family co-payments, to provide continued payments and assistance to child care providers in the case of decreased enrollment or closures related to coronavirus, and to ensure child care providers are able to remain open or reopen as appropriate and applicable: Pro-vided further, That States, Territories, and Tribes are encouraged to place conditions on payments to child care providers that ensure that child care providers use a portion of funds received to continue to pay the salaries and wages of staff: Provided further, That lead agencies shall, for the duration of the COVID–19 public health emergency, implement enrollment and eligibility policies that support the fixed costs of providing child care services by delinking provider reimbursement rates from an eligible child's absence and a provider's closure due to the COVID–19 public health emergency: Provided further, That the Secretary shall remind States that CCDBG State plans do not need to be amended prior to utilizing existing authorities in the Child Care and Development Block Grant Act for the purposes provided herein: Provided further, That States, Territories, and Tribes are authorized to use funds appropriated under this heading in this Act to provide child care assistance to health care sector employees, emergency responders, sanitation workers, farmworkers, and other workers deemed essential during the response to coronavirus by public officials, without regard to the income eligibility requirements of section 658P(4) of such Act: Provided further, That funds appropriated under this heading in this Act shall be available to eligible child care providers under section 658P(6) of the CCDBG Act, even if such providers were not receiving CCDBG assistance prior to the public health emergency as a result of the coronavirus, for the purposes of cleaning and sanitation, and other activities necessary to maintain or resume the operation of programs: Provided further, That no later than 60 days after the date of enactment of this Act, each State, Territory, and Tribe that receives funding under this heading in this Act shall submit to the Secretary a report, in such manner as the Secretary may require, describing how the funds appropriated under this heading in this Act will be spent and that no later than 90 days after the date of enactment of this Act, the Secretary shall submit to the Committees on Appropriations of the House of Representatives and the Senate, the Committee on Education and Labor of the House of Representatives, and the Com-mittee on Health, Education, Labor, and Pensions of the Senate a report summarizing such reports from the States, Territories, and Tribes: Provided further, That no later than October 31, 2021, each State, Territory, and Tribe that receives funding under this heading in this Act shall submit to the Secretary a report, in such manner as the Secretary may require, describing how the funds appropriated under this heading in this Act were spent and that no later than 60 days after receiving such reports from the States, Territories, and Tribes, the Secretary shall submit to the Committees on Appropriations of the House of Representatives and the Senate, the Committee on Education and Labor of the House of Representatives, and the Committee on Health, Education, Labor, and Pensions of the Senate a report summarizing such reports from the States, Territories, and Tribes: Provided further, That payments made under this heading in this Act may be obligated in this fiscal year or the succeeding two fiscal years: Provided further, That funds appropriated under this heading in this Act may be made available to restore amounts, either directly or through reimbursement, for obligations incurred to prevent, prepare for, and respond to coronavirus, prior to the date of enactment of this Act: Provided further, That such amount is designated by the Congress as being for an emergency requirement pursuant to section 251(b)(2)(A)(i) of the Balanced Budget and Emergency Deficit Control Act of 1985.

children and families services programs

For an additional amount for "Children and Families Services Programs", $1,590,000,000, to remain available until September 30, 2021, to prevent, prepare for, and respond to coronavirus, which shall be used as follows:

(1) $50,000,000 for Family Violence Prevention and Services grants as authorized by section 303(a) and 303(b) of the Family Violence Prevention and Services Act with such funds available to grantees without regard to matching requirements under section 306(c)(4) of such Act, of which $2,000,000 shall be for the National Domestic Violence Hotline: Provided, That the Secretary of Health and Human Services may make such funds available for providing temporary housing and assistance to victims of family, domestic, and dating violence;

(2) $20,000,000 for necessary expenses for community-based grants for the prevention of child abuse and neglect under section 209 of the Child Abuse Prevention and Treatment Act, which the Secretary shall make without regard to sections 203(b)(1) and 204(4) of such Act; and

(3) $20,000,000 for necessary expenses for the Child Abuse Prevention and Treatment Act State Grant program as authorized by Section 112 of such Act;

(4) $1,500,000,000 for necessary expenses for grants to carry out the Low-Income Household Drinking Water and Wastewater Assistance program, as described in section 190703 of division S of this Act.

Provided, That funds made available under this heading in this Act may be used for the purposes provided herein to reimburse costs incurred between January 20, 2020, and the date of award: Provided further, That funds appropriated by the CARES Act (P.L.116–136) to carry out the Community Services Block Grant Act (42 U.S.C. 9901 et seq.) and received by a State shall be made available to eligible entities (as defined in section 673(1)(A) of such Act (42 U.S.C. 9902(1)(A)) not later than either 30 days after such State receives such funds or 30 days after the date of the enactment of this Act, whichever occurs later: Provided further, That such amount is designated by the Congress as being for an emergency requirement pursuant to section 251(b)(2)(A)(i) of the Balanced Budget and Emergency Deficit Control Act of 1985.

Administration For Community Living

aging and disability services programs

For an additional amount for "Aging and Disability Services Programs", $100,000,000, to remain available until September 30, 2021, to prevent, prepare for, and respond to the coronavirus: Provided, That of the amount made available under this heading in this Act, $85,000,000 shall be for activities authorized under the Older Americans Act of 1965 ("OAA") and activities authorized under part B of title XX of the Social Security Act, including $20,000,000 for supportive services under part B of title III; $19,000,000 for nutrition services under subparts 1 and 2 of part C of title III; $1,000,000 for nutrition services under title VI; $20,000,000 for supportive services for family caregivers under part E of title III; $10,000,000 for evidence-based health promotion and disease prevention services under part D of title III; $10,000,000 for elder rights protection activities, including the long-term ombudsman program under title VI; and $5,000,000 shall be for grants to States to support the network of state-wide senior legal services, including existing senior legal hotlines, efforts to expand such hotlines to all interested States, and legal assistance to providers, in order to ensure seniors have access to legal assistance, with such fund allotted to States consistent with paragraphs (1) through (3) of section 304(a) of the OAA: Provided further, That State matching requirements under sections 304(d)(1)(D) and 373(g)(2) of the OAA shall not apply to funds made available under this heading: Provided further, That of the amount made available under this heading in this Act, $10,000,000 shall be for activities authorized in the Developmental Disabilities Assistance and Bill of Rights Act of 2000: Provided further, That of the amount made available under this heading in this Act, $5,000,000 shall be for activities authorized in the Assistive Technology Act of 2004: Provided further, That of the amount made available in the preceding proviso, $5,000,000 shall be for the purchase of equipment to allow interpreters to provide appropriate and essential services to the hearing-impaired community: Provided further, That for the purposes of the funding provided in the preceding proviso, during the emergency period described in section 1135(g)(1)(B) of the Social Security Act, for purposes of section 4(e)(2)(A) of the Assistive Technology Act of 2004, the term "targeted individuals and entities" (as that term is defined in section 3(16) of the Assistive Technology Act of 2004) shall be deemed to include American Sign Language certified interpreters who are providing interpretation services remotely for individuals with disabilities: Provided further, That during such emergency period, for the purposes of the previous two provisos, to facilitate the ability of individuals with disabilities to remain in their homes and practice social distancing, the Secretary shall waive the prohibitions on the use of grant funds for direct payment for an assistive technology device for an individual with a disability under sections 4(e)(2)(A) and 4(e)(5) of such Act: Provided further, That such amount is designated by the Congress as being for an emergency requirement pursuant to section 251(b)(2)(A)(i) of the Balanced Budget and Emergency Deficit Control Act of 1985.

Office Of The Secretary

public health and social services emergency fund

For an additional amount for "Public Health and Social Services Emergency Fund", $4,575,000,000, to remain available until September 30, 2024, to prevent, prepare for, and respond to coronavirus, domestically or internationally, including the development of necessary countermeasures and vaccines, prioritizing platform-based technologies with U.S.-based manufacturing capabilities, the purchase of vaccines, therapeutics, diagnostics, necessary medical supplies, as well as medical surge capacity, addressing blood supply chain, workforce modernization, telehealth access and infrastructure, initial advanced manufacturing, novel dispensing, enhancements to the U.S. Commissioned Corps, and other preparedness and response activities: Provided, That funds appropriated under this paragraph in this Act may be used to develop and demonstrate innovations and enhancements to manufacturing platforms to support such capabilities: Provided further, That the Secretary of Health and Human Services shall purchase vaccines developed using funds made available under this paragraph in this Act to respond to an outbreak or pandemic related to coronavirus in quantities determined by the Secretary to be adequate to address the public health need: Provided further, That products purchased by the Federal government with funds made available under this paragraph in this Act, including vaccines, therapeutics, and diagnostics, shall be purchased in accordance with Federal Acquisition Regulation guidance on fair and reasonable pricing: Provided further, That the Secretary may take such measures authorized under current law to ensure that vaccines, therapeutics, and diagnostics developed from funds provided in this Act will be affordable in the commercial market: Provided further, That in carrying out the previous proviso, the Secretary shall not take actions that delay the development of such products: Provided further, That products purchased with funds appropriated under this paragraph in this Act may, at the discretion of the Secretary of Health and Human Services, be deposited in the Strategic National Stockpile under section 319F–2 of the Public Health Service Act: Provided further, That funds appropriated under this paragraph in this Act may be transferred to, and merged with, the fund authorized by section 319F–4, the Covered Countermeasure Process Fund, of the Public Health Service Act: Provided further, That of the amount made available under this paragraph in this Act, $3,500,000,000 shall be available to the Biomedical Advanced Research and Development Authority for necessary expenses of advanced research, development, manufacturing, production, and purchase of vaccines and therapeutics: Provided further, That of the amount made available under this paragraph in this Act, $500,000,000 shall be available to the Biomedical Advanced Research and Development Authority for the construction, renovation, or equipping of U.S.-based next generation manufacturing facilities, other than facilities owned by the United States Government: Provided further, That of the amount made available under this paragraph in this Act, $500,000,000 shall be available to the Biomedical Advanced Research and Development Authority to promote innovation in antibacterial research and development: Provided further, That funds made available under this paragraph in this Act may be used for grants for the rent, lease, purchase, acquisition, construction, alteration, or renovation of non-Federally owned facilities to improve preparedness and response capability at the State and local level: Provided further, That funds appropriated under this paragraph in this Act may be used for the construction, alteration, renovation or equipping of non-Federally owned facilities for the production of vaccines, therapeutics, diagnostics, and medicines and other items purchased under section 319F–2(a) of the Public Health Service Act where the Secretary determines that such a contract is necessary to assure sufficient domestic production of such supplies: Provided further, That all construction, alteration, or renovation work, carried out, in whole or in part, with fund appropriated under this heading in this Act, the CARES Act (P.L. 116–136), or the Paycheck Protection Program and Health Care Enhancement Act (P.L. 116–139), shall be subject to the requirements of 42 U.S.C. 300s-1(b)(1)(I): Provided further, That not later than seven days after the date of enactment of this Act, and weekly thereafter until the public health emergency related to coronavirus is no longer in effect, the Secretary shall report to the Committees on Appropriations of the House of Representatives and the Senate on the current inventory of ventilators and personal protective equipment in the Strategic National Stockpile, including the numbers of face shields, gloves, goggles and glasses, gowns, head covers, masks, and respirators, as well as deployment of ventilators and personal protective equipment during the previous week, reported by state and other jurisdiction: Provided further, That after the date that a report is required to be submitted by the preceding proviso, amounts made available for "Department of Health and Human Services—Office of the Secretary—General Departmental Management" in Public Law 116–94 for salaries and expenses of the Immediate Office of the Secretary shall be reduced by $250,000 for each day that such report has not been submitted: Provided further, That not later than the first Monday in February of fiscal year 2021 and each fiscal year thereafter, the Secretary shall include in the annual budget submission for the Department, and submit to the Congress, the Secretary's request with respect to expenditures necessary to maintain the minimum level of relevant supplies in the Strategic National Stockpile, including in case of a significant pandemic, in consultation with the working group under section 319F(a) of the Public Health Service Act and the Public Health Emergency Medical Countermeasures Enterprise established under section 2811–1 of such Act: Provided further, That such amount is designated by the Congress as being for an emergency requirement pursuant to section 251(b)(2)(A)(i) of the Balanced Budget and Emergency Deficit Control Act of 1985.

For an additional amount for "Public Health and Social Services Emergency Fund", $100,000,000,000, to remain available until expended, to prevent, prepare for, and respond to coronavirus, for necessary expenses to make payments under the Health Care Provider Relief Fund as described in section 30611 of division C of this Act: Provided, That such amount is designated by the Congress as being for an emergency requirement pursuant to section 251(b)(2)(A)(i) of the Balanced Budget and Emergency Deficit Control Act of 1985.

For an additional amount for "Public Health and Social Services Emergency Fund", $75,000,000,000, to remain available until expended, to prevent, prepare for, and respond to coronavirus, for necessary expenses to carry out the COVID-19 National Testing and Contact Tracing Initiative, as described in subtitle D of division C of this Act: Provided, That such amount is designated by the Congress as being for an emergency requirement pursuant to section 251(b)(2)(A)(i) of the Balanced Budget and Emergency Deficit Control Act of 1985.

DEPARTMENT OF EDUCATION

State Fiscal Stabilization Fund

For an additional amount for "State Fiscal Stabilization Fund", $90,000,000,000, to remain available until September 30, 2022, to prevent, prepare for, and respond to coronavirus: Provided, That the Secretary of Education (referred to under this heading as "Secretary") shall make grants to the Governor of each State for support of elementary, secondary, and postsecondary education and, as applicable, early childhood education programs and services: Provided further, That of the amount made available, the Secretary shall first allocate up to one-half of 1 percent to the outlying areas and one-half of 1 percent to the Bureau of Indian Education ("BIE") for activities consistent with this heading under such terms and conditions as the Secretary may determine: Provided further, That the Secretary may reserve up to $30,000,000 for administration and oversight of the activities under this heading: Provided further, That the Secretary shall allocate 61 percent of the remaining funds made available to carry out this heading to the States on the basis of their relative population of individuals aged 5 through 24 and allocate 39 percent on the basis of their relative number of children counted under section 1124(c) of the Elementary and Secondary Education Act of 1965 (referred to under this heading as "ESEA") as State grants: Provided further, That State grants shall support statewide elementary, secondary, and postsecondary activities; subgrants to local educational agencies; and, subgrants to public institutions of higher education: Provided further, That States shall allocate 65 percent of the funds received under the sixth proviso as subgrants to local educational agencies in proportion to the amount of funds such local educational agencies received under part A of title I of the ESEA in the most recent fiscal year: Provided further, That States shall allocate 30 percent of the funds received under the sixth proviso as subgrants to public institutions of higher education, of which 75 percent shall be apportioned according to the relative share of students who received Pell

Grants who are not exclusively enrolled in distance education courses prior to the coronavirus emergency at the institution in the previous award year and 25 percent shall be apportioned according to the total enrollment of students at the institution who are not exclusively enrolled in distance education courses prior to the coronavirus emergency at the institution in the previous award year: Provided further, That the Governor shall return to the Secretary any funds received that the Governor does not award to local educational agencies and public institutions of higher education or otherwise commit within two years of receiving such funds, and the Secretary shall reallocate such funds to the remaining States in accordance with the sixth proviso: Provided further, That Governors shall use State grants and subgrants to maintain or restore State and local fiscal support for elementary, secondary and postsecondary education: Provided further, That funds for local educational agencies may be used for any activity authorized by the ESEA, including the Native Hawaiian Education Act and the Alaska Native Educational Equity, Support, and Assistance Act, the Individuals with Disabilities Education Act ("IDEA"), subtitle B of title VII of the McKinney-Vento Homeless Assistance Act , the Adult Education and Family Literacy Act or the Carl D. Perkins Career and Technical Education Act of 2006 ("the Perkins Act"): Provided further, That a State or local educational agency receiving funds under this heading may use the funds for activities coordinated with State, local, tribal, and territorial public health departments to detect, prevent, or mitigate the spread of infectious disease or otherwise respond to coronavirus; support online learning by purchasing educational technology and internet access for students, which may include assistive technology or adaptive equipment, that aids in regular and substantive educational interactions between students and their classroom instructor; provide ongoing professional development to staff in how to effectively provide quality online academic instruction; provide assistance for children and families to promote equitable participation in quality online learning; plan and implement activities related to summer learning, including providing classroom instruction or quality online learning during the summer months; plan for and coordinate during long-term closures, provide technology for quality online learning to all students, and how to support the needs of low-income students, racial and ethnic minorities, students with disabilities, English learners, students experiencing homelessness, and children in foster care, including how to address learning gaps that are created or exacerbated due to long-term closures; support the continuity of student engagement through social and emotional learning; and other activities that are necessary to maintain the operation of and continuity of services in local educational agencies, including maintaining employment of existing personnel, and reimbursement for eligible costs incurred during the national emergency: Provided further, That a public institution of higher education that receives funds under this heading shall use funds for education and general expenditures (including defraying expenses due to lost revenue, reimbursement for expenses already incurred, and payroll) and grants to students for expenses directly related to coronavirus and the disruption of campus operations (which may include emergency financial aid to students for food, housing, technology, health care, and child care costs that shall not be required to be repaid by such students) or for the acquisition of technology and services directly related to the need for distance education and the training of faculty and staff to use such technology and services: Provided further, That priority shall be given to under-resourced institutions, institutions with high burden due to the coronavirus, and institutions who did not possess distance education capabilities prior to the coronavirus emergency: Provided further, That any institution of higher education that is not otherwise eligible for a grant of at least $1,000,000 under this heading shall be eligible to receive an amount equal to whichever is lesser of the total loss of revenue and increased costs associated with the coronavirus or $1,000,000: Provided further, That an institution of higher education may not use funds received under this heading to increase its endowment or provide funding for capital outlays associated with facilities related to athletics, sectarian instruction, or religious worship: Provided further, That funds may be used to support hourly workers, such as education support professionals, classified school employees, and adjunct and contingent faculty: Provided further, That a Governor of a State desiring to receive an allocation under this heading shall submit an application at such time, in such manner, and containing such information as the Secretary may reasonably require: Provided further, That the Secretary shall issue a notice inviting applications not later than 15 days after the date of enactment of this Act: Provided further, That any State receiving funding under this heading shall maintain its percent of total spending on elementary, secondary, and postsecondary education in fiscal year 2019 for fiscal years 2020, 2021, and 2022: Provided further, That a State's application shall include assurances that the State will maintain support for elementary and secondary education in fiscal year 2020, fiscal year 2021, and fiscal year 2022 at least at the level of such support that is the average of such State's support for elementary and secondary education in the 3 fiscal years preceding the date of enactment of this Act: Provided further, That a State's application shall include assurances that the State will maintain State support for higher education (not including support for capital projects or for research and development or tuition and fees paid by students) in fiscal year 2020, fiscal year 2021, and fiscal year 2022 at least at the level of such support that is the average of such State's support for higher education (which shall include State and local government funding to institutions of higher education and state need-based financial aid) in the 3 fiscal years preceding the date of enactment of this Act, and that any such State's support for higher education funding, as calculated as spending for public higher education per full-time equivalent student, shall be the same in fiscal year 2022 as it was in fiscal year 2019: Provided further, That in such application, the Governor shall provide baseline data that demonstrates the State's current status in each of the areas described in such assurances in the preceding provisos: Provided further, That a State's application shall include assurances that the State will not construe any provisions under this heading as displacing any otherwise applicable provision of any collective-bargaining agreement between an eligible entity and a labor organization as defined by section 2(5) of the National Labor Relations Act (29 U.S.C. 152(5)) or analogous State law: Provided further, That a State's application shall include assurances that the State shall maintain the wages, benefits, and other terms and conditions of employment set forth in any collective-bargaining agreement between the eligible entity and a labor organization, as defined in the preceding proviso: Provided further, That a State's application shall include assurances that all students with disabilities are afforded their full rights under IDEA, including all rights and services outlined in individualized education programs ("IEPs"): Provided further, That a State receiving funds under this heading shall submit a report to the Secretary, at such time and in such manner as the Secretary may require, that describes the use of funds provided under this heading: Provided further, That no recipient of funds under this heading shall use funds to provide financial assistance to students to attend private elementary or secondary schools, unless such funds are used to provide special education and related services to children with disabilities whose IEPs require such placement, and where the school district maintains responsibility for providing such children a free appropriate public education, as authorized by IDEA: Provided further, That a local educational agency, State, institution of higher education, or other entity that receives funds under "State Fiscal Stabilization Fund", shall to the greatest extent practicable, continue to pay its employees and contractors during the period of any disruptions or closures related to coronavirus: Provided further, That the terms "elementary education" and "secondary education" have the meaning given such terms under State law: Provided further, That the term "institution of higher education" has the meaning given such term in section 101 of the Higher Education Act of 1965: Provided further, That the term "fiscal year" shall have the meaning given such term under State law: Provided further, That the term "State" means each of the 50 States, the District of Columbia, and the Commonwealth of Puerto Rico: Provided further, That such amount is designated by the Congress as being for an emergency requirement pursuant to section 251(b)(2)(A)(i) of the Balanced Budget and Emergency Deficit Control Act of 1985.

Higher Education

For an additional amount for "Higher Education", $10,150,000,000, to remain available until September 30, 2021, to prevent, prepare for, and respond to coronavirus, of which $11,000,000 shall be transferred to "National Technical Institute for the Deaf" to help defray expenses (which may include lost revenue, reimbursement for expenses already incurred, technology costs associated with a transition to distance education, sign language and captioning costs associated with a transition to distance education, faculty and staff trainings, and payroll) directly caused by coronavirus and to enable emergency financial aid to students for expenses directly related to coronavirus and the disruption of university operations (which may include food, housing, transportation, technology, health care, and child care), of which $20,000,000 shall be transferred to "Howard University" to help defray expenses (which may include lost revenue, reimbursement for expenses already incurred, technology costs associated with a transition to distance education, technology costs associated with a transition to distance education, faculty and staff trainings, and payroll) directly related to coronavirus and to enable grants to students for expenses directly related to coronavirus and the disruption of university operations (which may include food, housing, transportation, technology, health care, and child care), of which $11,000,000 shall be transferred to "Gallaudet University" to help defray expenses (which may include lost revenue, reimbursement for expenses already incurred, technology costs associated with a transition to distance education, sign language and captioning costs associated with a transition to distance education, faculty and staff trainings, and payroll) directly related to coronavirus and to enable grants to students for expenses directly related to coronavirus and the disruption of university operations (which may include food, housing, transportation, technology, health care, and child care), and of which the remaining amounts shall be used to carry out parts A and B of title III, parts A and B of title V, subpart 4 of part A of title VII, and part B of title VII of the Higher Education Act of 1965 ("HEA") as follows:

(1) $1,708,000,000 for parts A and B of title III, parts A and B of title V, and subpart 4 of part A of title VII of the HEA to address needs directly related to coronavirus: Provided, That such amount shall be allocated by the Secretary proportionally to such

programs covered under this paragraph and based on the relative share of funding appropriated to such programs in the Further Consolidated Appropriations Act, 2020 (Public Law 116–94) and distributed to institutions of higher education as follows:

(A) Except as otherwise provided in subparagraph (B), for eligible institutions under part B of title III and subpart 4 of part A of title VII of the Higher Education Act, the Secretary shall allot to each eligible institution an amount using the following formula:

(i) 70 percent according to a ratio equivalent to the number of Pell Grant recipients in attendance at such institution at the end of the school year preceding the beginning of that fiscal year and the total number of Pell Grant recipients at all such institutions;

(ii) 20 percent according to a ratio equivalent to the total number of students enrolled at such institution at the end of the school year preceding the beginning of that fiscal year and the number of students enrolled at all such institutions; and

(iii) 10 percent according to a ratio equivalent to the total endowment size at all eligible institutions at the end of the school year preceding the beginning of that fiscal year and the total endowment size at such institutions;

(B) For eligible institutions under section 326 of the Higher Education Act, the Secretary shall allot to each eligible institution an amount in proportion to the award received from funding for such institutions in the Further Consolidated Appropriations Act, 2020 (Public Law 116–94);

(C) For eligible institutions under section 316 of the Higher Education Act, the Secretary shall allot funding according to the formula in section 316(d)(3) of the Higher Education Act;

(D) Notwithstanding section 318(f) of the Higher Education Act, for eligible institutions under section 318 of the Higher Education Act, the Secretary shall allot funding according to the formula in section 318(e) of the Higher Education Act;

(E) Except as provided in subparagraphs (C) and (D), for eligible institutions under part A of title III of the Higher Education Act and parts A and B of title V, the Secretary shall issue an application for eligible institutions to demonstrate unmet need, and the Secretary shall allow eligible institutions to apply for funds under one of the programs for which they are eligible.

(2) $8,400,000,000 for part B of title VII of the HEA for institutions of higher education (as defined in section 101 or 102(c) of the HEA) to address needs directly related to coronavirus as follows:

(A) $7,000,000,000 shall be provided to private, non-profit institutions of higher education apportioning it—

(i) 75 percent according to the relative share of enrollment of Federal Pell Grant recipients who are not exclusively enrolled in distance education courses prior to the coronavirus emergency, and

(ii) 25 percent according to the relative share of the total equivalent enrollment of students who were not Federal Pell Grant recipients who are not exclusively enrolled in distance education courses prior to the coronavirus emergency.

(B) $1,400,000,000 shall be for institutions of higher education (as defined in section 101 of the Higher Education Act) with unmet need related to the coronavirus, including institutions of higher education that offer their courses and programs exclusively through distance education:

Provided, That funds shall be used to make payments to such institutions to provide emergency grants to students who attended such institutions at any point during the coronavirus emergency and for any component of the student's cost of attendance (as

defined under section 472 of the HEA), including food, housing, course materials, technology, health care, and child care): Provided further, That institutions of higher education may use such funds to defray expenses (including lost revenue, reimbursement for expenses already incurred, technology costs associated with a transition to distance education, faculty and staff trainings, and payroll) incurred by institutions of higher education: Provided further, That such payments shall not be used to increase endowments or provide funding for capital outlays associated with facilities related to athletics, sectarian instruction, or religious worship: Provided further, That any institution of higher education that is not otherwise eligible for a grant of at least $1,000,000 under paragraph (2)(A) of this heading and has a total enrollment of at least 500 students shall be eligible to receive an amount equal to whichever is the lesser of the total loss of revenue and increased costs associated with the coronavirus or $1,000,000: Provided further, That such amount is designated by the Congress as being for an emergency requirement pursuant to section 251(b)(2)(A)(i) of the Balanced Budget and Emergency Deficit Control Act of 1985.
General Provisions—Department Of Education

SEC. 10602.

Amounts made available to "Department of Education—Office of Inspector General" in title VIII of division B of Public Law 116–136 are hereby permanently rescinded, and an amount of additional new budget authority equivalent to the amount rescinded is hereby appropriated, to remain available until expended, for the same purposes and under the same authorities as they were originally appropriated, and shall be in addition to any other funds available for such purposes: Provided, That the amounts appropriated by this section may also be used for investigations and are available until expended: Provided further, That such amount is designated by the Congress as being for an emergency requirement pursuant to section 251(b)(2)(A)(i) of the Balanced Budget and Emergency Deficit Control Act of 1985.

SEC. 10603.

The Coronavirus Aid, Relief, and Economic Security Act (P.L. 116–136) is amended by striking section 18001(a)(3): Provided , That amounts repurposed by this section that were previously designated by the Congress as an emergency requirement pursuant to the Balanced Budget and Emergency Deficit Control Act of 1985 are designated by the Congress as an emergency requirement pursuant to section 251(b)(2)(A)(i) of the Balanced Budget and Emergency Deficit Control Act of 1985.

SEC. 10604.

Section 18005(a) of the Coronavirus Aid, Relief, and Economic Security Act (P.L. 116–136) is amended by inserting "with these funds only for children identified under section 1115(c) of the ESEA in the school district served by a local educational agency who are enrolled in private elementary schools and secondary schools" after "equitable services": Provided , That amounts repurposed by this section that were previously designated by the Congress as an emergency requirement pursuant to the Balanced Budget and Emergency Deficit Control Act of 1985 are designated by the Congress as an emergency requirement pursuant to section 251(b)(2)(A)(i) of the Balanced Budget and Emergency Deficit Control Act of 1985.

SEC. 10605.

Section 18004(c) of the Coronavirus Aid, Relief, and Economic Security Act (P.L.

116–136) is amended by striking "to cover any costs associated with significant changes to the delivery of instruction due to the coronavirus" and inserting "to defray expenses (including lost revenue, reimbursement for expenses already incurred, technology costs associated with a transition to distance education, faculty and staff trainings, payroll) incurred by institutions of higher education.": Provided , That amounts repurposed by this section that were previously designated by the Congress as an emergency requirement pursuant to the Balanced Budget and Emergency Deficit Control Act of 1985 are designated by the Congress as an emergency requirement pursuant to section 251(b)(2)(A)(i) of the Balanced Budget and Emergency Deficit Control Act of 1985.

SEC. 10606.
With respect to the allocation and award of funds under this title, the Secretary of Education is prohibited from—
(a) establishing a priority or preference not specified in this title; and
(b) imposing limits on the use of such funds not specified in this title.
RELATED AGENCIES
Corporation For National And Community Service
administrative provisions—corporation for national and community service

SEC. 10607.
(a) The remaining unobligated balances of funds as of September 30, 2020, from amounts provided to "Corporation for National and Community Service—Salaries and Expenses" in title IV of division A of the Further Consolidated Appropriations Act, 2020 (Public Law 116–94), are hereby permanently rescinded, and an amount of additional new budget authority equal to the unobligated balances rescinded is hereby appropriated on September 30, 2020, to remain available until September 30, 2021, for the same purposes and under the same authorities that they were originally made available in Public Law 116–94, which shall be in addition to any other funds available for such purposes: Provided, That such amount is designated by the Congress as being for an emergency requirement pursuant to section 251(b)(2)(A)(i) of the Balanced Budget and Emergency Deficit Control Act of 1985.
(b) The remaining unobligated balances of funds as of September 30, 2020, from amounts provided to "Corporation for National and Community Service—Operating Expenses" in title IV of division A of the Further Consolidated Appropriations Act, 2020 (Public Law 116–94), are hereby permanently rescinded, and an amount of additional new budget authority equal to the unobligated balances rescinded is hereby appropriated on September 30, 2020, to remain available until September 30, 2021, for the same purposes and under the same authorities that they were originally made available in Public Law 116–94, which shall be in addition to any other funds available for such purposes: Provided, That any amounts appropriated by the preceding proviso shall not be subject to the allotment requirements otherwise applicable under sections 129(a), (b), (d), and (e) of the National and Community Service Act of 1993: Provided further, That such amount is designated by the Congress as being for an emergency requirement pursuant to section 251(b)(2)(A)(i) of the Balanced Budget and Emergency Deficit Control Act of 1985.
(c) The remaining unobligated balances of funds as of September 30, 2020, from amounts provided to "Corporation for National and Community Service—Office of Inspector General" in title IV of division A of the Further Consolidated Appro-

priations Act, 2020 (Public Law 116–94), are hereby permanently rescinded, and an amount of additional new budget authority equal to the amount rescinded is hereby appropriated on September 30, 2020, to remain available until September 30, 2021, for the same purposes and under the same authorities that they were originally made available in Public Law 116–94, which shall be in addition to any other funds available for such purposes: Provided, That such amount is designated by the Congress as being for an emergency requirement pursuant to section 251(b)(2)(A)(i) of the Balanced Budget and Emergency Deficit Control Act of 1985.

(d) (1) Section 3514(b) of title III of division A of Public Law 116–136 is hereby repealed, and shall be applied hereafter as if such subsection had never been enacted.

(2) (A) IN GENERAL.—The budgetary effects of this subsection are designated as an emergency requirement pursuant to section 4(g) of the Statutory Pay-As-You-Go Act of 2010 (2 U.S.C. 933(g)).

(B) DESIGNATION IN THE SENATE.—In the Senate, this subsection is designated as an emergency requirement pursuant to section 4112(a) of H. Con. Res. 71 (115th Congress), the concurrent resolution on the budget for fiscal year 2018.

(C) CLASSIFICATION OF BUDGETARY EFFECTS.—Notwithstanding Rule 3 of the Budget Scorekeeping Guidelines set forth in the joint explanatory statement of the committee of conference accompanying Conference Report 105–217 and section 250(c)(7) and (c)(8) of the Balanced Budget and Emergency Deficit Control Act of 1985, the budgetary effects of this subsection—

(i) shall not be estimated for purposes of section 251 of such Act; and

(ii) shall be entered on the PAYGO scorecards maintained pursuant to section 4(d) of the Statutory Pay As-You-Go Act of 2010.

Institute Of Museum And Library Sciences

office of museum and library services: grants and administration

For an additional amount for "Institute of Museum and Library Services", $5,000,000, to remain available until September 30, 2021, to prevent, prepare for, and respond to coronavirus, including grants to States, territories, tribes, museums, and libraries, to expand digital network access, purchase internet accessible devices, provide technical support services, and for operational expenses: Provided, That any matching funds requirements for States, tribes, libraries, and museums are waived for grants provided with funds made available under this heading in this Act: Provided further, That such amount is designated by the Congress as being for an emergency requirement pursuant to section 251(b)(2)(A)(i) of the Balanced Budget and Emergency Deficit Control Act of 1985.

Railroad Retirement Board

limitation on administration

For an additional amount for "Limitation on Administration", $4,500,000, to remain available until September 30, 2021, to prevent, prepare for, and respond to coronavirus, including the expeditious dispensation of railroad unemployment insurance benefits, and to support full-time equivalents and overtime hours as needed to administer the Railroad Unemployment Insurance Act: Provided, That such amount is designated by the Congress as being for an emergency requirement pursuant to section 251(b)(2)(A)(i) of the Balanced Budget and Emergency Deficit Control Act of 1985.

limitation on the office of inspector general

For an additional amount for "Office of the Inspector General", $500,000, to remain available until expended, to prevent, prepare for, and respond to coronavirus, including salaries and expenses necessary for oversight, investigations and audits of the Railroad Retirement Board and railroad unemployment insurance benefits funded in this Act and Public Law 116–136: Provided, That such amount is designated by the Congress as being for an emergency requirement pursuant to section 251(b)(2)(A)(i) of the Balanced Budget and Emergency Deficit Control Act of 1985.

GENERAL PROVISIONS—THIS TITLE

SEC. 10608.

Notwithstanding any other provision of law, funds made available under each heading in this title shall only be used for the purposes specifically described under that heading.

SEC. 10609.

Funds appropriated by this title may be used by the Secretary of the Health and Human Services to appoint, without regard to the provisions of sections 3309 through 3319 of title 5 of the United States Code, candidates needed for positions to perform critical work relating to coronavirus for which—

(1) public notice has been given; and

(2) the Secretary has determined that such a public health threat exists.

SEC. 10610.

Funds made available by this title may be used to enter into contracts with individuals for the provision of personal services (as described in section 104 of part 37 of title 48, Code of Federal Regulations (48 CFR 37.104)) to support the prevention of, preparation for, or response to coronavirus, domestically and internationally, subject to prior notification to the Committees on Appropriations of the House of Representatives and the Senate: Provided, That such individuals may not be deemed employees of the United States for the purpose of any law administered by the Office of Personnel Management: Provided further, That the authority made available pursuant to this section shall expire on September 30, 2024.

SEC. 10611.

Not later than 30 days after the date of enactment of this Act, the Secretary of Health and Human Services shall provide a detailed spend plan of anticipated uses of funds made available to the Department of Health and Human Services in this Act, including estimated personnel and administrative costs, to the Committees on Appropriations of the House of Representatives and the Senate: Provided, That such plans shall be updated and submitted to such Committees every 60 days until September 30, 2024: Provided further, That the spend plans shall be accompanied by a listing of each contract obligation incurred that exceeds $5,000,000 which has not previously been reported, including the amount of each such obligation.

SEC. 10612.

No later than September 30, 2020, the remaining unobligated balances of funds made available through September 30, 2020, under the heading "National Institutes of Health" in the Further Consolidated Appropriations Act, 2020 (Public Law 116–94) are hereby permanently rescinded, and an amount of additional new budget authority equivalent to the amount rescinded from each account is hereby appropriated to that account, to remain available until September 30, 2021, and shall be available for the same purposes, in addition to other funds as may be available for such purposes, and under the same authorities for which the funds were originally provided in Public Law

116–94: Provided, That such amount is designated by the Congress as being for an emergency requirement pursuant to section 251(b)(2)(A)(i) of the Balanced Budget and Emergency Deficit Control Act of 1985.

SEC. 10613.

Funds made available in Public Law 113–235 to the accounts of the National Institutes of Health that were available for obligation through fiscal year 2015 and were obligated for multi-year research grants shall be available through fiscal year 2021 for the liquidation of valid obligations if the Director of the National Insitutes of Health determines the project suffered an interruption of activities attributable to SARS–CoV–2: Provided, That such amount is designated by the Congress as being for an emergency requirement pursuant to section 251(b)(2)(A)(i) of the Balanced Budget and Emergency Deficit Control Act of 1985.

SEC. 10614.

Of the funds appropriated by this title under the heading "Public Health and Social Services Emergency Fund", $75,000,000 shall be transferred to, and merged with, funds made available under the heading "Office of the Secretary, Office of Inspector General", and shall remain available until expended, for oversight of activities supported with funds appropriated to the Department of Health and Human Services in this Act: Provided, That the Inspector General of the Department of Health and Human Services shall consult with the Committees on Appropriations of the House of Representatives and the Senate prior to obligating such funds: Provided further, That the transfer authority provided by this section is in addition to any other transfer authority provided by law.

TITLE VII

—LEGISLATIVE BRANCH
HOUSE OF REPRESENTATIVES
For an additional amount for the "House of Representatives", $5,000,000, to remain available until September 30, 2021, for necessary expenses to prevent, prepare for, and respond to coronavirus: Provided, That the amounts made available under this heading in this Act shall be allocated in accordance with a spend plan submitted to the Committee on Appropriations of the House of Representatives by the Chief Administrative Officer and approved by such Committee: Provided further, That such amount is designated by the Congress as being for an emergency requirement pursuant to section 251(b)(2)(A)(i) of the Balanced Budget and Emergency Deficit Control Act of 1985.
Government Accountability Office
salaries and expenses
For an additional amount for "Salaries and Expenses", $30,000,000, to remain available until expended, for audits and investigations relating to COVID–19 or similar pandemics, as well as any related stimulus funding to assist the Nation's response to health and economic vulnerabilities to pandemics: Provided, That, not later than 90 days after the date of enactment of this Act, the Government Accountability Office shall submit to the Committees on Appropriations of the House of Representatives and the Senate a spend plan specifying funding estimates and a timeline for such audits and investigations: Provided further, That such amount is designated by the Congress as being for an emergency requirement pursuant to section 251(b)(2)(A)

(i) of the Balanced Budget and Emergency Deficit Control Act of 1985.

TITLE VIII

—DEPARTMENT OF STATE, FOREIGN OPERATIONS, AND RELATED PROGRAMS
DEPARTMENT OF STATE
Administration Of Foreign Affairs
office of inspector general
For an additional amount for "Office of Inspector General", $2,000,000, to remain available until September 30, 2022, for oversight of funds administered by the Department of State and made available to prevent, prepare for, and respond to coronavirus by this title and by prior acts: Provided, That such amount is designated by the Congress as being for an emergency requirement pursuant to section 251(b)(2)(A)(i) of the Balanced Budget and Emergency Deficit Control Act of 1985.
GENERAL PROVISIONS — THIS TITLE
(including transfer of funds)

SEC. 10801.
Section 21005 of the Emergency Appropriations for Coronavirus Health Response and Agency Operations (division B of Public Law 116–136) is amended by inserting at the end before the period "and is further amended by striking '$5,563,619' in the second proviso under the heading 'Repatriation Loans Program Account' and inserting in lieu thereof '$15,563,619'".

SEC. 10802.
Section 21009 of the Emergency Appropriations for Coronavirus Health Response and Agency Operations (division B of Public Law 116–136) is amended by striking "fiscal year 2020" and inserting in lieu thereof "fiscal years 2020 and 2021": Provided, That the amount provided by this section is designated by the Congress as being for an emergency requirement pursuant to section 251(b)(2)(A)(i) of the Balanced Budget and Emergency Deficit Control Act of 1985.

TITLE IX

TRANSPORTATION, HOUSING AND URBAN DEVELOPMENT, AND RELATED AGENCIES
DEPARTMENT OF TRANSPORTATION
Federal Aviation Administration
operations
For an additional amount for "Operations", $75,000,000, to remain available until September 30, 2022, to prevent, prepare for, and respond to coronavirus: Provided , That amounts made available under this heading in this Act shall be derived from the general fund, of which not less than $1,000,000 shall be for the Administrator to seek to enter into an agreement not later than 45 days after the date of enactment of this Act with a research organization established under chapter 1503 of title 36, United States Code, to conduct a study to determine whether the environmental controls systems in commercial airliners recirculate pathogens in the cabin air and to assess existing and potential technological solutions to reduce pathogen recirculation and to mitigate any elevated risk of exposure to pathogens in the cabin air: Provided further That

such amount is designated by the Congress as being for an emergency requirement pursuant to section 251(b)(2)(A)(i) of the Balanced Budget and Emergency Deficit Control Act of 1985.

Federal Highway Administration

highway infrastructure programs

For an additional amount for "Highway Infrastructure Programs", $15,000,000,000, to remain available until expended: Provided , That the funds made available under this heading shall be derived from the general fund, shall be in addition to any funds provided for fiscal year 2020 in this or any other Act for "Federal-aid Highways" under chapters 1 or 2 of title 23, United States Code, and shall not affect the distribution or amount of funds provided in any other Act: Provided further, That notwithstanding chapter 1 of title 23, United States Code, or any other provision of law, a State, territory, Puerto Rico, or Indian Tribe may use funds made available under this heading in this Act for activities eligible under section 133(b) of title 23, United States Code, for administrative and operations expenses, including salaries of employees (including those employees who have been placed on administrative leave) or contractors, information technology needs, and availability payments: Provided further, That of the funds made available under this heading, $14,775,000,000 shall be available for States, $150,000,000 shall be available for the Tribal Transportation Program, as described in section 202 of title 23, United States Code, $60,000,000 shall be available for the Puerto Rico Highway Program, as described in section 165(b)(2)(C)(iii) of such title; and $15,000,000 shall be available for under the Territorial Highway Program, as described in section 165(c)(6) of such title: Provided further, That for the purposes of funds made available under this heading the term "State" means any of the 50 States or the District of Columbia: Provided further, That the funds made available under this heading for States shall be apportioned to States in the same ratio as the obligation limitation for fiscal year 2020 was distributed among the States in accordance with the formula specified in section 120(a)(5) of division H of Public Law 116–94 and shall be apportioned not later than 30 days after the date of enactment of this Act: Provided further, That the funds made available under this heading shall be administered as if apportioned under chapter 1 of title 23, United States Code, except that activities eligible under the Tribal Transportation Program shall be administered as if allocated under chapter 2 of title 23, United States Code: Provided further, That funds apportioned to a State under this heading shall be suballocated within the State to areas described in subsection 133(d)(1)(A)(i) of title 23, United States Code, in the same ratio that funds suballocated to those areas for fiscal year 2020 bears to the total amount of funds apportioned to the State for the Federal-aid highway program under section 104 of such title for fiscal year 2020: Provided further, That of funds made available under this heading for activities eligible under section 133(b) of title 23, United States Code, any such activity shall be subject to the requirements of section 133(i) of such title: Provided further, That, except as provided in the following proviso, the funds made available under this heading for activities eligible under the Puerto Rico Highway Program and activities eligible under the Territorial Highway Program shall be administered as if allocated under sections 165(b) and 165(c), respectively, of such title: Provided further, That the funds made available under this heading for activities eligible under the Puerto Rico Highway Program shall not be subject to the requirements of sections 165(b)(2)(A) or 165(b)(2)(B) of such title: Provided further, That for amounts subject to the obligation limitation under the heading "Department of Transportation—Federal Highway Administration—Federal-aid Highways—(Limitation on Obligations)—(Highway Trust Fund)" in Public Law 116–94 for fiscal year 2020 that are obligated after the date of enactment of this Act, and for any amounts made available under this heading in this Act, the Federal share of the costs shall be, at the option of the State, District of Columbia, territory, Puerto Rico, or Indian Tribe, up to 100 percent, and may be available for administrative and operations expenses, including salaries of employees (including those employees who have been placed on administrative leave) or contractors, information technology needs, and availability payments: Provided further, That section 120(c) of Public Law 116–94 shall not apply for fiscal year 2020, and that amounts that would otherwise have been redistributed by section 120(c) shall be retained by States and shall be available for their original purpose until September 30, 2021, except that such amounts shall be subject to such redistribution in fiscal year 2021: Provided further, That amounts made available under section 147 of title 23, United States Code, for fiscal years 2019 and 2020 are available for the administrative and operating expenses of eligible entities related to the response to a coronavirus public health emergency beginning on January 20, 2020, reimbursement for administrative and operating costs to maintain service including the purchase of personal protective equipment, and paying the administrative leave of operations personnel due to reductions in service: Provided further, That funds made available for administrative and operating expenses authorized for fiscal year 2020 in Public Law 116–94 or in this Act under this heading are not required to be included in a transportation improvement program or a statewide transportation improvement program under sections 134 or 135 of title 23, United States Code, or chapter 53 of title 49, United States Code, as applicable: Provided further, That unless otherwise specified, applicable requirements under title 23, United States Code, shall apply to funds made available under this heading: Provided further, That the Administrator of the Federal Highway Administration may retain up to one half of one percent of the funds made available under this heading to fund the oversight by the Administrator of activities carried out with funds made available under this heading: Provided further, That such amount is designated by the Congress as being for an emergency requirement pursuant to section 251(b)(2)(A)(i) of the Balanced Budget and Emergency Deficit Control Act of 1985.

Federal Transit Administration
public transportation emergency relief
For an additional amount for "Public Transportation Emergency Relief", $15,750,000,000, to remain available until expended, to prevent, prepare for, and respond to coronavirus: Provided, That of the amounts appropriated under this heading in this Act—
(1) $11,750,000,000 shall be for grants to urbanized areas with populations over 3,000,000 and shall be allocated in the same ratio as funds were provided in fiscal year 2020: Provided, That 15 percent of the amounts provided in this paragraph shall be allocated as if such funds were provided under section 5307 of title 49, United States Code and apportioned in accordance with section 5338 of such title (other than subsection (b)(3) and (c)(1)(A)) and 85 percent of the amounts provided in this paragraph shall be allocated under section 5337 of such title and apportioned in accordance with such section: Provided further, That funds provided under section 5337 shall be added to funds apportioned under section 5307 for administration in accordance with provisions under section 5307: Provided further, That for urbanized

areas with multiple subrecipients, funds provided under section 5337 in this paragraph shall be distributed among subrecipients using the same ratio used to distribute funds made available for section 5337 in fiscal year 2020; and

(2) $4,000,000,000 shall be for grants to transit agencies that, as a result of coronavirus, require significant additional assistance to maintain basic transit services: Provided, That such funds shall be administered as if they were provided under section 5324 of title 49, United States Code: Provided further , That any recipient or subrecipient of funds under chapter 53 of title 49, United States Code, or an intercity bus service provider that has, between October 1, 2018 and January 20, 2020, partnered with a recipient or subrecipient in order to meet the requirements of section 5311(f) of such title shall be eligible to directly apply for funds under this paragraph: Provided further , That entities that are not recipients or subrecipients of funds under chapter 53 of title 49 but are eligible for grants under this heading in this Act shall be eligible to receive not more than 18.75 percent of the total funds provided under this paragraph: Provided further , That such entities shall use assistance provided under this heading only for workforce retention or, the recall or rehire of any laid off, furloughed, or terminated employee, associated with the provision of bus service: Provided further , That, the Secretary shall issue a Notice of Funding Opportunity not later than 30 days after the date of enactment of this Act and that such Notice of Funding Opportunity shall require application submissions not later than 45 days after the enactment of this Act: Provided further , That the Secretary shall make awards not later than 45 days after the application deadline: Provided further , That the Secretary shall require grantees to provide estimates of financial need, data on reduced ridership, and a spending plan for funds: Provided further , That when evaluating applications for assistance, the Secretary shall give priority to transit agencies with the largest revenue loss as a percentage of their operating expenses: Provided further , That if applications for assistance do not exceed available funds, the Secretary shall reserve the remaining amounts for grantees to prevent, prepare for, and respond to coronavirus and shall accept applications on a rolling basis: Provided further , That if amounts made available under this heading in this Act remain unobligated on December 31, 2021, such amounts shall be available for any purpose eligible under section 5324 of title 49, United States Code:

Provided further, That the provision of funds under this section shall not affect the ability of any other agency of the Government, including the Federal Emergency Management Agency, or State agency, a local governmental entity, organization, or person, to provide any other funds otherwise authorized by law: Provided further, That notwithstanding subsection (a)(1) or (b) of section 5307 of title 49, United States Code, subsection (a)(1) of section 5324 of such title, or any provision of chapter 53 of title 49, funds provided under this heading in this Act are available for the operating expenses of transit agencies related to the response to a coronavirus public health emergency, including, beginning on January 20, 2020, reimbursement for operating costs to maintain service and lost revenue due to the coronavirus public health emergency, including the purchase of personal protective equipment, and paying the administrative leave of operations or contractor personnel due to reductions in service: Provided further, That to the maximum extent possible, funds made available under this heading in this Act and in title XII of division B of the CARES Act (Public Law 116–136) shall be directed to payroll and public transit service, unless the recipient certifies to the Secretary they have not furloughed any employees: Provided further,

That such operating expenses are not required to be included in a transportation improvement program, long-range transportation plan, statewide transportation plan, or a statewide transportation improvement program: Provided further, That the Secretary shall not waive the requirements of section 5333 of title 49, United States Code, for funds appropriated under this heading in this Act: Provided further , That unless otherwise specified, applicable requirements under chapter 53 of title 49, United States Code, shall apply to funding made available under this heading in this Act, except that the Federal share of the costs for which any grant is made under this heading in this Act shall be, at the option of the recipient, up to 100 percent: Provided further, That the amount made available under this heading in this Act shall be derived from the general fund and shall not be subject to any limitation on obligations for transit programs set forth in any Act: Provided further, That not more than one-half of one percent of the funds for transit infrastructure grants provided under this heading in this Act shall be available for administrative expenses and ongoing program management oversight as authorized under sections 5334 and 5338(f)(2) of title 49, United States Code, and shall be in addition to any other appropriations for such purpose: Provided further, That such amount is designated by the Congress as being for an emergency requirement pursuant to section 251(b)(2)(A)(i) of the Balanced Budget and Emergency Deficit Control Act of 1985.

DEPARTMENT OF HOUSING AND URBAN DEVELOPMENT

Public And Indian Housing

tenant-based rental assistance

(including transfer of funds)

For an additional amount for "Tenant-Based Rental Assistance", $4,000,000,000, to remain available until expended, and to be used under the same authority and conditions as the additional appropriations for fiscal year 2020 under this heading in title XII of division B of the CARES Act (Public Law 116–136), except that any amounts provided for administrative expenses and other expenses of public housing agencies for their section 8 programs, including Mainstream vouchers, under this heading in the CARES Act (Public Law 116–136) and under this heading in this Act shall also be available for Housing Assistance Payments under section 8(o) of the United States Housing Act of 1937 (42 U.S.C. 1437f(o)): Provided, That amounts made available under this heading in this Act and under the same heading in title XII of division B of the CARES Act may be used to cover or reimburse allowable costs incurred to prevent, prepare for, and respond to coronavirus regardless of the date on which such costs were incurred: Provided further, That of the amounts made available under this heading in this Act, $500,000,000 shall be available for administrative expenses and other expenses of public housing agencies for their section 8 programs, including Mainstream vouchers: Provided further, That of the amounts made available under this heading in this Act, $2,500,000,000 shall be available for adjustments in the calendar year 2020 section 8 renewal funding allocations, including Mainstream vouchers, for public housing agencies that experience a significant increase in voucher per-unit costs due to extraordinary circumstances or that, despite taking reasonable cost savings measures, as determined by the Secretary, would otherwise be required to terminate rental assistance for families as a result of insufficient funding: Provided further, That of the amounts made available under this heading in this Act, $1,000,000,000 shall be used for incremental rental voucher assistance under section 8(o) of the United States Housing Act of 1937 for use by individuals and families who are—homeless, as defined under section 103(a) of the McKinney-Vento Homeless Assistance Act (42 U.S.C. 11302(a)); at risk of homelessness, as defined under section 401(1) of the McKinney-Vento Homeless Assistance Act (42 U.S.C. 11360(1)); or fleeing, or attempting to flee, domestic violence, dating violence, sexual assault, or stalking: Provided further, That the Secretary shall allocate amounts made available in the preceding proviso to public housing agencies not later than 60 days after the date of enactment of this Act, according to a formula that considers the ability of the public housing agency to use vouchers promptly and the need of geographical areas based on factors to be determined by the Secretary, such as risk of transmission of coronavirus, high numbers or rates of sheltered and unsheltered homelessness, and economic and housing market conditions: Provided further, That if a public housing authority elects not to administer or does not promptly issue all of its authorized vouchers within a reasonable period of time, the Secretary shall reallocate any unissued vouchers and associated funds to other public housing agencies according to the criteria in the preceding proviso: Provided further, That a public housing agency shall not reissue any vouchers under this heading in this Act for incremental rental voucher assistance when assistance for the family initially assisted is terminated: Provided further, That upon termination of incremental rental voucher assistance under this heading in this Act for one or more families assisted by a public housing agency, the Secretary shall reallocate amounts that are no longer needed by such public housing agency for assistance under this heading in this Act to another public housing agency for the renewal of vouchers previously authorized under this heading in this Act: Provided further, That amounts made available in this paragraph are in addition to any other amounts made available for such purposes: Provided further, That up to 0.5 percent of the amounts made available under this heading in this Act may be transferred, in aggregate, to "Department of Housing and Urban Development, Program Offices—Public and Indian Housing" to supplement existing resources for the necessary costs of administering and overseeing the obligation and expenditure of these amounts, to remain available until September 30, 2024: Provided further, That such amount is designated by the Congress as being for an emergency requirement pursuant to section 251(b)(2)(A)(i) of the Balanced Budget and Emergency Deficit Control Act of 1985.

public housing operating fund

(including transfer of funds)

For an additional amount for "Public Housing Operating Fund", as authorized by section 9(e) of the United States Housing Act of 1937 (42 U.S.C. 1437g(e)), $2,000,000,000, to remain available until September 30, 2021, and to be used under the same authority and conditions as the additional appropriations for fiscal year 2020 under this heading in title XII of division B of the CARES Act (Public Law 116–136): Provided, That amounts made available under this heading in this Act and under the same heading in title XII of division B of the CARES Act may be used to cover or reimburse allowable costs incurred to prevent, prepare for, and respond to coronavirus regardless of the date on which such costs were incurred: Provided further, That up to 0.5 percent of the amounts made available under this heading in this Act may be transferred, in aggregate, to "Department of Housing and Urban Development, Program Offices—Public and Indian Housing" to supplement existing resources for the necessary costs of administering and overseeing the obligation and expenditure of these amounts, to remain available until September 30, 2024: Provided further, That

such amount is designated by the Congress as being for an emergency requirement pursuant to section 251(b)(2)(A)(i) of the Balanced Budget and Emergency Deficit Control Act of 1985.

Community Planning And Development

housing opportunities for persons with aids

For an additional amount for "Housing Opportunities for Persons with AIDS", $15,000,000, to remain available until September 30, 2021, and to be used under the same authority and conditions as the additional appropriations for fiscal year 2020 under this heading in title XII of division B of the CARES Act (Public Law 116–136): Provided , That amounts provided under this heading in this Act that are allocated pursuant to section 854(c)(5) of the AIDS Housing Opportunity Act (42 U.S.C. 12901 et seq.) shall remain available until September 30, 2022: Provided further , That not less than $15,000,000 of the amount provided under this heading in this Act shall be allocated pursuant to the formula in section 854 of such Act using the same data elements as utilized pursuant to that same formula in fiscal year 2020: Provided further , That such amount is designated by the Congress as being for an emergency requirement pursuant to section 251(b)(2)(A)(i) of the Balanced Budget and Emergency Deficit Control Act of 1985.

community development fund

(including transfer of funds)

For an additional amount for "Community Development Fund", $5,000,000,000, to remain available until September 30, 2023, and to be used under the same authority and conditions as the additional appropriations for fiscal year 2020 under this heading in title XII of division B of the CARES Act (Public Law 116–136): Provided , That such amount made available under this heading in this Act shall be distributed pursuant to section 106 of the Housing and Community Development Act of 1974 (42 U.S.C. 5306) to grantees that received allocations pursuant to such formula in fiscal year 2020, and that such allocations shall be made within 30 days of enactment of this Act: Provided further , That in administering funds under this heading, an urban county shall consider needs throughout the entire urban county configuration to prevent, prepare for, and respond to coronavirus: Provided further , That up to $100,000,000 of amounts made available under this heading in this Act may be used to make new awards or increase prior awards to existing technical assistance providers: Provided further , That of the amounts made available under this heading in this Act, up to $25,000,000 may be transferred to "Department of Housing and Urban Development, Program Offices—Community Planning and Development" for necessary costs of administering and overseeing the obligation and expenditure of amounts under this heading in this Act, to remain available until September 30, 2028: Provided further , That such amount is designated by the Congress as being for an emergency requirement pursuant to section 251(b)(2)(A)(i) of the Balanced Budget and Emergency Deficit Control Act of 1985.

homeless assistance grants

(including transfer of funds)

For an additional amount for "Homeless Assistance Grants", $11,500,000,000, to remain available until September 30, 2025, for the Emergency Solutions Grants program as authorized under subtitle B of title IV of the McKinney-Vento Homeless Assistance Act (42 U.S.C. 11371 et seq.), as amended, and to be used under the same authority and conditions as the additional appropriations for fiscal year 2020 under this heading in title XII of division B of the CARES Act (Public Law 116–136): Provided , That $4,000,000,000 of the amount made available under this heading in this Act shall be distributed pursuant to 24 CFR 576.3 to grantees that received allocations pursuant to that same formula in fiscal year 2020, and that such allocations shall be made within 30 days of enactment of this Act: Provided further , That, in addition to amounts allocated in the preceding proviso, remaining amounts shall be allocated directly to a State or unit of general local government by the formula specified in the third proviso under this heading in title XII of division B of the CARES Act (Public Law 116–136): Provided further , That not later than 90 days after the date of enactment of this Act and every 60 days thereafter, the Secretary shall allocate a minimum of an additional $500,000,000, pursuant to the formula referred to in the preceding proviso, based on the best available data: Provided further , That up to 0.5 percent of the amounts made available under this heading in this Act may be transferred to "Department of Housing and Urban Development—Program Offices—Community Planning and Development" for necessary costs of administering and overseeing the obligation and expenditure of amounts under this heading in this Act, to remain available until September 30, 2030: Provided further , That funds made available under this heading in this Act and under this heading in title XII of division B of the CARES Act (Public Law 116–136) may be used for eligible activities the Secretary determines to be crit-ical in order to assist survivors of domestic violence, sexual assault, dating violence, and stalking or to assist homeless youth, age 24 and under: Provided further , That amounts repurposed by this paragraph that were previously designated by the Con-gress as an emergency requirement pursuant to the Balanced Budget and Emergency Deficit Control Act of 1985 are designated by the Congress as an emergency require-ment pursuant to section 251(b)(2)(A)(i) of the Balanced Budget and Emergency Deficit Control Act of 1985: Provided further, That such amount is designated by the Congress as being for an emergency requirement pursuant to section 251(b)(2)(A)(i) of the Balanced Budget and Emergency Deficit Control Act of 1985.

emergency rental assistance

For activities and assistance authorized in section 110201 of the "COVID–19 HERO Act", $100,000,000,000, to remain available until expended: Provided, That such amount is designated by the Congress as being for an emergency requirement pursuant to section 251(b)(2)(A)(i) of the Balanced Budget and Emergency Deficit Control Act of 1985.

Housing Programs

project-based rental assistance

For an additional amount for "Project-Based Rental Assistance", $750,000,000, to remain available until expended, and to be used under the same authority and conditions as the additional appropriations for fiscal year 2020 under this heading in title XII of division B of the CARES Act (Public Law 116–136): Provided , That such amount is designated by the Congress as being for an emergency requirement pursuant to section 251(b)(2)(A)(i) of the Balanced Budget and Emergency Deficit Control Act of 1985.

housing for the elderly

For an additional amount for "Housing for the Elderly", $500,000,000, to remain available until September 30, 2023, and to be used under the same authority and conditions as the additional appropriations for fiscal year 2020 under this heading in title XII of division B of the CARES Act (Public Law 116–136): Provided , That notwithstanding the first proviso under this heading in the CARES Act, $300,000,000 of the amount made available under this heading in this Act shall be for one-time grants for service coordinators, as authorized under section 676 of the Housing and Community Development Act of 1992 (42 U.S.C. 13632), and the continuation of existing congregate service grants for residents of assisted housing projects: Provided further , That such amount is designated by the Congress as being for an emergency requirement pursuant to section 251(b)(2)(A)(i) of the Balanced Budget and Emergency Deficit Control Act of 1985.

housing for persons with disabilities

For an additional amount for "Housing for Persons with Disabilities", $200,000,000, to remain available until September 30, 2023, and to be used under the same authority and conditions as the additional appropriations for fiscal year 2020 under this heading in title XII of division B of the CARES Act (Public Law 116–136): Provided , That such amount is designated by the Congress as being for an emergency requirement pursuant to section 251(b)(2)(A)(i) of the Balanced Budget and Emergency Deficit Control Act of 1985.

housing counseling assistance

For an additional amount for "Housing Counseling Assistance", for contracts, grants, and other assistance excluding loans, as authorized under section 106 of the Housing and Urban Development Act of 1968, $100,000,000, to remain available until September 30, 2022, including up to $8,000,000 for administrative contract services: Provided , That funds made available under this heading in this Act shall be used for providing counseling and advice to tenants and homeowners, both current and prospective, with respect to property maintenance, financial management or literacy, foreclosure and eviction mitigation, and such other matters as may be appropriate to assist them in improving their housing conditions, meeting their financial needs, and fulfilling the responsibilities of tenancy or homeownership; for program administration; and for housing counselor training: Provided further , That amounts made available under this heading in this Act may be used to purchase equipment and technology to deliver services through use of the Internet or other electronic or virtual means in response to the public health emergency related to the Coronavirus Disease 2019 (COVID–19) pandemic: Provided further , That for purposes of providing such grants from amounts provided under this heading, the Secretary may enter into multiyear agreements, as appropriate, subject to the availability of annual appropriations: Provided further , That such amount is designated by the Congress as being for an emergency requirement pursuant to section 251(b)(2)(A)(i) of the Balanced Budget and Emergency Deficit Control Act of 1985.

Fair Housing And Equal Opportunity

fair housing activities

For an additional amount for "Fair Housing Activities", $14,000,000, to remain available until September 30, 2022, and to be used under the same authority and conditions as the additional appropriations for fiscal year 2020 under this heading in title XII of division B of the CARES Act (Public Law 116–136): Provided , That of the funds made available under this heading in this Act, $4,000,000 shall be for Fair Housing Organization Initiative grants through the Fair Housing Initiatives Program (FHIP), made available to existing grantees, which may be used for fair housing activities and for technology and equipment needs to deliver services through use of the Internet or other electronic or virtual means in response to the public health emergency related to the Coronavirus Disease 2019 (COVID–19) pandemic: Provided further , That of the funds made available under this heading in this Act, $10,000,000 shall be for FHIP Education and Outreach grants made available to previously-funded national media grantees and State and local education and outreach grantees, to educate the public and the housing industry about fair housing rights and responsibilities during the COVID–19 pandemic: Provided further , That such grants in the preceding proviso shall be divided evenly between the national media campaign and education and outreach activities: Provided further , That such amount is designated by the Congress as being for an emergency requirement pursuant to section 251(b)(2)(A)(i) of the Balanced Budget and Emergency Deficit Control Act of 1985.

GENERAL PROVISIONS—THIS TITLE

(Including Rescissions)

SEC. 10901.

There is hereby appropriated from the General Fund of the Treasury, for payment to the Airport and Airway Trust Fund, an amount equal to the amount authorized by section 9502(c) of title 26, United States Code.

SEC. 10902.

Amounts previously made available in the Further Continuing Appropriations Act, 2013 (Public Law 113–6) for the heading "Department of Housing and Urban Development—Public and Indian Housing—Choice Neighborhoods Initiative" shall remain available for expenditure for the purpose of paying valid obligations incurred prior to the expiration of such amounts through September 30, 2021.

SEC. 10903.

The provision under the heading "Office of the Inspector General—Salaries and Expenses" in title XII of division B of the Coronavirus Aid, Relief, and Economic Security Act (Public Law 116–136) is amended by striking "with funds made available in this Act to" and inserting "by": Provided, That the amounts repurposed in this section that were previously designated by the Congress as an emergency requirement pursuant to the Balanced Budget and Emergency Deficit Control Act of 1985 are designated by the Congress as an emergency requirement pursuant to section 251(b)(2)(A)(i) of the Balanced Budget and Emergency Deficit Control Act of 1985.

SEC. 10904.

(a) Notwithstanding section 51309(a)(1)(B) of title 46, United States Code, for fiscal year 2020, the Secretary of Transportation may confer the degree of bachelor of science on an individual who has not passed the examination for a merchant marine officer's license due to intervening efforts to prevent, prepare for, and respond to coronavirus.

(b) The Secretary of Transportation may provide such individual up to 1 year after receipt of such degree to pass the examination for a merchant marine officer's license.

(c) Nothing in this section shall be construed to allow the provision of a license under section 7101 of title 46, United States Code, to an individual who has not passed the required examination.

SEC. 10905.

(a) Notwithstanding section 51506(a)(3) of title 46, United States Code, for fiscal year 2020, the Secretary of Transportation may allow a State maritime academy to waive a condition for graduation for an individual to pass the examination required for the issuance of a license under section 7101 of title 46, United States Code, due to intervening efforts to prevent, prepare for, and respond to coronavirus.

(b) The Secretary of Transportation may provide such individual up to 1 year after graduation to pass such examination.

(c) Nothing in this section shall be construed to allow the provision of a license under section 7101 of title 46, United States Code, to an individual who has not passed the required examination.

SEC. 10906.

Amounts made available under the headings "Project-Based Rental Assistance," "Housing for the Elderly" and "Housing for Persons With Disabilities" in title XII of division B of the CARES Act (Public Law 116–136) and under such headings in this title of this Act may be used, notwithstanding any other provision of law, to provide additional funds to maintain operations for such housing, for providing supportive services, and for taking other necessary actions to prevent, prepare for, and respond to coronavirus, including to actions to self-isolate, quarantine, or to provide other coronavirus infection control services as recommended by the Centers for Disease Control and Prevention, including providing relocation services for residents of such housing to provide lodging at hotels, motels, or other locations: Provided, That the amounts repurposed in this section that were previously designated by the Congress as an emergency requirement pursuant to the Balanced Budget and Emergency Deficit Control Act of 1985 are designated by the Congress as an emergency requirement pursuant to section 251(b)(2)(A)(i) of the Balanced Budget and Emergency Deficit Control Act of 1985.

TITLE X

GENERAL PROVISIONS—THIS DIVISION

SEC. 11001.

Not later than 30 days after the date of enactment of this Act, the head of each executive agency that receives funding in any division of this Act, or that received funding in the Coronavirus Preparedness and Response Supplemental Appropriations Act, 2020 (division A of Public Law 116–123), the Second Coronavirus Preparedness and Response Supplemental Appropriations Act, 2020 (division A of Public Law 116–127), the CARES Act (Public Law 116–136), or the Paycheck Protection Program and Health Care Enhancement Act (Public Law 116–139) shall provide a report detailing the anticipated uses of all such funding to the Committees on Appropriations of the House of Representatives and the Senate: Provided, That each report shall include estimated personnel and administrative costs, as well as the total amount of funding apportioned, allotted, obligated, and expended, to date: Provided further, That each such report shall be updated and submitted to such Committees every 60 days until all funds are expended or expire: Provided further, That reports submitted pursuant to this section shall satisfy the requirements of section 1701 of division A of Public Law 116–127.

SEC. 11002.

Each amount appropriated or made available by this Act is in addition to amounts otherwise appropriated for the fiscal year involved.

SEC. 11003.

No part of any appropriation contained in this Act shall remain available for obligation beyond the current fiscal year unless expressly so provided herein.

SEC. 11004.

Unless otherwise provided for by this Act, the additional amounts appropriated by this Act to appropriations accounts shall be available under the authorities and conditions applicable to such appropriations accounts for fiscal year 2020.

SEC. 11005.

Each amount designated in this Act by the Congress as being for an emergency requirement pursuant to section 251(b)(2)(A)(i) of the Balanced Budget and Emergency Deficit Control Act of 1985 shall be available (or rescinded or transferred, if applicable) only if the President subsequently so designates all such amounts and transmits such designations to the Congress.

SEC. 11006.

Any amount appropriated by this Act, designated by the Congress as an emergency requirement pursuant to section 251(b)(2)(A)(i) of the Balanced Budget and Emergency Deficit Control Act of 1985 and subsequently so designated by the President, and transferred pursuant to transfer authorities provided by this Act shall retain such designation.

SEC. 11007.

(a) Any contract or agreement entered into by an agency with a State or local government or any other non-Federal entity for the purposes of providing covered assistance, including any information and documents related to the performance of and compliance with such contract or agreement, shall be—

(1) deemed an agency record for purposes of section 552(f)(2) of title 5, United States Code; and

(2) subject to section 552 of title 5, United States Code (commonly known as the "Freedom of Information Act").

(b) In this section—

(1) the term "agency" has the meaning given the term in section 551 of title 5, United States Code; and

(2) the term "covered assistance"—

(A) means any assistance provided by an agency in accordance with an Act or amendments made by an Act to provide aid, assistance, or funding related to the outbreak of COVID-19 that is enacted before, on, or after the date of enactment of this Act; and

(B) includes any such assistance made available by an agency under—

(i) this Act;

(ii) the Paycheck Protection Program and Health Care Enhancement Act (Public Law 116–139), or an amendment made by that Act;

(iii) the CARES Act (Public Law 116–136), or an amendment made by that Act;

(iv) the Families First Coronavirus Response Act (Public Law 116–127), or an amendment made by that Act; or

(v) the Coronavirus Preparedness and Response Supplemental Appropriations Act, 2020 (Public Law 116–123), or an amendment made by that Act.

SEC. 11008.

(a) Notwithstanding any other provision of law and in a manner consistent with other provisions in any division of this Act, all laborers and mechanics employed by contractors and subcontractors on projects funded directly by or assisted in whole or in part by and through the Federal Government pursuant to any division of this Act shall be paid wages at rates not less than those prevailing on projects of a character similar in the locality as determined by the Secretary of Labor in accordance with subchapter IV of chapter 31 of title 40, United States Code. With respect to the labor standards specified in this section, the Secretary of Labor shall have the authority and functions set forth in Reorganization Plan Numbered 14 of 1950 (64 Stat. 1267; 5 U.S.C. App.) and section 3145 of title 40, United States Code.

(b) The amounts provided by this section are designated by the Congress as being for an emergency requirement pursuant to section 251(b)(2)(A)(i) of the Balanced Budget and Emergency Deficit Control Act of 1985.

BUDGETARY EFFECTS

SEC. 11009.

(a) Statutory PAYGO Emergency Designation.—The amounts provided under division B and each succeeding division are designated as an emergency requirement pursuant to section 4(g) of the Statutory Pay-As-You-Go Act of 2010 (2 U.S.C. 933(g)).

(b) Senate PAYGO Emergency Designation.—In the Senate, division B and each succeeding division are designated as an emergency requirement pursuant to section 4112(a) of H. Con. Res. 71 (115th Congress), the concurrent resolution on the budget for fiscal year 2018.

(c) Classification Of Budgetary Effects.—Notwithstanding Rule 3 of the Budget Scorekeeping Guidelines set forth in the joint explanatory statement of the committee of conference accompanying Conference Report 105–217 and section 250(c)(8) of the Balanced Budget and Emergency Deficit Control Act of 1985, the budgetary effects of division B and each succeeding division—

(1) shall not be estimated for purposes of section 251 of such Act; and

(2) shall be entered on the PAYGO scorecards maintained pursuant to section 4(d) of the Statutory Pay-As-You-Go Act of 2010.

(d) Ensuring No Within-Session Sequestration.—Solely for the purpose of calculating a breach within a category for fiscal year 2020 pursuant to section 251(a)(6) or section 254(g) of the Balanced Budget and Emergency Deficit Control Act of 1985, and notwithstanding any other provision of this division, the budgetary effects from this division shall be counted as amounts designated as being for an emergency requirement pursuant to section 251(b)(2)(A) of such Act.

This division may be cited as the "Coronavirus Recovery Supplemental Appropriations Act, 2020".

DIVISION B—REVENUE PROVISIONS

SHORT TITLE

SEC. 20001.
This division may be cited as the "COVID–19 Tax Relief Act of 2020".

TITLE I

—ECONOMIC STIMULUS

Subtitle A—2020 Recovery Rebate Improvements

DEPENDENTS TAKEN INTO ACCOUNT IN DETERMINING CREDIT AND REBATES

SEC. 20101.

(a) In General.—Section 6428(a)(2) of the Internal Revenue Code of 1986 is amended by striking "qualifying children (within the meaning of section 24(c))" and inserting "dependents (as defined in section 152)".

(b) Conforming Amendments.—

(1) Section 6428(g) of such Code is amended by striking "qualifying child" each place it appears and inserting "dependent".

(2) Section 6428(g)(2)(B) of such Code is amended by striking "such child" and inserting "such dependent".

(c) Effective Date.—The amendments made by this section shall take effect as if included in section 2201 of the CARES Act.

INDIVIDUALS PROVIDING TAXPAYER IDENTIFICATION NUMBERS TAKEN INTO ACCOUNT IN DETERMINING CREDIT AND REBATES

SEC. 20102.

(a) In General.—Section 6428(g) of the Internal Revenue Code of 1986, as amended by section 20101 of this Act, is amended to read as follows:

"(g) Identification Number Requirement.—

"(1) IN GENERAL.—The $1,200 amount in subsection (a)(1) shall be treated as being zero unless the taxpayer includes the TIN of the taxpayer on the return of tax for the taxable year.

"(2) JOINT RETURNS.—In the case of a joint return, the $2,400 amount in subsection (a)(1) shall be treated as being—

"(A) zero if the TIN of neither spouse is included on the return of tax for the taxable year, and

"(B) $1,200 if the TIN of only one spouse is so included.

"(3) DEPENDENTS.—A dependent shall not be taken into account under subsection (a)(2) unless the TIN of such dependent is included on the return of tax for the taxable year.

"(4) COORDINATION WITH CERTAIN ADVANCE PAYMENTS.—In the case of any payment made pursuant to subsection (f)(5)(B), a TIN shall be treated for purposes of this subsection as included on the taxpayer's return of tax if such TIN is provided pursuant to such subsection.

"(5) MATHEMATICAL OR CLERICAL ERROR AUTHORITY.—Any omission of a correct TIN required under this subsection shall be treated as a mathematical or clerical error for purposes of applying section 6213(g)(2) to such omission.".

(b) Effective Date.—The amendment made by this section shall take effect as if included in section 2201 of the CARES Act.

2020 RECOVERY REBATES NOT SUBJECT TO REDUCTION OR OFFSET WITH RESPECT TO PAST-DUE SUPPORT

SEC. 20103.

(a) In General.—Section 2201(d)(2) of the CARES Act is amended by inserting "(c)," before "(d)".

(b) Effective Date.—The amendment made by this section shall apply to credits and refunds allowed or made after the date of the enactment of this Act.

PROTECTION OF 2020 RECOVERY REBATES

SEC. 20104.

(a) In General.—Subsection (d) of section 2201 of the CARES Act, as amended by the preceding provisions of this Act, is amended—

(1) by redesignating paragraphs (1), (2), and (3) as subparagraphs (A), (B), and (C), and by moving such subparagraphs 2 ems to the right,

(2) by striking "Reduction Or Offset.—Any credit" and inserting "Reduction, Offset, Garnishment, Etc.—

"(1) IN GENERAL.—Any credit", and

(3) by adding at the end the following new paragraphs:

"(2) ASSIGNMENT OF BENEFITS.—

"(A) IN GENERAL.—Any applicable payment shall not be subject to transfer, assignment, execution, levy, attachment, garnishment, or other legal process, or the operation of any bankruptcy or insolvency law, to the same extent as payments described in section 207 of the Social Security Act (42 U.S.C. 407) without regard to subsection (b) thereof.

"(B) ENCODING OF PAYMENTS.—As soon as practicable after the date of the enactment of this paragraph, the Secretary of the Treasury shall encode applicable payments that are paid electronically to any account—

"(i) with a unique identifier that is reasonably sufficient to allow a financial institution to identify the payment as a payment protected under subparagraph (A), and

"(ii) pursuant to the same specifications as required for a benefit payment to which part 212 of title 31, Code of Federal regulations applies.

"(C) GARNISHMENT.—

"(i) ENCODED PAYMENTS.—Upon receipt of a garnishment order that applies to an account that has received an applicable payment that is encoded as provided in subparagraph (B), a financial institution shall follow the requirements and procedures set forth in part 212 of title 31, Code of Federal Regulations. This paragraph shall not alter the status of payments as tax refunds or other nonbenefit payments for purpose of any reclamation rights of the Department of Treasury or the Internal Revenue Service as per part 210 of title 31 of the Code of Federal Regulations.

"(ii) OTHER PAYMENTS.—If a financial institution receives a garnishment order (other than an order that has been served by the United States) that applies to an account into which an applicable payment that has not been encoded as provided in subparagraph (B) has been deposited on any date in the prior 60 days (including any date before the date of the enactment of this paragraph), the financial institution, upon the request of the account holder or for purposes of complying in good faith with a State order, State law, court order, or interpretation by a State Attorney General relating to garnishment order, may, but is not required to, treat the amount of the payment as exempt under law from garnishment without requiring the account holder to assert any right of garnishment exemption or requiring the consent of the judgment creditor.

"(iii) LIABILITY.—A financial institution that complies in good faith with clause (i) or that acts in good faith in reliance on clause (ii) shall not be liable under any Federal or State law, regulation, or court or other order to a creditor that initiates an order for any protected amounts, to an account holder for any frozen amounts or garnishment order applied.

"(D) DEFINITIONS.—For purposes of this paragraph—

"(i) ACCOUNT HOLDER.—The term 'account holder' means a natural person against whom a garnishment order is issued and whose name appears in a financial institution's records.

"(ii) APPLICABLE PAYMENT.—The term 'applicable payment' means any payment of credit or refund by reason of section 6428 of such Code (as so added) or by reason of subsection (c) of this section.

"(iii) GARNISHMENT.—The term 'garnishment' means execution, levy, attachment, garnishment, or other legal process.

"(iv) GARNISHMENT ORDER.—The term 'garnishment order' means a writ, order, notice, summons, judgment, levy, or similar written instruction issued by a court, a State or State agency, a municipality or municipal corporation, or a State child support enforcement agency, including a lien arising by operation of law for overdue child support or an order to freeze the assets in an account, to effect a garnishment against a debtor.".

(b) Effective Date.—The amendments made by this section shall take effect on the date of the enactment of this Act.

PAYMENTS TO REPRESENTATIVE PAYEES AND FIDUCIARIES

SEC. 20105.

(a) In General.—Section 6428(f) of the Internal Revenue Code of 1986 is amended by redesignating paragraph (6) as paragraph (7) and by inserting after paragraph (5) the following new paragraph:

"(6) PAYMENT TO REPRESENTATIVE PAYEES AND FIDUCIARIES.—

"(A) IN GENERAL.—In the case of any individual for which payment information is provided to the Secretary by the Commissioner of Social Security, the Railroad Retirement Board, or the Secretary of Veterans Affairs, the payment by the Secretary under paragraph (3) with respect to such individual may be made to such individual's representative payee or fiduciary and the entire payment shall be—

"(i) provided to the individual who is entitled to the payment, or

"(ii) used only for the benefit of the individual who is entitled to the payment.

"(B) APPLICATION OF ENFORCEMENT PROVISIONS.—

"(i) In the case of a payment described in subparagraph (A) which is made with respect to a social security beneficiary or a supplemental security income recipient, section 1129(a)(3) of the Social Security Act (42 U.S.C. 1320a–8(a)(3)) shall apply to such payment in the same manner as such section applies to a payment under title II or XVI of such Act.

"(ii) In the case of a payment described in subparagraph (A) which is made with respect to a railroad retirement beneficiary, section 13 of the Railroad Retirement Act (45 U.S.C. 231l) shall apply to such payment in the same manner as such section applies to a payment under such Act.

"(iii) In the case of a payment described in subparagraph (A) which is made with respect to a veterans beneficiary, sections 5502, 6106, and 6108 of title 38, United States Code, shall apply to such payment in the same manner as such sections apply to a payment under such title.".

(b) Effective Date.—The amendments made by this section shall take effect as if included in section 2201 of the CARES Act.

APPLICATION TO TAXPAYERS WITH RESPECT TO WHOM ADVANCE PAYMENT HAS ALREADY BEEN MADE

SEC. 20106.

In the case of any taxpayer with respect to whom refund or credit was made or allowed before the date of the enactment of this Act under subsection (f) of section 6428 of the Internal Revenue Code of 1986 (as added by the CARES Act), such subsection shall be applied separately with respect to the excess (if any) of—

(1) the advance refund amount determined under section 6428(f)(2) of such Code after the application of the amendments made by this subtitle, over

(2) the amount of such refund or credit so made or allowed.

Subtitle B—Additional Recovery Rebates To Individuals

ADDITIONAL RECOVERY REBATES TO INDIVIDUALS

SEC. 20111.

(a) In General.—Subchapter B of chapter 65 of the Internal Revenue Code of 1986 is amended by inserting after section 6428 the following new section:

"SEC. 6428A. ADDITIONAL RECOVERY REBATES TO INDIVIDUALS.

"(a) In General.—In the case of an eligible individual, there shall be allowed as a credit against the tax imposed by subtitle A for the first taxable year beginning in 2020 an amount equal to the additional rebate amount determined for such taxable year.

"(b) Additional Rebate Amount.—For purposes of this section, the term 'additional rebate amount' means, with respect to any taxpayer for any taxable year, the sum of—

"(1) $1,200 ($2,400 in the case of a joint return), plus

"(2) $1,200 multiplied by the number of dependents of the taxpayer for such taxable year (not in excess of 3 such dependents).

"(c) Eligible Individual.—For purposes of this section, the term 'eligible individual' means any individual other than—

"(1) any nonresident alien individual,

"(2) any individual with respect to whom a deduction under section 151 is allowable to another taxpayer for a taxable year beginning in the calendar year in which the individual's taxable year begins, and

"(3) an estate or trust.

"(d) Limitation Based On Modified Adjusted Gross Income.—The amount of the credit allowed by subsection (a) (determined without regard to this subsection and subsection (f)) shall be reduced (but not below zero) by 5 percent of so much of the taxpayer's modified adjusted gross income as exceeds—

"(1) $150,000 in the case of a joint return or a surviving spouse (as defined in section 2(a)),

"(2) $112,500 in the case of a head of household (as defined in section 2(b)), and

"(3) $75,000 in any other case.

"(e) Definitions And Special Rules.—

"(1) MODIFIED ADJUSTED GROSS INCOME.—For purposes of this subsection (other than this paragraph), the term 'modified adjusted gross income' means adjusted gross income determined without regard to sections 911, 931, and 933.

"(2) DEPENDENT DEFINED.—For purposes of this section, the term 'dependent' has the meaning given such term by section 152.

"(3) CREDIT TREATED AS REFUNDABLE.—The credit allowed by subsection (a) shall be treated as allowed by subpart C of part IV of subchapter A of chapter 1.

"(4) IDENTIFICATION NUMBER REQUIREMENT.—

"(A) IN GENERAL.—The $1,200 amount in subsection (b)(1) shall be treated as being zero unless the taxpayer includes the TIN of the taxpayer on the return of tax for the taxable year.

"(B) JOINT RETURNS.—In the case of a joint return, the $2,400 amount in subsection (b)(1) shall be treated as being—

"(i) zero if the TIN of neither spouse is included on the return of tax for the taxable year, and

"(ii) $1,200 if the TIN of only one spouse is so included.

"(C) DEPENDENTS.—A dependent shall not be taken into account under subsection (b)(2) unless the TIN of such dependent is included on the return of tax for the taxable year.

"(D) COORDINATION WITH CERTAIN ADVANCE PAYMENTS.—In the case of any payment made pursuant to subsection (g)(5)(A)(ii), a TIN shall be treated for purposes of this paragraph as included on the taxpayer's return of tax if such TIN is provided pursuant to such subsection.

"(f) Coordination With Advance Refunds Of Credit.—

"(1) REDUCTION OF REFUNDABLE CREDIT.—The amount of the credit which would (but for this paragraph) be allowable under subsection (a) shall be reduced (but not below zero) by the aggregate refunds and credits made or allowed to the taxpayer (or any dependent of the taxpayer) under subsection (g). Any failure to so reduce the credit shall be treated as arising out of a mathematical or clerical error and assessed according to section 6213(b)(1).

"(2) JOINT RETURNS.—In the case of a refund or credit made or allowed under subsection (g) with respect to a joint return, half of such refund or credit shall be treated as having been made or allowed to each individual filing such return.

"(g) Advance Refunds And Credits.—

"(1) IN GENERAL.—Subject to paragraph (5), each individual who was an eligible individual for such individual's first taxable year beginning in 2019 shall be treated as having made a payment against the tax imposed by chapter 1 for such taxable year in an amount equal to the advance refund amount for such taxable year.

"(2) ADVANCE REFUND AMOUNT.—For purposes of paragraph (1), the advance refund amount is the amount that would have been allowed as a credit under this section for such taxable year if this section (other than subsection (f) and this subsection) had applied to such taxable year.

"(3) TIMING AND MANNER OF PAYMENTS.—

"(A) TIMING.—The Secretary shall, subject to the provisions of this title, refund or credit any overpayment attributable to this section as rapidly as possible. No refund or credit shall be made or allowed under this subsection after December 31, 2020.

"(B) DELIVERY OF PAYMENTS.—Notwithstanding any other provision of law, the Secretary may certify and disburse refunds payable under this subsection electronically to any account to which the payee authorized, on or after January 1, 2018, the delivery of a refund of taxes under this title or of a Federal payment (as defined in section 3332 of title 31, United States Code).

"(C) WAIVER OF CERTAIN RULES.—Notwithstanding section 3325 of title 31, United States Code, or any other provision of law, with respect to any payment of a refund under this subsection, a disbursing official in the executive branch of the United States Government may modify payment information received from an officer or employee described in section 3325(a)(1)(B) of such title for the purpose of facilitating the accurate and efficient delivery of such payment. Except in cases of fraud or reckless neglect, no liability under sections 3325, 3527, 3528, or 3529 of title 31, United States Code, shall be imposed with respect to payments made under this subparagraph.

"(4) NO INTEREST.—No interest shall be allowed on any overpayment attributable to this section.

"(5) APPLICATION TO INDIVIDUALS WHO DO NOT FILE A RETURN OF TAX FOR 2019.—

"(A) IN GENERAL.—In the case of an individual who, at the time of any determination made pursuant to paragraph (3), has not filed a tax return for the year described in paragraph (1), the Secretary shall—

"(i) apply paragraph (1) by substituting '2018' for '2019', and

"(ii) in the case of a specified individual who has not filed a tax return for such individual's first taxable year beginning in 2018, determine the advance refund amount with respect to such individual without regard to subsections (d) and on the basis of information with respect to such individual which is provided by—

"(I) in the case of a specified social security beneficiary or a specified supplemental security income recipient, the Commissioner of Social Security,

"(II) in the case of a specified railroad retirement beneficiary, the Railroad Retirement Board, and

"(III) in the case of a specified veterans beneficiary, the Secretary of Veterans Affairs (in coordination with, and with the assistance of, the Commissioner of Social Security if appropriate).

"(B) SPECIFIED INDIVIDUAL.—For purposes of this paragraph, the term 'specified individual' means any individual who is—

"(i) a specified social security beneficiary,

"(ii) a specified supplemental security income recipient,

"(iii) a specified railroad retirement beneficiary, or

"(iv) a specified veterans beneficiary.

"(C) SPECIFIED SOCIAL SECURITY BENEFICIARY.—For purposes of this paragraph—

"(i) IN GENERAL.—The term 'specified social security beneficiary' means any individual who, for the last month that ends prior to the date of enactment of this section, is entitled to any monthly insurance benefit payable under title II of the Social Security Act (42 U.S.C. 401 et seq.), including payments made pursuant to sections 202(d), 223(g), and 223(i)(7) of such Act.

"(ii) EXCEPTION.—Such term shall not include any individual if such benefit is not payable for such month by reason of section 202(x) of the Social Security Act (42 U.S.C. 402(x)) or section 1129A of such Act (42 U.S.C. 1320a–8a).

"(D) SPECIFIED SUPPLEMENTAL SECURITY INCOME RECIPIENT.—For purposes of this paragraph—

"(i) IN GENERAL.—The term 'specified supplemental security income recipient' means any individual who, for the last month that ends prior to the date of enactment of this section, is eligible for a monthly benefit payable under title XVI of the Social Security Act (42 U.S.C. 1381 et seq.) (other than a benefit to an individual described in section 1611(e)(1)(B) of such Act (42 U.S.C. 1382(e)(1)(B)), including—

"(I) payments made pursuant to section 1614(a)(3)(C) of such Act (42 U.S.C. 1382c(a)(3)(C)),

"(II) payments made pursuant to section 1619(a) (42 U.S.C. 1382h) or subsections (a)

(4), (a)(7), or (p)(7) of section 1631 (42 U.S.C. 1383) of such Act, and

"(III) State supplementary payments of the type referred to in section 1616(a) of such Act (42 U.S.C. 1382e(a)) (or payments of the type described in section 212(a) of Public Law 93–66) which are paid by the Commissioner under an agreement referred to in such section 1616(a) (or section 212(a) of Public Law 93–66).

"(ii) EXCEPTION.—Such term shall not include any individual if such monthly benefit is not payable for such month by reason of subsection (e)(1)(A) or (e)(4) of section 1611 (42 U.S.C. 1382) or section 1129A of such Act (42 U.S.C. 1320a–8a).

"(E) SPECIFIED RAILROAD RETIREMENT BENEFICIARY.—For purposes of this paragraph, the term 'specified railroad retirement beneficiary' means any individual who, for the last month that ends prior to the date of enactment of this section, is entitled to a monthly annuity or pension payment payable (without regard to section 5(a)(ii) of the Railroad Retirement Act of 1974 (45 U.S.C. 231d(a)(ii))) under—

"(i) section 2(a)(1) of such Act (45 U.S.C. 231a(a)(1)),

"(ii) section 2(c) of such Act (45 U.S.C. 231a(c)),

"(iii) section 2(d)(1) of such Act (45 U.S.C. 231a(d)(1)), or

"(iv) section 7(b)(2) of such Act (45 U.S.C. 231f(b)(2)) with respect to any of the benefit payments described in subparagraph (C)(i).

"(F) SPECIFIED VETERANS BENEFICIARY.—For purposes of this paragraph—

"(i) IN GENERAL.—The term 'specified veterans beneficiary' means any individual who, for the last month that ends prior to the date of enactment of this section, is entitled to a compensation or pension payment payable under—

"(I) section 1110, 1117, 1121, 1131, 1141, or 1151 of title 38, United States Code,

"(II) section 1310, 1312, 1313, 1315, 1316, or 1318 of title 38, United States Code,

"(III) section 1513, 1521, 1533, 1536, 1537, 1541, 1542, or 1562 of title 38, United States Code, or

"(IV) section 1805, 1815, or 1821 of title 38, United States Code,

to a veteran, surviving spouse, child, or parent as described in paragraph (2), (3), (4)(A)(ii), or (5) of section 101, title 38, United States Code.

"(ii) EXCEPTION.—Such term shall not include any individual if such compensation or pension payment is not payable, or was reduced, for such month by reason of section 1505, 5313, or 5313B of title 38, United States Code.

"(G) SUBSEQUENT DETERMINATIONS AND REDETERMINATIONS NOT TAKEN INTO ACCOUNT.—For purposes of this section, any individual's status as a specified social security beneficiary, a specified supplemental security income recipient, a specified railroad retirement beneficiary, or a specified veterans beneficiary shall be unaffected by any determination or redetermination of any entitlement to, or eligibility for, any benefit, payment, or compensation, if such determination or redetermination occurs after the last month that ends prior to the date of enactment of this section.

"(H) PAYMENT TO REPRESENTATIVE PAYEES AND FIDUCIARIES.—

"(i) IN GENERAL.—If the benefit, payment, or compensation referred to in subparagraph (C)(i), (D)(i), (E), or (F)(i) with respect to any specified individual is paid to a representative payee or fiduciary, payment by the Secretary under paragraph (3) with respect to such specified individual shall be made to such individual's representative payee or fiduciary and the entire payment shall be used only for the benefit of the individual who is entitled to the payment.

"(ii) APPLICATION OF ENFORCEMENT PROVISIONS.—

"(I) In the case of a payment described in clause (i) which is made with respect to a specified social security beneficiary or a specified supplemental security income recipient, section 1129(a)(3) of the Social Security Act (42 U.S.C. 1320a–8(a)(3)) shall apply to such payment in the same manner as such section applies to a payment under title II or XVI of such Act.

"(II) In the case of a payment described in clause (i) which is made with respect to a specified railroad retirement beneficiary, section 13 of the Railroad Retirement Act (45 U.S.C. 231l) shall apply to such payment in the same manner as such section applies to a payment under such Act.

"(III) In the case of a payment described in clause (i) which is made with respect to a specified veterans beneficiary, sections 5502, 6106, and 6108 of title 38, United States Code, shall apply to such payment in the same manner as such sections apply to a payment under such title.

"(6) NOTICE TO TAXPAYER.—Not later than 15 days after the date on which the Secretary distributed any payment to an eligible taxpayer pursuant to this subsection, notice shall be sent by mail to such taxpayer's last known address. Such notice shall indicate the method by which such payment was made, the amount of such payment, and a phone number for the appropriate point of contact at the Internal Revenue Service to report any error with respect to such payment.

"(h) Regulations.—The Secretary shall prescribe such regulations or other guidance as may be necessary or appropriate to carry out the purposes of this section, including—

"(1) regulations or other guidance providing taxpayers the opportunity to provide the Secretary information sufficient to allow the Secretary to make payments to such taxpayers under subsection (g) (including the determination of the amount of such payment) if such information is not otherwise available to the Secretary, and

"(2) regulations or other guidance providing for the proper treatment of joint returns and taxpayers with dependents to ensure that an individual is not taken into account more than once in determining the amount of any credit under subsection (a) and any credit or refund under subsection (g).

"(i) Outreach.—The Secretary shall carry out a robust and comprehensive outreach program to ensure that all taxpayers described in subsection (h)(1) learn of their eligibility for the advance refunds and credits under subsection (g); are advised of the opportunity to receive such advance refunds and credits as provided under subsection (h)(1); and are provided assistance in applying for such advance refunds and credits. In conducting such outreach program, the Secretary shall coordinate with other government, State, and local agencies; federal partners; and community-based nonprofit organizations that regularly interface with such taxpayers.".

(b) Treatment Of Certain Possessions.—

(1) PAYMENTS TO POSSESSIONS WITH MIRROR CODE TAX SYSTEMS.—The Secretary of the Treasury shall pay to each possession of the United States which has a mirror code tax system amounts equal to the loss (if any) to that possession by reason of the amendments made by this section. Such amounts shall be determined by the Secretary of the Treasury based on information provided by the government of the respective possession.

(2) PAYMENTS TO OTHER POSSESSIONS.—The Secretary of the Treasury shall pay to each possession of the United States which does not have a mirror code tax system amounts estimated by the Secretary of the Treasury as being equal to the aggregate benefits (if any) that would have been provided to residents of such possession

by reason of the amendments made by this section if a mirror code tax system had been in effect in such possession. The preceding sentence shall not apply unless the respective possession has a plan, which has been approved by the Secretary of the Treasury, under which such possession will promptly distribute such payments to its residents.

(3) COORDINATION WITH CREDIT ALLOWED AGAINST UNITED STATES INCOME TAXES.—No credit shall be allowed against United States income taxes under section 6428A of the Internal Revenue Code of 1986 (as added by this section), nor shall any credit or refund be made or allowed under subsection (g) of such section, to any person—

(A) to whom a credit is allowed against taxes imposed by the possession by reason of the amendments made by this section, or

(B) who is eligible for a payment under a plan described in paragraph (2).

(4) MIRROR CODE TAX SYSTEM.—For purposes of this subsection, the term "mirror code tax system" means, with respect to any possession of the United States, the income tax system of such possession if the income tax liability of the residents of such possession under such system is determined by reference to the income tax laws of the United States as if such possession were the United States.

(c) Administrative Provisions.—

(1) DEFINITION OF DEFICIENCY.—Section 6211(b)(4)(A) of the Internal Revenue Code of 1986 is amended by striking "and 6428" and inserting "6428, and 6428A".

(2) MATHEMATICAL OR CLERICAL ERROR AUTHORITY.—Section 6213(g)(2) of such Code is amended—

(A) by inserting "or section 6428A (relating to additional recovery rebates to individuals)" before the comma at the end of subparagraph (H), and

(B) by striking "or 6428" in subparagraph (L) and inserting "6428, or 6428A".

(3) EXCEPTION FROM REDUCTION OR OFFSET.—Any credit or refund allowed or made to any individual by reason of section 6428A of the Internal Revenue Code of 1986 (as added by this section) or by reason of subsection (b) of this section shall not be—

(A) subject to reduction or offset pursuant to section 3716 or 3720A of title 31, United States Code,

(B) subject to reduction or offset pursuant to subsection (c), (d), (e), or (f) of section 6402 of the Internal Revenue Code of 1986, or

(C) reduced or offset by other assessed Federal taxes that would otherwise be subject to levy or collection.

(4) ASSIGNMENT OF BENEFITS.—

(A) IN GENERAL.—Any applicable payment shall not be subject to transfer, assignment, execution, levy, attachment, garnishment, or other legal process, or the operation of any bankruptcy or insolvency law, to the same extent as payments described in section 207 of the Social Security Act (42 U.S.C. 407) without regard to subsection (b) thereof.

(B) ENCODING OF PAYMENTS.—As soon as practicable after the date of the enactment of the paragraph, the Secretary of the Treasury shall encode applicable payments that are paid electronically to any account—

(i) with a unique identifier that is reasonably sufficient to allow a financial institution to identify the payment as a payment protected under subparagraph (A), and

(ii) pursuant to the same specifications as required for a benefit payment to which part 212 of title 31, Code of Federal regulations applies.

(C) GARNISHMENT.—

(i) ENCODED PAYMENTS.—Upon receipt of a garnishment order that applies to an account that has received an applicable payment that is encoded as provided in subparagraph (B), a financial institution shall follow the requirements and procedures set forth in part 212 of title 31, Code of Federal Regulations. This paragraph shall not alter the status of payments as tax refunds or other nonbenefit payments for purpose of any reclamation rights of the Department of Treasury or the Internal Revenue Serves as per part 210 of title 31 of the Code of Federal Regulations.

(ii) OTHER PAYMENTS.—If a financial institution receives a garnishment order (other than an order that has been served by the United States) that applies to an account into which an applicable payment that has not been encoded as provided in subparagraph (B) has been deposited on any date in the prior 60 days (including any date before the date of the enactment of this paragraph), the financial institution, upon the request of the account holder or for purposes of complying in good faith with a State order, State law, court order, or interpretation by a State Attorney General relating to garnishment order, may, but is not required to, treat the amount of the payment as exempt under law from garnishment without requiring the account holder to assert any right of garnishment exemption or requiring the consent of the judgment creditor.

(iii) LIABILITY.—A financial institution that complies in good faith with clause (i) or that acts in good faith in reliance on clause (ii) shall not be liable under any Federal or State law, regulation, or court or other order to a creditor that initiates an order for any protected amounts, to an account holder for any frozen amounts or garnishment order applied.

(D) DEFINITIONS.—For purposes of this paragraph—

(i) ACCOUNT HOLDER.—The term "account holder" means a natural person against whom a garnishment order is issued and whose name appears in a financial institution's records.

(ii) APPLICABLE PAYMENT.—The term "applicable payment" means any payment of credit or refund by reason of section 6428 of such Code (as so added) or by reason of subsection (c) of this section.

(iii) GARNISHMENT.—The term "garnishment" means execution, levy, attachment, garnishment, or other legal process.

(iv) GARNISHMENT ORDER.—The term "garnishment order" means a writ, order, notice, summons, judgment, levy, or similar written instruction issued by a court, a State or State agency, a municipality or municipal corporation, or a State child support enforcement agency, including a lien arising by operation of law for overdue child support or an order to freeze the assets in an account, to effect a garnishment against a debtor.

(5) TREATMENT OF CREDIT AND ADVANCE PAYMENTS.—For purposes of section 1324 of title 31, United States Code, any credit under section 6428A(a) of the Internal Revenue Code of 1986, any credit or refund under section 6428A(g) of such Code, and any payment under subsection (b) of this section, shall be treated in the same manner as a refund due from a credit provision referred to in subsection (b)(2) of such section 1324.

(6) AGENCY INFORMATION SHARING AND ASSISTANCE.—The Commissioner of Social Security, the Railroad Retirement Board, and the Secretary of Veterans

Affairs shall each provide the Secretary of the Treasury (or the Secretary's delegate) such information and assistance as the Secretary of the Treasury (or the Secretary's delegate) may require for purposes of making payments under section 6428A(g) of the Internal Revenue Code of 1986 to individuals described in paragraph (5)(A)(ii) thereof.

(7) CLERICAL AMENDMENT.—The table of sections for subchapter B of chapter 65 of the Internal Revenue Code of 1986 is amended by inserting after the item relating to section 6428 the following new item:

"SEC. 6428A. Additional recovery rebates to individuals.".

(d) Appropriations To Carry Out This Section.—

(1) IN GENERAL.—Immediately upon the enactment of this Act, the following sums are appropriated, out of any money in the Treasury not otherwise appropriated, for the fiscal year ending September 30, 2020—

(A) DEPARTMENT OF THE TREASURY.—

(i) For an additional amount for "Department of the Treasury—Bureau of Fiscal Services—Salaries and Expenses", $78,650,000, to remain available until September 30, 2021.

(ii) For an additional amount for "Department of the Treasury—Internal Revenue Service—Taxpayer Services", $298,700,000, to remain available until September 30, 2021.

(iii) For an additional amount for "Department of the Treasury—Internal Revenue Service—Enforcement", $37,200,000, to remain available until September 30, 2021.

(iv) For an additional amount for "Department of the Treasury—Internal Revenue Service—Operations Support", $185,000,000, to remain available until September 30, 2021.

(v) For an additional amount for "Department of the Treasury—Office of Treasury Inspector General for Tax Administration", $10,000,000, to remain available until September 30, 2024, for necessary expenses related to COVID–19 including carrying out investigations.

Amounts made available in appropriations under clauses (ii), (iii), and (iv) of this subparagraph may be transferred between such appropriations upon the advance notification of the Committees on Appropriations of the House of Representatives and the Senate. Such transfer authority is in addition to any other transfer authority provided by law.

(B) SOCIAL SECURITY ADMINISTRATION.—For an additional amount for "Social Security Administration—Limitation on Administrative Expenses", $40,500,000, to remain available until September 30, 2021: Provided, that $2,500,000, to remain available until September 30, 2024, shall be transferred to "Social Security Administration—Office of Inspector General" for necessary expenses in carrying out the provisions of the Inspector General Act of 1978.

(C) RAILROAD RETIREMENT BOARD.—For an additional amount for "Railroad Retirement Board—Limitation on Administration", $8,300, to remain available until September 30, 2021.

(2) REPORTS.—No later than 15 days after enactment of this Act, the Secretary of the Treasury shall submit a plan to the Committees on Appropriations of the House of Representatives and the Senate detailing the expected use of the funds provided by clauses (i) through (iv) paragraph (1)(A). Beginning 90 days after enactment of this Act, the Secretary of the Treasury shall submit a quarterly report to the Com-

mittees on Appropriations of the House of Representatives and the Senate detailing the actual expenditure of such funds and the expected expenditure of such funds in the subsequent quarter.

(e) Certain Requirements Related To Recovery Rebates And Additional Recovery Rebates.—

(1) SIGNATURES ON CHECKS AND NOTICES, ETC., BY THE DEPARTMENT OF THE TREASURY.—Any check issued to an individual by the Department of the Treasury pursuant to section 6428 or 6428A of the Internal Revenue Code of 1986, and any notice issued pursuant to section 6428(f)(6) or section 6428A(g)(6) of such Code, may not be signed by or otherwise bear the name, signature, image or likeness of the President, the Vice President or any elected official or cabinet level officer of the United States, or any individual who, with respect to any of the aforementioned individuals, bears any relationship described in subparagraphs (A) through (G) of section 152(d)(2) of the Internal Revenue Code of 1986.

(2) EFFECTIVE DATE.—Paragraph (1) shall apply to checks and notices issued after the date of the enactment of this Act.

(f) Reports To Congress.—Each week beginning after the date of the enactment of this Act and beginning before December 31, 2020, on Friday of such week, not later than 3 p.m. Eastern Time, the Secretary of the Treasury shall provide a written report to the Committee on Ways and Means of the House of Representatives and the Committee on Finance of the Senate. Such report shall include the following information with respect to payments made pursuant to each of sections 6428 and 6428A of the Internal Revenue Code of 1986:

(1) The number of scheduled payments sent to the Bureau of Fiscal Service for payment by direct deposit or paper check for the following week (stated separately for direct deposit and paper check).

(2) The total dollar amount of the scheduled payments described in paragraph (1).

(3) The number of direct deposit payments returned to the Department of the Treasury and the total dollar value of such payments, for the week ending on the day prior to the day on which the report is provided.

(4) The total number of letters related to payments under section 6428 or 6428A of such Code mailed to taxpayers during the week ending on the day prior to the day on which the report is provided.

Subtitle C—Earned Income Tax Credit

STRENGTHENING THE EARNED INCOME TAX CREDIT FOR INDIVIDUALS WITH NO QUALIFYING CHILDREN

SEC. 20121.

(a) Special Rules For 2020.—Section 32 of the Internal Revenue Code of 1986 is amended by adding at the end the following new subsection:

"(n) Special Rules For Individuals Without Qualifying Children.—In the case of any taxable year beginning after December 31, 2019, and before January 1, 2021—

"(1) DECREASE IN MINIMUM AGE FOR CREDIT.—

"(A) IN GENERAL.—Subsection (c)(1)(A)(ii)(II) shall be applied by substituting 'the applicable minimum age' for 'age 25'.

"(B) APPLICABLE MINIMUM AGE.—For purposes of this paragraph, the term 'applicable minimum age' means—

"(i) except as otherwise provided in this subparagraph, age 19, "(ii) in the case of a full-time student (other than a qualified former foster youth or a qualified homeless youth), age 25, and

"(iii) in the case of a qualified former foster youth or a qualified homeless youth, age 18.

"(C) FULL-TIME STUDENT.—For purposes of this paragraph, the term 'full-time student' means, with respect to any taxable year, an individual who is an eligible student (as defined in section 25A(b)(3)) during at least 5 calendar months during the taxable year.

"(D) QUALIFIED FORMER FOSTER YOUTH.—For purposes of this paragraph, the term 'qualified former foster youth' means an individual who—

"(i) on or after the date that such individual attained age 14, was in foster care provided under the supervision or administration of a State or tribal agency administering (or eligible to administer) a plan under part B or part E of the Social Security Act (without regard to whether Federal assistance was provided with respect to such child under such part E), and

"(ii) provides (in such manner as the Secretary may provide) consent for State and tribal agencies which administer a plan under part B or part E of the Social Security Act to disclose to the Secretary information related to the status of such individual as a qualified former foster youth.

"(E) QUALIFIED HOMELESS YOUTH.—For purposes of this paragraph, the term 'qualified homeless youth' means, with respect to any taxable year, an individual who—

"(i) is certified by a local educational agency or a financial aid administrator during such taxable year as being either an unaccompanied youth who is a homeless child or youth, or as unaccompanied, at risk of homelessness, and self-supporting. Terms used in the preceding sentence which are also used in section 480(d)(1) of the Higher Education Act of 1965 shall have the same meaning as when used in such section, and

"(ii) provides (in such manner as the Secretary may provide) consent for local educational agencies and financial aid administrators to disclose to the Secretary information related to the status of such individual as a qualified homeless youth.

"(2) INCREASE IN MAXIMUM AGE FOR CREDIT.—Subsection (c)(1)(A)(ii)(II) shall be applied by substituting 'age 66' for 'age 65'.

"(3) INCREASE IN CREDIT AND PHASEOUT PERCENTAGES.—The table contained in subsection (b)(1) shall be applied by substituting '15.3' for '7.65' each place it appears therein.

"(4) INCREASE IN EARNED INCOME AND PHASEOUT AMOUNTS.—

"(A) IN GENERAL.—The table contained in subsection (b)(2)(A) shall be applied—

"(i) by substituting '$9,720' for '$4,220', and

"(ii) by substituting '$11,490' for '$5,280'.

"(B) COORDINATION WITH INFLATION ADJUSTMENT.—Subsection (j) shall not apply to any dollar amount specified in this paragraph.".

(b) Information Return Matching.—As soon as practicable, the Secretary of the Treasury (or the Secretary's delegate) shall develop and implement procedures to use information returns under section 6050S (relating to returns relating to higher education tuition and related expenses) to check the status of individuals as full-time students for purposes of section 32(n)(1)(B)(ii) of the Internal Revenue Code of 1986 (as added by this section).

(c) Effective Date.—The amendment made by this section shall apply to taxable years beginning after December 31, 2019.

TAXPAYER ELIGIBLE FOR CHILDLESS EARNED INCOME CREDIT IN CASE OF QUALIFYING CHILDREN WHO FAIL TO MEET CERTAIN IDENTIFICATION REQUIREMENTS

SEC. 20122.

(a) In General.—Section 32(c)(1) of the Internal Revenue Code of 1986 is amended by striking subparagraph (F).

(b) Effective Date.—The amendment made by this section shall apply to taxable years beginning after the date of the enactment of this Act.

CREDIT ALLOWED IN CASE OF CERTAIN SEPARATED SPOUSES

SEC. 20123.

(a) In General.—Section 32(d) of the Internal Revenue Code of 1986 is amended—

(1) by striking "Married Individuals.—In the case of" and inserting the following: "Married Individuals.—

"(1) IN GENERAL.—In the case of", and

(2) by adding at the end the following new paragraph:

"(2) DETERMINATION OF MARITAL STATUS.—For purposes of this section—

"(A) IN GENERAL.—Except as provided in subparagraph (B), marital status shall be determined under section 7703(a).

"(B) SPECIAL RULE FOR SEPARATED SPOUSE.—An individual shall not be treated as married if such individual—

"(i) is married (as determined under section 7703(a)) and does not file a joint return for the taxable year,

"(ii) lives with a qualifying child of the individual for more than one-half of such taxable year, and

"(iii) (I) during the last 6 months of such taxable year, does not have the same principal place of abode as the individual's spouse, or

"(II) has a decree, instrument, or agreement (other than a decree of divorce) described in section 121(d)(3)(C) with respect to the individual's spouse and is not a member of the same household with the individual's spouse by the end of the taxable year.".

(b) Conforming Amendments.—

(1) Section 32(c)(1)(A) of such Code is amended by striking the last sentence.

(2) Section 32(c)(1)(E)(ii) of such Code is amended by striking "(within the meaning of section 7703)".

(3) Section 32(d)(1) of such Code, as amended by subsection (a), is amended by striking "(within the meaning of section 7703)".

(c) Effective Date.—The amendments made by this section shall apply to taxable years beginning after the date of the enactment of this Act.

ELIMINATION OF DISQUALIFIED INVESTMENT INCOME TEST

SEC. 20124.

(a) In General.—Section 32 of the Internal Revenue Code of 1986 is amended by striking subsection (i).

(b) Conforming Amendments.—

(1) Section 32(j)(1) of such Code is amended by striking "subsections (b)(2) and (i)(1)" and inserting "subsection (b)(2)".

(2) Section 32(j)(1)(B)(i) of such Code is amended by striking "subsections (b)(2)(A) and (i)(1)" and inserting "subsection (b)(2)(A)".

(3) Section 32(j)(2) of such Code is amended—

(A) by striking subparagraph (B), and

(B) by striking "ROUNDING.—" and all that follows through "If any dollar amount" and inserting the following: "ROUNDING.—If any dollar amount".

(c) Effective Date.—The amendments made by this section shall apply to taxable years beginning after the date of the enactment of this Act.

APPLICATION OF EARNED INCOME TAX CREDIT IN POSSESSIONS OF THE UNITED STATES

SEC. 20125.

(a) In General.—Chapter 77 of the Internal Revenue Code of 1986 is amended by adding at the end the following new section:

"SEC. 7530. APPLICATION OF EARNED INCOME TAX CREDIT TO POS-SESSIONS OF THE UNITED STATES.

"(a) Puerto Rico.—

"(1) IN GENERAL.—With respect to calendar year 2021 and each calendar year thereafter, the Secretary shall, except as otherwise provided in this subsection, make payments to Puerto Rico equal to—

"(A) the specified matching amount for such calendar year, plus

"(B) in the case of calendar years 2021 through 2025, the lesser of—

"(i) the expenditures made by Puerto Rico during such calendar year for education efforts with respect to individual taxpayers and tax return preparers relating to the earned income tax credit, or

"(ii) $1,000,000.

"(2) REQUIREMENT TO REFORM EARNED INCOME TAX CREDIT.—The Secretary shall not make any payments under paragraph (1) with respect to any calendar year unless Puerto Rico has in effect an earned income tax credit for taxable years beginning in or with such calendar year which (relative to the earned income tax credit which was in effect for taxable years beginning in or with calendar year 2019) increases the percentage of earned income which is allowed as a credit for each group of individuals with respect to which such percentage is separately stated or determined in a manner designed to substantially increase workforce participation.

"(3) SPECIFIED MATCHING AMOUNT.—For purposes of this subsection—

"(A) IN GENERAL.—The term 'specified matching amount' means, with respect to any calendar year, the lesser of—

"(i) the excess (if any) of—

"(I) the cost to Puerto Rico of the earned income tax credit for taxable years beginning in or with such calendar year, over

"(II) the base amount for such calendar year, or

"(ii) the product of 3, multiplied by the base amount for such calendar year.

"(B) BASE AMOUNT.—

"(i) BASE AMOUNT FOR 2020.—In the case of calendar year 2020, the term 'base amount' means the greater of—

"(I) the cost to Puerto Rico of the earned income tax credit for taxable years beginning in or with calendar year 2019 (rounded to the nearest multiple of $1,000,000), or

"(II) $200,000,000.

"(ii) INFLATION ADJUSTMENT.—In the case of any calendar year after 2021, the term 'base amount' means the dollar amount determined under clause (i) increased by an amount equal to—

"(I) such dollar amount, multiplied by—

"(II) the cost-of-living adjustment determined under section 1(f)(3) for such calendar year, determined by substituting 'calendar year 2020' for 'calendar year 2016' in subparagraph (A)(ii) thereof.

Any amount determined under this clause shall be rounded to the nearest multiple of $1,000,000.

"(4) RULES RELATED TO PAYMENTS AND REPORTS.—

"(A) TIMING OF PAYMENTS.—The Secretary shall make payments under paragraph (1) for any calendar year—

"(i) after receipt of the report described in subparagraph (B) for such calendar year, and

"(ii) except as provided in clause (i), within a reasonable period of time before the due date for individual income tax returns (as determined under the laws of Puerto Rico) for taxable years which began on the first day of such calendar year.

"(B) ANNUAL REPORTS.—With respect to calendar year 2021 and each calendar year thereafter, Puerto Rico shall provide to the Secretary a report which shall include—

"(i) an estimate of the costs described in paragraphs (1)(B)(i) and (3)(A)(i)(I) with respect to such calendar year, and

"(ii) a statement of such costs with respect to the preceding calendar year.

"(C) ADJUSTMENTS.—

"(i) IN GENERAL.—In the event that any estimate of an amount is more or less than the actual amount as later determined and any payment under paragraph (1) was determined on the basis of such estimate, proper payment shall be made by, or to, the Secretary (as the case may be) as soon as practicable after the determination that such estimate was inaccurate. Proper adjustment shall be made in the amount of any subsequent payments made under paragraph (1) to the extent that proper payment is not made under the preceding sentence before such subsequent payments.

"(ii) ADDITIONAL REPORTS.—The Secretary may require such additional periodic reports of the information described in subparagraph (B) as the Secretary determines appropriate to facilitate timely adjustments under clause (i).

"(D) DETERMINATION OF COST OF EARNED INCOME TAX CREDIT.—For purposes of this subsection, the cost to Puerto Rico of the earned income tax credit shall be determined by the Secretary on the basis of the laws of Puerto Rico and shall include reductions in revenues received by Puerto Rico by reason of such credit and refunds attributable to such credit, but shall not include any administrative costs with respect to such credit.

"(E) PREVENTION OF MANIPULATION OF BASE AMOUNT.—No payments shall be made under paragraph (1) if the earned income tax credit as in effect in Puerto Rico for taxable years beginning in or with calendar year 2019 is modified after the date of the enactment of this subsection.

"(b) Possessions With Mirror Code Tax Systems.—

"(1) IN GENERAL.—With respect to calendar year 2020 and each calendar year thereafter, the Secretary shall, except as otherwise provided in this subsection, make payments to the Virgin Islands, Guam, and the Commonwealth of the Northern Mariana Islands equal to—

"(A) 75 percent of the cost to such possession of the earned income tax credit for taxable years beginning in or with such calendar year, plus

"(B) in the case of calendar years 2020 through 2024, the lesser of—

"(i) the expenditures made by such possession during such calendar year for education efforts with respect to individual taxpayers and tax return preparers relating to such earned income tax credit, or

"(ii) $50,000.

"(2) APPLICATION OF CERTAIN RULES.—Rules similar to the rules of subparagraphs (A), (B), (C), and (D) of subsection (a)(4) shall apply for purposes of this subsection.

"(c) American Samoa.—

"(1) IN GENERAL.—With respect to calendar year 2020 and each calendar year thereafter, the Secretary shall, except as otherwise provided in this subsection, make payments to American Samoa equal to—

"(A) the lesser of—

"(i) 75 percent of the cost to American Samoa of the earned income tax credit for taxable years beginning in or with such calendar year, or

"(ii) $12,000,000, plus

"(B) in the case of calendar years 2020 through 2024, the lesser of—

"(i) the expenditures made by American Samoa during such calendar year for education efforts with respect to individual taxpayers and tax return preparers relating to such earned income tax credit, or

"(ii) $50,000.

"(2) REQUIREMENT TO ENACT AND MAINTAIN AN EARNED INCOME TAX CREDIT.—The Secretary shall not make any payments under paragraph (1) with respect to any calendar year unless American Samoa has in effect an earned income tax credit for taxable years beginning in or with such calendar year which allows a refundable tax credit to individuals on the basis of the taxpayer's earned income which is designed to substantially increase workforce participation.

"(3) INFLATION ADJUSTMENT.—In the case of any calendar year after 2020, the $12,000,000 amount in paragraph (1)(A)(ii) shall be increased by an amount equal to—

"(A) such dollar amount, multiplied by—

"(B) the cost-of-living adjustment determined under section 1(f)(3) for such calendar year, determined by substituting 'calendar year 2019' for 'calendar year 2016' in subparagraph (A)(ii) thereof.

Any increase determined under this clause shall be rounded to the nearest multiple of $100,000.

"(4) APPLICATION OF CERTAIN RULES.—Rules similar to the rules of subparagraphs (A), (B), (C), and (D) of subsection (a)(4) shall apply for purposes of this subsection.

"(d) Treatment Of Payments.—For purposes of section 1324 of title 31, United States Code, the payments under this section shall be treated in the same manner as a refund due from a credit provision referred to in subsection (b)(2) of such section.".

(b) Clerical Amendment.—The table of sections for chapter 77 of the Internal Revenue Code of 1986 is amended by adding at the end the following new item:

"SEC. 7529. Application of earned income tax credit to possessions of the United States.".

TEMPORARY SPECIAL RULE FOR DETERMINING EARNED INCOME FOR

PURPOSES OF EARNED INCOME TAX CREDIT

SEC. 20126.

(a) In General.—If the earned income of the taxpayer for the taxpayer's first taxable year beginning in 2020 is less than the earned income of the taxpayer for the preceding taxable year, the credit allowed under section 32 of the Internal Revenue Code of 1986 may, at the election of the taxpayer, be determined by substituting-—

(1) such earned income for the preceding taxable year, for

(2) such earned income for the taxpayer's first taxable year beginning in 2020.

(b) Earned Income.—

(1) IN GENERAL.—For purposes of this section, the term "earned income" has the meaning given such term under section 32(c) of the Internal Revenue Code of 1986.

(2) APPLICATION TO JOINT RETURNS.—For purposes of subsection (a), in the case of a joint return, the earned income of the taxpayer for the preceding taxable year shall be the sum of the earned income of each spouse for such preceding taxable year.

(c) Special Rules.—

(1) ERRORS TREATED AS MATHEMATICAL ERROR.—For purposes of section 6213 of the Internal Revenue Code of 1986, an incorrect use on a return of earned income pursuant to subsection (a) shall be treated as a mathematical or clerical error.

(2) NO EFFECT ON DETERMINATION OF GROSS INCOME, ETC.—Except as otherwise provided in this subsection, the Internal Revenue Code of 1986 shall be applied without regard to any substitution under subsection (a).

(d) Treatment Of Certain Possessions.—

(1) PAYMENTS TO POSSESSIONS WITH MIRROR CODE TAX SYSTEMS.—The Secretary of the Treasury shall pay to each possession of the United States which has a mirror code tax system amounts equal to the loss (if any) to that possession by reason of the application of the provisions of this section (other than this subsection) with respect to section 32 of the Internal Revenue Code of 1986. Such amounts shall be determined by the Secretary of the Treasury based on information provided by the government of the respective possession.

(2) PAYMENTS TO OTHER POSSESSIONS.—The Secretary of the Treasury shall pay to each possession of the United States which does not have a mirror code tax system amounts estimated by the Secretary of the Treasury as being equal to the aggregate benefits (if any) that would have been provided to residents of such possession by reason of the provisions of this section (other than this subsection) with respect to section 32 of the Internal Revenue Code of 1986 if a mirror code tax system had been in effect in such possession. The preceding sentence shall not apply unless the respective possession has a plan, which has been approved by the Secretary of the Treasury, under which such possession will promptly distribute such payments to its residents.

(3) MIRROR CODE TAX SYSTEM.—For purposes of this section, the term "mirror code tax system" means, with respect to any possession of the United States, the income tax system of such possession if the income tax liability of the residents of such possession under such system is determined by reference to the income tax laws of the United States as if such possession were the United States.

(4) TREATMENT OF PAYMENTS.—For purposes of section 1324 of title 31, United States Code, the payments under this section shall be treated in the same manner as a refund due from a credit provision referred to in subsection (b)(2) of such section.

Subtitle D—Child Tax Credit

CHILD TAX CREDIT IMPROVEMENTS FOR 2020

SEC. 20131.

(a) In General.—Section 24 of the Internal Revenue Code of 1986 is amended by adding at the end the following new subsection:

"(i) Special Rules For 2020.—In the case of any taxable year beginning in 2020—

"(1) REFUNDABLE CREDIT.—Subsection (h)(5) shall not apply and the increase determined under the first sentence of subsection (d)(1) shall be the amount determined under subsection (d)(1)(A) (determined without regard to subsection (h)(4)).

"(2) CREDIT AMOUNT.—Subsection (h)(2) shall not apply and subsection (a) shall be applied by substituting '$3,000 ($3,600 in the case of a qualifying child who has not attained age 6 as of the close of the calendar year in which the taxable year of the taxpayer begins)' for '$1,000'.

"(3) 17-YEAR-OLDS ELIGIBLE FOR TREATMENT AS QUALIFYING CHILDREN.—This section shall be applied—

"(A) by substituting 'age 18' for 'age 17' in subsection (c)(1), and

"(B) by substituting 'described in subsection (c) (determined after the application of subsection (i)(3)(A))' for 'described in subsection (c)' in subsection (h)(4)(A).".

(b) Advance Payment Of Credit.—

(1) IN GENERAL.—Chapter 77 of such Code is amended by inserting after section 7527 the following new section:

"SEC. 7527A. ADVANCE PAYMENT OF CHILD TAX CREDIT.

"(a) In General.—As soon as practicable after the date of the enactment of this Act, the Secretary shall establish a program for making advance payments of the credit allowed under subsection (a) of section 24 on a monthly basis (determined without regard to subsection (i)(4)) of such section), or as frequently as the Secretary determines to be administratively feasible, to taxpayers determined to be eligible for advance payment of such credit.

"(b) Limitation.—

"(1) IN GENERAL.—The Secretary may make payments under subsection (a) only to the extent that the total amount of such payments made to any taxpayer during the taxable year does not exceed an amount equal to the excess, if any, of—

"(A) subject to paragraph (2), the amount determined under subsection (a) of section 24 with respect to such taxpayer (determined without regard to subsection (i)(4)) of such section) for such taxable year, over

"(B) the estimated tax imposed by subtitle A, as reduced by the credits allowable under subparts A and C (other than section 24) of such part IV, with respect to such taxpayer for such taxable year, as determined in such manner as the Secretary deems appropriate.

"(2) APPLICATION OF THRESHOLD AMOUNT LIMITATION.—The program described in subsection (a) shall make reasonable efforts to apply the limitation of section 24(b) with respect to payments made under such program.

"(c) Application.—The advance payments described in this section shall only be made with respect to credits allowed under section 24 for taxable years beginning during 2020.".

(2) RECONCILIATION OF CREDIT AND ADVANCE CREDIT.—Section 24(i) of such Code, as amended by subsection (a), is amended by adding at the end the following new paragraph:

"(4) RECONCILIATION OF CREDIT AND ADVANCE CREDIT.—

"(A) IN GENERAL.—The amount of the credit allowed under this section for any taxable year shall be reduced (but not below zero) by the aggregate amount of any advance payments of such credit under section 7527A for such taxable year.

"(B) EXCESS ADVANCE PAYMENTS.—If the aggregate amount of advance payments under section 7527A for the taxable year exceeds the amount of the credit allowed under this section for such taxable year (determined without regard to subparagraph (A)), the tax imposed by this chapter for such taxable year shall be increased by the amount of such excess.".

(3) CLERICAL AMEMDMENT.—The table of sections for chapter 77 of such Code is amended by inserting after the item relating to section 7527 the following new item:

"SEC. 7527A. Advance payment of child tax credit.".

(c) Effective Date.—The amendments made by this section shall apply to taxable years beginning after December 31, 2019.

APPLICATION OF CHILD TAX CREDIT IN POSSESSIONS

SEC. 20132.

(a) In General.—Section 24 of the Internal Revenue Code of 1986 is amended by adding at the end the following new subsection:

"(i) Application Of Credit In Possessions.—

"(1) MIRROR CODE POSSESSIONS.—

"(A) IN GENERAL.—The Secretary shall pay to each possession of the United States with a mirror code tax system amounts equal to the loss to that possession by reason of the application of this section (determined without regard to this subsection) with respect to taxable years beginning after 2019. Such amounts shall be determined by the Secretary based on information provided by the government of the respective possession.

"(B) COORDINATION WITH CREDIT ALLOWED AGAINST UNITED STATES INCOME TAXES.—No credit shall be allowed under this section for any taxable year to any individual to whom a credit is allowable against taxes imposed by a possession with a mirror code tax system by reason of the application of this section in such possession for such taxable year.

"(C) MIRROR CODE TAX SYSTEM.—For purposes of this paragraph, the term 'mirror code tax system' means, with respect to any possession of the United States, the income tax system of such possession if the income tax liability of the residents of such possession under such system is determined by reference to the income tax laws of the United States as if such possession were the United States.

"(2) PUERTO RICO.—In the case of any bona fide resident of Puerto Rico (within the meaning of section 937(a))—

"(A) the credit determined under this section shall be allowable to such resident,

"(B) in the case of any taxable year beginning during 2020, the increase determined under the first sentence of subsection (d)(1) shall be the amount determined under subsection (d)(1)(A) (determined without regard to subsection (h)(4)),

"(C) in the case of any taxable year beginning after December 31, 2020, and before January 1, 2026, the increase determined under the first sentence of subsection (d)(1) shall be the lesser of—

"(i) the amount determined under subsection (d)(1)(A) (determined without regard to subsection (h)(4)), or "(ii) the dollar amount in effect under subsection (h)(5), and

"(D) in the case of any taxable year after December 31, 2025, the increase determined under the first sentence of subsection (d)(1) shall be the amount determined under subsection (d)(1)(A).

"(3) AMERICAN SAMOA.—

"(A) IN GENERAL.—The Secretary shall pay to American Samoa amounts estimated by the Secretary as being equal to the aggregate benefits that would have been provided to residents of American Samoa by reason of the application of this section for taxable years beginning after 2019 if the provisions of this section had been in effect in American Samoa.

"(B) DISTRIBUTION REQUIREMENT.—Subparagraph (A) shall not apply unless American Samoa has a plan, which has been approved by the Secretary, under which American Samoa will promptly distribute such payments to the residents of American Samoa in a manner which replicates to the greatest degree practicable the benefits that would have been so provided to each such resident.

"(C) COORDINATION WITH CREDIT ALLOWED AGAINST UNITED STATES INCOME TAXES.—

"(i) IN GENERAL.—In the case of a taxable year with respect to which a plan is approved under subparagraph (B), this section (other than this subsection) shall not apply to any individual eligible for a distribution under such plan.

"(ii) APPLICATION OF SECTION IN EVENT OF ABSENCE OF APPROVED PLAN.—In the case of a taxable year with respect to which a plan is not approved under subparagraph (B), rules similar to the rules of paragraph (2) shall apply with respect to bona fide residents of American Samoa (within the meaning of section 937(a)).

"(4) TREATMENT OF PAYMENTS.—The payments made under this subsection shall be treated in the same manner for purposes of section 1324(b)(2) of title 31, United States Code, as refunds due from the credit allowed under this section.".

(b) Effective Date.—The amendment made by this section shall apply to taxable years beginning after December 31, 2019.

Subtitle E—Dependent Care Assistance

REFUNDABILITY AND ENHANCEMENT OF CHILD AND DEPENDENT CARE TAX CREDIT

SEC. 20141.

(a) In General.—Section 21 of the Internal Revenue Code of 1986 is amended by adding at the end the following new subsection:

"(g) Special Rules For 2020.—In the case of any taxable year beginning after December 31, 2019, and before January 1, 2021—

"(1) CREDIT MADE REFUNDABLE.—In the case of an individual other than a nonresident alien, the credit allowed under subsection (a) shall be treated as a credit allowed under subpart C (and not allowed under this subpart).

"(2) INCREASE IN APPLICABLE PERCENTAGE.—Subsection (a)(2) shall be applied—

"(A) by substituting '50 percent' for '35 percent ', and

"(B) by substituting '$120,000' for '$15,000'.

"(3) INCREASE IN DOLLAR LIMIT ON AMOUNT CREDITABLE.—Subsection (c) shall be applied—

"(A) by substituting '$6,000' for '$3,000' in paragraph (1) thereof, and

"(B) by substituting 'twice the amount in effect under paragraph (1)' for '$6,000' in paragraph (2) thereof.".

(b) Conforming Amendment.—Section 1324(b)(2) of title 31, United States Code, is amended by inserting "21 (by reason of subsection (g) thereof)," before "25A".

(c) Coordination With Possession Tax Systems.—Section 21(g)(1) of the Internal Revenue Code of 1986 (as added by this section) shall not apply to any person—

(1) to whom a credit is allowed against taxes imposed by a possession with a mirror code tax system by reason of the application of section 21 of such Code in such possession for such taxable year, or

(2) to whom a credit would be allowed against taxes imposed by a possession which does not have a mirror code tax system if the provisions of section 21 of such Code had been in effect in such possession for such taxable year.

(d) Effective Date.—The amendments made by this section shall apply to taxable years beginning after December 31, 2019.

INCREASE IN EXCLUSION FOR EMPLOYER-PROVIDED DEPENDENT CARE ASSISTANCE

SEC. 20142.

(a) In General.—Section 129(a)(2) of the Internal Revenue Code of 1986 is amended by adding at the end the following new subparagraph:

"(D) SPECIAL RULE FOR 2020.—In the case of any taxable year beginning during 2020, subparagraph (A) shall be applied be substituting '$10,500 (half such dollar amount' for '$5,000 ($2,500".

(b) Effective Date.—The amendment made by this section shall apply to taxable years beginning after December 31, 2019.

(c) Retroactive Plan Amendments.—A plan or other arrangement that otherwise satisfies all applicable requirements of sections 106, 125, and 129 of the Internal Revenue Code of 1986 (including any rules or regulations thereunder) shall not fail to be treated as a cafeteria plan or dependent care flexible spending arrangement merely because such plan or arrangement is amended pursuant to a provision under this section and such amendment is retroactive, if—

(1) such amendment is adopted no later than the last day of the plan year in which the amendment is effective, and

(2) the plan or arrangement is operated consistent with the terms of such amendment during the period beginning on the effective date of the amendment and ending on the date the amendment is adopted.

Subtitle F—Flexibility For Certain Employee Benefits

INCREASE IN CARRYOVER FOR HEALTH FLEXIBLE SPENDING ARRANGE-MENTS

SEC. 20151.

(a) In General.—A plan or other arrangement that otherwise satisfies all of the applicable requirements of sections 106 and 125 of the Internal Revenue Code of 1986 (including any rules or regulations thereunder) shall not fail to be treated as a cafeteria plan or health flexible spending arrangement merely because such plan or arrangement permits participants to carry over an amount not in excess of $2,750 of unused benefits or contributions remaining in a health flexible spending arrangement from the plan year ending in 2020 to the plan year ending in 2021.

(b) Definitions.—Any term used in this section which is also used in section 106 or 125 of the Internal Revenue Code of 1986 or the rules or regulations thereunder shall have the same meaning as when used in such section or rules or regulations.

CARRYOVER FOR DEPENDENT CARE FLEXIBLE SPENDING ARRANGEMENTS

SEC. 20152.

(a) In General.—A plan or other arrangement that otherwise satisfies all applicable requirements of sections 106, 125, and 129 of the Internal Revenue Code of 1986 (including any rules or regulations thereunder) shall not fail to be treated as a cafeteria plan or dependent care flexible spending arrangement merely because such plan or arrangement permits participants to carry over (under rules similar to the rules applicable to health flexible spending arrangements) an amount, not in excess of the amount in effect under section 129(a)(2)(A) of such Code, of unused benefits or contributions remaining in a dependent care flexible spending arrangement from the plan year ending in 2020 to the plan year ending in 2021.

(b) Definitions.—Any term used in this section which is also used in section 106, 125, or 129 of the Internal Revenue Code of 1986 or the rules or regulations thereunder shall have the same meaning as when used in such section or rules or regulations.

CARRYOVER OF PAID TIME OFF

SEC. 20153.

(a) In General.—A plan that otherwise satisfies all applicable requirements of section 125 of the Internal Revenue Code of 1986 (including any rules or regulations thereunder) shall not fail to be treated as a cafeteria plan merely because such plan permits participants to carry over (under rules similar to the rules applicable to health flexible spending arrangements) any amount of paid time off (without limitation) from the plan year ending in 2020 to the plan year ending in 2021.

(b) Definitions.—Any term used in this section which is also used in section 125 of the Internal Revenue Code of 1986 or the rules or regulations thereunder shall have the same meaning as when used in such section or rules or regulations.

CHANGE IN ELECTION AMOUNT

SEC. 20154.

(a) In General.—A plan or other arrangement that otherwise satisfies all applicable requirements of sections 106 and 125 of the Internal Revenue Code of 1986 (including any rules or regulations thereunder) shall not fail to be treated as a cafeteria plan or health flexible spending arrangement merely because such plan or arrangement allows an employee to make, with respect to the remaining portion of a period of coverage within the applicable period—

(1) an election modifying the amount of such employee's contributions to such a health flexible spending arrangement (without regard to any change in status), or

(2) an election modifying the amount of such employee's elective paid time off.

Any election as modified under paragraph (1) shall not exceed the limitation applicable under section 125(i) for the taxable year.

(b) One-Time Application.—Paragraphs (1) and (2) of subsection (a) shall each apply to only 1 election change described in such paragraph with respect to an employee (in addition to any other election changes during a period of coverage permitted under the plan or arrangement without regard to this section).

(c) Applicable Period.—For purposes of this section, the term "applicable period" means the period beginning on the date of the enactment of this Act and ending on December 31, 2020.

(d) Definitions.—Any term used in this section which is also used in section 106 or 125 of the Internal Revenue Code of 1986 or the rules or regulations thereunder shall have the same meaning as when used in such section or rules or regulations.

EXTENSION OF GRACE PERIODS, ETC

SEC. 20155.

(a) In General.—A plan or other arrangement that otherwise satisfies all applicable requirements of sections 106, 125, or 129 of the Internal Revenue Code (including any rules or regulations thereunder) shall not fail to be treated as a cafeteria plan, health flexible spending arrangement, or dependent care flexible spending arrangement (whichever is applicable) merely because such plan or arrangement extends the grace period for the plan year ending in 2020 to 12 months after the end of such plan year, with respect to unused benefits or contributions remaining in a health flexible spending arrangement or a dependent care flexible spending arrangement.

(b) Post-Termination Reimbursements From Health FSAs.—A plan or other arrangement that otherwise satisfies all applicable requirements of sections 106 and 125 of the Internal Revenue Code of 1986 (including any rules or regulations thereunder) shall not fail to be treated as a cafeteria plan or health flexible spending arrangement merely because such plan or arrangement allows (under rules similar to the rules applicable to dependent care flexible spending arrangements) an employee who ceases participation in the plan during calendar year 2020 to continue to receive reimbursements from unused benefits or contributions through the end of the plan year (including any grace period, taking into account any modification of a grace period permitted under subsection (a)).

(c) Definitions.—Any term used in this section which is also used in section 106, 125, or 129 of the Internal Revenue Code of 1986 or the rules or regulations thereunder shall have the same meaning as when used in such section or rules or regulations.

PLAN AMENDMENTS

SEC. 20156.

A plan or other arrangement that otherwise satisfies all applicable requirements of sections 106, 125, and 129 of the Internal Revenue Code of 1986 (including any rules or regulations thereunder) shall not fail to be treated as a cafeteria plan, health flexible spending arrangement, or dependent care flexible spending arrangement merely because such plan or arrangement is amended pursuant to a provision under this subtitle and such amendment is retroactive, if—

(1) such amendment is adopted no later than the last day of the plan year in which the amendment is effective, and

(2) the plan or arrangement is operated consistent with the terms of such amendment during the period beginning on the effective date of the amendment and ending on the date the amendment is adopted.

Subtitle G—Deduction Of State And Local Taxes

ELIMINATION FOR 2020 AND 2021 OF LIMITATION ON DEDUCTION OF STATE AND LOCAL TAXES

SEC. 20161.

(a) In General.—Section 164(b)(6)(B) of the Internal Revenue Code of 1986 is amended by inserting "in the case of a taxable year beginning before January 1, 2020, or after December 31, 2021," before "the aggregate amount of taxes".

(b) Conforming Amendments.—Section 164(b)(6) of the Internal Revenue Code of 1986 is amended—

(1) by striking "For purposes of subparagraph (B)" and inserting "For purposes of this section",

(2) by striking "January 1, 2018" and inserting "January 1, 2022",

(3) by striking "December 31, 2017, shall" and inserting "December 31, 2021, shall", and

(4) by adding at the end the following: "For purposes of this section, in the case of State or local taxes with respect to any real or personal property paid during a taxable year beginning in 2020 or 2021, the Secretary shall prescribe rules which treat all or a portion of such taxes as paid in a taxable year or years other than the taxable year in which actually paid as necessary or appropriate to prevent the avoidance of the limitations of this subsection.".

(c) Effective Date.—The amendments made by this section shall apply to taxes paid or accrued in taxable years beginning after December 31, 2019.

TITLE II
—ADDITIONAL RELIEF FOR WORKERS

Subtitle A—Additional Relief
INCREASE IN ABOVE-THE-LINE DEDUCTION FOR CERTAIN EXPENSES OF ELEMENTARY AND SECONDARY SCHOOL TEACHERS

SEC. 20201.
(a) Increase.—Section 62(a)(2)(D) of the Internal Revenue Code of 1986 is amended by striking "$250" and inserting "$500".

(b) Conforming Amendments.—Section 62(d)(3) of the Internal Revenue Code of 1986 is amended—

(1) by striking "2015" and inserting "2020",

(2) by striking "$250" and inserting "$500", and

(3) in subparagraph (B), by striking "2014" and inserting "2019".

(c) Effective Date.—The amendments made by this section shall apply to taxable years beginning after December 31, 2019.

ABOVE-THE-LINE DEDUCTION ALLOWED FOR CERTAIN EXPENSES OF FIRST RESPONDERS

SEC. 20202.
(a) In General.—Section 62(a)(2) of the Internal Revenue Code of 1986 is amended by adding at the end the following new subparagraph:

"(F) CERTAIN EXPENSES OF FIRST RESPONDERS.—The deductions allowed by section 162 which consist of expenses, not in excess of $500, paid or incurred by a first responder—

"(i) as tuition or fees for the participation of the first responder in professional development courses related to service as a first responder, or

"(ii) for uniforms used by the first responder in service as a first responder.".

(b) First Responder Defined.—Section 62(d) of the Internal Revenue Code of 1986 is amended by adding at the end the following new paragraph:

"(4) FIRST RESPONDER.—For purposes of subsection (a)(2)(F), the term 'first responder' means, with respect to any taxable year, any employee who provides at least 1000 hours of service during such taxable year as a law enforcement officer, firefighter, paramedic, or emergency medical technician.".

(c) Inflation Adjustment.—Section 62(d)(3) of the Internal Revenue Code of 1986, as amended by the preceding provisions of this Act, is further amended by striking "the $500 amount in subsection (a)(2)(D)" and inserting "the $500 amount in each of subparagraphs (D) and (F) of subsection (a)(2)".

(d) Effective Date.—The amendments made by this section shall apply to taxable years beginning after December 31, 2019.

TEMPORARY ABOVE-THE-LINE DEDUCTION FOR SUPPLIES AND EQUIPMENT OF FIRST RESPONDERS AND COVID–19 FRONT LINE EMPLOYEES

SEC. 20203.

(a) In General.—Section 62(d) of the Internal Revenue Code of 1986, as amended by the preceding provisions of this Act, is amended by adding at the end of the following new paragraph:

"(5) TEMPORARY RULE FOR FIRST RESPONDERS AND COVID–19 FRONT LINE EMPLOYEES.—

"(A) IN GENERAL.—In the case of any taxable year beginning in 2020—

"(i) subsection (a)(2)(F)(ii) shall be applied by substituting 'uniforms, supplies, or equipment' for 'uniforms', and

"(ii) for purposes of subsection (a)(2)(F), the term 'first responder' shall include any COVID–19 front line employee.

"(B) COVID–19 FRONT LINE EMPLOYEE.—For purposes of this paragraph, the term 'COVID–19 front line employee' means, with respect to any taxable year, any individual who performs at least 1000 hours of essential work (as defined in the COVID–19 Heroes Fund Act except without regard to the time period during which such work is performed) during such taxable year as an employee in a trade or business of an employer.".

(b) Effective Date.—The amendment made by this section shall apply to taxable years beginning after December 31, 2019.

PAYROLL CREDIT FOR CERTAIN PANDEMIC-RELATED EMPLOYEE BENEFIT EXPENSES PAID BY EMPLOYERS

SEC. 20204.

(a) In General.—In the case of an employer, there shall be allowed as a credit against applicable employment taxes for each calendar quarter an amount equal to the applicable percentage of the qualified pandemic-related employee benefit expenses paid by such employer with respect to such calendar quarter.

(b) Limitations And Refundability.—

(1) DOLLAR LIMITATION PER EMPLOYEE.—The qualified pandemic-related employee benefit expenses which may be taken into account under subsection (a) with respect to any employee for any calendar quarter shall not exceed $5,000.

(2) CREDIT LIMITED TO CERTAIN EMPLOYMENT TAXES.—The credit allowed by subsection (a) with respect to any calendar quarter shall not exceed the applicable employment taxes for such calendar quarter (reduced by any credits allowed under subsections (e) and (f) of section 3111 of such Code, sections 7001 and 7003 of the

Families First Coronavirus Response Act, and section 2301 of the CARES Act, for such quarter) on the wages paid with respect to the employment of all the employees of the employer for such calendar quarter.

(3) REFUNDABILITY OF EXCESS CREDIT.—

(A) IN GENERAL.—If the amount of the credit under subsection (a) exceeds the limitation of paragraph (2) for any calendar quarter, such excess shall be treated as an overpayment that shall be refunded under sections 6402(a) and 6413(b) of the Internal Revenue Code of 1986.

(B) TREATMENT OF PAYMENTS.—For purposes of section 1324 of title 31, United States Code, any amounts due to an employer under this paragraph shall be treated in the same manner as a refund due from a credit provision referred to in subsection (b)(2) of such section.

(4) COORDINATION WITH GOVERNMENT GRANTS.—The qualified pandemic-related employee benefit expenses taken into account under this section by any employer shall be reduced by any amounts provided by and Federal, State, or local government for purposes of making or reimbursing such expenses.

(c) Qualified Pandemic-Related Employee Benefit Expenses.—For purposes of this section, the term "qualified pandemic-related employee benefit expenses" means any amount paid to or for the benefit of an employee in the employment of the employer if—

(1) such amount is excludible from the gross income of the employee under section 139 of the Internal Revenue Code of 1986 by reason of being a qualified disaster relief payment described in subsection (b)(1) of such section with respect to a qualified disaster described in subsection (c)(2) of such section which was declared by reason of COVID–19, and

(2) the employer elects (at such time and in such manner as the Secretary may provide) to treat such amount as a qualified pandemic-related employee benefit expense.

(d) Applicable Percentage.—For purposes of this section—

(1) IN GENERAL.—The term "applicable percentage" means—

(A) 50 percent, in the case of qualified pandemic-related employee benefit expenses paid with respect to an essential employee, and

(B) 30 percent, in any other case.

(2) ESSENTIAL EMPLOYEE.—The term "essential employee" means, with respect to any employer for any calendar quarter, any employee of such employer if a substantial portion of the services performed by such employee for such employer during such calendar quarter are essential work (as defined in the COVID–19 Heroes Fund Act except without regard to the time period during which such work is performed).

(e) Special Rules; Other Definitions.—

(1) APPLICATION OF CERTAIN NON-DISCRIMINATION RULES.—No credit shall be allowed under this section to any employer for any calendar quarter if qualified pandemic-related employee benefit expenses are provided by such employer to employees for such calendar quarter in a manner which discriminates in favor of highly compensated individuals (within the meaning of section 125) as to eligibility for, or the amount of, such benefit expenses. An employer may elect with respect to any calendar quarter to apply this paragraph separately with respect to essential employees and with respect to all other employees.

(2) DENIAL OF DOUBLE BENEFIT.—For purposes of chapter 1 of such Code, no deduction or credit (other than the credit allowed under this section) shall be allowed

for so much of qualified pandemic-related employee benefit expenses as is equal to the credit allowed under this section.

(3) THIRD PARTY PAYORS.—Any credit allowed under this section shall be treated as a credit described in section 3511(d)(2) of such Code.

(4) APPLICABLE EMPLOYMENT TAXES.—For purposes of this section, the term "applicable employment taxes" means the following:

(A) The taxes imposed under section 3111(a) of the Internal Revenue Code of 1986.

(B) So much of the taxes imposed under section 3221(a) of such Code as are attributable to the rate in effect under section 3111(a) of such Code.

(5) SECRETARY.—For purposes of this section, the term "Secretary" means the Secretary of the Treasury or the Secretary's delegate.

(6) CERTAIN TERMS.—

(A) IN GENERAL.—Any term used in this section which is also used in chapter 21 or 22 of such Code shall have the same meaning as when used in such chapter (as the case may be).

(B) CERTAIN PROVISIONS NOT TAKEN INTO ACCOUNT EXCEPT FOR PURPOSES OF LIMITING CREDIT TO EMPLOYMENT TAXES.—For purposes of subparagraph (A) (other than with respect to subsection (b)(2)), section 3121(b) of such Code shall be applied without regard to paragraphs (1), (5), (6), (7), (8), (10), (13), (18), (19), and (22) thereof (except with respect to services performed in a penal institution by an inmate thereof) and section 3231(e)(1) shall be applied without regard to the sentence that begins "Such term does not include remuneration".

(f) Certain Governmental Employers.—

(1) IN GENERAL.—The credit under this section shall not be allowed to the Federal Government or any agency or instrumentality thereof.

(2) EXCEPTION.—Paragraph (1) shall not apply to any organization described in section 501(c)(1) of the Internal Revenue Code of 1986 and exempt from tax under section 501(a) of such Code.

(g) Treatment Of Deposits.—The Secretary shall waive any penalty under section 6656 of such Code for any failure to make a deposit of applicable employment taxes if the Secretary determines that such failure was due to the anticipation of the credit allowed under this section.

(h) Regulations.—The Secretary shall prescribe such regulations or other guidance as may be necessary to carry out the purposes of this section, including regulations or other guidance—

(1) to allow the advance payment of the credit determined under subsection (a), subject to the limitations provided in this section, based on such information as the Secretary shall require,

(2) to provide for the reconciliation of such advance payment with the amount of the credit at the time of filing the return of tax for the applicable quarter or taxable year,

(3) for recapturing the benefit of credits determined under this section in cases where there is a subsequent adjustment to the credit determined under subsection (a), and

(4) with respect to the application of the credit to third party payors (including professional employer organizations, certified professional employer organizations, or agents under section 3504 of such Code), including to allow such payors to submit documentation necessary to substantiate eligibility for, and the amount of, the credit allowed under this section.

(i) Application Of Section.—This section shall apply only to qualified pandemic-related employee benefit expenses paid after March 12, 2020, and before January 1, 2021.

(j) Transfers To Certain Trust Funds.—There are hereby appropriated to the Federal Old-Age and Survivors Insurance Trust Fund and the Federal Disability Insurance Trust Fund established under section 201 of the Social Security Act (42 U.S.C. 401) and the Social Security Equivalent Benefit Account established under section 15A(a) of the Railroad Retirement Act of 1974 (45 U.S.C. 231n–1(a)) amounts equal to the reduction in revenues to the Treasury by reason of this section (without regard to this subsection). Amounts appropriated by the preceding sentence shall be transferred from the general fund at such times and in such manner as to replicate to the extent possible the transfers which would have occurred to such Trust Fund or Account had this section not been enacted.

Subtitle B—Tax Credits To Prevent Business Interruption

IMPROVEMENTS TO EMPLOYEE RETENTION CREDIT

SEC. 20211.

(a) Increase In Credit Percentage.—Section 2301(a) of the CARES Act is amended by striking "50 percent" and inserting "80 percent".

(b) Increase In Per Employee Limitation.—Section 2301(b)(1) of the CARES Act is amended by striking "for all calendar quarters shall not exceed $10,000." and inserting shall not exceed—

"(A) $15,000 in any calendar quarter, and

"(B) $45,000 in the aggregate for all calendar quarters.".

(c) Modification Of Threshold For Treatment As A Large Employer.—

(1) IN GENERAL.—Section 2301(c)(3)(A) of the CARES Act is amended—

(A) by striking "for which the average number of full-time employees (within the meaning of section 4980H of the Internal Revenue Code of 1986) employed by such eligible employer during 2019 was greater than 100" in clause (i) and inserting "which is a large employer", and

(B) by striking "for which the average number of full-time employees (within the meaning of section 4980H of the Internal Revenue Code of 1986) employed by such eligible employer during 2019 was not greater than 100" in clause (ii) and inserting "which is not a large employer".

(2) LARGE EMPLOYER DEFINED.—Section 2301(c) of the CARES Act is amended by redesignating paragraph (6) as paragraph (7) and by inserting after paragraph (5) the following new paragraph:

"(6) LARGE EMPLOYER.—The term 'large employer' means any eligible employer if—

"(A) the average number of full-time employees (as determined for purposes of determining whether an employer is an applicable large employer for purposes of section 4980H(c)(2) of the Internal Revenue Code of 1986) employed by such eligible employer during calendar year 2019 was greater than 1,500, and

"(B) the gross receipts (within the meaning of section 448(c) of the Internal Revenue Code of 1986) of such eligible employer during calendar year 2019 was greater than $41,500,000.".

(d) Phase-In Of Eligibility Based On Reduction In Gross Receipts.—

(1) DECREASE OF REDUCTION IN GROSS RECEIPTS NECESSARY TO QUALIFY FOR CREDIT.—Section 2301(c)(2)(B) of the CARES Act is amended—

(A) by striking "50 percent" in clause (i) and inserting "90 percent", and

(B) by striking "80 percent" in clause (ii) and inserting "90 percent".

(2) PHASE-IN OF CREDIT IF REDUCTION IN GROSS RECEIPTS IS LESS THAN 50 PERCENT.—Section 2301(c)(2) of the CARES Act is amended by adding at the end the following new subparagraph:

"(D) PHASE-IN OF CREDIT WHERE BUSINESS NOT SUSPENDED AND RE-DUCTION IN GROSS RECEIPTS LESS THAN 50 PERCENT.—

"(i) IN GENERAL.—In the case of any calendar quarter with respect to which an eligible employer would not be an eligible employer if subparagraph (B)(i) were applied by substituting '50 percent' for '90 percent', the amount of the credit allowed under subsection (a) shall be reduced by the amount which bears the same ratio to the amount of such credit (determined without regard to this subparagraph) as—

"(I) the excess gross receipts percentage point amount, bears to

"(II) 40 percentage points.

"(ii) EXCESS GROSS RECEIPTS PERCENTAGE POINT AMOUNT.—For purposes of this subparagraph, the term 'excess gross receipts percentage point amount' means, with respect to any calendar quarter, the excess of—

"(I) the lowest of the gross receipts percentage point amounts determined with respect to any calendar quarter during the period ending with such calendar quarter and beginning with the first calendar quarter during the period described in subparagraph (B), over

"(II) 50 percentage points.

"(iii) GROSS RECEIPTS PERCENTAGE POINT AMOUNTS.—For purposes of this subparagraph, the term 'gross receipts percentage point amount' means, with respect to any calendar quarter, the percentage (expressed as a number of percentage points) obtained by dividing—

"(I) the gross receipts (within the meaning of subparagraph (B)) for such calendar quarter, by

"(II) the gross receipts for the same calendar quarter in calendar year 2019.".

(3) GROSS RECEIPTS OF TAX-EXEMPT ORGANIZATIONS.—Section 2301(c)(2)(C) of the CARES Act is amended—

(A) by striking "of such Code, clauses (i) and (ii)(I)" and inserting of such Code—

"(i) clauses (i) and (ii)(I)",

(B) by striking the period at the end and inserting ", and", and

(C) by adding at the end the following new clause:

"(ii) any reference in this section to gross receipts shall be treated as a reference to gross receipts within the meaning of section 6033 of such Code.".

(e) Modification Of Treatment Of Health Plan Expenses.—

(1) IN GENERAL.—Section 2301(c)(5) of the CARES Act is amended to read as follows:

"(5) WAGES.—

"(A) IN GENERAL.—The term 'wages' means wages (as defined in section 3121(a) of the Internal Revenue Code of 1986) and compensation (as defined in section 3231(e) of such Code).

"(B) ALLOWANCE FOR CERTAIN HEALTH PLAN EXPENSES.—

"(i) IN GENERAL.—Such term shall include amounts paid or incurred by the eligible employer to provide and maintain a group health plan (as defined in section 5000(b)(1) of the Internal Revenue Code of 1986), but only to the extent that such amounts are excluded from the gross income of employees by reason of section 106(a) of such

Code.

"(ii) ALLOCATION RULES.—For purposes of this section, amounts treated as wages under clause (i) shall be treated as paid with respect to any employee (and with respect to any period) to the extent that such amounts are properly allocable to such employee (and to such period) in such manner as the Secretary may prescribe. Except as otherwise provided by the Secretary, such allocation shall be treated as properly made if made on the basis of being pro rata among periods of coverage.".

(2) CONFORMING AMENDMENT.—Section 2301(c)(3) of the CARES Act is amended by striking subparagraph (C).

(f) Qualified Wages Permitted To Include Amounts For Tip Replacement.—

(1) IN GENERAL.—Section 2301(c)(3)(B) of the CARES Act is amended by inserting "(including tips which would have been deemed to be paid by the employer under section 3121(q))" after "would have been paid".

(2) CONFORMING AMENDMENT.—Section 2301(h)(2) of the CARES Act is amended by inserting "45B or" before "45S".

(g) Certain Governmental Employers Eligible For Credit.—

(1) IN GENERAL.—Section 2301(f) of the CARES Act is amended to read as follows:

"(f) Certain Governmental Employers.—

"(1) IN GENERAL.—The credit under this section shall not be allowed to the Federal Government or any agency or instrumentality thereof.

"(2) EXCEPTION.—Paragraph (1) shall not apply to any organization described in section 501(c)(1) of the Internal Revenue Code of 1986 and exempt from tax under section 501(a) of such Code.

"(3) SPECIAL RULES.—In the case of any State government, Indian tribal government, or any agency, instrumentality, or political subdivision of the foregoing—

"(A) clauses (i) and (ii)(I) of subsection (c)(2)(A) shall apply to all operations of such entity, and

"(B) subclause (II) of subsection (c)(2)(A)(ii) shall not apply.".

(2) COORDINATION WITH APPLICATION OF CERTAIN DEFINITIONS.—

(A) IN GENERAL.—Section 2301(c)(5)(A) of the CARES Act, as amended by the preceding provisions of this Act, is amended by adding at the end the following: "For purposes of the preceding sentence (other than for purposes of subsection (b)(2)), wages as defined in section 3121(a) of the Internal Revenue Code of 1986 shall be determined without regard to paragraphs (1), (5), (6), (7), (8), (10), (13), (18), (19), and (22) of section 3212(b) of such Code (except with respect to services performed in a penal institution by an inmate thereof).".

(B) CONFORMING AMENDMENTS.—Sections 2301(c)(6) of the CARES Act is amended by striking "Any term" and inserting "Except as otherwise provided in this section, any term".

(h) Effective Date.—The amendments made by this section shall take effect as if included in section 2301 of the CARES Act.

PAYROLL CREDIT FOR CERTAIN FIXED EXPENSES OF EMPLOYERS SUBJECT TO CLOSURE BY REASON OF COVID–19

SEC. 20212.

(a) In General.—In the case of an eligible employer, there shall be allowed as a credit against applicable employment taxes for each calendar quarter an amount equal to 50 percent of the qualified fixed expenses paid or incurred by such employer during such calendar quarter.

(b) Limitations And Refundability.—

(1) LIMITATION.—The qualified fixed expenses which may be taken into account under subsection (a) by any eligible employer for any calendar quarter shall not exceed the least of—

(A) the qualified fixed expenses paid by the eligible employer in the same calendar quarter of calendar year 2019,

(B) $50,000, or

(C) the greater of—

(i) 25 percent of the wages paid with respect to the employment of all the employees of the eligible employer for such calendar quarter, or

(ii) 6.25 percent of the gross receipts of the eligible employer for calendar year 2019.

(2) CREDIT LIMITED TO CERTAIN EMPLOYMENT TAXES.—The credit allowed by subsection (a) with respect to any calendar quarter shall not exceed the applicable employment taxes for such calendar quarter (reduced by any credits allowed under subsections (e) and (f) of section 3111 of such Code, sections 7001 and 7003 of the Families First Coronavirus Response Act, section 2301 of the CARES Act, and section 20204 of this division, for such quarter) on the wages paid with respect to the employment of all the employees of the eligible employer for such calendar quarter.

(3) REFUNDABILITY OF EXCESS CREDIT.—

(A) IN GENERAL.—If the amount of the credit under subsection (a) exceeds the limitation of paragraph (2) for any calendar quarter, such excess shall be treated as an overpayment that shall be refunded under sections 6402(a) and 6413(b) of the Internal Revenue Code of 1986.

(B) TREATMENT OF PAYMENTS.—For purposes of section 1324 of title 31, United States Code, any amounts due to an employer under this paragraph shall be treated in the same manner as a refund due from a credit provision referred to in subsection (b)(2) of such section.

(c) Definitions.—For purposes of this section—

(1) APPLICABLE EMPLOYMENT TAXES.—The term "applicable employment taxes" means the following:

(A) The taxes imposed under section 3111(a) of the Internal Revenue Code of 1986.

(B) So much of the taxes imposed under section 3221(a) of such Code as are attributable to the rate in effect under section 3111(a) of such Code.

(2) ELIGIBLE EMPLOYER.—

(A) IN GENERAL.—The term "eligible employer" means any employer—

(i) which was carrying on a trade or business during calendar year 2020,

(ii) which had either—

(I) not more than 1,500 full-time equivalent employees (as determined for purposes of determining whether an employer is an applicable large employer for purposes of section 4980H(c)(2) of the Internal Revenue Code of 1986) for calendar year 2019, or

(II) not more than $41,500,000 of gross receipts in the last taxable year ending in 2019, and

(iii) with respect to any calendar quarter, for which—

(I) the operation of the trade or business described in clause (i) is fully or partially suspended during the calendar quarter due to orders from an appropriate governmental authority limiting commerce, travel, or group meetings (for commercial, social, religious, or other purposes) due to the coronavirus disease 2019 (COVID-19), or

(II) such calendar quarter is within the period described in subparagraph (B).

(B) SIGNIFICANT DECLINE IN GROSS RECEIPTS.—The period described in this subparagraph is the period—

(i) beginning with the first calendar quarter beginning after December 31, 2019, for which gross receipts (within the meaning of section 448(c) of the Internal Revenue Code of 1986) for the calendar quarter are less than 90 percent of gross receipts for the same calendar quarter in the prior year, and

(ii) ending with the calendar quarter following the first calendar quarter beginning after a calendar quarter described in clause (i) for which gross receipts of such employer are greater than 90 percent of gross receipts for the same calendar quarter in the prior year.

(C) TAX-EXEMPT ORGANIZATIONS.—In the case of an organization which is described in section 501(c) of the Internal Revenue Code of 1986 and exempt from tax under section 501(a) of such Code—

(i) clauses (i) and (iii)(I) of subparagraph (A) shall apply to all operations of such organization, and

(ii) any reference in this section to gross receipts shall be treated as a reference to gross receipts within the meaning of section 6033 of the Internal Revenue Code of 1986.

(D) PHASE-IN OF CREDIT WHERE BUSINESS NOT SUSPENDED AND REDUCTION IN GROSS RECEIPTS LESS THAN 50 PERCENT.—

(i) IN GENERAL.—In the case of any calendar quarter with respect to which an eligible employer would not be an eligible employer if subparagraph (B)(i) were applied by substituting "50 percent" for "90 percent", the amount of the credit allowed under subsection (a) shall be reduced by the amount which bears the same ratio to the amount of such credit (determined without regard to this subparagraph) as—

(I) the excess gross receipts percentage point amount, bears to

(II) 40 percentage points.

(ii) EXCESS GROSS RECEIPTS PERCENTAGE POINT AMOUNT.—For purposes of this subparagraph, the term "excess gross receipts percentage point amount" means, with respect to any calendar quarter, the excess of—

(I) the lowest of the gross receipts percentage point amounts determined with respect to any calendar quarter during the period ending with such calendar quarter and beginning with the first calendar quarter during the period described in subparagraph (B), over

(II) 50 percentage points.

(iii) GROSS RECEIPTS PERCENTAGE POINT AMOUNTS.—For purposes of this subparagraph, the term "gross receipts percentage point amount" means, with respect to any calendar quarter, the percentage (expressed as a number of percentage points) obtained by dividing—

(I) the gross receipts (within the meaning of subparagraph (B)) for such calendar quarter, by

(II) the gross receipts for the same calendar quarter in calendar year 2019.

(3) QUALIFIED FIXED EXPENSES.—

(A) IN GENERAL.—The term "qualified fixed expenses" means the payment or accrual, in the ordinary course of the eligible employer's trade or business, of any covered mortgage obligation, covered rent obligation, or covered utility payment. Such term shall not include the prepayment of any obligation for a period in excess of a month unless the payment for such period is customarily due in advance.

(B) APPLICATION OF DEFINITIONS.—The terms "covered mortgage obligation", "covered rent obligation", and "covered utility payment" shall each have the same meaning as when used in section 1106 of the CARES Act.

(4) SECRETARY.—The term "Secretary" means the Secretary of the Treasury or the Secretary's delegate.

(5) WAGES.—

(A) IN GENERAL.—The term "wages" means wages (as defined in section 3121(a) of the Internal Revenue Code of 1986) and compensation (as defined in section 3231(e) of such Code). For purposes of the preceding sentence (other than for purposes of subsection (b)(2)), wages as defined in section 3121(a) of such Code shall be determined without regard to paragraphs (1), (8), (10), (13), (18), (19), and (22) of section 3121(b) of such Code.

(B) ALLOWANCE FOR CERTAIN HEALTH PLAN EXPENSES.—

(i) IN GENERAL.—Such term shall include amounts paid or incurred by the eligible employer to provide and maintain a group health plan (as defined in section 5000(b)(1) of the Internal Revenue Code of 1986), but only to the extent that such amounts are excluded from the gross income of employees by reason of section 106(a) of such Code.

(ii) ALLOCATION RULES.—For purposes of this section, amounts treated as wages under clause (i) shall be treated as paid with respect to any employee (and with respect to any period) to the extent that such amounts are properly allocable to such employee (and to such period) in such manner as the Secretary may prescribe. Except as otherwise provided by the Secretary, such allocation shall be treated as properly made if made on the basis of being pro rata among periods of coverage.

(6) EMPLOYER.—The term "employer" means any employer (as defined in section 3401(d) of such Code) of at least one employee on any day in calendar year 2020.

(7) OTHER TERMS.—Except as otherwise provided in this section, any term used in this section which is also used in chapter 21 or 22 of the Internal Revenue Code of 1986 shall have the same meaning as when used in such chapter.

(d) Aggregation Rule.—All persons treated as a single employer under subsection (a) or (b) of section 52 of the Internal Revenue Code of 1986, or subsection (m) or (o) of section 414 of such Code, shall be treated as one employer for purposes of this section.

(e) Denial Of Double Benefit.—For purposes of chapter 1 of such Code, the gross income of any eligible employer, for the taxable year which includes the last day of any calendar quarter with respect to which a credit is allowed under this section, shall be increased by the amount of such credit.

(f) Certain Governmental Employers.—

(1) IN GENERAL.—The credit under this section shall not be allowed to the Federal Government, the government of any State, of the District of Columbia, or of any possession of the United States, any tribal government, or any political subdivision, agency, or instrumentality of any of the foregoing.

(2) EXCEPTION.—Paragraph (1) shall not apply to any organization described in section 501(c)(1) of the Internal Revenue Code of 1986 and exempt from tax under section 501(a) of such Code.

(g) Election Not To Have Section Apply.—This section shall not apply with respect to any eligible employer for any calendar quarter if such employer elects (at such time and in such manner as the Secretary may prescribe) not to have this section apply.

(h) Transfers To Certain Trust Funds.—There are hereby appropriated to the Federal Old-Age and Survivors Insurance Trust Fund and the Federal Disability Insurance

Trust Fund established under section 201 of the Social Security Act (42 U.S.C. 401) and the Social Security Equivalent Benefit Account established under section 15A(a) of the Railroad Retirement Act of 1974 (45 U.S.C. 231n–1(a)) amounts equal to the reduction in revenues to the Treasury by reason of this section (without regard to this subsection). Amounts appropriated by the preceding sentence shall be transferred from the general fund at such times and in such manner as to replicate to the extent possible the transfers which would have occurred to such Trust Fund or Account had this section not been enacted.

(i) Treatment Of Deposits.—The Secretary shall waive any penalty under section 6656 of such Code for any failure to make a deposit of applicable employment taxes if the Secretary determines that such failure was due to the anticipation of the credit allowed under this section.

(j) Third Party Payors.—Any credit allowed under this section shall be treated as a credit described in section 3511(d)(2) of such Code.

(k) Regulations And Guidance.—The Secretary shall issue such forms, instructions, regulations, and guidance as are necessary—

(1) to allow the advance payment of the credit under subsection (a), subject to the limitations provided in this section, based on such information as the Secretary shall require,

(2) regulations or other guidance to provide for the reconciliation of such advance payment with the amount of the credit at the time of filing the return of tax for the applicable quarter or taxable year,

(3) with respect to the application of the credit under subsection (a) to third party payors (including professional employer organizations, certified professional employer organizations, or agents under section 3504 of the Internal Revenue Code of 1986), including regulations or guidance allowing such payors to submit documentation necessary to substantiate the eligible employer status of employers that use such payors,

(4) for application of subsection (b)(1)(A) and subparagraphs (A)(ii)(II) and (B) of subsection (c)(2) in the case of any employer which was not carrying on a trade or business for all or part of the same calendar quarter in the prior year, and

(5) for recapturing the benefit of credits determined under this section in cases where there is a subsequent adjustment to the credit determined under subsection (a).

(l) Application Of Section.—This section shall apply only to qualified fixed expenses paid or accrued after March 12, 2020, and before January 1, 2021.

BUSINESS INTERRUPTION CREDIT FOR CERTAIN SELF-EMPLOYED INDIVIDUALS

SEC. 20213.
(a) Credit Against Tax.—In the case of an eligible self-employed individual, there shall be allowed as a credit against the tax imposed by chapter 1 of subtitle A of the Internal Revenue Code of 1986 for the taxpayer's first taxable year beginning in 2020 an amount equal to 90 percent of the eligible self-employed individual's qualified self-employment income.

(b) Limitations.—

(1) OVERALL LIMITATION.—The amount of qualified self-employment income taken into account under subsection (a) with respect to any eligible self-employed individual shall not exceed $45,000.

(2) LIMITATION BASED ON MODIFIED ADJUSTED GROSS INCOME.—

(A) IN GENERAL.—The amount of the credit allowed by subsection (a) (after application of paragraph (1)) shall be reduced (but not below zero) by 50 percent of so much of the taxpayer's modified adjusted gross income for the taxpayer's first taxable year beginning in 2020 as exceeds $60,000 ($120,000 in the case of a joint return).

(B) MODIFIED ADJUSTED GROSS INCOME.—For purposes of this section the term "modified adjusted gross income" means adjusted gross income determined without regard to sections 911, 931, and 933 of such Code.

(c) Eligible Self-Employed Individual.—For purposes of this section, the term "eligible self-employed individual" means an individual—

(1) who—

(A) regularly carries on one or more trades or businesses within the meaning of section 1402 of such Code, or

(B) is allocated income or loss described in section 702(a)(8) of such Code from any trade or business carried on by a partnership which is not excluded under section 1402 of such Code, and

(2) for whom gross self-employment income during the first taxable year beginning in 2020 is less than 90 percent of such individual's gross self-employment income during the first taxable year beginning in 2019.

(d) Qualified Self-Employment Income.—For purposes of this section—

(1) IN GENERAL.—The term "qualified self-employment income" means the product of—

(A) the specified gross self-employment income reduction for the first taxable year beginning in 2020, multiplied by

(B) the ratio of—

(i) self-employment income (as determined under section 1402(b) of such Code, but not below zero) for the first taxable year beginning in 2019, divided by

(ii) gross self-employment income for the first taxable year beginning in 2019.

(2) LIMITATION BASED ON MODIFIED ADJUSTED GROSS INCOME.—In the case of any taxpayer, qualified self-employment income shall not exceed the excess (if any) of—

(A) modified adjusted gross income for the first taxable year beginning in 2019, over

(B) modified adjusted gross income for the first taxable year beginning in 2020.

(3) SPECIFIED GROSS SELF-EMPLOYMENT INCOME REDUCTION.—For purposes of paragraph (1), the term "specified gross self-employment income reduction" means, with respect to a taxable year, the excess (if any) of—

(A) 90 percent of gross self-employment income for the taxable year preceding such taxable year, over

(B) gross self-employment income for such taxable year.

(e) Gross Self-Employment Income.—For purposes of this section, the term "gross self-employment income" means, with respect to any taxable year, the sum of—

(1) the eligible self-employed individuals' gross income derived from all trades or business carried on by such individual for purposes of determining net earnings from self-employment under section 1402 of such Code for such taxable year, and

(2) the eligible individual's distributive share of gross income (as determined under section 702(c) of such Code) from any trade or business carried on by a partnership for purposes of determining net earnings from self-employment under section 1402 of such Code (and which is not excluded under such section) for such taxable year.

(f) Special Rules.—

(1) CREDIT REFUNDABLE.—

(A) IN GENERAL.—The credit determined under this section shall be treated as a credit allowed to the taxpayer under subpart C of part IV of subchapter A of chapter 1 of such Code.

(B) TREATMENT OF PAYMENTS.—For purposes of section 1324 of title 31, United States Code, any refund due from the credit allowed under this section shall be treated in the same manner as a refund due from a credit provision referred to in subsection (b)(2) of such section.

(2) DOCUMENTATION.—No credit shall be allowed under this section unless the taxpayer maintains such documentation as the Secretary of the Treasury (or the Secretary's delegate) may prescribe to establish such individual as an eligible self-employed individual.

(3) DENIAL OF DOUBLE BENEFIT.—Qualified self-employment income shall be reduced by—

(A) the qualified sick leave equivalent amount for which a credit is allowed under section 7002(a) of the Families First Coronavirus Response Act and the qualified family leave equivalent amount for which a credit is allowed under section 7004(a) of such Act,

(B) the qualified wages for which a credit is allowed under section 2301 of the CARES Act,

(C) the amount of the credit allowed under section 6432 of the Internal Revenue Code of 1986 (as added by this Act), and

(D) except to the extent taken into account in determining gross self-employment income, amounts from a covered loan under section 7(a)(36) of the Small Business Act that are—

(i) forgiven pursuant to section 1106(b) of the CARES Act, and

(ii) paid or distributed to the eligible self-employed individual as payroll costs described in section 7(a)(36)(A)(viii)(I) of the Small Business Act.

(4) JOINT RETURNS.—

(A) IN GENERAL.—In the case of a joint return, the taxpayer shall be treated for purposes of this section as an eligible self-employed individual if either spouse is an eligible self-employed individual.

(B) APPLICATION OF MODIFIED ADJUSTED GROSS INCOME LIMITATION ON QUALIFIED SELF-EMPLOYMENT INCOME.—If the taxpayer filed a joint return for only one of the taxable years described in subsection (d)(2), such limitation shall apply in such manner as the Secretary of the Treasury (or the Secretary's delegate) may provide.

(5) ELECTION NOT TO HAVE SECTION APPLY.—This section shall not apply with respect to any taxpayer for any taxable year if such taxpayer elects (at such time and in such manner as the Secretary of the Treasury, or the Secretary's delegate, may prescribe) not to have this section apply.

(g) Application Of Credit In Certain Possessions.—

(1) PAYMENTS TO POSSESSIONS WITH MIRROR CODE TAX SYSTEMS.—The Secretary of the Treasury (or the Secretary's delegate) shall pay to each possession of the United States which has a mirror code tax system amounts equal to the loss (if any) to that possession by reason of the application of the provisions of this section. Such amounts shall be determined by the Secretary of the Treasury (or the Secretary's delegate) based on information provided by the government of the respective possession.

(2) PAYMENTS TO OTHER POSSESSIONS.—The Secretary of the Treasury (or the Secretary's delegate) shall pay to each possession of the United States which does not have a mirror code tax system amounts estimated by the Secretary of the Treasury (or the Secretary's delegate) as being equal to the aggregate benefits (if any) that would have been provided to residents of such possession by reason of the provisions of this section if a mirror code tax system had been in effect in such possession. The preceding sentence shall not apply unless the respective possession has a plan, which has been approved by the Secretary of the Treasury (or the Secretary's delegate), under which such possession will promptly distribute such payments to its residents.

(3) MIRROR CODE TAX SYSTEM.—For purposes of this section, the term "mirror code tax system" means, with respect to any possession of the United States, the income tax system of such possession if the income tax liability of the residents of such possession under such system is determined by reference to the income tax laws of the United States as if such possession were the United States.

(4) TREATMENT OF PAYMENTS.—For purposes of section 1324 of title 31, United States Code, the payments under this section shall be treated in the same manner as a refund due from a credit provision referred to in subsection (b)(2) of such section.

(h) Certain Terms.—Any term used in this section which is also used in chapter 2 of the Internal Revenue Code of 1986 shall have the same meaning as when used in such chapter.

(i) Regulations And Guidance.—The Secretary of the Treasury (or the Secretary's delegate) shall issue such forms, instructions, regulations, and guidance as are necessary or appropriate—

(1) to allow the advance payment of the credit under subsection (a) (including allowing use of the anticipated credit to offset estimated taxes) based on the taxpayer's good faith estimates of gross self-employment income and qualified self-employment income for the first taxable year beginning in 2020 and such other information as the Secretary of the Treasury (or the Secretary's delegate) shall require, subject to the limitations provided in this section,

(2) to provide for the reconciliation of such advance payment with the amount of the credit at the time of filing the return of tax for the taxpayer's first taxable year beginning in 2020,

(3) to provide for the application of this section to partners in partnerships, and

(4) to implement the purposes of this section.

Subtitle C—Credits For Paid Sick And Family Leave

EXTENSION OF CREDITS

SEC. 20221.

(a) In General.—Sections 7001(g), 7002(e), 7003(g), and 7004(e) of the Families First Coronavirus Response Act are each amended by striking "2020" and inserting "2021".

(b) Effective Date.—The amendments made by this section shall take effect as if included in the provisions of the Families First Coronavirus Response Act to which they relate.

REPEAL OF REDUCED RATE OF CREDIT FOR CERTAIN LEAVE

SEC. 20222.

(a) Payroll Credit.—Section 7001(b) of the Families First Coronavirus Response Act is amended by inserting "or any day on or after the date of the enactment of the COVID–19 Tax Relief Act of 2020" after "in the case of any day any portion of which is paid sick time described in paragraph (1), (2), or (3) of section 5102(a) of the Emergency Paid Sick Leave Act".

(b) Self-Employed Credit.—

(1) IN GENERAL.—Clauses (i) and (ii) of section 7002(c)(1)(B) of the Families First Coronavirus Response Act are each amended by inserting inserting "or any day on or after the date of the enactment of the COVID–19 Tax Relief Act of 2020" after "in the case of any day any portion of which is paid sick time described in paragraph (1), (2), or (3) of section 5102(a) of the Emergency Paid Sick Leave Act".

(2) CONFORMING AMENDMENT.—Section 7002(d)(3) of the Families First Coronavirus Response Act is amended by inserting inserting "or any day on or after the date of the enactment of the COVID–19 Tax Relief Act of 2020" after "in the case of any day any portion of which is paid sick time described in paragraph (1), (2), or (3) of section 5102(a) of the Emergency Paid Sick Leave Act".

(c) Effective Date.—The amendments made by this section shall apply to days on or after the date of the enactment of this Act.

INCREASE IN LIMITATIONS ON CREDITS FOR PAID FAMILY LEAVE

SEC. 20223.

(a) Increase In Overall Limitation On Qualified Family Leave Wages.—

(1) IN GENERAL.—Section 7003(b)(1)(B) of the Families First Coronavirus Response Act is amended by striking "$10,000" and inserting "$12,000".

(2) CONFORMING AMENDMENT.—Section 7004(d)(3) of the Families First Coronavirus Response Act is amended by striking "$10,000" and inserting "$12,000".

(b) Increase In Qualified Family Leave Equivalent Amount For Self-Employed Individuals.—Section 7004(c)(1)(A) of the Families First Coronavirus Response Act is amended by striking "50" and inserting "60".

(c) Effective Date.—The amendments made by this section shall take effect as if included in the provisions of the Families First Coronavirus Response Act to which they relate.

ELECTION TO USE PRIOR YEAR NET EARNINGS FROM SELF-EMPLOYMENT IN DETERMINING AVERAGE DAILY SELF-EMPLOYMENT INCOME

SEC. 20224.

(a) Credit For Sick Leave.—Section 7002(c) of the Families First Coronavirus Response Act is amended by adding at the end the following new paragraph:

"(4) ELECTION TO USE PRIOR YEAR NET EARNINGS FROM SELF-EMPLOYMENT INCOME.—In the case of an individual who elects (at such time and in such manner as the Secretary, or the Secretary's delegate, may provide) the application of this paragraph, paragraph (2)(A) shall be applied by substituting 'the prior taxable year' for 'the taxable year'".

(b) Credit For Family Leave.—Section 7004(c) of the Families First Coronavirus Response Act is amended by adding at the end the following new paragraph:

"(4) ELECTION TO USE PRIOR YEAR NET EARNINGS FROM SELF-EMPLOYMENT INCOME.—In the case of an individual who elects (at such time and in such manner as the Secretary, or the Secretary's delegate, may provide) the application of this paragraph, paragraph (2)(A) shall be applied by substituting 'the prior taxable year' for 'the taxable year'".

(c) Effective Date.—The amendments made by this section shall take effect as if included in the provisions of the Families First Coronavirus Response Act to which they relate.

FEDERAL, STATE, AND LOCAL GOVERNMENTS ALLOWED TAX CREDITS FOR PAID SICK AND PAID FAMILY AND MEDICAL LEAVE

SEC. 20225.

(a) In General.—Sections 7001(e) and 7003(e) of the Families First Coronavirus Response Act are each amended by striking paragraph (4).

(b) Coordination With Application Of Certain Definitions.—

(1) IN GENERAL.—Sections 7001(c) and 7003(c) of the Families First Coronavirus Response Act are each amended—

(A) by inserting ", determined without regard to paragraphs (1) through (22) of section 3121(b) of such Code " after "as defined in section 3121(a) of the Internal Revenue Code of 1986", and

(B) by inserting ", determined without regard to the sentence in paragraph (1) thereof which begins 'Such term does include remuneration'" after "as defined in section 3231(e) of the Internal Revenue Code".

(2) CONFORMING AMENDMENTS.—Sections 7001(e)(3) and 7003(e)(3) of the Families First Coronavirus Response Act are each amended by striking "Any term" and inserting "Except as otherwise provided in this section, any term".

(c) Effective Date.—The amendments made by this section shall take effect as if included in the provisions of the Families First Coronavirus Response Act to which they relate.

CERTAIN TECHNICAL IMPROVEMENTS

SEC. 20226.

(a) Coordination With Exclusion From Employment Taxes.—Sections 7001(c) and 7003(c) of the Families First Coronavirus Response Act, as amended by the preceding provisions of this Act, are each amended—

(1) by inserting "and section 7005(a) of this Act," after "determined without regard to paragraphs (1) through (22) of section 3121(b) of such Code", and

(2) by inserting "and without regard to section 7005(a) of this Act" after "which begins 'Such term does not include remuneration'".

(b) Clarification Of Applicable Railroad Retirement Tax For Paid Leave Credits.— Sections 7001(e) and 7003(e) of the Families First Coronavirus Response Act, as amended by the preceding provisions of this Act, are each amended by adding at the end the following new paragraph:

"(4) REFERENCES TO RAILROAD RETIREMENT TAX.—Any reference in this section to the tax imposed by section 3221(a) of the Internal Revenue Code of 1986 shall be treated as a reference to so much of such tax as is attributable to the rate in effect under section 3111(a) of such Code.".

(c) Clarification Of Treatment Of Paid Leave For Applicable Railroad Retirement Tax.—Section 7005(a) of the Families First Coronavirus Response Act is amended by adding the following sentence at the end of such subsection: "Any reference in this subsection to the tax imposed by section 3221(a) of such Code shall be treated as a reference to so much of the tax as is attributable to the rate in effect under section 3111(a) of such Code."

(d) Clarification Of Applicable Railroad Retirement Tax For Hospital Insurance Tax Credit.—Section 7005(b)(1) of the Families First Coronavirus Response Act is amended as follows:

"(1) IN GENERAL.—The credit allowed by section 7001 and the credit allowed by section 7003 shall each be increased by the amount of the tax imposed by section 3111(b) of the Internal Revenue Code of 1986 and so much of the taxes imposed under section 3221(a) of such Code as are attributable to the rate in effect under section 3111(b) of such Code on qualified sick leave wages, or qualified family leave wages, for which credit is allowed under such section 7001 or 7003 (respectively).".

(e) Effective Date.—The amendments made by this section shall take effect as if included in the provisions of the Families First Coronavirus Response Act to which they relate.

CREDITS NOT ALLOWED TO CERTAIN LARGE EMPLOYERS

SEC. 20227.

(a) Credit For Required Paid Sick Leave.—

(1) IN GENERAL.—Section 7001(a) of the Families First Coronavirus Response Act is amended by striking "In the case of an employer" and inserting "In the case of an eligible employer".

(2) ELIGIBLE EMPLOYER.—Section 7001(c) of the Families First Coronavirus Response Act, as amended by the preceding provisions of this Act, is amended by striking "For purposes of this section, the term" and all that precedes it and inserting the following:

"(c) Definitions.—For purposes of this section—

"(1) ELIGIBLE EMPLOYER.—The term 'eligible employer' means any employer other than an applicable large employer (as defined in section 4980H(c)(2), determined by substituting '500' for '50' each place it appears in subparagraphs (A) and (B) thereof and without regard to subparagraphs (D) and (F) thereof). For purposes of the preceding sentence, the Government of the United States, the government of any State or political subdivision thereof, or any agency or instrumentality of any of the foregoing shall not be treated as an applicable large employer.

"(2) QUALIFIED SICK LEAVE WAGES.—The term".

(b) Credit For Required Paid Family Leave.—

(1) IN GENERAL.—Section 7003(a) of the Families First Coronavirus Response Act is amended by striking "In the case of an employer" and inserting "In the case of an eligible employer".

(2) ELIGIBLE EMPLOYER.—Section 7003(c) of the Families First Coronavirus Response Act, as amended by the preceding provisions of this Act, is amended by striking "For purposes of this section, the term" and all that precedes it and inserting the following:

"(c) Definitions.—For purposes of this section—

"(1) ELIGIBLE EMPLOYER.—The term 'eligible employer' means any employer other than an applicable large employer (as defined in section 4980H(c)(2), determined by substituting '500' for '50' each place it appears in subparagraphs (A) and (B) thereof and without regard to subparagraphs (D) and (F) thereof). For purposes of the preceding sentence, the Government of the United States, the government of any State or political subdivision thereof, or any agency or instrumentality of any of the foregoing, shall not be treated as an applicable large employer.

"(2) QUALIFIED FAMILY LEAVE WAGES.—The term".

(c) Effective Date.—The amendments made by this section shall apply to wages paid after the date of the enactment of this Act.

Subtitle D—Other Relief

PAYROLL TAX DEFERRAL ALLOWED FOR RECIPIENTS OF CERTAIN LOAN FORGIVENESS

SEC. 20231.

(a) In General.—Section 2302(a) of the CARES Act is amended by striking paragraph (3).

(b) Effective Date.—The amendment made by this section shall take effect as if included in section 2302 of the CARES Act.

EMERGENCY FINANCIAL AID GRANTS

SEC. 20232.

(a) In General.—In the case of a student receiving a qualified emergency financial aid grant—

(1) such grant shall not be included in the gross income of such individual for purposes of the Internal Revenue Code of 1986, and

(2) such grant shall not be treated as described in subparagraph (A), (B), or (C) of section 25A(g)(2) of such Code.

(b) Definitions.—For purposes of this subsection, the term "qualified emergency financial aid grant" means—

(1) any emergency financial aid grant awarded by an institution of higher education under section 3504 of the CARES Act,

(2) any emergency financial aid grant from an institution of higher education made with funds made available under section 18004 of the CARES Act, and

(3) any other emergency financial aid grant made to a student from a Federal agency, a State, an Indian tribe, an institution of higher education, or a scholarship-granting organization (including a tribal organization, as defined in section 4 of the Indian Self-Determination and Education Assistance Act (25 U.S.C.5304)) for the purpose of providing financial relief to students enrolled at institutions of higher education in response to a qualifying emergency (as defined in section 3502(a)(4) of the CARES Act).

(c) Limitation.—This section shall not apply to that portion of any amount received which represents payment for teaching, research, or other services required as a condition for receiving the qualified emergency financial aid grant.

(d) Effective Date.—This section shall apply to qualified emergency financial aid grants made after March 26, 2020.

CERTAIN LOAN FORGIVENESS AND OTHER BUSINESS FINANCIAL ASSISTANCE UNDER CARES ACT NOT INCLUDIBLE IN GROSS INCOME

SEC. 20233.

(a) United States Treasury Program Management Authority.—For purposes of the Internal Revenue Code of 1986, no amount shall be included in gross income by reason of loan forgiveness described in section 1109(d)(2)(D) of the CARES Act.

(b) Emergency EIDL Grants.—For purposes of the Internal Revenue Code of 1986, any advance described in section 1110(e) of the CARES Act shall not be included in the gross income of the person that receives such advance.

(c) Subsidy For Certain Loan Payments.—For purposes of the Internal Revenue Code of 1986, any payment described in section 1112(c) of the CARES Act shall not be included in the gross income of the person on whose behalf such payment is made.

(d) Effective Date.—Subsections (a), (b), and (c) shall apply to taxable years ending after the date of the enactment of the CARES Act.

AUTHORITY TO WAIVE CERTAIN INFORMATION REPORTING REQUIRE-
MENTS

SEC. 20234.

The Secretary of the Treasury (or the Secretary's delegate) may provide an exception from any requirement to file an information return otherwise required by chapter 61 of the Internal Revenue Code of 1986 with respect to any amount excluded from gross income by reason of section 1106(i) of the CARES Act or section 20232 or 20233 of this Act.

CLARIFICATION OF TREATMENT OF EXPENSES PAID OR INCURRED WITH PROCEEDS FROM CERTAIN GRANTS AND LOANS

SEC. 20235.

(a) In General.—For purposes of the Internal Revenue Code of 1986 and notwithstanding any other provision of law, any deduction and the basis of any property shall be determined without regard to whether any amount is excluded from gross income under section 20233 of this Act or section 1106(i) of the CARES Act.

(b) Clarification Of Exclusion Of Loan Forgiveness.—Section 1106(i) of the CARES Act is amended to read as follows:

"(i) Taxability.—For purposes of the Internal Revenue Code of 1986, no amount shall be included in the gross income of the eligible recipient by reason of forgiveness of indebtedness described in subsection (b).".

(c) Effective Date.—Subsection (a) and the amendment made by subsection (b) shall apply to taxable years ending after the date of the enactment of the CARES Act.

REINSTATEMENT OF CERTAIN PROTECTIONS FOR TAXPAYER RETURN INFORMATION

SEC. 20236.

(a) In General.—Section 6103(a)(3) of the Internal Revenue Code of 1986, as amended by section 3516 of the CARES Act, is amended by striking "(13)(A), (13)(B), (13)(C), (13)(D)(i), (16)" and inserting "(13), (16)".

(b) Records Requirements.—Section 6103(p)(3)(A) of such Code, as so amended, is amended by striking "(12), (13)(A), (13)(B), (13)(C), (13)(D)(i)" and inserting "(12),".

(c) Application Of Safeguards.—Section 6103(p)(4) of such Code, as so amended, is amended by striking "(13)(A), (13)(B), (13)(C), (13)(D)(i)" each place it appears and inserting "(13)".

(d) Effective Date.—The amendments made by this section shall apply to disclosures made after the date of the enactment of the FUTURE Act (Public Law 116–91).

TITLE III

—NET OPERATING LOSSES

LIMITATION ON EXCESS BUSINESS LOSSES OF NON-CORPORATE TAXPAYERS RESTORED AND MADE PERMANENT

SEC. 20301.

(a) In General.—Section 461(l)(1) of the Internal Revenue Code of 1986 is amended to read as follows:

"(1) LIMITATION.—In the case of a taxpayer other than a corporation, any excess business loss of the taxpayer shall not be allowed.".

(b) Farming Losses.—Section 461 of such Code is amended by striking subsection (j).

(c) Effective Date.—The amendments made by this section shall apply to taxable years beginning after December 31, 2017.

CERTAIN TAXPAYERS ALLOWED CARRYBACK OF NET OPERATING LOSSES ARISING IN 2019 AND 2020

SEC. 20302.

(a) Carryback Of Losses Arising In 2019 And 2020.—

(1) IN GENERAL.—Section 172(b)(1)(D)(i) of the Internal Revenue Code of 1986 is amended to read as follows:

"(i) IN GENERAL.—In the case of any net operating loss arising in a taxable year beginning after December 31, 2018, and before January 1, 2021, and to which subparagraphs (B) and (C)(i) do not apply, such loss shall be a net operating loss carryback to each taxable year preceding the taxable year of such loss, but not to any taxable year beginning before January 1, 2018.".

(2) CONFORMING AMENDMENTS.—

(A) The heading for section 172(b)(1)(D) of such Code is amended by striking "2018, 2019, AND" and inserting "2019 AND".

(B) Section 172(b)(1)(D) of such Code is amended by striking clause (iii) and by redesignating clauses (iv) and (v) as clauses (iii) and (iv), respectively.

(C) Section 172(b)(1)(D)(iii) of such Code, as so redesignated, is amended by striking "(i)(I)" and inserting "(i)".

(D) Section 172(b)(1)(D)(iv) of such Code, as so redesignated, is amended—

(i) by striking "If the 5-year carryback period under clause (i)(I)" in subclause (I) and inserting "If the carryback period under clause (i)", and

(ii) by striking "2018 or" in subclause (II).

(b) Disallowed For Certain Taxpayers.—Section 172(b)(1)(D) of such Code, as amended by the preceding provisions of this Act, is amended by adding at the end the following new clauses:

"(v) CARRYBACK DISALLOWED FOR CERTAIN TAXPAYERS.—Clause (i) shall not apply with respect to any loss arising in a taxable year in which—

"(I) the taxpayer (or any related person) is not allowed a deduction under this chapter for the taxable year by reason of section 162(m) or section 280G, or

"(II) the taxpayer (or any related person) is a specified corporation for the taxable year.

"(vi) SPECIFIED CORPORATION.—For purposes of clause (v)—

"(I) IN GENERAL.—The term 'specified corporation' means, with respect to any taxable year, a corporation the aggregate distributions (including redemptions) of which during all taxable years ending after December 31, 2017, exceed the sum of applicable stock issued of such corporation and 5 percent of the fair market value of the stock of such corporation as of the last day of the taxable year.

"(II) APPLICABLE STOCK ISSUED.—The term 'applicable stock issued' means, with respect to any corporation, the aggregate fair market value of stock (as of the issue date of such stock) issued by the corporation during all taxable years ending after December 31, 2017, in exchange for money or property other than stock in such corporation.

"(III) CERTAIN PREFERRED STOCK DISREGARDED.—For purposes of subclause (I), stock described in section 1504(a)(4), and distributions (including redemptions) with respect to such stock, shall be disregarded.

"(vii) RELATED PERSON.—For purposes of clause (v), a person is a related person to a taxpayer if the related person bears a relationship to the taxpayer specified in section 267(b) or section 707(b)(1).".

(c) Effective Date.—The amendments made by this section shall take effect as if included in the enactment of section 2302(b) of the Coronavirus Aid, Relief, and Economic Security Act.

DIVISION C—HEALTH PROVISIONS

TITLE I

—MEDICAID PROVISIONS

COVID–19-RELATED TEMPORARY INCREASE OF MEDICAID FMAP

SEC. 30101.

(a) In General.—Section 6008 of the Families First Coronavirus Response Act (42 U.S.C. 1396d note) is amended—

(1) in subsection (a)—

(A) by inserting "(or, if later, June 30, 2021)" after "last day of such emergency period occurs"; and

(B) by striking "6.2 percentage points." and inserting "the percentage points specified in subsection (e). In no case may the application of this section result in the Federal medical assistance percentage determined for a State being more than 95 percent."; and

(2) by adding at the end the following new subsections:

"(e) Specified Percentage Points.—For purposes of subsection (a), the percentage points specified in this subsection are—

"(1) for each calendar quarter occurring during the period beginning on the first day of the emergency period described in paragraph (1)(B) of section 1135(g) of the Social Security Act (42 U.S.C. 1320b-5(g)) and ending on June 30, 2020, 6.2 percentage points;

"(2) for each calendar quarter occurring during the period beginning on July 1, 2020, and ending on June 30, 2021, 14 percentage points; and

"(3) for each calendar quarter, if any, occurring during the period beginning on July 1, 2021, and ending on the last day of the calendar quarter in which the last day of such emergency period occurs, 6.2 percentage points.

"(f) Clarifications.—

"(1) In the case of a State that treats an individual described in subsection (b)(3) as eligible for the benefits described in such subsection, for the period described in subsection (a), expenditures for medical assistance and administrative costs attributable to such individual that would not otherwise be included as expenditures under section 1903 of the Social Security Act shall be regarded as expenditures under the State plan approved under title XIX of the Social Security Act or for administration of such State plan.

"(2) The limitations on payment under subsections (f) and (g) of section 1108 of the Social Security Act (42 U.S.C. 1308) shall not apply to Federal payments made under section 1903(a)(1) of the Social Security Act (42 U.S.C. 1396b(a)(1)) attributable to the increase in the Federal medical assistance percentage under this section.

"(3) Expenditures attributable to the increased Federal medical assistance percentage under this section shall not be counted for purposes of the limitations under section 2104(b)(4) of such Act (42 U.S.C. 1397dd(b)(4)).

"(g) Scope Of Application.—An increase in the Federal medical assistance percentage for a State under this section shall not be taken into account for purposes of payments under part D of title IV of the Social Security Act (42 U.S.C. 651 et seq.).".

(b) Effective Date.—The amendments made by subsection (a) shall take effect and apply as if included in the enactment of section 6008 of the Families First Coronavirus Response Act (Public Law 116–127).

LIMITATION ON ADDITIONAL SECRETARIAL ACTION WITH RESPECT TO MEDICAID SUPPLEMENTAL PAYMENTS REPORTING REQUIREMENTS

SEC. 30102.

(a) In General.—Notwithstanding any other provision of law, during the period that begins on the date of enactment of this section and ends on the last day of the emergency period described in paragraph (1)(B) of section 1135(g) of the Social Security Act (42 U.S.C. 1320b–5(g)), the Secretary of Health and Human Services shall not take any action (through promulgation of regulation, issue of regulatory guidance, or otherwise) to—

(1) finalize or otherwise implement provisions contained in the proposed rule published on November 18, 2019, on pages 63722 through 63785 of volume 84, Federal Register (relating to parts 430, 433, 447, 455, and 457 of title 42, Code of Federal Regulations); or

(2) promulgate or implement any rule or provision similar to the provisions described in paragraph (1) pertaining to the Medicaid program established under title XIX of the Social Security Act (42 U.S.C. 1396 et seq.) or the State Children's Health Insurance Program established under title XXI of such Act (42 U.S.C. 1397aa et seq.).

(b) Continuation Of Other Secretarial Authority.—Nothing in this section shall be construed as prohibiting the Secretary during the period described in subsection (a) from taking any action (through promulgation of regulation, issuance of regulatory guidance, or other administrative action) to enforce a provision of law in effect as of the date of enactment of this section with respect to the Medicaid program established under title XIX of the Social Security Act (42 U.S.C. 1396 et seq.) or the State Children's Health Insurance Program established under title XXI of such Act (42 U.S.C. 1397aa et seq.), or to promulgate or implement a new rule or provision during such period with respect to such programs, other than a rule or provision described in subsection (a) and subject to the prohibition set forth in that subsection.

ADDITIONAL SUPPORT FOR MEDICAID HOME AND COMMUNITY-BASED SERVICES DURING THE COVID–19 EMERGENCY PERIOD

SEC. 30103.

(a) Increased FMAP.—

(1) IN GENERAL.—Notwithstanding section 1905(b) of the Social Security Act (42 U.S.C. 1396d(b)), in the case of an HCBS program State, the Federal medical assistance percentage determined for the State under section 1905(b) of such Act and, if applicable, increased under subsection (y), (z), or (aa) of section 1905 of such Act (42 U.S.C. 1396d), section 1915(k) of such Act (42 U.S.C. 1396n(k)), or section 6008(a) of the Families First Coronavirus Response Act (Public Law 116–127), shall be increased by 10 percentage points with respect to expenditures of the State under the State Medicaid program for home and community-based services that are provided during the HCBS program improvement period. In no case may the application of the previous sentence result in the Federal medical assistance percentage determined

for a State being more than 95 percent.

(2) DEFINITIONS.—In this section:

(A) HCBS PROGRAM IMPROVEMENT PERIOD.—The term "HCBS program improvement period" means, with respect to a State, the period—

(i) beginning on July 1, 2020; and

(ii) ending on June 30, 2021.

(B) HCBS PROGRAM STATE.—The term "HCBS program State" means a State that meets the condition described in subsection (b) by submitting an application described in such subsection, which is approved by the Secretary pursuant to subsection (c).

(C) HOME AND COMMUNITY-BASED SERVICES.—The term "home and community-based services" means home health care services authorized under paragraph (7) of section 1905(a) of the Social Security Act (42 U.S.C. 1396d(a)), personal care services authorized under paragraph (24) of such section, PACE services authorized under paragraph (26) of such section, services authorized under subsections (b), (c), (i), (j), and (k) of section 1915 of such Act (42 U.S.C. 1396n), such services authorized under a waiver under section 1115 of such Act (42 U.S.C. 1315), and such other services specified by the Secretary.

(b) Condition.—The condition described in this subsection, with respect to a State, is that the State submits an application to the Secretary, at such time and in such manner as specified by the Secretary, that includes, in addition to such other information as the Secretary shall require—

(1) a description of which activities described in subsection (d) that a state plans to implement and a description of how it plans to implement such activities;

(2) assurances that the Federal funds attributable to the increase under subsection (a) will be used—

(A) to implement the activities described in subsection (d); and

(B) to supplement, and not supplant, the level of State funds expended for home and community-based services for eligible individuals through programs in effect as of the date of the enactment of this section; and

(3) assurances that the State will conduct adequate oversight and ensure the validity of such data as may be required by the Secretary.

(c) Approval Of Application.—Not later than 90 days after the date of submission of an application of a State under subsection (b), the Secretary shall certify if the application is complete. Upon certification that an application of a State is complete, the application shall be deemed to be approved for purposes of this section.

(d) Activities To Improve The Delivery Of HCBS.—

(1) IN GENERAL.—A State shall work with community partners, such as Area Agencies on Aging, Centers for Independent Living, non-profit home and community-based services providers, and other entities providing home and community-based services, to implement—

(A) the purposes described in paragraph (2) during the COVID–19 public health emergency period; and

(B) the purposes described in paragraph (3) after the end of such emergency period.

(2) FOCUSED AREAS OF HCBS IMPROVEMENT.—The purposes described in this paragraph, with respect to a State, are the following:

(A) To increase rates for home health agencies and agencies that employ direct support professionals (including independent providers in a self-directed or consumer-directed model) to provide home and community-based services under the State Medicaid program, provided that any agency or individual that receives payment under such an increased rate increases the compensation it pays its home health workers or direct support professionals.

(B) To provide paid sick leave, paid family leave, and paid medical leave for home health workers and direct support professionals.

(C) To provide hazard pay, overtime pay, and shift differential pay for home health workers and direct support professionals.

(D) To provide home and community-based services to eligible individuals who are on waiting lists for programs approved under sections 1115 or 1915 of the Social Security Act (42 U.S.C. 1315, 1396n).

(E) To purchase emergency supplies and equipment, which may include items not typically covered under the Medicaid program, such as personal protective equipment, necessary to enhance access to services and to protect the health and well-being of home health workers and direct support professionals.

(F) To pay for the travel of home health workers and direct support professionals to conduct home and community-based services.

(G) To recruit new home health workers and direct support professionals.

(H) To support family care providers of eligible individuals with needed supplies and equipment, which may include items not typically covered under the Medicaid program, such as personal protective equipment, and pay.

(I) To pay for training for home health workers and direct support professionals that is specific to the COVID–19 public health emergency.

(J) To pay for assistive technologies, staffing, and other costs incurred during the COVID–19 public health emergency period in order to facilitate community integration and ensure an individual's person-centered service plan continues to be fully implemented.

(K) To prepare information and public health and educational materials in accessible formats (including formats accessible to people with low literacy or intellectual disabilities) about prevention, treatment, recovery and other aspects of COVID–19 for eligible individuals, their families, and the general community served by agencies described in subparagraph (A).

(L) To pay for American sign language interpreters to assist in providing home and community-based services to eligible individuals and to inform the general public about COVID–19.

(M) To allow day services providers to provide home and community-based services.

(N) To pay for other expenses deemed appropriate by the Secretary to enhance, expand, or strengthen Home and Community-Based Services, including retainer payments, and expenses which meet the criteria of the home and community-based settings rule published on January 16, 2014.

(3) PERMISSIBLE USES AFTER THE EMERGENCY PERIOD.—The purpose described in this paragraph, with respect to a State, is to assist eligible individuals who had to relocate to a nursing facility or institutional setting from their homes during the COVID–19 public health emergency period in—

(A) moving back to their homes (including by paying for moving costs, first month's rent, and other one-time expenses and start-up costs);

(B) resuming home and community-based services;

(C) receiving mental health services and necessary rehabilitative service to regain skills lost while relocated during the public health emergency period; and

(D) while funds attributable to the increased FMAP under this section remain available, continuing home and community-based services for eligible individuals who were served from a waiting list for such services during the public health emergency period.

(e) Reporting Requirements.—

(1) STATE REPORTING REQUIREMENTS.—Not later than December 31, 2022, any State with respect to which an application is approved by the Secretary pursuant to subsection (c) shall submit a report to the Secretary that contains the following information:

(A) Activities and programs that were funded using Federal funds attributable to such increase.

(B) The number of eligible individuals who were served by such activities and programs.

(C) The number of eligible individuals who were able to resume home and community-based services as a result of such activities and programs.

(2) HHS EVALUATION.—

(A) IN GENERAL.—The Secretary shall evaluate the implementation and outcomes of this section in the aggregate using an external evaluator with experience evaluating home and community-based services, disability programs, and older adult programs.

(B) EVALUATION CRITERIA.—For purposes of subparagraph (A), the external evaluator shall—

(i) document and evaluate changes in access, availability, and quality of home and community-based services in each HCBS program State;

(ii) document and evaluate aggregate changes in access, availability, and quality of home and community-based services across all such States; and

(iii) evaluate the implementation and outcomes of this section based on—

(I) the impact of this section on increasing funding for home and community-based services;

(II) the impact of this section on achieving targeted access, availability, and quality of home and community-based services; and

(III) promising practices identified by activities conducted pursuant to subsection (d) that increase access to, availability of, and quality of home and community-based services.

(C) DISSEMINATION OF EVALUATION FINDINGS.—The Secretary shall—

(i) disseminate the findings from the evaluations conducted under this paragraph to—

(I) all State Medicaid directors; and

(II) the Committee on Energy and Commerce of the House of Representatives, the Committee on Finance of the Senate, and the Special Committee on Aging of the Senate; and

(ii) make all evaluation findings publicly available in an accessible electronic format and any other accessible format determined appropriate by the Secretary.

(D) OVERSIGHT.—Each State with respect to which an application is approved by the Secretary pursuant to subsection (c) shall ensure adequate oversight of the expenditure of Federal funds pursuant to such increase in accordance with the Medicaid regulations, including section 1115 and 1915 waiver regulations and special terms and conditions for any relevant waiver or grant program.

(3) NON-APPLICATION OF THE PAPERWORK REDUCTION ACT.—Chapter 35

of title 44, United States Code (commonly referred to as the "Paperwork Reduction Act of 1995"), shall not apply to the provisions of this subsection.

(f) Additional Definitions.—In this section:

(1) COVID–19 PUBLIC HEALTH EMERGENCY PERIOD.—The term "COVID–19 public health emergency period" means the portion of the emergency period described in paragraph (1)(B) of section 1135(g) of the Social Security Act (42 U.S.C. 1320b–5(g)) beginning on or after the date of the enactment of this Act.

(2) ELIGIBLE INDIVIDUAL.—The term "eligible individual" means an individual who is eligible for or enrolled for medical assistance under a State Medicaid program.

(3) MEDICAID PROGRAM.—The term "Medicaid program" means, with respect to a State, the State program under title XIX of the Social Security Act (42 U.S.C. 1396 et seq.) (including any waiver or demonstration under such title or under section 1115 of such Act (42 U.S.C. 1315) relating to such title).

(4) SECRETARY.—The term "Secretary" means the Secretary of Health and Human Services.

(5) STATE.—The term "State" has the meaning given such term for purposes of title XIX of the Social Security Act (42 U.S.C. 1396 et seq.).

COVERAGE AT NO COST SHARING OF COVID–19 VACCINE AND TREATMENT

SEC. 30104.

(a) Medicaid.—

(1) IN GENERAL.—Section 1905(a)(4) of the Social Security Act (42 U.S.C. 1396d(a)(4)) is amended—

(A) by striking "and (D)" and inserting "(D)"; and

(B) by striking the semicolon at the end and inserting "; (E) during the portion of the emergency period described in paragraph (1)(B) of section 1135(g) beginning on the date of the enactment of the HEROES Act, a COVID–19 vaccine licensed under section 351 of the Public Health Service Act, or approved or authorized under sections 505 or 564 of the Federal Food, Drug, and Cosmetic Act, and administration of the vaccine; (F) during such portion of the emergency period described in paragraph (1)(B) of section 1135(g), items or services for the prevention or treatment of COVID–19, including drugs approved or authorized under such section 505 or such section 564 or, without regard to the requirements of section 1902(a)(10)(B) (relating to comparability), in the case of an individual who is diagnosed with or presumed to have COVID–19, during such portion of such emergency period during which such individual is infected (or presumed infected) with COVID–19, the treatment of a condition that may complicate the treatment of COVID–19;".

(2) PROHIBITION OF COST SHARING.—

(A) IN GENERAL.—Subsections (a)(2) and (b)(2) of section 1916 of the Social Security Act (42 U.S.C. 1396o) are each amended—

(i) in subparagraph (F), by striking "or" at the end;

(ii) in subparagraph (G), by striking "; and" and inserting ", or"; and

(iii) by adding at the end the following subparagraphs:

"(H) during the portion of the emergency period described in paragraph (1)(B) of section 1135(g) beginning on the date of the enactment of this subparagraph, a COVID–19 vaccine licensed under section 351 of the Public Health Service Act, or approved or authorized under section 505 or 564 of the Federal Food, Drug, and Cosmetic Act, and the administration of such vaccine, or

"(I) during such portion of the emergency period described in paragraph (1)(B) of section 1135(g), any item or service furnished for the treatment of COVID–19, including drugs approved or authorized under such section 505 or such section 564 or, in the case of an individual who is diagnosed with or presumed to have COVID–19, during the portion of such emergency period during which such individual is infected (or presumed infected) with COVID–19, the treatment of a condition that may complicate the treatment of COVID–19; and".

(B) APPLICATION TO ALTERNATIVE COST SHARING.—Section 1916A(b)(3)(B) of the Social Security Act (42 U.S.C. 1396o–1(b)(3)(B)) is amended—

(i) in clause (xi), by striking "any visit" and inserting "any service"; and

(ii) by adding at the end the following clauses:

"(xii) During the portion of the emergency period described in paragraph (1)(B) of section 1135(g) beginning on the date of the enactment of this clause, a COVID–19 vaccine licensed under section 351 of the Public Health Service Act, or approved or authorized under section 505 or 564 of the Federal Food, Drug, and Cosmetic Act, and the administration of such vaccine.

"(xiii) During such portion of the emergency period described in paragraph (1)(B) of section 1135(g), an item or service furnished for the treatment of COVID–19, including drugs approved or authorized under such section 505 or such section 564 or, in the case of an individual who is diagnosed with or presumed to have COVID–19, during such portion of such emergency period during which such individual is infected (or presumed infected) with COVID–19, the treatment of a condition that may complicate the treatment of COVID–19.".

(C) CLARIFICATION.—The amendments made by this subsection shall apply with respect to a State plan of a territory in the same manner as a State plan of one of the 50 States.

(b) State Pediatric Vaccine Distribution Program.—Section 1928 of the Social Security Act (42 U.S.C. 1396s) is amended—

(1) in subsection (a)(1)—

(A) in subparagraph (A), by striking "; and" and inserting a semicolon;

(B) in subparagraph (B), by striking the period and inserting "; and"; and

(C) by adding at the end the following subparagraph:

"(C) during the portion of the emergency period described in paragraph (1)(B) of section 1135(g) beginning on the date of the enactment of this subparagraph, each vaccine-eligible child (as defined in subsection (b)) is entitled to receive a COVID–19 vaccine from a program-registered provider (as defined in subsection (h)(7)) without charge for—

"(i) the cost of such vaccine; or

"(ii) the administration of such vaccine.";

(2) in subsection (c)(2)—

(A) in subparagraph (C)(ii), by inserting ", but, during the portion of the emergency period described in paragraph (1)(B) of section 1135(g) beginning on the date of the enactment of the HEROES Act, may not impose a fee for the administration of a COVID–19 vaccine" before the period; and

(B) by adding at the end the following subparagraph:

"(D) The provider will provide and administer an approved COVID–19 vaccine to a vaccine-eligible child in accordance with the same requirements as apply under the preceding subparagraphs to the provision and administration of a qualified pediatric vaccine to such a child."; and

(3) in subsection (d)(1), in the first sentence, by inserting ", including, during the portion of the emergency period described in paragraph (1)(B) of section 1135(g) beginning on the date of the enactment of the HEROES Act, with respect to a COVID–19 vaccine licensed under section 351 of the Public Health Service Act, or approved or authorized under section 505 or 564 of the Federal Food, Drug, and Cosmetic Act" before the period.

(c) CHIP.—

(1) IN GENERAL.—Section 2103(c) of the Social Security Act (42 U.S.C. 1397cc(c)) is amended by adding at the end the following paragraph:

"(11) COVERAGE OF COVID–19 VACCINES AND TREATMENT.—Regardless of the type of coverage elected by a State under subsection (a), child health assistance provided under such coverage for targeted low-income children and, in the case that the State elects to provide pregnancy-related assistance under such coverage pursuant to section 2112, such pregnancy-related assistance for targeted low-income pregnant women (as defined in section 2112(d)) shall include coverage, during the portion of the emergency period described in paragraph (1)(B) of section 1135(g) beginning on the date of the enactment of this paragraph, of—

"(A) a COVID–19 vaccine licensed under section 351 of the Public Health Service Act, or approved or authorized under section 505 or 564 of the Federal Food, Drug, and Cosmetic Act, and the administration of such vaccine; and

"(B) any item or service furnished for the treatment of COVID–19, including drugs approved or authorized under such section 505 or such section 564, or, in the case of an individual who is diagnosed with or presumed to have COVID–19, during the portion of such emergency period during which such individual is infected (or presumed infected) with COVID–19, the treatment of a condition that may complicate the treatment of COVID–19.".

(2) PROHIBITION OF COST SHARING.—Section 2103(e)(2) of the Social Security Act (42 U.S.C. 1397cc(e)(2)), as amended by section 6004(b)(3) of the Families First Coronavirus Response Act, is amended—

(A) in the paragraph header, by inserting "A COVID–19 VACCINE, COVID–19 TREATMENT," before "OR PREGNANCY-RELATED ASSISTANCE"; and

(B) by striking "visits described in section 1916(a)(2)(G), or" and inserting "services described in section 1916(a)(2)(G), vaccines described in section 1916(a)(2)(H) administered during the portion of the emergency period described in paragraph (1)(B) of section 1135(g) beginning on the date of the enactment of the HEROES Act, items or services described in section 1916(a)(2)(I) furnished during such emergency period, or".

(d) Conforming Amendments.—Section 1937 of the Social Security Act (42 U.S.C. 1396u–7) is amended—

(1) in subsection (a)(1)(B), by inserting ", under subclause (XXIII) of section 1902(a)(10)(A)(ii)," after "section 1902(a)(10)(A)(i)"; and

(2) in subsection (b)(5), by adding before the period the following: ", and, effective on the date of the enactment of the HEROES Act, must comply with subparagraphs (F) through (I) of subsections (a)(2) and (b)(2) of section 1916 and subsection (b)(3)(B) of section 1916A".

(e) Effective Date.—The amendments made by this section shall take effect on the date of enactment of this Act and shall apply with respect to a COVID–19 vaccine beginning on the date that such vaccine is licensed under section 351 of the Public Health Service Act (42 U.S.C. 262), or approved or authorized under section 505 or 564 of the Federal Food, Drug, and Cosmetic Act.

OPTIONAL COVERAGE AT NO COST SHARING OF COVID–19 TREATMENT AND VACCINES UNDER MEDICAID FOR UNINSURED INDIVIDUALS

SEC. 30105.

(a) In General.—Section 1902(a)(10) of the Social Security Act (42 U.S.C. 1396a(a) (10) is amended, in the matter following subparagraph (G), by striking "and any visit described in section 1916(a)(2)(G)" and inserting the following: ", any COVID–19 vaccine that is administered during any such portion (and the administration of such vaccine), any item or service that is furnished during any such portion for the treatment of COVID–19, including drugs approved or authorized under section 505 or 564 of the Federal Food, Drug, and Cosmetic Act, or, in the case of an individual who is diagnosed with or presumed to have COVID–19, during the period such individual is infected (or presumed infected) with COVID–19, the treatment of a condition that may complicate the treatment of COVID–19, and any services described in section 1916(a)(2)(G)".

(b) Definition Of Uninsured Individual.—

(1) IN GENERAL.—Subsection (ss) of section 1902 of the Social Security Act (42 U.S.C. 1396a) is amended to read as follows:

"(ss) Uninsured Individual Defined.—For purposes of this section, the term 'uninsured individual' means, notwithstanding any other provision of this title, any individual who is not covered by minimum essential coverage (as defined in section 5000A(f)(1) of the Internal Revenue Code of 1986)".

(2) EFFECTIVE DATE.—The amendment made by paragraph (1) shall take effect and apply as if included in the enactment of the Families First Coronavirus Response Act (Public Law 116–127).

(c) Clarification Regarding Emergency Services For Certain Individuals.—Section 1903(v)(2) of the Social Security Act (42 U.S.C. 1396b(v)(2)) is amended by adding at the end the following flush sentence:

"For purposes of subparagraph (A), care and services described in such subparagraph include any in vitro diagnostic product described in section 1905(a)(3)(B) (and the administration of such product), any COVID–19 vaccine (and the administration of such vaccine), any item or service that is furnished for the treatment of COVID–19, including drugs approved or authorized under section 505 or 564 of the Federal Food, Drug, and Cosmetic Act, or a condition that may complicate the treatment of COVID–19, and any services described in section 1916(a)(2)(G)".

(d) Inclusion Of COVID–19 Concern As An Emergency Condition.—Section 1903(v)(3) of the Social Security Act (42 U.S.C. 1396b(v)(3)) is amended by adding at the end the following flush sentence:

"Such term includes any indication that an alien described in paragraph (1) may have contracted COVID–19".

EXTENSION OF FULL FEDERAL MEDICAL ASSISTANCE PERCENTAGE TO INDIAN HEALTH CARE PROVIDERS

SEC. 30106.

Section 1905 of the Social Security Act (42 U.S.C. 1396d) is amended—

(1) in subsection (a), by amending paragraph (9) to read as follows:

"(9) clinic services furnished by or under the direction of a physician, without regard to whether the clinic itself is administered by a physician, including—

"(A) such services furnished outside the clinic by clinic personnel to an eligible individual who does not reside in a permanent dwelling or does not have a fixed home or mailing address; and

"(B) for the period beginning on July 1, 2020, and ending on June 30, 2021, such services provided outside the clinic on the basis of a referral from a clinic administered by an Indian Health Program (as defined in paragraph (12) of section 4 of the Indian Health Care Improvement Act, or an Urban Indian Organization as defined in paragraph (29) of section 4 of such Act that has a grant or contract with the Indian Health Service under title V of such Act;".

(2) in subsection (b), by inserting after "(as defined in section 4 of the Indian Health Care Improvement Act)" the following: "; for the period beginning on July 1, 2020, and ending on June 30, 2021, the Federal medical assistance percentage shall also be 100 per centum with respect to amounts expended as medical assistance for services which are received through an Urban Indian organization (as defined in section 4 of the Indian Health Care Improvement Act) that has a grant or contract with the Indian Health Service under title V of such Act; and, for such period, the Federal medical assistance percentage shall also be 100 per centum with respect to amounts expended as medical assistance for services provided to an individual who is eligible to receive services from the Indian Health Service and is eligible for assistance under the State plan, by a participating provider under the State plan whether provided directly or on the basis of a referral from the Indian Health Service, a Indian Health Service facility operated by an Indian tribe or tribal organization, or an Urban Indian organization (as defined in section 4 of such Act) that has a grant or contract with the Indian Health Service under title V of such Act".

MEDICAID COVERAGE FOR CITIZENS OF FREELY ASSOCIATED STATES

SEC. 30107.

(a) In General.—Section 402(b)(2) of the Personal Responsibility and Work Opportunity Reconciliation Act of 1996 (8 U.S.C. 1612(b)(2)) is amended by adding at the end the following new subparagraph:

"(G) MEDICAID EXCEPTION FOR CITIZENS OF FREELY ASSOCIATED STATES.—With respect to eligibility for benefits for the designated Federal program defined in paragraph (3)(C) (relating to the Medicaid program), section 401(a) and paragraph (1) shall not apply to any individual who lawfully resides in 1 of the 50 States or the District of Columbia in accordance with the Compacts of Free Association between the Government of the United States and the Governments of the Federated States of Micronesia, the Republic of the Marshall Islands, and the Republic of Palau and shall not apply, at the option of the Governor of Puerto Rico, the Virgin Islands, Guam, the Northern Mariana Islands, or American Samoa as communicated to the Secretary of Health and Human Services in writing, to any individual who lawfully resides in the respective territory in accordance with such Compacts.".

(b) Exception To 5–Year Limited Eligibility.—Section 403(d) of such Act (8 U.S.C. 1613(d)) is amended—

(1) in paragraph (1), by striking "or" at the end;

(2) in paragraph (2), by striking the period at the end and inserting "; or"; and

(3) by adding at the end the following new paragraph:

"(3) an individual described in section 402(b)(2)(G), but only with respect to the designated Federal program defined in section 402(b)(3)(C).".

(c) Definition Of Qualified Alien.—Section 431(b) of such Act (8 U.S.C. 1641(b)) is amended—

(1) in paragraph (6), by striking "; or" at the end and inserting a comma;

(2) in paragraph (7), by striking the period at the end and inserting ", or"; and

(3) by adding at the end the following new paragraph:

"(8) an individual who lawfully resides in the United States in accordance with a Compact of Free Association referred to in section 402(b)(2)(G), but only with respect to the designated Federal program defined in section 402(b)(3)(C) (relating to the Medicaid program).".

(d) Application To State Plans.—Section 1902(a)(10)(A)(i) of the Social Security Act (42 U.S.C. 1396a(a)(10)(A)(i)) is amended by inserting after subclause (IX) the following:

"(X) who are described in section 402(b)(2)(G) of the Personal Responsibility and Work Opportunity Reconciliation Act of 1996 and eligible for benefits under this title by reason of application of such section;".

(e) Conforming Amendments.—Section 1108 of the Social Security Act (42 U.S.C. 1308) is amended—

(1) in subsection (f), in the matter preceding paragraph (1), by striking "subsections (g) and (h) and section 1935(e)(1)(B)" and inserting "subsections (g), (h), and (i) and section 1935(e)(1)(B)"; and

(2) by adding at the end the following:

"(i) Exclusion Of Medical Assistance Expenditures For Citizens Of Freely Associated States.—Expenditures for medical assistance provided to an individual described in section 431(b)(8) of the Personal Responsibility and Work Opportunity Reconciliation Act of 1996 (8 U.S.C. 1641(b)(8)) shall not be taken into account for purposes of applying payment limits under subsections (f) and (g).".

(f) Effective Date.—The amendments made by this section shall apply to benefits for items and services furnished on or after the date of the enactment of this Act.

TEMPORARY INCREASE IN MEDICAID DSH ALLOTMENTS

SEC. 30108.

(a) In General.—Section 1923(f)(3) of the Social Security Act (42 U.S.C. 1396r–4(f)(3)) is amended—

(1) in subparagraph (A), by striking "and subparagraph (E)" and inserting "and subparagraphs (E) and (F)"; and

(2) by adding at the end the following new subparagraph:

"(F) TEMPORARY INCREASE IN ALLOTMENTS DURING CERTAIN PUBLIC HEALTH EMERGENCY.—The DSH allotment for any State for each of fiscal years 2020 and 2021 is equal to 102.5 percent of the DSH allotment that would be determined under this paragraph for the State for each respective fiscal year without application of this subparagraph, notwithstanding subparagraphs (B) and (C). For each fiscal year after fiscal year 2021, the DSH allotment for a State for such fiscal year is equal to the DSH allotment that would have been determined under this paragraph for such fiscal year if this subparagraph had not been enacted.

(b) DSH Allotment Adjustment For Tennessee.—Section 1923(f)(6)(A)(vi) of the Social Security Act (42 U.S.C. 1396r–4(f)(6)(A)(vi)) is amended—

(1) by striking "Notwithstanding any other provision of this subsection" and inserting the following:

"(I) IN GENERAL.—Notwithstanding any other provision of this subsection (except as provided in subclause (II) of this clause)"; and

(2) by adding at the end the following:

"(II) TEMPORARY INCREASE IN ALLOTMENTS.—The DSH allotment for Tennessee for each of fiscal years 2020 and 2021 shall be equal to $54,427,500.".

(c) Sense Of Congress.—It is the sense of Congress that a State should prioritize making payments under the State plan of the State under title XIX of the Social Security Act (42 U.S.C. 1396 et seq.) (or a waiver of such plan) to disproportionate share hospitals that have a higher share of COVID–19 patients relative to other such hospitals in the State.

EXTENSION OF EXISTING SECTION 1115 DEMONSTRATIONS

SEC. 30109.

(a) Applicability.—This section shall apply with respect to demonstrations operated by States pursuant to section 1115(a) of the Social Security Act (42 U.S.C. 1315(a)) to promote the objectives of title XIX or XXI of the Social Security Act with a project term set to end on or before February 28, 2021.

(b) Approval Of Extension.—Upon request by a State, the Secretary of Health and Human Services shall approve an extension of the waiver and expenditure authorities for a demonstration project described in subsection (a) for a period up to and including December 31, 2021, to ensure continuity of programs and funding during the emergency period described in section 1135(g)(1)(B) of the Social Security Act (42 U.S.C. 1320b–5(g)(1)(B)).

(c) Extension Terms And Conditions.— (1) The approval pursuant to this section shall extend the terms and conditions that applied to the demonstration project to the extension period. Financial terms and conditions shall continue at levels equivalent to the prior demonstration or program year. All demonstration program components shall be extended to operate through the end of the extension term. In its request for an extension, the State shall identify operational and programmatic changes necessary to continue and stabilize programs into the extension period and shall work with the Secretary of Health and Human Services to implement such changes.

(2) Notwithstanding the foregoing, the State may request, and the Secretary of Health and Human Services may approve, modifications to a demonstration project's terms and conditions to address the impact of the federally designated public health emergency with respect to COVID–19. Such modifications may, at the option of the State, become effective retroactive to the start of the calendar quarter in which the first day of the emergency period described in paragraph (1)(B) of section 1135(g) of the Social Security Act (42 U.S.C. 1320b–5(g)) occurs.

(d) Budget Neutrality.—Budget neutrality for extensions under this section shall be deemed to have been met at the conclusion of the extension period, and States receiving extensions under this section shall not be required to submit a budget neutrality analysis for the extension period.

(e) Expedited Application Process.—The Federal and State public notice and comment procedures or other time constraints otherwise applicable to demonstration project amendments shall be waived to expedite a State's extension request pursuant to this section. The Secretary of Health and Human Services shall approve the extension application within 45 days of a State's submission of its request, or such other timeframe as is mutually agreed to with the State.

(f) Continuation Of Secretarial Authority Under Declared Emergency.—This section does not restrict the Secretary of Health and Human Services from exercising existing flexibilities through demonstration projects operated pursuant to section 1115 of the Social Security Act (42 U.S.C. 1315) in conjunction with the COVID–19 public health emergency.

(g) Rule Of Construction.—Nothing in this section shall authorize the Secretary of Health and Human Service to approve or extend a waiver that fails to meet the requirements of section 1115 of the Social Security Act (42 U.S.C. 1315).

ALLOWING FOR MEDICAL ASSISTANCE UNDER MEDICAID FOR INMATES DURING 30-DAY PERIOD PRECEDING RELEASE

SEC. 30110.

(a) In General.—The subdivision (A) following paragraph (30) of section 1905(a) of the Social Security Act (42 U.S.C. 1396d(a)) is amended by inserting "and except during the 30-day period preceding the date of release of such individual from such public institution" after "medical institution".

(b) Report.—Not later than June 30, 2022, the Medicaid and CHIP Payment and Access Commission shall submit a report to Congress on the Medicaid inmate exclusion under the subdivision (A) following paragraph (30) of section 1905(a) of the Social Security Act (42 U.S.C. 1396d(a)). Such report may, to the extent practicable, include the following information:

(1) The number of incarcerated individuals who would otherwise be eligible to enroll for medical assistance under a State plan approved under title XIX of the Social Security Act (42 U.S.C. 1396 et seq.) (or a waiver of such a plan).

(2) Access to health care for incarcerated individuals, including a description of medical services generally available to incarcerated individuals.

(3) A description of current practices related to the discharge of incarcerated individuals, including how prisons interact with State Medicaid agencies to ensure that such individuals who are eligible to enroll for medical assistance under a State plan or waiver described in paragraph (1) are so enrolled.

(4) If determined appropriate by the Commission, recommendations for Congress, the Department of Health and Human Services, or States regarding the Medicaid inmate exclusion.

(5) Any other information that the Commission determines would be useful to Congress.

MEDICAID COVERAGE OF CERTAIN MEDICAL TRANSPORTATION

SEC. 30111.

(a) Continuing Requirement Of Medicaid Coverage Of Necessary Transportation.—

(1) REQUIREMENT.—Section 1902(a)(4) of the Social Security Act (42 U.S.C. 1396a(a)(4)) is amended—

(A) by striking "and including provision for utilization" and inserting "including provision for utilization"; and

(B) by inserting after "supervision of administration of the plan" the following: ", and, subject to section 1903(i), including a specification that the single State agency described in paragraph (5) will ensure necessary transportation for beneficiaries under the State plan to and from providers and a description of the methods that such agency will use to ensure such transportation".

(2) APPLICATION WITH RESPECT TO BENCHMARK BENEFIT PACKAGES AND BENCHMARK EQUIVALENT COVERAGE.—Section 1937(a)(1) of the Social

Security Act (42 U.S.C. 1396u–7(a)(1)) is amended—

(A) in subparagraph (A), by striking "subsection (E)" and inserting "subparagraphs (E) and (F)"; and

(B) by adding at the end the following new subparagraph:

"(F) NECESSARY TRANSPORTATION.—The State may only exercise the option under subparagraph (A)(i) if, subject to section 1903(i)(9) and in accordance with section 1902(a)(4), the benchmark benefit package or benchmark equivalent coverage described in such subparagraph (or the State)—

"(i) ensures necessary transportation for individuals enrolled under such package or coverage to and from providers; and

"(ii) provides a description of the methods that will be used to ensure such transportation.

(3) LIMITATION ON FEDERAL FINANCIAL PARTICIPATION.—Section 1903(i) of the Social Security Act (42 U.S.C. 1396b(i)) is amended by inserting after paragraph (8) the following new paragraph:

"(9) with respect to any amount expended for non-emergency transportation described in section 1902(a)(4), unless the State plan provides for the methods and procedures required under section 1902(a)(30)(A); or".

(4) EFFECTIVE DATE.—The amendments made by this subsection shall take effect on the date of the enactment of this Act and shall apply to transportation furnished on or after such date.

(b) Medicaid Program Integrity Measures Related To Coverage Of Nonemergency Medical Transportation.—

(1) GAO STUDY.—Not later than two years after the date of the enactment of this Act, the Comptroller General of the United States shall conduct a study, and submit to Congress, a report on coverage under the Medicaid program under title XIX of the Social Security Act of nonemergency transportation to medically necessary services. Such study shall take into account the 2009 report of the Office of the Inspector General of the Department of Health and Human Services, titled "Fraud and Abuse Safeguards for Medicaid Nonemergency Medical Transportation" (OEI–06–07–003200). Such report shall include the following:

(A) An examination of the 50 States and the District of Columbia to identify safeguards to prevent and detect fraud and abuse with respect to coverage under the Medicaid program of nonemergency transportation to medically necessary services.

(B) An examination of transportation brokers to identify the range of safeguards against such fraud and abuse to prevent improper payments for such transportation.

(C) Identification of the numbers, types, and outcomes of instances of fraud and abuse, with respect to coverage under the Medicaid program of such transportation, that State Medicaid Fraud Control Units have investigated in recent years.

(D) Identification of commonalities or trends in program integrity, with respect to such coverage, to inform risk management strategies of States and the Centers for Medicare & Medicaid Services.

(2) STAKEHOLDER WORKING GROUP.—

(A) IN GENERAL.—Not later than one year after the date of the enactment of this Act, the Secretary of Health and Human Services, through the Centers of Medicare & Medicaid Services, shall convene a series of meetings to obtain input from appropriate stakeholders to facilitate discussion and shared learning about the leading practices for improving Medicaid program integrity, with respect to coverage of nonemergency transportation to medically necessary services.

(B) TOPICS.—The meetings convened under subparagraph (A) shall—

(i) focus on ongoing challenges to Medicaid program integrity as well as leading practices to address such challenges; and

(ii) address specific challenges raised by stakeholders involved in coverage under the Medicaid program of nonemergency transportation to medically necessary services, including unique considerations for specific groups of Medicaid beneficiaries meriting particular attention, such as American Indians and tribal land issues or accommodations for individuals with disabilities.

(C) STAKEHOLDERS.—Stakeholders described in subparagraph (A) shall include individuals from State Medicaid programs, brokers for nonemergency transportation to medically necessary services that meet the criteria described in section 1902(a)(70)(B) of the Social Security Act (42 U.S.C. 1396a(a)(70)(B)), providers (including transportation network companies), Medicaid patient advocates, and such other individuals specified by the Secretary.

(3) GUIDANCE REVIEW.—Not later than 18 months after the date of the enactment of this Act, the Secretary of Health and Human Services, through the Centers for Medicare & Medicaid Services, shall assess guidance issued to States by the Centers for Medicare & Medicaid Services relating to Federal requirements for nonemergency transportation to medically necessary services under the Medicaid program under title XIX of the Social Security Act and update such guidance as necessary to ensure States have appropriate and current guidance in designing and administering coverage under the Medicaid program of nonemergency transportation to medically necessary services.

(4) NEMT TRANSPORTATION PROVIDER AND DRIVER REQUIREMENTS.—

(A) STATE PLAN REQUIREMENT.—Section 1902(a) of the Social Security Act (42 U.S.C. 1396a(a)) is amended—

(i) by striking "and" at the end of paragraph (85);

(ii) by striking the period at the end of paragraph (86) and inserting "; and"; and

(iii) by inserting after paragraph (86) the following new paragraph:

"(87) provide for a mechanism, which may include attestation, that ensures that, with respect to any provider (including a transportation network company) or individual driver of nonemergency transportation to medically necessary services receiving payments under such plan (but excluding any public transit authority), at a minimum—

"(A) each such provider and individual driver is not excluded from participation in any Federal health care program (as defined in section 1128B(f)) and is not listed on the exclusion list of the Inspector General of the Department of Health and Human Services;

"(B) each such individual driver has a valid driver's license;

"(C) each such provider has in place a process to address any violation of a State drug law; and

"(D) each such provider has in place a process to disclose to the State Medicaid program the driving history, including any traffic violations, of each such individual driver employed by such provider, including any traffic violations.".

(B) EFFECTIVE DATE.—

(i) IN GENERAL.—Except as provided in clause (ii), the amendments made by subparagraph (A) shall take effect on the date of the enactment of this Act and shall apply to services furnished on or after the date that is one year after the date of the enactment of this Act.

(ii) EXCEPTION IF STATE LEGISLATION REQUIRED.—In the case of a State plan for medical assistance under title XIX of the Social Security Act which the Secretary of Health and Human Services determines requires State legislation (other than legislation appropriating funds) in order for the plan to meet the additional requirement imposed by the amendments made by subparagraph (A), the State plan shall not be regarded as failing to comply with the requirements of such title solely on the basis of its failure to meet this additional requirement before the first day of the first calendar quarter beginning after the close of the first regular session of the State legislature that begins after the date of the enactment of this Act. For purposes of the previous sentence, in the case of a State that has a 2-year legislative session, each year of such session shall be deemed to be a separate regular session of the State legislature.

(5) ANALYSIS OF T-MSIS DATA.—Not later than one year after the date of the enactment of this Act, the Secretary of Health and Human Services, through the Centers for Medicare & Medicaid Services, shall analyze, and submit to Congress a report on, the nation-wide data set under the Transformed Medicaid Statistical Information System to identify recommendations relating to coverage under the Medicaid program under title XIX of the Social Security Act of nonemergency transportation to medically necessary services.

TITLE II

—MEDICARE PROVISIONS
HOLDING MEDICARE BENEFICIARIES HARMLESS FOR SPECIFIED COVID–19 TREATMENT SERVICES FURNISHED UNDER PART A OR PART B OF THE MEDICARE PROGRAM

SEC. 30201.

(a) In General.—Notwithstanding any other provision of law, in the case of a specified COVID–19 treatment service (as defined in subsection (b)) furnished during any portion of the emergency period described in paragraph (1)(B) of section 1135(g) of the Social Security Act (42 U.S.C. 1320b-5(g)) beginning on or after the date of the enactment of this Act to an individual entitled to benefits under part A or enrolled under part B of title XVIII of the Social Security Act (42 U.S.C. 1395 et seq.) for which payment is made under such part A or such part B, the Secretary of Health and Human Services (in this section referred to as the "Secretary") shall provide that—

(1) any cost-sharing required (including any deductible, copayment, or coinsurance) applicable to such individual under such part A or such part B with respect to such item or service is paid by the Secretary; and

(2) the provider of services or supplier (as defined in section 1861 of the Social Security Act (42 U.S.C. 1395x)) does not hold such individual liable for such requirement.

(b) Definition Of Specified COVID–19 Treatment Services.—For purposes of this section, the term "specified COVID–19 treatment service" means any item or service furnished to an individual for which payment may be made under part A or part B of title XVIII of the Social Security Act (42 U.S.C. 1395 et seq.) if such item or service is included in a claim with an ICD–10–CM code relating to COVID–19 (as described in the document entitled "ICD–10–CM Official Coding Guidelines - Supplement Coding encounters related to COVID–19 Coronavirus Outbreak" published on February 20, 2020, or as otherwise specified by the Secretary).

(c) Recovery Of Cost-Sharing Amounts Paid By The Secretary In The Case Of Supplemental Insurance Coverage.—

(1) IN GENERAL.—In the case of any amount paid by the Secretary pursuant to subsection (a)(1) that the Secretary determines would otherwise have been paid by a group health plan or health insurance issuer (as such terms are defined in section 2791 of the Public Health Service Act (42 U.S.C. 300gg–91)), a private entity offering a medicare supplemental policy under section 1882 of the Social Security Act (42 U.S.C. 1395ss), any other health plan offering supplemental coverage, a State plan under title XIX of the Social Security Act, or the Secretary of Defense under the TRICARE program, such plan, issuer, private entity, other health plan, State plan, or Secretary of Defense, as applicable, shall pay to the Secretary, not later than 1 year after such plan, issuer, private entity, other health plan, State plan, or Secretary of Defense receives a notice under paragraph (3), such amount in accordance with this subsection.

(2) REQUIRED INFORMATION.—Not later than 9 months after the date of the enactment of this Act, each group health plan, health insurance issuer, private entity, other health plan, State plan, and Secretary of Defense described in paragraph (1) shall submit to the Secretary such information as the Secretary determines necessary for purposes of carrying out this subsection. Such information so submitted shall be updated by such plan, issuer, private entity, other health plan, State plan, or Secretary of Defense, as applicable, at such time and in such manner as specified by the Secretary.

(3) REVIEW OF CLAIMS AND NOTIFICATION.—The Secretary shall establish a process under which claims for items and services for which the Secretary has paid an amount pursuant to subsection (a)(1) are reviewed for purposes of identifying if such amount would otherwise have been paid by a plan, issuer, private entity, other health plan, State plan, or Secretary of Defense described in paragraph (1). In the case such a claim is so identified, the Secretary shall determine the amount that would have been otherwise payable by such plan, issuer, private entity, other health plan, State plan, or Secretary of Defense and notify such plan, issuer, private entity, other health plan, State plan, or Secretary of Defense of such amount.

(4) ENFORCEMENT.—The Secretary may impose a civil monetary penalty in an amount determined appropriate by the Secretary in the case of a plan, issuer, private entity, other health plan, or State plan that fails to comply with a provision of this section. The provisions of section 1128A of the Social Security Act shall apply to a civil monetary penalty imposed under the previous sentence in the same manner as such provisions apply to a penalty or proceeding under subsection (a) or (b) of such section.

(d) Funding.—The Secretary shall provide for the transfer to the Centers for Medicare & Medicaid Program Management Account from the Federal Hospital Insurance Trust Fund and the Federal Supplementary Trust Fund (in such portions as the Secretary determines appropriate) $100,000,000 for purposes of carrying out this section.

(e) Report.—Not later than 3 years after the date of the enactment of this Act, the Inspector General of the Department of Health and Human Services shall submit to Congress a report containing an analysis of amounts paid pursuant to subsection (a)(1) compared to amounts paid to the Secretary pursuant to subsection (c).

(f) Implementation.—Notwithstanding any other provision of law, the Secretary may implement the provisions of this section by program instruction or otherwise.

ENSURING COMMUNICATIONS ACCESSIBILITY FOR RESIDENTS OF

SKILLED NURSING FACILITIES DURING THE COVID-19 EMERGENCY PERIOD

SEC. 30202.

(a) In General.—Section 1819(c)(3) of the Social Security Act (42 U.S.C. 1395i–3(c)(3)) is amended—

(1) in subparagraph (D), by striking "and" at the end;

(2) in subparagraph (E), by striking the period and inserting "; and"; and

(3) by adding at the end the following new subparagraph:

"(F) provide for reasonable access to the use of a telephone, including TTY and TDD services (as defined for purposes of section 483.10 of title 42, Code of Federal Regulations (or a successor regulation)), and the internet (to the extent available to the facility) and inform each such resident (or a representative of such resident) of such access and any changes in policies or procedures of such facility relating to limitations on external visitors.".

(b) COVID–19 Provisions.—

(1) GUIDANCE.—Not later than 15 days after the date of the enactment of this Act, the Secretary of Health and Human Service shall issue guidance on steps skilled nursing facilities may take to ensure residents have access to televisitation during the emergency period defined in section 1135(g)(1)(B) of the Social Security Act (42 U.S.C. 1320b–5(g)(1)(B)). Such guidance shall include information on how such facilities will notify residents of such facilities, representatives of such residents, and relatives of such residents of the rights of such residents to such televisitation, and ensure timely and equitable access to such televisitation.

(2) REVIEW OF FACILITIES.—The Secretary of Health and Human Services shall take such steps as determined appropriate by the Secretary to ensure that residents of skilled nursing facilities and relatives of such residents are made aware of the access rights described in section 1819(c)(3)(F) of the Social Security Act (42 U.S.C. 1395i–3(c)(3)(F)).

MEDICARE HOSPITAL INPATIENT PROSPECTIVE PAYMENT SYSTEM OUTLIER PAYMENTS FOR COVID-19 PATIENTS DURING CERTAIN EMERGENCY PERIOD

SEC. 30203.

(a) In General.—Section 1886(d)(5)(A) of the Social Security Act (42 U.S.C. 1395ww(d)(5)(A)) is amended—

(1) in clause (ii), by striking "For cases" and inserting "Subject to clause (vii), for cases";

(2) in clause (iii), by striking "The amount" and inserting "Subject to clause (vii), the amount";

(3) in clause (iv), by striking "The total amount" and inserting "Subject to clause (vii), the total amount"; and

(4) by adding at the end the following new clause:

"(vii) For discharges that have a primary or secondary diagnosis of COVID–19 and that occur during the period beginning on the date of the enactment of this clause and ending on the sooner of January 31, 2021, or the last day of the emergency period described in section 1135(g)(1)(B), the amount of any additional payment under clause (ii) for a subsection (d) hospital for such a discharge shall be determined as if—

"(I) clause (ii) was amended by striking 'plus a fixed dollar amount determined by the Secretary';

"(II) the reference in clause (iii) to 'approximate the marginal cost of care beyond the cutoff point applicable under clause (i) or (ii)' were a reference to 'approximate the marginal cost of care beyond the cutoff point applicable under clause (i), or, in the case of an additional payment requested under clause (ii), be equal to 100 percent of the amount by which the costs of the discharge for which such additional payment is so requested exceed the applicable DRG prospective payment rate'; and

"(III) clause (iv) does not apply.".

(b) Exclusion From Reduction In Average Standardized Amounts Payable To Hospitals Located In Certain Areas.—Section 1886(d)(3)(B) of the Social Security Act (42 U.S.C. 1395ww(d)(3)(B)) is amended by inserting before the period the following: ", other than additional payments described in clause (vii) of such paragraph".

(c) Application To Site Neutral IPPS Payment Rates.—Section 1886(m)(6)(B) of the Social Security Act (42 U.S.C. 1395ww(m)(6)(B)) is amended—

(1) in clause (i)—

(A) in the matter preceding subclause (I), by striking "In this paragraph" and inserting "Subject to clause (ii), in this paragraph";

(B) in subclause (I), by striking "clause (iii)" and inserting "clause (iv)"; and

(C) in subclause (II), by striking "clause (ii)" and inserting "clause (iii)";

(2) in clause (ii), in the matter preceding subclause (I), by striking "clause (iv)" and inserting "clause (v)";

(3) in clause (iii)(I), by striking "clause (ii)" and inserting "clause (iii)";

(4) in clause (iv), by striking "clause (ii)(I)" and inserting "clause (iii)(I)";

(5) by redesignating clauses (ii) through (iv) as clauses (iii) through (v), respectively; and

(6) by inserting after clause (i) the following new clause:

"(ii) EXCEPTION.—Notwithstanding clause (i), the term 'applicable site neutral payment rate' means—

"(I) for discharges that have a primary or secondary diagnosis of COVID–19 and that occur during any portion of the emergency period described in section 1135(g)(1)(B) occurring during a cost reporting period described in clause (i)(I), the greater of the blended payment rate specified in clause (iv) or the percent described in clause (iii)(II); and

"(II) for discharges that have a primary or secondary diagnosis of COVID–19 and that occur during any portion of the emergency period described in section 1135(g)(1)(B) occurring during a cost reporting period described in clause (i)(II), the percent described in clause (iii)(II).".

(d) Implementation.—Notwithstanding any other provision of law, the Secretary of Health and Human Services may implement the amendments made by this section by program instruction or otherwise.

COVERAGE OF TREATMENTS FOR COVID–19 AT NO COST SHARING UNDER THE MEDICARE ADVANTAGE PROGRAM

SEC. 30204.

(a) In General.—Section 1852(a)(1)(B) of the Social Security Act (42 U.S.C. 1395w–22(a)(1)(B)) is amended by adding at the end the following new clause:

"(vii) SPECIAL COVERAGE RULES FOR SPECIFIED COVID–19 TREATMENT SERVICES.—Notwithstanding clause (i), in the case of a specified COVID–19 treatment service (as defined in section 30201(b) of the HEROES Act) that is furnished during a plan year occurring during any portion of the emergency period defined in section 1135(g)(1)(B) beginning on or after the date of the enactment of this clause, a Medicare Advantage plan may not, with respect to such service, impose—

"(I) any cost-sharing requirement (including a deductible, copayment, or coinsurance requirement); and

"(II) in the case such service is a critical specified COVID–19 treatment service (including ventilator services and intensive care unit services), any prior authorization or other utilization management requirement.

A Medicare Advantage plan may not take the application of this clause into account for purposes of a bid amount submitted by such plan under section 1854(a)(6).".

(b) Implementation.—Notwithstanding any other provision of law, the Secretary of Health and Human Services may implement the amendments made by this section by program instruction or otherwise.

REQUIRING COVERAGE UNDER MEDICARE PDPS AND MA–PD PLANS, WITHOUT THE IMPOSITION OF COST SHARING OR UTILIZATION MANAGEMENT REQUIREMENTS, OF DRUGS INTENDED TO TREAT COVID–19 DURING CERTAIN EMERGENCIES

SEC. 30205.

(a) Coverage Requirement.—

(1) IN GENERAL.—Section 1860D–4(b)(3) of the Social Security Act (42 U.S.C. 1395w–104(b)(3)) is amended by adding at the end the following new subparagraph:

"(I) REQUIRED INCLUSION OF DRUGS INTENDED TO TREAT COVID–19.—

"(i) IN GENERAL.—Notwithstanding any other provision of law, a PDP sponsor offering a prescription drug plan shall, with respect to a plan year, any portion of which occurs during the period described in clause (ii), be required to—

"(I) include in any formulary—

"(aa) all covered part D drugs with a medically accepted indication (as defined in section 1860D–2(e)(4)) to treat COVID–19 that are marketed in the United States; and

"(bb) all drugs authorized under section 564 or 564A of the Federal Food, Drug, and Cosmetic Act to treat COVID–19; and

"(II) not impose any prior authorization or other utilization management requirement with respect to such drugs described in item (aa) or (bb) of subclause (I) (other than such a requirement that limits the quantity of drugs due to safety).

"(ii) PERIOD DESCRIBED.—For purposes of clause (i), the period described in this clause is the period during which there exists the public health emergency declared by the Secretary pursuant to section 319 of the Public Health Service Act on January 31, 2020, entitled 'Determination that a Public Health Emergency Exists Nationwide as the Result of the 2019 Novel Coronavirus' (including any renewal of such declaration pursuant to such section).".

(b) Elimination Of Cost Sharing.—

(1) ELIMINATION OF COST-SHARING FOR DRUGS INTENDED TO TREAT COVID–19 UNDER STANDARD AND ALTERNATIVE PRESCRIPTION DRUG COVERAGE.—Section 1860D–2 of the Social Security Act (42 U.S.C. 1395w–102) is amended—

(A) in subsection (b)—

(i) in paragraph (1)(A), by striking "The coverage" and inserting "Subject to paragraph (8), the coverage";

(ii) in paragraph (2)—

(I) in subparagraph (A), by inserting after "Subject to subparagraphs (C) and (D)" the following: "and paragraph (8)";

(II) in subparagraph (C)(i), by striking "paragraph (4)" and inserting "paragraphs (4) and (8)"; and

(III) in subparagraph (D)(i), by striking "paragraph (4)" and inserting "paragraphs (4) and (8)";

(iii) in paragraph (4)(A)(i), by striking "The coverage" and inserting "Subject to paragraph (8), the coverage"; and

(iv) by adding at the end the following new paragraph:

"(8) ELIMINATION OF COST-SHARING FOR DRUGS INTENDED TO TREAT COVID–19.—The coverage does not impose any deductible, copayment, coinsurance, or other cost-sharing requirement for drugs described in section 1860D–4(b)(3) (I)(i)(I) with respect to a plan year, any portion of which occurs during the period during which there exists the public health emergency declared by the Secretary pursuant to section 319 of the Public Health Service Act on January 31, 2020, entitled 'Determination that a Public Health Emergency Exists Nationwide as the Result of the 2019 Novel Coronavirus' (including any renewal of such declaration pursuant to such section)."; and

(B) in subsection (c), by adding at the end the following new paragraph:

"(4) SAME ELIMINATION OF COST-SHARING FOR DRUGS INTENDED TO TREAT COVID–19.—The coverage is in accordance with subsection (b)(8).".

(2) ELIMINATION OF COST-SHARING FOR DRUGS INTENDED TO TREAT COVID–19 DISPENSED TO INDIVIDUALS WHO ARE SUBSIDY ELIGIBLE INDIVIDUALS.—Section 1860D–14(a) of the Social Security Act (42 U.S.C. 1395w–114(a)) is amended—

(A) in paragraph (1)—

(i) in subparagraph (D)—

(I) in clause (ii), by striking "In the case of" and inserting "Subject to subparagraph (F), in the case of"; and

(II) in clause (iii), by striking "In the case of" and inserting "Subject to subparagraph (F), in the case of"; and

(ii) by adding at the end the following new subparagraph:

"(F) ELIMINATION OF COST-SHARING FOR DRUGS INTENDED TO TREAT COVID–19.—Coverage that is in accordance with section 1860D–2(b)(8)."; and

(B) in paragraph (2)—

(i) in subparagraph (B), by striking "A reduction" and inserting "Subject to subparagraph (F), a reduction";

(ii) in subparagraph (D), by striking "The substitution" and inserting "Subject to subparagraph (F), the substitution";

(iii) in subparagraph (E), by inserting after "Subject to" the following: "subparagraph (F) and"; and

(iv) by adding at the end the following new subparagraph:

"(F) ELIMINATION OF COST-SHARING FOR DRUGS INTENDED TO TREAT COVID–19.—Coverage that is in accordance with section 1860D–2(b)(8).".

(c) Implementation.—Notwithstanding any other provision of law, the Secretary of Health and Human Services may implement the amendments made by this section by program instruction or otherwise.

MODIFYING THE ACCELERATED AND ADVANCE PAYMENT PROGRAMS

UNDER PARTS A AND B OF THE MEDICARE PROGRAM DURING THE COVID–19 EMERGENCY

SEC. 30206.
(a) Special Repayment Rules.—
(1) PART A.—Section 1815(f)(2)(C) of the Social Security Act (42 U.S.C. 1395g(f)(2)(C)) is amended to read as follows:
"(C) In the case of an accelerated payment made under the program under subsection (e)(3) on or after the date of the enactment of the CARES Act and so made during the emergency period described in section 1135(g)(1)(B)—
"(i) such payment shall be treated as if such payment were made from the General Fund of the Treasury; and
"(ii) upon request of the hospital, the Secretary shall—
"(I) provide up to 1 year before claims are offset to recoup such payment;
"(II) provide that any such offset of a claim to recoup such payment shall not exceed 25 percent of the amount of such claim; and
"(III) allow not less than 2 years from the date of the first accelerated payment before requiring that the outstanding balance be paid in full.".
(2) PART B.—In carrying out the program described in section 421.214 of title 42, Code of Federal Regulations (or any successor regulation), in the case of a payment made under such program on or after the date of the enactment of the CARES Act (Public Law 116–136) and so made during the emergency period described in section 1135(g)(1)(B) of the Social Security Act (42 U.S.C. 1320b–5(g)(1)(B)), the Secretary of Health and Human Services shall—
(A) treat such payment as if such payment were made from the General Fund of the Treasury; and
(B) upon request of the entity receiving such payment—
(i) provide up to 1 year before claims are offset to recoup such payment;
(ii) provide that any such offset of a claim to recoup such payment shall not exceed 25 percent of the amount of such claim; and
(iii) allow not less than 2 years from the date of the first advance payment before requiring that the outstanding balance be paid in full.
(b) Interest Rates.—
(1) PART A.—Section 1815(d) of the Social Security Act (42 U.S.C. 1395g(d)) is amended by inserting before the period at the end the following: "(or, in the case of such a determination made with respect to a payment made on or after the date of the enactment of the CARES Act and during the emergency period described in section 1135(g)(1)(B) under the program under subsection (e)(3), at a rate of 1 percent)".
(2) PART B.—Section 1833(j) of the Social Security Act (42 U.S.C. 1395l(j)) is amended by inserting before the period at the end the following: "(or, in the case of such a determination made with respect to a payment made on or after the date of the enactment of the CARES Act and during the emergency period described in section 1135(g)(1)(B) under the program described in section 421.214 of title 42, Code of Federal Regulations (or any successor regulation), at a rate of 1 percent)".
(c) Report.—
(1) REPORTS DURING COVID–19 EMERGENCY.—Not later than 2 weeks after the date of the enactment of this section, and every 2 weeks thereafter during the emergency period described in section 1135(g)(1)(B) of the Social Security Act (42 U.S.C. 1320b–5(g)(1)(B)), the Secretary of Health and Human Services shall submit

to the Committee on Ways and Means and the Committee on Energy and Commerce of the House of Representatives, and the Committee on Finance of the Senate, a report that includes the following:

(A) The total amount of payments made under section 1815(e)(3) of the Social Security Act (42 U.S.C. 1395g(e)(3)) and under the program described in section 421.214 of title 42, Code of Federal Regulations (or any successor regulation) during the most recent 2-week period for which data is available that precedes the date of the submission of such report.

(B) The number of entities receiving such payments during such period.

(C) A specification of each such entity.

(2) REPORTS AFTER COVID–19 EMERGENCY.—

(A) IN GENERAL.—Not later than 6 months after the termination of the emergency period described in paragraph (1), and every 6 months thereafter until all specified payments (as defined in subparagraph (B)) have been recouped or repaid, the Secretary of Health and Human Services shall submit to the Committee on Ways and Means and the Committee on Energy and Commerce of the House of Representatives, and the Committee on Finance of the Senate, a report that includes the following:

(i) The total amount of all specified payments for which claims have been offset to recoup such payment or the balance has been repaid.

(ii) The amount of interest that has accrued with respect to all specified payments.

(B) SPECIFIED PAYMENTS.—For purposes of subparagraph (A), the term "specified payments" means all payments made under section 1815(e)(3) of the Social Security Act (42 U.S.C. 1395g(e)(3)) or under the program described in section 421.214 of title 42, Code of Federal Regulations (or any successor regulation) made on or after the date of the enactment of the CARES Act (Public Law 116–136) during the emergency period described in such subparagraph.

MEDICARE SPECIAL ENROLLMENT PERIOD FOR INDIVIDUALS RESIDING IN COVID–19 EMERGENCY AREAS

SEC. 30207.

(a) In General.—Section 1837(i) of the Social Security Act (42 U.S.C. 1395p(i)) is amended by adding at the end the following new paragraph:

"(5) (A) In the case of an individual who—

"(i) is eligible under section 1836 to enroll in the medical insurance program established by this part,

"(ii) did not enroll (or elected not to be deemed enrolled) under this section during an enrollment period, and

"(iii) during the emergency period (as described in section 1135(g)(1)(B)), resided in an emergency area (as described in such section),

there shall be a special enrollment period described in subparagraph (B).

"(B) The special enrollment period referred to in subparagraph (A) is the period that begins not later than July 1, 2020, and ends on the last day of the month in which the emergency period (as described in section 1135(g)(1)(B)) ends.".

(b) Coverage Period For Individuals Transitioning From Other Coverage.—Section 1838(e) of the Social Security Act (42 U.S.C. 1395q(e)) is amended—

(1) by striking "pursuant to section 1837(i)(3) or 1837(i)(4)(B)—" and inserting the following: pursuant to—

"(1) section 1837(i)(3) or 1837(i)(4)(B)—";

(2) by redesignating paragraphs (1) and (2) as subparagraphs (A) and (B), respectively,

and moving the indentation of each such subparagraph 2 ems to the right;

(3) by striking the period at the end of the subparagraph (B), as so redesignated, and inserting "; or"; and

(4) by adding at the end the following new paragraph:

"(2) section 1837(i)(5), the coverage period shall begin on the first day of the month following the month in which the individual so enrolls.".

(c) Funding.—The Secretary of Health and Human Services shall provide for the transfer from the Federal Hospital Insurance Trust Fund (as described in section 1817 of the Social Security Act (42 U.S.C. 1395i)) and the Federal Supplementary Medical Insurance Trust Fund (as described in section 1841 of such Act (42 U.S.C. 1395t)), in such proportions as determined appropriate by the Secretary, to the Social Security Administration, of $30,000,000, to remain available until expended, for purposes of carrying out the amendments made by this section.

(d) Implementation.—Notwithstanding any other provision of law, the Secretary of Health and Human Services may implement the amendments made by this section by program instruction or otherwise.

COVID–19 SKILLED NURSING FACILITY PAYMENT INCENTIVE PROGRAM

SEC. 30208.

(a) In General.—Section 1819 of the Social Security Act (42 U.S.C. 1395i–3) is amended by adding at the end the following new subsection:

"(k) COVID–19 Designation Program.—

"(1) IN GENERAL.—Not later than 2 weeks after the date of the enactment of this subsection, the Secretary shall establish a program under which a skilled nursing facility that makes an election described in paragraph (2)(A) and meets the requirements described in paragraph (2)(B) is designated (or a portion of such facility is so designated) as a COVID–19 treatment center and receives incentive payments under section 1888(e)(13).

"(2) DESIGNATION.—

"(A) IN GENERAL.—A skilled nursing facility may elect to be designated (or to have a portion of such facility designated) as a COVID–19 treatment center under the program established under paragraph (1) if the facility submits to the Secretary, at a time and in a manner specified by the Secretary, an application for such designation that contains such information as required by the Secretary and demonstrates that such facility meets the requirements described in subparagraph (B).

"(B) REQUIREMENTS.—The requirements described in this subparagraph with respect to a skilled nursing facility are the following:

"(i) The facility has a star rating with respect to staffing of 4 or 5 on the Nursing Home Compare website (as described in subsection (i)) and has maintained such a rating on such website during the 2-year period ending on the date of the submission of the application described in subparagraph (A).

"(ii) The facility has a star rating of 4 or 5 with respect to health inspections on such website and has maintained such a rating on such website during such period.

"(iii) During such period, the Secretary or a State has not found a deficiency with such facility relating to infection control that the Secretary or State determined immediately jeopardized the health or safety of the residents of such facility (as described in paragraph (1) or (2)(A) of subsection (h), as applicable).

"(iv) The facility provides care at such facility (or, in the case of an election made with respect to a portion of such facility, to provide care in such portion of such facility) only to eligible individuals.

"(v) The facility arranges for and transfers all residents of such facility (or such portion of such facility, as applicable) who are not eligible individuals to other skilled nursing facilities (or other portions of such facility, as applicable).

"(vi) The facility complies with the notice requirement described in paragraph (4).

"(vii) The facility meets the reporting requirement described in paragraph (5).

"(viii) Any other requirement determined appropriate by the Secretary.

"(3) DURATION OF DESIGNATION.—

"(A) IN GENERAL.—A designation of a skilled nursing facility (or portion of such facility) as a COVID–19 treatment center shall begin on a date specified by the Secretary and end upon the earliest of the following:

"(i) The revocation of such designation under subparagraph (B).

"(ii) The submission of a notification by such facility to the Secretary that such facility elects to terminate such designation.

"(iii) The termination of the program (as specified in paragraph (6)).

"(B) REVOCATION.—The Secretary may revoke the designation of a skilled nursing facility (or portion of such facility) as a COVID–19 treatment center if the Secretary determines that the facility is no longer in compliance with a requirement described in paragraph (2)(B).

"(4) RESIDENT NOTICE REQUIREMENT.—For purposes of paragraph (2)(B)(vi), the notice requirement described in this paragraph is that, not later than 72 hours before the date specified by the Secretary under paragraph (3)(A) with respect to the designation of a skilled nursing facility (or portion of such facility) as a COVID–19 treatment center, the facility provides a notification to each resident of such facility (and to appropriate representatives or family members of each such resident, as specified by the Secretary) that contains the following:

"(A) Notice of such designation.

"(B) In the case such resident is not an eligible individual (and, in the case such designation is made only with respect to a portion of such facility, resides in such portion of such facility)—

"(i) a specification of when and where such resident will be transferred (or moved within such facility);

"(ii) an explanation that, in lieu of such transfer or move, such resident may arrange for transfer to such other setting (including a home) selected by the resident; and

"(iii) if such resident so arranges to be transferred to a home, information on Internet resources for caregivers who elect to care for such resident at home.

"(C) Contact information for the State long-term care ombudsman (established under section 307(a)(12) of the Older Americans Act of 1965) for the applicable State.

"(5) REPORTING REQUIREMENT.—

"(A) IN GENERAL.—For purposes of paragraph (2)(B)(vii), the reporting requirement described in this paragraph is, with respect to a skilled nursing facility, that the facility reports to the Secretary, weekly and in such manner specified by the Secretary, the following (but only to the extent the information described in clauses (i) through (vii) is not otherwise reported to the Secretary weekly):

"(i) The number of COVID–19 related deaths at such facility.

"(ii) The number of discharges from such facility.

"(iii) The number of admissions to such facility.

"(iv) The number of beds occupied and the number of beds available at such facility.

"(v) The number of residents on a ventilator at such facility.

"(vi) The number of clinical and nonclinical staff providing direct patient care at such facility.

"(vii) Such other information determined appropriate by the Secretary.

"(B) NONAPPLICATION OF PAPERWORK REDUCTION ACT.—Chapter 35 of title 44, United States Code (commonly known as the 'Paperwork Reduction Act'), shall not apply to the collection of information under this paragraph.

"(6) DEFINITION.—For purposes of this subsection, the term 'eligible individual' means an individual who, during the 30-day period ending on the first day on which such individual is a resident of a COVID–19 treatment center (on or after the date such center is so designated), was furnished a test for COVID–19 that came back positive.

"(7) TERMINATION.—The program established under paragraph (1) shall terminate upon the termination of the emergency period described in section 1135(g)(1)(B).

"(8) PROHIBITION ON ADMINISTRATIVE AND JUDICIAL REVIEW.—There shall be no administrative or judicial review under section 1869, 1878, or otherwise of a designation of a skilled nursing facility (or portion of such facility) as a COVID–19 treatment center, or revocation of such a designation, under this subsection.".

(b) Payment Incentive.—Section 1888(e) of the Social Security Act (42 U.S.C. 1395yy(e)) is amended—

(1) in paragraph (1), in the matter preceding subparagraph (A), by striking "and (12)" and inserting "(12), and (13)"; and

(2) by adding at the end the following new paragraph:

"(13) ADJUSTMENT FOR COVID–19 TREATMENT CENTERS.—In the case of a resident of a skilled nursing facility that has been designated as a COVID–19 treatment center under section 1819(k) (or in the case of a resident who resides in a portion of such facility that has been so designated), if such resident is an eligible individual (as defined in paragraph (5) of such section), the per diem amount of payment for such resident otherwise applicable shall be increased by 20 percent to reflect increased costs associated with such residents.".

FUNDING FOR STATE STRIKE TEAMS FOR RESIDENT AND EMPLOYEE SAFETY IN SKILLED NURSING FACILITIES AND NURSING FACILITIES

SEC. 30209.

(a) In General.—Of the amounts made available under subsection (c), the Secretary of Health and Human Services (referred to in this section as the "Secretary") shall allocate such amounts among the States, in a manner that takes into account the percentage of skilled nursing facilities and nursing facilities in each State that have residents or employees who have been diagnosed with COVID–19, for purposes of establishing and implementing strike teams in accordance with subsection (b).

(b) Use Of Funds.—A State that receives funds under this section shall use such funds to establish and implement a strike team that will be deployed to a skilled nursing facility or nursing facility in the State with diagnosed or suspected cases of COVID–19 among residents or staff for the purposes of assisting with clinical care, infection control, or staffing.

(c) Authorization Of Appropriations.—For purposes of carrying out this section, there is authorized to be appropriated $500,000,000.

(d) Definitions.—In this section:

(1) NURSING FACILITY.—The term "nursing facility" has the meaning given such

term in section 1919(a) of the Social Security Act (42 U.S.C. 1396r(a)).

(2) SKILLED NURSING FACILITY.—The term "skilled nursing facility" has the meaning given such term in section 1819(a) of the Social Security Act (42 U.S.C. 1395i–3(a)).

PROVIDING FOR INFECTION CONTROL SUPPORT TO SKILLED NURSING FACILITIES THROUGH CONTRACTS WITH QUALITY IMPROVEMENT OR-GANIZATIONS

SEC. 30210.

(a) In General.—Section 1862(g) of the Social Security Act (42 U.S.C. 1395y(g)) is amended—

(1) by striking "The Secretary" and inserting "(1) The Secretary"; and

(2) by adding at the end the following new paragraph:

"(2) (A) The Secretary shall ensure that at least 1 contract with a quality improve-ment organization described in paragraph (1) entered into on or after the date of the enactment of this paragraph and before the end of the emergency period described in section 1135(g)(1)(B) (or in effect as of such date) includes the requirement that such organization provide to skilled nursing facilities with cases of COVID–19 (or facilities attempting to prevent outbreaks of COVID–19) infection control support described in subparagraph (B) during such period.

"(B) For purposes of subparagraph (A), the infection control support described in this subparagraph is, with respect to skilled nursing facilities described in such sub-paragraph, the development and dissemination to such facilities of protocols relating to the prevention or mitigation of COVID–19 at such facilities and the provision of training materials to such facilities relating to such prevention or mitigation.".

(b) Funding.—The Secretary of Health and Human Services shall provide for the transfer from the Federal Supplementary Medical Insurance Trust Fund (as described in section 1841 of the Social Security Act (42 U.S.C. 1395t)) and the Federal Hospital Insurance Trust Fund (as described in section 1817 of such Act (42 U.S.C. 1395i)), in such proportions as determined appropriate by the Secretary, to the Centers for Medicare & Medicaid Services Program Management Account, of $210,000,000, to remain available until expended, for purposes of entering into contracts with quality improvement organizations under part B of title XI of such Act (42 U.S.C. 1320c et seq.). Of the amount transferred pursuant to the previous sentence, not less that $110,000,000 shall be used for purposes of entering into such a contract that includes the requirement described in section 1862(g)(2)(A) of such Act (as added by subsection (a)).

REQUIRING LONG TERM CARE FACILITIES TO REPORT CERTAIN INFOR-MATION RELATING TO COVID–19 CASES AND DEATHS

SEC. 30211.

(a) In General.—The Secretary of Health and Human Services (in this section referred to as the "Secretary") shall, as soon as practicable, require that the information de-scribed in paragraph (1) of section 483.80(g) of title 42, Code of Federal Regulations, or a successor regulation, be reported by a facility (as defined for purposes of such section).

(b) Demographic Information.—The Secretary shall post the following information with respect to skilled nursing facilities (as defined in section 1819(a) of the Social Security Act (42 U.S.C. 1395i–3(a))) and nursing facilities (as defined in section

1919(a) of such Act (42 U.S.C. 1396r(a))) on the Nursing Home Compare website (as described in section 1819(i) of the Social Security Act (42 U.S.C. 1395i–3(i))), or a successor website, aggregated by State:

(1) The age, race/ethnicity, and preferred language of the residents of such skilled nursing facilities and nursing facilities with suspected or confirmed COVID–19 infections, including residents previously treated for COVID–19.

(2) The age, race/ethnicity, and preferred language relating to total deaths and COVID–19 deaths among residents of such skilled nursing facilities and nursing facilities.

(c) Confidentiality.—Any information reported under this section that is made available to the public shall be made so available in a manner that protects the identity of residents of skilled nursing facilities and nursing facilities.

(d) Implementation.—The Secretary may implement the provisions of this section be program instruction or otherwise.

FLOOR ON THE MEDICARE AREA WAGE INDEX FOR HOSPITALS IN ALL-URBAN STATES

SEC. 30212.

(a) In General.—Section 1886(d)(3)(E) of the Social Security Act (42 U.S.C. 1395ww(d)(3)(E)) is amended—

(1) in clause (i), in the first sentence, by striking "or (iii)" and inserting ", (iii), or (iv)"; and

(2) by adding at the end the following new clause:

"(iv) FLOOR ON AREA WAGE INDEX FOR HOSPITALS IN ALL-URBAN STATES.—

"(I) IN GENERAL.—For discharges occurring on or after October 1, 2021, the area wage index applicable under this subparagraph to any hospital in an all-urban State (as defined in subclause (IV)) may not be less than the minimum area wage index for the fiscal year for hospitals in that State, as established under subclause (II).

"(II) MINIMUM AREA WAGE INDEX.—For purposes of subclause (I), the Secretary shall establish a minimum area wage index for a fiscal year for hospitals in each all-urban State using the methodology described in section 412.64(h)(4) of title 42, Code of Federal Regulations, as in effect for fiscal year 2018.

"(III) WAIVING BUDGET NEUTRALITY.—Pursuant to the fifth sentence of clause (i), this subsection shall not be applied in a budget neutral manner.

"(IV) ALL-URBAN STATE DEFINED.—In this clause, the term 'all-urban State' means a State in which there are no rural areas (as defined in paragraph (2)(D)) or a State in which there are no hospitals classified as rural under this section.".

(b) Waiving Budget Neutrality.—

(1) TECHNICAL AMENDATORY CORRECTION.—Section 10324(a)(2) of Public Law 111–148 is amended by striking "third sentence" and inserting "fifth sentence".

(2) WAIVER.—Section 1886(d)(3)(E)(i) of the Social Security Act (42 U.S.C. 1395ww(d)(3)(E)(i)) is amended, in the fifth sentence—

(A) by striking "and the amendments" and inserting ", the amendments"; and

(B) by inserting ", and the amendments made by section 30212 of the HEROES Act" after "Care Act".

TITLE III

—PRIVATE INSURANCE PROVISIONS

Subtitle A—Health Plans

SPECIAL ENROLLMENT PERIOD THROUGH EXCHANGES; FEDERAL EX-
CHANGE OUTREACH AND EDUCATIONAL ACTIVITIES

SEC. 30301.

(a) Special Enrollment Period Through Exchanges.—Section 1311(c) of the Patient
Protection and Affordable Care Act (42 U.S.C. 18031(c)) is amended—

(1) in paragraph (6)—

(A) in subparagraph (C), by striking at the end "and";

(B) in subparagraph (D), by striking at the end the period and inserting "; and"; and

(C) by adding at the end the following new subparagraph:

"(E) subject to subparagraph (B) of paragraph (8), the special enrollment period
described in subparagraph (A) of such paragraph."; and

(2) by adding at the end the following new paragraph:

"(8) SPECIAL ENROLLMENT PERIOD FOR CERTAIN PUBLIC HEALTH EMER-
GENCY.—

"(A) IN GENERAL.—The Secretary shall, subject to subparagraph (B), require an
Exchange to provide—

"(i) for a special enrollment period during the emergency period described in section
1135(g)(1)(B) of the Social Security Act—

"(I) which shall begin on the date that is one week after the date of the enactment of
this paragraph and which, in the case of an Exchange established or operated by the
Secretary within a State pursuant to section 1321(c), shall be an 8-week period; and

"(II) during which any individual who is otherwise eligible to enroll in a qualified
health plan through the Exchange may enroll in such a qualified health plan; and

"(ii) that, in the case of an individual who enrolls in a qualified health plan through the
Exchange during such enrollment period, the coverage period under such plan shall
begin, at the option of the individual, on April 1, 2020, or on the first day of the month
following the day the individual selects a plan through such special enrollment period.

"(B) EXCEPTION.—The requirement of subparagraph (A) shall not apply to a
State-operated or State-established Exchange if such Exchange, prior to the date
of the enactment of this paragraph, established or otherwise provided for a special
enrollment period to address access to coverage under qualified health plans offered
through such Exchange during the emergency period described in section 1135(g)
(1)(B) of the Social Security Act.".

(b) Federal Exchange Outreach And Educational Activities.—Section 1321(c) of
the Patient Protection and Affordable Care Act (42 U.S.C. 18041(c)) is amended by
adding at the end the following new paragraph:

"(3) OUTREACH AND EDUCATIONAL ACTIVITIES.—

"(A) IN GENERAL.—In the case of an Exchange established or operated by the Secretary within a State pursuant to this subsection, the Secretary shall carry out outreach
and educational activities for purposes of informing potential enrollees in qualified
health plans offered through the Exchange of the availability of coverage under such
plans and financial assistance for coverage under such plans. Such outreach and educational activities shall be provided in a manner that is culturally and linguistically
appropriate to the needs of the populations being served by the Exchange (including
hard-to-reach populations, such as racial and sexual minorities, limited English pro-

ficient populations, and young adults).

"(B) LIMITATION ON USE OF FUNDS.—No funds appropriated under this paragraph shall be used for expenditures for promoting non-ACA compliant health insurance coverage.

"(C) NON-ACA COMPLIANT HEALTH INSURANCE COVERAGE.—For purposes of subparagraph (B):

"(i) The term 'non-ACA compliant health insurance coverage' means health insurance coverage, or a group health plan, that is not a qualified health plan.

"(ii) Such term includes the following:

"(I) An association health plan.

"(II) Short-term limited duration insurance.

"(D) FUNDING.—There are appropriated, out of any funds in the Treasury not otherwise appropriated, $25,000,000, to remain available until expended—

"(i) to carry out this paragraph; and—

"(ii) at the discretion of the Secretary, to carry out section 1311(i), with respect to an Exchange established or operated by the Secretary within a State pursuant to this subsection.".

(c) Implementation.—The Secretary of Health and Human Services may implement the provisions of (including amendments made by) this section through subregulatory guidance, program instruction, or otherwise.

EXPEDITED MEETING OF ACIP FOR COVID–19 VACCINES

SEC. 30302.

(a) In General.—Notwithstanding section 3091 of the 21st Century Cures Act (21 U.S.C. 360bbb–4 note), the Advisory Committee on Immunization Practices shall meet and issue a recommendation with respect to a vaccine that is intended to prevent or treat COVID–19 not later than 15 business days after the date on which such vaccine is licensed under section 351 of the Public Health Service Act (42 U.S.C. 262).

(b) Definition.—In this section, the term "Advisory Committee on Immunization Practices" means the Advisory Committee on Immunization Practices established by the Secretary of Health and Human Services pursuant to section 222 of the Public Health Service Act (42 U.S.C. 217a), acting through the Director of the Centers for Disease Control and Prevention.

COVERAGE OF COVID–19 RELATED TREATMENT AT NO COST SHARING

SEC. 30303.

(a) In General.—A group health plan and a health insurance issuer offering group or individual health insurance coverage (including a grandfathered health plan (as defined in section 1251(e) of the Patient Protection and Affordable Care Act)) shall provide coverage, and shall not impose any cost sharing (including deductibles, copayments, and coinsurance) requirements, for the following items and services furnished during any portion of the emergency period defined in paragraph (1)(B) of section 1135(g) of the Social Security Act (42 U.S.C. 1320b–5(g)) beginning on or after the date of the enactment of this Act:

(1) Medically necessary items and services (including in-person or telehealth visits in which such items and services are furnished) that are furnished to an individual who has been diagnosed with (or after provision of the items and services is diagnosed with) COVID–19 to treat or mitigate the effects of COVID–19.

(2) Medically necessary items and services (including in-person or telehealth visits

in which such items and services are furnished) that are furnished to an individual who is presumed to have COVID–19 but is never diagnosed as such, if the following conditions are met:

(A) Such items and services are furnished to the individual to treat or mitigate the effects of COVID–19 or to mitigate the impact of COVID–19 on society.

(B) Health care providers have taken appropriate steps under the circumstances to make a diagnosis, or confirm whether a diagnosis was made, with respect to such individual, for COVID–19, if possible.

(b) Items And Services Related To COVID–19.—For purposes of this section—

(1) not later than one week after the date of the enactment of this section, the Secretary of Health and Human Services, Secretary of Labor, and Secretary of the Treasury shall jointly issue guidance specifying applicable diagnoses and medically necessary items and services related to COVID–19; and

(2) such items and services shall include all items or services that are relevant to the treatment or mitigation of COVID–19, regardless of whether such items or services are ordinarily covered under the terms of a group health plan or group or individual health insurance coverage offered by a health insurance issuer.

(c) Enforcement.—

(1) APPLICATION WITH RESPECT TO PHSA, ERISA, AND IRC.—The provisions of this section shall be applied by the Secretary of Health and Human Services, Secretary of Labor, and Secretary of the Treasury to group health plans and health insurance issuers offering group or individual health insurance coverage as if included in the provisions of part A of title XXVII of the Public Health Service Act, part 7 of the Employee Retirement Income Security Act of 1974, and subchapter B of chapter 100 of the Internal Revenue Code of 1986, as applicable.

(2) PRIVATE RIGHT OF ACTION.—An individual with respect to whom an action is taken by a group health plan or health insurance issuer offering group or individual health insurance coverage in violation of subsection (a) may commence a civil action against the plan or issuer for appropriate relief. The previous sentence shall not be construed as limiting any enforcement mechanism otherwise applicable pursuant to paragraph (1).

(d) Implementation.—The Secretary of Health and Human Services, Secretary of Labor, and Secretary of the Treasury may implement the provisions of this section through sub-regulatory guidance, program instruction or otherwise.

(e) Terms.—The terms "group health plan"; "health insurance issuer"; "group health insurance coverage", and "individual health insurance coverage" have the meanings given such terms in section 2791 of the Public Health Service Act (42 U.S.C. 300gg–91), section 733 of the Employee Retirement Income Security Act of 1974 (29 U.S.C. 1191b), and section 9832 of the Internal Revenue Code of 1986, as applicable.

REQUIRING PRESCRIPTION DRUG REFILL NOTIFICATIONS DURING EMERGENCIES

SEC. 30304.

(a) ERISA.—

(1) IN GENERAL.—Subpart B of part 7 of subtitle B of title I of the Employee Retirement Income Security Act of 1974 (29 U.S.C. 1185 et seq.) is amended by adding at the end the following new section:

"SEC. 716. PROVISION OF PRESCRIPTION DRUG REFILL NOTIFICA-

TIONS DURING EMERGENCIES.

"(a) In General.—A group health plan, and a health insurance issuer offering health insurance coverage in connection with a group health plan, that provides benefits for prescription drugs under such plan or such coverage shall provide to each participant or beneficiary under such plan or such coverage who resides in an emergency area during an emergency period—

"(1) not later than 5 business days after the date of the beginning of such period with respect to such area (or, the case of the emergency period described in section 30304(d)(2) of the HEROES Act, not later than 5 business days after the date of the enactment of this section), a notification (written in a manner that is clear and understandable to the average participant or beneficiary)—

"(A) of whether such plan or coverage will waive, during such period with respect to such a participant or beneficiary, any time restrictions under such plan or coverage on any authorized refills for such drugs to enable such refills in advance of when such refills would otherwise have been permitted under such plan or coverage; and

"(B) in the case that such plan or coverage will waive such restrictions during such period with respect to such a participant or beneficiary, that contains information on how such a participant or beneficiary may obtain such a refill; and

"(2) in the case such plan or coverage elects to so waive such restrictions during such period with respect to such a participant or beneficiary after the notification described in paragraph (1) has been provided with respect to such period, not later than 5 business days after such election, a notification of such election that contains the information described in subparagraph (B) of such paragraph.

"(b) Emergency Area; Emergency Period.—For purposes of this section, an 'emergency area' is a geographical area in which, and an 'emergency period' is the period during which, there exists—

"(1) an emergency or disaster declared by the President pursuant to the National Emergencies Act or the Robert T. Stafford Disaster Relief and Emergency Assistance Act; and

"(2) a public health emergency declared by the Secretary pursuant to section 319 of the Public Health Service Act.".

(2) CLERICAL AMENDMENT.—The table of contents of the Employee Retirement Income Security Act of 1974 is amended by inserting after the item relating to section 714 the following:

"SEC. 715. Additional market reforms.

"SEC. 716. Provision of prescription drug refill notifications during emergencies.".

(b) PHSA.—Subpart II of part A of title XXVII of the Public Health Service Act (42 U.S.C. 300gg–11 et seq.) is amended by adding at the end the following new section:

"SEC. 2730. PROVISION OF PRESCRIPTION DRUG REFILL NOTIFICATIONS DURING EMERGENCIES.

"(a) In General.—A group health plan, and a health insurance issuer offering group or individual health insurance coverage, that provides benefits for prescription drugs under such plan or such coverage shall provide to each participant, beneficiary, or enrollee enrolled under such plan or such coverage who resides in an emergency area during an emergency period—

"(1) not later than 5 business days after the date of the beginning of such period with respect to such area (or, the case of the emergency period described in section 30304(d)(2) of the HEROES Act, not later than 5 business days after the date of the enactment of this section), a notification (written in a manner that is clear and understandable to the average participant, beneficiary, or enrollee)—

"(A) of whether such plan or coverage will waive, during such period with respect to such a participant, beneficiary, or enrollee, any time restrictions under such plan or coverage on any authorized refills for such drugs to enable such refills in advance of when such refills would otherwise have been permitted under such plan or coverage; and

"(B) in the case that such plan or coverage will waive such restrictions during such period with respect to such a participant, beneficiary, or enrollee, that contains information on how such a participant, beneficiary, or enrollee may obtain such a refill; and

"(2) in the case such plan or coverage elects to so waive such restrictions during such period with respect to such a participant, beneficiary, or enrollee after the notification described in paragraph (1) has been provided with respect to such period, not later than 5 business days after such election, a notification of such election that contains the information described in subparagraph (B) of such paragraph.

"(b) Emergency Area; Emergency Period.—For purposes of this section, an 'emergency area' is a geographical area in which, and an 'emergency period' is the period during which, there exists—

"(1) an emergency or disaster declared by the President pursuant to the National Emergencies Act or the Robert T. Stafford Disaster Relief and Emergency Assistance Act; and

"(2) a public health emergency declared by the Secretary pursuant to section 319.".

(c) IRC.—

(1) IN GENERAL.—Subchapter B of chapter 100 of the Internal Revenue Code of 1986 is amended by adding at the end the following new section:

"SEC. 9816. PROVISION OF PRESCRIPTION DRUG REFILL NOTIFICA-TIONS DURING EMERGENCIES.

"(a) In General.—A group health plan that provides benefits for prescription drugs under such plan shall provide to each participant or beneficiary enrolled under such plan who resides in an emergency area during an emergency period, not later than 5 business days after the date of the beginning of such period with respect to such area (or, the case of the emergency period described in section 30304(d)(2) of the HEROES Act, not later than 5 business days after the date of the enactment of this section)—

"(1) a notification (written in a manner that is clear and understandable to the average participant or beneficiary)—

"(A) of whether such plan will waive, during such period with respect to such a participant or beneficiary, any time restrictions under such plan on any authorized refills for such drugs to enable such refills in advance of when such refills would otherwise have been permitted under such plan; and

"(B) in the case that such plan will waive such restrictions during such period with respect to such a participant or beneficiary, that contains information on how such a participant or beneficiary may obtain such a refill; and

"(2) in the case such plan elects to so waive such restrictions during such period with respect to such a participant or beneficiary after the notification described in paragraph (1) has been provided with respect to such period, not later than 5 business days after such election, a notification of such election that contains the information described in subparagraph (B) of such paragraph.

"(b) Emergency Area; Emergency Period.—For purposes of this section, an 'emergency area' is a geographical area in which, and an 'emergency period' is the period during which, there exists—

"(1) an emergency or disaster declared by the President pursuant to the National Emergencies Act or the Robert T. Stafford Disaster Relief and Emergency Assistance Act; and

"(2) a public health emergency declared by the Secretary pursuant to section 319 of the Public Health Service Act.".

(2) CLERICAL AMENDMENT.—The table of sections for subchapter B of chapter 100 of the Internal Revenue Code of 1986 is amended by adding at the end the following new item:

"SEC. 9816. Provision of prescription drug refill notifications during emergencies.".

(d) Effective Date.—The amendments made by this section shall apply with respect to—

(1) emergency periods beginning on or after the date of the enactment of this Act; and

(2) the emergency period relating to the public health emergency declared by the Secretary of Health and Human Services pursuant to section 319 of the Public Health Service Act on January 31, 2020, entitled "Determination that a Public Health Emergency Exists Nationwide as the Result of the 2019 Novel Coronavirus".

IMPROVEMENT OF CERTAIN NOTIFICATIONS PROVIDED TO QUALIFIED BENEFICIARIES BY GROUP HEALTH PLANS IN THE CASE OF QUALIFYING EVENTS

SEC. 30305.

(a) Employee Retirement Income Security Act Of 1974.—

(1) IN GENERAL.—Section 606 of the Employee Retirement Income Security Act of 1974 (29 U.S.C. 1166) is amended—

(A) in subsection (a)(4), in the matter following subparagraph (B), by striking "under this subsection" and inserting "under this part in accordance with the notification requirements under subsection (c)"; and

(B) in subsection (c)—

(i) by striking "For purposes of subsection (a)(4), any notification" and inserting For purposes of subsection (a)(4)—

"(1) any notification";

(ii) by striking ", whichever is applicable, and any such notification" and inserting of subsection (a), whichever is applicable;

"(2) any such notification"; and

(iii) by striking "such notification is made" and inserting such notification is made; and

"(3) any such notification shall, with respect to each qualified beneficiary with respect to whom such notification is made, include information regarding any Exchange established under title I of the Patient Protection and Affordable Care Act through which such a qualified beneficiary may be eligible to enroll in a qualified health plan (as defined in section 1301 of the Patient Protection and Affordable Care Act), including—

"(A) the publicly accessible Internet website address for such Exchange;

"(B) the publicly accessible Internet website address for the Find Local Help directory maintained by the Department of Health and Human Services on the healthcare.gov Internet website (or a successor website);

"(C) a clear explanation that—

"(i) an individual who is eligible for continuation coverage may also be eligible to enroll, with financial assistance, in a qualified health plan offered through such Exchange, but, in the case that such individual elects to enroll in such continuation coverage and subsequently elects to terminate such continuation coverage before the period of such continuation coverage expires, such individual will not be eligible to enroll in a qualified health plan offered through such Exchange during a special enrollment period; and

"(ii) an individual who elects to enroll in continuation coverage will remain eligible to enroll in a qualified health plan offered through such Exchange during an open enrollment period and may be eligible for financial assistance with respect to enrolling in such a qualified health plan;

"(D) information on consumer protections with respect to enrolling in a qualified health plan offered through such Exchange, including the requirement for such a qualified health plan to provide coverage for essential health benefits (as defined in section 1302(b) of the Patient Protection and Affordable Care Act) and the requirements applicable to such a qualified health plan under part A of title XXVII of the Public Health Service Act; and

"(E) information on the availability of financial assistance with respect to enrolling in a qualified health plan, including the maximum income limit for eligibility for a premium tax credit under section 36B of the Internal Revenue Code of 1986.".

(2) EFFECTIVE DATE.—The amendments made by paragraph (1) shall apply with respect to qualifying events occurring on or after the date that is 14 days after the date of the enactment of this Act.

(b) Public Health Service Act.—

(1) IN GENERAL.—Section 2206 of the Public Health Service Act (42 U.S.C. 300bb–6) is amended—

(A) by striking "In accordance" and inserting the following:

"(a) In General.—In accordance";

(B) by striking "of such beneficiary's rights under this subsection" and inserting "of such beneficiary's rights under this title in accordance with the notification requirements under subsection (b)"; and

(C) by striking "For purposes of paragraph (4)," and all that follows through "such notification is made." and inserting the following:

"(b) Rules Relating To Notification Of Qualified Beneficiaries By Plan Administrator.—For purposes of subsection (a)(4)—

"(1) any notification shall be made within 14 days of the date on which the plan administrator is notified under paragraph (2) or (3) of subsection (a), whichever is applicable;

"(2) any such notification to an individual who is a qualified beneficiary as the spouse of the covered employee shall be treated as notification to all other qualified beneficiaries residing with such spouse at the time such notification is made; and

"(3) any such notification shall, with respect to each qualified beneficiary with respect to whom such notification is made, include information regarding any Exchange established under title I of the Patient Protection and Affordable Care Act through which such a qualified beneficiary may be eligible to enroll in a qualified health plan (as defined in section 1301 of the Patient Protection and Affordable Care Act), including—

"(A) the publicly accessible Internet website address for such Exchange;

"(B) the publicly accessible Internet website address for the Find Local Help directory maintained by the Department of Health and Human Services on the healthcare.gov Internet website (or a successor website);

"(C) a clear explanation that—

"(i) an individual who is eligible for continuation coverage may also be eligible to enroll, with financial assistance, in a qualified health plan offered through such Exchange, but, in the case that such individual elects to enroll in such continuation coverage and subsequently elects to terminate such continuation coverage before the period of such continuation coverage expires, such individual will not be eligible to enroll in a qualified health plan offered through such Exchange during a special enrollment period; and

"(ii) an individual who elects to enroll in continuation coverage will remain eligible to enroll in a qualified health plan offered through such Exchange during an open enrollment period and may be eligible for financial assistance with respect to enrolling in such a qualified health plan;

"(D) information on consumer protections with respect to enrolling in a qualified health plan offered through such Exchange, including the requirement for such a qualified health plan to provide coverage for essential health benefits (as defined in section 1302(b) of the Patient Protection and Affordable Care Act) and the requirements applicable to such a qualified health plan under part A of title XXVII; and

"(E) information on the availability of financial assistance with respect to enrolling in a qualified health plan, including the maximum income limit for eligibility for a premium tax credit under section 36B of the Internal Revenue Code of 1986.".

(2) EFFECTIVE DATE.—The amendments made by paragraph (1) shall apply with respect to qualifying events occurring on or after the date that is 14 days after the date of the enactment of this Act.

(c) Internal Revenue Code Of 1986.—

(1) IN GENERAL.—Section 4980B(f)(6) of the Internal Revenue Code of 1986 is amended—

(A) in subparagraph (D)—

(i) in clause (ii), by striking "under subparagraph (C)" and inserting "under clause (iii)"; and

(ii) by redesignating clauses (i) and (ii) as subclauses (I) and (II), respectively, and moving the margin of each such subclause, as so redesignated, 2 ems to the right;

(B) by redesignating subparagraphs (A) through (D) as clauses (i) through (iv), respectively, and moving the margin of each such clause, as so redesignated, 2 ems to the right;

(C) by striking "In accordance" and inserting the following:

"(A) IN GENERAL.—In accordance";

(D) by inserting after "of such beneficiary's rights under this subsection" the following: "in accordance with the notification requirements under subparagraph (C)"; and

(E) by striking "The requirements of subparagraph (B)" and all that follows through "such notification is made." and inserting the following:

"(B) ALTERNATIVE MEANS OF COMPLIANCE WITH REQUIREMENT FOR

NOTIFICATION OF MULTIEMPLOYER PLANS BY EMPLOYERS.—The requirements of subparagraph (A)(ii) shall be considered satisfied in the case of a multiemployer plan in connection with a qualifying event described in paragraph (3)(B) if the plan provides that the determination of the occurrence of such qualifying event will be made by the plan administrator.

"(C) RULES RELATING TO NOTIFICATION OF QUALIFIED BENEFICIARIES BY PLAN ADMINISTRATOR.—For purposes of subparagraph (A)(iv)—

"(i) any notification shall be made within 14 days (or, in the case of a group health plan which is a multiemployer plan, such longer period of time as may be provided in the terms of the plan) of the date on which the plan administrator is notified under clause (ii) or (iii) of subparagraph (A), whichever is applicable;

"(ii) any such notification to an individual who is a qualified beneficiary as the spouse of the covered employee shall be treated as notification to all other qualified beneficiaries residing with such spouse at the time such notification is made; and

"(iii) any such notification shall, with respect to each qualified beneficiary with respect to whom such notification is made, include information regarding any Exchange established under title I of the Patient Protection and Affordable Care Act through which such a qualified beneficiary may be eligible to enroll in a qualified health plan (as defined in section 1301 of the Patient Protection and Affordable Care Act), including—

"(I) the publicly accessible Internet website address for such Exchange;

"(II) the publicly accessible Internet website address for the Find Local Help directory maintained by the Department of Health and Human Services on the healthcare.gov Internet website (or a successor website);

"(III) a clear explanation that—

"(aa) an individual who is eligible for continuation coverage may also be eligible to enroll, with financial assistance, in a qualified health plan offered through such Exchange, but, in the case that such individual elects to enroll in such continuation coverage and subsequently elects to terminate such continuation coverage before the period of such continuation coverage expires, such individual will not be eligible to enroll in a qualified health plan offered through such Exchange during a special enrollment period; and

"(bb) an individual who elects to enroll in continuation coverage will remain eligible to enroll in a qualified health plan offered through such Exchange during an open enrollment period and may be eligible for financial assistance with respect to enrolling in such a qualified health plan;

"(IV) information on consumer protections with respect to enrolling in a qualified health plan offered through such Exchange, including the requirement for such a qualified health plan to provide coverage for essential health benefits (as defined in section 1302(b) of the Patient Protection and Affordable Care Act) and the requirements applicable to such a qualified health plan under part A of title XXVII of the Public Health Service Act; and

"(V) information on the availability of financial assistance with respect to enrolling in a qualified health plan, including the maximum income limit for eligibility for a premium tax credit under section 36B.".

(2) EFFECTIVE DATE.—The amendments made by paragraph (1) shall apply with respect to qualifying events occurring on or after the date that is 14 days after the date of the enactment of this Act.

(d) Model Notices.—Not later than 14 days after the date of the enactment of this Act, the Secretary of the Labor, in consultation with the Secretary of the Treasury and the Secretary of Health and Human Services, shall—

(1) update the model Consolidated Omnibus Budget Reconciliation Act of 1985 (referred to in this subsection as "COBRA") continuation coverage general notice and the model COBRA continuation coverage election notice developed by the Secretary of Labor for purposes of facilitating compliance of group health plans with the notification requirements under section 606 of the Employee Retirement Income Security Act of 1974 (29 U.S.C. 1166) to include the information described in paragraph (3) of subsection (c) of such section 606, as added by subsection (a)(1);

(2) provide an opportunity for consumer testing of each such notice, as so updated, to ensure that each such notice is clear and understandable to the average participant or beneficiary of a group health plan; and

(3) rename the model COBRA continuation coverage general notice and the model COBRA continuation coverage election notice as the "model COBRA continuation coverage and Affordable Care Act coverage general notice" and the "model COBRA continuation coverage and Affordable Care Act coverage election notice", respectively.
SOONER COVERAGE OF TESTING FOR COVID–19

SEC. 30306.
Section 6001(a) of division F of the Families First Coronavirus Response Act (42 U.S.C. 1320b–5 note) is amended by striking "beginning on or after" and inserting "beginning before, on, or after".

Subtitle B—Worker Health Coverage Protection
SHORT TITLE

SEC. 30311.
This subtitle may be cited as the "Worker Health Coverage Protection Act".
PRESERVING HEALTH BENEFITS FOR WORKERS

SEC. 30312.
(a) Premium Assistance For COBRA Continuation Coverage And Furloughed Continuation Coverage For Individuals And Their Families.—
(1) PROVISION OF PREMIUM ASSISTANCE.—
(A) REDUCTION OF PREMIUMS PAYABLE.—
(i) COBRA CONTINUATION COVERAGE.—In the case of any premium for a period of coverage during the period beginning on March 1, 2020, and ending on January 31, 2021 for COBRA continuation coverage with respect to any assistance eligible individual described in paragraph (3)(A), such individual shall be treated for purposes of any COBRA continuation provision as having paid the amount of such premium if such individual pays (and any person other than such individual's employer pays on behalf of such individual) 0 percent of the amount of such premium owed by such individual (as determined without regard to this subsection).
(ii) FURLOUGHED CONTINUATION COVERAGE.—In the case of any premium for a period of coverage during the period beginning on March 1, 2020, and ending on January 31, 2021 for coverage under a group health plan with respect to any assistance eligible individual described in paragraph (3)(B), such individual shall be treated for purposes of coverage under the plan offered by the plan sponsor in which the individual is enrolled as having paid the amount of such premium if such individual

pays (and any person other than such individual's employer pays on behalf of such individual) 0 percent of the amount of such premium owed by such individual (as determined without regard to this subsection).

(B) PLAN ENROLLMENT OPTION.—

(i) IN GENERAL.—Notwithstanding the COBRA continuation provisions, any assistance eligible individual who is enrolled in a group health plan offered by a plan sponsor may, not later than 90 days after the date of notice of the plan enrollment option described in this subparagraph, elect to enroll in coverage under a plan offered by such plan sponsor that is different than coverage under the plan in which such individual was enrolled at the time—

(I) in the case of any assistance eligible individual described in paragraph (3)(A), the qualifying event specified in section 603(2) of the Employee Retirement Income Security Act of 1974, section 4980B(f)(3)(B) of the Internal Revenue Code of 1986, section 2203(2) of the Public Health Service Act, or section 8905a of title 5, United States Code (except for the voluntary termination of such individual's employment by such individual), occurred, and such coverage shall be treated as COBRA continuation coverage for purposes of the applicable COBRA continuation coverage provision; or

(II) in the case of any assistance eligible individual described in paragraph (3)(B), the furlough period began with respect to such individual.

(ii) REQUIREMENTS.—Any assistance eligible individual may elect to enroll in different coverage as described in clause (i) only if—

(I) the employer involved has made a determination that such employer will permit such assistance eligible individual to enroll in different coverage as provided under this subparagraph;

(II) the premium for such different coverage does not exceed the premium for coverage in which such individual was enrolled at the time such qualifying event occurred or immediately before such furlough began;

(III) the different coverage in which the individual elects to enroll is coverage that is also offered to the active employees of the employer, who are not in a furlough period, at the time at which such election is made; and

(IV) the different coverage in which the individual elects to enroll is not—

(aa) coverage that provides only dental, vision, counseling, or referral services (or a combination of such services);

(bb) a qualified small employer health reimbursement arrangement (as defined in section 9831(d)(2) of the Internal Revenue Code of 1986);

(cc) a flexible spending arrangement (as defined in section 106(c)(2) of the Internal Revenue Code of 1986); or

(dd) benefits that provide coverage for services or treatments furnished in an on-site medical facility maintained by the employer and that consists primarily of first-aid services, prevention and wellness care, or similar care (or a combination of such care).

(C) PREMIUM REIMBURSEMENT.—For provisions providing the payment of such premium, see section 6432 of the Internal Revenue Code of 1986, as added by paragraph (14).

(2) LIMITATION OF PERIOD OF PREMIUM ASSISTANCE.—

(A) ELIGIBILITY FOR ADDITIONAL COVERAGE.—Paragraph (1)(A) shall not apply with respect to—

(i) any assistance eligible individual described in paragraph (3)(A) for months of coverage beginning on or after the earlier of—

(I) the first date that such individual is eligible for coverage under any other group health plan (other than coverage consisting of only dental, vision, counseling, or referral services (or a combination thereof), coverage under a flexible spending arrangement (as defined in section 106(c)(2) of the Internal Revenue Code of 1986), coverage of treatment that is furnished in an on-site medical facility maintained by the employer and that consists primarily of first-aid services, prevention and wellness care, or similar care (or a combination thereof)), or eligible for benefits under the Medicare program under title XVIII of the Social Security Act; or

(II) the earliest of—

(aa) the date following the expiration of the maximum period of continuation coverage required under the applicable COBRA continuation coverage provision; or

(bb) the date following the expiration of the period of continuation coverage allowed under paragraph (4)(B)(ii); or

(ii) any assistance eligible individual described in paragraph (3)(B) for months of coverage beginning on or after the earlier of—

(I) the first date that such individual is eligible for coverage under any other group health plan (other than coverage consisting of only dental, vision, counseling, or referral services (or a combination thereof), coverage under a flexible spending arrangement (as defined in section 106(c)(2) of the Internal Revenue Code of 1986), coverage of treatment that is furnished in an on-site medical facility maintained by the employer and that consists primarily of first-aid services, prevention and wellness care, or similar care (or a combination thereof)), or eligible for benefits under the Medicare program under title XVIII of the Social Security Act; or

(II) the first date that such individual is no longer in the furlough period.

(B) NOTIFICATION REQUIREMENT.—Any assistance eligible individual shall notify the group health plan with respect to which paragraph (1)(A) applies if such paragraph ceases to apply by reason of clause (i)(I) or (ii)(I) of subparagraph (A) (as applicable). Such notice shall be provided to the group health plan in such time and manner as may be specified by the Secretary of Labor.

(C) SPECIAL ENROLLMENT PERIOD FOLLOWING EXPIRATION OF PREMIUM ASSISTANCE.—Notwithstanding section 1311 of the Patient Protection and Affordable Care Act (42 U.S.C. 18031), the expiration of premium assistance pursuant to a limitation specified under subparagraph (A) shall be treated as a qualifying event for which any assistance eligible individual is eligible to enroll in a qualified health plan offered through an Exchange under title I of such Act (42 U.S.C. 18001 et seq.) during a special enrollment period.

(3) ASSISTANCE ELIGIBLE INDIVIDUAL.—For purposes of this section, the term "assistance eligible individual" means, with respect to a period of coverage during the period beginning on March 1, 2020, and ending on January 31, 2021—

(A) any individual that is a qualified beneficiary that—

(i) is eligible for COBRA continuation coverage by reason of a qualifying event specified in section 603(2) of the Employee Retirement Income Security Act of 1974, section 4980B(f)(3)(B) of the Internal Revenue Code of 1986, section 2203(2) of the Public Health Service Act, or section 8905a of title 5, United States Code (except for the voluntary termination of such individual's employment by such individual); and

(ii) elects such coverage; or

(B) any covered employee that is in a furlough period that remains eligible for coverage under a group health plan offered by the employer of such covered employee.

(4) EXTENSION OF ELECTION PERIOD AND EFFECT ON COVERAGE.—

(A) IN GENERAL.—For purposes of applying section 605(a) of the Employee Retirement Income Security Act of 1974, section 4980B(f)(5)(A) of the Internal Revenue Code of 1986, section 2205(a) of the Public Health Service Act, and section 8905a(c)(2) of title 5, United States Code, in the case of—

(i) an individual who does not have an election of COBRA continuation coverage in effect on the date of the enactment of this Act but who would be an assistance eligible individual described in paragraph (3)(A) if such election were so in effect; or

(ii) an individual who elected COBRA continuation coverage on or after March 1, 2020, and discontinued from such coverage before the date of the enactment of this Act,

such individual may elect the COBRA continuation coverage under the COBRA continuation coverage provisions containing such provisions during the period beginning on the date of the enactment of this Act and ending 60 days after the date on which the notification required under paragraph (7)(C) is provided to such individual.

(B) COMMENCEMENT OF COBRA CONTINUATION COVERAGE.—Any COBRA continuation coverage elected by a qualified beneficiary during an extended election period under subparagraph (A)—

(i) shall apply as if such qualified beneficiary had been covered as of the date of a qualifying event specified in section 603(2) of the Employee Retirement Income Security Act of 1974, section 4980B(f)(3)(B) of the Internal Revenue Code of 1986, section 2203(2) of the Public Health Service Act, or section 8905a of title 5, United States Code, except for the voluntary termination of such beneficiary's employment by such beneficiary, that occurs no earlier than March 1, 2020 (including the treatment of premium payments under paragraph (1)(A) and any cost-sharing requirements for items and services under a group health plan); and

(ii) shall not extend beyond the period of COBRA continuation coverage that would have been required under the applicable COBRA continuation coverage provision if the coverage had been elected as required under such provision.

(5) EXPEDITED REVIEW OF DENIALS OF PREMIUM ASSISTANCE.—In any case in which an individual requests treatment as an assistance eligible individual described in subparagraph (A) or (B) of paragraph (3) and is denied such treatment by the group health plan, the Secretary of Labor (or the Secretary of Health and Human Services in connection with COBRA continuation coverage which is provided other than pursuant to part 6 of subtitle B of title I of the Employee Retirement Income Security Act of 1974), in consultation with the Secretary of the Treasury, shall provide for expedited review of such denial. An individual shall be entitled to such review upon application to such Secretary in such form and manner as shall be provided by such Secretary, in consultation with the Secretary of Treasury. Such Secretary shall make a determination regarding such individual's eligibility within 15 business days after receipt of such individual's application for review under this paragraph. Either Secretary's determination upon review of the denial shall be de novo and shall be the final determination of such Secretary. A reviewing court shall grant deference to such Secretary's determination. The provisions of this paragraph, paragraphs (1) through (4), and paragraphs (7) through (9) shall be treated as provisions of title I of the Employee Retirement Income Security Act of 1974 for purposes of part 5 of subtitle B of such title.

(6) DISREGARD OF SUBSIDIES FOR PURPOSES OF FEDERAL AND STATE PRO-

GRAMS.—Notwithstanding any other provision of law, any premium assistance with respect to an assistance eligible individual under this subsection shall not be considered income, in-kind support, or resources for purposes of determining the eligibility of the recipient (or the recipient's spouse or family) for benefits or assistance, or the amount or extent of benefits or assistance, or any other benefit provided under any Federal program or any program of a State or political subdivision thereof financed in whole or in part with Federal funds.

(7) COBRA-SPECIFIC NOTICE.—

(A) GENERAL NOTICE.—

(i) IN GENERAL.—In the case of notices provided under section 606(a)(4) of the Employee Retirement Income Security Act of 1974 (29 U.S.C. 1166(4)), section 4980B(f)(6)(D) of the Internal Revenue Code of 1986, section 2206(4) of the Public Health Service Act (42 U.S.C. 300bb–6(4)), or section 8905a(f)(2)(A) of title 5, United States Code, with respect to individuals who, during the period described in paragraph (3), become entitled to elect COBRA continuation coverage, the requirements of such provisions shall not be treated as met unless such notices include an additional notification to the recipient a written notice in clear and understandable language of—

(I) the availability of premium assistance with respect to such coverage under this subsection; and

(II) the option to enroll in different coverage if the employer permits assistance eligible individuals described in paragraph (3)(A) to elect enrollment in different coverage (as described in paragraph (1)(B)).

(ii) ALTERNATIVE NOTICE.—In the case of COBRA continuation coverage to which the notice provision under such sections does not apply, the Secretary of Labor, in consultation with the Secretary of the Treasury and the Secretary of Health and Human Services, shall, in consultation with administrators of the group health plans (or other entities) that provide or administer the COBRA continuation coverage involved, provide rules requiring the provision of such notice.

(iii) FORM.—The requirement of the additional notification under this subparagraph may be met by amendment of existing notice forms or by inclusion of a separate document with the notice otherwise required.

(B) SPECIFIC REQUIREMENTS.—Each additional notification under subparagraph (A) shall include—

(i) the forms necessary for establishing eligibility for premium assistance under this subsection;

(ii) the name, address, and telephone number necessary to contact the plan administrator and any other person maintaining relevant information in connection with such premium assistance;

(iii) a description of the extended election period provided for in paragraph (4)(A);

(iv) a description of the obligation of the qualified beneficiary under paragraph (2)(B) and the penalty provided under section 6720C of the Internal Revenue Code of 1986 for failure to carry out the obligation;

(v) a description, displayed in a prominent manner, of the qualified beneficiary's right to a reduced premium and any conditions on entitlement to the reduced premium;

(vi) a description of the option of the qualified beneficiary to enroll in different coverage if the employer permits such beneficiary to elect to enroll in such different coverage under paragraph (1)(B); and

(vii) information regarding any Exchange established under title I of the Patient Protection and Affordable Care Act (42 U.S.C. 18001 et seq.) through which a qualified beneficiary may be eligible to enroll in a qualified health plan, including—

(I) the publicly accessible internet website address for such Exchange;

(II) the publicly accessible internet website address for the Find Local Help directory maintained by the Department of Health and Human Services on the healthcare.gov internet website (or a successor website);

(III) a clear explanation that—

(aa) an individual who is eligible for continuation coverage may also be eligible to enroll, with financial assistance, in a qualified health plan offered through such Exchange, but, in the case that such individual elects to enroll in such continuation coverage and subsequently elects to terminate such continuation coverage before the period of such continuation coverage expires, such termination does not initiate a special enrollment period (absent a qualifying event specified in section 603(2) of the Employee Retirement Income Security Act of 1974, section 4980B(f)(3)(B) of the Internal Revenue Code of 1986, section 2203(2) of the Public Health Service Act, or section 8905a of title 5, United States Code, with respect to such individual); and

(bb) an individual who elects to enroll in continuation coverage will remain eligible to enroll in a qualified health plan offered through such Exchange during an open enrollment period and may be eligible for financial assistance with respect to enrolling in such a qualified health plan;

(IV) information on consumer protections with respect to enrolling in a qualified health plan offered through such Exchange, including the requirement for such a qualified health plan to provide coverage for essential health benefits (as defined in section 1302(b) of such Act (42 U.S.C. 18022(b))) and the requirements applicable to such a qualified health plan under part A of title XXVII of the Public Health Service Act (42 U.S.C. 300gg et seq.);

(V) information on the availability of financial assistance with respect to enrolling in a qualified health plan, including the maximum income limit for eligibility for the premium tax credit under section 36B of the Internal Revenue Code of 1986; and

(VI) information on any special enrollment periods during which any assistance eligible individual described in paragraph (3)(A)(i) may be eligible to enroll, with financial assistance, in a qualified health plan offered through such Exchange (including a special enrollment period for which an individual may be eligible due to the expiration of premium assistance pursuant to a limitation specified under paragraph (2)(A)).

(C) NOTICE IN CONNECTION WITH EXTENDED ELECTION PERIODS.—In the case of any assistance eligible individual described in paragraph (3)(A) (or any individual described in paragraph (4)(A)) who became entitled to elect COBRA continuation coverage before the date of the enactment of this Act, the administrator of the applicable group health plan (or other entity) shall provide (within 60 days after the date of enactment of this Act) for the additional notification required to be provided under subparagraph (A) and failure to provide such notice shall be treated as a failure to meet the notice requirements under the applicable COBRA continuation provision.

(D) MODEL NOTICES.—Not later than 30 days after the date of enactment of this Act, with respect to any assistance eligible individual described in paragraph (3)(A)—

(i) the Secretary of Labor, in consultation with the Secretary of the Treasury and the Secretary of Health and Human Services, shall prescribe models for the additional notification required under this paragraph (other than the additional notification described in clause (ii)); and

(ii) in the case of any additional notification provided pursuant to subparagraph (A) under section 8905a(f)(2)(A) of title 5, United States Code, the Office of Personnel Management shall prescribe a model for such additional notification.

(8) FURLOUGH-SPECIFIC NOTICE.—

(A) IN GENERAL.—With respect to any assistance eligible individual described in paragraph (3)(B) who, during the period described in such paragraph, becomes eligible for assistance pursuant to paragraph (1)(A)(ii), the requirements of section 606(a)(4) of the Employee Retirement Income Security Act of 1974 (29 U.S.C. 1166(4)), section 4980B(f)(6)(D) of the Internal Revenue Code of 1986, section 2206(4) of the Public Health Service Act (42 U.S.C. 300bb–6(4)), or section 8905a(f)(2)(A) of title 5, United States Code, shall not be treated as met unless the group health plan administrator, in accordance with the timing requirement specified under subparagraph (B), provides to the individual a written notice in clear and understandable language of—

(i) the availability of premium assistance with respect to such coverage under this subsection;

(ii) the option of the qualified beneficiary to enroll in different coverage if the employer permits such beneficiary to elect to enroll in such different coverage under paragraph (1)(B); and

(iii) the information specified under paragraph (7)(B) (as applicable).

(B) TIMING SPECIFIED.—For purposes of subparagraph (A), the timing requirement specified in this subparagraph is—

(i) with respect to such an individual who is within a furlough period during the period beginning on March 1, 2020, and ending on the date of the enactment of this Act, 30 days after the date of such enactment; and

(ii) with respect to such an individual who is within a furlough period during the period beginning on the first day after the date of the enactment of this Act and ending on January 31, 2021, 30 days after the date of the beginning of such furlough period.

(C) MODEL NOTICES.—Not later than 30 days after the date of enactment of this Act, with respect to any assistance eligible individual described in paragraph (3)(B)—

(i) the Secretary of Labor, in consultation with the Secretary of the Treasury and the Secretary of Health and Human Services, shall prescribe models for the notification required under this paragraph (other than the notification described in clause (ii)); and

(ii) in the case of any notification provided pursuant to subparagraph (A) under section 8905a(f)(2)(A) of title 5, United States Code, the Office of Personnel Management shall prescribe a model for such notification.

(9) NOTICE OF EXPIRATION OF PERIOD OF PREMIUM ASSISTANCE.—

(A) IN GENERAL.—With respect to any assistance eligible individual, subject to subparagraph (B), the requirements of section 606(a)(4) of the Employee Retirement Income Security Act of 1974 (29 U.S.C. 1166(4)), section 4980B(f)(6)(D) of the Internal Revenue Code of 1986, section 2206(4) of the Public Health Service Act (42 U.S.C. 300bb–6(4)), or section 8905a(f)(2)(A) of title 5, United States Code, shall not be treated as met unless the employer of the individual, during the period specified under subparagraph (C), provides to such individual a written notice in clear and understandable language—

(i) that the premium assistance for such individual will expire soon and the prominent identification of the date of such expiration;

(ii) that such individual may be eligible for coverage without any premium assistance through—

(I) COBRA continuation coverage; or

(II) coverage under a group health plan;

(iii) that the expiration of premium assistance is treated as a qualifying event for which any assistance eligible individual is eligible to enroll in a qualified health plan offered through an Exchange under title I of such Act (42 U.S.C. 18001 et seq.) during a special enrollment period; and

(iv) the information specified in paragraph (7)(B)(vii).

(B) EXCEPTION.—The requirement for the group health plan administrator to provide the written notice under subparagraph (A) shall be waived in the case the premium assistance for such individual expires pursuant to clause (i)(I) or (ii)(I) of paragraph (2)(A).

(C) PERIOD SPECIFIED.—For purposes of subparagraph (A), the period specified in this subparagraph is, with respect to the date of expiration of premium assistance for any assistance eligible individual pursuant to a limitation requiring a notice under this paragraph, the period beginning on the day that is 45 days before the date of such expiration and ending on the day that is 15 days before the date of such expiration.

(D) MODEL NOTICES.—Not later than 30 days after the date of enactment of this Act, with respect to any assistance eligible individual—

(i) the Secretary of Labor, in consultation with the Secretary of the Treasury and the Secretary of Health and Human Services, shall prescribe models for the notification required under this paragraph (other than the notification described in clause (ii)); and

(ii) in the case of any notification provided pursuant to subparagraph (A) under section 8905a(f)(2)(A) of title 5, United States Code, the Office of Personnel Management shall prescribe a model for such notification.

(10) REGULATIONS.—The Secretary of the Treasury and the Secretary of Labor may jointly prescribe such regulations or other guidance as may be necessary or appropriate to carry out the provisions of this subsection, including the prevention of fraud and abuse under this subsection, except that the Secretary of Labor and the Secretary of Health and Human Services may prescribe such regulations (including interim final regulations) or other guidance as may be necessary or appropriate to carry out the provisions of paragraphs (5), (7), (8), (9), and (11).

(11) OUTREACH.—

(A) IN GENERAL.—The Secretary of Labor, in consultation with the Secretary of the Treasury and the Secretary of Health and Human Services, shall provide outreach consisting of public education and enrollment assistance relating to premium assistance provided under this subsection. Such outreach shall target employers, group health plan administrators, public assistance programs, States, insurers, and other entities as determined appropriate by such Secretaries. Such outreach shall include an initial focus on those individuals electing continuation coverage who are referred to in paragraph (7)(C). Information on such premium assistance, including enrollment, shall also be made available on websites of the Departments of Labor, Treasury, and Health and Human Services.

(B) ENROLLMENT UNDER MEDICARE.—The Secretary of Health and Human Services shall provide outreach consisting of public education. Such outreach shall target individuals who lose health insurance coverage. Such outreach shall include information regarding enrollment for benefits under title XVIII of the Social Security

Act (42 U.S.C. 1395 et seq.) for purposes of preventing mistaken delays of such enrollment by such individuals, including lifetime penalties for failure of timely enrollment.

(12) DEFINITIONS.—For purposes of this section:

(A) ADMINISTRATOR.—The term "administrator" has the meaning given such term in section 3(16)(A) of the Employee Retirement Income Security Act of 1974.

(B) COBRA CONTINUATION COVERAGE.—The term "COBRA continuation coverage" means continuation coverage provided pursuant to part 6 of subtitle B of title I of the Employee Retirement Income Security Act of 1974 (other than under section 609), title XXII of the Public Health Service Act, section 4980B of the Internal Revenue Code of 1986 (other than subsection (f)(1) of such section insofar as it relates to pediatric vaccines), or section 8905a of title 5, United States Code, or under a State program that provides comparable continuation coverage. Such term does not include coverage under a health flexible spending arrangement under a cafeteria plan within the meaning of section 125 of the Internal Revenue Code of 1986.

(C) COBRA CONTINUATION PROVISION.—The term "COBRA continuation provision" means the provisions of law described in subparagraph (B).

(D) COVERED EMPLOYEE.—The term "covered employee" has the meaning given such term in section 607(2) of the Employee Retirement Income Security Act of 1974.

(E) QUALIFIED BENEFICIARY.—The term "qualified beneficiary" has the meaning given such term in section 607(3) of the Employee Retirement Income Security Act of 1974.

(F) GROUP HEALTH PLAN.—The term "group health plan" has the meaning given such term in section 607(1) of the Employee Retirement Income Security Act of 1974.

(G) STATE.—The term "State" includes the District of Columbia, the Commonwealth of Puerto Rico, the Virgin Islands, Guam, American Samoa, and the Commonwealth of the Northern Mariana Islands.

(H) PERIOD OF COVERAGE.—Any reference in this subsection to a period of coverage shall be treated as a reference to a monthly or shorter period of coverage with respect to which premiums are charged with respect to such coverage.

(I) PLAN SPONSOR.—The term "plan sponsor" has the meaning given such term in section 3(16)(B) of the Employee Retirement Income Security Act of 1974.

(J) FURLOUGH PERIOD.—

(i) IN GENERAL.—The term "furlough period" means, with respect to an individual and an employer of such individual, a period—

(I) beginning with the first month beginning on or after March 1, 2020 and before January 31, 2021, during which such individual's employer reduces such individual's work hours (due to a lack of work, funds, or other nondisciplinary reason) to an amount that is less than 70 percent of the base month amount; and

(II) ending with the earlier of—

(aa) the first month beginning after January 31, 2021; or

(bb) the month following the first month during which work hours of such employee are greater than 80 percent of work hours of the base month amount.

(ii) BASE MONTH AMOUNT.—For purposes of clause (i), the term "base month amount" means, with respect to an individual and an employer of such individual, the greater of—

(I) such individual's work hours in the month prior (or in the case such individual had no work hours in the month prior and had work hours in the 3 months prior, the last month with work hours within the prior 3 months); and

(II) such individual's work hours during the period beginning January 1, 2020 and ending January 31, 2020.

(13) REPORTS.—

(A) INTERIM REPORT.—The Secretary of the Treasury and the Secretary of Labor shall jointly submit an interim report to the Committee on Education and Labor, the Committee on Ways and Means, and the Committee on Energy and Commerce of the House of Representatives and the Committee on Health, Education, Labor, and Pensions and the Committee on Finance of the Senate regarding the premium assistance provided under this subsection that includes—

(i) the number of individuals provided such assistance as of the date of the report; and

(ii) the total amount of expenditures incurred (with administrative expenditures noted separately) in connection with such assistance as of the date of the report.

(B) FINAL REPORT.—As soon as practicable after the last period of COBRA continuation coverage for which premium assistance is provided under this section, the Secretary of the Treasury and the Secretary of Labor shall jointly submit a final report to each Committee referred to in subparagraph (A) that includes—

(i) the number of individuals provided premium assistance under this section;

(ii) the average dollar amount (monthly and annually) of premium assistance provided to such individuals; and

(iii) the total amount of expenditures incurred (with administrative expenditures noted separately) in connection with premium assistance under this section.

(14) COBRA PREMIUM ASSISTANCE.—

(A) IN GENERAL.—Subchapter B of chapter 65 of the Internal Revenue Code of 1986 is amended by adding at the end the following new section:

"SEC. 6432. CONTINUATION COVERAGE PREMIUM ASSISTANCE.

"(a) In General.—The person to whom premiums are payable for continuation coverage under section 30312(a)(1) of the Worker Health Coverage Protection Act shall be allowed as a credit against the tax imposed by section 3111(a), or so much of the taxes imposed under section 3221(a) as are attributable to the rate in effect under section 3111(a), for each calendar quarter an amount equal to the premiums not paid by assistance eligible individuals for such coverage by reason of such section 30312(a)(1) with respect to such calendar quarter.

"(b) Person To Whom Premiums Are Payable.—For purposes of subsection (a), except as otherwise provided by the Secretary, the person to whom premiums are payable under such continuation coverage shall be treated as being—

"(1) in the case of any group health plan which is a multiemployer plan (as defined in section 3(37) of the Employee Retirement Income Security Act of 1974), the plan,

"(2) in the case of any group health plan not described in paragraph (1)—

"(A) which provides furlough continuation coverage described in section 30312(a)(1)(A)(ii) of the Worker Health Coverage Protection Act or subject to the COBRA continuation provisions contained in—

"(i) this title,

"(ii) the Employee Retirement Income Security Act of 1974,

"(iii) the Public Health Service Act, or

"(iv) title 5, United States Code, or

"(B) under which some or all of the coverage is not provided by insurance, the employer maintaining the plan, and

"(3) in the case of any group health plan not described in paragraph (1) or (2), the insurer providing the coverage under the group health plan.

"(c) Limitations And Refundability.—

"(1) CREDIT LIMITED TO CERTAIN EMPLOYMENT TAXES.—The credit allowed by subsection (a) with respect to any calendar quarter shall not exceed the tax imposed by section 3111(a), or so much of the taxes imposed under section 3221(a) as are attributable to the rate in effect under section 3111(a), for such calendar quarter (reduced by any credits allowed under subsections (e) and (f) of section 3111, sections 7001 and 7003 of the Families First Coronavirus Response Act, section 2301 of the CARES Act, and sections 20204 and 20212 of the COVID–19 Tax Relief Act of 2020 for such quarter) on the wages paid with respect to the employment of all employees of the employer.

"(2) REFUNDABILITY OF EXCESS CREDIT.—

"(A) CREDIT IS REFUNDABLE.—If the amount of the credit under subsection (a) exceeds the limitation of paragraph (1) for any calendar quarter, such excess shall be treated as an overpayment that shall be refunded under sections 6402(a) and 6413(b).

"(B) CREDIT MAY BE ADVANCED.—In anticipation of the credit, including the refundable portion under subparagraph (A), the credit may be advanced, according to forms and instructions provided by the Secretary, up to an amount calculated under subsection (a) through the end of the most recent payroll period in the quarter.

"(C) TREATMENT OF DEPOSITS.—The Secretary shall waive any penalty under section 6656 for any failure to make a deposit of the tax imposed by section 3111(a), or so much of the taxes imposed under section 3221(a) as are attributable to the rate in effect under section 3111(a), if the Secretary determines that such failure was due to the anticipation of the credit allowed under this section.

"(D) TREATMENT OF PAYMENTS.—For purposes of section 1324 of title 31, United States Code, any amounts due to an employer under this paragraph shall be treated in the same manner as a refund due from a credit provision referred to in subsection (b)(2) of such section.

"(3) LIMITATION ON REIMBURSEMENT FOR FURLOUGHED EMPLOYEES.— In the case of an individual who for any month is an assistance eligible individual described in section 30312(a)(3)(B) of the Worker Health Coverage Protection Act with respect to any coverage, the credit determined with respect to such individual under subsection (a) for any such month ending during a calendar quarter shall not exceed the amount of premium the individual would have paid for a full month of such coverage for the month preceding the first month for which an individual is such an assistance eligible individual.

"(d) Governmental Entities.—For purposes of this section, the term 'person' includes any governmental entity or Indian tribal government (as defined in section 139E(c)(1)).

"(e) Denial Of Double Benefit.—For purposes of chapter 1, the gross income of any person allowed a credit under this section shall be increased for the taxable year which includes the last day of any calendar quarter with respect to which such credit is allowed by the amount of such credit. No amount for which a credit is allowed under this section shall be taken into account as qualified wages under section 2301 of the CARES Act or as qualified health plan expenses under section 7001(d) or 7003(d) of the Families First Coronavirus Response Act.

"(f) Reporting.—Each person entitled to reimbursement under subsection (a) for any period shall submit such reports (at such time and in such manner) as the Secretary may require, including—

"(1) an attestation of involuntary termination of employment, reduction of hours, or furloughing, for each assistance eligible individual on the basis of whose termination, reduction of hours, or furloughing entitlement to reimbursement is claimed under subsection (a),

"(2) a report of the amount of payroll taxes offset under subsection (a) for the reporting period, and

"(3) a report containing the TINs of all covered employees, the amount of subsidy reimbursed with respect to each employee, and a designation with respect to each employee as to whether the subsidy reimbursement is for coverage of 1 individual or 2 or more individuals.

"(g) Regulations.—The Secretary shall issue such regulations or other guidance as may be necessary or appropriate to carry out this section, including—

"(1) the requirement to report information or the establishment of other methods for verifying the correct amounts of reimbursements under this section,

"(2) the application of this section to group health plans that are multiemployer plans (as defined in section 3(37) of the Employee Retirement Income Security Act of 1974),

"(3) to allow the advance payment of the credit determined under subsection (a), subject to the limitations provided in this section, based on such information as the Secretary shall require,

"(4) to provide for the reconciliation of such advance payment with the amount of the credit at the time of filing the return of tax for the applicable quarter or taxable year, and

"(5) with respect to the application of the credit to third party payors (including professional employer organizations, certified professional employer organizations, or agents under section 3504).".

(B) SOCIAL SECURITY TRUST FUNDS HELD HARMLESS.—There are hereby appropriated to the Federal Old-Age and Survivors Insurance Trust Fund and the Federal Disability Insurance Trust Fund established under section 201 of the Social Security Act (42 U.S.C. 401) and the Social Security Equivalent Benefit Account established under section 15A(a) of the Railroad Retirement Act of 1974 (45 U.S.C. 231n–1(a)) amounts equal to the reduction in revenues to the Treasury by reason of this section (without regard to this subparagraph). Amounts appropriated by the preceding sentence shall be transferred from the general fund at such times and in such manner as to replicate to the extent possible the transfers which would have occurred to such Trust Fund or Account had this section not been enacted.

(C) CLERICAL AMENDMENT.—The table of sections for subchapter B of chapter 65 of the Internal Revenue Code of 1986 is amended by adding at the end the following new item:

"SEC. 6432. Continuation coverage premium assistance.".

(D) EFFECTIVE DATE.—The amendments made by this paragraph shall apply to premiums to which subsection (a)(1)(A) applies.

(E) SPECIAL RULE IN CASE OF EMPLOYEE PAYMENT THAT IS NOT RE-QUIRED UNDER THIS SECTION.—

(i) IN GENERAL.—In the case of an assistance eligible individual who pays, with respect any period of coverage to which subsection (a)(1)(A) applies, the amount of the premium for such coverage that the individual would have (but for this Act) been required to pay, the person to whom such payment is payable shall reimburse such individual for the amount of such premium paid.

(ii) CREDIT OF REIMBURSEMENT.—A person to which clause (i) applies shall be allowed a credit in the manner provided under section 6432 of the Internal Revenue Code of 1986 for any payment made to the employee under such clause.

(iii) PAYMENT OF CREDITS.—Any person to which clause (i) applies shall make the payment required under such clause to the individual not later than 60 days after the date on which such individual elects continuation coverage under section 30312(a)(1) of the Worker Health Coverage Protection Act.

(15) PENALTY FOR FAILURE TO NOTIFY HEALTH PLAN OF CESSATION OF ELIGIBILITY FOR PREMIUM ASSISTANCE.—

(A) IN GENERAL.—Part I of subchapter B of chapter 68 of the Internal Revenue Code of 1986 is amended by adding at the end the following new section:

"SEC. 6720C. PENALTY FOR FAILURE TO NOTIFY HEALTH PLAN OF CESSATION OF ELIGIBILITY FOR CONTINUATION COVERAGE PREMIUM ASSISTANCE.

"(a) In General.—Except in the case of failure described in subsection (b) or (c), any person required to notify a group health plan under section 30312(a)(2)(B) of the Worker Health Coverage Protection Act who fails to make such a notification at such time and in such manner as the Secretary of Labor may require shall pay a penalty of $250.

"(b) Intentional Failure.—In the case of any such failure that is fraudulent, such person shall pay a penalty equal to the greater of—

"(1) $250, or

"(2) 110 percent of the premium assistance provided under section 30312(a)(1)(A) of such Act after termination of eligibility under such section.

"(c) Reasonable Cause Exception.—No penalty shall be imposed under this section with respect to any failure if it is shown that such failure is due to reasonable cause and not to willful neglect.".

(B) CLERICAL AMENDMENT.—The table of sections of part I of subchapter B of chapter 68 of such Code is amended by adding at the end the following new item:

"SEC. 6720C. Penalty for failure to notify health plan of cessation of eligibility for continuation coverage premium assistance.".

(16) COORDINATION WITH HCTC.—

(A) IN GENERAL.—Section 35(g)(9) of the Internal Revenue Code of 1986 is amended to read as follows:

"(9) CONTINUATION COVERAGE PREMIUM ASSISTANCE.—In the case of an assistance eligible individual who receives premium assistance for continuation coverage under section 30312(a)(1) of the Worker Health Coverage Protection Act for any month during the taxable year, such individual shall not be treated as an eligible individual, a certified individual, or a qualifying family member for purposes of this section or section 7527 with respect to such month.".

(B) EFFECTIVE DATE.—The amendment made by subparagraph (A) shall apply to taxable years ending after the date of the enactment of this Act.

(17) EXCLUSION OF CONTINUATION COVERAGE PREMIUM ASSISTANCE FROM GROSS INCOME.—

(A) IN GENERAL.—Part III of subchapter B of chapter 1 of the Internal Revenue Code of 1986 is amended by inserting after section 139H the following new section:

"SEC. 139I. CONTINUATION COVERAGE PREMIUM ASSISTANCE.

"In the case of an assistance eligible individual (as defined in subsection (a)(3) of section 30312 of the Worker Health Coverage Protection Act), gross income does not include any premium assistance provided under subsection (a)(1) of such section.".

(B) CLERICAL AMENDMENT.—The table of sections for part III of subchapter B of chapter 1 of such Code is amended by inserting after the item relating to section 139H the following new item:

"SEC. 139I. Continuation coverage premium assistance.".

(C) EFFECTIVE DATE.—The amendments made by this paragraph shall apply to taxable years ending after the date of the enactment of this Act.

(18) DEADLINES WITH RESPECT TO NOTICES.—Notwithstanding section 518 of the Employee Retirement Income Security Act of 1974 and section 7508A of the Internal Revenue Code of 1986, the Secretary of Labor and the Secretary of the Treasury, respectively, may not waive or extend any deadline with respect to the provision of notices described in paragraphs (7), (8), and (9).

(b) Rule Of Construction.—In all matters of interpretation, rules, and operational procedures, the language of this section shall be interpreted broadly for the benefit of workers and their families.

TITLE IV

—APPLICATION TO OTHER HEALTH PROGRAMS
PROHIBITION ON COPAYMENTS AND COST SHARING FOR TRICARE BENEFICIARIES RECEIVING COVID–19 TREATMENT

SEC. 30401.

(a) In General.—Section 6006(a) of the Families First Coronavirus Response Act (Public Law 116–127; 38 U.S.C. 1074 note) is amended by striking "or visits described in paragraph (2) of such section" and inserting ", visits described in paragraph (2) of such section, or medical care to treat COVID–19".

(b) Effective Date.—The amendment made by subsection (a) shall apply with respect to medical care furnished on or after the date of the enactment of this Act.

PROHIBITION ON COPAYMENTS AND COST SHARING FOR VETERANS RECEIVING COVID–19 TREATMENT FURNISHED BY DEPARTMENT OF VETERANS AFFAIRS

SEC. 30402.

(a) In General.—Section 6006(b) of the Families First Coronavirus Response Act (Public Law 116–127; 38 U.S.C. 1701 note) is amended by striking "or visits described in paragraph (2) of such section" and inserting ", visits described in paragraph (2) of such section, or hospital care or medical services to treat COVID–19".

(b) Effective Date.—The amendment made by subsection (a) shall apply with respect to hospital care and medical services furnished on or after the date of the enactment of this Act.

PROHIBITION ON COPAYMENTS AND COST SHARING FOR FEDERAL CIVILIAN EMPLOYEES RECEIVING COVID–19 TREATMENT

SEC. 30403.

(a) In General.—Section 6006(c) of the Families First Coronavirus Response Act (Public Law 116–127; 5 U.S.C. 8904 note) is amended by striking "or visits described in paragraph (2) of such section" and inserting ", visits described in paragraph (2) of such section, or hospital care or medical services to treat COVID–19".

(b) Effective Date.—The amendment made by subsection (a) shall apply with respect to hospital care and medical services furnished on or after the date of the enactment of this Act.

TITLE V

—PUBLIC HEALTH POLICIES
DEFINITIONS

SEC. 30501.

In this title:

(1) Except as inconsistent with the provisions of this title, the term "Secretary" means the Secretary of Health and Human Services.

(2) The term "State" refers to each of the 50 States and the District of Columbia.

(3) The term "Tribal", with respect to a department of health (or health department), includes—

(A) Indian Tribes that—

(i) are operating one or more health facilities pursuant to an agreement under the Indian Self-Determination and Education Assistance Act (25 U.S.C. 5301 et seq.); or

(ii) receive services from a facility operated by the Indian Health Services; and

(B) Tribal organizations and Urban Indian organizations.

Subtitle A—Supply Chain Improvements

MEDICAL SUPPLIES RESPONSE COORDINATOR

SEC. 30511.

(a) In General.—The President shall appoint a Medical Supplies Response Coordinator to coordinate the efforts of the Federal Government regarding the supply and distribution of critical medical supplies and equipment related to detecting, diagnosing, preventing, and treating COVID–19, including personal protective equipment, medical devices, drugs, and vaccines.

(b) Qualifications.—To qualify to be appointed as the Medical Supplies Response Coordinator, an individual shall be a senior government official with—

(1) health care training, including training related to infectious diseases or hazardous exposures; and

(2) a familiarity with medical supply chain logistics.

(c) Activities.—The Medical Supplies Response Coordinator shall—

(1) consult with State, local, territorial, and Tribal officials to ensure that health care facilities and health care workers have sufficient personal protective equipment and other medical supplies;

(2) evaluate ongoing needs of States, localities, territories, Tribes, health care facilities, and health care workers to determine the need for critical medical supplies and equipment;

(3) serve as a point of contact for industry for procurement and distribution of critical medical supplies and equipment, including personal protective equipment, medical devices, testing supplies, drugs, and vaccines;

(4) procure and distribute critical medical supplies and equipment, including personal protective equipment, medical devices, testing supplies, drugs, and vaccines;

(5) (A) establish and maintain an up-to-date national database of hospital capacity, including beds, ventilators, and supplies, including personal protective equipment, medical devices, drugs, and vaccines; and

(B) provide weekly reports to the Congress on gaps in such capacity and progress made toward closing the gaps;

(6) require, as necessary, industry reporting on production and distribution of personal protective equipment, medical devices, testing supplies, drugs, and vaccines and assess financial penalties as may be specified by the Medical Supplies Response Coordinator for failure to comply with such requirements for reporting on production and distribution;

(7) consult with the Secretary and the Administrator of the Federal Emergency Management Agency, as applicable, to ensure sufficient production levels under the Defense Production Act (50 U.S.C. 4501 et seq.); and

(8) monitor the prices of critical medical supplies and equipment, including personal protective equipment and medical devices, drugs, and vaccines related to detecting, diagnosing, preventing, and treating COVID–19 and report any suspected price gouging of such materials to the Federal Trade Commission and appropriate law enforcement officials.

INFORMATION TO BE INCLUDED IN LIST OF DEVICES DETERMINED TO BE IN SHORTAGE

SEC. 30512.

Section 506J(g)(2)(A) of the Federal Food, Drug, and Cosmetic Act, as added by section 3121 of the CARES Act (Public Law 116–136), is amended by inserting ", including the device identifier or national product code for such device, if applicable" before the period at the end.

EXTENDED SHELF LIFE DATES FOR ESSENTIAL DEVICES

SEC. 30513.

(a) In General.—The Federal Food, Drug, and Cosmetic Act is amended by inserting after section 506J (21 U.S.C. 356j) the following:

"SEC. 506K. EXTENDED SHELF LIFE DATES FOR ESSENTIAL DEVICES.

"(a) In General.—A manufacturer of a device subject to notification requirements under section 506J (in this section referred to as an 'essential device') shall—

"(1) submit to the Secretary data and information as required by subsection (b)(1);

"(2) conduct and submit the results of any studies required under subsection (b)(3); and

"(3) make any labeling change described in subsection (c) by the date specified by the Secretary pursuant to such subsection.

"(b) Notification.—

"(1) IN GENERAL.—The Secretary may issue an order requiring the manufacturer of any essential device to submit, in such manner as the Secretary may prescribe, data and information from any stage of development of the device (including pilot, investigational, and final product validation) that are adequate to assess the shelf life of the device to determine the longest supported expiration date.

"(2) UNAVAILABLE OR INSUFFICIENT DATA AND INFORMATION.—If the data and information referred to in paragraph (1) are not available or are insufficient, the Secretary may require the manufacturer of the device to—

"(A) conduct studies adequate to provide the data and information; and

"(B) submit to the Secretary the results, data, and information generated by such studies when available.

"(c) Labeling.—The Secretary may issue an order requiring the manufacturer of an essential device to make by a specified date any labeling change regarding the expiration period that the Secretary determines to be appropriate based on the data and information required to be submitted under this section or any other data and information available to the Secretary.

"(d) Confidentiality.—Nothing in this section shall be construed as authorizing the Secretary to disclose any information that is a trade secret or confidential information subject to section 552(b)(4) of title 5, United States Code, or section 1905 of title 18, United States Code.".

(b) Civil Monetary Penalty.—Section 303(f) of the Federal Food, Drug, and Cosmetic Act (21 U.S.C. 333(f)) is amended by adding at the end the following:

"(10) Civil Monetary Penalty With Respect To Extended Shelf Life Dates For Essential Devices.—If the manufacturer of a device subject to notification requirements under section 506J violates section 506K by failing to submit data and information as required under section 506K(b)(1), failing to conduct or submit the results of studies as required under section 506K(b)(3), or failing to make a labeling change as required under section 506K(c), such manufacturer shall be liable to the United States for a civil penalty in an amount not to exceed $10,000 for each such violation.".

(c) Emergency Use Eligible Products.—Subparagraph (A) of section 564A(a)(1) of the Federal Food, Drug, and Cosmetic Act (21 U.S.C. 360bbb–3a(a)(1)) is amended to read as follows:

"(A) is approved or cleared under this chapter, otherwise listed as a device pursuant to section 510(j), conditionally approved under section 571, or licensed under section 351 of the Public Health Service Act;".

AUTHORITY TO DESTROY COUNTERFEIT DEVICES

SEC. 30514.

(a) In General.—Section 801(a) of the Federal Food, Drug, and Cosmetic Act (21 U.S.C. 381(a)) is amended—

(1) in the fourth sentence, by inserting "or counterfeit device" after "counterfeit drug"; and

(2) by striking "The Secretary of the Treasury shall cause the destruction of" and all that follows through "liable for costs pursuant to subsection (c)." and inserting the following: "The Secretary of the Treasury shall cause the destruction of any such article refused admission unless such article is exported, under regulations prescribed by the Secretary of the Treasury, within 90 days of the date of notice of such refusal or within such additional time as may be permitted pursuant to such regulations, except that the Secretary of Health and Human Services may destroy, without the opportunity for export, any drug or device refused admission under this section, if such drug or device is valued at an amount that is $2,500 or less (or such higher amount as the Secretary of the Treasury may set by regulation pursuant to section 498(a)(1) of the Tariff Act of 1930 (19 U.S.C. 1498(a)(1))) and was not brought into compliance as described under subsection (b). The Secretary of Health and Human Services shall issue regulations providing for notice and an opportunity to appear before the Secretary of Health and Human Services and introduce testimony, as described in the first sentence of this subsection, on destruction of a drug or device under the seventh sentence of this subsection. The regulations shall provide that

prior to destruction, appropriate due process is available to the owner or consignee seeking to challenge the decision to destroy the drug or device. Where the Secretary of Health and Human Services provides notice and an opportunity to appear and introduce testimony on the destruction of a drug or device, the Secretary of Health and Human Services shall store and, as applicable, dispose of the drug or device after the issuance of the notice, except that the owner and consignee shall remain liable for costs pursuant to subsection (c).".

(b) Definition.—Section 201(h) of the Federal Food, Drug, and Cosmetic Act (21 U.S.C. 321(h)) is amended—

(1) by redesignating subparagraphs (1), (2), and (3) as clauses (A), (B), and (C), respectively; and

(2) after making such redesignations—

(A) by striking "(h) The term" and inserting "(h)(1) The term"; and

(B) by adding at the end the following:

"(2) The term 'counterfeit device' means a device which, or the container, packaging, or labeling of which, without authorization, bears a trademark, trade name, or other identifying mark, imprint, or symbol, or any likeness thereof, or is manufactured using a design, of a device manufacturer, packer, or distributor other than the person or persons who in fact manufactured, packed, or distributed such device and which thereby falsely purports or is represented to be the product of, or to have been packed or distributed by, such other device manufacturer, packer, or distributor.

"(3) For purposes of subparagraph (2)—

"(A) the term 'manufactured' refers to any of the following activities: manufacture, preparation, propagation, compounding, assembly, or processing; and

"(B) the term 'manufacturer' means a person who is engaged in any of the activities listed in clause (A).".

REPORTING REQUIREMENT FOR DRUG MANUFACTURERS

SEC. 30515.

(a) Establishments In A Foreign Country.—Section 510(i) of the Federal Food, Drug, and Cosmetic Act (21 U.S.C. 360(i)) is amended by inserting at the end the following new paragraph:

"(5) The requirements of paragraphs (1) and (2) shall apply to establishments within a foreign country engaged in the manufacture, preparation, propagation, compounding, or processing of any drug, including the active pharmaceutical ingredient, that is required to be listed pursuant to subsection (j). Such requirements shall apply regardless of whether the drug or active pharmaceutical ingredient undergoes further manufacture, preparation, propagation, compounding, or processing at a separate establishment or establishments outside the United States prior to being imported or offered for import into the United States.".

(b) Listing Of Drugs.—Section 510(j)(1) of the Federal Food, Drug, and Cosmetic Act (21 U.S.C. 360(j)(1)) is amended—

(1) in subparagraph (D), by striking "and" at the end;

(2) in subparagraph (E), by striking the period at the end and inserting "; and"; and

(3) by adding at the end the following new subparagraph:

"(F) in the case of a drug contained in the applicable list, a certification that the registrant has—

"(i) identified every other establishment where manufacturing is performed for the drug; and "(ii) notified each known foreign establishment engaged in the manufacture, preparation, propagation, compounding, or processing of the drug, including the active pharmaceutical ingredient, of the inclusion of the drug in the list and the obligation to register.".

(c) Quarterly Reporting On Amount Of Drugs Manufactured.—Section 510(j)(3) (A) of the Federal Food, Drug, and Cosmetic Act (as added by section 3112 of the CARES Act (Public Law 116–136)) is amended by striking "annually" and inserting "once during the month of March of each year, once during the month of June of each year, once during the month of September of each year, and once during the month of December of each year".

RECOMMENDATIONS TO ENCOURAGE DOMESTIC MANUFACTURING OF CRITICAL DRUGS

SEC. 30516.

(a) In General.—Not later than 14 days after the date of enactment of this Act, the Secretary shall enter into an agreement with the National Academies of Sciences, Engineering, and Medicine (referred to in this section as the "National Academies") under which, not later than 90 days after the date of entering into the agreement, the National Academies will—

(1) establish a committee of experts who are knowledgeable about drug and device supply issues, including—

(A) sourcing and production of critical drugs and devices;

(B) sourcing and production of active pharmaceutical ingredients in critical drugs;

(C) the raw materials and other components for critical drugs and devices; and

(D) the public health and national security implications of the current supply chain for critical drugs and devices;

(2) convene a public symposium to—

(A) analyze the impact of United States dependence on the foreign manufacturing of critical drugs and devices on patient access and care, including in hospitals and intensive care units; and

(B) recommend strategies to end United States dependence on foreign manufacturing to ensure the United States has a diverse and vital supply chain for critical drugs and devices to protect the Nation from natural or hostile occurrences; and

(3) submit a report on the symposium's proceedings to the Congress and publish a summary of such proceedings on the public website of the National Academies.

(b) Symposium.—In carrying out the agreement under subsection (a), the National Academies shall consult with—

(1) the Department of Health and Human Services, the Department of Homeland Security, the Department of Defense, the Department of Commerce, the Department of State, the Department of Veterans Affairs, the Department of Justice, and any other Federal agencies as appropriate; and

(2) relevant stakeholders, including drug and device manufacturers, health care providers, medical professional societies, State-based societies, public health experts, State and local public health departments, State medical boards, patient groups, health care distributors, wholesalers and group purchasing organizations, pharmacists, and other entities with experience in health care and public health, as appropriate.

(c) Definitions.—For the purposes of this section:

(1) The term "critical"—

(A) with respect to a device, refers to a device classified by the Food and Drug Administration as implantable, life-saving, and life-sustaining; or

(B) with respect to a drug, refers to a drug that is described in subsection (a) of section 506C of the Federal Food, Drug, and Cosmetic Act (21 U.S.C. 356c) (relating to notification of any discontinuance or interruption in the production of life-saving drugs).

(2) The terms "device" and "drug" have the meanings given to those terms in section 201 of the Federal Food, Drug, and Cosmetic Act (21 U.S.C. 321).

FAILURE TO NOTIFY OF A PERMANENT DISCONTINUANCE OR AN INTERRUPTION

SEC. 30517.

Section 301 of the Federal Food, Drug, and Cosmetic Act (21 U.S.C. 331) is amended by adding at the end the following:

"(fff) The failure of a manufacturer of a drug described in section 506C(a) or an active pharmaceutical ingredient of such a drug, without a reasonable basis as determined by the Secretary, to notify the Secretary of a permanent discontinuance or an interruption, and the reasons for such discontinuance or interruption, as required by section 506C.".

FAILURE TO DEVELOP RISK MANAGEMENT PLAN

SEC. 30518.

Section 301 of the Federal Food, Drug, and Cosmetic Act (21 U.S.C. 331), as amended by section 30517, is further amended by adding at the end the following:

"(ggg) The failure to develop, maintain, and implement a risk management plan, as required by section 506C(j).".

NATIONAL CENTERS OF EXCELLENCE IN CONTINUOUS PHARMACEUTICAL MANUFACTURING

SEC. 30519.

(a) In General.—Section 3016 of the 21st Century Cures Act (21 U.S.C. 399h) is amended to read as follows:

"SEC. 3016. NATIONAL CENTERS OF EXCELLENCE IN CONTINUOUS PHARMACEUTICAL MANUFACTURING.

"(a) In General.—The Secretary of Health and Human Services, acting through the Commissioner of Food and Drugs—

"(1) shall solicit and, beginning not later than 1 year after the date of enactment of the National Centers of Excellence in Continuous Pharmaceutical Manufacturing Act of 2019, receive requests from institutions of higher education to be designated as a National Center of Excellence in Continuous Pharmaceutical Manufacturing (in this section referred to as a 'National Center of Excellence') to support the advancement and development of continuous manufacturing; and

"(2) shall so designate any institution of higher education that—

"(A) requests such designation; and

"(B) meets the criteria specified in subsection (c).

"(b) Request For Designation.—A request for designation under subsection (a) shall be made to the Secretary at such time, in such manner, and containing such information as the Secretary may require. Any such request shall include a description of how the institution of higher education meets or plans to meet each of the criteria specified in subsection (c).

"(c) Criteria For Designation Described.—The criteria specified in this subsection with respect to an institution of higher education are that the institution has, as of the date of the submission of a request under subsection (a) by such institution—

"(1) physical and technical capacity for research and development of continuous manufacturing;

"(2) manufacturing knowledge-sharing networks with other institutions of higher education, large and small pharmaceutical manufacturers, generic and nonprescription manufacturers, contract manufacturers, and other entities;

"(3) proven capacity to design and demonstrate new, highly effective technology for use in continuous manufacturing;

"(4) a track record for creating and transferring knowledge with respect to continuous manufacturing;

"(5) the potential to train a future workforce for research on and implementation of advanced manufacturing and continuous manufacturing; and

"(6) experience in participating in and leading a continuous manufacturing technology partnership with other institutions of higher education, large and small pharmaceutical manufacturers (including generic and nonprescription drug manufacturers), contract manufacturers, and other entities—

"(A) to support companies with continuous manufacturing in the United States;

"(B) to support Federal agencies with technical assistance, which may include regulatory and quality metric guidance as applicable, for advanced manufacturing and continuous manufacturing;

"(C) with respect to continuous manufacturing, to organize and conduct research and development activities needed to create new and more effective technology, capture and disseminate expertise, create intellectual property, and maintain technological leadership;

"(D) to develop best practices for designing continuous manufacturing; and

"(E) to assess and respond to the workforce needs for continuous manufacturing, including the development of training programs if needed.

"(d) Termination Of Designation.—The Secretary may terminate the designation of any National Center of Excellence designated under this section if the Secretary determines such National Center of Excellence no longer meets the criteria specified in subsection (c). Not later than 60 days before the effective date of such a termination, the Secretary shall provide written notice to the National Center of Excellence, including the rationale for such termination.

"(e) Conditions For Designation.—As a condition of designation as a National Center of Excellence under this section, the Secretary shall require that an institution of higher education enter into an agreement with the Secretary under which the institution agrees—

"(1) to collaborate directly with the Food and Drug Administration to publish the reports required by subsection (g);

"(2) to share data with the Food and Drug Administration regarding best practices and research generated through the funding under subsection (f);

"(3) to develop, along with industry partners (which may include large and small biopharmaceutical manufacturers, generic and nonprescription manufacturers, and contract manufacturers) and another institution or institutions designated under this section, if any, a roadmap for developing a continuous manufacturing workforce;

"(4) to develop, along with industry partners and other institutions designated under this section, a roadmap for strengthening existing, and developing new, relationships with other institutions; and

"(5) to provide an annual report to the Food and Drug Administration regarding the institution's activities under this section, including a description of how the institution continues to meet and make progress on the criteria listed in subsection (c).

"(f) Funding.—

"(1) IN GENERAL.—The Secretary shall award funding, through grants, contracts, or cooperative agreements, to the National Centers of Excellence designated under this section for the purpose of studying and recommending improvements to continuous manufacturing, including such improvements as may enable the Centers—

"(A) to continue to meet the conditions specified in subsection (e); and

"(B) to expand capacity for research on, and development of, continuing manufacturing.

"(2) CONSISTENCY WITH FDA MISSION.—As a condition on receipt of funding under this subsection, a National Center of Excellence shall agree to consider any input from the Secretary regarding the use of funding that would—

"(A) help to further the advancement of continuous manufacturing through the National Center of Excellence; and

"(B) be relevant to the mission of the Food and Drug Administration.

"(3) AUTHORIZATION OF APPROPRIATIONS.—There is authorized to be appropriated to carry out this subsection $100,000,000, to remain available until expended.

"(4) RULE OF CONSTRUCTION.—Nothing in this section shall be construed as precluding a National Center for Excellence designated under this section from receiving funds under any other provision of this Act or any other Federal law.

"(g) Annual Review And Reports.—

"(1) ANNUAL REPORT.—Beginning not later than 1 year after the date on which the first designation is made under subsection (a), and annually thereafter, the Secretary shall—

"(A) submit to Congress a report describing the activities, partnerships and collaborations, Federal policy recommendations, previous and continuing funding, and findings of, and any other applicable information from, the National Centers of Excellence designated under this section; and

"(B) make such report available to the public in an easily accessible electronic format on the website of the Food and Drug Administration.

"(2) REVIEW OF NATIONAL CENTERS OF EXCELLENCE AND POTENTIAL DESIGNEES.—The Secretary shall periodically review the National Centers of Excellence designated under this section to ensure that such National Centers of Excellence continue to meet the criteria for designation under this section.

"(3) REPORT ON LONG-TERM VISION OF FDA ROLE.—Not later than 2 years after the date on which the first designation is made under subsection (a), the Secretary, in consultation with the National Centers of Excellence designated under this section, shall submit a report to the Congress on the long-term vision of the Department of Health and Human Services on the role of the Food and Drug Administration in supporting continuous manufacturing, including—

"(A) a national framework of principles related to the implementation and regulation of continuous manufacturing;

"(B) a plan for the development of Federal regulations and guidance for how advanced manufacturing and continuous manufacturing can be incorporated into the development of pharmaceuticals and regulatory responsibilities of the Food and Drug

Administration; and

"(C) appropriate feedback solicited from the public, which may include other institutions, large and small biopharmaceutical manufacturers, generic and nonprescription manufacturers, and contract manufacturers.

"(h) Definitions.—In this section:

"(1) ADVANCED MANUFACTURING.—The term 'advanced manufacturing' means an approach for the manufacturing of pharmaceuticals that incorporates novel technology, or uses an established technique or technology in a new or innovative way (such as continuous manufacturing where the input materials are continuously transformed within the process by two or more unit operations) that enhances drug quality or improves the manufacturing process.

"(2) CONTINUOUS MANUFACTURING.—The term 'continuous manufacturing'—

"(A) means a process where the input materials are continuously fed into and transformed within the process, and the processed output materials are continuously removed from the system; and

"(B) consists of an integrated process that consists of a series of two or more unit operations.

"(3) INSTITUTION OF HIGHER EDUCATION.—The term 'institution of higher education' has the meaning given such term in section 101(a) of the Higher Education Act of 1965 (20 U.S.C. 1001(a)).

"(4) SECRETARY.—The term 'Secretary' means the Secretary of Health and Human Services, acting through the Commissioner of Food and Drugs.".

(b) Transition Rule.—Section 3016 of the 21st Century Cures Act (21 U.S.C. 399h), as in effect on the day before the date of the enactment of this section, shall apply with respect to grants awarded under such section before such date of enactment.

VACCINE MANUFACTURING AND ADMINISTRATION CAPACITY

SEC. 30520.

(a) Enhancing Manufacturing Capacity.—

(1) IN GENERAL.—The Secretary, acting through the Director of the Biomedical Advanced Research and Development Authority, shall, as appropriate, award contracts, grants, and cooperative agreements, and enter into other transactions, to expand and enhance manufacturing capacity of vaccines and vaccine candidates to prevent the spread of SARS–CoV–2 and COVID–19.

(2) AUTHORIZATION OF APPROPRIATIONS.—To carry out this subsection, there are authorized to be appropriated such sums as may be necessary for fiscal years 2020 through 2024, to remain available until expended.

(b) Report On Vaccine Manufacturing And Administration Capacity.—

(1) IN GENERAL.—Not later than December 31, 2020, the Secretary shall submit to the Committee on Energy and Commerce of the House of Representatives and the Committee on Health, Education, Labor and Pensions of the Senate a report detailing—

(A) an assessment of the estimated supply of vaccines and ancillary medical products related to vaccine administration necessary to control and stop the spread of SARS–CoV–2 and COVID–19, domestically and internationally;

(B) an assessment of current and future domestic manufacturing capacity for vaccines or vaccine candidates to control or stop the spread of SARS–CoV–2 and COVID–19, vaccine candidates, and ancillary products related to the administration of such vaccines, including identification of any gaps in manufacturing capacity;

(C) activities conducted to expand and enhance manufacturing capacity for vaccines, vaccine candidates, and ancillary medical products to levels sufficient to control and stop the spread of SARS–CoV–2 and COVID–19, domestically and internationally, including a list and explanation of all contracts, grants, and cooperative agreements awarded, and other transactions entered into, for purposes of such expansion and enhancement and how such activities will help to meet future domestic manufacturing capacity needs;

(D) a plan for the ongoing support of enhanced manufacturing capacity for vaccines, vaccine candidates, and ancillary medical products sufficient to control and stop the spread of SARS–CoV–2 and COVID–19, domestically and internationally; and

(E) a plan to support the administration of vaccines approved or authorized by the Food and Drug Administration to control and stop the spread of SARS–CoV–2 and COVID–19, domestically and internationally, including Federal workforce enhancements necessary to administer such vaccines.

(2) ANCILLARY MEDICAL PRODUCTS.—For purposes of this subsection, "ancillary medical products" includes—

(A) vials;

(B) bandages;

(C) alcohol swabs;

(D) syringes;

(E) needles;

(F) gloves and other personal protective equipment; and

(G) other medical products the Secretary determines necessary for the administration of vaccines.

Subtitle B—Strategic National Stockpile Improvements

EQUIPMENT MAINTENANCE

SEC. 30531.

Section 319F–2 of the Public Health Service Act (42 U.S.C. 247d–6b) is amended—

(1) in subsection (a)(3)—

(A) in subparagraph (I), by striking "; and" and inserting a semicolon;

(B) in subparagraph (J), by striking the period at the end and inserting a semicolon; and

(C) by inserting the following new subparagraph at the end:

"(K) ensure the contents of the stockpile remain in good working order and, as appropriate, conduct maintenance services on such contents; and"; and

(2) in subsection (c)(7)(B), by adding at the end the following new clause:

"(ix) EQUIPMENT MAINTENANCE SERVICE.—In carrying out this section, the Secretary may enter into contracts for the procurement of equipment maintenance services.".

SUPPLY CHAIN FLEXIBILITY MANUFACTURING PILOT

SEC. 30532.

(a) In General.—Section 319F–2(a)(3) of the Public Health Service Act (42 U.S.C. 247d–6b(a)(3)), as amended by section 30531, is further amended by adding at the end the following new subparagraph:

"(L) enhance medical supply chain elasticity and establish and maintain domestic reserves of critical medical supplies (including personal protective equipment, ancillary medical supplies, and other applicable supplies required for the administration of drugs, vaccines and other biological products, and other medical devices (including diagnostic tests)) by—

"(i) increasing emergency stock of critical medical supplies;

"(ii) geographically diversifying production of such medical supplies;

"(iii) purchasing, leasing, or entering into joint ventures with respect to facilities and equipment for the production of such medical supplies; and

"(iv) working with distributors of such medical supplies to manage the domestic reserves established under this subparagraph by refreshing and replenishing stock of such medical supplies.".

(b) Reporting; Sunset.—Section 319F–2(a) of the Public Health Service Act (42 U.S.C. 247d–6b(a)) is amended by adding at the end the following:

"(6) REPORTING.—Not later than September 30, 2022, the Secretary shall submit to the Committee on Energy and Commerce of the House of Representatives and the Committee on Health, Education, Labor and Pensions of the Senate a report on the details of each purchase, lease, or joint venture entered into under paragraph (3) (L), including the amount expended by the Secretary on each such purchase, lease, or joint venture.

"(7) SUNSET.—The authority to make purchases, leases, or joint ventures pursuant to paragraph (3)(L) shall cease to be effective on September 30, 2023.".

(c) Funding.—Section 319F–2(f) of the Public Health Service Act (42 U.S.C. 247d–6b(f)) is amended by adding at the end the following:

"(3) SUPPLY CHAIN ELASTICITY.—

"(A) IN GENERAL.—For the purpose of carrying out subsection (a)(3)(L), there is authorized to be appropriated $500,000,000 for each of fiscal years 2020 through 2023, to remain available until expended.

"(B) RELATION TO OTHER AMOUNTS.—The amount authorized to be appropriated by subparagraph (A) for the purpose of carrying out subsection (a)(3)(L) is in addition to any other amounts available for such purpose.".

REIMBURSABLE TRANSFERS FROM STRATEGIC NATIONAL STOCKPILE

SEC. 30533.

Section 319F–2(a) of the Public Health Service Act (42 U.S.C. 247d–6b(a)), as amended, is further amended by adding at the end the following:

"(8) TRANSFERS AND REIMBURSEMENTS.—

"(A) IN GENERAL.—Without regard to chapter 5 of title 40, United States Code, the Secretary may transfer to any Federal department or agency, on a reimbursable basis, any drugs, vaccines and other biological products, medical devices, and other supplies in the stockpile if—

"(i) the transferred supplies are less than 6 months from expiry;

"(ii) the stockpile is able to replenish the supplies, as appropriate; and

"(iii) the Secretary decides the transfer is in the best interest of the United States Government.

"(B) USE OF REIMBURSEMENT.—Reimbursement derived from the transfer of supplies pursuant to subparagraph (A) may be used by the Secretary, without further appropriation and without fiscal year limitation, to carry out this section.

"(C) REPORT.—Not later than September 30, 2022, the Secretary shall submit to the Committee on Energy and Commerce of the House of Representatives and the Committee on Health, Education, Labor and Pensions of the Senate a report on each transfer made under this paragraph and the amount received by the Secretary in exchange for that transfer.

"(D) SUNSET.—The authority to make transfers under this paragraph shall cease to be effective on September 30, 2023.".

STRATEGIC NATIONAL STOCKPILE ACTION REPORTING

SEC. 30534.

(a) In General.—The Assistant Secretary for Preparedness and Response (in this section referred to as the "Assistant Secretary"), in coordination with the Administrator of the Federal Emergency Management Agency, shall—

(1) not later than 30 days after the date of enactment of this Act, issue a report to the Committee on Energy and Commerce of the House of Representatives and the Committee on Health, Education, Labor and Pensions of the Senate regarding all State, local, Tribal, and territorial requests for supplies from the Strategic National Stockpile related to COVID–19; and

(2) not less than every 30 days thereafter through the end of the emergency period (as such term is defined in section 1135(g)(1)(B) of the Social Security Act (42 U.S.C. 1320b–5(g)(1)(B))), submit to such committees an updated version of such report.

(b) Reporting Period.—

(1) INITIAL REPORT.—The initial report under subsection (a) shall address all requests described in such subsection made during the period—

(A) beginning on January 31, 2020; and

(B) ending on the date that is 30 days before the date of submission of the report.

(2) UPDATES.—Each update to the report under subsection (a) shall address all requests described in such subsection made during the period—

(A) beginning at the end of the previous reporting period under this section; and

(B) ending on the date that is 30 days before the date of submission of the updated report.

(c) Contents Of Report.—The report under subsection (a) (and updates thereto) shall include—

(1) the details of each request described in such subsection, including—

(A) the specific medical countermeasures, including devices such as personal protective equipment, and other materials requested; and

(B) the amount of such materials requested; and

(2) the outcomes of each request described in subsection (a), including—

(A) whether the request was wholly fulfilled, partially fulfilled, or denied;

(B) if the request was wholly or partially fulfilled, the fulfillment amount; and

(C) if the request was partially fulfilled or denied, a rationale for such outcome.

IMPROVED, TRANSPARENT PROCESSES FOR THE STRATEGIC NATIONAL STOCKPILE

SEC. 30535.

(a) In General.—Not later than January 1, 2021, the Secretary, in collaboration with the Assistant Secretary for Preparedness and Response and the Director of the Centers for Disease Control and Prevention, shall develop and implement improved, transparent processes for the use and distribution of drugs, vaccines and other biological products, medical devices, and other supplies (including personal protective equipment, ancillary medical supplies, and other applicable supplies required for the administration of drugs, vaccines and other biological products, diagnostic tests, and other medical devices) in the Strategic National Stockpile under section 319F–2 of the Public Health Service Act (42 U.S.C. 247d–6b) (in this section referred to as the "Stockpile").

(b) Processes.—The processes developed under subsection (a) shall include—

(1) the form and manner in which States, localities, Tribes, and territories are required to submit requests for supplies from the Stockpile;

(2) the criteria used by the Secretary in responding to such requests, including the reasons for fulfilling or denying such requests;

(3) what circumstances result in prioritization of distribution of supplies from the Stockpile to States, localities, Tribes, or territories;

(4) clear plans for future, urgent communication between the Secretary and States, localities, Tribes, and territories regarding the outcome of such requests; and

(5) any differences in the processes developed under subsection (a) for geographically related emergencies, such as weather events, and national emergencies, such as pandemics.

(c) Report To Congress.—Not later than January 1, 2021, the Secretary shall—

(1) submit a report to the Committee Energy and Commerce of the House of Representatives and the Committee on Health, Education, Labor and Pensions of the Senate regarding the improved, transparent processes developed under this section; and

(2) include in such report recommendations for opportunities for communication (by telebriefing, phone calls, or in-person meetings) between the Secretary and States, localities, Tribes, and territories regarding such improved, transparent processes.

GAO STUDY ON THE FEASIBILITY AND BENEFITS OF A STRATEGIC NATIONAL STOCKPILE USER FEE AGREEMENT

SEC. 30536.

(a) In General.— The Comptroller General of the United States shall conduct a study to investigate the feasibility of establishing user fees to offset certain Federal costs attributable to the procurement of single-source materials for the Strategic National Stockpile under section 319F–2 of the Public Health Service Act (42 U.S.C. 247d–6b) and distributions of such materials from the Stockpile. In conducting this study, the Comptroller General shall consider, to the extent information is available—

(1) whether entities receiving such distributions generate profits from those distributions;

(2) any Federal costs attributable to such distributions;

(3) whether such user fees would provide the Secretary with funding to potentially offset procurement costs of such materials for the Strategic National Stockpile; and

(4) any other issues the Comptroller General identifies as relevant.

(b) Report.—Not later than February 1, 2023, the Comptroller General of the United States shall submit to the Congress a report on the findings and conclusions of the study under subsection (a).

Subtitle C—Testing And Testing Infrastructure Improvements

COVID–19 TESTING STRATEGY

SEC. 30541.

(a) Strategy.—Not later than June 15, 2020, the Secretary shall update the COVID–19 strategic testing plan under the heading "Department of Health and Human Services—Office of the Secretary—Public Health and Social Service Emergency Fund" in title I of division B of the Paycheck Protection Program and Health Care Enhancement Act (Public Law 116–139, 134 Stat. 620, 626–627) and submit to the appropriate congressional committees such updated national plan identifying—

(1) what level of, types of, and approaches to testing (including predicted numbers of tests, populations to be tested, and frequency of testing and the appropriate setting whether a health care setting (such as hospital-based, high-complexity laboratory, point-of-care, mobile testing units, pharmacies or community health centers) or non-health care setting (such as workplaces, schools, or child care centers)) are necessary—

(A) to sufficiently monitor and contribute to the control of the transmission of SARS–CoV–2 in the United States;

(B) to ensure that any reduction in social distancing efforts, when determined appropriate by public health officials, can be undertaken in a manner that optimizes the health and safety of the people of the United States, and reduces disparities (including disparities related to race, ethnicity, sex, age, disability status, socioeconomic status, and geographic location) in the prevalence of, incidence of, and health outcomes with respect to, COVID–19; and

(C) to provide for ongoing surveillance sufficient to support contact tracing, case identification, quarantine, and isolation to prevent future outbreaks of COVID–19;

(2) specific plans and benchmarks, each with clear timelines, to ensure—

(A) such level of, types of, and approaches to testing as are described in paragraph (1), with respect to optimizing health and safety;

(B) sufficient availability of all necessary testing materials and supplies, including extraction and testing kits, reagents, transport media, swabs, instruments, analysis equipment, personal protective equipment if necessary for testing (including point-of-care testing), and other equipment;

(C) allocation of testing materials and supplies in a manner that optimizes public health, including by considering the variable impact of SARS–CoV–2 on specific States, territories, Indian Tribes, Tribal organizations, urban Indian organizations, communities, industries, and professions;

(D) sufficient evidence of validation for tests that are deployed as a part of such strategy;

(E) sufficient laboratory and analytical capacity, including target turnaround time for test results;

(F) sufficient personnel, including personnel to collect testing samples, conduct and analyze results, and conduct testing follow-up, including contact tracing, as appropriate; and

(G) enforcement of the Families First Coronavirus Response Act (Public Law 116–127) to ensure patients who are tested are not subject to cost sharing;

(3) specific plans to ensure adequate testing in rural areas, frontier areas, health professional shortage areas, and medically underserved areas (as defined in section 330I(a) of the Public Health Service Act (42 U.S.C. 254c–14(a))), and for underserved populations, Native Americans (including Indian Tribes, Tribal organizations, and urban Indian organizations), and populations at increased risk related to COVID–19;

(4) specific plans to ensure accessibility of testing to people with disabilities, older individuals, and individuals with underlying health conditions or weakened immune systems; and

(5) specific plans for broadly developing and implementing testing for potential immunity in the United States, as appropriate, in a manner sufficient—

(A) to monitor and contribute to the control of SARS–CoV–2 in the United States;

(B) to ensure that any reduction in social distancing efforts, when determined appropriate by public health officials, can be undertaken in a manner that optimizes the health and safety of the people of the United States; and

(C) to reduce disparities (including disparities related to race, ethnicity, sex, age, disability status, socioeconomic status, and geographic location) in the prevalence of, incidence of, and health outcomes with respect to, COVID–19.

(b) Coordination.—The Secretary shall carry out this section—

(1) in coordination with the Administrator of the Federal Emergency Management Agency;

(2) in collaboration with other agencies and departments, as appropriate; and

(3) taking into consideration the State plans for COVID–19 testing prepared as required under the heading "Department of Health and Human Services—Office of the Secretary—Public Health and Social Service Emergency Fund" in title I of division B of the Paycheck Protection Program and Health Care Enhancement Act (Public Law 116–139; 134 Stat. 620, 624).

(c) Updates.—

(1) FREQUENCY.—The updated national plan under subsection (a) shall be updated every 30 days until the end of the public health emergency first declared by the Secretary under section 319 of the Public Health Service Act (42 U.S.C. 247d) on January 31, 2020, with respect to COVID–19.

(2) RELATION TO OTHER LAW.—Paragraph (1) applies in lieu of the requirement (for updates every 90 days until funds are expended) in the second to last proviso under the heading "Department of Health and Human Services—Office of the Secretary—Public Health and Social Service Emergency Fund" in title I of division B of the Paycheck Protection Program and Health Care Enhancement Act (Public Law 116–139; 134 Stat. 620, 627).

(d) Appropriate Congressional Committees.—In this section, the term "appropriate congressional committees" means—

(1) the Committee on Appropriations and the Committee on Energy and Commerce of the House of Representatives; and

(2) the Committee on Appropriations and the Committee on Health, Education, Labor and Pensions and of the Senate.

CENTRALIZED TESTING INFORMATION WEBSITE

SEC. 30542.

The Secretary shall establish and maintain a public, searchable webpage, to be updated and corrected as necessary through a process established by the Secretary, on the website of the Department of Health and Human Services that—

(1) identifies all in vitro diagnostic and serological tests used in the United States to analyze clinical specimens for detection of SARS–CoV–2 or antibodies specific to SARS–CoV–2, including—

(A) those tests—

(i) that are approved, cleared, or authorized under section 510(k), 513, 515, or 564 of the Federal Food, Drug, and Cosmetic Act (21 U.S.C. 360(k), 360c, 360e, 360bbb–3);

(ii) that have been validated by the test's developers for use on clinical specimens and for which the developer has notified the Food and Drug Administration of the developer's intent to market the test consistent with applicable guidance issued by the Secretary; or

(iii) that have been developed and authorized by a State that has notified the Secretary of the State's intention to review tests intended to diagnose COVID–19; and

(B) other SARS–CoV–2-related tests that the Secretary determines appropriate in guidance, which may include tests related to the monitoring of COVID–19 patient status;

(2) provides relevant information, as determined by the Secretary, on each test identified pursuant to paragraph (1), which may include—

(A) the name and contact information of the developer of the test;

(B) the date of receipt of notification by the Food and Drug Administration of the developer's intent to market the test;

(C) the date of authorization for use of the test on clinical specimens, where applicable;

(D) the letter of authorization for use of the test on clinical specimens, where applicable;

(E) any fact sheets, manufacturer instructions, and package inserts for the test, including information on intended use;

(F) sensitivity and specificity of the test; and

(G) in the case of tests distributed by commercial manufacturers, the number of tests distributed and, if available, the number of laboratories in the United States with the required platforms installed to perform the test; and

(3) includes—

(A) a list of laboratories certified under section 353 of the Public Health Service Act (42 U.S.C. 263a; commonly referred to as "CLIA") that—

(i) meet the regulatory requirements under such section to perform high- or moderate-complexity testing; and

(ii) are authorized to perform SARS–CoV–2 diagnostic or serological tests on clinical specimens; and

(B) information on each laboratory identified pursuant to subparagraph (A), including—

(i) the name and address of the laboratory;

(ii) the CLIA certificate number;

(iii) the laboratory type;

(iv) the certificate type; and

(v) the complexity level.

MANUFACTURER REPORTING OF TEST DISTRIBUTION

SEC. 30543.

(a) In General.—A commercial manufacturer of an in vitro diagnostic or serological COVID–19 test shall, on a weekly basis, submit a notification to the Secretary regarding distribution of each such test, which notification—

(1) shall include the number of tests distributed and the entities to which the tests are distributed; and

(2) may include the quantity of such tests distributed by the manufacturer.

(b) Confidentiality.—Nothing in this section shall be construed as authorizing the Secretary to disclose any information that is a trade secret or confidential information subject to section 552(b)(4) of title 5, United States Code, or section 1905 of title 18, United States Code.

(c) Failure To Meet Requirements.—If a manufacturer fails to submit a notification as required under subsection (a), the following applies:

(1) The Secretary shall issue a letter to such manufacturer informing such manufacturer of such failure.

(2) Not later than 7 calendar days after the issuance of a letter under paragraph (1), the manufacturer to whom such letter is issued shall submit to the Secretary a written response to such letter—

(A) setting forth the basis for noncompliance; and

(B) providing information as required under subsection (a).

(3) Not later than 14 calendar days after the issuance of a letter under paragraph (1), the Secretary shall make such letter and any response to such letter under paragraph (2) available to the public on the internet website of the Food and Drug Administration, with appropriate redactions made to protect information described in subsection (b). The preceding sentence shall not apply if the Secretary determines that—

(A) the letter under paragraph (1) was issued in error; or

(B) after review of such response, the manufacturer had a reasonable basis for not notifying as required under subsection (a).

STATE TESTING REPORT

SEC. 30544.

For any State that authorizes (or intends to authorize) one or more laboratories in the State to develop and perform in vitro diagnostic COVID–19 tests, the head of the department or agency of such State with primary responsibility for health shall—

(1) notify the Secretary of such authorization (or intention to authorize); and

(2) provide the Secretary with a weekly report—

(A) identifying all laboratories authorized (or intended to be authorized) by the State to develop and perform in vitro diagnostic COVID–19 tests;

(B) including relevant information on all laboratories identified pursuant to subparagraph (A), which may include information on laboratory testing capacity;

(C) identifying all in vitro diagnostic COVID–19 tests developed and approved for clinical use in laboratories identified pursuant to subparagraph (A); and

(D) including relevant information on all tests identified pursuant to subparagraph (C), which may include—

(i) the name and contact information of the developer of any such test;

(ii) any fact sheets, manufacturer instructions, and package inserts for any such test, including information on intended use; and

(iii) the sensitivity and specificity of any such test.

STATE LISTING OF TESTING SITES

SEC. 30545.

Not later than 14 days after the date of enactment of this Act, any State receiving funding or assistance under this Act, as a condition on such receipt, shall establish and maintain a public, searchable webpage on the official website of the State that—

(1) identifies all sites located in the State that provide diagnostic or serological testing for SARS–CoV–2; and

(2) provides appropriate contact information for SARS–CoV–2 testing sites pursuant to paragraph (1).

REPORTING OF COVID–19 TESTING RESULTS

SEC. 30546.

(a) In General.—Every laboratory that performs or analyzes a test that is intended to detect SARS–CoV–2 or to diagnose a possible case of COVID–19 shall report daily the number of tests performed and the results from each such test to the Secretary of Health and Human Services and to the Secretary of Homeland Security, in such form and manner as such Secretaries may prescribe. Such information shall be made available to the public in a searchable, electronic format.

(b) Additional Reporting Requirements.—The Secretaries specified in subsection (a)—

(1) may specify additional reporting requirements under this section by regulation, including by interim final rule, or by guidance; and

(2) may issue such regulations or guidance without regard to the procedures otherwise required by section 553 of title 5, United States Code.

GAO REPORT ON DIAGNOSTIC TESTS

SEC. 30547.

(a) GAO Study.—Not later than 18 months after the date of enactment of this Act, the Comptroller General of the United States shall submit to the Committee on Energy and Commerce of the House of Representatives and the Committee on Health, Education, Labor and Pensions of the Senate a report describing the response of entities described in subsection (b) to the COVID-19 pandemic with respect to the development, regulatory evaluation, and deployment of diagnostic tests.

(b) Entities Described.—Entities described in this subsection include—

(1) laboratories, including public health, academic, clinical, and commercial laboratories;

(2) diagnostic test manufacturers;

(3) State, local, Tribal, and territorial governments; and

(4) the Food and Drug Administration, the Centers for Disease Control and Prevention, the Centers for Medicare & Medicaid Services, the National Institutes of Health, and other relevant Federal agencies, as appropriate.

(c) Contents.—The report under subsection (a) shall include—

(1) a description of actions taken by entities described in subsection (b) to develop, evaluate, and deploy diagnostic tests;

(2) an assessment of the coordination of Federal agencies in the development, regulatory evaluation, and deployment of diagnostic tests;

(3) an assessment of the standards used by the Food and Drug Administration to evaluate diagnostic tests;

(4) an assessment of the clarity of Federal agency guidance related to testing, including the ability for individuals without medical training to understand which diagnostic tests had been evaluated by the Food and Drug Administration;

(5) a description of—

(A) actions taken and clinical processes employed by States and territories that have authorized laboratories to develop and perform diagnostic tests not authorized, approved, or cleared by the Food and Drug Administration, including actions of such States and territories to evaluate the accuracy and sensitivity of such tests; and

(B) the standards used by States and territories when deciding when to authorize laboratories to develop or perform diagnostic tests;

(6) an assessment of the steps taken by laboratories and diagnostic test manufacturers to validate diagnostic tests, as well as the evidence collected by such entities to support validation; and

(7) based on available reports, an assessment of the accuracy and sensitivity of a representative sample of available diagnostic tests.

(d) Definition.—In this section, the term "diagnostic test" means an in vitro diagnostic product (as defined in section 809.3(a) of title 21, Code of Federal Regulations) for—

(1) the detection of SARS–CoV–2;

(2) the diagnosis of the virus that causes COVID–19; or

(3) the detection of antibodies specific to SARS–CoV–2, such as a serological test.

PUBLIC HEALTH DATA SYSTEM TRANSFORMATION

SEC. 30548.

Subtitle C of title XXVIII of the Public Health Service Act (42 U.S.C. 300hh–31 et seq.) is amended by adding at the end the following:

"SEC. 2822. PUBLIC HEALTH DATA SYSTEM TRANSFORMATION.

"(a) Expanding CDC And Public Health Department Capabilities.—

"(1) IN GENERAL.—The Secretary, acting through the Director of the Centers for Disease Control and Prevention, shall—

"(A) conduct activities to expand, enhance, and improve applicable public health data systems used by the Centers for Disease Control and Prevention, related to the interoperability and improvement of such systems (including as it relates to preparedness for, prevention and detection of, and response to public health emergencies); and

"(B) award grants or cooperative agreements to State, local, Tribal, or territorial public health departments for the expansion and modernization of public health data systems, to assist public health departments in—

"(i) assessing current data infrastructure capabilities and gaps to improve and increase consistency in data collection, storage, and analysis and, as appropriate, to improve dissemination of public health-related information;

"(ii) improving secure public health data collection, transmission, exchange, maintenance, and analysis;

"(iii) improving the secure exchange of data between the Centers for Disease Control and Prevention, State, local, Tribal, and territorial public health departments, public health organizations, and health care providers, including by public health officials in multiple jurisdictions within such State, as appropriate, and by simplifying and supporting reporting by health care providers, as applicable, pursuant to State law, including through the use of health information technology;

"(iv) enhancing the interoperability of public health data systems (including systems created or accessed by public health departments) with health information technology, including with health information technology certified under section 3001(c)(5);

"(v) supporting and training data systems, data science, and informatics personnel;

"(vi) supporting earlier disease and health condition detection, such as through near real-time data monitoring, to support rapid public health responses;

"(vii) supporting activities within the applicable jurisdiction related to the expansion and modernization of electronic case reporting; and

"(viii) developing and disseminating information related to the use and importance of public health data.

"(2) DATA STANDARDS.—In carrying out paragraph (1), the Secretary, acting through the Director of the Centers for Disease Control and Prevention, shall, as appropriate and in consultation with the Office of the National Coordinator for Health Information Technology, designate data and technology standards (including standards for interoperability) for public health data systems, with deference given to standards published by consensus-based standards development organizations with public input and voluntary consensus-based standards bodies.

"(3) PUBLIC-PRIVATE PARTNERSHIPS.—The Secretary may develop and utilize public-private partnerships for technical assistance, training, and related implementation support for State, local, Tribal, and territorial public health departments, and the Centers for Disease Control and Prevention, on the expansion and modernization of electronic case reporting and public health data systems, as applicable.

"(b) Requirements.—

"(1) HEALTH INFORMATION TECHNOLOGY STANDARDS.—The Secretary may not award a grant or cooperative agreement under subsection (a)(1)(B) unless the applicant uses or agrees to use standards endorsed by the National Coordinator for Health Information Technology pursuant to section 3001(c)(1) or adopted by the Secretary under section 3004.

"(2) WAIVER.—The Secretary may waive the requirement under paragraph (1) with respect to an applicant if the Secretary determines that the activities under subsection (a)(1)(B) cannot otherwise be carried out within the applicable jurisdiction.

"(3) APPLICATION.—A State, local, Tribal, or territorial health department applying for a grant or cooperative agreement under this section shall submit an application to the Secretary at such time and in such manner as the Secretary may require. Such application shall include information describing—

"(A) the activities that will be supported by the grant or cooperative agreement; and

"(B) how the modernization of the public health data systems involved will support or impact the public health infrastructure of the health department, including a description of remaining gaps, if any, and the actions needed to address such gaps.

"(c) Strategy And Implementation Plan.—Not later than 180 days after the date of enactment of this section, the Secretary, acting through the Director of the Centers for Disease Control and Prevention, shall submit to the Committee on Health, Education, Labor and Pensions of the Senate and the Committee on Energy and Commerce of the House of Representatives a coordinated strategy and an accompanying implementation plan that identifies and demonstrates the measures the Secretary will utilize to—

"(1) update and improve applicable public health data systems used by the Centers for Disease Control and Prevention; and

"(2) carry out the activities described in this section to support the improvement of State, local, Tribal, and territorial public health data systems.

"(d) Consultation.—The Secretary, acting through the Director of the Centers for Disease Control and Prevention, shall consult with State, local, Tribal, and territorial health departments, professional medical and public health associations, associations representing hospitals or other health care entities, health information technology experts, and other appropriate public or private entities regarding the plan and grant program to modernize public health data systems pursuant to this section. Activities under this subsection may include the provision of technical assistance and training related to the exchange of information by such public health data systems used by relevant health care and public health entities at the local, State, Federal, Tribal, and territorial levels, and the development and utilization of public-private partnerships for implementation support applicable to this section.

"(e) Report To Congress.—Not later than 1 year after the date of enactment of this section, the Secretary shall submit a report to the Committee on Health, Education, Labor and Pensions of the Senate and the Committee on Energy and Commerce of the House of Representatives that includes—

"(1) a description of any barriers to—
"(A) public health authorities implementing interoperable public health data systems and electronic case reporting;
"(B) the exchange of information pursuant to electronic case reporting; or
"(C) reporting by health care providers using such public health data systems, as appropriate, and pursuant to State law;
"(2) an assessment of the potential public health impact of implementing electronic case reporting and interoperable public health data systems; and
"(3) a description of the activities carried out pursuant to this section.
"(f) Electronic Case Reporting.—In this section, the term 'electronic case reporting' means the automated identification, generation, and bilateral exchange of reports of health events among electronic health record or health information technology systems and public health authorities.
"(g) Authorization Of Appropriations.—To carry out this section, there are authorized to be appropriated $450,000,000 to remain available until expended.".

PILOT PROGRAM TO IMPROVE LABORATORY INFRASTRUCTURE

SEC. 30549.

(a) In General.—The Secretary shall award grants to States and political subdivisions of States to support the improvement, renovation, or modernization of infrastructure at clinical laboratories (as defined in section 353 of the Public Health Service Act (42 U.S.C. 263a)) that will help to improve SARS–CoV–2 and COVID–19 testing and response activities, including the expansion and enhancement of testing capacity at such laboratories.
(b) Authorization Of Appropriations.—To carry out this section, there is authorized to be appropriated $1,000,000,000 to remain available until expended.

CORE PUBLIC HEALTH INFRASTRUCTURE FOR STATE, LOCAL, TRIBAL, AND TERRITORIAL HEALTH DEPARTMENTS

SEC. 30550.

(a) Program.—The Secretary, acting through the Director of the Centers for Disease Control and Prevention, shall establish a core public health infrastructure program consisting of awarding grants under subsection (b).
(b) Grants.—
(1) AWARD.—For the purpose of addressing core public health infrastructure needs, the Secretary—
(A) shall award a grant to each State health department; and
(B) may award grants on a competitive basis to State, local, Tribal, or territorial health departments.
(2) ALLOCATION.—Of the total amount of funds awarded as grants under this subsection for a fiscal year—
(A) not less than 50 percent shall be for grants to State health departments under paragraph (1)(A); and
(B) not less than 30 percent shall be for grants to State, local, Tribal, or territorial health departments under paragraph (1)(B).
(c) Use Of Funds.—A State, local, Tribal, or territorial health department receiving a grant under subsection (b) shall use the grant funds to address core public health infrastructure needs, including those identified in the accreditation process under subsection (g).

(d) Formula Grants To State Health Departments.—In making grants under subsection (b)(1)(A), the Secretary shall award funds to each State health department in accordance with—

(1) a formula based on population size; burden of preventable disease and disability; and core public health infrastructure gaps, including those identified in the accreditation process under subsection (g); and

(2) application requirements established by the Secretary, including a requirement that the State health department submit a plan that demonstrates to the satisfaction of the Secretary that the State's health department will—

(A) address its highest priority core public health infrastructure needs; and

(B) as appropriate, allocate funds to local health departments within the State.

(e) Competitive Grants To State, Local, Tribal, And Territorial Health Departments.—In making grants under subsection (b)(1)(B), the Secretary shall give priority to applicants demonstrating core public health infrastructure needs identified in the accreditation process under subsection (g).

(f) Maintenance Of Effort.—The Secretary may award a grant to an entity under subsection (b) only if the entity demonstrates to the satisfaction of the Secretary that—

(1) funds received through the grant will be expended only to supplement, and not supplant, non-Federal and Federal funds otherwise available to the entity for the purpose of addressing core public health infrastructure needs; and

(2) with respect to activities for which the grant is awarded, the entity will maintain expenditures of non-Federal amounts for such activities at a level not less than the level of such expenditures maintained by the entity for the fiscal year preceding the fiscal year for which the entity receives the grant.

(g) Establishment Of A Public Health Accreditation Program.—

(1) IN GENERAL.—The Secretary shall—

(A) develop, and periodically review and update, standards for voluntary accreditation of State, local, Tribal, and territorial health departments and public health laboratories for the purpose of advancing the quality and performance of such departments and laboratories; and

(B) implement a program to accredit such health departments and laboratories in accordance with such standards.

(2) COOPERATIVE AGREEMENT.—The Secretary may enter into a cooperative agreement with a private nonprofit entity to carry out paragraph (1).

(h) Report.—The Secretary shall submit to the Congress an annual report on progress being made to accredit entities under subsection (g), including—

(1) a strategy, including goals and objectives, for accrediting entities under subsection (g) and achieving the purpose described in subsection (g)(1)(A);

(2) identification of gaps in research related to core public health infrastructure; and

(3) recommendations of priority areas for such research.

(i) Definition.—In this section, the term "core public health infrastructure" includes—

(1) workforce capacity and competency;

(2) laboratory systems;

(3) testing capacity, including test platforms, mobile testing units, and personnel;

(4) health information, health information systems, and health information analysis;

(5) disease surveillance;

(6) contact tracing;

(7) communications;

(8) financing;

(9) other relevant components of organizational capacity; and

(10) other related activities.

(j) Authorization Of Appropriations.—To carry out this section, there are authorized to be appropriated $6,000,000,000, to remain available until expended.

CORE PUBLIC HEALTH INFRASTRUCTURE AND ACTIVITIES FOR CDC

SEC. 30551.

(a) In General.—The Secretary, acting through the Director of the Centers for Disease Control and Prevention, shall expand and improve the core public health infrastructure and activities of the Centers for Disease Control and Prevention to address unmet and emerging public health needs.

(b) Report.—The Secretary shall submit to the Congress an annual report on the activities funded through this section.

(c) Definition.—In this section, the term "core public health infrastructure" has the meaning given to such term in section 30550.

(d) Authorization Of Appropriations.—To carry out this section, there is authorized to be appropriated $1,000,000,000, to remain available until expended.

Subtitle D—Covid-19 National Testing And Contact Tracing Initiative

NATIONAL SYSTEM FOR COVID-19 TESTING, CONTACT TRACING, SURVEILLANCE, CONTAINMENT, AND MITIGATION

SEC. 30561.

(a) In General.—The Secretary, acting through the Director of the Centers for Disease Control and Prevention, and in coordination with State, local, Tribal, and territorial health departments, shall establish and implement a nationwide evidence-based system for—

(1) testing, contact tracing, surveillance, containment, and mitigation with respect to COVID-19;

(2) offering guidance on voluntary isolation and quarantine of individuals infected with, or exposed to individuals infected with, the virus that causes COVID-19; and

(3) public reporting on testing, contact tracing, surveillance, and voluntary isolation and quarantine activities with respect to COVID-19.

(b) Coordination; Technical Assistance.—In carrying out the national system under this section, the Secretary shall—

(1) coordinate State, local, Tribal, and territorial activities related to testing, contact tracing, surveillance, containment, and mitigation with respect to COVID-19, as appropriate; and

(2) provide technical assistance for such activities, as appropriate.

(c) Consideration.—In establishing and implementing the national system under this section, the Secretary shall take into consideration—

(1) the State plans referred to in the heading "Public Health and Social Services Emergency Fund" in title I of division B of the Paycheck Protection Program and Health Care Enhancement Act (Public Law 116–139); and

(2) the testing strategy submitted under section 30541.

(d) Reporting.—The Secretary shall—

(1) not later than December 31, 2020, submit to the Committee on Energy and Com-

merce of the House of Representatives and the Committee on Health, Education, Labor and Pensions a preliminary report on the effectiveness of the activities carried out pursuant to this subtitle; and

(2) not later than December 21, 2021, submit to such committees a final report on such effectiveness.

GRANTS

SEC. 30562.

(a) In General.—To implement the national system under section 30561, the Secretary, acting through the Director of the Centers for Disease Control and Prevention, shall, subject to the availability of appropriations, award grants to State, local, Tribal, and territorial health departments that seek grants under this section to carry out coordinated testing, contact tracing, surveillance, containment, and mitigation with respect to COVID–19, including—

(1) diagnostic and surveillance testing and reporting;

(2) community-based contact tracing efforts; and

(3) policies related to voluntary isolation and quarantine of individuals infected with, or exposed to individuals infected with, the virus that causes COVID–19.

(b) Flexibility.—The Secretary shall ensure that—

(1) the grants under subsection (a) provide flexibility for State, local, Tribal, and territorial health departments to modify, establish, or maintain evidence-based systems; and

(2) local health departments receive funding from State health departments or directly from the Centers for Disease Control and Prevention to contribute to such systems, as appropriate.

(c) Allocations.—

(1) FORMULA.—The Secretary, acting through the Director of the Centers for Disease Control and Prevention, shall allocate amounts made available pursuant to subsection (a) in accordance with a formula to be established by the Secretary that provides a minimum level of funding to each State, local, Tribal, and territorial health department that seeks a grant under this section and allocates additional funding based on the following prioritization:

(A) The Secretary shall give highest priority to applicants proposing to serve populations in one or more geographic regions with a high burden of COVID–19 based on data provided by the Centers for Disease Control and Prevention, or other sources as determined by the Secretary.

(B) The Secretary shall give second highest priority to applicants preparing for, or currently working to mitigate, a COVID–19 surge in a geographic region that does not yet have a high number of reported cases of COVID–19 based on data provided by the Centers for Disease Control and Prevention, or other sources as determined by the Secretary.

(C) The Secretary shall give third highest priority to applicants proposing to serve high numbers of low-income and uninsured populations, including medically underserved populations (as defined in section 330(b)(3) of the Public Health Service Act (42 U.S.C. 254b(b)(3))), health professional shortage areas (as defined under section 332(a) of the Public Health Service Act (42 U.S.C. 254e(a))), racial and ethnic minorities, or geographically diverse areas, as determined by the Secretary.

(2) NOTIFICATION.—Not later than the date that is one week before first awarding grants under this section, the Secretary shall submit to the Committee on Energy and

Commerce of the House of Representatives and the Committee on Health, Education, Labor and Pensions of the Senate a notification detailing the formula established under paragraph (1) for allocating amounts made available pursuant to subsection (a).

(d) Use Of Funds.—A State, local, Tribal, and territorial health department receiving a grant under this section shall, to the extent possible, use the grant funds for the following activities, or other activities deemed appropriate by the Director of the Centers for Disease Control and Prevention:

(1) TESTING.—To implement a coordinated testing system that—

(A) leverages or modernizes existing testing infrastructure and capacity;

(B) is consistent with the updated testing strategy required under section 30541;

(C) is coordinated with the State plan for COVID–19 testing prepared as required under the heading "Department of Health and Human Services—Office of the Secretary—Public Health and Social Service Emergency Fund" in title I of division B of the Paycheck Protection Program and Health Care Enhancement Act (Public Law 116–139; 134 Stat. 620, 624);

(D) is informed by contact tracing and surveillance activities under this subtitle;

(E) is informed by guidelines established by the Centers for Disease Control and Prevention for which populations should be tested;

(F) identifies how diagnostic and serological tests in such system shall be validated prior to use;

(G) identifies how diagnostic and serological tests and testing supplies will be distributed to implement such system;

(H) identifies specific strategies for ensuring testing capabilities and accessibility in medically underserved populations (as defined in section 330(b)(3) of the Public Health Service Act (42 U.S.C. 254b(b)(3))), health professional shortage areas (as defined under section 332(a) of the Public Health Service Act (42 U.S.C. 254e(a))), racial and ethnic minority populations, and geographically diverse areas, as determined by the Secretary;

(I) identifies how testing may be used, and results may be reported, in both health care settings (such as hospitals, laboratories for moderate or high-complexity testing, pharmacies, mobile testing units, and community health centers) and non-health care settings (such as workplaces, schools, childcare centers, or drive-throughs);

(J) allows for testing in sentinel surveillance programs, as appropriate; and

(K) supports the procurement and distribution of diagnostic and serological tests and testing supplies to meet the goals of the system.

(2) CONTACT TRACING.—To implement a coordinated contact tracing system that—

(A) leverages or modernizes existing contact tracing systems and capabilities, including community health workers, health departments, and Federally qualified health centers;

(B) is able to investigate cases of COVID–19, and help to identify other potential cases of COVID–19, through tracing contacts of individuals with positive diagnoses;

(C) establishes culturally competent and multilingual strategies for contact tracing, which may include consultation with and support for cultural or civic organizations with established ties to the community;

(D) provides individuals identified under the contact tracing program with information and support for containment or mitigation;

(E) enables State, local, Tribal, and territorial health departments to work with a nongovernmental, community partner or partners and State and local workforce development systems (as defined in section 3(67) of Workforce Innovation and Opportunity Act (29 U.S.C. 3102(67))) receiving grants under section 30566(b) of this Act to hire and compensate a locally-sourced contact tracing workforce, if necessary, to supplement the public health workforce, to—

(i) identify the number of contact tracers needed for the respective State, locality, territorial, or Tribal health department to identify all cases of COVID–19 currently in the jurisdiction and those anticipated to emerge over the next 18 months in such jurisdiction;

(ii) outline qualifications necessary for contact tracers;

(iii) train the existing and newly hired public health workforce on best practices related to tracing close contacts of individuals diagnosed with COVID–19, including the protection of individual privacy and cybersecurity protection; and

(iv) equip the public health workforce with tools and resources to enable a rapid response to new cases;

(F) identifies the level of contact tracing needed within the State, locality, territory, or Tribal area to contain and mitigate the transmission of COVID–19;

(G) establishes statewide mechanisms to integrate regular evaluation to the Centers for Disease Control and Prevention regarding contact tracing efforts, makes such evaluation publicly available, and to the extent possible provides for such evaluation at the county level; and

(H) identifies specific strategies for ensuring contact tracing activities in medically underserved populations (as defined in section 330(b)(3) of the Public Health Service Act (42 U.S.C. 254b(b)(3))), health professional shortage areas (as defined under section 332(a) of the Public Health Service Act (42 U.S.C. 254e(a))), racial and ethnic minority populations, and geographically diverse areas, as determined by the Secretary.

(3) SURVEILLANCE.—To strengthen the existing public health surveillance system that—

(A) leverages or modernizes existing surveillance systems within the respective State, local, Tribal, or territorial health department and national surveillance systems;

(B) detects and identifies trends in COVID–19 at the county level;

(C) evaluates State, local, Tribal, and territorial health departments in achieving surveillance capabilities with respect to COVID–19;

(D) integrates and improves disease surveillance and immunization tracking; and

(E) identifies specific strategies for ensuring disease surveillance in medically underserved populations (as defined in section 330(b)(3) of the Public Health Service Act (42 U.S.C. 254b(b)(3))), health professional shortage areas (as defined under section 332(a) of the Public Health Service Act (42 U.S.C. 254e(a))), racial and ethnic minority populations, and geographically diverse areas, as determined by the Secretary.

(4) CONTAINMENT AND MITIGATION.—To implement a coordinated containment and mitigation system that—

(A) leverages or modernizes existing containment and mitigation strategies within the respective State, local, Tribal, or territorial governments and national containment and mitigation strategies;

(B) may provide for, connect to, and leverage existing social services and support for individuals who have been infected with or exposed to COVID–19 and who are isolated or quarantined in their homes, such as through—

(i) food assistance programs;

(ii) guidance for household infection control;

(iii) information and assistance with childcare services; and

(iv) information and assistance pertaining to support available under the CARES Act (Public Law 116–136) and this Act;

(C) provides guidance on the establishment of safe, high-quality, facilities for the voluntary isolation of individuals infected with, or quarantine of the contacts of individuals exposed to COVID–19, where hospitalization is not required, which facilities should—

(i) be prohibited from making inquiries relating to the citizenship status of an individual isolated or quarantined; and

(ii) be operated by a non-Federal, community partner or partners that—

(I) have previously established relationships in localities;

(II) work with local places of worship, community centers, medical facilities, and schools to recruit local staff for such facilities; and

(III) are fully integrated into State, local, Tribal, or territorial containment and mitigation efforts; and

(D) identifies specific strategies for ensuring containment and mitigation activities in medically underserved populations (as defined in section 330(b)(3) of the Public Health Service Act (42 U.S.C. 254b(b)(3))), health professional shortage areas (as defined under section 332(a) of the Public Health Service Act (42 U.S.C. 254e(a))), racial and ethnic minority populations, and geographically diverse areas, as determined by the Secretary.

(e) Reporting.—The Secretary shall facilitate mechanisms for timely, standardized reporting by grantees under this section regarding implementation of the systems established under this section and coordinated processes with the reporting as required and under the heading "Department of Health and Human Services—Office of the Secretary—Public Health and Social Service Emergency Fund" in title I of division B of the Paycheck Protection Program and Health Care Enhancement Act (Public Law 116–139, 134 Stat. 620), including—

(1) a summary of county or local health department level information from the States receiving funding, and information from directly funded localities, territories, and Tribal entities, about the activities that will be undertaken using funding awarded under this section, including subgrants;

(2) any anticipated shortages of required materials for testing for COVID–19 under subsection (a); and

(3) other barriers in the prevention, mitigation, or treatment of COVID–19 under this section.

(f) Public Listing Of Awards.—The Secretary shall—

(1) not later than 7 days after first awarding grants under this section, post in a searchable, electronic format a list of all awards made by the Secretary under this section, including the recipients and amounts of such awards; and

(2) update such list not less than every 7 days until all funds made available to carry out this section are expended.

GUIDANCE, TECHNICAL ASSISTANCE, INFORMATION, AND COMMUNICATION

SEC. 30563.

(a) In General.— Not later than 14 days after the date of the enactment of this Act, the Secretary, in coordination with other Federal agencies, as appropriate, shall issue guidance, provide technical assistance, and provide information to States, localities, Tribes, and territories, with respect to the following:

(1) The diagnostic and serological testing of individuals identified through contact tracing for COVID–19, including information with respect to the reduction of duplication related to programmatic activities, reporting, and billing.

(2) Best practices regarding contact tracing, including the collection of data with respect to such contact tracing and requirements related to the standardization of demographic and syndromic information collected as part of contact tracing efforts.

(3) Best practices regarding COVID–19 disease surveillance, including best practices to reduce duplication in surveillance activities, identifying gaps in surveillance and surveillance systems, and ways in which the Secretary plans to effectively support State, local, Tribal and territorial health departments in addressing such gaps.

(4) Information on ways for State, local, Tribal, and territorial health departments to establish and maintain the testing, contact tracing, and surveillance activities described in paragraphs (1) through (3).

(5) The protection of any personally identifiable health information collected pursuant to this subtitle.

(6) Best practices regarding privacy and cybersecurity protection related to contact tracing, containment, and mitigation efforts.

(b) Guidance On Payment.—Not later than 14 days after the date of the enactment of this Act, the Secretary, in coordination with the Administrator of the Centers for Medicare & Medicaid Services, the Director of the Centers for Disease Control and Prevention, and in coordination with other Federal agencies, as appropriate, shall develop and issue to State, local, Tribal, and territorial health departments clear guidance and policies—

(1) with respect to the coordination of claims submitted for payment out of the Public Health and Social Services Emergency Fund for services furnished in a facility referred to in section 30562(d)(4)(C);

(2) identifying how an individual who is isolated or quarantined at home or in such a facility—

(A) incurs no out-of-pocket costs for any services furnished to such individual while isolated; and

(B) may receive income support for lost earnings or payments for expenses such as child care or elder care while such individual is isolated at home or in such a facility;

(3) providing information and assistance pertaining to support available under the CARES Act (Public Law 116–136) and this Act; and

(4) identifying State, local, Tribal, and territorial health departments or partner agencies that may provide social support services, such as groceries or meals, health education, internet access, and behavioral health services, to individuals who isolated or quarantined at home or in such a facility.

(c) Guidance On Testing.—Not later than 14 days after the date of the enactment of this Act, the Secretary, in coordination with the Commissioner of Food and Drugs, the Director of the National Institutes of Health, and the Director of the Centers for Disease Control and Prevention, and in coordination with other Federal agencies as appropriate, shall develop and issue to State, local, Tribal, and territorial health departments clear guidance and policies regarding—

(1) objective standards to characterize the performance of all diagnostic and serological tests for COVID–19 in order to independently evaluate tests continuously

over time;

(2) protocols for the evaluation of the performance of diagnostic and serological tests for COVID–19; and

(3) a repository of characterized specimens to use to evaluate the performance of those tests that can be made available for appropriate entities to use to evaluate performance.

(d) Communication.—The Secretary shall identify and publicly announce the form and manner for communication with State, local, Tribal, and territorial health departments for purposes of carrying out the activities addressed by guidance issued under subsections (a) and (b).

(e) Availability To Providers.—Guidance issued under subsection (a)(1) shall be issued to health care providers.

(f) Ongoing Provision Of Guidance And Technical Assistance.—Notwithstanding whether funds are available specifically to carry out this subtitle, guidance and technical assistance shall continue to be provided under this section.

RESEARCH AND DEVELOPMENT

SEC. 30564.

The Secretary, in coordination with the Director of the Centers for Disease Control and Prevention and in collaboration with the Director of the National Institutes of Health, the Director of the Agency for Healthcare Research and Quality, the Commissioner of Food and Drugs, and the Administrator of the Centers for Medicare & Medicaid Services, shall support research and development on more efficient and effective strategies—

(1) for the surveillance of SARS–CoV–2 and COVID–19;

(2) for the testing and identification of individuals infected with COVID–19; and

(3) for the tracing of contacts of individuals infected with COVID–19.

AWARENESS CAMPAIGNS

SEC. 30565.

The Secretary, acting through the Director of the Centers for Disease Control and Prevention and in coordination with other offices and agencies, as appropriate, shall award competitive grants or contracts to one or more public or private entities, including faith-based organizations, to carry out multilingual and culturally appropriate awareness campaigns. Such campaigns shall—

(1) be based on available scientific evidence;

(2) increase awareness and knowledge of COVID–19, including countering stigma associated with COVID–19;

(3) improve information on the availability of COVID–19 diagnostic testing; and

(4) promote cooperation with contact tracing efforts.

GRANTS TO STATE AND TRIBAL WORKFORCE AGENCIES

SEC. 30566.

(a) Definitions.—In this section:

(1) IN GENERAL.—Except as otherwise provided, the terms in this section have the meanings given the terms in section 3 of the Workforce Innovation and Opportunity Act (29 U.S.C. 3102).

(2) APPRENTICESHIP; APPRENTICESHIP PROGRAM.—The term "apprenticeship" or "apprenticeship program" means an apprenticeship program registered under the Act of August 16, 1937 (commonly known as the "National Apprenticeship Act")

(50 Stat. 664, chapter 663; 29 U.S.C. 50 et seq.), including any requirement, standard, or rule promulgated under such Act, as such requirement, standard, or rule was in effect on December 30, 2019.

(3) CONTACT TRACING AND RELATED POSITIONS.—The term "contact tracing and related positions" means employment related to contact tracing, surveillance, containment, and mitigation activities as described in paragraphs (2), (3), and (4) of section 30562(d).

(4) ELIGIBLE ENTITY.—The term "eligible entity" means—

(A) a State or territory, including the District of Columbia and Puerto Rico;

(B) an Indian Tribe, Tribal organization, Alaska Native entity, Indian-controlled organizations serving Indians, or Native Hawaiian organizations;

(C) an outlying area; or

(D) a local board, if an eligible entity under subparagraphs (A) through (C) has not applied with respect to the area over which the local board has jurisdiction as of the date on which the local board submits an application under subsection (c).

(5) ELIGIBLE INDIVIDUAL.—Notwithstanding section 170(b)(2) of the Workforce Innovation and Opportunity Act (29 U.S.C. 3225(b)(2)), the term "eligible individual" means an individual seeking or securing employment in contact tracing or related positions and is served by an eligible entity or community-based organization receiving funding under this section.

(6) SECRETARY.—The term "Secretary" means the Secretary of Labor.

(b) Grants.—

(1) IN GENERAL.—Subject to the availability of appropriations under subsection (g), the Secretary shall award national dislocated worker grants under section 170(b)(1)(B) of the Workforce Innovation and Opportunity Act (29 U.S.C. 3225(b)(1)(B)) to each eligible entity that seeks a grant to assist local boards and community-based organizations in carrying out activities under subsections (f) and (d), respectively, for the following purposes:

(A) To support the recruitment, placement, and training, as applicable, of eligible individuals seeking employment in contact tracing and related positions in accordance with the national system for COVID–19 testing, contact tracing, surveillance, containment, and mitigation established under section 30561.

(B) To assist with the employment transition to new employment or education and training of individuals employed under this section in preparation for and upon termination of such employment.

(2) TIMELINE.—The Secretary of Labor shall—

(A) issue application requirements under subsection (c) not later than 10 days after the date of enactment of this section; and

(B) award grants to an eligible entity under paragraph (1) not later than 10 days after the date on which the Secretary receives an application from such entity.

(c) Grant Application.—An eligible entity applying for a grant under this section shall submit an application to the Secretary, at such time and in such form and manner as the Secretary may reasonably require, which shall include a description of—

(1) how the eligible entity will support the recruitment, placement, and training, as applicable, of eligible individuals seeking employment in contact tracing and related positions by partnering with—

(A) a State, local, Tribal, or territorial health department; or

(B) one or more nonprofit or community-based organizations partnering with such health departments;

(2) how the activities described in paragraph (1) will support State efforts to address the demand for contact tracing and related positions with respect to—

(A) the State plans referred to in the heading "Public Health and Social Services Emergency Fund" in title I of division B of the Paycheck Protection Program and Health Care Enhancement Act (Public Law 116–139);

(B) the testing strategy submitted under section 30541; and

(C) the number of eligible individuals that the State plans to recruit and train under the plans and strategies described in subparagraphs (A) and (B);

(3) the specific strategies for recruiting and placement of eligible individuals from or residing within the communities in which they will work, including—

(A) plans for the recruitment of eligible individuals to serve as contact tracers and related positions, including dislocated workers, individuals with barriers to employment, veterans, new entrants in the workforce, or underemployed or furloughed workers, who are from or reside in or near the local area in which they will serve, and who, to the extent practicable—

(i) have experience or a background in industry-sectors and occupations such as public health, social services, customer service, case management, or occupations that require related qualifications, skills, or competencies, such as strong interpersonal and communication skills, needed for contact tracing or related positions, as described in section 30562(d)(2)(E)(ii); or

(ii) seek to transition to public health and public health related occupations upon the conclusion of employment in contact tracing or related positions; and

(B) how such strategies will take into account the diversity of such community, including racial, ethnic, socioeconomic, linguistic, or geographic diversity;

(4) the amount, timing, and mechanisms for distribution of funds provided to local boards or through subgrants as described in subsection (d);

(5) for eligible entities described in subparagraphs (A) through (C) of subsection (a) (4), a description of how the eligible entity will ensure the equitable distribution of funds with respect to—

(A) geography (such as urban and rural distribution);

(B) medically underserved populations (as defined in section 33(b)(3) of the Public Health Service Act (42 U.S.C. 254b(b)));

(C) health professional shortage areas (as defined under section 332(a) of the Public Health Service Act (42 U.S.C. 254e(a))); and

(D) the racial and ethnic diversity of the area; and

(6) for eligible entities who are local boards, a description of how a grant to such eligible entity would serve the equitable distribution of funds as described in paragraph (5).

(d) Subgrant Authorization And Application Process.—

(1) IN GENERAL.—An eligible entity may award a subgrant to one or more community-based organizations for the purposes of partnering with a State or local board to conduct outreach and education activities to inform potentially eligible individuals about employment opportunities in contact tracing and related positions.

(2) APPLICATION.—A community-based organization shall submit an application at such time and in such manner as the eligible entity may reasonably require, including—

(A) a demonstration of the community-based organization's established expertise and effectiveness in community outreach in the local area that such organization plans to serve;

(B) a demonstration of the community-based organization's expertise in providing employment or public health information to the local areas in which such organization plans to serve; and

(C) a description of the expertise of the community-based organization in utilizing culturally competent and multilingual strategies in the provision of services.

(e) Grant Distribution.—

(1) FEDERAL DISTRIBUTION.—

(A) USE OF FUNDS.— The Secretary of Labor shall use the funds appropriated to carry out this section as follows:

(i) Subject to clause (ii), the Secretary shall distribute funds among eligible entities in accordance with a formula to be established by the Secretary that provides a minimum level of funding to each eligible entity that seeks a grant under this section and allocates additional funding as follows:

(I) The formula shall give first priority based on the number and proportion of contact tracing and related positions that the State plans to recruit, place, and train individuals as a part of the State strategy described in subsection (c)(2)(A).

(II) Subject to subclause (I), the formula shall give priority in accordance with section 30562(c).

(ii) Not more than 2 percent of the funding for administration of the grants and for providing technical assistance to recipients of funds under this section.

(B) EQUITABLE DISTRIBUTION.—If the geographic region served by one or more eligible entities overlaps, the Secretary shall distribute funds among such entities in such a manner that ensures equitable distribution with respect to the factors under subsection (c)(5).

(2) ELIGIBLE ENTITY USE OF FUNDS.—An eligible entity described in subparagraphs (A) through (C) of subsection (a)(4)—

(A) shall, not later than 30 days after the date on which the entity receives grant funds under this section, provide not less than 70 percent of grant funds to local boards for the purpose of carrying out activities in subsection (f);

(B) may use up to 20 percent of such funds to make subgrants to community-based organizations in the service area to conduct outreach, to potential eligible individuals, as described in subsection (d);

(C) in providing funds to local boards and awarding subgrants under this subsection shall ensure the equitable distribution with respect to the factors described in subsection (c)(5); and

(D) may use not more than 10 percent of the funds awarded under this section for the administrative costs of carrying out the grant and for providing technical assistance to local boards and community-based organizations.

(3) LOCAL BOARD USE OF FUNDS.—A local board, or an eligible entity that is a local board, shall use—

(A) not less than 60 percent of the funds for recruitment and training for COVID–19 testing, contact tracing, surveillance, containment, and mitigation established under section 30561;

(B) not less than 30 of the funds to support the transition of individuals hired as contact tracers and related positions into an education or training program, or unsubsidized employment upon completion of such positions; and

2

(C) not more than 10 percent of the funds for administrative costs.

(f) Eligible Activities.—The State or local boards shall use funds awarded under this section to support the recruitment and placement of eligible individuals, training and employment transition as related to contact tracing and related positions, and for the following activities:

(1) Establishing or expanding partnerships with—

(A) State, local, Tribal, and territorial public health departments;

(B) community-based health providers, including community health centers and rural health clinics;

(C) labor organizations or joint labor management organizations;

(D) two-year and four-year institutions of higher education (as defined in section 101 of the Higher Education Act of 1965 (20 U.S.C. 1001)), including institutions eligible to receive funds under section 371(a) of the Higher Education Act of 1965 (20 U.S.C. 1067q(a)); and

(E) community action agencies or other community-based organizations serving local areas in which there is a demand for contact tracers and related positions.

(2) Providing training for contact tracing and related positions in coordination with State, local, Tribal, or territorial health departments that is consistent with the State or territorial testing and contact tracing strategy and ensuring that eligible individuals receive compensation while participating in such training.

(3) Providing eligible individuals with—

(A) adequate and safe equipment, environments, and facilities for training and supervision, as applicable;

(B) information regarding the wages and benefits related to contact tracing and related positions, as compared to State, local, and national averages;

(C) supplies and equipment needed by the program participants to support placement of an individual in contact tracing and related positions, as applicable;

(D) an individualized employment plan for each eligible individual, as applicable—

(i) in coordination with the entity employing the eligible individual in a contact tracing or related position; and

(ii) which shall include providing a case manager to work with each eligible individual to develop the plan, which may include—

(I) identifying employment and career goals, and setting appropriate achievement objectives to attain such goals; and

(II) exploring career pathways that lead to in-demand industries and sectors, including in public health and related occupations; and

(E) services for the period during which the individual is employed in a contact tracing and related position to ensure job retention, which may include—

(i) supportive services throughout the term of employment;

(ii) a continuation of skills training as related to employment as a contact tracer or related positions, that is conducted in collaboration with the employers of such participants;

(iii) mentorship services and job retention support for eligible individuals; or

(iv) targeted training for managers and workers working with eligible individuals (such as mentors), and human resource representatives;

(4) Supporting the transition and placement in unsubsidized employment for eligible individuals serving in the contact tracing or related positions after such positions are no longer necessary in the State or local area, including—

(A) any additional training and employment activities as described in section 170(d)(4) of the Workforce Innovation and Opportunity Act (29 U.S.C. 3225(d)(4));

(B) developing the appropriate combination of services to enable the eligible individual to achieve the employment and career goals identified under paragraph (3)(D)(ii)(I); and

(C) services to assist eligible individuals in maintaining employment for not less than 12 months after the completion of employment in contact tracing or related positions, as appropriate.

(5) Any other activities as described in subsections (a)(3) and (b) of section 134 of the Workforce Innovation and Opportunity Act (29 U.S.C. 3174).

(g) Limitation.—Notwithstanding section 170(d)(3)(A) of the Workforce Innovation and Opportunity Act (29 U.S.C. 3225(d)(3)(A)), a person may be employed in a contact tracing or related position using funds under this section for a period not greater than 2 years.

(h) Reporting By The Department Of Labor.—

(1) IN GENERAL.—Not later than 120 days of the enactment of this Act, and once grant funds have been expended under this section, the Secretary shall report to the Committee on Education and Labor of the House of Representatives and the Committee on Health, Education, Labor and Pensions of the Senate, and make publicly available a report containing a description of—

(A) the number of eligible individuals recruited, hired, and trained as contract tracers and related positions;

(B) the number of individuals successfully transitioned to unsubsidized employment or training at the completion of employment in contact tracing or related positions using funds under this subtitle;

(C) the number of such individuals who were unemployed prior to being hired, trained, or deployed as described in paragraph (1);

(D) the performance of each program supported by funds under this subtitle with respect to the indicators of performance under section 116 of the Workforce Innovation and Opportunity Act (29 U.S.C. 3141), as applicable;

(E) the number of individuals in unsubsidized employment within six months and 1 year, respectively, of the conclusion of employment in contact tracing or related positions and, of those, the number of individuals within a State, territorial, or local public health department in an occupation related to public health;

(F) any information on how eligible entities, local boards, or community-based organizations that received funding under this subsection were able to support the goals of the national system for COVID–19 testing, contact tracing, surveillance, containment, and mitigation established under section 30561 of this Act; and

(G) best practices for improving and increasing the transition of individuals employed in contract tracing or related positions to permanent, full-time employment.

(2) DISAGGREGATION.—All data reported under paragraph (1) shall be disaggregated by race, ethnicity, sex, age, and, with respect to individuals with barriers to employment, subpopulation of such individuals, except for when the number of participants in a category is insufficient to yield statistically reliable information or when the results would reveal personally identifiable information about an individual participant.

(i) Special Rule.—Any funds used for programs under this section that are used to fund an apprenticeship or apprenticeship program shall only be used for, or provided to, an apprenticeship or apprenticeship program that meets the definition of such term subsection (a) of this section, including any funds awarded for the purposes of grants, contracts, or cooperative agreements, or the development, implementation, or administration, of an apprenticeship or an apprenticeship program.

(j) Information Sharing Requirement For HHS.—The Secretary of Health and Human Services, acting through the Director of the Centers for Disease Control and Prevention, shall provide the Secretary of Labor, acting through the Assistant Secretary of the Employment and Training Administration, with information on grants under section 30562, including—

(1) the formula used to award such grants to State, local, Tribal, and territorial health departments;

(2) the dollar amounts of and scope of the work funded under such grants;

(3) the geographic areas served by eligible entities that receive such grants; and

(4) the number of contact tracers and related positions to be hired using such grants.

(k) Authorization Of Appropriations.—Of the amounts appropriated to carry out this subtitle, $500,000,000 shall be used by the Secretary of Labor to carry out subsections (a) through (h) of this section.

APPLICATION OF THE SERVICE CONTRACT ACT TO CONTRACTS AND GRANTS

SEC. 30567.

Contracts and grants which include contact tracing as part of the scope of work and that are awarded under this subtitle shall require that contract tracers and related positions are paid not less than the prevailing wage and fringe rates required under chapter 67 of title 41, United States Code (commonly known as the "Service Contract Act") for the area in which the work is performed. To the extent that a nonstandard wage determination is required to establish a prevailing wage for contact tracers and related positions for purposes of this subtitle, the Secretary of Labor shall issue such determination not later than 14 days after the date of enactment of this Act, based on a job description used by the Centers for Disease Control and Prevention and contractors or grantees performing contact tracing for State public health agencies.

AUTHORIZATION OF APPROPRIATIONS

SEC. 30568.

To carry out this subtitle, there are authorized to be appropriated $75,000,000,000, to remain available until expended.

Subtitle E—Demographic Data And Supply Reporting Related To Covid–19

COVID–19 REPORTING PORTAL

SEC. 30571.

(a) In General.—Not later than 15 days after the date of enactment of this Act, the Secretary shall establish and maintain an online portal for use by eligible health care entities to track and transmit data regarding their personal protective equipment and medical supply inventory and capacity related to COVID–19.

(b) Eligible Health Care Entities.—In this section, the term "eligible health care entity" means a licensed acute care hospital, hospital system, or long-term care facility with confirmed cases of COVID–19.

(c) Submission.—An eligible health care entity shall report using the portal under this section on a biweekly basis in order to assist the Secretary in tracking usage and need of COVID–related supplies and personnel in a regular and real-time manner.

(d) Included Information.—The Secretary shall design the portal under this section to include information on personal protective equipment and medical supply inventory and capacity related to COVID–19, including with respect to the following:

(1) PERSONAL PROTECTIVE EQUIPMENT.—Total personal protective equipment inventory, including, in units, the numbers of N95 masks and authorized equivalent respirator masks, surgical masks, exam gloves, face shields, isolation gowns, and coveralls.

(2) MEDICAL SUPPLY.—

(A) Total ventilator inventory, including, in units, the number of universal, adult, pediatric, and infant ventilators.

(B) Total diagnostic and serological test inventory, including, in units, the number of test platforms, tests, test kits, reagents, transport media, swabs, and other materials or supplies determined necessary by the Secretary.

(3) CAPACITY.—

(A) Case count measurements, including confirmed positive cases and persons under investigation.

(B) Total number of staffed beds, including medical surgical beds, intensive care beds, and critical care beds.

(C) Available beds, including medical surgical beds, intensive care beds, and critical care beds.

(D) Total number of COVID–19 patients currently utilizing a ventilator.

(E) Average number of days a COVID–19 patient is utilizing a ventilator.

(F) Total number of additionally needed professionals in each of the following categories: intensivists, critical care physicians, respiratory therapists, registered nurses, certified registered nurse anesthetists, and laboratory personnel.

(G) Total number of hospital personnel currently not working due to self-isolation following a known or presumed COVID–19 exposure.

(e) Access To Information Related To Inventory And Capacity.—The Secretary shall ensure that relevant agencies and officials, including the Centers for Disease Control and Prevention, the Assistant Secretary for Preparedness and Response, and the Federal Emergency Management Agency, have access to information related to inventory and capacity submitted under this section.

(f) Weekly Report To Congress.—On a weekly basis, the Secretary shall transmit information related to inventory and capacity submitted under this section to the appropriate committees of the House and Senate.

REGULAR CDC REPORTING ON DEMOGRAPHIC DATA

SEC. 30572.

Not later than 14 days after the date of enactment of this Act, the Secretary, in coordination with the Director of the Centers for Disease Control and Prevention, shall amend the reporting under the heading "Department of Health and Human Services—Office of the Secretary—Public Health and Social Service Emergency Fund" in title I of division B of the Paycheck Protection Program and Health Care Enhancement Act (Public Law 116–139; 134 Stat. 620, 626) on the demographic characteristics, including race, ethnicity, age, sex, gender, geographic region, and other relevant factors of individuals tested for or diagnosed with COVID–19, to include—

(1) providing technical assistance to State, local, and territorial health departments

to improve the collection and reporting of such demographic data;

(2) if such data is not so collected or reported, the reason why the State, local, or territorial department of health has not been able to collect or provide such information; and

(3) making a copy of such report available publicly on the website of the Centers for Disease Control and Prevention.

FEDERAL MODERNIZATION FOR HEALTH INEQUITIES DATA

SEC. 30573.

(a) In General.—The Secretary shall work with covered agencies to support the modernization of data collection methods and infrastructure at such agencies for the purpose of increasing data collection related to health inequities, such as racial, ethnic, socioeconomic, sex, gender, and disability disparities.

(b) Covered Agency Defined.—In this section, the term "covered agency" means each of the following Federal agencies:

(1) The Agency for Healthcare Research and Quality.

(2) The Centers for Disease Control and Prevention.

(3) The Centers for Medicare & Medicaid Services.

(4) The Food and Drug Administration.

(5) The Office of the National Coordinator for Health Information Technology.

(6) The National Institutes of Health.

(c) Authorization Of Appropriations.—There is authorized to be appropriated to each covered agency to carry out this section $4,000,000, to remain available until expended.

MODERNIZATION OF STATE AND LOCAL HEALTH INEQUITIES DATA

SEC. 30574.

(a) In General.—Not later than 6 months after the date of enactment of this Act, the Secretary, acting through the Director of the Centers for Disease Control and Prevention, shall award grants to State, local, and territorial health departments in order to support the modernization of data collection methods and infrastructure for the purposes of increasing data related to health inequities, such as racial, ethnic, socioeconomic, sex, gender, and disability disparities. The Secretary shall—

(1) provide guidance, technical assistance, and information to grantees under this section on best practices regarding culturally competent, accurate, and increased data collection and transmission; and

(2) track performance of grantees under this section to help improve their health inequities data collection by identifying gaps and taking effective steps to support States, localities, and territories in addressing the gaps.

(b) Report.—Not later than 1 year after the date on which the first grant is awarded under this section, the Secretary shall submit to the Committee on Energy and Commerce of the House of Representatives and the Committee on Health, Education, Labor and Pensions of the Senate an initial report detailing—

(1) nationwide best practices for ensuring States and localities collect and transmit health inequities data;

(2) nationwide trends which hinder the collection and transmission of health inequities data;

(3) Federal best practices for working with States and localities to ensure culturally competent, accurate, and increased data collection and transmission; and

(4) any recommended changes to legislative or regulatory authority to help improve and increase health inequities data collection.

(c) Final Report.—Not later than December 31, 2023, the Secretary shall—

(1) update and finalize the initial report under subsection (b); and

(2) submit such final report to the committees specified in such subsection.

(d) Authorization Of Appropriations.—There is authorized to be appropriated to carry out this section $100,000,000, to remain available until expended.

TRIBAL FUNDING TO RESEARCH HEALTH INEQUITIES INCLUDING COVID-19

SEC. 30575.

(a) In General.—Not later than 6 months after the date of enactment of this Act, the Director of the Indian Health Service, in coordination with Tribal Epidemiology Centers and other Federal agencies, as appropriate, shall conduct or support research and field studies for the purposes of improved understanding of Tribal health inequities among American Indians and Alaska Natives, including with respect to—

(1) disparities related to COVID-19;

(2) public health surveillance and infrastructure regarding unmet needs in Indian country and Urban Indian communities;

(3) population-based health disparities;

(4) barriers to health care services;

(5) the impact of socioeconomic status; and

(6) factors contributing to Tribal health inequities.

(b) Consultation, Confer, And Coordination.—In carrying out this section, the Director of the Indian Health Service shall—

(1) consult with Indian Tribes and Tribal organizations;

(2) confer with Urban Indian organizations; and

(3) coordinate with the Director of the Centers for Disease Control and Prevention and the Director of the National Institutes of Health.

(c) Process.—Not later than 60 days after the date of enactment of this Act, the Director of the Indian Health Service shall establish a nationally representative panel to establish processes and procedures for the research and field studies conducted or supported under subsection (a). The Director shall ensure that, at a minimum, the panel consists of the following individuals:

(1) Elected Tribal leaders or their designees.

(2) Tribal public health practitioners and experts from the national and regional levels.

(d) Duties.—The panel established under subsection (c) shall, at a minimum—

(1) advise the Director of the Indian Health Service on the processes and procedures regarding the design, implementation, and evaluation of, and reporting on, research and field studies conducted or supported under this section;

(2) develop and share resources on Tribal public health data surveillance and reporting, including best practices; and

(3) carry out such other activities as may be appropriate to establish processes and procedures for the research and field studies conducted or supported under subsection (a).

(e) Report.—Not later than 1 year after expending all funds made available to carry out this section, the Director of the Indian Health Service, in coordination with the panel established under subsection (c), shall submit an initial report on the results of the research and field studies under this section to—

(1) the Committee on Energy and Commerce and the Committee on Natural Resources of the House of Representatives; and

(2) the Committee on Indian Affairs and the Committee on Health, Education, Labor and Pensions of the Senate.

(f) Tribal Data Sovereignty.—The Director of the Indian Health Service shall ensure that all research and field studies conducted or supported under this section are tribally-directed and carried out in a manner which ensures Tribal-direction of all data collected under this section—

(1) according to Tribal best practices regarding research design and implementation, including by ensuring the consent of the Tribes involved to public reporting of Tribal data;

(2) according to all relevant and applicable Tribal, professional, institutional, and Federal standards for conducting research and governing research ethics;

(3) with the prior and informed consent of any Indian Tribe participating in the research or sharing data for use under this section; and

(4) in a manner that respects the inherent sovereignty of Indian Tribes, including Tribal governance of data and research.

(g) Final Report.—Not later than December 31, 2023, the Director of the Indian Health Service shall—

(1) update and finalize the initial report under subsection (e); and

(2) submit such final report to the committees specified in such subsection.

(h) Definitions.—In this section:

(1) The terms "Indian Tribe" and "Tribal organization" have the meanings given to such terms in section 4 of the Indian Self-Determination and Education Assistance Act (25 U.S.C. 5304).

(2) The term "Urban Indian organization" has the meaning given to such term in section 4 of the Indian Health Care Improvement Act (25 U.S.C. 1603).

(i) Authorization Of Appropriations.—There is authorized to be appropriated to carry out this section $25,000,000, to remain available until expended.

CDC FIELD STUDIES PERTAINING TO SPECIFIC HEALTH INEQUITIES

SEC. 30576.

(a) In General.—Not later than 90 days after the date of enactment of this Act, the Secretary, acting through the Centers for Disease Control and Prevention, in collaboration with State, local, and territorial health departments, shall complete (by the reporting deadline in subsection (b)) field studies to better understand health inequities that are not currently tracked by the Secretary. Such studies shall include an analysis of—

(1) the impact of socioeconomic status on health care access and disease outcomes, including COVID–19 outcomes;

(2) the impact of disability status on health care access and disease outcomes, including COVID–19 outcomes;

(3) the impact of language preference on health care access and disease outcomes, including COVID–19 outcomes;

(4) factors contributing to disparities in health outcomes for the COVID–19 pandemic; and

(5) other topics related to disparities in health outcomes for the COVID–19 pandemic, as determined by the Secretary.

(b) Report.—Not later than December 31, 2021, the Secretary shall submit to the Committee on Energy and Commerce of the House of Representatives and the Committee on Health, Education, Labor and Pensions of the Senate an initial report on the results of the field studies under this section.

(c) Final Report.—Not later than December 31, 2023, the Secretary shall—

(1) update and finalize the initial report under subsection (b); and

(2) submit such final report to the committees specified in such subsection.

(d) Authorization Of Appropriations.—There is authorized to be appropriated to carry out this section $25,000,000, to remain available until expended.

ADDITIONAL REPORTING TO CONGRESS ON THE RACE AND ETHNICITY RATES OF COVID–19 TESTING, HOSPITALIZATIONS, AND MORTALITIES

SEC. 30577.

(a) In General.—Not later than August 1, 2020, the Secretary shall submit to the Committee on Appropriations and the Committee on Energy and Commerce of the House of Representatives and the Committee on Appropriations and the Committee on Health, Education, Labor and Pensions of the Senate an initial report—

(1) describing the testing, positive diagnoses, hospitalization, intensive care admissions, and mortality rates associated with COVID–19, disaggregated by race, ethnicity, age, sex, gender, geographic region, and other relevant factors as determined by the Secretary;

(2) including an analysis of any variances of testing, positive diagnoses, hospitalizations, and deaths by demographic characteristics; and

(3) including proposals for evidenced-based response strategies to reduce disparities related to COVID–19.

(b) Final Report.—Not later than December 31, 2024, the Secretary shall—

(1) update and finalize the initial report under subsection (a); and

(2) submit such final report to the committees specified in such subsection.

(c) Coordination.—In preparing the report submitted under this section, the Secretary shall take into account and otherwise coordinate such report with reporting required under section 30572 and under the heading "Department of Health and Human Services—Office of the Secretary—Public Health and Social Service Emergency Fund" in title I of division B of the Paycheck Protection Program and Health Care Enhancement Act (Public Law 116–139; 134 Stat. 620, 626).

Subtitle F—Miscellaneous

TECHNICAL CORRECTIONS TO AMENDMENTS MADE BY CARES ACT

SEC. 30581.

(a) The amendments made by this section shall take effect as if included in the enactment of the CARES Act (Public Law 116–136).

(b) Section 3112 of division A of the CARES Act (Public Law 116–136) is amended—

(1) in subsection (a)(2)(A), by striking the comma before "or a permanent";

(2) in subsection (d)(1), by striking "and subparagraphs (A) and (B)" and inserting "as subparagraphs (A) and (B)"; and

(3) in subsection (e), by striking "Drug, Cosmetic Act" and inserting "Drug, and Cosmetic Act".

(c) Section 6001(a)(1)(D) of division F of the Families First Coronavirus Response Act (Public Law 116–127), as amended by section 3201 of division A of the CARES

Act (Public Law 116–136), is amended by striking "other test that".

(d) Subsection (k)(9) of section 543 of the Public Health Service Act (42 U.S.C. 290dd–2), as added by section 3221(d) of division A of the CARES Act (Public Law 116–136), is amended by striking "unprotected health information" and inserting "unsecured protected health information".

(e) Section 3401(2)(D) of division A of the CARES Act (Public Law 116–136), is amended by striking "Not Later than" and inserting "Not later than".

(f) Section 831(f) of the Public Health Service Act, as redesignated by section 3404(a)(6)(E) and amended by section 3404(a)(6)(G) of division A of the CARES Act (Public Law 116–136), is amended by striking "a health care facility, or a partnership of such a school and facility".

(g) Section 846(i) of the Public Health Service Act, as amended by section 3404(i)(8)(C) of division A of the CARES Act (Public Law 116–136), is amended by striking "871(b),," and inserting "871(b),".

(h) Section 3606(a)(1)(A) of division A of the CARES Act (Public Law 116–136) is amended by striking "In general" and inserting "IN GENERAL".

(i) Section 3856(b)(1) of division A of the CARES Act (Public Law 116–136) is amended to read as follows:

"(1) IN GENERAL.—Section 905(b)(4) of the FDA Reauthorization Act of 2017 (Public Law 115–52) is amended by striking 'Section 744H(e)(2)(B) of the Federal Food, Drug, and Cosmetic Act (21 U.S.C. 379j–52(e)(2)(B))' and inserting 'Section 744H(f)(2)(B) of the Federal Food, Drug, and Cosmetic Act, as redesignated by section 403(c)(1) of this Act,'.".

TITLE VI

—PUBLIC HEALTH ASSISTANCE

Subtitle A—Assistance To Providers And Health System
HEALTH CARE PROVIDER RELIEF FUND

SEC. 30611.

(a) In General.—Not later than 7 days after the date of enactment of this Act, the Secretary, acting through the Administrator of the Health Resources and Services Administration, shall establish a program under which the Secretary shall reimburse, through grants or other mechanisms, eligible health care providers for eligible expenses or lost revenues occurring during calendar quarters beginning on or after January 1, 2020, to prevent, prepare for, and respond to COVID–19, in an amount calculated under subsection (c).

(b) Quarterly Basis.—

(1) SUBMISSION OF APPLICATIONS.—The Secretary shall give applicants a period of 7 calendar days after the close of a quarter to submit applications under this section with respect to such quarter, except that the Secretary shall give applicants a period of 7 calendar days after the date of enactment of this Act to submit applications with respect to the quarter beginning on January 1, 2020, if the applicant has not previously submitted an application with the respect to such quarter.

(2) REVIEW AND PAYMENT.—The Secretary shall—

(A) review applications and make awards of reimbursement under this section on a quarterly basis; and

(B) award the reimbursements under this section for a quarter not later than 14 calendar days after the close of the quarter, except that the Secretary shall award the reimbursements under this section for the quarter beginning on January 1, 2020, not later than 14 calendar days after the date of enactment of this Act.

(c) Calculation.—

(1) IN GENERAL.—The amount of the reimbursement to an eligible health provider under this section with respect to a calendar quarter shall equal—

(A) the sum of—

(i) 100 percent of the eligible expenses, as described in subsection (d), of the provider during the quarter; and

(ii) subject to paragraph (3), 60 percent of the lost revenues, as described in subsection (e), of the provider during the quarter; less

(B) any funds that are—

(i) received by the provider during the quarter pursuant to the Coronavirus Preparedness and Response Supplemental Appropriations Act, 2020 (Public Law 116–123), the Families First Coronavirus Response Act (Public Law 116–127), the CARES Act (Public Law 116–136), or the Paycheck Protection Program and Health Care Enhancement Act (Public Law 116–139); and

(ii) not required to be repaid.

(2) CARRYOVER.—If the amount determined under paragraph (1)(B) for a calendar quarter with respect to an eligible health care provider exceeds the amount determined under subparagraph (A) with respect to such provider and quarter, the amount of such difference shall be applied in making the calculation under this subsection, over each subsequent calendar quarter for which the eligible health care provider seeks reimbursement under this section.

(3) LOST REVENUE LIMITATION.—If the amount determined under subsection (e) with respect to the lost revenue of an eligible health care provider for a calendar quarter does not exceed an amount that equals 10 percent of the net patient revenue (as defined in such subsection) of the provider for the corresponding quarter in 2019, the addend under paragraph (1)(A)(ii), in making the calculation under paragraph (1), is deemed to be zero.

(d) Eligible Expenses.—Subject to subsection (h)(1), expenses eligible for reimbursement under this section include expenses for—

(1) building or construction of temporary structures;

(2) leasing of properties;

(3) medical supplies and equipment including personal protective equipment;

(4) in vitro diagnostic tests, serological tests, or testing supplies;

(5) increased workforce and trainings;

(6) emergency operation centers;

(7) construction or retrofitting of facilities;

(8) mobile testing units;

(9) surge capacity;

(10) retention of workforce; and

(11) such other items and services as the Secretary determines to be appropriate, in consultation with relevant stakeholders.

(e) Lost Revenues.—

(1) IN GENERAL.—Subject to subsection (h)(1), for purposes of subsection (c)(1)(A)(ii), the lost revenues of an eligible health care provider, with respect to the calendar

quarter involved, shall be equal to—

(A) net patient revenue of the provider for the corresponding quarter in 2019 minus net patient revenue of the provider for such quarter; less

(B) the savings of the provider during the calendar quarter involved attributable to foregone wages, payroll taxes, and benefits of personnel who were furloughed or laid off by the provider during that quarter.

(2) NET PATIENT REVENUE DEFINED.—For purposes of paragraph (1)(A), the term "net patient revenue", with respect to an eligible health care provider and a calendar quarter, means the sum of—

(A) 200 percent of the total amount of reimbursement received by the provider during the quarter for all items and services furnished under a State plan or a waiver of a State plan under title XIX of the Social Security Act (42 U.S.C. 1396 et seq.);

(B) 125 percent of the total amount of reimbursement received by the provider during the quarter for all items and services furnished under title XVIII of the Social Security Act (42 U.S.C. 1395 et seq.); and

(C) 100 percent of the total amount of reimbursement not described in subparagraph (A) or (B) received by the provider during the quarter for all items and services.

(f) Insufficient Funds For A Quarter.—If there are insufficient funds made available to reimburse all eligible health care providers for all eligible expenses and lost revenues for a quarter in accordance with this section, the Secretary shall—

(1) prioritize reimbursement of eligible expenses; and

(2) using the entirety of the remaining funds, uniformly reduce the percentage of lost revenues otherwise applicable under subsection (c)(1)(A)(ii) to the extent necessary to reimburse a portion of the lost revenues of all eligible health care providers applying for reimbursement.

(g) Application.—A health care provider seeking reimbursement under this section for a calendar quarter shall submit to the Secretary an application that—

(1) provides documentation demonstrating that the health care provider is an eligible health care provider;

(2) includes a valid tax identification number of the health care provider;

(3) attests to the eligible expenses and lost revenues of the health care provider, as described in subsection (d), occurring during the calendar quarter;

(4) includes an itemized listing of each such eligible expense, including expenses incurred in providing uncompensated care;

(5) for purposes of subsection (c)(3), attests to whether the amount determined under subsection (e) with respect to the lost revenue of an eligible health care provider for a calendar quarter exceeds an amount that equals 10 percent of the net patient revenue (as defined in such subsection) of the provider for the corresponding quarter in 2019;

(6) includes projections of the eligible expenses and lost revenues of the health care provider, as described in subsection (c), for the calendar quarter that immediately follows the calendar for which reimbursement is sought; and

(7) indicates the dollar amounts described in each of subparagraphs (A) and (B) of subsection (e)(1) and subparagraphs (A), (B), and (C) of subsection (e)(2) for the calendar quarter.

(h) Limitations.—

(1) NO DUPLICATIVE REIMBURSEMENT.—The Secretary may not provide, and a health care provider may not accept, reimbursement under this section for expenses or losses with respect to which—

(A) the eligible health care provider is reimbursed from other sources; or

(B) other sources are obligated to reimburse the provider.

(2) NO EXECUTIVE COMPENSATION.—Reimbursement for eligible expenses (as described in subsection (e)) and lost revenues (as described in subsection (f)) shall not include compensation or benefits, including salary, bonuses, awards of stock, or other financial benefits, for an officer or employee described in section 4004(a)(2) of the CARES Act (Public Law 116–136).

(i) No Balance Billing As Condition Of Receipt Of Funds.—

(1) PROTECTING INDIVIDUALS ENROLLED IN HEALTH PLANS.—As a condition of receipt of reimbursement under this section, a health care provider, in the case such provider furnishes during the emergency period described in section 1135(g)(1)(B) of the Social Security Act (42 U.S.C. 1320b–5(g)(1)(B)) (whether before, on, or after, the date on which the provider submits an application under this section) a medically necessary item or service described in subparagraph (A), (B), or (C) of paragraph (3) to an individual who is described in such subparagraph (A), (B), or (C), respectively, and enrolled in a group health plan or group or individual health insurance coverage offered by a health insurance issuer (including grandfathered health plans as defined in section 1251(e) of the Patient Protection and Affordable Care Act (42 U.S.C. 18011(e)) and such provider is a nonparticipating provider with respect to such plan or coverage and such plan or coverage and such items and services would otherwise be covered under such plan if furnished by a participating provider—

(A) may not bill or otherwise hold liable such individual for a payment amount for such item or service that is more than the cost-sharing amount that would apply under such plan or coverage for such item or service if such provider furnishing such service were a participating provider with respect to such plan or coverage;

(B) shall reimburse such individual in a timely manner for any amount for such item or service paid by the individual to such provider in excess of such cost-sharing amount;

(C) shall submit any claim for such item or service directly to the plan or coverage; and

(D) shall not bill the individual for such cost-sharing amount until such individual is informed by the plan or coverage of the required payment amount.

(2) PROTECTING UNINSURED INDIVIDUALS.—As a condition of receipt of reimbursement under this section, a health care provider, in the case such reimbursement is with respect to expenses incurred in providing uncompensated care (as described in subsection (g)(4)) with respect to a medically necessary item or service described in subparagraph (A), (B), or (C) of paragraph (3) furnished during such emergency period (whether before, on, or after, the date on which the provider submits an application under this section) by the provider to an individual who is described in such subparagraph (A), (B), or (C), respectively—

(A) shall consider such reimbursement as payment in full with respect to such item or service so furnished to such individual;

(B) may not bill or otherwise hold liable such individual for any payment for such item or service so furnished to such individual; and

(C) shall reimburse such individual in a timely manner for any amount for such item or service paid by the individual to such provider.

(3) MEDICALLY NECESSARY ITEMS AND SERVICES DESCRIBED.—For purposes of this subsection, medically necessary items and services described in this paragraph are—

(A) medically necessary items and services (including in-person or telehealth visits in which such items and services are furnished) that are furnished to an individual who has been diagnosed with (or after provision of the items and services is diagnosed with) COVID–19 to treat or mitigate the effects of COVID–19;

(B) medically necessary items and services (including in-person or telehealth visits in which such items and services are furnished) that are furnished to an individual who is presumed, in accordance with paragraph (4), to have COVID–19 but is never diagnosed as such; and

(C) a diagnostic test (and administration of such test) as described in section 6001(a) of division F of the Families First Coronavirus Response Act (42 U.S.C. 1320b–5 note) administered to an individual.

(4) PRESUMPTIVE CASE OF COVID–19.—For purposes of paragraph (3)(B), an individual shall be presumed to have COVID–19 if the medical record documentation of the individual supports a diagnosis of COVID–19, even if the individual does not have a positive in vitro diagnostic test result in the medical record of the individual.

(5) PENALTY.—In the case of an eligible health care provider that is paid a reimbursement under this section and that is in violation of paragraph (1) or (2), in addition to any other penalties that may be prescribed by law, the Secretary may recoup from such provider up to the full amount of reimbursement the provider receives under this section.

(6) DEFINITIONS.—In this subsection:

(A) NONPARTICIPATING PROVIDER.—The term "nonparticipating provider" means, with respect to an item or service and group health plan or group or individual health insurance coverage offered by a health insurance issuer, a health care provider that does not have a contractual relationship directly or indirectly with the plan or issuer, respectively, for furnishing such an item or service under the plan or coverage.

(B) PARTICIPATING PROVIDER.—The term "participating provider" means, with respect to an item or service and group health plan or group or individual health insurance coverage offered by a health insurance issuer, a health care provider that has a contractual relationship directly or indirectly with the plan or issuer, respectively, for furnishing such an item or service under the plan or coverage.

(C) GROUP HEALTH PLAN, HEALTH INSURANCE COVERAGE.—The terms "group health plan", "health insurance issuer", "group health insurance coverage", and "individual health insurance coverage" shall have the meanings given such terms under section 2791 of the Public Health Service Act (42 U.S.C. 300gg–91).

(j) Reports.—

(1) AWARD INFORMATION.—In making awards under this section, the Secretary shall post in a searchable, electronic format, a list of all recipients and awards pursuant to funding authorized under this section.

(2) REPORTS BY RECIPIENTS.—Each recipient of an award under this section shall, as a condition on receipt of such award, submit reports and maintain documentation, in such form, at such time, and containing such information, as the Secretary determines is needed to ensure compliance with this section.

(3) PUBLIC LISTING OF AWARDS.—The Secretary shall—

(A) not later than 7 days after the date of enactment of this Act, post in a searchable, electronic format, a list of all awards made by the Secretary under this section, including the recipients and amounts of such awards; and

(B) update such list not less than every 7 days until all funds made available to carry out this section are expended.

(4) INSPECTOR GENERAL REPORT.—

(A) IN GENERAL.—Not later than 3 years after final payments are made under this section, the Inspector General of the Department of Health and Human Services shall transmit a final report on audit findings with respect to the program under this section to the Committee on Energy and Commerce and the Committee on Appropriations of the House of Representatives and the Committee on Health, Education, Labor and Pensions and the Committee on Appropriations of the Senate.

(B) RULE OF CONSTRUCTION.—Nothing in this paragraph shall be construed as limiting the authority of the Inspector General of the Department of Health and Human Services or the Comptroller General of the United States to conduct audits of interim payments earlier than the deadline described in subparagraph (A).

(k) Eligible Health Care Provider Defined.—In this section:

(1) IN GENERAL.—The term "eligible health care provider" means a health care provider described in paragraph (2) that provides diagnostic or testing services or treatment to individuals with a confirmed or presumptive diagnosis of COVID–19.

(2) HEALTH CARE PROVIDERS DESCRIBED.—A health care provider described in this paragraph is any of the following:

(A) A health care provider enrolled as a participating provider under a State plan approved under title XIX of the Social Security Act (42 U.S.C. 1396 et seq.) (or a waiver of such a plan).

(B) A provider of services (as defined in subsection (u) of section 1861 of the Social Security Act (42 U.S.C. 1395x)) or a supplier (as defined in subsection (d) of such section) that is enrolled as a participating provider of services or participating supplier under the Medicare program under title XVIII of such Act (42 U.S.C. 1395 et seq.).

(C) A public entity.

(D) Any other entity not described in this paragraph as the Secretary may specify.

(l) Funding.—

(1) AUTHORIZATION OF APPROPRIATIONS.—There is authorized to be appropriated for an additional amount to carry out this section $100,000,000,000, to remain available until expended.

(2) HEALTH CARE PROVIDER RELIEF FUND.—

(A) USE OF APPROPRIATED FUNDS.—

(i) IN GENERAL.—In addition to amounts authorized to be appropriated pursuant to paragraph (1), the unobligated balance of all amounts appropriated to the Health Care Provider Relief Fund shall be made available only to carry out this section.

(ii) AMOUNTS.—For purposes of clause (i), the following amounts are deemed to be appropriated to the Health Care Provider Relief Fund:

(I) The unobligated balance of the appropriation of $100,000,000,000 in the third paragraph under the heading "Department of Health and Human Services—Office of the Secretary—Public Health and Social Services Emergency Fund" in division B of the CARES Act (Public Law 116–136).

(II) The unobligated balance of the appropriation under the heading "Department of Health and Human Services—Office of the Secretary—Public Health and Social Services Emergency Fund" in division B of the Paycheck Protection Program and Health Care Enhancement Act (Public Law 116–139).

(B) LIMITATION.—Of the unobligated balances described in subparagraph (A)(ii), the Secretary may not make available more than $10,000,000,000 to reimburse eligible health care providers for expenses incurred in providing uncompensated care.

(C) FUTURE AMOUNTS.—Any appropriation enacted subsequent to the date of enactment of this Act that is made available for reimbursing eligible health care providers as described in subsection (a) shall be made available only to carry out this section.

PUBLIC HEALTH WORKFORCE LOAN REPAYMENT PROGRAM

SEC. 30612.

Part D of title III of the Public Health Service Act (42 U.S.C. 254b et seq.) is amended by adding at the end the following new subpart:

"Subpart XIII—Public Health Workforce

"SEC. 340J. LOAN REPAYMENT PROGRAM.

"(a) Establishment.—The Secretary of Health and Human Services shall establish a program to be known as the Public Health Workforce Loan Repayment Program (referred to in this section as the 'Program') to assure an adequate supply of and encourage recruitment of public health professionals to eliminate critical public health workforce shortages in local, State, territorial, and Tribal public health agencies.

"(b) Eligibility.—To be eligible to participate in the Program, an individual shall—

"(1) (A) be accepted for enrollment, or be enrolled, as a student in an accredited academic educational institution in a State or territory in the final semester or equivalent of a course of study or program leading to a public health degree, a health professions degree or certificate, or a degree in computer science, information science, information systems, information technology, or statistics and have accepted employment with a local, State, territorial, or Tribal public health agency, or a related training fellowship, as recognized by the Secretary, to commence upon graduation; or

"(B) (i) have graduated, during the preceding 10-year period, from an accredited educational institution in a State or territory and received a public health degree, a health professions degree or certificate, or a degree in computer science, information science, information systems, information technology, or statistics; and

"(ii) be employed by, or have accepted employment with, a local, State, territorial, or Tribal public health agency or a related training fellowship, as recognized by the Secretary;

"(2) be a United States citizen;

"(3) (A) submit an application to the Secretary to participate in the Program; and

"(B) execute a written contract as required in subsection (c); and

"(4) not have received, for the same service, a reduction of loan obligations under section 428K or 428L of the Higher Education Act of 1965 (20 U.S.C. 1078–11, 1078–12).

"(c) Contract.—The written contract referred to in subsection (b)(3)(B) between the Secretary and an individual shall contain—

"(1) an agreement on the part of the Secretary that the Secretary will repay, on behalf of the individual, loans incurred by the individual in the pursuit of the relevant degree or certificate in accordance with the terms of the contract;

"(2) an agreement on the part of the individual that the individual will serve in the full-time employment of a local, State, or Tribal public health agency or a related fellowship program in a position related to the course of study or program for which the contract was awarded for a period of time equal to the greater of—

"(A) 2 years; or

"(B) such longer period of time as determined appropriate by the Secretary and the individual;

"(3) an agreement, as appropriate, on the part of the individual to relocate to a priority service area (as determined by the Secretary) in exchange for an additional loan repayment incentive amount to be determined by the Secretary;

"(4) a provision that any financial obligation of the United States arising out of a contract entered into under this section and any obligation of the individual that is conditioned thereon, is contingent on funds being appropriated for loan repayments under this section;

"(5) a statement of the damages to which the United States is entitled, under this section for the individual's breach of the contract; and

"(6) such other statements of the rights and liabilities of the Secretary and of the individual as the Secretary determines appropriate, not inconsistent with this section.

"(d) Payments.—

"(1) IN GENERAL.—A loan repayment provided for an individual under a written contract referred to in subsection (b)(3)(B) shall consist of payment, in accordance with paragraph (2), for the individual toward the outstanding principal and interest on education loans incurred by the individual in the pursuit of the relevant degree in accordance with the terms of the contract.

"(2) EQUITABLE DISTRIBUTION.—In awarding contracts under this section, the Secretary shall ensure—

"(A) a certain percentage of contracts are awarded to individuals who are not already working in public health departments;

"(B) an equitable distribution of funds geographically; and

"(C) an equitable distribution among State, local, territorial, and Tribal public health departments.

"(3) PAYMENTS FOR YEARS SERVED.—For each year of service that an individual contracts to serve pursuant to subsection (c)(2), the Secretary may pay not more than $35,000 on behalf of the individual for loans described in paragraph (1). With respect to participants under the Program whose total eligible loans are less than $105,000, the Secretary shall pay an amount that does not exceed ⅓ of the eligible loan balance for each year of such service of such individual.

"(4) TAX LIABILITY.—For purposes of the Internal Revenue Code of 1986, a payment made under this section shall be treated in the same manner as an amount received under section 338B(g) of this Act, as described in section 108(f)(4) of such Code.

"(e) Postponing Obligated Service.—With respect to an individual receiving a degree or certificate from a health professions or other related school, the date of the initiation of the period of obligated service may be postponed as approved by the Secretary.

"(f) Breach Of Contract.—An individual who fails to comply with the contract entered into under subsection (c) shall be subject to the same financial penalties as provided for under section 338E of the Public Health Service Act (42 U.S.C. 254o) for breaches of loan repayment contracts under section 338B of such Act (42 U.S.C. section 254l–1).

"(g) Definition.—For purposes of this section, the term 'full-time' means full-time as such term is used in section 455(m)(3) of the Higher Education Act of 1965.

"(h) Authorization Of Appropriations.—There is authorized to be appropriated to carry out this section—

"(1) $100,000,000 for fiscal year 2020; and

"(2) $75,000,000 for fiscal year 2021.".

EXPANDING CAPACITY FOR HEALTH OUTCOMES

SEC. 30613.

(a) In General.—The Secretary, acting through the Administrator of the Health Resources and Services Administration, shall award grants to eligible entities to develop and expand the use of technology-enabled collaborative learning and capacity building models to respond to ongoing and real-time learning, health care information sharing, and capacity building needs related to COVID–19.

(b) Eligible Entities.—To be eligible to receive a grant under this section, an entity shall have experience providing technology-enabled collaborative learning and capacity building health care services—

(1) in rural areas, frontier areas, health professional shortage areas, or medically underserved area; or

(2) to medically underserved populations or Indian Tribes.

(c) Use Of Funds.—An eligible entity receiving a grant under this section shall use funds received through the grant—

(1) to advance quality of care in response to COVID–19, with particular emphasis on rural and underserved areas and populations;

(2) to protect medical personnel and first responders through sharing real-time learning through virtual communities of practice;

(3) to improve patient outcomes for conditions affected or exacerbated by COVID–19, including improvement of care for patients with complex chronic conditions; and

(4) to support rapid uptake by health care professionals of emerging best practices and treatment protocols around COVID–19.

(d) Optional Additional Uses Of Funds.—An eligible entity receiving a grant under this section may use funds received through the grant for—

(1) equipment to support the use and expansion of technology-enabled collaborative learning and capacity building models, including hardware and software that enables distance learning, health care provider support, and the secure exchange of electronic health information;

(2) the participation of multidisciplinary expert team members to facilitate and lead technology-enabled collaborative learning sessions, and professionals and staff assisting in the development and execution of technology-enabled collaborative learning;

(3) the development of instructional programming and the training of health care providers and other professionals that provide or assist in the provision of services through technology-enabled collaborative learning and capacity building models; and

(4) other activities consistent with achieving the objectives of the grants awarded under this section.

(e) Technology-Enabled Collaborative Learning And Capacity Building Model Defined.—In this section, the term "technology-enabled collaborative learning and capacity building model" has the meaning given that term in section 2(7) of the Expanding Capacity for Health Outcomes Act (Public Law 114–270; 130 Stat. 1395).

(f) Authorization Of Appropriations.—There is authorized to be appropriated to carry out this section $20,000,000, to remain available until expended.

ADDITIONAL FUNDING FOR MEDICAL RESERVE CORPS

SEC. 30614.

Section 2813 of the Public Health Service Act (42 U.S.C. 300hh–15) is amended by striking "$11,200,000 for each of fiscal years 2019 through 2023" and inserting "$31,200,000 for each of fiscal years 2020 and 2021 and $11,200,000 for each of fiscal years 2022 and 2023".

GRANTS FOR SCHOOLS OF MEDICINE IN DIVERSE AND UNDERSERVED AREAS

SEC. 30615.

Subpart II of part C of title VII of the Public Health Service Act is amended by inserting after section 749B of such Act (42 U.S.C. 293m) the following:

"SEC. 749C. SCHOOLS OF MEDICINE IN UNDERSERVED AREAS.

"(a) Grants.—The Secretary, acting through the Administrator of the Health Resources and Services Administration, may award grants to institutions of higher education (including multiple institutions of higher education applying jointly) for the establishment, improvement, and expansion of an allopathic or osteopathic school of medicine, or a branch campus of an allopathic or osteopathic school of medicine.

"(b) Priority.—In selecting grant recipients under this section, the Secretary shall give priority to institutions of higher education that—

"(1) propose to use the grant for an allopathic or osteopathic school of medicine, or a branch campus of an allopathic or osteopathic school of medicine, in a combined statistical area with fewer than 200 actively practicing physicians per 100,000 residents according to the medical board (or boards) of the State (or States) involved;

"(2) have a curriculum that emphasizes care for diverse and underserved populations; or

"(3) are minority-serving institutions described in the list in section 371(a) of the Higher Education Act of 1965.

"(c) Use Of Funds.—The activities for which a grant under this section may be used include—

"(1) planning and constructing—

"(A) a new allopathic or osteopathic school of medicine in an area in which no other school is based; or

"(B) a branch campus of an allopathic or osteopathic school of medicine in an area in which no such school is based;

"(2) accreditation and planning activities for an allopathic or osteopathic school of medicine or branch campus;

"(3) hiring faculty and other staff to serve at an allopathic or osteopathic school of medicine or branch campus;

"(4) recruitment and enrollment of students at an allopathic or osteopathic school of medicine or branch campus;

"(5) supporting educational programs at an allopathic or osteopathic school of medicine or branch campus;

"(6) modernizing infrastructure or curriculum at an existing allopathic or osteopathic school of medicine or branch campus thereof;

"(7) expanding infrastructure or curriculum at existing an allopathic or osteopathic school of medicine or branch campus; and

"(8) other activities that the Secretary determines further the development, improvement, and expansion of an allopathic or osteopathic school of medicine or branch campus thereof.

"(d) Definitions.—In this section:

"(1) The term 'branch campus' means a geographically separate site at least 100 miles from the main campus of a school of medicine where at least one student completes at least 60 percent of the student's training leading to a degree of doctor of medicine.

"(2) The term 'institution of higher education' has the meaning given to such term in section 101(a) of the Higher Education Act of 1965.

"(e) Authorization Of Appropriations.—To carry out this section, there is authorized to be appropriated $1,000,000,000, to remain available until expended.".

GAO STUDY ON PUBLIC HEALTH WORKFORCE

SEC. 30616.

(a) In General.—The Comptroller General of the United States shall conduct a study on the public health workforce in the United States during the COVID–19 pandemic.

(b) Topics.—The study under subsection (a) shall address—

(1) existing gaps in the Federal, State, local, Tribal, and territorial public health workforce, including—

(A) epidemiological and disease intervention specialists needed during the pandemic for contact tracing, laboratory technicians necessary for testing, community health workers for community supports and services, and other staff necessary for contact tracing, testing, or surveillance activities; and

(B) other personnel needed during the COVID–19 pandemic;

(2) challenges associated with the hiring, recruitment, and retention of the Federal, State, local, Tribal, and territorial public health workforce; and

(3) recommended steps the Federal Government should take to improve hiring, recruitment, and retention of the public health workforce.

(c) Report.—Not later than December 1, 2021, the Comptroller General shall submit to the Congress a report on the findings of the study conducted under this section.

LONGITUDINAL STUDY ON THE IMPACT OF COVID–19 ON RECOVERED PATIENTS

SEC. 30617.

Part A of title IV of the Public Health Service Act (42 U.S.C. 281 et seq.) is amended by adding at the end the following:

"SEC. 404O. LONGITUDINAL STUDY ON THE IMPACT OF COVID–19 ON RECOVERED PATIENTS.

"(a) In General.—The Director of NIH, in consultation with the Director of the Centers for Disease Control and Prevention, shall conduct a longitudinal study, over not less than 10 years, on the full impact of SARS–CoV–2 or COVID–19 on infected individuals, including both short-term and long-term health impacts.

"(b) Timing.—The Director of NIH shall begin enrolling patients in the study under this section not later than 6 months after the date of enactment of this section.

"(c) Requirements.—The study under this section shall—

"(1) be nationwide;

"(2) include diversity of enrollees to account for gender, age, race, ethnicity, geography, comorbidities, and underrepresented populations, including pregnant and lactating women;

"(3) study individuals with COVID–19 who experienced mild symptoms, such individuals who experienced moderate symptoms, and such individuals who experienced severe symptoms;

"(4) monitor the health outcomes and symptoms of individuals with COVID–19, or who had prenatal exposure to SARS–CoV–2 or COVID–19, including lung capacity and function, and immune response, taking into account any pharmaceutical interventions such individuals may have received;

"(5) monitor the mental health outcomes of individuals with COVID–19, taking into account any interventions that affected mental health; and

"(6) monitor individuals enrolled in the study not less frequently than twice per year after the first year of the individual's infection with SARS–CoV–2.

"(d) Public-Private Research Network.—For purposes of carrying out the study under this section, the Director of NIH may develop a network of public-private research partners, provided that all research, including the research carried out through any such partner, is available publicly.

"(e) Summaries Of Findings.—The Director of NIH shall make public a summary of findings under this section not less frequently than once every 3 months for the first 2 years of the study, and not less frequently than every 6 months thereafter. Such summaries may include information about how the findings of the study under this section compare with findings from research conducted abroad.

"(f) Authorization Of Appropriations.—There is authorized to be appropriated to carry out this section $200,000,000, to remain available until expended.".

RESEARCH ON THE MENTAL HEALTH IMPACT OF COVID–19

SEC. 30618.

(a) In General.—The Secretary, acting through the Director of the National Institute of Mental Health, shall conduct or support research on the mental health consequences of SARS–CoV–2 or COVID–19.

(b) Use Of Funds.—Research under subsection (a) may include the following:

(1) Research on the mental health impact of SARS–CoV–2 or COVID–19 on health care providers, including—

(A) traumatic stress;

(B) psychological distress; and

(C) psychiatric disorders.

(2) Research on the impact of SARS–CoV–2 or COVID–19 stressors on mental health over time.

(3) Research to strengthen the mental health response to SARS–CoV–2 or COVID–19, including adapting to and maintaining or providing additional services for new or increasing mental health needs.

(4) Research on the reach, efficiency, effectiveness, and quality of digital mental health interventions.

(5) Research on effectiveness of strategies for implementation and delivery of evidence-based mental health interventions and services for underserved populations.

(6) Research on suicide prevention.

(c) Research Coordination.—The Secretary shall coordinate activities under this section with similar activities conducted by national research institutes and centers of the National Institutes of Health to the extent that such institutes and centers have responsibilities that are related to the mental health consequences of SARS–CoV–2 or COVID–19.

(d) Authorization Of Appropriations.—To carry out this section, there is authorized to be appropriated $200,000,000, to remain available until expended.

EMERGENCY MENTAL HEALTH AND SUBSTANCE USE TRAINING AND TECHNICAL ASSISTANCE CENTER

SEC. 30619.
Subpart 3 of part B of title V of the Public Health Service Act (42 U.S.C. 290bb–31 et seq.) is amended by inserting after section 520A (42 U.S.C. 290bb–32) the following:

"SEC. 520B. EMERGENCY MENTAL HEALTH AND SUBSTANCE USE TRAINING AND TECHNICAL ASSISTANCE CENTER.
"(a) Establishment.—The Secretary, acting through the Assistant Secretary, shall establish or operate a center to be known as the Emergency Mental Health and Substance Use Training and Technical Assistance Center (referred to in this section as the 'Center') to provide technical assistance and support—
"(1) to public or nonprofit entities seeking to establish or expand access to mental health and substance use prevention, treatment, and recovery support services, and increase awareness of such services; and
"(2) to public health professionals, health care professionals and support staff, essential workers (as defined by a State, Tribe, locality, or territory), and members of the public to address the trauma, stress, and mental health needs associated with an emergency period.
"(b) Assistance And Support.—The assistance and support provided under subsection (a) shall include assistance and support with respect to—
"(1) training on identifying signs of trauma, stress, and mental health needs;
"(2) providing accessible resources to assist individuals and families experiencing trauma, stress, or other mental health needs during and after an emergency period;
"(3) providing resources for substance use disorder prevention, treatment, and recovery designed to assist individuals and families during and after an emergency period;
"(4) the provision of language access services, including translation services, interpretation, or other such services for individuals with limited English speaking proficiency or people with disabilities; and
"(5) evaluation and improvement, as necessary, of the effectiveness of such services provided by public or nonprofit entities.
"(c) Best Practices.—The Center shall periodically issue best practices for use by organizations seeking to provide mental health services or substance use disorder prevention, treatment, or recovery services to individuals during and after an emergency period.
"(d) Emergency Period.—In this section, the term 'emergency period' has the meaning given such term in section 1135(g)(1)(A) of the Social Security Act.
"(e) Authorization Of Appropriations.—There is authorized to be appropriated to carry out this section $20,000,000 for each of fiscal years 2020 and 2021.".
IMPORTANCE OF THE BLOOD AND PLASMA SUPPLY

SEC. 30620.
(a) In General.—Section 3226 of the CARES Act (Public Law 116–136) is amended—
(1) in the section heading after "BLOOD" by inserting "AND PLASMA"; and
(2) by inserting after "blood" each time it appears "and plasma".
(b) Conforming Amendment.—The item relating to section 3226 in the table of contents in section 2 of the CARES Act (Public Law 116–136) is amended to read as follows:

"SEC. 3226. Importance of the blood and plasma supply.".

Subtitle B—Assistance For Individuals And Families

REIMBURSEMENT FOR ADDITIONAL HEALTH SERVICES RELATING TO CORONAVIRUS

SEC. 30631.

Title V of division A of the Families First Coronavirus Response Act (Public Law 116–127) is amended under the heading "Department of Health and Human Services—Office of the Secretary—Public Health and Social Services Emergency Fund" by inserting ", or treatment related to SARS–CoV–2 or COVID–19 for uninsured individuals" after "or visits described in paragraph (2) of such section for uninsured individuals".

CENTERS FOR DISEASE CONTROL AND PREVENTION COVID–19 RESPONSE LINE

SEC. 30632.

(a) In General.—During the public health emergency declared by the Secretary pursuant to section 319 of the Public Health Service Act (42 U.S.C. 247d) on January 31, 2020 with respect to COVID–19, the Secretary, acting through the Director of the Centers for Disease Control and Prevention, shall maintain a toll-free telephone number to address public health queries, including questions concerning COVID–19.

(b) Authorization Of Appropriations.—To carry out this section, there is authorized to be appropriated $10,000,000, to remain available until expended.

GRANTS TO ADDRESS SUBSTANCE USE DURING COVID–19

SEC. 30633.

(a) In General.—The Assistant Secretary for Mental Health and Substance Use of the Department of Health and Human Services (in this section referred to as the "Assistant Secretary"), in consultation with the Director of the Centers for Disease Control and Prevention, shall award grants to States, political subdivisions of States, Tribes, Tribal organizations, and community-based entities to address the harms of drug misuse, including by—

(1) preventing and controlling the spread of infectious diseases, such as HIV/AIDS and viral hepatitis, and the consequences of such diseases for individuals with substance use disorder;

(2) connecting individuals at risk for or with a substance use disorder to overdose education, counseling, and health education; or

(3) encouraging such individuals to take steps to reduce the negative personal and public health impacts of substance use or misuse during the emergency period.

(b) Considerations.—In awarding grants under this section, the Assistant Secretary shall prioritize grants to applicants proposing to serve areas with—

(1) a high proportion of people who meet criteria for dependence on or abuse of illicit drugs who have not received any treatment;

(2) high drug overdose death rates;

(3) high telemedicine infrastructure needs; and

(4) high behavioral health and substance use disorder workforce needs.

(c) Definition.—In this section, the term "emergency period" has the meaning given to such term in section 1135(g)(1)(B) of the Social Security Act (42 U.S.C. 1320b–5(g)(1)(B))).

(d) Authorization Of Appropriations.—To carry out this section, there is authorized to be appropriated $10,000,000, to remain available until expended.

GRANTS TO SUPPORT INCREASED BEHAVIORAL HEALTH NEEDS DUE TO

COVID–19

SEC. 30634.

(a) In General.—The Secretary, acting through the Assistant Secretary of Mental Health and Substance Use, shall award grants to States, political subdivisions of States, Indian Tribes and Tribal organizations, community-based entities, and primary care and behavioral health organizations to address behavioral health needs caused by the public health emergency declared pursuant to section 319 of the Public Health Service Act (42 U.S.C. 247d) with respect to COVID–19.

(b) Use Of Funds.—An entity that receives a grant under subsection (a) may use funds received through such grant to—

(1) increase behavioral health treatment and prevention capacity, including to—

(A) promote coordination among local entities;

(B) train the behavioral health workforce, relevant stakeholders, and community members;

(C) upgrade technology to support effective delivery of health care services through telehealth modalities;

(D) purchase medical supplies and equipment for behavioral health treatment entities and providers;

(E) address surge capacity for behavioral health needs such as through mobile units; and

(F) promote collaboration between primary care and mental health providers; and

(2) support or enhance behavioral health services, including—

(A) emergency crisis intervention, including mobile crisis units, 24/7 crisis call centers, and medically staffed crisis stabilization programs;

(B) screening, assessment, diagnosis, and treatment;

(C) mental health awareness trainings;

(D) evidence-based suicide prevention;

(E) evidence-based integrated care models;

(F) community recovery supports;

(G) outreach to underserved and minority communities; and

(H) for front line health care workers.

(c) Priority.—The Secretary shall give priority to applicants proposing to serve areas with a high number of COVID–19 cases.

(d) Evaluation.—An entity that receives a grant under this section shall prepare and submit an evaluation to the Secretary at such time, in such manner, and containing such information as the Secretary may reasonably require, including—

(1) an evaluation of activities carried out with funds received through the grant; and

(2) a process and outcome evaluation.

(e) Authorization Of Appropriations.—To carry out this section, there is authorized to be appropriated $50,000,000 for each of fiscal years 2020 and 2021, to remain available until expended.

Subtitle C—Assistance To Tribes

IMPROVING STATE, LOCAL, AND TRIBAL PUBLIC HEALTH SECURITY

SEC. 30641.

Section 319C–1 of the Public Health Service Act (42 U.S.C. 247d–3a) is amended—

(1) in the section heading, by striking "AND LOCAL" and inserting ", LOCAL, AND

TRIBAL";

(2) in subsection (b)—

(A) in paragraph (1)—

(i) in subparagraph (B), by striking "or" at the end;

(ii) in subparagraph (C), by striking "and" at the end and inserting "or"; and

(iii) by adding at the end the following:

"(D) be an Indian Tribe, Tribal organization, or a consortium of Indian Tribes or Tribal organizations; and"; and

(B) in paragraph (2)—

(i) in the matter preceding subparagraph (A), by inserting ", as applicable" after "including";

(ii) in subparagraph (A)(viii)—

(I) by inserting "and Tribal" after "with State";

(II) by striking "(as defined in section 8101 of the Elementary and Secondary Education Act of 1965)" and inserting "and Tribal educational agencies (as defined in sections 8101 and 6132, respectively, of the Elementary and Secondary Education Act of 1965)"; and

(III) by inserting "and Tribal" after "and State";

(iii) in subparagraph (G), by striking "and tribal" and inserting "Tribal, and urban Indian organization"; and

(iv) in subparagraph (H), by inserting ", Indian Tribes, and urban Indian organizations" after "public health";

(3) in subsection (e), by inserting "Indian Tribes, Tribal organizations, urban Indian organizations," after "local emergency plans,";

(4) in subsection (g)(1), by striking "tribal officials" and inserting "Tribal officials";

(5) in subsection (h)—

(A) in paragraph (1)(A)—

(i) by striking "through 2023" and inserting "and 2020"; and

(ii) by inserting before the period "; and $690,000,000 for each of fiscal years 2021 through 2023 for awards pursuant to paragraph (3) (subject to the authority of the Secretary to make awards pursuant to paragraphs (4) and (5)) and paragraph (8), of which not less than $5,000,000 shall be reserved each fiscal year for awards under paragraph (8)";

(B) in subsection (h)(2)(B), by striking "tribal public" and inserting "Tribal public";

(C) in the heading of paragraph (3), by inserting "FOR STATES" after "AMOUNT"; and

(D) by adding at the end the following:

"(8) TRIBAL ELIGIBLE ENTITIES.—

"(A) DETERMINATION OF FUNDING AMOUNT.—

"(i) IN GENERAL.—The Secretary shall award at least 10 cooperative agreements under this section, in amounts not less than the minimum amount determined under clause (ii), to eligible entities described in subsection (b)(1)(D) that submits to the Secretary an application that meets the criteria of the Secretary for the receipt of such an award and that meets other reasonable implementation conditions established by the Secretary, in consultation with Indian Tribes, for such awards. If the Secretary receives more than 10 applications under this section from eligible entities described in subsection (b)(1)(D) that meet the criteria and conditions described in the previous sentence, the Secretary, in consultation with Indian Tribes, may make additional awards under this section to such entities.

"(ii) MINIMUM AMOUNT.—In determining the minimum amount of an award pursuant to clause (i), the Secretary, in consultation with Indian Tribes, shall first determine an amount the Secretary considers appropriate for the eligible entity.

"(B) AVAILABLE UNTIL EXPENDED.—Amounts provided to a Tribal eligible entity under a cooperative agreement under this section for a fiscal year and remaining unobligated at the end of such year shall remain available to such entity during the entirety of the performance period, for the purposes for which said funds were provided.

"(C) NO MATCHING REQUIREMENT.—Subparagraphs (B), (C), and (D) of paragraph (1) shall not apply with respect to cooperative agreements awarded under this section to eligible entities described in subsection (b)(1)(D)."; and

(6) by adding at the end the following:

"(l) Special Rules Related To Tribal Eligible Entities.—

"(1) MODIFICATIONS.—After consultation with Indian Tribes, the Secretary may make necessary and appropriate modifications to the program under this section to facilitate the use of the cooperative agreement program by eligible entities described in subsection (b)(1)(D).

"(2) WAIVERS.—

"(A) IN GENERAL.—Except as provided in subparagraph (B), the Secretary may waive or specify alternative requirements for any provision of this section (including regulations) that the Secretary administers in connection with this section if the Secretary finds that the waiver or alternative requirement is necessary for the effective delivery and administration of this program with respect to eligible entities described in subsection (b)(1)(D).

"(B) EXCEPTION.—The Secretary may not waive or specify alternative requirements under subparagraph (A) relating to labor standards or the environment.

"(3) CONSULTATION.—The Secretary shall consult with Indian Tribes and Tribal organizations on the design of this program with respect to such Tribes and organizations to ensure the effectiveness of the program in enhancing the security of Indian Tribes with respect to public health emergencies.

"(4) REPORTING.—

"(A) IN GENERAL.—Not later than 2 years after the date of enactment of this subsection, and as an addendum to the biennial evaluations required under subsection (k), the Secretary, in coordination with the Director of the Indian Health Service, shall—

"(i) conduct a review of the implementation of this section with respect to eligible entities described in subsection (b)(1)(D), including any factors that may have limited its success; and

"(ii) submit a report describing the results of the review described in clause (i) to—

"(I) the Committee on Indian Affairs, the Committee on Health, Education, Labor and Pensions, and the Committee on Appropriations of the Senate; and

"(II) the Subcommittee for Indigenous Peoples of the United States of the Committee on Natural Resources, the Committee on Energy and Commerce, and the Committee on Appropriations of the House of Representatives.

"(B) ANALYSIS OF TRIBAL PUBLIC HEALTH EMERGENCY INFRASTRUCTURE LIMITATION.—The Secretary shall include in the initial report submitted under subparagraph (A) a description of any public health emergency infrastructure limitation encountered by eligible entities described in subsection (b)(1)(D).".

PROVISION OF ITEMS TO INDIAN PROGRAMS AND FACILITIES

SEC. 30642.

(a) Strategic National Stockpile.—Section 319F–2(a)(3)(G) of the Public Health Service Act (42 U.S.C. 247d–6b(a)(3)(G)) is amended by inserting ", and, in the case that the Secretary deploys the stockpile under this subparagraph, ensure, in coordination with the applicable States and programs and facilities, that appropriate drugs, vaccines and other biological products, medical devices, and other supplies are deployed by the Secretary directly to health programs or facilities operated by the Indian Health Service, an Indian Tribe, a Tribal organization (as those terms are defined in section 4 of the Indian Self-Determination and Education Assistance Act (25 U.S.C. 5304)), or an inter-Tribal consortium (as defined in section 501 of the Indian Self-Determination and Education Assistance Act (25 U.S.C. 5381)) or through an urban Indian organization (as defined in section 4 of the Indian Health Care Improvement Act), while avoiding duplicative distributions to such programs or facilities" before the semicolon.

(b) Distribution Of Qualified Pandemic Or Epidemic Products To IHS Facilities.—Title III of the Public Health Service Act (42 U.S.C. 241 et seq.) is amended by inserting after section 319F–4 the following:

"SEC. 319F–5. DISTRIBUTION OF QUALIFIED PANDEMIC OR EPIDEMIC PRODUCTS TO INDIAN PROGRAMS AND FACILITIES.

"In the case that the Secretary distributes qualified pandemic or epidemic products (as defined in section 319F–3(i)(7)) to States or other entities, the Secretary shall ensure, in coordination with the applicable States and programs and facilities, that, as appropriate, such products are distributed directly to health programs or facilities operated by the Indian Health Service, an Indian Tribe, a Tribal organization (as those terms are defined in section 4 of the Indian Self-Determination and Education Assistance Act (25 U.S.C. 5304)), or an inter-Tribal consortium (as defined in section 501 of the Indian Self-Determination and Education Assistance Act (25 U.S.C. 5381)) or through an urban Indian organization (as defined in section 4 of the Indian Health Care Improvement Act), while avoiding duplicative distributions to such programs or facilities.".

HEALTH CARE ACCESS FOR URBAN NATIVE VETERANS

SEC. 30643.

Section 405 of the Indian Health Care Improvement Act (25 U.S.C. 1645) is amended—

(1) in subsection (a)(1), by inserting "urban Indian organizations," before "and tribal organizations"; and

(2) in subsection (c)—

(A) by inserting "urban Indian organization," before "or tribal organization"; and

(B) by inserting "an urban Indian organization," before "or a tribal organization".

PROPER AND REIMBURSED CARE FOR NATIVE VETERANS

SEC. 30644.

Section 405(c) of the Indian Health Care Improvement Act (25 U.S.C. 1645(c)) is amended by inserting before the period at the end the following: ", regardless of whether such services are provided directly by the Service, an Indian tribe, or tribal organization, through contract health services, or through a contract for travel described in section 213(b)".

AMENDMENT TO THE INDIAN HEALTH CARE IMPROVEMENT ACT

SEC. 30645.

Section 409 of the Indian Health Care Improvement Act (25 U.S.C. 1647b) is amended by inserting "or the Tribally Controlled Schools Act of 1988 (25 U.S.C. 2501 et seq.)" after "(25 U.S.C. 450 et seq.)".

DIVISION D—RETIREMENT PROVISIONS

SEC. 40001. SHORT TITLE.

This division may be cited as the "Emergency Pension Plan Relief Act of 2020".

TITLE I—RELIEF FOR MULTIEMPLOYER PENSION PLANS

SEC. 40101. SPECIAL PARTITION RELIEF.

(a) Appropriation.—Section 4005 of the Employee Retirement Income Security Act of 1974 (29 U.S.C. 1305) is amended by adding at the end the following:

"(i) (1) An eighth fund shall be established for partition assistance to multiemployer pension plans, as provided under section 4233A, and to pay for necessary administrative and operating expenses relating to such assistance.

"(2) There is appropriated from the general fund such amounts as necessary for the costs of providing partition assistance under section 4233A and necessary administrative and operating expenses. The eighth fund established under this subsection shall be credited with such amounts from time to time as the Secretary of the Treasury determines appropriate, from the general fund of the Treasury, and such amounts shall remain available until expended.".

(b) Special Partition Authority.—The Employee Retirement Income Security Act of 1974 (29 U.S.C. 1001 et seq.) is amended by inserting after section 4233 the following:

"SEC. 4233A. SPECIAL PARTITION RELIEF.

"(a) Special Partition Authority.—

"(1) IN GENERAL.—Upon the application of a plan sponsor of an eligible multiemployer plan for partition of the plan under this section, the corporation shall order a partition of the plan in accordance with this section.

"(2) INAPPLICABILITY OF CERTAIN REPAYMENT OBLIGATION.—A plan receiving partition assistance pursuant to this section shall not be subject to repayment obligations under section 4261(b)(2).

"(b) Eligible Plans.—

"(1) IN GENERAL.—For purposes of this section, a multiemployer plan is an eligible multiemployer plan if—

"(A) the plan is in critical and declining status (within the meaning of section 305(b)(6)) in any plan year beginning in 2020 through 2024;

"(B) a suspension of benefits has been approved with respect to the plan under section 305(e)(9) as of the date of the enactment of this section;

"(C) in any plan year beginning in 2020 through 2024, the plan is certified by the plan actuary to be in critical status (within the meaning of section 305(b)(2)), has a modified funded percentage of less than 40 percent, and has a ratio of active to inactive participants which is less than 2 to 3; or

"(D) the plan is insolvent for purposes of section 418E of the Internal Revenue Code of 1986 as of the date of enactment of this section, if the plan became insolvent after December 16, 2014, and has not been terminated by such date of enactment.

"(2) MODIFIED FUNDED PERCENTAGE.—For purposes of paragraph (1)(C), the term 'modified funded percentage' means the percentage equal to a fraction the numerator of which is current value of plan assets (as defined in section 3(26) of such Act) and the denominator of which is current liabilities (as defined in section 431(c)(6)(D) of such Code and section 304(c)(6)(D) of such Act).

"(c) Applications For Special Partition.—

"(1) GUIDANCE.—The corporation shall issue guidance setting forth requirements for special partition applications under this section not later than 120 days after the date of the enactment of this section. In such guidance, the corporation shall—

"(A) limit the materials required for a special partition application to the minimum necessary to make a determination on the application; and

"(B) provide for an alternate application for special partition under this section, which may be used by a plan that has been approved for a partition under section 4233 before the date of enactment of this section.

"(2) TEMPORARY PRIORITY CONSIDERATION OF APPLICATIONS.—

"(A) IN GENERAL.—The corporation may specify in guidance under paragraph (1) that, during the first 2 years following the date of enactment of this section, special partition applications will be provided priority consideration, if—

"(i) the plan is likely to become insolvent within 5 years of the date of enactment of this section;

"(ii) the corporation projects a plan to have a present value of financial assistance payments under section 4261 that exceeds $1,000,000,000 if the special partition is not ordered;

"(iii) the plan has implemented benefit suspensions under section 305(e)(9) as of the date of the enactment of this section; or

"(iv) the corporation determines it appropriate based on other circumstances.

"(B) NO EFFECT ON AMOUNT OF ASSISTANCE.—A plan that is approved for special partition assistance under this section shall not receive reduced special partition assistance on account of not receiving priority consideration under subparagraph (A).

"(3) ACTUARIAL ASSUMPTIONS AND OTHER INFORMATION.—The corporation shall accept assumptions incorporated in a multiemployer plan's determination that it is in critical status or critical and declining status (within the meaning of section 305(b)), or that the plan's modified funded percentage is less than 40 percent, unless such assumptions are clearly erroneous. The corporation may require such other information as the corporation determines appropriate for making a determination of eligibility and the amount of special partition assistance necessary under this section.

"(4) APPLICATION DEADLINE.—Any application by a plan for special partition assistance under this section shall be submitted no later than December 31, 2026, and any revised application for special partition assistance shall be submitted no later than December 31, 2027.

"(5) NOTICE OF APPLICATION.—Not later than 120 days after the date of enactment of this section, the corporation shall issue guidance requiring multiemployer plans to notify participants and beneficiaries that the plan has applied for partition under this section, after the corporation has determined that the application is complete. Such notice shall reference the special partition relief internet website described in subsection (p).

"(d) Determinations On Applications.—A plan's application for special partition under this section that is timely filed in accordance with guidance issued under subsection (c)(1) shall be deemed approved and the corporation shall issue a special partition order unless the corporation notifies the plan within 120 days of the filing of the application that the application is incomplete or the plan is not eligible under this section. Such notice shall specify the reasons the plan is ineligible for a special partition or information needed to complete the application. If a plan is denied partition under this subsection, the plan may submit a revised application under this section. Any revised application for special partition submitted by a plan shall be deemed approved unless the corporation notifies the plan within 120 days of the filing of the revised application that the application is incomplete or the plan is not eligible under this section. A special partition order issued by the corporation shall be effective no later than 120 days after a plan's special partition application is approved by the corporation or deemed approved.

"(e) Amount And Manner Of Special Partition Assistance.—

"(1) IN GENERAL.—The liabilities of an eligible multiemployer plan that the corporation assumes pursuant to a special partition order under this section shall be the amount necessary for the plan to meet its funding goals described in subsection (g).

"(2) NO CAP.—Liabilities assumed by the corporation pursuant to a special partition order under this section shall not be capped by the guarantee under section 4022A. The corporation shall have discretion on how liabilities of the plan are partitioned.

"(f) Successor Plan.—

"(1) IN GENERAL.—The plan created by a special partition order under this section is a successor plan to which section 4022A applies.

"(2) PLAN SPONSOR AND ADMINISTRATOR.—The plan sponsor of an eligible multiemployer plan prior to the special partition and the administrator of such plan shall be the plan sponsor and the administrator, respectively, of the plan created by the partition.

"(g) Funding Goals.—

"(1) IN GENERAL.—The funding goals of a multiemployer plan eligible for partition under this section are both of the following:

"(A) The plan will remain solvent over 30 years with no reduction in a participant's or beneficiary's accrued benefit (except to the extent of a reduction in accordance with section 305(e)(8) adopted prior to the plan's application for partition under this section).

"(B) The funded percentage of the plan (disregarding partitioned benefits) at the end of the 30-year period is projected to be 80 percent.

"(2) BASIS.—The funding projections under paragraph (1) shall be performed on a deterministic basis.

"(h) Restoration Of Benefit Suspensions.—An eligible multiemployer plan that is partitioned under this section shall—

"(1) reinstate any benefits that were suspended under section 305(e)(9) or section 4245(a), effective as of the first month the special partition order is effective, for participants or beneficiaries as of the effective date of the partition; and

"(2) provide payments equal to the amount of benefits previously suspended to any participants or beneficiaries in pay status as of the effective date of the special partition, payable in the form of a lump sum within 3 months of such effective date or in equal monthly installments over a period of 5 years, with no adjustment for interest.

"(i) Adjustment Of Special Partition Assistance.—

"(1) IN GENERAL.—Every 5 years, the corporation shall adjust the special partition assistance described in subsection (e) as necessary for the eligible multiemployer plan to satisfy the funding goals described in subsection (g). If the 30 year period described in subsection (g) has lapsed, in applying this paragraph, 5 years shall be substituted for 30 years.

"(2) SUBMISSION OF INFORMATION.—An eligible multiemployer plan that is the subject of a special partition order under subsection (a) shall submit such information as the corporation may require to determine the amount of the adjustment under paragraph (1).

"(3) CESSATION OF ADJUSTMENTS.—Adjustments under this subsection with respect to special partition assistance for an eligible multiemployer plan shall cease and the corporation shall permanently assume liability for payment of any benefits transferred to the successor plan (subject to subsection (l)) beginning with the first plan year that the funded percentage of the eligible multiemployer plan (disregarding partitioned benefits) is at least 80 percent and the plan's projected funded percentage for each of the next 10 years is at least 80 percent. Any accumulated funding deficiency of the plan (within the meaning of section 304(a)) shall be reduced to zero as of the first day of the plan year for which partition assistance is permanent under this paragraph.

"(j) Conditions On Plans During Partition.—

"(1) IN GENERAL.—The corporation may impose, by regulation, reasonable conditions on an eligible multiemployer plan that is partitioned under section (a) relating to increases in future accrual rates and any retroactive benefit improvements, allocation of plan assets, reductions in employer contribution rates, diversion of contributions to, and allocation of, expenses to other retirement plans, and withdrawal liability.

"(2) LIMITATIONS.—The corporation shall not impose conditions on an eligible multiemployer plan as a condition of or following receipt of such partition assistance under this section relating to—

"(A) any reduction in plan benefits (including benefits that may be adjusted pursuant to section 305(e)(8));

"(B) plan governance, including selection of, removal of, and terms of contracts with, trustees, actuaries, investment managers, and other service providers; or

"(C) any funding rules relating to the plan that is partitioned under this section.

"(3) CONDITION.—An eligible multiemployer plan that is partitioned under subsection (a) shall continue to pay all premiums due under section 4007 for participants and beneficiaries in the plan created by a special partition order until the plan year beginning after a cessation of adjustments applies under subsection (i).

"(k) Withdrawal Liability.—An employer's withdrawal liability for purposes of this title shall be calculated taking into account any plan liabilities that are partitioned under subsection (a) until the plan year beginning after the expiration of 15 calendar years from the effective date of the partition.

"(l) Cessation Of Partition Assistance.—If a plan that receives partition assistance under this section becomes insolvent for purposes of section 418E of the Internal Revenue Code of 1986, the plan shall no longer be eligible for assistance under this section and shall be eligible for assistance under section 4261.

"(m) Reporting.—An eligible multiemployer plan that receives partition assistance under this section shall file with the corporation a report, including the following information, in such manner (which may include electronic filing requirements) and at such time as the corporation requires:

"(1) The funded percentage (as defined in section 305(j)(2)) as of the first day of such plan year, and the underlying actuarial value of assets and liabilities taken into account in determining such percentage.

"(2) The market value of the assets of the plan (determined as provided in paragraph (1)) as of the last day of the plan year preceding such plan year.

"(3) The total value of all contributions made by employers and employees during the plan year preceding such plan year.

"(4) The total value of all benefits paid during the plan year preceding such plan year.

"(5) Cash flow projections for such plan year and the 9 succeeding plan years, and the assumptions used in making such projections.

"(6) Funding standard account projections for such plan year and the 9 succeeding plan years, and the assumptions relied upon in making such projections.

"(7) The total value of all investment gains or losses during the plan year preceding such plan year.

"(8) Any significant reduction in the number of active participants during the plan year preceding such plan year, and the reason for such reduction.

"(9) A list of employers that withdrew from the plan in the plan year preceding such plan year, the payment schedule with respect to such withdrawal liability, and the resulting reduction in contributions.

"(10) A list of employers that paid withdrawal liability to the plan during the plan year preceding such plan year and, for each employer, a total assessment of the withdrawal liability paid, the annual payment amount, and the number of years remaining in the payment schedule with respect to such withdrawal liability.

"(11) Any material changes to benefits, accrual rates, or contribution rates during the plan year preceding such plan year, and whether such changes relate to the conditions of the partition assistance.

"(12) Details regarding any funding improvement plan or rehabilitation plan and updates to such plan.

"(13) The number of participants and beneficiaries during the plan year preceding such plan year who are active participants, the number of participants and beneficiaries in pay status, and the number of terminated vested participants and beneficiaries.

"(14) The information contained on the most recent annual funding notice submitted by the plan under section 101(f).

"(15) The information contained on the most recent annual return under section 6058 of the Internal Revenue Code of 1986 and actuarial report under section 6059 of such Code of the plan.

"(16) Copies of the plan document and amendments, other retirement benefit or ancillary benefit plans relating to the plan and contribution obligations under such plans, a breakdown of administrative expenses of the plan, participant census data and distribution of benefits, the most recent actuarial valuation report as of the plan year, financial reports, and copies of the portions of collective bargaining agreements relating to plan contributions, funding coverage, or benefits, and such other information as the corporation may reasonably require.

Any information disclosed by a plan to the corporation that could identify individual employers shall be confidential and not subject to publication or disclosure.

"(n) Report To Congress.—

"(1) IN GENERAL.—Not later than 1 year after the date of enactment of this section and annually thereafter, the board of directors of the corporation shall submit to the Committee on Health, Education, Labor, and Pensions and the Committee on Finance of the Senate and the Committee on Education and Labor and the Committee on Ways and Means of the House of Representatives a detailed report on the implementation and administration of this section. Such report shall include—

"(A) information on the name and number of multiemployer plans that have applied for partition assistance under this section;

"(B) the name and number of such plans that have been approved for partition assistance under this section and the name and number of the plans that have not been approved for special partition assistance;

"(C) a detailed rationale for any decision by the corporation to not approve an application for special partition assistance;

"(D) the amount of special partition assistance provided to eligible multiemployer plans (including amounts provided on an individual plan basis and in the aggregate);

"(E) the name and number of the multiemployer plans that restored benefit suspensions and provided lump sum or monthly installment payments to participants or beneficiaries;

"(F) the amount of benefits that were restored and lump sum or monthly installment payments that were paid (including amounts provided on an individual plan basis and in the aggregate);

"(G) the name and number of the plans that received adjustments to partition assistance under subsection (i);

"(H) a list of, and rationale for, each reasonable condition imposed by the corporation on plans approved for special partition assistance under this section;

"(I) the contracts that have been awarded by the corporation to implement or administer this section;

"(J) the number, purpose, and dollar amounts of the contracts that have been awarded to implement or administer the section;

"(K) a detailed summary of the reports required under subsection (m); and

"(L) a detailed summary of the feedback received on the pension relief internet website established under subsection (p).

"(2) PBGC CERTIFICATION.—The board of directors of the corporation shall include with the report under paragraph (1) a certification and affirmation that the amount of special partition assistance provided to each plan under this section is the amount necessary to meet its funding goals under subsection (g), including, if applicable, any adjustment of special partition assistance as determined under subsection (i).

"(3) CONFIDENTIALITY.—Congress may publicize the reports received under paragraph (1) only after redacting all sensitive or proprietary information.

"(o) GAO Report.—Not later than 1 year after the first partition application is approved by the corporation under this section, and biennially thereafter, the Comptroller General of the United States shall submit to the Committee on Health, Education, Labor, and Pensions and the Committee on Finance of the Senate and the Committee on Education and Labor and the Committee on Ways and Means of the House of Representatives a detailed report on the actions of the corporation to implement and administer this section, including an examination of the contracts awarded by such corporation to carry out this section and an analysis of such corporation's compliance with subsections (e) and (g).

"(p) Special Partition Relief Website.—

"(1) ESTABLISHMENT.—Not later than 120 days after the date of enactment of this section, the corporation shall establish and maintain a user-friendly, public-facing internet website to foster greater accountability and transparency in the implementation and administration of this section.

"(2) PURPOSE.—The internet website established and maintained under paragraph (1) shall be a portal to key information relating to this section for multiemployer plan administrators and trustees, plan participants, beneficiaries, participating employers, other stakeholders, and the public.

"(3) CONTENT AND FUNCTION.—The internet website established under paragraph (1) shall—

"(A) describe the nature and scope of the special partition authority and assistance under this section in a manner calculated to be understood by the average plan participant;

"(B) include published guidance, regulations, and all other relevant information on the implementation and administration of this section;

"(C) include, with respect to plan applications for special partition assistance—

"(i) a general description of the process by which eligible plans can apply for special partition assistance, information on how and when the corporation will process and consider plan applications;

"(ii) information on how the corporation will address any incomplete applications as specified in under this section;

"(iii) a list of the plans that have applied for special partition assistance and, for each application, the date of submission of a completed application;

"(iv) the text of each plan's completed application for special partition assistance with appropriate redactions of personal, proprietary, or sensitive information;

"(v) the estimated date that a decision will be made by the corporation on each application;

"(vi) the actual date when such decision is made;

"(vii) the corporation's decision on each application; and

"(viii) as applicable, a detailed rationale for any decision not to approve a plan's application for special partition assistance;

"(D) provide detailed information on each contract solicited and awarded to implement or administer this section;

"(E) include reports, audits, and other relevant oversight and accountability information on this section, including the annual reports submitted by the board of directors of the corporation to Congress required under subsection (n), the Office of the Inspector General audits, correspondence, and publications, and the Government Accountability Office reports under subsection (o);

"(F) provide a clear means for multiemployer plan administrators, plan participants, beneficiaries, other stakeholders, and the public to contact the corporation and provide feedback on the implementation and administration of this section; and

"(G) be regularly updated to carry out the purposes of this subsection.

"(q) Office Of Inspector General.—There is authorized to be appropriated to the corporation's Office of Inspector General $24,000,000 for fiscal year 2020, which shall remain available through September 30, 2028, for salaries and expenses necessary for conducting investigations and audits of the implementation and administration of this section.

324

U.S. HOUSE OF REPRESENTATIVES DEMOCRATS

"(r) Application Of Excise Tax.—During the period that a plan is subject to a partition order under this section and prior to a cessation of adjustments pursuant to subsection (i)(3), the plan shall not be subject to section 4971 of the Internal Revenue Code of 1986.".

SEC. 40102. REPEAL OF BENEFIT SUSPENSIONS FOR MULTIEMPLOYER PLANS IN CRITICAL AND DECLINING STATUS.

(a) Amendment To Internal Revenue Code Of 1986.—Paragraph (9) of section 432(e) of the Internal Revenue Code of 1986 is repealed.

(b) Amendment To Employee Retirement Income Security Act Of 1974.—Paragraph (9) of section 305(e) of the Employee Retirement Income Security Act of 1974 (29 U.S.C. 1085(e)) is repealed.

(c) Effective Date.—The repeals made by this section shall not apply to plans that have been approved for a suspension of benefit under section 432(e)(9)(G) of the Internal Revenue Code of 1986 and section 305(e)(9)(G) of the Employee Retirement Income Security Act of 1974 (29 U.S.C. 1085(e)(9)(G)) before the date of the enactment of this Act.

SEC. 40103. TEMPORARY DELAY OF DESIGNATION OF MULTIEMPLOYER PLANS AS IN ENDANGERED, CRITICAL, OR CRITICAL AND DECLINING STATUS.

(a) In General.—Notwithstanding the actuarial certification under section 305(b)(3) of the Employee Retirement Income Security Act of 1974 and section 432(b)(3) of the Internal Revenue Code of 1986, if a plan sponsor of a multiemployer plan elects the application of this section, then, for purposes of section 305 of such Act and section 432 of such Code—

(1) the status of the plan for its first plan year beginning during the period beginning on March 1, 2020, and ending on February 28, 2021, or the next succeeding plan year (as designated by the plan sponsor in such election), shall be the same as the status of such plan under such sections for the plan year preceding such designated plan year, and

(2) in the case of a plan which was in endangered or critical status for the plan year preceding the designated plan year described in paragraph (1), the plan shall not be required to update its plan or schedules under section 305(c)(6) of such Act and section 432(c)(6) of such Code, or section 305(e)(3)(B) of such Act and section 432(e)(3)(B) of such Code, whichever is applicable, until the plan year following the designated plan year described in paragraph (1).

If section 305 of the Employee Retirement Income Security Act of 1974 and section 432 of the Internal Revenue Code of 1986 did not apply to the plan year preceding the designated plan year described in paragraph (1), the plan actuary shall make a certification of the status of the plan under section 305(b)(3) of such Act and section 432(b)(3) of such Code for the preceding plan year in the same manner as if such sections had applied to such preceding plan year.

(b) Exception For Plans Becoming Critical During Election.—If—

(1) an election was made under subsection (a) with respect to a multiemployer plan, and

(2) such plan has, without regard to such election, been certified by the plan actuary under section 305(b)(3) of the Employee Retirement Income Security Act of 1974 and section 432(b)(3) of the Internal Revenue Code of 1986 to be in critical status

for the designated plan year described in subsection (a)(1), then such plan shall be treated as a plan in critical status for such plan year for purposes of applying section 4971(g)(1)(A) of such Code, section 302(b)(3) of such Act (without regard to the second sentence thereof), and section 412(b)(3) of such Code (without regard to the second sentence thereof).

(c) Election And Notice.—

(1) ELECTION.—An election under subsection (a)—

(A) shall be made at such time and in such manner as the Secretary of the Treasury or the Secretary's delegate may prescribe and, once made, may be revoked only with the consent of the Secretary, and

(B) if made—

(i) before the date the annual certification is submitted to the Secretary or the Secretary's delegate under section 305(b)(3) of such Act and section 432(b)(3) of such Code, shall be included with such annual certification, and

(ii) after such date, shall be submitted to the Secretary or the Secretary's delegate not later than 30 days after the date of the election.

(2) NOTICE TO PARTICIPANTS.—

(A) IN GENERAL.—Notwithstanding section 305(b)(3)(D) of the Employee Retirement Income Security Act of 1974 and section 432(b)(3)(D) of the Internal Revenue Code of 1986, if the plan is neither in endangered nor critical status by reason of an election made under subsection (a)—

(i) the plan sponsor of a multiemployer plan shall not be required to provide notice under such sections, and

(ii) the plan sponsor shall provide to the participants and beneficiaries, the bargaining parties, the Pension Benefit Guaranty Corporation, and the Secretary of Labor a notice of the election under subsection (a) and such other information as the Secretary of the Treasury (in consultation with the Secretary of Labor) may require—

(I) if the election is made before the date the annual certification is submitted to the Secretary or the Secretary's delegate under section 305(b)(3) of such Act and section 432(b)(3) of such Code, not later than 30 days after the date of the certification, and

(II) if the election is made after such date, not later than 30 days after the date of the election.

(B) NOTICE OF ENDANGERED STATUS.—Notwithstanding section 305(b)(3)(D) of such Act and section 432(b)(3)(D) of such Code, if the plan is certified to be in critical status for any plan year but is in endangered status by reason of an election made under subsection (a), the notice provided under such sections shall be the notice which would have been provided if the plan had been certified to be in endangered status.

SEC. 40104. TEMPORARY EXTENSION OF THE FUNDING IMPROVEMENT AND REHABILITATION PERIODS FOR MULTIEMPLOYER PENSION PLANS IN CRITICAL AND ENDANGERED STATUS FOR 2020 OR 2021.

(a) In General.—If the plan sponsor of a multiemployer plan which is in endangered or critical status for a plan year beginning in 2020 or 2021 (determined after application of section 4) elects the application of this section, then, for purposes of section 305 of the Employee Retirement Income Security Act of 1974 and section 432 of the Internal Revenue Code of 1986—

(1) except as provided in paragraph (2), the plan's funding improvement period or rehabilitation period, whichever is applicable, shall be 15 years rather than 10 years, and

(2) in the case of a plan in seriously endangered status, the plan's funding improvement period shall be 20 years rather than 15 years.

(b) Definitions And Special Rules.—For purposes of this section—

(1) ELECTION.—An election under this section shall be made at such time, and in such manner and form, as (in consultation with the Secretary of Labor) the Secretary of the Treasury or the Secretary's delegate may prescribe.

(2) DEFINITIONS.—Any term which is used in this section which is also used in section 305 of the Employee Retirement Income Security Act of 1974 and section 432 of the Internal Revenue Code of 1986 shall have the same meaning as when used in such sections.

(c) Effective Date.—This section shall apply to plan years beginning after December 31, 2019.

SEC. 40105. ADJUSTMENTS TO FUNDING STANDARD ACCOUNT RULES.

(a) Adjustments.—

(1) AMENDMENT TO EMPLOYEE RETIREMENT INCOME SECURITY ACT OF 1974.—Section 304(b)(8) of the Employee Retirement Income Security Act of 1974 (29 U.S.C. 1084(b)) is amended by adding at the end the following new subparagraph:

"(F) RELIEF FOR 2020 AND 2021.—A multiemployer plan with respect to which the solvency test under subparagraph (C) is met as of February 29, 2020, may elect to apply this paragraph by substituting 'February 29, 2020' for 'August 31, 2008' each place it appears in subparagraphs (A)(i), (B)(i)(I), and (B)(i)(II) (without regard to whether such plan previously elected the application of this paragraph). The preceding sentence shall not apply to a plan with respect to which a partition order is in effect under section 4233A.".

(2) AMENDMENT TO INTERNAL REVENUE CODE OF 1986.—Section 431(b)(8) of the Internal Revenue Code of 1986 is amended by adding at the end the following new subparagraph:

"(F) RELIEF FOR 2020 AND 2021.—A multiemployer plan with respect to which the solvency test under subparagraph (C) is met as of February 29, 2020, may elect to apply this paragraph by substituting 'February 29, 2020' for 'August 31, 2008' each place it appears in subparagraphs (A)(i), (B)(i)(I), and (B)(i)(II) (without regard to whether such plan previously elected the application of this paragraph). The preceding sentence shall not apply to a plan with respect to which a partition order is in effect under section 4233A of the Employee Retirement Income Security Act of 1974.".

(b) Effective Dates.—

(1) IN GENERAL.—The amendments made by this section shall take effect as of the first day of the first plan year ending on or after February 29, 2020, except that any election a plan makes pursuant to this section that affects the plan's funding standard account for the first plan year beginning after February 29, 2020, shall be disregarded for purposes of applying the provisions of section 305 of the Employee Retirement Income Security Act of 1974 and section 432 of the Internal Revenue Code of 1986 to such plan year.

(2) RESTRICTIONS ON BENEFIT INCREASES.—Notwithstanding paragraph (1), the restrictions on plan amendments increasing benefits in sections 304(b)(8)(D) of such Act and 431(b)(8)(D) of such Code, as applied by the amendments made by this section, shall take effect on the date of enactment of this Act.

SEC. 40106. PBGC GUARANTEE FOR PARTICIPANTS IN MULTIEMPLOY-

ER PLANS.

Section 4022A(c)(1) of the Employee Retirement Income Security Act of 1974 (29 U.S.C. 1322a(c)(1)) is amended by striking subparagraphs (A) and (B) and inserting the following:

"(A) 100 percent of the accrual rate up to $15, plus 75 percent of the lesser of—

"(i) $70; or

"(ii) the accrual rate, if any, in excess of $15; and

"(B) the number of the participant's years of credited service.

For each calendar year after the first full calendar year following the date of the enactment of the Emergency Pension Plan Relief Act of 2020, the accrual rates in subparagraph (A) shall increase by the national average wage index (as defined in section 209(k)(1) of the Social Security Act). For purposes of this subsection, the rates applicable for determining the guaranteed benefits of the participants of any plan shall be the rates in effect for the calendar year in which the plan becomes insolvent under section 4245 or the calendar year in which the plan is terminated, if earlier.".

TITLE II—RELIEF FOR SINGLE EMPLOYER PENSION PLANS

SEC. 40201. EXTENDED AMORTIZATION FOR SINGLE EMPLOYER PLANS.

(a) 15-Year Amortization Under The Internal Revenue Code Of 1986.—Section 430(c) of the Internal Revenue Code of 1986 is amended by adding at the end the following new paragraph:

"(8) 15-YEAR AMORTIZATION.—With respect to plan years beginning after December 31, 2019—

"(A) the shortfall amortization bases for all plan years preceding the first plan year beginning after December 31, 2019 (and all shortfall amortization installments determined with respect to such bases) shall be reduced to zero, and

"(B) subparagraphs (A) and (B) of paragraph (2) shall each be applied by substituting '15-plan-year period' for '7-plan-year period'.".

(b) 15-Year Amortization Under The Employee Retirement Income Security Act Of 1974.—Section 303(c) of the Employee Retirement Income Security Act of 1974 (29 U.S.C. 1083(c)) is amended by adding at the end the following new paragraph:

"(8) 15-YEAR AMORTIZATION.—With respect to plan years beginning after December 31, 2019—

"(A) the shortfall amortization bases for all plan years preceding the first plan year beginning after December 31, 2019 (and all shortfall amortization installments determined with respect to such bases) shall be reduced to zero, and

"(B) subparagraphs (A) and (B) of paragraph (2) shall each be applied by substituting '15-plan-year period' for '7-plan-year period'.".

(c) Effective Date.—The amendments made by this section shall apply to plan years beginning after December 31, 2019.

SEC. 40202. EXTENSION OF PENSION FUNDING STABILIZATION PERCENTAGES FOR SINGLE EMPLOYER PLANS.

(a) Amendments To Internal Revenue Code Of 1986.—

(1) IN GENERAL.—The table contained in subclause (II) of section 430(h)(2)(C)(iv) of the Internal Revenue Code of 1986 is amended to read as follows:

"If the calendar year is: The applicable minimum percentage is: The applicable maximum percentage is:

If the calendar year is:	The applicable minimum percentage is:	The applicable maximum percentage is:
Any year in the period starting in 2012 and ending in 2019	90%	110%
Any year in the period starting in 2020 and ending in 2025	95%	105%
2026	90%	110%
2027	85%	115%
2028	80%	120%
2029	75%	125%
After 2029	70%	130%.".

(2) FLOOR ON 25-YEAR AVERAGES.—Subclause (I) of section 430(h)(2)(C)(iv) of such Code is amended by adding at the end the following: "Notwithstanding anything in this subclause, if the average of the first, second, or third segment rate for any 25-year period is less than 5 percent, such average shall be deemed to be 5 percent.".

(b) Amendments To Employee Retirement Income Security Act Of 1974.—

(1) IN GENERAL.—The table contained in subclause (II) of section 303(h)(2)(C)(iv) of the Employee Retirement Income Security Act of 1974 (29 U.S.C. 1083(h)(2)(C)(iv)(II)) is amended to read as follows:

"If the calendar year is: The applicable minimum percentage is: The applicable maximum percentage is:

If the calendar year is:	The applicable minimum percentage is:	The applicable maximum percentage is:
Any year in the period starting in 2012 and ending in 2019	90%	110%
Any year in the period starting in 2020 and ending in 2025	95%	105%
2026	90%	110%
2027	85%	115%
2028	80%	120%
2029	75%	125%
After 2029	70%	130%.".

(2) CONFORMING AMENDMENTS.—

(A) IN GENERAL.—Section 101(f)(2)(D) of such Act (29 U.S.C. 1021(f)(2)(D)) is amended—

(i) in clause (i) by striking "and the Bipartisan Budget Act of 2015" both places it appears and inserting ", the Bipartisan Budget Act of 2015, and the Emergency Pension Plan Relief Act of 2020", and

(ii) in clause (ii) by striking "2023" and inserting "2029".

(B) STATEMENTS.—The Secretary of Labor shall modify the statements required under subclauses (I) and (II) of section 101(f)(2)(D)(i) of such Act to conform to the amendments made by this section.

(3) FLOOR ON 25-YEAR AVERAGES.—Subclause (I) of section 303(h)(2)(C)(iv) of such Act (29 U.S.C. 1083(h)(2)(C)(iv)(II)) is amended by adding at the end the following: "Notwithstanding anything in this subclause, if the average of the first, second, or third segment rate for any 25-year period is less than 5 percent, such average shall be deemed to be 5 percent.".

(c) Effective Date.—The amendments made by this section shall apply with respect to plan years beginning after December 31, 2019.

TITLE III—OTHER RETIREMENT RELATED PROVISIONS

SEC. 40301. WAIVER OF REQUIRED MINIMUM DISTRIBUTIONS FOR 2019.

(a) In General.—Section 401(a)(9)(I)(i) of the Internal Revenue Code of 1986 is amended by striking "calendar year 2020" and inserting "calendar years 2019 and 2020".

(b) Eligible Rollover Distributions.—Section 402(c)(4) of such Code is amended by striking "2020" each place it appears in the last sentence and inserting "2019 or 2020".

(c) Conforming Amendments.—Section 401(a)(9)(I) of such Code is amended—

(1) by striking clause (ii) and redesignating clause (iii) as clause (ii), and

(2) by striking "calendar year 2020" in clause (ii)(II), as so redesignated, and inserting "calendar years 2019 and 2020".

(d) Effective Date.—The amendments made by this section shall take effect as if included in the enactment of section 2203 of the Coronavirus Aid, Relief, and Economic Security Act, except that subparagraph (c)(1) thereof shall be applied by substituting "December 31, 2018" for "December 31, 2019".

SEC. 40302. WAIVER OF 60-DAY RULE IN CASE OF ROLLOVER OF OTHERWISE REQUIRED MINIMUM DISTRIBUTIONS IN 2019 OR 2020.

(a) Qualified Trusts.—402(c)(3) of the Internal Revenue Code of 1986 is amended by adding at the end the following new subparagraph:

"(D) EXCEPTION FOR ROLLOVER OF OTHERWISE REQUIRED MINIMUM DISTRIBUTIONS IN 2019 OR 2020.—In the case of an eligible rollover distribution described in the second sentence of paragraph (4), subparagraph (A) shall not apply to any transfer of such distribution made before December 1, 2020.".

(b) Individual Retirement Accounts.—Section 408(d)(3) of such Code is amended by adding at the end the following new subparagraph:

"(J) WAIVER OF 60-DAY RULE AND ONCE PER-YEAR LIMITATION FOR CERTAIN 2019 AND 2020 ROLLOVERS.—In the case of a distribution during 2019 or 2020 to which, under subparagraph (E), this paragraph would not have applied had the minimum distribution requirements of section 401(a)(9) applied during such years, the 60-day requirement under subparagraph (A) and the limitation under subparagraph (B) shall not apply to such distribution to the extent the amount is paid into an individual retirement account, individual retirement annuity (other than an endowment contract), or eligible retirement plan (as defined in subparagraph (A)) as otherwise required under such subparagraph before December 1, 2020.".

(c) Effective Date.—The amendments made by this section shall apply to taxable years beginning after December 31, 2018.

SEC. 40303. EMPLOYEE CERTIFICATION AS TO ELIGIBILITY FOR INCREASED CARES ACT LOAN LIMITS FROM EMPLOYER PLAN.

(a) In General.—Section 2202(b) of the Coronavirus Aid, Relief, and Economic Security Act is amended by adding at the end the following new paragraph:

"(4) EMPLOYEE CERTIFICATION.—The administrator of a qualified employer plan may rely on an employee's certification that the requirements of subsection (a)(4)(A)(ii) are satisfied in determining whether the employee is a qualified individual for purposes of this subsection.".

(b) Effective Date.—The amendment made by this section shall take effect as if included in the enactment of section 2202(b) of the Coronavirus Aid, Relief, and Economic Security Act.

SEC. 40304. EXCLUSION OF BENEFITS PROVIDED TO VOLUNTEER FIREFIGHTERS AND EMERGENCY MEDICAL RESPONDERS MADE PERMANENT.

(a) In General.—Section 139B of the Internal Revenue Code of 1986 is amended by striking subsection (d).

(b) Effective Date.—The amendment made by this section shall apply to taxable years beginning after December 31, 2020.

SEC. 40305. APPLICATION OF SPECIAL RULES TO MONEY PURCHASE PENSION PLANS.

Section 2202(a)(6)(B) of the Coronavirus Aid, Relief, and Economic Security Act is amended by inserting ", and, in the case of a money purchase pension plan, a coronavirus-related distribution which is an in-service withdrawal shall be treated as meeting the distribution rules of section 401(a) of such Code" before the period.

SEC. 40306. GRANTS TO ASSIST LOW-INCOME WOMEN AND SURVIVORS OF DOMESTIC VIOLENCE IN OBTAINING QUALIFIED DOMESTIC RELATIONS ORDERS.

(a) Authorization Of Grant Awards.—The Secretary of Labor, acting through the Director of the Women's Bureau and in conjunction with the Assistant Secretary of the Employee Benefits Security Administration, shall award grants, on a competitive basis, to eligible entities to enable such entities to assist low-income women and survivors of domestic violence in obtaining qualified domestic relations orders and ensuring that those women actually obtain the benefits to which they are entitled through those orders.

(b) Definition Of Eligible Entity.—In this section, the term "eligible entity" means a community-based organization with proven experience and expertise in serving women and the financial and retirement needs of women.

(c) Application.—An eligible entity that desires to receive a grant under this section shall submit an application to the Secretary of Labor at such time, in such manner, and accompanied by such information as the Secretary of Labor may require.

(d) Minimum Grant Amount.—The Secretary of Labor shall award grants under this section in amounts of not less than $250,000.

(e) Use Of Funds.—An eligible entity that receives a grant under this section shall use the grant funds to develop programs to offer help to low-income women or survivors of domestic violence who need assistance in preparing, obtaining, and effectuating a qualified domestic relations order.

(f) Authorization Of Appropriations.—There is authorized to be appropriated to carry out this section $100,000,000 for fiscal year 2020 and each succeeding fiscal year.

SEC. 40307. MODIFICATION OF SPECIAL RULES FOR MINIMUM FUNDING STANDARDS FOR COMMUNITY NEWSPAPER PLANS.

(a) Amendment To Internal Revenue Code Of 1986.—Subsection (m) of section 430 of the Internal Revenue Code of 1986, as added by the Setting Every Community Up for Retirement Enhancement Act of 2019, is amended to read as follows:

"(m) Special Rules For Community Newspaper Plans.—

"(1) IN GENERAL.—An eligible newspaper plan sponsor of a plan under which no participant has had the participant's accrued benefit increased (whether because of service or compensation) after April 2, 2019, may elect to have the alternative standards described in paragraph (4) apply to such plan.

"(2) ELIGIBLE NEWSPAPER PLAN SPONSOR.—The term 'eligible newspaper plan sponsor' means the plan sponsor of—

"(A) any community newspaper plan, or

"(B) any other plan sponsored, as of April 2, 2019, by a member of the same controlled group of a plan sponsor of a community newspaper plan if such member is in the trade or business of publishing 1 or more newspapers.

"(3) ELECTION.—An election under paragraph (1) shall be made at such time and in such manner as prescribed by the Secretary. Such election, once made with respect to a plan year, shall apply to all subsequent plan years unless revoked with the consent of the Secretary.

"(4) ALTERNATIVE MINIMUM FUNDING STANDARDS.—The alternative standards described in this paragraph are the following:

"(A) INTEREST RATES.—

"(i) IN GENERAL.—Notwithstanding subsection (h)(2)(C) and except as provided in clause (ii), the first, second, and third segment rates in effect for any month for purposes of this section shall be 8 percent.

"(ii) NEW BENEFIT ACCRUALS.—Notwithstanding subsection (h)(2), for purposes of determining the funding target and normal cost of a plan for any plan year, the present value of any benefits accrued or earned under the plan for a plan year with respect to which an election under paragraph (1) is in effect shall be determined on the basis of the United States Treasury obligation yield curve for the day that is the valuation date of such plan for such plan year.

"(iii) UNITED STATES TREASURY OBLIGATION YIELD CURVE.—For purposes of this subsection, the term 'United States Treasury obligation yield curve' means, with respect to any day, a yield curve which shall be prescribed by the Secretary for such day on interest-bearing obligations of the United States.

"(B) SHORTFALL AMORTIZATION BASE.—

"(i) PREVIOUS SHORTFALL AMORTIZATION BASES.—The shortfall amortization bases determined under subsection (c)(3) for all plan years preceding the first plan year to which the election under paragraph (1) applies (and all shortfall amortization installments determined with respect to such bases) shall be reduced to zero under rules similar to the rules of subsection (c)(6).

"(ii) NEW SHORTFALL AMORTIZATION BASE.—Notwithstanding subsection (c)(3), the shortfall amortization base for the first plan year to which the election under paragraph (1) applies shall be the funding shortfall of such plan for such plan year (determined using the interest rates as modified under subparagraph (A)).

"(C) DETERMINATION OF SHORTFALL AMORTIZATION INSTALLMENTS.—

"(i) 30-YEAR PERIOD.—Subparagraphs (A) and (B) of subsection (c)(2) shall be applied by substituting '30-plan-year' for '7-plan-year' each place it appears.

"(ii) NO SPECIAL ELECTION.—The election under subparagraph (D) of subsection (c)(2) shall not apply to any plan year to which the election under paragraph (1) applies.

"(D) EXEMPTION FROM AT-RISK TREATMENT.—Subsection (i) shall not apply.

"(5) COMMUNITY NEWSPAPER PLAN.—For purposes of this subsection—

"(A) IN GENERAL.—The term 'community newspaper plan' means any plan to which this section applies maintained as of December 31, 2018, by an employer which—

"(i) maintains the plan on behalf of participants and beneficiaries with respect to employment in the trade or business of publishing 1 or more newspapers which were published by the employer at any time during the 11-year period ending on the date of the enactment of this subsection,

"(ii) (I) is not a company the stock of which is publicly traded (on a stock exchange or in an over-the-counter market), and is not controlled, directly or indirectly, by such a company, or

"(II) is controlled, directly or indirectly, during the entire 30-year period ending on the date of the enactment of this subsection by individuals who are members of the same family, and does not publish or distribute a daily newspaper that is carrier-distributed in printed form in more than 5 States, and

"(iii) is controlled, directly or indirectly—

"(I) by 1 or more persons residing primarily in a State in which the community newspaper has been published on newsprint or carrier-distributed,

"(II) during the entire 30-year period ending on the date of the enactment of this subsection by individuals who are members of the same family,

"(III) by 1 or more trusts, the sole trustees of which are persons described in subclause (I) or (II), or

"(IV) by a combination of persons described in subclause (I), (II), or (III).

"(B) NEWSPAPER.—The term 'newspaper' does not include any newspaper (determined without regard to this subparagraph) to which any of the following apply:

"(i) Is not in general circulation.

"(ii) Is published (on newsprint or electronically) less frequently than 3 times per week.

"(iii) Has not ever been regularly published on newsprint.

"(iv) Does not have a bona fide list of paid subscribers.

"(C) CONTROL.—A person shall be treated as controlled by another person if such other person possesses, directly or indirectly, the power to direct or cause the direction and management of such person (including the power to elect a majority of the members of the board of directors of such person) through the ownership of voting securities.

"(6) CONTROLLED GROUP.—For purposes of this subsection, the term 'controlled group' means all persons treated as a single employer under subsection (b), (c), (m), or (o) of section 414 as of the date of the enactment of this subsection.".

(b) Amendment To Employee Retirement Income Security Act Of 1974.—Subsection (m) of section 303 of the Employee Retirement Income Security Act of 1974 (29 U.S.C. 1083(m)), as added by the Setting Every Community Up for Retirement Enhancement Act of 2019, is amended to read as follows:

"(m) Special Rules For Community Newspaper Plans.—

"(1) IN GENERAL.—An eligible newspaper plan sponsor of a plan under which no participant has had the participant's accrued benefit increased (whether because of service or compensation) after April 2, 2019, may elect to have the alternative standards described in paragraph (4) apply to such plan.

"(2) ELIGIBLE NEWSPAPER PLAN SPONSOR.—The term 'eligible newspaper plan sponsor' means the plan sponsor of—

"(A) any community newspaper plan, or

"(B) any other plan sponsored, as of April 2, 2019, by a member of the same controlled group of a plan sponsor of a community newspaper plan if such member is in the trade or business of publishing 1 or more newspapers.

"(3) ELECTION.—An election under paragraph (1) shall be made at such time and in such manner as prescribed by the Secretary of the Treasury. Such election, once made with respect to a plan year, shall apply to all subsequent plan years unless revoked with the consent of the Secretary of the Treasury.

"(4) ALTERNATIVE MINIMUM FUNDING STANDARDS.—The alternative standards described in this paragraph are the following:

"(A) INTEREST RATES.—

"(i) IN GENERAL.—Notwithstanding subsection (h)(2)(C) and except as provided in clause (ii), the first, second, and third segment rates in effect for any month for purposes of this section shall be 8 percent.

"(ii) NEW BENEFIT ACCRUALS.—Notwithstanding subsection (h)(2), for purposes of determining the funding target and normal cost of a plan for any plan year, the present value of any benefits accrued or earned under the plan for a plan year with respect to which an election under paragraph (1) is in effect shall be determined on the basis of the United States Treasury obligation yield curve for the day that is the valuation date of such plan for such plan year.

"(iii) UNITED STATES TREASURY OBLIGATION YIELD CURVE.—For purposes of this subsection, the term 'United States Treasury obligation yield curve' means, with respect to any day, a yield curve which shall be prescribed by the Secretary of the Treasury for such day on interest-bearing obligations of the United States.

"(B) SHORTFALL AMORTIZATION BASE.—

"(i) PREVIOUS SHORTFALL AMORTIZATION BASES.—The shortfall amortization bases determined under subsection (c)(3) for all plan years preceding the first plan year to which the election under paragraph (1) applies (and all shortfall amortization installments determined with respect to such bases) shall be reduced to zero under rules similar to the rules of subsection (c)(6).

"(ii) NEW SHORTFALL AMORTIZATION BASE.—Notwithstanding subsection (c)(3), the shortfall amortization base for the first plan year to which the election under paragraph (1) applies shall be the funding shortfall of such plan for such plan year (determined using the interest rates as modified under subparagraph (A)).

"(C) DETERMINATION OF SHORTFALL AMORTIZATION INSTALLMENTS.—

"(i) 30-YEAR PERIOD.—Subparagraphs (A) and (B) of subsection (c)(2) shall be applied by substituting '30-plan-year' for '7-plan-year' each place it appears.

"(ii) NO SPECIAL ELECTION.—The election under subparagraph (D) of subsection (c)(2) shall not apply to any plan year to which the election under paragraph (1) applies.

"(D) EXEMPTION FROM AT-RISK TREATMENT.—Subsection (i) shall not apply.

"(5) COMMUNITY NEWSPAPER PLAN.—For purposes of this subsection—

"(A) IN GENERAL.—The term 'community newspaper plan' means a plan to which this section applies maintained as of December 31, 2018, by an employer which—

"(i) maintains the plan on behalf of participants and beneficiaries with respect to employment in the trade or business of publishing 1 or more newspapers which were published by the employer at any time during the 11-year period ending on the date of the enactment of this subsection,

"(ii) (I) is not a company the stock of which is publicly traded (on a stock exchange or in an over-the-counter market), and is not controlled, directly or indirectly, by such a company, or

"(II) is controlled, directly, or indirectly, during the entire 30-year period ending on the date of the enactment of this subsection by individuals who are members of the same family, and does not publish or distribute a daily newspaper that is carrier-distributed in printed form in more than 5 States, and

"(iii) is controlled, directly, or indirectly—

"(I) by 1 or more persons residing primarily in a State in which the community newspaper has been published on newsprint or carrier-distributed,

"(II) during the entire 30-year period ending on the date of the enactment of this subsection by individuals who are members of the same family,

"(III) by 1 or more trusts, the sole trustees of which are persons described in subclause (I) or (II), or

"(IV) by a combination of persons described in subclause (I), (II), or (III).

"(B) NEWSPAPER.—The term 'newspaper' does not include any newspaper (determined without regard to this subparagraph) to which any of the following apply:

"(i) Is not in general circulation.

"(ii) Is published (on newsprint or electronically) less frequently than 3 times per week.

"(iii) Has not ever been regularly published on newsprint.

"(iv) Does not have a bona fide list of paid subscribers.

"(C) CONTROL.—A person shall be treated as controlled by another person if such other person possesses, directly or indirectly, the power to direct or cause the direction and management of such person (including the power to elect a majority of the members of the board of directors of such person) through the ownership of voting securities.

"(6) CONTROLLED GROUP.—For purposes of this subsection, the term 'controlled group' means all persons treated as a single employer under subsection (b), (c), (m), or (o) of section 414 of the Internal Revenue Code of 1986 as of the date of the enactment of this subsection.

"(7) EFFECT ON PREMIUM RATE CALCULATION.—Notwithstanding any other provision of law or any regulation issued by the Pension Benefit Guaranty Corporation, in the case of a plan for which an election is made to apply the alternative standards described in paragraph (3), the additional premium under section 4006(a)(3)(E) shall be determined as if such election had not been made.".

(c) Effective Date.—The amendments made by this section shall apply to plan years ending after December 31, 2017.

SEC. 40308. MINIMUM RATE OF INTEREST FOR CERTAIN DETERMINATIONS RELATED TO LIFE INSURANCE CONTRACTS.

(a) Modification Of Minimum Rate For Purposes Of Cash Value Accumulation Test.—

(1) IN GENERAL.—Section 7702(b)(2)(A) of the Internal Revenue Code of 1986 is amended by striking "an annual effective rate of 4 percent" and inserting "the applicable accumulation test minimum rate".

(2) APPLICABLE ACCUMULATION TEST MINIMUM RATE.—Section 7702(b) of such Code is amended by adding at the end the following new paragraph:

"(3) APPLICABLE ACCUMULATION TEST MINIMUM RATE.—For purposes of paragraph (2)(A), the term 'applicable accumulation test minimum rate' means the lesser of—

"(A) an annual effective rate of 4 percent, or

"(B) the insurance interest rate (as defined in subsection (f)(11)) in effect at the time the contract is issued.".

(b) Modification Of Minimum Rate For Purposes Of Guideline Premium Requirements.—

(1) IN GENERAL.—Section 7702(c)(3)(B)(iii) of such Code is amended by striking

"an annual effective rate of 6 percent" and inserting "the applicable guideline premium minimum rate".

(2) APPLICABLE GUIDELINE PREMIUM MINIMUM RATE.—Section 7702(c) (3) of such Code is amended by adding at the end the following new subparagraph:

"(E) APPLICABLE GUIDELINE PREMIUM MINIMUM RATE.—For purposes of subparagraph (B)(iii), the term 'applicable guideline premium minimum rate' means the applicable accumulation test minimum rate (as defined in subsection (b)(3)) plus 2 percentage points.".

(c) Application Of Modified Minimum Rates To Determination Of Guideline Level Premium.—Section 7702(c)(4) of such Code is amended—

(1) by striking "4 percent" and inserting "the applicable accumulation test minimum rate", and

(2) by striking "6 percent" and inserting "the applicable guideline premium minimum rate".

(d) Insurance Interest Rate.—Section 7702(f) of such Code is amended by adding at the end the following new paragraph:

"(11) INSURANCE INTEREST RATE.—For purposes of this section—

"(A) IN GENERAL.—The term 'insurance interest rate' means, with respect to any contract issued in any calendar year, the lesser of—

"(i) the section 7702 valuation interest rate for such calendar year (or, if such calendar year is not an adjustment year, the most recent adjustment year), or

"(ii) the section 7702 applicable Federal interest rate for such calendar year (or, if such calendar year is not an adjustment year, the most recent adjustment year).

"(B) SECTION 7702 VALUATION INTEREST RATE.—The term 'section 7702 valuation interest rate' means, with respect to any adjustment year, the prescribed U.S. valuation interest rate for life insurance with guaranteed durations of more than 20 years (as defined in the National Association of Insurance Commissioners' Standard Valuation Law) as effective in the calendar year immediately preceding such adjustment year.

"(C) SECTION 7702 APPLICABLE FEDERAL INTEREST RATE.—The term 'section 7702 applicable Federal interest rate' means, with respect to any adjustment year, the average (rounded to the nearest whole percentage point) of the applicable Federal mid-term rates (as defined in section 1274(d) but based on annual compounding) effective as of the beginning of each of the calendar months in the most recent 60-month period ending before the second calendar year prior to such adjustment year.

"(D) ADJUSTMENT YEAR.—The term 'adjustment year' means the calendar year following any calendar year that includes the effective date of a change in the prescribed U.S. valuation interest rate for life insurance with guaranteed durations of more than 20 years (as defined in the National Association of Insurance Commissioners' Standard Valuation Law).

"(E) TRANSITION RULE.—Notwithstanding subparagraph (A), the insurance interest rate shall be 2 percent in the case of any contract which is issued during the period that—

"(i) begins on January 1, 2021, and

"(i) ends immediately before the beginning of the first adjustment year that beings after December 31, 2021.".

(e) Effective Date.—The amendments made by this section shall apply to contracts issued after December 31, 2020.

DIVISION E—CONTINUED ASSISTANCE TO UNEMPLOYED WORKERS

SEC. 50001. EXTENSION OF FEDERAL PANDEMIC UNEMPLOYMENT COMPENSATION.

(a) In General.—Section 2104(e) of the CARES Act (Public Law 116–136) is amended to read as follows:

"(e) Applicability.—

"(1) IN GENERAL.—An agreement entered into under this section shall apply to weeks of unemployment—

"(A) beginning after the date on which such agreement is entered into; and

"(B) ending on or before January 31, 2021.

"(2) TRANSITION RULE FOR INDIVIDUALS REMAINING ENTITLED TO REGULAR COMPENSATION AS OF JANUARY 31, 2021.—In the case of any individual who, as of the date specified in paragraph (1)(B), has not yet exhausted all rights to regular compensation under the State law of a State with respect to a benefit year that began before such date, Federal Pandemic Unemployment Compensation shall continue to be payable to such individual for any week beginning on or after such date for which the individual is otherwise eligible for regular compensation with respect to such benefit year.

"(3) TERMINATION.—Notwithstanding any other provision of this subsection, no Federal Pandemic Unemployment Compensation shall be payable for any week beginning after March 31, 2021.".

(b) Limitation On Application Of Transition Rule.—Section 2104(g) of such Act is amended by inserting "(except for subsection (e)(2))" after "the preceding provisions of this section".

(c) Disregard Of Federal Pandemic Unemployment Compensation For Certain Purposes.—Section 2104(h) of such Act is amended to read as follows:

"(h) Disregard Of Federal Pandemic Unemployment Compensation For Purposes Of All Federal And Federally Assisted Programs.—A Federal Pandemic Unemployment Compensation payment shall not be regarded as income and shall not be regarded as a resource for the month of receipt and the following 9 months, for purposes of determining the eligibility of the recipient (or the recipient's spouse or family) for benefits or assistance, or the amount or extent of benefits or assistance, under any Federal program or under any State or local program financed in whole or in part with Federal funds.".

SEC. 50002. EXTENSION AND BENEFIT PHASEOUT RULE FOR PANDEMIC UNEMPLOYMENT ASSISTANCE.

Section 2102(c) of the CARES Act (Public Law 116–136) is amended—

(1) in paragraph (1)—

(A) by striking "paragraph (2)" and inserting "paragraphs (2) and (3)"; and

(B) in subparagraph (A)(ii), by striking "December 31, 2020" and inserting "January 31, 2021"; and

(2) by redesignating paragraph (3) as paragraph (4); and

(3) by inserting after paragraph (2) the following:

"(3) TRANSITION RULE FOR INDIVIDUALS REMAINING ENTITLED TO PANDEMIC UNEMPLOYMENT ASSISTANCE AS OF JANUARY 31, 2021.—
"(A) IN GENERAL.—In the case of any individual who, as of the date specified in paragraph (1)(A)(ii), is receiving Pandemic Unemployment Assistance but has not yet exhausted all rights to such assistance under this section, Pandemic Unemployment Assistance shall continue to be payable to such individual for any week beginning on or after such date for which the individual is otherwise eligible for Pandemic Unemployment Assistance.
"(B) TERMINATION.—Notwithstanding any other provision of this subsection, no Pandemic Unemployment Assistance shall be payable for any week beginning after March 31, 2021.".

SEC. 50003. EXTENSION AND BENEFIT PHASEOUT RULE FOR PANDEMIC EMERGENCY UNEMPLOYMENT COMPENSATION.

Section 2107(g) of the CARES Act (Public Law 116–136) is amended to read as follows:
"(g) Applicability.—
"(1) IN GENERAL.—An agreement entered into under this section shall apply to weeks of unemployment—
"(A) beginning after the date on which such agreement is entered into; and
"(B) ending on or before January 31, 2021.
"(2) TRANSITION RULE FOR INDIVIDUALS REMAINING ENTITLED TO PANDEMIC EMERGENCY UNEMPLOYMENT COMPENSATION AS OF JANUARY 31, 2021.—In the case of any individual who, as of the date specified in paragraph (1)(A)(ii), is receiving Pandemic Emergency Unemployment Compensation but has not yet exhausted all rights to such assistance under this section, Pandemic Emergency Unemployment Compensation shall continue to be payable to such individual for any week beginning on or after such date for which the individual is otherwise eligible for Pandemic Emergency Unemployment Compensation.
"(3) TERMINATION.—Notwithstanding any other provision of this subsection, no Pandemic Emergency Unemployment Compensation shall be payable for any week beginning after March 31, 2021.".

SEC. 50004. EXTENSION OF FULL FEDERAL FUNDING OF THE FIRST WEEK OF COMPENSABLE REGULAR UNEMPLOYMENT FOR STATES WITH NO WAITING WEEK.

Section 2105(e)(2) of the CARES Act (Public Law 116–136) is amended by striking "December 31, 2020" and inserting "January 31, 2021".

SEC. 50005. EXTENSION OF EMERGENCY RELIEF AND TECHNICAL CORRECTIONS FOR GOVERNMENTAL ENTITIES AND NONPROFIT ORGANIZATIONS.

Section 903(i)(1) of the Social Security Act, as added by section 2103 of the CARES Act (Public Law 116–136), is amended—
(1) in subparagraph (A), by striking "during the applicable period" and inserting "with respect to the applicable period";
(2) in subparagraph (B), by striking "section 3309(a)(1)" and inserting "section 3309(a)";
(3) in subparagraph (C), by striking "shall be used exclusively" and all that follows through the end and inserting "shall be used exclusively to reduce the amounts re-

quired to be paid in lieu of contributions into the State unemployment fund pursuant to such section by governmental entities and other organizations described in section 3309(a) of such Code"; and

(4) in subparagraph (D), by striking "December 31, 2020" and inserting "January 31, 2021".

SEC. 50006. REDUCTION OF STATE ADMINISTRATIVE BURDEN IN DETERMINATION OF AMOUNT OF PANDEMIC UNEMPLOYMENT ASSISTANCE.

Section 2102(d) of the CARES Act (Public Law 116–136) is amended by adding at the end the following:

"(4) STATE FLEXIBILITY IN ESTABLISHING INCOME.—In determining the income of an individual for purposes of an application for assistance authorized under subsection (b), a State may rely on such wage and self-employment data as the State may elect, including any applicable data with respect to an individual's electronically mediated employment.".

SEC. 50007. EXTENSION OF TEMPORARY ASSISTANCE FOR STATES WITH ADVANCES.

Section 1202(b)(10)(A) of the Social Security Act (42 U.S.C. 1322(b)(10)(A)) is amended by striking "December 31, 2020" and inserting "June 30, 2021".

SEC. 50008. EXTENSION OF FULL FEDERAL FUNDING OF EXTENDED UNEMPLOYMENT COMPENSATION.

Section 4105 of the Families First Coronavirus Response Act (Public Law 116–127) is amended by striking "December 31, 2020" each place it appears and inserting "June 30, 2021".

SEC. 50009. EXTENSION OF TEMPORARY FINANCING OF SHORT-TIME COMPENSATION PAYMENTS IN STATES WITH PROGRAMS IN LAW.

Section 2108(b)(2) of the CARES Act (Public Law 116–136) is amended by striking "December 31, 2020" and inserting "January 31, 2021".

SEC. 50010. EXTENSION OF TEMPORARY FINANCING OF SHORT-TIME COMPENSATION AGREEMENTS.

Section 2109(d)(2) of the CARES Act (Public Law 116–136) is amended by striking "December 31, 2020" and inserting "January 31, 2021".

SEC. 50011. GRACE PERIOD FOR FULL FINANCING OF SHORT-TIME COMPENSATION PROGRAMS.

Section 2108(c) of the CARES Act (Public Law 116–136) is amended by striking "shall be eligible" and all that follows through the end and inserting the following:
"shall be eligible—

"(1) for payments under subsection (a) for weeks of unemployment beginning after the effective date of such enactment; and

"(2) for an additional payment equal to the total amount of payments for which the State is eligible pursuant to an agreement under section 2109 for weeks of unemployment before such effective date.".

DIVISION F—ASSISTANCE TO AGRICULTURAL PRODUCERS AND OTHER MATTERS RELATING TO AGRICULTURE

DEFINITIONS

SEC. 60001.

In this division:

(1) The term "COVID–19" means the disease caused by SARS–CoV–2, or any viral strain mutating therefrom with pandemic potential.

(2) The term "Secretary" means the Secretary of Agriculture.

TITLE I

—LIVESTOCK

ESTABLISHMENT OF TRUST FOR BENEFIT OF UNPAID CASH SELLERS OF LIVESTOCK

SEC. 60101.

The Packers and Stockyards Act, 1921, is amended by inserting after section 317 (7 U.S.C. 217a) the following new section:

"SEC. 318. STATUTORY TRUST ESTABLISHED; DEALER.

"(a) Establishment.—

"(1) IN GENERAL.—All livestock purchased by a dealer in cash sales and all inventories of, or receivables or proceeds from, such livestock shall be held by such dealer in trust for the benefit of all unpaid cash sellers of such livestock until full payment has been received by such unpaid cash sellers.

"(2) EXEMPTION.—Any dealer whose average annual purchases of livestock do not exceed $100,000 shall be exempt from the provisions of this section.

"(3) EFFECT OF DISHONORED INSTRUMENTS.—For purposes of determining full payment under paragraph (1), a payment to an unpaid cash seller shall not be considered to have been made if the unpaid cash seller receives a payment instrument that is dishonored.

"(b) Preservation Of Trust.—An unpaid cash seller shall lose the benefit of a trust under subsection (a) if the unpaid cash seller has not preserved the trust by giving written notice to the dealer involved and filing such notice with the Secretary—

"(1) within 30 days of the final date for making a payment under section 409 in the event that a payment instrument has not been received; or

"(2) within 15 business days after the date on which the seller receives notice that the payment instrument promptly presented for payment has been dishonored.

"(c) Notice To Lien Holders.—When a dealer receives notice under subsection (b) of the unpaid cash seller's intent to preserve the benefits of the trust, the dealer shall, within 15 business days, give notice to all persons who have recorded a security interest in, or lien on, the livestock held in such trust.

"(d) Cash Sales Defined.—For the purpose of this section, a cash sale means a sale in which the seller does not expressly extend credit to the buyer.

"(e) Purchase Of Livestock Subject To Trust.—

"(1) IN GENERAL.—A person purchasing livestock subject to a dealer trust shall receive good title to the livestock if the person receives the livestock—

"(A) in exchange for payment of new value; and

"(B) in good faith without notice that the transfer is a breach of trust.

"(2) DISHONORED PAYMENT INSTRUMENT.—Payment shall not be considered to have been made if a payment instrument given in exchange for the livestock is dishonored.

"(3) TRANSFER IN SATISFACTION OF ANTECEDENT DEBT.—A transfer of livestock subject to a dealer trust is not for value if the transfer is in satisfaction of an antecedent debt or to a secured party pursuant to a security agreement.

"(f) Enforcement.—Whenever the Secretary has reason to believe that a dealer subject to this section has failed to perform the duties required by this section or whenever the Secretary has reason to believe that it will be in the best interest of unpaid cash sellers, the Secretary shall do one or more of the following—

"(1) appoint an independent trustee to carry out the duties required by this section, preserve trust assets, and enforce the trust;

"(2) serve as independent trustee, preserve trust assets, and enforce the trust; or

"(3) file suit in the United States district court for the district in which the dealer resides to enjoin the dealer's failure to perform the duties required by this section, preserve trust assets, and to enforce the trust. Attorneys employed by the Secretary may, with the approval of the Attorney General, represent the Secretary in any such suit. Nothing herein shall preclude unpaid sellers from filing suit to preserve or enforce the trust.".

EMERGENCY ASSISTANCE FOR MARKET-READY LIVESTOCK AND POULTRY LOSSES

SEC. 60102.

(a) In General.—The Secretary shall make payments to covered producers to offset losses related to the intentional depopulation of market-ready livestock and poultry due to insufficient regional processing access related to the COVID–19 public health emergency, as determined by the Secretary.

(b) Payment Rate For Covered Producers.—

(1) PAYMENTS FOR FIRST 30-DAY PERIOD.—For a period of 30 days beginning, with respect to a covered producer, on the initial date of depopulation described in subsection (a) of the market-ready livestock or poultry of the covered producer, the Secretary shall reimburse such covered producer for 85 percent of the value of losses as determined under subsection (c).

(2) SUBSEQUENT 30-DAY PERIODS.—For each 30-day period subsequent to the 30-day period described in paragraph (1), the Secretary shall reduce the value of the losses as determined under subsection (c) with respect to a covered producer by 10 percent.

(c) Valuation.—In calculating the amount of losses for purposes of the payment rates under subsection (b), the Secretary shall use the average fair market value, as determined by the Secretary in collaboration with the Chief Economist of the Department of Agriculture and the Administrator of the Agricultural Marketing Service, for market-ready livestock, where applicable, and market-ready poultry, where applicable, during the period beginning March 1, 2020, and ending on the date of the enactment of this section. In no case shall a payment made under subsection (b) exceed the average market value of market-ready livestock or poultry on the date of depopulation.

(d) Packer-Owned Animals Excluded.—The Secretary may not make payments under this section for the losses of packer-owned animals.

(e) Definitions.—In this section:

(1) COVERED PRODUCER.—The term "covered producer" means a person or legal entity that assumes the production and market risks associated with the agricultural production of livestock and poultry (as such terms are defined in section 2(a) of the

Packers and Stockyards Act, 1921 (7 U.S.C. 183(a)).

(2) PACKER.—The term "packer" has the meaning given the term in section 201 of the Packers and Stockyards Act, 1921 (7 U.S.C. 191).

(3) SECRETARY.—The term "Secretary" means the Secretary of Agriculture.

(f) Funding.—There is appropriated, out of any funds in the Treasury not otherwise appropriated, such sums as may be necessary to carry out this section.

ANIMAL DISEASE PREVENTION AND MANAGEMENT RESPONSE

SEC. 60103.

Out of any amounts in the Treasury not otherwise appropriated, there is appropriated to carry out section 10409A of the Animal Health Protection Act (7 U.S.C. 8308A) $300,000,000, to remain available until expended.

TITLE II

—DAIRY

DAIRY DIRECT DONATION PROGRAM

SEC. 60201.

(a) Definitions.—In this section:

(1) ELIGIBLE DAIRY ORGANIZATION.—The term "eligible dairy organization" is defined in section 1431(a) of the Agricultural Act of 2014 (7 U.S.C. 9071(a)).

(2) ELIGIBLE DISTRIBUTOR.—The term "eligible distributor" means a public or private nonprofit organization that distributes donated eligible dairy products to recipient individuals and families.

(3) ELIGIBLE DAIRY PRODUCTS.—The term "eligible dairy products" means products primarily made from milk produced and processed within a Federal Milk Marketing Order.

(4) ELIGIBLE PARTNERSHIP.—The term "eligible partnership" means a partnership between an eligible dairy organization and an eligible distributor.

(b) Establishment And Purposes.—Not later than 45 days after the enactment of this Act, the Secretary shall establish and administer a direct dairy donation program for the purposes of—

(1) facilitating the timely donation of eligible dairy products and

(2) preventing and minimizing food waste.

(c) Donation And Distribution Plans.—

(1) IN GENERAL.—To be eligible to receive reimbursement under this section, an eligible partnership shall submit to the Secretary a donation and distribution plan that describes the process that the eligible partnership will use for the donation, processing, transportation, temporary storage, and distribution of eligible dairy products.

(2) REVIEW AND APPROVAL.—No later than 15 business days after receiving a plan described in paragraph (1), the Secretary shall—

(A) review such plan; and

(B) issue an approval or disapproval of such plan.

(d) Reimbursement.—

(1) IN GENERAL.—On receipt of appropriate documentation under paragraph (2), the Secretary shall reimburse an eligible dairy organization at a rate equal to the current Class I milk price multiplied by the volume of milk required to make the donated product.

(2) SPECIAL CASE.—In the case of donated Class I products, the Secretary shall

reimburse an eligible dairy organization at a rate equal to the current Class I milk price plus 5 percent multiplied by the volume of milk required to make the donated Class I product.

(3) DOCUMENTATION.—

(A) IN GENERAL.—An eligible dairy organization shall submit to the Secretary such documentation as the Secretary may require to demonstrate the eligible dairy product production and donation to the eligible distributor.

(B) VERIFICATION.—The Secretary may verify the accuracy of documentation submitted.

(3) RETROACTIVE REIMBURSEMENT.—In providing reimbursements under paragraph (1), the Secretary may provide reimbursements for milk costs incurred before the date on which the donation and distribution plan for the applicable participating partnership was approved by the Secretary.

(e) Prohibition On Resale Of Products.—

(1) IN GENERAL.—An eligible distributor that receives eligible dairy products donated under this section may not sell the products into commercial markets.

(2) PROHIBITION ON FUTURE PARTICIPATION.—An eligible distributor that the Secretary determines has violated paragraph (1) shall not be eligible for any future participation in the program established under this section.

(f) Reviews.—The Secretary shall conduct appropriate reviews or audits to ensure the integrity of the program established under this section.

(g) Publication Of Donation Activity.—The Secretary, acting through the Agricultural Marketing Service, shall publish on the publicly accessible website of such agency periodic reports containing donation activity under this section.

(h) Supplemental Reimbursements.—

(1) IN GENERAL.—The Secretary may make a supplemental reimbursement to an eligible dairy organization for an approved donation and distribution plan in accordance with the milk donation program established under section 1431 of the Agricultural Act of 2014 (7 U.S.C. 9071).

(2) REIMBURSEMENT CALCULATION.—A supplemental reimbursement described in paragraph (1) shall be equal to the value of—

(A) the sum of—

(i) the Class IV milk price for the applicable month, plus

(ii) 5 percent of the Class I price for the applicable month, multiplied by

(B) the volume of eligible milk under such approved donation plan.

(i) Funding.—Out of the amounts of the Treasury not otherwise appropriated, the Secretary shall use to carry out this section $500,000,000 to remain available until expended.

SUPPLEMENTAL DAIRY MARGIN COVERAGE PAYMENTS

SEC. 60202.

(a) In General.—The Secretary shall provide supplemental dairy margin coverage payments to eligible dairy operations described in subsection (b)(1) whenever the average actual dairy production margin (as defined in section 1401 of the Agricultural Act of 2014 (7 U.S.C. 9051)) for a month is less than the coverage level threshold selected by such eligible dairy operation under such section 1406.

(b) Eligible Dairy Operation Described.—

(1) IN GENERAL.—An eligible dairy operation described in this subsection is a dairy operation that—

(A) is located in the United States; and

(B) during a calendar year in which such dairy operation is a participating dairy operation (as defined in section 1401 of the Agricultural Act of 2014 (7 U.S.C. 9051)), has a production history established under the dairy margin coverage program under section 1405 of the Agricultural Act of 2014 (7 U.S.C. 9055) of less than 5 million pounds, as determined in accordance with subsection (c) of such section 1405.

(2) LIMITATION ON ELIGIBILITY.—An eligible dairy operation shall only be eligible for payments under this section during a calendar year in which such eligible dairy operation is enrolled in the dairy margin coverage (as defined in section 1401 of the Agricultural Act of 2014 (7 U.S.C. 9051)).

(c) Supplemental Production History Calculation.—For purposes of determining the production history of an eligible dairy operation under this section, such dairy operation's production history shall be equal to—

(1) the production volume of such dairy operation for the 2019 milk marketing year; minus

(2) the dairy margin coverage production history of such dairy operation established under section 1405 of the Agricultural Act of 2014 (7 U.S.C. 9055).

(d) Coverage Percentage.—

(1) IN GENERAL.—For purposes of calculating payments to be issued under this section during a calendar year, an eligible dairy operation's coverage percentage shall be equal to the coverage percentage selected by such eligible dairy operation with respect to such calendar year under section 1406 of the Agricultural Act of 2014 (7 U.S.C. 9056).

(2) 5-MILLION POUND LIMITATION.—

(A) IN GENERAL.—The Secretary shall not provide supplemental dairy margin coverage on an eligible dairy operation's actual production for a calendar year such that the total covered production history of such dairy operation exceeds 5 million pounds.

(B) DETERMINATION OF AMOUNT.—In calculating the total covered production history of an eligible dairy operation under subparagraph (A), the Secretary shall multiply the coverage percentage selected by such operation under section 1406 of the Agricultural Act of 2014 (7 U.S.C. 9056) by the sum of—

(i) the supplemental production history calculated under subsection (c) with respect to such dairy operation; and

(ii) the dairy margin coverage production history described in subsection (c)(2) with respect to such dairy operation.

(e) Premium Cost.—The premium cost for an eligible dairy operation under this section for a calendar year shall be equal to the product of multiplying—

(1) the Tier I premium cost calculated with respect to such dairy operation for such year under section 1407(b) of the Agricultural Act of 2014 (7 12 U.S.C. 9057(b)); by

(2) the production history calculation with respect to such dairy operation determined under subsection (c) (such that total covered production history does not exceed 5 million pounds).

(f) Regulations.—Not later than 45 days after the date of the enactment of this section, the Secretary shall issue regulations to carry out this section.

(g) Prohibition With Respect To Dairy Margin Coverage Enrollment.—The Secretary may not reopen or otherwise provide a special enrollment for dairy margin coverage (as defined in section 1401 of the Agricultural Act of 2014 (7 U.S.C. 9051)) for purposes of establishing eligibility for supplemental dairy margin coverage payments under this section.

(h) Retroactive Application For Calendar Year 2020.—The Secretary shall make payments under this section to eligible dairy operations described in subsection (b)(1) for months after and including January, 2020.

(i) Sunset.—The authority to make payments under this section shall terminate on December 31, 2023.

(j) Funding.—Out of any amounts in the Treasury not otherwise appropriated, there are made available such sums as may be necessary to carry out this program.

RECOURSE LOAN PROGRAM FOR COMMERCIAL PROCESSORS OF DAIRY PRODUCTS

SEC. 60203.

(a) In General.—The Secretary shall make recourse loans available to qualified applicants during the COVID–19 pandemic.

(b) Amount Of Loan.—

(1) IN GENERAL.—A recourse loan made under this section shall be provided to qualified applicants up to the value of the eligible dairy product inventory of the applicant as determined by the Secretary and consistent with subsection (c).

(2) VALUATION.—For purposes of making recourse loans under this section, the Secretary shall conduct eligible dairy product valuations to provide, to the maximum extent practicable, funds to continue the operations of qualified applicants.

(c) Inventory Used As Collateral.—Eligible dairy product inventory used as collateral for the recourse loan program under this section shall be pledged on a rotating basis to prevent spoilage of perishable products.

(d) Term Of Loan.—A recourse loan under this section may be made for a period as determined by the Secretary, except that no such recourse loan may end after the date that is 24 months after the date of the enactment of this section.

(e) Funding And Authorities.—Out of any amounts in the Treasury not otherwise appropriated, there is made available $500,000,000 to carry out this section.

(f) Definitions.—In this section:

(1) ELIGIBLE DAIRY PRODUCTS.—The term "eligible dairy products" means all dairy products whether in base commodity or finished product form.

(2) QUALIFIED APPLICANT.—The term "qualified applicant" means any commercial processors, packagers, merchants, marketers, wholesalers, and distributors of eligible dairy products impacted by COVID–19.

DAIRY MARGIN COVERAGE PREMIUM DISCOUNT FOR 3-YEAR SIGNUP

SEC. 60204.

The Secretary shall provide a 15 percent discount for the premiums described in subsections (b) and (c) of section 1407 of the Agricultural Act of 2014 (7 U.S.C. 9051) and the premium described in section 60202(e) for a dairy operation (as defined in 1401 of such Act (7 U.S.C. 9051)) that makes a 1-time, three-year election to enroll in dairy margin coverage under part I of subtitle D of such Act for calendar years 2021 through 2023.

TITLE III

—SPECIALTY CROPS AND OTHER COMMODITIES
SUPPORT FOR SPECIALTY CROP SECTOR

SEC. 60301.

Section 101(l) of the Specialty Crops Competitiveness Act of 2004 (7 U.S.C. 1621 note) is amended by adding at the end the following:

"(3) COVID–19 OUTBREAK RELIEF.—

"(A) IN GENERAL.—The Secretary shall make grants to States eligible to receive a grant under this section to assist State efforts to support the specialty crop sector for impacts related to the COVID–19 public health emergency.

"(B) FUNDING.—There is appropriated, out of any funds in the Treasury not otherwise appropriated, to carry out subparagraph (A) not less than $100,000,000, to remain available until expended.".

SUPPORT FOR LOCAL AGRICULTURAL MARKETS

SEC. 60302.

Section 210A(i) of the Agricultural Marketing Act of 1946 (7 U.S.C. 1627c(d)) is amended by adding at the end the following:

"(4) GRANTS FOR COVID–19 LOSSES.—

"(A) IN GENERAL.—In addition to grants made under the preceding provisions of this subsection, the Secretary shall make grants to eligible entities specified in subsection (d)(6)(B) to provide assistance in response to the COVID–19 pandemic.

"(B) MATCHING FUNDS APPLICABILITY.—The Secretary may not require a recipient of a grant under subparagraph (A) to provide any nonFederal matching funds.

"(F) FUNDING.—There is appropriated, out of any funds in the Treasury not otherwise appropriated, to carry out this paragraph, $50,000,000, to remain available until expended.".

SUPPORT FOR FARMING OPPORTUNITIES TRAINING AND OUTREACH

SEC. 60303.

Section 2501 of the Food, Agriculture, Conservation, and Trade Act of 1990 (7 U.S.C. 2279) is amended by adding at the end the following:

"(m) Additional Funding.—

"(1) IN GENERAL.—The Secretary shall make grants to, or enter into cooperative agreements or contracts with, eligible entities specified in subsection (c)(1) to provide training, outreach, and technical assistance on operations, financing, and marketing to beginning farmers and ranchers, socially disadvantaged farmers and ranchers, and veteran farmers and ranchers.

"(2) MATCHING FUNDS APPLICABILITY.—The Secretary may not require a recipient of a grant under this subsection to provide any nonFederal matching funds.

"(3) FUNDING.—There is appropriated, out of any funds in the Treasury not otherwise appropriated, to carry out this subsection, $50,000,000, to remain available until expended.".

SUPPORT FOR FARM STRESS PROGRAMS

SEC. 60304.

(a) In General.—The Secretary shall make grants to State departments of agriculture (or such equivalent department) to expand or sustain stress assistance programs for individuals who are engaged in farming, ranching, and other agriculture-related occupations, including—

(1) programs that meet the criteria specified in section 7522(b)(1) of the Food, Conservation, and Energy Act of 2008 (7 U.S.C. 5936(b)(1)); and

(2) any State initiatives carried out as of the date of the enactment of this Act that

provide stress assistance for such individuals.

(b) Grant Timing And Amount.—In making grants under subsection (a), not later than 60 days after the date of the enactment of this Act and subject to subsection (c), the Secretary shall—

(1) make awards to States submitting State plans that meet the criteria specified in paragraph (1)(A) of such subsection within the time period specified by the Secretary, in an amount not to exceed, $500,000 for each State; and

(2) of the amounts made available under subsection (f), allocate among such States, an amount to be determined by the Secretary.

(c) State Plan.—

(1) IN GENERAL.—A State department of agriculture seeking a grant under subsection (b) shall submit to the Secretary a State plan to initiate, expand, or sustain stress assistance programs described in subsection (a) that includes—

(A) a description of each activity and the estimated amount of funding to support each program and activity carried out through such a program;

(B) an estimated timeline for the operation of each such program and activity;

(C) the total amount of funding sought; and

(D) an assurance that the State department of agriculture will comply with the reporting requirement under subsection (e).

(2) GUIDANCE.—Not later than 20 days after the date of the enactment of this Act, the Secretary shall issue guidance for States with respect to the submission of a State plan under paragraph (1) and the allocation criteria under subsection (b).

(3) REALLOCATION.—If, after the first grants are awarded pursuant to allocation under subsection (b), any funds made available under subsection (f) to carry out this subsection remain unobligated, the Secretary shall—

(A) inform States that submit plans as described in subsection (b), of such availability; and

(B) reallocate such funds among such States, as the Secretary determines to be appropriate and equitable.

(d) Collaboration.—The Secretary may issue guidance to encourage State departments of agriculture to use funds provided under this section to support programs described in subsection (a) that are operated by—

(1) Indian tribes (as defined in section 4 of the Indian Self-Determination and Education Assistance Act (25 U.S.C. 5304));

(2) State cooperative extension services; and

(3) nongovernmental organizations.

(e) Reporting.—Not later than 180 days after the public health emergency declared under section 319 of the Public Health Services Act (42 U.S.C. 247d) on January 31, 2020, is terminated, each State receiving additional grants under subsection (b) shall submit a report to the Secretary describing—

(1) the activities conducted using such funds;

(2) the amount of funds used to support each such activity; and

(3) the estimated number of individuals served by each such activity.

(f) Funding.—Out of any money not otherwise appropriated, there is appropriated to carry out this section $28,000,000, to remain available until expended.

(g) State Defined.—In this section, the term "State" means—

(1) a State;

(2) the District of Columbia;

(3) the Commonwealth of Puerto Rico; and

(4) any other territory or possession of the United States.

SUPPORT FOR PROCESSED COMMODITIES

SEC. 60305.

(a) Renewable Fuel Reimbursement Program.—

(1) IN GENERAL.—The Secretary shall make payments in accordance with this subsection to eligible entities that experienced unexpected market losses as a result of the COVID–19 pandemic during the applicable period.

(2) DEFINITIONS.—In this section:

(A) APPLICABLE PERIOD.—The term "applicable period" means January 1, 2020, through May 1, 2020.

(B) ELIGIBLE ENTITY.—The term "eligible entity" means any domestic entity or facility that produced any qualified fuel in the calendar year 2019.

(C) QUALIFIED FUEL.—The term "qualified fuel" means any renewable fuel or advanced biofuel (as such terms are defined in section 211(o)(1) of the Clean Air Act), including renewable fuel from corn starch feedstock.

(3) AMOUNT OF PAYMENT.—The amount of the payment payable to an eligible entity shall be the sum of—

(A) $0.45 multiplied by the number of gallons of qualified fuel produced by the eligible entity during the applicable period; and

(B) if the Secretary determines that the eligible entity was unable to produce any qualified fuel throughout 1 or more calendar months during the applicable period due to the COVID–19 pandemic, $0.45 multiplied by 50 percent of the number of gallons produced by the eligible entity in the corresponding month or months in calendar year 2019.

(4) REPORT.—Not later than 180 days after the date of the enactment of this Act, the Secretary shall submit to the Committee on Agriculture of the House of Representatives and the Committee on Agriculture, Nutrition, and Forestry of the Senate a report on the payments made under this subsection, including the identity of each payment recipient and the amount of the payment paid to the payment recipient.

(5) FUNDING.—There is made available, out of any funds in the Treasury not otherwise appropriated, such sums as may be necessary for payments to eligible entities under this subsection.

(6) ADMINISTRATION.—

(A) IN GENERAL.—The Secretary shall use the funds, facilities, and authorities of the Commodity Credit Corporation to carry out this subsection.

(B) REGULATIONS.—

(i) IN GENERAL.—Except as otherwise provided in this subsection, not later than 30 days after the date of the enactment of this Act, the Secretary and the Commodity Credit Corporation, as appropriate, shall prescribe such regulations as are necessary to carry out this subsection.

(ii) PROCEDURE.—The promulgation of regulations under, and administration of, this subsection shall be made without regard to—

(I) the notice and comment provisions of section 553 of title 5, United States Code; and

(II) chapter 35 of title 44, United States Code (commonly known as the "Paperwork Reduction Act").

(b) Emergency Assistance For Textile Mills.—

(1) IN GENERAL.—The Secretary shall make emergency assistance available to domestic users of upland cotton and extra long staple cotton in the form of a payment in an amount determined under paragraph (2), regardless of the origin of such upland cotton or extra long staple cotton, during the 10-month period beginning on March 1, 2020.

(2) CALCULATION OF ASSISTANCE.—The amount of the assistance provided under paragraph (1) to a domestic user described in such paragraph shall be equal to 10 multiplied by the product of—

(A) the domestic user's historical monthly average consumption; and

(B) 6 cents per pound so consumed.

(3) ALLOWABLE USE.—Any emergency assistance provided under this section shall be made available only to domestic users of upland cotton and extra long staple cotton that certify that the assistance shall be used only for operating expenses.

(4) HISTORICAL MONTHLY AVERAGE CONSUMPTION DEFINED.—The term "historical monthly average consumption" means the average consumption for each month occurring during the period beginning on January 1, 2017, and ending on December 31, 2019.

(5) SUNSET.—The Secretary may not provide emergency assistance under this section on or after December 31, 2020.

(6) FUNDING.—There is made available, out of any funds in the Treasury not otherwise appropriated, such sums as may be necessary to carry out this section.

DIRECT PAYMENTS TO AGRICULTURAL PRODUCERS

SEC. 60306.

(a) In General.—The Secretary shall make direct payments to producers of specialty crops, livestock, and other commodities, to cover losses in response to the COVID–19 pandemic.

(b) Payment Calculations.—Payment under subsection (a), shall be calculated as follows:

(1) SPECIALTY CROPS, LIVESTOCK, AND OTHER COMMODITIES COVERED BY CORONAVIRUS FOOD ASSISTANCE PROGRAM.—In the case of losses of specialty crops, livestock, and other commodities incurred during the first quarter of calendar year 2020 and eligible to receive direct payments under the Department of Agriculture's final rule for the Coronavirus Food Assistance program of the Department of Agriculture, payments under subsection (a) shall be made to producers to ensure that they are compensated for 85 percent of the second quarter actual losses estimated by the Secretary.

(2) SPECIALTY CROPS, LIVESTOCK, AND OTHER COMMODITIES NOT COVERED BY CORONAVIRUS FOOD ASSISTANCE PROGRAM.—In the case of losses of specialty crops, livestock, and other commodities for which a producer is ineligible to receive direct payments under the program referred to in paragraph (1), payments under subsection (a) shall be equal to 85 percent of the actual losses estimated by the Secretary for the first and second quarters of calendar year 2020 for their commodity.

(c) Adjustment.—In calculating the amount of a payment under subsection (b)(2), the Secretary shall account for price differentiation factors for a given commodity based on location, specialized varieties, and farming practices such as certified organic products, by using—

(1) differentiated prices, as determined by the Risk Management Agency for purposes of the Federal crop insurance program under the Federal Crop Insurance Act (7

U.S.C. 1501 et seq.), when available; and

(2) other data from the Department of Agriculture and colleges and universities, to determine estimated prices.

(d) Adjusted Gross Income Limitations.—A payment under this section shall be deemed to be a covered benefit under section 1001D(b)(2) of the Food Security Act of 1985 (7 U.S.C. 1308–3a(b)(2)), unless at least 75 percent of the adjusted gross income of the recipient of the payment is derived from farming, ranching, or forestry-related activities.

(e) Payments.—The Secretary shall make payments under subsection (a) not later than 60 days after the date of the enactment of this section.

(f) Funding.—There is made available, out of any funds in the Treasury not otherwise appropriated, to carry out this section $16,500,000,000, to remain available until December 31, 2020.

(g) Notification.—Any obligation or expenditure under this section shall be subject to the requirements described in section 20 of the Commodity Credit Corporation Charter Act, as added by section 60402.

(h) Report To Congress.—Not later than one year after the date of the enactment of this Act, the Secretary shall submit to the Committee on Agriculture of the House of Representatives and the Committee on Agriculture, Nutrition, and Forestry of the Senate a report specifying how price losses were calculated for each crop and crop differentiation factor, and evaluating the implementation, costs, and general effectiveness of this section and the Coronavirus Food Assistance program of the Department of Agriculture.

TITLE IV

—COMMODITY CREDIT CORPORATION
EMERGENCY ASSISTANCE

SEC. 60401.

Section 5 of the Commodity Credit Corporation Charter Act (15 U.S.C. 714c) is amended by redesignating subsection (h) as subsection (j) and inserting the following:
"(h) Remove and dispose of or aid in the removal or disposition of surplus livestock and poultry due to significant supply chain interruption during an emergency period.
"(i) Aid agricultural processing plants to ensure supply chain continuity during an emergency period.".
CONGRESSIONAL NOTIFICATION

SEC. 60402.

The Commodity Credit Corporation Charter Act (15 U.S.C. 714 et seq.) is amended by adding at the end the following new section:

"SEC. 20. CONGRESSIONAL NOTIFICATION AND OVERSIGHT ON SPENDING.

"(a) In General.—The Secretary shall notify in writing, by first-class mail and electronic mail, the Committee on Agriculture of the House of Representatives and the Committee on Agriculture, Nutrition, and Forestry of the Senate at least 90 calendar days (not counting any day on which both the House of Representatives and Senate are not in session) in advance of any obligation or expenditure authorized under this Act.

"(b) Written Notice.—A written notice required under subsection (a) shall specify—

"(1) the commodities that will be affected;

"(2) the maximum financial benefit per commodity;

"(3) the nature of the support, including—

"(A) direct payments;

"(B) technical and financial assistance;

"(C) marketing assistance; and

"(D) purchases;

"(4) the expected legal entities or individuals that would receive financial benefits;

"(5) the intended policy goals;

"(6) the legal justification specifying the authority of this Act utilized; and

"(7) the projected impacts to commodity markets.

"(c) Monitoring Or Oversight.—The Comptroller General of the United States shall conduct monitoring and oversight of the exercise of authorities, the receipt, disbursement, and use of funds for which a report is required under subsection (a).

"(d) Reports.—In conducting monitoring and oversight under subsection (c), the Comptroller General shall publish reports regarding the ongoing monitoring and oversight efforts, which, along with any audits and investigations conducted by the Comptroller General, shall be submitted to the Committee on Agriculture of the House of Representatives and the Committee on Agriculture, Nutrition, and Forestry of the Senate and posted on the website of the Government Accountability Office—

"(1) not later than 90 days after the initial obligation or expenditure of funds subject to subsection (a), and every other month thereafter for as long as such obligations or expenditures continue; and

"(2) submit to the Committee on Agriculture of the House of Representatives and the Committee on Agriculture, Nutrition, and Forestry of the Senate additional reports as warranted by the findings of the monitoring and oversight activities of the Comptroller General.

"(e) Access To Information.—

"(1) RIGHT OF ACCESS.—In conducting monitoring and oversight activities under subsection (c), the Comptroller General shall have access to records, upon request, of any Federal, State, or local agency, contractor, grantee, recipient, or subrecipient pertaining to any obligations or expenditures subject to subsection (a), including private entities receiving such assistance.

"(2) COPIES.—The Comptroller General may make and retain copies of any records accessed under paragraph (1) as the Comptroller General determines appropriate.

"(3) INTERVIEWS.—In addition to such other authorities as are available, the Comptroller General or a designee of the Comptroller General may interview Federal, State, or local officials, contractor staff, grantee staff, recipients, or subrecipients pertaining to any obligations or expenditures subject to subsection (a), including private entities receiving such assistance.

"(4) INSPECTION OF FACILITIES.—As determined necessary by the Comptroller General, the Government Accountability Office may inspect facilities at which Federal, State, or local officials, contractor staff, grantee staff, or recipients or subrecipients carry out their responsibilities related to obligations or expenditures subject to subsection (a).

"(5) ENFORCEMENT.—Access rights under this subsection shall be subject to enforcement consistent with section 716 of title 31, United States Code.

"(f) Relationship To Existing Authority.—Nothing in this section shall be construed to limit, amend, supersede, or restrict in any manner any existing authority of the Comptroller General.

"(g) Exception To Waiting Period.—Subsection (a) shall not apply if, prior to obligating or spending any funding described in such subsection, the Secretary obtains approval in writing from at least three of the following individuals—

"(1) the Chair of the Committee on Agriculture of the House of Representatives,

"(2) the Ranking Member of the Committee on Agriculture of the House of Representatives,

"(3) the Chair of the Committee on Agriculture, Nutrition, and Forestry of the Senate; and

"(4) the Ranking Member of the Committee on Agriculture, Nutrition, and Forestry of the Senate.

"(h) Exclusion For Preexisting Authorizations.—This section shall not apply to obligations and expenditures authorized in the Agriculture Improvement Act of 2018 (Public Law 115–334).".

TITLE V

—CONSERVATION

EMERGENCY SOIL HEALTH AND INCOME PROTECTION PILOT PROGRAM

SEC. 60501.

(a) Definition Of Eligible Land.—In this section, the term "eligible land" means cropland that—

(1) is selected by the owner or operator of the land for proposed enrollment in the pilot program under this section; and

(2) as determined by the Secretary, had a cropping history or was considered to be planted during each of the 3 crop years preceding enrollment.

(b) Establishment.—

(1) IN GENERAL.—The Secretary shall establish a voluntary emergency soil health and income protection pilot program under which eligible land is enrolled through the use of contracts to assist owners and operators of eligible land to conserve and improve the soil, water, and wildlife resources of the eligible land.

(2) DEADLINE FOR PARTICIPATION.—Eligible land may be enrolled in the program under this section through December 31, 2021.

(c) Contracts.—

(1) REQUIREMENTS.—A contract described in subsection (b) shall—

(A) be entered into by the Secretary, the owner of the eligible land, and (if applicable) the operator of the eligible land; and

(B) provide that, during the term of the contract—

(i) the lowest practicable cost perennial conserving use cover crop for the eligible land, as determined by the applicable State conservationist after considering the advice of the applicable State technical committee, shall be planted on the eligible land;

(ii) subject to paragraph (4), the eligible land may be harvested for seed, hayed, or grazed outside the primary nesting season established for the applicable county;

(iii) the eligible land may be eligible for a walk-in access program of the applicable State, if any; and

(iv) a nonprofit wildlife organization may provide to the owner or operator of the eligible land a payment in exchange for an agreement by the owner or operator not to harvest the conserving use cover.

(2) PAYMENTS.—

(A) RENTAL RATE.—Except as provided in paragraph (4)(B)(ii), the annual rental rate for a payment under a contract described in subsection (b) shall be $70 per acre.

(B) ADVANCE PAYMENT.—At the request of the owner and (if applicable) the operator of the eligible land, the Secretary shall make all rental payments under a contract entered into under this section within 30 days of entering into such contract.

(C) COST SHARE PAYMENTS.—A contract described in subsection (b) shall provide that, during the term of the contract, the Secretary shall pay, of the actual cost of establishment of the conserving use cover crop under paragraph (1)(B)(i), not more than $30 per acre.

(3) TERM.—

(A) IN GENERAL.—Except as provided in subparagraph (B), each contract described in subsection (b) shall be for a term of 3 years.

(B) EARLY TERMINATION.—

(i) SECRETARY.—The Secretary may terminate a contract described in subsection (b) before the end of the term described in subparagraph (A) if the Secretary determines that the early termination of the contract is appropriate.

(ii) OWNERS AND OPERATORS.—An owner and (if applicable) an operator of eligible land enrolled in the pilot program under this section may terminate a contract described in subsection (b) before the end of the term described in subparagraph (A) if the owner and (if applicable) the operator pay to the Secretary an amount equal to the amount of rental payments received under the contract.

(4) HARVESTING, HAYING, AND GRAZING OUTSIDE APPLICABLE PERIOD.—The harvesting for seed, haying, or grazing of eligible land under paragraph (1)(B)(ii) outside of the primary nesting season established for the applicable county shall be subject to the conditions that—

(A) with respect to eligible land that is so hayed or grazed, adequate stubble height shall be maintained to protect the soil on the eligible land, as determined by the applicable State conservationist after considering the advice of the applicable State technical committee; and

(B) with respect to eligible land that is so harvested for seed—

(i) the eligible land shall not be eligible to be insured or reinsured under the Federal Crop Insurance Act (7 U.S.C. 1501 et seq.); and

(ii) the annual rental rate for a payment under a contract described in subsection (b) shall be $52.50 per acre.

(d) Acreage Limitation.—Not more than 5,000,000 total acres of eligible land may be enrolled under the pilot program under this section.

(e) Funding.—There is appropriated, out of any funds in the Treasury not otherwise appropriated, such sums as may be necessary to carry out this section.

TITLE VI

—NUTRITION
DEFINITIONS

SEC. 60601.
In this title:

(1) COVID-19 PUBLIC HEALTH EMERGENCY.—The term "COVID–19 public health emergency" means the public health emergency declared by the Secretary of Health and Human Services under section 319 of the Public Health Services Act (42 U.S.C. 247d) on January 31, 2020, with respect to COVID–19.

(2) SUPPLEMENTAL NUTRITION ASSISTANCE PROGRAM.—The term "supplemental nutrition assistance program" has the meaning given such term in section 3(t) of the Food and Nutrition Act of 2008 (7 U.S.C. 2012(t)).

ENHANCED PROJECTS TO HARVEST, PROCESS, PACKAGE, OR TRANSPORT DONATED COMMODITIES

SEC. 60602.

(a) Definitions.—In this section:

(1) EMERGENCY FEEDING ORGANIZATION.—The term "emergency feeding organization" has the meaning given the term in section 201A of the Emergency Food Assistance Act of 1983 (7 U.S.C. 7501).

(2) PROJECT.—The term "project" has the meaning given the term in section 203D(d)(1) of the Emergency Food Assistance Act of 1983 (7 U.S.C. 7507(d)(1)).

(3) PRIORITY AGRICULTURAL PRODUCT.—The term "priority agricultural product" means a dairy, meat, or poultry product, or a specialty crop—

(A) packaged or marketed for sale to commercial or food service industries;

(B) for which decreased demand exists for such a product due to the COVID–19 outbreak; and

(C) the repurposing of which would be impractical for grocery or retail sale.

(4) STATE.—The term "State" has the meaning given the term in section 203D of the Emergency Food Assistance Act of 1983 (7 U.S.C. 7507).

(5) STATE AGENCY.—The term "State agency" has the meaning given the term in section 203D of the Emergency Food Assistance Act of 1983 (7 U.S.C. 7507).

(b) Enhanced Projects.—

(1) IN GENERAL.—Subject to paragraphs (3) and (4), using funds made available under subsection (d), the Secretary may provide funds to States to pay for harvesting, processing, packaging, or transportation costs of carrying out a project.

(2) GUIDANCE.—Not later than 30 days after the date of enactment of this Act, the Secretary shall issue guidance to States—

(A) to carry out this section;

(B) to inform States of their allocations under paragraph (3); and

(C) to encourage States to carry out projects that work with agricultural producers, processors, and distributors with priority agricultural products.

(3) ALLOCATION.—

(A) ELIGIBILITY FOR ALLOCATION.—The Secretary shall allocate funds made available under subsection (d) based on the formula in effect under section 214(a) of the Emergency Food Assistance Act of 1983 (7 U.S.C. 7515(a)), among States that timely submit a State plan of operation for a project that includes—

(i) a list of emergency feeding organizations in the State that will operate the project in partnership with the State agency;

(ii) at the option of the State, a list of priority agricultural products located in the State that are for donation to emergency feeding organizations and ready for transport;

(iii) a description of how the project will meet the purposes described in section 203D(d)(3) of the Emergency Food Assistance Act of 1983 (7 U.S.C. 7507(d)(3)); and

(iv) a timeline of when the project will begin operating.

(B) REALLOCATION.—If the Secretary determines that a State will not expend all the funds allocated to the State under subparagraph (A), the Secretary shall reallocate the unexpended funds to other eligible States.

(C) REPORT.—Each State that receives funds allocated under this paragraph shall submit to the Secretary financial reports on a regular basis describing the use of the funds.

(4) USE OF FUNDS.—

(A) IN GENERAL.—A State that receives funds under section 203D(d)(5) of the Emergency Food Assistance Act of 1983 (7 U.S.C. 7507(d)(5)) may—

(i) receive funds under this section; and

(ii) use funds received under this section—

(I) to expand projects for which funds are received under such section 203D(d)(5);

(II) to carry out new projects with agricultural producers, processors, or distributors participating in projects for which funds are received under such section 203D(d)(5); and

(III) to carry out projects with agricultural producers, processors, or distributors not participating in projects for which funds are received under such section 203D(d)(5).

(B) FEDERAL SHARE.—Funds received under this section shall not be subject to the Federal share limitation described in section 203D(d)(2)(B) of the Emergency Food Assistance Act of 1983 (7 U.S.C. 7507(d)(2)(B)).

(c) Cooperative Agreements.—

(1) IN GENERAL.—A State agency that carries out a project using Federal funds received under this section may enter into cooperative agreements with State agencies of other States under section 203B(d) of the Emergency Food Assistance Act of 1983 (7 U.S.C. 7507(d)) to maximize the use of commodities donated under the project.

(2) SUBMISSION.—Not later than 15 days after entering into a cooperative agreement under paragraph (1), a State agency shall submit such agreement to the Secretary.

(d) Appropriation Of Funds.—Out of funds in the Treasury not otherwise appropriated, there is appropriated to carry out this section $25,000,000 to remain available until the September 30, 2021.

(e) Public Availability.—Not later than 10 days after the date of the receipt or issuance of each document listed in paragraphs (1), (2), or (3) of this subsection, the Secretary shall make publicly available on the website of the Department of Agriculture the following documents:

(1) Any guidance issued under subsection (b)(2).

(2) A State plan of operation or report submitted in accordance with subsection (b)(3).

(3) A cooperative agreement submitted in accordance with subsection (c).

EMERGENCY FOOD ASSISTANCE PROGRAM FLEXIBILITIES

SEC. 60603.

(a) In General.—Notwithstanding any other provision of law, the Secretary of Agriculture shall issue guidance to waive the non-Federal match requirement under section 204(a)(4)(A) of the Emergency Food Assistance Act of 1983 for funding appropriated in title I of division A of this Act for costs associated with the distribution of commodities.

(b) Public Availability.—The Secretary shall make available the guidance document issued under subsection (a) on the public website of the Department of Agriculture not later than 10 days after the date of the issuance of such guidance.

(c) Effective Period.—The authority under this section shall expire 30 days after the termination of the COVID–19 public health emergency.

FLEXIBILITIES FOR SENIOR FARMERS' MARKET PROGRAM

SEC. 60604.

(a) Authority To Modify Or Waive Rules.—Notwithstanding any other provision of law and if requested by a State agency, the Secretary of Agriculture may modify or waive any rule issued under section 4402 of the Farm Security and Rural Investment Act of 2002 (7 U.S.C. 3007) that applies to such State agency if the Secretary determines that—

(1) such State agency is unable to comply with such rule as a result of COVID–19, and

(2) the requested modification or waiver is necessary to enable such State agency to provide assistance to low-income seniors under such section.

(b) Public Availability.—Not later than 10 days after the date of the receipt or issuance of each document listed in paragraphs (1) and (2) of this subsection, the Secretary shall make publicly available on the website of the Department of Agriculture the following documents:

(1) Any request submitted by State agencies under subsection (a).

(2) The Secretary's approval or denial of each such request.

(c) Definition Of State Agency.—The term "State agency" has the meaning given such term in section 249.2 of 18 title 7 of the Code of Federal Regulations.

(d) Effective Period.—Subsection (a) shall be in effect during the period that begins on the date of the enactment of this Act and ends 30 days after the termination of the COVID–19 public health emergency.

FLEXIBILITIES FOR THE FOOD DISTRIBUTION PROGRAM ON INDIAN RESERVATIONS

SEC. 60605.

(a) Waiver Of Non-Federal Share Requirement.—Funds provided in division B of the Coronavirus Aid, Relief, and Economic Security Act (Public Law 116–136) for the food distribution program on Indian reservations authorized by section 4(b) of the Food and Nutrition Act of 2008 (7 U.S.C. 2013(b)) shall not be subject to the payment of the non-Federal share requirement described in section 4(b)(4)(A) of such Act (7 U.S.C. 2013(b)(4)(A)).

(b) Flexibilities For Certain Households.—

(1) IN GENERAL.—Notwithstanding any other provision of law, the Secretary of Agriculture may issue guidance to waive or adjust section 4(b)(2)(C) of the Food and Nutrition Act of 2008 (7 U.S.C. 2013(b)(2)(C)) for any Tribal organization (as defined in section 3(v) of such Act (7 U.S.C. 2012(v)), or for an appropriate State agency administering the program established under section 4(b) of such Act (7 U.S.C. 2013(b)), to ensure that households on the Indian reservation who are participating in the supplemental nutrition assistance program and who are unable to access approved retail food stores due to the outbreak of COVID–19 have access to commodities distributed under section 4(b) of such Act.

(2) PUBLIC AVAILABILITY.—The Secretary shall make available the guidance document issued under paragraph (1) on the public website of the Department of Agriculture not later than 10 days after the date of the issuance of such guidance.

(3) SUNSET.—The authority under this subsection shall expire 30 days after the termination of the COVID–19 public health emergency.

SUPPLEMENTAL NUTRITION ASSISTANCE PROGRAM

SEC. 60606.

(a) Value Of Benefits.—Notwithstanding any other provision of law, beginning on June 1, 2020, and for each subsequent month through September 30, 2021, the value of benefits determined under section 8(a) of the Food and Nutrition Act of 2008 (7 U.S.C. 2017(a)), and consolidated block grants for Puerto Rico and American Samoa determined under section 19(a) of such Act (7 U.S.C. 2028(a)), shall be calculated using 115 percent of the June 2019 value of the thrifty food plan (as defined in section 3 of such Act (7 U.S.C. 2012)) if the value of the benefits and block grants would be greater under that calculation than in the absence of this subsection.

(b) Minimum Amount.—

(1) IN GENERAL.—The minimum value of benefits determined under section 8(a) of the Food and Nutrition Act of 2008 (7 U.S.C. 2017(a)) for a household of not more than 2 members shall be $30.

(2) EFFECTIVENESS.—Paragraph (1) shall remain in effect until the date on which 8 percent of the value of the thrifty food plan for a household containing 1 member, rounded to the nearest whole dollar increment, is equal to or greater than $30.

(c) Requirements For The Secretary.—In carrying out this section, the Secretary shall—

(1) consider the benefit increases described in each of subsections (a) and (b) to be a "mass change";

(2) require a simple process for States to notify households of the increase in benefits;

(3) consider section 16(c)(3)(A) of the Food and Nutrition Act of 2008 (7 U.S.C. 2025(c)(3)(A)) to apply to any errors in the implementation of this section, without regard to the 120-day limit described in that section;

(4) disregard the additional amount of benefits that a household receives as a result of this section in determining the amount of overissuances under section 13 of the Food and Nutrition Act of 2008 (7 U.S.C. 2022); and

(5) set the tolerance level for excluding small errors for the purposes of section 16(c) of the Food and Nutrition Act of 2008 (7 U.S.C. 2025(c)) at $50 through September 30, 2021.

(d) Provisions For Impacted Workers.—Notwithstanding any other provision of law, the requirements under subsections (d)(1)(A)(ii) and (o) of section 6 of the Food and Nutrition Act of 2008 (7 U.S.C. 2015) shall not be in effect during the period beginning on June 1, 2020, and ending 2 years after the date of enactment of this Act.

(e) Administrative Expenses.—

(1) IN GENERAL.—For the costs of State administrative expenses associated with carrying out this section and administering the supplemental nutrition assistance program established under the Food and Nutrition Act of 2008 (7 U.S.C. 2011 et seq.), the Secretary shall make available $150,000,000 for fiscal year 2020 and $150,000,000 for fiscal year 2021.

(2) TIMING FOR FISCAL YEAR 2020.—Not later than 60 days after the date of the enactment of this Act, the Secretary shall make available to States amounts for fiscal year 2020 under paragraph (1).

(3) ALLOCATION OF FUNDS.—Funds described in paragraph (1) shall be made available as grants to State agencies for each fiscal year as follows:

(A) 75 percent of the amounts available for each fiscal year shall be allocated to States based on the share of each State of households that participate in the supplemental nutrition assistance program as reported to the Department of Agriculture for the most recent 12-month period for which data are available, adjusted by the Secretary (as of the date of the enactment of this Act) for participation in disaster programs under section 5(h) of the Food and Nutrition Act of 2008 (7 U.S.C. 2014(h)); and

(B) 25 percent of the amounts available for each fiscal year shall be allocated to States based on the increase in the number of households that participate in the supplemental nutrition assistance program as reported to the Department of Agriculture over the most recent 12-month period for which data are available, adjusted by the Secretary (as of the date of the enactment of this Act) for participation in disaster programs under section 5(h) of the Food and Nutrition Act of 2008 (7 U.S.C. 2014(h)).

(f) Snap Rules.—No funds (including fees) made available under this Act or any other Act for any fiscal year may be used to finalize, implement, administer, enforce, carry out, or otherwise give effect to—

(1) the final rule entitled "Supplemental Nutrition Assistance Program: Requirements for Able-Bodied Adults Without Dependents" published in the Federal Register on December 5, 2019 (84 Fed. Reg. 66782);

(2) the proposed rule entitled "Revision of Categorical Eligibility in the Supplemental Nutrition Assistance Program (SNAP)" published in the Federal Register on July 24, 2019 (84 Fed. Reg. 35570); or

(3) the proposed rule entitled "Supplemental Nutrition Assistance Program: Standardization of State Heating and Cooling Standard Utility Allowances" published in the Federal Register on October 3, 2019 (84 Fed. Reg. 52809).

(g) Certain Exclusions From SNAP Income.—A Federal pandemic unemployment compensation payment made to an individual under section 2104 of the CARES Act (Public Law 116–136) shall not be regarded as income and shall not be regarded as a resource for the month of receipt and the following 9 months, for the purpose of determining eligibility for such individual or any other individual for benefits or assistance, or the amount of benefits or assistance, under any programs authorized under the Food and Nutrition Act of 2008 (7 U.S.C. 2011 et seq.).

(h) Public Availability.—Not later than 10 days after the date of the receipt or issuance of each document listed below, the Secretary shall make publicly available on the website of the Department of Agriculture the following documents:

(1) Any State agency request to participate in the supplemental nutrition assistance program online program under section 7(k).

(2) Any State agency request to waive, adjust, or modify statutory or regulatory requirements under the Food and Nutrition Act of 2008 related to the COVID–19 outbreak.

(3) The Secretary's approval or denial of each such request under paragraphs (1) or (2).

(i) Funding.—There are hereby appropriated to the Secretary, out of any money not otherwise appropriated, such sums as may be necessary to carry out this section.

SNAP HOT FOOD PURCHASES

SEC. 60607.

During the period beginning 10 days after the date of the enactment of this Act and ending on the termination date of the COVID–19 public health emergency, the term "food", as defined in section 3 of the Food and Nutrition Act of 2008 (7 U.S.C. 2012), shall be deemed to exclude "hot foods or hot food products ready for immediate consumption other than those authorized pursuant to clauses (3), (4), (5), (7), (8), and (9) of this subsection," for purposes of such Act, except that such exclusion is limited to retail food stores authorized to accept and redeem supplemental nutrition assistance program benefits as of the date of enactment of this Act.

SNAP NUTRITION EDUCATION FLEXIBILITY

SEC. 60608.

(a) In General.—Notwithstanding any other provision of law, the Secretary may issue nationwide guidance to allow funding allocated under section 28 of the Food and Nutrition Act (7 U.S.C. 2036a) to be used for individuals distributing food in a non-congregate setting under commodity distribution programs and child nutrition programs administered by the Food and Nutrition Service of the Department of Agriculture in States affected by the COVID–19 outbreak, provided that any individuals who distribute school meals under—

(1) the school lunch program established under the Richard B. Russell National School Lunch Act (42 U.S.C. 1751 et seq.); and

(2) the school breakfast program established under section 4 of the Child Nutrition Act of 1966 (42 U.S.C. 1773);

using funds allocated under section 28 of the Food and Nutrition Act of 2008 (7 U.S.C. 2036a) supplement, not supplant, individuals who are employed by local educational authorities as of the date of enactment of this Act.

(b) Sunset.—The authority for this section shall expire 30 days after the COVID–19 public health emergency is terminated.

DIVISION G—ACCOUNTABILITY AND GOVERNMENT OPERATIONS

TITLE I—ACCOUNTABILITY

SEC. 70101. MEMBERSHIP OF THE PANDEMIC RESPONSE ACCOUNTABILITY COMMITTEE.

Section 15010(c) of the CARES Act (Public Law 116–136) is amended—

(1) in paragraph (1), by striking "and (D)" and inserting "(D), and (E)"; and

(2) in paragraph (2)(E), by inserting "of the Council" after "Chairperson".

SEC. 70102. CONGRESSIONAL NOTIFICATION OF CHANGE IN STATUS OF INSPECTOR GENERAL.

(a) Change In Status Of Inspector General Of Offices.—Section 3(b) of the Inspector General Act of 1978 (5 U.S.C. App.) is amended—

(1) by inserting ", is placed on paid or unpaid non-duty status," after "is removed from office";

(2) by inserting ", change in status," after "any such removal"; and

(3) by inserting ", change in status," after "before the removal".

(b) Change In Status Of Inspector General Of Designated Federal Entities.—Section 8G(e)(2) of the Inspector General Act of 1978 (5 U.S.C. App.) is amended—

(1) by inserting ", is placed on paid or unpaid non-duty status," after "office";

(2) by inserting ", change in status," after "any such removal"; and

(3) by inserting ", change in status," after "before the removal".

(c) Effective Date.—The amendments made by this section shall take effect 30 days after the date of the enactment of this Act.

SEC. 70103. PRESIDENTIAL EXPLANATION OF FAILURE TO NOMINATE AN INSPECTOR GENERAL.

(a) In General.—Subchapter III of chapter 33 of title 5, United States Code, is amended by inserting after section 3349d the following new section:

"§ 3349e. Presidential explanation of failure to nominate an Inspector General

"If the President fails to make a formal nomination for a vacant Inspector General position that requires a formal nomination by the President to be filled within the period beginning on the date on which the vacancy occurred and ending on the day that is 210 days after that date, the President shall communicate, within 30 days after the end of such period, to Congress in writing—

"(1) the reasons why the President has not yet made a formal nomination; and

"(2) a target date for making a formal nomination.".

(b) Clerical Amendment.—The table of sections for chapter 33 of title 5, United States Code, is amended by inserting after the item relating to 3349d the following new item:

"3349e. Presidential explanation of failure to nominate an Inspector General.".

(c) Effective Date.—The amendment made by subsection (a) shall take effect on the date of the enactment of this Act and shall apply to any vacancy first occurring on or after that date.

SEC. 70104. INSPECTOR GENERAL INDEPENDENCE.

(a) Short Title.—This section may be cited as the "Inspector General Independence Act".

(b) Amendment.—The Inspector General Act of 1978 (5 U.S.C. App.) is amended—

(1) in section 3(b)—

(A) by striking "An Inspector General" and inserting "(1) An Inspector General";

(B) by inserting after "by the President" the following: "in accordance with paragraph (2)"; and

(C) by inserting at the end the following new paragraph:

"(2) The President may remove an Inspector General only for any of the following grounds:

"(A) Permanent incapacity.

"(B) Inefficiency.

"(C) Neglect of duty.

"(D) Malfeasance.

"(E) Conviction of a felony or conduct involving moral turpitude.

"(F) Knowing violation of a law, rule, or regulation.

"(G) Gross mismanagement.

"(H) Gross waste of funds.

"(I) Abuse of authority."; and

(2) in section 8G(e)(2), by adding at the end the following new sentence: "An Inspector General may be removed only for any of the following grounds:

"(A) Permanent incapacity.

"(B) Inefficiency.

"(C) Neglect of duty.

"(D) Malfeasance.

"(E) Conviction of a felony or conduct involving moral turpitude.

"(F) Knowing violation of a law, rule, or regulation.

"(G) Gross mismanagement.

"(H) Gross waste of funds.

"(I) Abuse of authority.".

SEC. 70105. USPS INSPECTOR GENERAL OVERSIGHT RESPONSIBILITIES.

The Inspector General of the United States Postal Service shall—

(1) conduct oversight, audits, and investigations of projects and activities carried out with funds provided in division A of this Act to the United States Postal Service; and

(2) not less than 90 days after the Postal Service commences use of funding provided by division A of this Act, and annually thereafter, initiate an audit of the Postal Service's use of appropriations and borrowing authority provided by any division of this Act, including the use of funds to cover lost revenues, costs due to COVID–19, and expenditures, and submit a copy of such audit to the Committee on Homeland Security and Governmental Affairs of the Senate, the Committee on Oversight and Reform of the House of Representatives, and the Committees on Appropriations of the House of Representatives and the Senate.

TITLE II

—CENSUS MATTERS

MODIFICATION OF 2020 CENSUS DEADLINES AND TABULATION OF POPULATION

SEC. 70201.

(a) Deadline Modification.—Notwithstanding the timetables provided in sections 141(b) and (c) of title 13, United States Code, and section 22(a) of the Act entitled "An Act to provide for the fifteenth and subsequent decennial censuses and to provide for an apportionment of Representatives in Congress", approved June 18, 1929 (2 U.S.C. 2a(a)), for the 2020 decennial census of the population—

(1) the tabulation of total population by States required by section 141(a) of such title for the apportionment of Representatives in Congress among the several States shall be completed and reported by the Secretary to the President within 13 months after the decennial census date of April 1, 2020, and shall be made public by the Secretary no later than the date on which it is reported to the President;

(2) the President shall transmit to the Congress a statement showing the whole number of persons in each State, and the number of Representatives to which each State would be entitled under an apportionment of the then existing number of Representatives, as required by such section 22(a), and determined solely as described therein, within 14 days after receipt of the tabulation reported by the Secretary; and

(3) the tabulations of populations required by section 141(c) of such title shall be completed by the Secretary as expeditiously as possible after the census date of April 1, 2020, taking into account each State's deadlines for legislative apportionment or districting, and reported to the Governor of the State involved and to the officers or public bodies having responsibility for legislative apportionment or districting of such State, except that such tabulations of population of each State requesting a tabulation plan, and basic tabulations of population of each other State, shall be completed, reported, and transmitted to each respective State within 16 months after the decennial census date of April 1, 2020.

(b) Quality.—Data products and tabulations produced by the Bureau of the Census pursuant to sections 141(b) or (c) of title 13, United States Code, in connection with the 2020 decennial census shall meet the same or higher data quality standards as similar products produced by the Bureau of the Census in connection with the 2010 decennial census.

REPORTING REQUIREMENTS FOR 2020 CENSUS

SEC. 70202.

On the first day of each month during the period between the date of enactment of this Act and July 1, 2021, the Director of the Bureau of the Census shall submit, to the Committee on Oversight and Reform of the House of Representatives, the Committee on Homeland Security and Governmental Affairs of the Senate, and the Committees on Appropriations of the House and the Senate, a report regarding the 2020 decennial census of population containing the following information:

(1) The total number of field staff, sorted by category, hired by the Bureau compared to the number of field staff the Bureau estimated was necessary to carry out such census.

(2) Retention rates of such hired field staff.

(3) Average wait time for call center calls and average wait time for each language provided.

(4) Anticipated schedule of such census operations.

(5) Total tabulated responses, categorized by race and Hispanic origin.

(6) Total appropriations available for obligation for such census and a categorized list of total disbursements.

(7) Non-Response Follow-Up completion rates by geographic location.

(8) Update/Enumerate and Update/Leave completion rates by geographic location.

(9) Total spending to date on media, advertisements, and partnership specialists, including a geographic breakdown of such spending.

(10) Post-enumeration schedule and subsequent data aggregation and delivery progress.

PROVIDING BUREAU OF THE CENSUS ACCESS TO INFORMATION FROM INSTITUTIONS OF HIGHER EDUCATION

SEC. 70203.

(a) In General.—Notwithstanding any other provision of law, including section 444 of the General Education Provisions Act (commonly known as the "Family Educational Rights and Privacy Act of 1974"), an institution of higher education may, in furtherance of a full and accurate decennial census of population count, provide to the Bureau of the Census information requested by the Bureau for purposes of enumeration for the 2020 decennial census of population.

(b) Application.—

(1) INFORMATION.—Only information requested on the official 2020 decennial census of population form may be provided to the Bureau of the Census pursuant to this section. No institution of higher education may provide any information to the Bureau on the immigration or citizenship status of any individual.

(2) NOTICE REQUIRED.—Before information can be provided to the Bureau, the institution of higher education shall give public notice of the categories of information which it plans to provide and shall allow 10 days after such notice has been given for a student to inform the institution that any or all of the information designated should not be released without the student's prior consent. No institution of higher education shall provide the Bureau with the information of any individual who has objected to the provision of such information.

(3) USE OF INFORMATION.—Information provided to the Bureau pursuant to this section may only be used for the purposes of enumeration for the 2020 decennial

census of population.

(c) Definition Of Institution Of Higher Education.—In this section, the term "institution of higher education" has the meaning given that term in section 102 of the Higher Education Act of 1965 (20 U.S.C. 1002).

(d) Sunset.—The authority provided in this section shall expire at the conclusion of 2020 census operations.

LIMITATION ON TABULATION OF CERTAIN DATA

SEC. 70204.

(a) Limitation.—The Bureau of the Census may not compile or produce any data product or tabulation as part of, in combination with, or in connection with, the 2020 decennial census of population or any such census data produced pursuant to section 141(c) of title 13, United States Code, that is based in whole or in part on data that is not collected in such census.

(b) Exception.—The limitation in subsection (a) shall not apply to any data product or tabulation that is required by sections 141(b) or (c) of such title, that uses the same or substantially similar methodology and data sources as a decennial census data product produced by the Bureau of the Census before January 1, 2019, or that uses a methodology and data sources that the Bureau of the Census finalized and made public prior to January 1, 2018.

TITLE III

—FEDERAL WORKFORCE

COVID-19 TELEWORKING REQUIREMENTS FOR FEDERAL EMPLOYEES

SEC. 70301.

(a) Mandated Telework.—

(1) IN GENERAL.—Effective immediately upon the date of enactment of this Act, the head of any Federal agency shall require any employee of such agency who is authorized to telework under chapter 65 of title 5, United States Code, or any other provision of law to telework during the period beginning on the date of enactment of this Act and ending on December 31, 2020.

(2) DEFINITIONS.—In this subsection—

(A) the term "employee" means—

(i) an employee of the Library of Congress;

(ii) an employee of the Government Accountability Office;

(iii) a covered employee as defined in section 101 of the Congressional Accountability Act of 1995 (2 U.S.C. 1301), other than an applicant for employment;

(iv) a covered employee as defined in section 411(c) of title 3, United States Code;

(v) a Federal officer or employee covered under subchapter V of chapter 63 of title 5, United States Code; or

(vi) any other individual occupying a position in the civil service (as that term is defined in section 2101(1) of title 5, United States Code); and

(B) the term "telework" has the meaning given that term in section 6501(3) of such title.

(b) Telework Participation Goals.—Chapter 65 of title 5, United States Code, is amended as follows:

(1) In section 6502—

(A) in subsection (b)—

(i) in paragraph (4), by striking "and" at the end;

(ii) in paragraph (5), by striking the period at the end and inserting a semicolon; and

(iii) by adding at the end the following:

"(6) include annual goals for increasing the percent of employees of the executive agency participating in teleworking—

"(A) three or more days per pay period;

"(B) one or 2 days per pay period;

"(C) once per month; and

"(D) on an occasional, episodic, or short-term basis; and

"(7) include methods for collecting data on, setting goals for, and reporting costs savings to the executive agency achieved through teleworking, consistent with the guidance developed under section 70302 (c) of the HEROES Act."; and

(B) by adding at the end the following:

"(d) Notification For Reduction In Teleworking Participation.—Not later than 30 days before the date that an executive agency implements or modifies a teleworking plan that would reduce the percentage of employees at the agency who telework, the head of the executive agency shall provide written notification, including a justification for the reduction in telework participation and a description of how the agency will pay for any increased costs resulting from that reduction, to—

"(1) the Director of the Office of Personnel Management;

"(2) the Committee on Oversight and Reform of the House of Representatives; and

"(3) the Committee on Homeland Security and Governmental Affairs of the Senate.

"(e) Prohibition On Agency-Wide Limits On Teleworking.—An agency may not prohibit any delineated period of teleworking participation for all employees of the agency, including the periods described in subparagraphs (A) through (D) of subsection (b)(6). The agency shall make any teleworking determination with respect to an employee or group of employees at the agency on a case-by-case basis.".

(2) In section 6506(b)(2)—

(A) in subparagraph (F)(vi), by striking "and" at the end;

(B) in subparagraph (G), by striking the period at the end and inserting a semicolon; and

(C) by adding at the end the following:

"(H) agency cost savings achieved through teleworking, consistent with the guidance developed under section 2(c) of the Telework Metrics and Cost Savings Act; and

"(I) a detailed explanation of a plan to increase the Government-wide teleworking participation rate above such rate applicable to fiscal year 2016, including agency-level plans to maintain or imparove such rate for each of the teleworking frequency categories listed under subparagraph (A)(iii).".

(c) Guidance.—Not later than 90 days after the date of the enactment of this Act, the Director of the Office of Personnel Management, in collaboration with the Chief Human Capital Officer Council, shall establish uniform guidance for agencies on how to collect data on, set goals for, and report cost savings achieved through, teleworking. Such guidance shall account for cost savings related to travel, energy use, and real estate.

(d) Technical Correction.—Section 6506(b)(1) of title 5, United States Code, is amended by striking "with Chief" and inserting "with the Chief".

RETIREMENT FOR CERTAIN EMPLOYEES

SEC. 70302.

(a) CSRS.—Section 8336(c) of title 5, United States Code, is amended by adding at the end the following:

"(3) (A) In this paragraph—

"(i) the term 'affected individual' means an individual covered under this subchapter who—

"(I) is performing service in a covered position;

"(II) is diagnosed with COVID–19 before the date on which the individual becomes entitled to an annuity under paragraph (1) of this subsection or subsection (e), (m), or (n), as applicable;

"(III) because of the illness described in subclause (II), is permanently unable to render useful and efficient service in the employee's covered position, as determined by the agency in which the individual was serving when such individual incurred the illness; and

"(IV) is appointed to a position in the civil service that—

"(aa) is not a covered position; and

"(bb) is within an agency that regularly appoints individuals to supervisory or administrative positions related to the activities of the former covered position of the individual;

"(ii) the term 'covered position' means a position as a law enforcement officer, customs and border protection officer, firefighter, air traffic controller, nuclear materials courier, member of the Capitol Police, or member of the Supreme Court Police; and

"(iii) the term 'COVID–19' means the 2019 Novel Coronavirus or 2019-nCoV.

"(B) Unless an affected individual files an election described in subparagraph (E), creditable service by the affected individual in a position described in subparagraph (A)(i)(IV) shall be treated as creditable service in a covered position for purposes of this chapter and determining the amount to be deducted and withheld from the pay of the affected individual under section 8334.

"(C) Subparagraph (B) shall only apply if the affected employee transitions to a position described in subparagraph (A)(i)(IV) without a break in service exceeding 3 days.

"(D) The service of an affected individual shall no longer be eligible for treatment under subparagraph (B) if such service occurs after the individual—

"(i) is transferred to a supervisory or administrative position related to the activities of the former covered position of the individual; or

"(ii) meets the age and service requirements that would subject the individual to mandatory separation under section 8335 if such individual had remained in the former covered position.

"(E) In accordance with procedures established by the Director of the Office of Personnel Management, an affected individual may file an election to have any creditable service performed by the affected individual treated in accordance with this chapter without regard to subparagraph (B).

"(F) Nothing in this paragraph shall be construed to apply to such affected individual any other pay-related laws or regulations applicable to a covered position.".

(b) FERS.—

(1) IN GENERAL.—Section 8412(d) of title 5, United States Code, is amended—

(A) by redesignating paragraphs (1) and (2) as subparagraphs (A) and (B), respectively;

(B) by inserting "(1)" before "An employee"; and

(C) by adding at the end the following:

"(2) (A) In this paragraph—

"(i) the term 'affected individual' means an individual covered under this chapter who—

"(I) is performing service in a covered position;

"(II) is diagnosed with COVID–19 before the date on which the individual becomes entitled to an annuity under paragraph (1) of this subsection or subsection (e), as applicable;

"(III) because of the illness described in subclause (II), is permanently unable to render useful and efficient service in the employee's covered position, as determined by the agency in which the individual was serving when such individual incurred the illness; and

"(IV) is appointed to a position in the civil service that—

"(aa) is not a covered position; and

"(bb) is within an agency that regularly appoints individuals to supervisory or administrative positions related to the activities of the former covered position of the individual;

"(ii) the term 'covered position' means a position as a law enforcement officer, customs and border protection officer, firefighter, air traffic controller, nuclear materials courier, member of the Capitol Police, or member of the Supreme Court Police; and

"(iii) the term 'COVID–19' means the 2019 Novel Coronavirus or 2019-nCoV.

"(B) Unless an affected individual files an election described in subparagraph (E), creditable service by the affected individual in a position described in subparagraph (A)(i)(IV) shall be treated as creditable service in a covered position for purposes of this chapter and determining the amount to be deducted and withheld from the pay of the affected individual under section 8422.

"(C) Subparagraph (B) shall only apply if the affected employee transitions to a position described in subparagraph (A)(i)(IV) without a break in service exceeding 3 days.

"(D) The service of an affected individual shall no longer be eligible for treatment under subparagraph (B) if such service occurs after the individual—

"(i) is transferred to a supervisory or administrative position related to the activities of the former covered position of the individual; or

"(ii) meets the age and service requirements that would subject the individual to mandatory separation under section 8425 if such individual had remained in the former covered position.

"(E) In accordance with procedures established by the Director of the Office of Personnel Management, an affected individual may file an election to have any creditable service performed by the affected individual treated in accordance with this chapter without regard to subparagraph (B).

"(F) Nothing in this paragraph shall be construed to apply to such affected individual any other pay-related laws or regulations applicable to a covered position.".

(2) TECHNICAL AND CONFORMING AMENDMENTS.—

(A) Chapter 84 of title 5, United States Code, is amended—

(i) in section 8414(b)(3), by inserting "(1)" after "subsection (d)";

(ii) in section 8415—

(I) in subsection (e), in the matter preceding paragraph (1), by inserting "(1)" after "subsection (d)"; and

(II) in subsection (h)(2)(A), by striking "(d)(2)" and inserting "(d)(1)(B)";

(iii) in section 8421(a)(1), by inserting "(1)" after "(d)";

(iv) in section 8421a(b)(4)(B)(ii), by inserting "(1)" after "section 8412(d)";

(v) in section 8425, by inserting "(1)" after "section 8412(d)" each place it appears; and

(vi) in section 8462(c)(3)(B)(ii), by inserting "(1)" after "subsection (d)".

(B) Title VIII of the Foreign Service Act of 1980 (22 U.S.C. 4041 et seq.) is amended—

(i) in section 805(d)(5) (22 U.S.C. 4045(d)(5)), by inserting "(1)" after "or 8412(d)"; and

(ii) in section 812(a)(2)(B) (22 U.S.C. 4052(a)(2)(B)), by inserting "(1)" after "or 8412(d)".

(c) CIA Employees.—Section 302 of the Central Intelligence Agency Retirement Act (50 U.S.C. 2152) is amended by adding at the end the following:

"(d) Employees Disabled On Duty.—

"(1) DEFINITIONS.—In this subsection—

"(A) the term 'affected employee' means an employee of the Agency covered under subchapter II of chapter 84 of title 5, United States Code, who—

"(i) is performing service in a position designated under subsection (a);

"(ii) is diagnosed with COVID–19 before the date on which the employee becomes entitled to an annuity under section 233 of this Act or section 8412(d)(1) of title 5, United States Code;

"(iii) because of the illness described in clause (ii), is permanently unable to render useful and efficient service in the employee's covered position, as determined by the Director; and

"(iv) is appointed to a position in the civil service that is not a covered position but is within the Agency;

"(B) the term 'covered position' means a position as—

"(i) a law enforcement officer described in section 8331(20) or 8401(17) of title 5, United States Code;

"(ii) a customs and border protection officer described in section 8331(31) or 8401(36) of title 5, United States Code;

"(iii) a firefighter described in section 8331(21) or 8401(14) of title 5, United States Code;

"(iv) an air traffic controller described in section 8331(30) or 8401(35) of title 5, United States Code;

"(v) a nuclear materials courier described in section 8331(27) or 8401(33) of title 5, United States Code;

"(vi) a member of the United States Capitol Police;

"(vii) a member of the Supreme Court Police;

"(viii) an affected employee; or

"(ix) a special agent described in section 804(15) of the Foreign Service Act of 1980 (22 U.S.C. 4044(15)); and

"(C) the term 'COVID–19' means the 2019 Novel Coronavirus or 2019-nCoV.

"(2) TREATMENT OF SERVICE AFTER DISABILITY.—Unless an affected employee files an election described in paragraph (3), creditable service by the affected employee in a position described in paragraph (1)(A)(iv) shall be treated as creditable service in a covered position for purposes of this Act and chapter 84 of title 5, United States Code, including eligibility for an annuity under section 233 of this Act or 8412(d)(1) of title 5, United States Code, and determining the amount to be deducted and withheld from the pay of the affected employee under section 8422 of title 5, United States Code.

"(3) BREAK IN SERVICE.—Paragraph (2) shall only apply if the affected employee transitions to a position described in paragraph (1)(A)(iv) without a break in service exceeding 3 days.

"(4) LIMITATION ON TREATMENT OF SERVICE.—The service of an affected employee shall no longer be eligible for treatment under paragraph (2) if such service occurs after the employee is transferred to a supervisory or administrative position related to the activities of the former covered position of the employee.

"(5) OPT OUT.—An affected employee may file an election to have any creditable service performed by the affected employee treated in accordance with chapter 84 of title 5, United States Code, without regard to paragraph (2).".

(d) Foreign Service Retirement And Disability System.—Section 806(a)(6) of the Foreign Service Act of 1980 (22 U.S.C. 4046(a)(6)) is amended by adding at the end the following:

"(D) (i) In this subparagraph—

"(I) the term 'affected special agent' means an individual covered under this subchapter who—

"(aa) is performing service as a special agent;

"(bb) is diagnosed with COVID–19 before the date on which the individual becomes entitled to an annuity under section 811;

"(cc) because of the illness described in item (bb), is permanently unable to render useful and efficient service in the employee's covered position, as determined by the Secretary; and

"(dd) is appointed to a position in the Foreign Service that is not a covered position;

"(II) the term 'covered position' means a position as—

"(aa) a law enforcement officer described in section 8331(20) or 8401(17) of title 5, United States Code;

"(bb) a customs and border protection officer described in section 8331(31) or 8401(36) of title 5, United States Code;

"(cc) a firefighter described in section 8331(21) or 8401(14) of title 5, United States Code;

"(dd) an air traffic controller described in section 8331(30) or 8401(35) of title 5, United States Code;

"(ee) a nuclear materials courier described in section 8331(27) or 8401(33) of title 5, United States Code;

"(ff) a member of the United States Capitol Police;

"(gg) a member of the Supreme Court Police;

"(hh) an employee of the Agency designated under section 302(a) of the Central Intelligence Agency Retirement Act (50 U.S.C. 2152(a)); or

"(ii) a special agent; and

"(III) the term 'COVID–19' means the 2019 Novel Coronavirus or 2019-nCoV.

"(ii) Unless an affected special agent files an election described in clause (iv), creditable service by the affected special agent in a position described in clause (i)(I)(dd) shall be treated as creditable service as a special agent for purposes of this subchapter, including determining the amount to be deducted and withheld from the pay of the individual under section 805.

"(iii) Clause (ii) shall only apply if the special agent transitions to a position described in clause (i)(I)(dd) without a break in service exceeding 3 days.

"(iv) The service of an affected employee shall no longer be eligible for treatment under clause (ii) if such service occurs after the employee is transferred to a supervisory or administrative position related to the activities of the former covered position of the employee.

"(v) In accordance with procedures established by the Secretary, an affected special agent may file an election to have any creditable service performed by the affected special agent treated in accordance with this subchapter, without regard to clause (ii).".

(e) Implementation.—

(1) OFFICE OF PERSONNEL MANAGEMENT.—The Director of the Office of Personnel Management shall promulgate regulations to carry out the amendments made by subsections (a) and (b).

(2) CIA EMPLOYEES.—The Director of the Central Intelligence Agency shall promulgate regulations to carry out the amendment made by subsection (c).

(3) FOREIGN SERVICE RETIREMENT AND DISABILITY SYSTEM.—The Secretary of State shall promulgate regulations to carry out the amendment made by subsection (d).

(4) AGENCY REAPPOINTMENT.—The regulations promulgated to carry out the amendments made by this section shall ensure that, to the greatest extent possible, the head of each agency appoints affected employees or special agents to supervisory or administrative positions related to the activities of the former covered position of the employee or special agent.

(5) TREATMENT OF SERVICE.—The regulations promulgated to carry out the amendments made by this section shall ensure that the creditable service of an affected employee or special agent (as the case may be) that is not in a covered position pursuant to an election made under such amendments shall be treated as the same type of service as the covered position in which the employee or agent suffered the qualifying illness.

(f) Effective Date; Applicability.—The amendments made by this section—

(1) shall take effect on the date of enactment of this section; and

(2) shall apply to an individual who suffers an illness described in section 8336(c)(3)(A)(i)(II) or section 8412(d)(2)(A)(i)(II) of title 5, United States Code (as amended by this section), section 302(d)(1)(A)(ii) of the Central Intelligence Agency Retirement Act (as amended by this section), or section 806(a)(6)(D)(i)(I)(bb) of the Foreign Service Act of 1980 (as amended by this section), on or after the date that is 2 years after the date of enactment of this section.

PRESUMPTION OF ELIGIBILITY FOR WORKERS' COMPENSATION BENEFITS FOR FEDERAL EMPLOYEES DIAGNOSED WITH CORONAVIRUS

SEC. 70303.

(a) In General.—An employee who is diagnosed with COVID-19 during the period described in subsection (b)(2)(A) shall, with respect to any claim made by or on behalf of the employee for benefits under subchapter I of chapter 81 of title 5, United States Code, be deemed to have an injury proximately caused by exposure to coronavirus arising out of the nature of the employee's employment and be presumptively entitled to such benefits, including disability compensation, medical services, and survivor benefits.

(b) Definitions.—In this section—

(1) the term "coronavirus" means SARS- CoV-2 or another coronavirus with pandemic potential; and

(2) the term "employee"—

(A) means an employee as that term is defined in section 8101(1) of title 5, United States Code, (including an employee of the United States Postal Service, the Transportation Security Administration, or the Department of Veterans Affairs, including any individual appointed under chapter 73 or 74 of title 38, United States Code) employed in the Federal service at anytime during the period beginning on January 27, 2020, and ending on January 30, 2022—

(i) who carried out duties requiring contact with patients, members of the public, or co-workers; or

(ii) whose duties include a risk of exposure to the coronavirus; and

(B) does not include any employee otherwise covered by subparagraph (A) who is teleworking on a full-time basis during all of such period.

TITLE IV

—FEDERAL CONTRACTING PROVISIONS
MANDATORY TELEWORK

SEC. 70401.

(a) In General.—During the emergency period, the Director of the Office of Management and Budget shall direct agencies to allow telework for all contractor personnel to the maximum extent practicable. Additionally, the Director shall direct contracting officers to document any decision to not allow telework during the emergency period in the contract file.

(b) Emergency Period Defined.—In this section, the term "emergency period" means the period that—

(1) begins on the date that is not later than 15 days after the date of the enactment of this Act; and

(2) ends on the date that the public health emergency declared pursuant to section 319 of the Public Health Service Act (42 U.S.C. 247d) as result of COVID–19, including any renewal thereof, expires.

GUIDANCE ON THE IMPLEMENTATION OF SECTION 3610 OF THE CARES ACT

SEC. 70402.

Not later than 15 days after the date of the enactment of this Act, the Director of the Office of Management and Budget shall issue guidance to ensure uniform implementation across agencies of section 3610 of the CARES Act (Public Law 116–136). Any such guidance shall—

(1) limit the basic requirements for reimbursement to those included in such Act and the effective date for such reimbursement shall be January 31, 2020; and

(2) clarify that the term "minimum applicable contract billing rates" as used in such section includes the financial impact incurred as a consequence of keeping the employees or subcontractors of the contractor in a ready state (such as the base hourly wage rate of an employee, plus indirect costs, fees, and general and administrative expenses).

PAST PERFORMANCE RATINGS

SEC. 70403.

Section 1126 of title 41, United States Code, is amended by adding at the end the following new subsection:

"(c) Exception For Failure To Deliver Goods Or Complete Work Due To Covid–19.—
If the head of an executive agency determines that a contractor failed to deliver goods
or complete work as a result of measures taken as a result of COVID–19 under a contract with the agency by the date or within the time period imposed by the contract,
any information relating to such failure may not be—
"(1) included in any past performance database used by executive agencies for making
source selection decisions; or
"(2) evaluated unfavorably as a factor of past contract performance.".
ACCELERATED PAYMENTS

SEC. 70404.
Not later than 10 days after the date of the enactment of this Act and ending on the
expiration of the public health emergency declared pursuant to section 319 of the
Public Health Service Act (42 U.S.C. 247d) as a result of COVID–19, including any
renewal thereof, the Director of the Office of Management and Budget shall direct
contracting officers to establish an accelerated payment date for any prime contract
(as defined in section 8701 of title 41, United States Code) with payments due 15 days
after the receipt of a proper invoice.

TITLE V

—DISTRICT OF COLUMBIA
SPECIAL BORROWING BY THE DISTRICT OF COLUMBIA

SEC. 70501.
(a) Authorizing Borrowing Under Municipal Liquidity Facility Of Federal Reserve
Board And Similar Facilities Or Programs.—The Council of the District of Columbia (hereafter in this section referred to as the "Council") may by act authorize the
issuance of bonds, notes, and other obligations, in amounts determined by the Chief
Financial Officer of the District of Columbia to meet cash-flow needs of the District of
Columbia government, for purchase by the Board of Governors of the Federal Reserve
under the Municipal Liquidity Facility of the Federal Reserve or any other facility or
program of the Federal Reserve or another entity of the Federal government which
is established in response to the COVID–19 Pandemic.
(b) Requiring Issuance To Be Competitive With Other Forms Of Borrowing.—The
Council may authorize the issuance of bonds, notes, or other obligations under
subsection (a) only if the issuance of such bonds, notes, and other obligations is
competitive with other forms of borrowing in the financial market.
(c) Treatment As General Obligation.—Any bond, note, or other obligation issued
under subsection (a) shall, if provided in the act of the Council, be a general obligation of the District.
(d) Payments Not Subject To Appropriation.—No appropriation is required to pay—
(1) any amount (including the amount of any accrued interest or premium) obligated
or expended from or pursuant to subsection (a) for or from the sale of any bonds,
notes, or other obligation under such subsection;
(2) any amount obligated or expended for the payment of principal of, interest on, or
any premium for any bonds, notes, or other obligations issued under subsection (a);
(3) any amount obligated or expended pursuant to provisions made to secure any
bonds, notes, or other obligations issued under subsection (a); or
(4) any amount obligated or expended pursuant to commitments, including lines

of credit or costs of issuance, made or entered in connection with the issuance of any bonds, notes, or other obligations for operating or capital costs financed under subsection (a).

(e) Renewal.—Any bond, note, or other obligation issued under subsection (a) may be renewed if authorized by an act of the Council.

(f) Payment.—Any bonds, notes, or other obligations issued under subsection (a), including any renewal of such bonds, notes, or other obligations, shall be due and payable on such terms and conditions as are consistent with the terms and conditions of the Municipal Liquidity Facility or other facility or program referred to in subsection (a).

(g) Inclusion Of Payments In Annual Budget.—The Council shall provide in each annual budget for the District of Columbia government sufficient funds to pay the principal of and interest on all bonds, notes, or other obligations issued under subsection (a) of this section becoming due and payable during such fiscal year.

(h) Obligation To Pay.—The Mayor of the District of Columbia shall ensure that the principal of and interest on all bonds, notes, or other obligations issued under subsection (a) are paid when due, including by paying such principal and interest from funds not otherwise legally committed.

(i) Security Interest In District Revenues.—The Council may by act provide for a security interest in any District of Columbia revenues as additional security for the payment of any bond, note, or other obligation issued under subsection (a).

TITLE VI

—OTHER MATTERS

ESTIMATES OF AGGREGATE ECONOMIC GROWTH ACROSS INCOME GROUPS

SEC. 70601.

(a) Short Title.—This section may be cited as the "Measuring Real Income Growth Act of 2020".

(b) Definitions.—In this section:

(1) BUREAU.—The term "Bureau" means the Bureau of Economic Analysis of the Department of Commerce.

(2) GROSS DOMESTIC PRODUCT ANALYSIS.—The term "gross domestic product analysis"—

(A) means a quarterly or annual analysis conducted by the Bureau with respect to the gross domestic product of the United States; and

(B) includes a revision prepared by the Bureau of an analysis described in subparagraph (A).

(3) RECENT ESTIMATE.—The term "recent estimate" means the most recent estimate described in subsection (c) that is available on the date on which the gross domestic product analysis with which the estimate is to be included is conducted.

(c) Inclusion In Reports.—Beginning in 2020, in each gross domestic product analysis conducted by the Bureau, the Bureau shall include a recent estimate of, with respect to specific percentile groups of income, the total amount that was added to the economy of the United States during the period to which the recent estimate pertains, including in—

(1) each of the 10 deciles of income; and

(2) the highest 1 percent of income.

(d) Authorization Of Appropriations.—There are authorized to be appropriated to the Secretary of Commerce such sums as are necessary to carry out this section.

WAIVER OF MATCHING FUNDS REQUIREMENT FOR THE DRUG FREE COMMUNITIES SUPPORT PROGRAM

SEC. 70602.

The matching funds requirement under paragraphs (1)(A)(i), (1)(A)(iii), and (3)(D) of section 1032(b) of the Anti-Drug Abuse Act of 1988 (21 U.S.C. 1532(b)) may be modified or waived by the Administrator if a grantee or applicant is unable to meet the requirement as a result of the public health emergency declared pursuant to section 319 of the Public Health Service Act (42 U.S.C. 247d) as a result of COVID–19.

UNITED STATES POSTAL SERVICE BORROWING AUTHORITY

SEC. 70603.

Subsection (b)(2) of section 6001 of the Coronavirus Aid, Relief, and Economic Security Act (Public Law 116–136) is amended to read as follows:

"(2) the Secretary of the Treasury shall lend up to the amount described in paragraph (1) at the request of the Postal Service subject to the terms and conditions of the note purchase agreement between the Postal Service and the Federal Financing Bank in effect on September 29, 2018.".

DIVISION H—VETERANS AND SERVICEMEMBERS PROVISIONS

SEC. 80001. MODIFICATION OF PAY LIMITATION FOR CERTAIN HIGH-LEVEL EMPLOYEES AND OFFICERS OF THE DEPARTMENT OF VETERANS AFFAIRS.

(a) Modification.—Section 7404(d) of title 38, United States Code, is amended by inserting "and except for individuals appointed under 7401(4) and 7306 of this title," after "section 7457 of this title,".

(b) Waivers.—

(1) IN GENERAL.—The Secretary of Veterans Affairs may waive the limitation described in section 7404(d) of such title, as in effect on the day before the date of the enactment of this Act, on the amount of basic pay payable to individuals appointed under section 7401(4) or 7306 of such title for basic pay payable during the period—

(A) beginning on November 1, 2010; and

(B) ending on the day before the date of the enactment of this Act.

(2) FORM.—The Secretary shall prescribe the form for requesting a waiver under paragraph (1).

(3) TREATMENT OF WAIVER.—A decision not to grant a waiver under paragraph (1) shall not be treated as an adverse action and is not subject to further appeal, third-party review, or judicial review.

SEC. 80002. INCREASE OF AMOUNT OF CERTAIN DEPARTMENT OF VETERANS AFFAIRS PAYMENTS DURING EMERGENCY PERIOD RESULTING FROM COVID–19 PANDEMIC.

(a) In General.—During the covered period, the Secretary of Veterans Affairs shall apply each of the following provisions of title 38, United States Code, by substituting for each of the dollar amounts in such provision the amount equal to 125 percent of the dollar amount that was in effect under such provision on the date of the enactment of this Act:

(1) Subsections (l), (m), (r), and (t) of section 1114.
(2) Paragraph (1)(E) of section 1115.
(3) Subsection (c) of section 1311.
(4) Subsection (g) of section 1315.
(5) Paragraphs (1) and (2) of subsection (d) of section 1521.
(6) Paragraphs (2) and (4) of subsection (f) of section 1521.
(b) Treatment Of Amounts.—Any amount payable to an individual under subsection (a) in excess of the amount otherwise in effect shall be in addition to any other benefit or any other amount payable to that individual under any provision of law referred to in subsection (a) or any other provision of law administered by the Secretary of Veterans Affairs.
(c) Covered Period.—In this section, the covered period is the period that begins on the date of the enactment of this Act and ends 60 days after the last day of the emergency period (as defined in section 1135(g)(1) of the Social Security Act (42 U.S.C. 1320b-5(g)(1))) resulting from the COVID-19 pandemic.

SEC. 80003. PROHIBITION ON COPAYMENTS AND COST SHARING FOR VETERANS RECEIVING PREVENTIVE SERVICES RELATING TO COVID-19.

(a) Prohibition.—The Secretary of Veterans Affairs may not require any copayment or other cost sharing under chapter 17 of title 38, United States Code, for qualifying coronavirus preventive services. The requirement described in this subsection shall take effect with respect to a qualifying coronavirus preventive service on the specified date.
(b) Definitions.—In this section, the terms "qualifying coronavirus preventive service" and "specified date" have the meaning given those terms in section 3203 of the CARES Act (Public Law 116-136).

SEC. 80004. MODIFICATION OF CALCULATION OF AMOUNTS OF PER DIEM GRANTS.

Section 2012(a)(2)(B) of title 38, United States Code, is amended—
(1) in clause (i), by inserting "or (iii)" after "clause (ii)"; and
(2) by adding at the end the following new clause:
"(iii) With respect to a homeless veteran who has care of a minor dependent while receiving services from the grant recipient or eligible entity, the daily cost of care shall be the sum of the daily cost of care determined under subparagraph (A) plus, for each such minor dependent, an amount that equals 50 percent of such daily cost of care.".

SEC. 80005. EMERGENCY TREATMENT FOR VETERANS DURING COVID-19 EMERGENCY PERIOD.

(a) Emergency Treatment.—Notwithstanding section 1725 or 1728 of title 38, United States Code, or any other provision of law administered by the Secretary of Veterans Affairs pertaining to furnishing emergency treatment to veterans at non-Department facilities, during the period of a covered public health emergency, the Secretary of Veterans Affairs shall furnish to an eligible veteran emergency treatment at a non-Department facility in accordance with this section.
(b) Authorization Not Required.—The Secretary may not require an eligible veteran to seek authorization by the Secretary for emergency treatment furnished to the

veteran pursuant to subsection (a).

(c) Payment Rates.—

(1) DETERMINATION.—The rate paid for emergency treatment furnished to eligible veterans pursuant to subsection (a) shall be equal to the rate paid by the United States to a provider of services (as defined in section 1861(u) of the Social Security Act (42 U.S.C. 1395x(u))) or a supplier (as defined in section 1861(d) of such Act (42 U.S.C. 1395x(d))) under the Medicare program under title XI or title XVIII of the Social Security Act (42 U.S.C. 1301 et seq.), including section 1834 of such Act (42 U.S.C. 1395m), for the same treatment.

(2) FINALITY.—A payment in the amount payable under paragraph (1) for emergency treatment furnished to an eligible veteran pursuant to subsection (a) shall be considered payment in full and shall extinguish the veteran's liability to the provider of such treatment, unless the provider rejects the payment and refunds to the United States such amount by not later than 30 days after receiving the payment.

(d) Claims Processed By Third Party Administrators.—

(1) REQUIREMENT.—Not later than 30 days after the date of the enactment of this Act, the Secretary shall seek to award a contract to one or more entities, or to modify an existing contract, to process claims for payment for emergency treatment furnished to eligible veterans pursuant to subsection (a).

(2) PROMPT PAYMENT STANDARD.—Section 1703D of title 38, United States Code, shall apply with respect to claims for payment for emergency treatment furnished to eligible veterans pursuant to subsection (a).

(e) Primary Payer.—The Secretary shall be the primary payer with respect to emergency treatment furnished to eligible veterans pursuant to subsection (a), and with respect to the transportation of a veteran by ambulance. In any case in which an eligible veteran is furnished such emergency treatment for a non-service-connected disability described in subsection (a)(2) of section 1729 of title 38, United States Code, the Secretary shall recover or collect reasonable charges for such treatment from a health plan contract described in such section 1729 in accordance with such section.

(f) Application.—This section shall apply to emergency treatment furnished to eligible veterans during the period of a covered public health emergency, regardless of whether treatment was furnished before the date of the enactment of this Act.

(g) Definitions.—In this section:

(1) The term "covered public health emergency" means the declaration—

(A) of a public health emergency, based on an outbreak of COVID–19 by the Secretary of Health and Human Services under section 319 of the Public Health Service Act (42 U.S.C. 247d); or

(B) of a domestic emergency, based on an outbreak of COVID–19 by the President, the Secretary of Homeland Security, or a State or local authority.

(2) The term "eligible veteran" means a veteran enrolled in the health care system established under section 1705 of title 38, United States Code.

(3) The term "emergency treatment" means medical care or services rendered in a medical emergency of such nature that a prudent layperson reasonably expects that delay in seeking immediate medical attention would be hazardous to life or health.

(4) The term "non-Department facility" has the meaning given that term in section 1701 of title 38, United States Code.

SEC. 80006. FLEXIBILITY FOR THE SECRETARY OF VETERANS AFFAIRS IN CARING FOR HOMELESS VETERANS DURING A COVERED PUBLIC

HEALTH EMERGENCY.

(a) General Support.—

(1) USE OF FUNDS.—During a covered public health emergency, the Secretary of Veterans Affairs may use amounts appropriated or otherwise made available to the Department of Veterans Affairs to carry out sections 2011, 2012, and 2061 of title 38, United States Code, to provide to homeless veterans the following:

(A) Food.

(B) Shelter.

(C) Basic supplies (such as clothing, blankets, and toiletry items).

(D) Transportation.

(E) Communications equipment and required capabilities (such as smartphones, disposable phones, and phone service plans).

(F) Such other assistance as the Secretary determines appropriate.

(2) HOMELESS VETERANS ON LAND OF THE DEPARTMENT.—

(A) USE OF REVOLVING FUND.—During a covered public health emergency, the Secretary may use amounts in the revolving fund under section 8109(h) of title 38, United States Code, to alter parking facilities of the Department to facilitate the use of such facilities as temporary shelter locations for homeless veterans.

(B) PARTNERSHIPS.—During a covered public health emergency, the Secretary may partner with one or more organizations to manage land of the Department used by homeless veterans for sleeping.

(C) EQUIPMENT.—During a covered public health emergency, the Secretary shall not be responsible for furnishing outdoor equipment necessary for sleeping on land of the Department.

(b) Grant And Per Diem Program.—

(1) MAXIMUM PER DIEM RATE.—Notwithstanding paragraph (2) of section 2012(a) of title 38, United States Code, during a covered public health emergency, the maximum rate of per diem authorized under such section is 300 percent of the rate authorized for State homes for domiciliary care under subsection (a)(1)(A) of section 1741 of such title, as the Secretary may increase from time to time under subsection (c) of that section.

(2) USE OF PER DIEM PAYMENTS.—During a covered public health emergency, a recipient of a grant or an eligible entity under the grant and per diem program of the Department (in this subsection referred to as the "program") may use per diem payments under sections 2012 and 2061 of title 38, United States Code, to provide food and basic supplies for—

(A) homeless veterans in the program; and

(B) formerly homeless veterans in the community who experienced homelessness during the one-year period ending on the date of the enactment of this Act.

(3) ADDITIONAL TRANSITIONAL HOUSING.—

(A) IN GENERAL.—During a covered public health emergency, the Secretary may provide amounts for grants and per diem payments under the program for additional transitional housing beds to facilitate access to housing and services provided to homeless veterans.

(B) NOTICE; COMPETITION; PERIOD OF PERFORMANCE.—The Secretary may provide amounts under subparagraph (A)—

(i) without notice or competition; and

(ii) for a period of performance determined by the Secretary.

(4) INSPECTIONS AND LIFE SAFETY CODE REQUIREMENTS.—
(A) IN GENERAL.—During a covered public health emergency, the Secretary may waive any requirement under subsection (b) or (c) of section 2012 of title 38, United States Code, in order to allow the recipient of a grant or an eligible entity under the program—
(i) to quickly identify temporary alternate sites of care for homeless veterans that are suitable for habitation;
(ii) to facilitate social distancing or isolation needs; or
(iii) to facilitate activation or continuation of a program for which a grant has been awarded.
(B) LIMITATION.—The Secretary may waive a requirement pursuant to the authority provided by subparagraph (A) with respect to a facility of a recipient of a grant or an eligible entity under the program only if the facility meets applicable local safety requirements, including fire safety requirements.
(c) Health Care For Homeless Veterans.—
(1) COMMUNITY-BASED TREATMENT FACILITIES.—During a covered public health emergency, the Secretary may use amounts as authorized under subsection (a)(1) notwithstanding any requirement under subsection (a)(2) of section 2031 of title 38, United States Code, that community-based treatment facilities provide care, treatment, and rehabilitative services to veterans described in such section.
(2) REPORT TO CONGRESS ON REDUCTION OF CARE, TREATMENT, AND REHABILITATIVE SERVICES.—During a covered public health emergency, if the Secretary reduces the care, treatment, and rehabilitative services provided to homeless veterans under section 2031(a)(2) of title 38, United States Code, the Secretary shall submit to Congress monthly reports on the reduction of such care, treatment, and services for the duration of the covered public health emergency.
(3) INSPECTION AND LIFE SAFETY CODE REQUIREMENTS.—
(A) IN GENERAL.—During a covered public health emergency, the Secretary may waive any inspection or life safety code requirement under subsection (c) of section 2032 of title 38, United States Code—
(i) to allow quick identification of temporary alternate sites of care for homeless veterans that are suitable for habitation;
(ii) to facilitate social distancing or isolation needs; or
(iii) to facilitate the operation of housing under such section.
(B) LIMITATION.—The Secretary may waive a requirement pursuant to the authority provided by subparagraph (A) with respect to a residence or facility referred to in such section 2032 only if the residence or facility, as the case may be, meets applicable local safety requirements, including fire safety requirements.
(d) Access Of Homeless Veterans To Department Of Veterans Affairs Telehealth Services.—During a covered public health emergency, the Secretary may make available telehealth capabilities to homeless veterans who—
(1) are receiving services provided under chapter 20 of title 38, United States Code; or
(2) are participating in a program under such chapter.
(e) Definitions.—In this section:
(1) COVERED PUBLIC HEALTH EMERGENCY.—The term "covered public health emergency" means an emergency with respect to COVID–19 declared by a Federal, State, or local authority.
(2) HOMELESS VETERAN; VETERAN.—The terms "homeless veteran" and "vet-

eran" have the meanings given those terms in section 2002 of title 38, United States Code.

(3) PARKING FACILITY.—The term "parking facility" has the meaning given that term in section 8109(a) of such title.

(4) TELEHEALTH.—

(A) IN GENERAL.—The term "telehealth" means the use of electronic information and telecommunications technologies to support and promote long-distance clinical health care, patient and professional health-related education, public health, and health administration.

(B) TECHNOLOGIES.—For purposes of subparagraph (A), "telecommunications technologies" include video conferencing, the internet, streaming media, and terrestrial and wireless communications.

SEC. 80007. HUD–VASH PROGRAM.

The Secretary of Housing and Urban Development shall take such actions with respect to the supported housing program carried out under section 8(o)(19) of the United States Housing Act of 1937 (42 U.S.C. 1437f(o)(19)) in conjunction with the Department of Veterans Affairs (commonly referred to as "HUD–VASH"), and shall require public housing agencies administering assistance under such program to take such actions, as may be appropriate to facilitate the issuance and utilization of vouchers for rental assistance under such program during the period of the covered public health emergency (as such term is defined in section 1 of this Act), including the following actions:

(1) Establishing mechanisms and procedures providing for referral and application documents used under such program to be received by fax, electronic mail, drop box, or other means not requiring in-person contact.

(2) Establishing mechanisms and procedures for processing applications for participation in such program that do not require identification or verification of identity by social security number or photo ID in cases in which closure of governmental offices prevents confirmation or verification of identity by such means.

(3) Providing for waiver of requirements to conduct housing quality standard inspections with respect to dwelling units for which rental assistance is provided under such program.

SEC. 80008. EXTENSION OF LEASE PROTECTIONS FOR SERVICEMEMBERS UNDER STOP MOVEMENT ORDERS IN RESPONSE TO LOCAL, NATIONAL, OR GLOBAL EMERGENCY.

(a) Termination.—Subsection (a)(1) of section 305 of the Servicemembers Civil Relief Act (50 U.S.C. 3955) is amended—

(1) in subparagraph (A), by striking "; or" and inserting a semicolon;

(2) in subparagraph (B), by striking the period at the end and inserting "; or"; and

(3) by adding at the end the following new subparagraph:

"(C) the date of the lessee's stop movement order described in paragraph (1)(C) or (2)(C) of subsection (b), as the case may be.".

(b) Covered Leases.—

(1) LEASES OF PREMISES.—Paragraph (1) of subsection (b) of such section is amended—

(A) in subparagraph (A), by striking "; or" and inserting a semicolon;

(B) in subparagraph (B), by striking the period at the end and inserting "; or"; and

(C) by adding at the end the following new subparagraph:

"(C) the servicemember, while in military service—

"(i) executes a lease upon receipt of military orders for a permanent change of station or to deploy with a military unit, or as an individual in support of a military operation, for a period of not less than 90 days; and

"(ii) thereafter receives a stop movement order issued by the Secretary of Defense in response to a local, national, or global emergency, effective for an indefinite period or for a period of not less than 30 days, which prevents the servicemember or servicemember's dependents from occupying the lease for a residential, professional, business, agricultural, or similar purpose.".

(2) LEASES OF MOTOR VEHICLES.—Paragraph (2) of such subsection is amended—

(A) in subparagraph (A), by striking "; or" and inserting a semicolon;

(B) in subparagraph (B)(ii), by striking the period at the end and inserting "; or"; and

(C) by adding at the end the following new subparagraph:

"(C) the servicemember, while in military service—

"(i) executes a lease upon receipt of military orders described in subparagraph (B); and

"(ii) thereafter receives a stop movement order issued by the Secretary of Defense in response to a local, national, or global emergency, effective for an indefinite period or for a period of not less than 30 days, which prevents the servicemember, or the servicemember's dependents, from using the vehicle for personal or business transportation.".

(c) Effective Date Of Termination.—Paragraph (1) of subsection (d) of such section is amended to read as follows:

"(1) LEASE OF PREMISES.—

"(A) ENTRANCE TO MILITARY SERVICE, PERMANENT CHANGE OF STATION, OR DEPLOYMENT.—In the case of a lease described in subparagraph (A) or (B) of subsection (b)(1) that provides for monthly payment of rent, termination of the lease under subsection (a) is effective 30 days after the first date on which the next rental payment is due and payable after the date on which the notice under subsection (c) is delivered. In the case of any other lease described in subparagraphs (A) and (B) of subsection (b)(1) termination of the lease under subsection (a) is effective on the last day of the month following the month in which the notice is delivered.

"(B) STOP MOVEMENT ORDERS.—In the case of a lease described in subsection (b)(1)(C), termination of the lease under subsection (a) is effective on the date on which the requirements of subsection (c) are met for such termination.".

(d) Technical Correction.—Subsection (i) is amended, in the matter before paragraph (1), by inserting "In this section:" after "Definitions.—".

(e) Retroactive Application.—The amendments made by this section shall apply to stop movement orders issued on or after March 1, 2020.

SEC. 80009. TERMINATION OF TELEPHONE, MULTICHANNEL VIDEO PROGRAMMING, AND INTERNET ACCESS SERVICE CONTRACTS BY SERVICEMEMBERS WHO ENTER INTO CONTRACTS AFTER RECEIVING MILITARY ORDERS FOR PERMANENT CHANGE OF STATION BUT THEN RECEIVE STOP MOVEMENT ORDERS DUE TO AN EMERGENCY SITUATION.

(a) In General.—Section 305A(a)(1) of the Servicemembers Civil Relief Act (50 U.S.C.

3956) is amended—

(1) by striking "after the date the servicemember receives military orders to relocate for a period of not less than 90 days to a location that does not support the contract." and inserting "after—"; and

(2) by adding at the end the following new subparagraphs:

"(A) the date the servicemember receives military orders to relocate for a period of not less than 90 days to a location that does not support the contract; or

"(B) the date the servicemember, while in military service, receives military orders for a permanent change of station, thereafter enters into the contract, and then after entering into the contract receives a stop movement order issued by the Secretary of Defense in response to a local, national, or global emergency, effective for an indefinite period or for a period of not less than 30 days, which prevents the servicemember from using the services provided under the contract.".

(b) Retroactive Application.—The amendments made by this section shall apply to stop movement orders issued on or after March 1, 2020.

SEC. 80010. TERMINATION OF CONTRACTS FOR TELEPHONE, MULTI-CHANNEL VIDEO PROGRAMMING, OR INTERNET ACCESS SERVICE BY CERTAIN INDIVIDUALS UNDER SERVICEMEMBERS CIVIL RELIEF ACT.

Section 305A(a) of the Servicemembers Civil Relief Act (50 U.S.C. 3956(a)) is amended by adding at the end the following new paragraph:

"(4) ADDITIONAL INDIVIDUALS COVERED.—For purposes of this section, the following individuals shall be treated as a servicemember covered by paragraph (1):

"(A) A spouse or dependent of a servicemember who dies while in military service or a spouse or dependent of a member of the reserve components who dies while performing duty described in subparagraph (C).

"(B) A spouse or dependent of a servicemember who incurs a catastrophic injury or illness (as that term is defined in section 439(g) of title 37, United States Code), if the servicemember incurs the catastrophic injury or illness while in military service or performing duty described in subparagraph (C).

"(C) A member of the reserve components performing military service or performing full-time National Guard duty, active Guard and Reserve duty, or inactive-duty training (as such terms are defined in section 101(d) of title 10, United States Code).".

SEC. 80011. CLARIFICATION OF TERMINATION OF LEASES OF PREMISES AND MOTOR VEHICLES OF SERVICEMEMBERS WHO INCUR CATASTROPHIC INJURY OR ILLNESS OR DIE WHILE IN MILITARY SERVICE.

(a) Catastrophic Injuries And Illnesses.—Paragraph (4) of section 305(a) of the Servicemembers Civil Relief Act (50 U.S.C. 3955(a)), as added by section 545 of the National Defense Authorization Act for Fiscal Year 2020 (Public Law 116–92), is amended to read as follows:

"(4) CATASTROPHIC INJURY OR ILLNESS OF LESSEE.—

"(A) TERMINATION.—If the lessee on a lease described in subsection (b) incurs a catastrophic injury or illness during a period of military service or while performing covered service, during the one-year period beginning on the date on which the lessee incurs such injury or illness—

"(i) the lessee may terminate the lease; or

"(ii) in the case of a lessee who lacks the mental capacity to contract or to manage his or her own affairs (including disbursement of funds without limitation) due to such injury or illness, the spouse or dependent of the lessee may terminate the lease.

"(B) DEFINITIONS.—In this paragraph:

"(i) The term 'catastrophic injury or illness' has the meaning given that term in section 439(g) of title 37, United States Code.

"(ii) The term 'covered service' means full-time National Guard duty, active Guard and Reserve duty, or inactive-duty training (as such terms are defined in section 101(d) of title 10, United States Code).".

(b) Deaths.—Paragraph (3) of such section is amended by striking "The spouse of the lessee" and inserting "The spouse or dependent of the lessee".

SEC. 80012. DEFERRAL OF CERTAIN DEBTS ARISING FROM BENEFITS UNDER LAWS ADMINISTERED BY THE SECRETARY OF VETERANS AFFAIRS.

(a) In General.—During the covered period, the Secretary of Veterans Affairs may not—

(1) take any action to collect a covered debt (including the offset of any payment by the Secretary);

(2) record a covered debt;

(3) issue notice of a covered debt to a person or a consumer reporting agency;

(4) allow any interest to accrue on a covered debt; or

(5) apply any administrative fee to a covered debt.

(b) Exception.—Notwithstanding subsection (a), the Secretary may collect a payment regarding a covered debt (including interest or any administrative fee) from a person (or the fiduciary of that person) who elects to make such a payment during the covered period.

(c) Definitions.—In this section:

(1) The term "consumer reporting agency" has the meaning given that term in section 5701 of title 38, United States Code.

(2) The term "covered debt" means a debt—

(A) owed by a person (including a fiduciary) to the United States;

(B) arising from a benefit under a covered law; and

(C) that is not subject to recovery under—

(i) section 3729 of title 31, United States Code;

(ii) section 1729 of title 38, United States Code; or

(iii) Public Law 87–693 (42 U.S.C. 2651).

(3) The term "covered law" means any law administered by the Secretary of Veterans Affairs through—

(A) the Under Secretary for Health; or

(B) the Under Secretary for Benefits.

(4) The term "covered period" means—

(A) the COVID–19 emergency period; and

(B) the 60 days immediately following the date of the end of the COVID–19 emergency period.

(5) The term "COVID–19 emergency period" means the emergency period described in section 1135(g)(1)(B) of the Social Security Act (42 U.S.C. 1320b-5(g)(1)(B)).

SEC. 80013. TOLLING OF DEADLINES RELATING TO CLAIMS FOR BENEFITS ADMINISTERED BY SECRETARY OF VETERANS AFFAIRS.

(a) Required Tolling.—With respect to claims and appeals made by a claimant, the covered period shall be excluded in computing the following:

(1) In cases where an individual expresses an intent to file a claim, the period in which the individual is required to file the claim in order to have the effective date of the claim be determined based on the date of such intent, as described in section 3.155(b) (1) of title 38, Code of Federal Regulations.

(2) The period in which the claimant is required to take an action pursuant to section 5104C of title 38, United States Code.

(3) The period in which the claimant is required to appeal a change in service-connected or employability status or change in physical condition described in section 5112(b)(6) of such title.

(4) The period in which an individual is required to file a notice of appeal under section 7266 of such title.

(5) Any other period in which a claimant or beneficiary is required to act with respect to filing, perfecting, or appealing a claim, as determined appropriate by the Secretary of Veterans Affairs.

(b) Use Of Postmark Dates.—With respect to claims filed using nonelectronic means and appeals made during the covered period, the Secretary of Veterans Affairs and the Court of Appeals for Veterans Claims, as the case may be, shall administer the provisions of title 38, United States Code, as follows:

(1) In section 5110—

(A) in subsection (a)—

(i) in paragraph (1), by substituting "the earlier of the date of receipt of application therefor and the date of the postmark or other official proof of mailing date of the application therefor" for "the date of receipt of application therefor"; and

(ii) in paragraph (3), by substituting "the earlier of the date of receipt of the supplemental claim and the date of the postmark or other official proof of mailing date of the supplemental claim" for "the date of receipt of the supplemental claim"; and

(B) in subsection (b)(2)(A), by substituting "the earlier of the date of receipt of application and the date of the postmark or other official proof of mailing date of the application" for "the date of receipt of the application".

(2) In section 7266, without regard to subsection (d).

(c) Definitions.—In this section:

(1) The term "claimant" has the meaning given that term in section 5100 of title 38, United States Code.

(2) The term "covered period" means the period beginning on the date of the emergency period (as defined in section 1135(g)(1) of the Social Security Act (42 U.S.C. 1320b-5(g)(1))) resulting from the COVID–19 pandemic and ending 90 days after the last day of such emergency period.

SEC. 80014. PROVISION OF DEPARTMENT OF VETERANS AFFAIRS HOSPITAL CARE AND MEDICAL SERVICES TO CERTAIN VETERANS WHO ARE UNEMPLOYED OR LOST EMPLOYER-SPONSORED HEALTH CARE COVERAGE BY REASON OF A COVERED PUBLIC HEALTH EMERGENCY.

(a) In General.—During the 12-month period beginning on the date of the enactment of this Act, the Secretary of Veterans Affairs shall consider a covered veteran to be unable to defray the expenses of necessary care for purposes of section 1722 of title 38, United States Code, and shall furnish to such veteran hospital care and medical services under chapter 17 of title 38, United States Code.

(b) Covered Veteran.—For purposes of this section, a covered veteran is a veteran—

(1) who—

(A) is unemployed; or

(B) has lost access to a group health plan or group health insurance coverage by reason of a covered public health emergency; and

(2) whose projected attributable income for the 12-month period beginning on the date of application for hospital care or medical services under this section is not more than the amount in effect under section 1722(b) of title 38, United States Code.

(c) Definitions.—In this section:

(1) The term "covered public health emergency" means the declaration—

(A) of a public health emergency, based on an outbreak of COVID–19 by the Secretary of Health and Human Services under section 319 of the Public Health Service Act (42 U.S.C. 247d); or

(B) of a domestic emergency, based on an outbreak of COVID–19 by the President, the Secretary of Homeland Security, or State, or local authority.

(2) The terms "group health plan" and "group health insurance coverage" have the meaning given such terms in section 2701 of the Public Health Service Act (42 U.S.C. 300gg-3).

SEC. 80015. PROHIBITION ON COPAYMENTS AND COST SHARING FOR VETERANS RECEIVING COVID-19 TREATMENT FURNISHED BY DEPARTMENT OF VETERANS AFFAIRS.

(a) In General.—Section 6006(b) of the Families First Coronavirus Response Act (Public Law 116–127; 38 U.S.C. 1701 note) is amended by striking "or visits described in paragraph (2) of such section" and inserting ", visits described in paragraph (2) of such section, or hospital care or medical services to treat COVID–19".

(b) Effective Date.—The amendment made by subsection (a) shall take effect as if included in the enactment of the Families First Coronavirus Response Act (Public Law 116–127).

SEC. 80016. EXPANSION OF VET CENTER SERVICES TO VETERANS AND MEMBERS OF THE ARMED FORCES WHO PERFORM CERTAIN SERVICE IN RESPONSE TO COVERED PUBLIC HEALTH EMERGENCY.

Section 1712A of title 38, United States Code, is amended—

(1) by striking "clauses (i) through (iv)" both places it appears and inserting "clauses (i) through (v)";

(2) by striking "in clause (v)" both places it appears and inserting "in clause (vi)";

(3) in subsection (a)(1)(C)—

(A) by redesignating clauses (iv) and (v) as clauses (v) and (vi), respectively; and

(B) by inserting after clause (iii) the following new clause (iv):

"(iv) Any individual who is a veteran or member of the Armed Forces (including the reserve components), who, in response to a covered public health emergency, performed active service or State active duty for a period of at least 14 days."; and

(4) in subsection (h), by adding at the end the following new paragraphs:

"(4) The term 'active service' has the meaning given that term in section 101 of title 10.

"(5) The term 'covered public health emergency' means the declaration—

"(A) of a public health emergency, based on an outbreak of COVID–19, by the Secretary of Health and Human Services under section 319 of the Public Health Service Act (42 U.S.C. 247d); or

"(B) of a domestic emergency, based on an outbreak of COVID–19, by the President, the Secretary of Homeland Security, or a State or local authority.".

DIVISION I—SMALL BUSINESS PROVISIONS

SEC. 90001. AMENDMENTS TO THE PAYCHECK PROTECTION PROGRAM.

(a) Extension Of Covered Period.—Section 7(a)(36)(A)(iii) of the Small Business Act (15 U.S.C. 636(a)(36)(A)(iii)) is amended by striking "June 30, 2020" and inserting "December 31, 2020".

(b) Tribal Business Concerns.—Section 7(a)(36)(D) of the Small Business Act (15 U.S.C. 636(a)(36)(D)) is amended by striking "described in section 31(b)(2)(C)" each place it appears.

(c) Inclusion Of Critical Access Hospitals In The Paycheck Protection Program.—Section 7(a)(36)(D) of the Small Business Act (15 U.S.C. 636(a)(36)(D)) is amended by adding at the end the following new clause:

"(vii) INCLUSION OF CRITICAL ACCESS HOSPITALS.—During the covered period, any nonprofit organization that is a critical access hospital (as defined in section 1861(mm) of the Social Security Act (42 U.S.C. 1395x(mm))) shall be eligible to receive a covered loan, regardless of the status of such a hospital as a debtor in a case under chapter 11 of title 11, Unites States Code, or the status of any debts owed by such a hospital to the Federal Government.".

(d) Nonprofit Organizations.—Section 7(a)(36) of the Small Business Act (15 U.S.C. 636(a)(36))—

(1) in subparagraph (A)(vii), by striking "section 501(c)(3)" and inserting "section 501(c)"; and

(2) in subparagraph (D)—

(A) by striking "nonprofit organization," each place it appears;

(B) in clause (iv)—

(i) in subclause (II), by striking " and" at the end;

(ii) in subclause (III), by striking the period at the end and inserting "; and"; and

(iii) by adding at the end the following new subclause:

"(IV) any nonprofit organization."; and

(C) in clause (vi), by striking "a nonprofit organization and".

(e) Application To Certain Local News Media.—Section 7(a)(36)(D) of the Small Business Act (15 U.S.C. 636(a)(36)(D)) is amended—

(1) in clause (iii)—

(A) by striking "business concern that employs" and inserting the following: business concern that—

"(I) employs";

(B) in subclause (I), by striking the period at the end and inserting "; and"; and

(C) by adding at the end the following:

"(II) is assigned a North American Industry Classification System code beginning with 511110, 515112, or 515120 and the individual physical location at the time of disbursal does not exceed the size standard established by the Administrator for the applicable code shall be eligible to receive a covered loan for expenses associated with an individual physical location of that business concern to support the continued provision of local news, information, content, or emergency information, and, at the time of disbursal, the individual physical location.";

(2) in clause (iv) (as amended by subsection (d))—

(A) in subclause (III), by striking "and" at the end;

(B) in subclause (IV), by striking the period at the end and inserting "; and"; and

(C) by adding at the end the following:

"(V) an individual physical location of a business concern described in clause (iii) (II), if such concern shall not pay, distribute, or otherwise provide any portion of the covered loan to any other entity other than the individual physical location that is the intended recipient of the covered loan."; and

(3) by adding at the end the following new clause:

"(vii) ADDITIONAL REQUIREMENTS FOR NEWS BROADCAST ENTITIES.—

"(I) IN GENERAL.—With respect to an individual physical location of a business concern described in clause (iii)(II), each such location shall be treated as an independent, nonaffiliated entity for purposes of this paragraph.

"(II) DEMONSTRATION OF NEED.—Any such location that is a franchise or affiliate of, or owned or controlled by a parent company, investment company, or the management thereof, shall demonstrate, upon request of the Administrator, the need for a covered loan to support the continued provision of local news, information, content, or emergency information, and, at the time of disbursal, the individual physical location.

"(III) REPORT.—The Administrator and Secretary of the Treasury shall submit to the Committee on Small Business of the House of Representatives, the Committee on Small Business and Entrepreneurship of the Senate, and the Congressional Oversight Commission established under section 4020 of the CARES Act a report including information on loans made to an entity described under this clause.".

(f) Application Of Certain Terms Through Life Of Covered Loan.—Section 7(a)(36) of the Small Business Act (15 U.S.C. 636(a)(36)) is amended—

(1) in subparagraph (H), by striking "During the covered period, with" and inserting "With";

(2) in subparagraph (I), by striking "During the covered period, the" and inserting "The";

(3) in subparagraph (J), by striking "During the covered period, with" and inserting "With";

(4) in subparagraph (M)—

(A) in clause (ii), by striking "During the covered period, the" and inserting "The"; and

(B) in clause (iii), by striking "During the covered period, with" and inserting "With".

(g) Loan Maturity.—Section 7(a)(36)(K)(ii) of the Small Business Act (15 U.S.C. 636(a)(36)(K)(ii)) is amended by inserting "minimum maturity of 5 years" before "maximum maturity".

(h) Interest Calculation.—Section 7(a)(36)(L) of the Small Business Act (15 U.S.C. 636(a)(36)(L)) is amended by inserting ", calculated on a non-compounding, non-adjustable basis" after "4 percent".

(i) Funding For The Paycheck Protection Program.—

(1) IN GENERAL.—Section 7(a)(36)(S) of the Small Business Act (15 U.S.C. 636(a) (36)(S)) is amended to read as follows:

"(S) SET ASIDE FOR CERTAIN ENTITIES.—The Administrator shall provide for the cost to guarantee covered loans made under this paragraph—

"(i) a set aside of not less than 25 percent of each such amount for covered loans made to eligible recipients with 10 or fewer employees; and

"(ii) a set aside of 25 percent of each such amount for covered loans made to nonprofit organizations, of which not more than 12.5 percent of each such amount set aside may be used to make covered loans to nonprofit organizations with 500 or more employees.".

(2) SET ASIDE FOR COMMUNITY FINANCIAL INSTITUTIONS.—Of amounts appropriated by the Paycheck Protection Program and Health Care Enhancement Act (Public Law 116–139) under the heading "Small Business Administration—Business Loans Program Account, CARES Act" that have not been obligated or expended, the lesser of 25 percent of such amounts or $10,000,000,000 shall be set aside for the cost to guarantee covered loans made under section 7(a)(36) of the Small Business Act (15 U.S.C. 636(a)(36)) by community financial institutions (as such term is defined in subparagraph (A)(xi) of such section).

(3) AMOUNTS RETURNED.—Section 7(a)(36) of the Small Business Act (15 U.S.C. 636(a)(36)) is amended by adding at the end the following new subparagraph:

"(T) AMOUNTS RETURNED.—Any amounts returned to the Secretary of the Treasury due to the cancellation of a covered loan shall be solely used for the cost to guarantee covered loans made to eligible recipients with 10 or fewer employees.".

(j) Treatment Of Certain Criminal Violations.—

(1) IN GENERAL.—Section 7(a)(36) of the Small Business Act (15 U.S.C. 636(a)(36)), as amended by subsection (h), is further amended by adding at the end the following new subparagraph:

"(U) TREATMENT OF CERTAIN CRIMINAL VIOLATIONS.—

"(i) FINANCIAL FRAUD OR DECEPTION.—A entity that is a business, organization, cooperative, or enterprise may not receive a covered loan if an owner of 20 percent or more of the equity of such entity, during the 5-year period preceding the date on which such entity applies for a covered loan, has been convicted of a felony of financial fraud or deception under Federal, State, or Tribal law.

"(ii) ARRESTS OR CONVICTIONS.—An entity that is a business, organization, cooperative, or enterprise shall be an eligible recipient notwithstanding a prior arrest or conviction under Federal, State, or Tribal law of an owner of 20 percent or more of the equity of such entity, unless such owner is currently incarcerated.

"(iii) WAIVER.—The Administrator may waive the requirements of clause (i).".

(2) RULEMAKING.—Not later than 15 days after the date of enactment of this Act, the Administrator of the Small Business Administration shall make necessary revisions to any rules to carry out the amendment made by this subsection.

(k) Technical Assistance For Community Financial Institutions.—Section 7(a)(36) of the Small Business Act (15 U.S.C. 636(a)(36)), as amended by subsection (i), is further amended by adding at the end the following new subparagraph:

"(V) TECHNICAL ASSISTANCE FOR COMMUNITY FINANCIAL INSTITU-TIONS.—Of amounts appropriated to carry out this paragraph, the Secretary of the Treasury, in consultation with the Administrator, shall use $1,000,000,000 of such amounts to provide grants to community financial institutions, insured depository institutions with consolidated assets of less than $10,000,000,000, and credit unions with consolidated assets of less than $10,000,000,000, to ensure such institutions can update their systems (including updates related to compliance with the Bank Secrecy Act) and efficiently provide loans that are guaranteed under this paragraph.".

(l) Technical Amendment.—Section 7(a)(36)(G) of the Small Business Act (15 U.S.C.

636(a)(36)) is amended—

(1) in the subparagraph heading, by striking "BORROWER REQUIREMENTS" and all that follows through "eligible recipient applying" and inserting "BORROWER CERTIFICATION REQUIREMENTS.—An eligible recipient applying"; and

(2) by redesignating subclauses (I) through (IV) as clauses (i) through (iv), respectively.

SEC. 90002. COMMITMENTS FOR PAYCHECK PROTECTION PROGRAM.

Section 1102(b) of the CARES Act (Public Law 116–136) is amended by striking "June 30, 2020" and all that follows through the period at the end and inserting "December 31, 2020, the amount authorized for commitments for loans made under paragraph (36) of section 7(a) of the Small Business Act, as added by subsection (a), shall be $659,000,000,000. The amount authorized under this section for commitments for loans made under section 7(a)(36) of the Small Business Act shall be in addition to the amount authorized under the heading 'Small Business Administration—Business Loans Program Account' in the Financial Services and General Government Appropriations Act, 2020 (division C of Public Law 116–93) for commitments for general business loans made under section 7(a) of the Small Business Act.".

SEC. 90003. INCLUSION OF SCORE AND VETERAN BUSINESS OUTREACH CENTERS IN ENTREPRENEURIAL DEVELOPMENT PROGRAMS.

(a) In General.—Section 1103(a)(2) of the CARES Act (Public Law 116–136) is amended—

(1) in subparagraph (A), by striking "and" at the end;

(2) by adding at the end the following new subparagraphs:

"(C) a Veteran Business Outreach Center (as described under section 32(d) of the Small Business Act); and

"(D) the Service Corps of Retired Executives Association, or any successor or other organization, that receives a grant from the Administrator to operate the SCORE program established under section 8(b)(2)(A) of the Small Business Act;".

(b) Funding.—Section 1107(a)(4) of the CARES Act (Public Law 116–136) is amended—

(1) in subparagraph (A)—

(A) by striking "$240,000,000" and inserting "$220,000,000";

(B) by striking "and" at the end; and

(2) by adding at the end the following new subparagraphs:

"(C) $10,000,000 shall be for a Veteran Business Outreach Center described in section 1103(a)(2)(C) of this Act to carry out activities under such section; and

"(D) $10,000,000 shall be for the Service Corps of Retired Executives Association described in section 1103(a)(2)(D) of this Act to carry out activities under such section;".

SEC. 90004. AMENDMENTS TO PAYCHECK PROTECTION PROGRAM LOAN FORGIVENESS.

(a) Covered Period.—

(1) IN GENERAL.—Section 1106(a)(3) of the CARES Act (Public Law 116–136) is amended to read as follows:

"(3) the term 'covered period' means the period beginning on the date of the origination of a covered loan and ending on the earlier of—

"(A) the date that is 24 weeks after such date of origination; or

"(B) December 31, 2020;".

(2) EXEMPTION FOR REHIRES.—Section 1106(d)(5)(B) of such Act is amended by striking "June 30, 2020" each place it appears and inserting "December 31, 2020".

(b) Definition Of Expected Forgiveness Amount.—

(1) DEFINITION OF EXPECTED FORGIVENESS AMOUNT.—Section 1106(a)(7) of the CARES Act (Public Law 116–136) is amended—

(A) in subparagraph (C), by striking "and" at the end;

(B) in subparagraph (D), by striking "and" at the end; and

(C) by adding at the end the following new subparagraphs:

"(E) interest on any other debt obligations that were incurred before the covered period; and

"(F) any amount that was a loan made under subsection (b)(2) that was refinanced as part of a covered loan and authorized by section 7(a)(36)(F)(iv) of the Small Business Act; and".

(2) FORGIVENESS.—Section 1106(b) of the CARES Act (Public Law 116–136) is amended by adding at the end the following new paragraphs:

"(5) Any payment of interest on any other debt obligations that were incurred before the covered period.

"(6) Any amount that was a loan made under section 7(b)(2) of the Small Business Act that was refinanced as part of a covered loan and authorized by section 7(a)(36) (F)(iv) of such Act.".

(3) CONFORMING AMENDMENTS.—Section 1106 of the CARES Act (Public Law 116–136) is amended—

(A) in subsection (e)—

(i) in paragraph (2), by striking "payments on covered mortgage obligations, payments on covered lease obligations, and covered utility payments" and inserting "payments or amounts refinanced described under subsection (b) (other than payroll costs)";

(ii) in paragraph (3)(B), by striking ", make interest payments" and all that follows through "or make covered utility payments" and inserting ", make payments described under subsection (b), or that was refinanced as part of a covered loan and authorized by section 7(a)(36)(F)(iv) of the Small Business Act"; and

(B) in subsection (h), by striking "payments for payroll costs, payments on covered mortgage obligations, payments on covered lease obligations, or covered utility payments" each place it appears and inserting "payments or amounts refinanced described under subsection (b)".

(c) Application Requirements For Paycheck Protection Program Loan Forgiveness.—Section 1106(e) of the CARES Act (Public Law 116–136) is amended—

(1) in paragraph (3)(B), by striking "and" at the end;

(2) by redesignating paragraph (4) as paragraph (6); and

(3) by inserting after paragraph (3) the following new paragraphs:

"(4) information on the veteran status, gender, race, and ethnicity, as reported on Form 1919 of the Administration or any similar loan application form of the Administration, of the eligible recipient;

"(5) the number of full-time equivalent employees of the eligible recipient—

"(A) on February 15, 2020;

"(B) on the day the eligible recipient submitted an application for a covered loan; and

"(C) on the day the eligible recipient submitted an application for forgiveness of a covered loan under this section; and".

(d) Hold Harmless For Eligible Recipients.—Section 1106(d) of the CARES Act

(Public Law 116–136) is amended by adding at the end the following new paragraph:
"(7) EXEMPTION BASED ON EMPLOYEE AVAILABILITY.—During the period beginning on February 15, 2020 and ending on December 31, 2020, the amount of loan forgiveness under this section shall be determined without regard to a reduction in the number of full-time equivalent employees if an eligible recipient—
"(A) is unable rehire an individual who was an employee of the eligible recipient on or before February 15, 2020; or
"(B) is able to demonstrate an inability to find similarly qualified employees on or before December 31, 2020.".
(e) Prohibition On Limiting Forgiveness.—Section 1106(d) of the CARES Act (Public Law 116–136), as amended by subsection (c), is further amended by adding at the end the following new paragraph:
"(8) NO LIMITATIONS.—In carrying out this section, the Administrator may not limit the non-payroll portion of a forgivable covered loan amount.".
(f) Hold Harmless.—Section 1106(h) of the CARES Act (Public Law 116–136), is amended by striking "If a lender" and all that follows through "during covered period" inserting the following: "If a lender has received any documentation required under this Act related to payments made by an eligible recipient attesting that the eligible recipient has accurately verified such payments".

SEC. 90005. IMPROVED COORDINATION BETWEEN PAYCHECK PROTECTION PROGRAM AND EMPLOYEE RETENTION TAX CREDIT.

(a) Amendment To Paycheck Protection Program.—Section 1106(a)(8) of the Cares Act is amended by inserting ", except that such costs shall not include qualified wages taken into account in determining the credit allowed under section 2301 of this Act" before the period at the end.
(b) Amendments To Employee Retention Tax Credit.—
(1) IN GENERAL.—Section 2301(g) of the CARES Act is amended to read as follows:
"(g) Election To Not Take Certain Wages Into Account.—
"(1) IN GENERAL.—This section shall not apply to qualified wages paid by an eligible employer with respect to which such employer makes an election (at such time and in such manner as the Secretary may prescribe) to have this section not apply to such wages.
"(2) COORDINATION WITH PAYCHECK PROTECTION PROGRAM.—The Secretary, in consultation with the Administrator of the Small Business Administration, shall issue guidance providing that payroll costs paid or incurred during the covered period shall not fail to be treated as qualified wages under this section by reason of an election under paragraph (1) to the extent that a covered loan of the eligible employer is not forgiven by reason of a decision under section 1106(g). Terms used in the preceding sentence which are also used in section 1106 shall have the same meaning as when used in such section.".
(2) CONFORMING AMENDMENTS.—
(A) Section 2301 of the CARES Act is amended by striking subsection (j).
(B) Section 2301(l) of the CARES Act is amended by striking paragraph (3) and by redesignating paragraphs (4) and (5) as paragraphs (3) and (4), respectively.
(c) Effective Date.—The amendments made by this section shall take effect as if included in the provisions of the CARES Act to which they relate.

SEC. 90006. TAXABILITY OF SUBSIDY FOR CERTAIN LOAN PAYMENTS.

Section 1112 of the CARES Act (Public Law 116–136) is amended by inserting at the end the following new subsection:

"(g) Taxability.—For purposes of the Internal Revenue Code of 1986, any payment under this section shall not be included in the gross income of the taxpayer on whose behalf such payment is made.".

SEC. 90007. PROHIBITING CONFLICTS OF INTEREST FOR SMALL BUSINESS PROGRAMS UNDER THE CARES ACT.

Section 4019 of the CARES Act (Public Law 116–136) is amended—

(1) in subsection (a), by adding at the end the following:

"(7) SMALL BUSINESS ASSISTANCE.—The term 'small business assistance' means assistance provided under—

"(A) paragraph (36) of section 7(a) of the Small Business Act (15 U.S.C. 636(a)), as added by section 1102 of this Act;

"(B) subsection (b) or (c) of section 1103 of this Act;

"(C) section 1110 of this Act; or

"(D) section 1112 of this Act.";

(2) in subsection (b)—

(A) by inserting "or provisions relating to small business assistance" after "this subtitle"; and

(B) by inserting "or for any small business assistance" before the period at the end; and

(3) in subsection (c)—

(A) by inserting "or seeking any small business assistance" after "4003";

(B) by inserting "or small business assistance" after "that transaction";

(C) by inserting "or the Administrator of the Small Business Administration, as applicable," after "System"; and

(D) by inserting "or receive the small business assistance" after "in that transaction".

SEC. 90008. FLEXIBILITY IN DEFERRAL OF PAYMENTS OF 7(A) LOANS.

Section 7(a)(7) of the Small Business Act (15 U.S.C. 636(a)(7)) is amended—

(1) by striking "The Administration" and inserting "(A) IN GENERAL.—The Administrator";

(2) by inserting "and interest" after "principal"; and

(3) by adding at the end the following new subparagraphs:

"(B) DEFERRAL REQUIREMENTS.—With respect to a deferral provided under this paragraph, the Administrator—

"(i) shall require lenders under this subsection to provide full payment deferment relief (including payment of principal and interest) for a period of not less than 1 year; and

"(ii) may allow lenders under this subsection provide an additional deferment period if the borrower provides documentation justifying such additional deferment.

"(C) SECONDARY MARKET.—If an investor declines to approve a deferral or additional deferment requested by a lender under subparagraph (B), the Administrator shall exercise the authority to purchase the loan so that the borrower may receive full payment deferment relief (including payment of principal and interest) or an additional deferment as described under subparagraph (B).".

SEC. 90009. CERTAIN CRIMINAL VIOLATIONS AND DISASTER LOAN APPLICATIONS.

(a) In General.—The flush matter following subparagraph (E) of section 7(b)(2) of the Small Business Act (15 U.S.C. 636(b)(2)) is amended by striking the period at the end and inserting the following: ": Provided further, That any application for a loan or guarantee made pursuant to this paragraph (2) shall include a statement that an applicant is not ineligible for assistance under this paragraph solely because of the applicant's involvement in the criminal justice system."

(b) Rulemaking.—Not later than 15 days after the date of enactment of this Act, the Administrator of the Small Business Administration shall make necessary revisions to any rules to carry out the amendment made by this section.

SEC. 90010. TEMPORARY FEE REDUCTIONS.

(a) Administrative Fee Waiver.—

(1) IN GENERAL.—During the period beginning on the date of enactment of this Act and ending on September 30, 2021, and to the extent that the cost of such elimination or reduction of fees is offset by appropriations, with respect to each loan guaranteed under section 7(a) of the Small Business Act (15 U.S.C. 636(a)) (including a recipient of assistance under the Community Advantage Pilot Program of the Administration) for which an application is approved or pending approval on or after the date of enactment of this Act, the Administrator shall—

(A) in lieu of the fee otherwise applicable under section 7(a)(23)(A) of the Small Business Act (15 U.S.C. 636(a)(23)(A)), collect no fee or reduce fees to the maximum extent possible; and

(B) in lieu of the fee otherwise applicable under section 7(a)(18)(A) of the Small Business Act (15 U.S.C. 636(a)(18)(A)), collect no fee or reduce fees to the maximum extent possible.

(2) APPLICATION OF FEE ELIMINATIONS OR REDUCTIONS.—To the extent that amounts are made available to the Administrator for the purpose of fee eliminations or reductions under paragraph (1), the Administrator shall—

(A) first use any amounts provided to eliminate or reduce fees paid by small business borrowers under clauses (i) through (iii) of section 7(a)(18)(A) of the Small Business Act (15 U.S.C. 636(a)(18)(A)), to the maximum extent possible; and

(B) then use any amounts provided to eliminate or reduce fees under 7(a)(23)(A) of the Small Business Act (15 U.S.C. 636(a)(23)(A)).

(c) Temporary Fee Elimination For The 504 Loan Program.—

(1) IN GENERAL.—During the period beginning on the date of enactment of this section and ending on September 30, 2021, and to the extent the cost of such elimination in fees is offset by appropriations, with respect to each project or loan guaranteed by the Administrator pursuant to title V of the Small Business Investment Act of 1958 (15 U.S.C. 695 et seq.) for which an application is approved or pending approval on or after the date of enactment of this section—

(A) the Administrator shall, in lieu of the fee otherwise applicable under section 503(d)(2) of the Small Business Investment Act of 1958 (15 U.S.C. 697(d)(2)), collect no fee; and

(B) a development company shall, in lieu of the processing fee under section 120.971(a)(1) of title 13, Code of Federal Regulations (relating to fees paid by borrowers), or any successor thereto, collect no fee.

(2) REIMBURSEMENT FOR WAIVED FEES.—

(A) IN GENERAL.—To the extent that the cost of such payments is offset by appropriations, the Administrator shall reimburse each development company that does not collect a processing fee pursuant to paragraph (1)(B).

(B) AMOUNT.—The payment to a development company under subparagraph (A) shall be in an amount equal to 1.5 percent of the net debenture proceeds for which the development company does not collect a processing fee pursuant to paragraph (1)(B).

SEC. 90011. GUARANTEE AMOUNTS.
(a) 7(a) Loan Guarantees.—
(1) IN GENERAL.—Section 7(a)(2)(A) of the Small Business Act (15 U.S.C. 636(a)(2)(A)) is amended by striking "), such participation by the Administration shall be equal to" and all that follows through the period at the end and inserting "or the Community Advantage Pilot Program of the Administration), such participation by the Administration shall be equal to 90 percent of the balance of the financing outstanding at the time of disbursement of the loan.".
(2) TERMINATION.—Effective September 30, 2021, section 7(a)(2)(A) of the Small Business Act (15 U.S.C. 636(a)(2)(A)), as amended by paragraph (1), is amended to read as follows:
"(A) IN GENERAL.—Except as provided in subparagraphs (B), (D), (E), and (F), in an agreement to participate in a loan on a deferred basis under this subsection (including a loan made under the Preferred Lenders Program), such participation by the Administration shall be equal to—
"(i) 75 percent of the balance of the financing outstanding at the time of disbursement of the loan, if such balance exceeds $150,000; or
"(ii) 85 percent of the balance of the financing outstanding at the time of disbursement of the loan, if such balance is less than or equal to $150,000.".
(b) Express Loan Guarantee Amounts.—
(1) TEMPORARY MODIFICATION.—Section 7(a)(31)(A)(iv) of the Small Business Act (15 U.S.C. 636(a)(31)(A)(iv)) is amended by striking "with a guaranty rate of not more than 50 percent." and inserting the following: "with a guarantee rate—
"(I) for a loan in an amount less than or equal to $350,000, of not more than 90 percent; and
"(II) for a loan in an amount greater than $350,000, of not more than 75 percent.".
(2) PROSPECTIVE REPEAL.—Effective January 1, 2021, section 7(a)(31)(A)(iv) of the Small Business Act (15 U.S.C. 636(a)(31)), as amended by paragraph (1), is amended by striking "guarantee rate" and all that follows through the period at the end and inserting "guarantee rate of not more than 50 percent.".

SEC. 90012. MAXIMUM LOAN AMOUNT FOR 7(a) LOANS.
During the period beginning on the date of enactment of this section and ending on September 30, 2021, with respect to any loan guaranteed under section 7(a) of the Small Business Act (15 U.S.C. 636(a)) for which an application is approved or pending approval on or after the date of enactment of this section, the maximum loan amount shall be $10,000,000.

SEC. 90013. MAXIMUM LOAN AMOUNT FOR 504 LOANS.
(a) Temporary Increase.—During the period beginning on the date of enactment of this section and ending on September 30, 2021, with respect to each project or loan guaranteed by the Administrator pursuant to title V of the Small Business Investment Act of 1958 (15 U.S.C. 695 et seq.) for which an application is approved or pending approval on or after the date of enactment of this section, the maximum loan amount shall be $10,000,000.
(b) Permanent Increase For Small Manufacturers.—Effective on October 1, 2021,

section 502(2)(A)(iii) of the Small Business Investment Act of 1958 (15 U.S.C. 696(2)(A)(iii)) is amended by striking "$5,500,000" and inserting "$10,000,000".

(c) Low-Interest Refinancing Under The Local Development Business Loan Program.—

(1) REPEAL.—Section 521(a) of division E of the Consolidated Appropriations Act, 2016 (Public Law 114–113; 129 Stat. 2463; 15 U.S.C. 696 note) is repealed.

(2) REFINANCING.—Section 502(7) of the Small Business Investment Act of 1958 (15 U.S.C. 696(7)) is amended by adding at the end the following new subparagraph:

"(C) REFINANCING NOT INVOLVING EXPANSIONS.—

"(i) DEFINITIONS.—In this subparagraph—

"(I) the term 'borrower' means a small business concern that submits an application to a development company for financing under this subparagraph;

"(II) the term 'eligible fixed asset' means tangible property relating to which the Administrator may provide financing under this section; and

"(III) the term 'qualified debt' means indebtedness that—

"(aa) was incurred not less than 6 months before the date of the application for assistance under this subparagraph;

"(bb) is a commercial loan;

"(cc) the proceeds of which were used to acquire an eligible fixed asset;

"(dd) was incurred for the benefit of the small business concern; and

"(ee) is collateralized by eligible fixed assets; and

"(ii) AUTHORITY.—A project that does not involve the expansion of a small business concern may include the refinancing of qualified debt if—

"(I) the amount of the financing is not more than 90 percent of the value of the collateral for the financing, except that, if the appraised value of the eligible fixed assets serving as collateral for the financing is less than the amount equal to 125 percent of the amount of the financing, the borrower may provide additional cash or other collateral to eliminate any deficiency;

"(II) the borrower has been in operation for all of the 2-year period ending on the date the loan application is submitted; and

"(III) for a financing for which the Administrator determines there will be an additional cost attributable to the refinancing of the qualified debt, the borrower agrees to pay a fee in an amount equal to the anticipated additional cost.

"(iii) FINANCING FOR BUSINESS EXPENSES.—

"(I) FINANCING FOR BUSINESS EXPENSES.—The Administrator may provide financing to a borrower that receives financing that includes a refinancing of qualified debt under clause (ii), in addition to the refinancing under clause (ii), to be used solely for the payment of business expenses.

"(II) APPLICATION FOR FINANCING.— An application for financing under subclause (I) shall include—

"(aa) a specific description of the expenses for which the additional financing is requested; and

"(bb) an itemization of the amount of each expense.

"(III) CONDITION ON ADDITIONAL FINANCING.—A borrower may not use any part of the financing under this clause for non-business purposes.

"(iv) LOANS BASED ON JOBS.—

"(I) JOB CREATION AND RETENTION GOALS.—

"(aa) IN GENERAL.—The Administrator may provide financing under this subparagraph for a borrower that meets the job creation goals under subsection (d) or (e) of section 501.

"(bb) ALTERNATE JOB RETENTION GOAL.—The Administrator may provide financing under this subparagraph to a borrower that does not meet the goals described in item (aa) in an amount that is not more than the product obtained by multiplying the number of employees of the borrower by $75,000.

"(II) NUMBER OF EMPLOYEES.—For purposes of subclause (I), the number of employees of a borrower is equal to the sum of—

"(aa) the number of full- time employees of the borrower on the date on which the borrower applies for a loan under this subparagraph; and

"(bb) the product obtained by multiplying—

"(AA) the number of part-time employees of the borrower on the date on which the borrower applies for a loan under this subparagraph, by

"(BB) the quotient obtained by dividing the average number of hours each part time employee of the borrower works each week by 40.

"(vi) TOTAL AMOUNT OF LOANS.—The Administrator may provide not more than a total of $7,500,000,000 of financing under this subparagraph for each fiscal year.".

(d) Refinancing Senior Project Debt.—During the 1-year period beginning after the date of the enactment of this Act, a development company described under title V of the Small Business Investment Act of 1958 (15 U.S.C. 695 et seq.) is authorized to allow the refinancing of a senior loan on an existing project in an amount that, when combined with the outstanding balance on the development company loan, is not more than 90 percent of the total value of the senior loan. Proceeds of such refinancing can be used to support business operating expenses of such development company.

SEC. 90014. RECOVERY ASSISTANCE UNDER THE MICROLOAN PROGRAM.

(a) Loans To Intermediaries.—

(1) IN GENERAL.—Section 7(m) of the Small Business Act (15 U.S.C. 636(m)) is amended—

(A) in paragraph (3)(C)—

(i) by striking "and $6,000,000" and inserting "$10,000,000, in the aggregate,"; and

(ii) by inserting before the period at the end the following: ", and $4,500,000 in any of those remaining years";

(B) in paragraph (4)—

(i) in subparagraph (A), by striking "subparagraph (C)" each place that term appears and inserting "subparagraphs (C) and (G)";

(ii) in subparagraph (C), by amending clause (i) to read as follows:

"(i) IN GENERAL.—In addition to grants made under subparagraph (A) or (G), each intermediary shall be eligible to receive a grant equal to 5 percent of the total outstanding balance of loans made to the intermediary under this subsection if—

"(I) the intermediary provides not less than 25 percent of its loans to small business concerns located in or owned by one or more residents of an economically distressed area; or

"(II) the intermediary has a portfolio of loans made under this subsection—

"(aa) that averages not more than $10,000 during the period of the intermediary's participation in the program; or

"(bb) of which not less than 25 percent is serving rural areas during the period of the intermediary's participation in the program.";and

(iii) by adding at the end the following:

"(G) GRANT AMOUNTS BASED ON APPROPRIATIONS.—In any fiscal year in which the amount appropriated to make grants under subparagraph (A) is sufficient to provide to each intermediary that receives a loan under paragraph (1)(B)(i) a grant of not less than 25 percent of the total outstanding balance of loans made to the intermediary under this subsection, the Administration shall make a grant under subparagraph (A) to each intermediary of not less than 25 percent and not more than 30 percent of that total outstanding balance for the intermediary.";and

(C) by striking paragraph (7) and inserting the following:

"(7) PROGRAM FUNDING FOR MICROLOANS.—Under the program authorized by this subsection, the Administration may fund, on a competitive basis, not more than 300 intermediaries.".

(2) PROSPECTIVE AMENDMENT.—Effective on October 1, 2021, section 7(m)(3)(C) of the Small Business Act (15 U.S.C. 636(m)(3)(C)), as amended by paragraph (1)(A), is further amended—

(A) by striking "$10,000,000" and by inserting "$7,000,000"; and

(B) by striking "$4,500,000" and inserting "$3,000,000".

(b) Temporary Waiver Of Technical Assistance Grants Matching Requirements And Flexibility On Pre- And Post-Loan Assistance.—During the period beginning on the date of enactment of this section and ending on September 30, 2021, the Administration shall waive—

(1) the requirement to contribute non-Federal funds under section 7(m)(4)(B) of the Small Business Act (15 U.S.C. 636(m)(4)(B)); and

(2) the limitation on amounts allowed to be expended to provide information and technical assistance under clause (i) of section 7(m)(4)(E) of the Small Business Act (15 U.S.C. 636(m)(4)(E)) and enter into third-party contracts to provide technical assistance under clause (ii) of such section 7(m)(4)(E).

(c) Temporary Duration Of Loans To Borrowers.—

(1) IN GENERAL.—During the period beginning on the date of enactment of this section and ending on September 30, 2021, the duration of a loan made by an eligible intermediary under section 7(m) of the Small Business Act (15 U.S.C. 636(m))—

(A) to an existing borrower may be extended to not more than 8 years; and

(B) to a new borrower may be not more than 8 years.

(2) REVERSION.—On and after October 1, 2021, the duration of a loan made by an eligible intermediary to a borrower under section 7(m) of the Small Business Act (15 U.S.C. 636(m)) shall be 7 years or such other amount established by the Administrator.

(d) Funding.—Section 20 of the Small Business Act (15 U.S.C. 631 note) is amended by adding at the end the following:

"(h) Microloan Program.—For each of fiscal years 2021 through 2025, the Administration is authorized to make—

"(1) $80,000,000 in technical assistance grants, as provided in section 7(m); and

"(2) $110,000,000 in direct loans, as provided in section 7(m).".

(e) Authorization Of Appropriations.—In addition to amounts provided under the Consolidated Appropriations Act, 2020 (Public Law 116–93) for the program established under section 7(m) of the Small Business Act (15 U.S.C. 636(m)), there is authorized to be appropriated for fiscal year 2020, to remain available until expended—

(1) $50,000,000 to provide technical assistance grants under such section 7(m); and
(2) $7,000,000 to provide direct loans under such section 7(m).

SEC. 90015. CYBERSECURITY AWARENESS REPORTING.

Section 10 of the Small Business Act (15 U.S.C. 639) is amended by inserting after subsection (a) the following:

"(b) Cybersecurity Reports.—

"(1) ANNUAL REPORT.—Not later than 180 days after the date of enactment of this subsection, and every year thereafter, the Administrator shall submit a report to the appropriate congressional committees that includes—

"(A) an assessment of the information technology (as defined in section 11101 of title 40, United States Code) and cybersecurity infrastructure of the Administration;

"(B) a strategy to increase the cybersecurity infrastructure of the Administration;

"(C) a detailed account of any information technology equipment or interconnected system or subsystem of equipment of the Administration that was manufactured by an entity that has its principal place of business located in the People's Republic of China; and

"(D) an account of any cybersecurity risk or incident that occurred at the Administration during the 2-year period preceding the date on which the report is submitted, and any action taken by the Administrator to respond to or remediate any such cybersecurity risk or incident.

"(2) ADDITIONAL REPORTS.—If the Administrator determines that there is a reasonable basis to conclude that a cybersecurity risk or incident occurred at the Administration, the Administrator shall—

"(A) not later than 7 days after the date on which the Administrator makes that determination, notify the appropriate congressional committees of the cybersecurity risk or incident; and

"(B) not later than 30 days after the date on which the Administrator makes a determination under subparagraph (A)—

"(i) provide notice to individuals and small business concerns affected by the cybersecurity risk or incident; and

"(ii) submit to the appropriate congressional committees a report, based on information available to the Administrator as of the date which the Administrator submits the report, that includes—

"(I) a summary of information about the cybersecurity risk or incident, including how the cybersecurity risk or incident occurred; and

"(II) an estimate of the number of individuals and small business concerns affected by the cybersecurity risk or incident, including an assessment of the risk of harm to affected individuals and small business concerns.

"(3) RULE OF CONSTRUCTION.—Nothing in this subsection shall be construed to affect the reporting requirements of the Administrator under chapter 35 of title 44, United States Code, in particular the requirement to notify the Federal information security incident center under section 3554(b)(7)(C)(ii) of such title, or any other provision of law.

"(4) DEFINITIONS.—In this subsection:

"(A) APPROPRIATE CONGRESSIONAL COMMITTEES.—The term 'appropriate congressional committees' means—

"(i) the Committee on Small Business and Entrepreneurship of the Senate; and

"(ii) the Committee on Small Business of the House of Representatives.

"(B) CYBERSECURITY RISK; INCIDENT.—The terms 'cybersecurity risk' and 'incident' have the meanings given such terms, respectively, under section 2209(a) of the Homeland Security Act of 2002.".

SEC. 90016. REPORTING ON SMALL BUSINESS PROGRAMS UNDER THE CARES ACT.

(a) Definitions.—In this section—

(1) the terms "Administration" and "Administrator" mean the Small Business Administration and the Administrator thereof;

(2) the term "appropriate congressional committees" means—

(A) Committee on Appropriations and the Committee on Small Business and Entrepreneurship of the Senate; and

(B) the Committee on Appropriations and the Committee on Small Business of the House of Representatives;

(3) the term "covered assistance" means—

(A) loans made under section 7(a)(36) of the Small Business Act (15 U.S.C. 636(a)(36));

(B) an advance on a loan made under section 1110(e) of the CARES Act (Public Law 116–136);

(C) loans made under section 7(b)(2) of the Small Business Act (15 U.S.C. 636(b)(2)), including those made in accordance with section 1110 of the CARES Act (Public Law 116–136);

(D) loan forgiveness under section 1106 of the CARES Act (Public Law 116–136); and

(E) the payment of principal, interest, and fees under section 1112(c) of the CARES Act (Public Law 116–136);

(4) the term "covered loan" has the meaning given the term in section 1112(a) of the CARES Act (Public Law 116–136);

(5) the term "demographics" means veteran status, gender, race, and ethnicity, as reported on Form 1919 of the Administration or any similar loan application form of the Administration; and

(6) the term "State"—

(A) means any State of the United States, the District of Columbia, the Commonwealth of Puerto Rico, the United States Virgin Islands, Guam, American Samoa, the Commonwealth of the Northern Mariana Islands, and any possession of the United States; and

(B) includes an Indian tribe, as defined in section 4 of the Indian Self-Determination and Education Assistance Act (25 U.S.C. 450b).

(b) Daily Reporting.—

(1) IN GENERAL.—During the period beginning on the day after the date of enactment of this Act and ending on the date on which loan, advance, or payment activity described in this subsection related to COVID–19 has ceased, the Administrator shall, on a daily basis, report to Congress on—

(A) the total number and dollar amount of loans or advances, broken down by loans and grants approved and loans and grants disbursed, under—

(i) section 7(a)(36) of the Small Business Act (15 U.S.C. 636(a)(36));

(ii) section 1110(e) of the CARES Act (Public Law 116–136); and

(iii) section 7(b)(2) of the Small Business Act (15 U.S.C. 636(b)(2));

(B) for loans made under section 7(a)(36) of the Small Business Act (15 U.S.C. 636(a)(36))—

(i) the amount of remaining authority for the loans, in dollar amount and as a percentage; and

(ii) an estimate of the date on which the net and gross dollar amount of loans will reach the maximum amount authorized for commitments for such loans;

(C) for advances made under section 1110(e) of the CARES Act (Public Law 116–136)—

(i) the amount of remaining funds appropriated for the advances, in dollar amount and as a percentage; and

(ii) an estimate of the date on which the funds will be expended; and

(D) for loans made under section 7(b)(2) of the Small Business Act (15 U.S.C. 636(b)(2))—

(i) the amount of remaining authority for the loans, in dollar amount and as a percentage; and

(ii) an estimate of the date on which the net and gross dollar amount of loans will reach the maximum amount authorized for commitments for such loans.

(2) REPORTING ON DEBT RELIEF FOR MICROLOANS, 7(A) LOANS, AND 504 LOANS.—The Administrator shall include in each daily report submitted under paragraph (1), and update on a monthly basis until the date described in paragraph (1), with respect to payments made on covered loans under section 1112(c) of the CARES Act (Public Law 116–136)—

(A) the amount of remaining funds appropriated for the payments, in dollar amount and as a percentage; and

(B) an estimate of the date on which the funds will be expended.

(c) Weekly Reporting.—

(1) IN GENERAL.—Not later than 1 week after the date of enactment of this Act, and every week thereafter until the date on which loan, advance, or payment activity described in this subsection related to COVID–19 has ceased, the Administrator shall submit to Congress a report on—

(A) loans made under section 7(a)(36) of the Small Business Act (15 U.S.C. 636(a)(36)), which shall include—

(i) the number and dollar amount of loans approved for or disbursed to all borrowers, including a breakout of loans by State, congressional district, demographics, industry, and loan size;

(ii) the number and dollar amount of loans approved for or disbursed to business concerns assigned a North American Industry Classification System code beginning with 72, including a breakout of loans by State, congressional district, demographics, and loan size;

(iii) the number and dollar amount of loans approved for or disbursed to nonprofit organizations and veterans organizations (as those terms are defined in section 7(a)(36)(A) of the Small Business Act (15 U.S.C. 636(a)(36)(A)), including religious institutions, including a breakout of loans by State, congressional district, industry, and loan size;

(iv) for each category of borrowers described in clauses (i), (ii), and (iii)—

(I) the number of full-time equivalent employees at the time at which the borrower submits a loan application;

(II) the number of full-time equivalent employees at the time at which the borrower receives loan forgiveness under section 1106 of the CARES Act (Public Law 116–136); and

(III) the number of full-time equivalent employees expected for borrowers in the 6-month period following forgiveness of the loan;

(v) the number and dollar amount of loans fully forgiven under section 1106 of the CARES Act (Public Law 116–136), as compared to the number and dollar amount of loans made as of the date of the report;

(vi) the number and dollar amount of loans not fully forgiven under section 1106 of the CARES Act (Public Law 116–136), and the proportion of that dollar amount of loans that become term loans guaranteed by the Administration under section 7(a)(36) of the Small Business Act (15 U.S.C. 636(a)(36));

(vii) the total amount of the lender compensation fees paid to lenders; and

(viii) the total amount lenders paid in broker fees; and

(B) loans made under section 7(b)(2) of the Small Business Act (15 U.S.C. 636(b)(2)) and advances made under section 1110(e) of the CARES Act (Public Law 116–136), which shall include—

(i) the number and dollar amount of loans approved for or disbursed to all borrowers, including a breakout of loans by State, congressional district, demographics, industry, and loan size;

(ii) the number and dollar amount of advances approved for or disbursed to grantees, including a breakout of loans by State, congressional district, demographics, industry, and grant size;

(iii) the number and dollar amount of advances approved for or disbursed to private nonprofit organizations, including a breakout by State, congressional district, industry, and loan or grant size;

(iv) for each category of recipients, the number of full-time equivalent employees of the recipient at the time at which an application is submitted for the loan or advance, and the number of jobs created or retained because of the loan or advance;

(v) loan processing times, including processing times for application to approval and approval to disbursement; and

(vi) advance processing times, including the percentage of advances that were provided within 3 days of submission of the application, as required under section 1110(e)(1) of the CARES Act (Public Law 116–136).

(2) REPORTING ON DEBT RELIEF FOR MICROLOANS, 7(A) LOANS, AND 504 LOANS.—The Administrator shall include in each weekly report submitted under paragraph (1), and update on a monthly basis until the date described in paragraph (1), with respect to payments made on covered loans under section 1112(c) of the CARES Act (Public Law 116–136)—

(A) the total dollar amount approved and the total amount disbursed by the Administration and the number of borrowers receiving assistance under such section 1112(c), including a breakdown by—

(i) each type of covered loan described in subparagraph (A) and (B) of paragraph (1) and paragraph (2) of such section 1112(a); and

(ii) whether the borrower is—

(I) an existing borrower of a covered loan, as described in subparagraph (A) or (B) of such section 1112(c)(1); or

(II) a new borrower of a covered loan, as described in subparagraph (C) of such section 1112(c)(1);

(B) the total dollar amount approved and the total amount disbursed by the Administration by the Administration and number of borrowers receiving assistance under such section 1112(c) broken out by State and congressional district, including a breakdown by each type of covered loan described in subparagraph (A) and (B) of paragraph (1) and paragraph (2) of such section 1112(a); and

(C) the total number and amount of new covered loans by approval and disbursement broken out by lending institution, including a breakout of loans by State, congressional district, demographics, industry, and loan size.

(d) Report On Waste, Fraud And Abuse.—Not later than 30 days after the date of enactment of this Act, the Administrator and the Secretary of the Treasury shall submit to Congress a joint report on steps that the Administration and the Department of the Treasury are taking to identify and prevent potential instances of waste, fraud, and abuse relating to covered assistance, including borrower compliance with any loan deferment, relief, or forgiveness provided through covered assistance.

(e) Report On Jobs For The Debt Relief Program.—

(1) IN GENERAL.—To the extent practicable, with respect to each type of covered loan described in subparagraphs (A) and (B) of paragraph (1) and paragraph (2) of section 1112(a) of the CARES Act (Public Law 116–136), the Administrator shall submit to Congress a report on—

(A) the number of full-time equivalent employees—

(i) for existing borrowers of a covered loan, as described in subparagraph (A) or (B) of such section 1112(c)(1) at the start of the debt relief under such section 1112(c); and

(ii) for new borrowers of a covered loan, as described in subparagraph (C) of such section 1112(c)(1), at the time of application for the covered loan; and

(B) the number of jobs created or retained because of the covered loan or the debt relief.

(2) TIMING.—The Administrator shall, to the extent practicable, submit to Congress the report required under paragraph (1) not later than October 1, 2020, with an updated version submitted not later than January 31, 2021.

(f) Report On CARES Act Salaries And Expenses Funding.—Not later than 30 days after the date of enactment of this Act, the Administrator shall submit to the appropriate congressional committees a report that includes the plans of the Administrator to use the $675,000,000 provided in section 1107(a)(2) of the CARES Act (Public Law 116–136) for salaries and expenses, and the $2,100,000,000 provided in title II of the Paycheck Protection Program and Health Care Enhancement Act (Public Law 116–139) for salaries and expenses (including staff hired, the use of outside consultants, program improvements, and system upgrades), to carry out the provisions of title I of division A of the CARES Act (Public Law 116–136).

(g) Collection Of Additional Data.—The Administrator shall collect and make publically available—

(1) the number and dollar amount of loans approved and for or disbursed under 7(a)(36) of the Small Business Act (15 U.S.C. 636(a)(36)) to borrowers broken out by lending institution, including a breakout of loans made by the lending institution by State, congressional district, demographics, industry, and loan size, and the number and percent of loan applicants that were new or existing customers of the lender;

(2) the total amount of the lender compensation fees paid to each lender under such section 7(a)(36);

(3) the total amount each lender paid in broker fees under such section 7(a)(36); and

(4) to the extent practicable, detailed information on processing times for—

(A) loan approvals and loan disbursements under such section 7(a)(36); and

(B) notices of forgiveness of the loans under section 1106 of the CARES Act (Public Law 116–136) to borrowers.

(h) Format Of Reported Data.—Not later than 30 days after the date of enactment of this Act, the Administrator shall make available on a publicly available website in a standardized and downloadable format, and update on a monthly basis, any data contained in a report submitted under this section.

SEC. 90017. FUNDING FOR RESOURCES AND SERVICES IN LANGUAGES OTHER THAN ENGLISH.

Of the unobligated balances of amounts appropriated for salaries and expenses by section 1107(a)(2) of the CARES Act, $25,000,000 shall be made available to carry out the requirements of section 1111 of such Act.

SEC. 90018. DIRECT APPROPRIATION.

There is appropriated, out of amounts in the Treasury not otherwise appropriated, for the fiscal year ending September 30, 2020, to remain available until September 30, 2021—

(1) $500,000,000 under the heading "Small Business Administration—Business Loans Program Account" to carry out the requirements of sections 90010, 90011, and 90012 of this division; and

(2) $7,000,000 under the heading "Small Business Administration—Business Loans Program Account" to carry out the requirements of section 90014 of this division; and

(3) $50,000,000 under the heading "Small Business Administration—Entrepreneurial Development Programs" for technical assistance grants, as authorized under section 90014 of this division.

DIVISION J—SUPPORT FOR ESSENTIAL WORKERS, AT-RISK INDIVIDUALS, FAMILIES, AND COMMUNITIES

TITLE I—FAMILY CARE FOR ESSENTIAL WORKERS

SEC. 100101. FAMILY CARE FOR ESSENTIAL WORKERS.

(a) Increase In Funding.—

(1) IN GENERAL.—The amount specified in subsection (c) of section 2003 of the Social Security Act for purposes of subsections (a) and (b) of such section is deemed to be $12,150,000,000 for fiscal year 2020, of which $850,000,000 shall be obligated by States during calendar year 2020 in accordance with subsection (b) of this section.

(2) APPROPRIATION.—Out of any money in the Treasury of the United States not otherwise appropriated, there are appropriated $850,000,000 for fiscal year 2020 to carry out this section.

(b) Rules Governing Use Of Additional Funds.—

(1) IN GENERAL.—Funds are used in accordance with this subsection if—

(A) the funds are used for—

(i) child care services for a child of an essential worker; or

(ii) daytime care services or other adult protective services for an individual who—

(I) is a dependent, or a member of the household of, an essential worker; and

(II) requires the services;

(B) the funds are provided to reimburse an essential worker for the cost of obtaining the services (including child care services obtained on or after the date the Secretary of Health and Human Services declared a public health emergency pursuant to section 319 of the Public Health Service Act on January 31, 2020, entitled "Determination that a Public Health Emergency Exists Nationwide as the Result of the 2019 Novel Coronavirus"), to a provider of child care services, or to establish a temporary child care facility operated by a State or local government;

(C) eligibility for the funds or services, and the amount of funds or services provided, is not conditioned on a means test;

(D) the funds are used subject to the limitations in section 2005 of the Social Security Act, except that, for purposes of this subparagraph—

(i) paragraphs (3), (5), and (8) of section 2005(a) of such Act shall not apply; and

(ii) (I) the limitation in section 2005(a)(7) of such Act shall not apply with respect to any standard which the State involved determines would impede the ability of the State to provide emergency temporary care to a child, dependent, or household member referred to in subparagraph (A) of this paragraph; and

(II) if the State determines that such a standard would be so impeding, the State shall report the determination to the Secretary, separately from the annual report to the Secretary by the State;

(E) the funds are used to supplement, not supplant, State general revenue funds for child care assistance; and

(F) the funds are not used for child care costs that are—

(i) covered by funds provided under the Child Care and Development Block Grant Act of 1990 or section 418 of the Social Security Act; or

(ii) reimbursable by the Federal Emergency Management Agency.

(2) ESSENTIAL WORKER DEFINED.—In paragraph (1), the term "essential worker" means—

(A) a health sector employee;

(B) an emergency response worker;

(C) a sanitation worker;

(D) a worker at a business which a State or local government official has determined must remain open to serve the public during the emergency referred to in paragraph (1)(B); and

(E) any other worker who cannot telework, and whom the State deems to be essential during the emergency referred to in paragraph (1)(B).

TITLE II—PANDEMIC EMERGENCY ASSISTANCE AND SERVICES

SEC. 100201. FUNDING TO STATES, LOCALITIES, AND COMMUNITY-BASED ORGANIZATIONS FOR EMERGENCY AID AND SERVICES.

(a) Funding For States.—

(1) INCREASE IN FUNDING FOR SOCIAL SERVICES BLOCK GRANT PROGRAM.—

(A) APPROPRIATION.—Out of any money in the Treasury of the United States not otherwise appropriated, there are appropriated $9,600,000,000, which shall be available for payments under section 2002 of the Social Security Act.

(B) DEADLINE FOR DISTRIBUTION OF FUNDS.—Within 45 days after the date of the enactment of this Act, the Secretary of Health and Human Services shall distribute the funds made available by this paragraph, which shall be made available to States on an emergency basis for immediate obligation and expenditure.

(C) SUBMISSION OF REVISED PRE-EXPENDITURE REPORT.—Within 90 days after a State receives funds made available by this paragraph, the State shall submit to the Secretary a revised pre-expenditure report pursuant to title XX of the Social Security Act that describes how the State plans to administer the funds.

(D) OBLIGATION OF FUNDS BY STATES.—A State to which funds made available by this paragraph are distributed shall obligate the funds not later than December 31, 2020.

(E) EXPENDITURE OF FUNDS BY STATES.—A grantee to which a State (or a subgrantee to which a grantee) provides funds made available by this paragraph shall expend the funds not later than December 31, 2021.

(2) RULES GOVERNING USE OF ADDITIONAL FUNDS.—A State to which funds made available by paragraph (1)(B) are distributed shall use the funds in accordance with the following:

(A) PURPOSE.—

(i) IN GENERAL.—The State shall use the funds only to support the provision of emergency services to disadvantaged children, families, and households.

(ii) DISADVANTAGED DEFINED.—In this paragraph, the term "disadvantaged" means, with respect to an entity, that the entity—

(I) is an individual, or is located in a community, that is experiencing material hardship;

(II) is a household in which there is a child (as defined in section 12(d) of the Richard B. Russell National School Lunch Act) or a child served under section 11(a)(1) of such Act, who, if not for the closure of the school attended by the child during a public health emergency designation and due to concerns about a COVID–19 outbreak, would receive free or reduced price school meals pursuant to such Act;

(III) is an individual, or is located in a community, with barriers to employment; or

(IV) is located in a community that, as of the date of the enactment of this Act, is not experiencing a 56-day downward trajectory of—

(aa) influenza-like illnesses;

(bb) COVID-like syndromic cases;

(cc) documented COVID–19 cases; or

(dd) positive test results as a percentage of total COVID–19 tests.

(B) PASS-THROUGH TO LOCAL ENTITIES.—

(i) In the case of a State in which a county administers or contributes financially to the non-Federal share of the amounts expended in carrying out a State program funded under title IV of the Social Security Act, the State may pass funds so made available through to—

(I) the chief elected official of the city or urban county that administers the program; or

(II) local government and community-based organizations.

(ii) In the case of any other State, the State shall—

(I) pass the funds through to—

(aa)(AA) local governments that will expend or distribute the funds in consultation with community-based organizations with experience serving disadvantaged families or individuals; or

(BB) community-based organizations with experience serving disadvantaged families and individuals; and (bb) sub-State areas in proportions based on the population of disadvantaged individuals living in the areas; and

(II) report to the Secretary on how the State determined the amounts passed through pursuant to this clause.

(C) METHODS.—

(i) IN GENERAL.—The State shall use the funds only for—

(I) administering emergency services;

(II) providing short-term cash, non-cash, or in-kind emergency disaster relief;

(III) providing services with demonstrated need in accordance with objective criteria that are made available to the public;

(IV) operational costs directly related to providing services described in subclauses (I), (II), and (III);

(V) local government emergency social service operations; and

(VI) providing emergency social services to rural and frontier communities that may not have access to other emergency funding streams.

(ii) ADMINISTERING EMERGENCY SERVICES DEFINED.—In clause (i), the term "administering emergency services" means—

(I) providing basic disaster relief, economic, and well-being necessities to ensure communities are able to safely observe shelter-in-place and social distancing orders;

(II) providing necessary supplies such as masks, gloves, and soap, to protect the public against infectious disease; and

(III) connecting individuals, children, and families to services or payments for which they may already be eligible.

(D) PROHIBITIONS.—

(i) NO INDIVIDUAL ELIGIBILITY DETERMINATIONS BY GRANTEES OR SUBGRANTEES.—Neither a grantee to which the State provides the funds nor any subgrantee of such a grantee may exercise individual eligibility determinations for the purpose of administering short-term, non-cash, in-kind emergency disaster relief to communities.

(ii) APPLICABILITY OF CERTAIN SOCIAL SERVICES BLOCK GRANT FUNDS USE LIMITATIONS.—The State shall use the funds subject to the limitations in section 2005 of the Social Security Act, except that, for purposes of this clause, section 2005(a)(2) and 2005(a)(8) of such Act shall not apply.

(iii) NO SUPPLANTATION OF CERTAIN STATE FUNDS.—The State may use the funds to supplement, not supplant, State general revenue funds for social services.

(iv) BAN ON USE FOR CERTAIN COSTS REIMBURSABLE BY FEMA.—The State may not use the funds for costs that are reimbursable by the Federal Emergency Management Agency, under a contract for insurance, or by self-insurance.

(b) Funding For Federally Recognized Indian Tribes And Tribal Organizations.—

(1) GRANTS.—

(A) IN GENERAL.—Within 90 days after the date of the enactment of this Act, the Secretary of Health and Human Services shall make grants to federally recognized Indian Tribes and Tribal organizations.

(B) AMOUNT OF GRANT.—The amount of the grant for an Indian Tribe or Tribal organization shall bear the same ratio to the amount appropriated by paragraph (3) as the total amount of grants awarded to the Indian Tribe or Tribal organization under the Low-Income Home Energy Assistance Act of 1981 and the Community Service Block Grant for fiscal year 2020 bears to the total amount of grants awarded to all Indian Tribes and Tribal organizations under such Act and such Grant for the fiscal year.

(2) RULES GOVERNING USE OF FUNDS.—An entity to which a grant is made under paragraph (1) shall obligate the funds not later than December 31, 2020, and the funds shall be expended by grantees and subgrantees not later than December 31, 2021, and used in accordance with the following:

(A) PURPOSE.—

(i) IN GENERAL.—The grantee shall use the funds only to support the provision of emergency services to disadvantaged households.

(ii) DISADVANTAGED DEFINED.—In clause (i), the term "disadvantaged" means, with respect to an entity, that the entity—

(I) is an individual, or is located in a community, that is experiencing material hardship;

(II) is a household in which there is a child (as defined in section 12(d) of the Richard B. Russell National School Lunch Act) or a child served under section 11(a)(1) of such Act, who, if not for the closure of the school attended by the child during a public health emergency designation and due to concerns about a COVID–19 outbreak, would receive free or reduced price school meals pursuant to such Act;

(III) is an individual, or is located in a community, with barriers to employment; or

(IV) is located in a community that, as of the date of the enactment of this Act, is not experiencing a 56-day downward trajectory of—

(aa) influenza-like illnesses;

(bb) COVID-like syndromic cases;

(cc) documented COVID–19 cases; or

(dd) positive test results as a percentage of total COVID–19 tests.

(B) METHODS.—

(i) IN GENERAL.—The grantee shall use the funds only for—

(I) administering emergency services;

(II) providing short-term, non-cash, in-kind emergency disaster relief; and

(III) tribal emergency social service operations.

(ii) ADMINISTERING EMERGENCY SERVICES DEFINED.—In clause (i), the term "administering emergency services" means—

(I) providing basic economic and well-being necessities to ensure communities are able to safely observe shelter-in-place and social distancing orders;

(II) providing necessary supplies such as masks, gloves, and soap, to protect the public against infectious disease; and

(III) connecting individuals, children, and families to services or payments for which they may already be eligible.

(C) PROHIBITIONS.—

(i) NO INDIVIDUAL ELIGIBILITY DETERMINATIONS BY GRANTEES OR SUBGRANTEES.—Neither the grantee nor any subgrantee may exercise individual eligibility determinations for the purpose of administering short-term, non-cash, in-kind emergency disaster relief to communities.

(ii) BAN ON USE FOR CERTAIN COSTS REIMBURSABLE BY FEMA.—The grantee may not use the funds for costs that are reimbursable by the Federal Emergency Management Agency, under a contract for insurance, or by self-insurance.

(3) APPROPRIATION.—Out of any money in the Treasury of the United States not otherwise appropriated, there are appropriated to the Secretary of Health and Human Services $400,000,000 to carry out this subsection.

SEC. 100202. EMERGENCY ASSISTANCE TO OLDER FOSTER YOUTH.

(a) Funding Increases.—

(1) GENERAL PROGRAM.—The dollar amount specified in section 477(h)(1) of the Social Security Act for fiscal year 2020 is deemed to be $193,000,000.

(2) EDUCATION AND TRAINING VOUCHERS.—The dollar amount specified in section 477(h)(2) of such Act for fiscal year 2020 is deemed to be $78,000,000.

(b) Programmatic Flexibility.—With respect to the period that begins on March 1, 2020, and ends January 31, 2021:

(1) ELIMINATION OF AGE LIMITATIONS ON ELIGIBILITY FOR ASSISTANCE.—Eligibility for services or assistance under a State program operated pursuant to section 477 of the Social Security Act shall be provided without regard to the age of the recipient.

(2) SUSPENSION OF WORK AND EDUCATION REQUIREMENTS UNDER THE EDUCATION AND TRAINING VOUCHER PROGRAM.—Section 477(i)(3) of the Social Security Act shall be applied and administered without regard to any work or education requirement.

(3) AUTHORITY TO WAIVE LIMITATION ON PERCENTAGE OF FUNDS USED FOR HOUSING ASSISTANCE.—The Secretary of Health and Human Services (in this subsection referred to as the "Secretary") may apply and administer section 477 of the Social Security Act without regard to subsection (b)(3)(B) of such section.

(4) ELIMINATION OF EDUCATION AND EMPLOYMENT REQUIREMENTS FOR CERTAIN FOSTER YOUTH.—The Secretary may waive the applicability of subclauses (I) through (IV) of section 475(8)(B)(iv) of the Social Security Act.

(c) State Defined.—In subsection (a), the term "State" has the meaning given the term in section 1101(a) of the Social Security Act for purposes of title IV of such Act, and includes an Indian tribe, tribal organization, or tribal consortium with an application and plan approved under section 477(j) of such Act for fiscal year 2020.

SEC. 100203. EMERGENCY ASSISTANCE TO FAMILIES THROUGH HOME VISITING PROGRAMS.

(a) In General.—For purposes of section 511 of the Social Security Act, during the period that begins on February 1, 2020, and ends January 31, 2021—

(1) a virtual home visit shall be considered a home visit;

(2) funding for, and staffing levels of, a program conducted pursuant to such section shall not be reduced on account of reduced enrollment in the program; and

(3) funds provided for such a program may be used—

(A) to train home visitors in conducting a virtual home visit and in emergency preparedness and response planning for families served;

(B) for the acquisition by families enrolled in the program of such technological means as are needed to conduct and support a virtual home visit;

(C) to provide emergency supplies (such as diapers, formula, non-perishable food, water, hand soap and hand sanitizer) to families served; and

(D) to provide prepaid debit cards to an eligible family (as defined in section 511(k)(2) of such Act) for the purpose of enabling the family to meet the emergency needs of the family.

(b) Virtual Home Visit Defined.—In subsection (a), the term "virtual home visit" means a visit that is conducted solely by electronic means.

(c) Authority To Delay Deadlines.—

(1) IN GENERAL.—The Secretary of Health and Human Services may extend the

deadline by which a requirement of section 511 of the Social Security Act must be met, by such period of time as the Secretary deems appropriate.

(2) GUIDANCE.—The Secretary shall provide to eligible entities funded under section 511 of the Social Security Act information on the parameters used in extending a deadline under paragraph (1) of this subsection.

(d) Supplemental Appropriation.—In addition to amounts otherwise appropriated, out of any money in the Treasury of the United States not otherwise appropriated, there are appropriated to the Secretary of Health and Human Services $100,000,000, to enable eligible entities to conduct programs funded under section 511 of the Social Security Act pursuant to this section, which shall remain available for obligation not later than January 31, 2021.

TITLE III—PROGRAM FLEXIBILITY DURING THE PANDEMIC

SEC. 100301. EMERGENCY FLEXIBILITY FOR CHILD WELFARE PROGRAMS.

(a) In General.—With respect to the period that begins on March 1, 2020, and ends January 31, 2021:

(1) AUTHORITY OF STATES TO DETERMINE HOW DAILY ACTIVITIES MAY BE CONDUCTED REMOTELY.—The Secretary of Health and Human Services may allow a State to determine how daily activities under the State plan developed under part B of title IV of the Social Security Act and the State program funded under section 477 of such Act may be conducted through electronic means to comply with public health guidelines relating to social distancing, including conducting any required court proceedings pertaining to children in care. In making any such determination, the State shall work to ensure that the safety and health of each child in care remains paramount.

(2) COUNTING OF REMOTE CASEWORKER VISITS AS IN-PERSON VISITS.— In the case of a foster child who has attained 18 years of age and with respect to whom foster care maintenance payments are being made under a State plan approved under part E of title IV of the Social Security Act, caseworker contact with the child that includes visual and auditory contact and which is conducted solely by electronic means is deemed an in-person visit to the child by the caseworker for purposes of section 424(f)(1)(A) of such Act if the child is visited by the caseworker in person not less than once every 6 months while in such care.

(b) State Defined.—In subsection (a), the term "State" has the meaning given the term in section 1101(a) of the Social Security Act for purposes of title IV of such Act, and includes an Indian tribe, tribal organization, or tribal consortium with an application and plan approved under this section 477(j) of such Act for fiscal year 2020.

SEC. 100302. EMERGENCY FLEXIBILITY FOR CHILD SUPPORT PROGRAMS.

(a) In General.—With respect to the period that begins on March 1, 2020, and ends January 31, 2021:

(1) Sections 408(a)(2), 409(a)(5), and 409(a)(8) of the Social Security Act shall have no force or effect.

(2) Notwithstanding section 466(d) of such Act, the Secretary of Health and Human Services (in this subsection referred to as the "Secretary") may exempt a State from

any requirement of section 466 of such Act to respond to the COVID–19 pandemic, except that the Secretary may not exempt a State from any requirement to—

(A) provide a parent with notice of a right to request a review and, if appropriate, adjustment of a support order; or

(B) afford a parent the opportunity to make such a request.

(3) The Secretary may not impose a penalty or take any other adverse action against a State pursuant to section 452(g)(1) of such Act for failure to achieve a paternity establishment percentage of less than 90 percent.

(4) The Secretary may not find that the paternity establishment percentage for a State is not based on reliable data for purposes of section 452(g)(1) of such Act, and the Secretary may not determine that the data which a State submitted pursuant to section 452(a)(4)(C)(i) of such Act and which is used in determining a performance level is not complete or reliable for purposes of section 458(b)(5)(B) of such Act, on the basis of the failure of the State to submit OCSE Form 396 or 34 in a timely manner.

(5) The Secretary may not impose a penalty or take any other adverse action against a State for failure to comply with section 454A(g)(1)(A)(i) of such Act.

(6) The Secretary may not disapprove a State plan submitted pursuant to part D of title IV of such Act for failure of the plan to meet the requirement of section 454(1) of such Act, and may not impose a penalty or take any other adverse action against a State with such a plan that meets that requirement for failure to comply with that requirement.

(7) To the extent that a preceding provision of this section applies with respect to a provision of law applicable to a program operated by an Indian tribe or tribal organization (as defined in subsections (e) and (l) of section 4 of the Indian Self-Determination and Education Assistance Act (25 U.S.C. 450b)), that preceding provision shall apply with respect to the Indian tribe or tribal organization.

(b) State Defined.—In subsection (a), the term "State" has the meaning given the term in section 1101(a) of the Social Security Act for purposes of title IV of such Act.

SEC. 100303. EMERGENCY FLEXIBILITY FOR STATE TANF PROGRAMS.

(a) State Programs.—Sections 407(a), 407(e)(1), and 408(a)(7)(A) of the Social Security Act shall have no force or effect during the applicable period, and paragraphs (3), (9), (14), and (15) of section 409(a) of such Act shall not apply with respect to conduct engaged in during the period.

(b) Tribal Programs.—The minimum work participation requirements and time limits established under section 412(c) of the Social Security Act shall have no force or effect during the applicable period, and the penalties established under such section shall not apply with respect to conduct engaged in during the period.

(c) Penalty For Noncompliance.—

(1) IN GENERAL.—If the Secretary of Health and Human Services finds that a State or an Indian tribe has imposed a work requirement as a condition of receiving assistance, or a time limit on the provision of assistance, under a program funded under part A of title IV of the Social Security Act or any program funded with qualified State expenditures (as defined in section 409(a)(7)(B)(i) of such Act) during the applicable period, or has imposed a penalty for failure to comply with a work requirement during the period, the Secretary shall reduce the grant payable to the State under section 403(a)(1) of such Act or the grant payable to the tribe under section 412(a)(1) of such Act, as the case may be, for fiscal year 2021 by an amount equal to 5 percent of the State or tribal family assistance grant, as the case may be.

(2) APPLICABILITY OF CERTAIN PROVISIONS.—For purposes of section 409(d) of the Social Security Act, paragraph (1) of this subsection shall be considered to be included in section 409(a) of such Act.

(d) Definitions.—In this section:

(1) APPLICABLE PERIOD.—The term "applicable period" means the period that begins on March 1, 2020, and ends January 31, 2021.

(2) WORK REQUIREMENT.—The term "work requirement" means a requirement to engage in a work activity (as defined in section 407(d) of the Social Security Act) or other work-related activity as defined by a State or tribal program funded under part A of title IV of such Act.

(3) OTHER TERMS.—Each other term has the meaning given the term in section 419 of the Social Security Act.

DIVISION K—COVID–19 HERO ACT

SHORT TITLE; TABLE OF CONTENTS

SEC. 110001.

This division may be cited as the "COVID–19 Housing, Economic Relief, and Oversight Act" or the "COVID–19 HERO Act".

TITLE I

—PROVIDING MEDICAL EQUIPMENT FOR FIRST RESPONDERS AND ESSENTIAL WORKERS
COVID–19 EMERGENCY MEDICAL SUPPLIES ENHANCEMENT

SEC. 110101.

(a) Determination On Emergency Supplies And Relationship To State And Local Efforts.—

(1) DETERMINATION.—For the purposes of section 101 of the Defense Production Act of 1950 (50 U.S.C. 4511), the following materials shall be deemed to be scarce and critical materials essential to the national defense and otherwise meet the requirements of section 101(b) of such Act during the COVID–19 emergency period:

(A) Diagnostic tests, including serological tests, for COVID–19 and the reagents and other materials necessary for producing or conducting such tests.

(B) Personal protective equipment, including face shields, N–95 respirator masks, and any other masks determined by the Secretary of Health and Human Services to be needed to respond to the COVID–19 pandemic, and the materials to produce such equipment.

(C) Medical ventilators, the components necessary to make such ventilators, and medicines needed to use a ventilator as a treatment for any individual who is hospitalized for COVID–19.

(D) Pharmaceuticals and any medicines determined by the Food and Drug Administration or another Government agency to be effective in treating COVID–19 (including vaccines for COVID–19) and any materials necessary to produce or use such pharmaceuticals or medicines (including self-injection syringes or other delivery systems).

(E) Any other medical equipment or supplies determined by the Secretary of Health and Human Services or the Secretary of Homeland Security to be scarce and critical materials essential to the national defense for purposes of section 101 of the Defense Production Act of 1950 (50 U.S.C. 4511).

(2) EXERCISE OF TITLE I AUTHORITIES IN RELATION TO CONTRACTS BY STATE AND LOCAL GOVERNMENTS.—In exercising authorities under title I of the Defense Production Act of 1950 (50 U.S.C. 4511 et seq.) during the COVID–19 emergency period, the President (and any officer or employee of the United States to which authorities under such title I have been delegated)—

(A) may exercise the prioritization or allocation authority provided in such title I to exclude any materials described in paragraph (1) ordered by a State or local government that are scheduled to be delivered within 15 days of the time at which—

(i) the purchase order or contract by the Federal Government for such materials is made; or

(ii) the materials are otherwise allocated by the Federal Government under the authorities contained in such Act; and

(B) shall, within 24 hours of any exercise of the prioritization or allocation authority provided in such title I—

(i) notify any State or local government if the exercise of such authorities would delay the receipt of such materials ordered by such government; and

(ii) take such steps as may be necessary to ensure that such materials ordered by such government are delivered in the shortest possible period.

(3) UPDATE TO THE FEDERAL ACQUISITION REGULATION.—Not later than 15 days after the date of the enactment of this Act, the Federal Acquisition Regulation shall be revised to reflect the requirements of paragraph (2)(A).

(b) Engagement With The Private Sector.—

(1) SENSE OF CONGRESS.—The Congress—

(A) appreciates the willingness of private companies not traditionally involved in producing items for the health sector to volunteer to use their expertise and supply chains to produce essential medical supplies and equipment;

(B) encourages other manufacturers to review their existing capacity and to develop capacity to produce essential medical supplies, medical equipment, and medical treatments to address the COVID–19 emergency; and

(C) commends and expresses deep appreciation to individual citizens who have been producing personal protective equipment and other materials for, in particular, use at hospitals in their community.

(2) OUTREACH REPRESENTATIVE.—

(A) DESIGNATION.—Consistent with the authorities in title VII of the Defense Production Act of 1950 (50 U.S.C. 4551 et seq.), the Administrator of the Federal Emergency Management Agency, in consultation with the Secretary of Health and Human Services, shall designate or shall appoint, pursuant to section 703 of such Act (50 U.S.C. 4553), an individual to be known as the "Outreach Representative". Such individual shall—

(i) be appointed from among individuals with substantial experience in the private sector in the production of medical supplies or equipment; and

(ii) act as the Government-wide single point of contact during the COVID–19 emergency for outreach to manufacturing companies and their suppliers who may be interested in producing medical supplies or equipment, including the materials described under subsection (a).

(B) ENCOURAGING PARTNERSHIPS.—The Outreach Representative shall seek to develop partnerships between companies, in coordination with the Supply Chain Stabilization Task Force or any overall coordinator appointed by the President to oversee the response to the COVID–19 emergency, including through the exercise of the authorities under section 708 of the Defense Production Act of 1950 (50 U.S.C. 4558).

(c) Enhancement Of Supply Chain Production.—In exercising authority under title III of the Defense Production Act of 1950 (50 U.S.C. 4531 et seq.) with respect to materials described in subsection (a), the President shall seek to ensure that support is provided to companies that comprise the supply chains for reagents, components, raw materials, and other materials and items necessary to produce or use the materials described in subsection (a).

(d) Oversight Of Current Activity And Needs.—

(1) RESPONSE TO IMMEDIATE NEEDS.—

(A) IN GENERAL.—Not later than 7 days after the date of the enactment of this Act, the President, in coordination with the National Response Coordination Center of the Federal Emergency Management Agency, the Administrator of the Defense Logistics Agency, the Secretary of Health and Human Services, the Secretary of Veterans Affairs, and heads of other Federal agencies (as appropriate), shall submit to the appropriate congressional committees a report assessing the immediate needs described in subparagraph (B) to combat the COVID–19 pandemic and the plan for meeting those immediate needs.

(B) ASSESSMENT.—The report required by this paragraph shall include—

(i) an assessment of the needs for medical supplies or equipment necessary to address the needs of the population of the United States infected by the virus SARS–CoV–2 that causes COVID–19 and to prevent an increase in the incidence of COVID–19 throughout the United States, including diagnostic tests, serological tests, medicines that have been approved by the Food and Drug Administration to treat COVID–19, and ventilators and medicines needed to employ ventilators;

(ii) based on meaningful consultations with relevant stakeholders, an assessment of the need for personal protective equipment and other supplies (including diagnostic tests) required by—

(I) health professionals, health workers, and hospital staff;

(II) workers in industries and sectors described in the "Advisory Memorandum on Identification of Essential Critical Infrastructure Workers during the COVID–19 Response" issued by the Director of Cybersecurity and Infrastructure Security Agency of the Department of Homeland Security on April 17, 2020 (and any expansion of industries and sectors included in updates to such advisory memorandum); and

(III) other workers determined to be essential based on such consultation;

(iii) an assessment of the quantities of equipment and supplies in the Strategic National Stockpile (established under section 319F–2 of the Public Health Service Act ((42 U.S.C. 247d–6b(a)(1))) as of the date of the report, and the projected gap between the quantities of equipment and supplies identified as needed in the assessment under clauses (i) and (ii) and the quantities in the Strategic National Stockpile;

(iv) an identification of the industry sectors and manufacturers most ready to fulfill purchase orders for such equipment and supplies (including manufacturers that may be incentivized) through the exercise of authority under section 303(e) of the Defense Production Act of 1950 (50 U.S.C. 4533(e)) to modify, expand, or improve production processes to manufacture such equipment and supplies to respond immediately to a need identified in clause (i) or (ii);

(v) an identification of Government-owned and privately-owned stockpiles of such equipment and supplies not included in the Strategic National Stockpile that could be repaired or refurbished;

(vi) an identification of previously distributed critical supplies that can be redistributed based on current need;

(vii) a description of any exercise of the authorities described under paragraph (1)(E) or (2)(A) of subsection (a); and

(viii) an identification of critical areas of need, by county and by areas identified by the Indian Health Service, in the United States and the metrics and criteria for identification as a critical area.

(C) PLAN.—The report required by this paragraph shall include a plan for meeting the immediate needs to combat the COVID–19 pandemic, including the needs described in subparagraph (B). Such plan shall include—

(i) each contract the Federal Government has entered into to meet such needs, including the purpose of each contract, the type and amount of equipment, supplies, or services to be provided under the contract, the entity performing such contract, and the dollar amount of each contract;

(ii) each contract that the Federal Government intends to enter into within 14 days after submission of such report, including the information described in subparagraph (B) for each such contract; and

(iii) whether any of the contracts described in clause (i) or (ii) have or will have a priority rating under the Defense Production Act of 1950 (50 U.S.C. 4501 et seq.), including purchase orders pursuant to Department of Defense Directive 4400.1 (or any successor directive), subpart A of part 101 of title 45, Code of Federal Regulations, or any other applicable authority.

(D) ADDITIONAL REQUIREMENTS.—The report required by this paragraph, and each update required by subparagraph (E), shall include—

(i) any requests for equipment and supplies from State or local governments and Indian Tribes, and an accompanying list of the employers and unions consulted in developing these requests;

(ii) any modeling or formulas used to determine allocation of equipment and supplies, and any related chain of command issues on making final decisions on allocations;

(iii) the amount and destination of equipment and supplies delivered;

(iv) an explanation of why any portion of any contract, whether to replenish the Strategic National Stockpile or otherwise, will not be filled;

(v) of products procured under this section, the percentage of such products that are used to replenish the Strategic National Stockpile, that are targeted to COVID–19 hotspots, and that are used for the commercial market;

(vi) metrics, formulas, and criteria used to determine COVID–19 hotspots or areas of critical need for a State, county, or an area identified by the Indian Health Service;

(vii) production and procurement benchmarks, where practicable; and

(viii) results of the consultation with the relevant stakeholders required by subparagraph (B)(ii).

(E) UPDATES.—The President, in coordination with the National Response Coordination Center of the Federal Emergency Management Agency, the Administrator of the Defense Logistics Agency, the Secretary of Health and Human Services, the Secretary of Veterans Affairs, and heads of other Federal agencies (as appropriate), shall update such report every 14 days.

(F) PUBLIC AVAILABILITY.—The President shall make the report required by this paragraph and each update required by subparagraph (E) available to the public, including on a Government website.

(2) RESPONSE TO LONGER-TERM NEEDS.—

(A) IN GENERAL.—Not later than 14 days after the date of enactment of this Act, the President, in coordination with the National Response Coordination Center of the Federal Emergency Management Agency, the Administrator of the Defense Logistics Agency, the Secretary of Health and Human Services, the Secretary of Veterans Affairs, and heads of other Federal agencies (as appropriate), shall submit to the appropriate congressional committees a report containing an assessment of the needs described in subparagraph (B) to combat the COVID–19 pandemic and the plan for meeting such needs during the 6-month period beginning on the date of submission of the report.

(B) ASSESSMENT.—The report required by this paragraph shall include—

(i) an assessment of the elements describe in clauses (i) through (v) and clause (viii) of paragraph (1)(B); and

(ii) an assessment of needs related to COVID–19 vaccines and any additional services to address the COVID–19 pandemic, including services related to health surveillance to ensure that the appropriate level of contact tracing related to detected infections is available throughout the United States.

(C) PLAN.—The report required by this paragraph shall include a plan for meeting the longer-term needs to combat the COVID–19 pandemic, including the needs described in subparagraph (B). This plan shall include—

(i) a plan to exercise authorities under the Defense Production Act of 1950 (50 U.S.C. 4501 et seq.) necessary to increase the production of the medical equipment, supplies, and services that are essential to meeting the needs identified in subparagraph (B), including the number of N–95 respirator masks and other personal protective equipment needed, based on meaningful consultations with relevant stakeholders, by the private sector to resume economic activity and by the public and nonprofit sectors to significantly increase their activities;

(ii) results of the consultations with the relevant stakeholders required by clause (i) (II);

(iii) an estimate of the funding and other measures necessary to rapidly expand manufacturing production capacity for such equipment and supplies, including—

(I) any efforts to expand, retool, or reconfigure production lines;

(II) any efforts to establish new production lines through the purchase and installation of new equipment; or

(III) the issuance of additional contracts, purchase orders, purchase guarantees, or other similar measures;

(iv) each contract the Federal Government has entered into to meet such needs or expand such production, the purpose of each contract, the type and amount of equipment, supplies, or services to be provided under the contract, the entity performing such contract, and the dollar amount of each contract;

(v) each contract that the Federal Government intends to enter into within 14 days after submission of such report, including the information described in clause (iv) for each such contract;

(vi) whether any of the contracts described in clause (iv) or (v) have or will have a priority rating under the Defense Production Act of 1950 (50 U.S.C. 4501 et seq.), including purchase orders pursuant to Department of Defense Directive 4400.1 (or any successor directive), subpart A of part 101 of title 45, Code of Federal Regulations, or any other applicable authority; and

(vii) the manner in which the Defense Production Act of 1950 (50 U.S.C. 4501 et seq.) could be used to increase services necessary to combat the COVID–19 pandemic, including services described in subparagraph (B)(ii).

(D) UPDATES.—The President, in coordination with the National Response Coordination Center of the Federal Emergency Management Agency, the Administrator of the Defense Logistics Agency, the Secretary of Health and Human Services, the Secretary of Veterans Affairs, and heads of other Federal agencies (as appropriate), shall update such report every 14 days.

(E) PUBLIC AVAILABILITY.—The President shall make the report required by this subsection and each update required by subparagraph (D) available to the public, including on a Government website.

(3) REPORT ON EXERCISING AUTHORITIES UNDER THE DEFENSE PRODUCTION ACT OF 1950.—

(A) IN GENERAL.—Not later than 14 days after the date of the enactment of this Act, the President, in consultation with the Administrator of the Federal Emergency Management Agency, the Secretary of Defense, and the Secretary of Health and Human Services, shall submit to the appropriate congressional committees a report on the exercise of authorities under titles I, III, and VII of the Defense Production Act of 1950 (50 U.S.C. 4501 et seq.) prior to the date of such report.

(B) CONTENTS.—The report required under subparagraph (A) and each update required under subparagraph (C) shall include, with respect to each exercise of such authority—

(i) an explanation of the purpose of the applicable contract, purchase order, or other exercise of authority (including an allocation of materials, services, and facilities under section 101(a)(2) of the Defense Production Act of 1950 (50 U.S.C. 4511(a)(2));

(ii) the cost of such exercise of authority; and

(iii) if applicable—

(I) the amount of goods that were purchased or allocated;

(II) an identification of the entity awarded a contract or purchase order or that was the subject of the exercise of authority; and

(III) an identification of any entity that had shipments delayed by the exercise of any authority under the Defense Production Act of 1950 (50 U.S.C. 4501 et seq.).

(C) UPDATES.—The President shall update the report required under subparagraph (A) every 14 days.

(D) PUBLIC AVAILABILITY.—The President shall make the report required by this subsection and each update required by subparagraph (C) available to the public, including on a Government website.

(4) QUARTERLY REPORTING.—The President shall submit to Congress, and make available to the public (including on a Government website), a quarterly report detailing all expenditures made pursuant to titles I, III, and VII of the Defense Production Act of 1950 50 U.S.C. 4501 et seq.).

(5) SUNSET.—The requirements of this subsection shall terminate on the later of—

(A) December 31, 2021; or

(B) the end of the COVID–19 emergency period.

(e) Enhancements To The Defense Production Act Of 1950.—

(1) HEALTH EMERGENCY AUTHORITY.—Section 107 of the Defense Production Act of 1950 (50 U.S.C. 4517) is amended by adding at the end the following:
"(c) Health Emergency Authority.—With respect to a public health emergency declaration by the Secretary of Health and Human Services under section 319 of the Public Health Service Act, or preparations for such a health emergency, the Secretary of Health and Human Services and the Administrator of the Federal Emergency Management Agency are authorized to carry out the authorities provided under this section to the same extent as the President.".
(2) EMPHASIS ON BUSINESS CONCERNS OWNED BY WOMEN, MINORITIES, VETERANS, AND NATIVE AMERICANS.—Section 108 of the Defense Production Act of 1950 (50 U.S.C. 4518) is amended—
(A) in the heading, by striking "MODERNIZATION OF SMALL BUSINESS SUPPLIERS" and inserting "SMALL BUSINESS PARTICIPATION AND FAIR INCLUSION";
(B) by amending subsection (a) to read as follows:
"(a) Participation And Inclusion.—
"(1) IN GENERAL.—In providing any assistance under this Act, the President shall accord a strong preference for subcontractors and suppliers that are—
"(A) small business concerns; or
"(B) businesses of any size owned by women, minorities, veterans, and the disabled.
"(2) SPECIAL CONSIDERATION.—To the maximum extent practicable, the President shall accord the preference described under paragraph (1) to small business concerns and businesses described in paragraph (1)(B) that are located in areas of high unemployment or areas that have demonstrated a continuing pattern of economic decline, as identified by the Secretary of Labor."; and
(C) by adding at the end the following:
"(c) Minority Defined.—In this section, the term 'minority'—
"(1) has the meaning given the term in section 308(b) of the Financial Institutions Reform, Recovery, and Enforcement Act of 1989; and
"(2) includes any indigenous person in the United States, including any territories of the United States.".
(3) ADDITIONAL INFORMATION IN ANNUAL REPORT.—Section 304(f)(3) of the Defense Production Act of 1950 (50 U.S.C. 4534(f)(3)) is amended by striking "year." and inserting "year, including the percentage of contracts awarded using Fund amounts to each of the groups described in section 108(a)(1)(B) (and, with respect to minorities, disaggregated by ethnic group), and the percentage of the total amount expended during such fiscal year on such contracts.".
(4) DEFINITION OF NATIONAL DEFENSE.—Section 702(14) of the Defense Production Act of 1950 is amended by striking "and critical infrastructure protection and restoration" and inserting ", critical infrastructure protection and restoration, and health emergency preparedness and response activities".
(f) Securing Essential Medical Materials.—
(1) STATEMENT OF POLICY.—Section 2(b) of the Defense Production Act of 1950 (50 U.S.C. 4502) is amended—
(A) by redesignating paragraphs (3) through (8) as paragraphs (4) through (9), respectively; and
(B) by inserting after paragraph (2) the following:
"(3) authorities under this Act should be used when appropriate to ensure the availability of medical materials essential to national defense, including through measures

designed to secure the drug supply chain, and taking into consideration the importance of United States competitiveness, scientific leadership and cooperation, and innovative capacity;".

(2) STRENGTHENING DOMESTIC CAPABILITY.—Section 107 of the Defense Production Act of 1950 (50 U.S.C. 4517) is amended—

(A) in subsection (a), by inserting "(including medical materials)" after "materials"; and

(B) in subsection (b)(1), by inserting "(including medical materials such as drugs to diagnose, cure, mitigate, treat, or prevent disease that essential to national defense)" after "essential materials".

(3) STRATEGY ON SECURING SUPPLY CHAINS FOR MEDICAL ARTICLES.—Title I of the Defense Production Act of 1950 (50 U.S.C. 4511 et seq.) is amended by adding at the end the following:

"SEC. 109. STRATEGY ON SECURING SUPPLY CHAINS FOR MEDICAL MATERIALS.

"(a) In General.—Not later than 180 days after the date of the enactment of this section, the President, in consultation with the Secretary of Health and Human Services, the Secretary of Commerce, the Secretary of Homeland Security, and the Secretary of Defense, shall transmit a strategy to the appropriate Members of Congress that includes the following:

"(1) A detailed plan to use the authorities under this title and title III, or any other provision of law, to ensure the supply of medical materials (including drugs to diagnose, cure, mitigate, treat, or prevent disease) essential to national defense, to the extent necessary for the purposes of this Act.

"(2) An analysis of vulnerabilities to existing supply chains for such medical articles, and recommendations to address the vulnerabilities.

"(3) Measures to be undertaken by the President to diversify such supply chains, as appropriate and as required for national defense; and

"(4) A discussion of—

"(A) any significant effects resulting from the plan and measures described in this subsection on the production, cost, or distribution of vaccines or any other drugs (as defined under section 201 of the Federal Food, Drug, and Cosmetic Act (21 U.S.C. 321));

"(B) a timeline to ensure that essential components of the supply chain for medical materials are not under the exclusive control of a foreign government in a manner that the President determines could threaten the national defense of the United States; and

"(C) efforts to mitigate any risks resulting from the plan and measures described in this subsection to United States competitiveness, scientific leadership, and innovative capacity, including efforts to cooperate and proactively engage with United States allies.

"(b) Progress Report.—Following submission of the strategy under subsection (a), the President shall submit to the appropriate Members of Congress an annual progress report evaluating the implementation of the strategy, and may include updates to the strategy as appropriate. The strategy and progress reports shall be submitted in unclassified form but may contain a classified annex.

"(c) Appropriate Members Of Congress.—The term 'appropriate Members of Congress' means the Speaker, majority leader, and minority leader of the House of Representatives, the majority leader and minority leader of the Senate, the Chairman and

Ranking Member of the Committees on Armed Services and Financial Services of the House of Representatives, and the Chairman and Ranking Member of the Committees on Armed Services and Banking, Housing, and Urban Affairs of the Senate.".

(g) GAO Report.—

(1) IN GENERAL.—Not later than 270 days after the date of the enactment of this Act, and annually thereafter, the Comptroller General of the United States shall submit to the appropriate congressional committees a report on ensuring that the United States Government has access to the medical supplies and equipment necessary to respond to future pandemics and public health emergencies, including recommendations with respect to how to ensure that the United States supply chain for diagnostic tests (including serological tests), personal protective equipment, vaccines, and therapies is better equipped to respond to emergencies, including through the use of funds in the Defense Production Act Fund under section 304 of the Defense Production Act of 1950 (50 U.S.C. 4534) to address shortages in that supply chain.

(2) REVIEW OF ASSESSMENT AND PLAN.—

(A) IN GENERAL.—Not later than 30 days after each of the submission of the reports described in paragraphs (1) and (2) of subsection (d), the Comptroller General of the United States shall submit to the appropriate congressional committees an assessment of such reports, including identifying any gaps and providing any recommendations regarding the subject matter in such reports.

(B) MONTHLY REVIEW.—Not later than a month after the submission of the assessment under subparagraph (A), and monthly thereafter, the Comptroller General shall issue a report to the appropriate congressional committees with respect to any updates to the reports described in paragraph (1) and (2) of subsection (d) that were issued during the previous 1-month period, containing an assessment of such updates, including identifying any gaps and providing any recommendations regarding the subject matter in such updates.

(h) Definitions.—In this section:

(1) APPROPRIATE CONGRESSIONAL COMMITTEES.—The term "appropriate congressional committees" means the Committees on Appropriations, Armed Services, Energy and Commerce, Financial Services, Homeland Security, and Veterans' Affairs of the House of Representatives and the Committees on Appropriations, Armed Services, Banking, Housing, and Urban Affairs, Health, Education, Labor, and Pensions, Homeland Security and Governmental Affairs, and Veterans' Affairs of the Senate.

(2) COVID–19 EMERGENCY PERIOD.—The term "COVID–19 emergency period" means the period beginning on the date of enactment of this Act and ending after the end of the incident period for the emergency declared on March 13, 2020, by the President under Section 501 of the Robert T. Stafford Disaster Relief and Emergency Assistance Act (42 U.S.C. 4121 et seq.) relating to the Coronavirus Disease 2019 (COVID–19) pandemic.

(3) RELEVANT STAKEHOLDER.—The term "relevant stakeholder" means—

(A) representative private sector entities;

(B) representatives of the nonprofit sector; and

(C) representatives of labor organizations representing workers, including unions that represent health workers, manufacturers, public sector employees, and service sector workers.

(4) STATE.—The term "State" means each of the several States, the District of Co-

lumbia, the Commonwealth of Puerto Rico, and any territory or possession of the United States.

TITLE II

—PROTECTING RENTERS AND HOMEOWNERS FROM EVICTIONS AND FORECLOSURES
EMERGENCY RENTAL ASSISTANCE

SEC. 110201.

(a) Authorization Of Appropriations.—There is authorized to be appropriated to the Secretary of Housing and Urban Development (referred to in this section as the "Secretary") $100,000,000,000 for an additional amount for grants under the Emergency Solutions Grants program under subtitle B of title IV of the McKinney-Vento Homeless Assistance Act (42 U.S.C. 11371 et seq.), to remain available until expended (subject to subsections (d) and (n) of this section), to be used for providing short- or medium-term assistance with rent and rent-related costs (including tenant-paid utility costs, utility- and rent-arrears, fees charged for those arrears, and security and utility deposits) in accordance with paragraphs (4) and (5) of section 415(a) of such Act (42 U.S.C. 11374(a)) and this section.

(b) Definition Of At Risk Of Homelessness.—Notwithstanding section 401(1) of the McKinney-Vento Homeless Assistance Act (42 U.S.C. 11360(1)), for purposes of assistance made available with amounts made available pursuant to subsection (a), the term "at risk of homelessness" means, with respect to an individual or family, that the individual or family—

(1) has an income below 80 percent of the median income for the area as determined by the Secretary; and

(2) has an inability to attain or maintain housing stability or has insufficient resources to pay for rent or utilities due to financial hardships.

(c) Income Targeting And Calculation.—For purposes of assistance made available with amounts made available pursuant to subsection (a)—

(1) each recipient of such amounts shall use—

(A) not less than 40 percent of the amounts received only for providing assistance for individuals or families experiencing homelessness, or for persons or families at risk of homelessness who have incomes not exceeding 30 percent of the median income for the area as determined by the Secretary;

(B) not less than 70 percent of the amounts received only for providing assistance for individuals or families experiencing homelessness, or for persons or families at risk of homelessness who have incomes not exceeding 50 percent of the median income for the area as determined by the Secretary; and

(C) the remainder of the amounts received only for providing assistance to individuals or families experiencing homelessness, or for persons or families at risk of homelessness who have incomes not exceeding 80 percent of the median income for the area as determined by the Secretary, but such recipient may establish a higher percentage limit for purposes of subsection (b)(1), which shall not in any case exceed 120 percent of the area median income, if the recipient states that it will serve such population in its plan; and

(2) in determining the income of a household for homelessness prevention assistance—

(A) the calculation of income performed at the time of application for such assistance, including arrearages, shall consider only income that the household is currently receiving at such time and any income recently terminated shall not be included;

(B) any calculation of income performed with respect to households receiving ongoing assistance (such as medium-term rental assistance) 3 months after initial receipt of assistance shall consider only the income that the household is receiving at the time of such review; and

(C) the calculation of income performed with respect to households receiving assistance for arrearages shall consider only the income that the household was receiving at the time such arrearages were incurred.

(d) 3-Year Availability.—

(1) IN GENERAL.—Each recipient of amounts made available pursuant to subsection (a) shall—

(A) expend not less than 60 percent of such grant amounts within 2 years of the date that such funds became available to the recipient for obligation; and

(B) expend 100 percent of such grant amounts within 3 years of such date.

(2) REALLOCATION AFTER 2 YEARS.—The Secretary may recapture any amounts not expended in compliance with paragraph (1)(A) and reallocate such amounts to recipients in compliance with the formula referred to in subsection (h)(1)(A).

(e) Rent Restrictions.—

(1) INAPPLICABILITY.—Section 576.106(d) of title 24, Code of Federal Regulations, shall not apply with respect to homelessness prevention assistance made available with amounts made available under subsection (a).

(2) AMOUNT OF RENTAL ASSISTANCE.—In providing homelessness prevention assistance with amounts made available under subsection (a), the maximum amount of rental assistance that may be provided shall be the greater of—

(A) 120 percent of the higher of—

(i) the Fair Market Rent established by the Secretary for the metropolitan area or county; or

(ii) the applicable Small Area Fair Market Rent established by the Secretary; or

(B) such higher amount as the Secretary shall determine is needed to cover market rents in the area.

(f) Subleases.—A recipient shall not be prohibited from providing assistance authorized under subsection (a) with respect to subleases that are valid under State law.

(g) Housing Relocation Or Stabilization Activities.—A recipient of amounts made available pursuant to subsection (a) may expend up to 25 percent of its allocation for activities under section 415(a)(5) of the McKinney-Vento Homeless Assistance Act (42 U.S.C. 11374(a)(5)), except that notwithstanding such section, activities authorized under this subsection may be provided only for individuals or families who have incomes not exceeding 50 percent of the area median income and meet the criteria in subsection (b)(2) of this section or section 103 of the McKinney-Vento Homeless Assistance Act (42 U.S.C. 11302). This subsection shall not apply to rent-related costs that are specifically authorized under subsection (a) of this section.

(h) Allocation Of Assistance.—

(1) IN GENERAL.—In allocating amounts made available pursuant to subsection (a), the Secretary shall—

(A) (i) for any purpose authorized in this section—

(I) allocate 2 percent of such amount for Indian tribes and tribally designated housing entities (as such terms are defined in section 4 of the Native American Housing Assistance and Self-Determination Act of 1996 (25 U.S.C. 4103)) under the formula established pursuant to section 302 of such Act (25 U.S.C. 4152), except that 0.3 percent of the amount allocated under this clause shall be allocated for the Department of Hawaiian Home Lands; and

(II) allocate 0.3 percent of such amount for the Virgin Islands, Guam, American Samoa, and the Northern Mariana Islands;

(ii) not later than 30 days after the date of enactment of this Act, obligate and disburse the amounts allocated pursuant to clause (i) in accordance with such allocations and provide such recipient with any necessary guidance for use of the funds; and

(B) (i) not later than 7 days after the date of enactment of this Act and after setting aside amounts under subparagraph (A), allocate 50 percent of any such remaining amounts under the formula specified in subsections (a), (b), and (e) of section 414 of the McKinney-Vento Homeless Assistance Act (42 U.S.C. 11373) for, and notify, each State, metropolitan city, and urban county that is to receive a direct grant of such amounts; and

(ii) not later than 30 days after the date of enactment of this Act, obligate and disburse the amounts allocated pursuant to clause (i) in accordance with such allocations and provide such recipient with any necessary guidance for use of the funds; and

(C) (i) not later than 45 days after the date of enactment of this Act, allocate any remaining amounts for eligible recipients according to a formula to be developed by the Secretary that takes into consideration the formula referred to in subparagraph (A) and the need for emergency rental assistance under this section, including the severe housing cost burden among extremely low- and very low-income renters and disruptions in housing and economic conditions, including unemployment; and

(ii) not later than 30 days after the date of the allocation of such amounts pursuant to clause (i), obligate and disburse such amounts in accordance with such allocations.

(2) ALLOCATIONS TO STATES.—

(A) IN GENERAL.—Notwithstanding subsection (a) of section 414 of the McKinney-Vento Homeless Assistance Act (42 U.S.C. 11373(a)) and section 576.202(a) of title 24, Code of Federal Regulations, a State recipient of an allocation under this section may elect to use up to 100 percent of its allocation to carry out activities eligible under this section directly.

(B) REQUIREMENT.—Any State recipient making an election described in subparagraph (A) shall serve households throughout the entire State, including households in rural communities and small towns.

(3) ELECTION NOT TO ADMINISTER.—If a recipient other than a State elects not to receive funds under this section, such funds shall be allocated to the State recipient in which the recipient is located.

(4) PARTNERSHIPS, SUBGRANTS, AND CONTRACTS.—A recipient of a grant under this section may distribute funds through partnerships, subgrants, or contracts with an entity, such as a public housing agency (as such term is defined in section 3(b) of the United States Housing Act of 1937 (42 U.S.C. 1437a(b))), that is capable of carrying activities under this section.

(5) REVISION TO RULE.—The Secretary shall revise section 576.3 of tile 24, Code of Federal Regulations, to change the set aside for allocation to the territories to exactly 0.3 percent.

(i) Inapplicability Of Matching Requirement.—Subsection (a) of section 416 of the

McKinney-Vento Homeless Assistance Act (42 U.S.C. 11375(a)) shall not apply to any amounts made available pursuant to subsection (a) of this section.

(j) Reimbursement Of Eligible Activities.—Amounts made available pursuant to subsection (a) may be used by a recipient to reimburse expenditures incurred for eligible activities under this section after March 27, 2020.

(k) Prohibition On Prerequisites.—None of the funds made available pursuant to this section may be used to require any individual receiving assistance under the program under this section to receive treatment or perform any other prerequisite activities as a condition for receiving shelter, housing, or other services.

(l) Waivers And Alternative Requirements.—

(1) IN GENERAL.—

(A) AUTHORITY.—In administering the amounts made available pursuant to subsection (a), the Secretary may waive, or specify alternative requirements for, any provision of any statute or regulation that the Secretary administers in connection with the obligation by the Secretary or the use by the recipient of such amounts (except for requirements related to fair housing, nondiscrimination, labor standards, prohibition on prerequisites, minimum data reporting, and the environment), if the Secretary finds that good cause exists for the waiver or alternative requirement and such waiver or alternative requirement is necessary to expedite the use of funds made available pursuant to this section, to respond to public health orders or conditions related to the COVID-19 emergency, or to ensure that eligible individuals can attain or maintain housing stability.

(B) PUBLIC NOTICE.—The Secretary shall notify the public through the Federal Register or other appropriate means of any waiver or alternative requirement under this paragraph, and that such public notice shall be provided, at a minimum, on the internet at the appropriate Government website or through other electronic media, as determined by the Secretary.

(C) ELIGIBILITY REQUIREMENTS.—Eligibility for rental assistance or housing relocation and stabilization services shall not be restricted based upon the prior receipt of assistance under the program during the preceding three years.

(2) PUBLIC HEARINGS.—

(A) INAPPLICABILITY OF IN-PERSON HEARING REQUIREMENTS DURING THE COVID-19 EMERGENCY.—

(i) IN GENERAL.—A recipient under this section shall not be required to hold in-person public hearings in connection with its citizen participation plan, but shall provide citizens with notice, including publication of its plan for carrying out this section on the internet, and a reasonable opportunity to comment of not less than 5 days.

(ii) RESUMPTION OF IN-PERSON HEARING REQUIREMENTS.—After the period beginning on the date of enactment of this Act and ending on the date of the termination by the Federal Emergency Management Agency of the emergency declared on March 13, 2020, by the President under the Robert T. Stafford Disaster Relief and Emergency Assistance Act (42 U.S.C. 4121 et seq.) relating to the Coronavirus Disease 2019 (COVID-19) pandemic, and after the period described in subparagraph (B), the Secretary shall direct recipients under this section to resume pre-crisis public hearing requirements.

(B) VIRTUAL PUBLIC HEARINGS.—

(i) IN GENERAL.—During the period that national or local health authorities recommend social distancing and limiting public gatherings for public health reasons, a recipient may fulfill applicable public hearing requirements for all grants from funds made available pursuant to this section by carrying out virtual public hearings.

(ii) REQUIREMENTS.—Any virtual hearings held under clause (i) by a recipient under this section shall provide reasonable notification and access for citizens in accordance with the recipient's certifications, timely responses from local officials to all citizen questions and issues, and public access to all questions and responses.

(m) Consultation.—In addition to any other citizen participation and consultation requirements, in developing and implementing a plan to carry out this section, each recipient of funds made available pursuant to this section shall consult with the applicable Continuum or Continuums of Care for the area served by the recipient and organizations representing underserved communities and populations and organizations with expertise in affordable housing, fair housing, and services for people with disabilities.

(n) Administration.—

(1) BY SECRETARY.—Of any amounts made available pursuant to subsection (a)—

(A) not more than the lesser of 0.5 percent, or $15,000,000, may be used by the Secretary for staffing, training, technical assistance, technology, monitoring, research, and evaluation activities necessary to carry out the program carried out under this section, and such amounts shall remain available until September 30, 2024; and

(B) not more than $2,000,000 shall be available to the Office of the Inspector General for audits and investigations of the program authorized under this section.

(2) BY RECIPIENTS.—Notwithstanding section 576.108 of title 24 of the Code of Federal Regulations, with respect to amounts made available pursuant to this section, a recipient may use up to 10 percent of the recipient's grant for payment of administrative costs related to the planning and execution of activities.

HOMEOWNER ASSISTANCE FUND

SEC. 110202.

(a) Definitions.—In this section:

(1) FUND.—The term "Fund" means the Homeowner Assistance Fund established under subsection (b).

(2) SECRETARY.—The term "Secretary" means the Secretary of the Treasury.

(3) STATE.—The term "State" means any State of the United States, the District of Columbia, any territory of the United States, Puerto Rico, Guam, American Samoa, the Virgin Islands, and the Northern Mariana Islands.

(b) Establishment Of Fund.—There is established at the Department of the Treasury a Homeowner Assistance Fund to provide such funds as are made available under subsection (g) to State housing finance agencies for the purpose of preventing homeowner mortgage defaults, foreclosures, and displacements of individuals and families experiencing financial hardship after January 21, 2020.

(c) Allocation Of Funds.—

(1) ADMINISTRATION.—Of any amounts made available for the Fund, the Secretary of the Treasury may allocate, in the aggregate, an amount not exceeding 5 percent—

(A) to the Office of Financial Stability established under section 101(a) of the Emergency Economic Stabilization Act of 2008 (12 U.S.C. 5211(a)) to administer and oversee the Fund, and to provide technical assistance to States for the creation and implementation of State programs to administer assistance from the Fund; and

(B) to the Inspector General of the Department of the Treasury for oversight of the program under this section.

(2) FOR STATES.—The Secretary shall establish such criteria as are necessary to allocate the funds available within the Fund for each State. The Secretary shall allocate such funds among all States taking into consideration the number of unemployment claims within a State relative to the nationwide number of unemployment claims.

(3) SMALL STATE MINIMUM.—The amount allocated for each State shall not be less than $250,000,000.

(4) SET-ASIDE FOR INSULAR AREAS.—Notwithstanding any other provision of this section, of the amounts appropriated under subsection (g), the Secretary shall reserve $200,000,000 to be disbursed to Guam, American Samoa, the Virgin Islands, and the Northern Mariana Islands based on each such territory's share of the combined total population of all such territories, as determined by the Secretary. For the purposes of this paragraph, population shall be determined based on the most recent year for which data are available from the United States Census Bureau.

(5) SET-ASIDE FOR INDIAN TRIBES AND NATIVE HAWAIIANS.——

(A) INDIAN TRIBES.—Notwithstanding any other provision of this section, of the amounts appropriated under subsection (g), the Secretary shall use 5 percent to make grants in accordance with subsection (f) to eligible recipients for the purposes described in subsection (e)(1).

(B) NATIVE HAWAIIANS.— Of the funds set aside under subparagraph (A), the Secretary shall use 0.3 percent to make grants to the Department of Hawaiian Home Lands in accordance with subsection (f) for the purposes described in subsection (e)(1).

(d) Disbursement Of Funds.—

(1) ADMINISTRATION.—Except for amounts made available for assistance under subsection (f), State housing finance agencies shall be primarily responsible for administering amounts disbursed from the Fund, but may delegate responsibilities and sub-allocate amounts to community development financial institutions and State agencies that administer Low-Income Home Energy Assistance Program of the Department of Health and Human Services.

(2) NOTICE OF FUNDING.—The Secretary shall provide public notice of the amounts that will be made available to each State and the method used for determining such amounts not later than the expiration of the 14-day period beginning on the date of the enactment of this Act of enactment.

(3) SHFA PLANS.—

(A) ELIGIBILITY.—To be eligible to receive funding allocated for a State under the section, a State housing finance agency for the State shall submit to the Secretary a plan for the implementation of State programs to administer, in part or in full, the amount of funding the state is eligible to receive, which shall provide for the commencement of receipt of applications by homeowners for assistance, and funding of such applications, not later than the expiration of the 6-month period beginning upon the approval under this paragraph of such plan.

(B) MULTIPLE PLANS.—. A State housing finance agency may submit multiple plans, each covering a separate portion of funding for which the State is eligible.

(C) TIMING.— The Secretary shall approve or disapprove a plan within 30 days after the plan's submission and, if disapproved, explain why the plan could not be approved.

(D) DISBURSEMENT UPON APPROVAL.—The Secretary shall disburse to a State housing finance agency the appropriate amount of funding upon approval of the agency's plan.

(E) AMENDMENTS.—A State housing finance agency may subsequently amend a plan that has previously been approved, provided that any plan amendment shall be subject to the approval of the Secretary. The Secretary shall approve any plan amendment or disapprove such amendment explain why the plan amendment could not be approved within 45 days after submission to the Secretary of such amendment.

(F) TECHNICAL ASSISTANCE.—The Secretary shall provide technical assistance for any State housing finance agency that twice fails to have a submitted plan approved.

(4) PLAN TEMPLATES.—The Secretary shall, not later than 30 days after the date of the enactment of this Act, publish templates that States may utilize in drafting the plans required under paragraph (3)(A). The template plans shall include standard program terms and requirements, as well as any required legal language, which State housing finance agencies may modify with the consent of the Secretary.

(e) Permissible Uses Of Fund.—

(1) IN GENERAL.—Funds made available to State housing finance agencies pursuant to this section may be used for the purposes established under subsection (b), which may include—

(A) mortgage payment assistance, including financial assistance to allow a borrower to reinstate their mortgage or to achieve a more affordable mortgage payment, which may include principal reduction or rate reduction, provided that any mortgage payment assistance is tailored to a borrower's needs and their ability to repay, and takes into consideration the loss mitigation options available to the borrower;

(B) assistance with payment of taxes, hazard insurance, flood insurance, mortgage insurance, or homeowners' association fees;

(C) utility payment assistance, including electric, gas, water, and internet service, including broadband internet access service (as such term is defined in section 8.1(b) of title 47, Code of Federal Regulations (or any successor regulation));

(D) reimbursement of funds expended by a State or local government during the period beginning on January 21, 2020, and ending on the date that the first funds are disbursed by the State under the Fund, for the purpose of providing housing or utility assistance to individuals or otherwise providing funds to prevent foreclosure or eviction of a homeowner or prevent mortgage delinquency or loss of housing or critical utilities as a response to the coronavirus disease 2019 (COVID–19) pandemic; and

(E) any other assistance for homeowners to prevent eviction, mortgage delinquency or default, foreclosure, or the loss of essential utility services.

(2) TARGETING.—

(A) REQUIREMENT.—Not less than 60 percent of amounts made available for each State or other entity allocated amounts under subsection (c) shall be used for activities under paragraph (1) that assist homeowners having incomes equal to or less than 80 percent of the area median income.

(B) DETERMINATION OF INCOME.— In determining the income of a household for purposes of this paragraph, income shall be considered to include only income that the household is receiving at the time of application for assistance from the Fund and any income recently terminated shall not be included, except that for purposes of households receiving assistance for arrearages income shall include only the income that the household was receiving at the time such arrearages were incurred.

(C) LANGUAGE ASSISTANCE.—Each State housing finance agency or other entity allocated amounts under subsection (c) shall make available to each applicant for assistance from amounts from the Fund language assistance in any language that such language assistance is available in and shall provide notice to each such applicant that such language assistance is available.

(3) ADMINISTRATIVE EXPENSES.—Not more than 15 percent of the amount allocated to a State pursuant to subsection (c) may be used by a State housing financing agency for administrative expenses. Any amounts allocated to administrative expenses that are no longer necessary for administrative expenses may be used in accordance with paragraph (1).

(f) Tribal And Native Hawaiian Assistance.—

(1) DEFINITIONS.—In this subsection:

(A) DEPARTMENT OF HAWAIIAN HOME LANDS.—The term "Department of Hawaiian Home Lands" has the meaning given the term in section 801 of the Native American Housing Assistance and Self-Determination Act of 1996 (42 U.S.C. 4221).

(B) ELIGIBLE RECIPIENT.—The term "eligible recipient" means any entity eligible to receive a grant under section 101 of the Native American Housing Assistance and Self-Determination Act of 1996 (25 U.S.C. 4111).

(2) REQUIREMENTS.—

(A) ALLOCATION.—Except for the funds set aside under subsection (c)(5)(B), the Secretary shall allocate the funds set aside under subsection (c)(5)(A) using the allocation formula described in subpart D of part 1000 of title 24, Code of Federal Regulations (or any successor regulations).

(B) NATIVE HAWAIIANS.—The Secretary shall use the funds made available under subsection (c)(5)(B) in accordance with part 1006 of title 24, Code of Federal Regulations (or successor regulations).

(3) TRANSFER.—The Secretary shall transfer any funds made available under subsection (c)(5) that have not been allocated by an eligible recipient or the Department of Hawaiian Home Lands, as applicable, to provide the assistance described in subsection (e)(1) by December 31, 2030, to the Secretary of Housing and Urban Development to carry out the Native American Housing Assistance and Self-Determination Act of 1996 (25 U.S.C. 4101 et seq.).

(g) Funding.—There is appropriated, out of any funds in the Treasury not otherwise appropriated, to the Homeowner Assistance Fund established under subsection (b), $75,000,000,000, to remain available until expended or transferred or credited under subsection (i).

(h) Use Of Housing Finance Agency Innovation Fund For The Hardest Hit Housing Markets Funds.—A State housing finance agency may reallocate any administrative or programmatic funds it has received as an allocation from the Housing Finance Agency Innovation Fund for the Hardest Hit Housing Markets created pursuant to section 101(a) of the Emergency Economic Stabilization Act of 2008 (12 U.S.C. 5211(a)) that have not been otherwise allocated or disbursed as of the date of enactment of this Act to supplement any administrative or programmatic funds received from the Housing Assistance Fund. Such reallocated funds shall not be considered when allocating resources from the Housing Assistance Fund using the process established under subsection (c) and shall remain available for the uses permitted and under the terms and conditions established by the contract with Secretary created pursuant to subsection (d)(1) and the terms of subsection (i).

(i) Reporting Requirements.—The Secretary shall provide public reports not less frequently than quarterly regarding the use of funds provided by the Homeowner Assistance Fund. Such reports shall include the following data by State and by program within each State, both for the past quarter and throughout the life of the program—

(1) the amount of funds allocated;

(2) the amount of funds disbursed;

(3) the number of households and individuals assisted;

(4) the acceptance rate of applicants;

(5) the type or types of assistance provided to each household;

(6) whether the household assisted had a federally backed loan and identification of the Federal entity backing such loan;

(7) the average amount of funding provided per household receiving assistance and per type of assistance provided;

(8) the average number of monthly payments that were covered by the funding amount that a household received, as applicable, disaggregated by type of assistance provided;

(9) the income level of each household receiving assistance; and

(10) the outcome 12 months after the household has received assistance.

Each report under this subsection shall disaggregate the information provided under paragraphs (3) through (10) by State, zip code, racial and ethnic composition of the household, and whether or not the person from the household applying for assistance speaks English as a second language.

PROTECTING RENTERS AND HOMEOWNERS FROM EVICTIONS AND FORECLOSURES

SEC. 110203.

(a) Eviction Moratorium.—The CARES Act is amended by striking section 4024 (15 U.S.C. 9058; Public Law 116–136; 134 Stat. 492) and inserting the following new section:

"SEC. 4024. TEMPORARY MORATORIUM ON EVICTION FILINGS.

"(a) Congressional Findings.—The Congress finds that—

"(1) according to the 2018 American Community Survey, 36 percent of households in the United States—more than 43 million households—are renters;

"(2) in 2019 alone, renters in the United States paid $512 billion in rent;

"(3) according to the Joint Center for Housing Studies of Harvard University, 20.8 million renters in the United States spent more than 30 percent of their incomes on housing in 2018 and 10.9 million renters spent more than 50 percent of their incomes on housing in the same year;

"(4) according to data from the Department of Labor, more than 30 million people have filed for unemployment since the COVID-19 pandemic began;

"(5) the impacts of the spread of COVID-19, which is now considered a global pandemic, are expected to negatively impact the incomes of potentially millions of renter households, making it difficult for them to pay their rent on time; and

"(6) evictions in the current environment would increase homelessness and housing instability which would be counterproductive towards the public health goals of keeping individuals in their homes to the greatest extent possible.

"(b) Moratorium.—During the period beginning on the date of the enactment of this Act and ending 12 months after such date of enactment, the lessor of a covered dwelling located in such State may not make, or cause to be made, any filing with the court of jurisdiction to initiate a legal action to recover possession of the covered dwelling from the tenant for nonpayment of rent or other fees or charges.

"(c) Definitions.—For purposes of this section, the following definitions shall apply:

"(1) COVERED DWELLING.—The term 'covered dwelling' means a dwelling that is occupied by a tenant—

"(A) pursuant to a residential lease; or

"(B) without a lease or with a lease terminable at will under State law.

"(2) DWELLING.—The term 'dwelling' has the meaning given such term in section 802 of the Fair Housing Act (42 U.S.C. 3602) and includes houses and dwellings described in section 803(b) of such Act (42 U.S.C. 3603(b)).

"(d) Notice To Vacate After Moratorium Expiration Date.—After the expiration of the period described in subsection (b), the lessor of a covered dwelling may not require the tenant to vacate the covered dwelling by reason of nonpayment of rent or other fees or charges before the expiration of the 30-day period that begins upon the provision by the lessor to the tenant, after the expiration of the period described in subsection (b), of a notice to vacate the covered dwelling.".

(b) Mortgage Relief.—

(1) FORBEARANCE AND FORECLOSURE MORATORIUM FOR COVERED MORTGAGE LOANS.—Section 4022 of the CARES Act (15 U.S.C. 9056) is amended—

(A) by striking "Federally backed mortgage loan" each place such term appears and inserting "covered mortgage loan"; and

(B) in subsection (a)—

(i) by amending paragraph (2) to read as follows:

"(2) COVERED MORTGAGE LOAN.—The term 'covered mortgage loan' means any credit transaction that is secured by a mortgage, deed of trust, or other equivalent consensual security interest on a 1- to 4-unit dwelling or on residential real property that includes a 1- to 4-unit dwelling, except that it shall not include a credit transaction under an open end credit plan other than a reverse mortgage."; and

(ii) by adding at the end the following:

"(3) COVERED PERIOD.—With respect to a loan, the term 'covered period' means the period beginning on the date of enactment of this Act and ending 12 months after such date of enactment.".

(2) AUTOMATIC FORBEARANCE FOR DELINQUENT BORROWERS.—Section 4022(c) of the CARES Act (15 U.S.C. 9056(c)), as amended by paragraph (5) of this subsection, is further amended by adding at the end the following:

"(9) AUTOMATIC FORBEARANCE FOR DELINQUENT BORROWERS.—

"(A) IN GENERAL.—Notwithstanding any other law governing forbearance relief—

"(i) any borrower whose covered mortgage loan became 60 days delinquent between March 13, 2020, and the date of enactment of this paragraph, and who has not already received a forbearance under subsection (b), shall automatically be granted a 60-day forbearance that begins on the date of enactment of this paragraph, provided that a borrower shall not be considered delinquent for purposes of this paragraph while making timely payments or otherwise performing under a trial modification or other loss mitigation agreement; and

"(ii) any borrower whose covered mortgage loan becomes 60 days delinquent between the date of enactment of this paragraph and the end of the covered period, and who has not already received a forbearance under subsection (b), shall automatically be granted a 60-day forbearance that begins on the 60th day of delinquency, provided that a borrower shall not be considered delinquent for purposes of this paragraph while making timely payments or otherwise performing under a trial modification or other loss mitigation agreement.

"(B) INITIAL EXTENSION.—An automatic forbearance provided under subparagraph (A) shall be extended for up to an additional 120 days upon the borrower's request, oral or written, submitted to the borrower's servicer affirming that the borrower is experiencing a financial hardship that prevents the borrower from making timely payments on the covered mortgage loan due, directly or indirectly, to the COVID–19 emergency.

"(C) SUBSEQUENT EXTENSION.—A forbearance extended under subparagraph (B) shall be extended for up to an additional 180 days, up to a maximum of 360 days (including the period of automatic forbearance), upon the borrower's request, oral or written, submitted to the borrower's servicer affirming that the borrower is experiencing a financial hardship that prevents the borrower from making timely payments on the covered mortgage loan due, directly or indirectly, to the COVID–19 emergency.

"(D) RIGHT TO ELECT TO CONTINUE MAKING PAYMENTS.—With respect to a forbearance provided under this paragraph, the borrower of such loan may elect to continue making regular payments on the loan. A borrower who makes such election shall be offered a loss mitigation option pursuant to subsection (d) within 30 days of resuming regular payments to address any payment deficiency during the forbearance.

"(E) RIGHT TO SHORTEN FORBEARANCE.—At a borrower's request, any period of forbearance provided under this paragraph may be shortened. A borrower who makes such a request shall be offered a loss mitigation option pursuant to subsection (d) within 30 days of resuming regular payments to address any payment deficiency during the forbearance.

"(10) AUTOMATIC FORBEARANCE FOR CERTAIN REVERSE MORTGAGE LOANS.—

"(A) IN GENERAL.—When any covered mortgage loan which is also a federally-insured reverse mortgage loan, during the covered period, is due and payable due to the death of the last borrower or end of a deferral period or eligible to be called due and payable due to a property charge default, or if the borrower defaults on a property charge repayment plan, or if the borrower defaults for failure to complete property repairs, or if an obligation of the borrower under the Security Instrument is not performed, the mortgagee automatically shall be granted a six-month extension of—

"(i) the mortgagee's deadline to request due and payable status from the Department of Housing and Urban Development;

"(ii) the mortgage's deadline to send notification to the mortgagor or his or her heirs that the loan is due and payable;

"(iii) the deadline to initiate foreclosure;

"(iv) any reasonable diligence period related to foreclosure or the Mortgagee Optional Election;

"(v) if applicable, the deadline to obtain the due and payable appraisal; and

"(vi) any claim submission deadline, including the 6-month acquired property marketing period.

"(B) FORBEARANCE PERIOD.—The mortgagee shall not request due and payable status from the Secretary of Housing and Urban Development nor initiate foreclosure during this six-month period described under subparagraph (A), which shall be considered a forbearance period.

"(C) EXTENSION.—A forbearance provided under subparagraph (B) and related deadline extension authorized under subparagraph (A) shall be extended for an additional 180 days upon—

"(i) the borrower's request, oral or written, submitted to the borrower's servicer affirming that the borrower is experiencing a financial hardship that prevents the borrower from making payments on property charges, completing property repairs, or performing an obligation of the borrower under the Security Instrument due, directly or indirectly, to the COVID–19 emergency;

"(ii) a non-borrowing spouse's request, oral or written, submitted to the servicer affirming that the non-borrowing spouse has been unable to satisfy all criteria for the Mortgagee Optional Election program due, directly or indirectly, to the COVID-19 emergency, or to perform all actions necessary to become an eligible non-borrowing spouse following the death of all borrowers; or

"(iii) a successor-in-interest of the borrower's request, oral or written, submitted to the servicer affirming the heir's difficulty satisfying the reverse mortgage loan due, directly or indirectly, to the COVID-19 emergency.

"(D) CURTAILMENT OF DEBENTURE INTEREST.—Where any covered mortgage loan which is also a federally insured reverse mortgage loan is in default during the covered period and subject to a prior event which provides for curtailment of debenture interest in connection with a claim for insurance benefits, the curtailment of debenture interest shall be suspended during any forbearance period provided herein.".

(3) ADDITIONAL FORECLOSURE AND REPOSSESSION PROTECTIONS.—Section 4022(c) of the CARES Act (15 U.S.C. 9056(c)) is amended—

(A) in paragraph (2), by striking "may not initiate any judicial or non-judicial foreclosure process, move for a foreclosure judgment or order of sale, or execute a foreclosure-related eviction or foreclosure sale for not less than the 60-day period beginning on March 18, 2020" and inserting "may not initiate or proceed with any judicial or non-judicial foreclosure process, schedule a foreclosure sale, move for a foreclosure judgment or order of sale, execute a foreclosure related eviction or foreclosure sale for six months after the date of enactment of the COVID–19 HERO Act"; and

(B) by adding at the end the following:

"(3) REPOSSESSION MORATORIUM.—In the case of personal property, including any recreational or motor vehicle, used as a dwelling, no person may use any judicial or non-judicial procedure to repossess or otherwise take possession of such property for six months after date of enactment of this paragraph.".

(4) MORTGAGE FORBEARANCE REFORMS.—Section 4022 of the CARES Act (15 U.S.C. 9056) is amended—

(A) in subsection (b), by striking paragraphs (1), (2), and (3) and inserting the following:

"(1) IN GENERAL.—During the covered period, a borrower with a covered mortgage loan who has not obtained automatic forbearance pursuant to this section and who is experiencing a financial hardship that prevents the borrower from making timely payments on the covered mortgage loan due, directly or indirectly, to the COVID–19 emergency may request forbearance on the loan, regardless of delinquency status, by—

"(A) submitting a request, orally or in writing, to the servicer of the loan; and

"(B) affirming that the borrower is experiencing a financial hardship that prevents the borrower from making timely payments on the covered mortgage loan due, directly or indirectly, to the COVID–19 emergency.

"(2) DURATION OF FORBEARANCE.—

"(A) IN GENERAL.—Upon a request by a borrower to a servicer for forbearance under paragraph (1), such forbearance shall be granted by the servicer for the period requested by the borrower, up to an initial length of 180 days, the length of which shall be extended by the servicer, at the request of the borrower for the period or periods requested, for a total forbearance period of up to 12-months.

"(B) MINIMUM FORBEARANCE AMOUNTS.—For purposes of granting a forbearance under this paragraph, a servicer may grant an initial forbearance with a term of not less than 90 days, provided that it is automatically extended for an additional 90 days unless the servicer confirms the borrower does not want to renew the forbearance or that the borrower is no longer experiencing a financial hardship that prevents the borrower from making timely mortgage payments due, directly or indirectly, to the COVID–19 emergency.

"(C) RIGHT TO SHORTEN FORBEARANCE.—At a borrower's request, any period of forbearance described under this paragraph may be shortened. A borrower who makes such a request shall be offered a loss mitigation option pursuant to subsection (d) within 30 days of resuming regular payments to address any payment deficiency during the forbearance.

"(3) ACCRUAL OF INTEREST OR FEES.—A servicer shall not charge a borrower any fees, penalties, or interest (beyond the amounts scheduled or calculated as if the borrower made all contractual payments on time and in full under the terms of the mortgage contract) in connection with a forbearance, provided that a servicer may offer the borrower a modification option at the end of a forbearance period granted hereunder that includes the capitalization of past due principal and interest and escrow payments as long as the borrower's principal and interest payment under such modification remains at or below the contractual principal and interest payments owed under the terms of the mortgage contract before such forbearance period except as the result of a change in the index of an adjustable rate mortgage.

"(4) COMMUNICATION WITH SERVICERS.—Any communication between a borrower and a servicer described under this section may be made in writing or orally, at the borrower's choice.

"(5) COMMUNICATION WITH BORROWERS WITH A DISABILITY.—Upon request from a borrower, servicers shall communicate with borrowers who have a disability in the borrower's preferred method of communication. For purposes of this paragraph, the term 'disability' has the meaning given that term in the Fair Housing Act, the Americans with Disabilities Act of 1990, or the Rehabilitation Act of 1973."; and

(B) in subsection (c), by amending paragraph (1) to read as follows:

"(1) NO DOCUMENTATION REQUIRED.—A servicer of a covered mortgage loan shall not require any documentation with respect to a forbearance under this section other than the borrower's affirmation (oral or written) to a financial hardship that prevents the borrower from making timely payments on the covered mortgage loan due, directly or indirectly, to the COVID–19 emergency. An oral request for forbearance and oral affirmation of hardship by the borrower shall be sufficient for the borrower to obtain or extend a forbearance.".

(5) OTHER SERVICER REQUIREMENTS DURING FORBEARANCE.—Section

4022(c) of the CARES Act (15 U.S.C. 9056(c)), as amended by paragraph (3) of this subsection, is further amended by adding at the end the following:

"(4) FORBEARANCE TERMS NOTICE.—Within 30 days of a servicer of a covered mortgage loan providing forbearance to a borrower under subsection (b) or paragraph (9) or (10), or 10 days if the forbearance is for a term of less than 60 days, but only where the forbearance was provided in response to a borrower's request for forbearance or when an automatic forbearance was initially provided under paragraph (9) or (10), and not when an existing forbearance is automatically extended, the servicer shall provide the borrower with a notice in accordance with the terms in paragraph (5).

"(5) CONTENTS OF NOTICE.—The written notice required under paragraph (4) shall state in plain language—

"(A) the specific terms of the forbearance;

"(B) the beginning and ending dates of the forbearance;

"(C) that the borrower is eligible for up to 12 months of forbearance;

"(D) that the borrower may request an extension of the forbearance unless the borrower will have reached the maximum period at the end of the forbearance;

"(E) that the borrower may request that the initial or extended period be shortened at any time;

"(F) that the borrower should contact the servicer before the end of the forbearance period;

"(G) a description of the loss mitigation options that may be available to the borrower at the end of the forbearance period based on the borrower's specific loan;

"(H) information on how to find a housing counseling agency approved by the Department of Housing and Urban Development;

"(I) in the case of a forbearance provided pursuant to paragraph (9) or (10), that the forbearance was automatically provided and how to contact the servicer to make arrangements for further assistance, including any renewal; and

"(J) where applicable, that the forbearance is subject to an automatic extension including the terms of any such automatic extensions and when any further extension would require a borrower request.

"(6) TREATMENT OF ESCROW ACCOUNTS.—During any forbearance provided under this section, a servicer shall pay or advance funds to make disbursements in a timely manner from any escrow account established on the covered mortgage loan.

"(7) NOTIFICATION FOR BORROWERS.—During the period that begins 90 days after the date of the enactment of this paragraph and ends at the end of the covered period, each servicer of a covered mortgage loan shall be required to—

"(A) make available in a clear and conspicuous manner on their webpage accurate information, in English and Spanish, for borrowers regarding the availability of forbearance as provided under subsection (b); and

"(B) notify every borrower whose payments on a covered mortgage loan are delinquent in any oral communication with or to the borrower that the borrower may be eligible to request forbearance as provided under subsection (b), except that such notice shall not be required if the borrower already has requested forbearance under subsection (b).

"(8) CERTAIN TREATMENT UNDER RESPA.—As long as a borrower's payment on a covered mortgage loan was not more than 30 days delinquent on March 13, 2020, a servicer may not deem the borrower as delinquent while a forbearance granted under subsection (b) is in effect for purposes of the application of sections 6 and 10 of the Real Estate Settlement Procedures Act and any applicable regulations.".

(6) POST-FORBEARANCE LOSS MITIGATION.—

(A) AMENDMENT TO CARES ACT.—Section 4022 of the CARES Act (15 U.S.C. 9056) is amended by adding at the end the following:

"(d) Post-Forbearance Loss Mitigation.—

"(1) NOTICE OF AVAILABILITY OF ADDITIONAL FORBEARANCE.—With respect to any covered mortgage loan as to which forbearance under this section has been granted and not otherwise extended, including by automatic extension, a servicer shall, no later than 30 days before the end of the forbearance period, in writing, notify the borrower that additional forbearance may be available and how to request such forbearance, except that no such notice is required where the borrower already has requested an extension of the forbearance period, is subject to automatic extension pursuant to subsection (b)(2)(B), or no additional forbearance is available.

"(2) LOSS MITIGATION OFFER BEFORE EXPIRATION OF FORBEARANCE.— No later than 30 days before the end of any forbearance period that has not been extended or 30 days after a request by a consumer to terminate the forbearance, which time shall be before the servicer initiates or engages in any foreclosure activity listed in subsection (c)(2), including incurring or charging to a borrower any fees or corporate advances related to a foreclosure, the servicer shall, in writing—

"(A) offer the borrower a loss mitigation option, without the charging of any fees or penalties other than interest, such that the borrower's principal and interest payment remains the same as it was prior to the forbearance, subject to any adjustment of the index pursuant to the terms of an adjustable rate mortgage, and that either—

"(i) defers the payment of total arrearages, including any escrow advances, to the end of the existing term of the loan, without the charging or collection of any additional interest on the deferred amounts; or

"(ii) extends the term of the mortgage loan, and capitalizes, defers, or forgives all escrow advances and other arrearages;

provided, however, that the servicer may offer the borrower a loss mitigation option that reduces the principal and interest payment on the loan and capitalizes, defers, or forgives all escrow advances or arrearages if the servicer has information indicating that the borrower cannot resume the pre-forbearance mortgage payments; and

"(B) concurrent with the loss mitigation offer in subparagraph (A), notify the borrower that the borrower has the right to be evaluated for other loss mitigation options if the borrower is not able to make the payment under the option offered in subparagraph (A).

"(3) EVALUATION FOR LOSS MITIGATION PRIOR TO FORECLOSURE INITI-ATION.—Before a servicer may initiate or engage in any foreclosure activity listed in subsection (c)(2), including incurring or charging to a borrower any fees or corporate advances related to a foreclosure on the basis that the borrower has failed to perform under the loss mitigation offer in paragraph (2)(A) within the first 90 days after the option is offered, including a failure to accept the loss mitigation offer in paragraph (2)(A), the servicer shall—

"(A) unless the borrower has already submitted a complete application that the servicer is reviewing—

"(i) notify the borrower in writing of the documents and information, if any, needed by the servicer to enable the servicer to consider the borrower for all available loss mitigation options;

"(ii) exercise reasonable diligence to obtain the documents and information needed to complete the borrower's loss mitigation application;

"(B) upon receipt of a complete application or if, despite the servicer's exercise of reasonable diligence, the loss mitigation application remains incomplete sixty days after the notice in paragraph (2)(A) is sent, conduct an evaluation of the complete or incomplete loss mitigation application without reference to whether the borrower has previously submitted a complete loss mitigation application and offer the borrower all available loss mitigation options for which the borrower qualifies under applicable investor guidelines, including guidelines regarding required documentation.

"(4) EFFECT ON FUTURE REQUESTS FOR LOSS MITIGATION REVIEW.—An application, offer, or evaluation for loss mitigation under this section shall not be the basis for the denial of a borrower's application as duplicative or for a reduction in the borrower's appeal rights under Regulation X (12 C.F.R. 1024) in regard to any loss mitigation application submitted after the servicer has complied with the requirements of paragraphs (2) and (3).

"(5) SAFE HARBOR.—Any loss mitigation option authorized by the Federal National Mortgage Association, the Federal Home Loan Corporation, or the Federal Housing Administration that either—

"(A) defers the payment of total arrearages, including any escrow advances, to the end of the existing term of the loan, without the charging or collection of any additional interest on the deferred amounts, or

"(B) extends the term of the mortgage loan, and capitalizes, defers, or forgives all escrow advances and other arrearages, without the charging of any fees or penalties beyond interest on any amount capitalized into the loan principal,

shall be deemed to comply with the requirements of paragraph (1)(B).

"(6) HOME RETENTION OPTIONS FOR CERTAIN REVERSE MORTGAGE LOANS.—

"(A) IN GENERAL.—For a covered mortgage loan which is also a federally-insured reverse mortgage loan, a servicer's conduct shall be deemed to comply with this section provided that if the loan is eligible to be called due and payable due to a property charge default, the mortgagee shall, as a precondition to sending a due and payable request to the Secretary or initiating or continuing a foreclosure process—

"(i) make a good faith effort to communicate with the borrower regarding available home retention options to cure the property charge default, including encouraging the borrower to apply for home retention options; and

"(ii) consider the borrower for all available home retention options as allowed by the Secretary.

"(B) PERMISSIBLE REPAYMENT PLANS.—The Secretary shall amend its allowable home retention options to permit a repayment plan of up to 120 months in length, and to permit a repayment plan without regard to prior defaults on repayment plans.

"(C) LIMITATION ON INTEREST CURTAILMENT.—The Secretary may not curtail interest paid to mortgagees who engage in loss mitigation or home retention actions through interest curtailment during such loss mitigation or home retention review or during the period when a loss mitigation or home retention plan is in effect and ending 90 days after any such plan terminates.".

(B) AMENDMENT TO HOUSING ACT OF 1949.—Section 505 of the Housing Act of 1949 (42 U.S.C. 1475) is amended—

(i) by striking the section heading and inserting "LOSS MITIGATION AND FORE-CLOSURE PROCEDURES";

(ii) in subsection (a), by striking the section designation and all that follows through "During any" and inserting the following:

"SEC. 505. (a) Moratorium— (1) In determining a borrower's eligibility for relief, the Secretary shall make all eligibility decisions based on the borrower's household's income, expenses, and circumstances.

"(2) During any".

(iii) by redesignating subsection (b) as subsection (c); and

(iv) by inserting after subsection (a) the following new subsection:

"(b) Loan Modification.— (1) Notwithstanding any other provision of this title, for any loan made under section 502 or 504, the Secretary may modify the interest rate and extend the term of such loan for up to 30 years from the date of such modification.

"(2) At the end of any moratorium period granted under this section or under the COVID–19 HERO Act, the Secretary shall determine whether the borrower can reasonably resume making principal and interest payments after the Secretary modifies the borrower's loan obligations in accordance with paragraph (1).".

(7) MULTIFAMILY MORTGAGE FORBEARANCE.—Section 4023 of the CARES Act (15 U.S.C. 9057) is amended—

(A) by striking "Federally backed multifamily mortgage loan" each place such term appears and inserting "multifamily mortgage loan";

(B) in subsection (b), by striking "during" and inserting "due, directly or indirectly, to";

(C) in subsection (c)(1)—

(i) in subparagraph (A), by adding "and" at the end;

(ii) by striking subparagraphs (B) and (C) and inserting the following:

"(B) provide the forbearance for up to the end of the period described under section 4024(b).'; and

(D) by redesignating subsection (f) as subsection (g);

(E) by inserting after subsection (e) the following:

"(f) Treatment After Forbearance.—With respect to a multifamily mortgage loan provided a forbearance under this section, the servicer of such loan—

"(1) shall provide the borrower with a 12-month period beginning at the end of such forbearance to become current on the payments under such loan;

"(2) may not charge any late fees, penalties, or other charges with respect to payments on the loan that were due during the forbearance period, if such payments are made before the end of the 12-month period; and

"(3) may not report any adverse information to a credit rating agency (as defined under section 603 of the Fair Credit Reporting Act with respect to any payments on the loan that were due during the forbearance period, if such payments are made before the end of the 12-month period.).'; and

(F) in subsection (g), as so redesignated—

(i) in paragraph (2)—

(I) by striking "that—" and all that follows through "(A) is secured by" and inserting "that is secured by";

(II) by striking "; and" and inserting a period; and

(III) by striking subparagraph (B); and

(ii) by amending paragraph (5) to read as follows:

"(5) COVERED PERIOD.—With respect to a loan, the term 'covered period' has the meaning given that term under section 4022(a)(3).".

(8) RENTER PROTECTIONS DURING FORBEARANCE PERIOD.— A borrower that receives a forbearance pursuant to section 4022 or 4023 of the CARES Act (15 U.S.C. 9056 or 9057) may not, for the duration of the forbearance—

(A) evict or initiate the eviction of a tenant solely for nonpayment of rent or other fees or charges; or

(B) charge any late fees, penalties, or other charges to a tenant for late payment of rent.

(9) EXTENSION OF GSE PATCH.—

(A) NON-APPLICABILITY OF EXISTING SUNSET.—Section 1026.43(e)(4)(iii)(B) of title 12, Code of Federal Regulations, shall have no force or effect.

(B) EXTENDED SUNSET.—The special rules in section 1026.43(e)(4) of title 12, Code of Federal Regulations, shall apply to covered transactions consummated prior to June 1, 2022, or such later date as the Director of the Bureau of Consumer Financial Protection may determine, by rule.

(10) SERVICER SAFE HARBOR FROM INVESTOR LIABILITY.—

(A) SAFE HARBOR.—

(i) IN GENERAL.—A servicer of covered mortgage loans or multifamily mortgage loans shall be deemed not to have violated any duty or contractual obligation owed to investors or other parties regarding such mortgage loans on account of offering or implementing in good faith forbearance during the covered period or offering or implementing in good faith post-forbearance loss mitigation (including after the expiration of the covered period) in accordance with the terms of sections 4022 and 4023 of the CARES Act to borrowers, respectively, on covered or multifamily mortgage loans that it services and shall not be liable to any party who is owed such a duty or obligation or subject to any injunction, stay, or other equitable relief to such party on account of such offer or implementation of forbearance or post-forbearance loss mitigation.

(ii) OTHER PERSONS.—Any person, including a trustee of a securitization vehicle or other party involved in a securitization or other investment vehicle, who in good faith cooperates with a servicer of covered or multifamily mortgage loans held by that securitization or investment vehicle to comply with the terms of section 4022 and 4023 of the CARES Act, respectively, to borrowers on covered or multifamily mortgage loans owned by the securitization or other investment vehicle shall not be liable to any party who is owed such a duty or obligation or subject to any injunction, stay, or other equitable relief to such party on account of its cooperation with an offer or implementation of forbearance during the covered period or post-forbearance loss mitigation, including after the expiration of the covered period.

(B) STANDARD INDUSTRY PRACTICE.—During the covered period, notwithstanding any contractual restrictions, it is deemed to be standard industry practice for a servicer to offer forbearance or loss mitigation options in accordance with the terms of sections 4022 and 4023 of the CARES Act to borrowers, respectively, on all covered or multifamily mortgage loans it services.

(C) RULE OF CONSTRUCTION.—Nothing in this paragraph may be construed as affecting the liability of a servicer or other person for actual fraud in the servicing of a mortgage loan or for the violation of a State or Federal law.

(D) DEFINITIONS.—In this paragraph:

(i) COVERED MORTGAGE LOAN.—The term "covered mortgage loan" has the meaning given that term under section 4022(a) of the CARES Act.

(ii) COVERED PERIOD.—The term "covered period " has the meaning given that term under section 4023(g) of the CARES Act.

(iii) MULTIFAMILY MORTGAGE LOAN.—The term "multifamily mortgage loan" has the meaning given that term under section 4023(g) of the CARES Act.

(iv) SERVICER.—The term "servicer"—

(I) has the meaning given the term under section 6(i) of the Real Estate Settlement Procedures Act of 1974 (12 U.S.C. 2605(i)); and

(II) means a master servicer and a subservicer, as such terms are defined, respectively, under section 1024.31 of title 12, Code of Federal Regulations.

(v) SECURITIZATION VEHICLE.—The term "securitization vehicle" has the meaning give that term under section 129A(f) of the Truth in Lending Act (15 U.S.C. 1639a(f)).

(c) Bankruptcy Protections.—

(1) BANKRUPTCY PROTECTIONS FOR FEDERAL CORONAVIRUS RELIEF PAYMENTS.—Section 541(b) of title 11, United States Code, is amended—

(A) in paragraph (9), in the matter following subparagraph (B), by striking "or";

(B) in paragraph (10)(C), by striking the period at the end and inserting "; or"; and

(C) by inserting after paragraph (10) the following:

"(11) payments made under Federal law relating to the national emergency declared by the President under the National Emergencies Act (50 U.S.C. 1601 et seq.) with respect to the coronavirus disease 2019 (COVID–19).".

(2) PROTECTION AGAINST DISCRIMINATORY TREATMENT OF HOMEOWN-ERS IN BANKRUPTCY.—Section 525 of title 11, United States Code, is amended by adding at the end the following:

"(d) A person may not be denied any forbearance, assistance, or loan modification relief made available to borrowers by a mortgage creditor or servicer because the person is or has been a debtor, or has received a discharge, in a case under this title.".

(3) INCREASING THE HOMESTEAD EXEMPTION.—Section 522 of title 11, United States Code, is amended—

(A) in subsection (d)(1), by striking "$15,000" and inserting "$100,000"; and

(B) by adding at the end the following:

"(r) Notwithstanding any other provision of applicable nonbankruptcy law, a debtor in any State may exempt from property of the estate the property described in sub-section (d)(1) not to exceed the value in subsection (d)(1) if the exemption for such property permitted by applicable nonbankruptcy law is lower than that amount.".

(4) EFFECT OF MISSED MORTGAGE PAYMENTS ON DISCHARGE.—Section 1328 of title 11, United States Code, is amended by adding at the end the following:

"(i) A debtor shall not be denied a discharge under this section because, as of the date of discharge, the debtor did not make 6 or fewer payments directly to the holder of a debt secured by real property.

"(j) Notwithstanding subsections (a) and (b), upon the debtor's request, the court shall grant a discharge of all debts provided for in the plan that are dischargeable under subsection (a) if the debtor—

"(1) has made payments under a confirmed plan for at least 1 year; and

"(2) is experiencing or has experienced a material financial hardship due, directly or indirectly, to the coronavirus disease 2019 (COVID–19) pandemic.".

(5) EXPANDED ELIGIBILITY FOR CHAPTER 13.—Section 109(e) of title 11,

United States Code, is amended—

(A) by striking "$250,000" each place the term appears and inserting "$850,000"; and

(B) by striking "$750,000" each place the term appears and inserting "$2,600,000".

(6) EXTENDED CURE PERIOD FOR HOMEOWNERS HARMED BY COVID–19 PANDEMIC.—

(A) IN GENERAL.—Chapter 13 of title 11, United States Code, is amended by adding at the end thereof the following:

"§ 1331. Special provisions related to COVID–19 pandemic

"(a) Notwithstanding subsections (b)(2) and (d) of section 1322, if the debtor is experiencing or has experienced a material financial hardship due, directly or indirectly, to the coronavirus disease 2019 (COVID–19) pandemic, a plan may provide for the curing of any default within a reasonable time, not to exceed 7 years after the time that the first payment under the original confirmed plan was due, and maintenance of payments while the case is pending on any unsecured claim or secured claim on which the last payment is due after the expiration of such time. Any such plan provision shall not affect the applicable commitment period under section 1325(b).

"(b) For purposes of sections 1328(a) and 1328(b), any cure or maintenance payments under subsection (a) that are made after the end of the period during which the plan provides for payments (other than payments under subsection (a)) shall not be treated as payments under the plan.

"(c) Notwithstanding section 1329(c), a plan modified under section 1329 at the debtor's request may provide for cure or maintenance payments under subsection (a) over a period that is not longer than 7 years after the time that the first payment under the original confirmed plan was due.

"(d) Notwithstanding section 362(c)(2), during the period after the debtor receives a discharge and the period during which the plan provides for the cure of any default and maintenance of payments under the plan, section 362(a) shall apply to the holder of a claim for which a default is cured and payments are maintained under subsection (a) and to any property securing such claim.

"(e) Notwithstanding section 1301(a)(2), the stay of section 1301(a) terminates upon the granting of a discharge under section 1328 with respect to all creditors other than the holder of a claim for which a default is cured and payments are maintained under subsection (a).".

(B) TABLE OF CONTENTS.—The table of sections of chapter 13, title 11, United States Code, is amended by adding at the end thereof the following:

"SEC. 1331. Special provisions related to COVID–19 Pandemic.".

(C) APPLICATION.—The amendments made by this paragraph shall apply only to any case under title 11, United States Code, commenced before 3 years after the date of enactment of this Act and pending on or commenced after such date of enactment, in which a plan under chapter 13 of title 11, United States Code, was not confirmed before March 27, 2020.

LIQUIDITY FOR MORTGAGE SERVICERS AND RESIDENTIAL RENTAL PROPERTY OWNERS

SEC. 110204.

(a) In General.—Section 4003 of the CARES Act (15 U.S.C. 9042), is amended by adding at the end the following:

"(i) Liquidity For Mortgage Servicers.—

"(1) IN GENERAL.—Subject to paragraph (2), the Secretary shall ensure that servicers of covered mortgage loans (as defined under section 4022) and multifamily mortgage loans (as defined under section 4023) are provided the opportunity to participate in the loans, loan guarantees, or other investments made by the Secretary under this section. The Secretary shall ensure that servicers are provided with access to such opportunities under equitable terms and conditions regardless of their size.

"(2) MORTGAGE SERVICER ELIGIBILITY.—In order to receive assistance under subsection (b)(4), a mortgage servicer shall—

"(A) demonstrate that the mortgage servicer has established policies and procedures to use such funds only to replace funds used for borrower assistance, including to advance funds as a result of forbearance or other loss mitigation provided to borrowers;

"(B) demonstrate that the mortgage servicer has established policies and procedures to provide forbearance, post-forbearance loss mitigation, and other assistance to borrowers in compliance with the terms of section 4022 or 4023, as applicable;

"(C) demonstrate that the mortgage servicer has established policies and procedures to ensure that forbearance and post-forbearance assistance is available to all borrowers in a non-discriminatory fashion and in compliance with the Fair Housing Act, the Equal Credit Opportunity Act, and other applicable fair housing and fair lending laws; and

"(D) comply with the limitations on compensation set forth in section 4004.

"(3) MORTGAGE SERVICER REQUIREMENTS.—A mortgage servicer receiving assistance under subsection (b)(4) may not, while the servicer is under any obligation to repay funds provided or guaranteed under this section—

"(A) pay dividends with respect to the common stock of the mortgage servicer or purchase an equity security of the mortgage servicer or any parent company of the mortgage servicer if the security is listed on a national securities exchange, except to the extent required under a contractual obligation that is in effect on the date of enactment of this subsection; or

"(B) prepay any debt obligation.".

(b) Credit Facility For Residential Rental Property Owners.—

(1) IN GENERAL.—The Board of Governors of the Federal Reserve System shall—

(A) establish a facility, using amounts made available under section 4003(b)(4) of the CARES Act (15 U.S.C. 9042(b)(4)), to make long-term, low-cost loans to residential rental property owners as to temporarily compensate such owners for documented financial losses caused by reductions in rent payments; and

(B) defer such owners' required payments on such loans until after six months after the date of enactment of this Act.

(2) REQUIREMENTS.—A borrower that receives a loan under this subsection may not, for the duration of the loan—

(A) evict or initiate the eviction of a tenant solely for nonpayment of rent or other fees or charges;

(B) charge any late fees, penalties, or other charges to a tenant for late payment of rent; and

(C) with respect to a person or entity described under paragraph (4), discriminate on the basis of source of income.

(3) REPORT ON RESIDENTIAL RENTAL PROPERTY OWNERS.—The Board of Governors shall issue a report to the Congress containing the following, with respect to each property owner receiving a loan under this subsection:

(A) The number of borrowers that received assistance under this subsection.

(B) The average total loan amount that each borrower received.

(C) The total number of rental units that each borrower owned.

(D) The average rent charged by each borrower.

(4) REPORT ON LARGE RESIDENTIAL RENTAL PROPERTY OWNERS.—The Board of Governors shall issue a report to Congress that identifies any person or entity that in aggregate owns or holds a controlling interest in any entity that, in aggregate, owns—

(A) more than 100 rental units that are located within in a single Metropolitan Statistical Area;

(B) more than 1,000 rental units nationwide; or

(C) rental units in three or more States.

(c) Amendments To National Housing Act.—Section 306(g)(1) of the National Housing Act (12 U.S.C. 1721(a)) is amended—

(1) in the fifth sentence, by inserting after "issued" the following: ", subject to any pledge or grant of security interest of the Federal Reserve under section 4003(a) of the CARES Act (Public Law 116–136; 134 Stat. 470; 15 U.S.C. 9042(a)) and to any such mortgage or mortgages or any interest therein and the proceeds thereon, which the Association may elect to approve"; and

(2) in the sixth sentence—

(A) by striking "or (C)" and inserting "(C)"; and

(B) by inserting before the period the following: ", or (D) its approval and honoring of any pledge or grant of security interest of the Federal Reserve under section 4003(a) of the CARES Act and to any such mortgage or mortgages or any interest therein and proceeds thereon as".

RURAL RENTAL ASSISTANCE

SEC. 110205.

There is authorized to be appropriated for fiscal year 2020 $309,000,000 for rural rental assistance, which shall remain available until September 30, 2021, of which—

(1) up to $25,000,000 million may be used for an additional amount for rural housing vouchers for any low-income households (including those not receiving rental assistance) residing in a property financed with a section 515 loan which has been prepaid after September 30, 2005, or has matured after September 30, 2019; and

(2) the remainder shall be used for an additional amount for rural rental assistance agreements entered into or renewed pursuant to section 521(a)(2) of the Housing Act of 1949 (42 U.S.C. 1490a(a)(2)) to—

(A) supplement the rental assistance of households on whose behalf assistance is being provided; and

(B) provide rental assistance on behalf of households who are not being assisted with such rental assistance but who qualify for such assistance.

FUNDING FOR PUBLIC HOUSING AND TENANT-BASED RENTAL ASSISTANCE

SEC. 110206.

(a) Public Housing Operating Fund.—There is authorized to be appropriated for an additional amount for fiscal year 2020 for the Public Housing Operating Fund under section 9(e) of the United States Housing Act of 1937 (42 U.S.C. 1437g(e)) $2,000,000,000, to remain available until September 30, 2021.

(b) Tenant-Based Section 8 Rental Assistance.—There is authorized to be appropriated for an additional amount for fiscal year 2020 for the tenant-based rental assistance under section 8(o) of the United States Housing Act of 1937 (42 U.S.C. 1437f(o)) $3,000,000,000, to remain available until September 30, 2021, of which not more than $500,000,000 may be used for administrative fees under section 8(q) of such Act (42 U.S.C. 1437f(q)).

(c) Applicability Of Waivers.—Any waiver or alternative requirement made by the Secretary of Housing and Urban Development pursuant to the heading "Tenant-Based Rental Assistance" or "Public Housing Operating Fund" in title XII of division B of the CARES Act (Public Law 116–136) shall apply with respect to amounts made available pursuant to this section.

SUPPLEMENTAL FUNDING FOR SUPPORTIVE HOUSING FOR THE ELDERLY, SUPPORTIVE HOUSING FOR PERSONS WITH DISABILITIES, SUPPORTIVE HOUSING FOR PERSONS WITH AIDS, AND PROJECT-BASED SECTION 8 RENTAL ASSISTANCE

SEC. 110207.

(a) Authorization Of Appropriations.—There is authorized to be appropriated $500,000,000 for fiscal year 2020 for additional assistance for supportive housing for the elderly, of which—

(1) $200,000,000 shall be for rental assistance under section 202 of the Housing Act of 1959 (12 U.S.C. 1701q) or section 8 of the United States Housing Act of 1937 (42 U.S.C. 1437f), as appropriate, and for hiring additional staff and for services and costs, including acquiring personal protective equipment, to prevent, prepare for, or respond to the public health emergency relating to Coronavirus Disease 2019 (COVID-19) pandemic; and

(2) $300,000,000 shall be for grants under section 676 of the Housing and Community Development Act of 1992 (42 U.S.C. 13632) for costs of providing service coordinators for purposes of coordinating services to prevent, prepare for, or respond to the public health emergency relating to Coronavirus Disease 2019 (COVID-19).

Any provisions of, and waivers and alternative requirements issued by the Secretary pursuant to, the heading 'Department of Housing and Urban Development—Housing Programs—Housing for the Elderly' in title XII of division B of the CARES Act (Public Law 116–136) shall apply with respect to amounts made available pursuant to this subsection.

(b) Eligibility Of Supportive Housing For Persons With Disabilities.—Subsection (a) of section 676 of the Housing and Community Development Act of 1992 (42 U.S.C. 13632(a)) shall be applied, for purposes of subsection (a) of this section, by substituting "(G), and (H)" for " and (G)".

(c) Service Coordinators.—

(1) HIRING.—In the hiring of staff using amounts made available pursuant to this section for costs of providing service coordinators, grantees shall consider and hire, at all levels of employment and to the greatest extent possible, a diverse staff, including by race, ethnicity, gender, and disability status. Each grantee shall submit a report to the Secretary of Housing and Urban Development describing compliance with the preceding sentence not later than the expiration of the 120-day period that begins upon the termination of the emergency declared on March 13, 2020, by the President under the Robert T. Stafford Disaster Relief and Emergency Assistance Act (42 U.S.C. 4121 et seq.) relating to the Coronavirus Disease 2019 (COVID-19) pandemic.

(2) ONE-TIME GRANTS.—Grants made using amounts made available pursuant to subsection (a) for costs of providing service coordinators shall not be renewable.
(3) ONE-YEAR AVAILABILITY.—Any amounts made available pursuant to this section for costs of providing service coordinators that are allocated for a grantee and remain unexpended upon the expiration of the 12-month period beginning upon such allocation shall be recaptured by the Secretary.
(d) Funding For Supportive Housing For Persons With Disabilities.—There is authorized to be appropriated $200,000,000 for fiscal year 2020 for additional assistance for supportive housing for persons with disabilities under section 811 of the Cranston-Gonzalez National Affordable Housing Act (42 U.S.C. 8013). Any provisions of, and waivers and alternative requirements issued by the Secretary pursuant to, the heading "Department of Housing and Urban Development—Housing Programs—Housing for Persons With Disabilities" in title XII of division B of the CARES Act (Public Law 116–136) shall apply with respect to amounts made available pursuant to this subsection.
(e) Funding For Housing Opportunities For People With AIDS Program.—There is authorized to be appropriated $15,000,000 for fiscal year 2020 for additional assistance for the Housing Opportunities for Persons with AIDS program under the AIDS Housing Opportunity Act (42 U.S.C. 12901 et seq.). Any provisions of, and waivers and alternative requirements issued by the Secretary pursuant to, the heading "Department of Housing and Urban Development—Community Planning and Development—Housing Opportunities for Persons With AIDS" in title XII of division B of the CARES Act (Public Law 116–136) shall apply with respect to amounts made available pursuant to this subsection.
(f) Funding For Project-Based Section 8 Rental Assistance.—There is authorized to be appropriated $750,000,000 for fiscal year 2020 for additional assistance for project-based rental assistance under section 8 of the United States Housing Act of 1937 (42 U.S.C. 1437f). Any provisions of, and waivers and alternative requirements issued by the Secretary pursuant to, the heading "Department of Housing and Urban Development—Housing Programs—Project-Based Rental Assistance" in title XII of division B of the CARES Act (Public Law 116–136) shall apply with respect to amounts made available pursuant to this subsection.
FAIR HOUSING

SEC. 110208.
(a) Definition Of COVID–19 Emergency Period.— For purposes of this Act, the term "COVID–19 emergency period" means the period that begins upon the date of the enactment of this Act and ends upon the date of the termination by the Federal Emergency Management Agency of the emergency declared on March 13, 2020, by the President under the Robert T. Stafford Disaster Relief and Emergency Assistance Act (42 U.S.C. 4121 et seq.) relating to the Coronavirus Disease 2019 (COVID–19) pandemic.
(b) Fair Housing Activities.—
(1) AUTHORIZATION OF APPROPRIATIONS.—To ensure existing grantees have sufficient resource for fair housing activities and for technology and equipment needs to deliver services through use of the Internet or other electronic or virtual means in response to the public health emergency related to the Coronavirus Disease 2019 (COVID-19) pandemic, there is authorized to be appropriated $4,000,000 for Fair Housing Organization Initiative grants through the Fair Housing Initiatives Program

under section 561 of the Housing and Community Development Act of 1987 (42 U.S.C. 3616a).

(2) 3-YEAR AVAILABILITY.—Any amounts made available pursuant paragraph (1) that are allocated for a grantee and remain unexpended upon the expiration of the 3-year period beginning upon such allocation shall be recaptured by the Secretary.

(c) Fair Housing Education.—There is authorized to be appropriated $10,000,000 for the Office of Fair Housing and Equal Opportunity of the Department of Housing and Urban Development to carry out a national media campaign and local education and outreach to educate the public of increased housing rights during COVID–19 emergency period, that provides that information and materials used in such campaign are available—

(1) in the languages used by communities with limited English proficiency; and

(2) to persons with disabilities.

FUNDING FOR HOUSING COUNSELING SERVICES

SEC. 110209.

(a) Congressional Findings.—The Congress finds that—

(1) the spread of Coronavirus Disease 2019 (COVID–19), which is now considered a global pandemic, is expected to negatively impact the incomes of potentially millions of homeowners, renters, individuals experiencing homelessness, and individuals at risk of homelessness, making it difficult for them to pay their mortgages or rents on time;

(2) housing counseling is critical to ensuring that homeowners, renters, individuals experiencing homelessness, and individuals at risk of homelessness have the resources they need to manage financial hardships from the COVID-19 crisis;

(3) loan preservation and foreclosure mitigation services are also critical to address the needs of homeowners who lose employment and income because of the pandemic and who face serious delinquency or home loan default, or are in foreclosing proceedings during this period;

(4) evaluations from the National Foreclosure Mitigation Counseling program revealed that homeowners at risk of or facing foreclosure are better served when they have access to a housing counselor and a range of tools and resources to help them avoid losing their home and have the support they need to tailor the best possible response to their situation.

(b) Authorization Of Appropriations.—There is authorized to be appropriated to the Neighborhood Reinvestment Corporation (in this section referred to as the "Corporation") established under the Neighborhood Reinvestment Corporation Act (42 U.S.C. 8101 et seq.) $100,000,000 for fiscal year 2020 for housing counseling services, which shall remain available until September 30, 2023.

(c) Prioritization Of Housing Counseling Services.—Of any grant funds made available pursuant to subsection (b), not less than 40 percent shall be provided to counseling organizations that target counseling services to minority and low-income homeowners, renters, individuals experiencing homelessness, and individuals at risk of homelessness or provide such services in neighborhoods with high concentrations of minority and low-income homeowners, renters, individuals experiencing homelessness, and individuals at risk of homelessness.

(d) Eligible Uses.—Amounts made available pursuant to subsection (b) may be used in such amounts as the Corporation determines for costs of—

(1) public education and outreach;

(2) direct services, including the full range of services provided by housing counselors to assist homeowners, including manufactured homeowners, regardless of financing type, renters, individuals experiencing homelessness, and individuals at risk of homelessness, including the practices, tools, and innovations in foreclosure mitigation that were utilized in the National Foreclosure Mitigation Counseling Program, and financial capability, credit counseling, homeless counseling, and rental counseling;

(3) equipment and technology, including broadband internet and equipment upgrades needed to ensure timely and effective service delivery;

(4) training, including capacitating housing counseling staff in various modes of counseling, including rental and foreclosure, delivery of remote counseling utilizing improved technology, enhanced network security, and supportive options for the delivery of client services; and

(5) administration and oversight of the program in accordance with the Corporation's rate for program administration.

(e) Disbursement.—The Corporation shall disburse all grant funds made available pursuant to subsection (b) as expeditiously as possible, through grants to housing counseling intermediaries approved by the Department of Housing and Urban Development, State housing finance agencies, and NeighborWorks organizations. The aggregate amount provided to NeighborWorks organizations shall not exceed 15 percent of the total of grant funds made available pursuant to subsection (b).

TITLE III

—PROTECTING PEOPLE EXPERIENCING HOMELESSNESS
HOMELESS ASSISTANCE FUNDING

SEC. 110301.

(a) Emergency Homeless Assistance.—

(1) AUTHORIZATION OF APPROPRIATIONS.—There is authorized to be appropriated under the Emergency Solutions Grants program under subtitle B of title IV of the McKinney-Vento Homeless Assistance Act (42 U.S.C. 11371 et seq.) $11,500,000,000 for grants under such subtitle in accordance with this subsection to respond to needs arising from the public health emergency relating to Coronavirus Disease 2019 (COVID-19). Of such amounts made available, $4,000,000,000 shall be allocated in accordance with sections 413 and 414 of the McKinney-Vento Homeless Assistance Act (42 U.S.C. 11372, 11373).

(2) FORMULA.—Notwithstanding sections 413 and 414 of the McKinney-Vento Homeless Assistance Act (42 U.S.C. 11372, 11373), the Secretary of Housing and Urban Development (in this Act referred to as the "Secretary") shall allocate any amounts remaining after amounts are allocated pursuant to paragraph (1) in accordance with a formula to be established by the Secretary that takes into consideration the following factors:

(A) Risk of transmission of coronavirus in a jurisdiction.

(B) Whether a jurisdiction has a high number or rate of sheltered and unsheltered homeless individuals and families.

(C) Economic and housing market conditions in a jurisdiction.

(3) ELIGIBLE ACTIVITIES.—In addition to eligible activities under section 415(a) of the McKinney-Vento Homeless Assistance Act (42 U.S.C. 11374(a), amounts made available pursuant to paragraph (1) may also be used for costs of the following

activities:

(A) Providing training on infectious disease prevention and mitigation.

(B) Providing hazard pay, including for time worked before the effectiveness of this subparagraph, for staff working directly to prevent and mitigate the spread of coronavirus or COVID-19 among people experiencing or at risk of homelessness.

(C) Reimbursement of costs for eligible activities (including activities described in this paragraph) relating to preventing, preparing for, or responding to the coronavirus or COVID-19 that were accrued before the date of the enactment of this Act.

(D) Notwithstanding 24 CFR 576.102(a)(3), providing a hotel or motel voucher for a homeless individual or family.

Use of such amounts for activities described in this paragraph shall not be considered use for administrative purposes for purposes of section 418 of the McKinney-Vento Homeless Assistance Act (42 U.S.C. 11377).

(4) INAPPLICABILITY OF PROCUREMENT STANDARDS.—To the extent amounts made available pursuant to paragraph (1) are used to procure goods and services relating to activities to prevent, prepare for, or respond to the coronavirus or COVID-19, the standards and requirements regarding procurement that are otherwise applicable shall not apply.

(5) INAPPLICABILITY OF HABITABILITY AND ENVIRONMENTAL REVIEW STANDARDS.—Any Federal standards and requirements regarding habitability and environmental review shall not apply with respect to any emergency shelter that is assisted with amounts made available pursuant to paragraph (1) and has been determined by a State or local health official, in accordance with such requirements as the Secretary shall establish, to be necessary to prevent and mitigate the spread of coronavirus or COVID-19, such shelters.

(6) INAPPLICABILITY OF CAP ON EMERGENCY SHELTER ACTIVITIES.—Subsection (b) of section 415 of the McKinney-Vento Homeless Assistance Act shall not apply to any amounts made available pursuant to paragraph (1) of this subsection.

(7) INITIAL ALLOCATION OF ASSISTANCE.—Section 417(b) of the McKinney-Vento Homeless Assistance Act (42 U.S.C. 11376(b)) shall be applied with respect to amounts made available pursuant to paragraph (1) of this subsection by substituting "30-day" for "60-day".

(8) WAIVERS AND ALTERNATIVE REQUIREMENTS.—

(A) AUTHORITY.—In administering amounts made available pursuant to paragraph (1), the Secretary may waive, or specify alternative requirements for, any provision of any statute or regulation (except for any requirements related to fair housing, nondiscrimination, labor standards, and the environment) that the Secretary administers in connection with the obligation or use by the recipient of such amounts, if the Secretary finds that good cause exists for the waiver or alternative requirement and such waiver or alternative requirement is consistent with the purposes described in this subsection.

(B) NOTIFICATION.—The Secretary shall notify the public through the Federal Register or other appropriate means 5 days before the effective date of any such waiver or alternative requirement, and any such public notice may be provided on the Internet at the appropriate Government web site or through other electronic media, as determined by the Secretary.

(C) EXEMPTION.—The use of amounts made available pursuant to paragraph (1) shall not be subject to the consultation, citizen participation, or match requirements that otherwise apply to the Emergency Solutions Grants program, except that a recipient shall publish how it has and will utilize its allocation at a minimum on the Internet at the appropriate Government web site or through other electronic media.

(9) INAPPLICABILITY OF MATCHING REQUIREMENT.—Subsection (a) of section 416 of the McKinney-Vento Homeless Assistance Act (42 U.S.C. 11375(a)) shall not apply to any amounts made available pursuant to paragraph (1) of this subsection.

(10) PROHIBITION ON PREREQUISITES.—None of the funds authorized under this subsection may be used to require people experiencing homelessness to receive treatment or perform any other prerequisite activities as a condition for receiving shelter, housing, or other services.

(b) Continuum Of Care Program.—Due to the emergency relating to the Coronavirus Disease 2019 (COVID-19) pandemic, the Notice of Funding Availability (NOFA) for fiscal year 2020 for the Continuum of Care program under subtitle C of title IV of the McKinney-Vento Homeless Assistance Act (42 U.S.C. 11381 et seq.) shall have no force or effect and the Secretary of Housing and Urban Development shall distribute amounts made available for such fiscal year for such program based on the results of the competition for amounts made available for such program for fiscal year 2019 (FR-6300--25), except that grant amounts may be adjusted to account for changes in fair market rents.

EMERGENCY RENTAL ASSISTANCE VOUCHER PROGRAM

SEC. 110302.

(a) Authorization Of Appropriations.—There is authorized to be appropriated to the Secretary of Housing and Urban Development (in this section referred to as the "Secretary"), $1,000,000,000 for fiscal year 2020, to remain available until expended, for incremental emergency vouchers under subsection (b).

(b) Emergency Vouchers.—

(1) IN GENERAL.—The Secretary shall provide emergency rental assistance vouchers under this subsection, which shall be tenant-based rental assistance under section 8(o) the United States Housing Act of 1937 (42 U.S.C. 1437f(o)).

(2) SELECTION OF FAMILIES.—

(A) MANDATORY PREFERENCES.—Each public housing agency administering assistance under this section shall provide preference for such assistance to eligible families that are—

(i) homeless (as such term is defined in section 103(a) of the McKinney-Vento Homeless Assistance Act (42 U.S.C. 11302(a));

(ii) at risk of homelessness (as such term is defined in section 401 of the McKinney-Vento Homeless Assistance Act (42 U.S.C. 11360); or

(iii) fleeing, or attempting to flee, domestic violence, dating violence, sexual assault, or stalking.

(B) ALLOCATION.—In allocating amounts made available under this section, the Secretary shall—

(i) not later than 60 days after the date of the enactment of this Act, allocate at least 50 percent of such amounts to public housing agencies in accordance with a formula that considers—

(I) the capability of public housing agencies to promptly use emergency vouchers provided under this section; and

(II) the need for emergency vouchers provided under this section in the geographical area, based on factors determined by the Secretary, including risk of transmission of coronavirus, high numbers or rates of sheltered and unsheltered homelessness, and economic and housing market conditions;

(ii) allocate remaining amounts in accordance with a formula that considers—

(I) the criteria under clause (i) and the success of a public housing agency in promptly utilizing vouchers awarded under clause (i); and

(II) the capability of the public housing agency to create and manage structured partnerships with service providers for the delivery of appropriate community-based services; and

(iii) designate the number of vouchers under this section that each public housing agency that is awarded funds under this section is authorized to administer.

(C) ELECTION NOT TO ADMINISTER.—If a public housing agency elects not to administer amounts under this section, the Secretary shall award such amounts to other public housing agencies according to the criteria in subparagraph (B).

(D) FAILURE TO USE VOUCHERS PROMPTLY.—If a public housing agency fails to issue all of its authorized vouchers under this section on behalf of eligible families within a reasonable period of time as determined by the Secretary, the Secretary shall reallocate any unissued vouchers and associated funds to others public housing agencies according to the criteria under subparagraph (B)(ii).

(3) WAIVERS AND ALTERNATIVE REQUIREMENTS.—Any waiver or alternative requirement that the Secretary makes available to all public housing agencies in connection with assistance made available under the heading "Tenant-Based Rental Assistance" in title XII of division B of the CARES Act (Public Law 116–136; 134 Stat.601) shall apply to assistance under this section until the expiration of such waiver or alternative requirement.

(4) TERMINATION OF VOUCHERS UPON TURNOVER.—

(A) IN GENERAL.—A public housing agency may not reissue any vouchers made available under this section when assistance for the family initially assisted is terminated.

(B) REALLOCATION.—Upon termination of assistance for one or more families assisted by a public housing agency under this section, the Secretary shall reallocate amounts that are no longer needed by such public housing agency for assistance under this section to another public housing agency for the renewal of vouchers previously authorized under this section.

TITLE IV

—SUSPENDING NEGATIVE CREDIT REPORTING AND STRENGTHENING CONSUMER AND INVESTOR PROTECTIONS
REPORTING OF INFORMATION DURING MAJOR DISASTERS

SEC. 110401.

(a) In General.—The CARES Act (Public Law 116–136) is amended by striking section 4021 and inserting the following:

"SEC. 4021. REPORTING OF INFORMATION DURING MAJOR DISASTERS.

"(a) Purpose.—The purpose of this Act, and the amendments made by this Act, is to protect consumers' credit from negative impacts as a result of financial hardship due to the coronavirus disease (COVID–19) outbreak and future major disasters.

"(b) Reporting Of Information During Major Disasters.—

"(1) IN GENERAL.—The Fair Credit Reporting Act is amended by inserting after section 605B the following:

'§ 605C. Reporting of information during major disasters

'(a) Definitions.—In this section:

'(1) CONSUMER.—With respect to a covered period, the term 'consumer' shall only include a consumer who is a resident of the affected area covered by the applicable disaster or emergency declaration.

'(2) COVERED MAJOR DISASTER PERIOD.—The term 'covered major disaster period' means the period—

'(A) beginning on the date on which a major disaster is declared by the President under—

'(i) section 401 of the Robert T. Stafford Disaster Relief and Emergency Assistance Act (42 U.S.C. 5170), under which assistance is authorized under section 408 of such Act (42 U.S.C. 5174); or

'(ii) section 501 of such Act; and

'(B) ending on the date that is 120 days after the end of the incident period for such disaster.

'(3) COVERED PERIOD.—The term 'covered period' means the COVID–19 emergency period or a covered major disaster period.

'(4) COVID–19 EMERGENCY PERIOD.—The term 'COVID–19 emergency period' means the period beginning on March 13, 2020 (the date the President declared the emergency under section 501 of the Robert T. Stafford Disaster Relief and Emergency Assistance Act (42 U.S.C. 4121 et seq.) relating to the Coronavirus Disease 2019 (COVID-19) pandemic) and ending on the later of—

'(A) 120 days after the date of enactment of this section; or

'(B) 120 days after the end of the incident period for such emergency.

'(5) MAJOR DISASTER.—The term 'major disaster' means a major disaster declared by the President under—

'(A) section 401 of the Robert T. Stafford Disaster Relief and Emergency Assistance Act (42 U.S.C. 5170), under which assistance is authorized under section 408 of such Act (42 U.S.C. 5174); or

'(B) section 501 of such Act.

'(b) Moratorium On Furnishing Adverse Information During Covered Period.—No person may furnish any adverse item of information (except information related to a felony criminal conviction) relating to a consumer that was the result of any action or inaction that occurred during a covered period.

'(c) Information Excluded From Consumer Reports.—In addition to the information described in section 605(a), no consumer reporting agency may make any consumer report containing an adverse item of information (except information related to a felony criminal conviction) relating to a consumer that was the result of any action or inaction that occurred during a covered period.

'(d) Summary Of Rights.—Not later than 60 days after the date of enactment of this section, the Director of the Bureau shall update the model summary of rights under section 609(c)(1) to include a description of the right of a consumer to—

'(1) request the deletion of adverse items of information under subsection (e); and

'(2) request a consumer report or score, without charge to the consumer, under subsection (f).

'(e) Deletion Of Adverse Items Of Information Resulting From The Coronavirus Disease (COVID–19) Outbreak And Major Disasters.—

'(1) REPORTING.—

'(A) IN GENERAL.—Not later than 60 days after the date of enactment of this sub-section, the Director of the Bureau shall create a website for consumers to report, under penalty of perjury, economic hardship as a result of the coronavirus disease (COVID–19) outbreak or a major disaster for the purpose of providing credit report protections under this subsection.

'(B) DOCUMENTATION.—The Director of the Bureau shall—

'(i) not require any documentation from a consumer to substantiate the economic hardship; and

'(ii) provide notice to the consumer that a report under subparagraph (A) is under penalty of perjury.

'(C) REPORTING PERIOD.—A consumer may report economic hardship under subparagraph (A) during a covered period and for 60 days thereafter.

'(2) DATABASE.—The Director of the Bureau shall establish and maintain a secure database that—

'(A) is accessible to each consumer reporting agency described in section 603(p) and nationwide specialty consumer reporting agency for purposes of fulfilling their duties under paragraph (3) to check and automatically delete any adverse item of information (except information related to a felony criminal conviction) reported that occurred during a covered period with respect to a consumer; and

'(B) contains the information reported under paragraph (1).

'(3) DELETION OF ADVERSE ITEMS OF INFORMATION BY NATIONWIDE CONSUMER REPORTING AND NATIONWIDE SPECIALTY CONSUMER RE-PORTING AGENCIES.—

'(A) IN GENERAL.—Each consumer reporting agency described in section 603(p) and each nationwide specialty consumer reporting agency shall, using the informa-tion contained in the database established under paragraph (2), delete from the file of each consumer named in the database each adverse item of information (except information related to a felony criminal conviction) that was a result of an action or inaction that occurred during a covered period or in the 270-day period following the end of a covered period.

'(B) TIMELINE.—Each consumer reporting agency described in section 603(p) and each nationwide specialty consumer reporting agency shall check the database at least weekly and delete adverse items of information as soon as practicable after information that is reported under paragraph (1) appears in the database established under paragraph (2).

'(4) REQUEST FOR DELETION OF ADVERSE ITEMS OF INFORMATION.—

'(A) IN GENERAL.—A consumer who has filed a report of economic hardship with the Bureau may submit a request, without charge to the consumer, to a consumer reporting agency described in section 603(p) or nationwide specialty consumer reporting agency to delete from the consumer's file an adverse item of information (except information related to a felony criminal conviction) that was a result of an action or inaction that occurred during a covered period or in the 270-day period following the end of a covered period.

'(B) TIMING.—A consumer may submit a request under subparagraph (A), not later than the end of the 270-day period described in that subparagraph.

'(C) REMOVAL AND NOTIFICATION.—Upon receiving a request under this paragraph to delete an adverse item of information, a consumer reporting agency described in section 603(p) or nationwide specialty consumer reporting agency shall—

'(i) delete the adverse item of information (except information related to a felony criminal conviction) from the consumer's file; and

'(ii) notify the consumer and the furnisher of the adverse item of information of the deletion.

'(f) Free Credit Report And Scores.—

'(1) IN GENERAL.—During the period between the beginning of a covered period and ending 12-months after the end of the covered period, each consumer reporting agency described under section 603(p) and each nationwide specialty consumer reporting agency shall make all disclosures described under section 609 upon request by a consumer, by mail or online, without charge to the consumer and without limitation as to the number of requests. Such a consumer reporting agency shall also supply a consumer, upon request and without charge, with a credit score that—

'(A) is derived from a credit scoring model that is widely distributed to users by the consumer reporting agency for the purpose of any extension of credit or other transaction designated by the consumer who is requesting the credit score; or

'(B) is widely distributed to lenders of common consumer loan products and predicts the future credit behavior of a consumer.

'(2) TIMING.—A file disclosure or credit score under paragraph (1) shall be provided to the consumer not later than—

'(A) 7 days after the date on which the request is received if the request is made by mail; and

'(B) not later than 15 minutes if the request is made online.

'(3) ADDITIONAL REPORTS.—A file disclosure provided under paragraph (1) shall be in addition to any disclosure requested by the consumer under section 612(a).

'(4) PROHIBITION.—A consumer reporting agency that receives a request under paragraph (1) may not request or require any documentation from the consumer that demonstrates that the consumer was impacted by the coronavirus disease (COVID–19) outbreak or a major disaster (except to verify that the consumer is a resident of the affected area covered by the applicable disaster or emergency declaration) as a condition of receiving the file disclosure or score.

'(g) Posting Of Rights.—Not later than 30 days after the date of enactment of this section, each consumer reporting agency described under section 603(p) and each nationwide specialty consumer reporting agency shall prominently post and maintain a direct link on the homepage of the public website of the consumer reporting agency information relating to the right of consumers to—

'(1) request the deletion of adverse items of information (except information related to a felony criminal conviction) under subsection (e); and

'(2) request consumer file disclosures and scores, without charge to the consumer, under subsection (f).

'(h) Ban On Reporting Medical Debt Information Related To COVID–19 Or A Major Disaster.—

'(1) FURNISHING BAN.—No person shall furnish adverse information to a consumer reporting agency related to medical debt if such medical debt is with respect to medical expenses related to treatments arising from COVID–19 or a major disaster (whether or not the expenses were incurred during a covered period).

'(2) CONSUMER REPORT BAN.—No consumer reporting agency may make a consumer report containing adverse information related to medical debt if such medical debt is with respect to medical expenses related to treatments arising from COVID–19 or a major disaster (whether or not the expenses were incurred during a covered period).

'(i) Credit Scoring Models.—A person that creates and implements credit scoring models may not treat the absence, omission, or deletion of any information pursuant to this section as a negative factor or negative value in credit scoring models created or implemented by such person.'.

(2) TECHNICAL AND CONFORMING AMENDMENT.—The table of contents for the Fair Credit Reporting Act is amended by inserting after the item relating to section 605B the following:

'605C. Reporting of information during major disasters.'.

"SEC. 4021A. LIMITATIONS ON NEW CREDIT SCORING MODELS DURING THE COVID–19 EMERGENCY AND MAJOR DISASTERS.

"The Fair Credit Reporting Act (15 U.S.C. 1681 et seq.) is amended—

"(1) by adding at the end the following:

'§ 630. Limitations on new credit scoring models during the COVID–19 emergency and major disasters

'With respect to a person that creates and implements credit scoring models, such person may not, during a covered period (as defined under section 605C), create or implement a new credit scoring model (including a revision to an existing scoring model) if the new credit scoring model would identify a significant percentage of consumers as being less creditworthy when compared to the previous credit scoring models created or implemented by such person.'; and

(2) in the table of contents for such Act, by adding at the end the following new item:

'630. Limitations on new credit scoring models during the COVID–19 emergency and major disasters.'.

(b) Clerical Amendment.—The table of contents in section 2 of the CARES Act is amended by striking the item relating to section 4021 and inserting the following:

"SEC. 4021. Reporting of information during major disasters.

"SEC. 4021A. Limitations on new credit scoring models during the COVID–19 emergency and major disasters.".

(c) Conforming Amendment.—Subparagraph (F) of section 623(a)(1) of the Fair Credit Reporting Act (15 U.S.C. 1681s–2(a)(1)) is hereby repealed.

RESTRICTIONS ON COLLECTIONS OF CONSUMER DEBT DURING A NATIONAL DISASTER OR EMERGENCY

SEC. 110402.

(a) In General.—The Fair Debt Collection Practices Act (15 U.S.C. 1692 et seq.) is amended by inserting after section 812 (15 U.S.C. 1692j) the following:

"§ 812A. Restrictions on collections of consumer debt during a national disaster or emergency

"(a) Definitions.—In this section:

"(1) COVERED PERIOD.—The term 'covered period' means the period beginning on the date of enactment of this section and ending 120 days after the end of the incident period for the emergency declared on March 13, 2020, by the President under section 501 of the Robert T. Stafford Disaster Relief and Emergency Assistance Act (42 U.S.C. 4121 et seq.) relating to the Coronavirus Disease 2019 (COVID-19) pandemic.

"(2) CREDITOR.—The term 'creditor' means any person—

"(A) who offers or extends credit creating a debt or to whom a debt is owed; or

"(B) to whom any obligation for payment is owed.

"(3) DEBT.—The term 'debt'—

"(A) means any obligation or alleged obligation that is or during the covered period becomes past due, other than an obligation arising out of a credit agreement entered into after the effective date of this section, that arises out of a transaction with a consumer; and

"(B) does not include a mortgage loan.

"(4) DEBT COLLECTOR.—The term 'debt collector' means a creditor and any other person or entity that engages in the collection of debt, including the Federal Government and a State government, irrespective of whether the applicable debt is allegedly owed to or assigned to such creditor, person, or entity.

"(5) MORTGAGE LOAN.—The term 'mortgage loan' means a covered mortgage loan (as defined under section 4022 of the CARES Act) and a multifamily mortgage loan (as defined under section 4023 of the CARES Act).

"(b) Prohibitions.—

"(1) IN GENERAL.—Notwithstanding any other provision of law, no debt collector may, during a covered period—

"(A) enforce a security interest securing a debt through repossession, limitation of use, or foreclosure;

"(B) take or threaten to take any action to deprive an individual of their liberty as a result of nonpayment of or nonappearance at any hearing relating to an obligation owed by a consumer;

"(C) collect any debt, by way of garnishment, attachment, assignment, deduction, offset, or other seizure, from—

"(i) wages, income, benefits, bank, prepaid or other asset accounts; or

"(ii) any assets of, or other amounts due to, a consumer;

"(D) commence or continue an action to evict a consumer from real or personal property for nonpayment;

"(E) disconnect or terminate service from a utility service, including electricity, natural gas, telecommunications or broadband, water, or sewer, for nonpayment; or

"(F) threaten to take any of the foregoing actions.

"(2) RULE OF CONSTRUCTION.—Nothing in this section may be construed to prohibit a consumer from voluntarily paying, in whole or in part, a debt.

"(c) Limitation On Fees And Interest.—After the expiration of a covered period, a debt collector may not add to any past due debt any interest on unpaid interest, higher rate of interest triggered by the nonpayment of the debt, or fee triggered prior to the expiration of the covered period by the nonpayment of the debt.

"(e) Violations.—Any person or government entity that violates this section shall be liable to the applicable consumer as provided under section 813, except that, for purposes of applying section 813—

"(1) such person or government entity shall be deemed a debt collector, as such term is defined for purposes of section 813; and

"(2) each dollar figure in such section shall be deemed to be 10 times the dollar figure specified.

"(f) Tolling.—Any applicable time limitations for exercising an action prohibited under subsection (b) shall be tolled during a covered period.

"(g) Predispute Arbitration Agreements.—Notwithstanding any other provision of law, no predispute arbitration agreement or predispute joint-action waiver shall be valid or enforceable with respect to a dispute brought under this section, including a dispute as to the applicability of this section, which shall be determined under Federal law.".

(b) Clerical Amendment.—The table of contents for the Fair Debt Collection Practices Act is amended by inserting after the item relating to section 812 the following: "812A. Restrictions on collections of consumer debt during a national disaster or emergency.".

REPAYMENT PERIOD AND FORBEARANCE FOR CONSUMERS

SEC. 110403.

Section 812A of the Fair Debt Collection Practices Act (15 U.S.C. 1692 et seq.), as added by section 110402, is amended—

(1) by inserting after subsection (c) the following:

"(d) Repayment Period.—After the expiration of a covered period, a debt collector shall comply with the following:

"(1) DEBT ARISING FROM CREDIT WITH A DEFINED PAYMENT PERIOD.— For any debt arising from credit with a defined term, the debt collector shall extend the time period to repay any past due balance of the debt by—

"(A) 1 payment period for each payment that a consumer missed during the covered period, with the payments due in the same amounts and at the same intervals as the pre-existing payment schedule; and

"(B) 1 payment period in addition to the payment periods described under subparagraph (A).

"(2) DEBT ARISING FROM AN OPEN END CREDIT PLAN.—For debt arising from an open end credit plan, as defined in section 103 of the Truth in Lending Act (15 U.S.C. 1602), the debt collector shall allow the consumer to repay the past-due balance in a manner that does not exceed the amounts permitted by the methods described in section 171(c) of the Truth in Lending Act (15 U.S.C. 1666i–1(c)) and regulations promulgated under that section.

"(3) DEBT ARISING FROM OTHER CREDIT.—

"(A) IN GENERAL.—For debt not described under paragraph (2) or (3), the debt collector shall—

"(i) allow the consumer to repay the past-due balance of the debt in substantially equal payments over time; and

"(ii) provide the consumer with—

"(I) for past due balances of $2,000 or less, 12 months to repay, or such longer period as the debt collector may allow;

"(II) for past due balances between $2,001 and $5,000, 24 months to repay, or such longer period as the debt collector may allow; or

"(III) for past due balances greater than $5,000, 36 months to repay, or such longer period as the debt collector may allow.

"(B) ADDITIONAL PROTECTIONS.—The Director of the Bureau may issue rules to provide greater repayment protections to consumers with debts described under subparagraph (A).

"(C) RELATION TO STATE LAW.—This paragraph shall not preempt any State law that provides for greater consumer protections than this paragraph."; and

(2) by adding at the end the following:

"(h) Forbearance For Affected Consumers.—

"(1) FORBEARANCE PROGRAM.—Each debt collector that makes use of the credit facility described in paragraph (4) shall establish a forbearance program for debts available during the covered period.

"(2) AUTOMATIC GRANT OF FORBEARANCE UPON REQUEST.—Under a forbearance program required under paragraph (1), upon the request of a consumer experiencing a financial hardship due, directly or indirectly, to COVID–19, the debt collector shall grant a forbearance on payment of debt for such time as needed until the end of the covered period, with no additional documentation required other than the borrower's attestation to a financial hardship caused by COVID–19 and with no fees, penalties, or interest (beyond the amounts scheduled or calculated as if the borrower made all contractual payments on time and in full under the terms of the loan contract) charged to the borrower in connection with the forbearance.

"(3) EXCEPTION FOR CERTAIN MORTGAGE LOANS SUBJECT TO THE CARES ACT.—This subsection shall not apply to a mortgage loan subject to section 4022 or 4023 of the CARES Act.".

CREDIT FACILITY

SEC. 110404.

Section 812A(h) of the Fair Debt Collection Practices Act (15 U.S.C. 1692 et seq.), as added by section 110403, is amended by adding at the end the following:

"(4) CREDIT FACILITY.—The Board of Governors of the Federal Reserve System shall—

"(A) establish a facility, using amounts made available under section 4003(b)(4) of the CARES Act (15 U.S.C. 9042(b)(4)), to make long-term, low-cost loans to debt collectors to temporarily compensate such debt collectors for documented financial losses caused by forbearance of debt payments under this subsection; and

"(B) defer debt collectors' required payments on such loans until after consumers' debt payments resume.".

TITLE V

—FORGIVING STUDENT LOAN DEBT AND PROTECTING STUDENT BORROWERS

PAYMENTS FOR PRIVATE EDUCATION LOAN BORROWERS AS A RESULT OF THE COVID–19 NATIONAL EMERGENCY

SEC. 110501.

(a) In General.—Section 140 of the Truth in Lending Act (15 U.S.C. 1650) is amended by adding at the end the following new subsection:

"(h) COVID–19 National Emergency Private Education Loan Repayment Assistance.—

"(1) AUTHORITY.—

"(A) IN GENERAL.—Effective on the date of the enactment of this section, until the end of September 2021, the Secretary of the Treasury shall, for each borrower of a private education loan, pay the total amount due for such month on the loan, based on the payment plan selected by the borrower or the borrower's loan status.

"(B) LIMITATION ON PAYMENTS.—The maximum amount of aggregate payments that the Secretary of the Treasury may make under subparagraph (A) with respect to an individual borrower is $10,000.

"(2) NO CAPITALIZATION OF INTEREST.—With respect to any loan in repayment until the end of September 2021, interest due on a private education loan during such period shall not be capitalized at any time until the end of September 2021.

"(3) REPORTING TO CONSUMER REPORTING AGENCIES.—Until the end of the September 2021—

"(A) during the period in which the Secretary of the Treasury is making payments on a loan under paragraph (1), the Secretary shall ensure that, for the purpose of reporting information about the loan to a consumer reporting agency, any payment made by the Secretary is treated as if it were a regularly scheduled payment made by a borrower; and

"(B) no adverse credit information may be furnished to a consumer reporting agency for any private education loan.

"(4) NOTICE OF PAYMENTS AND PROGRAM.—Not later than 15 days following the date of enactment of this subsection, and monthly thereafter until the end of September 2021, the Secretary of the Treasury shall provide a notice to all borrowers of private education loans—

"(A) informing borrowers of the actions taken under this subsection;

"(B) providing borrowers with an easily accessible method to opt out of the benefits provided under this subsection; and

"(C) notifying the borrower that the program under this subsection is a temporary program and will end at the end of September 2021.

"(5) SUSPENSION OF INVOLUNTARY COLLECTION.—Until the end of September 2021, the holder of a private education loan shall immediately take action to halt all involuntary collection related to the loan.

"(6) MANDATORY FORBEARANCE.—During the period in which the Secretary of the Treasury is making payments on a loan under paragraph (1), the servicer of such loan shall grant the borrower forbearance as follows:

"(A) A temporary cessation of all payments on the loan other than the payments of interest and principal on the loan that are made under paragraph (1).

"(B) For borrowers who are delinquent but who are not yet in default before the date on which the Secretary begins making payments under paragraph (1), the retroactive application of forbearance to address any delinquency.

"(7) DATA TO IMPLEMENT.—Holders and servicers of private education loans shall report, to the satisfaction of the Secretary of the Treasury, the information necessary to calculate the amount to be paid under this subsection.".

(b) Appropriation.—Notwithstanding any other provision of law, there is appropriated to the Secretary of the Treasury, out of amounts in the Treasury not otherwise appropriated, $45,000,000,000 to carry out this title and the amendments made by this title.

ADDITIONAL PROTECTIONS FOR PRIVATE STUDENT LOAN BORROWERS

SEC. 110502.

(a) In General.—

(1) REPAYMENT PLAN AND FORGIVENESS TERMS.—Each private education loan holder who receives a monthly payment pursuant to section 140(h) of the Truth in Lending Act shall modify all private education loan contracts that it holds to provide for the same repayment plan and forgiveness terms available to Direct Loans borrowers under section 685.209(c) of title 34, Code of Federal Regulations, in effect as of January 1, 2020.

(2) TREATMENT OF STATE STATUTES OF LIMITATION.—For a borrower who has defaulted on a private education loan under the terms of the promissory note prior to any loan payment made or forbearance granted under section 140(h) of the Truth in Lending Act, no payment made or forbearance granted under such section 140(h) shall be considered an event that impacts the calculation of the applicable State statutes of limitation.

(3) PROHIBITION ON PRESSURING BORROWERS.—

(A) IN GENERAL.—A private education loan debt collector or creditor may not pressure a borrower to elect to apply any amount received pursuant to subsection (b) to any private education loan.

(B) VIOLATIONS.—A violation of this paragraph is deemed—

(i) an unfair, deceptive, or abusive act or practice under Federal law in connection with any transaction with a consumer for a consumer financial product or service under section 1031 of the Consumer Financial Protection Act of 2010 (12 U.S.C. 5531); and

(ii) with respect to a violation by a debt collector, an unfair or unconscionable means to collect or attempt to collect any debt under section 808 of the Federal Debt Collection Practices Act (15 U.S.C. 1692f).

(C) PRESSURE DEFINED.—In this paragraph, the term "pressure" means any communication, recommendation, or other similar communication, other than providing basic information about a borrower's options, urging a borrower to make an election described under subsection (b).

(b) Relief For Private Student Loan Borrowers As A Result Of The COVID–19 National Emergency.—

(1) STUDENT LOAN RELIEF AS A RESULT OF THE COVID–19 NATIONAL EMERGENCY.—Not later than 90 days after the end of September 2021, the Secretary of the Treasury shall carry out a program under which a borrower, with respect to the private education loans of such borrower, shall receive in accordance with paragraph (3) an amount equal to the lesser of—

(A) the total amount of each private education loan of the borrower; or

(B) $10,000, reduced by the aggregate amount of all payments made by the Secretary of the Treasury with respect to such borrower under section 140(h) of the Truth in Lending Act.

(2) NOTIFICATION OF BORROWERS.—Not later than 90 days after the end of September 2021, the Secretary of the Treasury shall notify each borrower of a private education loan of—

(A) the requirements to provide loan relief to such borrower under this section; and

(B) the opportunity for such borrower to make an election under paragraph (3)(A) with respect to the application of such loan relief to the private education loans of such borrower.

(3) DISTRIBUTION OF FUNDING.—

(A) ELECTION BY BORROWER.—Not later than 45 days after a notice is sent under paragraph (2), a borrower may elect to apply the amount determined with respect to such borrower under paragraph (1) to any private education loan of the borrower.

(B) AUTOMATIC PAYMENT.—

(i) IN GENERAL.—In the case of a borrower who does not make an election under subparagraph (A) before the date described in such subparagraph, the Secretary of the Treasury shall apply the amount determined with respect to such borrower under paragraph (1) in order of the private education loan of the borrower with the highest interest rate.

(ii) EQUAL INTEREST RATES.—In case of two or more private education loans described in clause (i) with equal interest rates, the Secretary of the Treasury shall apply the amount determined with respect to such borrower under paragraph (1) first to the loan with the highest principal.

(c) Definitions.—In this section:

(1) FAIR DEBT COLLECTION PRACTICES ACT TERMS.—The terms "creditor" and "debt collector" have the meaning given those terms, respectively, under section 803 of the Fair Debt Collection Practices Act (15 U.S.C. 1692a).

(2) PRIVATE EDUCATION LOAN.—The term "private education loan" has the meaning given the term in section 140 of the Truth in Lending Act (15 U.S.C. 1650).

TITLE VI

—STANDING UP FOR SMALL BUSINESSES, MINORITY-OWNED BUSINESSES, AND NON-PROFITS
RESTRICTIONS ON COLLECTIONS OF SMALL BUSINESS AND NONPROFIT DEBT DURING A NATIONAL DISASTER OR EMERGENCY

SEC. 110601.

(a) In General.—The Fair Debt Collection Practices Act (15 U.S.C. 1692 et seq.), as amended by section 110402, is further amended by inserting after section 812A the following:

"§ 812B. Restrictions on collections of small business and nonprofit debt during a national disaster or emergency

"(a) Definitions.—In this section:

"(1) COVERED PERIOD.—The term 'covered period' means the period beginning on the date of enactment of this section and ending 120 days after the end of the incident period for the emergency declared on March 13, 2020, by the President under section 501 of the Robert T. Stafford Disaster Relief and Emergency Assistance Act (42 U.S.C. 4121 et seq.) relating to the Coronavirus Disease 2019 (COVID-19) pandemic.

"(2) CREDITOR.—The term 'creditor' means any person—

"(A) who offers or extends credit creating a debt or to whom a debt is owed; or

"(B) to whom any obligation for payment is owed.

"(3) DEBT.—The term 'debt'—

"(A) means any obligation or alleged obligation that is or during the covered period becomes past due, other than an obligation arising out of a credit agreement entered into after the effective date of this section, that arises out of a transaction with a non-profit organization or small business; and

"(B) does not include a mortgage loan.

"(4) DEBT COLLECTOR.—The term 'debt collector' means a creditor and any other person or entity that engages in the collection of debt, including the Federal Government and a State government, irrespective of whether the applicable debt is allegedly owed to or assigned to such creditor, person, or entity.

"(5) MORTGAGE LOAN.—The term 'mortgage loan' means a covered mortgage loan (as defined under section 4022 of the CARES Act) and a multifamily mortgage loan (as defined under section 4023 of the CARES Act).

"(6) NONPROFIT ORGANIZATION.—The term 'nonprofit organization' means an organization that is described in section 501(c)(3) of the Internal Revenue Code of 1986 and that is exempt from taxation under section 501(a) of such Code.

"(7) SMALL BUSINESS.—The term 'small business' has the meaning given the term 'small business concern' in section 3 of the Small Business Act (15 U.S.C. 632).

"(b) Prohibitions.—

"(1) IN GENERAL.—Notwithstanding any other provision of law, no debt collector may, during a covered period—

"(A) enforce a security interest securing a debt through repossession, limitation of use, or foreclosure;

"(B) take or threaten to take any action to deprive an individual of their liberty as a result of nonpayment of or nonappearance at any hearing relating to an obligation owed by a small business or nonprofit organization;

"(C) collect any debt, by way of garnishment, attachment, assignment, deduction, offset, or other seizure, from—

"(i) wages, income, benefits, bank, prepaid or other asset accounts; or

"(ii) any assets of, or other amounts due to, a small business or nonprofit organization;

"(D) commence or continue an action to evict a small business or nonprofit organization from real or personal property for nonpayment;

"(E) disconnect or terminate service from a utility service, including electricity, natural gas, telecommunications or broadband, water, or sewer, for nonpayment; or

"(F) threaten to take any of the foregoing actions.

"(2) RULE OF CONSTRUCTION.—Nothing in this section may be construed to prohibit a small business or nonprofit organization from voluntarily paying, in whole or in part, a debt.

"(c) Limitation On Fees And Interest.—After the expiration of a covered period, a debt collector may not add to any past due debt any interest on unpaid interest, higher rate of interest triggered by the nonpayment of the debt, or fee triggered prior to the expiration of the covered period by the nonpayment of the debt.

"(e) Violations.—Any person or government entity that violates this section shall be liable to the applicable small business or nonprofit organization as provided under section 813, except that, for purposes of applying section 813—

"(1) such person or government entity shall be deemed a debt collector, as such term is defined for purposes of section 813; and

"(2) such small business or nonprofit organization shall be deemed a consumer, as such term is defined for purposes of section 813.

"(f) Tolling.—Any applicable time limitations for exercising an action prohibited under subsection (b) shall be tolled during a covered period.

"(g) Predispute Arbitration Agreements.—Notwithstanding any other provision of law, no predispute arbitration agreement or predispute joint-action waiver shall be valid or enforceable with respect to a dispute brought under this section, including a dispute as to the applicability of this section, which shall be determined under Federal law.".

(b) Clerical Amendment.—The table of contents for the Fair Debt Collection Practices Act, as amended by section 110402, is further amended by inserting after the item relating to section 812A the following:

"812B. Restrictions on collections of small business and nonprofit debt during a national disaster or emergency.".

REPAYMENT PERIOD AND FORBEARANCE FOR SMALL BUSINESSES AND

NONPROFIT ORGANIZATIONS

SEC. 110602.

Section 812B of the Fair Debt Collection Practices Act (15 U.S.C. 1692 et seq.), as added by section 110601, is amended—

(1) by inserting after subsection (c) the following:

"(d) Repayment Period.—After the expiration of a covered period, a debt collector shall comply with the following:

"(1) DEBT ARISING FROM CREDIT WITH A DEFINED PAYMENT PERIOD.— For any debt arising from credit with a defined term, the debt collector shall extend the time period to repay any past due balance of the debt by—

"(A) 1 payment period for each payment that a small business or nonprofit organization missed during the covered period, with the payments due in the same amounts and at the same intervals as the pre-existing payment schedule; and

"(B) 1 payment period in addition to the payment periods described under subparagraph (A).

"(2) DEBT ARISING FROM AN OPEN END CREDIT PLAN.—For debt arising from an open end credit plan, as defined in section 103 of the Truth in Lending Act (15 U.S.C. 1602), the debt collector shall allow the small business or nonprofit organization to repay the past-due balance in a manner that does not exceed the amounts permitted by the methods described in section 171(c) of the Truth in Lending Act (15 U.S.C. 1666i–1(c)) and regulations promulgated under that section.

"(3) DEBT ARISING FROM OTHER CREDIT.—

"(A) IN GENERAL.—For debt not described under paragraph (2) or (3), the debt collector shall—

"(i) allow the small business or nonprofit organization to repay the past-due balance of the debt in substantially equal payments over time; and

"(ii) provide the small business or nonprofit organization with—

"(I) for past due balances of $2,000 or less, 12 months to repay, or such longer period as the debt collector may allow;

"(II) for past due balances between $2,001 and $5,000, 24 months to repay, or such longer period as the debt collector may allow; or

"(III) for past due balances greater than $5,000, 36 months to repay, or such longer period as the debt collector may allow.

"(B) ADDITIONAL PROTECTIONS.—The Director of the Bureau may issue rules to provide greater repayment protections to small businesses and nonprofit organizations with debts described under subparagraph (A).

"(C) RELATION TO STATE LAW.—This paragraph shall not preempt any State law that provides for greater small business or nonprofit organization protections than this paragraph."; and

(2) by adding at the end the following:

"(h) Forbearance For Affected Small Businesses And Nonprofit Organizations.—

"(1) FORBEARANCE PROGRAM.—Each debt collector that makes use of the credit facility described in paragraph (4) shall establish a forbearance program for debts available during the covered period.

"(2) AUTOMATIC GRANT OF FORBEARANCE UPON REQUEST.—Under a forbearance program required under paragraph (1), upon the request of a small business or nonprofit organization experiencing a financial hardship due, directly or indirectly, to COVID–19, the debt collector shall grant a forbearance on payment of debt for such time as needed until the end of the covered period, with no additional documentation required other than the small business or nonprofit organization's attestation to a financial hardship caused by COVID–19 and with no fees, penalties, or interest (beyond the amounts scheduled or calculated as if the borrower made all contractual payments on time and in full under the terms of the loan contract) charged to the borrower in connection with the forbearance.

"(3) EXCEPTION FOR CERTAIN MORTGAGE LOANS SUBJECT TO THE CARES ACT.—This subsection shall not apply to a mortgage loan subject to section 4022 or 4023 of the CARES Act.".

CREDIT FACILITY

SEC. 110603.

Section 812B(h) of the Fair Debt Collection Practices Act (15 U.S.C. 1692 et seq.), as added by section 110602, is amended by adding at the end the following:

"(4) CREDIT FACILITY.—The Board of Governors of the Federal Reserve System shall—

"(A) establish a facility, using amounts made available under section 4003(b)(4) of the CARES Act (15 U.S.C. 9042(b)(4)), to make long-term, low-cost loans to debt collectors to temporarily compensate such debt collectors for documented financial losses caused by forbearance of debt payments under this subsection; and

"(B) defer debt collectors' required payments on such loans until after small businesses or nonprofit organizations' debt payments resume.".

MAIN STREET LENDING PROGRAM REQUIREMENTS

SEC. 110604.

(a) In General.—Section 4003(c)(3)(D)(ii) of the CARES Act (15 U.S.C. 9042(c)(3)(D)(ii)) is amended—

(1) by striking "Nothing in this subparagraph shall limit the discretion of the Board of Governors of the Federal Reserve System to" and inserting the following:

"(I) IN GENERAL.—The Board of Governors of the Federal Reserve System shall"; and

(2) by adding at the end the following:

"(II) REQUIREMENTS.—In carrying out subclause (I), the Board of Governors of the Federal Reserve System—

"(aa) shall make non-profit organizations eligible for any program or facility established under such subclause;

"(bb) shall create a low-cost loan option tailored to the unique needs of non-profit organizations, including the ability to defer payments and, solely for non-profit organizations that are ineligible to receive a covered loan under section 7(a)(36) of the Small Business Act (15 U.S.C. 636(a)(36)) and that predominantly serve low-income communities, as determined by the Federal Reserve, have the loans forgiven by the Department of the Treasury for a similar purpose to maintain payroll and operations provided under the Paycheck Protection Program, notwithstanding section 4003(d)(3) of the CARES Act;".

(b) Deadline.—Not later than the end of the 5-day period beginning on the date of enactment of this Act, the Board of Governors of the Federal Reserve System shall issue such rules or take such other actions as may be necessary to implement the requirements made by the amendments made by this section.

OPTIONS FOR SMALL BUSINESSES AND NON-PROFITS UNDER THE MAIN

STREET LENDING PROGRAM

SEC. 110605.

(a) In General.—Section (c)(3)(D)(ii)(II) of the CARES Act (15 U.S.C. 9042(c)(3)(D)(ii)(II)), as added by section 110604, is further amended by adding at the end the following:

"(cc) shall provide at least one low-cost loan option that small businesses and small non-profits are eligible for that does not have a minimum loan size;".

(b) Deadline.—Not later than the end of the 5-day period beginning on the date of enactment of this Act, the Board of Governors of the Federal Reserve System shall issue such rules or take such other actions as may be necessary to implement the requirements made by the amendments made by this section.

SAFE BANKING

SEC. 110606.

(a) Short Title; Purpose.—

(1) SHORT TITLE.—This section may be cited as the "Secure And Fair Enforcement Banking Act of 2020" or the "SAFE Banking Act of 2020".

(2) PURPOSE.—The purpose of this section is to increase public safety by ensuring access to financial services to cannabis-related legitimate businesses and service providers and reducing the amount of cash at such businesses.

(b) Safe Harbor For Depository Institutions.—

(1) IN GENERAL.—A Federal banking regulator may not—

(A) terminate or limit the deposit insurance or share insurance of a depository institution under the Federal Deposit Insurance Act (12 U.S.C. 1811 et seq.), the Federal Credit Union Act (12 U.S.C. 1751 et seq.), or take any other adverse action against a depository institution under section 8 of the Federal Deposit Insurance Act (12 U.S.C. 1818) solely because the depository institution provides or has provided financial services to a cannabis-related legitimate business or service provider;

(B) prohibit, penalize, or otherwise discourage a depository institution from providing financial services to a cannabis-related legitimate business or service provider or to a State, political subdivision of a State, or Indian Tribe that exercises jurisdiction over cannabis-related legitimate businesses;

(C) recommend, incentivize, or encourage a depository institution not to offer financial services to an account holder, or to downgrade or cancel the financial services offered to an account holder solely because—

(i) the account holder is a cannabis-related legitimate business or service provider, or is an employee, owner, or operator of a cannabis-related legitimate business or service provider;

(ii) the account holder later becomes an employee, owner, or operator of a cannabis-related legitimate business or service provider; or

(iii) the depository institution was not aware that the account holder is an employee, owner, or operator of a cannabis-related legitimate business or service provider;

(D) take any adverse or corrective supervisory action on a loan made to—

(i) a cannabis-related legitimate business or service provider, solely because the business is a cannabis-related legitimate business or service provider;

(ii) an employee, owner, or operator of a cannabis-related legitimate business or service provider, solely because the employee, owner, or operator is employed by, owns, or operates a cannabis-related legitimate business or service provider, as applicable; or

(iii) an owner or operator of real estate or equipment that is leased to a cannabis-related legitimate business or service provider, solely because the owner or operator of the real estate or equipment leased the equipment or real estate to a cannabis-related legitimate business or service provider, as applicable; or

(E) prohibit or penalize a depository institution (or entity performing a financial service for or in association with a depository institution) for, or otherwise discourage a depository institution (or entity performing a financial service for or in association with a depository institution) from, engaging in a financial service for a cannabis-related legitimate business or service provider.

(2) SAFE HARBOR APPLICABLE TO DE NOVO INSTITUTIONS.—Paragraph (1) shall apply to an institution applying for a depository institution charter to the same extent as such subsection applies to a depository institution.

(c) Protections For Ancillary Businesses.—For the purposes of sections 1956 and 1957 of title 18, United States Code, and all other provisions of Federal law, the proceeds from a transaction involving activities of a cannabis-related legitimate business or service provider shall not be considered proceeds from an unlawful activity solely because—

(1) the transaction involves proceeds from a cannabis-related legitimate business or service provider; or

(2) the transaction involves proceeds from—

(A) cannabis-related activities described in subsection (n)(4)(B) conducted by a cannabis-related legitimate business; or

(B) activities described in subsection (n)(13)(A) conducted by a service provider.

(d) Protections Under Federal Law.—

(1) IN GENERAL.—With respect to providing a financial service to a cannabis-related legitimate business or service provider within a State, political subdivision of a State, or Indian country that allows the cultivation, production, manufacture, sale, transportation, display, dispensing, distribution, or purchase of cannabis pursuant to a law or regulation of such State, political subdivision, or Indian Tribe that has jurisdiction over the Indian country, as applicable, a depository institution, entity performing a financial service for or in association with a depository institution, or insurer that provides a financial service to a cannabis-related legitimate business or service provider, and the officers, directors, and employees of that depository institution, entity, or insurer may not be held liable pursuant to any Federal law or regulation—

(A) solely for providing such a financial service; or

(B) for further investing any income derived from such a financial service.

(2) PROTECTIONS FOR FEDERAL RESERVE BANKS AND FEDERAL HOME LOAN BANKS.—With respect to providing a service to a depository institution that provides a financial service to a cannabis-related legitimate business or service provider (where such financial service is provided within a State, political subdivision of a State, or Indian country that allows the cultivation, production, manufacture, sale, transportation, display, dispensing, distribution, or purchase of cannabis pursuant to a law or regulation of such State, political subdivision, or Indian Tribe that has jurisdiction over the Indian country, as applicable), a Federal reserve bank or Federal Home Loan Bank, and the officers, directors, and employees of the Federal reserve bank or Federal Home Loan Bank, may not be held liable pursuant to any Federal law or regulation—

(A) solely for providing such a service; or

(B) for further investing any income derived from such a service.

(3) PROTECTIONS FOR INSURERS.—With respect to engaging in the business of insurance within a State, political subdivision of a State, or Indian country that allows the cultivation, production, manufacture, sale, transportation, display, dispensing, distribution, or purchase of cannabis pursuant to a law or regulation of such State, political subdivision, or Indian Tribe that has jurisdiction over the Indian country, as applicable, an insurer that engages in the business of insurance with a cannabis-related legitimate business or service provider or who otherwise engages with a person in a transaction permissible under State law related to cannabis, and the officers, directors, and employees of that insurer may not be held liable pursuant to any Federal law or regulation—

(A) solely for engaging in the business of insurance; or

(B) for further investing any income derived from the business of insurance.

(4) FORFEITURE.—

(A) DEPOSITORY INSTITUTIONS.—A depository institution that has a legal interest in the collateral for a loan or another financial service provided to an owner, employee, or operator of a cannabis-related legitimate business or service provider, or to an owner or operator of real estate or equipment that is leased or sold to a cannabis-related legitimate business or service provider, shall not be subject to criminal, civil, or administrative forfeiture of that legal interest pursuant to any Federal law for providing such loan or other financial service.

(B) FEDERAL RESERVE BANKS AND FEDERAL HOME LOAN BANKS.—A Federal reserve bank or Federal Home Loan Bank that has a legal interest in the collateral for a loan or another financial service provided to a depository institution that provides a financial service to a cannabis-related legitimate business or service provider, or to an owner or operator of real estate or equipment that is leased or sold to a cannabis-related legitimate business or service provider, shall not be subject to criminal, civil, or administrative forfeiture of that legal interest pursuant to any Federal law for providing such loan or other financial service.

(e) Rules Of Construction.—

(1) NO REQUIREMENT TO PROVIDE FINANCIAL SERVICES.—Nothing in this section shall require a depository institution, entity performing a financial service for or in association with a depository institution, or insurer to provide financial services to a cannabis-related legitimate business, service provider, or any other business.

(2) GENERAL EXAMINATION, SUPERVISORY, AND ENFORCEMENT AUTHORITY.—Nothing in this section may be construed in any way as limiting or otherwise restricting the general examination, supervisory, and enforcement authority of the Federal banking regulators, provided that the basis for any supervisory or enforcement action is not the provision of financial services to a cannabis-related legitimate business or service provider.

(f) Requirements For Filing Suspicious Activity Reports.—Section 5318(g) of title 31, United States Code, is amended by adding at the end the following:

"(5) REQUIREMENTS FOR CANNABIS-RELATED LEGITIMATE BUSINESSES.—

"(A) IN GENERAL.—With respect to a financial institution or any director, officer, employee, or agent of a financial institution that reports a suspicious transaction pursuant to this subsection, if the reason for the report relates to a cannabis-related legitimate business or service provider, the report shall comply with appropriate guidance issued by the Financial Crimes Enforcement Network. The Secretary shall ensure that the guidance is consistent with the purpose and intent of the SAFE Banking Act of 2020 and does not significantly inhibit the provision of financial services to a cannabis-related legitimate business or service provider in a State, political subdivision of a State, or Indian country that has allowed the cultivation, production, manufacture, transportation, display, dispensing, distribution, sale, or purchase of cannabis pursuant to law or regulation of such State, political subdivision, or Indian Tribe that has jurisdiction over the Indian country.

"(B) DEFINITIONS.—For purposes of this paragraph:

"(i) CANNABIS.—The term 'cannabis' has the meaning given the term 'marihuana' in section 102 of the Controlled Substances Act (21 U.S.C. 802).

"(ii) CANNABIS-RELATED LEGITIMATE BUSINESS.—The term 'cannabis-related legitimate business' has the meaning given that term in subsection (n) of the SAFE Banking Act of 2020.

"(iii) INDIAN COUNTRY.—The term 'Indian country' has the meaning given that term in section 1151 of title 18.

"(iv) INDIAN TRIBE.—The term 'Indian Tribe' has the meaning given that term in section 102 of the Federally Recognized Indian Tribe List Act of 1994 (25 U.S.C. 479a).

"(v) FINANCIAL SERVICE.—The term 'financial service' has the meaning given that term in subsection (n) of the SAFE Banking Act of 2020.

"(vi) SERVICE PROVIDER.—The term 'service provider' has the meaning given that term in subsection (n) of the SAFE Banking Act of 2020.

"(vii) STATE.—The term 'State' means each of the several States, the District of Columbia, Puerto Rico, and any territory or possession of the United States.".

(g) Guidance And Examination Procedures.—Not later than 180 days after the date of enactment of this Act, the Financial Institutions Examination Council shall develop uniform guidance and examination procedures for depository institutions that provide financial services to cannabis-related legitimate businesses and service providers.

(h) Annual Diversity And Inclusion Report.—The Federal banking regulators shall issue an annual report to Congress containing—

(1) information and data on the availability of access to financial services for minority-owned and women-owned cannabis-related legitimate businesses; and

(2) any regulatory or legislative recommendations for expanding access to financial services for minority-owned and women-owned cannabis-related legitimate businesses.

(i) GAO Study On Diversity And Inclusion.—

(1) STUDY.—The Comptroller General of the United States shall carry out a study on the barriers to marketplace entry, including in the licensing process, and the access to financial services for potential and existing minority-owned and women-owned cannabis-related legitimate businesses.

(2) REPORT.—The Comptroller General shall issue a report to the Congress—

(A) containing all findings and determinations made in carrying out the study required under paragraph (1); and

(B) containing any regulatory or legislative recommendations for removing barriers to marketplace entry, including in the licensing process, and expanding access to financial services for potential and existing minority-owned and women-owned cannabis-related legitimate businesses.

(j) GAO Study On Effectiveness Of Certain Reports On Finding Certain Persons.— Not later than 2 years after the date of the enactment of this Act, the Comptroller

General of the United States shall carry out a study on the effectiveness of reports on suspicious transactions filed pursuant to section 5318(g) of title 31, United States Code, at finding individuals or organizations suspected or known to be engaged with transnational criminal organizations and whether any such engagement exists in a State, political subdivision, or Indian Tribe that has jurisdiction over Indian country that allows the cultivation, production, manufacture, sale, transportation, display, dispensing, distribution, or purchase of cannabis. The study shall examine reports on suspicious transactions as follows:

(1) During the period of 2014 until the date of the enactment of this Act, reports relating to marijuana-related businesses.

(2) During the 1-year period after date of the enactment of this Act, reports relating to cannabis-related legitimate businesses.

(k) Banking Services For Hemp Businesses.—

(1) FINDINGS.—The Congress finds that—

(A) the Agriculture Improvement Act of 2018 (Public Law 115–334) legalized hemp by removing it from the definition of "marihuana" under the Controlled Substances Act;

(B) despite the legalization of hemp, some hemp businesses (including producers, manufacturers, and retailers) continue to have difficulty gaining access to banking products and services; and

(C) businesses involved in the sale of hemp-derived cannabidiol ("CBD") products are particularly affected, due to confusion about their legal status.

(2) FEDERAL BANKING REGULATOR HEMP BANKING GUIDANCE.—Not later than the end of the 90-day period beginning on the date of enactment of this Act, the Federal banking regulators shall jointly issue guidance to financial institutions—

(A) confirming the legality of hemp, hemp-derived CBD products, and other hemp-derived cannabinoid products, and the legality of engaging in financial services with businesses selling hemp, hemp-derived CBD products, and other hemp-derived cannabinoid products, after the enactment of the Agriculture Improvement Act of 2018; and

(B) to provide recommended best practices for financial institutions to follow when providing financial services and merchant processing services to businesses involved in the sale of hemp, hemp-derived CBD products, and other hemp-derived cannabinoid products.

(3) FINANCIAL INSTITUTION DEFINED.—In this section, the term "financial institution" means any person providing financial services.

(l) Application Of Safe Harbors To Hemp And CBD Products.—

(1) IN GENERAL.—Except as provided under paragraph (2), the provisions of this section (other than subsections (f) and (j)) shall apply to hemp (including hemp-derived cannabidiol and other hemp-derived cannabinoid products) in the same manner as such provisions apply to cannabis.

(2) RULE OF APPLICATION.—In applying the provisions of this section described under paragraph (1) to hemp, the definition of "cannabis-related legitimate business" shall be treated as excluding any requirement to engage in activity pursuant to the law of a State or political subdivision thereof.

(3) HEMP DEFINED.—In this subsection, the term "hemp" has the meaning given that term under section 297A of the Agricultural Marketing Act of 1946 (7 U.S.C. 1639o).

(m) Requirements For Deposit Account Termination Requests And Orders.—

(1) TERMINATION REQUESTS OR ORDERS MUST BE VALID.—

(A) IN GENERAL.—An appropriate Federal banking agency may not formally or informally request or order a depository institution to terminate a specific customer account or group of customer accounts or to otherwise restrict or discourage a depository institution from entering into or maintaining a banking relationship with a specific customer or group of customers unless—

(i) the agency has a valid reason for such request or order; and

(ii) such reason is not based solely on reputation risk.

(B) TREATMENT OF NATIONAL SECURITY THREATS.—If an appropriate Federal banking agency believes a specific customer or group of customers is, or is acting as a conduit for, an entity which—

(i) poses a threat to national security;

(ii) is involved in terrorist financing;

(iii) is an agency of the Government of Iran, North Korea, Syria, or any country listed from time to time on the State Sponsors of Terrorism list;

(iv) is located in, or is subject to the jurisdiction of, any country specified in clause (iii); or

(v) does business with any entity described in clause (iii) or (iv), unless the appropriate Federal banking agency determines that the customer or group of customers has used due diligence to avoid doing business with any entity described in clause (iii) or (iv), such belief shall satisfy the requirement under subparagraph (A).

(2) NOTICE REQUIREMENT.—

(A) IN GENERAL.—If an appropriate Federal banking agency formally or informally requests or orders a depository institution to terminate a specific customer account or a group of customer accounts, the agency shall—

(i) provide such request or order to the institution in writing; and

(ii) accompany such request or order with a written justification for why such termination is needed, including any specific laws or regulations the agency believes are being violated by the customer or group of customers, if any.

(B) JUSTIFICATION REQUIREMENT.—A justification described under subparagraph (A)(ii) may not be based solely on the reputation risk to the depository institution.

(3) CUSTOMER NOTICE.—

(A) NOTICE REQUIRED.—Except as provided under subparagraph (B) or as otherwise prohibited from being disclosed by law, if an appropriate Federal banking agency orders a depository institution to terminate a specific customer account or a group of customer accounts, the depository institution shall inform the specific customer or group of customers of the justification for the customer's account termination described under paragraph (2).

(B) NOTICE PROHIBITED.—

(i) NOTICE PROHIBITED IN CASES OF NATIONAL SECURITY.—If an appropriate Federal banking agency requests or orders a depository institution to terminate a specific customer account or a group of customer accounts based on a belief that the customer or customers pose a threat to national security, or are otherwise described under subsection (a)(2), neither the depository institution nor the appropriate Federal banking agency may inform the customer or customers of the justification for the customer's account termination.

(ii) NOTICE PROHIBITED IN OTHER CASES.—If an appropriate Federal banking agency determines that the notice required under subparagraph (A) may interfere with an authorized criminal investigation, neither the depository institution nor the appropriate Federal banking agency may inform the specific customer or group of customers of the justification for the customer's account termination.

(4) REPORTING REQUIREMENT.—Each appropriate Federal banking agency shall issue an annual report to the Congress stating—

(A) the aggregate number of specific customer accounts that the agency requested or ordered a depository institution to terminate during the previous year; and

(B) the legal authority on which the agency relied in making such requests and orders and the frequency on which the agency relied on each such authority.

(5) DEFINITIONS.—For purposes of this subsection:

(A) APPROPRIATE FEDERAL BANKING AGENCY.—The term "appropriate Federal banking agency" means—

(i) the appropriate Federal banking agency, as defined under section 3 of the Federal Deposit Insurance Act (12 U.S.C. 1813); and

(ii) the National Credit Union Administration, in the case of an insured credit union.

(B) DEPOSITORY INSTITUTION.—The term "depository institution" means—

(i) a depository institution, as defined under section 3 of the Federal Deposit Insurance Act (12 U.S.C. 1813); and

(ii) an insured credit union.

(n) Definitions.—In this Act:

(1) BUSINESS OF INSURANCE.—The term "business of insurance" has the meaning given such term in section 1002 of the Dodd-Frank Wall Street Reform and Consumer Protection Act (12 U.S.C. 5481).

(2) CANNABIS.—The term "cannabis" has the meaning given the term "marihuana" in section 102 of the Controlled Substances Act (21 U.S.C. 802).

(3) CANNABIS PRODUCT.—The term "cannabis product" means any article which contains cannabis, including an article which is a concentrate, an edible, a tincture, a cannabis-infused product, or a topical.

(4) CANNABIS-RELATED LEGITIMATE BUSINESS.—The term "cannabis-related legitimate business" means a manufacturer, producer, or any person or company that—

(A) engages in any activity described in subparagraph (B) pursuant to a law established by a State or a political subdivision of a State, as determined by such State or political subdivision; and

(B) participates in any business or organized activity that involves handling cannabis or cannabis products, including cultivating, producing, manufacturing, selling, transporting, displaying, dispensing, distributing, or purchasing cannabis or cannabis products.

(5) DEPOSITORY INSTITUTION.—The term "depository institution" means—

(A) a depository institution as defined in section 3(c) of the Federal Deposit Insurance Act (12 U.S.C. 1813(c));

(B) a Federal credit union as defined in section 101 of the Federal Credit Union Act (12 U.S.C. 1752); or

(C) a State credit union as defined in section 101 of the Federal Credit Union Act (12 U.S.C. 1752).

(6) FEDERAL BANKING REGULATOR.—The term "Federal banking regulator"

means each of the Board of Governors of the Federal Reserve System, the Bureau of Consumer Financial Protection, the Federal Deposit Insurance Corporation, the Federal Housing Finance Agency, the Financial Crimes Enforcement Network, the Office of Foreign Asset Control, the Office of the Comptroller of the Currency, the National Credit Union Administration, the Department of the Treasury, or any Federal agency or department that regulates banking or financial services, as determined by the Secretary of the Treasury.

(7) FINANCIAL SERVICE.—The term "financial service"—

(A) means a financial product or service, as defined in section 1002 of the Dodd-Frank Wall Street Reform and Consumer Protection Act (12 U.S.C. 5481);

(B) includes the business of insurance;

(C) includes, whether performed directly or indirectly, the authorizing, processing, clearing, settling, billing, transferring for deposit, transmitting, delivering, instructing to be delivered, reconciling, collecting, or otherwise effectuating or facilitating of payments or funds, where such payments or funds are made or transferred by any means, including by the use of credit cards, debit cards, other payment cards, or other access devices, accounts, original or substitute checks, or electronic funds transfers;

(D) includes acting as a money transmitting business which directly or indirectly makes use of a depository institution in connection with effectuating or facilitating a payment for a cannabis-related legitimate business or service provider in compliance with section 5330 of title 31, United States Code, and any applicable State law; and

(E) includes acting as an armored car service for processing and depositing with a depository institution or a Federal reserve bank with respect to any monetary instruments (as defined under section 1956(c)(5) of title 18, United States Code.

(8) INDIAN COUNTRY.—The term "Indian country" has the meaning given that term in section 1151 of title 18.

(9) INDIAN TRIBE.—The term "Indian Tribe" has the meaning given that term in section 102 of the Federally Recognized Indian Tribe List Act of 1994 (25 U.S.C. 479a).

(10) INSURER.—The term "insurer" has the meaning given that term under section 313(r) of title 31, United States Code.

(11) MANUFACTURER.—The term "manufacturer" means a person who manufactures, compounds, converts, processes, prepares, or packages cannabis or cannabis products.

(12) PRODUCER.—The term "producer" means a person who plants, cultivates, harvests, or in any way facilitates the natural growth of cannabis.

(13) SERVICE PROVIDER.—The term "service provider"—

(A) means a business, organization, or other person that—

(i) sells goods or services to a cannabis-related legitimate business; or

(ii) provides any business services, including the sale or lease of real or any other property, legal or other licensed services, or any other ancillary service, relating to cannabis; and

(B) does not include a business, organization, or other person that participates in any business or organized activity that involves handling cannabis or cannabis products, including cultivating, producing, manufacturing, selling, transporting, displaying, dispensing, distributing, or purchasing cannabis or cannabis products.

(14) STATE.—The term "State" means each of the several States, the District of Columbia, Puerto Rico, and any territory or possession of the United States.

(o) Discretionary Surplus Funds.—Section 7(a)(3)(A) of the Federal Reserve Act

(12 U.S.C. 289(a)(3)(A)) is amended by striking "$6,825,000,000" and inserting "$6,821,000,000".

TITLE VII

—EMPOWERING COMMUNITY FINANCIAL INSTITUTIONS
COMMUNITY DEVELOPMENT FINANCIAL INSTITUTIONS FUND

SEC. 110701.
(a) In General.—There is authorized to be appropriated to the Community Development Financial Institutions Fund, out of amounts in the general fund not otherwise appropriated, $2,000,000,000 for fiscal year 2020, for providing financial assistance and technical assistance under subparagraphs (A) and (B) of section 108(a)(1) of the Community Development Banking and Financial Institutions Act of 1994 (12 U.S.C. 4707(a)(1)), except that subsections (d) and (e) of such section 108 shall not apply to the provision of such assistance, for the Bank Enterprise Award program, and for financial assistance, technical assistance, training, and outreach programs designed to benefit Native American, Native Hawaiian, and Alaska Native communities and provided primarily through qualified community development lender organizations with experience and expertise in community development banking and lending in Indian country, Native American organizations, Tribes and Tribal organizations, and other suitable providers. Of the amount appropriated pursuant to this heading, not less than $800,000,000 shall be for providing financial assistance, technical assistance, awards, training, and outreach programs described above to recipients that are minority lending institutions.

(b) Definitions.—For purposes of this section:
(1) MINORITY LENDING INSTITUTION.—The term "minority lending institution" means any depository institution, loan fund, or other financial institution that—
(A) if a privately-owned institution, 51 percent is owned by one or more socially and economically disadvantaged individuals;
(B) if publicly-owned, 51 percent of the stock is owned by one or more socially and economically disadvantaged individuals; and
(C) in the case of a mutual institution, where the majority of the Board of Directors, account holders, and the community which it services is predominantly minority.
(2) MINORITY.—The term "minority" means any black American, Native American, Hispanic American, or Asian American.
ENSURING DIVERSITY IN COMMUNITY BANKING

SEC. 110702.
(a) Short Title.—This section may be cited as the "Ensuring Diversity in Community Banking Act of 2020".
(b) Community Development Financial Institution.—In this section, the term "community development financial institution" has the meaning given under section 103 of the Riegle Community Development and Regulatory Improvement Act of 1994 (12 U.S.C. 4702).
(c) Minority Depository Institution.—In this section, the term "minority depository institution" has the meaning given under section 308 of the Financial Institutions Reform, Recovery, and Enforcement Act of 1989 (12 U.S.C. 1463 note), as amended by this section.
(d) Inclusion Of Women's Banks In The Definition Of Minority Depository In-

stitution.—Section 308(b)(1) of the Financial Institutions Reform, Recovery, and Enforcement Act of 1989 (12 U.S.C. 1463 note) is amended—

(1) by redesignating subparagraphs (A), (B), and (C) as clauses (i), (ii), and (iii), respectively;

(2) by striking "means any" and inserting the following: means—

"(A) any"; and

(3) in clause (iii) (as so redesignated), by striking the period at the end and inserting "; or"; and

(4) by inserting at the end the following new subparagraph:

"(B) any bank described in clause (i), (ii), or (iii) of section 19(b)(1)(A) of the Federal Reserve Act—

"(i) more than 50 percent of the outstanding shares of which are held by 1 or more women; and

"(ii) the majority of the directors on the board of directors of which are women.".

(e) Establishment Of Impact Bank Designation.—

(1) IN GENERAL.—Each appropriate Federal banking agency shall establish a program under which a depository institution with total consolidated assets of less than $10,000,000,000 may elect to be designated as an impact bank if the total dollar value of the loans extended by such depository institution to low-income borrowers is greater than or equal to 50 percent of the assets of such bank.

(2) DESIGNATION.—Based on data obtained through examinations, an appropriate Federal banking agency shall submit a notification to a depository institution stating that the depository institution qualifies for designation as an impact bank.

(3) APPLICATION.—A depository institution that does not receive a notification described in paragraph (2) may submit an application to the appropriate Federal banking agency demonstrating that the depository institution qualifies for designation as an impact bank.

(4) ADDITIONAL DATA OR OVERSIGHT.—A depository institution is not required to submit additional data to an appropriate Federal banking agency or be subject to additional oversight from such an agency if such data or oversight is related specifically and solely for consideration for a designation as an impact bank.

(5) REMOVAL OF DESIGNATION.—If an appropriate Federal banking agency determines that a depository institution designated as an impact bank no longer meets the criteria for such designation, the appropriate Federal banking agency shall rescind the designation and notify the depository institution of such rescission.

(6) RECONSIDERATION OF DESIGNATION; APPEALS.—A depository institution may—

(A) submit to the appropriate Federal banking agency a request to reconsider a determination that such depository institution no longer meets the criteria for the designation; or

(B) file an appeal in accordance with procedures established by the appropriate Federal banking agency.

(7) RULEMAKING.—Not later than 1 year after the date of the enactment of this Act, the appropriate Federal banking agencies shall jointly issue rules to carry out the requirements of this paragraph, including by providing a definition of a low-income borrower.

(8) REPORTS.—Each appropriate Federal banking agency shall submit an annual report to the Congress containing a description of actions taken to carry out this

paragraph.

(9) FEDERAL DEPOSIT INSURANCE ACT DEFINITIONS.—In this subsection, the terms "depository institution" and "appropriate Federal banking agency" have the meanings given such terms, respectively, in section 3 of the Federal Deposit Insurance Act (12 U.S.C. 1813).

(f) Minority Depository Institutions Advisory Committees.—

(1) ESTABLISHMENT.—Each covered regulator shall establish an advisory committee to be called the "Minority Depository Institutions Advisory Committee".

(2) DUTIES.—Each Minority Depository Institutions Advisory Committee shall provide advice to the respective covered regulator on meeting the goals established by section 308 of the Financial Institutions Reform, Recovery, and Enforcement Act of 1989 (12 U.S.C. 1463 note) to preserve the present number of covered minority institutions, preserve the minority character of minority-owned institutions in cases involving mergers or acquisitions, provide technical assistance, and encourage the creation of new covered minority institutions. The scope of the work of each such Minority Depository Institutions Advisory Committee shall include an assessment of the current condition of covered minority institutions, what regulatory changes or other steps the respective agencies may be able to take to fulfill the requirements of such section 308, and other issues of concern to minority depository institutions.

(3) MEMBERSHIP.—

(A) IN GENERAL.—Each Minority Depository Institutions Advisory Committee shall consist of no more than 10 members, who—

(i) shall serve for one two-year term;

(ii) shall serve as a representative of a depository institution or an insured credit union with respect to which the respective covered regulator is the covered regulator of such depository institution or insured credit union; and

(iii) shall not receive pay by reason of their service on the advisory committee, but may receive travel or transportation expenses in accordance with section 5703 of title 5, United States Code.

(B) DIVERSITY.—To the extent practicable, each covered regulator shall ensure that the members of Minority Depository Institutions Advisory Committee of such agency reflect the diversity of depository institutions.

(4) MEETINGS.—

(A) IN GENERAL.—Each Minority Depository Institutions Advisory Committee shall meet not less frequently than twice each year.

(B) INVITATIONS.—Each Minority Depository Institutions Advisory Committee shall invite the attendance at each meeting of the Minority Depository Institutions Advisory Committee of—

(i) one member of the majority party and one member of the minority party of the Committee on Financial Services of the House of Representatives and the Committee on Banking, Housing, and Urban Affairs of the Senate; and

(ii) one member of the majority party and one member of the minority party of any relevant subcommittees of such committees.

(5) NO TERMINATION OF ADVISORY COMMITTEES.—The termination requirements under section 14 of the Federal Advisory Committee Act (5 U.S.C. app.) shall not apply to a Minority Depository Institutions Advisory Committee established pursuant to this section.

(6) DEFINITIONS.—In this paragraph:

(A) COVERED REGULATOR.—The term "covered regulator" means the Comptroller of the Currency, the Board of Governors of the Federal Reserve System, the Federal Deposit Insurance Corporation, and the National Credit Union Administration.

(B) COVERED MINORITY INSTITUTION.—The term "covered minority institution" means a minority depository institution (as defined in section 308(b) of the Financial Institutions Reform, Recovery, and Enforcement Act of 1989 (12 U.S.C. 1463 note)) or a minority credit union (as defined in section 1204(c) of the Financial Institutions Reform, Recovery, and Enforcement Act of 1989, as amended by this Act).

(C) DEPOSITORY INSTITUTION.—The term "depository institution" has the meaning given under section 3 of the Federal Deposit Insurance Act (12 U.S.C. 1813).

(D) INSURED CREDIT UNION.—The term "insured credit union" has the meaning given in section 101 of the Federal Credit Union Act (12 U.S.C. 1752).

(7) TECHNICAL AMENDMENT.—Section 308(b) of the Financial Institutions Reform, Recovery, and Enforcement Act of 1989 (12 U.S.C. 1463 note) is amended by adding at the end the following new paragraph:

"(3) DEPOSITORY INSTITUTION.—The term 'depository institution' means an 'insured depository institution' (as defined in section 3 of the Federal Deposit Insurance Act (12 U.S.C. 1813)) and an insured credit union (as defined in section 101 of the Federal Credit Union Act (12 U.S.C. 1752)).".

(g) Federal Deposits In Minority Depository Institutions.—

(1) IN GENERAL.—Section 308 of the Financial Institutions Reform, Recovery, and Enforcement Act of 1989 (12 U.S.C. 1463 note) is amended—

(A) by adding at the end the following new subsection:

"(d) Federal Deposits.—The Secretary of the Treasury shall ensure that deposits made by Federal agencies in minority depository institutions and impact banks are collateralized or insured, as determined by the Secretary. Such deposits shall include reciprocal deposits, as defined under section 29(i)(2) of the Federal Deposit Insurance Act (12 U.S.C. 1831f(i)(2))."; and

(B) in subsection (b), as amended by section 6(g), by adding at the end the following new paragraph:

"(4) IMPACT BANK.—The term 'impact bank' means a depository institution designated by an appropriate Federal banking agency pursuant to subsection (e) of the Ensuring Diversity in Community Banking Act of 2020.".

(2) TECHNICAL AMENDMENTS.—Section 308 of the Financial Institutions Reform, Recovery, and Enforcement Act of 1989 (12 U.S.C. 1463 note) is amended—

(A) in the matter preceding paragraph (1), by striking "section—" and inserting "section:"; and

(B) in the paragraph heading for paragraph (1), by striking "FINANCIAL" and inserting "DEPOSITORY".

(h) Minority Bank Deposit Program.—

(1) IN GENERAL.—Section 1204 of the Financial Institutions Reform, Recovery, and Enforcement Act of 1989 (12 U.S.C. 1811 note) is amended to read as follows:

"SEC. 1204. EXPANSION OF USE OF MINORITY BANKS AND MINORITY CREDIT UNIONS.

"(a) Minority Bank Deposit Program.—

"(1) ESTABLISHMENT.—There is established a program to be known as the 'Minority Bank Deposit Program' to expand the use of minority banks and minority credit unions.

"(2) ADMINISTRATION.—The Secretary of the Treasury, acting through the Fiscal Service, shall—

"(A) on application by a depository institution or credit union, certify whether such depository institution or credit union is a minority bank or minority credit union;

"(B) maintain and publish a list of all depository institutions and credit unions that have been certified pursuant to subparagraph (A); and

"(C) periodically distribute the list described in subparagraph (B) to—

"(i) all Federal departments and agencies;

"(ii) interested State and local governments; and

"(iii) interested private sector companies.

"(3) INCLUSION OF CERTAIN ENTITIES ON LIST.—A depository institution or credit union that, on the date of the enactment of this section, has a current certification from the Secretary of the Treasury stating that such depository institution or credit union is a minority bank or minority credit union shall be included on the list described under paragraph (2)(B).

"(b) Expanded Use Among Federal Departments And Agencies.—

"(1) IN GENERAL.—Not later than 1 year after the establishment of the program described in subsection (a), the head of each Federal department or agency shall develop and implement standards and procedures to ensure, to the maximum extent possible as permitted by law and consistent with principles of sound financial management, the use of minority banks and minority credit unions to hold the deposits of each such department or agency.

"(2) REPORT TO CONGRESS.—Not later than 2 years after the establishment of the program described in subsection (a), and annually thereafter, the head of each Federal department or agency shall submit to Congress a report on the actions taken to increase the use of minority banks and minority credit unions hold the deposits of each such department or agency.

"(c) Definitions.—For purposes of this section:

"(1) CREDIT UNION.—The term 'credit union' has the meaning given the term 'insured credit union' in section 101 of the Federal Credit Union Act (12 U.S.C. 1752).

"(2) DEPOSITORY INSTITUTION.—The term 'depository institution' has the meaning given in section 3 of the Federal Deposit Insurance Act (12 U.S.C. 1813).

"(3) MINORITY.—The term 'minority' means any Black American, Native American, Hispanic American, or Asian American.

"(4) MINORITY BANK.—The term 'minority bank' means a minority depository institution as defined in section 308 of this Act.

"(5) MINORITY CREDIT UNION.—The term 'minority credit union' means any credit union for which more than 50 percent of the membership (including board members) of such credit union are minority individuals, as determined by the National Credit Union Administration pursuant to section 308 of this Act.".

(2) CONFORMING AMENDMENTS.—The following provisions are amended by striking "1204(c)(3)" and inserting "1204(c)":

(A) Section 808(b)(3) of the Community Reinvestment Act of 1977 (12 U.S.C. 2907(b)(3)).

(B) Section 40(g)(1)(B) of the Federal Deposit Insurance Act (12 U.S.C. 1831q(g)(1)(B)).

(C) Section 704B(h)(4) of the Equal Credit Opportunity Act (15 U.S.C. 1691c–2(h)(4)).

(i) Diversity Report And Best Practices.—

(1) ANNUAL REPORT.—Each covered regulator shall submit to Congress an annual report on diversity including the following:

(A) Data, based on voluntary self-identification, on the racial, ethnic, and gender composition of the examiners of each covered regulator, disaggregated by length of time served as an examiner.

(B) The status of any examiners of covered regulators, based on voluntary self-identification, as a veteran.

(C) Whether any covered regulator, as of the date on which the report required under this section is submitted, has adopted a policy, plan, or strategy to promote racial, ethnic, and gender diversity among examiners of the covered regulator.

(D) Whether any special training is developed and provided for examiners related specifically to working with banks that serve communities that are predominantly minorities, low income, or rural, and the key focus of such training.

(2) BEST PRACTICES.—Each Office of Minority and Women Inclusion of a covered regulator shall develop, provide to the head of the covered regulator, and make publicly available best practices—

(A) for increasing the diversity of candidates applying for examiner positions, including through outreach efforts to recruit diverse candidate to apply for entry-level examiner positions; and

(B) for retaining and providing fair consideration for promotions within the examiner staff for purposes of achieving diversity among examiners.

(3) COVERED REGULATOR DEFINED.—In this subsection, the term "covered regulator" means the Comptroller of the Currency, the Board of Governors of the Federal Reserve System, the Federal Deposit Insurance Corporation, and the National Credit Union Administration.

(j) Investments In Minority Depository Institutions And Impact Banks.—

(1) CONTROL FOR CERTAIN INSTITUTIONS.—Section 7(j)(8)(B) of the Federal Deposit Insurance Act (12 U.S.C. 1817(j)(8)(B)) is amended to read as follows:

"(B) 'control' means the power, directly or indirectly—

"(i) to direct the management or policies of an insured depository institution; or

"(ii) (I) with respect to an insured depository institution, of a person to vote 25 per centum or more of any class of voting securities of such institution; or

"(II) with respect to an insured depository institution that is an impact bank (as designated pursuant to subsection (e) of the Ensuring Diversity in Community Banking Act of 2020) or a minority depository institution (as defined in section 308(b) of the Financial Institutions Reform, Recovery, and Enforcement Act of 1989), of an individual to vote 30 percent or more of any class of voting securities of such an impact bank or a minority depository institution.".

(2) RULEMAKING.—The appropriate Federal banking agency (as defined in section 3 of the Federal Deposit Insurance Act (12 U.S.C. 1813)) shall jointly issue rules for de novo minority depository institutions and de novo impact banks (as designated pursuant to subsection (e)) to allow 3 years to meet the capital requirements otherwise applicable to minority depository institutions and impact banks.

(3) REPORT.—Not later than 1 year after the date of the enactment of this Act, the appropriate Federal banking agencies shall jointly submit to Congress a report on—

(A) the principal causes for the low number of de novo minority depository institutions during the 10-year period preceding the date of the report;

(B) the main challenges to the creation of de novo minority depository institutions and de novo impact banks; and

(C) regulatory and legislative considerations to promote the establishment of de novo minority depository institutions and de novo impact banks.

(k) Report On Covered Mentor-Protege Programs.—

(1) REPORT.—Not later than 6 months after the date of the enactment of this Act and annually thereafter, the Secretary of the Treasury shall submit to Congress a report on participants in a covered mentor-protege program, including—

(A) an analysis of outcomes of such program;

(B) the number of minority depository institutions that are eligible to participate in such program but do not have large financial institution mentors; and

(C) recommendations for how to match such minority depository institutions with large financial institution mentors.

(2) DEFINITIONS.—In this subsection:

(A) COVERED MENTOR-PROTEGE PROGRAM.—The term "covered mentor-protege program" means a mentor-protege program established by the Secretary of the Treasury pursuant to section 45 of the Small Business Act (15 U.S.C. 657r).

(B) LARGE FINANCIAL INSTITUTION.—The term "large financial institution" means any entity—

(i) regulated by the Comptroller of the Currency, the Board of Governors of the Federal Reserve System, the Federal Deposit Insurance Corporation, or the National Credit Union Administration; and

(ii) that has total consolidated assets greater than or equal to $50,000,000,000.

(l) Custodial Deposit Program For Covered Minority Depository Institutions And Impact Banks.—

(1) IN GENERAL.—Not later than one year after the date of the enactment of this Act, the Secretary of the Treasury shall issue rules establishing a custodial deposit program under which a covered bank may receive deposits from a qualifying account.

(2) REQUIREMENTS.—In issuing rules under paragraph (1), the Secretary of the Treasury shall—

(A) ensure each covered bank participating in the program established under this subsection—

(i) has appropriate policies relating to management of assets, including measures to ensure the safety and soundness of each such covered bank; and

(ii) is compliant with applicable law; and

(B) ensure, to the extent practicable that the rules do not conflict with goals described in section 308(a) of the Financial Institutions Reform, Recovery, and Enforcement Act of 1989 (12 U.S.C. 1463 note).

(3) REPORT.—Each quarter, the Secretary of the Treasury shall submit to Congress a report on the implementation of the program established under this subsection including information identifying participating covered banks and the total amount of deposits received by covered banks under the program.

(4) DEFINITIONS.—In this subsection:

(A) COVERED BANK.—The term "covered bank" means—

(i) a minority depository institution that is well capitalized, as defined by the Federal Deposit Insurance Corporation or the National Credit Union Administration, as appropriate; or

(ii) a depository institution designated pursuant to subsection (e) that is well capitalized, as defined by the Federal Deposit Insurance Corporation.

(B) QUALIFYING ACCOUNT.—The term "qualifying account" means any account established in the Department of the Treasury that—

(i) is controlled by the Secretary; and

(ii) is expected to maintain a balance greater than $200,000,000 for the following 24-month period.

(m) Streamlined Community Development Financial Institution Applications And Reporting.—

(1) APPLICATION PROCESSES.—Not later than 12 months after the date of the enactment of this Act and with respect to any person having assets under $3,000,000,000 that submits an application for deposit insurance with the Federal Deposit Insurance Corporation that could also become a community development financial institution, the Federal Deposit Insurance Corporation, in consultation with the Administrator of the Community Development Financial Institutions Fund, shall—

(A) develop systems and procedures to record necessary information to allow the Administrator to conduct preliminary analysis for such person to also become a community development financial institution; and

(B) develop procedures to streamline the application and annual certification processes and to reduce costs for such person to become, and maintain certification as, a community development financial institution.

(2) IMPLEMENTATION REPORT.—Not later than 18 months after the date of the enactment of this Act, the Federal Deposit Insurance Corporation shall submit to Congress a report describing the systems and procedures required under paragraph (1).

(3) ANNUAL REPORT.—

(A) IN GENERAL.—Section 17(a)(1) of the Federal Deposit Insurance Act (12 U.S.C. 1827(a)(1)) is amended—

(i) in subparagraph (E), by striking "and" at the end;

(ii) by redesignating subparagraph (F) as subparagraph (G);

(iii) by inserting after subparagraph (E) the following new subparagraph:

"(F) applicants for deposit insurance that could also become a community development financial institution (as defined in section 103 of the Riegle Community Development and Regulatory Improvement Act of 1994), a minority depository institution (as defined in section 308 of the Financial Institutions Reform, Recovery, and Enforcement Act of 1989), or an impact bank (as designated pursuant to subsection (e) of the Ensuring Diversity in Community Banking Act of 2020); and".

(B) APPLICATION.—The amendment made by this paragraph shall apply with respect to the first report to be submitted after the date that is 2 years after the date of the enactment of this Act.

(n) Task Force On Lending To Small Business Concerns.—

(1) IN GENERAL.—Not later than 6 months after the date of the enactment of this Act, the Administrator of the Small Business Administration shall establish a task force to examine methods for improving relationships between the Small Business Administration and community development financial institutions, minority depository institutions, and Impact Banks to increase the volume of loans provided by such institutions to small business concerns (as defined under section 3 of the Small Business Act (15 U.S.C. 632)).

(2) REPORT TO CONGRESS.—Not later than 18 months after the establishment of

the task force described in paragraph (1), the Administrator of the Small Business Administration shall submit to Congress a report on the findings of such task force.
(o) Assistance To Minority Depository Institutions And Impact Banks.—The Secretary of the Treasury shall establish a program to provide assistance to a minority depository institution or an impact bank (as designated pursuant to subsection (e)) to support growth and development of such minority depository institutions and impact banks, including by providing assistance with obtaining or converting a charter, bylaw amendments, field-of-membership expansion requests, and online training and resources.

TITLE VIII

—PROVIDING ASSISTANCE FOR STATE, TERRITORY, TRIBAL, AND LOCAL GOVERNMENTS
EMERGENCY RELIEF FOR STATE, TERRITORIAL, TRIBAL, AND LOCAL GOVERNMENTS

SEC. 110801.
(a) Purchase Of COVID-19 Related Municipal Issuances.—Section 14(b) of the Federal Reserve Act (12 U.S.C. 355) is amended by adding at the end the following new paragraph:
"(3) Unusual And Exigent Circumstances.—Under unusual and exigent circumstances, to buy any bills, notes, revenue bonds, and warrants issued by any State, county, district, political subdivision, municipality, or entity that is a combination of any of the several States, the District of Columbia, or any of the territories and possessions of the United States. In this paragraph, the term 'State' means each of the several States, the District of Columbia, each territory and possession of the United States, and each federally recognized Indian Tribe.".
(b) Federal Reserve Authorization To Purchase COVID-19 Related Municipal Issuances.—Within 7 days after the date of the enactment of this subsection, the Board of Governors of the Federal Reserve System shall modify the Municipal Liquidity Facility (established on April 9, 2020, pursuant to section 13(3) of the Federal Reserve Act (12 U.S.C. 343(3))) to—
(1) ensure such facility is operational until December 31, 2021;
(2) allow for the purchase of bills, notes, bonds, and warrants with maximum maturity of 10 years from the date of such purchase;
(3) ensure that any purchases made are at an interest rate equal to the discount window primary credit interest rate most recently published on the Federal Reserve Statistical Release on selected interest rates (daily or weekly), commonly referred to as the "H.15 release" or the "Federal funds rate";
(4) ensure that an eligible issuer does not need to attest to an inability to secure credit elsewhere; and
(5) include in the list of eligible issuers for such purchases—
(A) any of the territories and possessions of the United States;
(B) a political subdivision of a State with a population of more than 50,000 residents; and
(C) an entity that is a combination of any of the several States, the District of Columbia, or any of the territories and possessions of the United States.
COMMUNITY DEVELOPMENT BLOCK GRANTS

SEC. 110802.

(a) Funding And Allocations.—

(1) AUTHORIZATION OF APPROPRIATIONS.—There is authorized to be appropriated $5,000,000,000 for assistance in accordance with this section under the community development block grant program under title I of the Housing and Community Development Act of 1974 (42 U.S.C. 5301 et seq.), which shall remain available until September 30, 2023.

(2) ALLOCATION.—Amounts made available pursuant to paragraph (1) shall be distributed pursuant to section 106 of such Act (42 U.S.C. 5306) to grantees and such allocations shall be made within 30 days after the date of the enactment of this Act.

(b) Time Limitation On Emergency Grant Payments.—Paragraph (4) of section 570.207(b) of the Secretary's regulations (24 C.F.R. 570.207(b)(4)) shall be applied with respect to grants with amounts made available pursuant to subsection (a), by substituting "121 consecutive months" for "3 consecutive months".

(c) Matching Of Amounts Used For Administrative Costs.—Any requirement for a State to match or supplement amounts expended for program administration of State grants under section 106(d) of the Housing and Community Development Act of 1974 (42 U.S.C. 5306(d)) shall not apply with respect to amounts made available pursuant to subsection (a).

(d) CAPER Information.—During the period that begins on the date of enactment of this Act and ends on the date of the termination by the Federal Emergency Management Agency of the emergency declared on March 13, 2020, by the President under the Robert T. Stafford Disaster Relief and Emergency Assistance Act (42 U.S.C. 4121 et seq.) relating to the Coronavirus Disease 2019 (COVID-19) pandemic, the Secretary shall make all information included in Consolidated Annual Performance and Evaluation Reports relating to assistance made available pursuant to this section publicly available on its website on a quarterly basis.

(e) Authority; Waivers.—Any provisions of, and waivers and alternative requirements issued by the Secretary pursuant to, the heading "Department of Housing and Urban Development—Community Planning and Development—Community Development Fund" in title XII of division B of the CARES Act (Public Law 116–136) shall apply with respect to amounts made available pursuant to subsection (a) of this section.

TITLE IX

—PROVIDING OVERSIGHT AND PROTECTING TAXPAYERS
MANDATORY REPORTS TO CONGRESS

SEC. 110901.

(a) Disclosure Of Transaction Reports.—Section 4026(b)(1)(A)(iii) of the CARES Act (Public Law 116–136) is amended—

(1) in subclause (IV)—

(A) by inserting "and the justification for such exercise of authority" after "authority"; and

(B) by striking "and" at the end;

(2) in subclause (V), by striking the period at the end and inserting "; and"; and

(3) by adding at the end the following:

"(VI) the identity of each recipient of a loan or loan guarantee described in subclause (I);

"(VII) the date and amount of each such loan or loan guarantee and the form in which each such loan or loan guarantee was provided;

"(VIII) the material terms of each such loan or loan guarantee, including—

"(aa) duration;

"(bb) collateral pledged and the value thereof;

"(cc) all interest, fees, and other revenue or items of value to be received in exchange for such loan or loan guarantee;

"(dd) any requirements imposed on the recipient with respect to employee compensation, distribution of dividends, or any other corporate decision in exchange for the assistance; and

"(ee) the expected costs to the Federal Government with respect to such loans or loan guarantees.".

(b) Reports By The Secretary Of The Treasury.—Section 4018 of the CARES Act (Public Law 116–136) is amended by adding at the end the following:

"(k) Reports By The Secretary.—Not later than 7 days after the last day of each month, the Secretary shall submit to the Special Inspector General, the Committee on Financial Services of the House of Representatives, and the Committee on Banking, Housing, and Urban Affairs of the Senate a report that includes the information specified in subparagraphs (A) through (E) of subsection (c)(1) with respect to the making, purchase, management, and sale of loans, loan guarantees, and other investments made by the Secretary under any program established by the Secretary under this Act.".

DISCRETIONARY REPORTS TO CONGRESS

SEC. 110902.

Section 4020(b) of the CARES Act (Public Law 116–136) is amended by adding at the end the following:

"(3) DISCRETIONARY REPORTS TO CONGRESS.—In addition to the reports required under paragraph (2), the Oversight Commission may submit other reports to Congress at such time, in such manner, and containing such information as the Oversight Commission determines appropriate.".

DEFINITION OF APPROPRIATE CONGRESSIONAL COMMITTEES

SEC. 110903.

(a) Pandemic Response Accountability Committee.—Section 15010(a)(2) of the CARES Act (Public Law 116–136) is amended—

(1) by redesignating subparagraphs (B) through (D) as subparagraphs (D) through (F), respectively; and

(2) by inserting after subparagraph (A) the following:

"(B) the Committee on Banking, Housing, and Urban Affairs of the Senate;

"(C) the Committee on Financial Services of the House of Representatives;".

(b) Oversight And Audit Authority.—Section 19010(a)(1) of the CARES Act (Public Law 116–136) is amended—

(1) by redesignating subparagraphs (B) through (G) as subparagraphs (D) through (I), respectively; and

(2) by inserting after subparagraph (A) the following:

"(B) the Committee on Banking, Housing, and Urban Affairs of the Senate;

"(C) the Committee on Financial Services of the House of Representatives;".

REPORTING BY INSPECTORS GENERAL

SEC. 110904.

(a) Definition Of Covered Agency.—In this section, the term "covered agency" means—

(1) the Department of the Treasury;

(2) the Federal Deposit Insurance Corporation;

(3) the Office of the Comptroller of the Currency;

(4) the Board of Governors of the Federal Reserve System;

(5) the National Credit Union Administration;

(6) the Bureau of Consumer Financial Protection;

(7) the Department of Housing and Urban Development;

(8) the Department of Agriculture, Rural Housing Service;

(9) the Securities and Exchange Commission; and

(10) the Federal Housing Finance Agency.

(b) Report.—The Inspector General of each covered agency shall include in each semiannual report submitted by the Inspector General the findings of the Inspector General on the effectiveness of—

(1) rulemaking by the covered agency related to COVID–19; and

(2) supervision and oversight by the covered agency of institutions and entities that participate in COVID–19-related relief, funding, lending, or other programs of the covered agency.

(c) Submission.—The Inspector General of each covered agency shall submit the information required to be included in each semiannual report under subsection (b) to—

(1) the Special Inspector General for Pandemic Recovery appointed under section 4018 of division A of the CARES Act (Public Law 116–136);

(2) the Pandemic Response Accountability Committee established under section 15010 of division B of the CARES Act (Public Law 116–136); and

(3) the Congressional Oversight Commission established under section 4020 of division A of the CARES Act (Public Law 116–136).

DIVISION L—FAMILIES, WORKERS, AND COMMUNITY SUPPORT PROVISIONS

TITLE I—AMENDMENTS TO EMERGENCY FAMILY AND MEDICAL LEAVE EXPANSION ACT AND EMERGENCY PAID SICK LEAVE ACT

Subtitle A—Emergency Family And Medical Leave Expansion Act Amendments

SEC. 120101. REFERENCES.

Except as otherwise expressly provided, whenever in this subtitle an amendment or repeal is expressed in terms of an amendment to, or repeal of, a section or other provision, the reference shall be considered to be made to a section or other provision of the Family and Medical Leave Act of 1993 (29 U.S.C. 2601 et seq.), as amended by the Emergency Family and Medical Leave Expansion Act (Public Law 116–127).

SEC. 120102. EMPLOYEE ELIGIBILITY AND EMPLOYER CLARIFICATION.

(a) Employee Eligibility.—Section 101(2) is amended by adding at the end the following:

"(F) ALTERNATIVE ELIGIBILITY FOR COVID–19 PUBLIC HEALTH EMERGENCY .—For the period beginning on the date of enactment of the HEROES Act and ending on December 31, 2022—

"(i) subparagraph (A)(i) shall be applied by substituting '90 days' for '12 months'; and

"(ii) subparagraph (A)(ii) shall not apply.".

(b) Employer Clarification.—Section 101(4) is amended by adding at the end the following:

"(C) CLARIFICATION.—Subparagraph (A)(i) shall not apply with respect to a public agency described in subparagraph (A)(iii).".

SEC. 120103. EMERGENCY LEAVE EXTENSION.

Section 102(a)(1)(F) is amended by striking "December 31, 2020" and inserting "December 31, 2021".

SEC. 120104. EMERGENCY LEAVE DEFINITIONS.

(a) Eligible Employee.—Section 110(a)(1) is amended in subparagraph (A), by striking "sections 101(2)(A) and 101(2)(B)(ii)" and inserting "section 101(2)".

(b) Employer Threshold.—Section 110(a)(1)(B) is amended by striking "fewer than 500 employees" and inserting "1 or more employees".

(c) Parent.—Section 110(a)(1) is amended by adding at the end the following:

"(C) PARENT.—In lieu of the definition in section 101(7), the term 'parent', with respect to an employee, means any of the following:

"(i) A biological, foster, or adoptive parent of the employee.

"(ii) A stepparent of the employee.

"(iii) A parent-in-law of the employee.

"(iv) A parent of a domestic partner of the employee.

"(v) A legal guardian or other person who stood in loco parentis to an employee when the employee was a child.".

(d) Qualifying Need Related To A Public Health Emergency.—Section 110(a)(2)(A) is amended to read as follows:

"(A) QUALIFYING NEED RELATED TO A PUBLIC HEALTH EMERGENCY.— The term 'qualifying need related to a public health emergency', with respect to leave, means that the employee is unable to perform the functions of the position of such employee due to a need for leave for any of the following:

"(i) To self-isolate because the employee is diagnosed with COVID–19.

"(ii) To obtain a medical diagnosis or care if such employee is experiencing the symptoms of COVID–19.

"(iii) To comply with a recommendation or order by a public official with jurisdiction or a health care provider to self isolate, without regard to whether such recommendation or order is specific to the employee, on the basis that the physical presence of the employee on the job would jeopardize the employee's health, the health of other employees, or the health of an individual in the household of the employee because of—

"(I) the possible exposure of the employee to COVID–19; or

"(II) exhibition of symptoms of COVID–19 by the employee.

"(iv) To care for or assist a family member of the employee, without regard to whether another individual other than the employee is available to care for or assist such family member, because—

"(I) such family member—

"(aa) is self-isolating because such family member has been diagnosed with COVID–19; or

"(bb) is experiencing symptoms of COVID–19 and needs to obtain medical diagnosis or care; or

"(II) a public official with jurisdiction or a health care provider makes a recommendation or order with respect to such family member, without regard to whether such determination is specific to such family member, that the presence of the family member in the community would jeopardize the health of other individuals in the community because of—

"(aa) the possible exposure of such family member to COVID–19; or

"(bb) exhibition of symptoms of COVID–19 by such family member.

"(v) To care for the son or daughter of such employee if the school or place of care has been closed, or the child care provider of such son or daughter is unavailable, due to COVID–19.

"(vi) To care for a family member who is incapable of self-care because of a mental or physical disability or is a senior citizen, without regard to whether another individual other than the employee is available to care for such family member, if the place of care for such family member is closed or the direct care provider is unavailable due to COVID–19.".

(e) Family Member.—Section 110(a)(2) is amended by adding at the end the following:

"(E) FAMILY MEMBER.—The term 'family member', with respect to an employee, means any of the following:

"(i) A parent of the employee.

"(ii) A spouse of the employee.

"(iii) A sibling of the employee.

"(iv) Next of kin of the employee or a person for whom the employee is next of kin.

"(v) A son or daughter of the employee.

"(vi) A grandparent or grandchild of the employee.

"(vii) A domestic partner of the employee.

"(viii) Any other individual related by blood or affinity whose close association with the employee is the equivalent of a family relationship.

"(F) DOMESTIC PARTNER.—

"(i) IN GENERAL.—The term 'domestic partner', with respect to an individual, means another individual with whom the individual is in a committed relationship.

"(ii) COMMITTED RELATIONSHIP DEFINED.—The term 'committed relationship' means a relationship between 2 individuals, each at least 18 years of age, in which each individual is the other individual's sole domestic partner and both individuals share responsibility for a significant measure of each other's common welfare. The term includes any such relationship between 2 individuals that is granted legal recognition by a State or political subdivision of a State as a marriage or analogous relationship, including a civil union or domestic partnership.".

SEC. 120105. REGULATORY AUTHORITIES.

(a) In General.—Section 110(a) is amended by striking paragraph (3).

(b) Force Or Effect Of Regulations.—Any regulation issued under section 110(a)(3), as in effect on the day before the date of the enactment of this Act, shall have no force or effect.

SEC. 120106. PAID LEAVE.

Section 110(b) of the Family and Medical Leave Act of 1993 is amended—

(1) in the heading, by striking "Relationship to";

(2) by amending paragraph (1) to read as follows:

"(1) EMPLOYEE ELECTION.—

"(A) IN GENERAL.—An employee may elect to substitute any vacation leave, personal leave, or medical or sick leave for paid leave under section 102(a)(1)(F) in accordance with section 102(d)(2)(B).

"(B) EMPLOYER REQUIREMENT.—An employer may not require an employee to substitute any leave described in subparagraph (A) for leave under section 102(a)(1)(F).

"(C) RELATIONSHIP TO OTHER FAMILY AND MEDICAL LEAVE.—Leave taken under subparagraph (F) of section 102(a)(1) shall not count towards the 12 weeks of leave to which an employee is entitled under subparagraphs (A) through (E) of such section.

"(D) RELATIONSHIP TO LIMITATION.—Compensation for any vacation leave, personal leave, or medical or sick leave that is substituted for leave under section 102(a)(1)(F) shall not count toward the limitation under paragraph (2)(B)(ii)."; and

(3) in paragraph (2)(A), by striking "that an employee takes" and all that follows through "10 days".

SEC. 120107. WAGE RATE.

Section 110(b)(2)(B) is amended—

(1) by amending clause (i)(I) to read as follows:

"(I) an amount that is not less than the greater of—

"(aa) the minimum wage rate in effect under section 6(a)(1) of the Fair Labor Standards Act of 1938 (29 U.S.C. 206(a)(1));

"(bb) the minimum wage rate in effect for such employee in the applicable State or locality, whichever is greater, in which the employee is employed; or

"(cc) two thirds of an employee's regular rate of pay (as determined under section 7(e) of the Fair Labor Standards Act of 1938 (29 U.S.C. 207(e)); and"; and

(2) in clause (ii), by striking "$10,000" and inserting "$12,000".

SEC. 120108. NOTICE.

Section 110(c) is amended by striking "for the purpose described in subsection (a)(2)(A)".

SEC. 120109. INTERMITTENT LEAVE.

Section 110 is amended by adding at the end the following:

"(e) Leave Taken Intermittently Or On A Reduced Work Schedule.—Leave under section 102(a)(1)(F) may be taken by an employee intermittently or on a reduced work schedule, without regard to whether the employee and the employer of the employee have an agreement with respect to whether such leave may be taken intermittently or on a reduced work schedule.".

SEC. 120110. CERTIFICATION.

Section 110 is further amended by adding at the end the following:

"(f) Certification.—

"(1) IN GENERAL.—If an employer requires that a request for leave under section

102(a)(1)(F) be certified, the employer may require documentation for certification not earlier than 5 weeks after the date on which the employee takes such leave.

"(2) SUFFICIENT CERTIFICATION.—The following documentation shall be sufficient for certification:

"(A) With respect to leave taken for the purposes described in clauses (i) through (iv) of subsection (a)(2)(A)—

"(i) a recommendation or order from a public official having jurisdiction or a health care provider that the employee or relevant family member has symptoms of COVID-19 or should self-isolate; or

"(ii) documentation or evidence, including an oral or written statement from an employee, that the employee or relevant family member has been exposed to COVID-19.

"(B) With respect to leave taken for the purposes described in clause (v) or (vi) of subsection (a)(2)(A), notice from the school, place of care, or child care or direct care provider of the son or daughter or other family member of the employee of closure or unavailability.".

SEC. 120111. AUTHORITY OF THE DIRECTOR OF THE OFFICE OF MANAGEMENT AND BUDGET TO EXCLUDE CERTAIN EMPLOYEES.

Section 110(a) is amended by striking paragraph (4).

SEC. 120112. TECHNICAL AMENDMENTS.

(a) Section 110(a)(1)(A) is amended by striking "(ii)" before "SPECIAL RULE" and inserting "(iii)".

(b) Section 19008 of the CARES Act is amended—

(1) by striking "—" after "amended";

(2) by striking paragraph (1); and

(3) by striking "(2)" before "by adding at the end".

SEC. 120113. AMENDMENTS TO THE EMERGENCY FAMILY AND MEDICAL LEAVE EXPANSION ACT.

The Emergency Family and Medical Leave Expansion Act (Public Law 116–127) is amended—

(1) in section 3103(b), by striking "Employees" and inserting, "Notwithstanding section 102(a)(1)(A) of the Family and Medical Leave Act of 1993 (29 U.S.C. 2612(a)(1)(A)), employees"; and

(2) by striking sections 3104 and 3105.

Subtitle B—Emergency Paid Sick Leave Act Amendments

SEC. 120114. REFERENCES.

Except as otherwise expressly provided, whenever in this subtitle an amendment or repeal is expressed in terms of an amendment to, or repeal of, a section or other provision, the reference shall be considered to be made to a section or other provision of division E of the Families First Coronavirus Response Act (Public Law 116–127).

SEC. 120115. PAID SICK TIME REQUIREMENT.

(a) Uses.—Section 5102(a) is amended to read as follows:

"(a) In General.—An employer shall provide to each employee employed by the employer paid sick time for any qualifying need related to a public health emergency (as defined in section 110(a)(2)(A) of the Family and Medical Leave Act of 1993 (29 U.S.C. 2620(a)(2)(A))".

(b) Recurrence.—Section 5102(b) is amended by striking "An" and inserting "During any 12-month period, an".

(c) Employers With Existing Policies.—Section 5102 is amended by striking subsection (f) and inserting the following:

"(f) Employers With Existing Policies.—With respect to an employer that provides paid leave on the day before the date of enactment of this Act—

"(1) the paid sick time under this Act shall be made available to employees of the employer in addition to such paid leave; and

"(2) the employer may not change such paid leave on or after such date of enactment to avoid being subject to paragraph (1).".

(d) Intermittent Leave.—Section 5102 is further amended by adding at the end the following:

"(g) Leave Taken Intermittently Or On A Reduced Work Schedule.—Leave under section 5102 may be taken by an employee intermittently or on a reduced work schedule, without regard to whether the employee and the employer of the employee have an agreement with respect to whether such leave may be taken intermittently or on a reduced work schedule.".

(e) Certification.—Section 5102 is further amended by adding at the end the following:

"(h) Certification.—If an employer requires that a request for paid sick time under this section be certified—

"(1) the documentation described in paragraph (2) of section 110(f) of the Family and Medical Leave Act of 1993 (29 U.S.C. 2620(f)) shall be sufficient for certification; and

"(2) an employer may not require such certification unless—

"(A) the employee takes not less than 3 consecutive days of paid sick time; and

"(B) the employer requires documents for such certification not earlier than 7 workdays after the employee returns to work after such paid sick time.".

(f) Notice.—Section 5102 is further amended by adding at the end the following:

"(i) Notice.—In any case where the necessity for leave under this section is foreseeable, an employee shall provide the employer with such notice of leave as is practicable.".

(g) Leave Transfer To New Employer.—Section 5102 is further amended by adding at the end the following:

"(j) Leave Transfer To New Employer.—A covered employee who begins employment with a new covered employer shall be entitled to the full amount of leave under section 5102 with respect to such employer.".

(h) Restoration To Position.—

(1) IN GENERAL.—Section 5102 is further amended by adding at the end the following:

"(k) Restoration To Position.—Any covered employee who takes paid sick time under this section, on return from such paid sick time, shall be entitled—

"(1) to be restored by the employer to the position of employment held by the employee when the leave commenced; or

"(2) if such position is not available, to be restored to an equivalent position with equivalent employment benefits, pay, and other terms and conditions of employment.".

(2) ENFORCEMENT.—Section 5105 is amended—

(A) by amending subsection (a) to read as follows:

"(a) Unpaid Sick Leave.—Subject to subsection (b), a violation of section 5102 shall be deemed a violation of section 7 of the Fair Labor Standards Act of 1938 (29 U.S.C.

207) and unpaid amounts shall be treated as unpaid overtime compensation under such section for the purposes of sections 15 and 16 of such Act (29 U.S.C. 215 and 216).”; and

(B) in subsection (b), by inserting “section 5102(k) or” before “section 5104”.

SEC. 120116. SUNSET.

Section 5109 is amended by striking “December 31, 2020” and inserting “December 31, 2021”.

SEC. 120117. DEFINITIONS.

(a) Employer.—Section 5110(2)(B) is amended—

(1) by striking “terms” and inserting “term”;

(2) by amending subclause (I) of clause (i) to read as follows:

“(I) means any person engaged in commerce or in any industry or activity affecting commerce that employs 1 or more employees;”; and

(3) by amending clause (ii) to read as follows:

“(ii) PUBLIC AGENCY AND NON-PROFIT ORGANIZATIONS.—For purposes of clause (i)(III) and (i)(I), a public agency and a nonprofit organization shall be considered to be a person engaged in commerce or in an industry or activity affecting commerce.”.

(b) FMLA Terms.—Section 5110(4) is amended to read as follows:

“(4) FMLA TERMS.—

“(A) SECTION 101.—The terms ‘health care provider’, ‘next of kin’, ‘son or daughter’, and ‘spouse’ have the meanings given such terms in section 101 of the Family and Medical Leave Act of 1993 (29 U.S.C. 2611).

“(B) SECTION 110.—The terms ‘child care provider’, ‘domestic partner’, ‘family member’, ‘parent’, and ‘school’ have the meanings given such terms in section 110(a)(2) of the Family and Medical and Leave Act of 1993.”.

(c) Paid Sick Time.—Section 5110(5) is amended—

(1) in subparagraph (A)—

(A) in clause (i), by striking “reason described in any paragraph of section 2(a)” and inserting “qualifying need related to a public health emergency”; and

(B) in clause (ii), by striking “exceed” and all that follows and inserting “exceed $511 per day and $5,110 in the aggregate.”;

(2) in subparagraph (B)—

(A) by striking the following:

“(B) REQUIRED COMPENSATION.—

“(i) IN GENERAL.—Subject to subparagraph (A)(ii),”; and inserting the following:

“(B) REQUIRED COMPENSATION.—Subject to subparagraph (A)(ii),”; and

(B) by striking clause (ii); and

(3) in subparagraph (C), by striking “ section 2(a)” and inserting “section 5102(a)”.

(d) Qualifying Need Related To A Public Health Emergency.—Section 5110 is amended by adding at the end the following:

“(1) QUALIFYING NEED RELATED TO A PUBLIC HEALTH EMERGENCY.—The term ‘qualifying need related to a public health emergency’ has the meaning given such term in section 110(a)(2)(A) of the Family and Medical Leave Act of 1993 (29 U.S.C. 2620(a)(2)(A)).”.

SEC. 120118. EMERGENCY PAID SICK LEAVE FOR EMPLOYEES OF THE DEPARTMENT OF VETERANS AFFAIRS AND THE TRANSPORTATION

SECURITY ADMINISTRATION FOR PURPOSES RELATING TO COVID–19.
Section 5110(1) is further amended—
(1) in subparagraph (E) by striking "or" after "Code;";
(2) by redesignating subparagraph (F) as subparagraph (H); and
(3) by inserting after subparagraph (E) the following:
"(F) notwithstanding sections 7421(a) or 7425(b) of title 38, United States Code, or any other provision of law, an employee of the Department of Veterans Affairs (including employees under chapter 74 of such title);
"(G) any employee of the Transportation Security Administration, including an employee under 111(d) of the Aviation and Transportation Security Act (49 U.S.C. 44935 note); or".

SEC. 120119. AUTHORITY OF THE DIRECTOR OF THE OFFICE OF MANAGEMENT AND BUDGET TO EXCLUDE CERTAIN EMPLOYEES.
Division E is amended by striking section 5112.

SEC. 120120. REGULATORY AUTHORITIES.
(a) In General.—Division E is amended by striking section 5111.
(b) Force Or Effect Of Regulations.—Any regulation issued under section 5111 of division E of the Families First Coronavirus Response Act (Public Law 116–127), as in effect on the day before the date of the enactment of this Act, shall have no force or effect.

TITLE II—COVID–19 WORKFORCE DEVELOPMENT RESPONSE ACTIVITIES

SEC. 120201. DEFINITIONS AND SPECIAL RULE.
(a) Definitions.—
(1) IN GENERAL.—Except as otherwise provided, the terms in this title have the meanings given the terms in section 3 of the Workforce Innovation and Opportunity Act (29 U.S.C. 3102).
(2) APPRENTICESHIP; APPRENTICESHIP PROGRAM.—The terms "apprenticeship" or "apprenticeship program" mean an apprenticeship program registered under the Act of August 16, 1937 (commonly known as the "National Apprenticeship Act") (50 Stat. 664, chapter 663; 29 U.S.C. 50 et seq.), including any requirement, standard, or rule promulgated under such Act, as such requirement, standard, or rule was in effect on December 30, 2019.
(3) CORONAVIRUS.—The term "coronavirus" means coronavirus as defined in section 506 of the Coronavirus Preparedness and Response Supplemental Appropriations Act, 2020 (Public Law 116–123).
(4) COVID–19 NATIONAL EMERGENCY.—The term "COVID–19 national emergency" means the national emergency declared by the President under the National Emergencies Act (50 U.S.C. 1601 et seq.) on March 13, 2020, with respect to the coronavirus.
(5) SECRETARY.—The term "Secretary" means the Secretary of Labor.
(b) Special Rule.—For purposes of this Act, in fiscal years 2020 and 2021, funds are authorized to be appropriated for activities under the Workforce Innovation and Opportunity Act, except that funds are only authorized to support apprenticeship programs as defined under subsection (a)(2) of this section, including any funds

awarded for the purposes of grants, contracts, or cooperative agreements, or the development, implementation, or administration, of an apprenticeship or an apprenticeship program.

SEC. 120202. JOB CORPS RESPONSE TO THE COVID–19 NATIONAL EMERGENCY.

In order to provide for the successful continuity of services and enrollment periods during the COVID–19 national emergency, additional flexibility shall be provided for Job Corps operators, providers of eligible activities, and practitioners, including the following:

(1) ELIGIBILITY.—Notwithstanding the age requirements for enrollment under section 144(a)(1) of the Workforce Innovation and Opportunity Act (29 U.S.C. 3194(a)(1)), an individual seeking to enroll in Job Corps and who turns 25 during the COVID–19 national emergency is eligible for such enrollment.

(2) ENROLLMENT LENGTH.—Notwithstanding section 146(b) of the Workforce Innovation and Opportunity Act (29 U.S.C. 3196(b)), an individual enrolled in Job Corps during the COVID–19 national emergency may extend their period of enrollment for more than 2 years as long as such extension does not exceed a 2-year, continuous period of enrollment after the COVID–19 national emergency.

(3) ADVANCED CAREER TRAINING PROGRAMS.—Notwithstanding paragraph (2), with respect to advanced career training programs under section 148(c) of the Workforce Innovation and Opportunity Act (29 U.S.C. 3198(c)) in which the enrollees may continue to participate for a period not to exceed 1 year in addition to the period of participation to which the enrollees would otherwise be limited, the COVID–19 national emergency shall not be considered as any portion of such additional 1-year participation period.

(4) COUNSELING, JOB PLACEMENT, AND ASSESSMENT.—The counseling, job placement, and assessment services described in section 149 of the Workforce Innovation and Opportunity Act (29 U.S.C. 3199) shall be available to former enrollees—

(A) whose enrollment was interrupted due to the COVID–19 national emergency;

(B) who graduated from Job Corps on or after January 1, 2020; or

(C) who graduated from Job Corps not later than 3 months after the COVID–19 national emergency.

(5) SUPPORT.—The Secretary shall provide additional support for the transition periods described in section 150 of the Workforce Innovation and Opportunity Act (29 U.S.C. 3200), including the following:

(A) TRANSITION ALLOWANCES.—The Secretary shall provide, subject to the availability of appropriations, for the provision of additional transition allowances as described in subsection (b) of such section 150 (29 U.S.C. 3200) for Job Corps students who graduate during the periods described in subparagraph (B) or (C) of paragraph (4) of this paragraph.

(B) TRANSITION SUPPORT.—The Secretary shall consider the period during the COVID–19 national emergency and the three month period following the conclusion of the COVID–19 national emergency as the period in which the provision of employment services as described in subsection (c) of such section 150 (29 U.S.C. 3200) shall be provided to graduates who have graduated in 2020.

SEC. 120203. NATIVE AMERICAN PROGRAMS RESPONDING TO THE COVID–19 NATIONAL EMERGENCY.

As a result of challenges faced by the COVID–19 national emergency, the Secretary may extend, by 1 fiscal year, the 4-year period for grants, contracts, and cooperative agreements that will be awarded in fiscal year 2021 under subsection (c) of section 166 of the Workforce Innovation and Opportunity Act (29 U.S.C. 3221) for funds under such grants, contracts, and cooperative agreements to be used to carry out the activities described in subsection (d) of such section through fiscal year 2025.

SEC. 120204. MIGRANT AND SEASONAL FARMWORKER PROGRAM RE-SPONSE.

(a) Competitive Grant Awards.—As a result of challenges faced by the COVID–19 national emergency, the Secretary may extend, by 1 fiscal year, the 4-year period for grants and contracts that will be awarded in fiscal year 2021 under subsection (a) of section 167 of the Workforce Innovation and Opportunity Act (29 U.S.C. 3222) for funds under such grants and contracts to be used to carry out the activities described in subsection (d) of such section through fiscal year 2025.

(b) Eligible Migrant And Seasonal Farmworker.—Notwithstanding the definition of "eligible seasonal farmworker" in section 167(i)(3) of the Workforce Innovation and Opportunity Act (29 U.S.C. 3222(i)(3)), an individual seeking to enroll in a program funded under section 167 of the Workforce Innovation and Opportunity Act (29 U.S.C. 3222) during the COVID–19 national emergency is eligible for such enrollment if such individual is a member of a family with a total family income equal to or less than 150 percent of the poverty line.

SEC. 120205. YOUTHBUILD ACTIVITIES RESPONDING TO THE COVID–19 NATIONAL EMERGENCY.

During the COVID–19 national emergency, the Secretary shall provide for flexibility for YouthBuild participants and entities carrying out YouthBuild programs, including the following:

(1) ELIGIBILITY.— Notwithstanding the age requirements for enrollment under section 171(e)(1)(A)(i) of the Workforce Innovation and Opportunity Act (29 U.S.C. 3226(e)(1)(A)(i)), an individual seeking to participate in a YouthBuild program and who turns 25 during the COVID–19 national emergency is eligible for such participation.

(2) PARTICIPATION LENGTH.—Notwithstanding section 171(e)(2) of the Workforce Innovation and Opportunity Act (29 U.S.C. 3226(e)(2)), the period of participation in a YouthBuild program may extend beyond 24 months for an individual participating in such program during the COVID–19 national emergency, as long as such extension does not exceed a 24 month, continuous period of enrollment after the COVID–19 national emergency.

SEC. 120206. APPRENTICESHIP SUPPORT DURING THE COVID–19 NATIONAL EMERGENCY.

Not later than 30 days after the date of enactment of this Act, the Secretary shall identify and disseminate strategies and tools to support virtual and online learning and training in apprenticeship programs.

TITLE III—COVID–19 EVERY WORKER PROTECTION ACT OF 2020

SEC. 120301. SHORT TITLE.

This title may be cited as the "COVID–19 Every Worker Protection Act of 2020".

SEC. 120302. EMERGENCY TEMPORARY AND PERMANENT STANDARDS.

(a) Emergency Temporary Standard.—

(1) IN GENERAL.—In consideration of the grave danger presented by COVID–19 and the need to strengthen protections for employees, notwithstanding the provisions of law and the Executive orders listed in paragraph (7), not later than 7 days after the date of enactment of this Act, the Secretary of Labor shall promulgate an emergency temporary standard to protect from occupational exposure to SARS–CoV–2—

(A) employees of health care sector employers;

(B) employees of employers in the paramedic and emergency medical services, including such services provided by firefighters and other emergency responders; and

(C) other employees at occupational risk of such exposure.

(2) CONSULTATION.—In developing the standard under this subsection, the Secretary of Labor—

(A) shall consult with—

(i) the Director of the Centers for Disease Control and Prevention;

(ii) the Director of the National Institute for Occupational Safety and Health; and

(B) may consult with the professional associations and representatives of the employees in the occupations and sectors described in subparagraphs (A) through (C) of paragraph (1).

(3) ENFORCEMENT DISCRETION.—If the Secretary of Labor determines it is not feasible for an employer to comply with a requirement of the standard promulgated under this subsection (such as a shortage of the necessary personal protective equipment), the Secretary may exercise discretion in the enforcement of such requirement if the employer demonstrates that the employer—

(A) is exercising due diligence to come into compliance with such requirement; and

(B) is implementing alternative methods and measures to protect employees.

(4) EXTENSION OF STANDARD.—Notwithstanding paragraphs (2) and (3) of section 6(c) of the Occupational Safety and Health Act of 1970 (29 U.S.C. 655(c)), the emergency temporary standard promulgated under this subsection shall be in effect until the date on which the final standard promulgated under subsection (b) is in effect.

(5) STATE PLAN ADOPTION.—With respect to a State with a State plan that has been approved by the Secretary of Labor under section 18 of the Occupational Safety and Health Act of 1970 (29 U.S.C. 667), not later than 14 days after the date of enactment of this Act, such State shall promulgate an emergency temporary standard that is at least as effective in protecting from occupational exposure to SARS–CoV–2 the employees in the occupations and sectors described in subparagraphs (A) through (C) of paragraph (1) as the emergency temporary standard promulgated under this subsection.

(6) EMPLOYER DEFINED.—For purposes of the standard promulgated under this subsection, the term "employer" (as defined in section 3 of the Occupational Safety and Health Act of 1970 (29 U.S.C. 652)) includes any State or political subdivision of a State, except for a State or political subdivision of a State already subject to the jurisdiction of a State plan approved under section 18(b) of the Occupational Safety and Health Act of 1970 (29 U.S.C. 667(b)).

(7) INAPPLICABLE PROVISIONS OF LAW AND EXECUTIVE ORDER.—The provisions of law and the Executive orders list in this paragraph are as follows:

(A) The requirements of chapter 6 of title 5, United States Code (commonly referred to as the "Regulatory Flexibility Act").

(B) Subchapter I of chapter 35 of title 44, United States Code (commonly referred to as the "Paperwork Reduction Act").

(C) The Unfunded Mandates Reform Act of 1995 (2 U.S.C. 1501 et seq.).

(D) Executive Order 12866 (58 Fed. Reg. 190; relating to regulatory planning and review), as amended.

(E) Executive Order 13771 (82 Fed. Reg. 9339, relating to reducing regulation and controlling regulatory costs).

(b) Permanent Standard.—Not later than 24 months after the date of enactment of this Act, the Secretary of Labor shall, pursuant to section 6 of the Occupational Safety and Health Act (29 U.S.C. 655), promulgate a final standard—

(1) to protect employees in the occupations and sectors described in subparagraphs (A) through (C) of subsection (a)(1) from occupational exposure to infectious pathogens, including novel pathogens; and

(2) that shall be effective and enforceable in the same manner and to the same extent as a standard promulgated under section 6(b) of the Occupational Safety and Health Act of 1970 (29 U.S.C. 655(b)).

(c) Requirements.—Each standard promulgated under this section shall include—

(1) a requirement that the employers of the employees in the occupations and sectors described in subparagraphs (A) through (C) of subsection (a)(1)—

(A) develop and implement a comprehensive infectious disease exposure control plan, with the input and involvement of employees or, where applicable, the representatives of employees, as appropriate, to address the risk of occupational exposure in such sectors and occupations; and

(B) record and report each work-related COVID–19 infection and death, as set forth in part 1904 of title 29, Code of Federal Regulations (as in effect on the date of enactment of this Act);

(2) no less protection for novel pathogens than precautions mandated by standards adopted by a State plan that has been approved by the Secretary of Labor under section 18 of the Occupational Safety and Health Act of 1970 (29 U.S.C. 667); and

(3) the incorporation, as appropriate, of—

(A) guidelines issued by the Centers for Disease Control and Prevention, the National Institute for Occupational Safety and Health, and the Occupational Safety and Health Administration which are designed to prevent the transmission of infectious agents in health care or other occupational settings; and

(B) relevant scientific research on novel pathogens.

(d) Anti-Retaliation.—

(1) POLICY.—Each standard promulgated under this section shall require employers to adopt a policy prohibiting the discrimination and retaliation described in paragraph (2) by any person (including an agent of the employer).

(2) PROHIBITION.—No employer (including an agent of the employer) shall discriminate or retaliate against an employee for—

(A) reporting to the employer, to a local, State, or Federal government agency, or to the media or on a social media platform—

(i) a violation of a standard promulgated pursuant to this Act;

(ii) a violation of an infectious disease exposure control plan described in subsection (c)(1); or

(iii) a good faith concern about a workplace infectious disease hazard;

(B) seeking assistance or intervention from the employer or a local, State, or Federal government agency with respect to such a report;

(C) voluntary use of personal protective equipment with a higher level of protection than is provided by the employer; or

(D) exercising any other right under the Occupational Safety and Health Act of 1970 (29 U.S.C. 651 et seq.).

(3) ENFORCEMENT.—This subsection shall be enforced in the same manner and to the same extent as any standard promulgated under section 6(b) of the Occupational Safety and Health Act of 1970 (29 U.S.C. 655(b)).

SEC. 120303. SURVEILLANCE, TRACKING, AND INVESTIGATION OF WORK-RELATED CASES OF COVID–19.

The Director of the Centers for Disease Control and Prevention, in conjunction with the Director of the National Institute for Occupational Safety and Health, shall—

(1) collect and analyze case reports, including information on the work status, occupation, and industry classification of an individual, and other data on COVID–19, to identify and evaluate the extent, nature, and source of COVID–19 among employees in the occupations and sectors described in subparagraphs (A) through (C) of section 120302(a)(1);

(2) investigate, as appropriate, individual cases of COVID–19 among such employees to evaluate the source of exposure and adequacy of infection and exposure control programs and measures;

(3) provide regular periodic reports on COVID–19 among such employees to the public; and

(4) based on such reports and investigations, make recommendations on needed actions or guidance to protect such employees.

TITLE IV—COMMUNITY AND FAMILY SUPPORT

SEC. 120401. MATCHING FUNDS WAIVER FOR FORMULA GRANTS AND SUBGRANTS UNDER THE FAMILY VIOLENCE PREVENTION AND SERVICES ACT.

(a) Waiver Of Matching Funds For Awarded Grants And Subgrants.—The Secretary of Health and Human Services shall waive—

(1) the non-Federal contributions requirement under subsection (c)(4) of section 306 of the Family Violence Prevention and Services Act (42 U.S.C. 10406) with respect to the grants and subgrants awarded in fiscal years 2019 and 2020 to each State (as defined in section 302 of such Act (42 U.S.C. 10402)) and the eligible entities within such State under such section or section 308 of such Act (42 U.S.C. 10408); and

(2) the reporting requirements required under such grants and subgrants that relate to such non-Federal contributions requirement.

(b) Waiver Of Matching Funds For Grants Awarded After Date Of Enactment.—

(1) IN GENERAL.—Subsection (c)(4) of section 306 of the Family Violence Prevention and Services Act (42 U.S.C. 10406) shall not apply to a qualified grant during the period of a public health emergency declared pursuant to section 319 of the Public Health Service Act (42 U.S.C. 247d) resulting from the COVID–19 pandemic.

(2) QUALIFIED GRANT DEFINED.—In this subsection, the term "qualified grant" means a grant or subgrant awarded—

(A) after the date of the enactment of this section; and

(B) under section 306, 308, or 309 of the Family Violence Prevention and Services Act (42 U.S.C. 10406; 10408; 10409).

SEC. 120402. DISTRIBUTION OF CERTAIN FUNDS APPROPRIATED FOR THE COMMUNITY SERVICES BLOCK GRANT ACT.

(a) Distribution Of CARES Act Funds To States.—Section 675B(b)(3) of the Community Services Block Grant Act (42 U.S.C. 9906(b)(3)) shall not apply with respect to funds appropriated by the CARES Act (Public Law 116–136) to carry out the Community Services Block Grant Act (42 U.S.C.9901 et seq.).

(b) Increased Poverty Line.—For purposes of carrying out the Community Services Block Grant Act (42 U.S.C. 9901 et seq.) with any funds appropriated for fiscal year 2020 for such Act, the term "poverty line" as defined in section 673(2) of such Act (42 U.S.C. 9902(2)) means 200 percent of the poverty line otherwise applicable under such section (excluding the last sentence of such section) without regard to this subsection.

SEC. 120403. USE OF LIHEAP SUPPLEMENTAL APPROPRIATIONS.

Notwithstanding the Low-Income Home Energy Assistance Act of 1981, with respect to amounts appropriated under title VI of division A of this Act to carry out the Low-Income Home Energy Assistance Act of 1981, each State, the Commonwealth of Puerto Rico, Guam, American Samoa, the Virgin Islands of the United States, the Commonwealth of the Northern Mariana Islands, and each Indian Tribe, as applicable, that receives an allotment of funds from such amounts—

(1) shall, in using such funds, for purposes of income eligibility, accept proof of job loss or severe income loss dated after February 29, 2020, such as a layoff or furlough notice or verification of application for unemployment benefits, as sufficient to demonstrate lack of income for an individual or household; and

(2) may use not more than 12.5 percent of such funds for administrative costs.

TITLE V—COVID-19 PROTECTIONS UNDER LONGSHORE AND HARBOR WORKERS' COMPENSATION ACT

SEC. 120501. COMPENSATION PURSUANT TO THE LONGSHORE AND HARBOR WORKERS' COMPENSATION ACT.

(a) Entitlement To Compensation.—

(1) IN GENERAL.—A covered employee who receives a diagnosis or is subject to an order described in paragraph (2)(B) and who provides notice of or files a claim relating to such diagnosis or order under section 12 or 13 of the Longshore and Harbor Workers' Compensation Act (33 U.S.C. 912, 913), respectively, shall—

(A) be deemed to have an injury arising out of or in the course of employment for which compensation is payable under the Longshore and Harbor Workers' Compensation Act (33 U.S.C. 901 et seq.); and

(B) be paid the compensation to which the employee is entitled under such Act (33 U.S.C. 901 et seq.).

(2) COVERED EMPLOYEE.—In this section, the term "covered employee" means an employee who—

(A) at any time during the period beginning on January 27, 2020, and ending on January 27, 2022, was engaged in maritime employment; and

(B) was—

(i) at any time during the period beginning on January 27, 2020, and ending on February 27, 2022, diagnosed with COVID–19; or

(ii) at any time during the period described in subparagraph (A), ordered not to return to work by the employee's employer or by a local, State, or Federal agency because of exposure, or the risk of exposure, to 1 or more individuals diagnosed with COVID–19 in the workplace.

(b) Reimbursement.—

(1) IN GENERAL.—

(A) ENTITLEMENT.—Subject to subparagraph (B), an employer of a covered employee or the employer's carrier shall be entitled to reimbursement for any compensation paid with respect to a notice or claim described in subsection (a), including disability benefits, funeral and burial expenses, medical or other related costs for treatment and care, and reasonable and necessary allocated claims expenses.

(B) SAFETY AND HEALTH REQUIREMENTS.—To be entitled to reimbursement under subparagraph (A)—

(i) an employer shall be in compliance with all applicable safety and health guidelines and standards that are related to the prevention of occupational exposure to COVID–19, including such guidelines and standards issued by the Occupational Safety and Health Administration, State plans approved under section 18 of the Occupational Safety and Health Act of 1970 (29 U.S.C. 667), the Coast Guard, and Federal, State or local public health authorities; and

(ii) a carrier—

(I) shall be a carrier for an employer that is in compliance with clause (i); and

(II) shall not adjust the experience rating or the annual premium of the employer based upon the compensation paid by the carrier with respect to a notice or claim described in subparagraph (A).

(2) REIMBURSEMENT PROCEDURES.—To receive reimbursement under paragraph (1)—

(A) a claim for such reimbursement shall be submitted to the Secretary of Labor—

(i) not later than one year after the final payment of compensation to a covered employee pursuant to this section; and

(ii) in the same manner as a claim for reimbursement is submitted in accordance with part 61 of title 20, Code of Federal Regulations (as in effect on the date of enactment of this Act); and

(B) an employer and the employer's carrier shall make, keep, and preserve such records, make such reports, and provide such information, as the Secretary of Labor determines necessary or appropriate to carry out this section.

(c) Special Fund.—

(1) IN GENERAL.—A reimbursement under paragraph (1) shall be paid out of the special fund established in section 44 of Longshore and Harbor Workers' Compensation Act (33 U.S.C. 944).

(2) FUNDING.—There are authorized to be appropriated, and there are appropriated, such funds as may be necessary to reimburse the special fund described in paragraph (1) for each reimbursement paid out of such fund under paragraph (1).

(d) Report.—Not later than 60 days after the end of fiscal year 2020, 2021, and 2022, the Secretary of Labor shall submit to the Committee on Education and Labor of the House of Representatives and the Committee on Health, Education, Labor and

Pensions of the Senate, an annual report enumerating—

(1) the number of claims filed pursuant to section (a)(1);

(2) of such filed claims—

(A) the number and types of claims approved under section 13 of the Longshore and Harbor Workers' Compensation Act (33 U.S.C. 913);

(B) the number and types of claims denied under such section;

(C) the number and types of claims pending under such section; and

(3) the amounts and the number of claims for reimbursement paid out of the special fund under subsection (c)(1) for the fiscal year for which the report is being submitted.

(e) Regulations.—The Secretary of Labor may promulgate such regulations as may be necessary to carry out this section.

(f) LHWCA Terms.—In this section, the terms "carrier", "compensation", "employee", and "employer" have the meanings given the terms in section 2 of the Longshore and Harbor Workers' Compensation Act (33 U.S.C. 902).

DIVISION M—CONSUMER PROTECTION AND TELECOM-MUNICATIONS PROVISIONS

TITLE I—COVID–19 PRICE GOUGING PREVENTION

SEC. 130101. SHORT TITLE.

This title may be cited as the "COVID–19 Price Gouging Prevention Act".

SEC. 130102. PREVENTION OF PRICE GOUGING.

(a) In General.—For the duration of a public health emergency declared pursuant to section 319 of the Public Health Service Act (42 U.S.C. 247d) as a result of confirmed cases of 2019 novel coronavirus (COVID–19), including any renewal thereof, it shall be unlawful for any person to sell or offer for sale a good or service at a price that—

(1) is unconscionably excessive; and

(2) indicates the seller is using the circumstances related to such public health emergency to increase prices unreasonably.

(b) Factors For Consideration.—In determining whether a person has violated subsection (a), there shall be taken into account, with respect to the price at which such person sold or offered for sale the good or service, factors that include the following:

(1) Whether such price grossly exceeds the average price at which the same or a similar good or service was sold or offered for sale by such person—

(A) during the 90-day period immediately preceding January 31, 2020; or

(B) during the period that is 45 days before or after the date that is one year before the date such good or service is sold or offered for sale under subsection (a).

(2) Whether such price grossly exceeds the average price at which the same or a similar good or service was readily obtainable from other similarly situated competing sellers before January 31, 2020.

(3) Whether such price reasonably reflects additional costs, not within the control of such person, that were paid, incurred, or reasonably anticipated by such person, or reasonably reflects the profitability of forgone sales or additional risks taken by such person, to produce, distribute, obtain, or sell such good or service under the circumstances.

(c) Enforcement.—

(1) ENFORCEMENT BY FEDERAL TRADE COMMISSION.—

(A) UNFAIR OR DECEPTIVE ACTS OR PRACTICES.—A violation of subsection (a) shall be treated as a violation of a regulation under section 18(a)(1)(B) of the Federal Trade Commission Act (15 U.S.C. 57a(a)(1)(B)) regarding unfair or deceptive acts or practices.

(B) POWERS OF COMMISSION.—The Commission shall enforce subsection (a) in the same manner, by the same means, and with the same jurisdiction, powers, and duties as though all applicable terms and provisions of the Federal Trade Commission Act (15 U.S.C. 41 et seq.) were incorporated into and made a part of this section. Any person who violates such subsection shall be subject to the penalties and entitled to the privileges and immunities provided in the Federal Trade Commission Act.

(2) EFFECT ON OTHER LAWS.—Nothing in this section shall be construed in any way to limit the authority of the Commission under any other provision of law.

(3) ENFORCEMENT BY STATE ATTORNEYS GENERAL.—

(A) IN GENERAL.—If the chief law enforcement officer of a State, or an official or agency designated by a State, has reason to believe that any person has violated or is violating subsection (a), the attorney general, official, or agency of the State, in addition to any authority it may have to bring an action in State court under its consumer protection law, may bring a civil action in any appropriate United States district court or in any other court of competent jurisdiction, including a State court, to—

(i) enjoin further such violation by such person;

(ii) enforce compliance with such subsection;

(iii) obtain civil penalties; and

(iv) obtain damages, restitution, or other compensation on behalf of residents of the State.

(B) NOTICE AND INTERVENTION BY THE FTC.—The attorney general of a State shall provide prior written notice of any action under subparagraph (A) to the Commission and provide the Commission with a copy of the complaint in the action, except in any case in which such prior notice is not feasible, in which case the attorney general shall serve such notice immediately upon instituting such action. The Commission shall have the right—

(i) to intervene in the action;

(ii) upon so intervening, to be heard on all matters arising therein; and

(iii) to file petitions for appeal.

(C) LIMITATION ON STATE ACTION WHILE FEDERAL ACTION IS PENDING.—If the Commission has instituted a civil action for violation of this section, no State attorney general, or official or agency of a State, may bring an action under this paragraph during the pendency of that action against any defendant named in the complaint of the Commission for any violation of this section alleged in the complaint.

(D) RELATIONSHIP WITH STATE-LAW CLAIMS.—If the attorney general of a State has authority to bring an action under State law directed at acts or practices that also violate this section, the attorney general may assert the State-law claim and a claim under this section in the same civil action.

(4) SAVINGS CLAUSE.—Nothing in this section shall preempt or otherwise affect any State or local law.

(d) Definitions.—In this section:

(1) COMMISSION.—The term "Commission" means the Federal Trade Commission.

(2) GOOD OR SERVICE.—The term "good or service" means a good or service offered in commerce, including—

(A) food, beverages, water, ice, a chemical, or a personal hygiene product;

(B) any personal protective equipment for protection from or prevention of contagious diseases, filtering facepiece respirators, medical equipment and supplies (including medical testing supplies), a drug as defined in section 201(g)(1) of the Federal Food, Drug, and Cosmetic Act (21 U.S.C. 321(g)(1)), cleaning supplies, disinfectants, sanitizers; or

(C) any healthcare service, cleaning service, or delivery service.

(3) STATE.—The term "State" means each of the several States, the District of Columbia, each commonwealth, territory, or possession of the United States, and each federally recognized Indian Tribe.

TITLE II—E-RATE SUPPORT FOR WI-FI HOTSPOTS, OTHER EQUIPMENT, AND CONNECTED DEVICES

SEC. 130201. E-RATE SUPPORT FOR WI-FI HOTSPOTS, OTHER EQUIPMENT, AND CONNECTED DEVICES DURING EMERGENCY PERIODS RELATING TO COVID-19.

(a) Regulations Required.—Not later than 7 days after the date of the enactment of this Act, the Commission shall promulgate regulations providing for the provision, from amounts made available from the Emergency Connectivity Fund established under subsection (i)(1), of support under section 254(h)(1)(B) of the Communications Act of 1934 (47 U.S.C. 254(h)(1)(B)) to an elementary school, secondary school, or library (including a Tribal elementary school, Tribal secondary school, or Tribal library) eligible for support under such section, for the purchase during an emergency period described in subsection (e) (including any portion of such a period occurring before the date of the enactment of this Act) of equipment described in subsection (c), advanced telecommunications and information services, or equipment described in such subsection and advanced telecommunications and information services, for use by—

(1) in the case of a school, students and staff of such school at locations that include locations other than such school; and

(2) in the case of a library, patrons of such library at locations that include locations other than such library.

(b) Tribal Issues.—

(1) RESERVATION FOR TRIBAL LANDS.—The Commission shall reserve not less than 5 percent of the amounts available to the Commission under subsection (i)(3) to provide support under the regulations required by subsection (a) to schools and libraries that serve persons who are located on Tribal lands.

(2) ELIGIBILITY OF TRIBAL LIBRARIES.—For purposes of determining the eligibility of a Tribal library for support under the regulations required by subsection (a), the portion of paragraph (4) of section 254(h) of the Communications Act of 1934 (47 U.S.C. 254(h)) relating to eligibility for assistance from a State library administrative agency under the Library Services and Technology Act shall not apply.

(c) Equipment Described.—The equipment described in this subsection is the following:

(1) Wi-Fi hotspots.

(2) Modems.

(3) Routers.

(4) Devices that combine a modem and router.

(5) Connected devices.

(d) Prioritization Of Support.—The Commission shall provide in the regulations required by subsection (a) for a mechanism to require a school or library to prioritize the provision of equipment described in subsection (c), advanced telecommunications and information services, or equipment described in such subsection and advanced telecommunications and information services, for which support is received under such regulations, to students and staff or patrons (as the case may be) that the school or library believes do not have access to equipment described in subsection (c), do not have access to advanced telecommunications and information services, or have access to neither equipment described in subsection (c) nor advanced telecommunications and information services, at the residences of such students and staff or patrons.

(e) Emergency Periods Described.—An emergency period described in this subsection is a period that—

(1) begins on the date of a determination by the Secretary of Health and Human Services pursuant to section 319 of the Public Health Service Act (42 U.S.C. 247d) that a public health emergency exists as a result of COVID–19; and

(2) ends on the June 30 that first occurs after the date on which such determination (including any renewal thereof) terminates.

(f) Treatment Of Equipment After Emergency Period.—The Commission shall provide in the regulations required by subsection (a) that, in the case of a school or library that purchases equipment described in subsection (c) using support received under such regulations, such school or library—

(1) may, after the emergency period with respect to which such support is received, use such equipment for such purposes as such school or library considers appropriate, subject to any restrictions provided in such regulations (or any successor regulation); and

(2) may not sell or otherwise transfer such equipment in exchange for any thing (including a service) of value, except that such school or library may exchange such equipment for upgraded equipment of the same type.

(g) Rule Of Construction.—Nothing in this section shall be construed to affect any authority the Commission may have under section 254(h)(1)(B) of the Communications Act of 1934 (47 U.S.C. 254(h)(1)(B)) to allow support under such section to be used for the purposes described in subsection (a) other than as required by such subsection.

(h) Procedural Matters.—

(1) PART 54 REGULATIONS.—Nothing in this section shall be construed to prevent the Commission from providing that the regulations in part 54 of title 47, Code of Federal Regulations (or any successor regulation), shall apply in whole or in part to support provided under the regulations required by subsection (a), shall not apply in whole or in part to such support, or shall be modified in whole or in part for purposes of application to such support.

(2) EXEMPTION FROM CERTAIN RULEMAKING REQUIREMENTS.—Subsections (b), (c), and (d) of section 553 of title 5, United States Code, shall not apply to

a regulation promulgated under subsection (a) of this section or a rulemaking to promulgate such a regulation.

(3) PAPERWORK REDUCTION ACT EXEMPTION.—A collection of information conducted or sponsored under the regulations required by subsection (a), or under section 254 of the Communications Act of 1934 (47 U.S.C. 254) in connection with support provided under such regulations, shall not constitute a collection of information for the purposes of subchapter I of chapter 35 of title 44, United States Code (commonly referred to as the Paperwork Reduction Act).

(i) Emergency Connectivity Fund.—

(1) ESTABLISHMENT.—There is established in the Treasury of the United States a fund to be known as the Emergency Connectivity Fund.

(2) AUTHORIZATION OF APPROPRIATIONS.—There is authorized to be appropriated to the Emergency Connectivity Fund $5,000,000,000 for fiscal year 2020, to remain available through fiscal year 2021.

(3) USE OF FUNDS.—Amounts in the Emergency Connectivity Fund shall be available to the Commission to provide support under the regulations required by subsection (a).

(4) RELATIONSHIP TO UNIVERSAL SERVICE CONTRIBUTIONS.—Support provided under the regulations required by subsection (a) shall be provided from amounts made available under paragraph (3) and not from contributions under section 254(d) of the Communications Act of 1934 (47 U.S.C. 254(d)).

(j) Definitions.—In this section:

(1) ADVANCED TELECOMMUNICATIONS AND INFORMATION SERVICES.—The term "advanced telecommunications and information services" means advanced telecommunications and information services, as such term is used in section 254(h) of the Communications Act of 1934 (47 U.S.C. 254(h)).

(2) COMMISSION.—The term "Commission" means the Federal Communications Commission.

(3) CONNECTED DEVICE.—The term "connected device" means a laptop computer, tablet computer, or similar device that is capable of connecting to advanced telecommunications and information services.

(4) LIBRARY.—The term "library" includes a library consortium.

(5) TRIBAL LAND.—The term "Tribal land" means—

(A) any land located within the boundaries of—

(i) an Indian reservation, pueblo, or rancheria; or

(ii) a former reservation within Oklahoma;

(B) any land not located within the boundaries of an Indian reservation, pueblo, or rancheria, the title to which is held—

(i) in trust by the United States for the benefit of an Indian Tribe or an individual Indian;

(ii) by an Indian Tribe or an individual Indian, subject to restriction against alienation under laws of the United States; or

(iii) by a dependent Indian community;

(C) any land located within a region established pursuant to section 7(a) of the Alaska Native Claims Settlement Act (43 U.S.C. 1606(a));

(D) Hawaiian Home Lands, as defined in section 801 of the Native American Housing Assistance and Self-Determination Act of 1996 (25 U.S.C. 4221); or

(E) those areas or communities designated by the Assistant Secretary of Indian Affairs of the Department of the Interior that are near, adjacent, or contiguous to reservations where financial assistance and social service programs are provided to Indians because of their status as Indians.

(6) TRIBAL LIBRARY.—The term "Tribal library" means, only during an emergency period described under subsection (e), a facility owned by an Indian Tribe, serving Indian Tribes, or serving American Indians, Alaskan Natives, or Native Hawaiian communities, including—

(A) a Tribal library or Tribal library consortium; or

(B) a Tribal government building, chapter house, longhouse, community center, or other similar public building.

(7) WI-FI.—The term "Wi-Fi" means a wireless networking protocol based on Institute of Electrical and Electronics Engineers standard 802.11 (or any successor standard).

(8) WI-FI HOTSPOT.—The term "Wi-Fi hotspot" means a device that is capable of—

(A) receiving mobile advanced telecommunications and information services; and

(B) sharing such services with another device through the use of Wi-Fi.

TITLE III—EMERGENCY BENEFIT FOR BROADBAND SERVICE

SEC. 130301. BENEFIT FOR BROADBAND SERVICE DURING EMERGENCY PERIODS RELATING TO COVID-19.

(a) Promulgation Of Regulations Required.—Not later than 7 days after the date of the enactment of this Act, the Commission shall promulgate regulations implementing this section.

(b) Requirements.—The regulations promulgated pursuant to subsection (a) shall establish the following:

(1) EMERGENCY BROADBAND BENEFIT.—During an emergency period, a provider shall provide an eligible household with an internet service offering, upon request by a member of such household. Such provider shall discount the price charged to such household for such internet service offering in an amount equal to the emergency broadband benefit for such household.

(2) VERIFICATION OF ELIGIBILITY.—To verify whether a household is an eligible household, a provider shall either—

(A) use the National Lifeline Eligibility Verifier; or

(B) rely upon an alternative verification process of the provider, if the Commission finds such process to be sufficient to avoid waste, fraud, and abuse.

(3) USE OF NATIONAL LIFELINE ELIGIBILITY VERIFIER.—The Commission shall—

(A) expedite the ability of all providers to access the National Lifeline Eligibility Verifier for purposes of determining whether a household is an eligible household; and

(B) ensure that the National Lifeline Eligibility Verifier approves an eligible household to receive the emergency broadband benefit not later than two days after the date of the submission of information necessary to determine if such household is an eligible household.

(4) EXTENSION OF EMERGENCY PERIOD.—An emergency period may be extended within a State or any portion thereof if the State, or in the case of Tribal land, a Tribal government, provides written, public notice to the Commission stipulating

that an extension is necessary in furtherance of the recovery related to COVID–19. The Commission shall, within 48 hours after receiving such notice, post the notice on the public website of the Commission.

(5) REIMBURSEMENT.—From the Emergency Broadband Connectivity Fund established in subsection (h), the Commission shall reimburse a provider in an amount equal to the emergency broadband benefit with respect to an eligible household that receives such benefit from such provider.

(6) REIMBURSEMENT FOR CONNECTED DEVICE.—A provider that, in addition to providing the emergency broadband benefit to an eligible household, supplies such household with a connected device may be reimbursed up to $100 from the Emergency Broadband Connectivity Fund established in subsection (h) for such connected device, if the charge to such eligible household is more than $10 but less than $50 for such connected device, except that a provider may receive reimbursement for no more than one connected device per eligible household.

(7) NO RETROACTIVE REIMBURSEMENT.—A provider may not receive a reimbursement from the Emergency Broadband Connectivity Fund for providing an internet service offering discounted by the emergency broadband benefit, or for supplying a connected device, that was provided or supplied (as the case may be) before the date of the enactment of this Act.

(8) CERTIFICATION REQUIRED.—To receive a reimbursement under paragraph (5) or (6), a provider shall certify to the Commission the following:

(A) That the amount for which the provider is seeking reimbursement from the Emergency Broadband Connectivity Fund for an internet service offering to an eligible household is not more than the normal rate.

(B) That each eligible household for which a provider is seeking reimbursement for providing an internet service offering discounted by the emergency broadband benefit—

(i) has not been and will not be charged—

(I) for such offering, if the normal rate for such offering is less than or equal to the amount of the emergency broadband benefit for such household; or

(II) more for such offering than the difference between the normal rate for such offering and the amount of the emergency broadband benefit for such household;

(ii) will not be required to pay an early termination fee if such eligible household elects to enter into a contract to receive such internet service offering if such household later terminates such contract; and

(iii) was not subject to a mandatory waiting period for such internet service offering based on having previously received broadband internet access service from such provider.

(C) A description of the process used by the provider to verify that a household is an eligible household, if the provider elects an alternative verification process under paragraph (2)(B), and that such verification process was designed to avoid waste, fraud, and abuse.

(9) AUDIT REQUIREMENTS.—The Commission shall adopt audit requirements to ensure that providers are in compliance with the requirements of this section and to prevent waste, fraud, and abuse in the emergency broadband benefit program established under this section.

(c) Eligible Providers.—Notwithstanding subsection (e) of this section, the Commission shall provide a reimbursement to a provider under this section without requiring such provider to be designated as an eligible telecommunications carrier under section 214(e) of the Communications Act of 1934 (47 U.S.C. 214(e)).

(d) Rule Of Construction.—Nothing in this section shall affect the collection, distribution, or administration of the Lifeline Assistance Program governed by the rules set forth in subpart E of part 54 of title 47, Code of Federal Regulations (or any successor regulation).

(e) Part 54 Regulations.—Nothing in this section shall be construed to prevent the Commission from providing that the regulations in part 54 of title 47, Code of Federal Regulations (or any successor regulation), shall apply in whole or in part to support provided under the regulations required by subsection (a), shall not apply in whole or in part to such support, or shall be modified in whole or in part for purposes of application to such support.

(f) Enforcement.—A violation of this section or a regulation promulgated under this section, including the knowing or reckless denial of an internet service offering discounted by the emergency broadband benefit to an eligible household that requests such an offering, shall be treated as a violation of the Communications Act of 1934 (47 U.S.C. 151 et seq.) or a regulation promulgated under such Act. The Commission shall enforce this section and the regulations promulgated under this section in the same manner, by the same means, and with the same jurisdiction, powers, and duties as though all applicable terms and provisions of the Communications Act of 1934 were incorporated into and made a part of this section.

(g) Exemptions.—

(1) NOTICE AND COMMENT RULEMAKING REQUIREMENTS.—Section 553 of title 5, United States Code, shall not apply to a regulation promulgated under subsection (a) or a rulemaking to promulgate such a regulation.

(2) PAPERWORK REDUCTION ACT REQUIREMENTS.—A collection of information conducted or sponsored under the regulations required by subsection (a) shall not constitute a collection of information for the purposes of subchapter I of chapter 35 of title 44, United States Code (commonly referred to as the Paperwork Reduction Act).

(h) Emergency Broadband Connectivity Fund.—

(1) ESTABLISHMENT.—There is established in the Treasury of the United States a fund to be known as the Emergency Broadband Connectivity Fund.

(2) AUTHORIZATION OF APPROPRIATIONS.—There is authorized to be appropriated to the Emergency Broadband Connectivity Fund $8,800,000,000 for fiscal year 2020, to remain available through fiscal year 2021.

(3) USE OF FUNDS.—Amounts in the Emergency Broadband Connectivity Fund shall be available to the Commission for reimbursements to providers under the regulations required by subsection (a).

(4) RELATIONSHIP TO UNIVERSAL SERVICE CONTRIBUTIONS.—Reimbursements provided under the regulations required by subsection (a) shall be provided from amounts made available under this subsection and not from contributions under section 254(d) of the Communications Act of 1934 (47 U.S.C. 254(d)), except the Commission may use such contributions if needed to offset expenses associated with the reliance on the National Lifeline Eligibility Verifier to determine eligibility of households to receive the emergency broadband benefit.

(i) Definitions.—In this section:

(1) BROADBAND INTERNET ACCESS SERVICE.—The term "broadband internet

access service" has the meaning given such term in section 8.1(b) of title 47, Code of Federal Regulations (or any successor regulation).

(2) CONNECTED DEVICE.—The term "connected device" means a laptop or desktop computer or a tablet.

(3) ELIGIBLE HOUSEHOLD.—The term "eligible household" means, regardless of whether the household or any member of the household receives support under subpart E of part 54 of title 47, Code of Federal Regulations (or any successor regulation), and regardless of whether any member of the household has any past or present arrearages with a provider, a household in which—

(A) at least one member of the household meets the qualifications in subsection (a) or (b) of section 54.409 of title 47, Code of Federal Regulations (or any successor regulation);

(B) at least one member of the household has applied for and been approved to receive benefits under the free and reduced price lunch program under the Richard B. Russell National School Lunch Act (42 U.S.C. 1751 et seq.) or the school breakfast program under section 4 of the Child Nutrition Act of 1966 (42 U.S.C. 1773); or

(C) at least one member of the household has experienced a substantial loss of income since February 29, 2020, documented by layoff or furlough notice, application for unemployment insurance benefits, or similar documentation.

(4) EMERGENCY BROADBAND BENEFIT.—The term "emergency broadband benefit" means a monthly discount for an eligible household applied to the normal rate for an internet service offering, in an amount equal to such rate, but not more than $50, or, if an internet service offering is provided to an eligible household on Tribal land, not more than $75.

(5) EMERGENCY PERIOD.—The term "emergency period" means a period that—

(A) begins on the date of a determination by the Secretary of Health and Human Services pursuant to section 319 of the Public Health Service Act (42 U.S.C. 247d) that a public health emergency exists as a result of COVID–19; and

(B) ends on the date that is 6 months after the date on which such determination (including any renewal thereof) terminates, except as such period may be extended under subsection (b)(4).

(6) INTERNET SERVICE OFFERING.—The term "internet service offering" means, with respect to a provider, broadband internet access service provided by such provider to a household, offered in the same manner, and on the same terms, as described in any of such provider's advertisements for broadband internet access service to such household, as on May 1, 2020.

(7) NORMAL RATE.—The term "normal rate" means, with respect to an internet service offering by a provider, the advertised monthly retail rate, as of May 1, 2020, including any applicable promotions and excluding any taxes or other governmental fees.

(8) PROVIDER.—The term "provider" means a provider of broadband internet access service.

SEC. 130302. ENHANCED LIFELINE BENEFITS DURING EMERGENCY PERIODS.

(a) Enhanced Minimum Service Standards For Lifeline Benefits During Emergency Periods.—During an emergency period—

(1) the minimum service standard for Lifeline supported mobile voice service shall provide an unlimited number of minutes per month;

(2) the minimum service standard for Lifeline supported mobile data service shall provide an unlimited data allowance each month and 4G speeds, where available; and

(3) the Basic Support Amount and Tribal Lands Support Amount, as described in section 54.403 of title 47, Code of Federal Regulations (or any successor regulation), shall be increased by an amount necessary, as determined by the Commission, to offset any incremental increase in cost associated with the requirements in paragraphs (1) and (2).

(b) Extension Of Emergency Period.—An emergency period may be extended within a State or any portion thereof for a maximum of six months, if the State, or in the case of Tribal land, a Tribal government, provides written, public notice to the Commission stipulating that an extension is necessary in furtherance of the recovery related to COVID–19. The Commission shall, within 48 hours after receiving such notice, post the notice on the public website of the Commission.

(c) Regulations.—The Commission shall adopt, on an expedited basis, any regulations needed to carry out this section.

(d) Emergency Period Defined.—In this section, the term "emergency period" means a period that—

(1) begins on the date of a determination by the Secretary of Health and Human Services pursuant to section 319 of the Public Health Service Act (42 U.S.C. 247d) that a public health emergency exists as a result of COVID–19; and

(2) ends on the date that is 6 months after the date on which such determination (including any renewal thereof) terminates, except as such period may be extended under subsection (b).

SEC. 130303. GRANTS TO STATES TO STRENGTHEN NATIONAL LIFELINE ELIGIBILITY VERIFIER.

(a) In General.—From amounts appropriated under subsection (d), the Commission shall, not later than 7 days after the date of the enactment of this Act, make a grant to each State, in an amount in proportion to the population of such State, for the purpose of connecting the database used by such State for purposes of the supplemental nutrition assistance program under the Food and Nutrition Act of 2008 (7 U.S.C. 2011 et seq.) to the National Lifeline Eligibility Verifier, so that the receipt by a household of benefits under such program is reflected in the National Lifeline Eligibility Verifier.

(b) Disbursement Of Grant Funds.—Funds under each grant made under subsection (a) shall be disbursed to the State receiving such grant not later than 7 days after the date of the enactment of this Act.

(c) Certification To Congress.—Not later than 21 days after the date of the enactment of this Act, the Commission shall certify to the Committee on Energy and Commerce of the House of Representatives and the Committee on Commerce, Science, and Transportation of the Senate that the grants required by subsection (a) have been made and that funds have been disbursed as required by subsection (b).

(d) Authorization Of Appropriations.—There is authorized to be appropriated $200,000,000 to carry out this section for fiscal year 2020, to remain available through fiscal year 2021.

SEC. 130304. DEFINITIONS.

In this title:

(1) COMMISSION.—The term "Commission" means the Federal Communications Commission.

(2) NATIONAL LIFELINE ELIGIBILITY VERIFIER.—The term "National Lifeline Eligibility Verifier" has the meaning given such term in section 54.400 of title 47, Code of Federal Regulations (or any successor regulation).

(3) STATE.—The term "State" has the meaning given such term in section 3 of the Communications Act of 1934 (47 U.S.C. 153).

TITLE IV—CONTINUED CONNECTIVITY

SEC. 130401. CONTINUED CONNECTIVITY DURING EMERGENCY PERIODS RELATING TO COVID-19.

Title VII of the Communications Act of 1934 (47 U.S.C. 601 et seq.) is amended by adding at the end the following:

"SEC. 723. CONTINUED CONNECTIVITY DURING EMERGENCY PERIODS RELATING TO COVID-19.

"(a) In General.—During an emergency period described in subsection (b), it shall be unlawful—

"(1) for a provider of advanced telecommunications service or voice service to—

"(A) terminate, reduce, or change such service provided to any individual customer or small business because of the inability of the individual customer or small business to pay for such service if the individual customer or small business certifies to such provider that such inability to pay is a result of disruptions caused by the public health emergency to which such emergency period relates; or

"(B) impose late fees on any individual customer or small business because of the inability of the individual customer or small business to pay for such service if the individual customer or small business certifies to such provider that such inability to pay is a result of disruptions caused by the public health emergency to which such emergency period relates;

"(2) for a provider of advanced telecommunications service to, during such emergency period—

"(A) employ a limit on the amount of data allotted to an individual customer or small business during such emergency period, except that such provider may engage in reasonable network management; or

"(B) charge an individual customer or small business an additional fee for exceeding the limit on the data allotted to an individual customer or small business; or

"(3) for a provider of advanced telecommunications service that had functioning Wi-Fi hotspots available to subscribers in public places on the day before the beginning of such emergency period to fail to make service provided by such Wi-Fi hotspots available to the public at no cost during such emergency period.

"(b) Waiver.—Upon a petition by a provider advanced telecommunications service or voice service, the provisions in subsection (a) may be suspended or waived by the Commission at any time, in whole or in part, for good cause shown.

"(c) Emergency Periods Described.—An emergency period described in this subsection is any portion beginning on or after the date of the enactment of this section of the duration of a public health emergency declared pursuant to section 319 of the Public Health Service Act (42 U.S.C. 247d) as a result of COVID-19, including any renewal thereof.

"(d) Definitions.—In this section:

"(1) ADVANCED TELECOMMUNICATIONS SERVICE.—The term 'advanced telecommunications service' means a service that provides advanced telecommunications capability (as defined in section 706 of the Telecommunications Act of 1996 (47 U.S.C. 1302)).

"(2) BROADBAND INTERNET ACCESS SERVICE.—The term 'broadband internet access service' has the meaning given such term in section 8.1(b) of title 47, Code of Federal Regulations (or any successor regulation).

"(3) INDIVIDUAL CUSTOMER.—The term 'individual customer' means an individual who contracts with a mass-market retail provider of advanced telecommunications service or voice service to provide service to such individual.

"(4) REASONABLE NETWORK MANAGEMENT.—The term 'reasonable network management'—

"(A) means the use of a practice that—

"(i) has a primarily technical network management justification; and

"(ii) is primarily used for and tailored to achieving a legitimate network management purpose, taking into account the particular network architecture and technology of the service; and

"(B) does not include other business practices.

"(5) SMALL BUSINESS.—The term 'small business' has the meaning given such term under section 601(3) of title 5, United States Code.

"(6) VOICE SERVICE.—The term 'voice service' has the meaning given such term under section 227(e)(8) of the Communications Act of 1934 (47 U.S.C. 227(e)(8)).

"(7) WI-FI.—The term 'Wi-Fi' means a wireless networking protocol based on Institute of Electrical and Electronics Engineers standard 802.11 (or any successor standard).

"(8) WI-FI HOTSPOT.—The term 'Wi-Fi hotspot' means a device that is capable of—

"(A) receiving mobile broadband internet access service; and

"(B) sharing such service with another device through the use of Wi-Fi.".

TITLE V—DON'T BREAK UP THE T–BAND

SEC. 130501. REPEAL OF REQUIREMENT TO REALLOCATE AND AUCTION T-BAND SPECTRUM.

(a) Repeal.—Section 6103 of the Middle Class Tax Relief and Job Creation Act of 2012 (47 U.S.C. 1413) is repealed.

(b) Clerical Amendment.—The table of contents in section 1(b) of such Act is amended by striking the item relating to section 6103.

TITLE VI—NATIONAL SUICIDE HOTLINE DESIGNATION

SEC. 130601. FINDINGS.

Congress finds the following:

(1) According to the American Foundation for Suicide Prevention, on average, there are 129 suicides per day in the United States.

(2) To prevent future suicides, it is critical to transition the cumbersome, existing 10-digit National Suicide Hotline to a universal, easy-to-remember, 3-digit phone number and connect people in crisis with life-saving resources.

(3) It is essential that people in the United States have access to a 3-digit national suicide hotline across all geographic locations.

(4) The designated suicide hotline number will need to be both familiar and recognizable to all people in the United States.

SEC. 130602. UNIVERSAL TELEPHONE NUMBER FOR NATIONAL SUICIDE PREVENTION AND MENTAL HEALTH CRISIS HOTLINE SYSTEM.

(a) In General.—Section 251(e) of the Communications Act of 1934 (47 U.S.C. 251(e)) is amended by adding at the end the following:

"(4) UNIVERSAL TELEPHONE NUMBER FOR NATIONAL SUICIDE PREVENTION AND MENTAL HEALTH CRISIS HOTLINE SYSTEM.—9-8-8 is designated as the universal telephone number within the United States for the purpose of the national suicide prevention and mental health crisis hotline system operating through the National Suicide Prevention Lifeline maintained by the Assistant Secretary for Mental Health and Substance Use under section 520E-3 of the Public Health Service Act (42 U.S.C. 290bb-36c) and through the Veterans Crisis Line maintained by the Secretary of Veterans Affairs under section 1720F(h) of title 38, United States Code.".

(b) Effective Date.—The amendment made by subsection (a) shall take effect on the date that is 1 year after the date of the enactment of this Act.

(c) Required Report.—Not later than 180 days after the date of the enactment of this Act, the Assistant Secretary for Mental Health and Substance Use and the Secretary of Veterans Affairs shall jointly submit a report that details the resources necessary to make the use of 9-8-8, as designated under paragraph (4) of section 251(e) of the Communications Act of 1934 (47 U.S.C. 251(e)), as added by subsection (a) of this section, operational and effective across the United States to—

(1) the Committee on Commerce, Science, and Transportation of the Senate;

(2) the Committee on Appropriations of the Senate;

(3) the Committee on Energy and Commerce of the House of Representatives; and

(4) the Committee on Appropriations of the House of Representatives.

SEC. 130603. STATE AUTHORITY OVER FEES.

(a) Authority.—

(1) IN GENERAL.—Nothing in this Act, any amendment made by this Act, the Communications Act of 1934 (47 U.S.C. 151 et seq.), or any Commission regulation or order may prevent the imposition and collection of a fee or charge applicable to a voice service specifically designated by a State, a political subdivision of a State, an Indian Tribe, or a village or regional corporation serving a region established pursuant to the Alaska Native Claims Settlement Act (43 U.S.C. 1601 et seq.) for the support or implementation of 9-8-8 services, if the fee or charge is held in a sequestered account to be obligated or expended only in support of 9-8-8 services, or enhancements of such services, as specified in the provision of State or local law adopting the fee or charge.

(2) USE OF 9-8-8 FEES.—A fee or charge collected under this subsection shall only be imposed, collected, and used to pay expenses that a State, a political subdivision of a State, an Indian Tribe, or a village or regional corporation serving a region established pursuant to the Alaska Native Claims Settlement Act (43 U.S.C. 1601 et seq.) is expected to incur that are reasonably attributable to—

(A) ensuring the efficient and effective routing of calls made to the 9-8-8 national suicide prevention and mental health crisis hotline to an appropriate crisis center; or

(B) the provision of acute mental health, crisis outreach, and stabilization services directly responding to the 9-8-8 national suicide prevention and mental health crisis hotline.

(b) Fee Accountability Report.—To ensure efficiency, transparency, and accountability in the collection and expenditure of a fee or charge for the support or implementation of 9–8–8 services, not later than 2 years after the date of the enactment of this Act, and annually thereafter, the Commission shall submit to the Committees on Commerce, Science, and Transportation and Appropriations of the Senate and the Committees on Energy and Commerce and Appropriations of the House of Representatives a report that—

(1) details the status in each State, political subdivision of a State, Indian Tribe, or village or regional corporation serving a region established pursuant to the Alaska Native Claims Settlement Act (43 U.S.C. 1601 et seq.) of the collection and distribution of such fees or charges, including a detailed report about how those fees or charges are being used to support 9–8–8 services; and

(2) includes findings on the amount of revenues obligated or expended by each State, political subdivision of a State, Indian Tribe, or village or regional corporation serving a region established pursuant to the Alaska Native Claims Settlement Act (43 U.S.C. 1601 et seq.) for any purpose other than the purpose for which any such fees or charges are specified.

(c) Definitions.—In this section:

(1) COMMISSION.—The term "Commission" means the Federal Communications Commission.

(2) STATE.—The term "State" has the meaning given that term in section 7 of the Wireless Communications and Public Safety Act of 1999 (47 U.S.C. 615b).

(3) VOICE SERVICE.—The term "voice service" has the meaning given that term in section 227(e)(8) of the Communications Act of 1934 (47 U.S.C. 227(e)(8)).

SEC. 130604. LOCATION IDENTIFICATION REPORT.

(a) In General.—Not later than 180 days after the date of the enactment of this Act, the Federal Communications Commission shall submit to the appropriate committees a report that examines the feasibility and cost of including an automatic dispatchable location that would be conveyed with a 9–8–8 call, regardless of the technological platform used and including with calls from multi-line telephone systems (as defined in section 6502 of the Middle Class Tax Relief and Job Creation Act of 2012 (47 U.S.C. 1471)).

(b) Definitions.—In this section:

(1) APPROPRIATE COMMITTEES.—The term "appropriate committees" means the following:

(A) The Committee on Commerce, Science, and Transportation of the Senate.

(B) The Committee on Health, Education, Labor, and Pensions of the Senate.

(C) The Committee on Energy and Commerce of the House of Representatives.

(2) DISPATCHABLE LOCATION.—The term "dispatchable location" means the street address of the calling party and additional information such as room number, floor number, or similar information necessary to adequately identify the location of the calling party.

SEC. 130605. REPORT ON CERTAIN TRAINING PROGRAMS.

(a) Sense Of The Congress.—It is the sense of the Congress that—

(1) youth who are lesbian, gay, bisexual, transgender, or queer (referred to in this section as "LGBTQ") are more than 4 times more likely to contemplate suicide than their peers;

(2) 1 in 5 LGBTQ youth and more than 1 in 3 transgender youth report attempting suicide this past year; and

(3) the Substance Abuse and Mental Health Services Administration must be equipped to provide specialized resources to this at-risk community.

(b) Report.—Not later than 180 days after the date of the enactment of this Act, the Assistant Secretary for Mental Health and Substance Use shall submit to the Committee on Commerce, Science, and Transportation of the Senate, the Committee on Health, Education, Labor, and Pensions of the Senate, and the Committee on Energy and Commerce of the House of Representatives a report that—

(1) details a strategy, to be developed in consultation with 1 or more organizations with expertise in suicide of LGBTQ youth as well as 1 or more organizations with expertise in suicide of other high risk populations, for the Substance Abuse and Mental Health Services Administration to offer, support, or provide technical assistance to training programs for National Suicide Prevention Lifeline counselors to increase competency in serving LGBTQ youth and other high risk populations; and

(2) includes recommendations regarding—

(A) the facilitation of access to services that are provided to specially trained staff and partner organizations for LGBTQ individuals and other high risk populations; and

(B) a strategy for optimally implementing an Integrated Voice Response, or other equally effective mechanism, to allow National Suicide Prevention Lifeline callers who are LGBTQ youth or members of other high risk populations to access specialized services.

TITLE VII—COVID-19 COMPASSION AND MARTHA WRIGHT PRISON PHONE JUSTICE

SEC. 130701. FINDINGS.

Congress finds the following:

(1) Prison, jails, and other confinement facilities in the United States have unique telecommunications needs due to safety and security concerns.

(2) Unjust and unreasonable charges for telephone and advanced communications services in confinement facilities negatively impact the safety and security of communities in the United States by damaging relationships between incarcerated persons and their support systems, thereby exacerbating recidivism.

(3) The COVID-19 pandemic has greatly intensified these concerns. Jails and prisons have become epicenters for the spread of the virus, with incarcerated persons concentrated in small, confined spaces and often without access to adequate health care. At Cook County jail alone, hundreds of incarcerated persons and jail staff have tested positive for the virus since its outbreak.

(4) To prevent the spread of the virus, many jails and prisons across the country suspended public visitation, leaving confinement facility communications services as the only way that incarcerated persons can stay in touch with their families.

(5) All people in the United States, including anyone who pays for confinement facility communications services, should have access to communications services at charges that are just and reasonable.

(6) Unemployment has risen sharply as a result of the COVID-19 pandemic, straining the incomes of millions of Americans and making it even more difficult for families of incarcerated persons to pay the high costs of confinement facility communications

services.

(7) Certain markets for confinement facility communications services are distorted due to reverse competition, in which the financial interests of the entity making the buying decision (the confinement facility) are aligned with the seller (the provider of confinement facility communications services) and not the consumer (the incarcerated person or a member of his or her family). This reverse competition occurs because site commission payments to the confinement facility from the provider of confinement facility communications services are the chief criterion many facilities use to select their provider of confinement facility communications services.

(8) Charges for confinement facility communications services that have been shown to be unjust and unreasonable are often a result of site commission payments that far exceed the costs incurred by the confinement facility in accommodating these services.

(9) Unjust and unreasonable charges have been assessed for both audio and video services and for both intrastate and interstate communications from confinement facilities.

(10) Though Congress enacted emergency legislation to allow free communications in Federal prisons during the pandemic, it does not cover communications to or from anyone incarcerated in State and local prisons or jails.

(11) Mrs. Martha Wright-Reed led a campaign for just communications rates for incarcerated people for over a decade.

(12) Mrs. Wright-Reed was the lead plaintiff in Wright v. Corrections Corporation of America, CA No. 00–293 (GK) (D.D.C. 2001).

(13) That case ultimately led to the Wright Petition at the Federal Communications Commission, CC Docket No. 96–128 (November 3, 2003).

(14) As a grandmother, Mrs. Wright-Reed was forced to choose between purchasing medication and communicating with her incarcerated grandson.

(15) Mrs. Wright-Reed passed away on January 18, 2015, before fully realizing her dream of just communications rates for all people.

SEC. 130702. REQUIREMENTS FOR CONFINEMENT FACILITY COMMUNICATIONS SERVICES, DURING THE COVID–19 PANDEMIC AND OTHER TIMES.

(a) In General.—Section 276 of the Communications Act of 1934 (47 U.S.C. 276) is amended by adding at the end the following:

"(e) Additional Requirements For Confinement Facility Communications Services.—

"(1) AUTHORITY.—

"(A) IN GENERAL.—All charges, practices, classifications, and regulations for and in connection with confinement facility communications services shall be just and reasonable, and any such charge, practice, classification, or regulation that is unjust or unreasonable is declared to be unlawful.

"(B) RULEMAKING REQUIRED.—Not later than 18 months after the date of the enactment of this subsection, the Commission shall issue rules to adopt, for the provision of confinement facility communications services, rates and ancillary service charges that are just and reasonable, which shall be the maximum such rates and charges that a provider of confinement facility communications services may charge for such services. In determining rates and charges that are just and reasonable, the Commission shall adopt such rates and charges based on the average industry costs of providing such services using data collected from providers of confinement facility communications services.

"(C) BIENNIAL REVIEW.—Not less frequently than every 2 years following the issuance of rules under subparagraph (B), the Commission shall—

"(i) determine whether the rates and ancillary service charges authorized by the rules issued under such subparagraph remain just and reasonable; and

"(ii) if the Commission determines under clause (i) that any such rate or charge does not remain just and reasonable, revise such rules so that such rate or charge is just and reasonable.

"(2) INTERIM RATE CAPS.—Until the Commission issues the rules required by paragraph (1)(B), a provider of confinement facility communications services may not charge a rate for any voice service communication using confinement facility communications services that exceeds the following:

"(A) For debit calling or prepaid calling, $0.04 per minute.

"(B) For collect calling, $0.05 per minute.

"(3) ASSESSMENT ON PER-MINUTE BASIS.—Except as provided in paragraph (4), a provider of confinement facility communications services—

"(A) shall assess all charges for a communication using such services on a per-minute basis for the actual duration of the communication, measured from communication acceptance to termination, rounded up to the next full minute, except in the case of charges for services that the confinement facility offers free of charge or for amounts below the amounts permitted under this subsection; and

"(B) may not charge a per-communication or per-connection charge for a communication using such services.

"(4) ANCILLARY SERVICE CHARGES.—

"(A) GENERAL PROHIBITION.—A provider of confinement facility communications services may not charge an ancillary service charge other than—

"(i) if the Commission has not yet issued the rules required by paragraph (1)(B), a charge listed in subparagraph (B) of this paragraph; or

"(ii) a charge authorized by the rules adopted by the Commission under paragraph (1).

"(B) PERMITTED CHARGES AND RATES.—If the Commission has not yet issued the rules required by paragraph (1)(B), a provider of confinement facility communications services may not charge a rate for an ancillary service charge in excess of the following:

"(i) In the case of an automated payment fee, 2.9 percent of the total charge on which the fee is assessed.

"(ii) In the case of a fee for single-call and related services, the exact transaction fee charged by the third-party provider, with no markup.

"(iii) In the case of a live agent fee, $5.95 per use.

"(iv) In the case of a paper bill or statement fee, $2 per use.

"(v) In the case of a third-party financial transaction fee, the exact fee, with no markup, charged by the third party for the transaction.

"(5) PROHIBITION ON SITE COMMISSIONS.—A provider of confinement facility communications services may not assess a site commission.

"(6) RELATIONSHIP TO STATE LAW.—A State or political subdivision of a State may not enforce any law, rule, regulation, standard, or other provision having the force or effect of law relating to confinement facility communications services that allows for higher rates or other charges to be assessed for such services than is permitted under any Federal law or regulation relating to confinement facility communications services.

"(7) DEFINITIONS.—In this subsection:

"(A) ANCILLARY SERVICE CHARGE.—The term 'ancillary service charge' means any charge a consumer may be assessed for the setting up or use of a confinement facility communications service that is not included in the per-minute charges assessed for individual communications.

"(B) AUTOMATED PAYMENT FEE.—The term 'automated payment fee' means a credit card payment, debit card payment, or bill processing fee, including a fee for a payment made by means of interactive voice response, the internet, or a kiosk.

"(C) COLLECT CALLING.—The term 'collect calling' means an arrangement whereby a credit-qualified party agrees to pay for charges associated with a communication made to such party using confinement facility communications services and originating from within a confinement facility.

"(D) CONFINEMENT FACILITY.—The term 'confinement facility'—

"(i) means a jail or a prison; and

"(ii) includes any juvenile, detention, work release, or mental health facility that is used primarily to hold individuals who are—

"(I) awaiting adjudication of criminal charges or an immigration matter; or

"(II) serving a sentence for a criminal conviction.

"(E) CONFINEMENT FACILITY COMMUNICATIONS SERVICE.—The term 'confinement facility communications service' means a service that allows incarcerated persons to make electronic communications (whether intrastate, interstate, or international and whether made using video, audio, or any other communicative method, including advanced communications services) to individuals outside the confinement facility, or to individuals inside the confinement facility, where the incarcerated person is being held, regardless of the technology used to deliver the service.

"(F) CONSUMER.—The term 'consumer' means the party paying a provider of confinement facility communications services.

"(G) DEBIT CALLING.—The term 'debit calling' means a presubscription or comparable service which allows an incarcerated person, or someone acting on an incarcerated person's behalf, to fund an account set up through a provider that can be used to pay for confinement facility communications services originated by the incarcerated person.

"(H) FEE FOR SINGLE-CALL AND RELATED SERVICES.—The term 'fee for single-call and related services' means a billing arrangement whereby communications made by an incarcerated person using collect calling are billed through a third party on a per-communication basis, where the recipient does not have an account with the provider of confinement facility communications services.

"(I) INCARCERATED PERSON.—The term 'incarcerated person' means a person detained at a confinement facility, regardless of the duration of the detention.

"(J) JAIL.—The term 'jail'—

"(i) means a facility of a law enforcement agency of the Federal Government or of a State or political subdivision of a State that is used primarily to hold individuals who are—

"(I) awaiting adjudication of criminal charges;

"(II) post-conviction and committed to confinement for sentences of one year or less; or

"(III) post-conviction and awaiting transfer to another facility; and

"(ii) includes—

"(I) city, county, or regional facilities that have contracted with a private company to manage day-to-day operations;

"(II) privately-owned and operated facilities primarily engaged in housing city, county, or regional incarcerated persons; and

"(III) facilities used to detain individuals pursuant to a contract with U.S. Immigration and Customs Enforcement.

"(K) LIVE AGENT FEE.—The term 'live agent fee' means a fee associated with the optional use of a live operator to complete a confinement facility communications service transaction.

"(L) PAPER BILL OR STATEMENT FEE.—The term 'paper bill or statement fee' means a fee associated with providing a consumer an optional paper billing statement.

"(M) PER-COMMUNICATION OR PER-CONNECTION CHARGE.—The term 'per-communication or per-connection charge' means a one-time fee charged to a consumer at the initiation of a communication.

"(N) PREPAID CALLING.—The term 'prepaid calling' means a calling arrangement that allows a consumer to pay in advance for a specified amount of confinement facility communications services.

"(O) PRISON.—The term 'prison'—

"(i) means a facility operated by a State or Federal agency that is used primarily to confine individuals convicted of felonies and sentenced to terms in excess of one year; and

"(ii) includes—

"(I) public and private facilities that provide outsource housing to State or Federal agencies such as State Departments of Correction and the Federal Bureau of Prisons; and

"(II) facilities that would otherwise be jails but in which the majority of incarcerated persons are post-conviction or are committed to confinement for sentences of longer than one year.

"(P) PROVIDER OF CONFINEMENT FACILITY COMMUNICATIONS SERVICES.—The term 'provider of confinement facility communications services' means any communications service provider that provides confinement facility communications services, regardless of the technology used.

"(Q) SITE COMMISSION.—The term 'site commission' means any monetary payment, in-kind payment, gift, exchange of services or goods, fee, technology allowance, or product that a provider of confinement facility communications services or an affiliate of a provider of confinement facility communications services may pay, give, donate, or otherwise provide to—

"(i) an entity that operates a confinement facility;

"(ii) an entity with which the provider of confinement facility communications services enters into an agreement to provide confinement facility communications services;

"(iii) a governmental agency that oversees a confinement facility;

"(iv) the State or political subdivision of a State where a confinement facility is located; or

"(v) an agent or other representative of an entity described in any of clauses (i) through (iv).

"(R) THIRD-PARTY FINANCIAL TRANSACTION FEE.—The term 'third-party financial transaction fee' means the exact fee, with no markup, that a provider of confinement facility communications services is charged by a third party to transfer money or process a financial transaction to facilitate the ability of a consumer to make an account payment via a third party.

"(S) VOICE SERVICE.—The term 'voice service'—

"(i) means any service that is interconnected with the public switched telephone network and that furnishes voice communications to an end user using resources from the North American Numbering Plan or any successor to the North American Numbering Plan adopted by the Commission under section 251(e)(1); and

"(ii) includes—

"(I) transmissions from a telephone facsimile machine, computer, or other device to a telephone facsimile machine; and

"(II) without limitation, any service that enables real-time, two-way voice communications, including any service that requires internet protocol-compatible customer premises equipment (commonly known as 'CPE') and permits out-bound calling, whether or not the service is one-way or two-way voice over internet protocol.".

(b) Conforming Amendment.—Section 276(d) of the Communications Act of 1934 (47 U.S.C. 276(d)) is amended by striking "inmate telephone service in correctional institutions" and inserting "confinement facility communications services (as defined in subsection (e)(7))".

(c) Existing Contracts.—

(1) IN GENERAL.—In the case of a contract that was entered into and under which a provider of confinement facility communications services was providing such services at a confinement facility on or before the date of the enactment of this Act—

(A) paragraphs (1) through (5) of subsection (e) of section 276 of the Communications Act of 1934, as added by subsection (a) of this section, shall apply to the provision of confinement facility communications services by such provider at such facility beginning on the earlier of—

(i) the date that is 60 days after such date of enactment; or

(ii) the date of the termination of the contract; and

(B) the terms of such contract may not be extended after such date of enactment, whether by exercise of an option or otherwise.

(2) DEFINITIONS.—In this subsection, the terms "confinement facility", "confinement facility communications service", and "provider of confinement facility communications services" have the meanings given such terms in paragraph (7) of subsection (e) of section 276 of the Communications Act of 1934, as added by subsection (a) of this section.

SEC. 130703. AUTHORITY.

Section 2(b) of the Communications Act of 1934 (47 U.S.C. 152(b)) is amended by inserting "section 276," after "227, inclusive,".

TITLE VIII—HEALTHCARE BROADBAND EXPANSION DURING COVID–19

SEC. 130801. EXPANSION OF RURAL HEALTH CARE PROGRAM OF FCC IN RESPONSE TO COVID–19.

(a) Promulgation Of Regulations Required.—Not later than 7 days after the date of the enactment of this Act, the Commission shall promulgate regulations modifying the requirements in subpart G of part 54 of title 47, Code of Federal Regulations, in the following manner:

(1) A health care provider not located in a rural area shall be treated as a rural health care provider for the purposes of the Healthcare Connect Fund Program.

(2) The discount rate for an eligible expense through the Healthcare Connect Fund Program (as described in section 54.611(a) of title 47, Code of Federal Regulations, or any successor regulation) shall be increased to 85 percent in funding years 2019, 2020, and 2021 for eligible equipment purchased or eligible services rendered in such funding years (including for eligible equipment, upfront payments, and multi-year commitments without limitation).

(3) A temporary, mobile, or satellite health care delivery site shall be treated as a health care provider or an eligible site of a health care provider for purposes of determining eligibility for the Healthcare Connect Fund Program or the Telecommunications Program.

(4) The waiver of the application window specified in section 54.621(a) of title 47, Code of Federal Regulations (or any successor regulation), for funding year 2019.

(5) The adoption and implementation of a rolling application process to allow a health care provider to apply for funding.

(6) The following changes to certain bidding requirements:

(A) A waiver of any requirement under section 54.622 of title 47, Code of Federal Regulations (or any successor regulation), for a health care provider upgrading an existing supported service at a particular location, effective as of the date of declaration of the public health emergency pursuant to section 319 of the Public Health Service Act (42 U.S.C. 247d) as a result of confirmed cases of COVID–19, if the health care provider maintains the same eligible service provider to provide the upgraded service at such location.

(B) Reduction of the 28-day waiting period described in section 54.622(g) of title 47, Code of Federal Regulations (or any successor regulation), to a 14-day waiting period.

(C) Modification of the requirements in section 54.622 of title 47, Code of Federal Regulations (or any successor regulation), to—

(i) provide that bid evaluation criteria may give additional consideration to the speed with which an eligible service provider can initiate service; and

(ii) encourage applicants to consider bids from different providers to provide service to different locations of such applicants, if considering bids in this manner would expedite the overall timeline for initiating or expanding service to individual locations.

(7) Issuance of a decision on each application for funding not later than 60 days after the date on which the application is filed.

(8) Release of funding not later than 30 days after the date on which an invoice is submitted with respect to an application that is approved, applicable services have been provided, and required invoices have been submitted as required under program rules.

(b) Additional Changes To Rural Health Care Program.—

(1) RELEASE OF FUNDING FOR OUTSTANDING FUNDING REQUESTS.—

(A) IN GENERAL.—The Commission shall ensure the release of funding for all requests (outstanding as of the date of the enactment of this Act) under the Rural Health Care Program not later than 60 days after the date of the enactment of this Act, except that for outstanding funding requests that are subject to a review of the applicable urban and rural rates, the Commission shall ensure the release of interim funding not later than 60 days after the date of the enactment of this Act, disbursed at 65 percent of the funding request, subject to a true-up following the completion of such review.

(B) LIMITATION.—This paragraph shall not apply to any party or successor-in-interest to any party to which the Commission, during the period beginning on the date that is 1 year before the date of the enactment of this Act and ending on January 31, 2020, has issued a Letter of Inquiry, Notice of Apparent Liability, or Forfeiture Order relating to the party's participation in the Rural Health Care Program, pursuant to section 503(b) of the Communications Act of 1934 (47 U.S.C. 503(b)).

(C) REQUIRED REPAYMENT.—In the case of an eligible service provider that receives funding through the Rural Health Care Program pursuant to this paragraph to which such provider is not entitled, the Commission shall require such provider to repay such funds.

(2) DELAY OF IMPLEMENTATION SCHEDULE.—The Commission shall—

(A) delay by one year the implementation of sections 54.604 and 54.605 of title 47, Code of Federal Regulations (or any successor regulation), as adopted in the Report and Order in the matter of Promoting Telehealth in Rural America (FCC 19–78) that was adopted by the Commission on August 1, 2019; and

(B) delay application of the new definition of "similar services" as described in paragraphs 14 to 20 of such Report and Order until the implementation of such sections.

(c) Effective Date Of Regulations.—The regulations required under subsection (a) shall take effect on the date on which such regulations are promulgated.

(d) Termination Of Regulations.—Except to the extent that the Commission determines that some or all of the regulations promulgated under subsection (a) should remain in effect (excluding any regulation promulgated under paragraph (1) of such subsection), such regulations shall terminate on the later of—

(1) the earlier of—

(A) the date that is 60 days after the termination of the declaration, or any renewal thereof, of the public health emergency pursuant to section 319 of the Public Health Service Act (42 U.S.C. 247d) as a result of confirmed cases of COVID–19; and

(B) the date of the expiration of the appropriation in subsection (f)(2); and

(2) the date that is 9 months after the date of the enactment of this Act.

(e) Exemptions.—

(1) NOTICE AND COMMENT RULEMAKING REQUIREMENTS.—Subsections (b), (c), and (d) of section 553 of title 5, United States Code, shall not apply to a regulation promulgated under subsection (a) or a rulemaking to promulgate such a regulation.

(2) PAPERWORK REDUCTION ACT REQUIREMENTS.—A collection of information conducted or sponsored under the regulations required by subsection (a), or under section 254 of the Communications Act of 1934 (47 U.S.C. 254) in connection with universal service support provided under such regulations, shall not constitute a collection of information for the purposes of subchapter I of chapter 35 of title 44, United States Code (commonly referred to as the Paperwork Reduction Act).

(f) Emergency Rural Health Care Connectivity Fund.—

(1) ESTABLISHMENT.—There is established in the Treasury of the United States a fund to be known as the Emergency Rural Health Care Connectivity Fund.

(2) AUTHORIZATION OF APPROPRIATIONS.—There is authorized to be appropriated to the Emergency Rural Health Care Connectivity Fund $2,000,000,000 for fiscal year 2020, to remain available through fiscal year 2022.

(3) USE OF FUNDS.—Amounts in the Emergency Rural Health Care Connectivity Fund shall be available to the Commission to carry out the Rural Health Care Program, as modified by the regulations promulgated under subsection (a).

(4) RELATIONSHIP TO UNIVERSAL SERVICE CONTRIBUTIONS.—Support provided under the regulations required by paragraphs (1) through (3) of subsection (a) shall be provided from amounts made available under paragraph (3) of this subsection and not from contributions under section 254(d) of the Communications Act of 1934 (47 U.S.C. 254(d)). Such support shall be in addition to, and not in replacement of, funds authorized by the Commission for the Rural Health Care Program as of the date of the enactment of this Act from contributions under section 254(d) of the Communications Act of 1934 (47 U.S.C. 254(d)).

(g) Definitions.—In this section:

(1) COMMISSION.—The term "Commission" means the Federal Communications Commission.

(2) ELIGIBLE EQUIPMENT.—The term "eligible equipment" means the equipment described in section 54.613 of title 47, Code of Federal Regulations (or any successor regulation).

(3) ELIGIBLE SERVICE PROVIDER.—The term "eligible service provider" means a provider described in section 54.608 of title 47, Code of Federal Regulations (or any successor regulation).

(4) FUNDING YEAR.—The term "funding year" has the meaning given such term in section 54.600(a) of title 47, Code of Federal Regulations (or any successor regulation).

(5) HEALTH CARE PROVIDER.—The term "health care provider" has the meaning given such term in section 54.600(b) of title 47, Code of Federal Regulations (or any successor regulation).

(6) HEALTHCARE CONNECT FUND PROGRAM.—The term "Healthcare Connect Fund Program" has the meaning given such term in section 54.602(b) of title 47, Code of Federal Regulations (or any successor regulation).

(7) MULTI-YEAR COMMITMENTS.—The term "multi-year commitments" means the commitments described in section 54.620(c) of title 47, Code of Federal Regulations (or any successor regulation).

(8) RURAL AREA.—The term "rural area" has the meaning given such term in section 54.600(e) of title 47, Code of Federal Regulations (or any successor regulation).

(9) RURAL HEALTH CARE PROGRAM.—The term "Rural Health Care Program" means the program described in subpart G of part 54 of title 47, Code of Federal Regulations (or any successor regulation).

(10) RURAL HEALTH CARE PROVIDER.—The term "rural health care provider" has the meaning given such term in section 54.600(f) of title 47, Code of Federal Regulations (or any successor regulation).

(11) TELECOMMUNICATIONS PROGRAM.—The term "Telecommunications Program" has the meaning given such term in section 54.602(a) of title 47, Code of Federal Regulations (or any successor regulation).

(12) UPFRONT PAYMENTS.—The term "upfront payments" means the payments described in section 54.616 of title 47, Code of Federal Regulations (or any successor regulation).

DIVISION N—GIVING RETIREMENT OPTIONS TO WORK-

ERS ACT

SEC. 140001. SHORT TITLE.
This division may be cited as the "Giving Retirement Options to Workers Act of 2020" or the "GROW Act".

SEC. 140002. COMPOSITE PLANS.
(a) Amendment To The Employee Retirement Income Security Act Of 1974.—
(1) IN GENERAL.—Title I of the Employee Retirement Income Security Act of 1974 (29 U.S.C. 1001 et seq.) is amended by adding at the end the following:
"PART 8—COMPOSITE PLANS AND LEGACY PLANS

"SEC. 801. COMPOSITE PLAN DEFINED.
"(a) In General.—For purposes of this Act, the term 'composite plan' means a pension plan—
"(1) which is a multiemployer plan that is neither a defined benefit plan nor a defined contribution plan;
"(2) the terms of which provide that the plan is a composite plan for purposes of this title with respect to which not more than one multiemployer defined benefit plan is treated as a legacy plan within the meaning of section 805, unless there is more than one legacy plan following a merger of composite plans under section 806;
"(3) which provides systematically for the payment of benefits—
"(A) objectively calculated pursuant to a formula enumerated in the plan document with respect to plan participants after retirement, for life; and
"(B) in the form of life annuities, except for benefits which under section 203(e) may be immediately distributed without the consent of the participant;
"(4) for which the plan contributions for the first plan year are at least 120 percent of the normal cost for the plan year;
"(5) which requires—
"(A) an annual valuation of the liability of the plan as of a date within the plan year to which the valuation refers or within one month prior to the beginning of such year;
"(B) an annual actuarial determination of the plan's current funded ratio and projected funded ratio under section 802(a);
"(C) corrective action through a realignment program pursuant to section 803 whenever the plan's projected funded ratio is below 120 percent for the plan year; and
"(D) an annual notification to each participant describing the participant's benefits under the plan and explaining that such benefits may be subject to reduction under a realignment program pursuant to section 803 based on the plan's funded status in future plan years; and
"(6) the board of trustees of which includes at least one retiree or beneficiary in pay status during each plan year following the first plan year in which at least 5 percent of the participants in the plan are retirees or beneficiaries in pay status.
"(b) Transition From A Multiemployer Defined Benefit Plan.—
"(1) IN GENERAL.—The plan sponsor of a defined benefit plan that is a multiemployer plan may, subject to paragraph (2), amend the plan to incorporate the features of a composite plan as a component of the multiemployer plan separate from the defined benefit plan component, except in the case of a defined benefit plan for which the plan actuary has certified under section 305(b)(3) that the plan is or will be in critical status for the plan year in which such amendment would become effective or for any

of the succeeding 5 plan years.

"(2) REQUIREMENTS.—Any amendment pursuant to paragraph (1) to incorporate the features of a composite plan as a component of a multiemployer plan shall—

"(A) apply with respect to all collective bargaining agreements providing for contributions to the multiemployer plan on or after the effective date of the amendment;

"(B) apply with respect to all participants in the multiemployer plan for whom contributions are made to the multiemployer plan on or after the effective date of the amendment;

"(C) specify that the effective date of the amendment is—

"(i) the first day of a specified plan year following the date of the adoption of the amendment, except that the plan sponsor may alternatively provide for a separate effective date with respect to each collective bargaining agreement under which contributions to the multiemployer plan are required, which shall occur on the first day of the first plan year beginning after the termination, or if earlier, the re-opening, of each such agreement, or such earlier date as the parties to the agreement and the plan sponsor of the multiemployer plan shall agree to; and

"(ii) not later than the first day of the fifth plan year beginning on or after the date of the adoption of the amendment;

"(D) specify that, as of the amendment's effective date, no further benefits shall accrue under the defined benefit component of the multiemployer plan; and

"(E) specify that, as of the amendment's effective date, the plan sponsor of the multiemployer plan shall be the plan sponsor of both the composite plan component and the defined benefit plan component of the plan.

"(3) SPECIAL RULES.—If a multiemployer plan is amended pursuant to paragraph (1)—

"(A) the requirements of this title and title IV shall be applied to the composite plan component and the defined benefit plan component of the multiemployer plan as if each such component were maintained as a separate plan; and

"(B) the assets of the composite plan component and the defined benefit plan component of the plan shall be held in a single trust forming part of the plan under which the trust instrument expressly provides—

"(i) for separate accounts (and appropriate records) to be maintained to reflect the interest which each of the plan components has in the trust, including separate accounting for additions to the trust for the benefit of each plan component, disbursements made from each plan component's account in the trust, investment experience of the trust allocable to that account, and administrative expenses (whether direct expenses or shared expenses allocated proportionally), and permits, but does not require, the pooling of some or all of the assets of the two plan components for investment purposes; and

"(ii) that the assets of each of the two plan components shall be held, invested, reinvested, managed, administered and distributed for the exclusive benefit of the participants and beneficiaries of each such plan component, and in no event shall the assets of one of the plan components be available to pay benefits due under the other plan component.

"(4) NOT A TERMINATION EVENT.—Notwithstanding section 4041A, an amendment pursuant to paragraph (1) to incorporate the features of a composite plan as a component of a multiemployer plan does not constitute termination of the multiemployer plan.

"(5) NOTICE TO THE SECRETARY.—

"(A) NOTICE.—The plan sponsor of a composite plan shall provide notice to the Secretary of the intent to establish the composite plan (or, in the case of a composite plan incorporated as a component of a multiemployer plan as described in paragraph (1), the intent to amend the multiemployer plan to incorporate such composite plan) at least 30 days prior to the effective date of such establishment or amendment.

"(B) CERTIFICATION.—In the case of a composite plan incorporated as a component of a multiemployer plan as described in paragraph (1), such notice shall include a certification by the plan actuary under section 305(b)(3) that the effective date of the amendment occurs in a plan year for which the multiemployer plan is not in critical status for that plan year and any of the succeeding 5 plan years.

"(6) REFERENCES TO COMPOSITE PLAN COMPONENT.—As used in this part, the term 'composite plan' includes a composite plan component added to a defined benefit plan pursuant to paragraph (1).

"(7) RULE OF CONSTRUCTION.—Paragraph (2)(A) shall not be construed as preventing the plan sponsor of a multiemployer plan from adopting an amendment pursuant to paragraph (1) because some collective bargaining agreements are amended to cease any covered employer's obligation to contribute to the multiemployer plan before or after the plan amendment is effective. Paragraph (2)(B) shall not be construed as preventing the plan sponsor of a multiemployer plan from adopting an amendment pursuant to paragraph (1) because some participants cease to have contributions made to the multiemployer plan on their behalf before or after the plan amendment is effective.

"(c) Coordination With Funding Rules.—Except as otherwise provided in this title, sections 302, 304, and 305 shall not apply to a composite plan.

"(d) Treatment Of A Composite Plan.—For purposes of this Act (other than sections 302 and 4245), a composite plan shall be treated as if it were a defined benefit plan unless a different treatment is provided for under applicable law.

"SEC. 802. FUNDED RATIOS; ACTUARIAL ASSUMPTIONS.

"(a) Certification Of Funded Ratios.—

"(1) IN GENERAL.—Not later than the one-hundred twentieth day of each plan year of a composite plan, the plan actuary of the composite plan shall certify to the Secretary, the Secretary of the Treasury, and the plan sponsor the plan's current funded ratio and projected funded ratio for the plan year.

"(2) DETERMINATION OF CURRENT FUNDED RATIO AND PROJECTED FUNDED RATIO.—For purposes of this section:

"(A) CURRENT FUNDED RATIO.—The current funded ratio is the ratio (expressed as a percentage) of—

"(i) the value of the plan's assets as of the first day of the plan year; to

"(ii) the plan actuary's best estimate of the present value of the plan liabilities as of the first day of the plan year.

"(B) PROJECTED FUNDED RATIO.—The projected funded ratio is the current funded ratio projected to the first day of the fifteenth plan year following the plan year for which the determination is being made.

"(3) CONSIDERATION OF CONTRIBUTION RATE INCREASES.—For purposes of projections under this subsection, the plan sponsor may anticipate contribution rate increases beyond the term of the current collective bargaining agreement and any agreed-to supplements, up to a maximum of 2.5 percent per year, compounded annually, unless it would be unreasonable under the circumstances to assume that contributions would increase by that amount.

"(b) Actuarial Assumptions And Methods.—For purposes of this part:

"(1) IN GENERAL.—All costs, liabilities, rates of interest and other factors under the plan shall be determined for a plan year on the basis of actuarial assumptions and methods—

"(A) each of which is reasonable (taking into account the experience of the plan and reasonable expectations);

"(B) which, in combination, offer the actuary's best estimate of anticipated experience under the plan; and

"(C) with respect to which any change from the actuarial assumptions and methods used in the previous plan year shall be certified by the plan actuary and the actuarial rationale for such change provided in the annual report required by section 103.

"(2) FAIR MARKET VALUE OF ASSETS.—The value of the plan's assets shall be taken into account on the basis of their fair market value.

"(3) DETERMINATION OF NORMAL COST AND PLAN LIABILITIES.—A plan's normal cost and liabilities shall be based on the most recent actuarial valuation required under section 801(a)(5)(A) and the unit credit funding method.

"(4) TIME WHEN CERTAIN CONTRIBUTIONS DEEMED MADE.—Any contributions for a plan year made by an employer after the last day of such plan year, but not later than two and one-half months after such day, shall be deemed to have been made on such last day. For purposes of this paragraph, such two and one-half month period may be extended for not more than six months under regulations prescribed by the Secretary of the Treasury.

"(5) ADDITIONAL ACTUARIAL ASSUMPTIONS.—Except where otherwise provided in this part, the provisions of section 305(b)(3)(B) shall apply to any determination or projection under this part.

"SEC. 803. REALIGNMENT PROGRAM.

"(a) Realignment Program.—

"(1) ADOPTION.—In any case in which the plan actuary certifies under section 802(a) that the plan's projected funded ratio is below 120 percent for the plan year, the plan sponsor shall adopt a realignment program under paragraph (2) not later than 210 days after the due date of the certification required under such section 802(a). The plan sponsor shall adopt an updated realignment program for each succeeding plan year for which a certification described in the preceding sentence is made.

"(2) CONTENT OF REALIGNMENT PROGRAM.—

"(A) IN GENERAL.—A realignment program adopted under this paragraph is a written program which consists of all reasonable measures, including options or a range of options to be undertaken by the plan sponsor or proposed to the bargaining parties, formulated, based on reasonably anticipated experience and reasonable actuarial assumptions, to enable the plan to achieve a projected funded ratio of at least 120 percent for the following plan year.

"(B) INITIAL PROGRAM ELEMENTS.—Reasonable measures under a realignment program described in subparagraph (A) may include any of the following:

"(i) Proposed contribution increases.

"(ii) A reduction in the rate of future benefit accruals, so long as the resulting rate is not less than 1 percent of the contributions on which benefits are based as of the start of the plan year (or the equivalent standard accrual rate as described in section

305(e)(6)).

"(iii) A modification or elimination of adjustable benefits of participants that are not in pay status before the date of the notice required under subsection (b)(1).

"(iv) Any other lawfully available measures not specifically described in this subparagraph or subparagraph (C) or (D) that the plan sponsor determines are reasonable.

"(C) ADDITIONAL PROGRAM ELEMENTS.—If the plan sponsor has determined that all reasonable measures available under subparagraph (B) will not enable the plan to achieve a projected funded ratio of at least 120 percent for the following plan year, such reasonable measures may also include—

"(i) a reduction of accrued benefits that are not in pay status by the date of the notice required under subsection (b)(1); or

"(ii) a reduction of any benefits of participants that are in pay status before the date of the notice required under subsection (b)(1) other than core benefits as defined in paragraph (4).

"(D) ADDITIONAL REDUCTIONS.—In the case of a composite plan for which the plan sponsor has determined that all reasonable measures available under subparagraphs (B) and (C) will not enable the plan to achieve a projected funded ratio of at least 120 percent for the following plan year, such reasonable measures may also include—

"(i) a further reduction in the rate of future benefit accruals without regard to the limitation applicable under subparagraph (B)(ii); or

"(ii) a reduction of core benefits;

provided that such reductions shall be equitably distributed across the participant and beneficiary population, taking into account factors, with respect to participants and beneficiaries and their benefits, that may include one or more of the factors listed in subclauses (I) through (X) of section 305(e)(9)(D)(vi), to the extent necessary to enable the plan to achieve a projected funded ratio of at least 120 percent for the following plan year, or at the election of the plan sponsor, a projected funded ratio of at least 100 percent for the following plan year and a current funded ratio of at least 90 percent.

"(3) ADJUSTABLE BENEFIT DEFINED.—For purposes of this part, the term 'adjustable benefit' means—

"(A) benefits, rights, and features under the plan, including post-retirement death benefits, 60-month guarantees, disability benefits not yet in pay status, and similar benefits;

"(B) any early retirement benefit or retirement-type subsidy (within the meaning of section 204(g)(2)(A)) and any benefit payment option (other than the qualified joint and survivor annuity); and

"(C) benefit increases that were adopted (or, if later, took effect) less than 60 months before the first day such realignment program took effect.

"(4) CORE BENEFIT DEFINED.—For purposes of this part, the term 'core benefit' means a participant's accrued benefit payable in the normal form of an annuity commencing at normal retirement age, determined without regard to—

"(A) any early retirement benefits, retirement-type subsidies, or other benefits, rights, or features that may be associated with that benefit; and

"(B) any cost-of-living adjustments or benefit increases effective after the date of retirement.

"(5) COORDINATION WITH CONTRIBUTION INCREASES.—

"(A) IN GENERAL.—A realignment program may provide that some or all of the benefit modifications described in the program will only take effect if the bargaining parties fail to agree to specified levels of increases in contributions to the plan, effective as of specified dates.

"(B) INDEPENDENT BENEFIT MODIFICATIONS.—If a realignment program adopts any changes to the benefit formula that are independent of potential contribution increases, such changes shall take effect not later than 180 days after the first day of the first plan year that begins following the adoption of the realignment program.

"(C) CONDITIONAL BENEFIT MODIFICATIONS.—If a realignment program adopts any changes to the benefit formula that take effect only if the bargaining parties fail to agree to contribution increases, such changes shall take effect not later than the first day of the first plan year beginning after the third anniversary of the date of adoption of the realignment program.

"(D) REVOCATION OF CERTAIN BENEFIT MODIFICATIONS.—Benefit modifications described in subparagraph (C) may be revoked, in whole or in part, and retroactively or prospectively, when contributions to the plan are increased, as specified in the realignment program, including any amendments thereto. The preceding sentence shall not apply unless the contribution increases are to be effective not later than the fifth anniversary of the first day of the first plan year that begins after the adoption of the realignment program.

"(b) Notice.—

"(1) IN GENERAL.—In any case in which it is certified under section 802(a) that the projected funded ratio is less than 120 percent, the plan sponsor shall, not later than 30 days after the date of the certification, provide notification of the current and projected funded ratios to the participants and beneficiaries, the bargaining parties, and the Secretary. Such notice shall include—

"(A) an explanation that contribution rate increases or benefit reductions may be necessary;

"(B) a description of the types of benefits that might be reduced; and

"(C) an estimate of the contribution increases and benefit reductions that may be necessary to achieve a projected funded ratio of 120 percent.

"(2) NOTICE OF BENEFIT MODIFICATIONS.—

"(A) IN GENERAL.—No modifications may be made that reduce the rate of future benefit accrual or that reduce core benefits or adjustable benefits unless notice of such reduction has been given at least 180 days before the general effective date of such reduction for all participants and beneficiaries to—

"(i) plan participants and beneficiaries;

"(ii) each employer who has an obligation to contribute to the composite plan; and

"(iii) each employee organization which, for purposes of collective bargaining, represents plan participants employed by such employers.

"(B) CONTENT OF NOTICE.—The notice under subparagraph (A) shall contain—

"(i) sufficient information to enable participants and beneficiaries to understand the effect of any reduction on their benefits, including an illustration of any affected benefit or subsidy, on an annual or monthly basis that a participant or beneficiary would otherwise have been eligible for as of the general effective date described in subparagraph (A); and

"(ii) information as to the rights and remedies of plan participants and beneficiaries as well as how to contact the Department of Labor for further information and assistance, where appropriate.

"(C) FORM AND MANNER.—Any notice under subparagraph (A)—

"(i) shall be provided in a form and manner prescribed in regulations of the Secretary of Labor;

"(ii) shall be written in a manner so as to be understood by the average plan participant.

"(3) MODEL NOTICES.—The Secretary shall—

"(A) prescribe model notices that the plan sponsor of a composite plan may use to satisfy the notice requirements under this subsection; and

"(B) by regulation enumerate any details related to the elements listed in paragraph (1) that any notice under this subsection must include.

"(4) DELIVERY METHOD.—Any notice under this part shall be provided in writing and may also be provided in electronic form to the extent that the form is reasonably accessible to persons to whom the notice is provided.

"SEC. 804. LIMITATION ON INCREASING BENEFITS.

"(a) Level Of Current Funded Ratios.—Except as provided in subsections (c), (d), and (e), no plan amendment increasing benefits or establishing new benefits under a composite plan may be adopted for a plan year unless—

"(1) the plan's current funded ratio is at least 110 percent (without regard to the benefit increase or new benefits);

"(2) taking the benefit increase or new benefits into account, the current funded ratio is at least 100 percent and the projected funded ratio for the current plan year is at least 120 percent;

"(3) in any case in which, after taking the benefit increase or new benefits into account, the current funded ratio is less than 140 percent and the projected funded ratio is less than 140 percent, the benefit increase or new benefits are projected by the plan actuary to increase the present value of the plan's liabilities for the plan year by not more than 3 percent; and

"(4) expected contributions for the current plan year are at least 120 percent of normal cost for the plan year, determined using the unit credit funding method and treating the benefit increase or new benefits as in effect for the entire plan year.

"(b) Additional Requirements Where Core Benefits Reduced.—If a plan has been amended to reduce core benefits pursuant to a realignment program under section 803(a)(2)(D), such plan may not be subsequently amended to increase core benefits unless the amendment—

"(1) increases the level of future benefit payments only; and

"(2) provides for an equitable distribution of benefit increases across the participant and beneficiary population, taking into account the extent to which the benefits of participants were previously reduced pursuant to such realignment program.

"(c) Exception To Comply With Applicable Law.—Subsection (a) shall not apply in connection with a plan amendment if the amendment is required as a condition of qualification under part I of subchapter D of chapter 1 of the Internal Revenue Code of 1986 or to comply with other applicable law.

"(d) Exception Where Maximum Deductible Limit Applies.—Subsection (a) shall not apply in connection with a plan amendment if and to the extent that contributions to the composite plan would not be deductible for the plan year under section 404(a) (1)(E) of the Internal Revenue Code of 1986 if the plan amendment is not adopted.

"(e) Exception For Certain Benefit Modifications.—Subsection (a) shall not apply in connection with a plan amendment under section 803(a)(5)(C), regarding conditional benefit modifications.

"(f) Treatment Of Plan Amendments.—For purposes of this section—

"(1) if two or more plan amendments increasing benefits or establishing new benefits are adopted in a plan year, such amendments shall be treated as a single amendment adopted on the last day of the plan year;

"(2) all benefit increases and new benefits adopted in a single amendment are treated as a single benefit increase, irrespective of whether the increases and new benefits take effect in more than one plan year; and

"(3) increases in contributions or decreases in plan liabilities which are scheduled to take effect in future plan years may be taken into account in connection with a plan amendment if they have been agreed to in writing or otherwise formalized by the date the plan amendment is adopted.

"SEC. 805. COMPOSITE PLAN RESTRICTIONS TO PRESERVE LEGACY PLAN FUNDING.

"(a) Treatment As A Legacy Plan.—

"(1) IN GENERAL.—For purposes of this part and parts 2 and 3, a defined benefit plan shall be treated as a legacy plan with respect to the composite plan under which the employees who were eligible to accrue a benefit under the defined benefit plan become eligible to accrue a benefit under such composite plan.

"(2) COMPONENT PLANS.—In any case in which a defined benefit plan is amended to add a composite plan component pursuant to section 801(b), paragraph (1) shall be applied by substituting 'defined benefit component' for 'defined benefit plan' and 'composite plan component' for 'composite plan'.

"(3) ELIGIBLE TO ACCRUE A BENEFIT.—For purposes of paragraph (1), an employee is considered eligible to accrue a benefit under a composite plan as of the first day in which the employee completes an hour of service under a collective bargaining agreement that provides for contributions to and accruals under the composite plan in lieu of accruals under the legacy plan.

"(4) COLLECTIVE BARGAINING AGREEMENT.—As used in this part, the term 'collective bargaining agreement' includes any agreement under which an employer has an obligation to contribute to a plan.

"(5) OTHER TERMS.—Any term used in this part which is not defined in this part and which is also used in section 305 shall have the same meaning provided such term in such section.

"(b) Restrictions On Acceptance By Composite Plan Of Agreements And Contributions.—

"(1) IN GENERAL.—The plan sponsor of a composite plan shall not accept or recognize a collective bargaining agreement (or any modification to such agreement), and no contributions may be accepted and no benefits may be accrued or otherwise earned under the agreement—

"(A) in any case in which the plan actuary of any defined benefit plan that would be treated as a legacy plan with respect to such composite plan has certified under section 305(b)(3) that such defined benefit plan is or will be in critical status for the plan year in which such agreement would take effect or for any of the succeeding 5 plan years; and

"(B) unless the agreement requires each employer who is a party to such agreement, including employers whose employees are not participants in the legacy plan, to provide contributions to the legacy plan with respect to such composite plan in a manner that satisfies the transition contribution requirements of subsection (d).

"(2) NOTICE.—Not later than 30 days after a determination by a plan sponsor of a composite plan that an agreement fails to satisfy the requirements described in paragraph (1), the plan sponsor shall provide notification of such failure and the reasons for such determination—

"(A) to the parties to the agreement;

"(B) to active participants of the composite plan who have ceased to accrue or otherwise earn benefits with respect to service with an employer pursuant to paragraph (1); and

"(C) to the Secretary, the Secretary of the Treasury, and the Pension Benefit Guaranty Corporation.

"(3) LIMITATION ON RETROACTIVE EFFECT.—This subsection shall not apply to benefits accrued before the date on which notice is provided under paragraph (2).

"(c) Restriction On Accrual Of Benefits Under A Composite Plan.—

"(1) IN GENERAL.—In any case in which an employer, under a collective bargaining agreement entered into after the date of enactment of the Giving Retirement Options to Workers Act of 2020, ceases to have an obligation to contribute to a multiemployer defined benefit plan, no employees employed by the employer may accrue or otherwise earn benefits under any composite plan, with respect to service with that employer, for a 60-month period beginning on the date on which the employer entered into such collective bargaining agreement.

"(2) NOTICE OF CESSATION OF OBLIGATION.—Within 30 days of determining that an employer has ceased to have an obligation to contribute to a legacy plan with respect to employees employed by an employer that is or will be contributing to a composite plan with respect to service of such employees, the plan sponsor of the legacy plan shall notify the plan sponsor of the composite plan of that cessation.

"(3) NOTICE OF CESSATION OF ACCRUALS.—Not later than 30 days after determining that an employer has ceased to have an obligation to contribute to a legacy plan, the plan sponsor of the composite plan shall notify the bargaining parties, the active participants affected by the cessation of accruals, the Secretary, the Secretary of the Treasury, and the Pension Benefit Guaranty Corporation of the cessation of accruals, the period during which such cessation is in effect, and the reasons therefor.

"(4) LIMITATION ON RETROACTIVE EFFECT.—This subsection shall not apply to benefits accrued before the date on which notice is provided under paragraph (3).

"(d) Transition Contribution Requirements.—

"(1) IN GENERAL.—A collective bargaining agreement satisfies the transition contribution requirements of this subsection if the agreement—

"(A) authorizes payment of contributions to a legacy plan at a rate or rates equal to or greater than the transition contribution rate established by the legacy plan under paragraph (2); and

"(B) does not provide for—

"(i) a suspension of contributions to the legacy plan with respect to any period of service; or

"(ii) any new direct or indirect exclusion of younger or newly hired employees of the employer from being taken into account in determining contributions owed to the legacy plan.

"(2) TRANSITION CONTRIBUTION RATE.—

"(A) IN GENERAL.—The transition contribution rate for a plan year is the contribution rate that, as certified by the actuary of the legacy plan in accordance with the principles in section 305(b)(3)(B), is reasonably expected to be adequate—

"(i) to fund the normal cost for the plan year;

"(ii) to amortize the plan's unfunded liabilities in level annual installments over 25 years, beginning with the plan year in which the transition contribution rate is first established; and

"(iii) to amortize any subsequent changes in the legacy plan's unfunded liability due to experience gains or losses (including investment gains or losses, gains or losses due to contributions greater or less than the contributions made under the prior transition contribution rate, and other actuarial gains or losses), changes in actuarial assumptions, changes to the legacy plan's benefits, or changes in funding method over a period of 15 plan years beginning with the plan year in which such change in unfunded liability is incurred.

The transition contribution rate for any plan year may not be less than the transition contribution rate for the plan year in which such rate is first established.

"(B) MULTIPLE RATES.—If different rates of contribution are payable to the legacy plan by different employers or for different classes of employees, the certification shall specify a transition contribution rate for each such employer.

"(C) RATE APPLICABLE TO EMPLOYER.—

"(i) IN GENERAL.—Except as provided by clause (ii), the transition contribution rate applicable to an employer for a plan year is the rate in effect for the plan year of the legacy plan that commences on or after 180 days before the earlier of—

"(I) the effective date of the collective bargaining agreement pursuant to which the employer contributes to the legacy plan; or

"(II) 5 years after the last plan year for which the transition contribution rate applicable to the employer was established or updated.

"(ii) EXCEPTION.—The transition contribution rate applicable to an employer for the first plan year beginning on or after the commencement of the employer's obligation to contribute to the composite plan is the rate in effect for the plan year of the legacy plan that commences on or after 180 days before such first plan year.

"(D) EFFECT OF LEGACY PLAN FINANCIAL CIRCUMSTANCES.—If the plan actuary of the legacy plan has certified under section 305 that the plan is in endangered or critical status for a plan year, the transition contribution rate for the following plan year is the rate determined with respect to the employer under the legacy plan's funding improvement or rehabilitation plan under section 305, if greater than the rate otherwise determined, but in no event greater than 75 percent of the sum of the contribution rates applicable to the legacy plan and the composite plan for the plan year.

"(E) OTHER ACTUARIAL ASSUMPTIONS AND METHODS.—Except as provided in subparagraph (A), the determination of the transition contribution rate for a plan year shall be based on actuarial assumptions and methods consistent with the minimum funding determinations made under section 304 (or, if applicable, section 305) with respect to the legacy plan for the plan year.

"(F) ADJUSTMENTS IN RATE.—The plan sponsor of a legacy plan from time to time may adjust the transition contribution rate or rates applicable to an employer under this paragraph by increasing some rates and decreasing others if the actuary certifies that such adjusted rates in combination will produce projected contribution income for the plan year beginning on or after the date of certification that is not less than would be produced by the transition contribution rates in effect at the time of the certification.

"(G) NOTICE OF TRANSITION CONTRIBUTION RATE.—The plan sponsor of a legacy plan shall provide notice to the parties to collective bargaining agreements pursuant to which contributions are made to the legacy plan of changes to the transition contribution rate requirements at least 30 days before the beginning of the plan year for which the rate is effective.

"(H) NOTICE TO COMPOSITE PLAN SPONSOR.—Not later than 30 days after a determination by the plan sponsor of a legacy plan that a collective bargaining agreement provides for a rate of contributions that is below the transition contribution rate applicable to one or more employers that are parties to the collective bargaining agreement, the plan sponsor of the legacy plan shall notify the plan sponsor of any composite plan under which employees of such employer would otherwise be eligible to accrue a benefit.

"(3) CORRECTION PROCEDURES.—Pursuant to standards prescribed by the Secretary, the plan sponsor of a composite plan shall adopt rules and procedures that give the parties to the collective bargaining agreement notice of the failure of such agreement to satisfy the transition contribution requirements of this subsection, and a reasonable opportunity to correct such failure, not to exceed 180 days from the date of notice given under subsection (b)(2).

"(4) SUPPLEMENTAL CONTRIBUTIONS.—A collective bargaining agreement may provide for supplemental contributions to the legacy plan for a plan year in excess of the transition contribution rate determined under paragraph (2), regardless of whether the legacy plan is in endangered or critical status for such plan year.

"(e) Nonapplication Of Composite Plan Restrictions.—

"(1) IN GENERAL.—The provisions of subsections (a), (b), and (c) shall not apply with respect to a collective bargaining agreement, to the extent the agreement, or a predecessor agreement, provides or provided for contributions to a defined benefit plan that is a legacy plan, as of the first day of the first plan year following a plan year for which the plan actuary certifies that the plan is fully funded, has been fully funded for at least three out of the immediately preceding 5 plan years, and is projected to remain fully funded for at least the following 4 plan years.

"(2) DETERMINATION OF FULLY FUNDED.—A plan is fully funded for purposes of paragraph (1) if, as of the valuation date of the plan for a plan year, the value of the plan's assets equals or exceeds the present value of the plan's liabilities, determined in accordance with the rules prescribed by the Pension Benefit Guaranty Corporation under sections 4219(c)(1)(D) and 4281 for multiemployer plans terminating by mass withdrawal, as in effect for the date of the determination, except the plan's reasonable assumption regarding the starting date of benefits may be used.

"(3) OTHER APPLICABLE RULES.—Except as provided in paragraph (2), actuarial determinations and projections under this section shall be based on the rules in section 305(b)(3) and section 802(b).

"SEC. 806. MERGERS AND ASSET TRANSFERS OF COMPOSITE PLANS.

"(a) In General.—Assets and liabilities of a composite plan may only be merged with, or transferred to, another plan if—

"(1) the other plan is a composite plan;

"(2) the plan or plans resulting from the merger or transfer is a composite plan;

"(3) no participant's accrued benefit or adjustable benefit is lower immediately after the transaction than it was immediately before the transaction; and

"(4) the value of the assets transferred in the case of a transfer reasonably reflects the value of the amounts contributed with respect to the participants whose benefits are being transferred, adjusted for allocable distributions, investment gains and losses, and administrative expenses.

"(b) Legacy Plan.—

"(1) IN GENERAL.—After a merger or transfer involving a composite plan, the legacy plan with respect to an employer that is obligated to contribute to the resulting composite plan is the legacy plan that applied to that employer immediately before the merger or transfer.

"(2) MULTIPLE LEGACY PLANS.—If an employer is obligated to contribute to more than one legacy plan with respect to employees eligible to accrue benefits under more than one composite plan and there is a merger or transfer of such legacy plans, the transition contribution rate applicable to the legacy plan resulting from the merger or transfer with respect to that employer shall be determined in accordance with the provisions of section 805(d)(2)(B).".

(2) PENALTIES.—

(A) CIVIL ENFORCEMENT OF FAILURE TO COMPLY WITH REALIGNMENT PROGRAM.—Section 502(a) of such Act (29 U.S.C. 1132(a)) is amended—

(i) in paragraph (10), by striking "or" at the end;

(ii) in paragraph (11), by striking the period at the end and inserting "; or"; and

(iii) by adding at the end the following:

"(12) in the case of a composite plan required to adopt a realignment program under section 803, if the plan sponsor—

"(A) has not adopted a realignment program under that section by the deadline established in such section; or

"(B) fails to update or comply with the terms of the realignment program in accordance with the requirements of such section,

by the Secretary, by an employer that has an obligation to contribute with respect to the composite plan, or by an employee organization that represents active participants in the composite plan, for an order compelling the plan sponsor to adopt a realignment program, or to update or comply with the terms of the realignment program, in accordance with the requirements of such section and the realignment program.".

(B) CIVIL PENALTIES.—Section 502(c) of such Act (29 U.S.C. 1132(c)) is amended—

(i) by moving paragraphs (8), (10), and (12) each 2 ems to the left;

(ii) by redesignating paragraphs (9) through (12) as paragraphs (12) through (15), respectively; and

(iii) by inserting after paragraph (8) the following:

"(9) The Secretary may assess against any plan sponsor of a composite plan a civil penalty of not more than $1,100 per day for each violation by such sponsor—

"(A) of the requirement under section 802(a) on the plan actuary to certify the plan's current or projected funded ratio by the date specified in such subsection; or

"(B) of the requirement under section 803 to adopt a realignment program by the deadline established in that section and to comply with its terms.

"(10) (A) The Secretary may assess against any plan sponsor of a composite plan a civil penalty of not more than $100 per day for each violation by such sponsor of the requirement under section 803(b) to provide notice as described in such section, except that no penalty may be assessed in any case in which the plan sponsor exercised reasonable diligence to meet the requirements of such section and—

"(i) the plan sponsor did not know that the violation existed; or

"(ii) the plan sponsor provided such notice during the 30-day period beginning on the first date on which the plan sponsor knew, or in exercising reasonable due diligence should have known, that such violation existed.

"(B) In any case in which the plan sponsor exercised reasonable diligence to meet the requirements of section 803(b)—

"(i) the total penalty assessed under this paragraph against such sponsor for a plan year may not exceed $500,000; and

"(ii) the Secretary may waive part or all of such penalty to the extent that the payment of such penalty would be excessive or otherwise inequitable relative to the violation involved.

"(11) The Secretary may assess against any plan sponsor of a composite plan a civil penalty of not more than $100 per day for each violation by such sponsor of the notice requirements under sections 801(b)(5) and 805(b)(2).".

(3) CONFORMING AMENDMENT.—The table of contents in section 1 of such Act (29 U.S.C. 1001 note) is amended by inserting after the item relating to section 734 the following:

"PART 8—COMPOSITE PLANS AND LEGACY PLANS

"SEC. 801. Composite plan defined.

"SEC. 802. Funded ratios; actuarial assumptions.

"SEC. 803. Realignment program.

"SEC. 804. Limitation on increasing benefits.

"SEC. 805. Composite plan restrictions to preserve legacy plan funding.

"SEC. 806. Mergers and asset transfers of composite plans.".

(b) Amendment To The Internal Revenue Code Of 1986.—

(1) IN GENERAL.—Part III of subchapter D of chapter 1 of the Internal Revenue Code of 1986 is amended by adding at the end the following:

"Subpart C—Composite Plans And Legacy Plans

"SEC. 437. Composite plan defined.

"SEC. 438. Funded ratios; actuarial assumptions.

"SEC. 439. Realignment program.

"SEC. 440. Limitation on increasing benefits.

"SEC. 440A. Composite plan restrictions to preserve legacy plan funding.

"SEC. 440B. Mergers and asset transfers of composite plans.

"SEC. 437. COMPOSITE PLAN DEFINED.

"(a) In General.—For purposes of this title, the term 'composite plan' means a pension plan—

"(1) which is a multiemployer plan that is neither a defined benefit plan nor a defined contribution plan,

"(2) the terms of which provide that the plan is a composite plan for purposes of this title with respect to which not more than one multiemployer defined benefit plan is treated as a legacy plan within the meaning of section 440A, unless there is more than one legacy plan following a merger of composite plans under section 440B,

"(3) which provides systematically for the payment of benefits—

"(A) objectively calculated pursuant to a formula enumerated in the plan document with respect to plan participants after retirement, for life, and

"(B) in the form of life annuities, except for benefits which under section 411(a)(11) may be immediately distributed without the consent of the participant,

"(4) for which the plan contributions for the first plan year are at least 120 percent of the normal cost for the plan year,

"(5) which requires—

"(A) an annual valuation of the liability of the plan as of a date within the plan year to which the valuation refers or within one month prior to the beginning of such year,

"(B) an annual actuarial determination of the plan's current funded ratio and project-ed funded ratio under section 438(a),

"(C) corrective action through a realignment program pursuant to section 439 whenever the plan's projected funded ratio is below 120 percent for the plan year, and

"(D) an annual notification to each participant describing the participant's benefits under the plan and explaining that such benefits may be subject to reduction under a realignment program pursuant to section 439 based on the plan's funded status in future plan years, and

"(6) the board of trustees of which includes at least one retiree or beneficiary in pay status during each plan year following the first plan year in which at least 5 percent of the participants in the plan are retirees or beneficiaries in pay status.

"(b) Transition From A Multiemployer Defined Benefit Plan.—

"(1) IN GENERAL.—The plan sponsor of a defined benefit plan that is a multiemploy-er plan may, subject to paragraph (2), amend the plan to incorporate the features of a composite plan as a component of the multiemployer plan separate from the defined benefit plan component, except in the case of a defined benefit plan for which the plan actuary has certified under section 432(b)(3) that the plan is or will be in critical status for the plan year in which such amendment would become effective or for any of the succeeding 5 plan years.

"(2) REQUIREMENTS.—Any amendment pursuant to paragraph (1) to incorporate the features of a composite plan as a component of a multiemployer plan shall—

"(A) apply with respect to all collective bargaining agreements providing for contri-butions to the multiemployer plan on or after the effective date of the amendment,

"(B) apply with respect to all participants in the multiemployer plan for whom con-tributions are made to the multiemployer plan on or after the effective date of the amendment,

"(C) specify that the effective date of the amendment is—

"(i) the first day of a specified plan year following the date of the adoption of the amendment, except that the plan sponsor may alternatively provide for a separate effective date with respect to each collective bargaining agreement under which con-tributions to the multiemployer plan are required, which shall occur on the first day of the first plan year beginning after the termination, or if earlier, the re-opening, of each such agreement, or such earlier date as the parties to the agreement and the plan sponsor of the multiemployer plan shall agree to, and

"(ii) not later than the first day of the fifth plan year beginning on or after the date of the adoption of the amendment,

"(D) specify that, as of the amendment's effective date, no further benefits shall accrue under the defined benefit component of the multiemployer plan, and

"(E) specify that, as of the amendment's effective date, the plan sponsor of the multiemployer plan shall be the plan sponsor of both the composite plan component and the defined benefit plan component of the plan.

"(3) SPECIAL RULES.—If a multiemployer plan is amended pursuant to paragraph (1)—

"(A) the requirements of this title shall be applied to the composite plan component and the defined benefit plan component of the multiemployer plan as if each such component were maintained as a separate plan, and

"(B) the assets of the composite plan component and the defined benefit plan component of the plan shall be held in a single trust forming part of the plan under which the trust instrument expressly provides—

"(i) for separate accounts (and appropriate records) to be maintained to reflect the interest which each of the plan components has in the trust, including separate accounting for additions to the trust for the benefit of each plan component, disbursements made from each plan component's account in the trust, investment experience of the trust allocable to that account, and administrative expenses (whether direct expenses or shared expenses allocated proportionally), and permits, but does not require, the pooling of some or all of the assets of the two plan components for investment purposes, and

"(ii) that the assets of each of the two plan components shall be held, invested, reinvested, managed, administered and distributed for the exclusive benefit of the participants and beneficiaries of each such plan component, and in no event shall the assets of one of the plan components be available to pay benefits due under the other plan component.

"(4) NOT A TERMINATION EVENT.—Notwithstanding section 4041A of the Employee Retirement Income Security Act of 1974, an amendment pursuant to paragraph (1) to incorporate the features of a composite plan as a component of a multiemployer plan does not constitute termination of the multiemployer plan.

"(5) NOTICE TO THE SECRETARY.—

"(A) NOTICE.—The plan sponsor of a composite plan shall provide notice to the Secretary of the intent to establish the composite plan (or, in the case of a composite plan incorporated as a component of a multiemployer plan as described in paragraph (1), the intent to amend the multiemployer plan to incorporate such composite plan) at least 30 days prior to the effective date of such establishment or amendment.

"(B) CERTIFICATION.—In the case of a composite plan incorporated as a component of a multiemployer plan as described in paragraph (1), such notice shall include a certification by the plan actuary under section 432(b)(3) that the effective date of the amendment occurs in a plan year for which the multiemployer plan is not in critical status for that plan year and any of the succeeding 5 plan years.

"(6) REFERENCES TO COMPOSITE PLAN COMPONENT.—As used in this subpart, the term 'composite plan' includes a composite plan component added to a defined benefit plan pursuant to paragraph (1).

"(7) RULE OF CONSTRUCTION.—Paragraph (2)(A) shall not be construed as preventing the plan sponsor of a multiemployer plan from adopting an amendment pursuant to paragraph (1) because some collective bargaining agreements are amended to cease any covered employer's obligation to contribute to the multiemployer plan before or after the plan amendment is effective. Paragraph (2)(B) shall not be construed as preventing the plan sponsor of a multiemployer plan from adopting an amendment pursuant to paragraph (1) because some participants cease to have contributions made to the multiemployer plan on their behalf before or after the plan amendment is effective.

"(c) Coordination With Funding Rules.—Except as otherwise provided in this title, sections 412, 431, and 432 shall not apply to a composite plan.

"(d) Treatment Of A Composite Plan.—For purposes of this title (other than sections 412 and 418E), a composite plan shall be treated as if it were a defined benefit plan unless a different treatment is provided for under applicable law.

"SEC. 438. FUNDED RATIOS; ACTUARIAL ASSUMPTIONS.

"(a) Certification Of Funded Ratios.—

"(1) IN GENERAL.—Not later than the one-hundred twentieth day of each plan year of a composite plan, the plan actuary of the composite plan shall certify to the Secretary, the Secretary of Labor, and the plan sponsor the plan's current funded ratio and projected funded ratio for the plan year.

"(2) DETERMINATION OF CURRENT FUNDED RATIO AND PROJECTED FUNDED RATIO.—For purposes of this section—

"(A) CURRENT FUNDED RATIO.—The current funded ratio is the ratio (expressed as a percentage) of—

"(i) the value of the plan's assets as of the first day of the plan year, to

"(ii) the plan actuary's best estimate of the present value of the plan liabilities as of the first day of the plan year.

"(B) PROJECTED FUNDED RATIO.—The projected funded ratio is the current funded ratio projected to the first day of the fifteenth plan year following the plan year for which the determination is being made.

"(3) CONSIDERATION OF CONTRIBUTION RATE INCREASES.—For purposes of projections under this subsection, the plan sponsor may anticipate contribution rate increases beyond the term of the current collective bargaining agreement and any agreed-to supplements, up to a maximum of 2.5 percent per year, compounded annually, unless it would be unreasonable under the circumstances to assume that contributions would increase by that amount.

"(b) Actuarial Assumptions And Methods.—For purposes of this part—

"(1) IN GENERAL.—All costs, liabilities, rates of interest, and other factors under the plan shall be determined for a plan year on the basis of actuarial assumptions and methods—

"(A) each of which is reasonable (taking into account the experience of the plan and reasonable expectations),

"(B) which, in combination, offer the actuary's best estimate of anticipated experience under the plan, and

"(C) with respect to which any change from the actuarial assumptions and methods used in the previous plan year shall be certified by the plan actuary and the actuarial rationale for such change provided in the annual report required by section 6058.

"(2) FAIR MARKET VALUE OF ASSETS.—The value of the plan's assets shall be taken into account on the basis of their fair market value.

"(3) DETERMINATION OF NORMAL COST AND PLAN LIABILITIES.—A plan's normal cost and liabilities shall be based on the most recent actuarial valuation required under section 437(a)(5)(A) and the unit credit funding method.

"(4) TIME WHEN CERTAIN CONTRIBUTIONS DEEMED MADE.—Any contributions for a plan year made by an employer after the last day of such plan year, but not later than two and one-half months after such day, shall be deemed to have been made on such last day. For purposes of this paragraph, such two and one-half month period may be extended for not more than six months under regulations prescribed by the Secretary.

"(5) ADDITIONAL ACTUARIAL ASSUMPTIONS.—Except where otherwise provided in this subpart, the provisions of section 432(b)(3)(B) shall apply to any determination or projection under this subpart.

"SEC. 439. REALIGNMENT PROGRAM.

"(a) Realignment Program.—

"(1) ADOPTION.—In any case in which the plan actuary certifies under section 438(a) that the plan's projected funded ratio is below 120 percent for the plan year, the plan sponsor shall adopt a realignment program under paragraph (2) not later than 210 days after the due date of the certification required under section 438(a). The plan sponsor shall adopt an updated realignment program for each succeeding plan year for which a certification described in the preceding sentence is made.

"(2) CONTENT OF REALIGNMENT PROGRAM.—

"(A) IN GENERAL.—A realignment program adopted under this paragraph is a written program which consists of all reasonable measures, including options or a range of options to be undertaken by the plan sponsor or proposed to the bargaining parties, formulated, based on reasonably anticipated experience and reasonable actuarial assumptions, to enable the plan to achieve a projected funded ratio of at least 120 percent for the following plan year.

"(B) INITIAL PROGRAM ELEMENTS.—Reasonable measures under a realignment program described in subparagraph (A) may include any of the following:

"(i) Proposed contribution increases.

"(ii) A reduction in the rate of future benefit accruals, so long as the resulting rate shall not be less than 1 percent of the contributions on which benefits are based as of the start of the plan year (or the equivalent standard accrual rate as described in section 432(e)(6)).

"(iii) A modification or elimination of adjustable benefits of participants that are not in pay status before the date of the notice required under subsection (b)(1).

"(iv) Any other legally available measures not specifically described in this subparagraph or subparagraph (C) or (D) that the plan sponsor determines are reasonable.

"(C) ADDITIONAL PROGRAM ELEMENTS.—If the plan sponsor has determined that all reasonable measures available under subparagraph (B) will not enable the plan to achieve a projected funded ratio of at least 120 percent the following plan year, such reasonable measures may also include—

"(i) a reduction of accrued benefits that are not in pay status by the date of the notice required under subsection (b)(1), or

"(ii) a reduction of any benefits of participants that are in pay status before the date of the notice required under subsection (b)(1) other than core benefits as defined in paragraph (4).

"(D) ADDITIONAL REDUCTIONS.—In the case of a composite plan for which the plan sponsor has determined that all reasonable measures available under subparagraphs (B) and (C) will not enable the plan to achieve a projected funded ratio of at least 120 percent for the following plan year, such reasonable measures may also include—

"(i) a further reduction in the rate of future benefit accruals without regard to the limitation applicable under subparagraph (B)(ii), or

"(ii) a reduction of core benefits,

provided that such reductions shall be equitably distributed across the participant and beneficiary population, taking into account factors, with respect to participants and beneficiaries and their benefits, that may include one or more of the factors listed in subclauses (I) through (X) of section 432(e)(9)(D)(vi), to the extent necessary to enable the plan to achieve a projected funded ratio of at least 120 percent for the following plan year, or at the election of the plan sponsor, a projected funded ratio of at least 100 percent for the following plan year and a current funded ratio of at least 90 percent.

"(3) ADJUSTABLE BENEFIT DEFINED.—For purposes of this subpart, the term 'adjustable benefit' means—

"(A) benefits, rights, and features under the plan, including post-retirement death benefits, 60-month guarantees, disability benefits not yet in pay status, and similar benefits,

"(B) any early retirement benefit or retirement-type subsidy (within the meaning of section 411(d)(6)(B)(i)) and any benefit payment option (other than the qualified joint and survivor annuity), and

"(C) benefit increases that were adopted (or, if later, took effect) less than 60 months before the first day such realignment program took effect.

"(4) CORE BENEFIT DEFINED.—For purposes of this subpart, the term 'core benefit' means a participant's accrued benefit payable in the normal form of an annuity commencing at normal retirement age, determined without regard to—

"(A) any early retirement benefits, retirement-type subsidies, or other benefits, rights, or features that may be associated with that benefit, and

"(B) any cost-of-living adjustments or benefit increases effective after the date of retirement.

"(5) COORDINATION WITH CONTRIBUTION INCREASES.—

"(A) IN GENERAL.—A realignment program may provide that some or all of the benefit modifications described in the program will only take effect if the bargaining parties fail to agree to specified levels of increases in contributions to the plan, effective as of specified dates.

"(B) INDEPENDENT BENEFIT MODIFICATIONS.—If a realignment program adopts any changes to the benefit formula that are independent of potential contribution increases, such changes shall take effect not later than 180 days following the first day of the first plan year that begins following the adoption of the realignment program.

"(C) CONDITIONAL BENEFIT MODIFICATIONS.—If a realignment program adopts any changes to the benefit formula that take effect only if the bargaining parties fail to agree to contribution increases, such changes shall take effect not later than the first day of the first plan year beginning after the third anniversary of the date of adoption of the realignment program.

"(D) REVOCATION OF CERTAIN BENEFIT MODIFICATIONS.—Benefit modifications described in paragraph (3) may be revoked, in whole or in part, and retroactively or prospectively, when contributions to the plan are increased, as specified in the realignment program, including any amendments thereto. The preceding sentence shall not apply unless the contribution increases are to be effective not later than the fifth anniversary of the first day of the first plan year that begins after the adoption of the realignment program.

"(b) Notice.—

"(1) IN GENERAL.—In any case in which it is certified under section 438(a) that the projected funded ratio is less than 120 percent, the plan sponsor shall, not later than 30 days after the date of the certification, provide notification of the current and projected funded ratios to the participants and beneficiaries, the bargaining parties, and the Secretary. Such notice shall include—

"(A) an explanation that contribution rate increases or benefit reductions may be necessary,

"(B) a description of the types of benefits that might be reduced, and

"(C) an estimate of the contribution increases and benefit reductions that may be necessary to achieve a projected funded ratio of 120 percent.

"(2) NOTICE OF BENEFIT MODIFICATIONS.—

"(A) IN GENERAL.—No modifications may be made that reduce the rate of future benefit accrual or that reduce core benefits or adjustable benefits unless notice of such reduction has been given at least 180 days before the general effective date of such reduction for all participants and beneficiaries to—

"(i) plan participants and beneficiaries,

"(ii) each employer who has an obligation to contribute to the composite plan, and

"(iii) each employee organization which, for purposes of collective bargaining, represents plan participants employed by such employers.

"(B) CONTENT OF NOTICE.—The notice under subparagraph (A) shall contain—

"(i) sufficient information to enable participants and beneficiaries to understand the effect of any reduction on their benefits, including an illustration of any affected benefit or subsidy, on an annual or monthly basis that a participant or beneficiary would otherwise have been eligible for as of the general effective date described in subparagraph (A), and

"(ii) information as to the rights and remedies of plan participants and beneficiaries as well as how to contact the Department of Labor for further information and assistance, where appropriate.

"(C) FORM AND MANNER.—Any notice under subparagraph (A)—

"(i) shall be provided in a form and manner prescribed in regulations of the Secretary of Labor,

"(ii) shall be written in a manner so as to be understood by the average plan participant.

"(3) MODEL NOTICES.—The Secretary shall—

"(A) prescribe model notices that the plan sponsor of a composite plan may use to satisfy the notice requirements under this subsection, and

"(B) by regulation enumerate any details related to the elements listed in paragraph (1) that any notice under this subsection must include.

"(4) DELIVERY METHOD.—Any notice under this part shall be provided in writing and may also be provided in electronic form to the extent that the form is reasonably accessible to persons to whom the notice is provided.

"SEC. 440. LIMITATION ON INCREASING BENEFITS.

"(a) Level Of Current Funded Ratios.—Except as provided in subsections (c), (d), and (e), no plan amendment increasing benefits or establishing new benefits under a composite plan may be adopted for a plan year unless—

"(1) the plan's current funded ratio is at least 110 percent (without regard to the benefit increase or new benefits),

"(2) taking the benefit increase or new benefits into account, the current funded ratio is at least 100 percent and the projected funded ratio for the current plan year is at least 120 percent,

"(3) in any case in which, after taking the benefit increase or new benefits into account, the current funded ratio is less than 140 percent or the projected funded ratio is less than 140 percent, the benefit increase or new benefits are projected by the plan actuary to increase the present value of the plan's liabilities for the plan year by not more than 3 percent, and

"(4) expected contributions for the current plan year are at least 120 percent of normal cost for the plan year, determined using the unit credit funding method and treating the benefit increase or new benefits as in effect for the entire plan year.

"(b) Additional Requirements Where Core Benefits Reduced.—If a plan has been amended to reduce core benefits pursuant to a realignment program under section 439(a)(2)(D), such plan may not be subsequently amended to increase core benefits unless the amendment—

"(1) increases the level of future benefit payments only, and

"(2) provides for an equitable distribution of benefit increases across the participant and beneficiary population, taking into account the extent to which the benefits of participants were previously reduced pursuant to such realignment program.

"(c) Exception To Comply With Applicable Law.—Subsection (a) shall not apply in connection with a plan amendment if the amendment is required as a condition of qualification under part I of subchapter D of chapter 1 or to comply with other applicable law.

"(d) Exception Where Maximum Deductible Limit Applies.—Subsection (a) shall not apply in connection with a plan amendment if and to the extent that contributions to the composite plan would not be deductible for the plan year under section 404(a)(1) (E) if the plan amendment is not adopted. The Secretary of the Treasury shall issue regulations to implement this paragraph.

"(e) Exception For Certain Benefit Modifications.—Subsection (a) shall not apply in connection with a plan amendment under section 439(a)(5)(C), regarding conditional benefit modifications.

"(f) Treatment Of Plan Amendments.—For purposes of this section—

"(1) if two or more plan amendments increasing benefits or establishing new benefits are adopted in a plan year, such amendments shall be treated as a single amendment adopted on the last day of the plan year,

"(2) all benefit increases and new benefits adopted in a single amendment are treated as a single benefit increase, irrespective of whether the increases and new benefits take effect in more than one plan year, and

"(3) increases in contributions or decreases in plan liabilities which are scheduled to take effect in future plan years may be taken into account in connection with a plan amendment if they have been agreed to in writing or otherwise formalized by the date the plan amendment is adopted.

"SEC. 440A. COMPOSITE PLAN RESTRICTIONS TO PRESERVE LEGACY PLAN FUNDING.

"(a) Treatment As A Legacy Plan.—

"(1) IN GENERAL.—For purposes of this subchapter, a defined benefit plan shall be treated as a legacy plan with respect to the composite plan under which the employees who were eligible to accrue a benefit under the defined benefit plan become eligible to accrue a benefit under such composite plan.

"(2) COMPONENT PLANS.—In any case in which a defined benefit plan is amended to add a composite plan component pursuant to section 437(b), paragraph (1) shall be applied by substituting 'defined benefit component' for 'defined benefit plan' and 'composite plan component' for 'composite plan'.

"(3) ELIGIBLE TO ACCRUE A BENEFIT.—For purposes of paragraph (1), an employee is considered eligible to accrue a benefit under a composite plan as of the first day in which the employee completes an hour of service under a collective bargaining agreement that provides for contributions to and accruals under the composite plan in lieu of accruals under the legacy plan.

"(4) COLLECTIVE BARGAINING AGREEMENT.—As used in this subpart, the term 'collective bargaining agreement' includes any agreement under which an employer has an obligation to contribute to a plan.

"(5) OTHER TERMS.—Any term used in this subpart which is not defined in this part and which is also used in section 432 shall have the same meaning provided such term in such section.

"(b) Restrictions On Acceptance By Composite Plan Of Agreements And Contributions.—

"(1) IN GENERAL.—The plan sponsor of a composite plan shall not accept or recognize a collective bargaining agreement (or any modification to such agreement), and no contributions may be accepted and no benefits may be accrued or otherwise earned under the agreement—

"(A) in any case in which the plan actuary of any defined benefit plan that would be treated as a legacy plan with respect to such composite plan has certified under section 432(b)(3) that such defined benefit plan is or will be in critical status for the plan year in which such agreement would take effect or for any of the succeeding 5 plan years, and

"(B) unless the agreement requires each employer who is a party to such agreement, including employers whose employees are not participants in the legacy plan, to provide contributions to the legacy plan with respect to such composite plan in a manner that satisfies the transition contribution requirements of subsection (d).

"(2) NOTICE.—Not later than 30 days after a determination by a plan sponsor of a composite plan that an agreement fails to satisfy the requirements described in paragraph (1), the plan sponsor shall provide notification of such failure and the reasons for such determination to—

"(A) the parties to the agreement,

"(B) active participants of the composite plan who have ceased to accrue or otherwise earn benefits with respect to service with an employer pursuant to paragraph (1), and

"(C) the Secretary of Labor, the Secretary of the Treasury, and the Pension Benefit Guaranty Corporation.

"(3) LIMITATION ON RETROACTIVE EFFECT.—This subsection shall not apply to benefits accrued before the date on which notice is provided under paragraph (2).

"(c) Restriction On Accrual Of Benefits Under A Composite Plan.—

"(1) IN GENERAL.—In any case in which an employer, under a collective bargaining agreement entered into after the date of enactment of the Giving Retirement Options to Workers Act of 2020, ceases to have an obligation to contribute to a multiemployer defined benefit plan, no employees employed by the employer may accrue or otherwise earn benefits under any composite plan, with respect to service with that employer, for a 60-month period beginning on the date on which the employer entered into such collective bargaining agreement.

"(2) NOTICE OF CESSATION OF OBLIGATION.—Within 30 days of determining that an employer has ceased to have an obligation to contribute to a legacy plan with respect to employees employed by an employer that is or will be contributing to a composite plan with respect to service of such employees, the plan sponsor of the legacy plan shall notify the plan sponsor of the composite plan of that cessation.

"(3) NOTICE OF CESSATION OF ACCRUALS.—Not later than 30 days after determining that an employer has ceased to have an obligation to contribute to a legacy plan, the plan sponsor of the composite plan shall notify the bargaining parties, the active participants affected by the cessation of accruals, the Secretary, the Secretary of Labor, and the Pension Benefit Guaranty Corporation of the cessation of accruals, the period during which such cessation is in effect, and the reasons therefor.

"(4) LIMITATION ON RETROACTIVE EFFECT.—This subsection shall not apply to benefits accrued before the date on which notice is provided under paragraph (3).

"(d) Transition Contribution Requirements.—

"(1) IN GENERAL.—A collective bargaining agreement satisfies the transition contribution requirements of this subsection if the agreement—

"(A) authorizes for payment of contributions to a legacy plan at a rate or rates equal to or greater than the transition contribution rate established under paragraph (2), and

"(B) does not provide for—

"(i) a suspension of contributions to the legacy plan with respect to any period of service, or

"(ii) any new direct or indirect exclusion of younger or newly hired employees of the employer from being taken into account in determining contributions owed to the legacy plan.

"(2) TRANSITION CONTRIBUTION RATE.—

"(A) IN GENERAL.—The transition contribution rate for a plan year is the contribution rate that, as certified by the actuary of the legacy plan in accordance with the principles in section 432(b)(3)(B), is reasonably expected to be adequate—

"(i) to fund the normal cost for the plan year,

"(ii) to amortize the plan's unfunded liabilities in level annual installments over 25 years, beginning with the plan year in which the transition contribution rate is first established, and

"(iii) to amortize any subsequent changes in the legacy plan's unfunded liability due to experience gains or losses (including investment gains or losses, gains or losses due to contributions greater or less than the contributions made under the prior transition contribution rate, and other actuarial gains or losses), changes in actuarial assumptions, changes to the legacy plan's benefits, or changes in funding method over a period of 15 plan years beginning with the plan year in which such change in unfunded liability is incurred.

The transition contribution rate for any plan year may not be less than the transition contribution rate for the plan year in which such rate is first established.

"(B) MULTIPLE RATES.—If different rates of contribution are payable to the legacy plan by different employers or for different classes of employees, the certification shall specify a transition contribution rate for each such employer.

"(C) RATE APPLICABLE TO EMPLOYER.—

"(i) IN GENERAL.—Except as provided by clause (ii), the transition contribution rate applicable to an employer for a plan year is the rate in effect for the plan year of the legacy plan that commences on or after 180 days before the earlier of—

"(I) the effective date of the collective bargaining agreement pursuant to which the employer contributes to the legacy plan, or

"(II) 5 years after the last plan year for which the transition contribution rate applicable to the employer was established or updated.

"(ii) EXCEPTION.—The transition contribution rate applicable to an employer for the first plan year beginning on or after the commencement of the employer's obligation to contribute to the composite plan is the rate in effect for the plan year of the legacy plan that commences on or after 180 days before such first plan year.

"(D) EFFECT OF LEGACY PLAN FINANCIAL CIRCUMSTANCES.—If the plan actuary of the legacy plan has certified under section 432 that the plan is in endangered or critical status for a plan year, the transition contribution rate for the following plan year is the rate determined with respect to the employer under the legacy plan's funding improvement or rehabilitation plan under section 432, if greater than the rate otherwise determined, but in no event greater than 75 percent of the sum of the contribution rates applicable to the legacy plan and the composite plan for the plan year.

"(E) OTHER ACTUARIAL ASSUMPTIONS AND METHODS.—Except as provided in subparagraph (A), the determination of the transition contribution rate for a plan year shall be based on actuarial assumptions and methods consistent with the minimum funding determinations made under section 431 (or, if applicable, section 432) with respect to the legacy plan for the plan year.

"(F) ADJUSTMENTS IN RATE.—The plan sponsor of a legacy plan from time to time may adjust the transition contribution rate or rates applicable to an employer under this paragraph by increasing some rates and decreasing others if the actuary certifies that such adjusted rates in combination will produce projected contribution income for the plan year beginning on or after the date of certification that is not less than would be produced by the transition contribution rates in effect at the time of the certification.

"(G) NOTICE OF TRANSITION CONTRIBUTION RATE.—The plan sponsor of a legacy plan shall provide notice to the parties to collective bargaining agreements pursuant to which contributions are made to the legacy plan of changes to the transition contribution rate requirements at least 30 days before the beginning of the plan year for which the rate is effective.

"(H) NOTICE TO COMPOSITE PLAN SPONSOR.—Not later than 30 days after a determination by the plan sponsor of a legacy plan that a collective bargaining agreement provides for a rate of contributions that is below the transition contribution rate applicable to one or more employers that are parties to the collective bargaining agreement, the plan sponsor of the legacy plan shall notify the plan sponsor of any composite plan under which employees of such employer would otherwise be eligible to accrue a benefit.

"(3) CORRECTION PROCEDURES.—Pursuant to standards prescribed by the Secretary of Labor, the plan sponsor of a composite plan shall adopt rules and procedures that give the parties to the collective bargaining agreement notice of the failure of such agreement to satisfy the transition contribution requirements of this subsection, and a reasonable opportunity to correct such failure, not to exceed 180 days from the date of notice given under subsection (b)(2).

"(4) SUPPLEMENTAL CONTRIBUTIONS.—A collective bargaining agreement may provide for supplemental contributions to the legacy plan for a plan year in excess of the transition contribution rate determined under paragraph (2), regardless of whether the legacy plan is in endangered or critical status for such plan year.

"(e) Nonapplication Of Composite Plan Restrictions.—

"(1) IN GENERAL.—The provisions of subsections (a), (b), and (c) shall not apply with respect to a collective bargaining agreement, to the extent the agreement, or a predecessor agreement, provides or provided for contributions to a defined benefit plan that is a legacy plan, as of the first day of the first plan year following a plan year for which the plan actuary certifies that the plan is fully funded, has been fully funded for at least three out of the immediately preceding 5 plan years, and is projected to remain fully funded for at least the following 4 plan years.

"(2) DETERMINATION OF FULLY FUNDED.—A plan is fully funded for purposes of paragraph (1) if, as of the valuation date of the plan for a plan year, the value of the plan's assets equals or exceeds the present value of the plan's liabilities, determined in accordance with the rules prescribed by the Pension Benefit Guaranty Corporation under sections 4219(c)(1)(D) and 4281 of Employee Retirement Income and Security Act for multiemployer plans terminating by mass withdrawal, as in effect for the date of the determination, except the plan's reasonable assumption regarding the starting date of benefits may be used.

"(3) OTHER APPLICABLE RULES.—Except as provided in paragraph (2), actuarial determinations and projections under this section shall be based on the rules in section 432(b)(3) and section 438(b).

"SEC. 440B. MERGERS AND ASSET TRANSFERS OF COMPOSITE PLANS.

"(a) In General.—Assets and liabilities of a composite plan may only be merged with, or transferred to, another plan if—

"(1) the other plan is a composite plan,

"(2) the plan or plans resulting from the merger or transfer is a composite plan,

"(3) no participant's accrued benefit or adjustable benefit is lower immediately after the transaction than it was immediately before the transaction, and

"(4) the value of the assets transferred in the case of a transfer reasonably reflects the value of the amounts contributed with respect to the participants whose benefits are being transferred, adjusted for allocable distributions, investment gains and losses, and administrative expenses.

"(b) Legacy Plan.—

"(1) IN GENERAL.—After a merger or transfer involving a composite plan, the legacy plan with respect to an employer that is obligated to contribute to the resulting composite plan is the legacy plan that applied to that employer immediately before the merger or transfer.

"(2) MULTIPLE LEGACY PLANS.—If an employer is obligated to contribute to more than one legacy plan with respect to employees eligible to accrue benefits under more than one composite plan and there is a merger or transfer of such legacy plans, the transition contribution rate applicable to the legacy plan resulting from the merger or transfer with respect to that employer shall be determined in accordance with the provisions of section 440A(d)(2)(B).".

(2) CLERICAL AMENDMENT.—The table of subparts for part III of subchapter D

of chapter 1 of the Internal Revenue Code of 1986 is amended by adding at the end the following new item:
"SUBPART C. COMPOSITE PLANS AND LEGACY PLANS
(c) Effective Date.—The amendments made by this section shall apply to plan years beginning after the date of the enactment of this Act.

SEC. 140003. APPLICATION OF CERTAIN REQUIREMENTS TO COMPOSITE PLANS.

(a) Amendments To The Employee Retirement Income Security Act Of 1974.—
(1) TREATMENT FOR PURPOSES OF FUNDING NOTICES.—Section 101(f) of the Employee Retirement Income Security Act of 1974 (29 U.S.C. 1021(f)) is amended—
(A) in paragraph (1) by striking "title IV applies" and inserting "title IV applies or which is a composite plan"; and
(B) by adding at the end the following:
"(5) APPLICATION TO COMPOSITE PLANS.—The provisions of this subsection shall apply to a composite plan only to the extent prescribed by the Secretary in regulations that take into account the differences between a composite plan and a defined benefit plan that is a multiemployer plan.".
(2) TREATMENT FOR PURPOSES OF ANNUAL REPORT.—Section 103 of the Employee Retirement Income Security Act of 1974 (29 U.S.C. 1023) is amended—
(A) in subsection (d) by adding at the end the following sentence: "The provisions of this subsection shall apply to a composite plan only to the extent prescribed by the Secretary in regulations that take into account the differences between a composite plan and a defined benefit plan that is a multiemployer plan.";
(B) in subsection (f) by adding at the end the following:
"(3) ADDITIONAL INFORMATION FOR COMPOSITE PLANS.—With respect to any composite plan—
"(A) the provisions of paragraph (1)(A) shall apply by substituting 'current funded ratio and projected funded ratio (as such terms are defined in section 802(a)(2))' for 'funded percentage' each place it appears; and
"(B) the provisions of paragraph (2) shall apply only to the extent prescribed by the Secretary in regulations that take into account the differences between a composite plan and a defined benefit plan that is a multiemployer plan."; and
(C) by adding at the end the following:
"(h) Composite Plans.—A multiemployer plan that incorporates the features of a composite plan as provided in section 801(b) shall be treated as a single plan for purposes of the report required by this section, except that separate financial statements and actuarial statements shall be provided under paragraphs (3) and (4) of subsection (a) for the defined benefit plan component and for the composite plan component of the multiemployer plan.".
(3) TREATMENT FOR PURPOSES OF PENSION BENEFIT STATEMENTS.—Section 105(a) of the Employee Retirement Income Security Act of 1974 (29 U.S.C. 1025(a)) is amended by adding at the end the following:
"(4) COMPOSITE PLANS.—For purposes of this subsection, a composite plan shall be treated as a defined benefit plan to the extent prescribed by the Secretary in regulations that take into account the differences between a composite plan and a defined benefit plan that is a multiemployer plan.".
(b) Amendments To The Internal Revenue Code Of 1986.—Section 6058 of the Inter-

nal Revenue Code of 1986 is amended by redesignating subsection (f) as subsection (g) and by inserting after subsection (e) the following:

"(f) Composite Plans.—A multiemployer plan that incorporates the features of a composite plan as provided in section 437(b) shall be treated as a single plan for purposes of the return required by this section, except that separate financial statements shall be provided for the defined benefit plan component and for the composite plan component of the multiemployer plan.".

(c) Effective Date.—The amendments made by this section shall apply to plan years beginning after the date of the enactment of this Act.

SEC. 140004. TREATMENT OF COMPOSITE PLANS UNDER TITLE IV.

(a) Definition.—Section 4001(a) of the Employee Retirement Income Security Act of 1974 (29 U.S.C. 1301(a)) is amended by striking the period at the end of paragraph (21) and inserting a semicolon and by adding at the end the following:

"(22) COMPOSITE PLAN.—The term 'composite plan' has the meaning set forth in section 801.".

(b) Composite Plans Disregarded For Calculating Premiums.—Section 4006(a) of such Act (29 U.S.C. 1306(a)) is amended by adding at the end the following:

"(9) The composite plan component of a multiemployer plan shall be disregarded in determining the premiums due under this section from the multiemployer plan.".

(c) Composite Plans Not Covered.—Section 4021(b)(1) of such Act (29 U.S.C. 1321(b)(1)) is amended by striking "Act" and inserting "Act, or a composite plan, as defined in paragraph (43) of section 3 of this Act".

(d) No Withdrawal Liability.—Section 4201 of such Act (29 U.S.C. 1381) is amended by adding at the end the following:

"(c) Contributions by an employer to the composite plan component of a multiemployer plan shall not be taken into account for any purpose under this title.".

(e) No Withdrawal Liability For Certain Plans.—Section 4201 of such Act (29 U.S.C. 1381) is further amended by adding at the end the following:

"(d) Contributions by an employer to a multiemployer plan described in the except clause of section 3(35) of this Act pursuant to a collective bargaining agreement that specifically designates that such contributions shall be allocated to the separate defined contribution accounts of participants under the plan shall not be taken into account with respect to the defined benefit portion of the plan for any purpose under this title (including the determination of the employer's highest contribution rate under section 4219), even if, under the terms of the plan, participants have the option to transfer assets in their separate defined contribution accounts to the defined benefit portion of the plan in return for service credit under the defined benefit portion, at rates established by the plan sponsor.

"(e) A legacy plan created under section 805 shall be deemed to have no unfunded vested benefits for purposes of this part, for each plan year following a period of 5 consecutive plan years for which—

"(1) the plan was fully funded within the meaning of section 805 for at least 3 of the plan years during that period, ending with a plan year for which the plan is fully funded;

"(2) the plan had no unfunded vested benefits for at least 3 of the plan years during that period, ending with a plan year for which the plan is fully funded; and

"(3) the plan is projected to be fully funded and to have no unfunded vested benefits for the following four plan years.".

(f) No Withdrawal Liability For Employers Contributing To Certain Fully Funded Legacy Plans.—Section 4211 of such Act (29 U.S.C. 1382) is amended by adding at the end the following:

"(g) No amount of unfunded vested benefits shall be allocated to an employer that has an obligation to contribute to a legacy plan described in subsection (e) of section 4201 for each plan year for which such subsection applies.".

(g) No Obligation To Contribute.—Section 4212 of such Act (29 U.S.C. 1392) is amended by adding at the end the following:

"(d) No Obligation To Contribute.—An employer shall not be treated as having an obligation to contribute to a multiemployer defined benefit plan within the meaning of subsection (a) solely because—

"(1) in the case of a multiemployer plan that includes a composite plan component, the employer has an obligation to contribute to the composite plan component of the plan;

"(2) the employer has an obligation to contribute to a composite plan that is maintained pursuant to one or more collective bargaining agreements under which the multiemployer defined benefit plan is or previously was maintained; or

"(3) the employer contributes or has contributed under section 805(d) to a legacy plan associated with a composite plan pursuant to a collective bargaining agreement but employees of that employer were not eligible to accrue benefits under the legacy plan with respect to service with that employer.".

(h) No Inference.—Nothing in the amendment made by subsection (e) shall be construed to create an inference with respect to the treatment under title IV of the Employee Retirement Income Security Act of 1974, as in effect before such amendment, of contributions by an employer to a multiemployer plan described in the except clause of section 3(35) of such Act that are made before the effective date of subsection (e) specified in subsection (h)(2).

(i) Effective Date.—

(1) IN GENERAL.—Except as provided in subparagraph (2), the amendments made by this section shall apply to plan years beginning after the date of the enactment of this Act.

(2) SPECIAL RULE FOR SECTION 414(k) MULTIEMPLOYER PLANS.—The amendment made by subsection (e) shall apply only to required contributions payable for plan years beginning after the date of the enactment of this Act.

SEC. 140005. CONFORMING CHANGES.

(a) Definitions.—Section 3 of the Employee Retirement Income Security Act of 1974 (29 U.S.C. 1002) is amended—

(1) in paragraph (35), by inserting "or a composite plan" after "other than an individual account plan"; and

(2) by adding at the end the following:

"(43) The term 'composite plan' has the meaning given the term in section 801(a).".

(b) Special Funding Rule For Certain Legacy Plans.—

(1) AMENDMENT TO EMPLOYEE RETIREMENT INCOME SECURITY ACT OF 1974.—Section 304(b) of the Employee Retirement Income Security Act of 1974 (29 U.S.C. 1084(b)) is amended by adding at the end the following:

"(9) SPECIAL FUNDING RULE FOR CERTAIN LEGACY PLANS.—In the case of a multiemployer defined benefit plan that has adopted an amendment under section 801(b), in accordance with which no further benefits shall accrue under the multiemployer defined benefit plan, the plan sponsor may combine the outstanding balance of all charge and credit bases and amortize that combined base in level annual installments (until fully amortized) over a period of 25 plan years beginning with the plan year following the date all benefit accruals ceased.".

(2) AMENDMENT TO INTERNAL REVENUE CODE OF 1986.—Section 431(b) of the Internal Revenue Code of 1986 is amended by adding at the end the following: "(9) SPECIAL FUNDING RULE FOR CERTAIN LEGACY PLANS.—In the case of a multiemployer defined benefit plan that has adopted an amendment under section 437(b), in accordance with which no further benefits shall accrue under the multiemployer defined benefit plan, the plan sponsor may combine the outstanding balance of all charge and credit bases and amortize that combined base in level annual installments (until fully amortized) over a period of 25 plan years beginning with the plan year following the date on which all benefit accruals ceased.".

(c) Benefits After Merger, Consolidation, Or Transfer Of Assets.—

(1) AMENDMENT TO EMPLOYEE RETIREMENT INCOME SECURITY ACT OF 1974.—Section 208 of the Employee Retirement Income Security Act of 1974 (29 U.S.C. 1058) is amended—

(A) by striking so much of the first sentence as precedes "may not merge" and inserting the following:

"(1) IN GENERAL.—Except as provided in paragraph (2), a pension plan may not merge, and"; and

(B) by striking the second sentence and adding at the end the following:

"(2) SPECIAL REQUIREMENTS FOR MULTIEMPLOYER PLANS.—Paragraph (1) shall not apply to any transaction to the extent that participants either before or after the transaction are covered under a multiemployer plan to which title IV of this Act applies or a composite plan.".

(2) AMENDMENTS TO INTERNAL REVENUE CODE OF 1986.—

(A) QUALIFICATION REQUIREMENT.—Section 401(a)(12) of the Internal Revenue Code of 1986 is amended—

(i) by striking "(12) A trust" and inserting the following:

"(12) BENEFITS AFTER MERGER, CONSOLIDATION, OR TRANSFER OF ASSETS.—

"(A) IN GENERAL.—Except as provided in subparagraph (B), a trust";

(ii) by striking the second sentence; and

(iii) by adding at the end the following:

"(B) SPECIAL REQUIREMENTS FOR MULTIEMPLOYER PLANS.—Subparagraph (A) shall not apply to any multiemployer plan with respect to any transaction to the extent that participants either before or after the transaction are covered under a multiemployer plan to which title IV of the Employee Retirement Income Security Act of 1974 applies or a composite plan.".

(B) ADDITIONAL QUALIFICATION REQUIREMENT.—Paragraph (1) of section 414(l) of such Code is amended—

(i) by striking "(1) IN GENERAL" and all that follows through "shall not constitute" and inserting the following:

"(1) BENEFIT PROTECTIONS: MERGER, CONSOLIDATION, TRANSFER.—

"(A) IN GENERAL.—Except as provided in subparagraph (B), a trust which forms a part of a plan shall not constitute"; and

(ii) by striking the second sentence; and

(iii) by adding at the end the following:

"(B) SPECIAL REQUIREMENTS FOR MULTIEMPLOYER PLANS.—Subparagraph (A) does not apply to any multiemployer plan with respect to any transaction to the extent that participants either before or after the transaction are covered under a multiemployer plan to which title IV of the Employee Retirement Income Security Act of 1974 applies or a composite plan.".

(d) Requirements For Status As A Qualified Plan.—

(1) REQUIREMENT THAT ACTUARIAL ASSUMPTIONS BE SPECIFIED.—Section 401(a)(25) of the Internal Revenue Code of 1986 is amended by inserting "(in the case of a composite plan, benefits objectively calculated pursuant to a formula)" after "definitely determinable benefits".

(2) MISSING PARTICIPANTS IN TERMINATING COMPOSITE PLAN.—Section 401(a)(34) of the Internal Revenue Code of 1986 is amended by striking ", a trust" and inserting "or a composite plan, a trust".

(e) Deduction For Contributions To A Qualified Plan.—Section 404(a)(1) of the Internal Revenue Code of 1986 is amended by redesignating subparagraph (E) as subparagraph (F) and by inserting after subparagraph (D) the following:

"(E) COMPOSITE PLANS.—

"(i) IN GENERAL.—In the case of a composite plan, subparagraph (D) shall not apply and the maximum amount deductible for a plan year shall be the excess (if any) of—

"(I) 160 percent of the greater of—

"(aa) the current liability of the plan determined in accordance with the principles of section 431(c)(6)(D), or

"(bb) the present value of plan liabilities as determined under section 438, over

"(II) the fair market value of the plan's assets, projected to the end of the plan year.

"(ii) SPECIAL RULES FOR PREDECESSOR MULTIEMPLOYER PLAN TO COMPOSITE PLAN.—

"(I) IN GENERAL.—Except as provided in subclause (II), if an employer contributes to a composite plan with respect to its employees, contributions by that employer to a multiemployer defined benefit plan with respect to some or all of the same group of employees shall be deductible under sections 162 and this section, subject to the limits in subparagraph (D).

"(II) TRANSITION CONTRIBUTION.—The full amount of a contribution to satisfy the transition contribution requirement (as defined in section 440A(d)) and allocated to the legacy defined benefit plan for the plan year shall be deductible for the employer's taxable year ending with or within the plan year.".

(f) Minimum Vesting Standards.—

(1) YEARS OF SERVICE UNDER COMPOSITE PLANS.—

(A) EMPLOYEE RETIREMENT INCOME SECURITY ACT OF 1974.—Section 203 of the Employee Retirement Income Security Act of 1974 (29 U.S.C. 1053) is amended by inserting after subsection (f) the following:

"(g) Special Rules For Computing Years Of Service Under Composite Plans.—

"(1) IN GENERAL.—In determining a qualified employee's years of service under a composite plan for purposes of this section, the employee's years of service under a legacy plan shall be treated as years of service earned under the composite plan. For purposes of such determination, a composite plan shall not be treated as a defined benefit plan pursuant to section 801(d).

"(2) QUALIFIED EMPLOYEE.—For purposes of this subsection, an employee is a qualified employee if the employee first completes an hour of service under the composite plan (determined without regard to the provisions of this subsection) within the 12-month period immediately preceding or the 24-month period immediately following the date the employee ceased to accrue benefits under the legacy plan.

"(3) CERTIFICATION OF YEARS OF SERVICE.—For purposes of paragraph (1), the plan sponsor of the composite plan shall rely on a written certification by the plan sponsor of the legacy plan of the years of service the qualified employee completed under the defined benefit plan as of the date the employee satisfies the requirements of paragraph (2), disregarding any years of service that had been forfeited under the rules of the defined benefit plan before that date.

"(h) Special Rules For Computing Years Of Service Under Legacy Plans.—

"(1) IN GENERAL.—In determining a qualified employee's years of service under a legacy plan for purposes of this section, and in addition to any service under applicable regulations, the employee's years of service under a composite plan shall be treated as years of service earned under the legacy plan. For purposes of such determination, a composite plan shall not be treated as a defined benefit plan pursuant to section 801(d).

"(2) QUALIFIED EMPLOYEE.—For purposes of this subsection, an employee is a qualified employee if the employee first completes an hour of service under the composite plan (determined without regard to the provisions of this subsection) within the 12-month period immediately preceding or the 24-month period immediately following the date the employee ceased to accrue benefits under the legacy plan.

"(3) CERTIFICATION OF YEARS OF SERVICE.—For purposes of paragraph (1), the plan sponsor of the legacy plan shall rely on a written certification by the plan sponsor of the composite plan of the years of service the qualified employee completed under the composite plan after the employee satisfies the requirements of paragraph (2), disregarding any years of service that has been forfeited under the rules of the composite plan.".

(B) INTERNAL REVENUE CODE OF 1986.—Section 411(a) of the Internal Revenue Code of 1986 is amended by adding at the end the following:

"(14) SPECIAL RULES FOR DETERMINING YEARS OF SERVICE UNDER COMPOSITE PLANS.—

"(A) IN GENERAL.—In determining a qualified employee's years of service under a composite plan for purposes of this subsection, the employee's years of service under a legacy plan shall be treated as years of service earned under the composite plan. For purposes of such determination, a composite plan shall not be treated as a defined benefit plan pursuant to section 437(d).

"(B) QUALIFIED EMPLOYEE.—For purposes of this paragraph, an employee is a qualified employee if the employee first completes an hour of service under the composite plan (determined without regard to the provisions of this paragraph) within the 12-month period immediately preceding or the 24-month period immediately following the date the employee ceased to accrue benefits under the legacy plan.

"(C) CERTIFICATION OF YEARS OF SERVICE.—For purposes of subparagraph (A), the plan sponsor of the composite plan shall rely on a written certification by the plan sponsor of the legacy plan of the years of service the qualified employee completed under the legacy plan as of the date the employee satisfies the requirements of subparagraph (B), disregarding any years of service that had been forfeited under the rules of the defined benefit plan before that date.

"(15) SPECIAL RULES FOR COMPUTING YEARS OF SERVICE UNDER LEGACY PLANS.—

"(A) IN GENERAL.—In determining a qualified employee's years of service under a legacy plan for purposes of this section, and in addition to any service under applicable regulations, the employee's years of service under a composite plan shall be treated as years of service earned under the legacy plan. For purposes of such determination, a composite plan shall not be treated as a defined benefit plan pursuant to section 437(d).

"(B) QUALIFIED EMPLOYEE.—For purposes of this paragraph, an employee is a qualified employee if the employee first completes an hour of service under the composite plan (determined without regard to the provisions of this paragraph) within the 12-month period immediately preceding or the 24-month period immediately following the date the employee ceased to accrue benefits under the legacy plan.

"(C) CERTIFICATION OF YEARS OF SERVICE.—For purposes of subparagraph (A), the plan sponsor of the legacy plan shall rely on a written certification by the plan sponsor of the composite plan of the years of service the qualified employee completed under the composite plan after the employee satisfies the requirements of subparagraph (B), disregarding any years of service that has been forfeited under the rules of the composite plan.".

(2) REDUCTION OF BENEFITS.—

(A) EMPLOYEE RETIREMENT INCOME SECURITY ACT OF 1974.—Section 203(a)(3)(E)(ii) of the Employee Retirement Income Security Act of 1974 (29 U.S.C. 1053(a)(3)(E)(ii)) is amended—

(i) in subclause (I) by striking "4244A" and inserting "305(e), 803,"; and

(ii) in subclause (II) by striking "4245" and inserting "305(e), 4245,".

(B) INTERNAL REVENUE CODE OF 1986.—Section 411(a)(3)(F) of the Internal Revenue Code of 1986 is amended—

(i) in clause (i) by striking "section 418D or under section 4281 of the Employee Retirement Income Security Act of 1974" and inserting "section 432(e) or 439 or under section 4281 of the Employee Retirement Income Security Act of 1974"; and

(ii) in clause (ii) by inserting "or 432(e)" after "section 418E".

(3) ACCRUED BENEFIT REQUIREMENTS.—

(A) EMPLOYEE RETIREMENT INCOME SECURITY ACT OF 1974.—Section 204(b)(1)(B)(i) of the Employee Retirement Income Security Act of 1974 (29 U.S.C. 1054(b)(1)(B)(i)) is amended by inserting ", including an amendment reducing or suspending benefits under section 305(e), 803, 4245 or 4281," after "any amendment to the plan".

(B) INTERNAL REVENUE CODE OF 1986.—Section 411(b)(1)(B)(i) of the Internal Revenue Code of 1986 is amended by inserting ", including an amendment reducing or suspending benefits under section 418E, 432(e) or 439, or under section 4281 of the Employee Retirement Income Security Act of 1974," after "any amendment to the plan".

(4) ADDITIONAL ACCRUED BENEFIT REQUIREMENTS.—

(A) EMPLOYEE RETIREMENT INCOME SECURITY ACT OF 1974.—Section 204(b)(1)(H)(v) of the Employee Retirement Income Security Act of 1974 (29 U.S.C. 1053(b)(1)(H)(v)) is amended by inserting before the period at the end the following: ", or benefits are reduced or suspended under section 305(e), 803, 4245, or 4281".

(B) INTERNAL REVENUE CODE OF 1986.—Section 411(b)(1)(H)(iv) of the Internal Revenue Code of 1986 is amended—

(i) in the heading by striking "BENEFIT" and inserting "BENEFIT AND THE SUS-PENSION AND REDUCTION OF CERTAIN BENEFITS"; and

(ii) in the text by inserting before the period at the end the following: ", or benefits are reduced or suspended under section 418E, 432(e), or 439, or under section 4281 of the Employee Retirement Income Security Act of 1974".

(5) ACCRUED BENEFIT NOT TO BE DECREASED BY AMENDMENT.—

(A) EMPLOYEE RETIREMENT INCOME SECURITY ACT OF 1974.—Section 204(g)(1) of the Employee Retirement Income Security Act of 1974 (29 U.S.C. 1053(g)(1)) is amended by inserting after "302(d)(2)" the following: ", 305(e), 803, 4245,".

(B) INTERNAL REVENUE CODE OF 1986.—Section 411(d)(6)(A) of the Internal Revenue Code of 1986 is amended by inserting after "412(d)(2)," the following: "418E, 432(e), or 439,".

(g) Certain Funding Rules Not Applicable.—

(1) EMPLOYEE RETIREMENT INCOME SECURITY ACT OF 1974.—Section 305 of the Employee Retirement Income Security Act of 1974 (29 U.S.C. 1085) is amended by adding at the end the following:

"(k) Legacy Plans.—Sections 302, 304, and 305 shall not apply to an employer that has an obligation to contribute to a plan that is a legacy plan within the meaning of section 805(a) solely because the employer has an obligation to contribute to a composite plan described in section 801 that is associated with that legacy plan.".

(2) INTERNAL REVENUE CODE OF 1986.—Section 432 of the Internal Revenue Code of 1986 is amended by adding at the end the following:

"(k) Legacy Plans.—Sections 412, 431, and 432 shall not apply to an employer that has an obligation to contribute to a plan that is a legacy plan within the meaning of section 440A(a) solely because the employer has an obligation to contribute to a composite plan described in section 437 that is associated with that legacy plan.".

(h) Termination Of Composite Plan.—Section 403(d) of the Employee Retirement Income Security Act of 1974 (29 U.S.C. 1103(d) is amended—

(1) in paragraph (1), by striking "regulations of the Secretary." and inserting "regulations of the Secretary, or as provided in paragraph (3)."; and

(2) by adding at the end the following:

"(3) Section 4044(a) of this Act shall be applied in the case of the termination of a composite plan by—

"(A) limiting the benefits subject to paragraph (3) thereof to benefits as defined in section 802(b)(3)(B); and

"(B) including in the benefits subject to paragraph (4) all other benefits (if any) of individuals under the plan that would be guaranteed under section 4022A if the plan were subject to title IV.".

(i) Good Faith Compliance Prior To Guidance.—Where the implementation of any provision of law added or amended by this division is subject to issuance of regulations by the Secretary of Labor, the Secretary of the Treasury, or the Pension Benefit Guaranty Corporation, a multiemployer plan shall not be treated as failing to meet the requirements of any such provision prior to the issuance of final regulations or other guidance to carry out such provision if such plan is operated in accordance with a reasonable, good faith interpretation of such provision.

SEC. 140006. EFFECTIVE DATE.

Unless otherwise specified, the amendments made by this division shall apply to plan years beginning after the date of the enactment of this Act.

DIVISION O—EDUCATION PROVISIONS AND OTHER PROGRAMS

TITLE I

—HIGHER EDUCATION PROVISIONS

DEFINITIONS

SEC. 150101.

In this title:

(1) AWARD YEAR.—The term "award year" has the meaning given the term in section 481(a) of the Higher Education Act of 1965 (20 U.S.C. 1088(a)).

(2) AUTHORIZING COMMITTEES.—The term "authorizing committees" has the meaning given the term in section 103 of the Higher Education Act of 1965 (20 U.S.C. 1003).

(3) FAFSA.—The term "FAFSA" means an application under section 483 of the Higher Education Act of 1965 (20 U.S.C. 1090) for Federal student financial aid.

(4) INSTITUTION OF HIGHER EDUCATION.—The term "institution of higher education" has the meaning given the term in section 102 of the Higher Education Act of 1965 (20 U.S.C. 1002).

(5) QUALIFYING EMERGENCY.—The term "qualifying emergency" has the meaning given the term in section 3502 of the CARES Act (Public Law 116–136), as amended by this Act.

(6) SECRETARY.—The term "Secretary" means the Secretary of Education.

Subtitle A—Cares Act Amendments

APPLICATION OF WAIVER TO PARTICIPATING NONPROFIT EMPLOYERS

SEC. 150102.

(a) In General.—Section 3503 of the CARES Act (Public Law 116–136) is amended—

(1) by redesignating subsection (b) as subsection (c); and

(2) by inserting after subsection (a) the following:

"(b) Waiver Of Non-Federal Share Requirement For Nonprofit Employers.—Notwithstanding any other provision of law, with respect to funds made available for award years 2019–2020 and 2020–2021, the Secretary shall waive any requirement that a nonprofit employer provide a non-Federal share to match Federal funds provided to such nonprofit employer under an agreement under section 443 of the Higher Education Act of 1965 (20 U.S.C. 1087–53).".

(b) Effective Date.—The amendments made by subsection (a) shall take effect as if included in the enactment of the CARES Act (Public Law 116–136).

EXTENSION OF FEDERAL WORK-STUDY DURING A QUALIFYING EMERGENCY

SEC. 150103.

(a) In General.—Section 3505 of the CARES Act (Public Law 116–136) is amended—

(1) in subsection (a)—

(A) by striking "(not to exceed one academic year)"; and

(B) by striking "such academic year" and inserting "such period"; and

(2) in subsection (b)—

(A) in paragraph (1), by inserting "first" before "occurred"; and

(B) in paragraph (3), by striking "for all or part of such academic year".

(b) Effective Date.—The amendments made by subsection (a) shall take effect as if included in the enactment of the CARES Act (Public Law 116–136).

CONTINUING EDUCATION AT AFFECTED FOREIGN INSTITUTIONS

SEC. 150104.

(a) In General.—Section 3510 of the CARES Act (Public Law 116–136) is amended—

(1) in subsection (a), by striking "national emergency declared" and inserting "national emergency related to the coronavirus declared";

(2) in subsection (b), by striking "qualifying emergency" and inserting "emergency or disaster affecting the institution as described in subsection (a)";

(3) in subsection (c), by striking "qualifying emergency" and inserting "applicable emergency or disaster as described in subsection (a)"; and

(4) in subsection (d)—

(A) in paragraph (1)—

(i) by striking "for the duration of a qualifying emergency and the following payment period," and inserting "with respect to a foreign institution, in the case of a public health emergency, major disaster or emergency, or national emergency related to the coronavirus declared by the applicable government authorities in the country in which the foreign institution is located, or in the case of a qualifying emergency,"; and

(ii) by inserting ", for the duration of the applicable emergency or disaster and the following payment period," after "1087a et seq.)"; and

(B) in paragraph (4)—

(i) by striking "qualifying emergency" and inserting "applicable emergency or disaster"; and

(ii) by striking the period at the end and inserting ", the name of the institution of higher education located in the United States that has entered into a written arrangement with such foreign institution, and information regarding the nature of such written arrangement, including which coursework or program requirements are accomplished at each respective institution.".

(b) Effective Date.—The amendments made by subsection (a) shall take effect as if included in the enactment of the CARES Act (Public Law 116–136).

FUNDING FOR HBCU CAPITAL FINANCING

SEC. 150105.

(a) In General.—Section 3512(d) of the CARES Act (Public Law 116–136) is amended by striking "$62,000,000" and inserting "such sums as may be necessary".

(b) Effective Date.—The amendment made by subsection (a) shall take effect as if included in the enactment of the CARES Act (Public Law 116–136).

WAIVER AUTHORITY FOR INSTITUTIONAL AID

SEC. 150106.

(a) In General.—Section 3517(a)(1)(D) of the CARES Act (Public Law 116–136) is amended by striking "(b), (c), and (g)" and inserting "(b) and (c)".

(b) Effective Date.—The amendment made by subsection (a) shall take effect as if included in the enactment of the CARES Act (Public Law 116–136).

SCOPE OF MODIFICATIONS TO REQUIRED AND ALLOWABLE USES

SEC. 150107.

(a) Amendment To Include Minority Science And Engineering Improvement Program.—Subsection (a) of section 3518 of the CARES Act (Public Law 116–136) is amended—

(1) by striking "part A or B of title III," and inserting "part A, part B, or subpart 1 of part E of title III,"; and

(2) by inserting "1067 et seq.;" after "1060 et seq.;".

(b) Amendment To Clarify Scope Of Authority.—Section 3518 of the CARES Act (Public Law 116–136) is amended by adding at the end the following new subsection: "(d) Scope Of Authority.—Notwithstanding subsection (a), the Secretary may not modify the required or allowable uses of funds for grants awarded under a statutory provision cited in subsection (a) in a manner that deviates from the overall purpose of the grant program, as provided in the general authorization, findings, or purpose of the grant program under the applicable statutory provision cited in such subsection.".

(c) Effective Date.—The amendments made by this section shall take effect as if included in the enactment of the CARES Act (Public Law 116–136).

Subtitle B—Financial Aid Access

EMERGENCY FINANCIAL AID GRANTS EXCLUDED FROM NEED ANALYSIS

SEC. 150108.

(a) Treatment Of Emergency Financial Aid Grants For Need Analysis.—Notwithstanding any provision of the Higher Education Act of 1965 (20 U.S.C. 1001 et seq.), emergency financial aid grants—

(1) shall not be included as income or assets (including untaxed income and benefits under section 480(b) of the Higher Education Act of 1965 (20 U.S.C. 1807vv(b))) in the computation of expected family contribution for any program funded in whole or in part under the Higher Education Act of 1965 (20 U.S.C. 1001 et seq.); and

(2) shall not be treated as estimated financial assistance for the purposes of section 471 or section 480(j) of the Higher Education Act of 1965 (20 U.S.C. 1087kk; 1087vv(j)).

(b) Definition.—In this section, the term "emergency financial aid grant" means—

(1) an emergency financial aid grant awarded by an institution of higher education under section 3504 of the CARES Act (Public Law 116–136);

(2) an emergency financial aid grant from an institution of higher education made with funds made available under section 18004 of the CARES Act (Public Law 116–136); and

(3) any other emergency financial aid grant to a student from a Federal agency, a State, an Indian tribe, an institution of higher education, or a scholarship-granting organization (including a tribal organization, as defined in section 4 of the Indian Self-Determination and Education Assistance Act (25 U.S.C. 5304)) for the purpose of providing financial relief to students enrolled at institutions of higher education in response to a qualifying emergency.

FACILITATING ACCESS TO FINANCIAL AID FOR RECENTLY UNEMPLOYED STUDENTS

SEC. 150109.

(a) Treatment As Dislocated Worker.—

(1) IN GENERAL.—Notwithstanding section 479(d)(1) of the Higher Education Act of 1965 (20 U.S.C. 1087ss(d)(1)), any individual who has applied for, or who is

receiving, unemployment benefits at the time of the submission of a FAFSA for a covered award year shall be treated as a dislocated worker for purposes of the need analysis under part F of title IV such Act (20 U.S.C. 1087kk et seq.) applicable to such award year.

(2) INFORMATION TO APPLICANTS AND INSTITUTIONS.—The Secretary—

(A) in consultation with institutions of higher education, shall carry out activities to inform applicants for Federal student financial aid under the Higher Education Act of 1965 (20 U.S.C. 1001 et seq.)—

(i) of the treatment of individuals who have applied for, or who are receiving, unemployment benefits as dislocated workers under paragraph (1); and

(ii) of the availability of means-tested Federal benefits for which such applicants may be eligible;

(B) shall carry out activities to inform institutions of higher education of the authority of such institutions, with explicit written consent of an applicant for Federal student financial aid under the Higher Education Act of 1965 (20 U.S.C. 1001 et seq.), to provide information collected from such applicant's FAFSA to an organization assisting the applicant in applying for and receiving Federal, State, local, or tribal assistance in accordance with section 312 of the Department of Defense and Labor, Health and Human Services, and Education Appropriations Act, 2019 and Continuing Appropriations Act, 2019 (Public Law 115–245); and

(C) in consultation with the Secretary of Labor, shall carry out activities to inform applicants for, and recipients of, unemployment benefits of the availability of Federal student financial aid under the Higher Education Act of 1965 (20 U.S.C. 1001 et seq.) and the treatment of such applicants and recipients as dislocated workers under paragraph (1).

(3) IMPLEMENTATION.—The Secretary shall implement this subsection not later than 30 days after the date of enactment of this Act.

(4) APPLICABILITY.—Paragraph (1) shall apply with respect to a FAFSA submitted on or after the earlier of—

(A) the date on which the Secretary implements this subsection under paragraph (3); or

(B) the date that is 30 days after the date of enactment of this Act.

(b) Professional Judgment Of Financial Aid Administrators.—The guidance of the Secretary titled "Update on the use of 'Professional Judgment' by Financial Aid Administrators" (DCL ID: GEN–09–05), as in effect on May 8, 2009, shall apply—

(1) to the exercise of professional judgement by financial aid administrators pursuant to section 479A of the Higher Education Act of 1965 (20 U.S.C. 1087tt) with respect to any FAFSA for a covered award year; and

(2) to the selection of institutions for program reviews pursuant to section 498A of the Higher Education Act of 1965 (20 U.S.C. 1099c–1) for a covered award year.

(c) Definitions.—In this section:

(1) COVERED AWARD YEAR.—The term "covered award year" means—

(A) an award year during which there is a qualifying emergency; and

(B) the first award year beginning after the end of such qualifying emergency.

(2) MEANS-TESTED FEDERAL BENEFIT.—The term "means-tested Federal benefit" includes the following:

(A) The supplemental security income program under title XVI of the Social Security Act (42 U.S.C. 1381 et seq.).

(B) The supplemental nutrition assistance program under the Food and Nutrition Act of 2008 (7 U.S.C. 2011 et seq.).

(C) The free and reduced price school lunch program established under the Richard B. Russell National School Lunch Act (42 U.S.C. 1751 et seq.).

(D) The program of block grants for States for temporary assistance for needy families established under part A of title IV of the Social Security Act (42 U.S.C. 601 et seq.).

(E) The special supplemental nutrition program for women, infants, and children established by section 17 of the Child Nutrition Act of 1966 (42 U.S.C. 1786).

(F) The Medicaid program under title XIX of the Social Security Act (42 U.S.C. 1396 et seq.).

(G) The tax credits provided under the following sections of the Internal Revenue Code of 1986 (title 26, United States Code):

(i) Section 25A (relating to American Opportunity and Lifetime Learning credits).

(ii) Section 32 (relating to earned income).

(iii) Section 36B (relating to refundable credit for coverage under a qualified health plan).

(iv) Section 6428 (relating to 2020 recovery rebates for individuals).

(H) Federal housing assistance programs, including tenant-based assistance under section 8(o) of the United States Housing Act of 1937 (42 U.S.C. 1437f(o)), and public housing, as defined in section 3(b)(1) of such Act (42 U.S.C. 1437a(b)(1)).

(I) Such other Federal means-tested benefits as may be identified by the Secretary.

STUDENT ELIGIBILITY FOR HIGHER EDUCATION EMERGENCY RELIEF FUND AND OTHER HIGHER EDUCATION FUNDS

SEC. 150110.

(a) In General.—With respect to student eligibility for receipt of funds provided under section 18004 of the CARES Act (Public Law 116–136) and under title VI of division A of this Act—

(1) the Secretary is prohibited from imposing any restriction on, or defining, the populations of students who may receive such funds other than a restriction based solely on the student's enrollment at the institution of higher education; and

(2) section 401(a) the Personal Responsibility and Work Opportunity Reconciliation Act of 1996 (8 U.S.C. 1611(a)) shall not apply.

(b) Effective Date.—Subsection (a) shall take effect as if included in the enactment of the CARES Act (Public Law 116–136), and an institution of higher education that provided funds to a student before the date of enactment of this Act shall not be penalized if such provision is consistent with such subsection and section 18004 of the CARES Act (Public Law 116–136).

DEFINITION OF DISTANCE EDUCATION

SEC. 150111.

(a) In General.—Except as otherwise provided in title IV of the Higher Education Act of 1965 (20 U.S.C. 1070 et seq.), for purposes of such title, the term "distance education" means education that uses technology—

(1) to deliver instruction to students enrolled at an institution of higher education who are separated from the instructor or instructors; and

(2) to support regular and substantive interaction between the students and the instructor or instructors, either synchronously or asynchronously.

(b) Technology.—For purposes of subsection (a), the technologies that may be used to offer distance education include—

(1) the internet;

(2) one-way and two-way transmissions through open broadcast, closed circuit, cable, microwave, broadband lines, fiber optics, satellite, or wireless communications devices;

(3) audio conferencing; and

(4) other media used in a course in conjunction with any of the technologies listed in paragraphs (1) through (3).

(c) Instructor.—For purposes of subsection (a), an instructor is an individual responsible for delivering course content and who meets the qualifications for instruction established by the institution of higher education's accrediting agency.

(d) Substantive Interaction.—For purposes of subsection (a), substantive interaction is engaging students in teaching, learning, and assessment, consistent with the content under discussion, and also includes at least two of the following:

(1) Providing direct instruction.

(2) Assessing or providing feedback on a student's coursework.

(3) Providing information or responding to questions about the content of a course or competency.

(4) Facilitating a group discussion regarding the content of a course or competency.

(5) Other instructional activities approved by the institution of higher education's or program's accrediting agency.

(e) Regular Interaction.—For purposes of subsection (a), an institution ensures regular interaction between a student and an instructor or instructors by, prior to the student's completion of a course or competency—

(1) providing the opportunity for substantive interactions with the student on a predictable and regular basis commensurate with the length of time and the amount of content in the course or competency; and

(2) monitoring the student's academic engagement and success and ensuring that an instructor is responsible for promptly and proactively engaging in substantive interaction with the student when needed, on the basis of such monitoring, or upon request by the student.

(f) Effective Date.—This section shall be effective for any semester (or the equivalent) that begins on or after August 15, 2020, and shall cease to be effective at the end of the 2020–2021 award year.

INSTITUTIONAL STABILIZATION PROGRAM

SEC. 150112.

(a) Authority To Participate.—Notwithstanding paragraph (1) or (2) of section 498(c) of the Higher Education Act of 1965 (20 U.S.C. 1099c(c)), an eligible institution described in subsection (b) may, in lieu of submitting a letter of credit in accordance with section 498(c)(3)(A) of such Act, submit an application under subsection (c)(1) to enter into a COVID–19 provisional program participation agreement in accordance with subsection (d) to provide the Secretary with satisfactory evidence of its financial responsibility.

(b) Eligible Institution Described.—An eligible institution described in this subsection is a private nonprofit institution of higher education that—

(1) either—

(A) has a composite score of less than 1.0 for the institutional fiscal year ending in 2019, as determined under section 668.171(b)(1) of title 34, Code of Federal Regulations; or

(B) on the date of an application under subsection (c)(1), has (or anticipates having) a composite score of less than 1.0 for the institutional fiscal year ending in 2020, as determined under section 668.171(b)(1) of title 34, Code of Federal Regulations;

(2) during award year 2018–2019—

(A) offered on-campus classes; and

(B) qualified for participation in a program under title IV of the Higher Education Act of 1965 (20 U.S.C. 1070 et seq.); and

(3) on the date of the application under subsection (c)(1), has a liquidity level of less than or equal to 180 days.

(c) Application.—

(1) IN GENERAL.—An eligible institution desiring to enter into a COVID–19 provisional program participation agreement under subsection (d), shall, not later than December 31, 2020, submit to the Secretary an application that includes—

(A) the estimated liquidity level of the eligible institution on the date of the application and an assurance that such liquidity level will be attested to in accordance with paragraph (2);

(B) an assurance that such eligible institution will submit a record-management plan in accordance with paragraph (3); and

(C) an assurance that such eligible institution will submit a teach-out plan in accordance with paragraph (4); and

(D) an assurance that such eligible institution will submit reports on teach-out agreements and sufficient progress made on such agreements in accordance with subsection (d)(3), as applicable.

(2) AUDITOR ATTESTATION.—Not later than 60 days after submitting an application under paragraph (1), an eligible institution shall submit to the Secretary an auditor attestation of the liquidity level of such eligible institution on the date such institution submitted such application pursuant to an audit conducted by a qualified independent organization or person in accordance with standards established by the American Institute of Certified Public Accountants.

(3) RECORD-MANAGEMENT PLAN.—

(A) IN GENERAL.—Not later than 60 days after submitting an application under paragraph (1), an eligible institution shall submit to the Secretary a record-management plan approved by the accrediting agency of such eligible institution that includes—

(i) a plan for the custody, including by the State authorizing agency, and the disposition of—

(I) a teach-out plan and teach-out agreement records, as applicable; and

(II) student records, including student transcripts, billing, and financial aid records;

(ii) an estimate of the costs necessary to carry out such record-management plan; and

(iii) a financial plan to provide funding for such costs.

(B) ASSURANCE.—An eligible institution that submits a record-management plan under subparagraph (A) shall include an assurance to the Secretary that, in the case of the closure of such eligible institution, such eligible institution—

(i) will release all financial holds placed on student records; and

(ii) for the 3-year period beginning on the date of the closure of such eligible institution, will not require a student enrolled in such eligible institution on the date of such closure (and students withdrawn from such eligible institution in the 120 days prior to such date) who requests the student records of such student to purchase such records or otherwise charge such student a fee with respect to such records.

(C) REPORT.—Not later than 60 days after submitting an application under paragraph (1), an eligible institution shall submit the record-management plan required under subparagraph (A) and the assurance under subparagraph (B) to the accrediting agency and State authorizing agency of such eligible institution.

(4) TEACH-OUT PLAN.—Not later than 60 days after submitting an application under paragraph (1), an eligible institution shall submit a teach-out plan approved by the accrediting agency of such eligible institution to the Secretary and the State authorizing agency of such eligible institution.

(5) LETTER OF CREDIT DURING PENDING APPLICATION.—Notwithstanding section 498(c)(3)(A) of the Higher Education Act of 1965 (20 U.S.C. 1099c(c)(3)(A)), the Secretary may not use the composite score of an eligible institution (as determined under section 668.171(b)(1) of title 34, Code of Federal Regulations) to require the eligible institution to submit a new letter of credit or increase the value of an existing letter of credit while the institution has an application pending under paragraph (1).

(6) NOTIFICATION OF APPLICATION AND STATUS.—The eligible institution shall notify the accrediting agency and State authorizing agency of such institution—

(A) that the institution has submitted an application under paragraph (1) to the Secretary not later than 10 days after submitting such application; and

(B) of the final acceptance or denial of such application not later than 5 days after receiving a final decision from the Secretary.

(7) APPLICATION DECISION.—The Secretary shall accept or deny an application under paragraph (1) not later than 10 days after the date on which an eligible institution completes all of the submission requirements under paragraphs (2), (3), and (4).

(d) COVID–19 Provisional Program Participation Agreement.—

(1) AUTHORITY TO ENTER AGREEMENT.—The Secretary may enter into a COVID–19 provisional program participation agreement under this subsection with an eligible institution that submits an application under subsection (c)(1) on or before December 31, 2020, only if the Secretary has received—

(A) an auditor attestation under subsection (c)(2) that such eligible institution has a liquidity level of less than or equal to 180 days on the date of the application of such eligible institution under subsection (c)(1);

(B) a record-management plan with respect to such eligible institution in accordance with subsection (c)(3); and

(C) a teach-out plan with respect to such eligible institution in accordance with subsection (c)(4).

(2) PARTICIPATION REQUIREMENTS.—In entering into a COVID–19 provisional program participation agreement with an eligible institution under this subsection, the Secretary shall require such eligible institution—

(A) if such eligible institution has a liquidity level of less than or equal to 90 days on the date of the application of such eligible institution under subsection (c)(1), to submit a teach-out agreement (or teach-out agreements, as applicable) to the Secretary and to the accrediting agency and State authorizing agency of the institution in accordance with paragraph (3);

(B) to report to the Secretary in accordance with paragraph (4);

(C) to meet the administrative capacity requirements under section 498(d) of the Higher Education Act of 1965 (20 U.S.C. 1099c(d)); and

(D) to meet the cash reserves requirements under section 498(c)(6)(A) of the Higher Education Act of 1965 (20 U.S.C. 1099c(c)(6)(A)).

(3) TEACH-OUT AGREEMENTS.—

(A) SUFFICIENT PROGRESS.—Not later than 30 days after the date on which an eligible institution described in paragraph (2)(A) enters into a COVID–19 provisional program participation agreement under this subsection, such eligible institution shall submit to the Secretary an interim teach-out agreement that provides for the equitable treatment of at least 75 percent of enrolled students and a reasonable opportunity for such students to complete their program of study.

(B) ADDENDUM REPORTS.—Not later than 15 days after the date on which an eligible institution submits an interim teach-out agreement in accordance with subparagraph (A), and every 15 days thereafter, such eligible institution shall submit to the Secretary a report that includes—

(i) the percentage of students enrolled in such eligible institution that are covered by a teach-out agreement;

(ii) the increase in the percentage of students covered by such an agreement, as compared to the most recently submitted report; and

(iii) such other information as the Secretary or accrediting agency of the eligible institution may require, including the progress of such eligible institution in meeting any benchmarks set by such accrediting agency related to the percentage of students that should be covered by such an agreement.

(C) TEACH-OUT AGREEMENT REQUIRED.—On the date agreed to by the eligible institution, the accrediting agency of such eligible institution, and the Secretary under a COVID–19 provisional program participation agreement under this subsection, such eligible institution shall submit to the Secretary and to the accrediting agency and State authorizing agency of the institution a teach-out agreement (or agreements, as applicable) that—

(i) provides for the equitable treatment of all enrolled students and a reasonable opportunity for such students to complete their program of study;

(ii) includes—

(I) a list of all students enrolled in such eligible institution on the date such eligible institution submitted an application under subsection (c)(1) (and students withdrawn from such eligible institution in the 120 days prior to such date), including the name, contact information, program of study, program requirements completed, and estimated date of program completion of each such student;

(II) the amount of any unearned tuition, account balances, student fees, and refunds due to each such student;

(III) a plan to notify each such student, in the case of the closure of such eligible institution, of—

(aa) the process for obtaining a closed school discharge under section 437(c)(1) of the Higher Education Act of 1965 (20 U.S.C. 1087(c)(1)), using standard language developed by the Secretary under subsection (f), and the benefits and consequences of such discharge;

(bb) if applicable, information on institutional and State refund policies;

(cc) the teach-out institution or institutions available to enroll such student;

(dd) the tuition and fees of the educational program offered by each such teach-out institution and the number and types of credit each such teach-out institution will accept prior to the enrollment of such student; and (ee) the record-management plan submitted in accordance with subsection (c)(3).

(D) DECREASE IN LIQUIDITY.—In the case of an eligible institution that enters into a COVID–19 provisional program participation agreement under this subsection and has a liquidity level of greater than 90 days on the date of the application of such eligible institution under subsection (c)(1), if the Secretary determines such eligible institution has declined such that the liquidity level of such eligible institution is consistently less than or equal to 90 days, the Secretary may require such eligible institution to submit a teach-out agreement (or agreements, as applicable) to the Secretary in accordance with subparagraph (C).

(4) REPORTING REQUIREMENTS.—

(A) ELIGIBLE INSTITUTIONS WITH A LIQUIDITY LEVEL OF LESS THAN OR EQUAL TO 90 DAYS.—In the case of an eligible institution described in paragraph (2)(A), the Secretary shall require such eligible institution to report to the Secretary the liquidity level and total student enrollment of such eligible institution not less than once every 15 days, until such eligible institution closes or no longer participates in a COVID–19 provisional program participation agreement under this subsection.

(B) ELIGIBLE INSTITUTIONS WITH A LIQUIDITY LEVEL OF GREATER THAN 90 DAYS.—In the case of an eligible institution that enters into a COVID–19 provisional program participation agreement under this subsection and has a liquidity level of greater than 90 days on the date of the application of such eligible institution under subsection (c)(1), the Secretary shall require such eligible institution to report to the Secretary the liquidity level and total student enrollment of such eligible institution not less than once every 30 days, until such eligible institution closes or no longer participates in a COVID–19 provisional program participation agreement under this subsection.

(C) ALL ELIGIBLE INSTITUTIONS.—All eligible institutions that enter into a COVID–19 provisional program participation agreement under this subsection shall comply with the reporting requirements under paragraph (2) of section 668.175(d) of title 34, Code of Federal Regulations (as such paragraph is in effect on the date of enactment of this section).

(5) LETTER OF CREDIT DURING AGREEMENT.—The Secretary may not require an eligible institution that enters into a COVID–19 provisional program participation agreement under this subsection to submit a new letter of credit or increase the value of an existing letter of credit for the duration of the agreement.

(6) DURATION OF AGREEMENT.—A COVID–19 provisional program participation agreement under this subsection may only be entered into for a period less than or equal to the period—

(A) beginning on the first date of the agreement; and

(B) ending on the last day of the first full award year that begins after the date described in subparagraph (A).

(7) RENEWAL.—

(A) IN GENERAL.—A COVID–19 provisional program participation agreement under this subsection may be renewed for 1 award year subsequent to the award year described in paragraph (6)(B), and shall expire no later than June 30, 2022.

(B) AUTHORITY TO EXTEND RENEWAL PERIOD.—Notwithstanding subparagraph (A), if the Secretary determines that an extension of renewal authority is in the best interest of the eligible institutions with a COVID–19 provisional program participation agreement under this subsection, the Secretary may permit COVID–19 provisional program participation agreement under this subsection to be renewed, on an annual basis, for not more than 3 total consecutive award years subsequent to the award year described in paragraph (6)(B), provided that no agreement under this subsection shall expire later than June 30, 2024.

(C) RECALCULATION OF LIQUIDITY.—An eligible institution desiring to renew a COVID–19 provisional program participation agreement shall—

(i) submit to the Secretary the liquidity level of the institution on the last day of the most recent fiscal year of the eligible institution, to be used for purposes of such an agreement; and

(ii) not later than 60 days after submitting such liquidity level under clause (i), have such liquidity level attested to in accordance with subsection (c)(2).

(8) DISCONTINUATION OF AGREEMENT.—The participation of an eligible institution in a COVID–19 provisional program participation agreement under this subsection—

(A) may be discontinued at any time at the request of the eligible institution;

(B) shall be discontinued by the Secretary if such eligible institution receives a composite score of 1.0 or greater for the most recent institutional fiscal year, as determined under section 668.171(b)(1) of title 34, Code of Federal Regulations; and

(C) shall have no affect on the eligibility of the institution to participate in a program participation agreement under section 487(a) of the Higher Education Act of 1965 (20 U.S.C. 1094) after the COVID–19 provisional program participation agreement under this subsection has expired or been discontinued.

(9) GRANTS TO PARTICIPATING INSTITUTIONS.—From the amounts authorized to be available, subject to appropriation, under subsection (j), the Secretary may award a grant to an eligible institution that enters into a COVID–19 provisional program participation agreement under this subsection to carry out the requirements of such agreement and provide for the increased economic stability of such eligible institution.

(10) REGULATORY AUTHORITY.—Except as otherwise provided in this subsection, the Secretary shall have the same authority with respect to a COVID–19 provisional program participation agreement under this subsection as the Secretary has with respect to a program participation agreement under subparagraphs (B), (F), and (G) of section 487(c)(1) (20 U.S.C. 1099(c)(1)).

(e) Participation In Title IV Program.—An eligible institution that enters into a COVID–19 provisional program participation agreement under subsection (d) may participate in programs under title IV of the Higher Education Act of 1965 (20 U.S.C. 1070 et seq.) only if such eligible institution submits to the Secretary (and the accrediting agency of such eligible institution, as applicable) the agreements and reports applicable to such eligible institution under paragraphs (3) and (4) of subsection (d).

(f) Standard Language.—Not later than 30 days after the date of the enactment of this section, the Secretary shall publish standard language relating to closed school discharges for purposes of subsection (d)(3)(C)(ii)(III)(aa).

(g) Reports To Congress.—Not later than 90 days after the date of the enactment of this section and every 90 days thereafter until the date on which every COVID–19 provisional program participation agreement under this subsection has expired or been terminated, or until June 30, 2024, whichever is earlier, the Secretary shall submit to the authorizing committees a report that includes a summary of each COVID–19 provisional program participation agreement entered into or renewed in the preceding 90 days by the Secretary under this section, including the name, total student enrollment, and liquidity level of the institution.

(h) Automatic Closed School Discharge.—

(1) AUTOMATIC DISCHARGE REQUIRED.—With respect to a borrower described in paragraph (2), the Secretary shall, without any further action by the borrower, discharge the liability of the borrower with respect to each of the borrower's loans (including the interest and collection fees) described in paragraph (2)(A) in accordance with this subsection.

(2) BORROWER REQUIREMENTS.—A borrower described in this subparagraph is a borrower who—

(A) was enrolled for a period of enrollment at an eligible institution that was participating in a COVID–19 provisional program participation agreement under subsection (d), and—

(i) was unable to complete such period of enrollment due to the closure of the institution; or

(ii) withdrew from the eligible institution—

(I) not more than 120 days before the closure of the eligible institution; or

(II) if the Secretary determines an extension of the 120-day period described in subclause (I) is necessary due to exceptional circumstances related to the closure of the institution, during the extended period determined by the Secretary;

(B) has one or more loans—

(i) made under title IV of the Higher Education Act of 1965 (20 U.S.C. 1070 et seq.) for a program of study at the eligible institution described in subparagraph (A); and

(ii) that have not been discharged by the Secretary pursuant to section 437(c)(1) or section 464(g)(1) of the Higher Education Act of 1965 (20 U.S.C. 1087(c)(1); 1087dd(g)(1)); and

(C) during the 3-year period beginning on the date of the closure of the eligible institution described in subparagraph (A), has not enrolled in any institution of higher education that participates in a program under title IV of the Higher Education Act of 1965 (20 U.S.C. 1070 et seq.).

(3) REPORT.—Beginning on the date that is 3 years after the date of enactment of this Act and every 180 days thereafter, the Secretary shall report to the authorizing committees the number of loans discharged in accordance with this subsection, and any amounts recovered by the Secretary in accordance with the authority of the Secretary to pursue claims under section 437(c)(1) or section 464(g)(1) of the Higher Education Act of 1965 (20 U.S.C. 1087(c)(1); 1087dd(g)(1)).

(i) Definitions.—In this section:

(1) LIQUIDITY LEVEL.—The term "liquidity level" means, with respect to an eligible institution, the number of days such eligible institution can operate based on available resources, as determined in accordance with the Financial Accounting Standards Board update entitled "No. 2016–14 Not-for-Profit Entities (Topic 958)" and dated August, 2016.

(2) TEACH-OUT AGREEMENT.—The term "teach-out agreement" means a written agreement between an eligible institution and one or more teach-out institutions that is in accordance with the requirements in section 496(c)(6) of the Higher Education Act of 1965 (20 U.S.C. 1099b(c)(6)) and that provides for the equitable treatment of students and a reasonable opportunity for students to complete their program of study if such eligible institution, or an institutional location that provides 100 percent

of at least one program offered by such eligible institution, ceases to operate or plans to cease operations before all such enrolled students have completed their program of study.

(3) TEACH-OUT INSTITUTION.—The term "teach-out institution" means an institution of higher education that—

(A) is not subject to a COVID–19 provisional program participation agreement under this section;

(B) shows no evidence of significant problems (including financial responsibility or administrative capability) that affect, as determined by the Secretary, the institution's ability to administer a program under title IV of the Higher Education Act of 1965 (20 U.S.C. 1070 et seq.);

(C) is not required to pay any material debt, as determined by the Secretary, or incur any material liability, as determined by the Secretary, arising from a judgment in a judicial proceeding, an administrative proceeding or determination, or settlement;

(D) is not involved in a lawsuit by a Federal or State authority for financial relief on claims related to the making of loans under part D of title IV of the Higher Education Act of 1965 (20 U.S.C. 1087a et seq.);

(E) has the necessary experience, resources, and capacity, including support services, to enroll students and provide an educational program of acceptable quality that is reasonably similar in content and delivery, and to the extent practicable, scheduling, to that provided by the eligible institution that enters into an agreement with such teach-out institution; and

(F) during the five most recent award years, has not been subject to a denial, withdrawal, suspension, or termination of accreditation by an accrediting agency or association recognized by the Secretary.

(4) TEACH-OUT PLAN.—The term "teach-out plan" means a written plan developed by an eligible institution that provides for the equitable treatment of students if such eligible institution, or an institutional location that provides 100 percent of at least one program offered by the eligible institution, ceases to operate or plans to cease operations before all enrolled students have completed their program of study.

(j) Authorization Of Appropriations.—There is authorized to be appropriated $300,000,000 to carry out subsection (d)(9).

Subtitle C—Federal Student Loan Relief

Part A—Temporary Relief For Federal Student Borrowers Under The CARES Act
EXPANDING LOAN RELIEF TO ALL FEDERAL STUDENT LOAN BORROWERS

SEC. 150113.

Section 3502(a) of division A of the Coronavirus Aid, Relief, and Economic Security Act (Public Law 116–136) is amended—

(1) by redesignating paragraphs (2) through (5) as paragraphs (3) through (6), respectively; and

(2) by inserting after paragraph (1) the following:

"(2) FEDERAL STUDENT LOAN.—The term 'Federal student loan' means a loan—

"(A) made under part D, part B, or part E of title IV of the Higher Education Act of 1965 (20 U.S.C. 1070 et seq.), and held by the Department of Education;

"(B) made, insured, or guaranteed under part B of such title, or made under part E of such title, and not held by the Department of Education; or

"(C) made under—

"(i) subpart II of part A of title VII of the Public Health Service Act (42 U.S.C. 292q et seq.); or

"(ii) part E of title VIII of the Public Health Service Act (42 U.S.C. 297a et seq.).".

EXTENDING THE LENGTH OF BORROWER RELIEF DUE TO THE CORONAVIRUS EMERGENCY

SEC. 150114.

Section 3513 of division A of the Coronavirus Aid, Relief, and Economic Security Act (Public Law 116–136) is amended—

(1) by amending subsection (a) to read as follows:

"(a) Suspension Of Payments.—

"(1) IN GENERAL.—During the period beginning on March 13, 2020, and ending on September 30, 2021, the Secretary or, as applicable, the Secretary of Health and Human Services, shall suspend all payments due on Federal student loans.

"(2) TRANSITION PERIOD.—For one additional 30-day period beginning on the day after the last day of the suspension period described in subsection (a), the Secretary or, as applicable, the Secretary of Health and Human Services, shall ensure that any missed payments on a Federal student loan by a borrower during such additional 30-day period—

"(A) do not result in collection fees or penalties associated with late payments; and

"(B) are not reported to any consumer reporting agency or otherwise impact the borrower's credit history.

"(3) PAYMENT REFUND IN LIEU OF RETROACTIVE APPLICABILITY.—

"(A) IN GENERAL.—By not later than 60 days after the date of enactment of the HEROES Act, the Secretary or, as applicable, the Secretary of Health and Human Services, shall, for each Federal student loan defined in subparagraph (B) or (C) of section 3502(a)(2)—

"(i) determine the amount of principal due on such loan (or that would have been due in the absence of being voluntarily paid by the holder of such loan) during the period beginning March 13, 2020, and ending on such date of enactment; and

"(ii) refund the amount of principal calculated under subparagraph (A), by—

"(I) paying the holder of the loan the amount of the principal calculated under subparagraph (A), to be applied to the loan balance for the borrower of such loan; or

"(II) if there is no outstanding balance or payment due on the loan as of the date on which the refund is to be provided, providing a payment in the amount of the principal calculated under subparagraph (A) directly to the borrower.

"(B) PRINCIPAL.—In this paragraph, the term 'principal' includes any late charges or fees.

"(4) RECERTIFICATION.—A borrower who is repaying a Federal student loan pursuant to in an income-contingent repayment plan under section 455(d)(1)(D) of the Higher Education Act of 1965 (20 U.S.C. 1087e(d)(1)(D)) or an income-based repayment plan under section 493C of such Act (20 U.S.C. 1098e) shall not be required to recertify the income or family size of the borrower under such plan prior to December 31, 2021.";

(2) in subsection (c), by striking "part D or B of title IV of the Higher Education Act of 1965 (20 U.S.C. 1087a et seq.; 1071 et seq.)" and inserting "part B, D, or E of title IV of the Higher Education Act of 1965 (20 U.S.C. 1087a et seq.; 1071 et seq.; 1087aa et seq.)";

(3) in subsection (d), by striking "During the period in which the Secretary suspends

payments on a loan under subsection (a), the Secretary" and inserting "During the period in which payments on a Federal student loan are suspended under subsection (a), the Secretary or, as applicable, the Secretary of Health and Human Services";

(4) in subsection (e), by striking "During the period in which the Secretary suspends payments on a loan under subsection (a), the Secretary" and inserting "During the period in which payments on a Federal student loan are suspended under subsection (a), the Secretary or, as applicable, the Secretary of Health and Human Services"; and

(5) in subsection (f), by striking "the Secretary" and inserting "the Secretary or, as applicable, the Secretary of Health and Human Services;".

NO INTEREST ACCRUAL

SEC. 150115.

Section 3513(b) of division A of the Coronavirus Aid, Relief, and Economic Security Act (Public Law 116–136) is amended to read as follows:

"(b) Providing Interest Relief.—

"(1) NO ACCRUAL OF INTEREST.—

"(A) IN GENERAL.—During the period described in subparagraph (D), interest on a Federal student loan shall not accrue or shall be paid by the Secretary (or the Secretary of Health and Human Services) during—

"(i) the repayment period of such loan;

"(ii) any period excluded from the repayment period of such loan (including any period of deferment or forbearance);

"(iii) any period in which the borrower of such loan is in a grace period; or

"(iv) any period in which the borrower of such loan is in default on such loan.

"(B) DIRECT LOANS AND DEPARTMENT OF EDUCATION HELD FFEL AND PERKINS LOANS.—For purposes of subparagraph (A), interest shall not accrue on a Federal student loan described in section 3502(a)(2)(A).

"(C) FFEL AND PERKINS LOANS NOT HELD BY THE DEPARTMENT OF EDUCATION AND HHS LOANS.—For purposes of subparagraph (A)—

"(i) in the case of a Federal student loan defined in section 3502(a)(2)(B), the Secretary shall pay, on a monthly basis, the amount of interest due on the unpaid principal of such loan to the holder of such loan, except that any payments made under this clause shall not affect payment calculations under section 438 of the Higher Education Act of 1965 (20 U.S.C. 1087–1); and

"(ii) in the case of a Federal student loan defined in section 3502(a)(2)(C), the Secretary of Health and Human Services shall pay, on a monthly basis, the amount of interest due on the unpaid principal of such loan to the holder of such loan.

"(D) PERIOD DESCRIBED.—

"(i) IN GENERAL.—The period described in this clause is the period beginning on March 13, 2020, and ending on the later of—

"(I) September 30, 2021; or

"(II) the day following the date of enactment of the HEROES Act that is 2 months after the national U–5 measure of labor underutilization shows initial signs of recovery.

"(ii) DEFINITIONS.—In this subparagraph:

"(I) NATIONAL U–5 MEASURE OF LABOR UNDERUTILIZATION.—The term 'national U–5 measure of labor underutilization' means the seasonally-adjusted, monthly U–5 measure of labor underutilization published by the Bureau of Labor Statistics.

"(II) INITIAL SIGNS OF RECOVERY.—The term 'initial signs of recovery' means that the average national U–5 measure of labor underutilization for months in the most recent 3-consecutive-month period for which data are available—

"(aa) is lower than the highest value of the average national U–5 measure of labor underutilization for a 3-consecutive-month period during the period beginning in March 2020 and the most recent month for which data from the Bureau of Labor Statistics are available by an amount that is equal to or greater than one-third of the difference between—

"(AA) the highest value of the average national U–5 measure of labor underutilization for a 3-consecutive-month period during such period; and

"(BB) the value of the average national U–5 measure of labor underutilization for the 3-consecutive-month period ending in February 2020; and

"(bb) has decreased for each month during the most recent 2 consecutive months for which data from the Bureau of Labor Statistics are available.

"(E) OTHER DEFINITIONS.—In this paragraph:

"(i) DEFAULT.—The term 'default'—

"(I) in the case of a Federal student loan made, insured, or guaranteed under part B or D of the Higher Education Act of 1965, has the meaning given such term in section 435(l) of the Higher Education Act of 1965 (20 U.S.C. 1085);

"(II) in the case of a Federal student loan made under part E of the Higher Education Act of 1965, has the meaning given such term in section 674.2 of title 34, Code of Federal Regulations (or successor regulations); or

"(III) in the case of a Federal student loan defined in section 3502(a)(2)(C), has the meaning given such term in section 721 or 835 of the Public Health Service Act (42 U.S.C. 292q, 297a), as applicable.

"(ii) GRACE PERIOD.—The term 'grace period' means—

"(I) in the case of a Federal student loan made, insured, or guaranteed under part B or D of the Higher Education Act of 1965, the 6-month period after the date the student ceases to carry at least one-half the normal full-time academic workload, as described in section 428(b)(7) of the Higher Education Act of 1965 (20 U.S.C. 1078(b)(7));

"(II) in the case of a Federal student loan made under part E of the Higher Education Act of 1965, the 9-month period after the date on which a student ceases to carry at least one-half the normal full-time academic workload, as described in section 464(c)(1)(A) of the Higher Education Act of 1965 (20 U.S.C. 1087dd(c)(1)(A)); and

"(III) in the case of a Federal student loan defined in section 3502(a)(2)(C), the 1-year period described in section 722(c) of the Public Health Service Act (42 U.S.C. 292r(c)) or the 9-month period described in section 836(b)(2) of such Act (42 U.S.C. 297b(b)(2)), as applicable.

"(iii) REPAYMENT PERIOD.—The term 'repayment period' means—

"(I) in the case of a Federal student loan made, insured, or guaranteed under part B or D of the Higher Education Act of 1965, the repayment period described in section 428(b)(7) of the Higher Education Act of 1965 (20 U.S.C. 1078(b)(7));

"(II) in the case of a Federal student loan made under part E of the Higher Education Act of 1965, the repayment period described in section 464(c)(4) of the Higher Education Act of 1965 (20 U.S.C. 1087dd(c)(4)); or

"(III) in the case of a Federal student loan defined in section 3502(2)(C), the repayment period described in section 722(c) or 836(b)(2) of the Public Health Service Act (42 U.S.C. 292r(c), 297b(b)(2)), as applicable.

"(2) INTEREST REFUND IN LIEU OF RETROACTIVE APPLICABILITY.—By not later than 60 days after the date of enactment of the HEROES Act, the Secretary or, as applicable, the Secretary of Health and Human Services, shall, for each Federal student loan defined in subparagraph (B) or (C) of section 3502(a)(2)—

"(A) determine the amount of interest due (or that would have been due in the absence of being voluntarily paid by the holder of such loan) on such loan during the period beginning March 13, 2020, and ending on such date of enactment; and

"(B) refund the amount of interest calculated under clause (i), by—

"(i) paying the holder of the loan the amount of the interest calculated under subparagraph (A), to be applied to the loan balance for the borrower of such loan; or

"(ii) if there is no outstanding balance or payment due on the loan as of the date on which the refund is to be provided, providing a payment in the amount of the interest calculated under clause (i) directly to the borrower.

"(3) SUSPENSION OF INTEREST CAPITALIZATION.—

"(A) IN GENERAL.—With respect to any Federal student loan, interest that accrued but had not been paid prior to March 13, 2020, and had not been capitalized as of such date, shall not be capitalized.

"(B) TRANSITION.—The Secretary or, as applicable, the Secretary of Health and Human Services, shall ensure that any interest on a Federal student loan that had been capitalized in violation of subparagraph (A) is corrected and the balance of principal and interest due for the Federal student loan is adjusted accordingly.".

NOTICE TO BORROWERS

SEC. 150116.

Section 3513(g) of division A of the Coronavirus Aid, Relief, and Economic Security Act (Public Law 116–136) is amended—

(1) in the matter preceding paragraph (1), by striking "the Secretary" and inserting "the Secretary or, as applicable, the Secretary of Health and Human Services,";

(2) in paragraph (1)(D), by striking the period and inserting a semicolon;

(3) in paragraph (2)—

(A) in the matter preceding subparagraph (A), by striking "August 1, 2020" and inserting "August 1, 2021"; and

(B) by amending subparagraph (B) to read as follows:

"(B) that—

"(i) a borrower of a Federal student loan made, insured, or guaranteed under part B or D of title IV of the Higher Education Act of 1965 may be eligible to enroll in an income-contingent repayment plan under section 455(d)(1)(D) of the Higher Education Act of 1965 (20 U.S.C. 1087e(d)(1)(D)) or an income-based repayment plan under section 493C of such Act (20 U.S.C. 1098e), including a brief description of such repayment plans; and

"(ii) in the case of a borrower of a Federal student loan defined in section 3502(a)(2)(C) or made under part E of title IV of the Higher Education of 1965, the borrower may be eligible to enroll in such a repayment plan if the borrower consolidates such loan with a loan described in clause (i) of this subparagraph, and receives a Federal Direct Consolidation Loan under part D of the Higher Education of 1965 (20 U.S.C. 1087a et seq.); and"; and

(C) by adding at the end the following:

"(3) in a case in which the accrual of interest on Federal student loans is suspended under subsection (b)(1) beyond September 30, 2021, during the 2-month period beginning on the date on which the national U–5 measure of labor underutilization shows initial signs of recovery (as such terms are defined in subsection (b)(1)(D)) carry out a program to provide not less than 6 notices by postal mail, telephone, or electronic communication to borrowers—

"(A) indicating when the interest on Federal student loans of the borrower will resume accrual and capitalization; and

"(B) the information described in paragraph (2)(B).".

WRITING DOWN BALANCES FOR FEDERAL STUDENT LOAN BORROWERS

SEC. 150117.

Section 3513 of division A of the Coronavirus Aid, Relief, and Economic Security Act (Public Law 116–136), as amended by this part, is further amended by adding at the end the following:

"(h) Writing Down Balances For Federal Student Loan Borrowers.—

"(1) IN GENERAL.—Not later than 30 days after the date of enactment of the HEROES Act, the Secretary shall cancel or repay an amount on the outstanding balance due (including the unpaid principal amount, any accrued interest, and any fees or charges) on the Federal student loans defined in subparagraphs (A) and (B) of section 3502(a)(2) of a borrower that is equal to the lesser of—

"(A) $10,000; or

"(B) the total outstanding balance due on such loans of the borrower.

"(2) APPLICATION.—Unless otherwise requested by the borrower in writing, a cancellation or repayment under paragraph (1) shall be applied —

"(A) in the case of a borrower whose loans have different applicable rates of interest, first toward the outstanding balance due on the loan with the highest applicable rate of interest among such loans; and

"(B) in the case of a borrower of loans that have the same applicable rates of interest, first toward the outstanding balance of principal due on the loan with the highest principal balance among such loans.

"(3) DATA TO IMPLEMENT.—Contractors of the Secretary, and holders of Federal student loans, shall report, to the satisfaction of the Secretary the information necessary to carry out this subsection.

"(4) TAXATION.—For purposes of the Internal Revenue Code of 1986, in the case of any cancellation or repayment of indebtedness under this subsection with respect to any borrower:

"(A) EXCLUSION FROM GROSS INCOME.—No amount shall be included in the gross income of such borrower by reason of such cancellation or repayment.

"(B) WAIVER OF INFORMATION REPORTING REQUIREMENTS.—Amounts excluded from gross income under subparagraph (A) shall not be required to be reported (and shall not be taken into account in determining whether any reporting requirement applies) under chapter 61 of such Code.".

IMPLEMENTATION

SEC. 150118.

Section 3513 of division A of the Coronavirus Aid, Relief, and Economic Security Act (Public Law 116–136), as amended by this part, is further amended by adding at the end the following:

"(i) Implementation.—

"(1) INFORMATION VERIFICATION.—

"(A) IN GENERAL.—To facilitate implementation of this section, information for the purposes described in subparagraph (B), shall be reported—

"(i) by the holders of Federal student loans defined in section 3502(a)(2)(B) to the satisfaction of the Secretary; and

"(ii) by the holders of Federal student loans defined in section 3502(a)(2)(C) to the satisfaction of the Secretary of Health and Human Services.

"(B) PURPOSES.—The purposes of the information reported under subparagraph (A) are to—

"(i) verify, at the borrower level, the payments that are provided or suspended under this section; and

"(ii) calculate the amount of any interest due to the holder for reimbursement of interest under subsection (b).

"(2) COORDINATION.—The Secretary shall coordinate with the Secretary of Health and Human Services to carry out the provisions of this section with respect to Federal student loans defined in section 3502(a)(2)(C).".

EFFECTIVE DATE

SEC. 150119.

This part, and the amendments made by this part, shall take effect as if enacted as part of the Coronavirus Aid, Relief, and Economic Security Act (Public Law 116–136).

Part B—Consolidation Loans And Public Service Loan Forgiveness

SPECIAL RULES RELATING TO FEDERAL DIRECT CONSOLIDATION LOANS

SEC. 150120.

(a) Special Rules Relating To Federal Direct Consolidation Loans And PSLF.—

(1) PUBLIC SERVICE LOAN FORGIVENESS OPTION ON CONSOLIDATION APPLICATION.—

(A) IN GENERAL.—During the period described in subsection (e), the Secretary shall—

(i) include, in any application for a Federal Direct Consolidation Loan under part D of title IV of the Higher Education Act of 1965 (20 U.S.C. 1087a et seq,), an option for the borrower to indicate that the borrower intends to participate in the public service loan forgiveness program under section 455(m) of such Act (20 U.S.C. 1087e(m)); and

(ii) for each borrower who submits an application for a Federal Direct Consolidation Loan, without regard to whether the borrower indicates the intention described in clause (i)—

(I) request that the borrower submit a certification of employment; and

(II) after receiving a complete certification of employment—

(aa) carry out the requirements of paragraph (2); and

(bb) inform the borrower of the number of qualifying monthly payments made on the component loans before consolidation that shall be deemed, in accordance with paragraph (2)(D), to be qualifying monthly payments made on the Federal Direct Consolidation Loan.

(B) HOLD HARMLESS.—The Secretary may not change or otherwise rescind a calculation made under paragraph (2)(D) after informing the borrower of the results of such calculation under subparagraph (A)(ii)(II)(bb).

(2) PROCESS TO DETERMINE QUALIFYING PAYMENTS FOR PURPOSES OF PSLF.—Upon receipt of a complete certification of employment under paragraph (1) (A)(ii)(II) of a borrower who receives a Federal Direct Consolidation Loan described in paragraph (1)(A), the Secretary shall—

(A) review the borrower's payment history to identify each component loan of such Federal Direct Consolidation Loan;

(B) for each such component loan—

(i) calculate the weighted factor of the component loan, which shall be the factor that represents the portion of such Federal Direct Consolidation Loan that is attributable to such component loan; and

(ii) determine the number of qualifying monthly payments made on such component loan before consolidation;

(C) calculate the number of qualifying monthly payments determined under sub-paragraph (B)(ii) with respect to a component loan that shall be deemed as qualifying monthly payments made on the Federal Direct Consolidation Loan by multiplying—

(i) the weighted factor of such component loan as determined under subparagraph (B)(i), by

(ii) the number of qualifying monthly payments made on such component loan as determined under subparagraph (B)(ii); and

(D) calculate the total number of qualifying monthly payments with respect to the component loans of the Federal Direct Consolidation Loan that shall be deemed as qualifying monthly payments made on such Federal Direct Consolidation Loan by—

(i) adding together the result of each calculation made under subparagraph (C) with respect to each such component loan; and

(ii) rounding the number determined under clause (i) to the nearest whole number.

(3) DEFINITIONS.—For purposes of this subsection:

(A) CERTIFICATION OF EMPLOYMENT.—The term "certification of employment", used with respect to a borrower, means a certification of the employment of the borrower in a public service job (as defined in section 455(m)(3)(B) of the Higher Education Act of 1965) on or after October 1, 2007.

(B) COMPONENT LOAN.—The term "component loan", used with respect to a Federal Direct Consolidation Loan, means each loan for which the liability has been discharged by the proceeds of the Federal Direct Consolidation Loan, which—

(i) may include a loan that is not an eligible Federal Direct Loan (as defined in section 455(m)(3)(A) of the Higher Education Act of 1965); and

(ii) in the case of a subsequent consolidation loan, only includes loans for which the liability has been directly discharged by such subsequent consolidation loan.

(C) FEDERAL DIRECT CONSOLIDATION LOAN.—The term "Federal Direct Consolidation Loan" means a Federal Direct Consolidation Loan made under part D of title IV of the Higher Education Act of 1965 (20 U.S.C. 1087a et seq.).

(D) QUALIFYING MONTHLY PAYMENT.—

(i) COMPONENT LOAN.—The term "qualifying monthly payment", used with respect to a component loan, means a monthly payment on such loan made by a borrower, during a period of employment in a public service job (as defined in section 455(m)(3)(B) of the Higher Education Act of 1965 (20 U.S.C. 1087e(m)(3)(B)) on or after October 1, 2007, pursuant to—

(I) a repayment plan under part B, D, or E of title IV of the Higher Education Act of 1965 (20 U.S.C. 1071 et seq.; 1087a et seq.; 1087aa et seq.); or

(II) in the case of a loan made under subpart II of part A of title VII of the Public Health Service Act or under part E of title VIII of the Public Health Service Act, a repayment plan under title VII or VIII of such Act.

(ii) FEDERAL DIRECT CONSOLIDATION LOAN.—The term "qualifying monthly payment", used with respect to a Federal Direct Consolidation Loan, means a monthly payment on such loan that counts as 1 of the 120 monthly payments described in section 455(m)(1)(A) of the Higher Education Act of 1965 (20 U.S.C. 1087e(m)(3)(B)).

(b) Special Rules Relating To Federal Direct Consolidation Loans And ICR And IBR.—

(1) IN GENERAL.—During the period described in subsection (e), with respect to a borrower who receives a Federal Direct Consolidation Loan and who intends to repay such loan under an income-contingent repayment plan under section 455(d)(1)(D) of the Higher Education Act of 1965 (20 U.S.C. 1087e(d)(1)(D)) or an income-based repayment plan under section 493C of such Act (20 U.S.C. 1098e), the Secretary shall—

(A) review the borrower's payment history to identify each component loan of such Federal Direct Consolidation Loan;

(B) for each such component loan—

(i) calculate the weighted factor of the component loan, which shall be the factor that represents the portion of such Federal Direct Consolidation Loan that is attributable to such component loan; and

(ii) determine the number of qualifying monthly payments made on such component loan before consolidation;

(C) calculate the number of qualifying monthly payments determined under subparagraph (B)(ii) with respect to a component loan that shall be deemed as qualifying monthly payments made on the Federal Direct Consolidation Loan by multiplying—

(i) the weighted factor of such component loan as determined under subparagraph (B)(i), by

(ii) the number of qualifying monthly payments made on such component loan as determined under subparagraph (B)(ii); and

(D) calculate and inform the borrower of the total number of qualifying monthly payments with respect to the component loans of the Federal Direct Consolidation Loan that shall be deemed as qualifying monthly payments made on such Federal Direct Consolidation Loan by—

(i) adding together the result of each calculation made under subparagraph (C) with respect to each such component loan; and

(ii) rounding the number determined under clause (i) to the nearest whole number.

(2) HOLD HARMLESS.—The Secretary may not change or otherwise rescind a calculation made under paragraph (1)(D) after informing the borrower of the results of such calculation under such paragraph.

(3) DEFINITIONS.—In this subsection:

(A) COMPONENT LOAN; FEDERAL DIRECT CONSOLIDATION LOAN.—The terms "component loan" and "Federal Direct Consolidation Loan" have the meanings given the terms in subsection (a).

(B) QUALIFYING PAYMENT.—

(i) COMPONENT LOANS.—Subject to clause (ii), the term "qualifying monthly payment", used with respect to a component loan, means a monthly payment on such loan made by a borrower pursuant to—

(I) a repayment plan under part B, D, or E of title IV of the Higher Education Act of 1965 (20 U.S.C. 1071 et seq., 1087a et seq., 1087aa et seq.); or

(II) in the case of a loan made under subpart II of part A of title VII of the Public Health Service Act (42 U.S.C. 292q et seq.) or under part E of title VIII of the Public Health Service Act (42 U.S.C. 297a et seq.), a repayment plan under title VII or VIII of such Act.

(ii) CLARIFICATION.—

(I) ICR.—For purposes of determining the number of qualifying monthly payments made on a component loan pursuant to an income-contingent repayment plan under section 455(d)(1)(D) of the Higher Education Act of 1965 (20 U.S.C. 1087e(d)(1)(D)), each month a borrower is determined to meet the requirements of section 455(e)(7)(B)(i) of such Act with respect to such loan shall be treated as such a qualifying monthly payment.

(II) IBR.—For purposes of determining the number of qualifying monthly payments made on a component loan pursuant to an income-based repayment plan under section 493C of such Act (20 U.S.C. 1098e), each month a borrower was determined to meet the requirements of subsection (b)(7)(B) of such section 493C with respect to such loan shall be treated as such a qualifying monthly payment.

(iii) FEDERAL DIRECT CONSOLIDATION LOANS.—The term "qualifying monthly payment", used with respect to a Federal Direct Consolidation Loan, means a monthly payment on such loan that counts as a monthly payment under an income-contingent repayment plan under section 455(d)(1)(D) of the Higher Education Act of 1965 (20 U.S.C. 1087e(d)(1)(D)), or an income-based repayment plan under section 493C of the Higher Education Act of 1965 (20 U.S.C. 1098e).

(c) Notification To Borrowers.—

(1) IN GENERAL.—During the period described in subsection (e), the Secretary and the Secretary of Health and Human Services shall undertake a campaign to alert borrowers of a loan described in paragraph (2)—

(A) on the benefits of consolidating such loans into a Federal Direct Consolidation Loan, including the benefits of the special rules under subsections (a) and (b) of this section; and

(B) under which servicers and holders of Federal student loans shall provide to borrowers such consumer information, and in such manner, as determined appropriate by the Secretaries, based on conducting consumer testing to determine how to make the information as meaningful to borrowers as possible.

(2) FEDERAL STUDENT LOANS.—A loan described in this paragraph is—

(A) a loan made under subpart II of part A of title VII of the Public Health Service Act or under part E of title VIII of such Act; or

(B) a loan made under part E of the Higher Education Act of 1965.

(d) Special Rule For Interest On Federal Direct Consolidation Loans.—Any Federal Direct Consolidation Loan for which the application is received during the period described in subsection (e), shall bear interest at an annual rate as calculated under section 455(b)(8)(D) of the Higher Education Act of 1965 (20 U.S.C. 1087e(b)(8)(D)), without regard to the requirement to round the weighted average of the interest rate to the nearest higher one-eighth of one percent.

(e) Period.—The period described in this clause is the period beginning on the date of enactment of this Act, and ending on the later of—

(1) September 30, 2021; or

(2) the day following the date of enactment of this Act that is 2 months after the national U–5 measure of labor underutilization shows initial signs of recovery (as such terms are defined in section 3513(b) of the Coronavirus Aid, Relief, and Economic Security Act (Public Law 116–136), as amended by this Act)).

(f) GAO Study On Implementation Of Special Rules On Consolidation.—Not later than 6 months after the date of enactment of this Act, the Comptroller General of the United States shall submit a report to the authorizing committees (defined in section 103 of the Higher Education Act of 1965 (20 U.S.C. 1003) on the implementation of this section, which shall include—

(1) information on borrowers who apply for or receive a Federal Direct Consolidation Loan under part D of the Higher Education Act of 1965 during the period described in subsection (e), disaggregated—

(A) by borrowers who intend to participate in the public service loan forgiveness program under section 455(m) of such Act (20 U.S.C. 1087e(m)); and

(B) by borrowers who intend to repay such loans on an income-contingent repayment plan under section 455(d)(1)(D) of the Higher Education Act of 1965 (20 U.S.C. 1087e(d)(1)(D)) or an income-based repayment plan under section 493C of such Act (20 U.S.C. 1098e);

(2) the extent to which the Secretary has established procedures for carrying out subsections (a) and (b);

(3) the extent to which the Secretary and the Secretary of Health and Human Services have carried out the notification to borrowers required under subsection (c); and

(4) recommendations on improving the implementation of this section to ensure increased borrower participation.

TREATMENT OF PSLF

SEC. 150121.

(a) Exception For Purposes Of PSLF Loan Forgiveness.—Section 455(m)(1)(B) of the Higher Education Act of 1965 (20 U.S.C. 1087e(m)(1)(B)) shall apply as if clause (i) were struck.

(b) Health Care Practitioner.—In section 455(m)(3)(B)(i) of the Higher Education Act of 1965 (20 U.S.C. 1087e(m)(3)(B)(i)), the term "full-time professionals engaged in health care practitioner occupations" includes an individual who—

(1) has a full-time job as a health care practitioner;

(2) provides medical services in such full-time job at a nonprofit hospital or public hospital or other nonprofit or public health care facility; and

(3) is prohibited by State law from being employed directly by such hospital or other health care facility.

Part C—Emergency Relief For Defrauded Borrowers

EMERGENCY RELIEF FOR DEFRAUDED BORROWERS

SEC. 150122.

(a) Emergency Relief.—An eligible borrower shall be entitled to relief on an eligible loan pursuant to this section.

(b) Definitions.—In this section:

(1) ELIGIBLE BORROWER.—The term "eligible borrower" means an individual—

(A) who—

(i) borrowed an eligible loan to finance the cost of enrollment at an institution of higher education that, according to findings by the Department of Education made on or before the date of enactment of this Act, made a false or misleading representation with the respect to the job placement rates of such institution of higher education; and

(ii) has not received the relief described in subsection (c)(1) on such eligible loan; or

(B) who—

(i) borrowed an eligible loan to finance the cost of enrollment at an institution of higher education that, according to findings by the Department of Education made on or before the date of enactment of this Act, made a false or misleading representation with respect to guaranteed employment or transferability of credits of such institution of higher education;

(ii) in an application to the Secretary for a defense to repayment of such eligible loan, has asserted that the borrower (or the dependent student on whose behalf the eligible borrowed such eligible loan) relied on such false or misleading representation in deciding to enroll in such institution of higher education; and

(iii) has not received the relief described in subsection (c)(1) on such eligible loan.

(2) ELIGIBLE LOAN.—The term "eligible loan" means a loan made, insured, or guaranteed under part B or D of title IV of the Higher Education Act of 1965 (20 U.S.C. 1071 et seq.; 1087a et seq.).

(c) Relief.—With respect to each eligible borrower, the Secretary shall—

(1) not later than 45 days after the date of enactment of this Act, with respect to each eligible loan of the borrower described in subsection (b)(1)—

(A) cancel or repay the full balance of interest and principal (including fees and charges) due on such loan; and

(B) return to the borrower an amount equal to the total amount of payments (including voluntary and involuntary payments) made on the loan by the borrower;

(2) not later than 60 days after the date of enactment of this section, report the cancellation or repayment under paragraph (1)(A) of each eligible loan to each consumer reporting agency to which the Secretary previously reported the status of the loan, so as to delete all adverse credit history assigned to the loan; and

(3) not later than 60 days after the date of enactment of this Act, no longer consider a borrower who has defaulted on a loan cancelled or repaid under this subsection to be in default on such loan.

(d) Notification.—Not later than 30 days after the date of enactment of this section, the Secretary shall notify (in writing) each eligible borrower of—

(1) the relief to which the borrower is entitled pursuant to subsection (c), and when the borrower will receive such relief;

(2) the borrower's eligibility to receive assistance under title IV of the Higher Education Act of 1965 (20 U.S.C. 1070 et seq.) after receiving relief pursuant to subsection (c); and

(3) any further relief to such borrower as the Secretary determines is appropriate.

(e) Expedient Adjudication Of State Attorney General Claims Relating To Defense To Repayment Of A Loan.—

(1) IN GENERAL.—The Secretary shall carry out the requirements of paragraph (2) with respect to each claim submitted to the Secretary on or before the date of enactment of this Act by a State attorney general on behalf of one or more individuals who—

(A) allege that the individual borrowed an eligible loan to finance the cost of enrollment at an institution of higher education whose act or omission the individual may assert as a defense to repayment on such loan under the Higher Education Act of 1965 (20 U.S.C. 1001 et seq.) or under applicable State law; and

(B) has not received the relief described in paragraph (2)(B) on such eligible loan.

(2) REQUIREMENTS.—The Secretary shall carry out the following with respect to each claim described in paragraph (1):

(A) Not later than 180 days after the date of enactment of this Act, adjudicate each such claim.

(B) For each claim for which the State attorney general proves the facts described in paragraph (1) by a preponderance of the evidence, with respect to each individual on whose behalf the claim was submitted, provide the following:

(i) Not later than 45 days after the date on which such claim is adjudicated, with respect to each eligible loan described in paragraph (1) of the individual—

(I) cancel or repay the full balance of interest and principal (including fees and charges) due on such loan; and

(II) return to the borrower an amount equal to the total amount of payments (including voluntary and involuntary payments) made on the loan by the borrower.

(ii) Not later than 60 days after the date on which such claim is adjudicated, report the cancellation or repayment under clause (i) of each eligible loan to each consumer reporting agency to which the Secretary previously reported the status of the loan, so as to delete all adverse credit history assigned to the loan.

(iii) Not later than 60 days after the date on which such claim is adjudicated, no longer consider a borrower who has defaulted on a loan cancelled or repaid under this subparagraph to be in default on such loan.

(C) Not later than 10 days after the date of adjudication under subparagraph (A), with respect to each claim submitted on behalf of not less than 20 individuals, provide detailed reports to the authorizing committees, which shall include—

(i) any evidence submitted by the State attorney general, which the Secretary relied upon in adjudicating the claim;

(ii) any evidence submitted by the State attorney general, which the Secretary did not rely upon in adjudicating the claim;

(iii) any other evidence the Secretary relied upon in adjudicating the claim;

(iv) a summary of all efforts to coordinate with the State attorney general to ensure a fair adjudication; and

(v) a detailed legal rationale for the Secretary's adjudication.

(D) For the duration of the adjudication of each claim—

(i) suspend any payments owed on any eligible loan that is the subject of such claim, including a suspension of any capitalization of interest;

(ii) suspend any involuntary collections on such loan, including collections under—

(I) a wage garnishment authorized under section 488A of the Higher Education Act of 1965 (20 U.S.C. 1095a) or section 3720D of title 31, United States Code;

(II) a reduction of tax refund by amount of debt authorized under section 3720A of title 31, United States Code, or section 6402(d) of the Internal Revenue Code of 1986;

(III) a reduction of any other Federal benefit payment by administrative offset authorized under section 3716 of title 31, United States Code (including a benefit payment due to an individual under the Social Security Act (42 U.S.C. 301 et seq.) or any other provision described in subsection (c)(3)(A)(i) of such section); or

(IV) any other involuntary collection activity by the Secretary; and

(iii) suspend any interest accrual on such loan.

(E) Not later than 10 days after the date of adjudication for which relief is provided under subparagraph (B), notify (in writing) each individual with respect to whom relief is provided of—

(i) the relief to which the individual is entitled pursuant to subparagraph (B), and when the individual will receive such relief;

(ii) the individual's eligibility to receive assistance under title IV of the Higher Education Act of 1965 (20 U.S.C. 1070 et seq.) after receiving relief pursuant to subparagraph (B); and

(iii) any further relief to such borrower as the Secretary determines is appropriate.

(f) Institutional Accountability.—With respect to each loan cancelled or repaid under this section, the Secretary shall initiate an appropriate proceeding to require the institution of higher education whose act or omission resulted in such cancellation or repayment to repay to the Secretary the amount so cancelled or repaid.

(g) Taxation.—For purposes of the Internal Revenue Code of 1986, in the case of any relief provided under subsection (c)(1) or (e)(2)(B) with respect to a borrower:

(1) EXCLUSION FROM GROSS INCOME; NO RECAPTURE OF TAX BENEFITS.—No amount shall be included in the gross income of such borrower by reason of such relief and section 111(b) such Code shall not apply with respect to such relief.

(2) WAIVER OF INFORMATION REPORTING REQUIREMENTS.—Amounts excluded from gross income under paragraph (1) shall not be required to be reported (and shall not be taken into account in determining whether any reporting requirement applies) under chapter 61 of such Code.

Subtitle D—Notifications And Reporting

NOTIFICATIONS AND REPORTING RELATING TO HIGHER EDUCATION

SEC. 150123.

(a) Notification Of Non-CARES Act Flexibilities.—

(1) NOTICE TO CONGRESS.—

(A) IN GENERAL.—Not later than two days before the date on which the Secretary grants a flexibility described in paragraph (4), the Secretary shall—

(i) submit to the authorizing committees a written notification of the Secretary's intent to grant such flexibility; and

(ii) publish the notification on a publicly accessible website of the Department of Education.

(B) ELEMENTS.—Each notification under subparagraph (A) shall—

(i) identify the provision of law, regulation, or subregulatory guidance to which the flexibility will apply;

(ii) identify any limitations on the flexibility, including any time limits;

(iii) identify the statutory authority under which the flexibility is provided;

(iv) identify the class of covered entities to which the flexibility will apply;

(v) identify whether a covered entity will need to request the flexibility or whether the flexibility will be applied without request;

(vi) in the case of a flexibility that requires a covered entity to request the flexibility, identify the factors the Secretary will consider in approving or denying the flexibility;

(vii) explain how the flexibility is expected to benefit the covered entity or class of covered entities to which it applies; and

(viii) explain the reasons the flexibility is necessary and appropriate due to COVID–19.

(2) QUARTERLY REPORTS.—Not later than 10 days after the end of each fiscal quarter for the duration of the qualifying emergency through the end of the first fiscal year beginning after the conclusion of such qualifying emergency, the Secretary shall submit to the authorizing committees a report that includes, with respect to flexibilities described in paragraph (4) that have been issued by the Secretary in the most recently ended fiscal quarter, the following:

(A) In the case of a flexibility that was issued by the Secretary without request from a covered entity, an explanation of all requirements, including reporting requirements, that the Secretary imposed on the covered entity as a condition of the flexibility.

(B) In the case of a flexibility for which a covered entity requested and received specific approval from the Secretary—

(i) identification of the covered entity that received the flexibility;

(ii) an explanation of the specific reasons for approval of the request;

(iii) a detailed description of the terms of the flexibility, including—

(I) a description of any limitations on the flexibility; and

(II) identification of each provision of law (including regulation and subregulatory guidance) that is waived or modified and, for each such provision, the statutory authority under which the flexibility was provided; and

(iv) a copy of the final document granting the flexibility.

(C) In the case of any request for a flexibility that was denied by the Secretary—

(i) identification of the covered entity or entities that were denied a flexibility;

(ii) a detailed description of the terms of the request for the flexibility; and

(iii) an explanation of the specific reasons for denial of the request.

(3) REPORT ON FLEXIBILITIES GRANTED BEFORE ENACTMENT.—Not later than 30 days after the date of enactment of this Act, the Secretary shall submit to the authorizing committees a report that—

(A) identifies each flexibility described in paragraph (4) that was granted by the Secretary between March 13, 2020, and the date of enactment of this Act; and

(B) with respect to each such flexibility, provides the information specified in paragraph (1)(B).

(4) FLEXIBILITY DESCRIBED.—A flexibility described in this paragraph is modification or waiver of any provision of the Higher Education Act of 1965 (20 U.S.C. 1001 et seq.) (including any regulation or subregulatory guidance issued under such a provision) that the Secretary determines to be necessary and appropriate to modify or waive due to COVID–19, other than a provision of the Higher Education Act of 1965 that the Secretary is specifically authorized to modify or waive pursuant to the CARES Act (Public Law 116–136).

(5) PRIVACY.—The Secretary shall ensure that any report or notification submitted under this subsection does not reveal personally identifiable information about an individual student.

(6) RULE OF CONSTRUCTION.—Nothing in this subsection shall be construed to authorize the Secretary to waive or modify any provision of law.

(b) Reports On Exercise Of CARES Act Waivers By Institutions Of Higher Education.—Not later than 30 days after the date of enactment of this Act, each institution of higher education that exercises an authority provided under section 3503(c) (as redesignated by section 150102 of this Act), section 3504, section 3505, section 3508(d), section 3509, or section 3517(b) of the CARES Act (Public Law 116–136) shall submit to the Secretary a report that describes the nature and extent of the institution's exercise of such authorities, including the number of students and amounts of aid provided under title IV of the Higher Education Act of 1965 (20 U.S.C. 1070 et seq.) affected by the exercise of such authorities, as applicable.

(c) Reports On Changes To Contracts And Agreements.—Not later than 10 days after the end of each fiscal quarter for the duration of the qualifying emergency through the end of the first fiscal year beginning after the conclusion of such qualifying emergency, the Secretary shall submit to the authorizing committees a report that includes, for the most recently ended fiscal quarter—

(1) a summary of all modifications to any contracts with Department of Education contractors relating to Federal student loans, including—

(A) the contractual provisions that were modified;

(B) the names of all contractors affected by the modifications; and

(C) estimates of any costs or savings resulting from the modifications;

(2) a summary of all amendments, addendums, or other modifications to program participation agreements with institutions of higher education under section 487 of the Higher Education Act of 1965 (20 U.S.C. 1094), any provisional program participation agreements entered into under such section, and any COVID–19 provisional program participation agreements entered into under section 150112 of this Act, including—

(A) any provisions of such agreements that were modified by the Department of Education; and

(B) the number of institutions of higher education that received such modifications or entered into such provisional agreements, disaggregated by—

(i) status as a four-year, two-year, or less-than-two-year public institution, private nonprofit institution, or proprietary institution; and

(ii) each category of minority-serving institution described in section 371(a) of the Higher Education Act (20 U.S.C. 1067q); and

(3) sample copies of program participation agreements (including provisional agreements), selected at random from among the agreements described in paragraph (2), including at least one agreement from each type of institution (whether a public institution, private nonprofit institution, or proprietary institution) that received a modified or provisional agreement.

(d) Report To Congress.—

(1) IN GENERAL.—Not later than 90 days after the date of enactment of this Act, the Secretary shall submit to the authorizing committees a report that includes the following:

(A) A summary of the reports received by the Secretary under subsection (b).

(B) A description of—

(i) the Secretary's use of the authority under section 3506 of the CARES Act (Public Law 116–136) to adjust subsidized loan usage limits, including the total number of students and the total amount of subsidized loans under title IV of the Higher Education Act of 1965 (20 U.S.C. 1070 et seq.) affected by the Secretary's use of such authority;

(ii) the Secretary's use of the authority under section 3507 of the CARES Act (Public Law 116–136) to exclude certain periods from the Federal Pell Grant duration limit, including the total number of students and the total amount of Federal Pell Grants under section 401 of the Higher Education Act of 1965 (20 U.S.C. 1070a) affected by the Secretary's use of such authority;

(iii) the Secretary's use of the authority under section 3508 of the CARES Act (Public Law 116–136) to waive certain requirements for the return of Federal funds, including—

(I) in the case of waivers issued to students under such section, the total number of students and the total amount of aid under title IV of the Higher Education Act of 1965 (20 U.S.C. 1070 et seq.) affected by the Secretary's use of such authority; and

(II) in the case of waivers issued to institutions of higher education under such section, the total number of students and the total amount of aid under title IV of the Higher Education Act of 1965 (20 U.S.C. 1070 et seq.) affected by the Secretary's use of such authority.

(C) A summary of the information required to be reported to the authorizing committees under sections 3510 and 3512 of the CARES Act (Public Law 116–136), as amended by this Act, regardless of whether such information has previously been reported to such committees as of the date of the report under this subsection.

(D) Information relating to the temporary relief for Federal student loan borrowers provided under section 3513 of the CARES Act (Public Law 116–136), including—

(i) with respect to the notifications required under subsection (g)(1) of such section—

(I) the total number of individual notifications sent to borrowers in accordance with such subsection, disaggregated by electronic, postal, and telephonic notifications;

(II) the total number of notifications described in clause (i) that were sent within the 15-day period specified in such subsection; and

(III) the actual costs to the Department of Education of making the notifications under such subsection;

(ii) the projected costs to the Department of Education of making the notifications required under subsection (g)(2) of such section;

(iii) the number of Federal student loan borrowers who have affirmatively opted-out of payment suspension under subsection (a) of such section;

(iv) the number of individual notifications sent to employers directing the employers to halt wage garnishment pursuant to subsection (e) of such section, disaggregated by electronic, postal, and telephonic notifications;

(v) the number of Federal student loan borrowers who have had their wages garnished pursuant to section 488A of the Higher Education Act of 1965 (20 U.S.C. 1095a) or section 3720D of title 31, United States Code, between March 13, 2020, and the date of the date of enactment of this Act;

(vi) the number of Federal student loan borrowers subject to interest capitalization as a result of consolidating Federal student loans since March 13, 2020, and the total amount of such interest capitalization;

(vii) the average daily call wait times and call drop rates, disaggregated by student loan servicer, for the period between March 13, 2020, and the date of enactment of this Act; and

(viii) the estimated or projected savings to the Department of Education for student loan servicing activities for the period beginning on March 13, 2020, and ending on September 30, 2020, due to lower reimbursement or contract costs per account for student loan servicers and private collection agencies resulting from the suspension of Federal student loan payments and halt to collection activities under the CARES Act (Public Law 116–136).

(E) Information relating to the special rules relating to Federal Direct Consolidation Loans under section 150120 of this Act, including—

(i) the number of borrowers who submitted an application for a Federal Direct Consolidation Loan;

(ii) the number of borrowers who received a Federal Direct Consolidation Loan; and

(iii) the wait time between submitting an application and receiving a Federal Direct Consolidation Loan.

(F) A summary of the information required to be reported to the authorizing committees under section 3517(c) and section 3518(c) of the CARES Act (Public Law 116–

136), as amended by this Act, regardless of whether such information has previously been reported to such committees as of the date of the report under this subsection. (G) A copy of any communication from the Department of Education to grantees and Federal student loan borrowers eligible for rights and benefits under section 3519 of the CARES Act (Public Law 116–136) to inform such grantees and borrowers of their eligibility for such rights and benefits.

(2) DUTY OF HHS.—The Secretary of Health and Human Services shall provide to the Secretary of Education the information necessary for the Secretary of Education to comply with paragraph (1)(D).

(e) Amendments To CARES Act Reporting Requirements.—

(1) REPORTING REQUIREMENT FOR HBCU CAPITAL FINANCING LOAN DEFERMENT.—Section 3512(c) of the CARES Act (Public Law 116–136) is amended by striking the period at the end and inserting ", the terms of the loans deferred, and the schedule for repayment of the deferred loan amount."

(2) REPORTING REQUIREMENT FOR INSTITUTIONAL AID MODIFICA-TIONS.—Section 3517(c) of the CARES Act (Public Law 116–136) is amended by striking the period at the end and inserting ", identifies the statutory provision waived or modified, and describes the terms of the waiver or modification received by the institution."

(3) REPORTING REQUIREMENT FOR GRANT MODIFICATIONS.—Section 3518(c) of the CARES Act (Public Law 116–136) is amended by striking the period at the end and inserting "and describes the terms of the modification received by the institution or other grant recipient."

(f) Definitions.—In this section:

(1) The term "covered entity" means an institution of higher education, a Federal contractor, a student, or any other entity that is subject to the Higher Education Act of 1965 (20 U.S.C. 1001 et seq.).

(2) The term "Federal student loan" means a loan described in section 3502(a)(2) of the CARES Act (Public Law 116–136), as amended by this Act.

TITLE II

—OTHER PROGRAMS

Subtitle A—Carl D. Perkins Career And Technical Education Act Of 2006 And Adult Education And Literacy Covid–19 National Emergency Response

DEFINITIONS

SEC. 150201.
In this subtitle:

(1) APPRENTICESHIP; APPRENTICESHIP PROGRAM.—The terms "appren-ticeship" and "apprenticeship program" mean an apprenticeship program registered under the Act of August 16, 1937 (commonly known as the "National Apprenticeship Act") (50 Stat. 664, chapter 663; 29 U.S.C. 50 et seq.), including any requirement, standard, or rule promulgated under such Act, as such requirement, standard, or rule was in effect on December 30, 2019.

(2) CORONAVIRUS.—The term "coronavirus" means coronavirus as defined in section 506 of the Coronavirus Preparedness and Response Supplemental Appropri-

ations Act, 2020 (Public Law 116–123).

(3) COVID–19 NATIONAL EMERGENCY.—The term "COVID–19 national emergency" means the national emergency declared by the President under the National Emergencies Act (50 U.S.C. 1601 et seq.) on March 13, 2020, with respect to the coronavirus.

(4) SECRETARY.—The term "Secretary" means the Secretary of Education.

COVID–19 CAREER AND TECHNICAL EDUCATION RESPONSE FLEXIBILITY

SEC. 150202.

(a) Retention Of Funds.—Notwithstanding section 133(b)(1) of the Carl D. Perkins Career and Technical Education Act of 2006 (29 U.S.C. 2353(b)(1)), with respect to an eligible recipient that, due to the COVID–19 national emergency, does not expend all of the amounts that the eligible recipient is allocated for academic year 2019–2020 under section 131 or 132 of the Carl D. Perkins Career and Technical Education Act of 2006 (20 U.S.C. 2351; 2352), the eligible agency that allocated such funds to the eligible recipient—

(1) may authorize the eligible recipient to retain such amounts to carry out, during academic year 2020–2021, any activities described in the application of eligible recipient submitted under section 134(b) of such Act (29 U.S.C. 2354(b)) that such eligible recipient had intended to carry out during academic year 2019–2020; and

(2) shall ensure that a retention of amounts by an eligible recipient under paragraph (1) has no impact on the allocation of amounts to such eligible recipient under section 131 or 132 of the Carl D. Perkins Career and Technical Education Act of 2006 (20 U.S.C. 2351; 2352) for academic year 2020–2021.

(b) Pooling Of Funds.—An eligible recipient may, in accordance with section 135(c) of the Carl D. Perkins Career and Technical Education Act of 2006 (20 U.S.C. 2355(c)), pool a portion of funds received under such Act with a portion of funds received under such Act available to one or more eligible recipients to support the transition from secondary education to postsecondary education or employment for CTE participants whose academic year was interrupted by the COVID–19 national emergency.

(c) Professional Development.—During the COVID–19 national emergency, section 3(40)(B) of the Carl D. Perkins Career and Technical Education Act of 2006 (20 U.S.C. 2302(40)(B)) shall apply as if "sustained (not stand-alone, 1-day, or short-term workshops), intensive, collaborative, job-embedded, data-driven, and classroom-focused," were struck.

(d) Definitions.—Except as otherwise provided, the terms in this section have the meanings given the terms in section 3 of the Carl D. Perkins Career and Technical Education Act of 2006 (20 U.S.C. 2302).

ADULT EDUCATION AND LITERACY RESPONSE ACTIVITIES

SEC. 150203.

(a) Online Service Delivery Of Adult Education And Literacy Activities.—During the COVID–19 national emergency, an eligible agency may use funds available to such agency under paragraphs (2) and (3) of section 222(a) of the Workforce Innovation and Opportunity Act (20 U.S.C. 3302(a)) for the administrative expenses of the eligible agency related to transitions to online service delivery of adult education and literacy activities.

(b) Secretarial Responsibilities.—Not later than 30 days after the date of enactment of this Act, the Secretary shall, in carrying out section 242(c)(2)(G) of the Workforce Innovation and Opportunity Act (29 U.S.C. 3332(c)(2)(G)), identify and disseminate to States strategies and virtual proctoring tools to—

(1) assess the progress of learners in adult education programs based upon valid research, as appropriate, and;

(2) measure the progress of such programs in meeting the State adjusted levels of performance described in section 116(b)(3) of the Workforce Innovation and Opportunity Act (29 U.S.C. 3141(b)(3)).

(c) Definitions.—Except as otherwise provided, the terms in this section have the meanings given the terms in section 203 of the Workforce Innovation and Opportunity Act (29 U.S.C. 3272).

GENERAL PROVISIONS

SEC. 150204.

Notwithstanding any other provision of law, if determined necessary and appropriate due to the COVID–19 national emergency by the Secretary, the Secretary may waive, for a period not to exceed academic year 2019–2020—

(1) upon the request of a State or Indian Tribe receiving funds under title I of the Carl D. Perkins Career and Technical Education Act of 2006 (20 U.S.C. 2321 et seq.), the requirements under section 421(b) of the General Education Provisions Act (20 U.S.C. 1225(b)) for the State or Indian Tribe with respect to such funds; and

(2) upon the request of an eligible agency receiving funds under the Adult Education and Family Literacy Act (29 U.S.C. 3271 et seq.), the requirements under section 421(b) of the General Education Provisions Act (20 U.S.C. 1225(b)) for that eligible agency with respect to such funds.

Subtitle B—Corporation For National And Community Service Covid–19 Response Activities

CORPORATION FOR NATIONAL AND COMMUNITY SERVICE PROVISIONS

SEC. 150205.

Section 3514(a)(2)(B) of the CARES Act is amended by inserting ", or the full value of the stipend under section 105(a) of title I of the Domestic Volunteer Service Act of 1973 (42 U.S.C. 4955), as amended," after "such subtitle".

NATIONAL SERVICE EXPANSION FEASIBILITY STUDY

SEC. 150206.

(a) Study Required.—The Corporation for National and Community Service shall conduct a study on the feasibility of increasing the capacity of national service programs across the country to respond to the COVID–19 national emergency, the corresponding public health crisis, and the economic and social impact to communities across the country.

(b) Scope Of Study.—The Corporation for National and Community Service shall examine new and existing programs, partnerships, organizations and grantees that could be utilized to respond to the COVID–19 national emergency as described in subsection (a), including—

(1) service opportunities related to food security, education, economic opportunity, and disaster or emergency response;

(2) partnerships with the Department of Health and Human Services, the Centers for Disease Control and Prevention, and public health departments in all 50 states and

territories to respond to public health needs related to COVID–19 such as testing, contact tracing, or related activities; and

(3) the capacity and ability of the State Commissions on National and Community Service to respond to the needs of state and local governments in each state or territory in which such State Commission is in operation.

(c) Required Aspects Of The Study.—In performing the study described in this section, the Corporation for National and Community Service shall examine the following aspects for each of the new or existing programs, partnerships, organizations and grantees as described in subsection (b), including—

(1) the cost and resources necessary related to expansion as described in paragraphs (1), (2) and (3) of subsection (b);

(2) the timeline for implementation of any expanded partnerships or expanded capacity as described in paragraphs (1), (2) and (3) of subsection (b);

(3) options to use existing corps programs overseen by the Corporation for National and Community Service for expanding such capacity, and the role of programs, such as AmeriCorps, AmeriCorps VISTA, AmeriCorps National Civilian Community Corps, or Senior Corps, for expanding capacity as described in paragraphs (1), (2) and (3) of subsection (b);

(4) the ability to increase diversity, including economic, racial, ethnic, and gender diversity, amongst national service volunteers and programs as part of any expansion activities;

(5) the geographic distribution of demand by state due to the economic or health related impacts of COVID–19 for national service volunteer opportunities across the country and the additional volunteer capacity needed to meet this demand, comparing existing demand for volunteer opportunities to expected or realized increases as a result of COVID–19; and

(6) whether any additional administrative capacity is needed to respond to increases in demand as described in paragraph (5), including through grantee organizational capacity or at the Corporation for National and Community Service.

(d) Reports To Congressional Committees.—Not later than 30 days after the date of enactment of this Act, the Chief Executive Officer of the Corporation for National and Community Service shall prepare and submit a report to the Committee on Education and Labor and the Committee on Appropriations of the House of Representatives, and the Committee on Health, Education, Labor, and Pensions and the Committee on Appropriations of the Senate, with recommendations on the role for the Corporation for National and Community Service in responding to the COVID–19 national emergency, including any recommendations for legislative, regulatory, and administrative changes based on findings related to the topics identified under subsection (b).
DEFINITIONS

SEC. 150207.

In this subtitle, the following definitions apply:

(1) DVSA TERMS.—The terms "Director" and "poverty line for a single individual" have the meaning given such terms in section 421 of the Domestic Volunteer Service Act of 1973 (42 U.S.C. 5061).

(2) COVID–19 NATIONAL EMERGENCY.—The term "COVID–19 national emergency" means the national emergency declared by the President under the National Emergencies Act (50 U.S.C. 1601 et seq.) on March 13, 2020, with respect to COVID–19.

(3) GRANTEE.—The term "grantee" means a recipient of a grant under the Domestic Volunteer Service Act of 1973 (42 U.S.C. 4950 et seq.) or the National and Community Service Act of 1990 (42 U.S.C. 12501 et seq.) to run a program.

(4) PROGRAM.—The term "program" means a program funded under the Domestic Volunteer Service Act of 1973 (42 U.S.C. 4950 et seq.) or the National and Community Service Act of 1990 (42 U.S.C. 12501 et seq.).

(5) STATE COMMISSION ON NATIONAL AND COMMUNITY SERVICE.—The term "State Commission on National and Community Service" has the meaning given such term in section 101 of the National and Community Service Act (42 U.S.C. 12511).

DIVISION P—ACCESS ACT

SHORT TITLE; TABLE OF CONTENTS

SEC. 160001.

This Act may be cited as the "American Coronavirus/COVID-19 Election Safety and Security Act" or the "ACCESS Act".

REQUIREMENTS FOR FEDERAL ELECTION CONTINGENCY PLANS IN RESPONSE TO NATURAL DISASTERS AND EMERGENCIES

SEC. 160002.

(a) In General.—

(1) ESTABLISHMENT.—Not later than 30 days after the date of the enactment of this Act, each State and each jurisdiction in a State which is responsible for administering elections for Federal office shall establish and make publicly available a contingency plan to enable individuals to vote in elections for Federal office during a state of emergency, public health emergency, or national emergency which has been declared for reasons including—

(A) a natural disaster; or

(B) an infectious disease.

(2) UPDATING.—Each State and jurisdiction shall update the contingency plan established under this subsection not less frequently than every 5 years.

(b) Requirements Relating To Safety.—The contingency plan established under subsection (a) shall include initiatives to provide equipment and resources needed to protect the health and safety of poll workers and voters when voting in person.

(c) Requirements Relating To Recruitment Of Poll Workers.—The contingency plan established under subsection (a) shall include initiatives by the chief State election official and local election officials to recruit poll workers from resilient or unaffected populations, which may include—

(1) employees of other State and local government offices; and

(2) in the case in which an infectious disease poses significant increased health risks to elderly individuals, students of secondary schools and institutions of higher education in the State.

(d) Enforcement.—

(1) ATTORNEY GENERAL.—The Attorney General may bring a civil action against any State or jurisdiction in an appropriate United States District Court for such declaratory and injunctive relief (including a temporary restraining order, a permanent or temporary injunction, or other order) as may be necessary to carry out the

requirements of this section.

(2) PRIVATE RIGHT OF ACTION.—

(A) IN GENERAL.—In the case of a violation of this section, any person who is aggrieved by such violation may provide written notice of the violation to the chief election official of the State involved.

(B) RELIEF.—If the violation is not corrected within 20 days after receipt of a notice under subparagraph (A), or within 5 days after receipt of the notice if the violation occurred within 120 days before the date of an election for Federal office, the aggrieved person may, in a civil action, obtain declaratory or injunctive relief with respect to the violation.

(C) SPECIAL RULE.—If the violation occurred within 5 days before the date of an election for Federal office, the aggrieved person need not provide notice to the chief election official of the State involved under subparagraph (A) before bringing a civil action under subparagraph (B).

(e) Definitions.—

(1) ELECTION FOR FEDERAL OFFICE.—For purposes of this section, the term "election for Federal office" means a general, special, primary, or runoff election for the office of President or Vice President, or of Senator or Representative in, or Delegate or Resident Commissioner to, the Congress.

(2) STATE.—For purposes of this section, the term "State" includes the District of Columbia, the Commonwealth of Puerto Rico, Guam, American Samoa, the United States Virgin Islands, and the Commonwealth of the Northern Mariana Islands.

(f) Effective Date.—This section shall apply with respect to the regularly scheduled general election for Federal office held in November 2020 and each succeeding election for Federal office.

EARLY VOTING AND VOTING BY MAIL

SEC. 160003.

(a) Requirements.—Title III of the Help America Vote Act of 2002 (52 U.S.C. 21081 et seq.) is amended by adding at the end the following new subtitle:

"Subtitle C—Other Requirements

"SEC. 321. EARLY VOTING.

"(a) Requiring Allowing Voting Prior To Date Of Election.—

"(1) IN GENERAL.—Each State shall allow individuals to vote in an election for Federal office during an early voting period which occurs prior to the date of the election, in the same manner as voting is allowed on such date.

"(2) LENGTH OF PERIOD.—The early voting period required under this subsection with respect to an election shall consist of a period of consecutive days (including weekends) which begins on the 15th day before the date of the election (or, at the option of the State, on a day prior to the 15th day before the date of the election) and ends on the date of the election.

"(b) Minimum Early Voting Requirements.—Each polling place which allows voting during an early voting period under subsection (a) shall—

"(1) allow such voting for no less than 10 hours on each day;

"(2) have uniform hours each day for which such voting occurs; and

"(3) allow such voting to be held for some period of time prior to 9:00 a.m (local time) and some period of time after 5:00 p.m. (local time).

"(c) Location Of Polling Places.—

"(1) PROXIMITY TO PUBLIC TRANSPORTATION.—To the greatest extent practicable, a State shall ensure that each polling place which allows voting during an early voting period under subsection (a) is located within walking distance of a stop on a public transportation route.

"(2) AVAILABILITY IN RURAL AREAS.—The State shall ensure that polling places which allow voting during an early voting period under subsection (a) will be located in rural areas of the State, and shall ensure that such polling places are located in communities which will provide the greatest opportunity for residents of rural areas to vote during the early voting period.

"(d) Standards.—

"(1) IN GENERAL.—The Commission shall issue standards for the administration of voting prior to the day scheduled for a Federal election. Such standards shall include the nondiscriminatory geographic placement of polling places at which such voting occurs.

"(2) DEVIATION.—The standards described in paragraph (1) shall permit States, upon providing adequate public notice, to deviate from any requirement in the case of unforeseen circumstances such as a natural disaster, terrorist attack, or a change in voter turnout.

"(e) Ballot Processing And Scanning Requirements.—

"(1) IN GENERAL.—The State shall begin processing and scanning ballots cast during early voting for tabulation at least 14 days prior to the date of the election involved.

"(2) LIMITATION.—Nothing in this subsection shall be construed to permit a State to tabulate ballots in an election before the closing of the polls on the date of the election.

"(f) Effective Date.—This section shall apply with respect to the regularly scheduled general election for Federal office held in November 2020 and each succeeding election for Federal office.

"SEC. 322. PROMOTING ABILITY OF VOTERS TO VOTE BY MAIL.

"(a) Uniform Availability Of Absentee Voting To All Voters.—

"(1) IN GENERAL.—If an individual in a State is eligible to cast a vote in an election for Federal office, the State may not impose any additional conditions or requirements on the eligibility of the individual to cast the vote in such election by absentee ballot by mail.

"(2) ADMINISTRATION OF VOTING BY MAIL.—

"(A) PROHIBITING IDENTIFICATION REQUIREMENT AS CONDITION OF OBTAINING BALLOT.—A State may not require an individual to provide any form of identification as a condition of obtaining an absentee ballot, except that nothing in this paragraph may be construed to prevent a State from requiring a signature of the individual or similar affirmation as a condition of obtaining an absentee ballot.

"(B) PROHIBITING REQUIREMENT TO PROVIDE NOTARIZATION OR WITNESS SIGNATURE AS CONDITION OF OBTAINING OR CASTING BALLOT.—A State may not require notarization or witness signature or other formal authentication (other than voter attestation) as a condition of obtaining or casting an absentee ballot.

"(C) DEADLINE FOR RETURNING BALLOT.—A State may impose a deadline for requesting the absentee ballot and related voting materials from the appropriate State or local election official and for returning the ballot to the appropriate State or local election official.

"(3) APPLICATION FOR ALL FUTURE ELECTIONS.—At the option of an individual, a State shall treat the individual's application to vote by absentee ballot by mail in an election for Federal office as an application to vote by absentee ballot by mail in all subsequent Federal elections held in the State.

"(b) Due Process Requirements For States Requiring Signature Verification.—

"(1) REQUIREMENT.—

"(A) IN GENERAL.—A State may not impose a signature verification requirement as a condition of accepting and counting an absentee ballot submitted by any individual with respect to an election for Federal office unless the State meets the due process requirements described in paragraph (2).

"(B) SIGNATURE VERIFICATION REQUIREMENT DESCRIBED.—In this subsection, a 'signature verification requirement' is a requirement that an election official verify the identification of an individual by comparing the individual's signature on the absentee ballot with the individual's signature on the official list of registered voters in the State or another official record or other document used by the State to verify the signatures of voters.

"(2) DUE PROCESS REQUIREMENTS.—

"(A) NOTICE AND OPPORTUNITY TO CURE DISCREPANCY.—If an individual submits an absentee ballot and the appropriate State or local election official determines that a discrepancy exists between the signature on such ballot and the signature of such individual on the official list of registered voters in the State or other official record or document used by the State to verify the signatures of voters, such election official, prior to making a final determination as to the validity of such ballot, shall—

"(i) make a good faith effort to immediately notify the individual by mail, telephone, and (if available) electronic mail that—

"(I) a discrepancy exists between the signature on such ballot and the signature of the individual on the official list of registered voters in the State, and

"(II) if such discrepancy is not cured prior to the expiration of the 10-day period which begins on the date the official notifies the individual of the discrepancy, such ballot will not be counted; and

"(ii) cure such discrepancy and count the ballot if, prior to the expiration of the 10-day period described in clause (i)(II), the individual provides the official with information to cure such discrepancy, either in person, by telephone, or by electronic methods.

"(B) NOTICE AND OPPORTUNITY TO PROVIDE MISSING SIGNATURE.—If an individual submits an absentee ballot without a signature, the appropriate State or local election official, prior to making a final determination as to the validity of the ballot, shall—

"(i) make a good faith effort to immediately notify the individual by mail, telephone, and (if available) electronic mail that—

"(I) the ballot did not include a signature, and

"(II) if the individual does not provide the missing signature prior to the expiration of the 10-day period which begins on the date the official notifies the individual that the ballot did not include a signature, such ballot will not be counted; and

"(ii) count the ballot if, prior to the expiration of the 10-day period described in clause (i)(II), the individual provides the official with the missing signature on a form proscribed by the State.

"(C) OTHER REQUIREMENTS.—An election official may not make a determination that a discrepancy exists between the signature on an absentee ballot and the signature of the individual who submits the ballot on the official list of registered voters in the State or other official record or other document used by the State to verify the signatures of voters unless—

"(i) at least 2 election officials make the determination; and

"(ii) each official who makes the determination has received training in procedures used to verify signatures.

"(3) REPORT.—

"(A) IN GENERAL.—Not later than 120 days after the end of a Federal election cycle, each chief State election official shall submit to Congress a report containing the following information for the applicable Federal election cycle in the State:

"(i) The number of ballots invalidated due to a discrepancy under this subsection.

"(ii) Description of attempts to contact voters to provide notice as required by this subsection.

"(iii) Description of the cure process developed by such State pursuant to this subsection, including the number of ballots determined valid as a result of such process.

"(B) FEDERAL ELECTION CYCLE DEFINED.—For purposes of this subsection, the term 'Federal election cycle' means the period beginning on January 1 of any odd numbered year and ending on December 31 of the following year.

"(c) Methods And Timing For Transmission Of Ballots And Balloting Materials To Voters.—

"(1) METHOD FOR REQUESTING BALLOT.—In addition to such other methods as the State may establish for an individual to request an absentee ballot, the State shall permit an individual to submit a request for an absentee ballot online. The State shall be considered to meet the requirements of this paragraph if the website of the appropriate State or local election official allows an absentee ballot request application to be completed and submitted online and if the website permits the individual—

"(A) to print the application so that the individual may complete the application and return it to the official; or

"(B) request that a paper copy of the application be transmitted to the individual by mail or electronic mail so that the individual may complete the application and return it to the official.

"(2) ENSURING DELIVERY PRIOR TO ELECTION.—If an individual requests to vote by absentee ballot in an election for Federal office, the appropriate State or local election official shall ensure that the ballot and relating voting materials are received by the individual prior to the date of the election so long as the individual's request is received by the official not later than 5 days (excluding Saturdays, Sundays, and legal public holidays) before the date of the election, except that nothing in this paragraph shall preclude a State or local jurisdiction from allowing for the acceptance and processing of ballot requests submitted or received after such required period.

"(3) SPECIAL RULES IN CASE OF EMERGENCY PERIODS.—

"(A) AUTOMATIC MAILING OF ABSENTEE BALLOTS TO ALL VOTERS.—If the area in which an election is held is in an area in which an emergency or disaster which is described in subparagraph (A) or (B) of section 1135(g)(1) of the Social Security Act (42 U.S.C. 1320b-5(g)(1)) is declared during the period described in subparagraph (C)—

"(i) paragraphs (1) and (2) shall not apply with respect to the election; and

"(ii) not later than 2 weeks before the date of the election, the appropriate State or local election official shall transmit by mail absentee ballots and balloting materials for the election to all individuals who are registered to vote in such election or, in the case of any State that does not register voters, all individuals who are in the State's central voter file (or if the State does not keep a central voter file, to all individuals who are eligible to vote in such election).

"(B) AFFIRMATION.—If an individual receives an absentee ballot from a State or local election official pursuant to subparagraph (A) and returns the voted ballot to the official, the ballot shall not be counted in the election unless the individual includes with the ballot a signed affirmation that—

"(i) the individual has not and will not cast another ballot with respect to the election; and

"(ii) acknowledges that a material misstatement of fact in completing the ballot may constitute grounds for conviction of perjury.

"(C) PERIOD DESCRIBED.—The period described in this subparagraph with respect to an election is the period which begins 120 days before the date of the election and ends 30 days before the date of the election.

"(D) APPLICATION TO NOVEMBER 2020 GENERAL ELECTION.—Because of the public health emergency declared pursuant to section 319 of the Public Health Service Act (42 U.S.C. 247d) resulting from the COVID–19 pandemic, the special rules set forth in this paragraph shall apply with respect to the regularly scheduled general election for Federal office held in November 2020 in each State.

"(d) Accessibility For Individuals With Disabilities.—The State shall ensure that all absentee ballots and related voting materials in elections for Federal office are accessible to individuals with disabilities in a manner that provides the same opportunity for access and participation (including with privacy and independence) as for other voters.

"(e) Uniform Deadline For Acceptance Of Mailed Ballots.—A State may not refuse to accept or process a ballot submitted by an individual by mail with respect to an election for Federal office in the State on the grounds that the individual did not meet a deadline for returning the ballot to the appropriate State or local election official if—

"(1) the ballot is postmarked, signed, or otherwise indicated by the United States Postal Service to have been mailed on or before the date of the election; and

"(2) the ballot is received by the appropriate election official prior to the expiration of the 10-day period which begins on the date of the election.

"(f) Alternative Methods Of Returning Ballots.—

"(1) IN GENERAL.—In addition to permitting an individual to whom a ballot in an election was provided under this section to return the ballot to an election official by mail, the State shall permit the individual to cast the ballot by delivering the ballot at such times and to such locations as the State may establish, including—

"(A) permitting the individual to deliver the ballot to a polling place on any date on which voting in the election is held at the polling place; and

"(B) permitting the individual to deliver the ballot to a designated ballot drop-off location.

"(2) PERMITTING VOTERS TO DESIGNATE OTHER PERSON TO RETURN BALLOT.—The State—

"(A) shall permit a voter to designate any person to return a voted and sealed absentee ballot to the post office, a ballot drop-off location, tribally designated building, or election office so long as the person designated to return the ballot does not receive any form of compensation based on the number of ballots that the person has returned and no individual, group, or organization provides compensation on this basis; and

"(B) may not put any limit on how many voted and sealed absentee ballots any designated person can return to the post office, a ballot drop off location, tribally designated building, or election office.

"(g) Ballot Processing And Scanning Requirements.—

"(1) IN GENERAL.—The State shall begin processing and scanning ballots cast by mail for tabulation at least 14 days prior to the date of the election involved.

"(2) LIMITATION.—Nothing in this subsection shall be construed to permit a State to tabulate ballots in an election before the closing of the polls on the date of the election.

"(h) Rule Of Construction.—Nothing in this section shall be construed to affect the authority of States to conduct elections for Federal office through the use of polling places at which individuals cast ballots.

"(i) No Effect On Ballots Submitted By Absent Military And Overseas Voters.—Nothing in this section may be construed to affect the treatment of any ballot submitted by an individual who is entitled to vote by absentee ballot under the Uniformed and Overseas Citizens Absentee Voting Act (52 U.S.C. 20301 et seq.).

"(j) Effective Date.—This section shall apply with respect to the regularly scheduled general election for Federal office held in November 2020 and each succeeding election for Federal office.

"SEC. 323. ABSENTEE BALLOT TRACKING PROGRAM.

"(a) Requirement.—Each State shall carry out a program to track and confirm the receipt of absentee ballots in an election for Federal office under which the State or local election official responsible for the receipt of voted absentee ballots in the election carries out procedures to track and confirm the receipt of such ballots, and makes information on the receipt of such ballots available to the individual who cast the ballot, by means of online access using the Internet site of the official's office.

"(b) Information On Whether Vote Was Counted.—The information referred to under subsection (a) with respect to the receipt of an absentee ballot shall include information regarding whether the vote cast on the ballot was counted, and, in the case of a vote which was not counted, the reasons therefor.

"(c) Use Of Toll-Free Telephone Number By Officials Without Internet Site.—A program established by a State or local election official whose office does not have an Internet site may meet the requirements of subsection (a) if the official has established a toll-free telephone number that may be used by an individual who cast an absentee ballot to obtain the information on the receipt of the voted absentee ballot as provided under such subsection.

"(d) Effective Date.—This section shall apply with respect to the regularly scheduled general election for Federal office held in November 2020 and each succeeding election for Federal office.

"SEC. 324. RULES FOR COUNTING PROVISIONAL BALLOTS.

"(a) Statewide Counting Of Provisional Ballots.—

"(1) IN GENERAL.—For purposes of section 302(a)(4), notwithstanding the precinct or polling place at which a provisional ballot is cast within the State, the appropriate election official shall count each vote on such ballot for each election in which the individual who cast such ballot is eligible to vote.

"(2) EFFECTIVE DATE.—This subsection shall apply with respect to the regularly scheduled general election for Federal office held in November 2020 and each succeeding election for Federal office.

"(b) Uniform And Nondiscriminatory Standards.—

"(1) IN GENERAL.—Consistent with the requirements of section 302, each State shall establish uniform and nondiscriminatory standards for the issuance, handling, and counting of provisional ballots.

"(2) EFFECTIVE DATE.—This subsection shall apply with respect to the regularly scheduled general election for Federal office held in November 2020 and each succeeding election for Federal office.

"SEC. 325. COVERAGE OF COMMONWEALTH OF NORTHERN MARIANA ISLANDS.

"In this subtitle, the term 'State' includes the Commonwealth of the Northern Mariana Islands.

"SEC. 326. MINIMUM REQUIREMENTS FOR EXPANDING ABILITY OF INDIVIDUALS TO VOTE.

"The requirements of this subtitle are minimum requirements, and nothing in this subtitle may be construed to prevent a State from establishing standards which promote the ability of individuals to vote in elections for Federal office, so long as such standards are not inconsistent with the requirements of this subtitle or other Federal laws.".

(b) Conforming Amendment Relating To Issuance Of Voluntary Guidance By Election Assistance Commission.—Section 311(b) of such Act (52 U.S.C. 21101(b)) is amended—

(1) by striking "and" at the end of paragraph (2);

(2) by striking the period at the end of paragraph (3) and inserting "; and"; and

(3) by adding at the end the following new paragraph:

"(4) in the case of the recommendations with respect to subtitle C, June 30, 2020.".

(c) Enforcement.—

(1) COVERAGE UNDER EXISTING ENFORCEMENT PROVISIONS.—Section 401 of such Act (52 U.S.C. 21111) is amended by striking "and 303" and inserting "303, and subtitle C of title III".

(2) AVAILABILITY OF PRIVATE RIGHT OF ACTION.—Title IV of such (52 U.S.C. 21111 et seq.) is amended by adding at the end the following new section:

"SEC. 403. PRIVATE RIGHT OF ACTION FOR VIOLATIONS OF CERTAIN REQUIREMENTS.

"(a) In General.—In the case of a violation of subtitle C of title III, section 402 shall not apply and any person who is aggrieved by such violation may provide written notice of the violation to the chief election official of the State involved.

"(b) Relief.—If the violation is not corrected within 20 days after receipt of a notice under subsection (a), or within 5 days after receipt of the notice if the violation occurred within 120 days before the date of an election for Federal office, the aggrieved person may, in a civil action, obtain declaratory or injunctive relief with respect to the violation.

"(c) Special Rule.—If the violation occurred within 5 days before the date of an election for Federal office, the aggrieved person need not provide notice to the chief election official of the State involved under subsection (a) before bringing a civil

action under subsection (b).".
(d) Clerical Amendment.—The table of contents of such Act is amended—
(1) by adding at the end of the items relating to title III the following:

"Subtitle C—Other Requirements

"SEC. 321. Early voting.

"SEC. 322. Promoting ability of voters to vote by mail.

"SEC. 323. Absentee ballot tracking program.

"SEC. 324. Rules for counting provisional ballots.

"SEC. 325. Coverage of Commonwealth of Northern Mariana Islands.

"SEC. 326. Minimum requirements for expanding ability of individuals to vote."; and

(2) by adding at the end of the items relating to title IV the following new item:

"SEC. 403. Private right of action for violations of certain requirements. ".
PERMITTING USE OF SWORN WRITTEN STATEMENT TO MEET IDENTIFI-
CATION REQUIREMENTS FOR VOTING

SEC. 160004.
(a) Permitting Use Of Statement.—Subtitle C of title III of the Help America Vote Act of 2002, as added by section 160003(a), is amended—
(1) by redesignating sections 325 and 326 as sections 326 and 327; and
(2) by inserting after section 324 the following new section:

"SEC. 325. PERMITTING USE OF SWORN WRITTEN STATEMENT TO MEET IDENTIFICATION REQUIREMENTS.
"(a) Use Of Statement.—
"(1) IN GENERAL.—Except as provided in subsection (c), if a State has in effect a requirement that an individual present identification as a condition of casting a ballot in an election for Federal office, the State shall permit the individual to meet the requirement—
"(A) in the case of an individual who desires to vote in person, by presenting the appropriate State or local election official with a sworn written statement, signed by the individual under penalty of perjury, attesting to the individual's identity and attesting that the individual is eligible to vote in the election; or
"(B) in the case of an individual who desires to vote by mail, by submitting with the ballot the statement described in subparagraph (A).
"(2) DEVELOPMENT OF PRE-PRINTED VERSION OF STATEMENT BY COM-MISSION.—The Commission shall develop a pre-printed version of the statement described in paragraph (1)(A) which includes a blank space for an individual to provide a name and signature for use by election officials in States which are subject to paragraph (1).
"(3) PROVIDING PRE-PRINTED COPY OF STATEMENT.—A State which is subject to paragraph (1) shall—
"(A) make copies of the pre-printed version of the statement described in paragraph (1)(A) which is prepared by the Commission available at polling places for election officials to distribute to individuals who desire to vote in person; and
"(B) include a copy of such pre-printed version of the statement with each blank

absentee or other ballot transmitted to an individual who desires to vote by mail.

"(b) Requiring Use Of Ballot In Same Manner As Individuals Presenting Identification.—An individual who presents or submits a sworn written statement in accordance with subsection (a)(1) shall be permitted to cast a ballot in the election in the same manner as an individual who presents identification.

"(c) Exception For First-Time Voters Registering By Mail.—Subsections (a) and (b) do not apply with respect to any individual described in paragraph (1) of section 303(b) who is required to meet the requirements of paragraph (2) of such section.".

(b) Requiring States To Include Information On Use Of Sworn Written Statement In Voting Information Material Posted At Polling Places.—Section 302(b)(2) of such Act (52 U.S.C. 21082(b)(2)), is amended—

(1) by striking "and" at the end of subparagraph (E);

(2) by striking the period at the end of subparagraph (F) and inserting "; and"; and

(3) by adding at the end the following new subparagraph:

"(G) in the case of a State that has in effect a requirement that an individual present identification as a condition of casting a ballot in an election for Federal office, information on how an individual may meet such requirement by presenting a sworn written statement in accordance with section 303A.".

(c) Clerical Amendment.—The table of contents of such Act, as amended by section 160003, is amended—

(1) by redesignating the items relating to sections 325 and 326 as relating to sections 326 and 327; and

(2) by inserting after the item relating to section 324 the following new item:

"SEC. 325. Permitting use of sworn written statement to meet identification requirements.".

(d) Effective Date.—The amendments made by this section shall apply with respect to elections occurring on or after the date of the enactment of this Act.

VOTING MATERIALS POSTAGE

SEC. 160005.

(a) Prepayment Of Postage On Return Envelopes.—

(1) IN GENERAL.—Subtitle C of title III of the Help America Vote Act of 2002, as added by section 160003(a) and as amended by section 160004(a), is further amended—

(A) by redesignating sections 326 and 327 as sections 327 and 328; and

(B) by inserting after section 325 the following new section:

"SEC. 326. PREPAYMENT OF POSTAGE ON RETURN ENVELOPES FOR VOTING MATERIALS.

"(a) Provision Of Return Envelopes.—The appropriate State or local election official shall provide a self-sealing return envelope with—

"(1) any voter registration application form transmitted to a registrant by mail;

"(2) any application for an absentee ballot transmitted to an applicant by mail; and

"(3) any blank absentee ballot transmitted to a voter by mail.

"(b) Prepayment Of Postage.—Consistent with regulations of the United States Postal Service, the State or the unit of local government responsible for the administration of the election involved shall prepay the postage on any envelope provided under subsection (a).

"(c) No Effect On Ballots Or Balloting Materials Transmitted To Absent Military And

Overseas Voters.—Nothing in this section may be construed to affect the treatment of any ballot or balloting materials transmitted to an individual who is entitled to vote by absentee ballot under the Uniformed and Overseas Citizens Absentee Voting Act (52 U.S.C. 20301 et seq.).".

(2) CLERICAL AMENDMENT.—The table of contents of such Act, as amended by section 160004(c), is amended—

(A) by redesignating the items relating to sections 326 and 327 as relating to sections 327 and 328; and

(B) by inserting after the item relating to section 325 the following new item:

"**SEC. 326. Prepayment of postage on return envelopes for voting materials**".

(b) Role Of United States Postal Service.—

(1) IN GENERAL.—Chapter 34 of title 39, United States Code, is amended by adding after section 3406 the following:

"§ 3407. Voting materials

"(a) Any voter registration application, absentee ballot application, or absentee ballot with respect to any election for Federal office shall be carried expeditiously, with postage on the return envelope prepaid by the State or unit of local government responsible for the administration of the election.

"(b) As used in this section—

"(1) the term 'absentee ballot' means any ballot transmitted by a voter by mail in an election for Federal office, but does not include any ballot covered by section 3406; and

"(2) the term 'election for Federal office' means a general, special, primary, or runoff election for the office of President or Vice President, or of Senator or Representative in, or Delegate or Resident Commissioner to, the Congress.

"(c) Nothing in this section may be construed to affect the treatment of any ballot or balloting materials transmitted to an individual who is entitled to vote by absentee ballot under the Uniformed and Overseas Citizens Absentee Voting Act (52 U.S.C. 20301 et seq.).".

(2) CLERICAL AMENDMENT.—The table of sections for chapter 34 of such title is amended by inserting after the item relating to section 3406 the following:

"3407. Voting materials.".

REQUIRING TRANSMISSION OF BLANK ABSENTEE BALLOTS UNDER UOCAVA TO CERTAIN VOTERS

SEC. 160006.

(a) In General.—The Uniformed and Overseas Citizens Absentee Voting Act (52 U.S.C. 20301 et seq.) is amended by inserting after section 103B the following new section:

"**SEC. 103C. TRANSMISSION OF BLANK ABSENTEE BALLOTS TO CERTAIN OTHER VOTERS.**

"(a) In General.—

"(1) STATE RESPONSIBILITIES.—Subject to the provisions of this section, each State shall transmit blank absentee ballots electronically to qualified individuals who request such ballots in the same manner and under the same terms and conditions under which the State transmits such ballots electronically to absent uniformed services voters and overseas voters under the provisions of section 102(f), except that no such marked ballots shall be returned electronically.

"(2) REQUIREMENTS.—Any blank absentee ballot transmitted to a qualified individual under this section—

"(A) must comply with the language requirements under section 203 of the Voting Rights Act of 1965 (52 U.S.C. 10503); and

"(B) must comply with the disability requirements under section 508 of the Rehabilitation Act of 1973 (29 U.S.C. 794d).

"(3) AFFIRMATION.—The State may not transmit a ballot to a qualified individual under this section unless the individual provides the State with a signed affirmation in electronic form that—

"(A) the individual is a qualified individual (as defined in subsection (b));

"(B) the individual has not and will not cast another ballot with respect to the election; and

"(C) acknowledges that a material misstatement of fact in completing the ballot may constitute grounds for conviction of perjury.

"(4) CLARIFICATION REGARDING FREE POSTAGE.—An absentee ballot obtained by a qualified individual under this section shall be considered balloting materials as defined in section 107 for purposes of section 3406 of title 39, United States Code.

"(5) PROHIBITING REFUSAL TO ACCEPT BALLOT FOR FAILURE TO MEET CERTAIN REQUIREMENTS.—A State shall not refuse to accept and process any otherwise valid blank absentee ballot which was transmitted to a qualified individual under this section and used by the individual to vote in the election solely on the basis of the following:

"(A) Notarization or witness signature requirements.

"(B) Restrictions on paper type, including weight and size.

"(C) Restrictions on envelope type, including weight and size.

"(b) Qualified Individual.—

"(1) IN GENERAL.—In this section, except as provided in paragraph (2), the term 'qualified individual' means any individual who is otherwise qualified to vote in an election for Federal office and who meets any of the following requirements:

"(A) The individual—

"(i) has previously requested an absentee ballot from the State or jurisdiction in which such individual is registered to vote; and

"(ii) has not received such absentee ballot at least 2 days before the date of the election.

"(B) The individual—

"(i) resides in an area of a State with respect to which an emergency or public health emergency has been declared by the chief executive of the State or of the area involved within 5 days of the date of the election under the laws of the State due to reasons including a natural disaster, including severe weather, or an infectious disease; and

"(ii) has not previously requested an absentee ballot.

"(C) The individual expects to be absent from such individual's jurisdiction on the date of the election due to professional or volunteer service in response to a natural disaster or emergency as described in subparagraph (B).

"(D) The individual is hospitalized or expects to be hospitalized on the date of the election.

"(E) The individual is an individual with a disability (as defined in section 3 of the Americans with Disabilities Act of 1990 (42 U.S.C. 12102)) and resides in a State which does not offer voters the ability to use secure and accessible remote ballot marking. For purposes of this subparagraph, a State shall permit an individual to self-certify that the individual is an individual with a disability.

"(2) EXCLUSION OF ABSENT UNIFORMED SERVICES AND OVERSEAS VOTERS.—The term 'qualified individual' shall not include an absent uniformed services voter or an overseas voter.

"(c) State.—For purposes of this section, the term 'State' includes the District of Columbia, the Commonwealth of Puerto Rico, Guam, American Samoa, the United States Virgin Islands, and the Commonwealth of the Northern Mariana Islands.

"(d) Effective Date.—This section shall apply with respect to the regularly scheduled general election for Federal office held in November 2020 and each succeeding election for Federal office.".

(b) Conforming Amendment.—Section 102(a) of such Act (52 U.S.C. 20302(a)) is amended—

(1) by striking "and" at the end of paragraph (10);

(2) by striking the period at the end of paragraph (11) and inserting "; and"; and

(3) by adding at the end the following new paragraph:

"(12) meet the requirements of section 103C with respect to the provision of blank absentee ballots for the use of qualified individuals described in such section.".

(c) Clerical Amendments.—The table of contents of such Act is amended by inserting the following after section 103:

"SEC. 103A. Procedures for collection and delivery of marked absentee ballots of absent overseas uniformed services voters.

"SEC. 103B. Federal voting assistance program improvements.

"SEC. 103C. Transmission of blank absentee ballots to certain other voters.".
VOTER REGISTRATION

SEC. 160007.

(a) Requiring Availability Of Internet For Voter Registration.—

(1) REQUIRING AVAILABILITY OF INTERNET FOR REGISTRATION.—The National Voter Registration Act of 1993 (52 U.S.C. 20501 et seq.) is amended by inserting after section 6 the following new section:

"SEC. 6A. INTERNET REGISTRATION.

"(a) Requiring Availability Of Internet For Online Registration.—

"(1) AVAILABILITY OF ONLINE REGISTRATION AND CORRECTION OF EXISTING REGISTRATION INFORMATION.—Each State, acting through the chief State election official, shall ensure that the following services are available to the public at any time on the official public websites of the appropriate State and local election officials in the State, in the same manner and subject to the same terms and conditions as the services provided by voter registration agencies under section 7(a):

"(A) Online application for voter registration.

"(B) Online assistance to applicants in applying to register to vote.

"(C) Online completion and submission by applicants of the mail voter registration application form prescribed by the Election Assistance Commission pursuant to section 9(a)(2), including assistance with providing a signature as required under subsection (c).

"(D) Online receipt of completed voter registration applications.

"(b) Acceptance Of Completed Applications.—A State shall accept an online voter registration application provided by an individual under this section, and ensure that the individual is registered to vote in the State, if—

"(1) the individual meets the same voter registration requirements applicable to individuals who register to vote by mail in accordance with section 6(a)(1) using the mail voter registration application form prescribed by the Election Assistance Commission pursuant to section 9(a)(2); and

"(2) the individual meets the requirements of subsection (c) to provide a signature in electronic form (but only in the case of applications submitted during or after the second year in which this section is in effect in the State).

"(c) Signature Requirements.—

"(1) IN GENERAL.—For purposes of this section, an individual meets the requirements of this subsection as follows:

"(A) In the case of an individual who has a signature on file with a State agency, including the State motor vehicle authority, that is required to provide voter registration services under this Act or any other law, the individual consents to the transfer of that electronic signature.

"(B) If subparagraph (A) does not apply, the individual submits with the application an electronic copy of the individual's handwritten signature through electronic means.

"(C) If subparagraph (A) and subparagraph (B) do not apply, the individual executes a computerized mark in the signature field on an online voter registration application, in accordance with reasonable security measures established by the State, but only if the State accepts such mark from the individual.

"(2) TREATMENT OF INDIVIDUALS UNABLE TO MEET REQUIREMENT.—If an individual is unable to meet the requirements of paragraph (1), the State shall—

"(A) permit the individual to complete all other elements of the online voter registration application;

"(B) permit the individual to provide a signature at the time the individual requests a ballot in an election (whether the individual requests the ballot at a polling place or requests the ballot by mail); and

"(C) if the individual carries out the steps described in subparagraph (A) and subparagraph (B), ensure that the individual is registered to vote in the State.

"(3) NOTICE.—The State shall ensure that individuals applying to register to vote online are notified of the requirements of paragraph (1) and of the treatment of individuals unable to meet such requirements, as described in paragraph (2).

"(d) Confirmation And Disposition.—

"(1) CONFIRMATION OF RECEIPT.—Upon the online submission of a completed voter registration application by an individual under this section, the appropriate State or local election official shall send the individual a notice confirming the State's receipt of the application and providing instructions on how the individual may check the status of the application.

"(2) NOTICE OF DISPOSITION.—Not later than 7 days after the appropriate State or local election official has approved or rejected an application submitted by an individual under this section, the official shall send the individual a notice of the disposition of the application.

"(3) METHOD OF NOTIFICATION.—The appropriate State or local election official shall send the notices required under this subsection by regular mail and—

"(A) in the case of an individual who has provided the official with an electronic mail address, by electronic mail; and

"(B) at the option of an individual, by text message.

"(e) Provision Of Services In Nonpartisan Manner.—The services made available under subsection (a) shall be provided in a manner that ensures that, consistent with section 7(a)(5)—

"(1) the online application does not seek to influence an applicant's political preference or party registration; and

"(2) there is no display on the website promoting any political preference or party allegiance, except that nothing in this paragraph may be construed to prohibit an applicant from registering to vote as a member of a political party.

"(f) Protection Of Security Of Information.—In meeting the requirements of this section, the State shall establish appropriate technological security measures to prevent to the greatest extent practicable any unauthorized access to information provided by individuals using the services made available under subsection (a).

"(g) Accessibility Of Services.—A state shall ensure that the services made available under this section are made available to individuals with disabilities to the same extent as services are made available to all other individuals.

"(h) Use Of Additional Telephone-Based System.—A State shall make the services made available online under subsection (a) available through the use of an automated telephone-based system, subject to the same terms and conditions applicable under this section to the services made available online, in addition to making the services available online in accordance with the requirements of this section.

"(i) Nondiscrimination Among Registered Voters Using Mail And Online Registration.—In carrying out this Act, the Help America Vote Act of 2002, or any other Federal, State, or local law governing the treatment of registered voters in the State or the administration of elections for public office in the State, a State shall treat a registered voter who registered to vote online in accordance with this section in the same manner as the State treats a registered voter who registered to vote by mail.".

(2) SPECIAL REQUIREMENTS FOR INDIVIDUALS USING ONLINE REGISTRATION.—

(A) TREATMENT AS INDIVIDUALS REGISTERING TO VOTE BY MAIL FOR PURPOSES OF FIRST-TIME VOTER IDENTIFICATION REQUIREMENTS.—Section 303(b)(1)(A) of the Help America Vote Act of 2002 (52 U.S.C. 21083(b)(1)(A)) is amended by striking "by mail" and inserting "by mail or online under section 6A of the National Voter Registration Act of 1993".

(B) REQUIRING SIGNATURE FOR FIRST-TIME VOTERS IN JURISDICTION.— Section 303(b) of such Act (52 U.S.C. 21083(b)) is amended—

(i) by redesignating paragraph (5) as paragraph (6); and

(ii) by inserting after paragraph (4) the following new paragraph:

"(5) SIGNATURE REQUIREMENTS FOR FIRST-TIME VOTERS USING ONLINE REGISTRATION.—

"(A) IN GENERAL.—A State shall, in a uniform and nondiscriminatory manner, require an individual to meet the requirements of subparagraph (B) if—

"(i) the individual registered to vote in the State online under section 6A of the National Voter Registration Act of 1993; and

"(ii) the individual has not previously voted in an election for Federal office in the State.

"(B) REQUIREMENTS.—An individual meets the requirements of this subparagraph if—

"(i) in the case of an individual who votes in person, the individual provides the appropriate State or local election official with a handwritten signature; or

"(ii) in the case of an individual who votes by mail, the individual submits with the ballot a handwritten signature.

"(C) INAPPLICABILITY.—Subparagraph (A) does not apply in the case of an individual who is—

"(i) entitled to vote by absentee ballot under the Uniformed and Overseas Citizens Absentee Voting Act (52 U.S.C. 20302 et seq.);

"(ii) provided the right to vote otherwise than in person under section 3(b)(2)(B)(ii) of the Voting Accessibility for the Elderly and Handicapped Act (52 U.S.C. 20102(b)(2)(B)(ii)); or

"(iii) entitled to vote otherwise than in person under any other Federal law.".

(C) CONFORMING AMENDMENT RELATING TO EFFECTIVE DATE.—Section 303(d)(2)(A) of such Act (52 U.S.C. 21083(d)(2)(A)) is amended by striking "Each State" and inserting "Except as provided in subsection (b)(5), each State".

(3) CONFORMING AMENDMENTS.—

(A) TIMING OF REGISTRATION.—Section 8(a)(1) of the National Voter Registration Act of 1993 (52 U.S.C. 20507(a)(1)) is amended—

(i) by striking "and" at the end of subparagraph (C);

(ii) by redesignating subparagraph (D) as subparagraph (E); and

(iii) by inserting after subparagraph (C) the following new subparagraph:

"(D) in the case of online registration through the official public website of an election official under section 6A, if the valid voter registration application is submitted online not later than the lesser of 28 days, or the period provided by State law, before the date of the election (as determined by treating the date on which the application is sent electronically as the date on which it is submitted); and".

(B) INFORMING APPLICANTS OF ELIGIBILITY REQUIREMENTS AND PENALTIES.—Section 8(a)(5) of such Act (52 U.S.C. 20507(a)(5)) is amended by striking "and 7" and inserting "6A, and 7".

(b) Use Of Internet To Update Registration Information.—

(1) UPDATES TO INFORMATION CONTAINED ON COMPUTERIZED STATE-WIDE VOTER REGISTRATION LIST.—

(A) IN GENERAL.—Section 303(a) of the Help America Vote Act of 2002 (52 U.S.C. 21083(a)) is amended by adding at the end the following new paragraph:

"(6) USE OF INTERNET BY REGISTERED VOTERS TO UPDATE INFORMATION.—

"(A) IN GENERAL.—The appropriate State or local election official shall ensure that any registered voter on the computerized list may at any time update the voter's registration information, including the voter's address and electronic mail address, online through the official public website of the election official responsible for the maintenance of the list, so long as the voter attests to the contents of the update by providing a signature in electronic form in the same manner required under section 6A(c) of the National Voter Registration Act of 1993.

"(B) PROCESSING OF UPDATED INFORMATION BY ELECTION OFFICIALS.—If a registered voter updates registration information under subparagraph (A), the appropriate State or local election official shall—

"(i) revise any information on the computerized list to reflect the update made by the voter; and "(ii) if the updated registration information affects the voter's eligibility to vote in an election for Federal office, ensure that the information is processed with respect to the election if the voter updates the information not later than the lesser of 7 days, or the period provided by State law, before the date of the election.

"(C) CONFIRMATION AND DISPOSITION.—

"(i) CONFIRMATION OF RECEIPT.—Upon the online submission of updated registration information by an individual under this paragraph, the appropriate State or local election official shall send the individual a notice confirming the State's receipt of the updated information and providing instructions on how the individual may check the status of the update.

"(ii) NOTICE OF DISPOSITION.—Not later than 7 days after the appropriate State or local election official has accepted or rejected updated information submitted by an individual under this paragraph, the official shall send the individual a notice of the disposition of the update.

"(iii) METHOD OF NOTIFICATION.—The appropriate State or local election official shall send the notices required under this subparagraph by regular mail and—

"(I) in the case of an individual who has requested that the State provide voter registration and voting information through electronic mail, by electronic mail; and

"(II) at the option of an individual, by text message.".

(B) CONFORMING AMENDMENT RELATING TO EFFECTIVE DATE.—Section 303(d)(1)(A) of such Act (52 U.S.C. 21083(d)(1)(A)) is amended by striking "subparagraph (B)," and inserting "subparagraph (B) and subsection (a)(6),".

(2) ABILITY OF REGISTRANT TO USE ONLINE UPDATE TO PROVIDE INFORMATION ON RESIDENCE.—Section 8(d)(2)(A) of the National Voter Registration Act of 1993 (52 U.S.C. 20507(d)(2)(A)) is amended—

(A) in the first sentence, by inserting after "return the card" the following: "or update the registrant's information on the computerized Statewide voter registration list using the online method provided under section 303(a)(6) of the Help America Vote Act of 2002"; and

(B) in the second sentence, by striking "returned," and inserting the following: "returned or if the registrant does not update the registrant's information on the computerized Statewide voter registration list using such online method,".

(c) Same Day Registration.—

(1) IN GENERAL.—Subtitle C of title III of the Help America Vote Act of 2002, as added by section 160003(a) and as amended by sections 160004(a) and 160005(a), is further amended—

(A) by redesignating sections 327 and 328 as sections 328 and 329; and

(B) by inserting after section 326 the following new section:

"SEC. 327. SAME DAY REGISTRATION.

"(a) In General.—

"(1) REGISTRATION.—Each State shall permit any eligible individual on the day of a Federal election and on any day when voting, including early voting, is permitted for a Federal election—

"(A) to register to vote in such election at the polling place using a form that meets the requirements under section 9(b) of the National Voter Registration Act of 1993 (or, if the individual is already registered to vote, to revise any of the individual's voter registration information); and

"(B) to cast a vote in such election.

"(2) EXCEPTION.—The requirements under paragraph (1) shall not apply to a State in which, under a State law in effect continuously on and after the date of the enactment of this section, there is no voter registration requirement for individuals in the State with respect to elections for Federal office.

"(b) Eligible Individual.—For purposes of this section, the term 'eligible individual' means, with respect to any election for Federal office, an individual who is otherwise qualified to vote in that election.

"(c) Effective Date.—Each State shall be required to comply with the requirements of subsection (a) for the regularly scheduled general election for Federal office occurring in November 2020 and for any subsequent election for Federal office.".

(2) CLERICAL AMENDMENT.—The table of contents of such Act, as added by section 160003 and as amended by sections 160004 and 160005, is further amended—

(A) by redesignating the items relating to sections 327 and 328 as relating to sections 328 and 329; and

(B) by inserting after the item relating to section 326 the following new item:

"SEC. 327. Same day registration.".

(d) Prohibiting State From Requiring Applicants To Provide More Than Last 4 Digits Of Social Security Number.—

(1) FORM INCLUDED WITH APPLICATION FOR MOTOR VEHICLE DRIVER'S LICENSE.—Section 5(c)(2)(B)(ii) of the National Voter Registration Act of 1993 (52 U.S.C. 20504(c)(2)(B)(ii)) is amended by striking the semicolon at the end and inserting the following: ", and to the extent that the application requires the applicant to provide a Social Security number, may not require the applicant to provide more than the last 4 digits of such number;".

(2) NATIONAL MAIL VOTER REGISTRATION FORM.—Section 9(b)(1) of such Act (52 U.S.C. 20508(b)(1)) is amended by striking the semicolon at the end and inserting the following: ", and to the extent that the form requires the applicant to provide a Social Security number, the form may not require the applicant to provide more than the last 4 digits of such number;".

(3) EFFECTIVE DATE.—The amendments made by this subsection shall apply with respect to the regularly scheduled general election for Federal office held in November 2020 and each succeeding election for Federal office.

ACCOMMODATIONS FOR VOTERS RESIDING IN INDIAN LANDS

SEC. 160008.

(a) Accommodations Described.—

(1) DESIGNATION OF BALLOT PICKUP AND COLLECTION LOCATIONS.—Given the widespread lack of residential mail delivery in Indian Country, an Indian Tribe may designate buildings as ballot pickup and collection locations with respect to an election for Federal office at no cost to the Indian Tribe. An Indian Tribe may designate one building per precinct located within Indian lands. The applicable State or political subdivision shall collect ballots from those locations. The applicable State or political subdivision shall provide the Indian Tribe with accurate precinct maps for all precincts located within Indian lands 60 days before the election.

(2) PROVISION OF MAIL-IN AND ABSENTEE BALLOTS.—The State or political subdivision shall provide mail-in and absentee ballots with respect to an election for Federal office to each individual who is registered to vote in the election who resides on Indian lands in the State or political subdivision involved without requiring a

residential address or a mail-in or absentee ballot request.

(3) USE OF DESIGNATED BUILDING AS RESIDENTIAL AND MAILING ADDRESS.—The address of a designated building that is a ballot pickup and collection location with respect to an election for Federal office may serve as the residential address and mailing address for voters living on Indian lands if the tribally designated building is in the same precinct as that voter. If there is no tribally designated building within a voter's precinct, the voter may use another tribally designated building within the Indian lands where the voter is located. Voters using a tribally designated building outside of the voter's precinct may use the tribally designated building as a mailing address and may separately designate the voter's appropriate precinct through a description of the voter's address, as specified in section 9428.4(a)(2) of title 11, Code of Federal Regulations.

(4) LANGUAGE ACCESSIBILITY.—In the case of a State or political subdivision that is a covered State or political subdivision under section 203 of the Voting Rights Act of 1965 (52 U.S.C. 10503), that State or political subdivision shall provide absentee or mail-in voting materials with respect to an election for Federal office in the language of the applicable minority group as well as in the English language, bilingual election voting assistance, and written translations of all voting materials in the language of the applicable minority group, as required by section 203 of the Voting Rights Act of 1965 (52 U.S.C. 10503), as amended by subsection (b).

(5) CLARIFICATION.—Nothing in this section alters the ability of an individual voter residing on Indian lands to request a ballot in a manner available to all other voters in the State.

(6) DEFINITIONS.—In this section:

(A) ELECTION FOR FEDERAL OFFICE.—The term "election for Federal office" means a general, special, primary or runoff election for the office of President or Vice President, or of Senator or Representative in, or Delegate or Resident Commissioner to, the Congress.

(B) INDIAN.—The term "Indian" has the meaning given the term in section 4 of the Indian Self-Determination and Education Assistance Act (25 U.S.C. 5304).

(C) INDIAN LANDS.—The term "Indian lands" includes—

(i) any Indian country of an Indian Tribe, as defined under section 1151 of title 18, United States Code;

(ii) any land in Alaska owned, pursuant to the Alaska Native Claims Settlement Act (43 U.S.C. 1601 et seq.), by an Indian Tribe that is a Native village (as defined in section 3 of that Act (43 U.S.C. 1602)) or by a Village Corporation that is associated with an Indian Tribe (as defined in section 3 of that Act (43 U.S.C. 1602));

(iii) any land on which the seat of the Tribal Government is located; and

(iv) any land that is part or all of a Tribal designated statistical area associated with an Indian Tribe, or is part or all of an Alaska Native village statistical area associated with an Indian Tribe, as defined by the Census Bureau for the purposes of the most recent decennial census.

(D) INDIAN TRIBE.—The term "Indian Tribe" has the meaning given the term "Indian tribe" in section 4 of the Indian Self-Determination and Education Assistance Act (25 U.S.C. 5304).

(E) TRIBAL GOVERNMENT.—The term "Tribal Government" means the recognized governing body of an Indian Tribe.

(7) ENFORCEMENT.—

(A) ATTORNEY GENERAL.—The Attorney General may bring a civil action in an appropriate district court for such declaratory or injunctive relief as is necessary to carry out this subsection.

(B) PRIVATE RIGHT OF ACTION.—

(i) A person or Tribal Government who is aggrieved by a violation of this subsection may provide written notice of the violation to the chief election official of the State involved.

(ii) An aggrieved person or Tribal Government may bring a civil action in an appropriate district court for declaratory or injunctive relief with respect to a violation of this subsection, if—

(I) that person or Tribal Government provides the notice described in clause (i); and

(II) (aa) in the case of a violation that occurs more than 120 days before the date of an election for Federal office, the violation remains and 90 days or more have passed since the date on which the chief election official of the State receives the notice under clause (i); or

(bb) in the case of a violation that occurs 120 days or less before the date of an election for Federal office, the violation remains and 20 days or more have passed since the date on which the chief election official of the State receives the notice under clause (i).

(iii) In the case of a violation of this section that occurs 30 days or less before the date of an election for Federal office, an aggrieved person or Tribal Government may bring a civil action in an appropriate district court for declaratory or injunctive relief with respect to the violation without providing notice to the chief election official of the State under clause (i).

(b) Bilingual Election Requirements.—Section 203 of the Voting Rights Act of 1965 (52 U.S.C. 10503) is amended—

(1) in subsection (b)(3)(C), by striking "1990" and inserting "2010"; and

(2) by striking subsection (c) and inserting the following:

"(c) Provision Of Voting Materials In The Language Of A Minority Group.—

"(1) IN GENERAL.—Whenever any State or political subdivision subject to the prohibition of subsection (b) of this section provides any registration or voting notices, forms, instructions, assistance, or other materials or information relating to the electoral process, including ballots, it shall provide them in the language of the applicable minority group as well as in the English language.

"(2) EXCEPTIONS.—

"(A) In the case of a minority group that is not American Indian or Alaska Native and the language of that minority group is oral or unwritten, the State or political subdivision shall only be required to furnish, in the covered language, oral instructions, assistance, translation of voting materials, or other information relating to registration and voting.

"(B) In the case of a minority group that is American Indian or Alaska Native, the State or political subdivision shall only be required to furnish in the covered language oral instructions, assistance, or other information relating to registration and voting, including all voting materials, if the Tribal Government of that minority group has certified that the language of the applicable American Indian or Alaska Native language is presently unwritten or the Tribal Government does not want written translations in the minority language.

"(3) WRITTEN TRANSLATIONS FOR ELECTION WORKERS.—Notwithstanding paragraph (2), the State or political division may be required to provide written translations of voting materials, with the consent of any applicable Indian Tribe, to election workers to ensure that the translations from English to the language of a minority group are complete, accurate, and uniform.".

(c) Effective Date.—This section and the amendments made by this section shall apply with respect to the regularly scheduled general election for Federal office held in November 2020 and each succeeding election for Federal office.

PAYMENTS BY ELECTION ASSISTANCE COMMISSION TO STATES TO ASSIST WITH COSTS OF COMPLIANCE

SEC. 160009.

(a) Availability Of Grants.—Subtitle D of title II of the Help America Vote Act of 2002 (52 U.S.C. 21001 et seq.) is amended by adding at the end the following new part:

"PART 7—PAYMENTS TO ASSIST WITH COSTS OF COMPLIANCE WITH ACCESS ACT

"SEC. 297. PAYMENTS TO ASSIST WITH COSTS OF COMPLIANCE WITH ACCESS ACT.

"(a) Availability And Use Of Payments.—

"(1) IN GENERAL.—The Commission shall make a payment to each eligible State to assist the State with the costs of complying with the American Coronavirus/ COVID–19 Election Safety and Security Act and the amendments made by such Act, including the provisions of such Act and such amendments which require States to pre-pay the postage on absentee ballots and balloting materials.

"(2) PUBLIC EDUCATION CAMPAIGNS.—For purposes of this part, the costs incurred by a State in carrying out a campaign to educate the public about the requirements of the American Coronavirus/COVID–19 Election Safety and Security Act and the amendments made by such Act shall be included as the costs of complying with such Act and such amendments.

"(b) Primary Elections.—

"(1) PAYMENTS TO STATES.—In addition to any payments under subsection (a), the Commission shall make a payment to each eligible State to assist the State with the costs incurred in voluntarily electing to comply with the American Coronavirus/ COVID–19 Election Safety and Security Act and the amendments made by such Act with respect to primary elections for Federal office held in the State in 2020.

"(2) STATE PARTY-RUN PRIMARIES.—In addition to any payments under paragraph (1), the Commission shall make payments to each eligible political party of the State for costs incurred by such parties to send absentee ballots and return envelopes with prepaid postage to eligible voters participating in such primaries during 2020.

"(c) Pass-Through Of Funds To Local Jurisdictions.—

"(1) IN GENERAL.—If a State receives a payment under this part for costs that include costs incurred by a local jurisdiction or Tribal government within the State, the State shall pass through to such local jurisdiction or Tribal government a portion of such payment that is equal to the amount of the costs incurred by such local jurisdiction or Tribal government.

"(2) TRIBAL GOVERNMENT DEFINED.—In this subsection, the term 'Tribal Government' means the recognized governing body of an Indian tribe (as defined in section 4 of the Indian Self-Determination and Education Assistance Act (25 U.S.C. 5304).

"(d) Schedule Of Payments.—As soon as practicable after the date of the enactment

602	U.S. House of Representatives Democrats

of this part and not less frequently than once each calendar year thereafter, the Commission shall make payments under this part.

"(e) Coverage Of Commonwealth Of Northern Mariana Islands.—In this part, the term 'State' includes the Commonwealth of the Northern Mariana Islands.

"(f) Limitation.—No funds may be provided to a State under this part for costs attributable to the electronic return of marked ballots by any voter.

"SEC. 297A. AMOUNT OF PAYMENT.

"(a) In General.—Except as provided in section 297C, the amount of a payment made to an eligible State for a year under this part shall be determined by the Commission.

"(b) Continuing Availability Of Funds After Appropriation.—A payment made to an eligible State or eligible unit of local government under this part shall be available without fiscal year limitation.

"SEC. 297B. REQUIREMENTS FOR ELIGIBILITY.

"(a) Application.—Except as provided in section 297C, each State that desires to receive a payment under this part for a fiscal year, and each political party of a State that desires to receive a payment under section 297(b)(2), shall submit an application for the payment to the Commission at such time and in such manner and containing such information as the Commission shall require.

"(b) Contents Of Application.—Each application submitted under subsection (a) shall—

"(1) describe the activities for which assistance under this part is sought; and

"(2) provide such additional information and certifications as the Commission determines to be essential to ensure compliance with the requirements of this part.

"SEC. 297C. SPECIAL RULES FOR PAYMENTS FOR ELECTIONS SUBJECT TO EMERGENCY RULES.

"(a) Submission Of Estimated Costs.—If the special rules in the case of an emergency period under section 322(c)(3) apply to an election, not later than the applicable deadline under subsection (c), the State shall submit to the Commission a request for a payment under this part, and shall include in the request the State's estimate of the costs the State expects to incur in the administration of the election which are attributable to the application of such special rules to the election.

"(b) Payment.—Not later than 7 days after receiving a request from the State under subsection (a), the Commission shall make a payment to the State in an amount equal to the estimate provided by the State in the request.

"(c) Applicable Deadline.—The applicable deadline under this paragraph with respect to an election is—

"(1) with respect to the regularly scheduled general election for Federal office held in November 2020, 15 days after the date of the enactment of this part; and

"(2) with respect to any other election, 15 days after the emergency or disaster described in section 322(c)(3) is declared.

"SEC. 297D. AUTHORIZATION OF APPROPRIATIONS.

"There are authorized to be appropriated for payments under this part—

"(1) in the case of payments made under section 297C, such sums as may be necessary for fiscal year 2020 and each succeeding fiscal year; and

"(2) in the case of any other payments, such sums as may be necessary for fiscal year 2020.

"SEC. 297E. REPORTS.

"(a) Reports By Recipients.—Not later than 6 months after the end of each fiscal year for which an eligible State received a payment under this part, the State shall submit a report to the Commission on the activities conducted with the funds provided during the year.

"(b) Reports By Commission To Committees.—With respect to each fiscal year for which the Commission makes payments under this part, the Commission shall submit a report on the activities carried out under this part to the Committee on House Administration of the House of Representatives and the Committee on Rules and Administration of the Senate.".

(b) Clerical Amendment.—The table of contents of such Act is amended by adding at the end of the items relating to subtitle D of title II the following:

"PART 7—PAYMENTS TO ASSIST WITH COSTS OF COMPLIANCE WITH ACCESS ACT

"SEC. 297. Payments to assist with costs of compliance with Access Act.

"SEC. 297A. Amount of payment.

"SEC. 297B. Requirements for eligibility.

"SEC. 297C. Authorization of appropriations.

"SEC. 297D. Reports.".

GRANTS TO STATES FOR CONDUCTING RISK-LIMITING AUDITS OF RESULTS OF ELECTIONS

SEC. 160010.

(a) Availability Of Grants.—Subtitle D of title II of the Help America Vote Act of 2002 (52 U.S.C. 21001 et seq.), as amended by section 160009(a), is further amended by adding at the end the following new part:

"PART 8—GRANTS FOR CONDUCTING RISK-LIMITING AUDITS OF RESULTS OF ELECTIONS

"SEC. 298. GRANTS FOR CONDUCTING RISK-LIMITING AUDITS OF RESULTS OF ELECTIONS.

"(a) Availability Of Grants.—The Commission shall make a grant to each eligible State to conduct risk-limiting audits as described in subsection (b) with respect to the regularly scheduled general elections for Federal office held in November 2020 and each succeeding election for Federal office.

"(b) Risk-Limiting Audits Described.—In this part, a 'risk-limiting audit' is a post-election process—

"(1) which is conducted in accordance with rules and procedures established by the chief State election official of the State which meet the requirements of subsection (c); and

"(2) under which, if the reported outcome of the election is incorrect, there is at least a predetermined percentage chance that the audit will replace the incorrect outcome with the correct outcome as determined by a full, hand-to-eye tabulation of all votes validly cast in that election that ascertains voter intent manually and directly from voter-verifiable paper records.

"(c) Requirements For Rules And Procedures.—The rules and procedures established for conducting a risk-limiting audit shall include the following elements:

"(1) Rules for ensuring the security of ballots and documenting that prescribed procedures were followed.

"(2) Rules and procedures for ensuring the accuracy of ballot manifests produced by election agencies.

"(3) Rules and procedures for governing the format of ballot manifests, cast vote records, and other data involved in the audit.

"(4) Methods to ensure that any cast vote records used in the audit are those used by the voting system to tally the election results sent to the chief State election official and made public.

"(5) Procedures for the random selection of ballots to be inspected manually during each audit.

"(6) Rules for the calculations and other methods to be used in the audit and to determine whether and when the audit of an election is complete.

"(7) Procedures and requirements for testing any software used to conduct risk-limiting audits.

"(d) Definitions.—In this part, the following definitions apply:

"(1) The term 'ballot manifest' means a record maintained by each election agency that meets each of the following requirements:

"(A) The record is created without reliance on any part of the voting system used to tabulate votes.

"(B) The record functions as a sampling frame for conducting a risk-limiting audit.

"(C) The record contains the following information with respect to the ballots cast and counted in the election:

"(i) The total number of ballots cast and counted by the agency (including undervotes, overvotes, and other invalid votes).

"(ii) The total number of ballots cast in each election administered by the agency (including undervotes, overvotes, and other invalid votes).

"(iii) A precise description of the manner in which the ballots are physically stored, including the total number of physical groups of ballots, the numbering system for each group, a unique label for each group, and the number of ballots in each such group.

"(2) The term 'incorrect outcome' means an outcome that differs from the outcome that would be determined by a full tabulation of all votes validly cast in the election, determining voter intent manually, directly from voter-verifiable paper records.

"(3) The term 'outcome' means the winner of an election, whether a candidate or a position.

"(4) The term 'reported outcome' means the outcome of an election which is determined according to the canvass and which will become the official, certified outcome unless it is revised by an audit, recount, or other legal process.

"SEC. 298A. ELIGIBILITY OF STATES.

"A State is eligible to receive a grant under this part if the State submits to the Commission, at such time and in such form as the Commission may require, an application containing—

"(1) a certification that, not later than 5 years after receiving the grant, the State will conduct risk-limiting audits of the results of elections for Federal office held in the State as described in section 298;

"(2) a certification that, not later than one year after the date of the enactment of this section, the chief State election official of the State has established or will establish the rules and procedures for conducting the audits which meet the requirements of section 298(c);

"(3) a certification that the audit shall be completed not later than the date on which the State certifies the results of the election;

"(4) a certification that, after completing the audit, the State shall publish a report on the results of the audit, together with such information as necessary to confirm that the audit was conducted properly;

"(5) a certification that, if a risk-limiting audit conducted under this part leads to a full manual tally of an election, State law requires that the State or election agency shall use the results of the full manual tally as the official results of the election; and

"(6) such other information and assurances as the Commission may require.

"SEC. 298B. AUTHORIZATION OF APPROPRIATIONS.

"There are authorized to be appropriated for grants under this part $20,000,000 for fiscal year 2020, to remain available until expended.".

(b) Clerical Amendment.—The table of contents of such Act, as amended by section 160009(b), is further amended by adding at the end of the items relating to subtitle D of title II the following:

"PART 8—GRANTS FOR CONDUCTING RISK-LIMITING AUDITS OF RESULTS OF ELECTIONS

"SEC. 298. Grants for conducting risk-limiting audits of results of elections.

"SEC. 298A. Eligibility of States.

"SEC. 298B. Authorization of appropriations.

(c) GAO Analysis Of Effects Of Audits.—

(1) ANALYSIS.—Not later than 6 months after the first election for Federal office is held after grants are first awarded to States for conducting risk-limiting audits under part 8 of subtitle D of title II of the Help America Vote Act of 2002 (as added by subsection (a)) for conducting risk-limiting audits of elections for Federal office, the Comptroller General of the United States shall conduct an analysis of the extent to which such audits have improved the administration of such elections and the security of election infrastructure in the States receiving such grants.

(2) REPORT.—The Comptroller General of the United States shall submit a report on the analysis conducted under subsection (a) to the appropriate congressional committees.

ADDITIONAL APPROPRIATIONS FOR THE ELECTION ASSISTANCE COMMISSION

SEC. 160011.

(a) In General.—In addition to any funds otherwise appropriated to the Election Assistance Commission for fiscal year 2020, there is authorized to be appropriated $3,000,000 for fiscal year 2020 in order for the Commission to provide additional assistance and resources to States for improving the administration of elections.

(b) Availability Of Funds.—Amounts appropriated pursuant to the authorization under this subsection shall remain available without fiscal year limitation.

DEFINITION

SEC. 160012.

(a) Definition Of Election For Federal Office .—Title IX of the Help America Vote Act of 2002 (52 U.S.C. 21141 et seq.) is amended by adding at the end the following new section:

"SEC. 907. ELECTION FOR FEDERAL OFFICE DEFINED.

"For purposes of titles I through III, the term 'election for Federal office' means a general, special, primary, or runoff election for the office of President or Vice President, or of Senator or Representative in, or Delegate or Resident Commissioner to, the Congress.".

(b) Clerical Amendment.—The table of contents of such Act is amended by adding at the end of the items relating to title IX the following new item:

"SEC. 907. Election for Federal office defined.".

DIVISION Q—COVID-19 HEROES FUND

SHORT TITLE

SEC. 170001.

This Act may be cited as the "COVID-19 Heroes Fund Act of 2020".

TITLE I—PROVISIONS RELATING TO STATE, LOCAL, TRIBAL, AND PRIVATE SECTOR WORKERS

SEC. 170101. DEFINITIONS.

In this title:

(1) COVID-19 PUBLIC HEALTH EMERGENCY.—The term "COVID-19 Public Health Emergency" means the public health emergency first declared on January 31, 2020, by the Secretary of Health and Human Services under section 319 of the Public Health Service Act (42 U.S.C. 247d) with respect to COVID-19.

(2) EMPLOYEE.—Except as provided in paragraph (3)(C)(iii), the term "employee" means an individual (not employed by an entity excluded from the definition of the term "employer" for purposes of this title under paragraph (3)(B)) who is—

(A) an employee, as defined in section 3(e) of the Fair Labor Standards Act of 1938 (29 U.S.C. 203(e)), except that a reference in such section 3(e) to an employer shall be considered to be a reference to an employer described in clauses (i)(I) and (ii) of paragraph (3)(A);

(B) a State employee described in section 304(a) of the Government Employee Rights Act of 1991 (42 U.S.C. 2000e-16c(a)); or

(C) an employee of a Tribal employer.

(3) EMPLOYER.—

(A) IN GENERAL.—The term "employer" means, except as provided in subparagraph (B), a person who is—

(i) (I) a covered employer, as defined in subparagraph (C);

(II) an entity employing a State employee described in section 304(a) of the Government Employee Rights Act of 1991; or

(III) a Tribal employer; and

(ii) engaged in commerce (including government), or an industry or activity affecting commerce (including government).

(B) EXCLUSION OF EXECUTIVE, LEGISLATIVE, AND JUDICIAL ENTITIES COVERED UNDER TITLE II.—The term "employer" does not include—

(i) any agency, as defined in section 201(1), except, only as provided in section 102(g)(2), the VA Office of Geriatrics & Extended Care of the Veterans Health Administration; or

(ii) the Postal Regulatory Commission.

(C) COVERED EMPLOYER.—

(i) IN GENERAL.—In subparagraph (A)(i)(I), the term "covered employer"—

(I) means any person engaged in commerce (including government), or in any industry or activity affecting commerce (including government), who employs 1 or more employees;

(II) includes—

(aa) any person who acts directly or indirectly in the interest of (within the meaning of section 3(d) of the Fair Labor Standards Act of 1938 (29 U.S.C. 203(d)) an employer in relation to any of the employees of such employer; and

(bb) any successor in interest of an employer;

(III) except as provided in subparagraph (B), includes any public agency, as defined in section 3(x) of the Fair Labor Standards Act of 1938 (29 U.S.C. 203(x));

(IV) includes any person described in subclause (I) who conducts business as a not-for-profit organization;

(V) includes—

(aa) an entity or person that contracts directly with a State, locality, Tribal government, or the Federal Government, to provide care (which may include items and services) through employees of such entity or person to individuals under the Medicare program under title XVIII of the Social Security Act (42 U.S.C. 1395 et seq.), under a State Medicaid plan under title XIX of such Act (42 U.S.C. 1396 et seq.) or under a waiver of such plan, or under any other program established or administered by a State, locality, Tribal government, or the Federal Government;

(bb) a subcontractor of an entity or person described in item (aa);

(cc) an individual client (or a representative on behalf of an individual client), an entity, or a person, that employs an individual to provide care (which may include items and services) to the individual client under a self-directed service delivery model through a program established or administered by a State, locality, Tribal government, or the Federal Government; or

(dd) an individual client (or a representative on behalf of an individual client) that, on their own accord, employs an individual to provide care (which may include items and services) to the individual client using the individual client's own finances;

(VI) includes the United States Postal Service;

(VII) includes a nonappropriated fund instrumentality under the jurisdiction of the Armed Forces; and

(VIII) includes, only with respect to section 102(g)(2), the VA Office of Geriatrics & Extended Care of the Veterans Health Administration.

(ii) PUBLIC AGENCY.—For purposes of this title, a public agency shall be considered to be a person engaged in commerce or in an industry or activity affecting commerce.

(iii) DEFINITION OF EMPLOYEE.—For purposes of clause (i), the term "employee" has the meaning given such term in section 3(e), except such term does not include any individual employed by entity excluded from the definition of the term "employer" for purposes of this title under subparagraph (B).

(D) PREDECESSORS.—Any reference in this paragraph to an employer shall include a reference to any predecessor of such employer.

(E) DEFINITION OF COMMERCE.—For purposes of this paragraph, the terms "commerce" and "industry or activity affecting commerce"—

(i) mean any activity, business, or industry in commerce or in which a labor dispute would hinder or obstruct commerce or the free flow of commerce;

(ii) include commerce and any industry affecting commerce, as such terms are defined in paragraphs (1) and (3) of section 501 of the Labor Management Relations Act, 1947 (29 U.S.C. 142(1) and (3)); and

(iii) include commerce, as defined in section 3(b) of the Fair Labor Standards Act of 1938 (29 U.S.C. 203(b)) and as described in section 2(a) of such Act (29 U.S.C. 202(a)).

(4) EMPLOYER PAYROLL TAXES.—The term "employer payroll taxes" means—

(A) taxes imposed under sections 3111(b), 3221(a) (but only to the extent attributable to the portion of such tax attributable to the tax imposed by section 3111(b)), 3221(b), and 3301 of the Internal Revenue Code of 1986; and

(B) taxes imposed by a State or local government on an employer with respect to amounts paid by such employer for work by employees.

(5) ESSENTIAL WORK.—The term "essential work" means any work that—

(A) is performed during the period that begins on January 27, 2020 and ends 60 days after the last day of the COVID–19 Public Health Emergency;

(B) is not performed while teleworking from a residence;

(C) involves—

(i) regular in-person interactions with—

(I) patients;

(II) the public; or

(III) coworkers of the individual performing the work; or

(ii) regular physical handling of items that were handled by, or are to be handled by—

(I) patients;

(II) the public; or

(III) coworkers of the individual performing the work; and

(D) is in any of the following areas:

(i) First responder work, in the public sector or private sector, including services in response to emergencies that have the potential to cause death or serious bodily injury, such as police, fire, emergency medical, protective, child maltreatment, domestic violence, and correctional services (including activities carried out by employees in fire protection activities, as defined in section 3(y) of the Fair Labor Standards Act of 1938 (29 U.S.C. 203(y)) and activities of law enforcement officers, as defined in section 1204(6) of the Omnibus Crime Control and Safe Streets Act of 1968 (34 U.S.C. 10284(6)).

(ii) Health care work physically provided in inpatient settings (including hospitals and other inpatient post-acute care settings such as nursing homes, inpatient rehabilitation facilities, and other related settings) and other work physically performed in such inpatient settings that supports or is in furtherance of such health care work physically provided in inpatient settings.

(iii) Health care work physically provided in outpatient settings (including at physician offices, community health centers, rural health clinics and other clinics, hospital outpatient departments, freestanding emergency departments, ambulatory surgical centers, and other related settings), and other work physically performed in such inpatient settings that supports or is in furtherance of such health care work physically provided in outpatient settings.

(iv) Pharmacy work, physically performed in pharmacies, drug stores, or other retail facilities specializing in medical goods and supplies.

(v) Any work physically performed in a facility that performs medical testing and diagnostic services, including laboratory processing, medical testing services, or related activities.

(vi) Home and community-based work, including home health care, residential care, assistance with activities of daily living, and any services provided by direct care workers (as defined in section 799B of the Public Health Service Act (42 U.S.C. 295p)), personal care aides, job coaches, or supported employment providers, and any other provision of care to individuals in their homes by direct service providers, personal care attendants, and home health aides.

(vii) Biomedical research regarding SARS–CoV–2 and COVID–19 that involves the handling of hazardous materials such as COVID–19 samples.

(viii) Behavioral health work requiring physical interaction with individuals, including mental health services and substance use disorder prevention, treatment, and recovery services.

(ix) Nursing care and residential care work physically provided in a facility.

(x) Family care, including child care services, in-home child care services such as nanny services, and care services provided by family members to other family members.

(xi) Social services work, including social work, case management, social and human services, child welfare, family services, shelter and services for people who have experienced intimate partner violence or sexual assault, services for individuals who are homeless, child services, community food and housing services, and other emergency social services.

(xii) Public health work conducted at State, local, territorial, and Tribal government public health agencies, including epidemiological activities, surveillance, contact tracing, data analysis, statistical research, health education, and other disease detection, prevention, and response methods.

(xiii) Tribal vital services, as defined by the Commissioner of the Administration for Native Americans in consultation with Tribal governments and after conferring with urban Indian organizations.

(xiv) Grocery work physically performed at grocery stores, supermarkets, convenience stores, corner stores, drug stores, retail facilities specializing in medical goods and supplies, bodegas, and other locations where individuals purchase non-prepared food items.

(xv) Restaurant work, including carry-out, drive-thru, or food delivery work, requiring physical interaction with individuals or food products.

(xvi) Food production work involving the physical interaction with food products, including all agricultural work, farming, fishing, forestry, ranching, processing, canning, slaughtering, packaging, baking, butchering, and other food production work, such as any service or activity included within the provisions of section 3(f) of the Fair Labor Standards Act of 1938 (29 U.S.C. 203(f)), or section 3121(g) of the Internal Revenue Code of 1986, and the handling, planting, drying, packing, packaging, processing, freezing, or grading prior to delivery for storage of any agricultural or horticultural commodity in its unmanufactured state.

(xvii) Transportation work, including—

(I) any services in public transportation, as defined in section 5302(14) of title 49, United States Code;

(II) any private transportation of people, such as transportation provided by air, rail, bus, taxicab, personal car or truck, non-motorized vehicle, or otherwise, including all services performed by individuals working in or on such vehicles, vehicle depots, or transit facilities;

(III) any private transportation of goods in bulk, including transportation via heavy or light truck, rail, air, or otherwise;

(IV) any public or private transportation of mail or packages;

(V) any private transportation of food or other goods to individuals, including in a personal car or truck, non-motorized vehicle, or otherwise;

(VI) any services in passenger rail transportation, including commuter rail, intercity passenger rail, or Amtrak, including services performed by employees of contractors of such entities;

(VII) any services in the transportation of persons, property, or mail by an aircraft of an air carrier conducting operations under part 121 of title 14, Code of Federal Regulations (or successor regulations), or a foreign air carrier within, to, or from the United States, either on board an aircraft or on the ground at an airport, including services performed by employees of contractors of air carriers, or foreign air carriers, as described in section 4111(3) of the CARES Act (Public Law 116–136);

(VIII) any services as an aircraft mechanic or technician who performs maintenance, repair, or overhaul work on an aircraft of an air carrier conducting operations under such part 121 or foreign air carrier within the United States;

(IX) services as maritime workers who qualify as seamen under section 10101(3) of title 46, United States Code, and other maritime employees including—

(aa) longshoremen, harbor workers and shipbuilders covered under section 2(3) of the Longshore and Harbor Workers' Compensation Act (33 U.S.C. 902(3)) involved in the transportation of merchandise or passengers by water; and

(bb) shipbuilders and ship repairers who are working for an employer performing shipbuilding or ship repair work under contract or subcontract to the Departments of Defense, Energy or Homeland Security for military or other national security purposes; and

(X) services as maritime transportation workers supporting or enabling transportation functions, including such services as—

(aa) barge workers, tug operators, and port and facility security personnel;

(bb) marine dispatchers; and

(cc) workers who repair and maintain marine vessels (including the equipment and infrastructure that enables operations that encompass movement of cargo and passengers).

(xviii) Work physically performed in a warehouse or other facility in warehousing (including all services performed by individuals picking, sorting, packing, and shipping in warehouses), storage, distribution, or call center support facilities, and other essential operational support functions that are necessary to accept, store, and process goods, and that facilitate the goods' transportation and delivery.

(xix) Cleaning work and building maintenance work physically performed on the grounds of a facility, including all custodial or janitorial services, security services, and repair and maintenance services.

(xx) Work in the collection, removal, transport, storage, or disposal of residential, industrial, or commercial solid waste and recycling, including services provided by individuals who drive waste or recycling trucks, who pick up waste or recycling from residential or commercial locations, or who work at waste or recycling centers or landfills.

(xxi) Work in the gathering, processing, disseminating, and delivery of news and information that serves the public interest to the public through mass media, including television, radio, and newspapers.

(xxii) Any work performed by an employee of a State, locality, or Tribal government, that is determined to be essential work by the highest authority of such State, locality, or Tribal government.

(xxiii) Educational work, school nutrition work, and other work required to operate a school facility, including early childhood programs, preschool programs, elementary and secondary education, and higher education.

(xxiv) Laundry work, including work in laundromats, laundry service companies, and dry cleaners.

(xxv) Elections work physically performed at polling places or otherwise amongst the public, including public-sector elections personnel and private-sector elections personnel.

(xxvi) Hazardous materials management, response, and cleanup work associated with any other essential work covered under this paragraph, including health care waste (including medical, pharmaceuticals, and medical material production), and testing operations (including laboratories processing test kits).

(xxvii) Disinfection work for all facilities and modes of transportation involved in other essential work covered under this paragraph.

(xxviii) Work in critical clinical research, development, and testing necessary for COVID–19 response that involves physical interaction with hazardous materials, such as samples of COVID–19.

(xxix) Work in mortuary, funeral, cremation, burial, cemetery, and related services.

(xxx) Work requiring physical interactions with patients in physical therapy, occupational therapy, speech-language pathology, and respiratory therapy and other therapy services.

(xxxi) Dental care work requiring physical interaction with patients.

(xxxii) Work performed by employees of the U.S. Postal Service.

(xxxiii) Work at hotel and commercial lodging facilities that are used for COVID–19 mitigation and containment measures.

(6) ESSENTIAL WORKER.—

(A) IN GENERAL.—The term "essential worker" means an individual, whose work and duties include essential work, and who is—

(i) an employee of an employer; or

(ii) an individual performing any services or labor for remuneration for an employer, regardless of whether the individual is classified as an independent contractor by the employer.

(B) IMMIGRATION STATUS.—Such term includes an individual regardless of the individual's immigration status.

(7) ESSENTIAL WORK EMPLOYER.—The term "essential work employer" means an employer who employs, or provides remuneration for services or labor to, an essential worker.

(8) FLSA TERMS.—The terms "employ", "person", "regular rate", and "State" have the meanings given the terms in section 3 of the Fair Labor Standards Act of 1938 (29 U.S.C. 203).

(9) HIGHLY-COMPENSATED ESSENTIAL WORKER.—The term "highly-compensated essential worker" means an essential worker who is paid the equivalent of $200,000 or more per year by an essential work employer.

(10) LARGE ESSENTIAL WORK EMPLOYER.—The term "large essential work employer" means an essential work employer who has more than 500 individuals who are employed by the employer or are otherwise providing services or labor for remuneration for the employer.

(11) SELF-DIRECTED CARE WORKER.—The term "self-directed care worker" means an individual employed to provide care (which may include items and services) to an individual client—

(A) under a self-directed service delivery model through a program established or administered by a State, locality, Tribal government, or the Federal Government; or

(B) on the individual client's own accord and using the individual client's own finances.

(12) TRIBAL EMPLOYER.—The term "Tribal employer" means—

(A) any Tribal government, a subdivision of a Tribal government (determined in accordance with section 7871(d) of the Internal Revenue Code), or an agency or instrumentality of a Tribal government or subdivision thereof;

(B) any Tribal organization (as the term "tribal organization" is defined in section 4(l) of the Indian Self-Determination and Education Assistance Act (25 U.S.C. 5304(l));

(C) any corporation if more than 50 percent (determined by vote and value) of the outstanding stock of such corporation is owned, directly or indirectly, by any entity described in subparagraph (A) or (B); or

(D) any partnership if more than 50 percent of the value of the capital and profits interests of such partnership is owned, directly or indirectly, by any entity described in subparagraph (A) or (B).

(13) TRIBAL GOVERNMENT.—The term "Tribal government" means the recognized governing body of any Indian or Alaska Native tribe, band, nation, pueblo, village, community, component band, or component reservation individually identified (including parenthetically) in the list published most recently as of the date of enactment of this Act pursuant to section 104 of the Federally Recognized Indian Tribe List Act of 1994 (25 U.S.C. 5131).

(14) WORK.—The term "work" means employment by, or engagement in providing labor or services for, an employer.

SEC. 170102. PANDEMIC PREMIUM PAY FOR ESSENTIAL WORKERS.

(a) In General.— Beginning 3 days after an essential work employer receives a grant under section 104 from the Secretary of the Treasury, the essential work employer shall—

(1) be required to comply with subsections (b) through (h); and

(2) be subject to the enforcement requirements of section 105.

(b) Pandemic Premium Pay.—

(1) IN GENERAL.—An essential work employer receiving a grant under section 104 shall, in accordance with this subsection, provide each essential worker of the essential work employer with premium pay at a rate equal to $13 for each hour of work performed by the essential worker for the employer from January 27, 2020, until the date that is 60 days after the last day of the COVID–19 Public Health Emergency.

(2) MAXIMUM AMOUNTS.—The total amount of all premium pay under this subsection that an essential work employer is required to provide to an essential worker, including through any retroactive payment under paragraph (3), shall not exceed—

(A) for an essential worker who is not a highly-compensated essential worker, $10,000 reduced by employer payroll taxes with respect to such premium pay; or

(B) for a highly-compensated essential worker, $5,000 reduced by employer payroll taxes with respect to such premium pay.

(3) RETROACTIVE PAYMENT.—For all work performed by an essential worker during the period from January 27, 2020, through the date on which the essential work employer of the worker receives a grant under this title, the essential work employer shall use a portion of the amount of such grant to provide such worker with premium pay under this subsection for such work at the rate provided under paragraph (1). Such amount shall be provided to the essential worker as a lump sum in the next paycheck (or other payment form) that immediately follows the receipt of the grant by the essential work employer. In any case where it is impossible for the employer to arrange for payment of the amount due in such paycheck (or other payment form), such amounts shall be paid as soon as practicable, but in no event later than the second paycheck (or other payment form) following the receipt of the grant by the essential work employer.

(4) NO EMPLOYER DISCRETION.—An essential work employer receiving a grant under section 104 shall not have any discretion to determine which portions of work performed by an essential worker qualify for premium pay under this subsection, but shall pay such premium pay for any increment of time worked by the essential worker for the essential work employer up to the maximum amount applicable to the essential worker under paragraph (2).

(c) Prohibition On Reducing Compensation And Displacement.—

(1) IN GENERAL.—Any payments made to an essential worker as premium pay under subsection (b) shall be in addition to all other compensation, including all wages, remuneration, or other pay and benefits, that the essential worker otherwise receives from the essential work employer.

(2) REDUCTION OF COMPENSATION.—An essential work employer receiving a grant under section 104 shall not, during the period beginning on the date of enactment of this Act and ending on the date that is 60 days after the last day of the COVID–19 Public Health Emergency, reduce or in any other way diminish, any other compensation, including the wages, remuneration, or other pay or benefits, that the essential work employer provided to the essential worker on the day before the date of enactment of this Act.

(3) DISPLACEMENT.—An essential work employer shall not take any action to displace an essential worker (including partial displacement such as a reduction in hours, wages, or employment benefits) for purposes of hiring an individual for an equivalent position at a rate of compensation that is less than is required to be provided to an essential worker under paragraph (2).

(d) Demarcation From Other Compensation.—The amount of any premium pay paid under subsection (b) shall be clearly demarcated as a separate line item in each paystub or other document provided to an essential worker that details the remuneration the essential worker received from the essential work employer for a particular period of time. If any essential worker does not otherwise regularly receive any such paystub or other document from the employer, the essential work employer shall provide such paystub or other document to the essential worker for the duration of the period in which the essential work employer provides premium pay under subsection (b).

(e) Exclusion From Wage-Based Calculations.—Any premium pay under subsection (b) paid to an essential worker under this section by an essential work employer receiving a grant under section 104 shall be excluded from the amount of remuneration for work paid to the essential worker for purposes of—

(1) calculating the essential worker's eligibility for any wage-based benefits offered by the essential work employer;

(2) computing the regular rate at which such essential worker is employed under section 7 of the Fair Labor Standards Act of 1938 (29 U.S.C. 207); and

(3) determining whether such essential worker is exempt from application of such section 7 under section 13(a)(1) of such Act (29 U.S.C. 213(a)(1)).

(f) Essential Worker Death.—

(1) IN GENERAL.—In any case in which an essential worker of an essential work employer receiving a grant under section 104 exhibits symptoms of COVID–19 and dies, the essential work employer shall pay as a lump sum to the next of kin of the essential worker for premium pay under subsection (b)—

(A) for an essential worker who is not a highly-compensated essential worker, the amount determined under subsection (b)(2)(A) minus the total amount of any premium pay the worker received under subsection (b) prior to the death; or

(B) for a highly-compensated essential worker, the amount determined under subsection (b)(2)(B) minus the amount of any premium pay the worker received under subsection (b) prior to the death.

(2) TREATMENT OF LUMP SUM PAYMENTS.—

(A) TREATMENT AS PREMIUM PAY.—For purposes of this title, any payment made under this subsection shall be treated as a premium pay under subsection (b).

(B) TREATMENT FOR PURPOSES OF INTERNAL REVENUE CODE OF 1986.—For purposes of the Internal Revenue Code of 1986, any payment made under this subsection shall be treated as a payment for work performed by the essential worker.

(g) Application To Self-Directed Care Workers Funded Through Medicaid Or The Veteran-Directed Care Program.—

(1) MEDICAID.—In the case of an essential work employer receiving a grant under section 104 that is a covered employer described in section 101(3)(C)(i)(V) who, under a State Medicaid plan under title XIX of the Social Security Act (42 U.S.C. 1396 et seq.) or under a waiver of such plan, has opted to receive items or services using a self-directed service delivery model, the preceding requirements of this section, including the requirements to provide premium pay under subsection (b) (including a lump sum payment in the event of an essential worker death under subsection (f)) and the requirements of sections 104 and 105, shall apply to the State Medicaid agency responsible for the administration of such plan or waiver with respect to self-directed care workers employed by that employer. In administering payments made under this title to such self-directed care workers on behalf of such employers, a State Medicaid agency shall—

(A) exclude and disregard any payments made under this title to such self-directed workers from the individualized budget that applies to the items or services furnished to the individual client employer under the State Medicaid plan or waiver;

(B) to the extent practicable, administer and provide payments under this title directly to such self-directed workers through arrangements with entities that provide financial management services in connection with the self-directed service delivery models used under the State Medicaid plan or waiver; and

(C) ensure that individual client employers of such self-directed workers are provided notice of, and comply with, the prohibition under section 105(b)(1)(B).

(2) VETERAN-DIRECTED CARE PROGRAM.—In the case of an essential work

employer that is a covered employer described in section 101(3)(C)(i)(V) who is a veteran participating in the Veteran Directed Care program administered by the VA Office of Geriatrics & Extended Care of the Veterans Health Administration, the preceding requirements of this section and sections 104 and 105, shall apply to such VA Office of Geriatrics & Extended Care with respect to self-directed care workers employed by that employer. Paragraph (1) of this subsection shall apply to the administration by the VA Office of Geriatrics & Extended Care of payments made under this title to such self-directed care workers on behalf of such employers in the same manner as such requirements apply to State Medicaid agencies.

(3) PENALTY ENFORCEMENT.—The Secretary of Labor shall consult with the Secretary of Health and Human Services and the Secretary of Veterans Affairs regarding the enforcement of penalties imposed under section 105(b)(2) with respect to violations of subparagraph (A) or (B) of section 105(b)(1) that involve self-directed workers for which the requirements of this section and sections 104 and 105 are applied to a State Medicaid agency under paragraph (1) or the VA Office of Geriatrics & Extended Care under paragraph (2).

(h) Interaction With Stafford Act.—Nothing in this section shall nullify, supersede, or otherwise change a State's ability to seek reimbursement under section 403 of the Robert T. Stafford Disaster Relief and Emergency Assistance Act (42 U.S.C. 5170b) for the costs of premium pay based on pre-disaster labor policies for eligible employees.

(i) Calculation Of Paid Leave Under FFCRA And FMLA.—

(1) FAMILIES FIRST CORONAVIRUS RESPONSE ACT.—Section 5110(5)(B) of the Families First Coronavirus Response Act (29 U.S.C. 2601 note) is amended by adding at the end the following:

"(iii) PANDEMIC PREMIUM PAY.—Compensation received by an employee under section 102(b) of the COVID–19 Heroes Fund Act of 2020 shall be included as remuneration for employment paid to the employee for purposes of computing the regular rate at which such employee is employed.".

(2) FAMILY AND MEDICAL LEAVE ACT OF 1993.—Section 110(b)(2)(B) of the Family and Medical Leave Act of 1993 (29 U.S.C. 2620(b)(2)(B)) is amended by adding at the end the following:

"(iii) PANDEMIC PREMIUM PAY.—Compensation received by an employee under section 102(b) of the COVID–19 Heroes Fund Act of 2020 shall be included as remuneration for employment paid to the employee for purposes of computing the regular rate at which such employee is employed.".

SEC. 170103. COVID–19 HEROES FUND.

(a) Establishment.—There is established in the Treasury of the United States a fund to be known as the "COVID–19 Heroes Fund" (referred to in this section as the "Fund"), consisting of amounts appropriated to the fund under section 107.

(b) Fund Administration.—The Fund shall be administered by the Secretary of the Treasury.

(c) Use Of Funds.—Amounts in the Fund shall be available to the Secretary of the Treasury for carrying out section 104.

SEC. 170104. COVID–19 HEROES FUND GRANTS.

(a) Grants.—

(1) FOR PANDEMIC PREMIUM PAY.—The Secretary of the Treasury shall award a grant to each essential work employer that applies for a grant, in accordance with

this section, for the purpose of providing premium pay to essential workers under section 102(b), including amounts paid under section 102(f).

(2) ELIGIBILITY.—

(A) ELIGIBLE EMPLOYERS GENERALLY.—Any essential work employer shall be eligible for a grant under paragraph (1).

(B) SELF-DIRECTED CARE WORKERS.—A self-directed care worker employed by an essential work employer other than an essential work employer described in section 102(g), shall be eligible to apply for a grant under paragraph (1) in the same manner as an essential work employer. Such a worker shall provide premium pay to himself or herself in accordance with this section, including the recordkeeping and refund requirements of this section.

(b) Amount Of Grants.—

(1) IN GENERAL.—The maximum amount available for making a grant under subsection (a)(1) to an essential work employer shall be equal to the sum of—

(A) the amount obtained by multiplying $10,000 by the number of essential workers the employer certifies, in the application submitted under subsection (c)(1), as employing, or providing remuneration to for services or labor, who are paid wages or remuneration by the employer at a rate that is less than the equivalent of $200,000 per year; and

(B) the amount obtained by multiplying $5,000 by the number of highly-compensated essential workers the employer certifies, in the application submitted under subsection (c)(1), as employing, or providing remuneration to for services or labor, who are paid wages or remuneration by the employer at a rate that is equal to or greater than the equivalent of $200,000 per year.

(2) NO PARTIAL GRANTS.—The Secretary of the Treasury shall not award a grant under this section in an amount less than the maximum described in paragraph (1).

(c) Grant Application And Disbursal.—

(1) APPLICATION.—Any essential work employer seeking a grant under subsection (a)(1) shall submit an application to the Secretary of the Treasury at such time, in such manner, and complete with such information as the Secretary may require.

(2) NOTICE AND CERTIFICATION.—

(A) IN GENERAL.—The Secretary of the Treasury shall, within 15 days after receiving a complete application from an essential work employer eligible for a grant under this section—

(i) notify the employer of the Secretary's findings with respect to the requirements for the grant; and

(ii) (I) if the Secretary finds that the essential work employer meets the requirements under this section for a grant under subsection (a), provide a certification to the employer—

(aa) that the employer has met such requirements;

(bb) of the amount of the grant payment that the Secretary has determined the employer shall receive based on the requirements under this section; or

(II) if the Secretary finds that the essential work employer does not meet the requirements under this section for a grant under subsection (a), provide a notice of denial stating the reasons for the denial and provide an opportunity for administrative review by not later than 10 days after the denial.

(B) TRANSFER.—Not later than 7 days after making a certification under subparagraph (A)(ii) with respect to an essential work employer, the Secretary of the Treasury shall make the appropriate transfer to the employer of the amount of the grant.

(d) Use Of Funds.—

(1) IN GENERAL.—An essential work employer receiving a grant under this section shall use the amount of the grant solely for the following purposes:

(A) Providing premium pay under section 102(b) to essential workers in accordance with the requirements for such payments under such section, including providing payments described in section 102(f) to the next of kin of essential workers in accordance with the requirements for such payments under such section.

(B) Paying employer payroll taxes with respect to premium pay amounts described in subparagraph (A), including such payments described in section 102(f).

Each dollar of a grant received by an essential work employer under this title shall be used as provided in subparagraph (A) or (B) or returned to the Secretary of the Treasury.

(2) NO OTHER USES AUTHORIZED.—An essential work employer who uses any amount of a grant for a purpose not required under paragraph (1) shall be—

(A) considered to have misused funds in violation of section 102; and

(B) subject to the enforcement and remedies provided under section 105.

(3) REFUND.—

(A) IN GENERAL.—If an essential work employer receives a grant under this section and, for any reason, does not provide every dollar of such grant to essential workers in accordance with the requirements of this title, then the employer shall refund any such dollars to the Secretary of the Treasury not later than June 30, 2021. Any amounts returned to the Secretary shall be deposited into the Fund and be available for any additional grants under this section.

(B) REQUIREMENT FOR NOT REDUCING COMPENSATION.—An essential work employer who is required to refund any amount under this paragraph shall not reduce or otherwise diminish an eligible worker's compensation or benefits in response to or otherwise due to such refund.

(e) Recordkeeping.—An essential work employer that receives a grant under this section shall—

(1) maintain records, including payroll records, demonstrating how each dollar of funds received through the grant were provided to essential workers; and

(2) provide such records to the Secretary of the Treasury or the Secretary of Labor upon the request of either such Secretary.

(f) Recoupment.—In addition to all other enforcement and remedies available under this title or any other law, the Secretary of the Treasury shall establish a process under which the Secretary shall recoup the amount of any grant awarded under subsection (a)(1) if the Secretary determines that the essential work employer receiving the grant—

(1) did not provide all of the dollars of such grant to the essential workers of the employer;

(2) did not, in fact, have the number of essential workers certified by the employer in accordance with subparagraphs (A) and (B) of subsection (b)(1);

(3) did not pay the essential workers for the number of hours the employer claimed to have paid; or

(4) otherwise misused funds or violated this title.

(g) Special Rule For Certain Employees Of Tribal Employers.—Essential workers of Tribal employers who receive funds under title II shall not be eligible to receive funds from grants under this section.

(h) Tax Treatment.—

(1) EXCLUSION FROM INCOME.—For purposes of the Internal Revenue Code of 1986, any grant received by an essential work employer under this section shall not be included in the gross income of such essential work employer.

(2) DENIAL OF DOUBLE BENEFIT.—

(A) IN GENERAL.—In the case of an essential work employer that receives a grant under this section—

(i) amounts paid under subsections (b) or (f) of section 102 shall not be taken into account as wages for purposes of sections 41, 45A, 51, or 1396 of the Internal Revenue Code of 1986 or section 2301 of the CARES Act (Public Law 116–136); and

(ii) any deduction otherwise allowable under such Code for applicable payments during any taxable year shall be reduced (but not below zero) by the excess (if any) of—

(I) the aggregate amounts of grants received under this section; over

(II) the sum of any amount refunded under subsection (d) plus the aggregate amount of applicable payments made for all preceding taxable years.

(B) APPLICABLE PAYMENTS.—For purposes of this paragraph, the term "applicable payments" means amounts paid as premium pay under subsections (b) or (f) of section 102 and amounts paid for employer payroll taxes with respect to such amounts.

(C) AGGREGATION RULE.—Rules similar to the rules of subsections (a) and (b) of section 52 of the Internal Revenue Code of 1986 shall apply for purposes of this section.

(3) INFORMATION REPORTING.—The Secretary of the Treasury shall submit to the Commissioner of Internal Revenue statements containing—

(A) the name and tax identification number of each essential work employer receiving a grant under this section;

(B) the amount of such grant; and

(C) any amounts refunded under section (d)(3).

(i) Reports.—

(1) IN GENERAL.—Not later than 30 days after obligating the last dollar of the funds appropriated under this title, the Secretary of the Treasury shall submit a report, to the Committees of Congress described in paragraph (2), that—

(A) certifies that all funds appropriated under this title have been obligated; and

(B) indicates the number of pending applications for grants under this section that will be rejected due to the lack of funds.

(2) COMMITTEES OF CONGRESS.—The Committees of Congress described in this paragraph are—

(A) the Committee on Ways and Means of the House of Representatives;

(B) the Committee on Education and Labor of the House of Representatives;

(C) the Committee on Finance of the Senate; and

(D) the Committee on Health, Education, Labor, and Pensions of the Senate.

SEC. 170105. ENFORCEMENT AND OUTREACH.

(a) Duties Of Secretary Of Labor.—The Secretary of Labor shall—

(1) have authority to enforce the requirements of section 102, in accordance with subsections (b) through (e);

(2) conduct outreach as described in subsection (f); and

(3) coordinate with the Secretary of the Treasury as needed to carry out the Secretary of Labor's responsibilities under this section.

(b) Prohibited Acts, Penalties, And Enforcement.—

(1) PROHIBITED ACTS.—It shall be unlawful for a person to—

(A) violate any provision of section 102 applicable to such person; or

(B) discharge or in any other manner discriminate against any essential worker because such essential worker has filed any complaint or instituted or caused to be instituted any proceeding under or related to this title, or has testified or is about to testify in any such proceeding.

(2) ENFORCEMENT AND PENALTIES.—

(A) PREMIUM PAY VIOLATIONS.—A violation described in paragraph (1)(A) shall be deemed a violation of section 7 of the Fair Labor Standards Act of 1938 (29 U.S.C. 207) and unpaid amounts required under this section shall be treated as unpaid overtime compensation under such section 7 for the purposes of sections 15 and 16 of such Act (29 U.S.C. 215 and 216).

(B) DISCHARGE OR DISCRIMINATION.—A violation of paragraph (1)(B) shall be deemed a violation of section 15(a)(3) of the Fair Labor Standards Act of 1938 (29 U.S.C. 215(a)(3)).

(c) Investigation.—

(1) IN GENERAL.—To ensure compliance with the provisions of section 102, including any regulation or order issued under that section, the Secretary of Labor shall have the investigative authority provided under section 11(a) of the Fair Labor Standards Act of 1938 (29 U.S.C. 211(a)). For the purposes of any investigation provided for in this subsection, the Secretary of Labor shall have the subpoena authority provided for under section 9 of such Act (29 U.S.C. 209).

(2) STATE AGENCIES.—The Secretary of Labor may, for the purpose of carrying out the functions and duties under this section, utilize the services of State and local agencies in accordance with section 11(b) of the Fair Labor Standards Act of 1938 (29 U.S.C. 211(b)).

(d) Essential Worker Enforcement.—

(1) RIGHT OF ACTION.—An action alleging a violation of paragraph (1) or (2) of subsection (b) may be maintained against an essential work employer receiving a grant under section 104 in any Federal or State court of competent jurisdiction by one or more essential workers or their representative for and on behalf of the essential workers, or the essential workers and others similarly situated, in the same manner, and subject to the same remedies (including attorney's fees and costs of the action), as an action brought by an employee alleging a violation of section 7 or 15(a)(3), respectively, of the Fair Labor Standards Act of 1938 (29 U.S.C. 207, 215(a)(3)).

(2) NO WAIVER.—In an action alleging a violation of paragraph (1) or (2) of subsection (b) brought by one or more essential workers or their representative for and on behalf of the persons as described in paragraph (1), to enforce the rights in section 102, no court of competent jurisdiction may grant the motion of an essential work employer receiving a grant under section 104 to compel arbitration, under chapter 1 of title 9, United States Code, or any analogous State arbitration statute, of the claims involved. An essential worker's right to bring an action described in paragraph (1) or subsection (b)(2)(A) on behalf of similarly situated essential workers to enforce such rights may not be subject to any private agreement that purports to require the essential workers to pursue claims on an individual basis.

(e) Recordkeeping.—An essential work employer receiving a grant under section 104 shall make, keep, and preserve records pertaining to compliance with section 102 in accordance with section 11(c) of the Fair Labor Standards Act of 1938 (29 U.S.C. 211(c)) and in accordance with regulations prescribed by the Secretary of Labor.

(f) Outreach And Education.—Out of amounts appropriated to the Secretary of the Treasury under section 107 for a fiscal year, the Secretary of the Treasury shall transfer, to the Secretary of Labor, an amount equal to 0.50 percent of such funds, of which the Secretary of Labor shall use—

(1) 0.25 percent of such funds for outreach to essential work employers and essential workers regarding the premium pay under section 102; and

(2) 0.25 percent of such funds to implement an advertising campaign encouraging large essential work employers to provide the same premium pay provided for by section 102 using the large essential work employers' own funds and without utilizing grants under this title.

(g) Clarification Of Enforcing Official.—Nothing in the Government Employee Rights Act of 1991 (42 U.S.C. 2000e–16a et seq.) or section 3(e)(2)(C) of the Fair Labor Standards Act of 1938 (29 U.S.C. 203(e)(2)(C)) shall be construed to prevent the Secretary of Labor from carrying out the authority of the Secretary under this section in the case of State employees described in section 304(a) of the Government Employee Rights Act of 1991 (42 U.S.C. 2000e–16c(a)).

SEC. 170106. FUNDING FOR THE DEPARTMENT OF THE TREASURY OFFICE OF INSPECTOR GENERAL.

There is appropriated, out of money in the Treasury not otherwise appropriated, to the Office of the Inspector General of the Department of the Treasury, $1,000,000 to carry out audits, investigations, and other oversight activities authorized under the Inspector General Act of 1978 (5 U.S.C. App.) that are related to the provisions of, and amendments made by, this title, to remain available until December 31, 2022.

SEC. 170107. AUTHORIZATION AND APPROPRIATIONS.

There is authorized to be appropriated, and there is hereby appropriated, $180,000,000,000 to carry out this title, to remain available until expended, to carry out this title.

TITLE II—PROVISIONS RELATING TO FEDERAL EMPLOYEES AND COVID–19

SEC. 170201. DEFINITIONS.

In this title—

(1) the term "agency"—

(A) means—

(i) each agency, office, or other establishment in the executive, legislative, or judicial branch of the Federal Government, including—

(I) an Executive agency, as that term is defined in section 105 of title 5, United States Code;

(II) a military department, as that term is defined in section 102 of title 5, United States Code;

(III) the Federal Aviation Administration;

(IV) the Transportation Security Administration;

(V) the Department of Veterans Affairs; and

(VI) the Government Accountability Office;

(ii) the District of Columbia courts and the District of Columbia Public Defender Service; and

(iii) (I) an Indian tribe or tribal organization carrying out a contract or compact under the Indian Self-Determination and Education Assistance Act (25 U.S.C. 5301 et seq.);

(II) an Indian tribe or tribal organization that receives a grant under the Tribally Controlled Schools Act of 1988 (25 U.S.C. 2501 et seq.); and

(III) an urban Indian organization that receives a grant or carries out a contract under title V of the Indian Health Care Improvement Act (25 U.S.C. 1651 et seq.); and

(B) does not include—

(i) the United States Postal Service or the Postal Regulatory Commission; or

(ii) a nonappropriated fund instrumentality under the jurisdiction of the Armed Forces;

(2) the term "covered duty"—

(A) means duty that requires—

(i) an employee to have regular or routine contact with the public; or

(ii) the reporting of an employee to a worksite at which—

(I) social distancing is not possible, consistent with the regularly assigned duties of the position of the employee; and

(II) other preventative measures with respect to COVID–19 are not available; and

(B) does not include duty that an employee performs while teleworking from a residence;

(3) the term "covered period" means the period beginning on the date on which the Secretary of Health and Human Services declared a public health emergency under section 319 of the Public Health Service Act (42 U.S.C. 247d) with respect to COVID–19 and ending on the date that is 60 days after the date on which that public health emergency terminates; and

(4) the term "employee"—

(A) means an employee of an agency;

(B) includes—

(i) any employee of an agency who occupies a position within the General Schedule under subchapter III of chapter 53 of title 5, United States Code;

(ii) any employee of an agency whose pay is fixed and adjusted from time to time in accordance with prevailing rates under subchapter IV of chapter 53 of title 5, United States Code, or by a wage board or similar administrative authority serving the same purpose;

(iii) an official or employee of an Indian tribe, tribal organization, or urban Indian organization described in paragraph (1)(A)(iii);

(iv) each employee of the Department of Veterans Affairs, including an employee appointed under chapter 74 of title 38, United States Code, without regard to whether section 7421(a) of that title, section 7425(b) of that title, or any other provision of chapter 74 of that title is inconsistent with that inclusion; and

(v) any other individual occupying a position in the civil service, as that term is defined in section 2101 of title 5, United States Code; and

(C) does not include—

(i) a member of the uniformed services, as that term is defined in section 2101 of title 5, United States Code;

(ii) an employee of an agency who occupies a position within the Executive Schedule under any of sections 5312 through 5316 of title 5, United States Code;

(iii) an individual in a Senior Executive Service position, unless the individual is a career appointee, as those terms are defined in section 3132(a) of title 5, United States Code;

(iv) an individual serving in a position of a confidential or policy-determining character under Schedule C of subpart C of part 213 of title 5, Code of Federal Regulations, or any successor regulations;

(v) a member of the Senate or House of Representatives, a Delegate to the House of Representatives, or the Resident Commissioner from Puerto Rico; or

(vi) an employee of the personal office of an individual described in clause (v), of a leadership office of the Senate or the House of Representatives, of a committee of the Senate or the House of Representatives, or of a joint committee of Congress.

SEC. 170202. PANDEMIC DUTY DIFFERENTIAL.

(a) In General.—There is established a schedule of pay differentials for covered duty as follows:

(1) An employee is entitled to pay for that covered duty at the rate of basic pay, which includes any differential or other premium pay paid for regularly scheduled work of the employee other than the differential established under this section, of the employee plus premium pay of $13 per hour.

(2) The total amount of premium pay paid to an employee under paragraph (1) shall be—

(A) with respect to an employee whose annual rate of basic pay is less than $200,000, not more than $10,000 reduced by employer payroll taxes (as defined in section 101(4)) with respect to such premium pay; and

(B) with respect to an employee whose annual rate of basic pay is not less than $200,000, not more than $5,000 reduced by employer payroll taxes (as so defined) with respect to such premium pay.

(b) Pay.—

(1) IN GENERAL.—With respect to the covered period, an employee is entitled to be paid the applicable differential established under subsection (a) for any period, including any period during the covered period that precedes the date of enactment of this Act, in which the employee is carrying out covered duty, subject to the applicable limitations under that subsection.

(2) RETROACTIVE PAYMENT.—With respect to a payment earned by an employee under this section for a period during the covered period that precedes the date of enactment of this Act, the employee shall be paid that payment in a lump sum payment as soon as is practicable after that date of enactment.

(c) Guidance And Regulations.—

(1) EXECUTIVE BRANCH.—

(A) IN GENERAL.—The Office of Personnel Management shall develop criteria for agencies in the executive branch of the Federal Government regarding the means by which to determine the eligibility of an employee in such an agency for the pay differential established under this section, which shall—

(i) be based on—

(I) the duties performed by the employee;

(II) the setting in which the employee performs the duties described in subclause

(I); and

(III) the interactions with the public required in order for the employee to perform the duties described in subclause (I); and

(ii) apply equally to all such agencies.

(B) REGULATIONS.—The Office of Personnel Management may prescribe regulations implementing the pay differential under this section with respect to employees in the executive branch of the Federal Government.

(2) OTHER BRANCHES, CERTAIN DC EMPLOYEES, AND CERTAIN TRIBAL OFFICIALS.—

(A) IN GENERAL.—The employing authority for each agency that is not in the executive branch of the Federal Government—

(i) shall develop criteria regarding the means by which to determine the eligibility of an employee in such an agency for the pay differential established under this section; and

(ii) may prescribe regulations implementing the pay differential under this section with respect to employees in the applicable agency.

(B) CONSISTENCY WITH OPM GUIDANCE AND REGULATIONS.—Any criteria developed, and regulations prescribed, by an agency under subparagraph (A) shall, to the extent practicable, be comparable to any criteria developed and regulations prescribed by the Office of Personnel Management under paragraph (1).

SEC. 170203. LIMITATION ON PREMIUM PAY.

(a) In General.—Notwithstanding subsections (a) and (b) of section 5547 of title 5, United States Code, or a provision of any other Federal, State, or Tribal law that imposes a limitation on the amount of premium pay (including any premium pay paid under section 202 and any overtime pay paid for covered duty) that may be payable to an employee, an employee may be paid such premium pay to the extent that the payment does not cause the aggregate of basic pay and such premium pay for service performed in that calendar year by that employee to exceed the annual rate of basic pay payable for level II of the Executive Schedule, as of the end of the calendar year.

(b) Applicability Of Aggregate Limitation On Pay.—In determining whether a payment to an employee is subject to the limitation under section 5307(a) of title 5, United States Code, a payment described in subsection (a) shall not apply.

(c) Applicability Of CARES Act.—The authority provided under this section shall be considered to be in addition to, and not a replacement for, the authority provided under section 18110 of title VIII of the CARES Act (Public Law 116–136).

(d) Retroactive Effect.—This section shall take effect as if enacted on the date on which the covered period began.

SEC. 170204. AUTHORIZATION AND APPROPRIATION.

There is authorized to be appropriated, and there is hereby appropriated, out of any money in the Treasury not otherwise appropriated, $10,000,000,000, to remain available until expended, for the offices and agencies described in subsection (b) of this section to carry out section 170202 and section 170203 of this title and to make transfers authorized under subsection (a) of this section.

(a) Offices And Agencies.—The offices and agencies described in this subsection are—

(1) the Office of the Sergeant at Arms and Doorkeeper of the Senate;

(2) the Office of the Clerk of the House of Representatives;

(3) the Office of the Sergeant at Arms of the House of Representatives;

(4) the Office of the Chief Administrative Officer of the House of Representatives;

(5) the Office of the Attending Physician;

(6) the Capitol Police;

(7) the Office of the Architect of the Capitol;

(8) the Library of Congress;

(9) the Government Publishing Office;

(10) the Government Accountability Office;

(11) the Office of Personnel Management;

(12) the Administrative Office of the United States Courts; and

(13) the District of Columbia Courts.

(b) Transfer Authority.—

(1) OPM.—The Office of Personnel Management may transfer funds made available under this section to other Federal agencies within the executive branch to reimburse such agencies for costs incurred to implement this title.

(2) AOUSC.—The Administrative Office of the United States Courts may transfer funds made available under this section to other entities within the judicial branch to reimburse the entities for costs incurred to implement this title.

(3) DC COURTS.—The District of Columbia Courts may transfer funds made available under this section to the District of Columbia Public Defender Service to reimburse the agency for costs incurred to implement this title.

TITLE III—COORDINATION OF BENEFITS WITH OTHER PROGRAMS AND LAWS

SEC. 170301. COORDINATION WITH OTHER BENEFITS.

(a) Disregard For Purposes Of Federal And State Programs.—Any payment provided under this Act shall not be regarded as income and shall not be regarded as a resource for the month of receipt and the following 12 months, for purposes of determining the eligibility of the recipient (or the recipient's spouse or family) for benefits or assistance, or the amount or extent of benefits or assistance, under any Federal program or under any State or local program financed in whole or in part with Federal funds.

(b) Amounts Not Taken Into Account For Purposes Of Premium Tax Credit.—

(1) IN GENERAL.—For purposes of determining modified adjusted gross income under section 36B(d)(2)(B) of the Internal Revenue Code of 1986, adjusted gross income shall be reduced by any amounts received under subsection (b), including pursuant to subsection (f), of section 170102 or by reason of section 170202.

(2) EXCEPTION.—Paragraph (1) shall not apply to the extent such reduction results in an amount of household income (as defined in section 36B(d)(2)(A) of such Code) of a taxpayer that is less than 100 percent of the poverty line (as defined in section 36B(d)(3) of such Code) for a family of the size involved (as determined under the rules of section 36B(d)(1) of such Code).

(3) REPORTING.—

(A) IN GENERAL.—Any employer that makes an applicable payment during a calendar year shall include as a separately stated item on any written statement required under section 6051 of the Internal Revenue Code of 1986 or any return or statement required by the Secretary of the Treasury (or the Secretary's delegate) with respect to nonemployee compensation the aggregate amount of each type of applicable payments so made.

(B) APPLICABLE PAYMENTS.—For purposes of this paragraph, the term "applicable payments" means—

(i) amounts paid as premium pay under section 170102(b), including amounts paid pursuant to section 170102(f); and

(ii) amounts paid by reason of section 170202.

(c) Employment Tax Treatment For Amounts Paid Through Grants.—

(1) IN GENERAL.—For purposes of section 3111(a) of the Internal Revenue Code of 1986, any amounts required to be paid by reason of this Act shall not be considered wages.

(2) RAILROAD RETIREMENT TAXES.—For purposes of section 3221(a) of the Internal Revenue Code of 1986, the amount of tax imposed under such section for any calendar year in which an employer is required to pay amounts under this Act shall be equal to the sum of—

(A) the product of the rate in effect under section 3111(a) of such Code and the compensation (reduced by any amounts required to be paid by reason of this Act) paid during any calendar year by such employer for services rendered to such employer; and

(B) the product of the rate in effect under section 3111(b) of such Code and the compensation paid during any calendar year by such employer for services rendered to such employer.

(3) SELF-EMPLOYED INDIVIDUALS.—

(A) IN GENERAL.—In the case of the tax imposed by section 1401(a) of the Internal Revenue Code of 1986, the self-employment income for any taxable year in which the individual received a payment required to be made under this Act shall be reduced by 50 percent of the amount of payments so made.

(B) REGULATORY AUTHORITY.—The Secretary of the Treasury (or the Secretary's delegate) shall prescribe regulations or other guidance for the application of sections 164(f) and 1402(a)(12) of the Internal Revenue Code of 1986 with respect to amounts to which subparagraph (A) applies.

(4) TRANSFERS TO TRUST FUNDS.—There are hereby appropriated to the Federal Old Age and Survivors Insurance Trust Fund and the Federal Disability Insurance Trust Fund established under section 201 of the Social Security Act (42 U.S.C. 401) and the Social Security Equivalent Benefit Account established under section 15A(a) of the Railroad Retirement Act of 1974 (45 U.S.C. 231n–1(a)) amounts equal to the reduction in revenues to the Treasury by reason of this subsection (without regard to this paragraph). Amounts appropriated by the preceding sentence shall be transferred from the general fund at such times and in such manner as to replicate to the extent possible the transfers which would have occurred to such Trust Fund or Account had this section not been enacted.

SEC. 170302. CLARIFICATION OF COORDINATION WITH OTHER LAWS.

(a) Essential Workers Rights And Benefits.—Nothing in this Act shall be construed to allow noncompliance with or in any way to diminish, and shall instead be construed to be in addition to, the rights or benefits that an essential worker is entitled to under any—

(1) Federal, State, or local law, including regulation;

(2) collective bargaining agreement; or

(3) employer policy.

(b) Title 5.—Nothing in this Act shall be construed to affect the application of the provisions of sections 5343 or 5545 of title 5, United States Code, with respect to pay differentials for duty involving unusual physical hardship or hazard, or environmental differentials.

SEC. 170303. APPLICABILITY OF FAIR LABOR STANDARDS ACT OF 1938 TO SOVEREIGN TRIBAL EMPLOYERS.

The receipt of any funds through a grant under section 104, or any funds under title II, by a sovereign Tribal employer, as defined in section 101(12), shall not expand, constrict, or alter the application of the Fair Labor Standards Act of 1938 (29 U.S.C. 201 et seq.) to such sovereign Tribal employer.

DIVISION R—CHILD NUTRITION AND RELATED PRO-GRAMS

SHORT TITLE

SEC. 180001.

This division may be cited as the "Child Nutrition and Related Programs Recovery Act".

EMERGENCY COSTS FOR CHILD NUTRITION PROGRAMS DURING COVID–19 PANDEMIC

SEC. 180002.

(a) Use Of Certain Appropriations To Cover Emergency Operational Costs Under School Meal Programs.—

(1) IN GENERAL.—

(A) REQUIRED ALLOTMENTS.—Notwithstanding any other provision of law, the Secretary shall allocate to each State that participates in the reimbursement program under paragraph (3) such amounts as may be necessary to carry out reimbursements under such paragraph for each reimbursement month, including, subject to paragraph (4)(B), administrative expenses necessary to make such reimbursements.

(B) GUIDANCE WITH RESPECT TO PROGRAM.—Not later than 10 days after the date of the enactment of this section, the Secretary shall issue guidance with respect to the reimbursement program under paragraph (3).

(2) REIMBURSEMENT PROGRAM APPLICATION.—To participate in the reimbursement program under paragraph (3), not later than 30 days after the date described in paragraph (1), a State shall submit an application to the Secretary that includes a plan to calculate and disburse reimbursements under the reimbursement program under paragraph (3).

(3) REIMBURSEMENT PROGRAM.—Using the amounts allocated under paragraph (1)(A), a State participating in the reimbursement program under this paragraph shall make reimbursements for emergency operational costs for each reimbursement month as follows:

(A) For each new school food authority in the State for the reimbursement month, an amount equal to 55 percent of the amount equal to—

(i) the average monthly amount such new school food authority was reimbursed under the reimbursement sections for meals and supplements served by such new school food authority during the alternate period; minus

(ii) the amount such new school food authority was reimbursed under the reimbursement sections for meals and supplements served by such new school food authority during such reimbursement month.

(B) For each school food authority not described in subparagraph (A) in the State for the reimbursement month, an amount equal to 55 percent of—

(i) the amount such school food authority was reimbursed under the reimbursement sections for meals and supplements served by such school food authority for the month beginning one year before such reimbursement month; minus

(ii) the amount such school food authority was reimbursed under the reimbursement sections for meals and supplements served by such school food authority during such reimbursement month.

(4) TREATMENT OF FUNDS.—

(A) AVAILABILITY.—Funds allocated to a State under paragraph (1)(A) shall remain available until March 30, 2021.

(B) ADMINISTRATIVE EXPENSES.—A State may reserve not more than 1 percent of the funds allocated under paragraph (1)(A) for administrative expenses to carry out this subsection.

(C) UNEXPENDED BALANCE.—On September 30, 2021, any amounts allocated to a State under paragraph (1)(A) or reimbursed to a school food authority or new school food authority under paragraph (3) that are unexpended by such State, school food authority, or new school food authority shall revert to the Secretary.

(5) REPORTS.—Each State that carries out a reimbursement program under paragraph (3) shall, not later than September 30, 2021, submit a report to the Secretary that includes a summary of the use of such funds by the State and each school food authority and new school food authority in such State.

(b) Use Of Certain Appropriations To Cover Child And Adult Care Food Program Child Care Operational Emergency Costs During COVID–19 Pandemic.—

(1) IN GENERAL.—

(A) REQUIRED ALLOTMENTS.—Notwithstanding any other provision of law, the Secretary shall allocate to each State that participates in the reimbursement program under paragraph (3) such amounts as may be necessary to carry out reimbursements under such paragraph for each reimbursement month, including, subject to paragraph (4)(C), administrative expenses necessary to make such reimbursements.

(B) GUIDANCE WITH RESPECT TO PROGRAM.—Not later than 10 days after the date of the enactment of this section, the Secretary shall issue guidance with respect to the reimbursement program under paragraph (3).

(2) REIMBURSEMENT PROGRAM APPLICATION.—To participate in the reimbursement program under paragraph (3), not later than 30 days after the date described in paragraph (1), a State shall submit an application to the Secretary that includes a plan to calculate and disburse reimbursements under the reimbursement program under paragraph (3).

(3) REIMBURSEMENT AMOUNT.—Using the amounts allocated under paragraph (1)(A), a State participating in the reimbursement program under this paragraph shall make reimbursements for child care operational emergency costs for each reimbursement month as follows:

(A) For each new covered institution in the State for the reimbursement month, an amount equal to 55 percent of—

(i) the average monthly amount such covered institution was reimbursed under subsection (c) and subsection (f) of section 17 of the Richard B. Russell National School

Lunch Act (42 U.S.C. 1766) for meals and supplements served by such new covered institution during the alternate period; minus

(ii) the amount such covered institution was reimbursed under such section for meals and supplements served by such new covered institution during such reimbursement month.

(B) For each covered institution not described in subparagraph (A) in the State for the reimbursement month, an amount equal to 55 percent of—

(i) the amount such covered institution was reimbursed under subsection (c) and subsection (f) of section 17 of the Richard B. Russell National School Lunch Act (42 U.S.C. 1766) for meals and supplements served by such covered institution during the month beginning one year before such reimbursement month; minus

(ii) the amount such covered institution was reimbursed under such section for meals and supplements served by such covered institution during such reimbursement month.

(C) For each new sponsoring organization of a family or group day care home in the State for the reimbursement month, an amount equal to 55 percent of—

(i) the average monthly amount such new sponsoring organization of a family or group day care home was reimbursed under section 17(f)(3)(B) of the Richard B. Russell National School Lunch Act (42 U.S.C. 1766(f)(3)(B)) for administrative funds for the alternate period; minus

(ii) the amount such new sponsoring organization of a family or group day care home was reimbursed under such section for administrative funds for the reimbursement month.

(D) For each sponsoring organization of a family or group day care home not described in subparagraph (C) in the State for the reimbursement month, an amount equal to 55 percent of—

(i) the amount such sponsoring organization of a family or group day care home was reimbursed under section 17(f)(3)(B) of the Richard B. Russell National School Lunch Act (42 U.S.C. 1766(f)(3)(B)) for administrative funds for the month beginning one year before such reimbursement month; minus

(ii) the amount such sponsoring organization of a family or group day care home was reimbursed under such section for administrative funds for such reimbursement month.

(4) TREATMENT OF FUNDS.—

(A) AVAILABILITY.—Funds allocated to a State under paragraph (1)(A) shall remain available until March 30, 2021.

(B) UNAFFILIATED CENTER.—In the case of a covered institution or a new covered institution that is an unaffiliated center that is sponsored by a sponsoring organization and receives funds for a reimbursement month under subparagraph (A) or (B), such unaffiliated center shall provide to such sponsoring organization an amount of such funds as agreed to by the sponsoring organization and the unaffiliated center, except such amount may not be greater be than 15 percent of such funds.

(C) ADMINISTRATIVE EXPENSES.—A State may reserve not more than 1 percent of the funds allocated under paragraph (1)(A) for administrative expenses to carry out this subsection.

(D) UNEXPENDED BALANCE.—On September 30, 2021, any amounts allocated to a State under paragraph (1)(A) or reimbursed to a new covered institution, covered institution, new sponsoring organization of a family or group day care home, or sponsoring organization of a family or group day care home that are unexpended by such State, new covered institution, covered institution, new sponsoring organization of a family or group day care home, or sponsoring organization of a family or group day care home, shall revert to the Secretary.

(5) REPORTS.—Each State that carries out a reimbursement program under paragraph (3) shall, not later than September 30, 2021, submit a report to the Secretary that includes a summary of the use of such funds by the State and each new covered institution, covered institution, new sponsoring organization of a family or group day care home, or sponsoring organization of a family or group day care home.

(c) Definitions.—In this section:

(1) ALTERNATE PERIOD.—The term "alternate period" means the period beginning January 1, 2020 and ending February 29, 2020.

(2) EMERGENCY OPERATIONAL COSTS.—The term "emergency operational costs" means the costs incurred by a school food authority or new school food authority—

(A) during a public health emergency;

(B) that are related to the ongoing operation, modified operation, or temporary suspension of operation (including administrative costs) of such school food authority or new school food authority; and

(C) except as provided under subsection (a), that are not reimbursed under a Federal grant.

(3) CHILD CARE OPERATIONAL EMERGENCY COSTS.—The term "child care operational emergency costs" means the costs under the child and adult care food program under section 17 of the Richard B. Russell National School Lunch Act (42 U.S.C. 1766) incurred by a new covered institution, covered institution, new sponsoring organization of a family or group day care home, or sponsoring organization of a family or group day care home—

(A) during a public health emergency;

(B) that are related to the ongoing operation, modified operation, or temporary suspension of operation (including administrative costs) of such new covered institution, covered institution, new sponsoring organization of a family or group day care home, sponsoring organization of a family or group day care home, or sponsoring organization of an unaffiliated center; and

(C) except as provided under subsection (b), that are not reimbursed under a Federal grant.

(4) COVERED INSTITUTION.—The term "covered institution" means—

(A) an institution (as defined in section 17(a)(2) of the Richard B. Russell National School Lunch Act (42 U.S.C. 1766(a)(2))); and

(B) a family or group day care home.

(5) NEW COVERED INSTITUTION.—The term "new covered institution" means a covered institution for which no reimbursements were made for meals and supplements under section 17(c) or (f) of the Richard B. Russell National School Lunch Act (42 U.S.C. 1766) with respect to the previous reimbursement period.

(6) NEW SCHOOL FOOD AUTHORITY.—The term "new school food authority" means a school food authority for which no reimbursements were made under the reimbursement sections with respect to the previous reimbursement period.

(7) NEW SPONSORING ORGANIZATION OF A FAMILY OR GROUP DAY CARE.—The term "new sponsoring organization of a family or group day care"

means a sponsoring organization of a family or group day care home for which no reimbursements for administrative funds were made under section 17(f)(3)(B) of the Richard B. Russell National School Lunch Act (42 U.S.C. 1766(f)(3)(B)) for the previous reimbursement period.

(8) PREVIOUS REIMBURSEMENT PERIOD.—The term "previous reimbursement period" means the period beginning March 1, 2019 and ending June 30, 2019.

(9) PUBLIC HEALTH EMERGENCY.—The term "public health emergency" means a public health emergency declared pursuant to section 319 of the Public Health Service Act (42 U.S.C. 247d) resulting from the COVID–19 pandemic.

(10) REIMBURSEMENT MONTH.—The term "reimbursement month" means March 2020, April 2020, May 2020, and June 2020.

(11) REIMBURSEMENT SECTIONS.—The term "reimbursement sections" means—
(A) section 4(b), section 11(a)(2), section 13, and section 17A(c) of the Richard B. Russell National School Lunch Act (42 U.S.C. 1753(b); 42 U.S.C. 1759a(a)(2); 42 U.S.C. 1761; 42 U.S.C. 1766a(c)); and
(B) section 4 of the Child Nutrition Act (42 U.S.C. 1773).

(12) SECRETARY.—The term "Secretary" means the Secretary of Agriculture.

(13) STATE.— The term "State" has the meaning given such term in section 12(d)(8) of the Richard B. Russell National School Lunch Act (42 U.S.C. 1760(d)(8)).

AMENDMENTS TO THE PANDEMIC EBT ACT

SEC. 180003.

Section 1101 of the Families First Coronavirus Response Act (Public Law 116–127) is amended—

(1) in subsection (a)—
(A) by striking "fiscal year 2020" and inserting "fiscal years 2020 and 2021";
(B) by striking "during which the school would otherwise be in session"; and
(C) by inserting "until the school reopens" after "assistance";

(2) in subsection (b)—
(A) by inserting "and State agency plans for child care covered children in accordance with subsection (i)" after "with eligible children";
(B) by inserting ", a plan to enroll children who become eligible children during a public health emergency designation" before ", and issuances";
(C) by striking "in an amount not less than the value of meals at the free rate over the course of 5 school days" and inserting "in accordance with subsection (h)(1)"; and
(D) by inserting "and for each child care covered child in the household" before the period at the end;

(3) in subsection (c), by inserting "or child care center" after "school";

(4) by amending subsection (e) to read as follows:

"(e) Release Of Information.—Notwithstanding any other provision of law, the Secretary of Agriculture may authorize—

"(1) State educational agencies and school food authorities administering a school lunch program under the Richard B. Russell National School Lunch Act (42 U.S.C. 1751 et seq.) to release to appropriate officials administering the supplemental nutrition assistance program such information as may be necessary to carry out this section with respect to eligible children; and

"(2) State agencies administering a child and adult care food program under section 17 of the Richard B. Russell National School Lunch Act (42 U.S.C. 1766) to release to appropriate officials administering the supplemental nutrition assistance program such information as may be necessary to carry out this section with respect to child care covered children.";

(5) by amending subsection (g) to read as follows:

"(g) Availability Of Commodities.—

"(1) IN GENERAL.—Subject to paragraph (2), during fiscal year 2020, the Secretary of Agriculture may purchase commodities for emergency distribution in any area of the United States during a public health emergency designation.

"(2) PURCHASES.—Funds made available to carry out this subsection on or after the date of the enactment of the Child Nutrition and Related Programs Recovery Act may only be used to purchase commodities for emergency distribution—

"(A) under commodity distribution programs and child nutrition programs that were established and administered by the Food and Nutrition Service on or before the day before the date of the enactment of the Families First Coronavirus Response Act (Public Law 116–127); or

"(B) to Tribal organizations (as defined in section 3 of the Food and Nutrition Act of 2008 (7 U.S.C. 2012)), that are not administering the food distribution program established under section 4(b) of the Food and Nutrition Act of 2008 (7 U.S.C. 2013(b)).".

(6) by redesignating subsections (h) and (i) as subsections (l) and (m);

(7) by inserting after subsection (g) the following:

"(h) Amount Of Benefits.—

"(1) IN GENERAL.—A household shall receive benefits under this section in an amount equal to 1 breakfast and 1 lunch at the free rate for each eligible child or child care covered child in such household for each day.

"(2) TREATMENT OF NEWLY ELIGIBLE CHILDREN.—In the case of a child who becomes an eligible child during a public health emergency designation, the Secretary and State agency shall—

"(A) if such child becomes an eligible child during school year 2019–2020, treat such child as if such child was an eligible child as of the date the school in which the child is enrolled closed; and

"(B) if such child becomes an eligible child after school year 2019–2020, treat such child as an eligible child as of the first day of the month in which such child becomes so eligible.

"(i) Child Care Covered Child Assistance.—

"(1) IN GENERAL.—During fiscal years 2020 and 2021, in any case in which a child care center is closed for at least 5 consecutive days during a public health emergency designation, each household containing at least 1 member who is a child care covered child attending the child care center shall be eligible until the schools in the State in which such child care center is located reopen, as determined by the Secretary, to receive assistance pursuant to—

"(A) a State agency plan approved under subsection (b) that includes—

"(i) an application by the State agency seeking to participate in the program under this subsection; and

"(ii) a State agency plan for temporary emergency standards of eligibility and levels of benefits under the Food and Nutrition Act of 2008 (7 U.S.C. 2011 et seq.) for households with child care covered children; or

"(B) an addendum application described in paragraph (2).

"(2) ADDENDUM APPLICATION.—In the case of a State agency that submits a plan to the Secretary of Agriculture under subsection (b) that does not include an application or plan described in clauses (i) and (ii) of paragraph (1)(A), such State agency may apply to participate in the program under this subsection by submitting to the Secretary of Agriculture an addendum application for approval that includes a State agency plan described in such clause (ii).

"(3) REQUIREMENTS FOR PARTICIPATION.—A State agency may not participate in the program under this subsection if—

"(A) the State agency plan submitted by such State agency under subsection (b) with respect to eligible children is not approved by the Secretary under such subsection; or

"(B) the State agency plan submitted by such State agency under subsection (b) or this subsection with respect to child care covered children is not approved by the Secretary under either such subsection.

"(4) AUTOMATIC ENROLLMENT.—

"(A) IN GENERAL.—Subject to subparagraph (B), the Secretary shall deem a child who is less than 6 years of age to be a child care covered child eligible to receive assistance under this subsection if—

"(i) the household with such child attests that such child is a child care covered child;

"(ii) such child resides in a household that includes an eligible child;

"(iii) such child receives cash assistance benefits under the temporary assistance for needy families program under part A of title IV of the Social Security Act (42 U.S.C. 601 et seq.);

"(iv) such child receives assistance under the Child Care and Development Block Grant Act of 1990 (42 U.S.C. 9857 et seq.);

"(v) such child is—

"(I) enrolled as a participant in a Head Start program authorized under the Head Start Act (42 U.S.C. 9831 et seq.);

"(II) a foster child whose care and placement is the responsibility of an agency that administers a State plan under part B or E of title IV of the Social Security Act (42 U.S.C. 621 et seq.);

"(III) a foster child who a court has placed with a caretaker household; or

"(IV) a homeless child or youth (as defined in section 725(2) of the McKinney-Vento Homeless Assistance Act (42 U.S.C. 11434a(2)));

"(vi) such child participates in the special supplemental nutrition program for women, infants, and children under section 17 of the Child Nutrition Act of 1966 (42 U.S.C. 1786);

"(vii) through the use of information obtained by the State agency for the purpose of participating in the supplemental nutrition assistance program under the Food and Nutrition Act of 2008 (7 U.S.C. 2011 et seq.), the State agency elects to treat as a child care covered child each child less than 6 years of age who is a member of a household that receives supplemental nutrition assistance program benefits under such Act; or

"(viii) the State in which such child resides determines that such child is a child care covered child, using State data approved by the Secretary.

"(B) ACCEPTANCE OF ANY FORM OF AUTOMATIC ENROLLMENT.—

"(i) ONE CATEGORY.—For purposes of deeming a child to be a child care covered child under subparagraph (A), a State agency may not be required to show that a child meets more than one requirement specified in clauses (i) through (viii) of such subparagraph.

"(ii) DEEMING REQUIREMENT.—If a State agency submits to the Secretary information that a child meets any one of the requirements specified in clauses (i) through

(viii) of subparagraph (A), the Secretary shall deem such child a child care covered child under such subparagraph.

"(j) Exclusions.—The provisions of section 16 of the Food and Nutrition Act of 2008 (7 U.S.C. 2025) relating to quality control shall not apply with respect to assistance provided under this section.

"(k) Feasibility Analysis.—

"(1) IN GENERAL.—Not later than 30 days after the date of the enactment of the Child Nutrition and Related Programs Recovery Act, the Secretary shall submit to the Education and Labor Committee and the Agriculture Committee of the House of Representatives and the Committee on Agriculture, Nutrition, and Forestry of the Senate a report on—

"(A) the feasibility of implementing the program for eligible children under this section using an EBT system in Puerto Rico, the Commonwealth of the Northern Mariana Islands, and American Samoa similar to the manner in which the supplemental nutrition assistance program under the Food and Nutrition Act of 2008 is operated in the States, including an analysis of-—

"(i) the current nutrition assistance program issuance infrastructure;

"(ii) the availability of—

"(I) an EBT system, including the ability for authorized retailers to accept EBT cards; and

"(II) EBT cards;

"(iii) the ability to limit purchases using nutrition assistance program benefits to food for home consumption; and

"(iv) the availability of reliable data necessary for the implementation of such program under this section for eligible children and child care covered children, including the names of such children and the mailing addresses of their households; and

"(B) the feasibility of implementing the program for child care covered children under subsection (i) in Puerto Rico, the Commonwealth of the Northern Mariana Islands, and American Samoa, including with respect to such program each analysis specified in clauses (i) through (iv) of subparagraph (A).

"(2) CONTINGENT AVAILABILITY OF PARTICIPATION.—Beginning 30 days after the date of the enactment of the Child Nutrition and Related Programs Recovery Act, Puerto Rico, the Commonwealth of the Northern Mariana Islands, and American Samoa may each—

"(A) submit a plan under subsection (b), unless the Secretary makes a finding, based on the analysis provided under paragraph (1)(A), that the implementation of the program for eligible children under this section is not feasible in such territories; and

"(B) submit a plan under subsection (i), unless the Secretary makes a finding, based on the analysis provided under paragraph (1)(B), that the implementation of the program for child care covered children under subsection (i) is not feasible in such territories.";

(8) in subsection (l), as redesigned by paragraph (7)—

(A) by redesignating paragraph (1) as paragraph (3);

(B) by redesignating paragraphs (2) and (3) as paragraphs (5) and (6), respectively;

(C) by inserting before paragraph (3) (as so redesignated) the following:

"(1) The term 'child care center' means an organization described in subparagraph (A) or (B) of section 17(a)(2) of the Richard B. Russell National School Lunch Act (42 U.S.C. 1766(a)(2)) and a family or group day care home.

"(2) The term 'child care covered child' means a child served under section 17 of the Richard B. Russell National School Lunch Act (42 U.S.C. 1766) who, if not for the closure of the child care center attended by the child during a public health emergency designation and due to concerns about a COVID–19 outbreak, would receive meals under such section at the child care center."; and

(D) by inserting after paragraph (3) (as so redesignated) the following:

"(4) The term 'free rate' means—

"(A) with respect to a breakfast, the rate of a free breakfast under the school breakfast program under section 4 of the Child Nutrition Act of 1966 (42 U.S.C. 1773); and

"(B) with respect to a lunch, the rate of a free lunch under the school lunch program under the Richard B. Russell National School Lunch Act (42 U.S.C. 1771 et seq.)."; and

(9) in subsection (m), as redesignated by paragraph (7), by inserting "(including all administrative expenses)" after "this section".

FRESH PRODUCE FOR KIDS IN NEED

SEC. 180004.

Section 2202(f)(1) of the Families First Coronavirus Response Act (Public Law 116–127) is amended by adding at the end the following:

"(E) The fresh fruit and vegetable program under section 19 of the Richard B. Russell National School Lunch Act (42 U.S.C. 1769a).".

WIC BENEFIT FLEXIBILITY DURING COVID–19 ACT

SEC. 180005.

(a) In General.—

(1) AUTHORITY TO INCREASE AMOUNT OF CASH-VALUE VOUCHER.— During the COVID–19 public health emergency declared under section 319 of the Public Health Service Act (42 U.S.C. 247d) and in response to challenges related to such public health emergency, the Secretary may increase the amount of a cash-value voucher under a qualified food package to an amount less than or equal to $35.

(2) APPLICATION OF INCREASED AMOUNT OF CASH-VALUE VOUCHER TO STATE AGENCIES.—

(A) NOTIFICATION.—An increase to the amount of a cash-value voucher under paragraph (1) shall apply to any State agency that notifies the Secretary of the intent to use such an increased amount, without further application.

(B) USE OF INCREASED AMOUNT.—A State agency that notifies the Secretary under subparagraph (A) may use or not use the increased amount described in such subparagraph during the period beginning on the date of the notification by the State agency under such subparagraph and ending September 30, 2020.

(3) APPLICATION PERIOD.—An increase to the amount of a cash-value voucher under paragraph (1) may only apply during the period beginning on the date of the enactment of this section and ending on September 30, 2020.

(4) SUNSET.—The authority to make an increase to the amount of a cash-value voucher under paragraph (1) or to use such an increased amount under paragraph (2)(B) shall terminate on September 30, 2020.

(b) Definitions.—

(1) CASH-VALUE VOUCHER.—The term "cash-value voucher" has the meaning given the term in section 246.2 of title 7, Code of Federal Regulations.

(2) QUALIFIED FOOD PACKAGE.—The term "qualified food package" means the following food packages under section 246.10(e) of title 7, Code of Federal Regula-

tions:

(A) Food Package IV–Children 1 through 4 years.

(B) Food Package V–Pregnant and partially (mostly) breastfeeding women.

(C) Food Package VI–Postpartum women.

(D) Food Package VII–Fully breastfeeding.

(3) SECRETARY.—The term "Secretary" means the Secretary of Agriculture.

(4) STATE AGENCY.—The term "State agency" has the meaning given the term in section 17(b) of the Child Nutrition Act of 1966 (42 U.S.C. 1786(b)).

CALCULATION OF PAYMENTS AND REIMBURSEMENTS FOR CERTAIN CHILD NUTRITION PROGRAMS

SEC. 180006.

(a) Richard B. Russell National School Lunch Act.—

(1) NUTRITION PROMOTION.—Notwithstanding any other provision of law, for purposes of making a payment to a State under section 5 of the Richard B. Russell National School Lunch Act (42 U.S.C. 1754), the Secretary shall deem the number of lunches served by school food authorities in such State during the 2020 period to be equal to the greater of the following:

(A) The number of lunches served by such school food authorities in such State during the 2019 period.

(B) The number of lunches served by such school food authorities in such State during the 2020 period.

(2) COMMODITY ASSISTANCE.—Notwithstanding any other provision of law, for purposes of providing commodity assistance to a State under section 6(c)(1)(C) of the Richard B. Russell National School Lunch Act (42 U.S.C. 1755(c)(1)(C)) or cash assistance in lieu of such commodity assistance under section 16 of such Act (42 U.S.C. 1765) the Secretary shall deem the number of lunches served by school food authorities in such State during the 2020 period to be equal to the greater of the following:

(A) The number of lunches served by such school food authorities in such State during the 2019 period.

(B) The number of lunches served by such school food authorities in such State during the 2020 period.

(3) SPECIAL ASSISTANCE PAYMENTS.—Notwithstanding any other provision of law, in determining the number of meals served by a school for purposes of making special assistance payments to a State with respect to a school under subparagraph (B), clause (ii) or (iii) of subparagraph (C), or subparagraph (E)(i)(II) of section 11(a)(1) of the Richard B. Russell National School Lunch Act (42 U.S.C. 1759a(a)(1)), the Secretary shall deem the number of meals served by such school during the 2020 period to be equal to the greater of the following:

(A) The number of meals served by such school during the 2019 period.

(B) The number of meals served by such school during the 2020 period.

(b) Child Nutrition Act Of 1966.—

(1) STATE ADMINISTRATIVE EXPENSES.—Notwithstanding any other provision of law, for purposes of making payments to a State under section 7(a) of the Child Nutrition Act of 1966 (42 U.S.C. 1776(a)), the Secretary shall deem the number of meals and supplements served by such school food authorities in such State during the 2020 period to be equal to the greater of the following:

(A) The number of meals and supplements served by such school food authorities in such State during the 2019 period.

(B) The number of meals and supplements served by such school food authorities in such State during the 2020 period.

(2) TEAM NUTRITION NETWORK.—Notwithstanding any other provision of law, for purposes of making allocations to a State under section 19(d) of the Child Nutrition Act of 1966 (42 U.S.C. 1788(d)), the Secretary shall deem the number of lunches served by school food authorities in such State during the 2020 period to be equal to the greater of the following:

(A) The number of lunches served by such school food authorities in such State during the 2019 period.

(B) The number of lunches served by such school food authorities in such State during the 2020 period.

(c) Definitions.—In this section:

(1) SECRETARY.—The term "Secretary" means the Secretary of Agriculture.

(2) 2019 PERIOD.—The term "2019 period" means the period beginning March 1, 2019 and ending June 30, 2019.

(3) 2020 PERIOD.—The term "2020 period" means the period beginning March 1, 2020 and ending June 30, 2020.

REPORTING ON WAIVER AUTHORITY

SEC. 180007.

(a) In General.—Not later than 10 days after the date of the receipt or issuance of each document listed in paragraph (1), (2), or (3) of this subsection, the Secretary of Agriculture shall make publicly available on the website of the Department of Agriculture the following documents:

(1) Any request submitted by State agencies for a qualified waiver.

(2) The Secretary's approval or denial of each such request.

(3) Any guidance issued by the Secretary with respect to a qualified waiver.

(b) Inclusion Of Date With Guidance.—With respect to the guidance described in subsection (a)(3), the Secretary of Agriculture shall include the date on which such guidance was issued on the publicly available website of the Department of Agriculture on such guidance.

(c) Qualified Waiver Defined.—In this section, the term "qualified waiver" means a waiver under section 2102, 2202, 2203, or 2204 of the Families First Coronavirus Response Act (Public Law 116–127).

DIVISION S—OTHER MATTERS

TITLE I—HEALTH CARE ACCESS FOR URBAN NATIVE VETERANS ACT

SEC. 190101. SHORT TITLE.

This title may be cited as the "Health Care Access for Urban Native Veterans Act".

SEC. 190102. SHARING ARRANGEMENTS WITH FEDERAL AGENCIES.

Section 405 of the Indian Health Care Improvement Act (25 U.S.C. 1645) is amended—

(1) in subsection (a)(1), by inserting "urban Indian organizations," before "and tribal organizations"; and

(2) in subsection (c)—

(A) by inserting "urban Indian organization," before "or tribal organization"; and

(B) by inserting "an urban Indian organization," before "or a tribal organization".

TITLE II—TRIBAL SCHOOL FEDERAL INSURANCE PARITY

SEC. 190201. SHORT TITLE.
This title may be cited as the "Tribal School Federal Insurance Parity Act".

SEC. 190202. AMENDMENT TO THE INDIAN HEALTH CARE IMPROVE-MENT ACT.
Section 409 of the Indian Health Care Improvement Act (25 U.S.C. 1647b) is amended by inserting "or the Tribally Controlled Schools Act of 1988 (25 U.S.C. 2501 et seq.)" after "(25 U.S.C. 450 et seq.)".

TITLE III—PRC FOR NATIVE VETERANS ACT

SEC. 190301. SHORT TITLE.
This title may be cited as the "Proper and Reimbursed Care for Native Veterans Act" or the "PRC for Native Veterans Act".

SEC. 190302. CLARIFICATION OF REQUIREMENT OF DEPARTMENT OF VETERANS AFFAIRS AND DEPARTMENT OF DEFENSE TO REIMBURSE INDIAN HEALTH SERVICE FOR CERTAIN HEALTH CARE SERVICES.
Section 405(c) of the Indian Health Care Improvement Act (25 U.S.C. 1645) is amended by inserting before the period at the end the following: ", regardless of whether such services are provided directly by the Service, an Indian tribe, or tribal organization, through contract health services, or through a contract for travel described in section 213(b)".

TITLE IV—WILDLIFE-BORNE DISEASE PREVENTION

SEC. 190401. SHORT TITLE.
This title may be cited as the "Wildlife-Borne Disease Prevention Act of 2020".

SEC. 190402. MEASURES TO ADDRESS SPECIES THAT POSE A RISK TO HUMAN HEALTH.
(a) Species That Pose A Risk To Human Health.—
(1) IN GENERAL.—The Secretaries shall, in consultation with the Director of the Centers for Disease Control, the United States Geological Survey, and other relevant Federal agencies, identify wildlife species (or larger taxonomic groups, if appropriate) that could pose a biohazard risk to human health, and perform a risk analysis with respect to each such species for the purposes of determining whether such species is injurious within the meaning of section 42 of title 18, United States Code.
(2) DRAFT LIST.—The Secretaries shall, not later than 90 days after the date of enactment of this Act, publish a draft of the list required by paragraph (1).
(3) FINAL LIST.—The Secretaries shall, not later than 1 year after the date of enactment of this Act, publish a final list required by paragraph (1).
(b) International Assistance.—The Secretaries shall, in consultation with the Secretary of State, provide assistance to foreign countries to end the trade of wildlife that poses a risk to humans because of transmission of pathogens that cause disease.
(c) Inspections And Interdiction.—The Secretary of the Interior shall complete de-

velopment on the electronic permitting system of the United States Fish and Wildlife Service and provide for law enforcement inspection and interdiction of any injurious wildlife species.

(d) Authorization Of Appropriation.—There is authorized to be appropriated $21,000,000 to remain available until expended for fiscal year 2020 to carry out this section.

(e) Secretaries.—In this section the term "Secretaries" means the Secretary of Commerce, acting through the Assistant Administrator for Fisheries, and the Secretary of the Interior, acting through the Director of the United States Fish and Wildlife Service.

SEC. 190403. TRADE OF INJURIOUS SPECIES AND SPECIES THAT POSE A RISK TO HUMAN HEALTH.

Section 42 of title 18, United States Code, is amended—

(1) in subsection (a)—

(A) in paragraph (1)—

(i) by inserting "or any interstate transport between States within the continental United States," after "shipment between the continental United States, the District of Columbia, Hawaii, the Commonwealth of Puerto Rico, or any possession of the United States,"; and

(ii) by striking "to be injurious to human beings, to the interests of agriculture" and inserting "to be injurious to or to transmit a pathogen that can cause disease in humans, to be injurious to the interests of agriculture"; and

(B) by adding at the end the following:

"(6) In the case of an emergency posing a significant risk to the health of humans, the Secretary of the Interior may designate a species by interim final rule. At the time of publication of the regulation in the Federal Register, the Secretary shall publish therein detailed reasons why such regulation is necessary, and in the case that such regulation applies to a native species, the Secretary shall give actual notice of such regulation to the State agency in each State in which such species is believed to occur. Any regulation promulgated under the authority of this paragraph shall cease to have force and effect at the close of the 365-day period following the date of publication unless, during such 365-day period, the rulemaking procedures which would apply to such regulation without regard to this paragraph are complied with. If at any time after issuing an emergency regulation the Secretary determines, on the basis of the best appropriate data available to the Secretary, that substantial evidence does not exist to warrant such regulation, the Secretary shall withdraw it.

"(7) Not more than 90 days after receiving a petition of an interested person under section 553(e) of title 5, United States Code, to determine that a species is injurious under this section, the Secretary of the Interior shall determine whether such petition has scientific merit. If the Secretary determines a petition has scientific merit, such Secretary shall make a determination regarding such petition not more than 12 months after the date such Secretary received such petition."; and

(2) by amending subsection (b) to read as follows:

"(b) Any person who knowingly imports, ships, or transports any species in violation of subsection (a) of this section and who reasonably should have known that the species at issue in such violation is a species listed in subsection (a) of this section, or in any regulation issued pursuant thereto, shall be fined under this title or imprisoned not more than six months, or both.".

SEC. 190404. NATIONAL WILDLIFE HEALTH CENTER.

(a) Wildlife Disease Surveillance.—The Director shall establish and maintain a national database of wildlife disease, including diseases that cause a human health risk, at the National Wildlife Health Center. The Director, acting through such Center, shall, with respect to wildlife disease—

(1) develop, validate, and deploy diagnostic tests;

(2) provide diagnostic services to Federal, State, and Tribal natural resource management agencies; and

(3) provide confirmatory testing of diagnostic results.

(b) Strategies For Mitigation.—The Director shall—

(1) develop a framework for wildlife disease experts in the United States to conduct risk assessments of wildlife diseases;

(2) communicate risk factors associated with wildlife diseases to the public;

(3) develop strategies to mitigate the threat posed by wildlife disease; and

(4) in coordination with the Director of the United States Fish and Wildlife Service—

(A) monitor wildlife disease threats to evaluate the risk posed by and impact of such diseases on the United States, conduct research and development to create statistically supported sampling frameworks for broad-scale surveillance of wildlife disease threats;

(B) conduct research on human dimensions of wildlife disease transmission and on effective outreach to stakeholders to help manage wildlife disease;

(C) conduct statistical modeling to understand and predict wildlife disease movement; and

(D) make recommendations to the Secretary of the Interior on wildlife species to be listed as injurious under section 42 of title 18, United States Code.

(c) International Surveillance.—The Director, in coordination with the Administrator for the United States Agency for International Development, may strengthen global capacity for wildlife health monitoring to enhance early detection of diseases that have the capacity to jump the species barrier and pose a risk to the United States, including by providing funding for—

(1) academic, governmental, and nongovernmental partner entities working to prevent wildlife disease outbreaks, emerging pathogens of wildlife origin, and epidemics or pandemics;

(2) building wildlife disease diagnostic capacity and monitoring systems in countries with areas that pose a high risk for animal-to-human transmission of disease; and

(3) providing technical assistance through training, data sharing, and performing testing in countries with areas that pose a high risk for animal-to-human transmission of disease.

(d) Director.—In this section, the term "Director" means the Director of the United States Geological Survey.

(e) Wildlife Disease.—In this section, the term "wildlife disease" means a disease-causing agent in wildlife that potentially poses a threat to human health.

SEC. 190405. SURVEILLANCE BY STATES, TRIBES, TERRITORIES, AND INSULAR AREAS.

(a) Wildlife Disease Surveillance, Research, Management, And Education.—The Director or the United States Fish and Wildlife Service shall establish a grant program to provide onetime funding to the States, the District of Columbia, Tribes, and the territories and insular areas of the United States to conduct epidemiological surveillance, research, management, and education relating to emerging wildlife disease.

TITLE V—PANDEMIC RELIEF FOR AVIATION WORKERS AND PASSENGERS

SEC. 190501. PANDEMIC RELIEF FOR AVIATION WORKERS.

(a) Applicability Of Assurance Regarding Furloughs.—Section 4114(a)(1) of the Coronavirus Aid, Relief, and Economic Security Act (Public Law 116–136) is amended by striking "September 30, 2020" and inserting "the date on which such financial assistance is fully exhausted by the air carrier or contractor".

(b) Protection Of Collective Bargaining Agreement.—Section 4115 of such Act is amended—

(1) in subsection (a) by striking "(a) In General.—"; and

(2) by striking subsection (b).

SEC. 190502. TRANSPARENCY OF FINANCIAL ASSISTANCE.

(a) Disclosure Of Financial Assistance.—Not later than 72 hours after issuance of financial assistance by the Secretary of the Treasury pursuant to section 4112(a) of the Coronavirus Aid, Relief, and Economic Security Act (Public Law 116–136), the Secretary shall publish on the website of the Department of the Treasury and shall submit to the congressional committees of jurisdiction—

(1) a plain-language description of the financial assistance, including the date of application, date of application approval, and identity of the recipient of financial assistance;

(2) the amount of the financial assistance; and

(3) a copy of any contract or assurances, if applicable, and other relevant documentation regarding the financial assistance.

(b) Trade Secrets.—Notwithstanding any other provision of law, the Secretary may redact, from a disclosure under subsection (a), any trade secret other than the amount of or conditions attached to the issuance of financial assistance.

(c) Definitions.—In this section:

(1) CONGRESSIONAL COMMITTEES OF JURISDICTION.—The term "congressional committees of jurisdiction" means the Committee on Transportation and Infrastructure and the Committee on Financial Services of the House of Representatives and the Committee on Commerce, Science, and Transportation and the Committee on Banking, Housing, and Urban Affairs of the Senate.

(2) TRADE SECRET DEFINED.—The term "trade secret" means any financial or business information provided by the recipient of financial assistance under section 4112(a) of the Coronavirus Aid, Relief, and Economic Security Act (Public Law 116–136), if—

(A) such recipient has taken reasonable measures to keep such information secret; and

(B) the information derives independent economic value, actual or potential, from not being generally known to, and not being readily ascertainable through proper means by, another person who can obtain economic value from the disclosure or use of the information.

(d) Savings Provision.—Nothing in this section shall be construed as eliminating or abridging any reporting requirement under the Coronavirus Aid, Relief, and Economic Security Act (Public Law 116–136).

SEC. 190503. AIR CARRIER MAINTENANCE OUTSOURCING.

(a) In General.—A passenger air carrier receiving a loan, loan guarantee, or other investment under section 4003 of the Coronavirus Aid, Relief, and Economic Security Act (Public Law 116–136) may not apply the proceeds of such assistance toward a contract for heavy maintenance work at a facility located outside of the United States if such contract would increase the ratio of maintenance work performed outside of the United States to all maintenance work performed by or on behalf of such air carrier at all locations.

(b) Definition Of Heavy Maintenance Work.—In this section, the term "heavy maintenance work" has the meaning given the term in section 44733(g) of title 49, United States Code.

SEC. 190504. NATIONAL AVIATION PREPAREDNESS PLAN.

(a) In General.—The Secretary of Transportation, in coordination with the Secretary of Health and Human Services, the Secretary of Homeland Security, and the heads of such other Federal departments or agencies as the Secretary considers appropriate, shall develop a national aviation preparedness plan for communicable disease outbreaks.

(b) Contents Of Plan.—A plan developed under subsection (a) shall, at a minimum—

(1) provide airports and air carriers with an adaptable and scalable framework with which to align the individual plans of such airports and air carriers and provide appropriate guidance as to each individual plan;

(2) improve coordination among airports, air carriers, U.S. Customs and Border Protection, the Centers for Disease Control and Prevention, other appropriate Federal entities, and State and local governments or health agencies on developing policies that increase the effectiveness of screening, quarantining, and contact-tracing with respect to inbound international passengers;

(3) ensure that at-risk employees are equipped with appropriate personal protective equipment to reduce the likelihood of exposure to pathogens in the event of a pandemic;

(4) ensure aircraft and enclosed facilities owned, operated, or used by an air carrier or airport are cleaned, disinfected, and sanitized frequently in accordance with Centers for Disease Control and Prevention guidance; and

(5) incorporate all elements referenced in the recommendation of the Comptroller General of the United States to the Secretary of Transportation contained in the report titled "Air Travel and Communicable Diseases: Comprehensive Federal Plan Needed for U.S. Aviation System's Preparedness" issued in December 2015 (GAO–16–127).

(c) Consultation.—When developing a plan under subsection (a), the Secretary of Transportation shall consult with aviation industry and labor stakeholders, including representatives of—

(1) air carriers;

(2) small, medium, and large hub airports;

(3) labor organizations that represent airline pilots, flight attendants, air carrier airport customer service representatives, and air carrier maintenance, repair, and overhaul workers;

(4) the labor organization certified under section 7111 of title 5, United States Code, as the exclusive bargaining representative of air traffic controllers of the Federal Aviation Administration;

(5) the labor organization certified under such section as the exclusive bargaining rep-

resentative of airway transportation systems specialists and aviation safety inspectors of the Federal Aviation Administration; and

(6) such other stakeholders as the Secretary considers appropriate.

(d) Report.—Not later than 30 days after the plan is developed under subsection (a), the Secretary shall submit to the appropriate committees of Congress such plan.

(e) Definition Of At-Risk Employees.—In this section, the term "at-risk employees" means—

(1) individuals whose job duties require interaction with air carrier passengers on a regular and continuing basis that are employees of—

(A) air carriers;

(B) air carrier contractors;

(C) airports; and

(D) Federal departments or agencies; and

(2) air traffic controllers and systems safety specialists of the Federal Aviation Administration.

SEC. 190505. WORKING AND TRAVEL CONDITIONS.

For the duration of the national emergency declared by the President under the National Emergencies Act (50 U.S.C. 1601 et seq.) related to the pandemic of SARS–CoV–2 or coronavirus disease 2019 (COVID–19), an air carrier operating under part 121 of title 14, Code of Federal Regulations, shall—

(1) require each passenger and cabin crewmember to wear a mask or protective face covering while on board an aircraft of the air carrier;

(2) require each flight crewmember to wear a mask or protective face covering while on board an aircraft but outside the flight deck;

(3) submit to the Administrator of the Federal Aviation Administration a proposal to permit flight crew members of the air carrier to wear a mask or protective face covering while at their stations in the flight deck, including a safety risk assessment with respect to such proposal;

(4) provide flight and cabin crewmembers, airport customer service agents, and other employees whose job responsibilities involve interaction with passengers with masks or protective face coverings, gloves, and hand sanitizer and wipes with sufficient alcohol content;

(5) ensure aircraft, including the cockpit and cabin, operated by such carrier are cleaned, disinfected, and sanitized after each use in accordance with Centers for Disease Control and Prevention guidance;

(6) ensure enclosed facilities owned, operated, or used by such air carrier, including facilities used for flight or cabin crewmember training or performance of indoor maintenance, repair, or overhaul work, are cleaned, disinfected, and sanitized frequently in accordance with Centers for Disease Control and Prevention guidance;

(7) provide air carrier employees whose job responsibilities involve cleaning, disinfecting, and sanitizing aircraft or enclosed facilities described in paragraphs (5) and (6) with masks or protective face coverings and gloves, and ensure that each contractor of the air carrier provides employees of such contractor with such materials; and

(8) establish guidelines, or adhere to applicable guidelines, for notifying employees of a confirmed COVID–19 diagnosis of an employee of such air carrier and for identifying other air carrier employees whom such employee contacted in the 48-hour period before the employee developed symptoms.

SEC. 190506. PROTECTION OF CERTAIN FEDERAL AVIATION ADMINISTRATION EMPLOYEES.

(a) In General.—For the duration of the national emergency declared by the President under the National Emergencies Act (50 U.S.C. 1601 et seq.) related to the pandemic of SARS–CoV–2 or coronavirus disease 2019 (COVID–19), in order to maintain the safe and efficient operation of the air traffic control system, the Administrator of the Federal Aviation Administration shall—

(1) provide air traffic controllers and airway transportation systems specialists of the Administration with masks or protective face coverings, gloves, and hand sanitizer and wipes with sufficient alcohol content;

(2) ensure air traffic control facilities are cleaned, disinfected, and sanitized frequently in accordance with Centers for Disease Control and Prevention guidance; and

(3) provide employees of the Administration whose job responsibilities involve cleaning, disinfecting, and sanitizing facilities described in paragraph (2) with masks or protective face coverings and gloves, and ensure that each contractor of the Administration provides employees of such contractor with such materials.

(b) Source Of Equipment.—The items described in subsection (a)(1) may be procured or provided under such subsection through any sources available to the Administrator.

TITLE VI—AMTRAK AND RAIL WORKERS

SEC. 190601. AMTRAK COVID–19 REQUIREMENTS.

(a) In General.—For the duration of the national emergency declared by the President under the National Emergencies Act (50 U.S.C. 1601 et seq.) related to the pandemic of SARS–CoV–2 or coronavirus disease (COVID–19), Amtrak shall—

(1) require each passenger and employee of Amtrak, including engineers, conductors, and onboard service workers, to wear a mask or other protective face covering while onboard an Amtrak train;

(2) take such actions as are reasonable to ensure passenger compliance with the requirement under paragraph (1);

(3) provide masks or protective face coverings, gloves, and hand sanitizer and sanitizing wipes with sufficient alcohol content to—

(A) conductors, engineers, and onboard service workers;

(B) ticket agents, station agents, and red cap agents; and

(C) any other employees whose job responsibilities include interaction with passengers;

(4) ensure Amtrak trains, including the locomotive cab and passenger cars, are cleaned, disinfected, and sanitized frequently in accordance with guidance issued by the Centers for Disease Control and Prevention and ensure that employees whose job responsibilities include such cleaning, disinfecting, or sanitizing are provided masks or protective face coverings and gloves;

(5) ensure stations and enclosed facilities that Amtrak owns and operates including facilities used for training or the performance of indoor maintenance, repair, or overhaul work, are cleaned, disinfected, and sanitized frequently in accordance with guidance issued by the Centers for Disease Control and Prevention and ensure that employees whose job responsibilities include such cleaning, disinfecting, or sanitizing are provided masks or protective face coverings and gloves;

(6) take such actions as are reasonable to ensure that stations or facilities served or used by Amtrak that Amtrak does not own are cleaned, disinfected, and sanitized frequently in accordance with Centers for Disease Control and Prevention guidance;

(7) ensure that each contractor of Amtrak provides masks or protective face coverings and gloves to employees of such contractor whose job responsibilities include those described in paragraphs (4) and (5); and

(8) establish guidelines, or adhere to existing applicable guidelines, for notifying employees of a confirmed diagnosis of COVID–19 of an employee of Amtrak.

(b) Availability.—If Amtrak is unable to acquire any of the items necessary to comply with paragraphs (3), (4), and (5) of subsection (a) due to market unavailability, Amtrak shall—

(1) prepare and make public documentation demonstrating what actions have been taken to acquire such items; and

(2) continue efforts to acquire such items until such items become available.

SEC. 190602. ADDITIONAL ENHANCED BENEFITS UNDER THE RAILROAD UNEMPLOYMENT INSURANCE ACT.

(a) In General.—Section 2(a)(5)(A) of the Railroad Unemployment Insurance Act (45 U.S.C. 352(a)(5)(A) is amended—

(1) by striking "July 31, 2020" and inserting "December 31, 2020, and for any registration periods during a period of continuing unemployment which began on or before December 31, 2020"; and

(2) by adding at the end "No recovery benefit under this section shall be payable for any registration period beginning on or after July 1, 2021."

(b) Additional Appropriations.—Section 2(a)(5)(B) of the Railroad Unemployment Insurance Act (45 U.S.C. 352(a)(5)(B) is amended by adding at the end the following: "In addition to the amount appropriated by the preceding sentence, out of any funds in the Treasury not otherwise appropriated, there are appropriated $1,000,000,000 to cover the cost of recovery benefits provided under subparagraph (A), to remain available until expended.".

(c) Disregard Of Recovery Benefits For Purposes Of All Federal And Federally Assisted Programs.—Section 2(a)(5) of the Railroad Unemployment Insurance Act (45 U.S.C. 352(a)(5)) is amended by adding at the end the following:

"(C) A recovery benefit payable under subparagraph (A) shall not be regarded as income and shall not be regarded as a resource for the month of receipt and the following 9 months, for purposes of determining the eligibility of the recipient (or the recipient's spouse or family) for benefits or assistance, or the amount or extent of benefits or assistance, under any Federal program or under any State or local program financed in whole or in part with Federal funds.".

(d) Clarification On Authority To Use Funds.—Funds appropriated under either the first or second sentence of subparagraph (B) of section 2(a)(5) of the Railroad Unemployment Insurance Act shall be available to cover the cost of recovery benefits provided under such section 2(a)(5) by reason of the amendments made by subsection (a) as well as to cover the cost of such benefits provided under such section 2(a)(5) as in effect on the day before the date of enactment of this Act.

SEC. 190603. TREATMENT OF PAYMENTS FROM THE RAILROAD UNEMPLOYMENT INSURANCE ACCOUNT.

(a) In General.—Section 256(i)(1) of the Balanced Budget and Emergency Deficit

Control Act of 1985 (2 U.S.C. 906(i)(1)) is amended—

(1) in subparagraph (B), by striking "and" at the end;

(2) in subparagraph (C), by inserting "and" at the end; and

(3) by inserting after subparagraph (C) the following new subparagraph:

"(D) any payment made from the Railroad Unemployment Insurance Account (established by section 10 of the Railroad Unemployment Insurance Act) for the purpose of carrying out the Railroad Unemployment Insurance Act, and funds appropriated or transferred to or otherwise deposited in such Account,".

(b) Effective Date.—The treatment of payments made from the Railroad Unemployment Insurance Account pursuant to the amendment made by subsection (a) shall take effect 7 days after the date of enactment of this Act and shall apply only to obligations incurred on or after such effective date for such payments.

SEC. 190604. TECHNICAL CORRECTION FOR EXTENDED UNEMPLOYMENT BENEFITS UNDER THE RAILROAD UNEMPLOYMENT INSURANCE ACT.

Section 2(c)(2)(D)(iii) of the Railroad Unemployment Insurance Act (45 U.S.C. 352(c)(2)(D)(iii)) is amended by striking "July 1, 2019" and inserting "July 15, 2019".

SEC. 190605. TECHNICAL CORRECTION.

Section 22002 of Public Law 116–136 is amended by striking "Railway Retirement Act of 1974" and inserting "Railroad Retirement Act of 1974".

SEC. 190606. CLARIFICATION OF OVERSIGHT AND IMPLEMENTATION OF RELIEF FOR WORKERS AFFECTED BY CORONAVIRUS ACT.

(a) Audits, Investigations, And Oversight.—Notwithstanding section 2115 of the Relief for Workers Affected by Coronavirus Act (subtitle A of title II of division A of Public Law 116–136), the authority of the Inspector General of the Department of Labor to carry out audits, investigations, and other oversight activities that are related to the provisions of such Act shall not extend to any activities related to sections 2112, 2113, or 2114 of such Act. Such authority with respect to such sections shall belong to the Inspector General of the Railroad Retirement Board.

(b) Operating Instructions Or Other Guidance.—Notwithstanding section 2116(b) of the Relief for Workers Affected by Coronavirus Act (subtitle A of title II of division A of Public Law 116–136), the authority of the Secretary of Labor to issue any operating instructions or other guidance necessary to carry out the provisions of such Act shall not extend to any activities related to sections 2112, 2113, or 2114 of such Act. Such authority with respect to such sections shall belong to the Railroad Retirement Board.

TITLE VII—ENERGY AND ENVIRONMENT PROVISIONS

SEC. 190701. HOME ENERGY AND WATER SERVICE CONTINUITY.

Any entity receiving financial assistance pursuant to any division of this Act shall, to the maximum extent practicable, establish or maintain in effect policies to ensure that no home energy service or public water system service to a residential customer, which is provided or regulated by such entity, is or remains disconnected or interrupted during the emergency period described in section 1135(g)(1)(B) of the Social Security Act because of nonpayment, and all reconnections of such public water system service are conducted in a manner that minimizes risk to the health of individuals receiving such service. For purposes of this section, the term "home energy service" means a service to provide home energy, as such term is defined in section 2603 of the Low-Income Home Energy Assistance Act of 1981, or service provided by an electric utility, as such term is defined in section 3 of the Public Utility Regulatory Policies Act of 1978, and the term "public water system" has the meaning given that term in section 1401 of the Safe Drinking Water Act. Nothing in this section shall be construed to require forgiveness of any debt incurred or owed to an entity or to absolve an individual of any obligation to an entity for service, nor to preempt any State or local law or regulation governing entities that provide such services to residential customers.

SEC. 190702. ENVIRONMENTAL JUSTICE GRANT PROGRAMS.

(a) Environmental Justice Grants.—The Administrator of the Environmental Protection Agency shall continue to carry out—

(1) the Environmental Justice Small Grants Program and the Environmental Justice Collaborative Problem-Solving Cooperative Agreement Program, as those programs are in existence on the date of enactment of this Act; and

(2) the Community Action for a Renewed Environment grant programs I and II, as in existence on January 1, 2012.

(b) Use Of Funds For Grants In Response To COVID–19 Pandemic.—With respect to amounts appropriated by division A of this Act that are available to carry out the programs described in subsection (a), the Administrator of the Environmental Protection Agency may only award grants under such programs for projects that will investigate or address the disproportionate impacts of the COVID–19 pandemic in environmental justice communities.

(c) Authorization Of Appropriations.—There is authorized to be appropriated to carry out the programs described in subsection (a) $50,000,000 for fiscal year 2020, and such sums as may be necessary for each fiscal year thereafter.

(d) Distribution.—Not later than 30 days after amounts are made available pursuant to subsection (c), the Administrator of the Environmental Protection Agency shall make awards of grants under each of the programs described in subsection (a).

SEC. 190703. LOW-INCOME HOUSEHOLD DRINKING WATER AND WASTEWATER ASSISTANCE.

(a) Authorization Of Appropriations.—There is authorized to be appropriated $1,500,000,000 to the Secretary to carry out this section.

(b) Low-Income Household Drinking Water And Wastewater Assistance.—The Secretary shall make grants to States and Indian Tribes to assist low-income households, particularly those with the lowest incomes, that pay a high proportion of household income for drinking water and wastewater services, by providing funds to owners or operators of public water systems or treatment works to reduce rates charged to such households for such services.

(c) Nonduplication Of Effort.—In carrying out this section, the Secretary, States, and Indian Tribes, as applicable, shall, as appropriate and to the extent practicable, use existing processes, procedures, policies, and systems in place to provide assistance to low-income households, including by using existing application and approval processes.

(d) Allotment.—

(1) IN GENERAL.—Except as provided in paragraph (2), the Secretary shall allot amounts appropriated pursuant to this section to a State or Indian Tribe based on

the following:

(A) The percentage of households in the State, or under the jurisdiction of the Indian Tribe, with income equal to or less than 150 percent of the Federal poverty line.

(B) The percentage of such households in the State, or under the jurisdiction of the Indian Tribe, that spend more than 30 percent of monthly income on housing.

(C) The extent to which the State or Indian Tribe has been affected by the public health emergency, including the rate of transmission of COVID–19 in the State or area over which the Indian Tribe has jurisdiction, the number of COVID–19 cases compared to the national average, and economic disruptions resulting from the public health emergency.

(2) RESERVED FUNDS.—The Secretary shall reserve not more than 10 percent of the amounts appropriated pursuant to this section for allotment to States and Indian Tribes based on the economic disruptions to the States and Indian Tribes resulting from the emergency described in the emergency declaration issued by the President on March 13, 2020, pursuant to section 501(b) of the Robert T. Stafford Disaster Relief and Emergency Assistance Act (42 U.S.C. 5191(b)), during the period covered by such emergency declaration and any subsequent major disaster declaration under section 401 of such Act (42 U.S.C. 5170) that supersedes such emergency declaration.

(e) Determination Of Low-Income Households.—

(1) MINIMUM DEFINITION OF LOW-INCOME.—In determining whether a household is considered low-income for the purposes of this section, a State or Indian Tribe—

(A) shall ensure that, at a minimum—

(i) all households with income equal to or less than 150 percent of the Federal poverty line are included as low-income households; and

(ii) all households with income equal to or less than 60 percent of the State median income are included as low-income households;

(B) may include households that have been adversely economically affected by job loss or severe income loss related to the public health emergency; and

(C) may include other households, including households in which 1 or more individuals are receiving—

(i) assistance under the State program funded under part A of title IV of the Social Security Act (42 U.S.C. 601 et seq.);

(ii) supplemental security income payments under title XVI of the Social Security Act (42 U.S.C. 1381 et seq.);

(iii) supplemental nutrition assistance program benefits under the Food and Nutrition Act of 2008 (7 U.S.C. 2011 et seq.); or

(iv) payments under section 1315, 1521, 1541, or 1542 of title 38, United States Code, or under section 306 of the Veterans' and Survivors' Pension Improvement Act of 1978.

(2) HOUSEHOLD DOCUMENTATION REQUIREMENTS.—States and Indian Tribes shall—

(A) to the maximum extent practicable, seek to limit the income history documentation requirements for determining whether a household is considered low-income for the purposes of this section; and

(B) for the purposes of income eligibility, accept proof of job loss or severe income loss dated after February 29, 2020, such as a layoff or furlough notice or verification of application of unemployment benefits, as sufficient to demonstrate lack of income

U.S. House of Representatives Democrats

for an individual or household.

(f) Applications.—Each State or Indian Tribe desiring to receive a grant under this section shall submit an application to the Secretary, in such form as the Secretary shall require.

(g) Utility Responsibilities.—Owners or operators of public water systems or treatment works receiving funds pursuant to this section for the purposes of reducing rates charged to low-income households for service shall—

(1) conduct outreach activities designed to ensure that such households are made aware of the rate assistance available pursuant to this section;

(2) charge such households, in the normal billing process, not more than the difference between the actual cost of the service provided and the amount of the payment made by the State or Indian Tribe pursuant to this section; and

(3) within 45 days of providing assistance to a household pursuant to this section, notify in writing such household of the amount of such assistance.

(h) State Agreements With Drinking Water And Wastewater Providers.—To the maximum extent practicable, a State that receives a grant under this section shall enter into agreements with owners and operators of public water systems, owners and operators of treatment works, municipalities, nonprofit organizations associated with providing drinking water, wastewater, and other social services to rural and small communities, and Indian Tribes, to assist in identifying low-income households and to carry out this section.

(i) Administrative Costs.—A State or Indian Tribe that receives a grant under this section may use up to 8 percent of the granted amounts for administrative costs.

(j) Federal Agency Coordination.—In carrying out this section, the Secretary shall coordinate with the Administrator of the Environmental Protection Agency and consult with other Federal agencies with authority over the provision of drinking water and wastewater services.

(k) Audits.—The Secretary shall require each State and Indian Tribe receiving a grant under this section to undertake periodic audits and evaluations of expenditures made by such State or Indian Tribe pursuant to this section.

(l) Reports To Congress.—The Secretary shall submit to Congress a report on the results of activities carried out pursuant to this section—

(1) not later than 1 year after the date of enactment of this section; and

(2) upon disbursement of all funds appropriated pursuant to this section.

(m) Definitions.—In this section:

(1) INDIAN TRIBE.—The term "Indian Tribe" means any Indian Tribe, band, group, or community recognized by the Secretary of the Interior and exercising governmental authority over a Federal Indian reservation.

(2) MUNICIPALITY.—The term "municipality" has the meaning given such term in section 502 of the Federal Water Pollution Control Act (33 U.S.C. 1362).

(3) PUBLIC HEALTH EMERGENCY.—The term "public health emergency" means the public health emergency described in section 1135(g)(1)(B) of the Social Security Act (42 U.S.C. 1320b–5).

(4) PUBLIC WATER SYSTEM.—The term "public water system" has the meaning given such term in section 1401 of the Safe Drinking Water Act (42 U.S.C. 300f).

(5) SECRETARY.—The term "Secretary" means the Secretary of Health and Human Services.

(6) STATE.—The term "State" means a State, the District of Columbia, the Com-

monwealth of Puerto Rico, the Virgin Islands of the United States, Guam, American Samoa, and the Commonwealth of the Northern Mariana Islands.

(7) TREATMENT WORKS.—The term "treatment works" has the meaning given that term in section 212 of the Federal Water Pollution Control Act (33 U.S.C. 1292).

SEC. 190704. HOME WATER SERVICE CONTINUITY.

(a) Continuity Of Service.—Any entity receiving financial assistance under division A of this Act shall, to the maximum extent practicable, establish or maintain in effect policies to ensure that, with respect to any service provided by a public water system or treatment works to an occupied residence, which service is provided or regulated by such entity—

(1) no such service is or remains disconnected or interrupted during the emergency period because of nonpayment;

(2) all reconnections of such service are conducted in a manner that minimizes risk to the health of individuals receiving such service; and

(3) no fees for late payment of bills for such service are charged or accrue during the emergency period.

(b) Effect.—Nothing in this section shall be construed to require forgiveness of outstanding debt owed to an entity or to absolve an individual of any obligation to an entity for service.

(c) Definitions.—In this section:

(1) EMERGENCY PERIOD.—The term "emergency period" means the emergency period described in section 1135(g)(1)(B) of the Social Security Act (42 U.S.C. 1320b–5).

(2) PUBLIC WATER SYSTEM.—The term "public water system" has the meaning given such term in section 1401 of the Safe Drinking Water Act (42 U.S.C. 300f).

(3) TREATMENT WORKS.—The term "treatment works" has the meaning given that term in section 212 of the Federal Water Pollution Control Act (33 U.S.C. 1292).

TITLE VIII—DEATH AND DISABILITY BENEFITS FOR PUBLIC SAFETY OFFICERS IMPACTED BY COVID–19

SEC. 190801. SHORT TITLE.

This title may be cited as the "Public Safety Officer Pandemic Response Act of 2020".

SEC. 190802. DEATH AND DISABILITY BENEFITS FOR PUBLIC SAFETY OFFICERS IMPACTED BY COVID–19.

Section 1201 of the Omnibus Crime Control and Safe Streets Act of 1968 (34 U.S.C. 10281) is amended by adding at the end the following new subsection:

"(o) For purposes of this part:

"(1) COVID–19 shall be presumed to constitute a personal injury within the meaning of subsection (a), sustained in the line of duty by a public safety officer and directly and proximately resulting in death, unless such officer is shown to have performed no line of duty activity or action within the 45 days immediately preceding a diagnosis of, or positive test for COVID–19.

"(2) The Attorney General shall accept claims, including supplemental claims, under this section from an individual who—

"(A) was serving as a public safety officer and was injured or disabled in the line of duty as a result of the terrorist attacks on the United States that occurred on September 11, 2001, or in the aftermath of such attacks developed a condition described in section 3312(a) of the Public Health Service Act (42 U.S.C. 300mm–22(a)); and

"(B) was diagnosed with COVID–19 during the period described in paragraph (3), which, in combination with the injury or disability described in subparagraph (A), permanently and totally disabled or directly and proximately resulted in the death of the individual.

In assessing a claim under this paragraph, the presumption of causation described in paragraph (1) shall apply.

"(3) The presumption described in paragraph (1) shall apply with respect to a diagnosis of COVID–19 beginning on January 20, 2020, and ending on the date that is one year after the emergency period (as such term is defined in section 1135(g) of the Social Security Act (42 U.S.C. 1320b–5(g))) based on the COVID–19 public health emergency ends.

"(4) The term 'COVID–19' means a disease caused by severe acute respiratory syndrome coronavirus 2 (SARS–CoV–2).

"(p) In determining whether the personal injury resulting from COVID–19 was a catastrophic injury, the Attorney General's inquiry shall be limited to whether the individual is permanently prevented from performing any gainful work as a public safety officer.".

TITLE IX—VICTIMS OF CRIME ACT AMENDMENTS

SEC. 190901. SHORT TITLE.

This title may be cited as the "Victims of Crime Act Fix Act of 2020".

SEC. 190902. DEPOSITS OF FUNDING INTO THE CRIME VICTIMS FUND.

Section 1402(b) of the Victims of Crime Act of 1984 (34 U.S.C. 20101(b)) is amended—

(1) in paragraph (4), by striking "and" at the end;

(2) in paragraph (5), by striking the period at the end and inserting "; and"; and

(3) by adding at the end the following:

"(6) any funds that would otherwise be deposited in the general fund of the Treasury collected as pursuant to—

"(A) a deferred prosecution agreement; or

"(B) a non-prosecution agreement.".

SEC. 190903. WAIVER OF MATCHING REQUIREMENT.

(a) In General.—Notwithstanding any other provision of VOCA, during the COVID–19 emergency period and for the period ending one year after the date on which such period expires or is terminated, the Attorney General, acting through the Director of the Office for Victims of Crime, may not impose any matching requirement as a condition of receipt of funds under any program to provide assistance to victims of crimes authorized under the Victims of Crime Act of 1984 (34 U.S.C. 20101 et seq.).

(b) Definition.—In this section, the term "COVID–19 emergency period" means the period beginning on the date on which the President declared a national emergency under the National Emergencies Act (50 U.S.C. 1601 et seq.) with respect to the Coronavirus Disease 2019 (COVID–19) and ending on the date that is 30 days after the date on which the national emergency declaration is terminated.

(c) Application.—This section shall apply with respect to—

(1) applications submitted during the period described under subsection (a), including applications for which funds will be distributed after such period; and

(2) distributions of funds made during the period described under subsection (a), including distributions made pursuant to applications submitted before such period.

TITLE X—JABARA-HEYER NO HATE ACT

SEC. 191001. SHORT TITLE.

This title may be cited as the "Jabara-Heyer National Opposition to Hate, Assault, and Threats to Equality Act of 2020" or the "Jabara-Heyer NO HATE Act".

SEC. 191002. FINDINGS.

Congress finds the following:

(1) The incidence of violence known as hate crimes or crimes motivated by bias poses a serious national problem.

(2) According to data obtained by the Federal Bureau of Investigation, the incidence of such violence increased in 2017, the most recent year for which data is available.

(3) In 1990, Congress enacted the Hate Crime Statistics Act (Public Law 101–275; 28 U.S.C. 534 note) to provide the Federal Government, law enforcement agencies, and the public with data regarding the incidence of hate crime. The Hate Crimes Statistics Act and the Matthew Shepard and James Byrd, Jr. Hate Crimes Prevention Act (division E of Public Law 111–84; 123 Stat. 2835) have enabled Federal authorities to understand and, where appropriate, investigate and prosecute hate crimes.

(4) A more complete understanding of the national problem posed by hate crime is in the public interest and supports the Federal interest in eradicating bias-motivated violence referenced in section 249(b)(1)(C) of title 18, United States Code.

(5) However, a complete understanding of the national problem posed by hate crimes is hindered by incomplete data from Federal, State, and local jurisdictions through the Uniform Crime Reports program authorized under section 534 of title 28, United States Code, and administered by the Federal Bureau of Investigation.

(6) Multiple factors contribute to the provision of inaccurate and incomplete data regarding the incidence of hate crime through the Uniform Crime Reports program. A significant contributing factor is the quality and quantity of training that State and local law enforcement agencies receive on the identification and reporting of suspected bias-motivated crimes.

(7) The problem of crimes motivated by bias is sufficiently serious, widespread, and interstate in nature as to warrant Federal financial assistance to States and local jurisdictions.

(8) Federal financial assistance with regard to certain violent crimes motivated by bias enables Federal, State, and local authorities to work together as partners in the investigation and prosecution of such crimes.

SEC. 191003. DEFINITIONS.

In this title:

(1) HATE CRIME.—The term "hate crime" means an act described in section 245, 247, or 249 of title 18, United States Code, or in section 901 of the Civil Rights Act of 1968 (42 U.S.C. 3631).

(2) PRIORITY AGENCY.—The term "priority agency" means—

(A) a law enforcement agency of a unit of local government that serves a population of not less than 100,000, as computed by the Federal Bureau of Investigation; or

(B) a law enforcement agency of a unit of local government that—

(i) serves a population of not less than 50,000 and less than 100,000, as computed by the Federal Bureau of Investigation; and

(ii) has reported no hate crimes through the Uniform Crime Reports program in each of the 3 most recent calendar years for which such data is available.

(3) STATE.—The term "State" has the meaning given the term in section 901 of title I of the Omnibus Crime Control and Safe Streets Act of 1968 (34 U.S.C. 10251).

(4) UNIFORM CRIME REPORTS.—The term "Uniform Crime Reports" means the reports authorized under section 534 of title 28, United States Code, and administered by the Federal Bureau of Investigation that compile nationwide criminal statistics for use—

(A) in law enforcement administration, operation, and management; and

(B) to assess the nature and type of crime in the United States.

(5) UNIT OF LOCAL GOVERNMENT.—The term "unit of local government" has the meaning given the term in section 901 of title I of the Omnibus Crime Control and Safe Streets Act of 1968 (34 U.S.C. 10251).

SEC. 191004. REPORTING OF HATE CRIMES.

(a) Implementation Grants.—

(1) IN GENERAL.—The Attorney General may make grants to States and units of local government to assist the State or unit of local government in implementing the National Incident-Based Reporting System, including to train employees in identifying and classifying hate crimes in the National Incident-Based Reporting System.

(2) PRIORITY.—In making grants under paragraph (1), the Attorney General shall give priority to States and units of local government with larger populations.

(b) Reporting.—

(1) COMPLIANCE.—

(A) IN GENERAL.—Except as provided in subparagraph (B), in each fiscal year beginning after the date that is 3 years after the date on which a State or unit of local government first receives a grant under subsection (a), the State or unit of local government shall provide to the Attorney General, through the Uniform Crime Reporting system, information pertaining to hate crimes committed in that jurisdiction during the preceding fiscal year.

(B) EXTENSIONS; WAIVER.—The Attorney General—

(i) may provide a 120-day extension to a State or unit of local government that is making good faith efforts to comply with subparagraph (A); and

(ii) shall waive the requirements of subparagraph (A) if compliance with that subparagraph by a State or unit of local government would be unconstitutional under the constitution of the State or of the State in which the unit of local government is located, respectively.

(2) FAILURE TO COMPLY.—If a State or unit of local government that receives a grant under subsection (a) fails to substantially comply with paragraph (1) of this subsection, the State or unit of local government shall repay the grant in full, plus reasonable interest and penalty charges allowable by law or established by the Attorney General.

SEC. 191005. GRANTS FOR STATE-RUN HATE CRIME HOTLINES.

(a) Grants Authorized.—

(1) IN GENERAL.—The Attorney General shall make grants to States to create State-run hate crime reporting hotlines.

(2) GRANT PERIOD.—A grant made under paragraph (1) shall be for a period of not more than 5 years.

(b) Hotline Requirements.—A State shall ensure, with respect to a hotline funded by a grant under subsection (a), that—

(1) the hotline directs individuals to—

(A) law enforcement if appropriate; and

(B) local support services;

(2) any personally identifiable information that an individual provides to an agency of the State through the hotline is not directly or indirectly disclosed, without the consent of the individual, to—

(A) any other agency of that State;

(B) any other State;

(C) the Federal Government; or

(D) any other person or entity;

(3) the staff members who operate the hotline are trained to be knowledgeable about—

(A) applicable Federal, State, and local hate crime laws; and

(B) local law enforcement resources and applicable local support services; and

(4) the hotline is accessible to—

(A) individuals with limited English proficiency, where appropriate; and

(B) individuals with disabilities.

(c) Best Practices.—The Attorney General shall issue guidance to States on best practices for implementing the requirements of subsection (b).

SEC. 191006. INFORMATION COLLECTION BY STATES AND UNITS OF LOCAL GOVERNMENT.

(a) Definitions.—In this section:

(1) APPLICABLE AGENCY.—The term "applicable agency", with respect to an eligible entity that is—

(A) a State, means—

(i) a law enforcement agency of the State; and

(ii) a law enforcement agency of a unit of local government within the State that—

(I) is a priority agency; and

(II) receives a subgrant from the State under this section; and

(B) a unit of local government, means a law enforcement agency of the unit of local government that is a priority agency.

(2) COVERED AGENCY.—The term "covered agency" means—

(A) a State law enforcement agency; or

(B) a priority agency.

(3) ELIGIBLE ENTITY.—The term "eligible entity" means—

(A) a State; or

(B) a unit of local government that has a priority agency.

(b) Grants.—

(1) IN GENERAL.—The Attorney General may make grants to eligible entities to assist covered agencies within the jurisdiction of the eligible entity in conducting law enforcement activities or crime reduction programs to prevent, address, or otherwise

respond to hate crime, particularly as those activities or programs relate to reporting hate crimes through the Uniform Crime Reports program, including—

(A) adopting a policy on identifying, investigating, and reporting hate crimes;

(B) developing a standardized system of collecting, analyzing, and reporting the incidence of hate crime;

(C) establishing a unit specialized in identifying, investigating, and reporting hate crimes;

(D) engaging in community relations functions related to hate crime prevention and education such as—

(i) establishing a liaison with formal community-based organizations or leaders; and

(ii) conducting public meetings or educational forums on the impact of hate crimes, services available to hate crime victims, and the relevant Federal, State, and local laws pertaining to hate crimes; and

(E) providing hate crime trainings for agency personnel.

(2) SUBGRANTS.—A State that receives a grant under paragraph (1) may award a subgrant to a priority agency of a unit of local government within the State for the purposes under that paragraph.

(c) Information Required Of States And Units Of Local Government.—

(1) IN GENERAL.—For each fiscal year in which an eligible entity receives a grant under subsection (b), the eligible entity shall—

(A) collect information from each applicable agency summarizing the law enforcement activities or crime reduction programs conducted by the agency to prevent, address, or otherwise respond to hate crime, particularly as those activities or programs relate to reporting hate crimes through the Uniform Crime Reports program; and

(B) submit to the Attorney General a report containing the information collected under subparagraph (A).

(2) SEMIANNUAL LAW ENFORCEMENT AGENCY REPORT.—

(A) IN GENERAL.—In collecting the information required under paragraph (1)(A), an eligible entity shall require each applicable agency to submit a semiannual report to the eligible entity that includes a summary of the law enforcement activities or crime reduction programs conducted by the agency during the reporting period to prevent, address, or otherwise respond to hate crime, particularly as those activities or programs relate to reporting hate crimes through the Uniform Crime Reports program.

(B) CONTENTS.—In a report submitted under subparagraph (A), a law enforcement agency shall, at a minimum, disclose—

(i) whether the agency has adopted a policy on identifying, investigating, and reporting hate crimes;

(ii) whether the agency has developed a standardized system of collecting, analyzing, and reporting the incidence of hate crime;

(iii) whether the agency has established a unit specialized in identifying, investigating, and reporting hate crimes;

(iv) whether the agency engages in community relations functions related to hate crime, such as—

(I) establishing a liaison with formal community-based organizations or leaders; and

(II) conducting public meetings or educational forums on the impact of hate crime, services available to hate crime victims, and the relevant Federal, State, and local laws pertaining to hate crime; and

(v) the number of hate crime trainings for agency personnel, including the duration

of the trainings, conducted by the agency during the reporting period.
(d) Compliance And Redirection Of Funds.—
(1) IN GENERAL.—Except as provided in paragraph (2), beginning not later than 1 year after the date of enactment of this title, an eligible entity receiving a grant under subsection (b) shall comply with subsection (c).
(2) EXTENSIONS; WAIVER.—The Attorney General—
(A) may provide a 120-day extension to an eligible entity that is making good faith efforts to collect the information required under subsection (c); and
(B) shall waive the requirements of subsection (c) for a State or unit of local government if compliance with that subsection by the State or unit of local government would be unconstitutional under the constitution of the State or of the State in which the unit of local government is located, respectively.

SEC. 191007. REQUIREMENTS OF THE ATTORNEY GENERAL.

(a) Information Collection And Analysis; Report.—In order to improve the accuracy of data regarding the incidence of hate crime provided through the Uniform Crime Reports program, and promote a more complete understanding of the national problem posed by hate crime, the Attorney General shall—
(1) collect and analyze the information provided by States and units of local government under section 191006 for the purpose of developing policies related to the provision of accurate data obtained under the Hate Crime Statistics Act (Public Law 101–275; 28 U.S.C. 534 note) by the Federal Bureau of Investigation; and
(2) for each calendar year beginning after the date of enactment of this title, publish and submit to Congress a report based on the information collected and analyzed under paragraph (1).
(b) Contents Of Report.—A report submitted under subsection (a) shall include—
(1) a qualitative analysis of the relationship between—
(A) the number of hate crimes reported by State law enforcement agencies or priority agencies through the Uniform Crime Reports program; and
(B) the nature and extent of law enforcement activities or crime reduction programs conducted by those agencies to prevent, address, or otherwise respond to hate crime; and
(2) a quantitative analysis of the number of State law enforcement agencies and priority agencies that have—
(A) adopted a policy on identifying, investigating, and reporting hate crimes;
(B) developed a standardized system of collecting, analyzing, and reporting the incidence of hate crime;
(C) established a unit specialized in identifying, investigating, and reporting hate crimes;
(D) engaged in community relations functions related to hate crime, such as—
(i) establishing a liaison with formal community-based organizations or leaders; and
(ii) conducting public meetings or educational forums on the impact of hate crime, services available to hate crime victims, and the relevant Federal, State, and local laws pertaining to hate crime; and
(E) conducted hate crime trainings for agency personnel during the reporting period, including—
(i) the total number of trainings conducted by each agency; and
(ii) the duration of the trainings described in clause (i).

SEC. 191008. ALTERNATIVE SENTENCING.

Section 249 of title 18, United States Code, is amended by adding at the end the following:

"(e) Supervised Release.—If a court includes, as a part of a sentence of imprisonment imposed for a violation of subsection (a), a requirement that the defendant be placed on a term of supervised release after imprisonment under section 3583, the court may order, as an explicit condition of supervised release, that the defendant undertake educational classes or community service directly related to the community harmed by the defendant's offense.".

TITLE XI—PRISONS AND JAILS

SEC. 191101. SHORT TITLE.

This title may be cited as the "Pandemic Justice Response Act".

SEC. 191102. EMERGENCY COMMUNITY SUPERVISION ACT.

(a) Findings.—Congress finds the following:

(1) As of the date of introduction of this Act, the novel coronavirus has spread to all 50 States, the District of Columbia, and 3 territories.

(2) The Centers for Disease Control and Prevention have projected that between 160,000,000 and 214,000,000 people could be infected by the novel coronavirus in the United States over the course of the pandemic.

(3) Although the United States has less than 5 percent of the world's population, the United States holds approximately 21 percent of the world's prisoners and leads the world in the number of individuals incarcerated, with nearly 2,200,000 people incarcerated in State and Federal prisons and local jails.

(4) Studies have shown that individuals age out of crime starting around 25 years of age, and released individuals over the age of 50 have a very low recidivism rate.

(5) According to public health experts, incarcerated individuals are particularly vulnerable to being gravely impacted by the novel corona virus pandemic because—

(A) they have higher rates of underlying health issues than members of the general public, including higher rates of respiratory disease, heart disease, diabetes, obesity, HIV/AIDS, substance abuse, hepatitis, and other conditions that suppress immune response; and

(B) the close conditions and lack of access to hygiene products in prisons make these institutions unusually susceptible to viral pandemics.

(6) The spread of communicable disease in the United States generally constitutes a serious, heightened threat to the safety of incarcerated individuals, and there is a serious threat to the general public that prisons may become incubators of community spread of communicable viral disease.

(b) Definitions.—In this section:

(1) COVERED HEALTH CONDITION.—The term "covered health condition" with respect to an individual, means the individual—

(A) is pregnant;

(B) has chronic lung disease or asthma;

(C) has congestive heart failure or coronary artery disease;

(D) has diabetes;

(E) has a neurological condition that weakens the ability to cough or breathe;

(F) has HIV;

(G) has sickle cell anemia;

(H) has cancer; or

(I) has a weakened immune system.

(2) COVERED INDIVIDUAL.—The term "covered individual"—

(A) means an individual who—

(i) is a juvenile (as defined in section 5031 of title 18, United States Code);

(ii) is 50 years of age or older;

(iii) has a covered health condition; or

(iv) is within 12 months of release from incarceration; and

(B) includes an individual described in subparagraph (A) who is serving a term of imprisonment for an offense committed before November 1, 1987.

(3) NATIONAL EMERGENCY RELATING TO A COMMUNICABLE DISEASE.— The term "national emergency relating to a communicable disease" means—

(A) an emergency involving Federal primary responsibility determined to exist by the President under the section 501(b) of the Robert T. Stafford Disaster Relief and Emergency Assistance Act (42 U.S.C. 5191(b)) with respect to a communicable disease; or

(B) a national emergency declared by the President under the National Emergencies Act (50 U.S.C. 1601 et seq.) with respect to a communicable disease.

(c) Placement Of Certain Individuals In Community Supervision.—

(1) AUTHORITY.—Except as provided in paragraph (2), beginning on the date on which a national emergency relating to a communicable disease is declared and ending on the date that is 60 days after such national emergency expires or is terminated—

(A) notwithstanding any other provision of law, the Director of the Bureau of Prisons shall place in community supervision all covered individuals who are in the custody of the Bureau of Prisons; and

(B) the district court of the United States for each judicial district shall place in community supervision all covered individuals who are in the custody and care of the United States Marshals Service.

(2) EXCEPTIONS.—

(A) BUREAU OF PRISONS.—In carrying out paragraph (1)(A), the Director—

(i) may not place in community supervision any individual determined, by clear and convincing evidence, to be likely to pose a specific and substantial risk of causing bodily injury to or using violent force against the person of another;

(ii) shall place in the file of each individual described in clause (i) documentation of such determination, including the evidence used to make the determination; and

(iii) not later than 180 days after the date on which the national emergency relating to a communicable disease expires, shall provide a report to Congress documenting—

(I) the demographic data (including race, gender, age, offense of conviction, and criminal history level) of the individuals denied placement in community supervision under clause (i); and

(II) the justification for the denials described in subclause (I).

(B) DISTRICT COURTS.—In carrying out paragraph (1)(B), each district court of the United States—

(i) shall conduct an immediate and expedited review of the detention orders of all covered individuals in the custody and care of the United States Marshals Service, which may be conducted sua sponte and ex parte, without—

(I) appearance by the defendant or any party; or

(II) requiring a petition, motion, or other similar document to be filed;

(ii) may not place in community supervision any individual if the court determines, after a hearing and the attorney for the Government shows by clear and convincing evidence based on individualized facts, that detention is necessary because the individual's release will pose a specific and substantial risk that the individual will cause bodily injury or use violent force against the person of another and that no conditions of release will reasonably mitigate that risk;

(iii) in carrying out clauses (i) and (ii), may—

(I) rely on evidence presented in prior court proceedings; and

(II) if the court determines it necessary, request additional information from the parties to make the determination.

(3) LIMITATION ON COMMUNITY SUPERVISION PLACEMENT.—In placing covered individuals into community supervision under this section, the Director of the Bureau of Prisons and the district court of the United States for each judicial district shall take into account and prioritize placements that enable adequate social distancing, which include home confinement or other forms of low in-person-contact supervised release.

(d) Limitation On Pre-Trial Detention.—

(1) NO BOND CONDITIONS ON RELEASE.—Notwithstanding section 3142 of title 18, United States Code, beginning on the date on which a national emergency relating to a communicable disease is declared and ending on the date that is 60 days after such national emergency expires or is terminated, in imposing conditions of release, the judicial officer may not require payment of cash bail, proof of ability to pay an unsecured bond, execution of a bail bond, a solvent surety to co-sign a secured or unsecured bond, or posting of real property.

(2) LIMITATION.—

(A) IN GENERAL.—Beginning on the date on which a national emergency relating to a communicable disease is declared and ending on the date that is 60 days after such national emergency expires or is terminated, at any initial appearance hearing, detention hearing, hearing on a motion for pretrial release, or any other hearing where the attorney for the Government is seeking the detention or continued detention of any individual, the judicial officer shall order the pretrial release of the individual on personal recognizance or on a condition or combination of conditions under section 3142(c) of title 18, United States Code, unless the attorney for the Government shows by clear and convincing evidence based on individualized facts that detention is necessary because the individual's release will pose a specific and substantial risk that the individual will cause bodily injury or use violent force against the person of another and that no conditions of release will reasonably mitigate that risk.

(B) REQUIRED CONSIDERATION OF CERTAIN FACTORS.—If the judicial officer finds that the attorney for the Government has made the requisite showing under subparagraph (A), the judicial officer shall take into consideration, in determining whether detention is necessary—

(i) whether the individual's age or medical condition renders them especially vulnerable; and

(ii) whether detention will compromise the individual's access to adequate medical treatment, access to medications, or ability to privately consult with counsel and meaningfully prepare a defense.

(C) JUVENILES.—

(i) IN GENERAL.—Beginning on the date on which a national emergency relating to a communicable disease is declared and ending on the date that is 60 days after such national emergency expires or is terminated, notwithstanding sections 5031 through 5035 of title 18, United States Code, and except as provided under clause (ii), in the case of a juvenile alleged to have committed an act of juvenile delinquency, the judicial officer shall release the juvenile to their parent, guardian, custodian, or other responsible party (including the director of a shelter-care facility) upon their promise to bring such juvenile before the appropriate court when requested by the judicial officer.

(ii) EXCEPTION.—A juvenile alleged to have committed an act of juvenile delinquency may be detained pending trial only if, at a hearing at which the juvenile is represented by counsel, the attorney for the Government shows by clear and convincing evidence based on individualized facts that detention is necessary because the juvenile's release will pose a specific and substantial risk that the juvenile will use violent force against a reasonably identifiable person and that no conditions of release will reasonably mitigate that risk, except that in no case may a judicial officer order the detention of a juvenile if it will compromise the juvenile's access to adequate medical treatment, access to medications, or ability to privately consult with counsel and meaningfully prepare a defense.

(iii) LEAST RESTRICTIVE DETENTION.—In the case that the judicial officer orders the detention of a juvenile under clause (ii), the judicial officer shall order the detention of the juvenile in the least restrictive and safest environment possible, taking the national emergency relating to a communicable disease into consideration.

(iv) CONTENTS OF DETENTION ORDER.—In the case that the judicial officer orders the detention of a juvenile under clause (ii), the judicial officer shall issue a written detention order that includes—

(I) findings of fact;

(II) the reasons for the detention;

(III) a description of the risk identified under clause (ii);

(IV) an explanation of why no conditions will reasonably mitigate the risk identified under clause (ii);

(V) a statement that detention will not compromise the juvenile's access to adequate medical treatment, access to medications, or ability to privately consult with counsel and meaningfully prepare a defense; and

(VI) a statement establishing that the detention environment is the least restrictive and safest possible in accordance with the requirement under clause (iii).

(e) Limitation On Supervised Release.—Beginning on the date on which a national emergency relating to a communicable disease is declared and ending on the date that is 60 days after such national emergency expires, the Office of Probation and Pretrial Services of the Administrative Office of the United States Courts shall take measures to prevent the spread of the communicable disease among individuals under supervision by—

(1) suspending the requirement that individuals determined to be a lower risk of re-offending, or any other individuals determined to be appropriate by the supervising probation officer, report in person to their probation or parole officer;

(2) identifying individuals who have successfully completed not less than 18 months of supervision and transferring such individuals to administrative supervision or petitioning the court to terminate supervision, as appropriate; and

(3) suspending the request for detention and imprisonment as a sanction for viola-

tions of probation, supervised release, or parole.

(f) Prohibition.—No individual who is granted placement in community supervision, termination of supervision, placement on administrative supervision, or pre-trial release shall be re-incarcerated, placed on supervision or active supervision, or ordered detained pre-trial only as a result of the expiration of the national emergency relating to a communicable disease.

(g) Prohibition On Technical Violations And Certain Mandatory Revocations Of Probation Or Supervised Release.—

(1) RESENTENCING IN CASES OF PROBATION AND SUPERVISED RELEASE.—

(A) IN GENERAL.—Beginning on the date on which a national emergency relating to a communicable disease is declared and ending on the date that is 60 days after such national emergency expires, and notwithstanding section 3582(b) of title 18, United States Code, a court shall order the resentencing of a defendant who is serving a term of imprisonment resulting from a revocation of probation, or supervised release for a Grade C violation for conduct under section 7B1.1(c)(3)(B) of the United States Sentencing Guidelines, upon motion of the defendant.

(B) RESENTENCING.—The court shall order the resentencing of a defendant described in subparagraph (A) as follows:

(i) In the case of a revoked sentence of probation, the court shall resentence the defendant to probation, the duration of which shall be equal to the period of time remaining on the term of probation originally imposed at the time the defendant was most recently placed in custody, unless the court determines that decreasing the length of the term of probation is in the interest of justice.

(ii) In the case of a revoked term of supervised release, the court shall continue the defendant on supervised release, the duration of which shall be equal to the period of time the defendant had remaining on supervised release when the defendant was most recently placed in custody, unless the court determines that decreasing the term of supervised release is in the interest of justice.

(2) RESENTENCING IN CASES OF PAROLE.—

(A) IN GENERAL.—Beginning on the date on which a national emergency relating to a communicable disease is declared and ending on the date that is 60 days after such national emergency expires, the court shall order the resentencing of a defendant who is serving a term of imprisonment resulting from a technical violation of the defendant's parole.

(B) RESENTENCING.—The court shall resentence the defendant to parole, the duration of which shall be equal to the period of time remaining on the defendant's term of parole at the time the defendant was most recently placed in custody, unless the court determines that decreasing the length of the term of parole is in the interest of justice.

(3) HEARING.—The court may grant, but not deny, a motion without a hearing under this section.

(4) NO MANDATORY REVOCATION.—

(A) IN GENERAL.—Beginning on the date on which a national emergency relating to a communicable disease is declared and ending on the date that is 60 days after such national emergency expires, a court is not required to revoke a defendant's probation or supervised release under sections 3565(b) and 3583(g) of title 18, United States Code, based on a finding that the defendant refused to comply with drug treatment.

(B) DISSEMINATION OF POLICY CHANGE.—Not later than 10 days after the date of enactment of this title, the Judicial Conference of the United States shall issue and disseminate to all district courts of the United States a temporary policy change suspending mandatory revocation of probation or supervised release for refusal to comply with drug testing.

(5) PROMPT DETERMINATION.—Any motion under this subsection shall be determined promptly.

(6) COUNSEL.—To effectuate the purposes of this subsection, counsel shall be appointed as early as possible to represent any indigent defendant.

(7) DEFINITIONS.—In this subsection, the term "defendant" includes individuals adjudicated delinquent under the Federal Juvenile Delinquency Act and applies to persons serving time in official detention for a revocation of juvenile probation or supervised release.

SEC. 191103. COURT AUTHORITY TO REDUCE SENTENCES AND TEMPORARY RELEASE DURING COVID–19 EMERGENCY PERIOD.

(a) Court Authority To Reduce Sentences.—

(1) IN GENERAL.—Notwithstanding section 3582 of title 18, United States Code, the court shall, during the covered emergency period, upon motion of a covered individual (as such term is defined in section 191102(b)) or on the court's own motion, reduce a term of imposed imprisonment on that individual, unless the government shows, by clear and convincing evidence, that the individual poses a risk of serious, imminent injury to a reasonably identifiable person.

(2) SENTENCE REDUCTION DEEMED AUTHORIZED.—Any sentence that is reduced under this subsection is deemed to be authorized under section 3582(c)(1) (B) of title 18, United States Code.

(3) RULE OF CONSTRUCTION.—In addition to the reduction of sentences authorized under this subsection, the court may continue to reduce and modify sentences under section 3582 of title 18, United States Code, during the covered emergency period.

(4) SPECIAL RULE.—During the covered emergency period, a covered individual who is serving a term of imprisonment for an offense committed before November 1, 1987, who would not otherwise be eligible to file a motion under section 3582(c)(1) (A) of title 18, United States Code, is eligible to file such a motion and for relief under such section. Any motion for relief filed in accordance with this paragraph before the expiration or termination of the covered emergency period shall not disqualify such motion based solely on such expiration or termination.

(b) Court Authority To Authorize Temporary Release Of Persons Awaiting Designation Or Transportation To A Bureau Of Prisons Facility.—Notwithstanding sections 3582 and 3621 of title 18, United States Code, during the covered emergency period, the court, upon motion of an individual (including individuals adjudicated delinquent under the Federal Juvenile Delinquency Act) awaiting designation or transportation to a Bureau of Prisons or other facility for service of sentence or official detention, or on the court's own motion, may order the temporary release of the individual, for a limited period ending not later than the expiration or termination of the COVID–19 emergency, if such release is for the purpose of avoiding or mitigating the risks associated with imprisonment during the covered emergency period, either generally with respect to the individual's place of imprisonment or specifically with respect to the individual.

(c) Hearing Requirement.—The court may grant, but not deny, a motion without a hearing under this section. Any motion under this section shall be determined promptly.

(d) Effective Representation During National Emergency.—

(1) ACCESS TO COURT.—During the covered emergency period, any procedural requirement under section 3582(c)(1)(A) of title 18, United States Code, that would delay a defendant from directly petitioning the court shall not apply, and the defendant may petition the court directly for relief.

(2) APPOINTMENT OF COUNSEL.—The court shall appoint counsel for indigent defendants or prisoners, at no cost to the defendant or prisoner, as early as possible to effectuate the purposes of this section and the purposes of section 3582(c)(1)(A) of title 18, United States Code.

(3) ACCESS TO MEDICAL RECORDS.—

(A) IN GENERAL.—In order to expedite proceedings under this section and proceedings under 3582(c)(1)(A) of title 18, United States Code, during the covered emergency period, the Director of the Bureau of Prisons shall promptly release all medical records in the possession of the Bureau of Prisons to a prisoner who requests them on their own behalf, or to the counsel of record for a prisoner upon submission to the court of an affidavit, signed by such counsel under penalty of perjury, that such counsel has reason to believe that the prisoner has a covered health condition (as such term is defined in section 191102(b)) or a condition that would entitle them to relief under section 3582(c)(1)(A) of title 18, United States Code.

(B) INDIVIDUALS IN THE CUSTODY OF THE U.S. MARSHALS SERVICE.—In order to expedite proceedings under this section, in the case of an individual who is in the custody or care of the U.S. Marshals Service, the Director of the U.S. Marshals Service shall facilitate the provision of any medical records of the individual to the individual or the counsel of record of the individual, upon request of the individual or counsel.

SEC. 191104. EXEMPTION FROM EXHAUSTING ADMINISTRATIVE REMEDIES DURING COVERED EMERGENCY PERIOD.

Section 7 of the Civil Rights of Institutionalized Persons Act (42 U.S.C. 1997e) is amended by adding at the end the following:

"(i) Covered Emergency Period.—

"(1) RELIEF WITHOUT EXHAUSTING ADMINISTRATIVE REMEDIES.—Notwithstanding the other provisions of this section, during the covered emergency period, a prisoner may commence, without exhausting all administrative remedies, an action relating to conditions of imprisonment under which the prisoner is at significant risk of harm or under which the prisoner's access to counsel has been impaired. If the court determines the prisoner is reasonably likely to prevail, the court may order such appropriate relief, limited in time and scope, as may be necessary to prevent or remedy the significant risk of harm or provide access to counsel.

"(2) RETALIATION PROHIBITED.—Section 6 shall apply in the case of retaliation against a prisoner who files an administrative claim or lawsuit during the covered emergency period or attempts to so file.

"(3) DEFINITIONS.—For purposes of this subsection, the term 'covered emergency period' has the meaning given the term in section 12003 of the CARES Act (Public Law 116–136).".

SEC. 191105. INCREASING AVAILABILITY OF HOME DETENTION FOR ELDERLY OFFENDERS.

(a) Good Conduct Time Credits For Certain Elderly Nonviolent Offenders.—Section 231(g)(5)(A)(ii) of the Second Chance Act of 2007 (34 U.S.C. 60541(g)(5)(A)(ii)) is amended by striking "to which the offender was sentenced" and inserting "reduced by any credit toward the service of the prisoner's sentence awarded under section 3624(b) of title 18, United States Code".

(b) Increasing Eligibility For Home Detention For Certain Elderly Nonviolent Offenders.—During the covered emergency period an offender who is in the custody of the Bureau of Prisons shall be considered an eligible elderly offender under section 231(g) of the Second Chance Act of 2007 (34 U.S.C. 60541(g)) if the offender—

(1) is not less than 50 years of age;

(2) has served 1/2 of the term of imprisonment reduced by any credit toward the service of the prisoner's sentence awarded under section 3624(b) of title 18, United States Code; and

(3) is otherwise described in such section 231(g)(5)(A).

SEC. 191106. EFFECTIVE ASSISTANCE OF COUNSEL IN THE DIGITAL ERA ACT.

(a) Prohibition On Monitoring.—Not later than 180 days after the date of the enactment of this title, the Attorney General shall create a program or system, or modify any program or system that exists on the date of enactment of this title, through which an incarcerated person sends or receives an electronic communication, to exclude from monitoring the contents of any privileged electronic communication. In the case that the Attorney General creates a program or system in accordance with this subsection, the Attorney General shall, upon implementing such system, discontinue using any program or system that exists on the date of enactment of this title through which an incarcerated person sends or receives a privileged electronic communication, except that any program or system that exists on such date may continue to be used for any other electronic communication.

(b) Retention Of Contents.—A program or system or a modification to a program or system under subsection (a) may allow for retention by the Bureau of Prisons of, and access by an incarcerated person to, the contents of electronic communications, including the contents of privileged electronic communications, of the person until the date on which the person is released from prison.

(c) Attorney-Client Privilege.—Attorney-client privilege, and the protections and limitations associated with such privilege (including the crime fraud exception), applies to electronic communications sent or received through the program or system established or modified under subsection (a).

(d) Accessing Retained Contents.—Contents retained under subsection (b) may only be accessed by a person other than the incarcerated person for whom such contents are retained under the following circumstances:

(1) ATTORNEY GENERAL.—The Attorney General may only access retained contents if necessary for the purpose of creating and maintaining the program or system, or any modification to the program or system, through which an incarcerated person sends or receives electronic communications. The Attorney General may not review retained contents that are accessed pursuant to this paragraph.

(2) INVESTIGATIVE AND LAW ENFORCEMENT OFFICERS.—

(A) WARRANT.—

(i) IN GENERAL.—Retained contents may only be accessed by an investigative or law enforcement officer pursuant to a warrant issued by a court pursuant to the procedures described in the Federal Rules of Criminal Procedure.

(ii) APPROVAL.—No application for a warrant may be made to a court without the express approval of a United States Attorney or an Assistant Attorney General.

(B) PRIVILEGED INFORMATION.—

(i) REVIEW.—Before retained contents may be accessed pursuant to a warrant obtained under subparagraph (A), such contents shall be reviewed by a United States Attorney to ensure that privileged electronic communications are not accessible.

(ii) BARRING PARTICIPATION.—A United States Attorney who reviews retained contents pursuant to clause (i) shall be barred from—

(I) participating in a legal proceeding in which an individual who sent or received an electronic communication from which such contents are retained under subsection (b) is a defendant; or

(II) sharing the retained contents with an attorney who is participating in such a legal proceeding.

(3) MOTION TO SUPPRESS.—In a case in which retained contents have been accessed in violation of this subsection, a court may suppress evidence obtained or derived from access to such contents upon motion of the defendant.

(e) Definitions.—In this section—

(1) the term "agent of an attorney or legal representative" means any person employed by or contracting with an attorney or legal representative, including law clerks, interns, investigators, paraprofessionals, and administrative staff;

(2) the term "contents" has the meaning given such term in 2510 of title 18, United States Code;

(3) the term "electronic communication" has the meaning given such term in section 2510 of title 18, United States Code, and includes the Trust Fund Limited Inmate Computer System;

(4) the term "monitoring" means accessing the contents of an electronic communication at any time after such communication is sent;

(5) the term "incarcerated person" means any individual in the custody of the Bureau of Prisons or the United States Marshals Service who has been charged with or convicted of an offense against the United States, including such an individual who is imprisoned in a State institution; and

(6) the term "privileged electronic communication" means—

(A) any electronic communication between an incarcerated person and a potential, current, or former attorney or legal representative of such a person; and

(B) any electronic communication between an incarcerated person and the agent of an attorney or legal representative described in subparagraph (A).

SEC. 191107. COVID–19 CORRECTIONAL FACILITY EMERGENCY RESPONSE ACT OF 2020.

Title I of the Omnibus Crime Control and Safe Streets Act of 1968 (34 U.S.C. 10101 et seq.) is amended by adding at the end the following:

"PART OO—PANDEMIC CORRECTIONAL FACILITY EMERGENCY RESPONSE

"SEC. 3061. FINDINGS; PURPOSES.

"(a) Immediate Release Of Vulnerable And Low-Risk Individuals.—The purpose of the grant program under section 3062 is to provide for the testing, initiation and transfer to treatment in the community, and provision of services in the community, by States and units of local government as they relate to preventing, detecting, and stopping the spread of COVID–19 in correctional facilities.

"(b) Pretrial Citation And Release.—

"(1) FINDINGS.—Congress finds as follows:

"(A) With the dramatic growth in pretrial detention resulting in county and city correctional facilities regularly exceeding capacity, such correctional facilities may serve to rapidly increase the spread of COVID–19, as facilities that hold large numbers of individuals in congregant living situations may promote the spread of COVID–19.

"(B) While individuals arrested and processed at local correctional facilities may only be held for hours or days, exposure to large number of individuals in holding cells and courtrooms promotes the spread of COVID–19.

"(C) Pretrial detainees and individuals in correctional facilities are then later released into the community having being exposed to COVID–19.

"(2) PURPOSE.—The purpose of the grant program under section 3065 is to substantially increase the use of risk-based citation release for all individuals who do not present a public safety risk.

"SEC. 3062. IMMEDIATE RELEASE OF VULNERABLE AND LOW-RISK INDIVIDUALS.

"(a) Authorization.—The Attorney General shall carry out a grant program to make grants to States and units of local government that operate correctional facilities, to establish and implement policies and procedures to prevent, detect, and stop the presence and spread of COVID–19 among arrestees, detainees, inmates, correctional facility staff, and visitors to the facilities.

"(b) Program Eligibility.—

"(1) IN GENERAL.—Eligible applicants under this section are States and units of local government that release or have a plan to release the persons described in paragraph (2) from custody in order to ensure that, not later than 90 days after enactment of this section, the total population of arrestees, detainees, and inmates at a correctional facility does not exceed the number established under subsection (c).

"(2) PERSONS DESCRIBED.—A person described in this paragraph is a person who—

"(A) does not pose a risk of serious, imminent injury to a reasonably identifiable person; or

"(B) is—

"(i) 50 years of age or older;

"(ii) a juvenile;

"(iii) an individual with serious chronic medical conditions, including heart disease, cancer, diabetes, HIV, sickle cell anemia, a neurological disease that interferes with the ability to cough or breathe, chronic lung disease, asthma, or respiratory illness;

"(iv) a pregnant woman;

"(v) an individual who is immunocompromised or has a weakened immune system; or

"(vi) an individual who has a health condition or disability that makes them vulnerable to COVID–19.

"(c) Target Correctional Population.—

"(1) TARGET POPULATION.—An eligible applicant shall establish individualized, facility-specific target capacities at each correction facility that will receive funds under this section that reflect the maximum number of individuals who may be incarcerated safely in accordance with the Centers for Disease Control and Prevention guidelines for correctional facilities pertaining to COVID–19, with consideration given to Centers for Disease Control and Prevention guidelines pertaining to community-based physical distancing, hygiene, and sanitation. A correctional facility receiving funds under this section may not use isolation in a punitive or non-medical manner as a way of achieving specific target capacities established under this paragraph.

"(2) CERTIFICATION.—An eligible applicant shall include in its application for a grant under this section a certification by a public health professional who is certified in epidemiology or infectious diseases that each correctional facility that will receive funds under this section in its jurisdiction meets the appropriate target capacity standard established under paragraph (1).

"(d) Authorized Uses.—Funds awarded pursuant to this section shall be used by grantees (including acting through nonprofit entities) to—

"(1) test all arrestees, detainees, and inmates, and initiate treatment for COVID–19, and transfer such an individual for an appropriate treatment at external medical facility, as needed;

"(2) test for COVID–19—

"(A) correctional facility staff;

"(B) volunteers;

"(C) visitors, including family members and attorneys;

"(D) court personnel that have regular contact with arrestees, detainees, and inmates;

"(E) law enforcement officers who transport arrestees, detainees, and inmates; and

"(F) personnel outside the correctional facility who provide medical treatment to arrestees, detainees, and inmates;

"(3) curtail booking and in-facility processing for individuals who have committed technical parole or probation violations; and

"(4) provide transition and reentry support services to individuals released pursuant to this section, including programs that—

"(A) increase access to and participation in reentry services;

"(B) promote a reduction in recidivism rates;

"(C) facilitate engagement in educational programs, job training, or employment;

"(D) place reentering individuals in safe and sanitary temporary transitional housing;

"(E) facilitate the enrollment of reentering individuals with a history of substance use disorder in medication-assisted treatment and a referral to overdose prevention services, mental health services, or other medical services; and

"(F) facilitate family reunification or support services, as needed.

"(e) Authorization Of Appropriations.—There is authorized to be appropriated $500,000,000 to carry out this section and section 3065 for each of fiscal years 2020 and 2021.

"SEC. 3063. JUVENILE SPECIFIC SERVICES.

"(a) In General.—The Attorney General, acting through the Administrator of the Office Juvenile Justice and Delinquency Prevention, consistent with section 261 of the Juvenile Justice and Delinquency Prevention Act of 1974 (34 U.S.C. 11171), is authorized to make grants to States and units of local government or combinations thereof to assist them in planning, establishing, operating, coordinating, and evaluating projects directly, or through grants and contracts with public and private agencies and nonprofit entities (as such term is defined under section 408(5)(A) of the Juvenile Justice and Delinquency Prevention Act of 1974 (34 U.S.C. 11296(5) (A))), for the development of more effective education, training, research, prevention, diversion, treatment, and rehabilitation programs in the area of juvenile delinquency and programs to improve the juvenile justice system, consistent with subsection (b).

"(b) Use Of Grant Funds.—Grants under this section shall be used for the exclusive purpose of providing juvenile specific services that—

"(1) provide rapid mass testing for COVID–19 in juvenile facilities, notification of the results of such tests to juveniles and authorized family members or legal guardians, and include policies and procedures for non-punitive quarantine that does not involve solitary confinement, and provide for examination by a doctor for any juvenile who tests positive for COVID–19;

"(2) examine all pre- and post-adjudication release processes and mechanisms applicable to juveniles and begin employing these as quickly as possible;

"(3) provide juveniles in out of home placements with continued access to appropriate education;

"(4) provide juveniles with access to legal counsel through confidential visits or teleconferencing;

"(5) provide staff and juveniles with appropriate personal protective equipment, hand washing facilities, toiletries, and medical care to reduce the spread of the virus;

"(6) provide juveniles with frequent and no cost calls home to parents, legal guardians, and other family members;

"(7) advance policies and procedures for juvenile delinquency program proceedings (including court proceedings) and probation conditions so that in-person reporting requirements for juveniles are replaced with virtual or telephonic appearances without penalty;

"(8) expand opportunities for juveniles to participate in community based services and social services through videoconferencing or teleconferencing; or

"(9) place a moratorium on all requirements for juveniles to attend and pay for court and probation-ordered programs, community service, and labor, that violate any applicable social distancing or stay at home order.

Each element described in paragraph (1) through (9) shall be trauma-informed, reflect the science of adolescent development, and be designed to meet the needs of at-risk juveniles and juveniles who come into contact with the justice system.

"(c) Definitions.—Terms used in this section have the meanings given such terms in the Juvenile Justice and Delinquency Prevention Act of 1974. The term 'juvenile' has the meaning given such term in section 1809 of this Act.

"(d) Authorization Of Appropriations.—There is authorized to be appropriated to carry out this section $75,000,000 for each of fiscal years 2020 and 2021.

"SEC. 3064. RAPID COVID–19 TESTING.

"(a) In General.—The Attorney General shall make grants to grantees under section 3062 for the exclusive purpose of providing for rapid COVID–19 testing of arrestees, detainees, and inmates who are exiting the custody of a correctional facility prior to returning to the community.

"(b) Use Of Funds.—Grants provided under this section may be used for any of the following:

"(1) Purchasing or leasing medical devices authorized by the U.S. Food and Drug Administration to detect COVID–19 that produce results in less than one hour.

"(2) Purchasing or securing COVID–19 testing supplies and personal protective equipment used by the correctional facility to perform such tests.

"(3) Contracting with medical providers to administer such tests.

"(c) Authorization Of Appropriations.—There is authorized to be appropriated to carry out this section $25,000,000 for each of fiscal years 2020 and 2021.

"SEC. 3065. PRETRIAL CITATION AND RELEASE.

"(a) Authorization.—The Attorney General shall make grants under this section to eligible applicants for the purposes set forth in section 3061(b)(2).

"(b) Program Eligibility.—Eligible applicants under this section are States and units of local government that implement or continue operation of a program described in subsection (c)(1) and not fewer than 2 of the other programs enumerated in such subsection.

"(c) Use Of Grant Funds.—A grantee shall use amounts provided as a grant under this section for programs that provide for the following:

"(1) Adopting and operating a cite-and-release process for individuals who are suspected of committing misdemeanor and felony offenses and who do not pose a risk of serious, imminent injury to a reasonably identifiable person.

"(2) Curtailing booking and in-facility processing for individuals who have committed technical parole or probation violations.

"(3) Ensuring that defense counsel is appointed at the earliest hearing that could result in pretrial detention so that low-risk defendants are not unnecessarily further exposed to COVID–19.

"(4) Establishing early review of charges by an experienced prosecutor, so only arrestees and detainees who will be charged are detained.

"(5) Providing appropriate victims' services supports and safety-focused residential accommodations for victims and community members who have questions or concerns about releases described in this subsection.

"SEC. 3066. REPORT.

"(a) In General.—Not later than 6 months after the date on which grants are initially made under this part, and biannually thereafter during the grant period, the Attorney General shall submit to Congress a report on the program, which shall include—

"(1) the number of grants made, the number of grantees, and the amount of funding distributed to each grantee pursuant to this part;

"(2) the location of each correctional facility where activities are carried out using grant amounts;

"(3) the number of persons in the custody of correctional facilities where activities are carried out using grant amounts, including incarcerated persons released on parole, community supervision, good time or early release, clemency or commutation, as a result of the national emergency under the National Emergencies Act (50 U.S.C. 1601 et seq.) declared by the President with respect to the Coronavirus Disease 2019 ('COVID–19'), disaggregated by type of offense, age, race, sex, and ethnicity; and

"(4) for each facility receiving funds under section 3062—

"(A) the total number of tests for COVID–19 performed;

"(B) the results of such COVID–19 tests (confirmed positive or negative);

"(C) the total number of probable COVID–19 infections;

"(D) the total number of COVID–19-related hospitalizations, the total number of intensive care unit admissions, and the duration of each such hospitalization;

"(E) recoveries from COVID–19; and

"(F) COVID–19 deaths,

disaggregated by race, ethnicity, age, disability, sex, pregnancy status, and whether the individual is a staff member of or incarcerated at the facility.

"(b) Privacy.—Data reported under this section shall be reported in accordance with applicable privacy laws and regulations.

"SEC. 3067. NO MATCHING REQUIRED.

"The Attorney General shall not require grantees to provide any matching funds with respect to the use of funds under this part.

"SEC. 3068. DEFINITION.

"For purposes of this part:

"(1) CORRECTIONAL FACILITY.—The term 'correctional facility' includes a juvenile facility.

"(2) COVERED EMERGENCY PERIOD.—The term 'covered emergency period' has the meaning given the term in section 12003 of the CARES Act (Public Law 116–136).

"(3) COVID–19.—The term 'COVID–19' means a disease caused by severe acute respiratory syndrome coronavirus 2 (SARS–CoV–2).

"(4) DETAINEE; ARRESTEE; INMATE.—The terms 'detainee', 'arrestee', and 'inmate' each include juveniles.".

SEC. 191108. MORATORIUM ON FEES AND FINES.

(a) In General.—During the covered emergency period, and for fiscal years 2020, 2021, and 2022, the Attorney General is authorized make grants to State and local courts that comply with the requirement under subsection (b) to ensure that such recipients are able to continue operations.

(b) Requirement To Impose Moratorium On Imposition And Collection Of Fees And Fines.—To be eligible for a grant under this section, a court shall implement a moratorium on the imposition and collection (including by a unit of local government or a State) of fees and fines imposed by that court—

(1) not later than 120 day after the date of the enactment of this section;

(2) retroactive to a period beginning 30 days prior the covered emergency period; and

(3) continuing for an additional 90 days after the date the covered emergency period terminates.

(c) Grant Amount.—In making grants under this section, the Attorney General shall—

(1) give preference to applicants that implement a moratorium on the imposition and collection of fines and fees related to juvenile delinquency proceedings for each of fiscal years 2020 through 2022; and

(2) make such grants in amounts that are proportionate to the number of individuals in the jurisdiction of the court.

(d) Use Of Funds.—Funds made available under this section may be used to ensure that the recipient is able to continue court operations during the covered emergency period.

(e) No Matching Requirement.—There is no matching requirement for grants under this section.

(f) Definitions.—In this section:

(1) The term "fees"—

(A) means monetary fees that are imposed for the costs of fine surcharges or court administrative fees; and

(B) includes additional late fees, payment-plan fees, interest added if an individual is unable to pay a fine in its entirety, collection fees, and any additional amounts that do not include the fine.

(2) The term "fines" means monetary fines imposed as punishment.

(g) Authorization Of Appropriations.—There is authorized to be appropriated to carry out this section $150,000,000 for each of fiscal years 2020 through 2022.

SEC. 191109. DEFINITION.

In this title, the term "covered emergency period" has the meaning given the term in section 12003 of the CARES Act (Public Law 116–136).

SEC. 191110. SEVERABILITY.

If any provision of this title or any amendment made by this title, or the application of a provision or amendment to any person or circumstance, is held to be invalid, the remainder of this title and the amendments made by this title, and the application of the provisions and amendments to any other person not similarly situated or to other circumstances, shall not be affected by the holding.

TITLE XII—IMMIGRATION MATTERS

SEC. 191201. EXTENSION OF FILING AND OTHER DEADLINES.

(a) New Deadlines For Extension Or Change Of Status Or Other Benefits.—

(1) FILING DELAYS.—In the case of an alien who was lawfully present in the United States on January 26, 2020, the alien's application for an extension or change of nonimmigrant status, application for renewal of employment authorization, or any other application for extension or renewal of a period of authorized stay, shall be considered timely filed if the due date of the application is within the period described in subsection (d) and the application is filed not later than 60 days after it otherwise would have been due.

(2) DEPARTURE DELAYS.—In the case of an alien who was lawfully present in the United States on January 26, 2020, the alien shall not be considered to be unlawfully present in the United States during the period described in subsection (d).

(3) SPECIFIC AUTHORITY.—

(A) IN GENERAL.—With respect to any alien whose immigration status, employment authorization, or other authorized period of stay has expired or will expire during the period described in subsection (d), during the one-year period beginning on the date of the enactment of this title, or during both such periods, the Secretary of Homeland Security shall automatically extend such status, authorization, or period of stay until the date that is 90 days after the last day of whichever of such periods ends later.

(B) EXCEPTION.—If the status, authorization, or period of stay referred to in subparagraph (A) is based on a grant of deferred action, or a grant of temporary protected status under section 244 of the Immigration and Nationality Act (8 U.S.C. 1254a), the extension under such subparagraph shall be for a period not less than the period for which deferred action or temporary protected status originally was granted by the Secretary of Homeland Security.

(b) Immigrant Visas.—

(1) EXTENSION OF VISA EXPIRATION.—Notwithstanding the limitations under section 221(c) of the Immigration and Nationality Act (8 U.S.C. 1201(c)), in the case of any immigrant visa issued to an alien that expires or expired during the period described in subsection (d), the period of validity of the visa is extended until the

date that is 90 days after the end of such period.

(2) ROLLOVER OF UNUSED VISAS.—

(A) IN GENERAL.—For fiscal years 2021 and 2022, the worldwide level of family-sponsored immigrants under subsection (c) of section 201 of the Immigration and Nationality Act (8 U.S.C. 1151), the worldwide level of employment-based immigrants under subsection (d) of such section, and the worldwide level of diversity immigrants under subsection (e) of such section shall each be increased by the number computed under subparagraph (B) with respect to each of such worldwide levels.

(B) COMPUTATION OF INCREASE.—For each of the worldwide levels described in subparagraph (A), the number computed under this subparagraph is the difference (if any) between the worldwide level established for the previous fiscal year under the applicable subsection of section 201 of the Immigration and Nationality Act (8 U.S.C. 1151) and the number of visas that were, during the previous fiscal year, issued and used as the basis for an application for admission into the United States as an immigrant described in the applicable subsection.

(C) CLARIFICATIONS.—

(i) ALLOCATION AMONG PREFERENCE CATEGORIES.—The additional visas made available for fiscal years 2021 and 2022 as a result of the computations made under subparagraphs (A) and (B) shall be proportionally allocated as set forth in subsections (a), (b), and (c) of section 203 of the Immigration and Nationality Act (8 U.S.C. 1153).

(ii) ELIMINATION OF FALL ACROSS.—For fiscal years 2021 and 2022, the number computed under subsection (c)(3)(C) of section 201 of the Immigration and Nationality Act (8 U.S.C. 1151), and the number computed under subsection (d)(2)(C) of such section, are deemed to equal zero.

(c) Voluntary Departure.—Notwithstanding section 240B of the Immigration and Nationality Act (8 U.S.C. 1229c), if a period for voluntary departure under such section expires or expired during the period described in subsection (d), such voluntary departure period is extended until the date that is 90 days after the end of such period.

(d) Period Described.—The period described in this subsection—

(1) begins on the first day of the public health emergency declared by the Secretary of Health and Human Services under section 319 of the Public Health Service Act (42 U.S.C. 247d) with respect to COVID–19; and

(2) ends 90 days after the date on which such public health emergency terminates.

SEC. 191202. TEMPORARY ACCOMMODATIONS FOR NATURALIZATION OATH CEREMONIES DUE TO PUBLIC HEALTH EMERGENCY.

(a) Remote Oath Ceremonies.—Not later than 30 days after the date of the enactment of this title, the Secretary of Homeland Security shall establish procedures for the administration of the oath of renunciation and allegiance under section 337 of the Immigration and Nationality Act (8 U.S.C. 1448) using remote videoconferencing, or other remote means for individuals who cannot reasonably access remote videoconferencing, as an alternative to an in-person oath ceremony.

(b) Eligible Individuals.—Notwithstanding section 310(b) of the Immigration and Nationality Act (8 U.S.C. 1421(b)), an individual may complete the naturalization process by participating in a remote oath ceremony conducted pursuant to subsection (a) if such individual—

(1) has an approved application for naturalization;

(2) is unable otherwise to complete the naturalization process due to the cancellation

U.S. House of Representatives Democrats

or suspension of in-person oath ceremonies during the public health emergency declared by the Secretary of Health and Human Services under section 319 of the Public Health Service Act (42 U.S.C. 247d) with respect to COVID–19; and

(3) elects to participate in a remote oath ceremony in lieu of waiting for in-person ceremonies to resume.

(c) Additional Requirements.—Upon establishing the procedures described in subsection (a), the Secretary of Homeland Security shall—

(1) without undue delay, provide written notice to individuals described in subsection (b)(1) of the option of participating in a remote oath ceremony in lieu of a participating in an in-person ceremony;

(2) to the greatest extent practicable, ensure that remote oath ceremonies are administered to individuals who elect to participate in such a ceremony not later than 30 days after the individual so notifies the Secretary; and

(3) administer oath ceremonies to all other eligible individuals as expeditiously as possible after the end of the public health emergency referred to in subsection (b)(2).

(d) Availability Of Remote Option.—The Secretary of Homeland Security shall begin administering remote oath ceremonies on the date that is 60 days after the date of the enactment of this title and shall continue administering such ceremonies until a date that is not earlier than 90 days after the end of the public health emergency referred to in subsection (b)(2).

(e) Clarification.—Failure to appear for a remote oath ceremony shall not create a presumption that the individual has abandoned his or her intent to be naturalized.

(f) Report To Congress.—Not later than 180 days after the end of the public health emergency referred to in subsection (b)(2), the Secretary of Homeland Security shall submit a report to Congress that identifies, for each State and political subdivision of a State, the number of—

(1) individuals who were scheduled for an in-person oath ceremony that was cancelled due to such public health emergency;

(2) individuals who were provided written notice pursuant to subsection (c)(1) of the option of participating in a remote oath ceremony;

(3) individuals who elected to participate in a remote oath ceremony in lieu of an in-person public ceremony;

(4) individuals who completed the naturalization process by participating in a remote oath ceremony; and

(5) remote oath ceremonies that were conducted within the period described in subsection (d).

SEC. 191203. TEMPORARY PROTECTIONS FOR ESSENTIAL CRITICAL INFRASTRUCTURE WORKERS.

(a) Protections For Essential Critical Infrastructure Workers.—During the period described in subsection (e), an alien described in subsection (d) shall be deemed to be in a period of deferred action and authorized for employment for purposes of section 274A of the Immigration and Nationality Act (8 U.S.C. 1324a).

(b) Employer Protections.—During the period described in subsection (e), the hiring, employment, or continued employment of an alien described in subsection (d) is not a violation of section 274A(a) of the Immigration and Nationality Act (8 U.S.C. 1324a(a)).

(c) Clarification.—Nothing in this section shall be deemed to require an alien described in subsection (d), or such alien's employer—

(1) to submit an application for employment authorization or deferred action, or register with, or pay a fee to, the Secretary of Homeland Security or the head of any other Federal agency; or

(2) to appear before an agent of the Department of Homeland Security or any other Federal agency for an interview, examination, or any other purpose.

(d) Aliens Described.—An alien is described in this subsection if the alien—

(1) on the date of the enactment of this title—

(A) is physically present in the United States; and

(B) is inadmissible to, or deportable from, the United States; and

(2) engaged in essential critical infrastructure labor or services in the United States prior to the period described in subsection (e) and continues to engage in such labor or services during such period.

(e) Period Described.—The period described in this subsection—

(1) begins on the first day of the public health emergency declared by the Secretary of Health and Human Services under section 319 of the Public Health Service Act (42 U.S.C. 247d) with respect to COVID–19; and

(2) ends 90 days after the date on which such public health emergency terminates.

(f) Essential Critical Infrastructure Labor Or Services.—For purposes of this section, the term "essential critical infrastructure labor or services" means labor or services performed in an essential critical infrastructure sector, as described in the "Advisory Memorandum on Identification of Essential Critical Infrastructure Workers During COVID–19 Response", revised by the Department of Homeland Security on April 17, 2020.

SEC. 191204. SUPPLEMENTING THE COVID RESPONSE WORKFORCE.

(a) Expedited Green Cards For Certain Physicians In The United States.—

(1) IN GENERAL.—During the period described in paragraph (3), an alien described in paragraph (2) may apply to acquire the status of an alien lawfully admitted to the United States for permanent residence consistent with section 201(b)(1) of the Immigration and Nationality Act (8 U.S.C. 1151(b)(1)).

(2) ALIEN DESCRIBED.—An alien described in this paragraph is an alien physician (and the spouse and children of such alien) who—

(A) has an approved immigrant visa petition under section 203(b)(2)(B)(ii) of the Immigration and Nationality Act (8 U.S.C. 1153(b)(2)(B)(ii)) and has completed the service requirements for a waiver under such section on or before the date of the enactment of this title; and

(B) provides a statement to the Secretary of Homeland Security attesting that the alien is engaged in or will engage in the practice of medicine or medical research involving the diagnosis, treatment, or prevention of COVID–19.

(3) PERIOD DESCRIBED.—The period described in this paragraph is the period beginning on the date of the enactment of this title and ending 180 days after the termination of the public health emergency declared by the Secretary of Health and Human Services under section 319 of the Public Health Service Act (42 U.S.C. 247d), with respect to COVID–19.

(b) Expedited Processing Of Nonimmigrant Petitions And Applications.—

(1) IN GENERAL.—In accordance with the procedures described in paragraph (2), the Secretary of Homeland Security shall expedite the processing of applications and petitions seeking employment or classification of an alien as a nonimmigrant to practice medicine, provide healthcare, engage in medical research, or participate in a

graduate medical education or training program involving the diagnosis, treatment, or prevention of COVID–19.

(2) APPLICATIONS OR PETITIONS FOR NEW EMPLOYMENT OR CHANGE OF STATUS.—

(A) INITIAL REVIEW.—Not later than 15 days after the Secretary of Homeland Security receives an application or petition for new employment or change of status described in paragraph (1), the Secretary shall conduct an initial review of such application or petition and, if additional evidence is required, shall issue a request for evidence.

(B) DECISION.—

(i) IN GENERAL.—The Secretary of Homeland Security shall issue a final decision on an application or petition described in paragraph (1) not later than 30 days after receipt of such application or petition, or, if a request for evidence is issued, not later than 15 days after the Secretary receives the applicant or petitioner's response to such request.

(ii) E-MAIL.—In addition to delivery through regular mail services, decisions described in clause (i) shall be transmitted to the applicant or petitioner via electronic mail, if the applicant or petitioner provides the Secretary of Homeland Security with an electronic mail address.

(3) TERMINATION.—This subsection shall take effect on the date of the enactment of this title and shall cease to be effective on the date that is 180 days after the termination of the public health emergency declared by the Secretary of Health and Human Services under section 319 of the Public Health Service Act (42 U.S.C. 247d), with respect to COVID–19.

(c) Emergency Visa Processing.—

(1) VISA PROCESSING.—

(A) IN GENERAL.—The Secretary of State shall prioritize the processing of applications submitted by aliens who are seeking a visa based on an approved nonimmigrant petition to practice medicine, provide healthcare, engage in medical research, or participate in a graduate medical education or training program involving the diagnosis, treatment, or prevention of COVID–19.

(B) INTERVIEW.—

(i) IN GENERAL.—The Secretary of State shall ensure that visa appointments are scheduled for aliens described in subparagraph (A) not later than 7 business days after the alien requests such an appointment.

(ii) SUSPENSION OF ROUTINE VISA SERVICES.—If routine visa services are unavailable in the alien's home country—

(I) the U.S. embassy or consulate in the alien's home country shall—

(aa) conduct the visa interview with the alien via video-teleconferencing technology; or

(bb) grant an emergency visa appointment to the alien not later than 10 business days after the alien requests such an appointment; or

(II) the alien may seek a visa appointment at any other U.S. embassy or consulate where routine visa services are available, and such embassy or consulate shall make every reasonable effort to provide the alien with an appointment within 10 business days after the alien requests such an appointment.

(2) INTERVIEW WAIVERS.—Except as provided in section 222(h)(2) of the Immigration and Nationality Act (8 U.S.C. 1202(h)(2)), the Secretary of State shall waive

the interview of any alien seeking a nonimmigrant visa based on an approved petition described in paragraph (1)(A), if—

(A) such alien is applying for a visa—

(i) not more than 3 years after the date on which such alien's prior visa expired;

(ii) in the visa classification for which such prior visa was issued; and

(iii) at a consular post located in the alien's country of residence or, if otherwise required by regulation, country of nationality; and

(B) the consular officer has no indication that such alien has failed to comply with the immigration laws and regulations of the United States.

(3) TERMINATION.—This subsection shall take effect on the date of the enactment of this title and shall cease to be effective on the date that is 180 days after the termination of the public health emergency declared by the Secretary of Health and Human Services under section 319 of the Public Health Service Act (42 U.S.C. 274d), with respect to COVID–19.

(d) Improving Mobility Of Nonimmigrant COVID–19 Workers.—

(1) LICENSURE.—Notwithstanding section 212(j)(2) of the Immigration and Nationality Act (8 U.S.C. 1182(j)(2)), for the period described in paragraph (6), the Secretary of Homeland Security may approve a petition for classification as a nonimmigrant described under section 101(a)(15)(H)(i)(b) of such Act, filed on behalf of a physician for purposes of performing direct patient care if such physician possesses a license or other authorization required by the State of intended employment to practice medicine, or is eligible for a waiver of such requirement pursuant to an executive order, emergency rule, or other action taken by the State to modify or suspend regular licensing requirements in response to the COVID–19 public health emergency.

(2) TEMPORARY LIMITATIONS ON AMENDED H–1B PETITIONS.—

(A) IN GENERAL.—Notwithstanding any other provision of law, the Secretary of Homeland Security shall not require an employer of a nonimmigrant alien described in section 101(a)(15)(H)(i)(b) of the Immigration and Nationality Act (8 U.S.C. 1101(a)(15)(H)(i)(b)) to file an amended or new petition under section 214(a) of such Act (8 U.S.C. 1184(a)) if upon transferring such alien to a new area of employment, the alien will practice medicine, provide healthcare, or engage in medical research involving the diagnosis, treatment, or prevention of COVID–19.

(B) CLARIFICATION ON TELEMEDICINE.—Nothing in the Immigration and Nationality Act or any other provision of law shall be construed to require an employer of a nonimmigrant alien described in section 101(a)(15)(H)(i)(b) of the Immigration and Nationality Act (8 U.S.C. 1101(a)(15)(H)(i)(b)) to file an amended or new petition under section 214(a) of such Act (8 U.S.C. 1184(a)) if the alien is a physician or other healthcare worker who will provide remote patient care through the use of real-time audio-video communication tools to consult with patients and other technologies to collect, analyze, and transmit medical data and images.

(3) PERMISSIBLE WORK ACTIVITIES FOR J–1 PHYSICIANS.—

(A) IN GENERAL.—Notwithstanding any other provision of law, the diagnosis, treatment, or prevention of COVID–19 shall be considered an integral part of a graduate medical education or training program and a nonimmigrant described in section 101(a)(15)(J) of the Immigration and Nationality Act (8 U.S.C. 1101(a)(15)(J)) who is participating in such a program—

(i) may be redeployed to a new rotation within the host training institution as needed to engage in COVID–19 work; and

(ii) may receive compensation for such work.

(B) OTHER PERMISSIBLE EMPLOYMENT ACTIVITIES.—A nonimmigrant described in section 101(a)(15)(J) of the Immigration and Nationality Act (8 U.S.C. 1101(a)(15)(J)) who is participating in a graduate medical education or training program may engage in work outside the scope of the approved program, if—

(i) the work involves the diagnosis, treatment, or prevention of COVID–19;

(ii) the alien has maintained lawful nonimmigrant status and has otherwise complied with the terms of the education or training program; and

(iii) the program sponsor approves the additional work by annotating the nonimmigrant's Certificate of Eligibility for Exchange Visitor (J–1) Status (Form DS–2019) and notifying the Immigration and Customs Enforcement Student and Exchange Visitor Program of the approval of such work.

(C) CLARIFICATION ON TELEMEDICINE.—Section 214(l)(1)(D) of the Immigration and Nationality Act (8 U.S.C. 1184(l)(1)(D)) may be satisfied through the provision of care to patients located in areas designated by the Secretary of Health and Human Services as having a shortage of health care professionals, through the physician's use of real-time audio-video communication tools to consult with patients and other technologies to collect, analyze, and transmit medical data and images.

(4) PORTABILITY OF O–1 NONIMMIGRANTS.—A nonimmigrant who was previously issued a visa or otherwise provided nonimmigrant status under section 101(a)(15)(O)(i) of the Immigration and Nationality Act (8 U.S.C. 1101(a)(15)(O)(i)), and is seeking an extension of such status, is authorized to accept new employment under the terms and conditions described in section 214(n) of such Act (8 U.S.C. 1184(n)).

(5) INCREASING THE ABILITY OF PHYSICIANS TO CHANGE NONIMMIGRANT STATUS.—

(A) CHANGE OF NONIMMIGRANT CLASSIFICATION.—Section 248(a) of the Immigration and Nationality Act (8 U.S.C. 1184(l)), is amended—

(i) in paragraph (1), by inserting "and" after the comma at the end;

(ii) by striking paragraphs (2) and (3); and

(iii) by redesignating paragraph (4) as paragraph (2).

(B) ADMISSION OF NONIMMIGRANTS.—Section 214(l)(2)(A) of the Immigration and Nationality Act (8 U.S.C. 1184(l)(2)(A)) is amended by striking "Notwithstanding section 248(a)(2), the" and inserting "The".

(6) TERMINATION.—This subsection shall take effect on the date of the enactment of this title and except as provided in paragraphs (2)(B), (3)(C), (4), and (5), shall cease to be effective on that date that is 180 days after the termination of the public health emergency declared by the Secretary of Health and Human Services under section 319 of the Public Health Service Act (42 U.S.C. 247d), with respect to COVID–19.

(e) Conrad 30 Program.—

(1) PERMANENT AUTHORIZATION.—Section 220(c) of the Immigration and Nationality Technical Corrections Act of 1994 (Public Law 103–416; 8 U.S.C. 1182 note) is amended by striking "and before September 30, 2015".

(2) ADMISSION OF NONIMMIGRANTS.—Section 214(l) of the Immigration and Nationality Act (8 U.S.C. 1184(l)), is amended—

(A) in paragraph (1)(B)—

(i) by striking "30" and inserting "35"; and

(ii) by inserting ", except as provided in paragraph (4)" before the semicolon at the end; and

(B) by adding at the end the following:

"(4) ADJUSTMENT IN WAIVER NUMBERS.—

"(A) INCREASES.—

"(i) IN GENERAL.—Except as provided in clause (ii), if in any fiscal year, not less than 90 percent of the waivers provided under paragraph (1)(B) are utilized by States receiving at least 5 such waivers, the number of such waivers allotted to each State shall increase by 5 for each subsequent fiscal year.

"(ii) EXCEPTION.—If 45 or more waivers are allotted to States in any fiscal year, an increase of 5 waivers in subsequent fiscal years shall be provided only in the case that not less than 95 percent of such waivers are utilized by States receiving at least 1 waiver.

"(B) DECREASES.—If in any fiscal year in which there was an increase in waivers, the total number of waivers utilized is 5 percent lower than in the previous fiscal year, the number of such waivers allotted to each State shall decrease by 5 for each subsequent fiscal year, except that in no case shall the number of waivers allotted to each State drop below 35.".

(f) Temporary Portability For Physicians And Critical Healthcare Workers In Response To COVID–19 Public Health Emergency.—

(1) IN GENERAL.—Not later than 30 days after the date of the enactment of this title, the Secretary of Homeland Security, in consultation with the Secretary of Labor and the Secretary of Health and Human Services, shall establish emergency procedures to provide employment authorization to aliens described in paragraph (2), for purposes of facilitating the temporary deployment of such aliens to practice medicine, provide healthcare, or engage in medical research involving the diagnosis, treatment, or prevention of COVID–19.

(2) ALIENS DESCRIBED.—An alien described in this paragraph is an alien who is—

(A) physically present in the United States;

(B) maintaining lawful nonimmigrant status that authorizes employment with a specific employer incident to such status; and

(C) working in the United States in a healthcare occupation essential to COVID–19 response, as determined by the Secretary of Health and Human Services.

(3) EMPLOYMENT AUTHORIZATION.—

(A) APPLICATION.—

(i) IN GENERAL.—The Secretary of Homeland Security may grant employment authorization to an alien described in paragraph (2) if such alien submits an Application for Employment Authorization (Form I–765 or any successor form), which shall include—

(I) evidence of the alien's current nonimmigrant status;

(II) copies of the alien's academic degrees and any licenses, credentials, or other documentation confirming authorization to practice in the alien's occupation; and

(III) any other evidence determined necessary by the Secretary of Homeland Security to establish by a preponderance of the evidence that the alien meets the requirements of paragraph (2).

(ii) CONVERSION OF PENDING APPLICATIONS.—The Secretary of Homeland Security shall establish procedures for the adjudication of any employment authorization applications for aliens described in paragraph (2) that are pending on the date of the enactment of this title, and the issuance of employment authorization documents in connection with such applications in accordance with the terms and conditions of this subsection, upon request by the applicant.

(B) FEES.—The Secretary of Homeland Security shall collect a fee for the processing of applications for employment authorization as provided under this paragraph.

(C) REQUEST FOR EVIDENCE.—If all required initial evidence has been submitted under this subsection but such evidence does not establish eligibility, the Secretary of Homeland Security shall issue a request for evidence not later than 15 days after receipt of the application for employment authorization.

(D) DECISION.—The Secretary of Homeland Security shall issue a final decision on an application for employment authorization under this subsection not later than 30 days after receipt of such application, or, if a request for evidence is issued, not later than 15 days after the Secretary receives the alien's response to such request.

(E) EMPLOYMENT AUTHORIZATION CARD.—An employment authorization document issued under this subsection shall—

(i) be valid for a period of not less than 1 year;

(ii) include the annotation "COVID–19"; and

(iii) notwithstanding any other provision of law, allow the bearer of such document to engage in employment during its validity period, with any United States employer to perform services described in paragraph (1).

(F) RENEWAL.—Subject to paragraph (5), the Secretary of Homeland Security may renew an employment authorization document issued under this subsection in accordance with procedures established by the Secretary.

(G) CLARIFICATIONS.—

(i) MAINTENANCE OF STATUS.—Notwithstanding a reduction in hours or cessation of work with the employer that petitioned for the alien's underlying nonimmigrant status, an alien granted employment authorization under this subsection, and the spouse and children of such alien shall, for the period of such authorization, be deemed—

(I) to be lawfully present in the United States; and

(II) to have continuously maintained the alien's underlying nonimmigrant status for purposes of an extension of such status, a change of nonimmigrant status under section 248 of the Immigration and Nationality Act (8 U.S.C. 1258), or adjustment of status under section 245 of such Act (8 U.S.C. 1255).

(ii) LIMITATIONS.—An employment authorization document described in subparagraph (E) may not be—

(I) utilized by the alien to engage in any employment other than that which is described in paragraph (1); or

(II) accepted by an employer as evidence of authorization under section 274A(b)(1)(C) of the Immigration and Nationality Act (8 U.S.C. 1324a(b)(1)(C)), to engage in employment other than that which is described in paragraph (1).

(4) TREATMENT OF TIME SPENT ENGAGING IN COVID–19-RELATED WORK.—Notwithstanding any other provision of law, time spent by an alien physician engaged in direct patient care involving the diagnosis, treatment, or prevention of COVID–19 shall count towards—

(A) the 5 years that an alien is required to work as a full-time physician for purposes of a national interest waiver under section 203(b)(2)(B)(ii) of the Immigration and Nationality Act (8 U.S.C. 1153(b)(2)(B)(ii)); and

(B) the 3 years that an alien is required to work as a full-time physician for purposes of a waiver of the 2-year foreign residence requirement under section 212(e) of the

Immigration and Nationality Act (8 U.S.C. 1182(e)), as provided in section 214(l) of such Act (8 U.S.C. 1184(l)).

(5) EXTENSION OR TERMINATION.—The procedures described in paragraph (1) shall take effect on the date that is 30 days after the date of the enactment of this title and shall remain in effect until 180 days after the termination of the public health emergency declared by the Secretary of Health and Human Services under section 319 of the Public Health Service Act (42 U.S.C. 247d), with respect to COVID–19.

(g) Special Immigrant Status For Nonimmigrant COVID–19 Workers And Their Families.—

(1) IN GENERAL.—The Secretary of Homeland Security may grant a petition for special immigrant classification to an alien described in paragraph (2) (and the spouse and children of such alien) if the alien files a petition for special immigrant status under section 204 of the Immigration and Nationality Act (8 U.S.C. 1154) for classification under section 203(b)(4) of such Act (8 U.S.C. 1153(b)(4)).

(2) ALIENS DESCRIBED.—An alien is described in this paragraph if, during the period beginning on the date that the COVID–19 public health emergency was declared by the Secretary of Health and Human Services under section 319 of the Public Health Service Act (42 U.S.C. 247d) and ending 180 days after the termination of such emergency, the alien was—

(A) authorized for employment in the United States and maintaining a nonimmigrant status; and

(B) engaged in the practice of medicine, provision of healthcare services, or medical research involving the diagnosis, treatment, or prevention of COVID–19 disease.

(3) PRIORITY DATE.—Subject to paragraph (5), immigrant visas under paragraph (1) shall be made available to aliens in the order in which a petition on behalf of each such alien is filed with the Secretary of Homeland Security, except that an alien shall maintain any priority date that was assigned with respect to an immigrant visa petition or application for labor certification that was previously filed on behalf of such alien.

(4) PROTECTIONS FOR SURVIVING SPOUSES AND CHILDREN.—

(A) SURVIVING SPOUSES AND CHILDREN.—Notwithstanding the death of an alien described in paragraph (2), the Secretary of State may approve an application for an immigrant visa, and the Secretary of Homeland Security may approve an application for adjustment of status to lawful permanent resident, filed by or on behalf of a spouse or child of such alien.

(B) AGE-OUT PROTECTION.—For purposes of an application for an immigrant visa or adjustment of status filed by or on behalf of a child of an alien described in paragraph (2), the determination of whether the child satisfies the age requirement under section 101(b)(1) of the Immigration and Nationality Act (8 U.S.C. 1101(b)(1)) shall be made using the age of the child on the date the immigrant visa petition under paragraph (1) was approved.

(C) CONTINUATION OF NONIMMIGRANT STATUS.—A spouse or child of an alien described in paragraph (2) shall be considered to have maintained lawful nonimmigrant status until the earlier of the date—

(i) on which the Secretary of Homeland Security accepts for filing, an application for adjustment of status based on a petition described in paragraph (1); or

(ii) that is 2 years after the date of the principal nonimmigrant's death.

(5) NUMERICAL LIMITATIONS.—

(A) IN GENERAL.—The total number of principal aliens who may be provided special immigrant status under this subsection may not exceed 4,000 per year for each of the 3 fiscal years beginning after the date of the enactment of this title.

(B) EXCLUSION FROM NUMERICAL LIMITATIONS.—Aliens provided special immigrant status under this subsection shall not be counted against any numerical limitations under section 201(d), 202(a), or 203(b)(4) of the Immigration and Nationality Act (8 U.S.C. 1151(d), 1152(a), or 1153(b)(4)).

(C) CARRY FORWARD.—If the numerical limitation specified in subparagraph (A) is not reached during a given fiscal year referred to in such subparagraph, the numerical limitation specified in such subparagraph for the following fiscal year shall be increased by a number equal to the difference between—

(i) the numerical limitation specified in subparagraph (A) for the given fiscal year; and

(ii) the number of principal aliens provided special immigrant status under this subsection during the given fiscal year.

SEC. 191205. ICE DETENTION.

(a) Reviewing ICE Detention.—During the public health emergency declared by the Secretary of Health and Human Services under section 319 of the Public Health Service Act (42 U.S.C. 247d) with respect to COVID–19, the Secretary of Homeland Security shall review the immigration files of all individuals in the custody of U.S. Immigration and Customs Enforcement to assess the need for continued detention. The Secretary of Homeland Security shall prioritize for release on recognizance or alternatives to detention individuals who are not subject to mandatory detention laws, unless the individual is a threat to public safety or national security.

(b) Access To Electronic Communications And Hygiene Products.—During the period described in subsection (c), the Secretary of Homeland Security shall ensure that—

(1) all individuals in the custody of U.S. Immigration and Customs Enforcement—

(A) have access to telephonic or video communication at no cost to the detained individual;

(B) have access to free, unmonitored telephone calls, at any time, to contact attorneys or legal service providers in a sufficiently private space to protect confidentiality;

(C) are permitted to receive legal correspondence by fax or email rather than postal mail; and

(D) are provided sufficient soap, hand sanitizer, and other hygiene products; and

(2) nonprofit organizations providing legal orientation programming or know-your-rights programming to individuals in the custody of U.S. Immigration and Customs Enforcement are permitted broad and flexible access to such individuals—

(A) to provide group presentations using remote videoconferencing; and

(B) to schedule and provide individual orientations using free telephone calls or remote videoconferencing.

(c) Period Described.—The period described in this subsection—

(1) begins on the first day of the public health emergency declared by the Secretary of Health and Human Services under section 319 of the Public Health Service Act (42 U.S.C. 247d) with respect to COVID–19; and

(2) ends 90 days after the date on which such public health emergency terminates.

TITLE XIII—CORONAVIRUS RELIEF FUND AMENDMENTS

SEC. 191301. CONGRESSIONAL INTENT RELATING TO TRIBAL GOVERN-

MENTS ELIGIBLE FOR CORONAVIRUS RELIEF FUND PAYMENTS.

(a) Purpose.—The purpose of this section and the amendments made by subsection (b) is to affirm the April 27, 2020, memorandum and decision of the United States District Court for the District of Columbia in Confederated Tribes of the Chehalis Reservation et al v. Mnuchin (Case No. 1:20–cv–01002) and clarify the intent of Congress that only Federally recognized Tribal Governments are eligible for payments from the Coronavirus Relief Fund established in section 601 of the Social Security Act, as added by section 5001(a) of the Coronavirus Aid, Relief, and Economic Security Act (Public Law 116–136).

(b) Eligible Tribal Governments.—Effective as if included in the enactment of the Coronavirus Aid, Relief, and Economic Security Act (Public Law 116–136), section 601 of the Social Security Act, as added by section 5001(a) of the Coronavirus Aid, Relief, and Economic Security Act, is amended—

(1) in subsection (c)(7), by striking "Indian Tribes" and inserting "Tribal Governments"; and

(2) in subsection (g)—

(A) by striking paragraph (1);

(B) by redesignating paragraphs (2) through (5) as paragraphs (1) through (4), respectively; and

(C) by striking paragraph (4) (as redesignated by subparagraph (B)) and inserting the following:

"(4) TRIBAL GOVERNMENT.—The term 'Tribal Government' means the recognized governing body of any Indian or Alaska Native tribe, band, nation, pueblo, village, community, component band, or component reservation, individually identified (including parenthetically) in the list published most recently as of the date of enactment of this Act pursuant to section 104 of the Federally Recognized Indian Tribe List Act of 1994 (25 U.S.C. 5131).".

(c) Rules Relating To Payments Made Before The Date Of Enactment Of This Act.—

(1) PAYMENTS MADE TO INELIGIBLE ENTITIES.—The Secretary of the Treasury shall require any entity that was not eligible to receive a payment from the amount set aside for fiscal year 2020 under subsection (a)(2)(B) of section 601 of the Social Security Act, as added by section 5001(a) of the Coronavirus Aid, Relief, and Economic Security Act (Public Law 116–136) and after the application of the amendments made by subsection (a) clarifying congressional intent relating to eligibility for such a payment, to return the full payment to the Department.

(2) DISTRIBUTION OF PAYMENTS RETURNED BY INELIGIBLE ENTITIES.—The Secretary of the Treasury shall distribute payments returned under paragraph (1), without further appropriation or fiscal year limitation and not later than 7 days after receiving any returned funds as required under paragraph (1) to Tribal Governments eligible for payments under such section 601 of the Social Security Act, as amended by subsection (a), in accordance with subsection (c)(7) of such Act.

(3) LIMITATION ON SECRETARIAL AUTHORITY.—The Secretary of the Treasury is prohibited from requiring an entity that is eligible for a payment from the amount set aside for fiscal year 2020 under subsection (a)(2)(B) of section 601 of the Social Security Act, as amended by subsection(a), and that received a payment before the date of enactment of this Act, from requiring the entity to return all or part of the payment except to the extent authorized under section 601(f) of such Act in the case of a determination by the Inspector General of the Department of the Treasury that

the Tribal government failed to comply with the use of funds requirements of section 601(d) of such Act.

SEC. 191302. REDISTRIBUTION OF AMOUNTS RECOVERED OR RE-COUPED FROM PAYMENTS FOR TRIBAL GOVERNMENTS; REPORTING REQUIREMENTS.

Effective as if included in the enactment of the Coronavirus Aid, Relief, and Economic Security Act (Public Law 116–136), section 601(c)(7) of the Social Security Act, as added by section 5001(a) of the Coronavirus Aid, Relief, and Economic Security Act, is amended—

(1) by striking "From the amount" and inserting the following:

"(A) IN GENERAL.—From the amount"; and

(2) by adding at the end the following:

"(B) REDISTRIBUTION OF FUNDS.—

"(i) REQUIREMENT.—In carrying out the requirement under subparagraph (A) to ensure that all amounts available under subsection (a)(2)(B) for fiscal year 2020 are distributed to Tribal governments, the Secretary shall redistribute any amounts from payments for Tribal Governments that are recovered through recoupment activities carried out by the Inspector General of the Department of the Treasury under subsection (f), without further appropriation, using a procedure and methodology determined by the Secretary in consultation with Tribal Governments, to Tribal Governments that apply for payments from such amounts.

"(ii) REPAYMENT.—In carrying out the recoupment activities by the Inspector General of the Department of the Treasury under subsection (f), Treasury shall not impose any additional fees, penalties, or interest payments on Tribal Governments associated with any amounts that are recovered.

"(C) DISCLOSURE AND REPORTING REQUIREMENTS.—

"(i) DISCLOSURE OF FUNDING FORMULA AND METHODOLOGY.—Not later than 24 hours before any payments for Tribal Governments are distributed by the Secretary pursuant to the requirements under subparagraph (A) and subparagraph (B), the Secretary shall publish on the website of the Department of the Treasury—

"(I) a detailed description of the funding allocation formula; and

"(II) a detailed description of the procedure and methodology used to determine the funding allocation formula.

"(ii) REPORT TO CONGRESS.—No later than 7 days after payments for Tribal Governments are distributed by the Secretary pursuant to the requirements under subparagraph (A) or subparagraph (B), the Secretary shall submit to the Committees on Appropriations of the House of Representatives and the Senate, the Chair and Ranking Members of the House Committee on Natural Resources and the Chair and Vice-Chair of the Senate Committee on Indian Affairs a report summarizing—

"(I) an overview of actions taken by the Secretary in carrying out the requirements under subparagraph (A) and subparagraph (B); and

"(II) the date and amount of all fund disbursements, broken down by individual Tribal Government recipients.".

SEC. 191303. USE OF RELIEF FUNDS.

Effective as if included in the Coronavirus, Aid, Relief, and Economic Security Act (Public Law 116–136), section 601 of the Social Security Act, as added by section 5001(a) of such Act, is amended by striking subsection (d) and inserting the following:

"(d) Use Of Funds.—A State, Tribal government, and unit of local government shall use the funds provided under a payment made under this section to

"(1) cover only those costs of the State, Tribal government, or unit of local government that—

"(A) Are necessary expenditures incurred due to the public health emergency with respect to the coronavirus disease 2019 (COVID–19);

"(B) were not accounted for in the budget most recently approved as of the date of enactment of this section for the State or government; and

"(C) were incurred during the period that begins on January 31, 2020, and ends on December 31, 2020; or

"(2) Replace lost, delayed, or decreased revenues, stemming from the public health emergency with respect to the coronavirus disease (COVID–19).".

TITLE XIV—RURAL DIGITAL OPPORTUNITY

SEC. 191401. ACCELERATION OF RURAL DIGITAL OPPORTUNITY FUND PHASE I AUCTION.

With respect to the Rural Digital Opportunity Fund Phase I auction (in this section referred to as the "auction") provided for in the Report and Order in the matter of Rural Digital Opportunity Fund and Connect America Fund adopted by the Federal Communications Commission (in this section referred to as the "Commission") on January 30, 2020 (FCC 20–5), the Commission shall modify the framework for the auction adopted in such Report and Order as follows:

(1) The Commission shall begin accepting long-form applications before the auction, not later than the earlier of the date that is 30 days after the date on which the Commission begins accepting short-form applications or July 31, 2020, from such applicants as are willing to commit to the schedule described in paragraph (3)(B) for deployment of networks capable of providing symmetrical Gigabit performance service.

(2) If the long-form applications accepted pursuant to paragraph (1) indicate that, for any census block or census block group identified in the Preliminary List of Eligible Areas released by the Commission on March 17, 2020, there is only 1 qualified applicant willing to commit to provide symmetrical Gigabit performance service pursuant to the schedule described in paragraph (3)(B), the Commission shall, not later than the earlier of September 30, 2020, or 30 days before the start of the auction—

(A) award to such applicant Rural Digital Opportunity Fund Phase I support for such census block or census block group, at 100 percent of the reserve price (in this paragraph referred to as the "award");

(B) remove such census block or census block group from the auction; and

(C) reduce the budget for the auction by 75 percent of the amount of the award and reduce the budget for the Rural Digital Opportunity Fund Phase II auction provided for in such Report and Order by 25 percent of the amount of the award.

(3) The Commission shall require an applicant submitting a long-form application pursuant to paragraph (1) to—

(A) not later than 30 days after the date on which such applicant submits such long-form application, provide a letter of commitment from a bank meeting the Commission's eligibility requirements stating that the bank would provide a letter of credit to such applicant if such applicant becomes a winning bidder and is awarded support; and

(B) commit to—

(i) begin construction not later than 6 months following funding authorization; and

(ii) begin to make service available not later than 1 year following funding authorization.

(4) If an applicant to which an award of support has been made under paragraph (2)(A) for a census block or census block group fails to meet the requirements of paragraph (3) with respect to such award of support, the Commission shall revoke such award of support and include such census block or census block group for competitive bidding in the Rural Digital Opportunity Fund Phase II auction provided for in such Report and Order.

(5) The Commission shall require an applicant to which an award of support has been made under paragraph (2)(A) to meet the deployment schedule to which the applicant committed under paragraph (3)(B).

SEC. 191402. ENSURING THE FCC CREATES ACCURATE SERVICE MAPS.

(a) Authorization Of Appropriations.—Title VIII of the Communications Act of 1934 (47 U.S.C. 641 et seq.) is amended by adding at the end the following:

"SEC. 807. AUTHORIZATION OF APPROPRIATIONS.

"There is authorized to be appropriated to the Commission to carry out this title—

"(1) $25,000,000 for fiscal year 2020; and

"(2) $9,000,000 for each of the fiscal years 2021 through 2027.".

(b) Deadline For Creation Of Maps.—Section 802(c)(1) of the Communications Act of 1934 (47 U.S.C. 642(c)(1)) is amended by striking "create" and inserting "create, not later than October 1, 2020".

TITLE XV—FOREIGN AFFAIRS PROVISIONS

Subtitle A—Matters Relating To The Department Of State

SEC. 191501. MITIGATION PLAN TO ASSIST FEDERAL VOTERS OVERSEAS IMPACTED BY COVID-19.

(a) In General.—Not later than 60 days after the date of the enactment of this Act, the Secretary of State, in consultation with the Secretary of Defense, shall submit to the appropriate congressional committees a plan to mitigate the effects of limited or curtailed diplomatic pouch capacities or other operations constraints at United States diplomatic and consular posts, due to coronavirus, on overseas voters (as such term is defined in section 107(5) of the Uniformed and Overseas Citizens Absentee Voting Act (52 U.S.C. 20310(5))) seeking to return absentee ballots and other balloting materials under such Act with respect to elections for Federal office held in 2020. Such plan shall include steps to—

(1) restore or augment diplomatic pouch capacities;

(2) facilitate using the Army Post Office, Fleet Post Office, the United States mails, or private couriers, if available;

(3) mitigate other operations constraints affecting eligible overseas voters; and

(4) develop specific outreach plans to educate eligible overseas voters about accessing all available forms of voter assistance prior to the date of the regularly scheduled general election for Federal office.

(b) Report On Efforts To Assist And Inform Federal Voters Overseas.—Not later than 90 days before the date of the regularly scheduled general election for Federal office held in November 2020, the Secretary of State, in consultation with the Secretary of Defense, shall report to the appropriate congressional committees on the implementation of efforts to carry out the plan submitted pursuant to subsection (a).

(c) Appropriate Congressional Committees Defined.—In this section, the term "appropriate congressional committees" means—

(1) the Committee on Foreign Affairs and the Committee on Armed Services of the House of Representatives; and

(2) the Committee on Foreign Relations and the Committee on Armed Services of the Senate.

SEC. 191502. REPORT ON EFFORTS OF THE CORONAVIRUS REPATRIATION TASK FORCE.

(a) In General.—Not later than the date specified in subsection (b), the Secretary of State shall submit to the Committee on Foreign Affairs of the House of Representatives and the Committee on Foreign Relations of the Senate a report evaluating the efforts of the Coronavirus Repatriation Task Force of the Department of State to repatriate United States citizens and legal permanent residents in response to the 2020 coronavirus outbreak. The report shall identify—

(1) the most significant impediments to repatriating such persons;

(2) the lessons learned from such repatriations; and

(3) any changes planned to future repatriation efforts of the Department of State to incorporate such lessons learned.

(b) Deadline.—The date specified in this subsection is the earlier of—

(1) the date that is 90 days after the date on which the Coronavirus Repatriation Task Force of the Department of State is disbanded; or

(2) September 30, 2020.

Subtitle B—Global Health Security Act Of 2020

SEC. 191503. SHORT TITLE.

This subtitle may be cited as the "Global Health Security Act of 2020".

SEC. 191504. FINDINGS.

Congress finds the following:

(1) In December 2009, President Obama released the National Strategy for Countering Biological Threats, which listed as one of seven objectives "Promote global health security: Increase the availability of and access to knowledge and products of the life sciences that can help reduce the impact from outbreaks of infectious disease whether of natural, accidental, or deliberate origin".

(2) In February 2014, the United States and nearly 30 other nations launched the Global Health Security Agenda (GHSA) to address several high-priority, global infectious disease threats. The GHSA is a multi-faceted, multi-country initiative intended to accelerate partner countries' measurable capabilities to achieve specific targets to prevent, detect, and respond to infectious disease threats, whether naturally occurring, deliberate, or accidental.

(3) In 2015, the United Nations adopted the Sustainable Development Goals (SDGs), which include specific reference to the importance of global health security as part of SDG 3 "ensure healthy lives and promote well-being for all at all ages" as follows:

"strengthen the capacity of all countries, in particular developing countries, for early warning, risk reduction and management of national and global health risks".

(4) On November 4, 2016, President Obama signed Executive Order 13747, "Advancing the Global Health Security Agenda to Achieve a World Safe and Secure from Infectious Disease Threats".

(5) In October 2017 at the GHSA Ministerial Meeting in Uganda, the United States and more than 40 GHSA member countries supported the "Kampala Declaration" to extend the GHSA for an additional 5 years to 2024.

(6) In December 2017, President Trump released the National Security Strategy, which includes the priority action: "Detect and contain biothreats at their source: We will work with other countries to detect and mitigate outbreaks early to prevent the spread of disease. We will encourage other countries to invest in basic health care systems and to strengthen global health security across the intersection of human and animal health to prevent infectious disease outbreaks".

(7) In September 2018, President Trump released the National Biodefense Strategy, which includes objectives to "strengthen global health security capacities to prevent local bioincidents from becoming epidemics", and "strengthen international preparedness to support international response and recovery capabilities".

SEC. 191505. STATEMENT OF POLICY.

It is the policy of the United States to—

(1) promote global health security as a core national security interest;

(2) advance the aims of the Global Health Security Agenda;

(3) collaborate with other countries to detect and mitigate outbreaks early to prevent the spread of disease;

(4) encourage other countries to invest in basic resilient and sustainable health care systems; and

(5) strengthen global health security across the intersection of human and animal health to prevent infectious disease outbreaks and combat the growing threat of antimicrobial resistance.

SEC. 191506. GLOBAL HEALTH SECURITY AGENDA INTERAGENCY REVIEW COUNCIL.

(a) Establishment.—The President shall establish a Global Health Security Agenda Interagency Review Council (in this section referred to as the "Council") to perform the general responsibilities described in subsection (c) and the specific roles and responsibilities described in subsection (e).

(b) Meetings.—The Council shall meet not less than four times per year to advance its mission and fulfill its responsibilities.

(c) General Responsibilities.—The Council shall be responsible for the following activities:

(1) Provide policy-level recommendations to participating agencies on Global Health Security Agenda (GHSA) goals, objectives, and implementation.

(2) Facilitate interagency, multi-sectoral engagement to carry out GHSA implementation.

(3) Provide a forum for raising and working to resolve interagency disagreements concerning the GHSA.

(4) (A) Review the progress toward and work to resolve challenges in achieving United States commitments under the GHSA, including commitments to assist other

countries in achieving the GHSA targets.

(B) The Council shall consider, among other issues, the following:

(i) The status of United States financial commitments to the GHSA in the context of commitments by other donors, and the contributions of partner countries to achieve the GHSA targets.

(ii) The progress toward the milestones outlined in GHSA national plans for those countries where the United States Government has committed to assist in implementing the GHSA and in annual work-plans outlining agency priorities for implementing the GHSA.

(iii) The external evaluations of United States and partner country capabilities to address infectious disease threats, including the ability to achieve the targets outlined within the WHO Joint External Evaluation (JEE) tool, as well as gaps identified by such external evaluations.

(d) Participation.—The Council shall consist of representatives, serving at the Assistant Secretary level or higher, from the following agencies:

(1) The Department of State.

(2) The Department of Defense.

(3) The Department of Justice.

(4) The Department of Agriculture.

(5) The Department of Health and Human Services.

(6) The Department of Labor.

(7) The Department of Homeland Security.

(8) The Office of Management and Budget.

(9) The United States Agency for International Development.

(10) The Environmental Protection Agency.

(11) The Centers for Disease Control and Prevention.

(12) The Office of Science and Technology Policy.

(13) The National Institutes of Health.

(14) The National Institute of Allergy and Infectious Diseases.

(15) Such other agencies as the Council determines to be appropriate.

(e) Specific Roles And Responsibilities.—

(1) IN GENERAL.—The heads of agencies described in subsection (d) shall—

(A) make the GHSA and its implementation a high priority within their respective agencies, and include GHSA-related activities within their respective agencies' strategic planning and budget processes;

(B) designate a senior-level official to be responsible for the implementation of this Act;

(C) designate, in accordance with subsection (d), an appropriate representative at the Assistant Secretary level or higher to participate on the Council;

(D) keep the Council apprised of GHSA-related activities undertaken within their respective agencies;

(E) maintain responsibility for agency-related programmatic functions in coordination with host governments, country teams, and GHSA in-country teams, and in conjunction with other relevant agencies;

(F) coordinate with other agencies that are identified in this section to satisfy programmatic goals, and further facilitate coordination of country teams, implementers, and donors in host countries; and

(G) coordinate across GHSA national plans and with GHSA partners to which the

United States is providing assistance.

(2) ADDITIONAL ROLES AND RESPONSIBILITIES.—In addition to the roles and responsibilities described in paragraph (1), the heads of agencies described in subsection (d) shall carry out their respective roles and responsibilities described in subsections (b) through (i) of section 3 of Executive Order 13747 (81 Fed. Reg. 78701; relating to Advancing the Global Health Security Agenda to Achieve a World Safe and Secure from Infectious Disease Threats), as in effect on the day before the date of the enactment of this Act.

SEC. 191507. UNITED STATES COORDINATOR FOR GLOBAL HEALTH SECURITY.

(a) In General.—The President shall appoint an individual to the position of United States Coordinator for Global Health Security, who shall be responsible for the coordination of the interagency process for responding to global health security emergencies. As appropriate, the designee shall coordinate with the President's Special Coordinator for International Disaster Assistance.

(b) Congressional Briefing.—Not less frequently than twice each year, the employee designated under this section shall provide to the appropriate congressional committees a briefing on the responsibilities and activities of the individual under this section.

SEC. 191508. SENSE OF CONGRESS.

It is the sense of the Congress that, given the complex and multisectoral nature of global health threats to the United States, the President—

(1) should consider appointing an individual with significant background and expertise in public health or emergency response management to the position of United States Coordinator for Global Health Security, as required by [section 191505(a)], who is an employee of the National Security Council at the level of Deputy Assistant to the President or higher; and

(2) in providing assistance to implement the strategy required under [section 191507(a)], should—

(A) coordinate, through a whole-of-government approach, the efforts of relevant Federal departments and agencies to implement the strategy;

(B) seek to fully utilize the unique capabilities of each relevant Federal department and agency while collaborating with and leveraging the contributions of other key stakeholders; and

(C) utilize open and streamlined solicitations to allow for the participation of a wide range of implementing partners through the most appropriate procurement mechanisms, which may include grants, contracts, cooperative agreements, and other instruments as necessary and appropriate.

SEC. 191509. STRATEGY AND REPORTS.

(a) Strategy.—The United States Coordinator for Global Health Security (appointed under [section 191505(a)]) shall coordinate the development and implementation of a strategy to implement the policy aims described in [section 191503], which shall—

(1) set specific and measurable goals, benchmarks, timetables, performance metrics, and monitoring and evaluation plans that reflect international best practices relating to transparency, accountability, and global health security;

(2) support and be aligned with country-owned global health security policy and investment plans developed with input from key stakeholders, as appropriate;

(3) facilitate communication and collaboration, as appropriate, among local stakeholders in support of a multi-sectoral approach to global health security;

(4) support the long-term success of programs by building the capacity of local organizations and institutions in target countries and communities;

(5) develop community resilience to infectious disease threats and emergencies;

(6) leverage resources and expertise through partnerships with the private sector, health organizations, civil society, nongovernmental organizations, and health research and academic institutions; and

(7) support collaboration, as appropriate, between United States universities, and public and private institutions in target countries and communities to promote health security and innovation.

(b) Coordination.—The President, acting through the United States Coordinator for Global Health Security, shall coordinate, through a whole-of-government approach, the efforts of relevant Federal departments and agencies in the implementation of the strategy required under subsection (a) by—

(1) establishing monitoring and evaluation systems, coherence, and coordination across relevant Federal departments and agencies; and

(2) establishing platforms for regular consultation and collaboration with key stakeholders and the appropriate congressional committees.

(c) Strategy Submission.—

(1) IN GENERAL.—Not later than 180 days after the date of the enactment of this Act, the President, in consultation with the head of each relevant Federal department and agency, shall submit to the appropriate congressional committees the strategy required under subsection (a) that provides a detailed description of how the United States intends to advance the policy set forth in [section 191503] and the agency-specific plans described in paragraph (2).

(2) AGENCY-SPECIFIC PLANS.—The strategy required under subsection (a) shall include specific implementation plans from each relevant Federal department and agency that describes—

(A) the anticipated contributions of the department or agency, including technical, financial, and in-kind contributions, to implement the strategy; and

(B) the efforts of the department or agency to ensure that the activities and programs carried out pursuant to the strategy are designed to achieve maximum impact and long-term sustainability.

(d) Report.—

(1) IN GENERAL.—Not later than 1 year after the date on which the strategy required under subsection (a) is submitted to the appropriate congressional committees under subsection (c), and not later than October 1 of each year thereafter, the President shall submit to the appropriate congressional committees a report that describes the status of the implementation of the strategy.

(2) CONTENTS.—The report required under paragraph (1) shall—

(A) identify any substantial changes made in the strategy during the preceding calendar year;

(B) describe the progress made in implementing the strategy;

(C) identify the indicators used to establish benchmarks and measure results over time, as well as the mechanisms for reporting such results in an open and transparent manner;

(D) contain a transparent, open, and detailed accounting of expenditures by relevant

Federal departments and agencies to implement the strategy, including, to the extent practicable, for each Federal department and agency, the statutory source of expenditures, amounts expended, partners, targeted populations, and types of activities supported;

(E) describe how the strategy leverages other United States global health and development assistance programs;

(F) assess efforts to coordinate United States global health security programs, activities, and initiatives with key stakeholders;

(G) incorporate a plan for regularly reviewing and updating strategies, partnerships, and programs and sharing lessons learned with a wide range of stakeholders, including key stakeholders, in an open, transparent manner; and

(H) describe the progress achieved and challenges concerning the United States Government's ability to advance the Global Health Security Agenda across priority countries, including data disaggregated by priority country using indicators that are consistent on a year-to-year basis and recommendations to resolve, mitigate, or otherwise address the challenges identified therein.

(e) Form.—The strategy required under subsection (a) and the report required under subsection (d) shall be submitted in unclassified form but may contain a classified annex.

SEC. 191510. COMPLIANCE WITH THE FOREIGN AID TRANSPARENCY AND ACCOUNTABILITY ACT OF 2016.

Section 2(3) of the Foreign Aid Transparency and Accountability Act of 2016 (Public Law 114–191; 22 U.S.C. 2394c note) is amended—

(1) in subparagraph (C), by striking "and" at the end;

(2) in subparagraph (D), by striking the period at the end and inserting "; and"; and

(3) by adding at the end the following:

"(E) the Global Health Security Act of 2020.".

SEC. 191511. DEFINITIONS.

In this subtitle:

(1) APPROPRIATE CONGRESSIONAL COMMITTEES.—The term "appropriate congressional committees" means—

(A) the Committee on Foreign Affairs and the Committee on Appropriations of the House of Representatives; and

(B) the Committee on Foreign Relations and the Committee on Appropriations of the Senate.

(2) GLOBAL HEALTH SECURITY.—The term "global health security" means activities supporting epidemic and pandemic preparedness and capabilities at the country and global levels in order to minimize vulnerability to acute public health events that can endanger the health of populations across geographical regions and international boundaries.

SEC. 191512. SUNSET.

This subtitle (other than section 191507), and the amendments made by this subtitle, shall cease to be effective on December 31, 2024.

Subtitle C—Securing America From Epidemics Act

SEC. 191513. FINDINGS.

Congress finds the following:

(1) Due to increasing population and population density, human mobility, and ecological change, emerging infectious diseases pose a real and growing threat to global health security.

(2) While vaccines can be the most effective tools to protect against infectious disease, the absence of vaccines for a new or emerging infectious disease with epidemic potential is a major health security threat globally, posing catastrophic potential human and economic costs.

(3) The 1918 influenza pandemic infected 500,000,000 people, or about one-third of the world's population at the time, and killed 50,000,000 people—more than died in the First World War.

(4) The economic cost of an outbreak can be devastating. The estimated global cost today, should an outbreak of the scale of the 1918 influenza pandemic strike, is 5 percent of global gross domestic product.

(5) Even regional outbreaks can have enormous human costs and substantially disrupt the global economy and cripple regional economies. The 2014 Ebola outbreak in West Africa killed more than 11,000 and cost $2,800,000,000 in losses in the affected countries alone.

(6) The ongoing novel coronavirus outbreak reflects the pressing need for quick and effective vaccine and countermeasure development.

(7) While the need for vaccines to address emerging epidemic threats is acute, markets to drive the necessary development of vaccines to address them—a complex and expensive undertaking—are very often critically absent. Also absent are mechanisms to ensure access to those vaccines by those who need them when they need them.

(8) To address this global vulnerability and the deficit of political commitment, institutional capacity, and funding, in 2017, several countries and private partners launched the Coalition for Epidemic Preparedness Innovations (CEPI). CEPI's mission is to stimulate, finance, and coordinate development of vaccines for high-priority, epidemic-potential threats in cases where traditional markets do not exist or cannot create sufficient demand.

(9) Through funding of partnerships, CEPI seeks to bring priority vaccines candidates through the end of phase II clinical trials, as well as support vaccine platforms that can be rapidly deployed against emerging pathogens.

(10) CEPI has funded multiple partners to develop vaccine candidates against the novel coronavirus, responding to this urgent, global requirement.

(11) Support for and participation in CEPI is an important part of the United States own health security and biodefense and is in the national interest, complementing the work of many Federal agencies and providing significant value through global partnership and burden-sharing.

SEC. 191514. AUTHORIZATION FOR UNITED STATES PARTICIPATION.

(a) In General.—The United States is hereby authorized to participate in the Coalition for Epidemic Preparedness Innovations.

(b) Privileges And Immunities.—The Coalition for Epidemic Preparedness Innovations shall be considered a public international organization for purposes of section 1 of the International Organizations Immunities Act (22 U.S.C. 288).

(c) Reports To Congress.—Not later than 180 days after the date of the enactment of this Act, the President shall submit to the appropriate congressional committees a report that includes the following:

(1) The United States planned contributions to the Coalition for Epidemic Pre-

paredness Innovations and the mechanisms for United States participation in such Coalition.

(2) The manner and extent to which the United States shall participate in the governance of the Coalition.

(3) How participation in the Coalition supports relevant United States Government strategies and programs in health security and biodefense, to include—

(A) the Global Health Security Strategy required by section 7058(c)(3) of division K of the Consolidated Appropriations Act, 2018 (Public Law 115–141);

(B) the applicable revision of the National Biodefense Strategy required by section 1086 of the National Defense Authorization Act for Fiscal Year 2017 (6 U.S.C. 104); and

(C) any other relevant decision-making process for policy, planning, and spending in global health security, biodefense, or vaccine and medical countermeasures research and development.

(d) Appropriate Congressional Committees.—In this section, the term "appropriate congressional committees" means—

(1) the Committee on Foreign Affairs and the Committee on Appropriations of the House of Representatives; and

(2) the Committee on Foreign Relations and the Committee on Appropriations of the Senate.

Subtitle D—Other Matters

SEC. 191515. AUTHORIZATION TO EXTEND MILLENNIUM CHALLENGE COMPACTS.

Notwithstanding the limitation in section 609(j) the Millennium Challenge Act of 2003 (22 U.S.C. 7708), the Millennium Challenge Corporation may extend any compact in effect as of January 29, 2020, for up to one additional year to account for delays related to the spread of coronavirus, if the Corporation provides to the Committee on Foreign Affairs of the House of Representatives and the Committee on Foreign Relations of the Senate a justification prior to providing any such extension.

DIVISION T—ADDITIONAL OTHER MATTERS

SEC. 200001. APPLICATION OF LAW.

Notwithstanding any other provision of law, the prohibition under section 213 of the Public Works and Economic Development Act of 1965 (42 U.S.C. 3153) shall not apply with respect to applications for grants made under this Act or Public Law 116–136.

SEC. 200002. DISASTER RECOVERY OFFICE.

(a) In General.—Section 601(d)(2) of the Public Works and Economic Development Act of 1965 (42 U.S.C. 3211(d)(2)) is amended—

(1) by striking "(2) RELEASE.—" and inserting the following:

"(2) RELEASE.—

"(A) IN GENERAL.—"; and

(2) by adding at the end the following:

"(B) REVOLVING LOAN FUND PROGRAM.—The Secretary may release, subject to terms and conditions the Secretary determines appropriate, the Federal Government's interest in connection with a grant under section 209(d) not less than 7 years after final disbursement of the grant, if—

"(i) the recipient has carried out the terms of the award in a satisfactory manner;

"(ii) any proceeds realized from the release of the Federal Government's interest will be used for one or more activities that continue to carry out the economic development purposes of this Act; and

"(iii) the recipient shall provide adequate assurance to the Secretary that at all times after release of the Federal Government's interest in connection with the grant, the recipient will be responsible for continued compliance with the requirements of section 602 in the same manner it was responsible prior to release of the Federal Government's interest and that the recipient's failure to comply shall result in the Secretary taking appropriate action, including, but not limited to, rescission of the release and recovery of the Federal share of the grant.".

(b) Office Of Disaster Recovery.—Title V of the Public Works and Economic Development Act of 1965 (42 U.S.C. 3191 et seq.) is amended by adding at the end the following:

"SEC. 508. OFFICE OF DISASTER RECOVERY.

"(a) In General.—The Secretary shall create an Office of Disaster Recovery to direct and implement the Agency's post-disaster economic recovery responsibilities pursuant to sections 209(c)(2) and 703.

"(b) Authorization.—The Secretary is authorized to appoint and fix the compensation of such temporary personnel as may be necessary to implement disaster recovery measures, without regard to the provisions of title 5, United States Code, governing appointments in the competitive service.".

(c) Clerical Amendment.—The table of contents for the Public Works and Economic Development Act of 1965 is amended by inserting after the item relating to section 507 the following new item:

"SEC. 508. Office of Disaster Recovery. ".

SEC. 200003. APPLICATION OF BUY AMERICAN.

Chapter 83 of title 41, United States Code, shall not apply with respect to purchases made in response to the emergency declared by the President on March 13, 2020, under section 501 of the Robert T. Stafford Disaster Relief and Emergency Assistance Act (42 U.S.C. 5191) and under any subsequent major disaster declaration under section 401 of such Act that supersedes such emergency declaration.

SEC. 200004. PREMIUM PAY AUTHORITY.

(a) In General.—If services performed during calendar year 2020 or 2021 are determined by the head of the agency to be primarily related to response or recovery operations arising out of an emergency or major disaster declared pursuant to the Robert T. Stafford Disaster Relief and Emergency Assistance Act (42 U.S.C. 5121 et seq.), any premium pay that is funded, either directly or through reimbursement, by the Federal Emergency Management Agency shall be exempted from the aggregate of basic pay and premium pay calculated under section 5547(a) of title 5, United States Code, and any other provision of law limiting the aggregate amount of premium pay payable on a biweekly or calendar year basis.

(b) Overtime Authority.—Any overtime that is funded for such services described in subsection (a), either directly or through reimbursement, by the Federal Emergency Management Agency shall be exempted from any annual limit on the amount of overtime payable in a calendar or fiscal year.

(c) Applicability Of Aggregate Limitation On Pay.—In determining whether an employee's pay exceeds the applicable annual rate of basic pay payable under section 5307 of title 5, United States Code, the head of an Executive agency shall not include pay exempted under this section.

(d) Limitation Of Pay Authority.—Pay exempted from otherwise applicable limits under subsection (a) shall not cause the aggregate pay earned for the calendar year in which the exempted pay is earned to exceed the rate of basic pay payable for a position at level II of the Executive Schedule under section 5313 of title 5, United States Code.

(e) Effective Date.—This section shall take effect as if enacted on January 1, 2020.

SEC. 200005. COST SHARE.

Assistance provided under the emergency declaration issued by the President on March 13, 2020, pursuant to section 501(b) of the Robert T. Stafford Disaster Relief and Emergency Assistance Act (42 U.S.C. 5191(b)), and under any subsequent major disaster declaration under section 401 of such Act (42 U.S.C. 5170) that supersedes such emergency declaration, shall be at a 100 percent Federal cost share.

SEC. 200006. CLARIFICATION OF ASSISTANCE.

(a) In General.—For the emergency declared on March 13, 2020 by the President under section 501 of the Robert T. Stafford Disaster Relief and Emergency Assistance Act (42 U.S.C. 5191), the President may provide assistance for activities, costs, and purchases of States or local governments or the owners or operators of eligible private nonprofit organizations, including—

(1) activities eligible for assistance under sections 301, 415, 416, and 426 of the Robert T. Stafford Disaster Relief and Emergency Assistance Act (42 U.S.C. 5141, 5182, 5183, 5189d);

(2) backfill costs for first responders and other essential employees who are ill or quarantined;

(3) increased operating costs for essential government services due to such emergency, including costs for implementing continuity plans, and sheltering or housing for first responders, emergency managers, health providers and other essential employees;

(4) costs of providing guidance and information to the public and for call centers to disseminate such guidance and information;

(5) costs associated with establishing and operating virtual services;

(6) costs for establishing and operating remote test sites;

(7) training provided specifically in anticipation of or in response to the event on which such emergency declaration is predicated;

(8) personal protective equipment and other critical supplies for first responders and other essential employees;

(9) medical equipment, regardless of whether such equipment is used for emergency or inpatient care;

(10) public health costs, including provision and distribution of medicine and medical supplies;

(11) costs associated with maintaining alternate care facilities or related facilities currently inactive but related to future needs tied to the ongoing pandemic event;

(12) costs of establishing and operating shelters and providing services, including transportation, that help alleviate the need of individuals for shelter, including individuals transitioning out of detention; and

(13) costs of procuring and distributing food to individuals affected by the pandemic through networks established by State, local, or Tribal governments or other organizations, including restaurants and farms, and for the purchase of food directly from food producers and farmers.

(b) Application To Subsequent Major Disaster.—The activities described in subsection (a) may also be eligible for assistance under any major disaster declared by the President under section 401 of such Act (42 U.S.C. 5170) that supersedes the emergency declaration described in such subsection.

(c) Financial Assistance For Funeral Expenses.—For any emergency or major disaster described in subsection (a) or subsection (b), the President shall provide financial assistance to an individual or household to meet disaster-related funeral expenses under section 408(e)(1) of such Act (42 U.S.C. 5174(e)).

(d) Advanced Assistance.—In order to facilitate activities under this section, the Administrator of the Federal Emergency Management Agency may provide assistance in advance to an eligible applicant if a failure to do so would prevent the applicant from carrying out such activities.

(e) Rule Of Construction.—Nothing in this section shall be construed to make ineligible any assistance that would otherwise be eligible under section 403, 408, or 502 of such Act (42 U.S.C. 5170b, 5174, 5192).

SEC. 200007. SAFETY UPGRADES IN GSA FACILITIES.

(a) Facility Safety Upgrades.—Not later than 60 days after the date of enactment of this Act, the Administrator of the General Services Administration shall take such actions as are necessary to prevent airborne transmission of COVID–19 through air conditioning, heating, ventilating, and water systems in facilities owned or leased by the General Services Administration to ensure safe and healthy indoor environments for Federal employees.

(b) Priorities.—Any projects carried out by the Administrator to carry out this section shall prioritize indoor air and water environmental quality in facilities and energy-saving building technologies and products.

SEC. 200008. NON-FEDERAL TENANTS IN GSA FACILITIES.

(a) Prohibition On Referral To Debt Collection Agencies.—Administrator of the General Services Administration may not refer any non-Federal tenants of facilities owned by the Administration to a debt collection agency during the national emergency declared by the President under the National Emergencies Act (50 U.S.C. 1601 et seq.) relating to COVID–19.

(b) Report On Rent Deferral Requests.—Not later than 30 days after the date of enactment of this Act, the Administrator of the General Services Administration shall submit to Congress a report containing all requests for rent deferrals related to COVID–19 from non-Federal tenants of facilities owned by the Administration.

SEC. 200009. TRANSIT COVID–19 REQUIREMENTS.

(a) In General.—For the duration of the national emergency declared by the President under the National Emergencies Act (50 U.S.C. 1601 et seq.) related to the pandemic of SARS–CoV–2 or coronavirus disease 2019 (COVID–19), recipients of funds under section 5307 of title 49, United States Code, that serve an urbanized area with a population of at least 500,000 individuals and that provided a minimum of 20,000,000 unlinked passenger trips in the most recent year for which data is available shall—

(1) require each passenger to wear a mask or protective face covering while on board

a public transportation vehicle;

(2) provide masks or protective face coverings, gloves, and hand santizer and wipes with sufficient alcohol content to operators, station managers, and other employees or contractors whose job responsibilities include interaction with passengers;

(3) ensure public transportation vehicles operated by such public transportation provider are cleaned, disinfected, and sanitized frequently in accordance with Centers for Disease Control and Prevention guidance and ensure that employees or contractors whose job responsibilities involve such cleaning, disinfecting, or sanitizing are provided masks or protective face coverings and gloves;

(4) ensure stations and enclosed facilities owned, operated, or used by such public transportation provider, including facilities used for training or performance of indoor maintenance, repair, or overhaul work, are cleaned, disinfected, and sanitized frequently in accordance with Centers for Disease Control and Prevention guidance and ensure that employees or contractors whose job responsibilities include such cleaning, disinfecting, or sanitizing are provided masks or other protective face coverings and gloves; and

(5) establish guidelines, or adhere to applicable guidelines, for notifying employees of a confirmed COVID–19 diagnosis of an employee of such public transportation provider.

(b) Implementation.—The implementation of the requirement under subsection (a) (1) shall be carried out in a manner determined by the provider of public transportation.

(c) Availability.—If a provider of public transportation is unable to acquire any of the items needed to comply with paragraph (2), (3), or (4) of subsection (a) due to market unavailability, such provider shall—

(1) prepare and make public documentation demonstrating what actions have been taken to acquire such items; and

(2) continue efforts to acquire such items until they become available.

SEC. 200010. REGULATION OF ANCHORAGE AND MOVEMENT OF VESSELS DURING NATIONAL EMERGENCY.

Section 70051 of title 46, United States Code, is amended—

(1) in the section heading by inserting "or public health emergency" after "national emergency";

(2) by inserting "or whenever the Secretary of Health and Human Services determines a public health emergency exists," after "international relations of the United States";

(3) by inserting "or to ensure the safety of vessels and persons in any port and navigable waterway," after "harbor or waters of the United States";

(4) by inserting "or public health emergency," after "subversive activity"; and

(5) by inserting "or to ensure the safety of vessels and persons in any port and navigable waterway," after "injury to any harbor or waters of the United States,".

SEC. 200011. MSP OPERATING VESSELS.

Notwithstanding part 296 of title 46, Code of Federal Regulations, until December 31, 2020, or upon the written determination of the Secretary of Transportation until June 31, 2021, the operator of a vessel operating such vessel under an MSP Operating Agreement (as such term is defined in section 296.2 of title 46, Code of Federal Regulations)—

(1) shall not be required to comply with any requirement with respect to operating

days (as such term is defined in such section) contained in such agreement; and
(2) shall maintain such vessel in a state of operational readiness, including through the employment of the vessel's crew complement, until the applicable date.

SEC. 200012. EXTENSION OF PERIOD OF PERFORMANCE FOR LIBRARY OF CONGRESS SEVERABLE SERVICE CONTRACTS.

(a) Extension.—Notwithstanding sections 3902(a) and 3904(b) of title 41, United States Code, if the performance or delivery of services procured under a severable service contract of the Library of Congress is delayed or otherwise affected by the COVID–19 Pandemic—
(1) the period for the performance or delivery of services under the contract may be extended for an additional period not exceeding 12 months; and
(2) funds shall remain available for obligation and expenditure under the contract until the performance or delivery of the services is completed.
(b) Contracts Covered.—This section applies with respect to contracts for services procured for a period beginning in fiscal year 2019 or fiscal year 2020.

SEC. 200013. COVERAGE OF COMMUTING EXPENSES UNDER AUTHORITY OF ARCHITECT OF THE CAPITOL TO MAKE EXPENDITURES IN RESPONSE TO EMERGENCIES.

(a) Coverage Of Commuting Expenses.—Section 1305(a)(2) of the Legislative Branch Appropriations Act, 2010 (2 U.S.C. 1827(a)(2)) is amended by inserting after "refreshments," the following: "transportation and other related expenses incurred by employees in commuting between their residence and their place of employment,".
(b) Effective Date.—The amendment made by subsection (a) shall apply with respect to fiscal year 2020 and each succeeding fiscal year.

SEC. 200014. REPORTS ON SUICIDE AMONG MEMBERS OF THE ARMED FORCES DURING THE COVID–19 PUBLIC HEALTH EMERGENCY.

(a) Report Required.—Not later than 90 days after the date of the enactment of this Act, and monthly thereafter through December 31, 2021, the Secretary of Defense shall submit to the congressional defense committees a report on suicide among members of the Armed Forces during the covered public health emergency.
(b) Elements.—Each report under subsection (a) shall include, with respect to the months covered by the report, the following:
(1) Incidents of suicide, attempted suicide, and suicidal ideation by a member of the Armed Forces, including the reserve components, listed by Armed Force.
(2) The incidents identified under paragraph (1) that occurred during a period of active service by a member in support of—
(A) a contingency operation; or
(B) an operation in response to a covered public health emergency.
(3) With respect to the member involved in each incident identified under paragraph (2):
(A) Gender.
(B) Age.
(C) Rank.
(D) Method of suicide or attempted suicide.
(4) Elements of a research agenda for the Department of Defense to establish suicide prevention treatment and risk communication for members of the Armed Forces that is—

(A) evidence-based;

(B) effective; and

(C) designed to apply to a covered public health emergency.

(c) Definitions.—In this section:

(1) The terms "active service", "congressional defense committees", and "contingency operation" have the meanings given those terms in section 101 of title 10, United States Code.

(2) The term "covered public health emergency" means the declaration—

(A) of a public health emergency, based on an outbreak of COVID–19, by the Secretary of Health and Human Services under section 319 of the Public Health Service Act (42 U.S.C. 247d); or

(B) of a domestic emergency, based on an outbreak of COVID–19, by the President or the Secretary of Homeland Security.

SEC. 200015. MODIFICATION TO MAINTENANCE OF EFFORT REQUIREMENT FOR TEMPORARY INCREASE IN MEDICAID FMAP.

(a) In General.—Section 6008(b)(1) of the Families First Coronavirus Response Act (42 U.S.C. 1396d note) is amended by inserting ", or as signed into State law on April 15, 2020, and taking effect in State law on April 3, 2020" after "January 1, 2020".

(b) Effective Date.—The amendment made by subsection (a) shall take effect as if included in the enactment of the Families First Coronavirus Response Act.

Coronavirus Aid, Relief, and Economic Security Act H. R. 748
The CARES Act is the largest spending bill in the history of the United States. Signed into law by President Donald Trump on March 27, 2020, this $2.2 trillion bill appropriates money to help the United States recover from the impacts of COVID-19 (the coronavirus). Read the contents of the bill to learn how the money was allocated.

Gun Violence Prevention and Community Safety Act of 2020 H.R.5717
This bill makes various changes to the federal framework governing the sale, transfer, and possession of firearms and ammunition. It includes a licensing requirement for all firearms, restricts firearm types and capacities, removes civil liabilities, and creates so-called Red Flag laws for teh confiscation of legally owned firearms.

Take Responsibility for Workers and Families Act H.R.6379
Read the overview, summary, and the complete text of the Democratic plan to recover from the COVID-19 crisis. The bill, H.R. 6379 contains substantial spending for multiple sectors of the economy. This bill also includes items unrelated to addressing the financial and life impacts of the crisis.

The FBI Confidential Source Failure by U.S. Department of Justice
Read the Office of the Inspector General's report on the FBI's deficiencies in its handling of classified human sources. This Inspector General identified multiple areas that the Federal Bureau of Investigation failed to properly vet confidential secret sources used for investigation. The Inspector discovered that FBI analysts were pressured into not identifying red flags about these sources, possibly tainting the counterintelligence investigation of the Trump campaign. This information was used to secure warrants for monitoring Trump campaign officials.

The Clinton Email Server Report by U.S. State Department
The U.S. Justice Department assigned Robert Mueller and a team of agents in the spring of 2017 to investigate accusations of collusion between President Donald Trump and Russian operatives. This is the complete text of the declassified, redacted report.

The Mueller Report by Robert Mueller
The U.S. Justice Department assigned Robert Mueller and a team of agents in the spring of 2017 to investigate accusations of collusion between President Donald Trump and Russian operatives. This is the complete text of the declassified, redacted report.

Other Books by Sastrugi Press

2024 Total Eclipse State Series by Aaron Linsdau
Sastrugi Press has published state-specific and country guides for the 2024 total eclipse crossing over North America. Check the Sastrugi Press website for the available eclipse books for Texas, Arkansas, Oklahoma, Missouri, Kentucky, Illinois, Indiana, Ohio, Pennsylvania, New York, Vermont, New Hampshire, Maine, Mexico, and Canada.
www.sastrugipress.com/eclipse

50 Wildlife Hotspots by Moose Henderson
Find out where to find animals and photograph them in Grand Teton National Park from a professional wildlife photographer. This unique guide shares the secret locations with the best chance at spotting wildlife.

Adventure Expedition One by Aaron Linsdau and Terry Williams M.D.
How do you set off on your first epic expedition? Where should you even start? This book has practical advice to help you begin planning your first trek. Dreaming, planning, training, doing, and returning alive are all covered in this guide.

Alaska: Illustrated Guide for the Curious by Nikki Mann and Jeff Wohl
This friendly, illustrated field guide presents interesting and educational information on Alaska's most common land and marine creatures and their habitats. With this book you can learn bear safety, edible berries, tracking, how glaciers are shaping Alaska, the creatures in a tidepool, and so much more. Curious explorers of all ages will enjoy referencing this vibrant guide as you explore the wonder of Alaska.

Along the Sylvan Trail by Julianne Couch
Along the Sylvan Trail dips into the lives of linked characters as they confront futures that aren't clearly dictated by conventional planning. The conflicts of the small town change and pressure residents of Sylvan Grove to look beyond their world to the outside.

Antarctic Tears by Aaron Linsdau
What would make someone give up a high-paying career to ski alone across Antarctica to the South Pole? This inspirational true story will make readers both cheer and cry. Fighting skin-freezing temperatures, infections, and emotional breakdown, Aaron Linsdau exposes the harsh realities of the world's largest wilderness. Discover what drives someone to the brink of destruction to pursue a dream.

Cache Creek by Susan Marsh
Five minutes from the hubbub of Jackson's town square, Cache Creek offers the chance for hikers to immerse themselves in wild nature. It is a popular hiking, biking, and cross-country ski area on the outskirts of Jackson Hole, Wyoming.

Cloudshade by Lori Howe, Ph.D.
The poems of Cloudshade breathe with the vivid, fragrant essence of life in every season on America's high plains. Extraordinarily relatable, the poems of Cloudshade swing wide a door to life in the West, both for

lovers of poetry and for those who don't normally read poems.

The Diary of a Dude Wrangler by Struthers Burt

The dude ranch world of Struthers Burt was a romantic destination in the early twentieth century. They transported people back to the Wild West. These ranches were and still are popular destinations. Experience the old west through this dude rancher's writing.

Journeys to the Edge by Randall Peeters, Ph.D.

What is it like to climb Mount Everest? Is it possible for you to actually make the ascent? It requires dreaming big and creating a personal vision to climb the mountains in your life. Randall Peeters shares his successes and failures and gives you some directly applicable guidelines on how you can create a vision for your life.

Lost at Windy Corner by Aaron Linsdau

Windy Corner on Denali has claimed lives, fingers, and toes. What would make someone brave lethal weather, crevasses, and slick ice to attempt to summit North America's highest mountain? The author shares the lessons Denali teaches on managing goals and risks. Apply the message to build resilience and overcome adversity.

Sagebrush Alley by Patricia Jones

What's worse than having a stalker? Being pursued by a second one who has already killed. Attempting to complete her studies, Dana Cameron has to avoid becoming a murder victim. She becomes tangled in a struggle for life trapped in a claustrophobic nightmare.

Sleeping Dogs Don't Lie by Michael McCoy

A young Native American boy is taken from his home after tragedy strikes, grows up in middle America, and through his first real adult summer searches for Wyoming artifacts, falls in with the subversive Dog Soldiers Resurrected, and attempts single-handedly to solve the mystery behind the murder of his treasured coworker.

So I Said by Gerry Spence

The collected sayings of Gerry Spence prods readers into thinking about their own vision of the world. As a lawyer with decades of experience in defending the defenseless, he's fought against giants. His insights provide a grander vision of how the nearly invisible world of the justice system in *So I Said*.

The Burqa Cave by Dean Petersen

Still haunted by Iraq, Tim Ross finds solace teaching high school in Wyoming. That is, until freshman David Jenkins reveals the murder of a lost local girl. Will Tim be able to overcome his demons to stop the murderer?

Voices at Twilight by Lori Howe, Ph.D.

Voices at Twilight is a guide that takes readers on a visual tour of twelve past and present Wyoming ghost towns. Contained within are travel directions, GPS coordinates, and tips for intrepid readers.www.sastrugi-press.com

Do you enjoy classic literature? Sastrugi Press has a classic series just for you. Visit our webpage and find more quality books like this one at www.sastrugipress.com/classics/.

Visit Sastrugi Press on the web at www.sastrugipress.com to purchase the above titles in bulk. They are also available from your local bookstore or online retailers in print, e-book, or audiobook form. Thank you for choosing Sastrugi Press.

www.sastrugipress.com
"Turn the Page Loose"